Information Security and Ethics:
Concepts, Methodologies, Tools, and Applications

Hamid Nemati
The University of North Carolina at Greensboro, USA

Volume IV

INFORMATION SCIENCE REFERENCE
Hershey • New York

Assistant Executive Editor:	Meg Stocking
Acquisitions Editor:	Kristin Klinger
Development Editor:	Kristin Roth
Senior Managing Editor:	Jennifer Neidig
Managing Editor:	Sara Reed
Typesetter:	Jennifer Neidig, Sara Reed, Sharon Berger, Diane Huskinson, Laurie Ridge, Jamie Snavely, Michael Brehm, Jeff Ash, Elizabeth Duke, Steve Whiskeyman
Cover Design:	Lisa Tosheff
Printed at:	Yurchak Printing Inc.

Published in the United States of America by
Information Science Reference (an imprint of IGI Global)
701 E. Chocolate Avenue, Suite 200
Hershey PA 17033
Tel: 717-533-8845
Fax: 717-533-8661
E-mail: cust@igi-global.com
Web site: http://www.igi-global.com/reference

and in the United Kingdom by
Information Science Reference (an imprint of IGI Global)
3 Henrietta Street
Covent Garden
London WC2E 8LU
Tel: 44 20 7240 0856
Fax: 44 20 7379 0609
Web site: http://www.eurospanonline.com

Library of Congress Cataloging-in-Publication Data

Information security and ethics : concepts, methodologies, tools and applications / Hamid Nemati, editor.
       p. cm.
   Summary: "This compilation serves as the ultimate source on all theories and models associated with information privacy and safeguard practices to help anchor and guide the development of technologies, standards, and best practices to meet these challenges"--Provided by publisher.
   Includes bibliographical references and index.
   ISBN-13: 978-1-59904-937-3 (hardciver)
   ISBN-13: 978-1-59904-938-0 (ebook)
  1. Computer security. 2. Information technology--Security measures. 3. Information technology--Moral and ethical aspects. I. Nemati, Hamid R., 1958-
   QA76.9.A25I54152 2008
   005.8--dc22
                              2007031962

British Cataloguing in Publication Data
A Cataloguing in Publication record for this book is available from the British Library.

Additional Research Collections found in the
"Contemporary Research in Information Science and Technology"
Book Series

Data Mining and Warehousing: Concepts, Methodologies, Tools, and Applications
John Wang, Montclair University, USA • 6-volume set • ISBN 978-1-59904-951-9

Electronic Commerce: Concepts, Methodologies, Tools, and Applications
S. Ann Becker, Florida Institute of Technology, USA • 4-volume set • ISBN 978-1-59904-943-4

Electronic Government: Concepts, Methodologies, Tools, and Applications
Ari-Veikko Anttiroiko, University of Tampere, Finland • 6-volume set • ISBN 978-1-59904-947-2

End-User Computing: Concepts, Methodologies, Tools, and Applications
Steve Clarke, University of Hull, UK • 4-volume set • ISBN 978-1-59904-945-8

Global Information Technologies: Concepts, Methodologies, Tools, and Applications
Felix Tan, Auckland University of Technology, New Zealand • 6-volume set • ISBN 978-1-59904-939-7

Information Communication Technologies: Concepts, Methodologies, Tools, and Applications
Craig Van Slyke, University of Central Florida, USA • 6-volume set • ISBN 978-1-59904-949-6

Information Security and Ethics: Concepts, Methodologies, Tools, and Applications
Hamid Nemati, The University of North Carolina at Greensboro, USA • 6-volume set • ISBN 978-1-59904-937-3

Intelligent Information Technologies: Concepts, Methodologies, Tools, and Applications
Vijayan Sugumaran, Oakland University, USA • 4-volume set • ISBN 978-1-59904-941-0

Knowledge Management: Concepts, Methodologies, Tools, and Applications
Murray E. Jennex, San Diego State University, USA • 6-volume set • ISBN 978-1-59904-933-5

Multimedia Technologies: Concepts, Methodologies, Tools, and Applications
Syad Mahbubur Rahman, Minnesota State University, USA • 3-volume set • ISBN 978-1-59904-953-3

Online and Distance Learning: Concepts, Methodologies, Tools, and Applications
Lawrence Tomei, Robert Morris University, USA • 6-volume set • ISBN 978-1-59904-935-9

Virtual Technologies: Concepts, Methodologies, Tools, and Applications
Jerzy Kisielnicki, Warsaw University, Poland • 3-volume set • ISBN 978-1-59904-955-7

<u>Free institution-wide online access with the purchase of a print collection!</u>

INFORMATION SCIENCE REFERENCE
Hershey · New York
Order online at www.igi-global.com or call 717-533-8845 ext.10
Mon–Fri 8:30am–5:00 pm (est) or fax 24 hours a day 717-533-8661

List of Contributors

Contents
by Volume

Section 1. Fundamental Concepts and Theories

This section serves as a foundation for this exhaustive reference tool by addressing crucial theories essential to the understanding of information security and ethics. Chapters found within these pages provide an excellent framework in which to position information security and ethics within the field of information science and technology. Insight regarding the critical incorporation of security measures into online and distance learning systems is addressed, while crucial stumbling blocks of information management are explored. With 45 chapters comprising this foundational section, the reader can learn and chose from a compendium of expert research on the elemental theories underscoring the information security and ethics discipline.

Section 2. Development and Design Methodologies

This section provides in-depth coverage of conceptual architecture frameworks to provide the reader with a comprehensive understanding of the emerging technological developments within the field of information security and ethics. Research fundamentals imperative to the understanding of developmental processes within information management are offered. From broad examinations to specific discussions on security tools, the research found within this section spans the discipline while offering detailed, specific discussions. From basic designs to abstract development, these chapters serve to expand the reaches of development and design technologies within the information security and ethics community. This section includes over 28 contributions from researchers throughout the world on the topic of information security and privacy within the information science and technology field.

Section 3. Tools and Technologies

This section presents an extensive coverage of various tools and technologies available in the field of information security and ethics that practitioners and academicians alike can utilize to develop different techniques. These chapters enlighten readers about fundamental research on the many methods used to facilitate and enhance the integration of security controls exploring defense strategies for information warfare—an increasingly pertinent research arena. It is through these rigorously researched chapters that the reader is provided with countless examples of the up-and-coming tools and technologies emerging from the field of information security and ethics. With more than 32 chapters, this section offers a broad treatment of some of the many tools and technologies within the IT security community.

Section 4. Utilization and Application

This section discusses a variety of applications and opportunities available that can be considered by practitioners in developing viable and effective information security programs and processes. This section includes more than 47 chapters which review certain legal aspects of forensic investigation and additional self-regulatory measures that can be leveraged to investigate cyber crime in forensic investigations. Further chapters investigate issues affecting the selection of personal firewall software in organizations. Also considered in this section are the challenges faced when utilizing information security and ethics with healthcare systems. Contributions included in this section provide excellent coverage of today's global community and how research into information security and ethics is impacting the social fabric of our present-day global village.

Section 5. Organizational and Social Implications

This section includes a wide range of research pertaining to the social and organizational impact of information security technologies around the world. Chapters introducing this section critically analyze the links between computing and cultural diversity as well as the natural environment. Additional chapters included in this section examine the link between ethics and IT and the influence of gender on ethical considerations in the IT environment. Also investigating a concern within the field of information security is research which provides an introductory overview of identity management as it relates to data networking and enterprise information management systems. With 32 chapters, the discussions presented in this section offer research into the integration of security technology as well as implementation of ethical considerations for all organizations.

Section 6. Managerial Impact

This section presents contemporary coverage of the social implications of information security and ethics, more specifically related to the corporate and managerial utilization of information sharing technologies and applications, and how these technologies can be facilitated within organizations. Core ideas such as training and continuing education of human resources in modern organizations are discussed through these 12 chapters. Issues such as strategic planning related to the organizational elements and information security program requirements that are necessary to build a framework in order to institu-

tionalize and sustain information systems as a core business process are discussed. Equally as crucial, chapters within this section examine the internal, external/environmental, and behavioral dimensions of information privacy, while analyzing findings for e-entrepreneurship and e-business ethics. Concluding this section is research which examines growth of the Internet and the effects of the wide availability of toolsets and documentation, making malware development easy. Security issues such as phishing, pharming, spamming, spoofing, spyware, and hacking incidents are explained while offering security options to defend against these increasingly more complex breeches of security and privacy.

Section 7. Critical Issues

This section contains 43 chapters addressing issues such as computer ethics, identify theft, e-fraud, social responsibility, cryptography, and online relationships, to name a few. Within the chapters, the reader is presented with an in-depth analysis of the most current and relevant issues within this growing field of study. Studies of the effects of technological innovation in the light of theories of regulation are revealed while analytical frameworks for new forms of information warfare which are threatening commercial and government computing systems are discussed. Crucial questions are addressed and alternatives offered such as the notion of social responsibility and its relationship to the information. Closing this section with a discussion of the mutual influence between culture and technology on a broad inter- and transcultural level concludes this section offering the research endless options for further research.

Section 8. Emerging Trends

This section highlights research potential within the field of information security and ethics while exploring uncharted areas of study for the advancement of the discipline. Introducing this section are chapters that set the stage for future research directions and topical suggestions for continued debate. Discussions regarding the Normal Accident Theory and the Theory of High Reliability Organizations are offered. Another debate which currently finds itself at the forefront of research which discusses three major ethical theories, Lockean liberalism, consequentialism, and Kantian deontology and the implication of these three theories as they are applied to intellectual property rights in digitally distributed media. Found in these 20 chapters concluding this exhaustive multi-volume set are areas of emerging trends and suggestions for future research within this rapidly expanding discipline.

Preface

Emphasis on knowledge and information is one of the key factors that differentiate the intelligent business enterprise of the 21st century. In order to harness knowledge and information to improve effectiveness, enterprises of the new millennium must capture, manage and utilize information with rapid speed in an effort to keep pace with the continually changing technology. Information security and ethical considerations of technology are important means by which organizations can better manage and secure information. Not easily defined, the field of information security and ethics embodies a plethora of categories within the field of information science and technology.

Over the past two decades, numerous researchers have developed a variety of techniques, methodologies, and measurement tools that have allowed them to develop, deliver and at the same time evaluate the effectiveness of several areas of information security and ethics. The explosion of these technologies and methodologies have created an abundance of new, state-of-art literature related to all aspects of this expanding discipline, allowing researchers and practicing educators to learn about the latest discoveries within the field.

Rapid technological changes, combined with a much greater interest in discovering innovative techniques to manage information security in today's modern organizations, have led researchers and practitioners to continually search for literature that will help them stay abreast of the far-reaching effects of these changes, as well as to facilitate the development and deliverance of more ground-breaking methodologies and techniques utilizing new technological innovation. In order to provide the most comprehensive, in-depth, and recent coverage of all issues related to information security and ethics, as well as to offer a single reference source on all conceptual, methodological, technical and managerial issues, as well as the opportunities, future challenges, and emerging trends related to this subject, Information Science Reference is pleased to offer a six-volume reference collection on this rapidly growing discipline, in order to empower students, researchers, academicians, and practitioners with a comprehensive understanding of the most critical areas within this field of study.

This collection, *Information Security and Ethics: Concepts, Methodologies, Tools, and Applications* is organized in eight distinct sections, providing the most wide-ranging coverage of topics such as: (1) Fundamental Concepts and Theories; (2) Development and Design Methodologies; (3) Tools and Technologies; (4) Utilization and Application; (5) Organizational and Social Implications; (6) Managerial Impact; (7) Critical Issues; and (8) Emerging Trends. The following provides a summary of what is covered in each section of this multi volume reference collection:

Section 1, **Fundamental Concepts and Theories**, serves as a foundation for this exhaustive reference tool by addressing crucial theories essential to the understanding of information security and ethics. Chapters such as, *Leadership Style, Anonymity, and the Discussion of an Ethical Issue in an Electronic Context* by Surinder S. Kahai and Bruce J. Avolio as well as *Information Security Management* by Mariana Hentea provide an excellent framework in which to position information security and ethics within the field of information science and technology. *Privacy and Security in E-Learning* by George Yee, Yuefei Xu, Larry Korba and Khalil El-Khatib offers excellent insight into the critical incorporation of security measures into online and distance learning systems, while chapters such as, *A Unified Information Security Management Plan* by Mari W. Buch and Chelley Vician address some of the basic, yet crucial stumbling blocks of information management. With 45 chapters comprising this foundational section, the reader can learn and chose from a compendium of expert research on the elemental theories underscoring the information security and ethics discipline.

Section 2, **Development and Design Methodologies**, provides in-depth coverage of conceptual architecture frameworks to provide the reader with a comprehensive understanding of the emerging technological developments within the field of information security and ethics. *Framework for Secure Information Management in Critical Systems* by Rajgopal Kannan, S. Sitharama Iyengar, and A. Durresi offers research fundamentals imperative to the understanding of research and developmental processes within information management. From broad examinations to specific discussions on security tools such as, Tsau Young Lin's, *Chinese Wall Security Policy Model: Granular Computing on DAC Model* the research found within this section spans the discipline while offering detailed, specific discussions. From basic designs to abstract development, chapters such as *Do Information Security Policies Reduce the Incidence of Security Breaches: An Exploratory Analysis* by Neil F. Doherty and Heather Fulford, and *Potential Security Issues in a Peer-to-Peer Network from a Database Perspective* by Sridhar Asvathanarayanan serve to expand the reaches of development and design technologies within the information security and ethics community. This section includes over 28 contributions from researchers throughout the world on the topic of information security and privacy within the information science and technology field.

Section 3, **Tools and Technologies**, presents an extensive coverage of various tools and technologies available in the field of information security and ethics that practitioners and academicians alike can utilize to develop different techniques. Chapters such as Paloma Díaz, Daniel Sanz, Susana Montero and Ignacio Aedo's *Integrating Access Policies into the Development Process of Hypermedia Web Systems* enlightens readers about fundamental research on one of the many methods used to facilitate and enhance the integration of security controls in hypermedia systems whereas chapters like, *A National Information Infrastructure Model for Information Warfare Defence?* by Vernon Stagg and Matthew Warren explore defense strategies for information warfare—an increasingly pertinent research arena. It is through these rigorously researched chapters that the reader is provided with countless examples of the up-and-coming tools and technologies emerging from the field of information security and ethics. With more than 32 chapters, this section offers a broad treatment of some of the many tools and technologies within the IT security community.

Section 4, **Utilization and Application**, discusses a variety of applications and opportunities available that can be considered by practitioners in developing viable and effective information security programs and processes. This section includes more than 47 chapters such as *Law, CyberCrime and Digital Forensics: Trailing Digital Suspects* by Andreas Mitrakas and Damián Zaitch which reviews certain legal aspects of forensic investigation, the overall legal framework in the EU and U.S. and additional self-regulatory measures that can be leveraged upon to investigate cyber crime in forensic investigations. Additional chapters such as Sunil Hazari's *Perceptions of End-Users on the Requirements in Personal Firewall Software: An Exploratory Study* investigates issues affecting selection of personal firewall software in organizations. Also considered in this section are the challenges faced when utilizing information security and ethics with healthcare systems as outlined by Christina Ilioudi and Athina Lazakidou's, *Security in Health Information Systems*. Contributions included in this section provide excellent coverage of today's global community and how research into information security and ethics is impacting the social fabric of our present-day global village.

Section 5, **Organizational and Social Implications**, includes a wide range of research pertaining to the social and organizational impact of information security technologies around the world. Introducing this section is Barbara Paterson's chapter, *We Cannot Eat Data: The Need for Computer Ethics to Address the Cultural and Ecological Impacts of Computing,* which critically analyzes the links between computing and cultural diversity as well as the natural environment. Additional chapters included in this section such as *Gender Influences on Ethical Considerations in the IT Environment* by Jessica Leong examine the link between ethics and IT and the influence of gender on ethical considerations in the IT environment. Also investigating a concern within the field of information security is Katherine M. Hollis and David M. Hollis' *Identity Management: A Comprehensive Approach to Ensuring a Secure Network Infrastructure,* which provides an introductory overview of identity management as it relates to data networking and enterprise information management systems. With 32 chapters the discussions presented in this section offer research into the integration of security technology as well as implementation of ethical considerations for all organizations.

Section 6, **Managerial Impact**, presents contemporary coverage of the social implications of information security and ethics, more specifically related to the corporate and managerial utilization of information sharing technologies and applications, and how these technologies can be facilitated within organizations. Core ideas such as training and continuing education of human resources in modern organizations are discussed through these 12 chapters. *A Security Blueprint for E-Business Applications* by Jun Du, Yuan-Yuan Jiao and Jianxin (Roger) Jiao discusses strategic planning related to the organizational elements and information security program requirements that are necessary to build a framework in order to institutionalize and sustain information systems as a core business process. Equally as crucial, chapters such as *Online Information Privacy and Its Implications for E-Entrepreneurship and E-Business Ethics* by Carmen Gould and Fang Zhao contain a comprehensive examination of the internal, external/environmental, and behavioral dimensions of information privacy, as well as a description of findings for e-entrepreneurship and e-business ethics. Concluding this section is a chapter by Raj Sharman, K. Pramod Krishna, H. Raghov Rao and Shambhu Upadhyaya, *Malware and Antivirus Deployment for Enterprise Security.* This chapter examines growth of the Internet and the effects of the wide availability of toolsets and documentation, making malware development easy. As blended threats continue to combine multiple types of attacks into single and more dangerous payloads, newer threats are emerging. These professors explore phishing, pharming, spamming, spoofing, spyware, and hacking incidents while offering security options to defend against these increasingly more complex breeches of security and privacy.

Section 7, **Critical Issues**, contains 43 chapters addressing issues such as computer ethics, identify theft, e-fraud, social responsibility, cryptography, and online relationships, to name a few. Within the chapters, the reader is presented with an in-depth analysis of the most current and relevant issues within this growing field of study. Carolyn Currie's, *Integrity and Security in the E-Century* studies the effects of technological innovation in the light of theories of regulation that postulate a struggle between attempts to control innovation and further innovation and regulation while *Hacker Wars: E-Collaboration by Vandals and Warriors* by Richard Baskerville develops an analytical framework for new forms of information warfare that may threaten commercial and government computing systems by using e-collaboration in new ways. Crucial questions are addressed such as that presented in Bernd Carsten Stahl's chapter, *What is the Social Responsibility in the Information Age? Maximising Profits?* which analyzes the notion of social responsibility and its relationship to the information age while expressing some of the normative questions of the information age. *Culture and Technology: A Mutual-Shaping Approach* by Thomas Herdin, Wolfgang Hofkirchner and Ursula Maier-Rabler closes this section with a discussion of the mutual influence between culture and technology on a broad inter- and transcultural level.

The concluding section of this authoritative reference tool, **Emerging Trends**, highlights research potential within the field of information security and ethics while exploring uncharted areas of study for the advancement of the discipline. Introducing this section is a chapter entitled, *Security Engineering for Ambient Intelligence: A Manifesto,* by A. Maña, C. Rudolph, G. Spanoudakis, V. Lotz, F. Massacci, M. Melideo, and J. S. López-Cobo which sets the stage for future research directions and topical suggestions for continued debate. Providing an alternative view of security in our post 9/11 world is *Information Technology as a Target and Shield in the Post 9/11 Environment* by Laura Lally. This chapter draws upon normal accident theory and the theory of high reliability organizations to examine the potential impacts of information technology being used as a target in terrorist and other malicious attacks, while arguing that IT can also be used as a shield to prevent further attacks and mitigate their impact if they should occur. Another debate which currently finds itself at the forefront of research within this field is presented by Kai Kristian Kimppa's research, *Intellectual Property Rights - or Rights to the Immaterial - in Digitally Distributable Media Gone All Wrong* which discusses three major ethical theories, Lockean liberalism, consequentialism, and Kantian deontology and the implication of these three theories as they are applied to intellectual property rights in digitally distributed media. Found in these 20 chapters concluding this exhaustive multi-volume set are areas of emerging trends and suggestions for future research within this rapidly expanding discipline.

Although the primary organization of the contents in this multi-volume is based on its eight sections, offering a progression of coverage of the important concepts, methodologies, technologies, applications, social issues, and emerging trends, the reader can also identify specific contents by utilizing the extensive indexing system listed at the end of each volume. Furthermore to ensure that the scholar, researcher and educator have access to the entire contents of this multi volume set as well as additional coverage that could not be include in the print version of this publication, the publisher will provide unlimited multi-user electronic access to the online aggregated database of this collection for the life of edition, free of charge when a library purchases a print copy. This aggregated database provides far more contents than what can be included in the print version in addition to continual updates. This unlimited access, coupled with the continuous updates to the database ensures that the most current research is accessible knowledge seekers.

Information security and ethics as a discipline has witnessed fundamental changes during the past two decades, allowing information seekers around the globe to have access to information which two decades ago, was inaccessible. In addition to this transformation, many traditional organizations and business enterprises have taken advantage of the technologies offered by the development of information security systems in order to expand and augment their existing programs. This has allowed practitioners and researchers to serve their customers, employees and stakeholders more effectively and efficiently in the modern virtual world. With continued technological innovations in information and communication technology and with on-going discovery and research into newer and more innovative techniques and applications, the information security and ethics discipline will continue to witness an explosion of information within this rapidly evolving field.

The diverse and comprehensive coverage of information security and ethics in this six-volume authoritative publication will contribute to a better understanding of all topics, research, and discoveries in this developing, significant field of study. Furthermore, the contributions included in this multi-volume collection series will be instrumental in the expansion of the body of knowledge in this enormous field, resulting in a greater understanding of the fundamentals while fueling the research initiatives in emerging fields. We at Information Science Reference, along with the editor of this collection, and the publisher hope that this multi-volume collection will become instrumental in the expansion of the discipline and will promote the continued growth of information security and ethics.

Chapter 4.25
Privacy and Trust in Agent-Supported Distributed Learning[1]

Larry Korba
*National Research Council
Canada, Canada*

George Yee
*National Research Council
Canada, Canada*

Yuefei Xu
*National Research Council
Canada, Canada*

Ronggong Song
*National Research Council
Canada, Canada*

Andrew S. Patrick
*National Research Council
Canada, Canada*

Khalil El-Khatib
*National Research Council
Canada, Canada*

ABSTRACT

The objective of this chapter is to explore the challenges, issues, and solutions associated with satisfying requirements for privacy and trust in agent-supported distributed learning (ADL). Accordingly, the first section will present the background, context, and challenges. The second section will delve into the requirements for privacy and trust as seen in legislation and standards. The third section will look at available technologies for satisfying these requirements. The fourth section will discuss an often-ignored area—that of building trustworthy user interfaces for distributed-learning systems. Finally, the chapter will end with conclusions and suggestions for further research.

INTRODUCTION

Background and Context

One of the key characteristics of our information economy is the requirement for lifelong learning. Industrial and occupational changes, global competition, and the explosion of information technologies have highlighted the need for skills, knowledge, and training. Focused on attracting and retaining staff, companies have placed an emphasis on training to bolster soft and hard skills to meet new corporate challenges. In many cases, career training has been placed in the hands of employees, with the understanding that employees must be able to keep ahead of technological change and perform innovative problem solving. One way of meeting the demand for these new skills (especially in information technology) is through online distance learning, which also offers the potential for continuous learning. Moreover, distance learning provides answers for the rising costs of tuition, the shortage of qualified training staff, the high cost of campus maintenance, and the need to reach larger learner populations. Key trends for corporate distance learning, germane to privacy and trust, include the following (Hodgins, 2000):

- Learners may access courseware using many different computing devices, from different locations, via different networks (i.e., the distance-learning system is distributed).
- Distance-learning technology will overtake classroom training to meet the needs for "know what" and "know how" training.
- Distance learning will offer more user personalization, whereas courseware will dynamically change based on learner preferences or needs. In other words, distance-learning applications of the future will be intelligent and adaptive.
- Corporate training is becoming knowledge management. This is the general trend in the digital economy. With knowledge management, employee competencies are assets, which increase in value through training. This trend has pushed the production of training that is more task specific than generic. Changes in corporate strategic directions are often reflected as changes in distance-learning requirements prompted by the need to train staff for those new directions.
- Distance learning is moving toward open standards.

Most distance-learning innovations have focused on course development and delivery, with little or no consideration to privacy and security as required elements. However, it is clear from the above trends that there will be a growing need for high levels of confidentiality, privacy, and trust in distance-learning applications, and that security technologies must be put in place to meet these needs. The savvy of consumers regarding their rights to privacy is increasing, and new privacy legislations have recently been introduced by diverse jurisdictions. It is also clear that confidentiality is vital for information concerning distance-learning activities undertaken by corporate staff. While corporations may advertise their learning approaches to skills and knowledge development in order to attract staff, they do not want competitors to learn the details of training provided, which could compromise their strategic directions.

Privacy, Trust, and Security in Distance Learning

We explain here what we mean by "privacy," "trust," and "security" in the context of distance learning. A learner's "privacy" represents the conditions under which he or she is willing to share personal and other valued information with others. Thus, information is private where conditions exist for its sharing. Privacy is violated where the underlying conditions for sharing are violated. A learner's "trust" is his or her level of confidence in the ability of the distance-learning system to comply with the conditions the learner has stated (privacy preferences) for sharing information, function as expected for distance learning, and act in the learner's best interest when made vulnerable. "Security" refers to the electronic means (e.g., encrypted traffic) used by a distance-learning system to comply with the learner's privacy preferences, and function correctly without being compromised by an attack.

The focus of this chapter is on a distance learner's privacy and trust: the requirements for privacy, the issues faced in providing for privacy, the standards and technologies available (security) for ensuring that privacy preferences are followed, and the technologies available (human factors design techniques) that promote trust. This means, for example, that we will not be just concerned with such issues as learner authentication, or even data integrity, unless it concerns the integrity of private data.

Agent-Supported Distributed Learning (ADL)

By agent-supported distributed learning, we mean a distance-learning system that has the following characteristics:

- Distance learning is carried out via a network (including a wireless network).
- The components of the distance-learning system are distributed across a network.
- Software agents act on behalf of the learner or the provider of the distance-learning system to provide or enhance functionality, e.g., retrieval of learning material. These agents may be mobile or stationary or autonomous or dependent on some other party for their actions.

In the literature, a few authors (the number of authors is not extensive) have written on the use of agents for distance learning.

Santos and Rodriguez (2002) discussed an agent architecture that provides knowledge-based facilities for distance education. Their approach is to take advantage of recent standardization activities to integrate information from different sources (in standardized formats) in order to improve the learning process, both detecting learner problems and recommending new contents that can be more suitable for the learner's skills and abilities. They accomplish this by using a suite of different agents, such as a "learning content agent," a "catalog agent," a "competency agent," a "certification agent," a "profile agent," and a "learner agent."

Rosié et al. (2002) looked at the application of the Semantic Web together with personal agents in distance education. They saw the following possibilities of such a combination: (a) enable sharing of knowledge bases regardless of how the information is presented, (b) allow access to services of other information systems that are offered through the Semantic Web, and (c) allow reuse of already stored data without the need to learn the relations and terminology of the knowledge base creator.

Koyama et al. (2001) proposed the use of a multifunctional agent for distance learning that would collect the learner's learning material requirements, perform management, do information analysis, determine the learner's understanding of a particular domain, handle the teaching material, and communicate with the learners. The distance-learning system would be built on the WWW, and this agent would reside in a Web server. Koyama et al. also proposed a fairly elaborate "judgment algorithm" that monitors the learner's progress and learning time and does learner testing in conjunction with learner requirements, learner personal history, and the existence of "re-learning items" in order to decide appropriate learning materials for the learner.

Finally, Cristea and Okamoto (2000) described an agent-managed adaptive distance-learning system for teaching English that adapts over time to a

Figure 1. LTSA system components

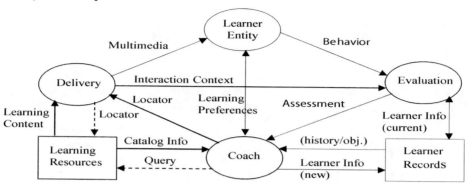

learner's needs and preferences in order to improve future learning performance. They use two agents, a Global agent (GA) and a personal agent (PA), to manage two student models, a global student model (GS) and an individual student model (IS), respectively. The GS contains global student information, such as the common mistakes, favorite pages, favorite lessons, search patterns, and so on. The IS contains personal student information, such as the last page accessed, grades for all tests taken, mistakes and their frequency, the order of access of texts inside each lesson, and so on. The PA manages the user information and extracts from it useful material for user guidance. The PA also requests information from the GA and collaborates with other PAs to obtain more specific information (e.g., what material other learners have used in a similar situation) than is available from the GA. In short, the PA acts as a personal assistant to the learner to provide guidance as to what material the learner should be studying. The GA averages information from several users to fill in the general student model. Its role is to give the PAs condensed information that might show trends and patterns. The GA cannot contact the learner directly unless the PA requests it.

It is noteworthy that privacy and trust issues abound in the above paper references. Yet none of the above authors even mentioned, let alone considered, such issues. However, we refer the interested reader to El-Khatib et al. (2003) who

discussed privacy, security, and trust issues in e-learning from the perspectives of standards, requirements, and technology.

As shown by the above reference papers, apart from El-Khatib et al. (2003), every author has a different agent architecture for agent-supported distance learning. We show here how a standard set of agents for distance learning can be derived from IEEE P1484.1/D9: the Learning Technology Systems Architecture (LTSA) (IEEE LTSC, 2001).

LTSA-Based Architectural Model for ADL

The LTSA prescribes processes, storage areas, and information flows for e-learning. Figure 1 shows the relationships between these elements. The solid arrows represent data flows; the dashed arrows represent control flows. The overall operation is as follows: *Learning Preferences,* including the learning styles, strategies, methods, etc., are initially passed from the *learner entity* to the *Coach* process; the *Coach* reviews the set of incoming information, such as performance *history,* future *objectives,* and searches *Learning Resources,* via *Query,* for appropriate learning content; the *Coach* extracts *Locator*s for the content from the *Catalog Info* and passes them to *Delivery,* which uses them to retrieve the content for delivery to the learner as *multimedia; multimedia* represents

Table 1. Derivation of a LTSA-based agent architecture for distance learning

LTSA Components	LTSA-Based Agent Architecture	Agent Owners
Learner entity L	earner agent(s)	Learning entity
Delivery process D	elivery agent(s) L	earning entity
Evaluation process	Evaluation agent(s) D	istance-learning system
Coach process	Coach agent(s) D	istance-learning system
Information flow (both data and control)	Message flow	
Storage areas S	torage areas	

learning content, to which the learner exhibits a certain *behavior*; this behavior is evaluated and results in an *Assessment* or *Learner Information* such as performance; *Learner Information* is stored in *Learner Records*; and *Interaction Context* provides the context used to interpret the learner's behavior.

An agent architecture for distance learning can be derived from this model simply by mapping each LTSA process to one or more agents that are then responsible for implementing the process, mapping the information flows (both data and control) to messaging flows, and letting the storage areas stay the same. This mapping is defined by the first two columns of Table 1. The third column of Table 1 shows the agent owners, the parties on whose behalf the agents act.

It may be necessary or convenient to have more than one agent implement a process for reasons of improved modularity, performance, or system organization. For example, a single delivery agent may get overloaded if it has to deal with too many learners. Rather, several delivery agents could be employed, wherein each agent deals with a certain number (determined through analysis or experimentation) of learners, and moreover, could be distributed to reduce communication bottleneck. As another example, improved modularity may be obtained through the use of several delivery

agents in which each agent is specialized to retrieve specific material. If the learning material concerns software engineering, such a division of labor could be one agent for retrieving material on requirements specification, another agent for design specification, and a third agent for testing. Figure 2 illustrates the LTSA-based agent architecture.

Scenarios

To further strengthen the concept of agent-supported distance learning, we list here some typical scenarios or use cases of an agent-supported distance-learning system. The first three scenarios are from Santos and Rodriguez (2002), but using the agent types derived from the LTSA:

- A coach agent may ask an evaluation agent for the previous week's learner monitoring information. The evaluation agent will search and retrieve this information and give it to the coach agent, who will analyze the information to determine if the learner needs help.
- A coach agent may ask a learner agent for the learner's preference information in order to send material availability notifications to

delivery agents for forwarding to learner agents.

- Coach agents can request information on learner preferences from learner agents and learner skills and attained certifications from other coach agents. Using this information, the coach agents can then make recommendations to the learner regarding new skills in which the learner might be interested, in order to achieve a new certification.

- A learner agent may ask a coach agent for the availability of specific learning material. The coach agent then asks the learner agent for the learner's preferences and uses this, together with the information on specific learning material, to query the learning resources for the availability of the material.

- An evaluation agent checks with a learner agent to determine if it can go ahead with monitoring the learner's performance on specific learning material. The learner agent checks its stored learner privacy preferences and gets back to the evaluation agent with the answer.

- A coach agent queries learning resources for the suppliers of particular learning material. Using this information, the coach agent then queries the reputation or trustworthiness (assumed contained in learning resources) of the suppliers and rejects the learning material that is from untrustworthy suppliers.

The last two use cases constitute a foretaste of how agents can be used to maintain privacy and guard against disreputable content suppliers. We will deal with solutions for privacy and trust in the following sections.

Challenges and Issues

We highlight here some of the challenges and issues associated with satisfying the requirements for privacy and trust in agent-supported distance learning. The challenges and issues arise from first identifying the requirements and then looking at how to satisfy the requirements. Requirements can come from privacy legislation, standards, or popular usage (as in de facto standards). We examine the first two of these in the section entitled "Privacy Legislation and Standards."

Challenges and issues arise from looking at how to satisfy the privacy requirements, as set out in the Privacy Principles, within an agent-supported distance-learning system. For example, how can agents be used to satisfy the Limiting Collection Principle? How can agents be used to satisfy the Safeguards Principle? Other issues are from a learner's trust point of view and involve the perceived trustability of the system (see section entitled "Promoting Trust in ADL Systems"). For example, how can a learner be assured that specific requested learning content is reliable? How can a learner be convinced that his or her privacy is actually being protected according to his or her expressed wishes? In order for the learner to fully learn from an ADL system, she must accept and trust the system. Therefore, it is paramount that answers be found for these questions.

State of Privacy and Trust Research for ADL

It is safe to say that privacy and trust research for ADL is still in its infancy. Privacy and trust issues for distributed systems in general have only recently started to receive attention from researchers, and ADL is a distributed system. In addition, a search through both IEEE and ACM databases in April, 2003, found only about half a dozen papers on ADL alone (four of these papers are described above) and no papers on privacy and trust for ADL. Luckily, some privacy and trust research for other distributed systems (e.g., online banking) may be applied to ADL. Indeed, we will mostly follow this approach in the sections below.

Figure 2. LTSA-based agent architecture for distance learning

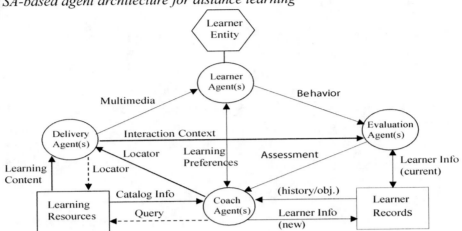

PRIVACY LEGISLATION AND STANDARDS

Privacy Legislation

Jurisdictions in countries throughout North America and Europe have realized the need to protect consumer privacy and have enacted privacy legislation for this purpose. In these countries, where there is privacy legislation, individual control is required for the use of personal information, including the collection, use, disclosure, retention, and disposal of personal data by organizations that may handle that information. Privacy principles have been developed to expose the implications of privacy laws or privacy policy adopted by online organizations. In Canada, 10 Privacy Principles (CSA 1) (see Table 2), incorporated in the *Personal Information Protection and Electronic Documents Act* of Canada (Department of Justice), spell out the requirements for use of personal information. These principles may be implemented in computer systems to varying degrees due to the nature of each principle or the underlying application. For example, Principle 1 is largely manual, but portions of it can still be implemented to facilitate its compliance. As a set of privacy requirements, the Privacy Principles serve as a reference to determine how well an ADL system meets these requirements.

From Privacy Legislation to Design Guidelines

The privacy legislation mentioned in subsection "Privacy Legislation" acknowledges that an e-learner should practice full control over the collection, use, disclosure, retention, and disposal of his or her personal information. The legislation also lists the principles that any online system that handles personal information, including distance-learning systems, should observe in order to comply with the legislation. These principles form, in fact, guidelines for deriving system designs. In the following sections, we will revisit each of the Privacy Principles and derive the privacy design guidelines for the LTSA-based ADL architecture presented in subsection "LTSA Based Architectural Model for ADL."

Data Collection

One of the most important principles of the Privacy Principles is the principle *Identifying Purposes*, also referred to as the principle of Notice (Langheinrich, 2001) or Feedback (Bellotti & Sellen, 1993). Complying with this principle requires that parts of the system that collect personal information announce to the learner their collection practices. This includes the data the learner or the learner's agent is asked to provide,

Table 2. The 10 privacy principles used in Canada

Principle	Description
1. Accountability	An organization is responsible for personal information under its control and shall designate an individual or individuals accountable for the organization's compliance with the privacy principles.
2. Identifying purposes	The purposes for which personal information is collected shall be identified by the organization at or before the time the information is collected.
3. Consent	The knowledge and consent of the individual are required for the collection, use, or disclosure of personal information, except when inappropriate.
4. Limiting collection	The collection of personal information shall be limited to that which is necessary for the purposes identified by the organization. Information shall be collected by fair and lawful means.
5. Limiting use, disclosure, and retention	Personal information shall not be used or disclosed for purposes other than those for which it was collected, except with the consent of the individual or as required by the law. In addition, personal information shall be retained only as long as necessary for fulfillment of those purposes.
6. Accuracy	Personal information shall be as accurate, complete, and up-to-date as is necessary for the purposes for which it is to be used.
7. Safeguards	Security safeguards appropriate to the sensitivity of the information shall be used to protect personal information.
8. Openness	An organization shall make readily available to individuals specific information about its policies and practices relating to the management of personal information.
9. Individual access	Upon request, an individual shall be informed of the existence, use, and disclosure of his or her personal information and shall be given access to that information. An individual shall be able to challenge the accuracy and completeness of the information and have it amended as appropriate.
10. Challenging compliance	An individual shall be able to address a challenge concerning compliance with the above principles to the designated individual or individuals accountable for the organization's compliance.

as well as the data that can be collected without the knowledge of the learner. In the LTSA ADL architecture, both the *evaluation agent* and *coach agent* may collect personal information to derive the learning requirements and progress of the learner. Therefore, both agents are required to inform the *learner agent* about their data collection practices. Depending on the degree of privacy of the requested data, the *learner agent* may directly release the data if it was not classified as private by the learner, or the agent might warn the learner about the data collection, and solicit the learner's feedback before releasing any information (*Consent* principle).

A closely related principle to the principle of *Identifying Purposes* is the principle of *Openness*, which requires the system to make readily available information about the policies and practices relating to the management of personal information. A distance-learning system can announce the privacy policies in a widely known URL, easily accessible to agents and learners.

Data Storage and Transmission

The *Safeguards* principle requires security safeguards be placed on any system component that handles a learner's private information. Fulfilling this principle requires the deployment of safeguards in every part of the system where private information might be exposed; in the LTSA ADL architecture, this includes the data storage facility for the learner record and the networking infrastructure over which these records are transmitted. With safeguards in place, the *Individual Access* principle requires the distance-learning system to implement mechanisms to allow learners (or their agents) access to their records.

While the privacy principles refer directly to data that are collected, transmitted, or stored, there might still be other forms of privacy threats that are not directly related to the data collected. The physical location of the learner is an example of information that could be classified as private, and exposed if the learning content was delivered directly between the delivery agent and learner agent. Such location information may be as valuable as the content of the learning material itself, and some learners may require some form of privacy for their location information.

Privacy and Security in Data Storage

A distance-learning system may gather any type of information from learners for a number of purposes ranging from regulating access to the learning content (authentication, authorization), to billing (accounting), to content customization or service adaptation. Systems, in general, that collect and store private information should implement appropriate security measures to protect the privacy and security of this information. Data storage facilities are usually like honeypots for hackers, and most systems make protection of these facilities a top priority. Typical security measures include authentication and authorization mechanisms that guard access to the stored data. These security measures are usually proportional to the sensitivity and value of the information they protect. A system that stores medical records usually has higher security mechanisms in place than a system that stores records of favorite movies.

Privacy and Security During Data Transmission

With the open structure of the Internet and the readily available, easy-to-use tools for monitoring network activity; it is possible for a relative novice to extract vital information simply by analyzing the traffic patterns between the communicating entities. Some may consider that technologies such as secure sockets layers or virtual private networks would provide all of the safeguards one may require for network privacy. While these technologies may protect the data transferred between parties from network snoopers relatively well, a number of passive attack techniques can reveal sensitive information about the participating communicators (Raymond, 2000). Timing and communication pattern attacks, for example, extract information about the timing of communications, the locations of the communicating parties, and the amount of information being shared. By examining the pattern, timing, origin, and destination of communications, a snooper can deduce relationships between parties. For some activities in an organization, it is vital to safeguard this information. For instance, a company may have secretly chosen a new strategic initiative wherein specialized training is required for several key members of a development team. As per a recent trend, the company may have chosen to purchase a course from an online training company. In order to maintain confidentiality concerning the new strategic direction, the company would want to ensure that it would be very difficult for anyone to determine that it has a relationship with the online training company. Indeed, the distance-learning company may wish to distinguish its offerings from the competition by providing customers with the option of allowing students and employers to keep their network interactions confidential.

Limiting Data Collection, Processing, and Retention

A privacy legislation compliant distance-learning system must limit data collection to the minimum necessary information required to complete the purposes identified by the system. Coach and evaluation agents must collect this information from the learner by fair and lawful means. In addition, this information can only be processed or disclosed for the purpose for which it was collected, unless the learner has otherwise consented, or when it is required or permitted by law. Additionally, the system may retain a learner's information only for the period of time required to fulfill the purpose for which it was collected.

Accountability and Challenging Compliance

Because the distance-learning system deals with private information about learners, the provider of the system should be held responsible for the management and protection of this information. In fulfilling this requirement, the provider is required to designate an individual who is accountable for the system's compliance with the Privacy Principles. In addition, the provider should clearly outline the procedures that a learner would follow in case of questions or enquiries with respect to the provider's privacy practices. The provider should also outline the dispute resolution mechanism in case of complaints.

Location Privacy

While some distance-learning systems give learners the freedom to select the time and learning content according to their preferences and convenience, service mobility in distance learning offers learners additional freedom: a learner agent can access the distance-learning service anywhere using any available device. Wireless communication and device mobility complement service mobility, as through this technology, learning content can be delivered to a learner agent running on mobile computing devices, such as Personal Digital Assistants (PDA) and Internet-enabled cellular phones. Using these mobile devices, learners can receive learning content anywhere, at any time, while traveling, commuting, or waiting in line.

Location privacy is of particular importance for mobile distance-learning systems and can be considered as an extension to network privacy. With the convenience of delivering learning content to mobile devices, there is the potential of jeopardizing the location privacy of the learner. Some learners might be reluctant to reveal the location from which they are accessing learning content and consider this information private. Compiling this location information may provide useful information about the mobility pattern of the learner, which could be useful for a third party interested in the mobility aspect of learners.

Privacy and Trust Requirements from Distributed-Learning Standards

Standardization and compatibility are important factors for consideration by distance-learning vendors and users looking to sell or purchase portable content and interchangeable components on the market. Emerging standards for distance learning and education are having major influences on the development of distance-learning systems. Such standards include the IEEE Learning Technology Standards Committee, the IMS Global Learning

Table 3. Featured elements of IEEE P1484 on security and Privacy

Model	Specification	Model	Specification
Session-View Security Model	D	Nonrepudiation Model I	
Security P arameter N egotiation Model	D	Repudiation Model	I
Security Extension Model D	P	rivacy Model N	
Access Control Model D	C	onfidentiality Model N	
Identification Model I	E	ncryption Model	N
Authentication Model O	D	ata Integrity Model	N
De-identification Model	O	Validation of Certificates	N
Authorization Model	I	Digital Signature Model	N
Delegation Model I			

D = Defined: The model or requirements are defined or provided.

I = Implementation-dependent: The detailed methods are dependent on implementations.

O = Outside the scope: The methods are outside the standard.

N = Nonspecified: The standard does not specify the model and requirements.

Consortium, the Aviation Industry CBT Committee, the Alliance of Remote Instructional Authoring and Distribution Networks for Europe, and the Advanced Distributed Learning-Sharable Content Object Reference Model. The privacy and security requirements are also important parts addressed in many of these standards. We consider here the IEEE P1484 and MIS LIP in more detail.

IEEE P1484

The IEEE P1484 is a standard for learning technology proposed by the Learning Technology Standards Committee (LTSC) of the IEEE Computer Society. The specification of Public and Private Information (PAPI) for Learners (P1484.2, 2000) outlines privacy and security requirements that are more specific than privacy legislation. It defines the elements for recording descriptive information related to the learning process, learner relationships, learner preferences, learner performance, and portfolios. It categorizes the security and privacy concerns from the points of view of different stakeholders, such as developer, institution, regulator, and user.

Specifically for the privacy concerns, the P1484.2 requires that the security techniques, including physical security, confidentiality, etc.,

are to be used to provide privacy protection. Further, the institutional administrators and users may all act as privacy policy makers to mandate privacy-related policies, which are implemented via a variety of security techniques, technologies, processes, and procedures.

Table 3 lists the featured elements of IEEE P1484 relating to security and privacy.

IMS LIP

The IMS Global Learning Consortium (IMS GLC) is an organization working on developing open specifications for distributed learning. It addresses key problems and challenges in distributed-learning environments with a series of reference specifications, including Meta-data Specifications, Enterprise Specification, Content & Packaging Specification, Question & Test Specification, Simple Sequencing Specification, and Learner Information Package Specification. Among these, the IMS Learner Information Package (IMS LIP) Specification addresses the interoperability of learner information systems with other systems that support the Internet learning environment. In this standard, "learner information" is defined as the collection of information about a learner or learning provider. The typical sorts of learner information include education record, training log, professional development record, lifelong learning record, and community service record (e.g., work and training experience). The ways of organizing learner information are specified in this standard so that learning systems can be more responsive to the specific needs of each user.

In order to maintain the privacy and security of the learner information, the IMS LIP specification specifies a learner information server to be responsible for exchanging learner's data with other information servers or other systems (e.g., a delivery system). The server is required to support an information owner, defining what part of the information is shared with other systems.

The IMS LIP treats data privacy and integrity as essential requirements. Although the standard does not define any details of implementation mechanisms or architectures that could be employed to support learner privacy protection, its final specification V1.0 (IMS GLC, 2001) provides the following structures to support the implementation of "any suitable architecture" for learner privacy protection:

- *Privacy and data protection metastructure:* Within a learner information tree structure, each tree node and leaf has an associated set of privacy description, which defines the concerns of privacy level, access rights, and data integrity. The granularity of information is the smallest set of data, where there is no further breakdown of independent privacy data.
- *"SecurityKey" data structure:* The security keys for the learner include password, public key, and digital signatures. In this structure, the password and security codes are used for communication. The structure can allow for public key encryption, data authenticity, and password-based access control on learner information.

PRIVACY-ENHANCING TECHNOLOGIES FOR ADL

Policy-Based Privacy and Trust Management

Policy-based management approaches have been used effectively to manage and control large distributed systems. In such a system, policies are usually expressed in terms of authorization, obligation, delegation, or refrain imperatives over subject, object, and actions. These policies are expressed using a policy specification language, such as Ponder or XACL, introduced in the next section.

While policies expressed using Ponder or XACL can be compiled and enforced in the system, other policy languages can be used simply to inform the user about the practices adopted by the system. These policies depend on other mechanisms for implementation and enforcement. An example of such a policy language is the Platform for Privacy Preferences Project (P3P) (P3P: The Platform for Privacy Preferences Project, 2001), developed by the World Wide Web Consortium (W3C). Subsection "P3P" elaborates more on the P3P and its use in meeting the privacy requirements.

Additionally, different system administrators might create policies, at different times and at different granularities. Naturally, conflicts can occur between policies, calling for some sort of mechanism to detect policy conflicts and to resolve them. Thus, a facility for policy specification and negotiation would be beneficial for distance-learning systems, with which the learner and distance-learning provider can identify policy conflicts and negotiate a resolution. A mechanism for policy negotiation is presented in the subsection entitled "Negotiation of Privacy Policy."

Ponder

In a policy-based distance-learning system, the system administrator might specify some basic policies for the general operation of the system, and additional policies might be added based on the preferences of the parties. There would be sets of policies for each of the parties in the system (administrator, teacher, student) as well as for the interaction between these parties. In addition, governments and other regulatory bodies may have privacy laws or regulations (Privacy Technology Review). These may be translated into electronic policies and added to the general policies (Korba, 2002).

Ponder (Damianou et al., 2001; Dulay et al., 2001) is a declarative, object-oriented language for specifying security and management policies for distributed network management. A policy has three parts: subject, object, and action. Ponder uses the following terms as listed: *subject* refers to users or principals, *target* refers to a resource, and *action* refers to an operation by the subject on the target.

Using Ponder, a system administrator can define the following access control policies:

- *Authorization policy:* Defining what activities a subject can perform on an object.
- *Delegation policies:* Permitting an authorized subject to delegate some of his or her authorities to other subjects.
- *Information-filtering policies:* Defining filters on the result of performed actions.
- *Refrain policies:* Defining actions that a subject must refrain from performing, even though he or she might be allowed to do so.

In addition to policies, Ponder allows for the definition of roles with certain policies, which allows for easy management. A similar access

control model and specification language is the XML Access Control Language (XACL) (Kudo & Hada, 2000) developed by the IBM Tokyo Research Library. Using XACL, a system administrator can write policies that specify who has access to XML documents. Polices can be defined with fine granularity applicable even to single elements within the document. XACL is usually combined with the Security SAML, which allows a business to issue an authentication, authorization, or attribute assertion for consumers or other businesses.

Interestingly, while a policy-based approach makes it possible to specify and manage privacy aspects of system operation, there is a challenge in implementing the actual controls within or around the objects. Consider the principle of Limiting Collection. This principle may be readily expressed as obligation policies. Unfortunately, in implementation, limiting the extent of collection of personal information is difficult, if not impossible. For instance, an organization may specify that it will collect names of students strictly for the purpose of managing record keeping during course execution. Yet it is difficult to imagine a system that would prevent collection of other information regarding the students' behavior during course execution, or the data mining of other information sources for further information about the user for any purpose the organization chooses. Indeed, especially for the principles of Limiting Collection and Limiting Use, rather than automated means of compliance, trust and audit approaches are the most obvious recourse.

P3P

P3P enables Web sites to express their privacy policies in a standard format that can be automatically retrieved and interpreted by software acting on behalf of or under the control of a user (i.e., a user agent). P3P defines a machine-readable format (XML) for data collection practices, such as listed:

- What information does the Web site gather and for what purpose?
- How can the user gain access to the information related to his or her privacy?
- How long is this information kept?
- Is this information revealed to other companies, and if so, for what purpose?

A user usually applies the P3P exchange language (APPEL) to express preferences (rules) over the P3P policies. Based on these preferences, a user agent can make automated or semi-automated decisions regarding the acceptability of machine-readable privacy policies from P3P-enabled Web sites. This allows P3P-enabled client software or user agents to retrieve Web site privacy policies and to compare them against the user's privacy preferences. If the user's privacy preferences are satisfied by the privacy policy of the Web site, then the user may proceed with the service; otherwise, the user might be warned that the Web site does not conform to his or her privacy preferences.

Negotiation of Privacy Policy

In policy-based privacy and trust management, policies must reflect the wishes of the distance-learning consumer as well as the distance-learning provider. Yee and Korba (2003) described an agent-based approach for the negotiation of privacy policies between a distance-learning consumer and a distance-learning provider [Yee and Korba (2003-1) present the approach for any e-service]. They examined negotiation under certainty and uncertainty (where the offers and counteroffers are known or unknown, respectively) and proposed a scheme for resolving the uncertainty using the experience of others who have undergone similar negotiation. The choice of whom to call upon for negotiation experience is resolved through the identification of common interest and reputation.

In this work, fixed nonautonomous user agents act on behalf of the learner. Similar provider agents act on behalf of the provider. The learner and the provider each must provide negotiation input to their respective agents. These agents facilitate the negotiation process through (a) conducting timely presentation and edit of the separate privacy policies, (b) providing access to reputations and negotiation experience, and (c) carrying out communications with the other party's agent. The decision to employ nonautonomous agents is justified by the fact that privacy is an inexact concept that depends on many factors, including culture and education level, so that it would be extremely difficult to build an autonomous agent that learners would trust to carry out privacy negotiations.

The scheme proposed for a negotiator to resolve negotiation uncertainty using the experience of others is summarized as follows:

Given: Stored negotiation experience of others (a data structure for this experience was given previously in this paper); stored reputation for the owners of the negotiation experience (a method to calculate the reputation from past transactions is given in this paper)

Perform the following steps in order:
1. Identify which parties are reputable by asking a reputation agent for parties with reputations that exceed a predetermined threshold. Call the resulting set *A*.
2. Among the parties in *A*, identify parties those that have the same interest as the negotiator. Call the resulting set *B*.
3. Among the parties in *B*, identify parties that have negotiated the same item as the negotiator is currently negotiating. Call the resulting set *C*.

4. Retrieve the negotiation experience of parties in C, corresponding to the item under negotiation. The negotiator can then use this experience (negotiation alternatives and offers) to resolve his or her uncertainty.

The authors have also implemented a working prototype of privacy policy negotiation that incorporates the above scheme for negotiating in uncertainty.

Trust Mechanisms for ADL

It is easy to imagine that students and teachers, whether young or old, will thrive in a distance-learning environment that provides mutual trust, respect, freedom, as well as individual respect. Trust will be the crucial factor for the success of distance learning. In the following, we investigate what mechanisms can be used to create the trusted interaction between the learner and the provider based on their underlying requirements.

Trust is also an important topic in information security research. It has absorbed many researchers, and series of papers have been published in recent years (Mass, 2001). The most common trust mechanisms are related to digital certificate-based approaches and policy-based trust management systems.

Digital Certificate-Based Mechanisms

Digital certificate-based mechanisms are based on the notion that "certificates represent a trusted party." The key concept behind these mechanisms is the digital certificate. A certification authority issues a digital certificate to identify whether or not a public key truly belongs to the claimed owner. Normally, a certificate consists of a public key, the certificate information, and the digital signature of the certificate authority. The certificate information contains the user's name and other pertinent identification data; the digital signature authenticates the user as the owner of the public key.

The most common approaches in use today are based on X.509/PKIX and PGP.

- *X.509/PKIX* (PKI = Public-Key Infrastructure) defines a framework for the provision of authentication services. This is a hierarchically structured PKI and is spanned by a tree with a Root Certificate Authority (RCA). In this structure, the trust is centered at the root and then transferred hierarchically to all the users in the network via certificate authorities (CA).

- *PGP* (An Open Specification for Pretty Good Privacy) presents a way to digitally sign and encrypt information "objects" without the overhead of a PKI infrastructure. In PGP, anyone can decide who to trust. Unlike X.509/PKIX certificates, which come from a professional CA, PGP implements a mechanism called a "Web of Trust," wherein multiple key holders sign each certificate attesting the validity of the certificate.

In an ADL system, these mechanisms are very useful in order to establish one agent's credentials when doing transactions with another agent on the Internet. The key risk here is that one agent must have confidence and default trust on the authenticity of the public key. There are still, however, many uncertainties that challenge certificate-based mechanisms (Ellison & Schneier, 2000). For example, why and how can one agent trust a PKI vendor? There are also questions related to a vendor's authentication rules before issuing a certificate to an agent. In practice, this kind of mechanism needs to be adjusted to offer different types of security and privacy protection depending on the application, for both the learner (agents) side and the service provider (agents) side.

Policy-Based Trust Management Systems

Besides certificate-based trust mechanisms, policy-based trust management systems have the goal of providing standard, general-purpose mechanisms for managing trust. Examples of trust management systems include KeyNote (Blaze, Feigenbaum, Ioannidis, & Keromytis, 1999) and REFEREE (Chu, 1997). Both were designed to be easily integrated into applications.

KeyNote provides a kind of unified approach to specifying and interpreting security policies, credentials, and relationships. There are five key concepts or components in this system:

- *Actions:* The operations with security consequences that are to be controlled by the system
- *Principals:* The entities that can be authorized to perform actions
- *Policies:* The specifications of actions that principals are authorized to perform
- *Credentials:* The vehicles that allow principals to delegate authorization to other principals
- *Compliance Checker:* A service used to determine how an action requested by principals should be handled, given a policy and a set of credentials

REFEREE (Rule-Controlled Environment for Evaluation of Rules and Everything Else) is a trust management system for making access decisions relating to Web documents, developed by Yang-Hua Chu and based on PolicyMaker (Blaze, Feigenbaum, & Lacy, 1996). It uses PICS labels (Resnick & Miller, 1996), which specify some properties of an Internet resource, as the "prototypical credential." It introduces the idea of "programmable credentials" to examine statements made by other credentials and fetch information from the network before making decisions.

These systems have a number of advantages on specifying and controlling authorization, especially where it is advantageous to distribute (rather than centralize) trust policy. Another advantage is that an application can simply ask the compliance checker whether a requested action should be allowed or not. Generally, these mechanisms provide more general solutions to the trust problem than public key certificate mechanisms, and they establish the trust on resource and service provision.

Building trust must be recognized as a key factor in using and developing interactions between agents, thus important for agent-based distance-learning systems and applications. The approaches and technologies we discussed provide trust decision and enforcement mechanisms for interactive distance learning with different foci and advantages. In practice, the certificate-based mechanisms and policy-based mechanisms are to be combined and tailored to provide solutions to fulfill the privacy and security requests from the learner and service provider. There is some research that has appeared in recent years in this regard; for example, Xu & Korba (2002) discussed and presented a trust model for distributed distance learning based on public key cryptography.

Secure Distributed Logs

Secure distributed logs allow a record to be kept of transactions that have taken place between a service user and a service provider. The logs are distributed by virtue of the fact that they may be stored by different applications operating on different computers. And, they may be stored within or managed by different agents within an ADL environment. Details of transaction including the times of their occurrences would be "logged" and the resulting record secured using cryptographic techniques, to provide assurance that any modification, deletion, or insertion would be detectable. For distance learning, the use of secure distributed logs has important implications for privacy. In fact they support the Privacy Principles of (1) Accountability, (5) Limiting Use, Disclosure, and Retention, and (10) Challenging Compliance. In the case of Principles (1) and (5), the existence of a secured record of transactions allows verification that conformance to each principle has been maintained. In the case of Principle (10), the existence of a record assists in challenging compliance by showing where compliance has wavered.

Pseudonym Systems

Pseudonym systems were introduced by Chaum in 1985 (Chaum, 1985) as a way of allowing a user to interact with multiple organizations anonymously. The primary goal of pseudonym systems is to hide the user's identity. Of course, a good pseudonym system can also authenticate users; control abuse by intruders, users, services, or applications; provide accountability measures for users; etc.

In pseudonym systems, each organization may know a user by the different aliases, but these aliases cannot be linked to the true identity of the user, i.e., two organizations cannot easily combine their databases to build a dossier on the user. The pseudonyms are formed in such a way that the user can prove a statement known as a private credential to an organization. Private credentials indicate a relationship with another party. The user can obtain the credential from one organization using one of his pseudonyms and demonstrate possession of the credential to another organization, without revealing his first pseudonym to the second organization.

In the literature (Lysyanskaya et al., 1999; Chaum, 1986; Chaum, 1985; Private Credentials, 2000; Samuels et al., 2000; Chen, 1995), several models for pseudonym systems are proposed and developed. In these models, a certificate authority (CA) is needed only to enable a user to prove to an organization that his pseudonym actually corresponds to a public key of a real user. As

well, there must be some stake in the secrecy of the corresponding secret key, such that the user can only share a private credential issued to that pseudonym by sharing his secret key. As long as the CA does not refuse service, a cheating CA cannot harm the system except by introducing some invalid users into the system.

In pseudonym systems, each user must first register with the CA, revealing the user's true identity and public key, as well as demonstrating possession of the corresponding secret key, i.e., the user gets a public key identity certificate from the CA. After registration, the user contacts an organization, and together, they compute a pseudonym for the user. The user then may open accounts with many different organizations using different, unlinkable pseudonyms. However, all pseudonyms are related to each other, i.e., there exists an identity extractor that can compute a user's public and secret keys.

An organization may issue a private credential to a user known by a pseudonym. A private credential may be single use or multiple use, and may also have an expiration date. Single-use private credentials are similar to e-cash, in that they can only be used once in an anonymous transaction. Some e-cash protocols protect against double spending by violating the anonymity of double spenders, but generally, they do not protect against transfer of the e-cash. A private credential should be usable only by the user to whom it was issued.

The private credential has the following properties (Private Credentials, 2000):

- *Anonymity:* Anonymity is the state of being unidentifiable within a subject set, the anonymity set based on the definition of Pfitzmann et al. (2000). It serves as the base case for privacy protection.
- *Control:* Full anonymity may not be beneficial to anyone, especially in the situation that at least one of the parties in a transaction has a legitimate need to verify previous

contacts, the affiliation and eligibility of the other party, the authenticity of personal data of the other party, and so on.

- *Credential Sharing Implies Secret Key Sharing:* The users who have valid credentials might want to help their friends to obtain whatever privileges the credential brings improperly. They could do so by revealing their secret keys to their friends such that their friends could successfully impersonate them in all regards.

- *Unlinkability of Pseudonyms:* This means that within the system, these pseudonyms are no more and no less related than they are related concerning the a priori knowledge. Without unlinkability, all of an individual's past and future transactions become traceable as soon as the individual is identified in a single one of these instances.

- *Unforgeability of Credentials:* A credential may not be issued to a user without the organization's cooperation.

- *Selective Disclosure:* The holder of private credentials can show the private credentials' attributes without revealing any other information about the private credentials.

- *Re-Issuance:* This means that the CA can refresh a previously issued private credential without knowing the attributes it contains. The attributes can even be updated before the private credential is recertified.

- *Dossier-Resistance:* A private credential can be presented to an organization in such a way that the organization is left with no mathematical evidence of the transaction. This is like waving a passport when passing customs. Alternatively, a private credential can be shown in such a way that the verifier is left with self-authenticating evidence of a message or a part of the disclosed property.

- *Pseudonym as a Public Key for Signatures and Encryption:* Additionally, there is an optional feature of a pseudonym system: the ability to sign with one's pseudonym, as well as encrypt and decrypt messages.

Privacy protection requires that each individual have the power to decide how his or her personal data are collected and used, how they are modified, and to what extent the data can be linked; only in this way can individuals remain in control over their personal data. When using private credentials, organizations cannot learn more about a private credential holder than what he or she voluntarily discloses, even if they conspire and have access to unlimited computing resources. Individuals can ensure the validity, timeliness, and relevance of their data.

Private credentials are beneficial in any authentication-based environment in which there is no strict need to identify individuals at each and every occasion. Private credentials do more than protect privacy: they minimize the risk of identity fraud. More generally, private credentials are not complementary to identity certificates but encompass them as a special case. Thus, pseudonym systems can subsume systems based on identity certificates.

Pseudonym systems are very useful, especially in electronic commerce environments, including agent-supported distributed-learning environments. The reason is that the accountability and anonymity are essential properties for fair exchange in e-commerce transactions. Clearly, anonymity is intended to hide a user's identity, whereas accountability is intended to expose the user's identity, thereby holding the user responsible for his or her activities. The pseudonym system is an effective solution for that. In fact, e-commerce systems implementing an effective pseudonym framework do not require further measures to meet the legislative requirements for privacy in many countries.

Pseudonym techniques can be implemented using proxies or sets of agents, etc. Actually, the Janus Personalized Web Anonymizer and the Identity Protector of the Privacy Incorporate Software Agent project (PISA, 2001; Borking et al., 1999) are all pseudonym techniques. These approaches could be applied to agent-supported distributed-learning environments to provide pseudonymity.

However, private credentials alone do not protect against wiretapping and traffic analysis. On networks such as the Internet, one can transmit from a computer that is part of a network located behind a firewall and deploy the pseudonymous services such as MIX network or Onion Routing network.

Network Privacy

The Internet is designed to allow computers to interconnect easily and to assure that network connections will be maintained even when various links may be damaged. This same versatility makes it easy to compromise data privacy in networked applications. Recently, traffic analyses have become significant threats to personal data on the Internet. For instance, networks may be sniffed for unencrypted packets, threatening the confidentiality of data. Research and development, however, have led to techniques that provide varying levels of private communication between parties. In this section, we concisely describe some of the more commonly known network privacy technologies: anonymous communication networks.

The primary goal of an anonymous communication network is to protect user communication against traffic analysis. Simon (1996) proposed a formal model for an anonymous communication network. It is assumed that parties can communicate anonymously. In the simplest of such models, parties can send individual messages to one another anonymously. A stronger assumption is that parties receiving anonymous messages can also reply to them. An intermediate model allows one or more parties to broadcast messages efficiently and thus to reply to anonymous ones without jeopardizing that anonymity. However, Simon's model assumes that reliable, synchronous communication is possible. While this simplifying assumption may be unrealistic, it is not actually exploited in his proposed protocol. Rather, the assumption of synchrony serves to discretize time, abstracting the issue of communications delays without preventing adversaries from taking advantage of them, because messages arriving during the same time period are queued in arbitrary order, to make it appear as though any one of them might have arrived first.

Anonymous communication has been studied fairly extensively. For example, in order to enable unobservable communication between users of the Internet, Chaum (1981) introduced MIX networks in 1981. A MIX network consists of a set of MIX nodes. A MIX node is a processor that accepts a number of messages as input, changes their appearance and timing using some cryptographic transformation, and outputs a randomly permuted list of function evaluations of the input items, without revealing the relationship between input and output elements. MIXes can be used to prevent traffic analysis in roughly the following manner:

1. The message will be sent through a series of MIX nodes, say i_1, i_2, ..., i_d. The user encrypts the message with an encryption key for MIX node i_d, encrypts the result with the key from MIX node i_{d-1}, and so on with the remaining keys.
2. The MIX nodes receive a certain number of these messages, which they decrypt, randomly reorder, and send to the next MIX node in the routes.

Based on Chaum's MIX networks, Wei Dai described a theoretical architecture that would provide protection against traffic analysis based on a distributed system of anonymizing packet forwarders. The architecture is called Pipenet (Dai, 2000). Pipenet consists of a cloud of packet forwarding nodes distributed around the Internet; packets from a client would be encrypted multiple times and flow through a chain of these nodes. Pipenet is an idealized architecture and has never been built. Pipenet's serious disadvantage is that its packet loss or delay would be extremely bad.

Like the Pipenet architecture, the Onion Routing network (Goldschlag et al., 1996, 1999) has been proposed and implemented in various forms. It provides a more mature approach for protection of user anonymity against traffic analysis. The primary goal of Onion Routing is to provide strongly private communications in real time over a public network at reasonable cost and efficiency. In Onion Routing, instead of making socket connections directly to a responding machine, initiating applications make connections through a sequence of machines called onion routers. The onion routing network allows the connection between the initiator and responder to remain anonymous. These connections are called anonymous socket connections or anonymous connections. Onion Routing builds anonymous connections within a network of onion routers, which are, roughly, real-time Chaum MIXes. While Chaum's MIXes could store messages for an indefinite amount of time while waiting to receive an adequate number of messages to mix together, a Core Onion Router is designed to pass information in real time, which limits mixing and potentially weakens the protection. Large volumes of traffic can improve the protection of real-time MIXes. Thus, with Onion Routing, a user directs his or her applications to contact application proxies that form the entrance to the cloud of nodes. The application proxy will then send an onion packet through a string of Onion Routers in order to create a route through the cloud. The application proxy will then forward the application data along this route through the

cloud, to exit on the other side, and be delivered to the responder the user wishes to connect.

The Freedom network (Back et al., 2001; Boucher et al., 2000) was an anonymity network implemented on a worldwide scale and in use as a commercial privacy service from early 1999 to October 2001. It was composed of a set of nodes called Anonymous Internet Proxies (AIP) that ran on top of the existing Internet. It not only used layers of encryption, similar to the MIX network and Onion Routing, but it also allowed users to engage in a wide variety of pseudonymous activities, such as multiple pseudonyms, hiding the users' real IP address, e-mail anonymity, and other identifying information, etc. A key difference between the Freedom Network and Onion Routing is that the last node replaces the missing IP source address, which was removed by the sender, with a special IP address called the wormhole IP address.

As a lighter-weight alternative to MIXes, Reiter and Rubin proposed Crowds system (Reiter et al., 1998, 1999) in 1998. The goal of the Crowds system is to make browsing anonymous, so that information about either the user or what information the user retrieves is hidden from Web servers and other parties. The Crowds system can be seen as a peer-to-peer relaying network in which all participants forward messages. The approach is based on the idea of "blending into a crowd," i.e., hiding one's actions within the actions of many others. To execute Web transactions in this model, a user first joins a crowd of other users. The user's initial request to a Web server is first passed to a random member of the crowd. That member can either submit the request directly to the end server or forward it to another randomly chosen member, and in the latter case, the next member independently chooses to forward or submit the request. The messages are forwarded to the final destination with probability p and to some other members with probability $1 - p$. Finally, the request is submitted to the server by a random member, thus preventing the end server from identifying

NEW YORK INSTITUTE OF
TECHNOLOGY

its true initiator. Even crowd members cannot identify the initiator of the request, because the initiator is indistinguishable from a member who simply passed on a request from another. Crowds system can prevent a Web server from learning any potentially identifying information about the user, including the user's IP address or domain name. Crowds also can prevent Web servers from learning a variety of other information, such as the page that referred the user to its site or the user's computing platform.

Recently, Freedman and Morris (Freedman et al., 2002) proposed a peer-to-peer anonymous network called Tarzan. In comparison with the Onion Routing and Freedom network, Tarzan uses the same basic idea to mix traffic but achieves IP-level anonymity by generic and transparent packet forwarding, and also sender anonymity like the Crowds system by its peer-to-peer architecture that removes any notion of an entry point into the anonymizing layer. In Tarzan, the system is designed to involve sequences of MIX relays chosen from a large pool of volunteer participants. All participants are equal peers—i.e., they are all potential originators as well as relayers of traffic. The packets are routed through tunnels involving sequences of Tarzan peers using MIX-style layered encryption. One of the ends of the tunnel is a Tarzan peer running a client application; another is a server-side pseudonymous network address translator to change the private address to a public address.

The above network-based approaches could be used to protect the users' privacy against the traffic analysis attacks and satisfy the requirements of the privacy protection for network transaction in the agent-supported distributed-learning environments. One example is the anonymous communications for mobile agents (Korba et al., 2002) proposed in MATA'02. It may appear that anonymity networks are a dramatic approach to take for a distance-learning environment. Yet consider the growth in the number of companies

providing and taking advantage of outsourced technical training. Companies use this training to retool their workforces for new initiatives. Competitors would gain information regarding the plans of others if they could pinpoint the key people taking courses from distance-learning providers. In this situation, it is easy to see that anonymous networking would be a value-added service that would be provided by the distance-learning service provider.

As a closing remark, threats against these anonymous communication networks have been discussed in the literature (Raymond, 2000; Song et al., 2002). Generally, it is a tough problem to achieve *unconditional* untraceability and anonymity for real-time services on the Internet, especially when we assume a strong attacker model.

Privacy-Enhancing Agent Architecture

Recently there has been some effort expended in the development of privacy-enhancing techniques for agent-based systems. The Privacy Incorporated Software Agent (PISA, 2001) is an EU-funded research project under the fifth EU Framework. Its goal is research and demonstration of intelligent software agent-based techniques to protect users' privacy. Its architecture includes a model and some privacy-supporting measures described as follows.

PISA Model

In order to protect the user's privacy, a PISA agent should have the following features:

- The privacy-enhancing techniques (PET), mechanisms, and interfaces.
- The legal mechanisms to protect personal data according to the Data Directive (the European Community privacy laws).

Figure 3. Structure of PISA agent

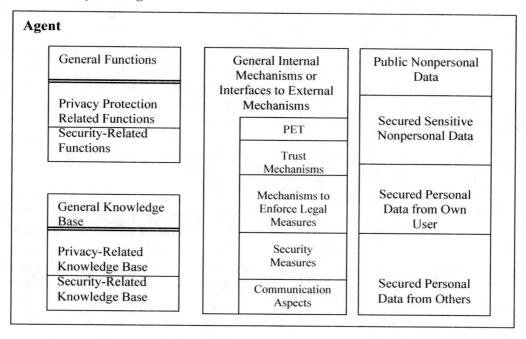

Figure 4. Model of PISA system

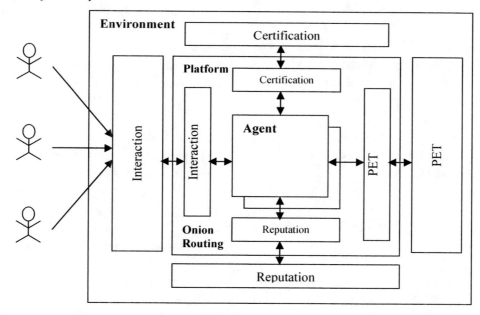

In the PISA system, the structure relationship of the privacy protection-related functions and mechanisms is illustrated in Figure 3.The privacy protection function of PISA consists of several privacy-enhancing technologies, e.g., pseudonyms, identity protectors, anonymous communication networks, trust mechanisms, security environments, etc. Figure 4 depicts the model of PISA in its environment.

Privacy-Supporting Measures

In the PISA system, the following privacy-enhancing technologies are required for building the privacy protection into intelligent software agents:

- *Anonymity versus Pseudonymity:* Anonymity provides better security, but a pseudonym is best for privacy protection and accountability. Also, the pseudonym-based business models are more attractive than anonymity-based ones.
- *Certificates:* The certificate forms the basis of the security solutions, including authentication, secure communication, and data storage, etc.
- *Agent Practices Statement (APS):* The APS describes the privacy policy of the agent.
- *Secure Communications:* The secure communication includes authentication, integrity, and confidentiality of the communication messages.
- *Anonymous Communication:* Anonymous communication provides the privacy protection against the traffic analysis, e.g., Onion Routing.
- *Human Computer Interface:* Its purposes are the usage of information groups and the way the user links his or her personal data with privacy preferences.
- *Deleting and Updating Personal Data:* PISA must be able to view, delete, and update its personal data upon request of the data subject.

Many technical measures may be put in place to protect user privacy. Because the user is ultimately in control of these features, measures to assure that the user understands and trusts that security and privacy measures are operating according to expectations are required.

PROMOTING TRUST IN ADL SYSTEMS

In this section, we focus on how to persuade the individual learner to trust and accept ADL systems and thereby be comfortable using them. We begin by discussing the impact of privacy, security, and trust in the learning process. We follow this by presenting an important component that engenders trust in ADL—the design of trustable user interfaces.

The Impact of Privacy, Security, and Trust on the Learning Process

In the above sections, privacy and security were discussed in terms of legislation, standards, and technology. Yet, the greatest challenge in the adoption of ADL may be learner acceptance of ADL technology. Holt et al. (2001) reported a number of obstacles to e-learning, including learner anxiety and resistance to computers brought about by the concerns for the privacy and security of a learner's data. They indicate that this may potentially lead to other negative implications, including alienation, inadequacy, loss of responsibility, and damage to self-image. Fraser, Holt, and Mackintosh (2000) studied computer-related anxiety and psychological impacts of computers. They identified two trends in e-learning. First, some students were anxious about security, privacy, information overload, lost of data, cost, and keeping up with technology. Second, some anxieties are relatively unrelated—anxiety about privacy and security versus anxiety about keeping up with technology, for example. Holt et al. (2001) further noted that familiarity with a particular issue was generally associated with lower anxiety for that issue and concluded that education may be part of the answer. Holt and Fraser (2003) stated that e-learners might experience "information anxiety" or a feeling of dread when overwhelmed and unable to understand an avalanche of data from diverse sources. Thumlert (1997) suggested that information overload may add to stress and promote faulty thinking.

Hiltz and Turoff (1985) reported some ways of dealing with information overload and improving user acceptance for computer-mediated communication systems (CMCSs). Some of their conclusions apply to e-learning systems as well. They based their conclusions on observations, user surveys, and controlled experiments. We apply some of their conclusions to e-learning as follows:

1. Perceptions of information overload may peak at intermediate levels of use, when communication volume has built up but users have not had a chance to develop information handling skills.
2. Users learn to self-organize communication flows that might initially appear overwhelming. Individuals have different preferences. Instead of imposing a single solution for all, systems should offer options for information handling and organization.
3. User evaluation and feedback are necessary for understanding what kinds of structures or features would be useful for preventing e-learning information overload.
4. Anonymity can improve user acceptance of e-learning systems by allowing users the opportunity to submit their concerns online without revealing their identities. This is analogous to the anonymous office suggestion box.

Friedman et al. (1999) formed a panel, as part of the 1999 ACM SIGCHI Conference on Human Factors in Computing Systems, to discuss the impact of electronic media on trust and accountability. Friedman observed that trust presupposes relationships among persons that must be distinguished from our concepts of technical system reliability. Friedman called for researchers and designers in the CHI community to play a critical role in creating conditions that are favorable to instilling trust in online transactions. These conditions applied to e-learning include ways to help users assess the types and sizes of risks that they are taking in using e-learning systems and, in the absence of face-to-face interactions, facilitate the development of goodwill among users and institutions in the e-learning community.

Holt and Fraser (2003) conducted a survey to more closely examine aspects of information technology that may lead to anxiety in different users. They found that the highest anxiety levels are associated with privacy, security, and loss of data. They also asked their respondents what measures would alleviate anxieties over loss of data, keeping up with software, keeping up with hardware, and so on. The responses indicated that more training, better online tutorials, and better reference materials would lessen the anxiety. These authors then explored the relationship between knowledge about a particular factor and anxiety with that factor. They found that more knowledge led to reductions in anxiety for loss of data, software currency, and hardware currency. However, anxiety about privacy increased with knowledge about privacy issues (sometimes better not to know). Among comments received in the survey on how to reduce anxiety, a repeated suggestion was to optimize the learner's control over software (particular agents) and access to information. The comments also expressed concerns over the security risks in file sharing and the use of video (partially due to performance issues).

As part of future investigation, Holt and Fraser (2003) suggested some possible steps for reducing learner anxiety over security and privacy. First, with the increasing power of the learner's computer, one can put more functionality and information under the learner's control to satisfy the learner's need for enhanced privacy and sense of control and security. Second, the student model (for e-learning) would be accessible for student inspection and reside primarily on the local computer, although this might contribute to information overload. Third, the learner would be the owner of all software agents that are directly involved in the e-learning process. Although these suggestions may seem to be reasonable, we need to be cautious and refer to the second and third points stated above by Hiltz and Turoff (1985). Not all users are the same, and some users may not want to have such control. Obtaining user feedback on the proposed measures would be of paramount importance.

Design of Trustable User Interfaces for ADL

Users and Their Agents

ADL services have the potential to be very valuable to learners. Software agents in an education situation can aid information exchange; monitor learner progress and performance; support decision making; and provide a convenient interface to a rich, complex set of information. In addition, agents can provide privacy protection if the agents operate on behalf of their users in an anonymous or pseudonymous fashion. Agent systems introduce some new human-factor concerns, however, that must be addressed before the systems will be usable and accepted. Not only will an agent system have to be "trustworthy," meaning to operate correctly and reliably, but it will also have to be "trustable," meaning to be *perceived* as trustworthy, usable, and acceptable to the user. This section examines the human side of trust and reviews what is necessary to make agent systems trustable.

Introducing agents into a learning environment creates a new level of indirection. That is, when using agents to perform a task, there is an indirect relationship between the users (e.g., learners or teachers) and the tasks or information with which they are working. Instead of manipulating the information directly, the user delegates this task to an agent, who reports back when the work is done. This indirection can make users less trusting and more risk averse than other nonagent services. Thus, the design of trustable systems is even more important when agents are used, and research recently conducted in our lab has looked at design factors that can address these concerns.

Increasing Trust and Reducing Risk

The issue of building trust when users are interacting with technical systems has most often been studied in the context of e-commerce transactions and was recently extended to agent scenarios (Patrick, 2002). When purchasing items over the Web, for example, users must make decisions about the trustability of the vendor and the technology with which they are interacting. A number of factors seem to be important in influencing those trust decisions. One of the most important factors for building feelings of trust is the visual design of the interface. Users often make rapid trust decisions based on a shallow analysis of the appearance of a WWW site, for example (Fogg et al., 2002). A visual appearance that is clean, uses pleasing colors and graphics, is symmetrical, and is professional looking is usually rated as more trustable. Other design factors that can build trust are the amount of information provided to the user, such as the information on how a system operates and the status of any processing. This transparency of operations can be particularly important for agent systems, where users have given up direct observability and control. Predictable performance can also be an important factor, with systems that respond rapidly and consistently, instilling higher levels of trust.

Research on human decision making has shown that people assess both the trustability and the risk of a particular situation, and then weigh the two against each other to decide on an action (e.g., Grandison & Soloman, 2000; Lee, Kim, & Moon, 2000; Rotter, 1980). Trustability can be low, for example, if the perceived risk is also relatively low. On the other hand, a system might need to be very trustable if the perceived risk is very high. For agent systems, one of the key factors that contributes to the assessment of risk is the level of autonomy granted to the agent (Lieberman, 2002). If the agent is empowered to take significant actions on behalf of the user, this will obviously be seen as a riskier situation that will require higher levels of trust than situations where an agent merely provides information or advice. Another risk factor is the number of alternatives available to the user. For example, a service available only from one vendor or via one interaction technique (e.g., no telephone or postal address provided) will often be considered by a user to be a higher-risk transaction.

Trust and risk assessments are not made in isolation. Instead, the *context* plays a role, where context can include the environment, conditions, and background in which the assessment is made (e.g., Dey & Abowd, 2000). In understanding context, a useful distinction can be made between *internal* and *external* context, where internal context is set by the thoughts and opinions of an individual, while external context is set by the physical environment. The internal context for building trustable agents includes such factors as a user's general ability to trust. For example, research has demonstrated that some users have a higher baseline willingness to trust, and this influences their trustability assessments in specific situations (e.g., Cranor et al., 1999; Rotter, 1980). In a parallel fashion, users also have a baseline risk perception bias, where different users can assess the same situation as more or less risky. Another internal context factor is experience. Individual users will have had different experiences, and these will affect the trust and risk assessments that they make. In addition, these experiences may be direct or indirect, with the latter including reports or reputations about a service or vendor. Other internal contextual factors are the cultures or groups that the users belong to. Different groups may have different expectations or requirements in the areas of trust and risk, and these will have to be taken into account.

The most important external context factor for ADL services is the *activity* being performed by the user. If an activity is casual, such as reading course material or doing background research, users will likely make different trustability decisions than if they were working on an activity that was important to them, such as taking an exam. Another important contextual factor is the amount of personal information that is involved in the activity. An electronic transaction that involves a student's marks, for example, includes personal and sensitive information so that the student and instructor may require higher levels of trust and lower degrees of risk before they are comfortable with such a service.

Building Usable Privacy Protection

It is not enough to increase feelings of trust and reduce perceptions of risk. Service designers must also ensure that their systems are usable and effective. Building usable privacy systems involves supporting specific activities or experiences of the potential users. These users' needs have recently been summarized into four categories: comprehension, consciousness, control, and consent (Patrick & Kenny, 2003).

Comprehension refers to the user understanding the nature of private information, the risks inherent in sharing such information, and how their private information is handled by various parties. Design factors that can support comprehension include training, documentation, help messages, and tutorial materials. Designers can also use familiar metaphors or mental models so that users can draw on related knowledge to aid understanding. The layout of the interface can also support comprehension, such as when a left-to-right arrangement is used to convey the correct order of sequential operations.

Consciousness refers to the user being aware of, and paying attention to, some aspect or feature at the desired time. Design techniques that support consciousness include alarms, alert messages, and pop-up windows. Interface assistants, such as the animated help character in Microsoft Office, are also attempts to make users aware of important information at the time it is needed. Users can also be reminded of some features of function by the strategic placement of a control element on an interface screen, as is seen when similar functions are arranged together. Other methods to draw users' attention to something can include changing the appearance, either by using a new color or font or by introducing animation or movement. Sound is also a powerful technique to make the user pay attention to a particular activity or event. Privacy-aware designers should use these techniques to ensure that the users are aware of the privacy features of a system, and that they are paying attention to all the relevant information when they perform a privacy-sensitive operation.

Control means the ability to perform a behavior necessary to use the interface. Supporting control means building interfaces that are obvious and easy to use. Door handles that reflect the behavior that is required, such as push plates for doors that open outwards and metal loops for doors that open inwards, are good examples of obvious controls. Another useful technique is mapping, where the display or arrangement of the controls is somehow related to the real-world objects they manipulate. This might be seen, for example, when light switches are arranged on a wall in a pattern that reflects how the light fixtures are installed on the ceiling. In the privacy domain, the concept of control is important for ensuring that users actually have the ability to manipulate their private information and their privacy preferences. Thus, a good interface design for an ADL system might include easy-to-use controls for monitoring a student's progress or viewing a teacher's course notes.

Consent refers to users agreeing to some service or action. It is most common that there is a requirement for *informed consent*, which means that the user fully understands all the information relevant to making the agreement. Supporting informed consent implies supporting the comprehension and conscious factors listed above, because the users must both understand and be aware of the relevant information when the agreement is made. In the privacy domain, consent to the processing of personal information is often obtained when a user enrolls for a service. At that time, users are often presented with a large, legally worded user agreement that specifies how their personal information will be handled. It is well known that users often ignore these agreement documents and proceed to using the service without considering or understanding the privacy implications. This is not what is meant by informed consent, and in our laboratory, we are experimenting with interface designs that allow users to make informed decisions in the appropriate context.

In summary, much is known about building trustable user interfaces, and this knowledge can be applied to agent-supported distributed-learning environments. Interface design techniques, properly used, can increase users' feelings of trust and reduce their perceptions of risk. In addition, paying attention to users' privacy needs in the areas of comprehension, consciousness, control, and consent, and ensuring these needs are satisfied by the service, will be an important step for building an environment that is usable and trusted.

CONCLUSIONS AND FURTHER RESEARCH

Within this chapter, we have described many aspects associated with building privacy into agent-supported distributed learning. We describe how the LTSA model may be applied to ADL environments. Probing deeper into privacy requirements, we started with the privacy principles to interpret the technologies that may be applied to ADL to provide privacy. Trust and policy systems, policy negotiation, ways of reducing learner anxiety, trustable human–computer interfaces, secure distributed logging, anonymity systems, and network confidentiality approaches can all play a role in meeting privacy requirements in ADL implementations. We also present a privacy architecture for agent-based e-commerce that may be applied to ADL. However, it is clear that not all of these technologies would be required for every learning environment. For instance, an agent-based learning environment designed for delivering most undergraduate university or community college courses would probably not require network confidentiality or pseudonyms. On the other hand, such privacy features would be highly advantageous for e-learning environments meeting training objectives that target important new corporate strategic directions. For instance, key research staff may undertake specialized technical training closely aligned with corporate strategy. Corporations would want an e-learning service that provides a high level of confidentiality and privacy as would be provided by integrating the technologies described in this chapter. Indeed, such security technologies could be adapted for other e-business areas such as healthcare, manufacturing, business-to-business commerce, as well as general e-commerce applications.

ENDNOTES

[1] NRC Document Number: NRC 46505

REFERENCES

Advanced Distributed Learning. Retrieved March 3, 2003 from the World Wide Web: http://www.adlnet.org

Alliance of Remote Instructional Authoring and Distribution Networks for Europe. Retrieved March 3, 2003 from the World Wide Web: http://www.ariadne-eu.org

Aviation Industry CBT Committee. Retrieved March 3, 2002 from the World Wide Web: http://aicc.org

Back, A., Goldberg, I., & Shostack, A. (2001, May). Freedom 2.1. Security issues and analysis.

Bellotti, V., & Sellen, A. (1993). Designing for privacy in ubiquitous computing environments. In *Proceedings of European Conference on Computer-Supported Cooperative Work, ECSCW '93*. Milan, Italy.

Blaze, M., Feigenbaum, J., & Lacy, J. (1996). Decentralized trust management. In *Proceedings of the 17th IEEE Symposium on Security and Privacy* (pp. 164–173), IEEE Computer Society.

Blaze, M., Feigenbaum, J., Ioannidis, J., & Keromytis, A. D. (1999). The KeyNote Trust-Management System Version 2, *Request For Comments (RFC) 2704*. Retrieved February 22, 2002 from the World Wide Web: http://www.ietf.org/rfc/rfc2704.txt?number=2704

Borking, J. J., Eck, B. M. A., & Siepel, P. (1999). Intelligent software agents and privacy. Registratiekamer, The Hague, Achtergrondstudies en Verkenningen 13.

Boucher, P., Shostack, A., & Goldberg, I. (2000). Freedom Systems 2.0.

Chaum, D. (1981). Untraceable electronic mail, return address, and digital pseudonyms. *Communications of the ACM, 24*(2), 84–88.

Chaum, D. (1985). Security without identification: Transaction systems to make big brother obsolete. *Communication of the ACM, 28*(10), 1030–1044.

Chaum, D., & Evertse, J. (1986). A secure and privacy-protecting protocol for transmitting personal information between organizations. In *Advances in Cryptology—CRYPTO'86, LNCS 0263* (pp. 118–167). Heidelberg: Springer-Verlag.

Chen, L. (1995). Access with pseudonyms. In E. Dawson, & J. Golic (Eds.), Cryptography: *Policy and algorithms—Lecture Notes in Computer Science* (Vol. 1029) (pp. 232–243). Heidelberg: Springer-Verlag.

Chu, Y. (1997). *REFEREE: Trust management for Web applications.* Retrieved April 1, 2002 from the World Wide Web: http://www.w3.org/PICS/Trust-Mgt/presentation/97-04-08-referee-www6/

Cranor, L. F., Reagle, J., & Ackerman, M. S. (1999). *Beyond concern: Understanding net users' attitudes about online privacy.* AT&T Labs—Research Technical Report TR 99.4.3; http://www.research.att.com/library/trs/TRs/99/99.4/

Cristea, A. I., & Okamoto, T. (2000). Student model-based, agent-managed, adaptive distance learning environment for academic English teaching. In *Proceedings, International Workshop on Advanced Learning Technologies (IWALT 2000).*

CSA 1 Canadian Standards Association Ten Privacy Principles. Available at http://www.csa.ca/standards/privacy/code/Default.asp?language=English

Dai, W. (2000). Pipenet 1.1. Available at http://www.eskimo.com/~weidai/pipenet.txt

Damianou, N., Dulay, N., Lupu, E., & Sloman, M. (2001). The Ponder Specification Language. *Workshop on Policies for Distributed Systems and Networks (Policy2001).* HP Labs Bristol.

Department of Justice. *Privacy provisions highlights.* Retrieved April 4, 2002 from the World Wide Web: http://canada.justice.gc.ca/en/news/nr/1998/attback2.html

Dey, A. K., & Abowd, G. D. (2000). Towards a better understanding of context and context-awareness. *CHI 2000, Workshop on the What, Who, Where and How of Context Awareness.* ftp://ftp.cc.gatech.edu/pub/gvu/tr/1999/99-22.pdf

Dulay, N., Lupu, E., Sloman, M., & Damianou, N. (2001). A policy deployment model for the Ponder Language. An extended version of the paper in *Proceedings of the IEEE/IFIP International Symposium on Integrated Network Management (IM 2001).* Seattle. IEEE Press.

El-Khatib, K., Korba, L., Xu, Y., & Yee, G. (2003). Privacy and security in e-learning. *International Journal of Distance Education Technologies, 1*(4), October–December.

Ellison, C., & Schneier, B. (2000). Ten risks of PKI: What you're not being told about Public Key Infrastructure. *Computer Security Journal, XVI*(1).

Fogg, B. J., Marable, L., Stanford, J., & Tauber, E. R. (2002). How do people evaluate a web site's credibility? Results from a large study. *Consumer Webwatch News*. Retrieved from the World Wide Web: http://www.consumerwebwatch.org/news/report3_credibilityresearch/stanfordPTL_TOC.htm

Fraser, J. H., Holt, P., & Mackintosh, J. (2000). Health issues in human–computer interactions in electronic learning environments. *EdMedia2000 Conference*, Montreal, Quebec.

Freedman, M. J., & Morris, R. (2002, November). Tarzan: A peer-to-peer anonymizing network layer. In *Proceedings of the ninth ACM Conference on Computer and Communications Security (CCS'02)* (pp. 193–206).

Friedman, B., Thomas, J. C., Grudin, J., Nass, C., Nissenbaum, H., Schlager, M., & Schneiderman, B. (1999). Trust me, I'm accountable: Trust and accountability online. In *CHI'99 Extended Abstracts on Human Factors in Computer Systems*, Panel Session (pp. 79–80). New York: ACM Press.

Goldschlag, D., Reed, M., & Syverson, P. (1999). Onion Routing for anonymous and private Internet connections. *Communications of the ACM, 42*(2), 39–41.

Goldschlag, D., Reed, M., & Syverson, P. (1996). Hiding routing information. In R. Anderson (Ed.), *Information hiding: First International Workshop, LNCS 1174* (pp. 137–150). Heidelberg: Springer-Verlag.

Grandison, T., & Sloman, M. (2000). A survey of trust in Internet applications. *IEEE Communications Surveys, Fourth Quarter 2000*; http://www.comsoc.org/livepubs/surveys/public/2000/dec/grandison.html

Hiltz, S. R., & Turoff, M. (1985). Structuring computer-mediated communication systems to avoid information overload. *Communications of the ACM, 28*(7), July.

Hodgins, H. W. (2000). *Into the future: A vision paper, Commission on Technology & Adult Learning*. Retrieved April 1, 2002 from the World Wide Web: http://www.learnativity.com/download/MP7.PDF

Holt, P., & Fraser, J. (2003). Anxiety and design issues for e-learning. In *Proceedings of Ed-Media 2003*, Honolulu, Hawaii.

Holt, P., Abaza, M., Brehaut, W., Lin, O., Jelica, G., Stauffer, K., Leung, S., Shata, O., & Wang, H. (2001). Towards a multimedia distributed learning environment. In *Proceedings of the Seventh International Conference on Distributed Multimedia Systems (DMS 01)* (pp. 32–41).

IEEE Learning Technology Standards Committee (LTSC). Retrieved March 3, 2002 from the World Wide Web: http://ltsc.ieee.org/index.html

IEEE LTSC. (2001). *IEEE P1484.1/D9 Draft standard for learning technology—Learning technology systems architecture (LTSA)*. Retrieved March 3, 2002 from the World Wide Web: http://ltsc.ieee.org/doc/wg1/IEEE_1484_01_D09_LTSA.pdf

IEEE P1484.2. (2000). Retrieved March 3, 2002 from the World Wide Web: http://ltsc.ieee.org/wg2/papi_learner_07_main.pdf

IMS Global Learning Consortium. (2001). *Final specification of IMS Learner Information Package Information Model*, Version 1.0. Retrieved March 3, 2002 from the World Wide Web: http://imsproject.org

IMS Global Learning Consortium. March 3, 2002: http://imsproject.org

Korba, L. (2002). Privacy in distributed electronic commerce. *Proceedings of the 35th Hawaii International Conference on System Science (HICSS)*, Hawaii.

Korba, L., Song, R., & Yee, G. (2002). Anonymous communications for mobile agents. In *Proceedings of the Fourth International Workshop on Mobile Agents for Telecommunication Applications (MATA'02), LNCS 2521* (pp. 171–181). Barcelona, Spain. Oct. 2002. NRC 44948.

Koyama, A., Barolli, L., Tsuda, A., & Cheng, Z. (2001). An agent-based personalized distance learning system. In *Proceedings, 15ᵗʰ International Conference on Information Networking*.

Kudo, M., & Hada, S. (2000). XML document security based on provisional authorization. In *Seventh ACM Conference on Computer and Communication Security (CCS 2000)*.

Langheinrich, M. (2001). Privacy by design—Principles of privacy-aware ubiquitous systems. In *Proceedings of Ubicomp 2001* (pp. 273–291).

Lee, J., Kim, J., & Moon, J. Y. (2000). What makes Internet users visit cyber stores again? Key design factors for customer loyalty. *Proceedings of CHI '2000* (pp. 305–312). The Hague, Amsterdam.

Lieberman, H. (2002). Interfaces that give and take advice. In J. M. Carroll (Ed.), *Human–computer interaction in the new millennium*. New York: ACM Press.

Lysyanskaya, A., Rivest, R., & Sahai, A. (1999). Pseudonym systems. *Selected areas in cryptography: Sixth Annual International Workshop, SAC'99, LNCS 1758* (pp. 184–200). Heidelberg: Springer-Verlag.

An Open Specification for Pretty Good Privacy. Retrieved January 22, 2002 from the World Wide Web: http://www.ietf.org/html.charters/openpgp-charter.html

Patrick, A. S. (2002). Building trustworthy software agents. *IEEE Internet Computing, 6*(6), 46–53.

Patrick, A. S., & Kenny, S. (2003). From privacy legislation to interface design: Implementing information privacy in human-computer interfaces. *Proceedings of Privacy Enhancing Technologies Workshop* (PET2003), Dresden, Germany, March 26-28. LNCS 2760. NRC 45787.

Privacy Technology Review. Retrieved March 3, 2003 from the World Wide Web: http://www.health-canada.ca/ohih-bsi/available/tech/tech_e.html

Public-Key Infrastructure. Retrieved January 22, 2002 from the World Wide Web: http://www.ietf.org/html.charters/pkix-harter.html

P3P: The Platform for Privacy Preferences Project. (2001). In S. Garfinkel, & G. Spafford (Eds.), *Web security, privacy & commerce* (2nd ed.) (pp. 699–707). Sebastopol, CA: O'Reilly & Associates, Inc.

Raymond, J. (2000). Traffic analysis: Protocols, attacks, design issues, and open problems. In H. Federrath (Ed.), Anonymity 2000, Volume 2009 of *Lecture Notes in Computer Science* (pp. 10–29). Heidelberg: Springer-Verlag.

Resnick, P., & Miller, J. (1996). PICS: Internet access controls without censorship. *Communications of the ACM, 39*, 87–93.

Rosié, M., Stankov, S., & Glavinié, V. (2002). Application of Semantic Web and personal agents in distance education system. In *Proceedings, IEEE MELECON 2002,* May 7–9, Cairo, Egypt.

Rotter, J. B. (1980). Interpersonal trust, trustworthiness, and gullibility. *American Psychologist, 35*(1), 1–7.

Samuels, R., & Hawco, E. (2000). Untraceable Nym Creation on the Freedom 2.0 Network. Zero-Knowledge Systems Inc., white paper.

Santos, J. M., & Rodriguez, J. S. (2002). Towards an agent architecture to provide knowledge-based facilities for distance education. *Proceedings, 24ᵗʰ Int. Conf. Information Technology Interfaces (ITI2002)*, June 24–27. Cavtat, Croatia.

Simon, D. R. (1996). Anonymous communication and anonymous cash. In *Advances in cryptology—CRYPTO '96, LNCS 1109* (pp. 61–73). Heidelberg: Springer-Verlag.

Song, R., & Korba, L. (2002). Review of network-based approaches for privacy. *Proceedings of the 14ᵗʰ Annual Canadian Information Technology Security Symposium*, Ottawa, Canada, May. NRC 44905.

Thumlert, K. (1997). *Hypertextuality and socio-cultural contexts for education.* Retrieved April 3, 2003 from the World Wide Web: http://home1.gte.net/grnjeans/htext.htm

Xu, Y., & Korba, L. (2002). A trust model for distributed e-learning service control. In *Proceeding of the World Conference on E-Learning in Corporate, Government, Healthcare & Higher Education (E-Learn2002)*, Montreal, Canada, Oct. 15–19.

Yee, G., & Korba, L. (2003). The negotiation of privacy policies in distance education. *Proceedings, 14th IRMA International Conference*, Philadelphia, Pennsylvania, May 18–21. NRC Paper Number: NRC 44985.

Yee, G., & Korba, L. (2003-1). Bilateral e-services negotiation under uncertainty. *Proceedings, 2003 Symposium on Applications and the Internet (Saint 2003)*, Orlando, Florida, January 27–31. NRC Paper Number: NRC 44964.

Chapter 4.26
Better Securing an Infrastructure for Telework

Loreen Marie Butcher-Powell
Bloomsburg University, USA

ABSTRACT

The XYZ Hardware Company, Inc. infrastructure features high volumes of sensitive and confidential corporate data relevant to internal and external transactions. From 1999 to the middle of 2004, XYZ has utilized the Operationally Critical Threat, Asset, and Vulnerability Evaluation^{SM} (OCTAVE^{SM}) Model version 1e to protect its network. The OCTAVE^{SM} Model has proven to be helpful for XYZ by identifying over 198 potential security breaches. However, in 2004, when XYZ began to enhance its existing network infrastructure to include telework, 210 security breaches occurred. These breaches cost the company over $350,000 in lost profits between July and December of 2004. To safeguard their network, upper management wanted to invest the money in a series of gener-alized training including working ethics, virus scanning, and backing up files. However, instead, XYZ'S chief information officer (CIO) invested over $100,000 in research in order to modify their existing protection strategy, to better safeguard their new telework infrastructure by identifying its specific strengths and weakness in an effort to create more concentrated and specialized training at the root of the problem.

ORGANIZATIONAL BACKGROUND

XYZ Hardware Company Incorporated (XYZ), located in Pennsylvania, USA, is a wholesale distributor for more than 160 of the best-known hardware product companies including Amerock, Broan, Classic Brass, 3M, Stanley, and Dupont. The company was founded in the early 1950s. The company employs over 430 and is regarded as one of the most technology-oriented companies in its line of business. In 2001, XYZ was awarded a national Cisco Technology Award in recognition of its innovative Internet and corporate network usage supporting internal operations and cus-

Table 1. Activities for Processes 1, 2, and 3

Process	Activity	Description
1, 2, 3	Identify assets and related priorities	Participants (including senior managers, operational area managers and staff members) identify the assets used by the organization via a questionnaire. The participants then select the assets that are most critical to the organization via a questionnaire and discuss their rationale for selecting those assets via a workshop forum (Alberts & Dorofee, 2003).
1, 2, 3	Identify areas of concern	Via a workshop, participants identify scenarios that threaten their most critical assets based on typical sources and outcomes of threats. The participants also discuss, via a workshop, the potential impact of scenarios on the organization (Alberts & Dorofee, 2003).
1, 2, 3	Identify security requirements for critical assets	The participants identify the security requirements for their most critical assets via a workshop. In addition, they examine trade-offs among the requirements and select the most important requirement via a workshop (Alberts & Dorofee, 2003).
1, 2, 3	Capture knowledge of current security practices and organizational vulnerabilities	The participants complete paper questionnaires in which they indicate which practices are currently followed by the organization's personnel and which are not (Alberts & Dorofee, 2003).

tomer relationships. Furthermore, in 2004, XYZ enhanced it network communications to accommodate telework. As a result of telework communications, over 210 security breaches occurred between July and December of 2004. To safeguard their network, XYZ'S Chief Information Officer (CIO) wants to invest over $100,000 in research in order to modify their existing protection strategy, the Operationally Critical Threat, Asset, and Vulnerability Evaluation[SM] (OCTAVE[SM]) Model version 1e along with the OCTAVE[SM] Catalog of Practices, to better safeguard their new telework infrastructure by identifying its specific strengths and weakness in an effort to create more concentrated and specialized training at the root of the problem. Meanwhile, the upper management wants to invest the money in a series of generalized training courses including working ethics, virus scanning, and backing up files.

SETTING THE STAGE

The OCTAVE[SM] Model developed by Carnegie Mellon University (CMU) Software Engineering Institute (SEI) is a repeatable methodological approach for identifying and managing information security risks of actual threats including disclosure of a critical asset, modification of a critical asset, loss or destruction of a critical asset, or interruption of access to a critical asset, via an organizational self-assessment (Alberts & Dorofee, 2003).

The OCTAVE[SM] Model's Catalog of Practices are currently used as a measurement for what XYZ is currently doing well with respect to physical security or current security practices, as well as its organizational vulnerabilities. The OCTAVE[SM] Model's Catalog of Practices comprised a collection of strategic and operational security practices (Allen, 2001; British Standards Institution, 1995;

Gramm-Leach Biley Act of 1999, 2000; Health Insurance Portability and Accountability Act [HIPAA] of 1996, 1998; Swanson & Guttman, 1996). Strategic practices focus on organizational issues at the policy level. Strategic practices included issues that are business-related as well as those that require organization-wide planning and participation (Alberts & Dorofee, 2003). The operational practices focus on technology-related concerns including issues related to how workers interact with and protect technology (Alberts & Dorofee, 2003).

The purpose of the OCTAVE[SM] Model & Catalog of Practices is to create a comprehensive protection strategy that reduces the overall risk of an organization's information assets via the use of a systematic, context-driven approach (Allen, 2001). A risk is defined as a threat that results in a negative impact on an organization through the disclosure of a critical asset, the modification of a critical asset, the loss or destruction of a critical asset, or the interruption of access to a critical asset (Alberts & Dorofee, 2003). The OCTAVE[SM] Model categorizes threats into four groups:

- network-based threats,
- physical threats,
- system threats, and
- other problems.

Network-based threats are deliberate or accidental actions involving an individual using an organization's network access. Physical threats come from the utilization of systems, hardware, software, or information with ill intent. System threats are problems such as viruses, trojan horses, and trap doors within an organization's information systems. Other problems are the result of natural disasters, terrorist threats, or any asset-altering event that is outside an organization's control (Alberts & Dorofee, 2003).

"An asset is defined as something of value to an organization" (Alberts & Dorofee, 2003, p. 103). In general, information technology assets are a combination of systems, software, hardware, information, and people. Systems are combinations of information, software, and hardware that are used to process and store information. Software consists of applications and services such as operating systems, database applications, networking software, office applications, e-mail applications, and security applications that process, store, and transmit information. Hardware is made up of physical devices such as servers, routers, and remote computers. Information consists of electronic and paper data or intellectual properties that are used to meet an organization's mission. People are individuals inside the organization that are difficult to replace because they possess a unique skill such as knowledge or experience (Alberts & Dorofee, 2003).

A systematic, context-driven approach is defined as a consecutive step-by-step methodology that is broken down into phases, processes and activities (Alberts & Dorofee, 2003). The OCTAVE[SM] Model contains the following three phases:

- Build Asset-Based Threat Profiles (Phase 1)
- Identify Infrastructure Vulnerabilities (Phase 2)
- Develop Security Strategies/Plans (Phase 3)

Phase 1: Build Asset-Based Threat Profiles

The goal of Phase 1 is to:

- create an organization-wide listing of information-related assets including systems, software, hardware, information, and people that are used throughout the organization;
- identify current security practices including system updates and usage policies, software policies, and hardware configuration, and

Table 2. Activities for Process 4

Process	Activity	Description
4	Select critical assets	An analysis team consisting of knowledgeable organizational personnel from IT and other departments utilizes the information obtained from the activities in Processes 1, 2, and 3 in order to determine which assets will have a large adverse impact on the organization if their security requirements are violated. Those with the greatest impact to the organization are called critical assets. The analysis team will then select the top five critical assets (Alberts & Dorofee, 2003).
4	Refine security requirements for critical assets	The analysis team creates or refines the security requirements for the organization's top five critical assets. In addition, the team selects the most important security requirement for each of the five critical assets (Alberts & Dorofee, 2003).
4	Identify threats to critical assets	The analysis team identifies the threats to each of the top five critical assets by mapping the areas of concern for each critical asset to a generic threat profile. Then the analysis team performs a gap analysis to determine additional threats to the top five critical assets (Alberts & Dorofee, 2003).

usage policies that are used by the organization; and

* identify organizational vulnerabilities including potential threats that are present in the organization (Alberts & Dorofee, 2003).

To accomplish Phase 1's goal, multiple processes and activities are needed. Phase 1 contains four processes consisting of the following:

* Identify Enterprise Knowledge (Process 1)
* Identify Operational Area Knowledge (Process 2)
* Identify Staff Knowledge (Process 3)
* Establish Security Requirements (Process 4)

Process 1: Identify Enterprise Knowledge

The goal of this process is to identify senior managers' perceptions regarding key assets and their values, threats to key assets, indicators of risk, and current protection strategies employed by the organization through several activities (Alberts & Dorofee, 2003). This process's activities are listed in Table 2.

Process 2: Identify Operational Area Knowledge

The goal of Process 2 is to identify operational managers' perceptions regarding key assets and their values, threats to key assets, indicators of risk, and current protection strategies employed by the organization through various activities (Alberts & Dorofee, 2003). The activities are defined in Table 2.

Process 3: Identify Staff Knowledge

The goal of this process is to identify staff-level employees' perceptions regarding key assets and their values, threats to key assets, indicators of risk, and current protection strategies employed by the organization through multiple activities (Alberts & Dorofee, 2003). The activities are listed in Table 1.

Table 3. Activities for Processes 5 and 6

Process	Activity	Description
5	Identify key classes of components	The analysis team establishes the system(s) of interest for each of the top five critical assets identified in Phase 1. The team then breaks the systems of interest down into classes including servers, desktop components, laptop components, networking devices, security components, and storage devices (Alberts & Dorofee, 2003).
5	Identify infrastructure components to examine	The analysis team selects systems to evaluate. The team selects one or more specific systems of interest from each class to evaluate. In addition, the team also selects an approach and specific tools including network topology diagrams and computer prioritization lists for evaluating vulnerabilities (Alberts & Dorofee, 2003).
6	Review technology vulnerabilities and summarize results	The IT staff members or external experts run vulnerability evaluations via network mapping tools on specific systems of interest. The results of the evaluation are presented for each system of interest to the analysis team. The analysis team reviews and refines the information (Alberts & Dorofee, 2003).

Process 4: Establish Security Requirements

This process integrates the specific organizational perspectives that have been identified in Processes 1, 2, and 3. Its goal is to consolidate the information collected in Processes 1, 2, and 3 in order to produce one organizational view of assets, threats, protection strategies, risk indicators, and security requirements via several activities (Allen, Alberts, Behrens, Laswell, & Wilson, 2000). Table 2 defines Process 4's activities.

Phase 2: Identify Infrastructure Vulnerabilities

The goal of Phase 2 is to build upon Phase 1 by conducting an evaluation of an organization's information infrastructure determining the adequacy of its security measures and identifying its security vulnerabilities. Vulnerabilities are weaknesses in an information system, security

practices and procedures, administrative and internal controls, or physical layout that can be exploited to gain unauthorized access to information or to disrupt information processing (Allen, 2001).

To accomplish the goal of Phase 2, two processes are needed. Phase 2's two processes are:

- Identify Key Components (Process 5)
- Evaluate Selected Components (Process 6)

Process 5: Identify Key Components

The goal of Process 5 is to utilize the critical assets previously identified in Phase 1 to set the scope for an examination of the organization's computer infrastructure via a network topology diagram and computer prioritization lists (Alberts & Dorofee, 2003). Network topology diagrams "are electronic or paper documents that are used to display the logical or physical mapping of

Table 4. Activities for Process 7

Process	Activity	Description
7	Identify the impact of threats to critical assets	The analysis team prepares a narrative that describes how a threat affects the organization (Alberts & Dorofee, 2003).
7	Create risk evaluation criteria	The analysis team creates impact values including high, medium, and low to evaluate the risks to the organization (Alberts & Dorofee, 2003).
7	Evaluate the impact of threats to critical assets	The analysis team reviews each risk and assigns it an impact value (Alberts & Dorofee, 2003).

Table 5. Activities for Process 8

Process	Activity	Description
8	Review risk information	The analysis team reviews the following information obtained throughout the OCTAVE^{SM} Model's Phases: • Threats to critical assets • Areas of concern for the critical assets • Current security practices and organizational vulnerabilities • Potential impacts of threats • Technology vulnerabilities for specific systems of interest • Recommended action resulting from the infrastructure vulnerability evaluation (Alberts & Dorofee, 2003).
8	Create protection strategy	The analysis team creates a proposed protection strategy by defining methods to be deployed for enabling, initiating, implementing, and maintaining security within an organization (Alberts & Dorofee, 2003).
8	Create mitigation plans	The analysis team creates a risk mitigation plan by defining the activities required to lessen the threats to critical assets (Alberts & Dorofee, 2003).
8	Create action lists	The analysis team creates an action list by defining any action that personnel within an organization can make or learn without specialized training or policy changes (Alberts & Dorofee, 2003).

a network" (Alberts & Dorofee, 2003, p. 142). Computer prioritization lists are "records of the computer inventory owned by an organization" (Alberts & Dorofee, 2003, p. 142). Computer prioritization lists are used to verify, prioritize, and examine the physical inventory.

Process 6: Evaluate Selected Components

The goal of Process 6 is to evaluate selected infrastructure components such as servers, workstations, and firewalls by using a technology vulnerability evaluation software tool to perform a vulnerability evaluation (Allen et al., 2000). Process 6 requires all technology vulnerability evaluation tools to be benchmarked against the Common Vulnerabilities and Exposures (CVE) dictionary. CVE is a commonly used dictionary that provides common names for publicly known mapping tools (MITRE Corporation, 2003).

A network mapping tool is "software used to search a network, identify the physical connectivity of systems and networking components" (Alberts & Dorofee, 2003, p. 142). XYZ utilizes Nessus.com (2004) for their free mapping software tool. It has been effective in testing the physical connectivity of firewalls.

To accomplish the goals of Processes 5 and 6 several activities are needed. Table 3 lists and defines each of these activities.

Phase 3: Develop Security Strategies and Plans

The goal of Phase 3 is to utilize the information obtained in Phase 2 to aid in creating a protection strategy and a mitigation plan addressing the risks to critical assets (Alberts, Behrens, Pethia & Wilson, 1999). To accomplish Phase 3's goal, several processes and activities are needed. Phase 3 contains two processes consisting of the following:

- Conduct Risk Analysis (Process 7)
- Develop Protection Strategy (Process 8)

Process 7: Conduct Risk Analysis

The goal of Process 7 is to create a risk profile by identifying the impact of threats to critical assets via a risk evaluation (Allen et al., 2000). A risk profile is created for each important asset by descriptive disclosure, modification, loss, destruction, and interruption of the impact of each outcome (Alberts & Dorofee, 2003).

Process 8: Develop Protection Strategy

The goal of Process 8 is to utilize the information obtained throughout the entire OCTAVE[SM] Model to develop a comprehensive protection strategy for an organization (Alberts & Dorofee, 2001). To accomplish the goals of Processes 7 and 8, several activities must be performed. Table 4 lists and defines each of the activities for Process 7, and Table 5 lists and defines each activity for Process 8.

Effectiveness of the OCTAVE[SM] Model

Each phase of the OCTAVE[SM] Model has generated significant results that were needed to complete the next phase of the model (Alberts et al., 1999). Research by Tremer (2001) illustrated that the OCTAVE[SM] Model was the most effective countermeasure for eliminating external threats, and it should be incorporated into any company's overall security strategy and policy. XYZ agrees with his research because they have also had tremendous success using the OCTAVE[SM] Model to safeguard its original network infrastructure. However, this model has not been effective since XYZ employed a telework infrastructure.

XYZ's Telework Infrastructure

On July 1, 2004 the XYZ began to utilize telework communications to support its sales and marketing staff in geographically dispersed residential locations throughout the East Coast of the United States of America. XYZ's telework communication elements include laptops, the Internet, a Citrix client, a firewall, and various routers which are used to access the XYZ data warehouse server, an AS400, a back office server, and two Citrix servers. XYZ's telework infrastructure is similar to any typical telework infrastructure. For example, each teleworker is provided with a laptop that contains locally installed programs such as Microsoft Office, the XYZ Sales at Work program, Norton AntiVirus protection and an Internet browser. Each laptop uses a Citrix client and Microsoft's Point-to-Point transfer protocol (PPTP) to enable remote access to the corporate network. The Citrix Client is also installed and configured to accept TCP/IP connections on the corporate network as needed.

XYZ's corporate policies do not mandate a specific access method for any teleworker's Internet connection. Therefore, each teleworker is required to obtain an Internet connection for his or her laptop via common public accommodations including a dial-up Internet Service Provider (ISP), a cable modem connection, or a digital subscriber line (DSL).

Once an Internet connection is established, the teleworker executes the Citrix client software installed on his or her laptop to begin the authentication process. The Citrix client software is designed to authenticate a teleworker's laptop through the corporate network security installations. The client contains a designated Internet protocol (IP) address, and a valid logon password needed to establish a peer-to-peer relationship to the XYZ corporate network. The peer-to-peer relationship is established by utilizing client software to connect to the XYZ firewall via tunneling. Tunneling is the encapsulating of the protocol information for the transmission of data via the Internet to a private network. A firewall is a system or collection of systems that enforce an access control policy among networks (Holden, 2004).

XYZ utilizes the Corporate Server 3.0 firewall. This firewall sits between its internal network and the Internet communications environment. The XYZ firewall serves as a gateway, blocking an unauthorized remote user from accessing the corporation's network if the remote user does not have a valid IP address (Herscovitz, 1999). Because the firewall functions on the network and transport layers of the Open Systems Intercon-

nection (OSI) Reference Model, remote users are able to authenticate to the firewall, receive an IP address that is valid for the local subnet, and then authenticate to the XYZ Citrix server as if they were physically connected to the XYZ in-house network. To better understand the connection protocol, a short description of the OSI model is rendered below.

The OSI reference model was created by the International Standards Organization (ISO) to define a set of protocols to support communication between computer systems. It consists of seven layers. Each layer is specified to perform a set of well-defined functions in order to minimize the interaction between layers. Each horizontal layer is defined according to the services it supports, and the layers are arranged vertically with the highest layer of abstraction located at the top and the lowest at the bottom. Table 1, in Appendix A, contains an explanation of the seven layers of the OSI model. Table 2, in Appendix A, contains an explanation of the hybrid OSI/TCP/IP model.

Once authenticated, a browser link interface, similar to the one found on the in-house XYZ workstation desktops, appears on the teleworker's screen. The browser link interface contains shortcuts linking to Microsoft Office Suite, Microsoft Office Outlook, Instant Messenger, access to onsite corporate printers, as well as access to networked drives including the AS400, the data warehouse server, and the back office server. The AS400 contains customer service information including customers' orders, numbers, pricing, and history. The data warehouse server contains a "Sales at Work" program. The "Sales at Work" program is a synchronized teleworker database containing up-to-date information regarding teleworkers' daily sales and associated activities. The back office server contains contingency files and other shared files and resources for use by network users. Additional information regarding the XYZ physical network structure is illustrated in Figure 1 of Appendix B.

CASE DESCRIPTION

From 1999 to mid 2004, XYZ has utilized the OCTAVE^{SM} Model version 1e to protect its network. The OCTAVE^{SM} Model has proven to be helpful for XYZ by identifying over 198 potential security breaches. Additionally, XYZ had only one minor security break-in that was the result of a disgruntled employee.

However, in 2004, XYZ began to enhance their existing network infrastructure to include telework. As a result, 210 security breaches that cost the company over $350,000 in lost profits occurred between July and December of 2004. Upon closer analyses of these security breaches, it was determined that all were caused by teleworker or the teleworker's computer.

Telework refers to an approved working arrangement whereby a teleworker officially performs his/her assigned job tasks on a regular basis in a specified work area including a home, a client's office, a telework center, or on the road (ITAC, 2003). Telework offers substantial savings of physical facility related costs including rent, storage, and electricity. It also enables companies to expand labor pools without geographic restrictions (Hirsch, 2004; Langlois, 2002; Mehlman, 2002; Motskula, 2001). However, with the increased benefits afforded by teleworking, there are increased security risks including viruses and data tampering (Atwood, 2004; Hirsch, 2004; Motskula, 2001; Quirk, 2002; Rubens, 2004). Viruses are malicious programs that are usually transmitted by means of various types of files including executable files. Viruses can shut down a PC and an entire network, delete files, and change files. Data tampering are the threats of data being altered in unauthorized ways, either accidentally or intentionally (Holden, 2004).

Existing research stated that the severities of security threats in a telework infrastructure are often related to the computer literacy of the teleworker accessing the network rather than the actual corporate network (Hirsch, 2004; Langlois, 2002; Mehlman, 2002; Motskula, 2001). For example, a white paper provided by Teleworker.org (2003) suggested that teleworkers using a high speed Internet connection, such as a cable modem or digital subscriber line (DSL), create an even higher security risk for telework infrastructures. Because high speed Internet connections are always connected to the network, this increases the chance of the teleworker's computer being discovered by hackers running automated port scans. An automated port scan consists of an intruder sending a request to a host name or a range of IP addresses followed by a port number to see if any services including file transfer protocol (FTP), telnet and hypertext transfer protocol (HTTP) are listening on that port. Table 6, in Appendix C, contains a list of commonly used ports and their associated services. Automated port scans are typically carried out by hackers trying to gain large amounts of information about a particular network so that an attack can be planned (Holden, 2004).

As described above, the XYZ network allows access and transmission of data across the Internet for electronic usages including electronic mail, database access and manipulation, online order processing, Web browsing, and remote file transfer. Substantial security threats, including viruses and data tampering, have been reported by the XYZ organization as a result of tits telework infrastructure. Telework has made the XYZ network vulnerable to security threats. For example, an outside intruder may find it simpler to attack a less fortified teleworker's laptop that is logged on to the corporation network rather than directly attacking the XYZ network itself (Hirsch, 2002).

Additionally, not all of the XYZ teleworkers' laptops are protected at all times by the corporate network. Consequently, if a teleworker's laptop is not connected to the XYZ network, it could be used for Web surfing, new software programs that are not related to work, old software reconfiguration, opening of e-mail attachments, and downloading of Internet files. Therefore, the laptop is not compliant with the corporate standards, thereby decreasing the effectiveness of any security software and increasing the risk of virus infection.

Problems Facing the Organization

Understanding the security risks of XYZ teleworkers are important in order to secure its telework infrastructure (Hirsch, 2004; Langlois, 2002; Mehlman, 2002; Motskula, 2001). Kadakia (2001) stated that the OCTAVE[SM] Model has proved to be both a balanced technology and a management model that can be formatted for all systems including telework. XYZ believed that modifying the OCTAVE[SM] Model would help predict and eliminate possible telework security risks, aid in construction a descriptive plan for securing a telework infrastructure, and eliminate unnecessary training by focusing on the more important training for teleworkers. In an effort to modify the OCTAVE[SM] Model, XYZ has begun to employ a Dephi process to develop and validate a specific set of criteria necessary for successful inclusion of telework-based activities. The Delphi process has currently aided in the modification of the OCTAVE[SM] Model by involving the teleworker in Phase 1, 2, and 3, cataloging of known XYZ intrusion scenarios since telework (a total of 210 intrusions; 67 intrusions were identified from computer ineffectiveness and 143 intrustions were attributed to teleworker incompetency), and creating a Catalog of Practices for teleworkers.

While modifications to the OCTAVE[SM] Model are still being conducted, preliminary results have indicated that the most important competency that teleworkers should develop is the ability to correctly utilize virus canners and backup procedures on their computer and on the shared network drives ($M = 4.55$, $SD = 0.87$) and correctly learn how to utilize and maintain firewalls ($M = 4.54$, $SD = 0.94$). In addition, the use of spyware and the understanding of operating systems controls ($M = 4.15$, $SD = 1.01$) were considered important skills for teleworkers to possess. It is expected that further outcomes and modifications will result in a better-proposed corporate security plan that will include specifically targeted education and training for teleworkers on a yearly basis.

Was the $100,000 investment in modifying the OCTAVE[SM] Model to include telework worthwhile since the preliminary results yielded the same type of training that upper management suggested in the beginning?

ACKNOWLEDGMENTS

Special permission to use the OCTAVE[SM] Model © 2004 by Carnegie Mellon University, in Nova Southeastern University (Loreen Butcher-Powell) is granted by the Software Engineering Institute.

REFERENCES

Alberts, C., Behrens, S. G., Pethia, R. D., & Wilson, W. R. (1999). *Operationally Critical Threat, Asset, and Vulnerability Evaluation (OCTAVE^SM) Framework, Version 1.0. (CMU/SEI-00-TR-017).* Retrieved April 29, 2006, from http://www.sei.cmu.edu/publications/documents/99.reports/99tr017/99tr017abstract.html

Alberts, C., & Dorofee, A. (2001). *Volume 1: Introduction. OCTAVE method implementation guide V2.0.* Retrieved April 29, 2006, from http://www.cert.org/octave/omig.html

Alberts, C., & Dorofee, A. (2003). *Managing information security risks: The OCTAVE^SM approach.* Upper Saddle River, NJ: Addison-Wesley.

Allen, J. (2001). *The CERT guide to system and network security practices.* Boston: Addison-Wesley.

Allen, J., Alberts, C., Behrens, S., Laswell, B., & Wilson, W. R. (2000). *Improving security of network systems.* Retrieved April 29, 2006, from http://www.stsc.hill.af.mil/crosstalk/2000/oct/allen.asp

Atwood, S. (2004). Data protection: Protecting your remote office data using replication technologies. *Disaster Recovery Journal, 17*(2), 20.

British Standards Institution. (1995). *Information security management, Part 1: Code of practice for information security management of systems BS7799: Part 1.* London: British Standards.

Carlson, P. A. (2000). Information technology and the emergence of a worker-centered organization. *ACM Journal of Computer Documentation, 24*(4), 204-212.

Gramm-Leach-Bliley Act of 1999. (2000, June). Interagency guidelines establishing standards for safeguarding customer information and rescission of Year 2000 standards for safety and soundness: Proposed rule. *Federal Register, 65*(123), 39471-39489.

Health Insurance Portability and Accountability Act [HIPAA] of 1996. (1998, August). Security standards and electronic signature standards: Proposed rule. *Federal Register, 63*(155), 43242-43280.

Herscovitz, E. (1999). Secure virtual private networks: The future of data communications. *International Journal of Network Management, 12*(1), 213-220.

Hirsch, J. (2002). *Telecommuting: Security policies and procedures for the "Work-From-Home" workforce.* Retrieved April 29, 2006, from http://www.teleworker.org/articles/telework_security.html

Holden, G. (2004). *Guide to firewalls and network security.* Boston: Thomson Learning.

International Telework Association & Council (ITAC). (2004). Retrieved April 29, 2006, from http://www.workingfromanywhere.org/resouces/abouttelework.htm

IT Director.com. (2002). TCP/IP and OSI. Retrieved April 29, 2006, from http://whatis. techtarget.com/originalContent/0,289142,sid7_gci851291,00.html

Kadakia, R. (2001). *Collaborative security in an outsourced, cross-agency Web system.* Retrieved April 29, 2006, from http://www.sans.org/rr/papers/53/547.pdf

Langlois, G. (2003). *HR launches telecommuting pilot program.* Retrieved April 29, 2006, from http://www.georgetown.edu/publications/bluegray/2002/0923/features/A010923C.htm

Mehlman, B. P. (2002). *Telework and the future of American competitiveness.* Retrieved April 29, 2006, from http://www.technology.gov/Speeches/BPM_020923_Telework.htm

MITRE Corporation. (2003). Retrieved April 29, 2006, from http://www.cve.mitre.org/

Motskula, P. (2001). *Securing teleworking as an ISP service.* Retrieved April 29, 2006, from http://www.telework2001.fi/Motskula.rtf

Nessus.com. (2004). Retrieved April 29, 2006, from http://www.nessus.org/

Nilles, J. (1998). *Managing telework: Strategies for managing the virtual workforce.* New York: John Wiley & Sons/Upside Series.

Quirk, K. P. (2002). *Telework in the Information Age.* Retrieved April 29, 2006, from http://www.accts.com/telework.htm

Rubens, P. (2004). *What you need to tell teleworkers.* Retrieved April 29, 2006, from http://networking.earthWeb.com/netsecur/article.php/3306781

Soy, S. (1998). *The case study as a research method.* Retrieved April 29, 2006, from http://www.gslis.utexas.edu/~ssoy/usesusers/l391d1b.htm

Swanson, M., & Guttman, B. (1996). *Generally accepted principles and practices for securing Information Technology systems.* Retrieved April 29, 2006, from http://csrc.nist.gov/publications/nistpubs/800-14/800-14.pdf

Teleworker.org. (2004). Retrieved April 29, 2006, from http://www.teleworker.org/articles/telecommuting_security.html

Tremer, P. (2001). *Toward global security.* Retrieved April 29, 2006, from http://www.sans.org/rr/papers/48/428.pdf

This work was previously published in Journal of Cases on Information Technology, Vol. 8, Issue 4, edited by M. Khosrow-Pour, pp. 71-86, copyright 2006 by IGI Publishing, formerly Idea Group Publishing (an imprint of IGI Global).

APPENDIX A

OSI Reference Model & TCP/IP Model

Table 1. Open systems interconnection reference model

Layer	Name	Description
7	Application	• used for applications specifically written to run over the network • handles network access, flow control, and error recovery
6	Presentation	• responsible for protocol conversion, character conversion, data encryption/decryption, expanding graphics commands, data compression • sets standards for different systems to provide seamless communication from multiple protocol stacks
5	Session	• establishes, maintains, and ends sessions across the network • responsible for name recognition (identification) so only the designated parties can participate in the session
4	Transport	• manages the flow control of data between parties across the network • provides error-checking to guarantee error-free data delivery, with no losses or duplications
3	Network	• translates logical network address and names to their physical address • responsible for addressing, determining routes for sending, managing network problems such as packet switching, data congestion, and routing
2	Data Link	• responsible for error-free transfer of frames to other computers via the Physical Layer • this layer defines the methods used to transmit and receive data on the network.
1	Physical	• transmits raw bit stream over physical cable • defines cables, cards, physical aspects, Network interface card (NIC) attachments to hardware • defines techniques to transfer bit stream to cable (IT Director.com, 2002)

Table 1A. Open systems interconnection reference model and TCP/IP model

OSI Layer	TCP/IP Layer	TCP/IP Function
Application(Layer 1) Presentation (Layer 2) Session (Layer 3)	Application	FTP, Telnet, SMTP, HTTP.
Transport (Layer 4)	Transport (Host-to-Host)	TCP, UDP
Network (Layer 5)	Internet	IP, ICMP
Data Link (Layer 6) Physical (Layer 7)	Subnet (Network Access)	Ethernet, Token (IT Director. com, 2002)

APPENDIX B

Figure 1. The XYZ network infrastructure

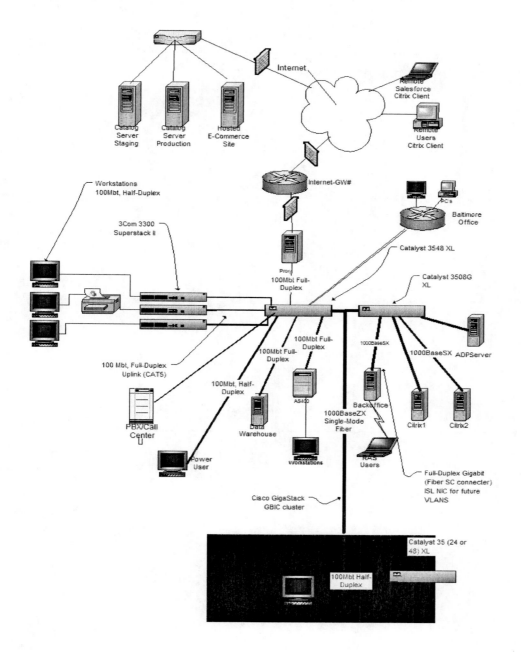

APPENDIX C

Commonly Used Ports and Associated Services

Table 6. Commonly used ports and associated services

Service	Associated Port
File Transfer Protocol (FTP) Data	20
FTP	21
Telnet	23
Simple Mail Transfer Protocol (SMTP)	25
Domain Name Service (DNS)	53
Hyper Text Transfer Protocol (HTTP)	80
Post Office Protocol – Version3 (POP3)	110
Network News Transfer Protocol (NNTP)	119
Internet Message Access Protocol (IMAP)	143
Simple Network Management Protocol (SNMP)	161 and 162
Hyper Text Transfer Protocol over Secure Socket Layer (HTTPS)	443
Usenet	532
Proxy	3128, 8008, 8088 and 8080

Chapter 4.27
A Method of Assessing Information System Security Controls

Malcolm R. Pattinson
University of South Australia, Australia

ABSTRACT

This chapter introduces a method of assessing the state of an organization's information system security by evaluating the effectiveness of the various IS controls that are in place. It describes how the Goal Attainment Scaling (GAS) methodology (Kiresuk, Smith & Cardillo, 1994) was used within a South Australian Government Agency and summarises the results of this research. The major purpose of this research was to investigate whether the GAS methodology is a feasible method of assessing the state of security of an organization's information systems. Additional objectives of this research were to determine the suitability of the GAS methodology as a self-evaluation tool and its usefulness in determining the extent of compliance with a mandated IS security standard.

INTRODUCTION

Information System (IS) security has become a critical issue for most organizations today, particularly those that have a large investment in information technology (IT). However, management and internal auditors still ask, "Is our information secure?" or "Do we have the necessary blend of controls in place to withstand the various threats to our information?" These questions are still very difficult to answer and in the past, management has sought answers by conducting computer security reviews and risk analyses by both internal and external security

Figure 1. Sample GAS follow-up guide

DATA CONFIDENTIALITY
Objective: To ensure that only authorised people have access to classified information.

LEVEL OF ATTAINMENT OF IS CONTROL	CLEAN DESK POLICY	CONTROL THE ENTRY AND SUPERVISION OF SERVICE PERSONNEL FROM EXTERNAL ORGANISATIONS	PHYSICAL ACCESS CONTROLS FOR OFF-SITE REMOVABLE STORAGE MEDIA
Much more than Acceptable level	Diskettes are stored in cabinets when they are not being used. Sensitive data media are stored in locked fire-resistant cabinets when not required & desks are cleared of all papers when desk is vacated.	Service people do NOT have easy physical access to any IT equipment (incl. workstations) & they must wear identity badges. All entry is logged and log is periodically audited. Also, they are escorted at all times.	Stored in fireproof, lockable cabinets. Physical access is restricted to authorised personnel only. Approval required to remove. Transported by professional security organisation.
Somewhat more than Acceptable level	Diskettes are stored in cabinets when they are not being used. Sensitive data media are stored in locked fire-resistant cabinets when not required.	Service people do NOT have easy physical access to any IT equipment (incl. workstations) & they must wear identity badges. All entry is logged and log is periodically audited.	Stored in fireproof, lockable cabinets. Physical access is restricted to authorised personnel only. Approval required to remove.
Acceptable level	Diskettes are stored in cabinets when they are not being used.	Service people do NOT have easy physical access to any IT equipment (incl. workstations).	Stored in fireproof, lockable cabinets. Physical access is restricted to authorised personnel only.
Somewhat less than Acceptable level	Diskettes are stored in a lockable diskette box on the desk or similar when not being used.	Service people have easy physical access to workstations but NOT network server(s) and comms. equipment.	Stored in fireproof, lockable cabinets but physical access is NOT strictly controlled.
Much less than Acceptable level	In general, desks are NOT cleared of papers and diskettes when the desk is vacated.	Service people have easy physical access to ALL IT equipment (incl. workstations).	NOT stored in fireproof, lockable cabinets and physical access is NOT strictly controlled.

specialists. These projects are typically expensive, time-consuming and resource-intensive because they were originally designed for use in large organizations with mainframe computers. With the advent of client-server technology and distributed computing via networks there is a need for a self-assessment technique or measuring device that is inexpensive and easy-to-use whilst providing management with a reliable indication of just how effective their IS security controls are.

This chapter describes a program evaluation methodology (Isaac & Michael, 1995; Owen, 1993) known as Goal Attainment Scaling (GAS) (Kiresuk, Smith & Cardillo, 1994), which has been used predominantly in the disciplines of health, social work and education and applies it within the discipline of IS security. Whilst traditionally the GAS methodology has been used to detect positive or negative changes in a patient's mental health, this application of GAS attempts to assess the changes in the "health and safety" of a computer system over time. More specifically, this chapter describes how the GAS methodology was used to evaluate IS security within a South Australian government agency by assessing the state, condition and quality of IS security controls in place.

ASSESSING INFORMATION SYSTEM SECURITY CONTROLS

An IS security control can take many forms. It can be a hardware device or a computer program or indeed a management process. In all cases its purpose is to prevent, avoid, detect or prepare for breaches of security that threaten the confidentiality, integrity or availability of information processed by computer systems. But how can the effectiveness of such a control be measured? The Australian Standard for Risk Management (Standards Australia/Standards New Zealand, 1999) defines the effectiveness of a control as a measure of how well the control objectives (and/or risk objectives) are met (i.e., how the risk of not achieving these objectives is reduced). For example, a typical control/risk objective is to prevent, or at least minimise, security breaches. In this case, it could be argued that the true effectiveness of a control of this nature is a measure of the number of threats that occur in spite of its presence. In other words, a control's effectiveness is a measure of the number of security breaches that it prevents. For example, if no security breaches occur, then it could be claimed that the controls that relate to that threat are 100% effective. However, there are two problems with this argument. Firstly, there is rarely a one-to-one relationship between a threat and a control. To explain this, consider the threat of unauthorised access to sensitive information. This is controlled by a number of physical controls such as locks, security guards and alarm systems and also by a number of logical controls such as passwords, encryption and authentication software. As such, it is difficult to isolate any of these controls and establish its sole effectiveness in preventing unauthorised access.

The second problem with attempting to assess the effectiveness of a control by measuring the number of security breaches it prevents relates to the fortuitous nature of threats. The occurrence of some threats is often unpredictable and independent of the controls in place. For example, some premises without locks may never have a break-in, whilst others with numerous locks may have two or three each year. There is a degree of luck involved. Therefore, the fact that no security breaches occur may be just good fortune and not a measure of how many breaches were prevented or a measure of the effectiveness of the controls in place.

The approach described in this chapter concentrates on assessing or evaluating the state, quality or condition of the controls that are in place. It does *not* assess the effectiveness of controls by measuring the number of security breaches that have occurred or have been prevented. As stated earlier, this "quality" or "condition" can relate to a number of characteristics of the control in question. For example, a control can be measured in terms of how well it has been implemented, that is, its "implemented-ness". As an analogy, compare this to assessing the effectiveness of a raincoat in preventing a person from getting wet. The obvious approach would be to measure how wet the wearer gets when it rains. Alternatively, one could get an indication of its effectiveness by assessing the raincoat in terms of its quality, that is, how well is it made? If it is designed well and made from high quality materials it is likely to be effective. Another option could be to assess the raincoat in terms of how well it is being applied, that is, is it being used properly? This may also give an indication of how effective it is. The point being made here is that the effectiveness of a raincoat, or indeed a management control, can be measured in more than one way.

WHAT IS GOAL ATTAINMENT SCALING (GAS)?

The GAS methodology is a program evaluation methodology used to evaluate the effectiveness of a program or project (Kiresuk et al., 1994). A program evaluation methodology is a process of determining how well a particular program is achieving or has achieved its stated aims and objectives. Kiresuk and Lund (1982) state that program evaluation is a process of establishing "...the degree to which an organization is doing what it is supposed to do and achieving what it is supposed to achieve" (p. 227).

One of the essential components of the GAS methodology is the evaluation instrument. This is primarily a table or matrix whereby the columns represent objectives to be assessed and the rows represent levels of attainment of those objectives. Kiresuk et al. (1994) refer to these objectives as goals or scales within a GAS Follow-up Guide. The rows represent contiguous descriptions of the degree of expected goal outcome. These can

range from the best-case level of goal attainment to the worst case, with the middle row being the most likely level of goal attainment. The sample GAS Follow-up Guide in Figure 1 is a portion of one of seven follow-up guides that comprised the complete evaluation tool used in the case study described herein.

The GAS goals that are being evaluated are, in fact, IS controls. This is an important concept because these types of "operational" GAS goals can be evaluated as either an outcome or a process (refer to "Evaluating Processes or Outcomes" in the Discussion section).

HOW GAS WAS USED IN A CASE STUDY

The case study organization referred to in this chapter was a South Australian government agency whose major function is to manage deceased estates. It has a total staff of 120. The IT department consists of four people, one of whom is the IT Manager, who is responsible for IS security within the agency. The IT facilities consist of a 150-workstation local area network (LAN) bridged to a mid-range computer system that runs their major Trust Accounting system. The hardware facilities and the software development function have been outsourced to various third party organizations. Although this agency is considered "small" relative to other South Australian government agencies, the issue of IS security is perhaps more important than with most other agencies because of the due diligence associated with the management of funds held in trust.

This case study comprised three phases, namely:

1. Develop the GAS evaluation instrument.
2. Use the GAS evaluation instrument.
3. Analyse the evaluation results and report to management.

Phase 1: Develop the GAS Evaluation Instrument

The GAS evaluation instrument developed in this phase of the case study was to represent all aspects of IS security for an organization. Because IS security is such a wide domain, the instrument needed more than a single follow-up guide. Consequently, it was necessary to develop a set of GAS follow-up guides, one for each category of IS security. The resulting GAS evaluation instrument, comprising seven follow-up guides, was developed in accordance with the nine-step process (Kiresuk et al., 1994, pp. 7-9). The titles for each of the steps are not identical to the titles of the Kiresuk et al. (1994) method, but have been modified to suit the IS security environment and in accordance with the case study agency's preference. Furthermore, step nine became redundant since all controls were addressed in each step. The nine steps are as follows:

1. Identify the security areas to be focused on.
2. Translate the selected security areas into several controls.
3. Choose a brief title for each control.
4. Select an indicator for each control.
5. Specify the minimal acceptable level of attainment for each control.
6. Review the acceptable levels of attainment.
7. Specify the "somewhat more" and "somewhat less" than acceptable levels of attainment.
8. Specify the "much more" and "much less" than acceptable levels of attainment.
9. Repeat these scaling steps for each of the controls in each follow-up guide.

Each of these Phase 1 steps is described in detail below:

Step 1: Identify the security areas to be focused on.

For the purpose of this research, the issues to be focused on included all aspects of IS security within an organization. It would be quite acceptable to focus on a specific category of IS security, but the case study agency agreed to address the whole IS security spectrum. IS security is a wide domain and it was necessary to define categories that were a manageable size. Rather than "re-invent the wheel," all that was necessary was to refer to any number of published standards on computer security. For example, the Standard AS/NZS ISO/IEC 17799 (Standards Australia/Standards New Zealand, 2001) breaks down IS security into 10 categories and 36 sub-categories. This case study adopted a mandated government standard comprising seven IS security categories defined by the South Australian Government Information Technology Security Standards document (South Australian Government, 1994b) as follows:

- The Organization
- Authentication
- Access Control
- Data Integrity
- Data Confidentiality
- Data Availability
- Audit

Step 2: Translate the selected security areas into several controls.

For each IS security category, the project team selected a set of IS controls that were considered most relevant, important and suitable for evaluation. Each of the selected IS controls would eventually be represented by a column in a GAS follow-up guide. The eventual number of IS controls selected ranged between 3 and 10 per follow-up guide, giving a total of 39.

This task of selecting an appropriate set of IS controls is critical to the success of using the GAS methodology. With this in mind, it is advisable that this evaluation methodology be complemented by an independent audit of all controls, particularly those compliance-driven controls that are excluded from the GAS follow-up guides because of their difficulty to scale.

Step 3: Choose a brief title for each control.

This step required that an abbreviated title be devised for each IS control selected in the previous step so that the eventual user of the GAS follow-up guides would easily recognise the control being evaluated.

Step 4: Select an indicator for each control.

This step relates to the criteria used to measure an IS control. The indicator is an element of measurement chosen to indicate the level of attainment of the IS control. For example, one IS control was "Establish formal policy with respect to software licences and use of unauthorised software". A possible indicator in determining the level of attainment of this control is the amount or extent of progress made towards developing such a document (e.g., fully developed, partly developed or not started). An alternative indicator could be the frequency of occurrence of the IS control. For example, the control "Regular reviews of software and data content of critical systems" could be measured by the frequency with which a review is conducted (e.g., annually or every six months).

Step 5: Specify the minimal acceptable level of attainment for each control.

This step required the development of narrative for the "zero" or middle cell for each control within each follow-up guide. This description represents the *minimum* level of acceptance (by management) of an IS control compared to the traditional "expected level of outcome" as per the Kiresuk et al. (1994) GAS methodology.

Step 6: Review the acceptable levels of attainment.

The objective of this step is to confirm the relevance and understandability of the descriptions by potential users. It is also important that these descriptions represented minimal acceptable levels of attainment of IS controls by agency management.

Step 7: Specify the "somewhat more" and "somewhat less" than acceptable levels of attainment.

This step required that narrative be developed that described the "somewhat more" and "somewhat less" than the minimum level of acceptance scenarios for each IS control.

Step 8: Specify the "much more" and "much less" than acceptable levels of attainment.

This step required that narrative be developed, as in Step 7, but which described the "much more" and "much less" than the minimum level of acceptance scenarios for each IS control.

Figure 2. Non-weighted GAS T-scores

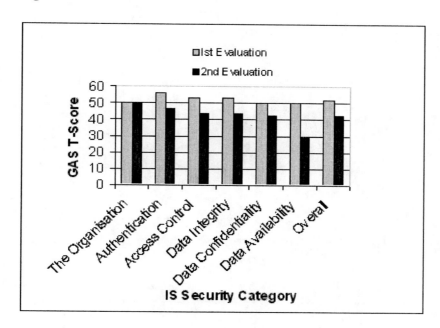

Step 9: Repeat these scaling steps for each of the controls in each follow-up guide.

Redundant.

Phase 2: Use the GAS Evaluation Instrument

This phase involved the use of the individualised GAS instrument by conducting a pre-treatment evaluation of IS security within the agency followed by a post-treatment evaluation 15 months later using the same GAS instrument without modification. The reference to "treatment" in this case study was the implementation and maintenance of IS controls in response to the first evaluation. This phase formed a very small component of this whole research because the GAS methodology requires that most of the time and effort is spent on developing the instrument so that it is quick and easy to use.

The ease and speed with which this data collection process was conducted on both occasions is not only testimony to the efficiency of the GAS methodology, but satisfies Love's (1991) essential characteristics of a Rapid Assessment Instrument (RAI) when used in a self study situation. He states, "They must be short, easy to read, easy to complete, easy to understand, easy to score, and easy to interpret" (p. 106).

Phase 3: Analyse the Evaluation Results and Report to Management

This phase involved the analysis of the data collected during the second phase. Raw scores were converted into GAS T-scores for each of the seven follow-up guides in accordance with the Kiresuk et al. (1994) methodology.

A GAS T-score is a linear transformation of the average of the raw scores in each follow-up guide using the formula documented by Kiresuk et al. (1994) and presented below:

Figure 3. Weighted GAS T-scores

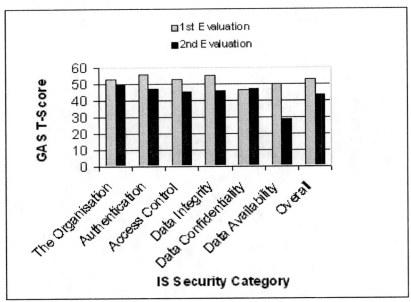

$$T - score = 50 + \frac{10 \sum w_i x_i}{\sqrt{(1-p) \sum w_i{}' + p (\sum w_i)^2}}$$

where x_i is the outcome score for the ith scale with a weight of w_i, and p is the weighted average inter-correlation of the scale scores and commonly set at 0.3. Scores on the individual scales between -2 and +2 each are assumed to have a theoretical distribution with a mean of zero and a standard deviation of 1. This formula then produces T-scores with a mean of 50 and a standard deviation of 10 when each scaled control is scored using the -2 to +2 scale.

For both the pre-treatment and the post-treatment evaluations, two T-scores were calculated for each follow-up guide, a non-weighted T-score and a weighted T-score. GAS T-scores for weighted controls were generated for the purpose of seeing what difference weighting actually made. GAS T-scores were then compared, interpreted and written up in business report form for management of the agency.

Figure 2 shows the non-weighted GAS T-scores for the pre-treatment and post-treatment evaluations. The "treatment" here is the action taken (or not taken) by management in response to the pre-treatment evaluation results. Figure 3 shows the weighted GAS T-scores for the pre-treatment and post-treatment evaluations. Both charts highlight the negative change in the rating of the level of security over the 15 months between evaluations.

A GAS T-score of 50 or more indicates that, on average, the controls specified within a GAS follow-up guide for a particular IS security category are considered acceptable to management. If these controls are representative of all controls specified for this IS security category within the adopted standard, then it can be argued that the controls in place are generally compliant with the standard. The extent of compliance is reflected in the amount by which the score is greater than 50. Conversely, a GAS T-score of less than 50 for a particular IS security category indicates that, in general, the IS controls in place are *not* acceptable to management and therefore (it could be argued) they are not compliant with the adopted standard.

In the first or pre-treatment evaluation the non-weighted GAS T-scores were all greater than or equal to 50. This means that, on average, the controls within each IS security category are considered to be acceptable relative to the government standards on which they are based. That is, on average across the scaled data cells, the IS controls are considered compliant with those standards provided the levels of attainment have been set correctly.

The second or post-treatment evaluation, conducted 15 months after the first, showed a significant decline in the GAS T-scores for each of the IS security categories and for overall security, using both weighted and non-weighted controls. In particular, the IS category "Data Availability" showed a dramatic decline in the supposed level of security since the first evaluation.

In summary, the overall results indicated that the level of IS security within the agency had dropped between the two evaluations in all IS categories except one, which showed no change. In fact, the overall results shown in Figures 2 and 3 for both weighted and non-weighted GAS T-scores indicate a substantial negative change in the state of IS controls between the first and second evaluations.

DISCUSSION

This section discusses the following major issues associated with this research:

- The nature of information system security
- Using a baseline standard to select controls
- Evaluating processes or outcomes
- The need for an independent audit
- The need for GAS training
- Evaluating a non-human service
- Criticisms of GAS

The Nature of Information System Security

Information system security relates to the adequacy of management controls to prevent, avoid, detect, deter and recover from a whole range of threats that could cause damage or disruption to computer systems. Total security is rarely achieved because it requires that the risk of every possible threat is zero, and for this to be the case, the computer system would not be functional. This is impractical and a balance needs to be struck between the impact that the threat will have on the business and the cost of the controls necessary to minimise risks. Therefore the aim of management should be to reduce the risks to an acceptable level and not to eliminate them. But what is an acceptable level of risk? This is a complex question and the answer is different for each organization, depending on a number of factors such as management's propensity to take risks and the sensitivity of the information stored and processed. These risk objectives should be established as a result of conducting a risk analysis before controls are selected and implemented. The methodology presented herein does not purport to measure or assess risk, but instead, it evaluates the condition or state or quality of IS controls that have been put in place. Consequently, the methodology does not attempt to determine the extent to which the controls in place achieve the risk objectives of the organization. It does, however, attempt to indicate the level of IS security relative to acceptable IS control benchmarks that are set by management as part of the methodology. This assumes that these acceptable levels of IS controls are in tune with the organization's risk objectives.

The GAS methodology outlined herein gives an indication only of the state of security of each individual IS security category and the state of overall IS security by the aggregation of all categories. If an IS security category receives a very high score, this does not necessarily mean that all controls within the category are adequate. Similarly, if overall IS security is considered adequate, this does not mean that there are not areas of weakness that need attention. This "weakest link in the chain" argument is particularly relevant in relation to security controls in general and is a possible criticism of the methodology.

Using a Baseline Standard to Select Controls

When the GAS methodology is used in collaboration with a set of IS security standards, the goal setting process described by Kiresuk et al. (1994) is assisted by the existence of a complete set of documented security objectives and controls from which to select as GAS goals. This does not necessarily compromise the methodology by reducing the effort of the goal setter because much care and attention is still necessary to select operational objectives, that is, IS controls, which are relevant and important to the organization. However, this effort will depend to a large extent on how relevant the set of IS security standards are to the organization.

Standards, in general, can either be generic or specific depending on the audience for which they are developed. IS security standards are no different. Examples of generic IS security standards are AS/NZS 17799 (Standards Australia/Standards New Zealand, 2001), AS/NZS 4360 (Standards Australia/Standards New Zealand, 1999) and the Control Objectives for Information and related Technology (COBIT) (Information Systems Audit and Control Foundation (ISACF), 2000). These standards and guidelines were developed by teams of people from various industries with different knowledge bases for organizations in general. On the other hand, more specific standards have been developed in-house. For example, the standards used by the case study agency were developed for whole-of-government (South Australian Government, 1994b). Although this is not organization specific, since whole-of-government consists of approximately 140 agencies, at least they are South Australian government specific. It is reasonable to assume that the more specific an IS security standard is to an organization, the less chance there is of it containing irrelevant controls.

Irrespective of the degree of relevance of the set of IS security standards, the goal setter must decide which controls are important, which controls are objective-driven and how many controls will constitute a valid representation of the issue being evaluated. Some standards were found to be easier to work with than others. For example, the Australian/New Zealand Standard AS/NZS 17799 (Standards Australia/Standards New Zealand, 2001) provides a descriptive objective for each IS security category. Furthermore, objective-driven controls were not too difficult to identify simply by envisaging how their level of attainment could be scaled.

The problem of determining whether a selection of controls is a valid representation of the IS security category being evaluated can be in conflict with the desire to make the evaluation instrument a manageable size. The temptation is to include all objective-driven controls, thus eliminating the risk of omitting an important one. Kiresuk et al. (1994) suggest that the initial number of scaleable GAS goals for a single GAS follow-up guide is between 3 and 10.

More research needs to be done in this area of GAS goal setting for IS security because the "weakest link" phenomenon applies. For example, a suburban house may be considered to be adequately safeguarded against theft because it has multi-layered controls in the form of infrared sensors, window and door deadlocks and a guard dog. However, if valuables are not put in a safe, then they are most vulnerable to theft when visitors are in the house. The non-existence of this control represents the weakest link in the control set.

Evaluating Processes or Outcomes

Kiresuk et al. (1994) point out that "GAS is appropriate only for outcome variables" (p. 31) and "In GAS, it is outcomes that are scaled" (p. 30). However, they accept that in certain circumstances the process or procedures undertaken to achieve the stated GAS goal may well be the operational objective. For example, consider the IS security control "Conduct an audit of physical access controls". If we were evaluating outcomes we could use as an indicator of measurement it would be the number of incidences of unauthorised physical access. On the other hand, if we were evaluating processes we might use as an indicator of measurement, it would be the frequency with which the audit is conducted. This equates to measuring the process put in place to achieve a goal rather than measuring an outcome of the process.

In order to implement GAS it is necessary to identify items to be evaluated as GAS goals. Are they to be outcomes, processes, enabling outcomes or some other form of output? One could be excused for thinking that the items to be evaluated in a goal-oriented evaluation of IS security controls would be control objectives such as "To reduce the number of viruses introduced" or "To minimise the number of unauthorised accesses to classified information," or "To reduce the number of accidental input errors". Objectives of this nature are certainly a valid item to assess. In contrast, this research focuses on evaluating the IS controls in place to achieve the objectives rather than evaluating the control objectives. This decision was made because the GAS methodology requires that the subject of evaluation (the GAS goal) be an objective that is scalable. The above-mentioned control objectives are certainly scalable but only in terms of the extent of security breaches that occur. In these cases the indicators of performance would need to relate to the number of breaches which actually occurred after the controls were put in place (or to be more accurate, the number of breaches which were prevented,

avoided or detected). For example, one would have to estimate or record the number of viruses introduced or the number of unauthorised accesses that occurred or the number of accidental input errors that occurred. Alternatively, breaches of security could be measured by the impact on the business when they do occur. For example, the effect of a computer virus can range from "a bit of a laugh" to hundreds of thousands of dollars lost because the computer system was made inoperable for a significant period of time, causing hundreds of people to become unproductive.

Measurements of this nature may seem to be the most effective means of evaluating the extent to which the types of control objectives mentioned above have been attained; that is, to measure the outcome or impact of having implemented the IS control. However, there are problems associated with the measurement of security breaches. Firstly, accurate information pertaining to security breaches can be very difficult to collect for a variety of reasons. Management is often very reluctant to release information that may reflect on their management style. Security is a management responsibility and if there are too many incidents of security breaches, management may be viewed negatively. Guest (1962) referred to this problem when conducting studies of organization behaviour at the management level. He claims that managers are often reluctant to provide accurate information to external parties for fear of it being leaked to competitors or that it may upset a delicate power struggle occurring within. Further to this, it may not be prudent for details regarding security breaches to be made public in situations where the organization is, for example, a custodian of people's money or other personal valuables. Banks and financial institutions must maintain customer confidence or risk losing patronage.

Another problem with measuring security breaches to ascertain the state of an organization's information security is equally contentious. It relates to the number of occurrences of breach or the extent of damage caused by the breach not necessarily reflecting the quality of the controls in place. Security breaches can occur at any time. They do not necessarily occur more often when fewer controls are in place. Take, for example, natural disasters like fire, flood, earthquake or terrorist attack. These threats are an act of God and an organization with numerous high quality controls is just as vulnerable as an organization which has very few.

Consequently, the evaluation approach used herein has *not* attempted to measure security breaches as a means of assessing the state of IS security, but instead, has focused on the evaluation of the IS controls in place. This amounts to evaluating a process that will contribute to an outcome.

The Need for an Independent Audit

It is important to appreciate that the GAS methodology espoused in this chapter is *not* an audit of the organization's IS controls. An IS audit would test inputs, processes, outputs and business operations for conformance against a standard, whereas the GAS methodology measures stakeholder perceptions of the current situation. Hence, it is recommended that the results be validated by conducting an independent audit of the controls.

The author is *not* questioning whether GAS can be used as a singular assessment method. However, it is generally accepted that alternate evaluation methods should be used to cross-validate (triangulate) data to increase the degree of inference about relationships (de Vries et al., 1992; Love, 1991; Patton, 1990, 1997; Steckler et al.,1992; all as cited in FIPPM, 1999). Another recent study (Robertson-Mjaanes, 1999) examined, among other things, the validity of GAS, and concluded that the best use of GAS may *not* be as a singular method. It was suggested that it is more suited when used to integrate and summarise the results obtained from other progress monitoring

and outcome measuring methods as opposed to being used as a single assessment method.

Whether GAS is shown to be highly suitable or otherwise does *not* mean that it should be used on its own without an independent third party assessment to confirm results. In striving to increase the quality of outcome assessment (although in this research, the outcomes are in fact processes) it is important to complement the results of a GAS evaluation with another measure/assessment process. This is the advice given by Kiresuk et al. (1994), regardless of the domain in which it is being used. This is particularly relevant in the evaluation of any prevention program like a program to prevent human injury on the roads (see FIPPM, 1999), or indeed, a program of controls put in place to prevent breaches of IS security as in this research. This is because prevention programs of this type are seldom foolproof or 100% effective and furthermore, it is difficult to attribute a null result to causality of the intervention. The point is that there are an infinite number of controls that can be put in place and therefore choices have to be made as to which ones and how many. Consequently, it is important that more than one evaluation method is deployed to confirm that the best selection of controls and processes is made in order to maximise the effectiveness of the program.

It is important that some form of continuous monitoring occurs. One such approach is to adopt a global rating system whereby an overall assessment of the situation can be obtained. One such program is the Global Assessment Scale described by Hargreaves and Attkisson (Attkisson, Hargreaves, Horowitz & Sorensen, 1978), used in the evaluation of mental health programs. In the domain of IS security, continuous monitoring by an independent third party could be achieved by utilising the services of external auditors who currently have the responsibility of auditing IS controls. This would serve as a check on evaluator bias and generally help to improve the validity of the evaluation process.

As with the upstream petroleum environmental application (Malavazos & Sharp, 1997) the full third party assessment (e.g., consultant ecologist research over 12 months) can be highly time-consuming and expensive. In any case, prevention is more cost-effective, because during the course of the third party review the organization may have to endure high-risk operations to be properly tested. All of these considerations do not obviate the need for third party independent review and application of safe standards. However, they do heighten the need for regular, frequent, low cost self-evaluations to reduce the cost and risk of the fully-fledged review.

The Need for GAS Training

The training of potential GAS goal setters is a critical component of the GAS methodology if a meaningful result is to be achieved. The GAS methodology is reported to have been used in hundreds of organizations and for many different purposes (Kiresuk et al., 1994). From these, Kiresuk et al. (1994) have concluded, "Effective training must be provided to staff who will be employing the technique, time must be allowed for the staff to use the technique properly, and administrative support must be available to sustain the implementation" (p. 6). In fact, proper training is considered such an important issue that Kiresuk et al. (1994)devoted a whole chapter to topics such as curriculum design, skills to be developed, GAS goal setting, GAS goal scoring and the costs of training.

Evaluating a Non-Human Service

An important question is whether the same arguments for GAS's success in evaluating human service programs can be extended to a study where the program being evaluated is a management "program" (or plan) where the subjects are not individuals but procedures or activities. In the

evaluation of a health or education program, the GAS methodology measures the outcomes of a program by assessing the impact that the program has on individuals; that is, the "condition" of the individuals. In contrast, this research uses a GAS-based methodology to measure the process of implementing and maintaining a set of IS controls by assessing the state of these controls. The most significant difference between an evaluation of a human service compared to a non-human service appears to be that the recipient of human service may also be involved in the goal setting process. In the case of a non-human service, this does not happen because the recipient is the organization, not a human being. However, stakeholders or representatives of the organization should be involved in the goal setting process. Notwithstanding the limited number of non-human service test cases in which GAS has been applied, the author believes that the methodology warrants further investigation in these situations to ascertain its usefulness and relevance. At this stage it would be incorrect to assume that the success of GAS in the evaluation of human service delivery programs automatically applies to non-human service programs.

Criticisms of GAS

Using the GAS methodology for the evaluation of IS security has its shortcomings and problems and is subject to criticism in the following areas:

- The approach does not offer solutions to poor IS security or recommend management action to improve IS security. This is the next step in the risk management process. This study is concerned with answering the management question "How secure are the ISs?" and does not attempt to address what should be done about them.
- The approach does not necessarily *audit* the security of ISs. It is a measure of stakeholder perceptions of the current situation.

However, for more accurate results, it is recommended that an independent person audits the IS controls.

- Evaluation results are not necessarily foolproof and conclusions based on GAS summary scores need to be conservative. The domain of security and management controls is subject to a form of the weakest link phenomenon. In other words, an organization is only as secure as the weakest control. The GAS methodology generates an average score for each follow-up guide and since each follow-up guide consists of between three and ten controls, this means that strong controls could hide weak controls. For this reason it is recommended that all low scoring controls be followed up individually.

- Self-assessment approaches, by their very nature, often have a credibility problem in terms of evaluator bias and a lack of objectivity. This is particularly likely to occur in situations where (a) the evaluator is involved in the creation of the measuring device or (b) the evaluator is the person responsible for IS security within the organization. Irrespective of the conduct of the self-assessment approach, Love (1991) advocates that one of the key elements of any self-study process is that the achievement of standards or objectives should be confirmed by external evaluators (p. 81). For this reason it is recommended that independent persons, preferably external to the organization, audit the validity of the GAS instrument and the evaluation process.

- Sets of GAS scales are only individualised scales to detect change in the target organization and are *not* for generalisation across different organizations.

CONCLUSION

This research showed that the GAS methodology, combined with a generally-accepted IS security standard, is not only a feasible approach for evaluating IS security but is also useful for assessing the level of compliance with that standard. This has particular relevance for public sector organizations that have a responsibility to comply with common whole-of-government standards.

In addition, this research highlighted a number of attributes of the GAS methodology that contribute to its suitability as a self-evaluation methodology when used to evaluate IS security. The most relevant of these attributes is the fact that the GAS evaluation instrument is developed by stakeholders within the organization and used periodically by other stakeholders to monitor the level of IS security against an established standard.

RECOMMENDATIONS

This research has spawned the following key recommendations relating to the use of the GAS methodology when used to assess IS security:

- A set of formally documented IS security standards should be used as a basis for developing the GAS evaluation instrument. This will:
- assist in identifying the IS security categories to be evaluated;
- ensure that the IS controls selected are truly representative of all the controls within a particular IS security category; and
- assist goal setters in developing an appropriate scale of GAS goals that are measurable.

- A generic or core instrument for whole-of-government should be developed before individual agencies develop their own individualised instruments. This core instrument, based on whole-of-government IS security standards, should then be used as a starting point for individual agencies.
- IS security should be assessed against a baseline set of controls such as a policy document or a set of standards. This implies that GAS should be used to measure the extent of compliance with a baseline set of controls, rather than attempting to assess the adequacy of existing controls.
- The selection of IS controls and the subsequent goal setting process is not only the most difficult aspect of the GAS methodology, but it is also the most important. It is therefore recommended that an independent person audit the IS controls and the five descriptive levels of attainment of each control.
- The selection of controls to be included in each GAS follow-up guide is a critical process that can determine the validity of the evaluation results. In order to select a truly representative set of controls for the IS security category being assessed, it is recommended that objective-driven controls are chosen in preference to compliance-driven controls.

CHAPTER SUMMARY

This chapter has described how an established and well-accepted methodology in one discipline can be adapted to a totally different discipline and still maintain its merit. Although this research is limited and quite specific as a single case study, it has extended the research of Malavazos

and Sharp (1997), who used the methodology to assess the environmental performance of the petroleum industry. This research also extended the research of von Solms, van de Haar, von Solms and Caelli (1994), who claimed that "...no information security self-evaluation tool, known to the authors, exists currently" (p. 149). At that time, they were not aware of any internationally accepted IS security standards. Since then, a number of such standards have been published (e.g., AS/NZS 17799, BS7799). As a consequence, it seems that it is now time for IS security research to concentrate on validating existing techniques and developing new techniques.

This research needs to be extended to enable the following questions to be answered:

- Is it suitable for different sized organizations?
- Is it suitable in organizations with multiple IT platforms?
- How can staff be trained to overcome the need for a GAS methodologist?
- Is the effort in developing a GAS measuring instrument a better utilisation of time and resources than actually taking preventative action?

REFERENCES

Attkisson, C.C., Hargreaves, W.A., Horowitz, M.J., & Sorensen, J.E. (Eds.). (1978). Evaluation of human service programs. New York: Academic Press.

FIPPM. (1999). Evaluating injury prevention initiatives. Developed by Flinders Institute of Public Policy and Management (FIPPM), Research Centre for Injury Studies, Flinders University, South Australia, 1-8.

Guest, R.H. (1962). Organizational change: The effect of successful leadership. London: Tavistock Publications.

Information Systems Audit and Control Foundation (ISACF). (2000). Control Objectives for Information and related Technology (COBIT) (3rd ed.). USA.

Isaac, S., & Michael, W.B. (1995). Handbook in research and evaluation (3rd ed.). San Diego,CA: Edits Publishers.

Kiresuk, T.J., & Lund, S.H. (1982). Goal attainment scaling: A medical-correctional application. Medicine and Law, 1, 227-251.

Kiresuk, T.J., Smith, A., & Cardillo, J.E. (Eds.). (1994). Goal attainment scaling: Applications, theory and measurement. NJ, USA: Erlbaum Inc.

Love, A.J. (1991). Internal evaluation: Building organizations from within. Newbury Park, USA: Sage Publications.

Malavazos, M., & Sharp, C.A. (1997, October). Goal attainment scaling: Environmental impact evaluation in the Upstream Petroleum Industry. Proceedings of Australasian Evaluation Society 1997 International Conference, Adelaide, South Australia, 333-340.

Owen, J.M. (1993). Program evaluation: Forms and approaches. NSW, Australia: Allen & Unwin.

Robertson-Mjaanes, S.L. (1999). An evaluation of goal s as an intervention monitoring and outcome evaluation technique. Dissertation at University of Wisconsin-Madison, published by UMI Dissertation Services.

South Australian Government. (1994a, July). South Australian government information technology security guidelines (vol. 1).

South Australian Government. (1994b, December). South Australian government information technology security standards in an outsourced environment (vol. 1).

Standards Australia/Standards New Zealand. (1999). Risk management, AS/NZS 4360:1999. Strathfield, NSW, Australia: Standards Association of Australia.

Standards Australia/Standards New Zealand. (2001). Information technology - Code of practice for information security management, AS/NZS ISO/IEC 17799:2001.

von Solms, R., van de Haar, H., von Solms, S.H., & Caelli, W.J. (1994). A framework for information security evaluation. Information and Management, 26(3), 143-153.

Chapter 4.28
Electronic Banking and Information Assurance Issues:
Survey and Synthesis

Manish Gupta
State University of New York, USA

Raghav Rao
State University of New York, USA

Shambhu Upadhyaya
State University of New York, USA

ABSTRACT

Information assurance is a key component in e-banking services. This article investigates the information assurance issues and tenets of e-banking security that would be needed for design, development, and assessment of an adequate electronic security infrastructure. The technology terminology and frameworks presented in the article are with the view to equip the reader with a glimpse of the state-of-art technologies that may help toward learning and better decisions regarding electronic security.

INTRODUCTION

The Internet has emerged as the dominant medium in enabling banking transactions. Adoption of e-banking has witnessed an unprecedented increase over the last few years. Twenty percent of Internet users now access online banking services, a total that will reach 33% by 2006, according to the Online Banking Report. By 2010, more than 55 million U.S. households will use online banking and e-payments services, which are tipped as "growth areas." The popularity of online banking is projected to grow from 22 million households in 2002 to 34 million in 2005, according to Financial Insite, publisher of the Online Banking Report[1] newsletter.

Electronic banking uses computer and electronic technology as a substitute for checks and other paper transactions. E-banking is initiated through devices such as cards or codes to gain access to an account. Many financial institutions use an automated teller machine (ATM) card and a personal identification number (PIN) for this purpose. Others use home banking, which involves installing a thick client on a home PC and using a secure dial-up network to access account information; others allow banking via the Internet. This article will discuss the information assurance issues (Maconachy, Schou, & Ragsdale, 2002) that are associated with e-banking infrastructure. We hope that this chapter will allow information technology (IT) managers to understand information assurance issues in e-banking in a holistic manner, and that it will help them make recommendations and take actions to ensure security of e-banking components.

INTERNET/WEB BANKING

A customer links to the Internet from his or her PC. The Internet connection is made through a public Web server. When the customer brings up the desired bank's Web page, the customer goes through the front-end interface to the bank's Web server, which, in turn, interfaces with the legacy systems to pull data out at the customer's request. Pulling legacy data is the most difficult part of Web banking. While connection to a direct dial access (DDA) system is fairly straightforward, doing wire transfer transactions or loan applications requires much more sophisticated functionality. A separate e-mail server may be used for customer service requests and other e-mail correspondence. There are also other middleware products that provide security to ensure that the customer's account

information is secured, as well as products that convert information into an HTML format. In addition, many of the Internet banking vendors provide consulting services to assist banks with Web site design and overall architecture. Some systems store financial information and records on client PCs but use the Internet connections to transmit information from the bank to the customer's PC. For example, the Internet version of Intuit's *BankNOW* runs off-line at the client and connects to the bank via the Internet only to transmit account and transaction information (Walsh, 1999).

In this section, we discuss some of the key nodal points in Internet banking. The following points are the foundations and principal aspects of e-banking: Web site and service hosting, possibly through providers; application software that includes middleware; regulations surrounding e-banking and standards that allow different organizations and platforms to communicate over the Internet.

Web Site and Banking Service Hosting

Banks have the option of hosting Web sites in-house or outsourcing either to service bureaus or core processing vendors with expertise in Internet banking. Whether outsourced or packaged, Internet banking architectures generally consist of the following components: Web servers; transaction servers; application servers; and data storage and access servers. Vendors such as *Online Resources*[2] offer a package of Web banking services that includes the design and hosting of a financial institution's Web site and the implementation of a transactional Web site. Online's connection makes use of the bank's underlying ATM network for transactions and real-time bill payment. In addition, optional modules are generally available for bill payment, bill presentment, brokerage, loan application/approval, small business, and credit cards. The fact that multiple options of Web host-

Figure 1. Architectural pieces of Internet banking (Starita, 1999)

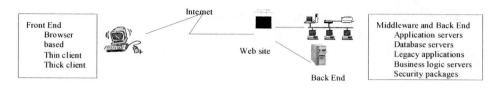

ing exist also brings with them issues in security and privacy—a topic that will be considered in a later section.

The components that form a typical Internet banking initiative are shown in Figure 1.

- *Internet Banking Front-End:* The front-end is often the client-side browser access to the bank's Web server. Client-side, thin-client access to the bank's Web server: This model allows the customer to download a thin-client software product from the bank's Web site and may allow storing financial data locally. Client-side, thick-client access to the bank's Web server: This is the model used when supporting personal financial management packages as tools to access account data and execute transactions. It is important to note that these models are not mutually exclusive of each other (Starita, 1999).

- *Internet Banking Transaction Platforms:* The Internet banking transaction platform is the technology component that supports transactional processes and interfaces between the front-end user interface and the back-end core processors for functions like account information retrieval, account update, and so forth. In general, the transactional platform defines two main things: (1) the functional capabilities of the Internet banking offering (i.e., whether it offers bill payment or credit card access); and (2) the method of access or interface between the front-end and back-end legacy processors (Starita, 1999).

Internet Banking Platforms and Applications

Most of the Internet plumbing to present data onto Web interfaces from data sources is offered by Internet banking application software vendors, who link legacy systems to allow access to account data and transaction execution. Most players position themselves as end-to-end solution providers by including a proprietary front-end software product, integration with other front-end software, or Web design services.

Some of the solutions are middleware platforms with plug-in applications to provide bill payment, bill presentment, brokerage, loan, small business, and/or credit card functionality. Most vendors use Open Financial Exchange standard (OFX) to connect to different delivery channels such as Interactive Voice Response (IVRs), Personal Finance Managers (PFMs), and the Internet. Middleware tools are designed to handle Internet-delivered core banking and bill payment transactions (Walsh, 2002). Middleware platforms provide a link between financial institutions' legacy host systems and customers using browser-based HTML interfaces and OFX-enabled personal financial management software (Walsh, 2002).

Middleware is designed for financial institutions that require a platform that translates messages between collections of separate processing systems that house core processing functions. Core processing systems include bill payment, credit card, brokerage, loans, and insurance. Electronic bill payment and presentment is widely believed to be the compelling application that brings large volumes of customers to the Internet channel to handle their finances. There are two kinds of Web sites: nontransactional and transactional. The nontransactional sites, commonly known as promotional Web sites, publish content with information about bank products and allow customers to investigate targeted areas such as college loans or retirement planning. These sites give basic information on bank products and do not allow any transactions. Banks can collect information to start to develop customer profiles by recording where a customer visits on the Web site and comparing it with demographic information to develop personalized marketing strategies.

Transactional sites link to back-end processing systems and include basic functionality such as the ability to view recent transactions and account histories, download information into PFM software, and transfer funds between existing accounts. As banks become more sophisticated with transactional capabilities, such things as electronic bill payment or moving of funds outside of the bank become possible. Integrating with a third-party processor such as Checkfree or Travelers Express most often does this. Bill presentment is also part of transactional capability; however, it is being done on a limited basis through a small number of pilots. Some banks allow customers to apply for loans, mortgages, and other products online, although much of the back-end process is still done manually. In transactional Web sites, every page must be composed dynamically and must offer continual updates on products and pricing.

Standards Compliance

Standards play a vital role in seamless flow and integration of information across channels and help to reduce risk emanating from diverse platforms and standards. In addition to the challenge of integrating Internet banking products into the bank's own IT environment, many Internet banking functions involve third-party participation. This poses a significant integration question: What is the best way to combine separate technology systems with third parties in a cost-effective way in order to enable each participant to maintain control over its data and maintain autonomy from other participants? The response from the technology marketplace has been to establish Internet banking standards to define interactions and the transfer of information between multiple parties (Bohle, 2001). The premise of a standard is that everyone would use it in the same consistent fashion; unfortunately, that is not the scenario in the current Internet banking environment. One of the problems for the lackluster performance of e-banking arguably is the industry's failure to attend to the payments infrastructure (Orr, 2002). One initiative that does show promise is by the National Institute of Standards and Technology, which has developed a proposed standard—Security Requirements for Cryptographic Modules—that will require role-based authentication and authorization (FIPS, 1992). Some of the standards pervasive in current e-banking models are the ADMS standard, the GOLD standard, and the OFX standard.

INFORMATION ASSURANCE

Web banking sites include financial calculators; e-mail addresses/customer service information; new account applications; transactions such as account balance checks, transfers, and bill payment; bill presentment/payment; cash management; loan applications; small business; credit card; and so forth. The modes by which they can be accessed include online service provider or portal site, direct-dial PC banking program, Internet-bank Web sites, WebTV, and personal financial manager. Depending on the functionality of the Web sites, different information assurance requirements are found.

Table 1. Standards in e-banking models

- *The ADMS Standard:* Access Device Messaging System (ADMS) is a proprietary standard developed and supported by Visa Interactive. From September 1998, this standard has been made obsolete for GOLD standard.

- *The GOLD Standard:* The GOLD standard is an electronic banking standard developed and supported by Integrion to facilitate the exchange of information between participants in electronic banking transactions. Integrion is a PC direct-dial and Internet banking vendor developed as a consortium with 16 member banks, IBM and Visa Interactive (through acquisition) in an equal equity partnership. IBM is the technology provider for the Integrion consortium.

- *The OFX Standard:* Open Financial Exchange (OFX) is a standard developed cooperatively by Microsoft, Intuit and Checkfree. Recently, Microsoft launched its OFX version 2.0 without the involvement of its partners, Checkfree and Intuit. OFX v.2.0 is developed with XML to enable OFX to be used for bill presentment. Though OFX can be considered as a much better solution for inter-operability needs of banks, it imposes problems of incompatibility between older OFX versions.

- *The IFX Standard:* Interactive Financial Exchange (IFX) initiative was launched in early 1998 by BITS (the Banking Industry Technology Secretariat) in order to ensure convergence between OFX and another proposed specification, GOLD, propounded by Integrion Financial Network. According to the IFX forum, IFX specification provides a robust and scalable framework for the exchange of financial data and instructions independent of a particular network technology or computing platform.

- *XML as standard:* XML language is often perceived as a solution to the problem of standards incompatibility. XML appears as an ideal tool for multi-banking, multi-service Internet banking applications.

Some examples of exploitation of information assurance issues in the Web-banking arena include the following:

- Many ATMs of Bank of America were made unavailable in January 2003 by the SQL Slammer worm, which also affected other financial services like Washington Mutual[3,4].
- Barclays suffered an embarrassing incident when it was discovered that after logging out of its online service, an account immediately could be re-accessed using the *back* button on a Web browser. If a customer accessed their Barclays account on a public terminal, the next user could thereby view banking details of the previous customer. According to the bank, when customers join the online banking service, they are given a booklet that tells them to clear the cache to prevent this from happening. However, this procedure shifts the responsibility for security to the end user[5].

Security and Privacy Issues

In their annual joint study in April 2002, the FBI and the Computer Security Institute noted that the combined financial losses for 223 of 503 companies that responded to their survey (Computer Crime and Security Survey) was $455 million for year 2002 (Junnarkar, 2002). Security and integrity of online transactions are the most important technical issues that a bank offering Web services will need to tackle. The Internet bank Web sites handle security in different ways. They can choose either public or private networks. The Integrion consortium, for example, uses the private IBM/AT&T Global Network for all Internet network traffic (Walsh, 1999). Server security is another important issue, usually accomplished by server certificates and SSL authentication. Banks must look at three kinds of security (Walsh, 1999): communications security; systems security, from the applications/authorization server; and information security.

From a user's perspective, security must accomplish privacy, integrity authentication, access

Figure 2. E-banking security infrastructure

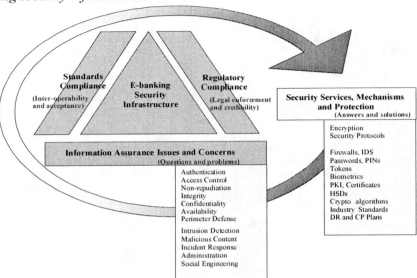

control, and non-repudiation. Security becomes an even more important issue when dealing with international banks, since only up to 128K encryption is licensed for export. Currently, most Internet bank Web sites use a combination of encryption, firewalls, and communications lines to ensure security. The basic level of security starts with an SSL-compliant browser. The SSL protocol provides data security between a Web browser and the Web server, and is based on public key cryptography licensed from security systems. Security has been one of the biggest roadblocks that have kept consumers from fully embracing Internet banking. Even after the advent of highly secure sites with the aid of 128K encryption, a virtually invulnerable encryption technology, the perception among some consumers is that Internet banking is unsafe. They apprehend privacy violations, as the bank keeps track of all transactions, and they are unsure of who has access to privileged data about their personal net worth. The basic security concerns that face financial institutions offering banking services and products through the Internet are summarized in Figure 2 and are discussed next.

Authentication

Authentication relates to assurance of identity of person or originator of data. Reliable customer authentication is imperative for financial institutions engaging in any form of electronic banking or commerce. Strong customer authentication practices are necessary to enforce anti-money laundering measures and help financial institutions detect and reduce identity theft. Customer interaction with financial institutions is migrating from physical recognition and paper-based documentation to remote electronic access and transaction initiation. The risks of doing business with unauthorized or masquerading individuals in an electronic banking environment could be devastating, which can result in financial loss and intangible losses like reputation damage, disclosure of confidential information, corruption of data, or unenforceable agreements.

There is a gamut of authentication tools and methodologies that financial institutions use to authenticate customers. These include the use of passwords and personal identification numbers (PINs), digital certificates using a public key infrastructure (PKI), physical devices such as smart cards or other types of tokens, database comparisons, and biometric identifiers. The level of risk protection afforded by each of these tools varies and is evolving as technology changes. Multi-factor authentication methods are more difficult to compromise than single factor systems. Properly designed and implemented multifactor authentication methods are more reliable indicators of authentication and stronger fraud deterrents. Broadly, the authentication methodologies can be classified, based on what a user knows (passwords, PINs), what a user has (smart card, magnetic card), and what a user is (fingerprint, retina, voiceprint, signature).

The issues that face banks using the Internet as a channel are the risks and risk management controls of a number of existing and emerging authentication tools necessary to initially verify the identity of new customers and authenticate existing customers that access electronic banking services. Besides, effective authentication framework and implementation provides banks with a foundation to enforce electronic transactions and agreements.

- *Account Origination and Customer Verification:* With the growth in electronic banking and commerce, financial institutions need to deploy reliable methods of originating new customer accounts online. Customer identity verification during account origination is important in reducing the risk of identity theft, fraudulent account applications, and unenforceable account agreements or transactions. There are significant risks when financial institutions accept new customers through the Internet or other electronic channels because of the absence of the tangible cues that banks traditionally use to identify individuals (FDIC, 2001).

- *Monitoring and Reporting:* Monitoring systems play a vital role in detecting unauthorized access to computer systems and customer accounts. A sound authentication system should include audit features that can assist in the detection of fraud, unusual activities (e.g., money laundering), compromised passwords, or other unauthorized activities (FDIC, 2001. In addition, financial institutions are required to report suspicious activities to appropriate regulatory and law enforcement agencies as required by 31 CFR 103.18.

Access Control

Access control refers to the regulating of access to critical business assets. Access control provides a policy-based control of who can access specific systems, what they can do within them, and when and from where they are allowed access. One of the primary modes of access control is based on roles. A role can be thought of as a set of transactions that a user or set of users can perform within the context of an organization. For example, the roles in a bank include teller, loan officer, and accountant, each of whom can perform different functions. Role-based access control (RBAC) policy bases access control decisions on the functions that a user is allowed to perform within an organization. In many applications, RBAC is concerned more with access to functions and information than strictly with access to information.

The applicability of RBAC to commercial systems is apparent from its widespread use. Nash and Poland (1990) discuss the application of role-based access control to cryptographic authentication devices commonly used in the banking industry. Even the Federal Information Processing Standard (FIPS) has provisions for support for role-based access and administration.

Non-Repudiation

Non-repudiation refers to the need for each party involved in a transaction to not go back on their word; that is, not break the electronic contract (Pfleeger, 1997). Authentication forms the basis for non-repudiation. It requires strong and substantial evidence of the identity of the signer of a message and of message integrity sufficient to prevent a party from successfully denying the origin, submission, or delivery of the message and the integrity of its contents. This is important for an e-banking environment where, in all electronic transactions, including ATMs (cash machines), all parties to a transaction must be confident that the transaction is secure; that the parties are who they say they are (authentication), and that the transaction is verified as final. Essentially, banks must have mechanisms that ensure that a party cannot subsequently repudiate (reject) a transaction. There are several ways to ensure non-repudiation, which include digital signatures, which not only validate the sender but also "time stamps" the transaction, so it cannot be claimed subsequently that the transaction was not authorized or not valid.

Integrity

Ensuring integrity means maintaining data consistency and protecting from unauthorized data alteration (Pfleeger, 1997). Integrity is very critical for Internet banking applications, as transactions have information that is consumer and business sensitive. To achieve integrity, data integrity mechanisms can be used. These typically involve the use of secret-key or public-key-based algorithms that allow the recipient a piece of protected data to verify that the data have not been modified in transit. The mechanisms are presented further in a later section.

Confidentiality and Privacy

Privacy and security concerns are not unique to banking systems. Privacy and confidentiality are related but are distinct concepts. Protection of personally identifiable information like banking

records must be ensured for consumers. Information Privacy (NIIAC, 1995) is the ability of an individual to control the use and dissemination of information that relates to him or her. Confidentiality (NIIAC, 1995) is a tool for protecting privacy. Sensitive information is accorded a confidential status that mandates specific controls, including strict limitations on access and disclosure. Those handling the information must adhere to these controls. Information confidentiality refers to ensuring that customer information is secured and hidden as it is transported through the Internet environment. Information not only must be protected wherever it is stored (e.g., on computer disks, backup tape, and printed form), but also in transit through the Internet.

Availability

Availability in this context means that legitimate users have access when they need it. With Internet banking, one of the strongest selling propositions is 24/7 availability; therefore, it becomes even more critical for e-banks. Availability applies both to data and to services. Expectations of availability include presence of a service in usable form, capacity to meet service needs, timeliness of service, fair allocation, fault tolerance, controlled concurrency, and deadlock management. One example where availability is compromised is the denial of service attack. On the Internet, a denial of service (DoS) attack is an incident in which a user or organization is deprived of the services of a resource they would normally expect to have. When there are enormous transactions on the Internet bank's Web site, the losses that may arise owing to unavailability are severe in terms of financial losses and reputation losses. Typically, the loss of service is the inability of a particular network service, such as email, to be available or the temporary loss of all network connectivity and services. It becomes imperative and crucial for IT managers in the Internet banking world to better understand the kind of denial of attacks possible. Some of the common and well-known types of denial of service attacks (IESAC, 2003) are the following:

- *SYN Attack:* It floods the server with open SYN connections, without completing the TCP handshake. TCP handshake is a three-step process to negotiate connection between two computers. The first step is for initiating the computer to send SYN (for *synchronize*) packet.
- *Teardrop Attack:* It exploits the way that the Internet Protocol (IP) requires a packet that is too large for the next router to handle be divided into fragments. Here, the attacker's IP puts a confusing offset value in the second or later fragment of the packet. It can cause the system to crash.
- *Smurf Attack:* In this attack, the perpetrator spoofs the source IP address and broadcasts ping requests to a multitude of machines to overwhelm the victim.

Perimeter Defense

Perimeter defense refers to the separation of an organization's computer systems from the outside world (IETF, 2000). This must allow free sharing of certain information with clients, partners, suppliers, and so on, while also protecting critical data from them. A security bulwark around network and information assets of any bank can be achieved to a certain extent by implementing firewalls and correctly performing tuning and configuration of firewalls.

Today, with the kind of traffic generated toward Web-banking sites for all kinds of purposes, from balance enquiries to interbank fund transfers, implementation of screening routers to ensure incoming and outgoing traffic would add another layer of security. In this age of systems being hijacked for cyber-attacks, it is also important that screen routers detect and prevent outgoing traffic that attempts to gain entry to systems like

spoofing IP addresses. Further, the periphery of the corporate computer infrastructure can be bolstered by implementing VPN solutions to ensure privacy of data flowing through the firewall into the public domain.

Probes and scans often are used techniques that are exploited to learn about exposures and vulnerabilities on the network systems. A probe is characterized by unusual attempts to gain access to a system or to discover information about the system. Probes are sometimes followed by a more serious security event, but often they are the result of curiosity or confusion. A scan is simply a large number of probes done using an automated tool. Scans can sometimes be the result of a misconfiguration or other error, but they are often a prelude to a more directed attack on systems that the intruder has found to be vulnerable.

Intrusion Detection

Intrusion detection refers to the ability to identify an attempt to access systems and networks in a fashion that breaches security policies. The Internet banking scenario, where most of business these days is carried out over public domain Internet and where a banking Web site becomes a single point interface for information as well as transactions, gives hackers enough motivation to intrude into Internet banks' systems. To safeguard from such unwanted activities, organizations need to be able to recognize and distinguish, at a minimum, the following (Gartner, 1999): internal and external intrusion attempts; human versus automated attacks; unauthorized hosts connecting to the network from inside and outside the perimeter; unauthorized software being loaded on systems; and all access points into the corporate network.

Intrusion detection systems (IDS) allow organizations to protect their systems from the threats that come with increasing network connectivity and reliance on information systems. Given the level and nature of modern network security threats, the question for security professionals should not be whether to use intrusion detection, but which intrusion detection features and capabilities to use. IDSs have gained acceptance as a necessary addition to every organization's security infrastructure. IDS products can provide worthwhile indications of malicious activity and spotlight security vulnerabilities, thus providing an additional layer of protection. Without them, network administrators have little chance of knowing about, much less assessing and responding to, malicious and invalid activity. Properly configured, IDSs are especially useful for monitoring the network perimeter for attacks originating from outside and for monitoring host systems for unacceptable insider activity.

Security Event Detection

Security event detection refers to the use of logs and other audit mechanisms to capture information about system and application access, types of access, network events, intrusion attempts, viruses, and so forth. Logging is an important link in the analysis of attack and real-time alerts of any kind of suspicious activity on the Internet bank Web site. For proper tracking of unusual events and attempts of intrusion, the following logs should be collected: basic security logs, network event logging, log authentication failures, log access violations, log attempts to implant viruses and other malicious code, and log abnormal activity. This strongly implies that the technical department that is analyzing logs to identify unusual behavior must be aware of business initiatives. In addition, it has to be ensured that audit logs are retained long enough to satisfy legal requirements. Also, at a minimum, investigation of security breaches should be allowed for up to 14 days after any given attack (IETF, 2000). Today, data mining techniques can interpret millions of items of log data and reveal any unobserved attempts to breach an ebank's Web site. For this,

it has to be ensured that logs do not overwrite themselves causing loss of data. For analysis of events at a site, documentation of automated systems that identify what the logs mean should be maintained. Understanding the nature of attempts such as whether an attack was from within the organization or from outside or whether it was just a false alarm is critical to security.

Malicious Content

Malicious content refers to programs of any type that are introduced into a system to cause damage or steal information. Malicious content includes viruses, Trojan horses, hacker tools, and network sniffers. While common in multiple domains, this is as important in the e-banking world, as well. Malicious code brings with it the potential to create serious technical and economic impact by crashing e-mail servers and networks, causing millions of dollars of damage in lost productivity.

Some of the common forms of malicious contents are the following:

- *Virus:* A virus is a computer program that runs on a system without being asked to do so, created to infect other computer programs with copies of itself. Pioneer virus researcher Fred Cohen has defined a virus as "a program that can 'infect' other programs by modifying them to include a, possibly evolved, copy of it."
- *Worm:* A worm has the ability to spread over a network and, thus, can take advantage of the Internet to do its work. Worms reside in memory and duplicate themselves throughout the network without user intervention.
- *Trojan Horse:* A Trojan horse is the name applied to a malicious computer program disguised as a seemingly innocent activity such as initiating a screen saver, accessing an e-mail attachment, or downloading executable files from an untrusted Web site. Some

of the widely manifested malicious codes are Stoned, Yankee, Michelangelo, Joshi, Lehigh, Jerusalem, MBDF (for Macintosh), Melissa, Concept, LoveBug (ILOVEYOU), ShapeShift, Fusion, Accessiv, Emporer, Sircam, Nimda, and Badtrans.

Protection against malicious codes like viruses, worms, Trojan horses, and so forth could be effectively dealt with by installing security protection software that thwarts and mitigates the effects of codes. However, such software provides only a level of defense and is not by itself sufficient. Recommendations for e-banking IT infrastructure include (Noakes, 2001):

- Install detection and protection solutions for all forms of malicious code, not just an antivirus solution.
- Ensure that all users are aware of and follow safe behavior practices—do not open attachments that have not been scanned, do not visit untrusted Web sites, and so forth.
- Ensure that users are aware of how easy data may be stolen automatically just by visiting a Web site. Install an effective solution. Keep it current with the latest signatures as new forms of malicious code are identified.
- Use anti-spammers, harden operating systems, configure stricter firewall rules, and so forth.

Security Services, Mechanisms, and Security Protection

Security risks are unlike privacy risks; they originate outside the Financial Service Provider (FSP) and change rapidly with advances in technology (DeLotto, 1999). In December 2000, IATF released guidelines that require all covered institutions to secure their clients' personal information against any reasonably foreseeable internal or external threats to their security, confidentiality, and integrity. By July 1, 2001, FSPs were expected to develop customer information security programs that ensured the security and confidentiality of customer information, protected against any anticipated threats or hazards to the security or integrity of customer information, and protected against unauthorized access to or use of customer information that could result in substantial harm or inconvenience to customers.

The services and mechanisms that are prevalent in an e-banking environment are presented below in order to provide an understanding of key issues and terms involved.

Encryption

Encryption is the process of using a key to scramble readable text into unreadable cyphertext. Encryption on the Internet, in general, and e-banking, in particular, have many uses, from the secure transmission of credit card numbers via the Web to protecting the privacy of personal e-mail messages. Authentication also uses encryption by using a key or key pair to verify the integrity of a document and its origin. The Data Encryption Standard (DES) has been endorsed by the National Institute of Standards and Technology (NIST) since 1975 and is the most readily available encryption standard. Rivest, Shamir, and Adleman (RSA) encryption is a public-key encryption system; it is a patented technology in the United States and, thus, is not available without a license. RSA encryption is growing in popularity and is considered quite secure from brute force attacks. Another encryption mechanism is Pretty Good Privacy (PGP), which allows users to encrypt information stored on their system as well as to send and receive encrypted e-mail. Encryption mechanisms rely on keys or passwords. The longer the password, the more difficult the encryption is to break. VPNs employ encryption to provide secure transmissions over public networks such as the Internet.

Security Protocol Services

The Internet is viewed as an insecure place. Many of the protocols used in the Internet do not provide any security. Today's businesses, particularly the banking sector, must integrate security protocols into their e-commerce infrastructure to protect customer information and privacy. Some of the most common protocols are discussed briefly in Appendix A.

Firewalls and Intrusion Detection Systems

A firewall is a collection of hardware and software designed to examine a stream of network traffic and service requests. Its purpose is to eliminate from the stream those packets or requests that fail to meet the security criteria established by the organization. A simple firewall may consist of a filtering router, configured to discard packets that arrive from unauthorized addresses or that represent attempts to connect to unauthorized service ports. Firewalls can filter packets based on their source and destination addresses and port numbers. This is known as address filtering. Firewalls also can filter specific types of network traffic. This is also known as protocol filtering, because the decision to forward or reject traffic is dependent upon the protocol used (e.g., HTTP, ftp, or telnet). Firewalls also can filter traffic by packet attribute or state. But a firewall cannot prevent individual users with modems from dialing into or out of the network, bypassing the firewall altogether (Odyssey, 2001). In this age of systems being hijacked, it is also important that firewalls and screen routers detect and prevent outgoing traffic that attempts to compromise the integrity of the systems. A Network Intrusion Detection System (NIDS) analyzes network traffic for attacks. It examines individual packets within the data stream to identify threats from authorized users, backdoor attacks, and hackers who have

thwarted the control systems to exploit network connections and access valuable data. NIDS adds a new level of visibility into the nature and characteristics of the network. They provide information about the use and usage of the network. Host Based IDS/Event Log Viewers are a kind of IDS that monitors event logs from multiple sources for suspicious activity. Host IDS is best placed to detect computer misuse from trusted insiders and those who have infiltrated the network. The technology and logical schemes used by these systems often are based on knowledge-based misuse detection (Allan, 2002). Knowledge-based detection methods use information about known security policy, known vulnerabilities, and known attacks on the systems they monitor. This approach compares network activity or system audit data to a database of known attack signatures or other misuse indicators, and pattern matches produce alarms of various sorts. Behavior-based detection (Allan, 2002) methods use information about repetitive and usual behavior on the systems they monitor. Also called *anomaly detection,* this approach notes events that diverge from expected (based on repetitive and usual) usage patterns. One technique is threshold detection (Allan, 2002) in which certain attributes of user and system behavior are expressed in terms of counts, with some level established as permissible. Another technique is to perform statistical analysis (Allan, 2002) on the information, build statistical models of the environment, and look for patterns of anomalous activity.

Passwords and Personal Identification Numbers (PINs)

The most common authentication method for existing customers requesting access to electronic banking systems is the entry of a user name and a secret string of characters such as a password or PIN. User IDs combined with passwords or PINs are considered a single-factor authentication technique. There are three aspects of passwords that contribute to the security they provide: secrecy, length and composition, and system controls. In the present Internet banking scenario, there are policies, for customers as well as employees, set by banks for passwords to ensure effective authentication, like prohibiting using public e-mail IDs as user IDs, ensuring that there are no user IDs with no password, ensuring that policies exist and can be automatically enforced concerning minimum password length, password format (i.e., which characters make up a valid password), expiration and renewal of passwords, uniqueness of passwords, not allowing the use of real words for passwords, and so forth.

Tokens

The use of a token represents authentication using something the customer possesses. Typically, a token is part of a two-factor authentication process, complemented by a password as the other factor. There are many benefits to the use of tokens. The authentication process cannot be completed unless the device is present. Static passwords or biometric identifiers used to activate the token may be authenticated locally by the device itself. This process avoids the transmission of shared secrets over an open network such as the Internet.

Digital Certificates and Public Key Infrastructure (PKI)

A financial institution may use a PKI system to authenticate customers to their own electronic banking product. Institutions may also use the infrastructure to provide authentication services to customers who wish to transact business over the Internet with other entities or to identify employees and commercial partners seeking access to the business' internal systems. A properly implemented and maintained PKI may provide a strong means of customer identification over open

networks such as the Internet. By combining a variety of hardware components, system software, policies, practices, and standards, PKI can provide for authentication, data integrity, and defenses against customer repudiation, and confidentiality (Odyssey, 2001). The certificate authority (CA), which may be the financial institution or its service provider, plays a key role by attesting with a digital certificate that a particular public key and the corresponding private key belong to a specific individual or system. It is important when issuing a digital certificate that the registration process for initially verifying the identity of customers is adequately controlled. The CA attests to the individual's identity by signing the digital certificate with its own private key, known as the *root key*. Each time the customer establishes a communication link with the financial institution, a digital signature is transmitted with a digital certificate. These electronic credentials enable the institution to determine that the digital certificate is valid, identify the individual as a customer, and confirm that transactions entered into the institution's computer system were performed by that customer. PKI, as the most reliable model for security and trust on the Internet, offers a comprehensive e-security solution for Internet banking. Unlike the other security models, PKI is a standards compliant, most credible trust framework, highly scalable and modular. PKI comprehensively satisfies the security requirements of e-banking (Odyssey, 2001).

A brief discussion on the processes and mechanisms used in PKI to address common security concerns follows:

- *Authentication:* The customer requests the Registration Authority (RA) for a certificate. The Registration Authority validates the customer's credentials. After valid credentials are ensured, the RA passes the certificate request to the Certification Authority (CA). CA then issues the certificates. A digital certificate can be stored on the browser on the user's computer, on a floppy disk, on a smart card, or on other hardware tokens.

- *Confidentiality:* The customer generates a random session key at his or her end. The session key is sent to the bank, encrypting it with the bank's public key. The bank decrypts the encrypted session key with its private key. The session key is employed for further transactions.

- *Integrity:* The message is passed through a suitable hashing algorithm to obtain a message digest or hash. The hash, encrypted with the sender's private key, is appended to the message. The receiver, upon receiving the message, passes it through the same hashing algorithm. The digest the receiver obtains is compared with the received and decrypted digest. If the digests are the same, it implies that the data have not been tampered with in transit.

- *Non-Repudiation:* The hash is encrypted with the sender's private key to yield the sender's digital signature. Since the hash is encrypted with the sender's private key (which is accessible only to the sender), it provides an indisputable means of non-repudiation.

- The use of digital signatures and certificates in Internet banking has provided the trust and security needed to carry out banking transactions across open networks like the Internet. PKI, being a universally accepted standards compliant security model, provides for the establishment of a global trust chain. (Odyssey, 2001).

Biometrics

A biometric identifier measures an individual's unique physical characteristic or behavior and compares it to a stored digital template to authenticate that individual. A biometric identifier representing "something the user is" can be created from sources such as a customer's voice, fingerprints, hand or face geometry, the iris or retina in an eye, or the way a customer signs a document or enters keyboard strokes (FDIC, 2001). The success of a biometric identifier rests on the ability of the digitally stored characteristic to relate typically to only one individual in a defined population. Although not yet in widespread use by financial institutions for authenticating existing customers, biometric identifiers are being used in some cases for physical access control.

Banks could use a biometric identifier for a single or multi-factor authentication process. ATMs that implement biometrics like iris-scan technologies are examples of the use of a biometric identifier to authenticate users. The biometric identifier may be used for authentication instead of the PIN. A customer can use a PIN or password to supplement the biometric identifier, making it part of a more secure two-factor authentication process. Financial institutions also may use biometric identifiers for automating existing processes. Another application would be a financial institution that allows customer to reset a password over the telephone with voice-recognition software that authenticates the customer. An authentication process that relies on a single biometric identifier may not work for everyone in a financial institution's customer base. Introducing a biometric method of authentication requires physical contact with each customer to capture initially the physical identifier, which further buttresses the initial customer verification process. But this process may increase the deployment costs.

Hardware Security Devices (HSDs)

This mechanism is an extension to usage of tokens for authentication. Using hardware devices for authentication provides "hacker-resistant" and "snooping-proof" two-factor authentication, which results in easy-to-use, effective user identification (Grand, 2001). To access protected

Table 2. End-user involvement with the security issues

Security issues with direct user focus	User-focused mechanisms that are available	User-transparent mechanisms/technology
Authentication	Passwords, PINs tokens, HSDs, Biometrics	Radius, TACACS, PKI, ISAKMP
Access Control	Roles, User Discretion, Hard-coded systems	
Confidentiality	Training	Encryption
Integrity	Encryption (hashing)	
Malicious Content	Training	Mail/Spam filters, anti-virus
Non-repudiation	Use of PKI, and authentication mechanisms	
Incident Response	Training	
Social Engineering	Training	
Security issues with system-only focus		
Availability	IDSs, Firewall, redundancy, fault-tolerance, application-level security rules	
Security Event, Intrusion Detection	IDSs, probes, firewalls	
Perimeter Defense	Firewalls, IDSs,	
Administration	Depends on the system policies as well as administrators.	

Table 3. IA issues

E-banking Specific Issues	Generic Issues (in E-banking)
E-banking related regulations, Banking and E-banking standards and frameworks, banking-specific protocol services.	Authentication, Access Control, Integrity, Availability, Perimeter Defense, Security Event Detection, Malicious Content, Incident Response, Social Engineering, Administration.

resources, the user simply combines his or her secret PIN (something the user knows) with the code generated by the user's token (something the user has). The result is a unique, one-time-use code that is used to positively identify, or authenticate, the user (Grand, 2001). Some central server validates the code. The goal is to provide acceleration, secure key management.

A hardware security module is a hardware-based security device that generates, stores, and protects cryptographic keys. There are universal criteria for rating these devices. The criteria are documented in a Federal Information Processing Standard (FIPS) called FIPS 140-1 to 140-4—Security for Cryptographic Modules. Such hardware devices generate tokens that are dynamic, one-time passwords through the use of a mathematical function. Passwords generated by tokens are different each time the user requests one, so an intercepted password is useless, as it will never be used again. Acceptance and credibility of the devices is reflected in the increasing number of devices in use.

Industry Standards and Frameworks

Industry standards for financial transactions over the Internet are an absolute necessity for ensuring various security aspects of business as well as consumer confidence. There have been a constant search and a development of standards for e-banking infrastructural tenets like authentication, access control, non-repudiation, and so forth. Some of the standards developed and advocated by different industry players and their proponents are briefly discussed in Appendix B, which will provide an overall understanding of the evolution and prevalence of some of the standards.

User and E-Banking Focus on Security Issues

To summarize, Table 2 presents issues over which the user has direct control or with which the user has involvement, and issues that are commonly left for the systems to handle.

CONCLUSIONS

It should be noted that the discussion of e-banking information assurance (IA) issues also has included several generic IA issues. To illustrate this, Table 3 briefly categorizes e-banking-specific information assurance issues and generic issues separately. Some issues may be more significant than in other areas. We have made an attempt to comprehensively discuss all the areas in the article.

Security for financial transactions is of vital importance to financial institutions providing or planning to provide service delivery to customers over the Internet, as well as to suppliers of products, services, and solutions for Internet-based e-commerce. The actual and perceived threats to Internet-based banking define the need for a set of interrelated security services to provide protection to all parties who can benefit from Web banking in a secure environment. Such services may be specific to counter particular threats or may be pervasive throughout an Internet-based environment to provide the levels of protection needed.

There are also requirements that the entire e-commerce environment be constructed from components that recognize the need for security services and provide means for overall security integration, administration, and management. These services that offer the security from an infrastructure standpoint are found throughout the e-commerce network and computing infrastructure. Financial institutions should carry out, as a matter of corporate security policy, identification of likely targets, which should include all systems that are open to the public network, such as routers, firewalls, Web servers, modem banks' Web sites, and internal unsecured systems such as desktops. They should regularly revise and update their policies on auditing, risk assessment, standards, and key management. Vulnerability assessment and identification of likely targets and the recognition of systems most vulnerable to attack are critical in the e-banking arena. Accurate identification of vulnerable and attractive systems will contribute to prioritization when addressing problem areas.

ACKNOWLEDGMENTS

The authors would like to thank John Walp and Shamik Banerjee for their contributions and help with this chapter, and the anonymous referees for their comments that have improved this chapter. We would also like to thank the NSA for the Center for Information Assurance recognition and the Department of Defense for two student fellowships. The research of the second author was supported in part by National Science Foundation (NSF) under grant 990735, and the research of the third author was supported in part by the U.S. Air Force Research Lab, Rome, New York, under Contract F30602-00-10505.

REFERENCES

Allan, A. (2002). *Technology overview. Intrusion detection systems (IDSs): Perspective.* Gartner Research Report (DPRO-95367).

Basel Committee (2001). *Risk management Principles for electronic banking.* Basel Committee Publication No. 82.

Bohle, K. (2001). Integration of Internet payment systems—What's the problem? *ePSO (E-payments systems Observatory)——Newsletter.* Retrieved March 1, 2003, from *http://epso.jrc.es/newsletter/vol11/ 5.html*

Burt, S. (2002). Online banking: Striving for compliance in cyberspace. *Bankers Systems Inc.* Retrieved September 5, 2002, from *http://www.bankers systems.com/compliance/article13.html*

DeLotto, R. (1999). *Competitive intelligence for the e-financial service provider.* Gartner Group Research Report.

Dittrich, D. (1999). *Incident response steps.* Lecture series at University of Washington.

FDIC (Federal Deposit Insurance Corporation) (2001). Authentication in electronic banking. *Financial Institution Letters.*

FIPS (Federal Information Processing Standard). (1992). *Security requirements for cryptographic modules.* Federal Information Processing Standard 140-1. National Institute of Standards and Technology.

GartnerGroup RAS Services. (1999). *Intrusion detection systems.* R-08-7031.

Glaessner, T., Kellermann, T., & McNevin, V. (2002). *Electronic security: Risk mitigation in financial transactions. Public policy issues.* The World Bank.

Grand, J. (2001). *Authentication tokens: Balancing the security risks with business requirements.* Cambridge, MA: Stake, Inc.

IESAC (2003). Transactional security. *Institution of Engineers, Saudi Arabian Center.* Retrieved January 12, 2003, from *http://www.iepsac.org/papers/p04c04a.htm*

Internet Security Task Force (2000). Initial recommendations for conducting secure ebusiness. Retrieved January 12, 2003, from *http://www.ca.com/ISTF/recomme ndations.htm*

Junnarkar, S. (2002). Online banks: Prime targets for attacks. *e-Business ZDTech News Update.*

Maconachy, W.V., Schou, C.D., Ragsdale, D., & Welch, D. (2001, June 5-6). A model for information assurance: An integrated approach. *Proceedings of the 2001 IEEE Workshop on Information Assurance and Security,* United States Military Academy, West Point, NY.

Marchany, R. (1998). *Internet security & incident response: Scenarios & tactics.* Retrieved February 2, 2003, from *https://courseware.vt.edu/marchany/InternetSecurity/Class*

NIIAC (The National Information Infrastructure Advisory Council) (1995). *Common ground: Fundamental principles for the national information infrastructure.*

Noakes, K. (2001). *Virus and malicious code protection products: Perspective.* Fry Technology Overview, Gartner Research Group, DPRO-90840.

OCC (Office of the Comptroller of the Currency) (1998). *OCC bulletin 98-3 Technology risk management.* PC Banking.

OCC (Office of the Comptroller of the Currency) (2001). *AL 2001-4 OCC advisory letter.*

Odyssey Technologies (2001). *PKI for Internet banking.* Retrieved August 23, 2002, from *http://www.odysseytec.com*

Orr, B. (2002). Infrastructure, not innovation. *ABA Banking Online Journal.* Retrieved August 8, 2002, from *http://www.banking.com/aba/infra structure.asp*

Pfleeger, C.P. (1997). *Security in computing.* Upper Saddle River, NJ: Prentice Hall.

Poland, K.R., & Nash, M.J. (1990). Some conundrums concerning separation of duty. *IEEE Symposium on Computer Security and Privacy.*

Starita, L. (1999). *Online banking: A strategic perspective.* Context Overview Report (R-08-7031-Gartner).

United States Senate (2002). Financial services modernization act: Provisions of GLB act. *The United States Senate.* Retrieved August 8, 2002, from *http://www.senate.gov/~banking/conf/grm-leach.htm*

Walsh, E. (1999). *Technology overview: Internet banking: Perspective.* DPRO-90293, Gartner.

Walsh, E. (2002). *Product report: S1 corporate suite e-banking software.* DPRO-95913 Gartner Research Group.

ENDNOTES

[1] http://www.*epaynews.com/statistics/bank-stats.html*

[2] *http://www.orcc.com*

[3] Robert Lemos, Staff Writer, CNET news. com, *Counting the Cost of Slammer,* Retrieved March 31, 2003, from *http://news. com.com/2100-1001-982955.html*

[4] Reuters, Seattle (Washington), *CNN.com, Technology news, Feb 5, 2003.* Retrieved March 8, 2003, from *http://www.cnn. com/2003/TECH/internet/02/05/virus. spread.reut/*

[5] Atomic Tangarine Inc, *NPV: Information Security,* Retrieved March 21, 2003, from *www.ttivanguard.com/risk/netpresent-value.pdf*

[6] The latest version of the specifications, EMV 2000 version 4.0, published December 2000, *http://www. emvco.com/*).

[7] CEN/ISSS was created in mid-1997 by CEN (European Committee for Standardization) and ISSS (Information Society Standardization) to provide a comprehensive and integrated range of standardization-oriented services and products.

This work was previously published in Advanced Topics in End User Computing, Vol. 4, edited by M. Mahood, pp. 233-256, copyright 2005 by IGI Publishing, formerly Idea Group Publishing (an imprint of IGI Global).

APPENDIX A: COMMON SECURITY PROTOCOL SERVICES

Protocol	Description
Secure Sockets Layer (SSL)	Originally developed by Netscape, the SSL security protocol provides data encryption, server authentication, message integrity, and optional client authentication for a TCP/IP connection. SSL has been universally accepted on the World Wide Web for authenticated and encrypted communication between clients and servers. However, SSL consumes large amounts of the Web server's processing power due to the massive cryptographic computations that take place when a secure session is initiated. If many secure sessions are initiated simultaneously, then the Web server quickly becomes overburdened. The results are slow response times, dropped connections, and failed transactions.
Secure Shell (SSH)	SSH Secure Shell is the de facto standard for remote logins. It solves an important security problem on the Internet of password hacking. Typical applications include secure use of networked applications, remote system administration, automated file transfers, and access to corporate resources over the Internet.
AS1 and AS2	AS1 provides S/MIME encryption and security over SMTP (Simple Mail Transfer Protocol) through object signature and object encryption technology. AS2 goes a step further than AS1 by supporting S/MIME over HTTP and HTTPS. Both AS1 and AS2 provide data authentication, proving that the sender and receiver are indeed the people or company that they claim to be.
Digital Certificates	Digital certificates are used to authenticate the identity of trading partners, ensuring partners are really who they say they are. In addition to data authentication, digital signatures support non-repudiation, proving that a specific message did come from a known sender at a specific time. A digital signature is a digital code that can be sent with electronically transmitted message and it uniquely identifies the sender. It is based on digital certificates. This prevents partners from claiming that they didn't send or receive a particular message or transaction.
Pretty Good Privacy (PGP)	PGP is a freely available encryption program that uses public key cryptography to ensure privacy over FTP, HTTP and other protocols. PGP is the de-facto standard software for the encryption of e-mail and works on virtually every platform. But PGP suffers from absence of Trust management and it is not standards compliant though it could provide for integrity, authentication, non-repudiation and confidentiality. PGP also provides tools and utilities for creating, certifying, and managing keys.
Secure Multipurpose Internet Mail Extension (S/MIME)	S/MIME addresses security concerns such as privacy, integrity, authentication and non-repudiation, through the use of signed receipts. S/MIME provides a consistent way to send and receive secure MIME data. Based on the MIME standard, S/MIME provides authentication, message integrity, non-repudiation of origin (using digital signatures) and data confidentiality (using encryption) for electronic messaging applications. Since its development by RSA in 1996, S/MIME has been widely recognized and widely used standard for messaging. The technology for S/MIME is primarily built on the Public Key Cryptographic Standard, which provides cryptographic interoperability. Two key features of S/MIME are the digital signature and the digital envelope. Digital signatures ensure that a message has not been tampered with during transit. Digital signatures also provide non-repudiation so senders can't deny that they sent the message.
Secure HTTP (S-HTTP)	S-HTTP is an extension to HTTP, which provides a number of security features, including Client/Server Authentication, Spontaneous Encryption and Request/Response Non-repudiation. S-HTTP allows the secure exchange of files on the World Wide Web. Each S-HTTP file is either encrypted, contains a digital certificate, or both. For a given document, S-HTTP is an alternative to another well-known security protocol, Secure Sockets Layer (SSL). A major difference is that S-HTTP allows the client to send a certificate to authenticate the user whereas, using SSL, only the server can be authenticated. S-HTTP is more likely to be used in situations where the server represents a bank and requires authentication from the user that is more secure than a userid and password.
Simple Key management for Internet Protocols (SKIP)	It is a manifestation of IP-Level Cryptography that secures the network at the IP packet level. Any networked application gains the benefits of encryption, without requiring modification. SKIP is unique in that an Internet host can send an encrypted packet to another host without requiring a prior message exchange to set up a secure channel. SKIP is particularly well suited to IP networks, as both are stateless protocols.
Encapsulating Security Payload (ESP)	ESP is security protocol that provides data confidentiality and protection with optional authentication and replay-detection services. ESP completely encapsulates user data. ESP can be used either by itself or in conjunction with AH. ESP may be implemented with AH, as discussed in next paragraph, in a nested fashion through the use of tunnel mode. Security services can be provided between a pair of communicating hosts, between a pair of communicating security gateways, or between a security gateway and a host, depending on the implementation. ESP may be used to provide the same security services, and it also provides a confidentiality (encryption) service. Specifically, ESP does not protect any IP header fields unless those fields are encapsulated by ESP (tunnel mode).
Authentication Header (AH)	A security protocol that provides authentication and optional replay-detection services. AH is embedded in the data to be protected (a full IP datagram, for example). AH can be used either by itself or with Encryption Service Payload (ESP). The IP Authentication Header is used to provide connectionless integrity and data origin authentication for IP datagrams, and to provide protection against replays. AH provides authentication for as much of the IP header as possible, as well as for upper level protocol data. However, some IP header fields may change in transit and the value of these fields, when the packet arrives at the receiver, may not be predictable by the sender. The values of such fields cannot be protected by AH. Thus the protection provided to the IP header by AH is somewhat piecemeal and not complete.

APPENDIX B: SOME INDUSTRY STANDARDS AND FRAMEWORKS IN E-BANKING

Standard	Description
SET	Secure Electronic Transaction (SET) is a system for ensuring the security of financial transactions on the Internet. It was supported initially by Mastercard, Visa, Microsoft, Netscape, and others. With SET, a user is given an *electronic wallet* (digital certificate) and a transaction is conducted and verified using a combination of digital certificates and digital signatures among the purchaser, a merchant, and the purchaser's bank in a way that ensures privacy and confidentiality. SET makes use of Netscape's Secure Sockets Layer (SSL), Microsoft's Secure Transaction Technology (STT), and Terisa System's Secure Hypertext Transfer Protocol (S-HTTP). SET uses some but not all aspects of a public key infrastructure (PKI). SET provides authentication, integrity, non-repudiation and confidentiality.
HBCI	HBCI is a specification for the communication between intelligent customer systems and the corresponding computing centers for the exchange of home banking transactions. The transmission of data is done by a net data interface, which is based on flexible delimiter syntax.
EMV[1]	Specifications by Europay, MasterCard and Visa that define a set of requirements to ensure interoperability between chip cards and terminals on a global basis, regardless of the manufacturer, the financial institution, or where the card is used.
CEPS	The Common Electronic Purse Specifications (CEPS) define requirements for all components needed by an organization to implement a globally interoperable electronic purse program, while maintaining full accountability and auditability. CEPS, which were made available in March of 1999, outline overall system security, certification and migration. CEPS have paved the way for the creation of an open, de facto, global electronic purse standard (http://www.cepsco.com/).
XMLPay	XMLPay is a standard proposed/developed by Ariba and Verisign. It defines an XML syntax for payment transaction requests, responses and receipts in a payment processing network. The intended users are Internet merchants and merchant aggregators who need to deal with multiple electronic payment mechanisms (credit/debit card, purchase card, electronic cheque and automated clearing house payment). The supported operations include funds authorization and capture, sales and repeat sales, and voiding of transactions.
ECML	The Electronic Commerce Modeling Language ECML is a specification that describes the format for data fields that need to be filled at checkout in an online transaction. The fields defined include shipping information, billing information, recipient information, payment card information and reference fields. Version 2.0 describes these fields in XML syntax.
W3C standard on micropayments	The W3C standard on micropayments has originated from IBM's standardization efforts. It covers the payment function for payment of digital goods. The Micropayment initiative specifies how to provide in a Web page all the information necessary to initialize a micropayment and transfer this information to the wallet for processing. The W3C Ecommerce/Micropayment Activity is now closed.
Passport	Microsoft Passport is an online user-authentication service. Passport's primary service is user authentication, referred to as the Passport single sign-in (SSI) service. Passport also offers two other optional services: Passport express purchase (EP), which lets users store credit card and billing/shipping address information in their optional Passport wallet profiles to expedite checkout at participating e-commerce sites, and Kids Passport (source: Microsoft Passport Technical White Paper).
eWallet project of CEN/ISSS[2]	CEN/ISSS Electronic Commerce Workshop initiated the eWallet project in mid-2001 assuming a need for standardization in the field. CEN/ISSS has chosen a flexible working definition considering an eWallet as "a collection of confidential data of a personal nature or relating to a role carried our by an individual, managed so as to facilitate completion of electronic transactions".
SEMPER	Secure Electronic Market Place for Europe (SEMPER) was produced by an EU supported project under a special program, undertaken by a 20 partner consortium led by IBM. It is a definition of an open and system independent architecture for Electronic Commerce. The project was concluded in 1999. Based on access via a browser, the architecture specifies common functions to be supported by applications which include Exchange of certificates, Exchange of signed offer/order, Fair contract signing, Fair payment for receipt, and Provision of delivery information.
IOTP	The Internet Open Trading Protocol (IOTP) is defined as an interoperable framework for Internet commerce. It is optimized for the case where the buyer and the merchant do not have a prior acquaintance. IOTP is payment system independent. It can encapsulate and support several of leading payment systems.
SEPP	Secure Electronic Payment Process is a protocol developed by MasterCard and Netscape to provide authentication, integrity and payment confidentiality. It uses DES for confidentiality and 512, 768, 1024 or 2048 bit RSA and 128 bit MD5 hashing. RSA encrypts DES key to encrypt hash of account numbers. It uses up to three public keys, one for signing, one for key exchange, one for certificate renewal. Besides, SEPP uses X.509 certificates with CMS at top of hierarchy[26].
STT	Secure Transaction Technology was developed by Visa and Microsoft to provide authentication, integrity and confidentiality to the Internet based transactions. It is based on 64 bit DES or 64 bit RC4 (24-bit salt) for confidentiality and 512, 768, 1024 or 2048 bit RSA for encryption with 160 bit SHA hashing. It uses two public keys, one for signing, one for key exchange. It has credentials similar to certificates but with account details and higher level signatures, though they are not certificates.
JEPI	(Joint Electronic Payment Initiative) CommerceNet and the W3 Consortium are jointly initiating a multi-industry project to develop an Internet payment negotiation protocol. The project explores the technology required to provide negotiation over multiple payment instruments, protocols and transports. Examples of payment instruments include credit cards, debit cards, electronic cash and checks. Payment protocols include STT and SEPP (amongst others). Payment transport encompasses the message transmission mechanism: S-HTTP, SSL, SMTP, and TCP/IP are all categorized as transport technologies that can be used for payment.

---

[1] The latest version of the specifications, EMV 2000 version 4.0, was published in December 2000 (http://www.emvco.com/).

[2] CEN/ISSS was created in mid-1997 by CEN (European Committee for Standardization) and ISSS(Information Society Standardization) to provide with a comprehensive and integrated range of standardization-oriented services and products

Chapter 4.29
Security, Privacy, and Trust in Mobile Systems

Marco Cremonini
Università di Milano, Italy

Ernesto Damiani
Università di Milano, Italy

Sabrina De Capitani di Vimercati
Università di Milano, Italy

Pierangela Samarati
Università di Milano, Italy

INTRODUCTION

Access to general purpose information and communication technology (ICT) is not equally distributed on our planet: developed countries represent about 70% of all Internet users, while its percentage of Internet hosts has raised from 90% in 2000 to about 99% in 2002.

Things change dramatically if we look at mobile and wireless technology: developing countries already represent about 40% of mobile connections in 2000, with a foreseen growth rate that is faster in developing countries than in developed ones in the period 2000-2005 (mainly due to India and the People's Republic of China). This trend is driven by the new perspectives offered by mobile electronic technology applications that provide an alternative to poor telecommunication infrastructures still common in many developing countries. The technological evolution in wireless data communications is introducing a rich landscape of new services relying on three main technologies:

- proximity (or personal) area networks (PANs), composed of personal and wearable devices capable of automatically setting up transient communication environments (also known as *ad hoc* networks);
- wireless local area network technologies (WLANs); and
- a third generation of mobile telecommunications (3G), gradually replacing General Packet Radio Service (GPRS) and the related

set of technologies collectively called "2.5 Generation" (2.5G).

PAN is a new technology bringing the "always connected" principle to the personal space. On the other hand, 3G systems and WLANs have coexisted for a while; what is new is their interconnection, aimed at decoupling terminals and applications from the access method. 3G mobile networks already provide video-capable bandwidth, global roaming for voice and data, and access to Internet-rich online content.

Thanks to their increasing integration, PANs, WLANs, and 3G networks will extend the user's connectivity in a complementary and hierarchical manner; in the fullness of time, they will provide all the functionalities of an *Integrated Services Multimedia Network* (ISMN), enabling a whole set of new business models and applications.

The fusion of these technologies will eventually result in an ultimate ubiquitous wireless system that will be operated from anywhere, including homes, business locations, vehicles, and even commercial aircrafts.

However, although wireless communications provide great flexibility and mobility, they often come at the expense of security. Indeed, wireless communications rely on open and public transmission media that expose new vulnerabilities in addition to the security threats found in wired networks. A number of specific open issues and even inherent dangers, some of which had been already identified and described in the early stages of wireless technology adoption, are yet to be solved (Howard, 2000). For instance, with wireless communications, important and vital information is often placed on a mobile device that is vulnerable to theft and loss. In addition, information is transmitted over the unprotected airwaves, and finally, 3G networks are getting smaller and more numerous, causing opportunities for hackers and other abusers to increase.

BACKGROUND

2G and 2.5G Mobile Authentication

GSM 2G systems introduced the *Subscriber Identity Module* (SIM) cards containing the user's identity and an authentication key (i.e., a shared secret key) supposed to last for the entire duration of the subscription. SIM-based authentication does not require any user action, other than entering the familiar four-digit *Personal Identification Number* (PIN) into the terminal. With GSM, a temporary user identity is allocated by the area operator where the user is located and is reassigned to another user as soon as the original requestor leaves the area. With the advent of 2.5G systems, enhanced by the *General Packet Radio Service* (GPRS), overlaying, certificates-based authentication became possible (Smith, 2002).

3G Authentication and On-the-Air Confidentiality

In the design of 3G systems like UMTS, a new security architecture was introduced (Blanchard, 2000). The new approach maintained backward compatibility with GSM, while trying to overcome some perceived weaknesses of 2G systems. Like in 2G systems, 3G systems identify users by means of the identity stored in the SIM. Differently from 2G systems, 3G authentication was designed with the following features:

- **Mutual Authentication:** Both the user and the network operator are identified in the authentication exchange.
- **Key Freshness:** Assurance that authentication information and keys are not being reused.
- **Integrity of Signaling:** Protection of service messages, for example, during the encryption algorithm negotiation.

- **Strong Encryption:** Strong cryptography, obtained via a combination of key length and algorithm design, is performed inside the core network rather than at the periphery.

Early Identity Management Systems

Starting from the late '80s, many examples of *Identity Management (IM)* systems have been proposed. In 1985, Chaum (1985) considered a device that helps the user with payment transactions and upholds the user's privacy. Clark (1993) proposed the *digital individual*, the individual's data shadow in the computer system which can be compared to user's identity.

Digital security and, more generally, digital identity management have grown fast in recent years, especially in mobile scenarios where personal communication and new computing devices will generate new security and integrity requirements for users and service information (Jendrike et al., 2002; Roussos & Patel, 2002).

MOBILE IDENTITY MANAGEMENT

Personal Identity Management in 3G Mobile Systems

Privacy and security issues related to mobile systems have been often described in terms of traditional security functionalities (e.g., access control, integrity, authentication, non repudiation, availability, and confidentiality). However, recent developments in ICT-based business models revealed the necessity to approach the concept of privacy and security more broadly, embracing not only the technical aspects, but also socioeconomic issues (Kagal, Parker, Chen, Joshi, & Finin, 2003). The ongoing transition from monolithic and localized systems, mainly based on single technology and weakly opened to integration,

towards multi-application, multi-access, multi-player, distributed, and heterogeneous scenarios, is generating a context in which mobile applications and systems could play a strategic role. In other words, technology and business must be strongly Internet-worked with users' social dynamics, standards, policy, and regulation to create a digital identity management framework where digital identity is conceived as "an electronic representation of individuals' or organizations' sensitive information" (Damiani, De Capitani di Vimercati, & Samarati, 2003). Support offered by this framework is crucial for building and maintaining trust relationships in today's globally interconnected society because it:

- offers adequate security and availability;
- permits the presentation of a different subset of the users' identity depending on the ongoing and perceived application and communication context;
- guarantees that identity, personal data, and user profile (including location-based information) are safeguarded and no thefts will happen.

A *Digital Identity Management Framework* is realized by taking into consideration both the architecture of the framework, and those external elements that may influence an identity manager (e.g., regulations, standards, and so on). In particular, with respect to the framework's architecture, the following main elements can be recognized.

User

The service requestor associated with a profile. The digital identity management framework should let the user keep her desired level of privacy depending on the situation, presenting multiple user "appearances" in different circumstances. In a mobile scenario, a portable user identity might include the following information:

- *Profile information* that consists of a number of static (e.g., date of birth, place of birth) and dynamic (e.g., technical skills and role) attributes.
- *Usage preferences* (e.g., browser settings) and other personal preferences that do not depend on the system (e.g., UK or U.S. English spelling).
- *Behavioral information* that may be derived by an history of previous interactions with the system.

Service Provider

The supplier of network services and applications.

Context

The particular situation in which users interact with the system. It includes the channel information (e.g., device and network features), the location information (e.g., cell, country, town), and time information.

Communication

This is based on well-known mechanisms to enable anonymity and confidentiality. With regard to anonymity, it is interesting to see that is possible for users to remain anonymous even in a world of SIM-based authentication. The authentication step is not repeated when roaming, because a user holds a reusable, temporary identification provided by the local mobile network. At the network level, therefore, mobile users have no fixed device address and, in principle, are identified only by the location.

Device

The terminal that provides the physical layer services (e.g., a radio interface) used to communicate data and to interact with context and service providers. Moreover, the device becomes the physical place where the user profile, context, and communication could be revealed and analyzed. For this reason, the terminal must be able to change the information it discloses much in the same way as the user.

The relevant external aspect that may most influence the Digital Identity Management Framework is as follows.

Shared Principles

Mobile privacy and identity management are realized to implement the following main principles:

- **Confidentiality:** Information must be accessible only by the intended receiver. Confidentiality can be split into three main elements: confidentiality of the message content, protection of location information, and support for sender/receiver anonymity.
- **Integrity:** Transmission of information is carried out by means of cryptographical mechanisms to identify and detect tampered data.
- **Notice:** An alert service must be available to draw the user's attention to situations in which privacy and security could be affected. Notice mechanisms should be manual whenever automatic solutions could compromise the user's security.
- **Data collection:** Users should be able to actively manage their own data, deciding whether and which identity is presented to devices and applications (Ceravolo, 2003). Data collection must be inspired to the principle of data minimization, by which data should only be collected for a specific purpose.

Wireless Heterogeneous Environments: Toward Ubiquitous Networking

One of the most challenging goals in the field of mobile services is the integration of different wireless technologies, like 2.5 or 3G cellular networks and WiFi (IEEE 802.11b and 802.11g) into the more general landscape of *ubiquitous networking*. Ubiquitous networking is aimed at addressing the users' need of seamlessly roaming from one connection mode to the other without impairing their ongoing operations. Accordingly, multimode cards (e.g., LAN-WLAN-GPRS cards) have been launched on the market and are becoming increasingly affordable. In particular, the advent of 3G is likely to make those multimode cards rapidly evolve to the LAN-WLAN-3G setting thus transforming portable devices—cellular phones, laptops, and PDAs—in *multimode devices*.

However, to foster effective mobility and ubiquitous computing through networks built on different wireless technologies, many fundamental issues need to be taken into consideration. An important one is the integration at link level between WiFi and GPRS/3G, which could result in a uniform network level. Realizing a uniform network layer between WiFi and GPRS/3G, in turn, may facilitate *transparent mobility*, that is, the possibility for users to automatically switch from one wireless network to another (possibly based on a different technology) without any detriment to ongoing Internet transactions or application service provision. There are many high-value mobile application services that will greatly benefit from transparent mobility such as telemedicine, Intelligent Transport Systems (ITS), and mobile Geographical Information Systems (mGIS).

More precisely, transparent mobility is characterized by successfully migrating live TCP connections during the handoffs through different wireless technologies (WLAN à GPRS/3G handoff and GPRS/3G à WLAN handoff). To do

this, not only is a seamless inter-network handoff mechanism sufficient, but also the connectivity (as devices keep moving across environments while still minimizing any disruption to ongoing flows during switchovers) is another important aspect.

A mechanism that enables this has to exhibit a low handoff latency, incur little or no data loss (even in highly mobile environments), scale to large inter-networks, adapt to different environments, and act as a conjuncture between heterogeneous environments and technologies without compromising on key issues related to security reliability (Vidales, Patanapongpibul, & Chakravorty, 2003). For all these reasons, transparent mobility is indeed one of the most challenging goals of ubiquitous computing in wireless heterogeneous environments.

Network technologies that are actively used for such systems are: *Mobile IPv4* (MIPv4) and *Mobile IPv6* (MIPv6) (Chakravorty, Vidales, Subramanian, Pratt, & Crowcroft, 2003). MIPv4 is the network technology traditionally used to foster seamless roaming for ubiquitous computing systems, mainly due to its compatibility with the wired IP-based network infrastructure. Nevertheless, MIPv4 limitations have forced the development of overly complex systems and protocols. MIPv6 promises to overcome some of MIPv4 limitations and improve security, although it has other disadvantages in high mobility scenarios (Chakravorty et al., 2003; Perkins, 1996). An IETF working group, called *Seamoby* (Kempf, 2002), has been formed aiming to resolve complex interactions of parameters and protocols needed for seamless handoffs and context transfers between nodes in an IP access network.

Multihop Hotspots

Hotspot providers in public areas represent key components of a heterogeneous wireless infrastructure for mobile users, which could be used to access WLAN services while moving. *Multi-*

hop hotspots, in particular, are hotspots through which users could roam seamlessly. Considering heterogeneous environments, users could hop through hotspots that are either physically contiguous, thus directly switching from one hotspot to another, or through a sequence of multimode handoffs between hotspots and GPRS/3G cells (Balachandran, Voelker, & Bahl, 2003).

With respect to security, hotspots still have significant open issues. One is *authentication* that is currently implemented with different and incompatible techniques by commercial WiFi networks. For instance, since hotspots are often under the control of different providers, users will have to repeat the authentication procedure (possibly different for each hotspot) at each hotspot location. Also, some commercial hotspot providers offer access to users through preestablished accounts, while others offer scratch-off cards containing a one-time login and password. A uniform and shared authentication infrastructure is fundamental for effective multihop mobility since highly mobile users cannot be required to cope with different authentication schemes, mechanisms, and configurations at each handoff. Clearly, the goal of providing fast and seamless authentication, while simultaneously ensuring user accountability, raises several research problems that are today still unsolved:

- **Ease of Access:** Single-Sign-On (SSO) features encompassing multihop hotspots are needed to support transparent mobility and reduce the latency.
- **Identity Management:** The mobile identity a user presents to each network provider could change according to context-related information such as provider reputation, QoS, location, or another contextual attribute.
- **Third-Party Authenticators:** Should authentication be delegated to dedicated third parties offering such a service for the whole multihop infrastructure?

MOBILE USER RECOVERY

VanderMeer, Dutta, Ramamritham, and Navathe (2003) addressed the problem of recovering Internet transactions initiated by mobile users. The issue is new and relevant since it presents many differences with respect to classical database transaction recovery techniques. Also, it appears extremely important in the context we have considered, since there is not only the case of recovery after a network failure, but there is the peculiar situation of recovery user activity after a handoff. This aspect is an additional novel issue to the most general problem of mobile user recovery.

This issue also has significant links with security and privacy since mobile user transactions and mechanisms for recovery could carry security risk and be targets of network attacks and subversion attempts. If network attacks would eventually succeed, it will be possible for an intruder, for example, to subvert the recovery mechanism and then recover transactions of other users, possibly gaining their privileges. By attacking a recovery mechanism, it could also be possible to access transactions' state information that still could let intruders impersonate users or gather sensitive information. Denial-of-service towards recovery systems is another threat that might severely impair the benefits of the infrastructure for ubiquitous computing and transparent mobility.

Security research in this area is still at the beginning since even operational features, like mobile user recovery, are in their initial stages. Despite this, the issue looks extremely important for the future evolution of ubiquitous computing and transparent mobility (VanderMeer et al., 2003). Several important issues that may affect security arise:

- **Secure Storage and Access to Logs and Recovery Procedures:** There could be different choices, from storing logs and procedures locally to the device, storing them at network gateways or at specialized recovery hosts. Indeed, a support to recovery features from the network infrastructure is needed. This introduces security issues related to trust relationships and authentication, with third parties or networked components in charge of user sessions recovery.

- **Trustworthy Generation, Management, and Usage of Users, Logs and State Information:** State information must be protected from tampering and disclosure since network components in charge of generating and storing state information are possible points of attacks.

FUTURE TRENDS

Ubiquitous computing in wireless heterogeneous environments and the ever-increasing interoperability between heterogeneous technologies are some of the most relevant trends in the field of mobile systems. However, such systems need operational features and security requirements that still have to be provided (Vidales et al., 2003). For instance, two interesting and fundamental open issues are the following:

- **Link-Switch Decision Rule-Base:** Current schemes that regulate handoffs operate based on link layer information, such as signal strength. However, this could be insufficient to assist the handoff process in heterogeneous environments. Signal quality, costs, and security requirements might be other parameters that need to be evaluated to decide the handoff.
- **Context-Awareness:** A mobile device context involves aspects such as physical context variables (e.g., device location, movement direction, velocity, and so on), application characteristics, and of course, user-based preferences. Context-awareness is necessary to take informed decisions about switching to a different network and provider.

CONCLUSION

The amount of mobile computing is expected to increase dramatically in the near future. As the users' demands increase with the offered services of mobile communication systems, the main expectation on such systems will be that they provide access to any service, anywhere, at anytime. Indeed, in today's highly connected and highly mobile environments, the secure transmission of information is imperative for every enterprise, and will grow in significance as mobile devices, networks, and applications continue to advance. However, the promise of mobile computing technologies further increases privacy and security concerns. In this article we have discussed the need for privacy and security in mobile systems and have presented technological trends that highlight that this issue is of growing concern.

ACKNOWLEDGMENTS

This work was supported in part by the European Union within the PRIME Project in the FP6/IST Programme under contract IST-2002-507591 and by the Italian Ministry of Research Funds for Basic Research (FIRB) within the KIWI and MAPS projects.

REFERENCES

Balachandran, A., Voelker, G. M., & Bahl, P. (2003). Wireless hotspot: Current challenges and future directions. *Proceedings of ACM WMASH'03*.

Blanchard, C. (2000). *Security for the third generation (3G) mobile system*. Retrieved from http://www.isrc.rhul.ac.uk/useca/OtherPublications/3G UMTS%20Security.pdf

Ceravolo, P. (2003). Managing identities via interactions between ontologies. *Proceedings of the Workshop on Metadata for Security,* Catania, Italy.

Chakravorty, R., Vidales, P., Subramanian, K., Pratt, I., & Crowcroft, J. (2003). Practical experiences with wireless integration using MobileIPv6. *Proceedings of ACM MOBICOM 2003.*

Chaum, D. (1985). Security without identification: Transaction systems to make big brother obsolete. *Communications of ACM, 28*(10), 1030-1044.

Clark, R. (1993). Computer matching and digital identity. *Proceedings of the Conference on Computers, Freedom & Privacy*, San Francisco, CA.

Damiani, E., De Capitani di Vimercati, & Samarati, P. (2003). Managing multiple and dependable identities. *IEEE Internet Computing, 7*(6), 29-37.

Howard, P. (2000). 3G security overview. *Proceedings of the IIR Fraud and Security Conference.* Retrieved from http://www.isrc.rhul.ac.uk/useca/OtherPublications/IIR-overview.pdf

Jendricke, U., Kreutzer, M., & Zugenmaier, A. (2002). Mobile identity management. *Proceedings of the Workshop on Security in Ubiquitous Computing (UBICOMP2002).*

Kagal, L., Parker, J., Chen, H., Joshi, A., & Finin, T. (2003). *Security, privacy and trust in mobile computing environments.* Boca Raton, FL: CRC Press.

Kempf, J. (2002). Problem description: Reason for doing context transfers between nodes in an IP access network. *IETF Request for Comments*, RFC 3374.

Perkins, C. E., & Johnson, D. B. (1996). Mobility support in IPv6. *Proceedings of ACM MOBICOM.*

Roussos, G., & Patel, U. (2002). Mobile identity management. *Proceedings of Mobile Business 2002.*

Smith, R. (2002). *Authentication: From passwords to public keys.* San Francisco: Addison-Wesley.

VanderMeer, D. A. D., Dutta, K., Ramamritham, K., & Navathe, S.B. (2003). Mobile user recovery in the context of Internet transactions. *IEEE Transactions on Mobile Computing, 2*(2), 132-146.

Vidales, P., Patanapongpibul, L., & Chakravorty, R. (2003). Ubiquitous networking in heterogeneous environments. *Proceedings of the 8th IEEE Mobile Multimedia Communications (MoMuC 2003).*

KEY TERMS

3G: The third generation of mobile communications technology.

Digital Identity Management System: A system related to the definition and lifecycle of digital identities and profiles as well as environments for exchanging and validating this information.

Multihop Hotspots: Hotspots through which users could roam seamlessly.

Privacy: Socially defined ability of an individual to determine whether, when, and to whom personal information is to be released.

Security: The combination of integrity, availability, and secrecy.

Ubiquitous Computing: A vision where computers are made available throughout the physical environment, but effectively invisible to the users.

Wireless Local Area Network: Local area network that uses radio waves as its carrier.

Chapter 4.30
Seamlessly Securing Web Services by a Signing Proxy

Mario Jeckle
University of Applied Sciences, Furtwangen, Germany

Ingo Melzer
DaimlerChrysler Research & Technology, Germany

ABSTRACT

Web services offer a way for very different systems to collaborate independent of the programming language used or the involved operating systems. Their basis is the XML-based SOAP protocol, which can be used over any protocol that is able to transport a byte stream. Due to the fact that Web services do not depend on any operating system and there is no burden of a underlying paradigm, they are ideal for the integration of even completely inhomogeneous systems. However, SOAP does not (and does not have to) deal with security issues, which is nevertheless important for the involved systems. This article describes an add-on for existing Internet proxies to achieve user and developer transparent security features for Web services. This approach allows corporate firewalls to handle authentication. A first step is to add corporate signatures to all outgoing SOAP messages to enable a corporate trust relationship. A second improvement is to use proxy authentication as defined in RFC 2616 and RFC 2617 to add personal signatures assuming that the proxy has access to some key management system.

INTRODUCTION

Today's computer systems are extremely inhomogeneous, which can be a real burden when collaboration is desired or even required. A possible solution to this problem is Web services, which offer a great possibility for companies and institutions to implement general interfaces to their heterogeneous systems. This allows others, humans or computer systems, to access important information to enable a better cooperation.

However, at the same time, the introduction of Web services for accessing possibly critical business systems may offer other users of the Internet the possibility to gain access to those systems. Most of the time, Web service deployment is based on the well-known HTTP protocol as transport media. Content of this type is normally not inspected or filtered by most firewalls at all. The efficiency of a firewall is therefore significantly reduced. Also, SOAP, the lightweight XML-based protocol of Web services, does not come with any security features, although a firewall or proxy is a commonly used security facility.

However, this does not constitute SOAP-based Web Services as a general security hole. SOAP is not secure or insecure — security is simply not its job! According to SOAP's underlying philosophy, the application has to take care of this topic. Taking XML's co-standards encrypting and digitally signing into account, arbitrary SOAP calls could be secured with respect to privacy, authentication, non-reputation, and integrity of the transmitted data. Based on this, the receiver is able to grant authorization to the system's access. Since the creation of a secured message requires modifications to the message itself by adding security information, the application creating the SOAP payload is required to be modified as well.

An alternative to changing numerous business systems to introduce security at this protocol layer is presented here. For reasonable secured and closed environments like today's intranets behind corporate firewalls, it is possible to concentrate the handling of digital signatures at a single point within the network's structure. The machine devoted to this task could sign and encrypt if desired all outbound Web service calls, and vice versa, decrypt and check the inbound calls as part of corporate's security infrastructure. Therefore, the inclusion of such a facility will disburden applications and even leverage the usage of security mechanisms. As an option, such a facility could reside on a firewall or proxy machine.

Such an add-on to the proxies can be a service that signs all outgoing SOAP calls with a signature owned by the company or encrypts selective message contents to be readable only for the desired reader. On the other side, the firewall of the other partner will block all SOAP calls that do not have an appropriate signature or cannot be decrypted successfully. The key issue of authorization based on authentication can therefore be eased significantly whenever a call passes an enterprise's boundary.

This article first illustrates a typical infrastructure for most Web services. It also provides the necessary basics of Web services security and digital XML signatures. Based on this, the most important steps for implementing such a proxy for Web services, which will be termed a *signing proxy,* to achieve a federated or corporate trust are shown.

Secondly, this step will be improved to add personal signatures. For this goal, it is necessary that the proxy is able to identify each user, which can be achieved by using proxy authentication as described in RFC 2616 and RFC2617 (Fielding, 1999; Franks, 1999). If a key management system is installed and the proxy has access to this system, it can add a second signature to the SOAP header that belongs to the calling user.

Additionally, using the XML co-standard XML-Encryption, it is possible to add privacy to the Web services application by encrypting the outgoing messages. However, due to the fact that it is very difficult to do this transparently for all users, encryption plays only a minor role in this article.

INFRASTRUCTURE

The technical basis of the Web service philosophy is grounded on the idea of enabling various systems to exchange structured information in a decentralized, distributed environment dynamically forming an extremely loosely coupled system. In essence this led to the definition of lightweight platform-independent protocols for synchronous remote procedure calls as well as asynchronous document exchange using XML encoding via

Code 1.

```
POST /axis/theService/ HTTP/1.1 Content-Type: text/xml;
charset=utf-8 Accept: application/soap+xml
Host: 10.0.0.1:8080
Content-Length: nnn

<?xml version="1.0" ?>
<env:Envelope xmlns:env="http://www.w3.org/2002/06/soap-envelope">
 <env:Header>
    <ns1:DeliveryNotification
    env:mustUnderstand="true"
    env:role="http://www.w3.org/2003/05/soap-envelope/role/ultimateReceiver"
       xmlns:ns1="urn:xmlns:dcx.com:research">
       <ns1:SendTo URI="MailTo:jd@dcx.com"/>
    </n1:DeliveryNotification>
 </env:Header>
 <env:Body>
    <ns2:QuoteRequest>
       <ns2:ID>7492653</ns2:ID>
       <ns2:Amount>10000</ns2:Amount>
       <ns2:DeliverTo>DCX ...</ns2:DeliverTo>
    <!-- more details omitted for brevity ... -->
    </ns2:QuoteRequest>
 </env:Body>
</env:Envelope>
```

well-known Internet protocols such as HTTP.

After some introductory approaches, which were popularized under the name *XML-RPC* (Winer, 1999), the seminal *SOAP* (at the time of its definition the acronym originally abbreviated the *Simple Object Access Protocol*. In the standardized version SOAP is no longer an acronym.) protocol, which has recently been standardized by the World Wide Web Consortium (Gudgin, 2003a; 2003b), establishes a transport-protocol agnostic framework for Web services that could be extended by the user on the basis of XML techniques.

The SOAP protocol consists of two integral parts: A messaging framework defining how to encode and send messages, and an extensibility model for extending this framework by its user.

First a brief introduction of the messaging framework is given before showing the value of the extensibility mechanisms to accomplish the goals defined above.

Technically speaking, SOAP resides in the protocol stack above a physical wire protocol such as HTTP, FTP, or TCP. Although the specification does not limit SOAP to HTTP-based transfers, this protocol binding is currently the most prominent one and is widely used for Web Service access. But it should be noted that the approach introduced by this article is designed to operate completely independent of the chosen transport protocol and resides solely on the SOAP layer.

All application data intended to be sent over a network using the SOAP protocol must be transferred into an XML representation. To accomplish this SOAP defines two message-encoding styles. Therefore the specification introduces rules for encoding arbitrary graphs into XML. Most prominent specialization of this approach is the *RPC style* introduced by the specification itself, which allows the exchange of messages that map conveniently to definitions and invocations of method and procedure calls in commonly used programming languages. As introduced before, SOAP is by nature protocol agnostic and can be deployed for message exchange using a variety of underlying protocols. Therefore a formal set of rules for carrying a SOAP message within or on top of another protocol needs to be defined for every respective transport protocol. This is done by the official SOAP specification for HTTP as well as SMTP.

Inside the SOAP protocol the classical pattern of a message body carrying the payload and an encapsulating envelope containing some descriptive data and meta-information is retained. Additionally, SOAP allows the extension of the header content by the use of XML elements not defined by the SOAP specification itself. For distinguishing these elements from those predefined by the specification the user has to take care that they are located in a different XML namespace.

Code 1 on page 3 shows a complete SOAP message accompanied with the transport protocol specific data necessary when using the HTTP binding. Additionally, a user defined header residing in a non-W3C and thus non- normative namespace is shown as part of the SOAP Header element.

In contrast to the payload, which is intended to be sent to the receiver of the SOAP message clearly identified by HTTP's Host header, SOAP headers may or may not be created for processing by the ultimate receiver. Specifically, they are only processed by machines identified by the predefined role attribute. By doing so the extension framework offers the possibility of partly processing a message along its path from the sender to the ultimate receiver. These intermediate processing steps could fulfill arbitrary tasks, ranging from problem oriented ones like reformatting, preprocessing, or even fulfilling parts of the requests to more infrastructural services such as filtering, caching, or transaction handling. In all cases the presence of a node capable of (specification compliant) processing of a SOAP message is prescribed. This is especially true since an intermediary addressed

by the role attribute is required to remove the processed header after executing the requested task. Additionally, the specification distinguishes between headers optionally to be processed (e.g., caching) and those that are interspersed to trigger necessary message behavior. The latter ones must additionally be equipped with the attribute mustUnderstand. If a header addressed to an intermediary flagged by this attribute cannot be processed, the SOAP node is forced to raise an exception and resubmit the message to the sender. Thus it is ensured that all headers mandatory to be processed are consumed by the respective addressees and removed afterwards.

SECURITY FOR WEB SERVICES

As it is deployed nowadays security is a rather a vertical issues spanning all protocol layers than an insulated issue. Since SOAP is designed to serve as a true protocol providing services to applications residing on top of it and concurrently using services supplied by lower layer protocols, security has to be also addressed at this layer. Due to the protocol independent design of SOAP this layer cannot rely on security mechanisms such as SSL/TLS, SHTTP or S-MIME probably provided by underlying layers; even this limitation may be irrelevant in some practical applications.

Furthermore, existing security provided by other protocols is often limited to certain message exchange patterns like synchronous communication (e.g., SSL) and is therefore not compatible with SOAP's assumption of autonomy from underlying protocols.

Three of the most important issues when dealing with security are message integrity, authorization, and authentication. The signing proxy presented in this article addresses these requirements. Another important security issue is privacy. It is not fully covered in this article, because methods to obtain privacy cannot be applied transparently for the users and do not keep

Code 2.

```
<?xml version="1.0"?>
<env:Envelope
 xmlns:env="http://www.w3.org/2002/06/soap-envelope"
 xmlns:wsse="http://schemas.xmlsoap.org/ws/2002/04/secext"
 xmlns:xenc="http://www.w3.org/2001/04/xmlenc#">
 <env:Header>
    <ns1:DeliveryNotification
    env:mustUnderstand="true"
    env:role="http://www.w3.org/2003/05/soap-envelope/role/ultimateReceiver"
    xmlns:ns1="urn:xmlns:dcx.com:research">
  <ns1:SendTo URI="MailTo:jd@dcx.com"/>
    </ns1:DeliveryNotification>
    <wsse:Security>
        <xenc:ReferenceList>
            <xenc:DataReference URI="#bodyID"/>
        </xenc:ReferenceList>
    </wsse:Security>
 </env:Header>
 <env:Body>
    <xenc:EncryptedData Id="bodyID">
        <ds:KeyInfo>
            <ds:KeyName>CN=John Doe, C=DE</ds:KeyName>
        </ds:KeyInfo>
        <xenc:CipherData> <xenc:CipherValue>dGhlIHF1aWNrIGJyb3duIGZv...
            ..</xenc:CipherValue>
 </xenc:CipherData>
    </xenc:EncryptedData>
 </env:Body>
</env:Envelope>
```

validating XML/SOAP documents, which causes some more problems to be solved.

However, if encryption between the outgoing proxy and the firewall of the receiver is desired, it is possible (after an initial corporate key exchange) to build a system like the basic signing proxy for that results in a real security proxy.

SOAP does not address security issues; it has not been designed to do this. The job has been left to other (mostly XML-based) standards. This section briefly introduces the most important standards necessary for building the signing proxy that provide more secure SOAP calls.

However, due to the fact that the additional security starts at the proxy and the intranet is usually not completely trustworthy, additional steps for this part of the route are necessary. The easiest solution is usually to access the proxy using SSL. There are nodes between the client and the proxy that have to be able to read the traffic, so a point-to-point encryption is a good solution.

XML ENCRYPTION

Imamura (2002) defines a process for encrypting data that is represented as an XML document under consideration of XML's structural constraints formulated by Bray (2004) and Cowan (2004). These structuring principles are respected in a two-folded manner. First, XML encryption ensures that the outcome of an encryption process is still a well-formed XML document, whereas validity with respect to a XML schema or a document type definition has to be sacrificed for security's sake. Basically, it is not possible to

Code 3.

```xml
<?xml version="1.0"?>
<env:Envelope
 xmlns:env="http://www.w3.org/2002/06/soap-envelope">
 <env:Header>
    <ns1:DeliveryNotification
    env:mustUnderstand="true"
    env:role="http://www.w3.org/2003/05/soap-envelope/role/ultimateReceiver"
        xmlns:ns1="urn:xmlns:dcx.com:research">
        <ns1:SendTo URI="MailTo:jd@dcx.com"/>
    </ns1:DeliveryNotification>
    <wsse:Security
        xmlns:wsse="http://schemas.xmlsoap.org/ws/2002/04/secext">
        <wsse:UsernameToken Id="MyID">
            <wsse:Username>John</wsse:Username>
        </wsse:UsernameToken>
        <ds:Signature>
            <ds:SignedInfo>
                <ds:CanonicalizationMethod
                    Algorithm="http://www.w3.org/2001/10/xml-exc-c14n#"/>
                <ds:SignatureMethod
                    Algorithm="http://www.w3.org/2000/09/xmldsig#hmac-sha1"/>
                <ds:Reference URI="#MsgBody">
                  <ds:DigestMethod
                      Algorithm="http://www.w3.org/2000/09/xmldsig#sha1"/>
                <ds:DigestValue>LyLsF0Pi4wPU...</ds:DigestValue>
                </ds:Reference>
            </ds:SignedInfo>
            <ds:SignatureValue>DJbchm5g...</ds:SignatureValue>
            <ds:KeyInfo>
                <wsse:SecurityTokenReference>
                    <wsse:Reference URI="#MyID"/>
                </wsse:SecurityTokenReference>
            </ds:KeyInfo>
        </ds:Signature>
    </wsse:Security>
 </env:Header>
 <env:Body Id="MsgBody">
    <ns2:QuoteRequest>
        <ns2:ID>7492653</ns2:ID>
        <ns2:Amount>10000</ns2:Amount>
        <ns2:DeliverTo>DCX ...</ns2:DeliverTo>
    <!— more details omitted for brevity ... —>
    </ns2:QuoteRequest>
 </env:Body>
</env:Envelope>
```

retain schema validity for encrypted contents. An attempt to represent encrypted content adhering to the type constraints of the original type would significantly curb the possibilities to lexically represent the encrypted data.

Second, XML encryption is designed to take XML's nature as data format into account. This is done by allowing the partial encryption of an XML, which offers to encryption only parts of an XML tree, that is, single elements.

Furthermore, the standard itself does not recommend or even define specific methods for encrypting XML encoded data. The application of particular algorithms and types of obfuscation such as asymmetric or symmetric cryptography is completely discounted by official W3C standards document.

Rather than defining ways of securing XML content, XML encryption establishes an open and extensible framework to apply cryptographic methods to a XML document to assure privacy. By doing so, arbitrary algorithms of unrestrained types can be used to secure the content.

This is guaranteed by a number of metadata elements that describe the usage of encryption for interoperability's sake without revealing trustworthy data.

Code 2 shows the XML document presented in Nadalin (2004) with encryption applied solely to the SOAP body. The encrypted content of the respective subelements is stored in the Cipher-Value element.

XML SIGNATURE

RFC3275 defines in Eastlake (2002) how a digital document can be signed and how the result can be represented in XML. Whereas this specification is not limited to XML documents, it is still especially useful for XML documents, because the result is also an XML document. Using XPath, it is possible to locate and identify only certain parts of an XML file to be signed. This is essentially the same mechanism that was discussed for XML encryption to allow partial application of cryptography.

Since the singing process can be traced back to an application of encryption the framework is quite similar to the one introduced before. Essentially, signing is done by applying asymmetric encryption of a message digest, which results from the application a one-way hash function to the parts to be signed.

Code 3 again shows the document presented in the introductory section with a digital signature applied to the body (i.e., the element and all its enclosed descendants) of the SOAP message.

It should be noted that since encryption and digital signatures serve different purposes with respect to security, both can be used in conjunction. Particularly, both standardized frameworks are designed to be interoperable.

A typical architecture for digital signatures to a Web Service is shown by Figure 1. For simplicity reasons, the firewalls are simplified on both sides.

Firewalls that parse HTTP are more and more frequently used. This changes both the Web service and client side. The according change is shown for one side in Figure 2.

WEB SERVICE SECURITY

Since SOAP adds an additional layer of semantics on top of XML signatures and encrypted content cannot be applied in a naive manner, particularly with regard to encryption this means only parts of the SOAP message that are not required to be readable by intermediaries are allowed to be encrypted. Otherwise either every possible intermediary, which could be arbitrarily any machine on the Web, must be in the position to decrypt the message in order to process the headers or the headers cannot be processed at all. On the other hand, the usage of security mechanisms creates some descriptive meta-information that has to be expressed appropriately.

In order to facilitate interoperability of SOAP and the security mechanisms discussed before, the standard WS-Security defines how to apply digital signatures to and encrypt the content of SOAP documents.

WS-Security (Nadalin, 2004) is designed as an extension of SOAP to add security relevant information into the header of each message. It is a combination of XML Signature and XML

Figure 1. Applying Digital Signatures to Web Services

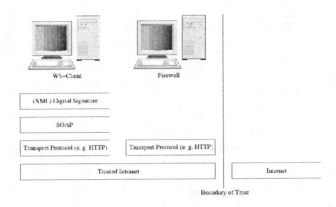

Figure 2. Applying Firewalls to Secure Network Transfers

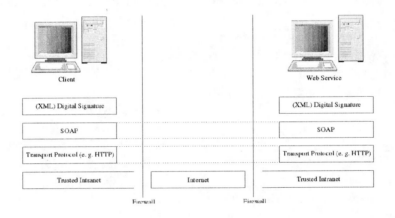

Figure 3. Signing Proxy Inserted into Web Service Infrastructure

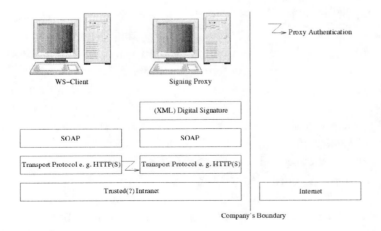

Encryption. The specification can be found at *http://www.oasis-open.org/committees/tc_home. php?wg_abbrev=wss*

By its very nature WS-Security does not define additional security mechanisms or message semantics. It solely describes syntactic constraints on how to place the information related to security inside a SOAP message.

Both examples given in the previous sections are coded according to principles set out by these standards.

SECURITY PROXY FOR WEB SERVICES

Due to the fact that SOAP does not care about security, it is necessary to develop solutions that add required security features. An ideal solution hides the additional effort such that users and even developers of Web services do not even notice the additions. This also means that an integration into existing systems in possible without changing a single Web service. The solution described in this section reaches these goals by means of a SOAP security proxy and a SOAP firewall.

INTERCEPTING OUTGOING SOAP MESSAGES

Proxies are commonly used in an HTTP environment. They reduce network traffic by caching techniques and allow controlling Web usage by blocking specific sites or pages with explicit content. Given richer and thus stricter settings a firewall may intercept also content which is operated on a higher level than plain transport protocols like SOAP messages are.

Such a SOAP proxy acts as an intermediary, receiving the SOAP request before it is sent over the Internet to the requesting receiver. The header of the SOAP message can be expanded by security credentials. It is advisable to use an existing standard like WS-Security for this step to gain an easier interoperability. The message is thereafter sent to the next destination within the message path.

If the intranet is not completely trustworthy, it is possible to apply a point-to-point encryption between the Web services client and the proxy using SSL. This does not cause problems, because there should not be any intermediaries between those two.

It is important to keep in mind that the outgoing call is still a valid SOAP message. The receiver can use the additional information, but it is also valid to simply ignore it.

The installation of such a signing proxy into the architecture shown in Figure 3 moves the responsibility of creating signatures to the proxy service as shown in Figure 2.

Assuming that the signing proxy has access to some key management system or even a public key infrastructure, shore PKI, this system can be further improved. Using proxy authentication as described in RFC 2616 and RFC 2617 (Fielding, 1999; Franks, 1999), the proxy is able to identify the individual users and also add their personal signatures.

PROCESSING INCOMING SOAP MESSAGES

The firewall of the receiver intercepts the incoming SOAP message. In addition to the usual steps that are always executed, it authenticates the message using the information that has been added to the header by the proxy of the sender. Thereafter, a check if the sender has permission to use the requested Web service is performed. The security credentials could be removed to make the whole process completely transparent for both sides, but this is not necessary since they do not bother the receiver and might still be useful.

INTEGRATION INTO EXISTING INFRASTRUCTURE

One of the main advantages of the presented approach is the small number of changes that have to be made by users and administrators. The users only have to change their proxy settings to contact the signing proxy, which contacts the regular proxy. The administrator should modify the firewall rules to enforce valid signatures in the SOAP header. Proxy authentication has to be enabled if personal signatures are desired.

But by introducing the signing proxy all applications are enabled to participate instantly in a secured environment, not requiring any changes to the application code. On the contrary, security code can be moved from many application layers (i.e., from the application layer of many applications) to one single location. Hence also the amount of auditing and maintenance could be centralized and thus lowered.

As a consequence of this the proposed approach could be transparently integrated into existing processes without requiring changes to the workflow or even the supporting business applications. Hence the signing proxy forms a plug-in solution that could easily be deployed at existing sites and be expanded to further partners.

Since the inner nature of the signing proxy is hidden by the usage of a standard communication infrastructure (i.e., HTTP and SOAP), interoperability problems are conceptually impossible.

Since currently most practical Web service applications are concentrated to closed and trusted communities (e.g., B2B communication), the communication path connecting the application with the signing proxy is always part of a trusted intranet and can thus be regarded as secured a priori. If the intranet cannot be trusted, the situation changes only very little — SSL can be used and the proxy is accessed using HTTPS.

Due to the fact that most calls can be regarded to be symmetric—a SOAP message is sent to the Web service and thereafter a SOAP message is sent back to the caller—those changes have to be made on both sides.

In a larger environment, it can be useful to install a policy server to get a single point of administration for each intranet.

As mentioned earlier, in addition to corporate trust, it is possible to also add personal signatures. There are two prerequisites for this step. Firstly, the proxy has to be able to identity the different users, which requires the use of proxy authentication. The other requirement for adding personal signatures is the use of an expanded key management system like a PKI that can be accessed by the proxy and grants access to the users' private keys. This is a dangerous requirement because the confidentiality of private keys is extremely important and faults in this area can destroy people's trust in the whole system.

SUMMARY

Securing Web services is an important and not impossible task. Due to the fact that this issue has been left out of the SOAP specification, it is important to apply security steps that are appropriate to the given environment.

This article demonstrates how to develop a proxy service to automatically add security features to Web services without saddling the users with this burden.

In addition, the given approach only uses open standards like WS-Security. This allows an easy integration into existing systems or infrastructures. Also, since these formats are, like SOAP, XML based, it is possible to allow this add-on and still keep valid XML/SOAP documents.

The improvement has been done in two steps. First, the proxy is enhanced to add a corporate signature to all outgoing calls proving that the origin lies within the company. This is a rather simple step, because the spoken private key can be used for all outgoing messages.

The other improvement has been to also add personal signatures. For this step, it has been necessary to identify all users, which has been done using proxy authentication. If the proxy is then able to access a PKI, the personal signatures can also be added to the SOAP header.

Advantages:

- platform-independence — (high interoperability)
- transparent integration even into existing systems
- smooth integration into existing processes
- usage-only open standards
- plug-in security
- central administration of security policies
- ideal for B2B (trust)
- also usable on personal basis (assuming proxy authentication and PKI)

REFERENCES

Bray, T., Paoli, J., Sperberg-McQueen, C.M., Maler, E., & Yergeau, F. (Eds.). (2004). *Extensible Markup Language (XML) 1.0* (3rd ed.). World Wide Web Consortium.

Cowan, J., & Tobin, R. (Eds.). (2004). *XML information set* (2nd ed.). World Wide Web Consortium.

Eastlake, D., Reagle, J., & Solo, D. (2002). *RFC 3275: XML-Signature syntax and processing*. Internet Engineering Task Force.

Fielding, R., Gettys, J., Mogul, J., Frystyck, H., Masinter, L., Leach, & Berners-Lee, T. (1999). *RFC 2616: HyperText Transport Protocol*. Internet Engineering Task Force.

Franks, J., Hallam-Baker, P., Lawrence, S., Leach, P., Luotonen, A., & Stewart, L. (1999). *RFC 2617: HTTP authentication: Basic digest and access authentication*. Internet Engineering Task Force.

Gudgin, M., Hadley, M., Mendelsohn, N., Moreau, J.-J., & Nielsen, H.F. (2003a). *SOAP Version 1.2 Part 1: Messaging framework*. World Wide Web Consortium.

Gudgin, M., Hadley, M., Mendelsohn, N., Moreau, J.-J., & Nielsen, H.F. (2003b). *SOAP Version 1.2 Part 2: Adjuncts*. World Wide Web Consortium.

Imamura, T., Dillaway, B., & Simon, E. (Eds.). (2002). *XML encryption syntax and processing*. World Wide Web Consortium.

Nadalin, A., Kaler, C., Hallam-Baker, P., & Monzillo, R. (Eds.). (2004). *Web services security – SOAP message security 1.0*. Oasis.

Winer, D. (1999). *XML-RPC specification*.

This work was previously published in International Journal of Web Services Research, Vol. 1, No. 3, edited by Zhang, pp. 88-100, copyright 2004 by IGI Publishing, formerly Idea Group Publishing (an imprint of IGI Global).

Chapter 4.31
A TAM Analysis of an Alternative High–Security User Authentication Procedure

Merrill Warkentin
Mississippi State University, USA

Kimberly Davis
Mississippi State University, USA

Ernst Bekkering
Northeastern State University, USA

ABSTRACT

The objective of information system security management is information assurance, which means to maintain confidentiality (privacy), integrity, and availability of information resources for authorized organizational end users. User authentication is a foundation procedure in the overall pursuit of these objectives, and password procedures historically have been the primary method of user authentication. There is an inverse relationship between the level of security provided by a password procedure and ease of recall for users. The longer the password and the more variability in its characters, the higher the level of security is that is provided by the password, because it is more difficult to violate or crack. However, such a password tends to be more difficult for an end user to remember, particularly when the password does not spell a recognizable word or when it includes non-alphanumeric characters such as punctuation marks or other symbols. Conversely, when end users select their own more easily remembered passwords, the passwords also may be cracked more easily. This study presents a new approach to entering passwords that combines a high level of security with easy recall for the end user. The Check-Off Password System (COPS) is more secure than self-selected passwords and high-protection, assigned-password procedures. The present study investigates tradeoffs between using COPS and three traditional password procedures, and provides a preliminary assessment of the efficacy of COPS. The study offers evidence that COPS is a valid alternative to current user authentication systems. End users perceive all tested password procedures to have equal usefulness, but the perceived ease of use of COPS passwords equals that of an established high-security password, and the new interface does not negatively affect user performance compared to a high-security password. Further research will be conducted to investigate long-term benefits.

BACKGROUND

Despite continuing improvements in computer and network technology, computer security continues to be a concern. One of the leading causes of security breaches is the lack of effective user authentication, primarily due to poor password system management (The SANS Institute, 2003), and the ease with which certain types of passwords may be cracked by computer programs. Yet even with today's high-speed computers, an eight-character password can be very secure, indeed. If a Pentium 4 processor can test 8 million combinations per second, it would take more than 13 years on average to break an eight-character password (Lemos, 2002). However, the potential for password security has not been fully realized, and a security breach can compromise significantly the security of information systems, other computer systems, data, and Web sites. Furthermore, the increasing degree to which confidential and proprietary data are stored and transmitted electronically makes security a foremost concern in today's age of technology. This is true not only in civilian use, but also in government and military use.

A primary objective of information system security is the maintenance of confidentiality, which is achieved in part by limiting access to valuable information resources. Historically, user authentication has been the primary method of protecting proprietary and/or confidential data by preventing unauthorized access to computerized systems. User authentication is a foundation procedure in the overall pursuit of secure systems, but in a recent e-mail to approximately one million people, Bill Gates (chairman of Microsoft Corporation) referred to passwords as "the weak link" in computer security, noting that most passwords are either easy to guess or difficult to remember ("Gates Pledges Better Software Security," 2003). Gates correctly identified a classic tradeoff that system and network administrators must face when considering various password procedures for adoption. Specifically, there is an inverse relationship between the level of security provided by a password procedure and the ease of recall for end users. When end users select their own easily remembered passwords, the passwords are easier to crack than longer passwords with a greater variety of characters. The longer the password and the more variability in the characters, the higher the level of security provided by such a password. However, human memory has significant limitations, and such passwords tend to be more difficult for end users to remember. Typically, human short-term memory can store only seven plus or minus two (7 ± 2) "chunks" of information (Miller, 1956), and alphanumeric characters such as punctuation marks and other symbols are not easily combined in a chunk with other characters. For example, the letters b, a, n, and d can be stored easily together as a single chunk, but it is difficult for humans to combine symbols such as the vertical bar (|) and tilde ($\sim$) with other characters to form a chunk. The problem of striking a balance between security and ability to remember passwords will become more acute as the number of passwords per user increases.

In a survey with 3,050 distinct respondents (Rainbow Technologies Inc., 2003), the following picture emerged:

- Respondents used, on average, almost 5½ passwords
- 23.9% of respondents used eight or more passwords
- More than 80% were required to change passwords at work at least once a year
- 54% reported writing down a password at least once
- 9% reported always writing down their passwords
- More than half had to reset business passwords at least once a year, because they forgot or misplaced the password

The 352 participants in the present study reported using an average of 3.9 passwords at the time of the study and 4.53 passwords in the prior six months. Furthermore, 35.5% reported writing down at least one password. Clearly, the use of multiple passwords constitutes a burden to users.

PASSWORD STRATEGIES

Because of these tradeoffs and because methods and technologies employed by crackers are improving constantly, new security strategies with improved password procedures are required. Traditional methods include allowing users to select their own passwords and assigning passwords to them, both of which may be subject to restrictions on password length and character choices. The efficacy of both systems depends on the ability of end users to recall such passwords without writing them down. The Federal Information Processing Standards (FIPS) publication 112 includes guidelines for different levels of password security (National Institute of Standards and Technology, 1985). At the highest level, these guidelines include passwords with six to eight characters composed from the full 95 printable character ASCII set. Furthermore, the guidelines specify using an automated password generator, individual ownership of passwords, use of non-printing keyboards, encrypted password storage, and encrypted communications with message numbering. The theoretical number of passwords using the FIPS procedure is approximately 6.7×10^{15} ($= 95^8 + 95^7 + 95^6$). However, to utilize the full set of characters, all printable non-alphanumeric characters must be included in the set and have an equal chance of selection as the alphanumeric characters. But passwords with non-alphanumeric characters can be hard to remember. Consider, for example, passwords such as " ,swFol=; " or " >_F<"Yjz ." To avoid having to use such awkward passwords, we have devised a new password interface for user authentication. (The FIPS procedure is one of the four procedures investigated in this study.)

When allowed to select their own password, users tend to select passwords that may be easy to remember but also may be easy to crack. On the other hand, when they are assigned a cryptographically strong password, users generally will find them difficult to remember and will frequently record them in writing. To remedy these potential security problems, various strategies currently are used. Some organizations attempt to reduce the number of passwords needed by using a single system sign on (SSO) (Boroditsky & Pleat, 2001). Others are researching the possibility of using graphical mechanisms (Bolande, 2000; Pinkas & Sander, 2002) or combining passwords with keystroke dynamics (Monrose, Reiter, & Wetzel, 1999). Organizations can instruct their members in the proper selection of passwords to varying degrees, from simple instructions regarding the minimum number of positions and the minimum variability of characters to extensive instructions and even feedback mechanisms where weak passwords are rejected immediately (Bergadano, Crispo, & Ruffo, 1998; Jianxin, 2001). Weirich and Sasse (2001) advocate proper instruction and motivation of users, as well as a flexible approach depending on the organization and type of work for which the security is needed. The self-selec-

Table 1. Examples of passwords used in current password procedures

Self-Selected	Spafford	FIPS
fido	academia	li&SqA<
101565 (birthdate)	trench	EUg`=M=
mustang	deluge	JVe*,UuB
corvette	garfield	lX+]HpM?
2895 (lastfour of SSN)	heinlein	*R(AO-3P
mary	irishman	&`qe2P\H
john	hm iration	,WU$&TTW
newyork	marvin	U&#==f9Z
godawgs81 (sportsfan)	napoleon	GB<X(DE)
chevy1	oxford	_so`yor$
march241981	password	$4Y,*T6R
Jesus1	rascal	Lh_<Mr,
covergirl1	saxon	`(WCpod{
holein1 (golffan)	william	2]`p<ren
Bullocks	yellowstone	s@5A:L7>

tion procedure ("Self") is the second of four procedures investigated in this study. Users were required to include at least one letter and at least one number in their password and were required to select passwords of at least six but not more than 14 characters in length. The third procedure utilizes system-assigned passwords from the list of common passwords found in Spafford's Technical Report (1988), typically spelling common words that are relatively easily remembered ("Spafford"). Table 1 shows some examples of passwords that might be used under the three primary password procedures in use today.

In a study of password usage, Adams and Sasse (1999) identified the following four factors that negatively influence the use of passwords:

1.   The need to remember multiple passwords due to the use of different passwords for different systems and the requirement to change passwords at intervals;
2.   Lack of user awareness regarding the requirements for secure password content
3.   Perceived lack of compatibility of passwords with work practices
4.   Unrealistic user perception of organizational security and information sensitivity

Though the latter three factors can be remedied with organizational measures such as review of password policies and user education, the first factor is grounded in the limitations of human memory. Since the number of secure systems used by each individual is bound to increase rather than decrease over time, resulting in the need to remember more passwords, memory limitations must be accommodated.

HUMAN MEMORY

A heuristic for the capacity of the human short-term memory system states that an individual can recall seven plus or minus two (7 ± 2) chunks of information (Miller, 1956). This rule of thumb only applies to information to be recalled for relatively brief periods without rehearsal. Information can be maintained for longer periods of time, but elaborate rehearsal is required for transfer to long-term memory (Hewett, 1999; Newell & Simon, 1972). A recent model describes a *working memory*, which is part of the larger memory system and not distinct from long-term memory (Anderson, 1994). In this model, memory limitations also depend on the ability to retrieve information from long-

Table 2. Examples of COPS passwords with user-tailored modifications

Original COPS Password	User-Tailored COPS Password	
TRLOHASM	HAL STORM	HARM BOLTS
	HALF STORM	FARM SLOTH
	HARM LOTS	SLAM THROW
	MARSH LOT	RAM SLOTH
GDRHISTE	RED SIGHT	WED RIGHTS
	SHRED TWIG	DREG THIS
	SHRED GIFT	THE GIRDS
	RIGHTS RED	DR EIGHTS
MROTPSCA	WORST CAMP	CRAFTS MOP
	CATS PROM	RAMP COST
	CRAP MOST	CAM SPORT
	CRAB STOMP	FARM PC TO
ENTMAOPL	MENTAL POW	PETAL MONK
	NAME PLOT	PANT MOLE
	LAMP TONE	PANEL TOM
	TAP MELON	LAMB PET ON
RMTOCALG	CLOG MART	GRAM CLOT
	MALT VCR GO	CART GLOM
	TRAM CLOG	TRACK GLOM
	GRAM COLT	TRACY GLOM
SAGNTPHI	PATH SIGN	SNAP BIGHT
	GAP HINTS	HANG SPIT
	HANG PITS	PANT WHIGS
	ZAP NIGHTS	PAST NIGH
TASHMREN	SMART HEN	FARMS THEN
	TRASH MEN	HARM VENTS
	MATH FERNS	WHEN SMART
	MASH RENT	MARSH NEWT

term storage to working memory. Regardless of the cognitive model, a capacity limitation exists. The proposed password procedure addresses this memory capacity limitation by using a password that may be easier to remember than FIPS-compliant passwords, although the input mechanism may be more cognitively challenging.

CHECK-OFF PASSWORD SYSTEM (COPS)

Traditional password procedures either assign an ordered series (sequence) of characters, which may or may not spell something meaningful to the user, or allow users to select their own ordered sequence of characters. In either case, the order of the characters is significant and must be maintained. A strength of the Check-Off Password System (COPS), the fourth procedure in this investigation, is that the order of characters within the password is irrelevant, and, therefore, the user can choose to remember them in many ways. A COPS password is assigned to each user and consists of a set of eight different characters (the "COPS password") selected from the 16 most commonly used letters in the American alphabet (AskOxford. com, 2002) (the "COPS Superset"), including all five major vowels (E A R I O T N S L C U D P M H G). The user may form any word or words by rearranging these eight characters (similar to an anagram) and may use any of the characters repeatedly in doing so. For example, suppose a user were issued the characters "ULATSREG," which we will refer to as the "Example Password." Using the characters in the Example Password, one user might form the compound word "STAR-GLUE" in order to remember the eight characters, whereas another user may select "GLUERATS," "SLUGTEARS," or "RESTGULAG." In other words, while the Example Password (and every COPS password) consists of a random selection of 8 alphabetic characters without repetition, users may reorder those characters (and use characters more than once) to form their own password to facilitate recall. The user even may use characters not found in the COPS Superset (B F Y W K V X Z J Q) to form a memorizable password, since

Figure 1. Representative COPS selection grid

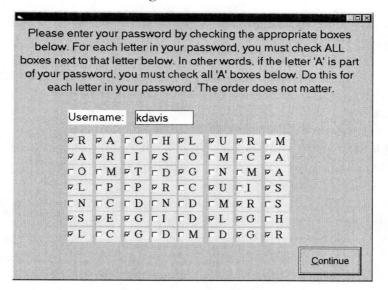

those characters will not be included on the input interface (the COPS selection grid), as described later. For example, by using the "B" character, a music aficionado could form the password "GREATBLUES" from the Example Password. In addition to users tapping their imagination to form a memorable password, an automated password generator with a facility for suggesting words from a dictionary could be used. Table 2 shows some additional examples of COPS passwords with several user-tailored modifications.

To authenticate the user, COPS presents an 8-by-7 grid of checkboxes, each adjacent to a character randomly selected from the COPS Superset. The user checks off only the boxes adjacent to characters contained in the COPS password. Because the grid contains 56 checkboxes generated from only 16 characters (the COPS Superset), characters will typically appear more than once. On average, each character in the COPS Superset will appear in a grid 3.5 times (56 ̦16), ranging from a minimum of zero times (even if such character appears in the COPS password) to a maximum of 56 times, although each of those extremes would be a rare occurrence. Thus, users must check off a given letter in a COPS password an average of 3.5 times, as follows.

Consider the Example Password again ("ULATSREG"). To enter the password, the user would be presented with a grid such as the one shown in Figure 1, which demonstrates a failed attempt to enter the Example Password. To successfully enter the Example Password in such grid, the user would need to check the box adjacent to every "U" appearing in the grid (i.e., three "U" checkboxes would need to be checked), and the user would need to check the box for every "L" appearing in the grid (i.e., four "L" checkboxes), and so forth. In Figure 1, the user has neglected to check off the "S" box in the fifth row of the eighth column, which will result in a failed login attempt. When the user fails to successfully check all of the necessary boxes, he or she will be presented with a new grid in a randomized layout, which will almost certainly be different than the preceding layout. The user must reattempt the COPS procedure with the same password and a new grid.

Without the ever-changing grid interface, the number of possible combinations would be no higher than C(16,8) or 12,870, because the presence of one instance of a character would determine the result for all other instances of the same character. In other words, if one "T" is selected, all other boxes with a "T" on the same interface should also be selected. A cracker could manually try to enter all 12,870 combinations, although time considerations would make this impractical. But this assumes that the cracker is a human who is able to see the letters next to each checkbox. A computer could run through combinations much faster, but the lack of knowledge of which letters appear on the grid (due to the lack of sight) causes the number of possible combinations to increase to 2^{56} or 7.2×10^{16}. For the computer, the number of possible combinations is higher than the 12,870 combinations for humans, because the universe of possible combinations is based on 56 checkboxes rather than letters appearing on the grid. Optical Character Recognition (OCR) could overcome this limitation of computers and is currently effectively counteracted online by major organizations such as AltaVista, PayPal, Yahoo (Pinkas & Sander, 2002) and Ticketmaster (Ticketmaster, 2003) by using a Reverse Turing Test (Coates, Baird, & Fateman, 2001). As long as the layouts are randomly generated and OCR cannot be used effectively, the number of possible combinations with 56 check-off boxes either selected or not selected will remain 2^{56} or 7.2×10^{16}. Unlike self-selected, Spafford, and FIPS passwords, COPS passwords achieve both a high level of security and a high degree of memorability—neither goal of password procedures is made paramount at the expense of the other. In other words, the COPS paradigm achieves the "best of both worlds" in terms of security and memorability.

RESEARCH QUESTIONS

Given these issues, an investigation into the COPS password system was undertaken in order to assess its efficacy in an end-user environment. Would the COPS system be perceived as useful and easy to use? Would users be inclined to use the COPS system, given the presumed relative tradeoff in its use? From these research questions, the following specific research hypotheses were developed.

- **Hypothesis 1:** All password procedures are perceived to be equally useful.
- **Hypothesis 2:** All password procedures are perceived to be equally easy to use.
- **Hypothesis 3:** Users will be equally inclined to use each of the password procedures.

METHODOLOGY

For this investigation, the authors devised and executed a controlled experiment in which the participants took a pre-survey to characterize their perceptions about the usefulness of passwords and their preferences and intention to use passwords in general. The participants then used one of the four password procedures under investigation, followed by a post-survey regarding their perceptions of the password procedure they used in the experiment. This research methodology is based on the theoretical foundations of the Technology Acceptance Model, from which the survey instrument was derived in a modified form.

Applicability of TAM

In new technology implementations, the Technology Acceptance Model (TAM) indicates that Perceived Ease of Use (PEOU) and Perceived Usefulness (PU) are considered antecedents of Behavioral Intent to Use (BI), which in turn is an antecedent to actual use (Davis, 1989). Although the semi-self-selected passwords using COPS are relatively easy to remember, the system also requires user input that is more cognitively challenging than traditional password systems. If only one check-off box is erroneously missed or selected, an entirely new check-off grid is generated and must be completed, thereby increasing the cognitive load of the activity. This may cause the system user to become frustrated, resulting in a low Perceived Ease of Use of the password procedure. If the user had a choice, such frustration might generate resistance to adopting the technology. The end user typically does not have a choice, however, of which password procedure is employed for user authentication. The selection of user authentication measures is the purview of system administrators, not end users. One might query, therefore, why researchers should be interested in end users' "intention to use" password procedures and why TAM is relevant to determining the potential for the widespread adoption of COPS.

Although system or network administrators are responsible for the selection and adoption of password procedures to protect the systems they manage, such decisions are not made in a vacuum. They are not at liberty to select the most cryptographically secure password procedure, if users are unable to efficiently and effectively use such a system. Imagine at one extreme a password system that is impossible to crack but also impossible to use. Obviously, implementation of that system is infeasible. Also, an extremely secure password procedure can generate user resistance and complaints, and lead to a high incidence of passwords being reset. At the other extreme is a password procedure that is extremely easy to use but also extremely easy to crack. Such a system also is not likely to be a system administrator's preferred choice. A system administrator must weigh the multiple objectives of a password system (including security and usability) in determining the most suitable password procedures to use for the protection of different computer systems. Therefore, PEOU and PU, as measured from the user's perspective, are indirect factors affecting the *system administrator's* adoption of a password procedure. Thus, it is imperative that we test the PEOU and PU of COPS from the user's perspective in order to evaluate its potential as an alternative to current user authentication methods. In order to preliminarily evaluate the efficacy of COPS, a controlled empirical study comparing user perceptions of COPS and existing alternatives was conducted.

Scale Development and Modification

A formal process was observed to develop measurement scales with reliability and validity within the TAM framework. A large inventory of existing TAM scale items was gathered from existing literature and adjusted for use in this password procedure study. During this process, the authors were confronted with the contrast between password procedures and other technologies in which the TAM model has been used to research user acceptance. In previous studies, ease of use and usefulness were considered assets of the technology. For example, if a menu clearly enables a user to attach a file to an e-mail with one click, it might be deemed easy to use. For a password procedure, however, ease of use may be a liability if it allows unauthorized users to easily crack the password procedure and obtain unauthorized access to a computer system or confidential data. Moreover, it is never easier to access a system that requires a password than a system that does not require a password. Similarly, the usefulness of a password protection procedure may not be apparent to the user, unlike the functionality of e-mail or other software. This requires some modification of the traditional TAM scales.

For example, an original Davis (1989) TAM instrument item stated, "Electronic mail enables me to accomplish tasks more quickly" (p. 324). If we simply had modified existing TAM indicators by substituting password procedures for the technology being tested, the instrument items would not have measured properly the Usefulness or Ease of Use in this context. For example, users always would strongly disagree with the statement, "This password system enables me to log on to computers more quickly," because password systems, by their very nature, require more time and make it more difficult to logon to computers. It was critical, therefore, to measure the constructs in terms of the absence of a negative, specifically the absence of inconvenience and frustration to the user. The above question was, therefore, modified as follows: "I can efficiently access computers even when I must use this password procedure." Similarly, the traditional TAM question, "Using this technology saves me time," was modified to read, "Using this password procedure does not take too much time."

Furthermore, password procedures do not facilitate end-user activity by producing a tangible benefit such as improved communication or increased efficiency in completing a task. The primary benefit of password procedures is maintaining the security of confidential data or proprietary applications. Such security is achieved by limiting access to authorized users through user authentication methods such as password procedures. Whether the purpose of such security is to protect a user's own data or an employer's data, password procedures frequently may be viewed by the user as a hindrance rather than a facilitator to accomplishing a task. While in the long run the user may recognize the necessity of password procedures for maintaining security, passwords often may be viewed as a necessary evil that otherwise impairs the user's immediate need for legitimate and authorized access to protected data or applications. Therefore, we determined that it was necessary to modify traditional TAM indicators designed to measure perceived usefulness of technologies *in general* to properly measure perceived usefulness *in this context* (see Table 3 for the resulting instrument items).

With these differences in mind, we made appropriate adjustments to standard TAM survey instrument items and developed a pre-test research instrument to measure attitudes toward password procedures in general and a post-test research instrument to measure attitudes toward the particular password procedure to which a user was exposed during the study. We generated a list of 14 potential items to measure PU, 16 potential items to measure PEOU, and five potential items to measure BI. Because all items were generated using well-established scales, all participants in our study responded to all items in the pre-survey

before exposure to a password procedure, and then responded again to all items in the post-survey after exposure to one of the four password procedures being tested. All items were measured on a five-point Likert scale ranging from *strongly disagree* to *strongly agree*.

Data Collection

The study was conducted as a controlled experiment in a large computer facility with 40 stations, where 352 participants were exposed to one of the following four password procedures: (1) self-selected passwords with limited restrictions;, (2) system-assigned passwords from the list of common passwords found in Spafford's Technical Report (1988); (3) system-assigned passwords compliant with the FIPS standard for high protection (National Institute of Standards and Technology, 1985); and (4) system-assigned passwords in the Check-Off Password System (COPS). The size of the groups was almost equal, with n = 90 for COPS, n = 88 for self-selected passwords, and n = 87 for FIPS and Spafford passwords. All participants were experienced system users who used an average of 3.90 passwords at the time of the study and 4.53 passwords in the six months prior.

Each study participant signed an implied consent form and then received a disk containing a compiled program written in Visual Basic. All disks were numbered and contained only one of four versions of the program. Each version of the program incorporated the pre-test instrument to measure attitudes toward password procedures in general, a login procedure using one of the four password procedures, and the post-test instrument to measure attitudes toward that particular password procedure. The different versions of the program were randomly distributed to participants (with randomization accomplished by using randomization functions in Microsoft Excel), so that participants were randomly exposed to the different password procedures. These random-

Table 3. Pre- and post-test instrument items

Item	Pre-Test Instrument Item	Post-Test Instrument Item	Status
PU1	Password procedures effectively protect my confidential information.	This password procedure would effectively protect my confidential information.	Eliminated
PU2	Password procedures enable computers to limit access to authorized users.	This password procedure would enable computers to limit access to authorized users.	Eliminated
PU3	I find password procedures useful.	I would find this password procedure useful.	Eliminated
PU4	Using password procedures to maintain security is a good idea.	Using this password procedure to maintain security would be a good idea.	Eliminated
PU5	Using password procedures is generally important for using computers.	Using this password procedure would be generally important for using computers.	Eliminated
PU6	Using password procedures is important to me for using computers.	Using this password procedure would be important to me for using computers.	Eliminated
PU7	Using password procedures enhances my security when working with computers.	Using this password procedure would enhance my security when working with computers.	Retained
PU8	I find password procedures useful for protecting my confidential information.	I would find this password procedure useful for protecting my confidential information.	Eliminated
PU9	Using password procedures improves the security of my confidential information.	Using this password procedure would improve the security of my confidential information.	Retained
PU10	Password procedures are an effective way to maintain security.	This password procedure would be an effective way to maintain security.	Retained
PU11	Password procedures improve the security of computers.	This password procedure would improve the security of computers.	Retained
PU12	I find password procedures useful for limiting access to confidential information.	I would find this password procedure useful for limiting access to confidential information.	Retained
PU13	Using password procedures for security is important to me.	Using this password procedure for security would be important to me.	Retained
PU14	Overall, I find password procedures useful.	Overall, I would find this password procedure useful.	Retained
PEOU1	Using password procedures is an easy method for maintaining security.	Using this password procedure would be an easy method for maintaining security.	Eliminated
PEOU2	Using password procedures does not take too much time.	Using this password procedure would not take too much time.	Eliminated
PEOU3	Password procedures make it difficult to use computers.	This password procedure would make it difficult to use computers.	Eliminated
PEOU4	Password procedures make it easier for me to maintain security.	This password procedure would make it easier for me to maintain security.	Eliminated
PEOU5	When I use password procedures, computers behave in unexpected ways.	When I used this password procedure, the computer behaved in unexpected ways.	Eliminated
PEOU6	Using password procedures requires a lot of mental effort.	Using this password procedure would require a lot of mental effort.	Eliminated
PEOU7	I can efficiently access computers even when I must use password procedures.	I could efficiently access computers even if I must use this password procedure.	Retained
PEOU8	I make mistakes frequently when I use password procedures.	I made mistakes frequently when I used this password procedure.	Eliminated
PEOU9	I find it easy to correct my mistakes while using password procedures.	I found it easy to correct my mistakes while using this password procedure.	Retained
PEOU10	I often become confused when I use password procedures.	I often became confused when I used this password procedure.	Eliminated
PEOU11	It is easy for me to become skillful at using password procedures.	It would be easy for me to become skillful at using this password procedure.	Retained
PEOU12	Learning to use password procedures is easy for me.	Learning to use this password procedure was easy for me.	Retained
PEOU13	Passwords are easy to remember.	This password was easy to remember.	Retained
PEOU14	Passwords are easy to enter.	This password was easy to enter.	Retained
PEOU15	Using password procedures is frustrating.	Using this password procedure was frustrating.	Eliminated
PEOU16	Overall, password procedures are easy to use.	Overall, this password procedure was easy to use.	Retained
BI1	I do not mind using password procedures when they are required.	I would not mind using this password procedure if it were required.	Eliminated
BI2	Whenever possible, I will avoid using computers that require password procedures.	Whenever possible, I would avoid using computers that require this password procedure.	Eliminated
BI3	I intend to choose password procedures for security over other procedures if I am given a choice.	I intend to choose this password procedure for security over other procedures if I am given a choice.	Retained
BI4	I would prefer using computers that use password procedures.	I would prefer using computers that use this password procedure.	Retained
BI5	I intend to use password procedures.	I intend to use this password procedure.	Retained

ized disks with no indication of the version were distributed sequentially as participants arrived at the lab. Participants eTxecuted the program from the disk, and at the end of the session, all data were automatically captured to a text file with the text files transferred to the researcher's hard disk after completion.

Each program started with a brief general description of the purpose of the study. Participants were informed that they would be using only one of four possible password procedures, and that they would have the option to stop trying if they were unable to successfully enter the correct password within five attempts, in which case the

Table 4. Factor analysis of PU, PEOU, and BI

		Component		
		PU	PEOU	BI
PU7	Using password procedures enhances my security when working with computers.	.799	.082	.171
PU9	Using password procedures improves the security of my confidential information.	.852	.028	.015
PU10	Password procedures are an effective way to maintain security.	.803	.116	.003
PU11	Password procedures improve the security of computers.	.795	.161	.011
PU12	I find password procedures useful for limiting access to confidential information.	.790	.121	.016
PU13	Using password procedures for security is important to me.	.747	.117	.279
PU14	Overall, I find password procedures useful.	.782	.155	.204
PEOU7	I can efficiently access computers even when I must use password procedures.	.121	.570	.059
PEOU9	I find it easy to correct my mistakes while using password procedures.	.046	.653	.028
PEOU11	It is easy for me to become skillful at using password procedures.	.137	.711	.208
PEOU12	Learning to use password procedures is easy for me.	.130	.766	.181
PEOU13	Passwords are easy to remember.	.071	.693	.216
PEOU14	Passwords are easy to enter.	.045	.530	.127
PEOU16	Overall, password procedures are easy to use.	.181	.626	.371
BI3	I intend to choose password procedures for security over other procedures if I am given a choice.	.102	.236	.620
BI4	I would prefer using computers that use password procedures.	.081	.220	.812
BI5	I intend to use password procedures.	.113	.226	.797

participants were presented immediately with the post-test survey instrument. After completing the pre-test survey reflecting general attitudes, participants received instructions for using the password procedure contained on their disk. Instructions for each procedure were different only to the extent necessary due to differences in the procedure to be used. After successfully entering their password (or electing to stop trying after five failed attempts), participants completed the post-test survey regarding the procedure they had just used and answered general demographic questions. Upon completion, disks were immediately returned to the researchers. Participants experienced minimal waiting time to receive their disks, and, once received, there was no further delay.

Scale Purification

Following data collection, we used the pre-test survey responses to generate the measurement scales. First, all items hypothesized to reflect one of the constructs were used to generate a unidimensional scale for each construct. Items were eliminated based on changes in coefficient Alpha and their effect on unidimensionality. A list of pre-test and post-test instrument items and their status of inclusion or elimination is provided in Table 3.

The scale for PU retained seven items and had a coefficient Alpha of 0.91. The scale for PEOU also retained seven items and had a coefficient Alpha of 0.80. In his classic work, Davis (1989) noted that this construct may contain three clusters relating to physical effort, mental effort, and ease of learning. Consistent with his findings, each cluster appears to be represented by two items in our scale, with overall ease of use as the seventh item. Finally, the scale for BI retained three items, with a coefficient Alpha of 0.71. All three scales were unidimensional. Testing for discriminant validity between the three constructs was performed with a Varimax

Table 5. ANOVA for PU

	Tests of Between-Subjects Effects Dependent Variable: Perceived Usefulness				
Source	**Type III Sum of Squares**	**df**	**Mean Square**	**F**	**Sig.**
Corrected Model	200.966(a)	3	66.989	2.236	.084
Intercept	243442.351	1	243,442.351	8125.086	.000
Password Procedure	200.966	3	66.989	2.236	.084
Error	10426.713	348	29.962		
Total	254071.000	352			
Corrected Total	10627.679	351			

R Squared = 0.019 (Adjusted R Squared = 0.010)

rotation of all items in the scales, yielding clear loading on the hypothesized construct without any cross-loadings (see Table 4).

RESULTS AND DISCUSSION

According to the TAM literature, PEOU and PU influence BI. Real-world user authentication, however, is accomplished with password procedures that are mandated by the organization or its technical staff, not adopted by user choice. Password procedure usage results indirectly from users' needs to use computer systems. In addition, one of our procedures (COPS) is experimental and not currently available for real-life application. Therefore, the full TAM model, which includes actual use, cannot be evaluated. In this chapter, we will limit our analysis to a discussion of differences between the four password procedures in terms of PEOU, PU, and BI, but not actual use, which was impossible to observe. To measure the effect of each procedure, we used summated scales constructed from the responses to the individual items. Since all items were worded positively, no reversal of negative scoring was needed. The ANOVA model for PU revealed an absence of statistically significant differences between the four procedures (p = 0.84).

The results show that end users do not perceive any procedure to be more useful than another (see Table 5) but do consider passwords in general to be useful, considering the high average mean scores for the our procedures (COPS 25.6, FIPS 26.0, Spafford 26.0, and Self 27.6 on a scale raging from 7 to 35). This absence of differences between procedures may be related to the fact that using passwords is generally mandated by system administrators rather than chosen by users, but could also be related to lack of user awareness regarding the protection that each procedure offers. Users generally are not aware of the ease with which self-selected or Spafford passwords can be cracked. Similarly, users generally do not reflect on the level of computing resources necessary to compromise passwords with the number of permutations offered by FIPS and COPS, and the amount of time required to be successful. In order not to influence our participants and possibly skew the responses with the impressive differences in the level of security provided by the different password procedures, we did not provide any information regarding this issue.

There were significant differences (p = 0.00) between password procedures for PEOU, but only between the two groups with low and high levels of security (and consequently different levels of effort needed to use them). Considering our large sample of 352 participants, average summated scores for COPS (21.82) and FIPS (22.0) are remarkably close, and the difference is statistically negligible (p=.995). The average scores for the

Table 6. Difference of means for PEOU*

	Password Procedure	N	Subset 1	Subset 2
	COPS	90	21.81	
	FIPS	87	22.00	
Tukey HSD	Spafford	87		29.38
	Self-selected	88		29.41
	Significance (Alpha = .05)		.995	1.000

* Scale of 7-35, with higher scores indicating higher PEOU.

lower-security Spafford (29.38) and self-selected passwords (29.41) are much higher than their high-security counterparts and not (p = 1.00) different from each other. Interestingly, the specific forms of the password procedures used appear to be irrelevant (see Table 6).

The same pattern (p = 0.00) can be found in the average summated scores for BI. Users are more inclined to use self-selected (11.1) or Spafford (10.46) passwords than either COPS or FIPS, but have no clear preference (p = .443) between the self-selected and Spafford passwords. Users are less inclined to use either COPS (8.29) or FIPS (8.84), but without a clear preference (p = .591) between those two procedures. The pattern is evident from Table 7. Of equal interest to system administrators may be the response to item BI1 ("I would not mind using this password procedure if it were required"), not included in the scale. The average summated score for COPS (3.17) is not statistically significantly (p= .056) different from FIPS (3.53).

In contrast with differences in PEOU and BI, examination of demographic information revealed no influence of gender (p = .186), or computer ownership (p = .244) on intent to use any of the procedures. Finally, performance measures revealed that COPS and FIPS require a statistically equal (p = .29) number of attempts to successfully enter the correct password (3.17 and 2.83 attempts, respectively), and that users are equally likely (p = .92) to abandon the procedure after repeated failed attempts. We did find a statistically significant difference in completion time for each attempt, between COPS (84.0 seconds) and all other procedures (Spafford 9.3 seconds, self-selected 10.3 seconds, FIPS 17.9 seconds). Indeed, participants required substantially more time (over a minute longer) to login using the COPS password than any of the other passwords. This finding is not shocking, however, in light of the fact that the Spafford, self-selected, and FIPS passwords involve the *familiar* task of entering characters in a textbox using a keyboard, while COPS involves a *new* task of selecting checkboxes using a mouse. We surmise that the time required to login using a COPS password would significantly diminish over time as users

Table 7. Difference of means for BI*

	Password procedure	N	Subset 1	Subset 2
	COPS	90	8.29	
	FIPS	87	8.84	
Tukey HSD	Spafford	87		10.46
	Self-selected	88		11.11
	Significance (Alpha=.05)		.591	.441

*Scale of 3-15, with higher scores indicating higher BI

acquire practice and familiarity with the task. Moreover, it is interesting that the substantial difference in completion time did not result in a significant difference in PEOU between COPS and FIPS, which may indicate that the difficulty of logging in using COPS is commensurate with the difficulty of logging in using FIPS, albeit for different reasons. In the case of FIPS passwords, the difficulty of remembering odd characters such as the vertical bar (|) and tilde (~) and locating them on the keyboard presumably reduced its PEOU scores.

Having empirically established that for high security systems COPS and FIPS are not distinguishable from a usability point of view, we will briefly discuss the security levels afforded by both. Initially, COPS and FIPS seem to afford a fairly comparable level of security, considering the total number of combinations (7.2×10^{16} vs. 6.7×10^{15}). This similarity is illusory, however, if users of FIPS are allowed to select their own passwords to make them easier to remember. Theoretically, this applies even more if restrictions other than minimum password length are placed on password selection, since each restriction decreases the total search space for a given password length. Character-selection restrictions reduce the search space of combinations by a very significant amount, in some cases by more than 90%. For instance, the FAA can be considered to be an organization with high security requirements, especially after September 11, 2001. Government documents are no longer freely posted on the World Wide Web (WWW), but a copy of the FAA Policy on Password Administration (2002) is cached on Google. Restrictions on password selection include using at least three of four characteristics: two or more numeric characters, two or more upper-case non-numeric characters, two or more lower-case non-numeric characters, and one or more special characters. For the best combination, the search space of combinations decreases by an astonishing

99.8% ($95^3 \times 33 \times 26^4 / 95^8 = 1.3 \times 10^{13} / 6.6 \times 10^{15} = 0.19\%$ of original combinations left).

Computers continue to increase in speed. Soon, we may reach the point where a reduced search space can be effectively covered in a brute force attack. At that point, system administrators are no longer able to balance security and usability concerns, and allowing users to select their own passwords may not be an option. Before we reach that point, easier-to-remember passwords such as COPS need to be researched and introduced in the field.

CONCLUSION

This study has demonstrated that end users perceive password procedures equally useful regardless of the specific procedure used. Further, though the study also shows that users perceive easy-to-remember passwords as easier to use than high security passwords and, therefore, are more inclined to use them, the mathematical and practical difficulty of hacking the high-security password procedures makes them more attractive to system administrators. A classic tradeoff is found to exist between ease of use and effectiveness of various password systems. Procedures that are easier for end users likely are also easier for hackers to compromise.

The study establishes that at least one acceptable alternative exists for the current guidelines for high security passwords as defined in FIPS 112—namely, the Check-Off Password System (COPS). If system administrators wish to use password procedures with protection levels equal to or exceeding the high security guidelines of FIPS 112, passwords from the full 95-character set should be assigned and not chosen, or an alternative password procedure such as COPS should be used. COPS can provide a secure alternative to FIPS passwords, which are difficult to remember for many users. COPS is more secure than FIPS by a factor of 10 (7.2 x 10^{16} vs. 6.7 x 10^{15}), and, despite the additional time required to enter a COPS password, PEOU is equal for both procedures. Moreover, as the number of passwords per user increases (because the number of secure systems they must access multiplies), improved memorability becomes an increasingly strong advantage of COPS passwords.

Future research efforts should include conducting longitudinal studies to establish the efficacy of COPS for more realistic applications in which passwords are used to access systems repeatedly over time. In particular, future studies should examine whether training end users how to use COPS passwords has an impact on its PEOU, and whether the time required to login using the COPS password procedure significantly decreases with proper training and repeated usage to the point where the login time is comparable to that of the FIPS password procedure. Will users be more able to remember the COPS password than the alternative high-security password (FIPS) for realistic periods of time?

The PEOU and PU of COPS also should be evaluated from the perspective of system administrators, who are ultimately responsible for the selection and adoption of password procedures to protect the systems they manage. Because system operators are more knowledgeable about security risks and the degree to which security measures may be compromised using available cracking tools, we might expect system operators (as opposed to end users) to appreciate more the increased security afforded by COPS passwords, which may lead to a significantly higher PU for COPS than traditional password procedures. Future studies could also examine a lower-security version of COPS by reducing the number of check-off boxes on the interface, which would reduce the cognitive load of the input mechanism, while still providing greater practical security than self-selected passwords.

ACKNOWLEDGMENT

This research is supported by the Mississippi State University Center for Computer Security Research and funded by the U.S. National Security Agency (NSA), grant number DUE-0209869.

REFERENCES

Adams, A., & Sasse, M.A. (1999). Users are not the enemy. *Communications of the ACM, 42*(12), 40-46.

Ames, B.B. (2002). PC developers worry about security. *Design News, 57*(16), 29.

Anderson, J.R. (1994). *Cognitive psychology and its implications.* New York: W.H. Freeman.

Bergadano, F., Crispo, B., & Ruffo, G. (1998). High dictionary compression for proactive password checking. *ACM Transactions on Information and System Security (TISSEC), 1*(1), 3-25.

Bolande, H. (2000). Forget passwords, what about pictures? Retrieved September 18, 2002, from *http://zdnet.com.com/2102-11-525841.html*

Boroditsky, M., & Pleat, B. (2001). Security @ the Edge—Making security and usability a reality with SSO. *Passlogix.* Retrieved September 18, 2002, from *http://www.passlogix.com/media/pdfs/security_at_the_edge.pdf*

Burrows, J. H. (1985). Password usage: Federal information processing standards publication 112. *National Institute of Standards and Technology.* Retrieved September 18, 2002, from *http://www.itl.nist.gov/fipspubs/fip112.htm*

Coates, A.L., Baird, H.S., & Fateman, R.J. (2001). Pessimal print: A reverse turing test. *Proceedings of the Sixth International Conference on Document Analysis and Recognition*, Seattle, WA.

Davis, F.D. (1989). Perceived usefulness, perceived ease of use, and user acceptance of information technology. *MIS Quarterly, 13*(3), 318.

Federal Aviation Administration (FAA), U.S. Department of Transportation (2002). Password administration (Internatl document N 1370.38, dated 3/25/2002, cancelled 3/24/2003). Retrieved April 8, 2003, from *http://216.239.39.100/ search?q=cache:UcqXFyMXIPYC:www2.faa. gov/aio/common/documents/HTMLfiles/N137038. htm+faa-8* (originally at *http://www2.faa.gov/aio/ common/documents/N137038.pdf*)

Gates pledges better software security. *CNN.com/ Technology*. Retrieved January 21, 2003, from *http://www.cnn.com/2003/TECH/biztech/01/25/ microsoft.security.ap/*

Hewett, T.T. (1999). Cognitive factors in design (tutorial session): Basic phenomena in human memory and problem solving. *Proceedings of the Third Conference on Creativity & Cognition*, Loughborough, United Kingdom.

Jianxin, J.Y. (2001). A note on proactive password checking. *Proceedings of the 2001 Workshop on New Security Paradigms*, Cloudcroft, NM.

Lemos, R. (2002). Passwords: The weakest link? Retrieved September 18, 2002 from *http://news. com.com/2009-1001-916719.html*

Miller, G.A. (1956). The magical number seven, plus or minus two: Some limits on our capacity for processing information. *Psychological Review, 63*, 81-97.

Monrose, F., Reiter, M.K., & Wetzel, S. (1999). Password hardening based on keystroke dynamics. *Proceedings of the 6th ACM Conference on Computer and Communications Security*, Singapore.

Newell, A., & Simon, H.A. (1972). *Human problem solving*. Englewood Cliffs, NJ: Prentice-Hall.

Password usage survey results: June 2003 (2003). *SafeNet*. Retrieved August 7, 2003, from *http:// mktg.rainbow.com/mk/get/pwsurvey03*

Pinkas, B., & Sander, T. (2002). Securing passwords against dictionary attacks. *Proceedings of the 9th ACM Conference on Computer and Communications Security*, Washington, D.C.

Spafford, E.H. (1988). *The Internet worm program: An analysis (Purdue Technical Report CSD-TR-823)*. West Lafayette, IN: Purdue University.

The twenty most critical Internet security vulnerabilities (updated): The experts consensus (2002). *SANS*. Retrieved May 2, 2002, from *http://www. sans.org/top20.htm*

The twenty most critical Internet security vulnerabilities (updated) (2003). *SANS*. Retrieved August 7, 2003, from *http://www.sans.org/top20*

Ticketmaster—Read this first (2003). *Ticketmaster*. Retrieved January 23, 2003, from *https://www. ticketmaster.com/checkout/reserve*

Weirich, D., & Sasse, M.A. (2001). Pretty good persuasion: A first step towards effective password security in the real world. *Proceedings of the Workshop on New Security Paradigms*, Cloudcroft, NM.

What is the frequency of the letters of the alphabet in English? (2002). *AskOxford.com*. Retrieved September 29, 2002, from *http://www.askoxford. com/asktheexperts/faq/aboutwords/frequency*

This work was previously published in Advanced Topics in End User Computing, Vol. 4, edited by M. Mahmood, pp. 280-300, copyright 2005 by IGI Publishing (formerly Idea Group Publishing), an imprint of IGI Global.

Chapter 4.32
IT Security Governance and Centralized Security Controls

Merrill Warkentin
Mississippi State University, USA

Allen C. Johnston
University of Louisiana-Monroe, USA

ABSTRACT

Every enterprise must establish and maintain information technology (IT) governance procedures that will ensure the execution of the firm's security policies and procedures. This chapter presents the problem and the framework for ensuring that the organization's policies are implemented over time. Since many of these policies require human involvement (employee and customer actions, for example), the goals are met only if such human activities can be influenced and monitored and if positive outcomes are rewarded while negative actions are sanctioned. This is the challenge to IT governance. One central issue in the context of IT security governance is the degree to which IT security controls should be centralized or decentralized. This issue is discussed in the context of enterprise security management.

INTRODUCTION

Information system security management goals can only be achieved if the policies and procedures are complete, accurate, available, and ultimately executed or put into action. Organizations must be conscious of the hazards associated with the diffusion of technology throughout the firm and must reflect this awareness through the purposeful creation of policy. Furthermore, it is prudent that organizations take the appropriate measures to maximize the transfer of policy into effective

Figure 1. Security policy — procedure — practice

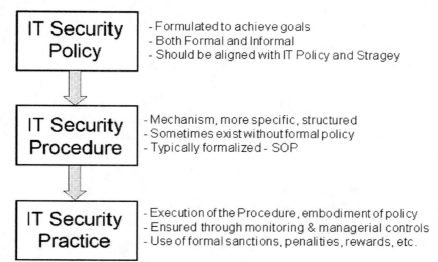

security management practices. This can only happen with an effective organizational design or structure and with adherence to proper information assurance procedures. Stakeholder compliance is only possible with the enforcement of internal controls to ensure that the organization's policies and procedures are executed.

The goals of IT security are to ensure the confidentiality, integrity and the availability of data within a system. The data should be accurate and available to the appropriate people, when they need it, and in the appropriate condition. Perfect security is not feasible — instead IT security managers strive to provide a level of assurance consistent with the value of the data they are asked to protect.

It is within their structures and governance procedures that organizations are able to address the issues of responsibility, accountability, and coordination toward the achievement of their purpose and goals. As organizations evolve to position themselves appropriately within their domains of interest, their governance posture evolves. These changes are reflected in the IT component of the organization as well. Within this mode of flux, however, one thing remains constant

— a desire to obtain and maintain a high level of information assurance. In this context, the roles of IT governance and organizational design in fulfilling the security management commitment are presented and presented.

Policies-procedures-practice. An organization's information security is only as good as the policies and procedures designed to maintain it, and such policies and procedures must also be put into practice (or executed). If managers, developers, and users are not aware of such policies and procedures, they will not be effectively executed. Of critical importance to the assurance of information security is the establishment of an enterprise training program with verifiable training protocols to ensure that all personnel (new and existing) are fully aware of such polices and procedures so that they can be put into practice on a daily basis.

IT GOVERNANCE

Governance encompasses those activities that ensure that the organization's plans are executed and its policies are implemented. *Planning* leads to *strategies* that are embodied in *policies* that are translated into *procedures*, which are executed and enforced through the *governance* process. One might say that governance is the method to ensure that policies and procedures are put into practice.

To support the goals of corporate governance, there must be a formalized process to guide the acquisition, management, and utilization of all strategic corporate assets, including its information resources. *IT governance describes the distribution of IT decision-making responsibilities within the firm and focuses on the procedures and practices necessary to create and support strategic IT decisions.*

The IT Governance Institute (2003) states that the purpose of IT governance is to direct IT endeavors and to ensure that IT's performance meets the following objectives: strategic alignment, value delivery, risk management, and performance measurement. Risk management ensures the appropriate management of IT-related risks, including the identification and implementation of appropriate IT security measures. Activity and performance monitoring and measurement are critical to ensure that objectives are realized, but require feedback loops and positive measures to proactively address deviation of goals.

The *IT Governance Institute* (ITGI*) (http://www.itgi.org/) has established the *Control Objectives for Information and related Technology* (COBIT) to facilitate in conducting all audits. This methodology is especially helpful in establishing the scope and plan for IT audits, and can guide managers in identifying appropriate controls and selecting effective infrastructure processes. This methodology of IT governance and control can also aid in maintaining compliance with the Sarbanes-Oxley Act and other applicable legislation. It can help a firm to establish assessment criteria for automated controls within key business processes and to gauge the performance of their application support activities (ITGI, 2003). Furthermore, it is designed to help ensure alignment between

technology investments and business strategies. (For an expanded discussion of COBIT, see Dhillon and Mishra (2006).)

IT Architecture

IT governance can be effective only if the enterprise organizes its information technology (hardware, software, procedures) in a manner consistent with its organizational and technical requirements. There are numerous formalized approaches to establishing an appropriate configuration for the organization's information resources. Such configurations are termed the "IT architecture" and are intended to efficiently and effectively support IT governance mandates as articulated in policy and procedure and enacted in practice.

The *Institute of Electrical and Electronic Engineers* (IEEE) describes an architecture as a dynamic structure of related components, whose design and maturation are governed by an established set of principles and guidelines. In building construction, the blueprint establishes the design, and the building is the actual embodiment of that design. In IT, the architecture establishes the design of the infrastructure, whereas the actual hardware and software installation is the embodiment of that design.

INFORMATION SYSTEMS CENTRALIZATION

For any enterprise function (whether production, billing, R&D, or others), there are various trade-offs in terms of the degree of centralization of managerial control. Certain functions (such as supply-chain management and purchasing) are subject to greater scale economies and are always operated more efficiently if they are highly centralized. Other organizational functions (such as customer support) may operate better when the function is decentralized for greater flexibility and attention to individual needs of the constituents.

However, most functions exhibit some level of trade-offs between highly centralized and highly decentralized control. Information systems or IT functions are also subject to this continuum.

The components of an organization's *information system* (IS) include hardware (such as storage servers), software components (application servers, etc.), data resources (often maintained in data servers), and personnel who build and maintain the system. These resources may be highly centralized in one IT department, highly decentralized (in the control of all the organization's departments), or somewhere along the continuum between the two extremes. The degree to which the IS is centralized or decentralized comprises one of the most fundamental characteristics of a firm's IT architecture or structure. A key role of IT managers is determining the IT architecture for the organization's information system, and one of the most important aspects of the architecture is the degree of centralization. The focus of this chapter is primarily on control and decision-making centralization, rather than on the physical location of IT assets.

Centralized Information Systems

In centralized information systems, the information resources and decisions regarding their acquisition and control are concentrated in one particular business unit that provides IT services to the whole firm. The main characteristics of a centralized approach include control, efficiency, and economy. Some centralized IS have always been centralized, while others have resulted from a cost-saving regrouping of an organization's IS to one particular location.

The primary advantage of centralized systems is centralized control using established technology and vendors (Kroenke & Hatch, 1994). Hardware and software standards save time and money in purchasing, installation, and support, and enable greater inter-operability of systems and sharing of data between divisions and departments.

Enterprise resource planning (ERP) and other enterprise-class applications require seamless intra-organizational data exchange.

This uniformity is built on a formal assessment of technology requirements and a professional evaluation of various technology choices, resulting in lower technical risks. Approved system components will typically function together more easily, with few surprising system compatibility issues. Centralized IT departments are typically staffed by highly trained and qualified IT professionals who employ structured systems design and maintenance procedures, leading to highly reliable systems. Professional IT managers often excel at selecting superior IT staff members.

Further, centralization enables efficiency gains that include reduced duplication of effort, resources, and expertise. Savings are realized through joint purchasing procedures and sharing of system resources (such as storage solutions, output devices, etc.). Further efficiencies are realized from the enterprise-wide administration of contracts and service agreements, licenses, and asset management.

There are other advantages of highly centralized IS architectures. Training costs can be minimized when the IT staff can specialize in a small set of hardware and software components. Planning is easier when all IT resources are under one group's control, and IT alignment can be more easily accomplished. An organization can afford key niche IT professionals with specialized skills within a large IT division more easily than if IT staff is dispersed throughout the enterprise with smaller budgets.

However, centralized systems may entail an initial cost disadvantage (Kroenke & Hatch, 1994), given the high salaries of systems professionals, the added bureaucracy, and the inflexibility of such systems, which can cause costs to escalate (Robson, 1997). Because of their propensity to command large budgets, centralized centers may be perceived within the organization as cost centers (rather than profit centers). Centralized operations may also slow various tasks when contrasted with decentralized systems where each business unit has its own autonomous system for local tasks (Robson, 1997). Autonomy to perform IT-related functions is synonymous with decision-making authority and can provide expedited responses to pressing matters. Reliance on single central components (servers, etc.) may increase the vulnerability of the entire system should any of those central components fail. Furthermore, central systems are isolated from customers and real business concerns, leading to a lack of responsiveness and personal attention to individual groups. Relationships between the centralized support unit and other business units within the same organization become more formalized and less flexible. Anytime decision-making authority is taken away from the departments and given to the organization, disparities between the goals of decision-making activities and their resultant outcomes may occur. This is because the knowledge of the unique requirements of the departmental or individual elements is either absent or undervalued.

Decentralized Information Systems

Decentralized systems provide the individual units with autonomy over their own IT resources without regard to other units. The primary advantages of the decentralized approach are the added flexibility and empowerment of individual business units. Response times to business demands are often faster. The proximity to the users and their actual information requirements can lead to closer fit, and the added involvement of end users in system development can lead to superior systems designs.

Start-up costs are relatively low in decentralized information systems (Kroenke & Hatch, 1994). Furthermore, it is far easier to customize and scale system components to individual departmental needs. There is increased autonomy (Hodgkinson, 1996), leading to increased flexibil-

ity and responsiveness. This enables far greater motivation and involvement of users as they perceive a sense of ownership (Robson, 1997). The redundancy of multiple computer systems may increase the reliability of the entire system — if one component fails, others may fill the gap. Finally, a decentralized approach reduces the conflicts that may arise when departments must compete for centralized IT resources.

Obviously decentralized IT management is more appropriate for organizations comprised of highly diverse business units that operate in very different marketplaces with very different business needs. If each unit is subject to different regulations, competitive pressures, and technology environments, then a centralized system may severely limit each unit's effectiveness. But a decentralized approach (which can still achieve information sharing through networking) will allow each unit each unit to react to its unique environment.

Because the locus of decision making is at the point of impact, decentralized systems typically have increased accountability, motivation, and management responsiveness (Hodgkinson, 1996). The increased understanding and customer focus is not without its costs, however. The lack of centralized control can lead to conflicts and policy clashes — sourcing from multiple vendors can certainly create incompatible systems, and inefficiencies can result from a high degree of duplication of resources, effort, and expertise. Additionally, the autonomous actions of the individual units (and perhaps the users within the units) can have disastrous results if the motivation or efficacy for compliance with the policies and procedures of the organization is missing. In other words, the facilitation of autonomy through decentralized managerial control may present a scenario in which increased decision-making authority and IT support activities are necessitated, but the desire or expertise necessary to adequately fulfill the requirements is lacking.

Table 1. Categories of threats to information systems (Source: Johnston et a.l, 2004; Adapted from Whitman, 2003)

Protection Mechanism	"TechUnit" (centralized)	"MedUnit" (decentralized)
Password	The centralized password management policy requires end users to maintain a single userid and password for access to all systems. Additionally, end users are required to adhere to specific password standards.	The decentralized password management approach allows users to establish their own unique password schemes. There are no specific requirements.
Media backup	IT management personnel are solely responsible for initiating and monitoring all data redundancy procedures.	IT personnel, as well as end users, actively participate in media backup efforts.
Virus protection software	Antivirus activities are initiated and supported for all end users and computational systems by IT personnel only.	IT personnel, as well as end users, actively participate in antivirus efforts.
Employee education	Formal training programs such as workshops and Intranet support webs are developed and implemented by IT personnel only.	End users are responsible for handling their specific training requirements.
Audit procedures	IT personnel monitor all relevant system and network logs.	End users are asked to monitor their respective systems for inappropriate activity.
Consistent security policy	IT personnel establish security policy for the entire FBU.	End users are instrumental in the establishment of security policy. Each unit within FBU #2 may have its own security policy.
Firewall	IT personnel maintain a single firewall for the entire FBU.	End users are asked to maintain personal firewalls for their respective systems.
Monitor computer usage	IT personnel are solely responsible for the monitoring of computer usage and resource allocation.	End users may monitor computer usage for their respective systems.
Control of workstations	Only IT personnel have administrative rights to computing resources. End user access is restricted.	End users have either Power-User or Administrator accounts on their respective workstations depending on their requirements.
Host intrusion detection	IT personnel are solely responsible for host intrusion detection.	End users are asked to maintain their own host intrusion detection mechanisms, such as ZoneAlarm®.

Centralization in IT Security Management

There are numerous information assurance mechanisms that may be deployed and managed in manner consistent with a desired level of centralization. For instance, firewall protection can be administered at the enterprise level by one administrator or a single unit within the organization. Alternatively, decentralized firewall protection, in which the individual user maintains a personal firewall solution, may be appropriate for environments characterized by a highly autonomous end user community. Another example of a security technology that can be deployed and managed in either a centralized or decentralized manner is an antivirus solution. While most organizations would probably choose to integrate antivirus protection into their enterprise level protection strategies, it is possible to deploy antivirus protection at the end-user level. In fact, for many organizations that allow mobile computing or remote connectivity, reliance on end users to appropriately manage an antivirus solution is commonplace. The same scenario is repeated for those security technologies that have not yet matured to the level of an enterprise-level solution, such as antispyware technology.

Currently, it is difficult to argue that the centralized IT security management strategy is undeniably more effective in providing the best protection to all organizations. When considered from the standpoint of prevention, detection, and remediation, it could be argued that each of these lines of defense could be addressed more immediately and precisely at the individual level. Unfortunately, there are no definitive answers to this problem because of the element of the human condition and its associated complexities. While many solutions may appear on the surface to be best suited for enterprise-level management, issues of culture, competency, and/or politics may force individual level management.

CASE STUDY

A comparative case study of two units within one enterprise (Johnston et al., 2004) compares the results of malware exposure under two types of IT security governance. The first, TechUnit, can be characterized as a centralized organization in terms of its IT environment, including its IT security governance. MedUnit, however, has a highly decentralized structure in which individual users maintain a high degree of control over their IT resources, including the responsibility for security-related activities. See Table 1 for details of the key differences.

The practice of centralized IT security management provided TechUnit with a highly effective framework from which to address issues specific to the Blaster and Sobig.F worms. As stated by the director of IT, "All of our PCs have antivirus software and multiple layers of protection and, in terms of the worms (Sobig.F and Blaster), it was all hands-off to the users" (Johnston et al., 2004, p. 8). This is a consistent theme among the other IT personnel. The only actions taken by TechUnit IT personnel to deal with the worms were slight modifications to their firewall and e-mail server filter. There were only a few observations of Blaster or Sobig.F worm activity in TechUnit's computing environment. These instances were identified and resolved solely by IT personnel with no impact in terms of cost, time, philosophy, or credibility (user confidence). The IT director noted, "If we have done our job properly, the impact is minimal, if at all felt, to the user community." Perhaps the minimal amount of end-user interaction required by TechUnit's IT personnel to deal with the worms could help to explain the notable absence of specific knowledge of the worms' functionality. Notably, the level of specific knowledge of the Blaster and Sobig.F worms increased as the level of management decreased and the degree of user interaction increased.

A decentralized approach to IT security management is one in which there is a high level of autonomy for end users in dealing with the security of their respective computing resources. The IT environment of MedUnit is highly reflective of such an approach. Although certain protection mechanisms are deployed in a manner consistent with centralized IT security management, such as the use of virus protection software, the majority of IT security management practices are decentralized described as follows.

MedUnit's users dictate IT security management policy and procedures. As explained by the MedUnit systems analyst, "While we have some end users that are technically savvy, it makes supporting those that aren't, very difficult. [End users] dictate what is going to happen. If several [end users] want something to happen, it's going to happen" (Johnston et al., 2004, p. 9). When faced with a malicious epidemic such as Blaster and Sobig.F, this approach to security management is not effective in the discovery or eradication of the worms. "We were hit pretty hard. It just hit us all of a sudden. For about two weeks, we could expect to come to work every morning and patch systems" (p. 9).

CONCLUSION AND FUTURE RESEARCH

In the current climate, the security of information systems needs to be properly managed in order to ensure availability of resources. Organizations planning their IT security management strategies can benefit from the findings of this research. While the decentralized approach and federal governance architecture facilitate meeting end-user requirements, security may need to be increasingly centrally managed. This is not necessarily contradictory to improving functionality for end users, since under the decentralized approach, end users are expected to take an active role in activities such as auditing and intrusion detection. This takes time and effort, and an end user's failure to practice these functions can potentially compromise the whole network for all users. Users may consider high IT activity in security breach remediation as a positive sign of service, but this may not last with repetitive loss of network availability. If MedUnit is indicative of security management under a decentralized approach, we expect a shift towards more centrally managed security in the future, considering the increasing external security threats. Further research is necessary to examine how to combine adequate security with realistic expectations regarding end-user involvement in security practices. This study examines two polar opposites of centralization and decentralization in IT security management. Future research endeavors can include varying levels of centralization across a larger number of FBUs.

REFERENCES

Hodgkinson, S. (1996). The role of the corporate IT function in the Federal IT organization. In M. Earl, *Information management: The organizational dimension*. Oxford, UK: Oxford University Press.

IEEE Std. 1471.2000. *Recommended practice for architectural description.* New York: IEEE.

ITGI®- IT Governance Institute. (2003). *Board briefing on IT governance.* Retrieved September 6, 2004, from www.ITgovernance.org/resources. htm

Johnston, A. C., Schmidt, M.B., & Bekkering, E. (2004, April). IT security management practices: Successes and failures in coping with Blaster and Sobig.F. *Proceedings of the 2004 ISOneWorld International Conference,* Las Vegas, NV (pp. 1-12).

Kroenke, D., & Hatch, R. (1994). *Management information systems.* Watsonville, CA: McGraw-Hill.

Mishra, S., & Dhillon, G. (2006). The impact of the Sarbanes-Oxley (SOX) Act on information security governance. In M. Warkentin & R. Vaughn (Eds.), *Enterprise information security assurance and system security: Managerial and technical issues* (pp. 62-79) . Hershey, PA: Idea Group Publishing.

Robson, W. (1997). *Strategic management and information systems: An integrated approach.* London: Pitman Publishing.

Whitman, M. E. (2003). Enemy at the gate: Threats to information security. *Communications of the ACM, 46*(8), 91-95.

This work was previously published in Enterprise Information Systems Assurance and Systems Security: Managerial and Technical Issues, edited by M. Warkentin, pp. 16-24, copyright 2006 by IGI Publishing, formerly Idea Group Publishing (an imprint of IGI Global).

Chapter 4.33
Securing E-Learning Systems:
A Case of Insider Cyber Attacks and Novice IT Management in a Small University

Michelle Ramim
Nova Southeastern University, USA

Yair Levy
Nova Southeastern University, USA

ABSTRACT

The growing use of e-learning systems has been documented by numerous studies (Levy, 2005). Yet in spite of this enormous growth, little attention has been given to the issue of security of e-learning systems both in research and in practice. Security of e-learning systems has a unique challenge as these systems are accessed and managed via the Internet by thousands of users over hundreds of networks. However, the Internet can pose security threats such as unauthorized access, hacking/cracking, obtaining sensitive information, and altering data and configuration, as well as enabling academic misconduct incidents (Freeh, 2000; Ramim, 2005; Sridhar & Bhasker, 2003). At the same time, cyber attacks have proliferated significantly in recent years. As a result, proper IT policies and procedures, in particular ones related to security of information systems, have become critical for organizations. This case study was written from the IS consultant's point of view and addresses the issues related to insider cyber attacks combined with novice IT management knowledge in a small university. After a year of substantial growth to its online learning program, the university in this case study experienced a devastating event that halted all academic activities enabled by the institution's e-learning system. This case reveals that internal cyber attack as well as lack of proper IT policies and procedures all resulted in multiple instances of damage to the e-learning system. The case provides detailed documentation on the security audit performed as well as stimulation for class discussions on actions to be taken as a result of the insider's cyber attack. Additionally, this case study attempts to provide a starting point on discussions in the area of security related to e-learning systems. It is hoped that this case study will stimulate discussions among practitioners and researchers related to e-learning systems security, and that it will help prevent such incidents from occurring at other academic institutions.

ORGANIZATIONAL BACKGROUND

Knowledgeville University (KU)[1] is a small higher education institution with mostly minority students in the Southeastern US. KU provides undergraduate and master's degrees in nine academic programs. The student body is about 1,200 students with most students attending full-time courses. However, a substantial number of students (20%) are enrolled on a part-time basis in the online learning program, which is enabled by KU's e-learning system. KU began to use its e-learning system during the 2001-2002 academic year. KU's IT department has been managing the technical administration of this program while a faculty member was appointed to recruit, coach, and encourage other faculty members to integrate their curricula into the e-learning system. A year later, during the 2002-2003 academic year, KU had 84 courses using the e-learning system. KU had about 120 faculty members of which, at that time, 42 were using the e-learning system on a daily basis.

KU's e-learning system is a proprietary, fully developed comprehensive online course management system (WebCT). Since 2001, online courses have been an important part of KU's vision by enabling students' learning in a flexible "any time, any place" mode. Consequently, online courses have been explored by KU's administration as a new opportunity for reaching distant and local working students, as well as a new revenue stream. The online courses have become a competitive edge for KU among other small academic institutions in the region. KU's president, Dr. Lopez[2], has committed to the success of the online learning program by incorporating the participation of faculty members in teaching online courses as part of their tenure and promotion review criteria. Additionally, Dr. Lopez has provided department chairs with incentives to help stimulate even further the use of the e-learning system both for on-campus courses and for fully online courses. Moreover, Dr. Lopez has allocated a moderate budget for the purchase of laptops for faculty members and for selected bright students who participate in online learning courses. Dr. Lopez also developed a set of strategies by which students, faculty, and administrators will incorporate the use of technology and the Internet in most of the daily activities on campus, quite apart from the online learning program. In every on-campus classroom building, KU now houses several multimedia classrooms and computer labs. The library purchased access to multiple electronic databases as well as acquiring several kiosk stations with Internet connection for students' use. Each full-time faculty member was provided with a computer system and basic software package. Residential halls were equipped with several kiosk stations in the lobby and a small computer lab in each hall. The president's office conducted annual surveys to assess students' and faculty members' technology skills. Consequently, as of the Fall 2002 term, all students were required to enroll in a technology course during their freshman year. Faculty who demonstrated low technology skills were encouraged to participate in technology training sessions provided by the Human Resources (HR) department. The use of the institution's e-mail system was regularly promoted during registration events. Although registration was not Web-enabled, Dr. Lopez hoped that Internet registration would be in place by 2005.

SETTING THE STAGE

KU's IT department was comprised of an IT director, Mrs. Rodriguez; a network administrator; two technicians who supported the entire institution; an IS consultant, Ms. Maya; a Webmaster; and a telecommunication subcontractor. Aside from Ms. Maya, all employees had been with the department for several years (4-10) and enjoyed interacting with the rest of KU's employees on a first-name basis. Mrs. Rodriguez reported directly to Dr.

Figure 1. KU's IT department organizational chart

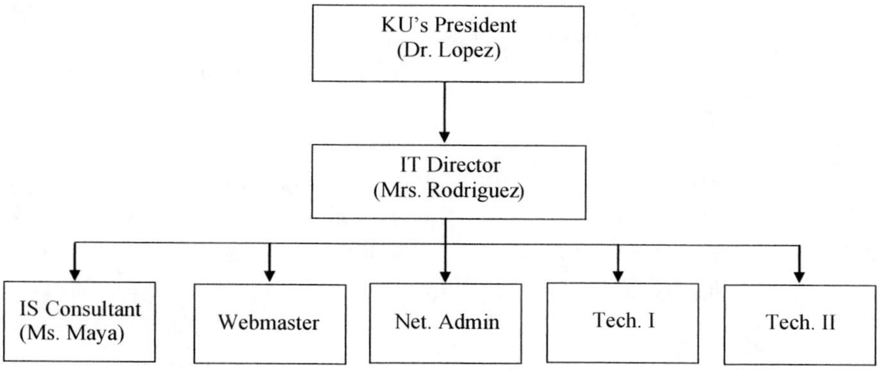

Lopez, KU's president. With 10 years' employment with KU, she was the most senior in the department. However, she had very minimal IT knowledge and had been promoted to the position of the IT director primarily due to her seniority. Mrs. Rodriguez's specific knowledge was in the area of accounting and finance, where she was very instrumental in helping implement the HR and student management systems. Mr. Perez had been KU's network administrator; over the course of several months he came late to work, took extensive lunch breaks, and had overall low performance. As a result, Mr. Perez was asked to leave, and Mrs. Rodriguez assumed his responsibilities until a new network administrator could be hired. See Figure 1 for KU's IT department organizational chart.

KU's IT department has four primary functions:

1. To provide technical support and orientation to students
2. To support and maintain the computer laboratories throughout campus as well as in the library
3. To provide technical support and various IT training to faculty members as well as to maintain faculty members' computers, software, and Web sites
4. To support and maintain the university's administration computing and the IT equipment of all KU's systems/functions (i.e., registration, tuition payments, financial aid, bookstore's point of sale, cafeteria's point of sale, grade reporting system, e-learning system, KU's Web site, financial reporting, human resources, and IT training)

Most of the equipment in KU's IT department had been donated from various equipment providers (i.e., Dell, HP, Cisco, etc.) where it was outdated and inadequate to perform most of the IT tasks required. KU's IT network infrastructure consisted of the following hardware:

*   An HP mainframe where the institution's administrative datacenter and main computing were hosted (student registration, financial aid, student housing, etc.)
*   An e-mail server
*   A server that hosted faculty members' Web pages as well as KU's Web site, and additional faculty members' server-end software used for teaching purposes
*   A server that hosted the e-learning system application (WebCT)
*   A server that hosted human resources application and data (payroll system)

- A server that hosted the library application and databases
- A server that hosted the bookstore point of sale application and data
- A server that hosted the cafeteria's point of sale application and data
- A server that hosted student access and a special debit card system
- A server that hosted server-end music software (used mainly by the music department)
- Two network-enabled HP printers that provided executive reports
- A dedicated T1 line connecting KU to the Internet
- Multiple Cisco switches and 16 port hubs

KU's IT department had no security policies and procedures as most of the activities in the department lacked formality. There was no evidence of a physical security mechanism in the server farm. Additionally, there were no mechanisms for network security in place. Moreover, technology manuals, warranties, and certificates were dispersed in various areas in the IT office.

CASE DESCRIPTION

In late 2002, KU experienced a cyber attack to its e-learning system that resulted in the server that hosted the e-learning system application shutting down in the middle of the semester, putting a halt to students' and faculty members' academic work. In order to assist in understanding the issues addressed in this case, the following section will provide an overview of insider cyber attacks, followed by a description of the approach to the problem proposed by Ms. Maya in the days following the cyber attack. Moreover, a review of the e-learning security audit process conducted, as well as the audit results and action plans, are discussed.

Insider Cyber Threats and Attacks

The knowledge-based economy has been mainly powered by technology-enabled communication and systems (Zang, Zhao, Zhou & Nunamaker, 2004). Additionally, enterprisewide systems and global communication have increasingly become an integral part of today's organizations (Hamin, 2000). Corporations have increased their dependency on enterprisewide systems and global communication networks (Garfinkel, Gopal & Goes, 2002; Magklaras & Furnell, 2002). E-learning systems have been getting increased attention and have become center-stage systems in many organizations (Levy, 2006). Hamin (2002) noted that the dependency on information systems has caused organizations to "become more exposed and vulnerable to an expanding array of computer security risks or harms and inevitably to various kinds of computer misuse" (p. 105). At the same time, newer technologies along with industry regulations (i.e., Sarbanes-Oxley Act) promote substantial investment in IT security products and such investment is predicted to reach $13.5 billion by 2006 (Hale & Brusil, 2004; Schultz, 2003). However, it has been observed that most small to mid-size business organizations do not employ a security management program (Keller, Powell, Horstmann, Predmore, & Crawford, 2005). Moreover, the latest report of the Computer Security Institute (CSI/FBI) (Gordon, Martin, William, & Richardson, 2004) states that nearly 66% of all cyber-security breach incidents, in the 280 organizations who responded to the survey, were conducted from inside the organization by authorized users. Additionally, an overwhelming 72% of organizations reported that they have no policy insurance to help them manage cyber-security risks (Gordon et al., 2004). However, most literature in the area of cyber security has been focusing on threats and attacks caused by an outsider imposed on the organization's network or systems (Magklaras & Furnell, 2002). Hamin (2002) defines *insider threats* as "threats from computer misuse within the workplace ... [as] it is generally concerned with the harms committed by employees against organizations for which they work" (p. 106). He further elaborates that under this definition the term *employees* actually refers to current, former, and temporary workers, as well as other individuals with close knowledge of the computer systems of the organization. For example, such individuals may include consultants or independent contractors working for the organization, system maintenance technicians from outside vendors who maintain the organization's network and/or systems, or suppliers (Hamin, 2002). Magklaras and Furnell (2002) provided a definition of the term *misuse* as "to use (something) in a wrong way or for a wrong purpose" (p. 63). By extending this definition, they defined *IT misuser* as an individual who is using the available resources in an unacceptable way and for an unapproved purpose (Magklaras & Furnell, 2002). Moreover, the term *insider* is not classified by the physical sense of the term, rather by its logical sense. As such, this study will define an *insider cyber misuser* (or *insider cyber attacker*) as a current, former, and/or temporary employee (including consultants, contractors, suppliers, maintenance technicians, etc.) who is using available computing resources either from inside the organization's networks or via the Internet in an unacceptable way and for an unapproved purpose in order to intentionally cause harm to the organization's networks or systems. This definition is also in full agreement with the description of *insider cyber attacker* provided by the former FBI director, Mr. Freeh, in his congressional testimony on "cybercrime" before the U.S. Senate Committee on Judiciary, Subcommittee for the Technology, Terrorism, and Government Information (Freeh, 2000).

The Days Following the Cyber Attack...

Within one day of the cyber attack against KU's e-learning system, faculty members and students mounted complaints to KU's IT department and eventually to the institution's president. During an emergency president's meeting, Dr. Lopez demanded from Mrs. Rodriguez an immediate audit of the technology network and a comprehensive report about the status of the e-learning system, along with immediate actions to restore the system. Following the meeting, Dr. Lopez assured both students and faculty members that a ramification plan was underway to save the semester's work and bring the e-learning system back to operation.

Mrs. Rodriguez solicited a proposal for a security audit from the IS consultant, Ms. Maya, who specialized in e-learning systems as well as crisis recovery management. Ms. Maya interviewed the IT director about the recent sequence of events, basic facts about the institution's network components, and types of hardware/software comprising the e-learning system. The following day, Ms. Maya submitted a proposal to Mrs. Rodriguez that included details about the scope of a proposed audit, a general outline of the proposed audit process, and a projected timetable as well as a projected report about the network audit and status of the e-learning system. Several days following KU's cyber attack, Ms. Maya was invited to perform the security audit.

During the audit phase that lasted a week, Ms. Maya visited KU's campus several times. Some of her activities included:

- Interviews of numerous personnel from KU's IT department and faculty members who have used the e-learning system as part of forensic computing. Also, interview Mrs. Rodriguez about past and present incidents with employees related to negative performance, low morale, or other employee behavioral issues.

- Visit to KU's server farm in order to observe the network physical space, review relevant manuals, and technology-related documents provided by Mrs. Rodriguez, and perform some tests on the server hosting the e-learning system application.
- Perform a security audit on the server hosting the e-learning system application.
- Create a comprehensive report about the security audit outcomes.
- Create a two-phase comprehensive action plan and recommendations for further action based on two criteria: (a) mission-critical issues, and (b) non-mission-critical issues.

The E-Learning Security Audit Process

Goan (1999) discussed various issues related to cyber attack processes. He provided a set of recommendations which were followed in this audit process. He advocated the use of audit trains in which logs of system activities are reviewed. Additional audit mechanisms that Goan (1999) recommended include monitoring operating system commands: "Looking for hidden processes, checking log files, and testing for known backdoor passwords are among the multitudes of manual techniques that system administrators may engage in via available system commands" (p. 50). Sandhu and Samarati (1996) also proposed an audit methodology similar to the one proposed by Goan (1999) that includes collection of data about the system's activities to find traces of the intruder or perpetrator. Furthermore, Goan (1999) maintained that "evidence must be gathered and analyzed in a timely fashion so as to improve the chances of detecting an intrusion before significant damage is done or before the trail left by the intruder becomes cold" (p. 50). This recommendation is effective in enabling early detection of cyber threats before damage is inflicted, or before a threat materializes as an attack. Oftentimes the cyber-attacker may survey the network over a period of time before setting up a malicious action (Hamin, 2000). Therefore, the audit methodology employed in this case also included collecting data about the system activities and analyses following the methodologies proposed by Goan (1999) as well as Sandhu and Samarati (1996).

The audit performed by Ms. Maya attempted to uncover the attacker's activities after the fact. As in this case, cyber attack audit is often used to provide legal evidence to the court system (Hamin, 2000). Consequently, cyber attack audit mechanisms can be utilized forensically in order to apply severe penalties to criminals, rather than as a preventative measure (Hamin, 2000; Schneier & Kelsey, 1999). In line with the recommendations provided by Goan (1999) as well as Sandhu and Samarati (1996), a number of system tools, log files (event logs) and access control mechanisms were reviewed on the server hosting the e-learning system. The findings were reported to Mrs. Rodriguez and Dr. Lopez.

The Audit Results

The security audit findings and the two recommended action plans were presented by Ms. Maya, the IS consultant, to KU's president, Dr. Lopez, and KU's IT director, Mrs. Rodriguez, about two weeks following the discovery of a cyber attack against KU's e-learning system. During an interview with Mrs. Rodriguez, it was revealed that the network administrator had been dismissed a few weeks prior to the cyber attack. Consequently, Mrs. Rodriguez was filling in the network administrator position. Not having had formal training in server and network administration, Mrs. Rodriguez did not maintain the current functions of the network. Although the former network administrator, Mr. Perez, had provided the administrator account usernames and passwords to Mrs. Rodriguez, no effort had been made to remove them from the systems—to change passwords or alter access permissions on the systems. Neither the server nor the network was protected by a firewall mechanism. The server farm did not appear to have a physical security system to its entrance. Servers were not securely attached to a server rack and server screens were not systemically locked down.

The server hosting the e-learning system application appeared to be unlocked on the system level. The http server application, Microsoft's Internet Information Server (MS-IIS), appeared intact. The server operating system was functioning and appeared to be intact as well. During the assessment of the e-learning server, Ms. Maya was able to log in using the "admin" information provided by Mrs. Rodriguez, which was the same information as used by the former network administrator, Mr. Perez. It appeared that the e-learning system application had been uninstalled from the server (on the C drive) remotely. The whole C drive had only 2GB disk space, while three other partitions of the hard drive (F, G, and H) were found empty with 1GB of free space on the F drive and 2GB of free space on the G and H drives. There were backups of only two of the 84 courses, dating back six weeks, according to Mrs. Rodriguez. It appears that there was a tape backup software installed on the server, but no scheduled backup was set. There were records of several previous manual backups done up to a few days before Mr. Perez left KU.

Based on the account of Mrs. Rodriguez, there were approximately 84 courses using the e-learning system. Additionally, 42 faculty members were regularly using the e-learning system. It was unknown how many students were enrolled in these courses or had access to the e-learning system; however, that information could be retrieved from the student information system that was running on another server and had not been attacked. The e-learning system application's centralized user database was fully corrupted on the

8989 port, and could not be recovered. Additional observations included the server settings on port 8989 that were not configured properly and the administrator e-mail for errors, which was not configured at all. There was no license key set for the e-learning system on the existing server. Also, there was no virus scan or net shield on the server. It appears that there was no uninterrupted power supply (UPS) system on the server in case the power was to shut down.

An inspection of the server system log files showed numerous entries for the "admin" account logging remotely via the Internet. The log files also confirmed the suspicion that the user of the "admin" account had uninstalled the e-learning system application remotely and a time stamp for this activity was present in the log files. A trace of the IP number was performed to the source perpetrator who used the "admin" user. Based on this information, it was concluded that Mr. Perez, the former network administrator, was associated with the intentional cyber attack on KU's e-learning system.

Following a massive search by Ms. Maya and the two technicians in KU's IT department, several tapes of manual backups were found. Some of the backup tapes included specific backups of the e-learning system performed by Mr. Perez several weeks before his departure from KU. It appeared that these tapes included backups of the 84 online courses lost during the cyber attack. However, these backups had been done about three weeks prior to the day of the cyber attack. As such, if restored properly on a new e-learning system, three weeks' worth of academic work (from the date of the backup to the date of the cyber attack) would be lost, aside from the delays and slowing of student productivity during the two weeks of the security assessment and recovery.

CURRENT CHALLENGES/ PROBLEMS FACING THE ORGANIZATION

Can KU Save the Term?

Based on the security audit and development of the audit outcomes report it was evident that KU was challenged to bring the e-learning program back on track. During a meeting with KU's president, Dr. Lopez, and KU's IT director, Mrs. Rodriguez, Ms. Maya expressed some reservations on KU's ability to rebound quickly from this incident. She noted that it might take some time to develop an action plan in order to reinstate the e-learning system. Additionally, Ms. Maya, noted that it may take longer to order new equipment, receive it, install it, and bring it up to a production level. Moreover, the backups that were found for the e-learning courses could be restorable. However, these backup copies were several weeks old and would require additional time to restore. As such, KU was facing major challenges as part of their recovery process. What are the different action plans Ms. Maya can propose to help KU recover the e-learning system? What actions will be needed in the short run and what actions will be needed in the long run to help KU recover? Will they be able to save the current academic term?

Will KU Reorganize the IT Department?

It appears that KU's IT department currently may lack the knowledge and skills needed to operate this department. Although understaffing of universities' IT departments appears to be a major issue for small and medium higher educational institutions (Ross, Tyran, Auer, Junell, & Williams, 2005), KU's current situation is not limited to staff shortage only. KU's president, Dr. Lopez, noted that a reorganization of their university's IT department is indispensable. However, given the long history of KU's IT director, Mrs. Rodriguez and her dedication to work, reorganization of the department may bring some new challenges both for Mrs. Rodriguez and Dr. Lopez. Additionally, Dr. Lopez does believe that Mrs. Rodriguez is a trusted and devoted employee. However, evidently her ability and skills to serve in the capacity of overseeing KU's whole IT operation may be questionable. Moreover, the overall reputation of KU's IT department was drastically eroded over the course of this incident. Furthermore, faculty members and students were discussing other potential failures. Concerns about privacy of students' records were conveyed by the faculty senate to the president. Will KU's president, Dr. Lopez, be able to reorganize the IT department without losing a trusted and devoted individual such as Mrs. Rodriguez? What policies and procedural changes will KU's IT department need to undertake as a result of this incident? Will this incident impact other KU's departments? Should KU file charges or seek legal actions against the former employee that conducted these acts?

The Lessons Learned

This case illustrates the importance of proper policies and procedures as well as proper IT knowledge by key individuals in the IT department of small universities. Moreover, although most attacks reported in the U.S. are performed by insiders, most of the security attention has been given in previous literature to attacks performed by outside perpetrators. This case addresses the issue of insider cyber attacks by providing some theoretical background on the term including clarification of the term "insider attacker." This case also highlights the need for formal policies and procedures in the IT department. In order to avoid such devastating consequences, IT departments should have clear policies and procedures (e.g., ones provided by CERT.org or US-CERT.gov) for various threats as well as for attack types.

Finally, this case supports the need for academic institutions to engage in creating proactive security safeguards for e-learning systems. Literature already noted that academic institutions should develop strategies to overcome challenges unique to e-learning systems (Zhang et al., 2004). However, very few institutions actually do so due to various challenges. One of these challenges relates to the limited security of e-learning systems resulting from untrained IT personnel in academic institutions, as seen in this case study. Another challenge related to the limited security of such systems is the tight budget under which IT departments of some academic institutions operate. Often, academic institutions are "too busy handling day-to-day IT operations to devote [adequate] resources to disaster planning" (Ross et al., 2005, p. 47). Moreover, lack of proper funding to academic institutions' IT departments has been causing IT directors to cut down on the number of qualified employees, that is, reduce overall staff, or hire unqualified employees. Levy and Ramim (2004) proposed eight key elements that are needed for successful e-learning programs. Three of these key elements are budget and funding, a high quality support and development team, as well as policies and procedures (Levy & Ramim, 2004). As this case study demonstrates, the consequences of limited IT knowledge combined with a lack of proper policies and procedures for IT-related issues such as employee discharge can be devastating to small academic institutions. Nevertheless, academic institutions should be open to embracing changes related to their current e-learning system's security strategy even though they are renowned for their resistance to IT changes (Chae & Poole, 2005; Wang, & Paper, 2005).

ACKNOWLEDGMENT

The authors would like to thank the editor-in-chief, Dr. Mehdi Khosrow-Pour, the accepting associate editor Dr. Ira Yermish, and the four anonymous referees for their careful review, constructive comments, and valuable suggestions.

REFERENCES

CERT® Coordination Center (CERT/CC). (n.d.). Retrieved April 28, 2006, from http://www.CERT.org

Chae, B., & Poole, M. S. (2005). Enterprise system development in higher education. *Journal of Cases on Information Technology, 7*(2), 82-101.

Freeh, J. L. (2000). Congressional testimony of FBI director on "cybercrime." Testimony before the U.S. Senate Committee on Judiciary, Subcommittee for the Technology, Terrorism, and Government Information. Retrieved April 28, 2006, from http://www.fbi.gov/congress/congress00/cyber032800.htm

Garfinkel, R., Gopal, R., & Goes, P. (2002). Privacy protection of binary confidential data against deterministic, stochastic, and insider threat. *Management Science 48*(6), 749-764.

Goan, T. (1999). A cop on the beat: Collecting and appraising intrusive evidence. *Communications of the ACM, 42*(7), 46-53.

Gordon, L. A., Martin, P. L., William, L., & Richardson, R. (2004). CSI/FBI computer crime and security survey. Computer Security Institute 2004. Retrieved April 28, 2006, from http://i.cmpnet.com/gocsi/db_area/pdfs/fbi/FBI2004.pdf

Hale, J., & Brusil, P. J. (2004). Guest editorial: Security management: Two sides of the same coin. *Journal of Network and Systems Management, 12*(1), 1-8.

Hamin, Z. (2000). Insider cyber-threats: Problems and perspectives. *International Review of Law, Computers & Technology, 14*(1), 105-113.

Keller, S., Powell, A., Horstmann, B., Predmore, C., & Crawford, M. (2005). Information security threats and practices in small businesses. *Information Systems Management, 22*(2), 7-20.

Levy, Y. (2005). A case study of management skills comparison in online and on-campus MBA programs. *International Journal of Information and Communications Technology Education, 1*(3), 1-20.

Levy, Y. (2006). *Assessing the value of e-learning systems*. Hershey, PA: Information Science Publishing.

Levy, Y., & Ramim, M. (2004). Financing expensive technologies in an era of decreased funding: Think Big... Start Small... Build Fast... In C. Howard, K. Schuenk, & R. Discenza (Eds.), *Distance learning and university effectiveness: Changing educational paradigms for online learning* (pp. 278-301). Hershey, PA: Idea Group Publishing.

Magklaras, G. B., & Furnell, S. M. (2002). Insider threat prediction tool: Evaluating the probability of IT misuse. *Computers & Security, 21*(1), 62-73.

Ramim, M. (2005, April 7-9). Towards an understanding and definition of academic misconduct in online learning environments. In *Proceedings of IEEE SoutheastCon 2005* (pp. 641-650), Fort Lauderdale, Florida.

Ross, S. C., Tyran, C. K., Auer, D. J., Junell, J. M., & Williams, T. G. (2005). Up in smoke: Rebuilding after an IT disaster. *Journal of Cases on Information Technology, 7*(2), 31-49.

Sandhu, R., & Samarati, P. (1996). Authentication, access control, and audit. *ACM Computing Surveys, 28*(1), 241-243.

Schneier, B., & Kelsey, J. (1999). Secure audit logs to support computer forensics. *ACM Transactions on Information and System Security, 2*(2), 159-176.

Schultz, E. (2003). IDS products lead sales surge. *Computers & Security, 22*(8), 660.

Sridhar, V., & Bhasker, B. (2003). Managing information security on a shoestring budget. *Annals of Cases on Information Technology, 5*(1), 151-167.

United States Computer Emergency Readiness Team (US-CERT). (n.d.). Retrieved April 28, 2006, from http://www.us-cert.gov/

U.S. Department of Justice. (2002). Fraud and related activity in connection with computers. Retrieved April 28, 2006, from http://www.usdoj.gov/criminal/cybercrime/1030_new.html

Wang, B., & Paper, D. (2005). A case of an IT-enabled organizational change intervention: The missing pieces. *Journal of Cases on Information Technology, 7*(1), 34-52.

Zhang, D. J., Zhao, L., Zhou, L., & Nunamaker, J. F. (2004). Can e-learning replace classroom learning? *Communications of the ACM, 47*(5), 75-79.

ENDNOTES

[1] The name of the university discussed in this case is concealed due to the sensitivity of the issues addressed. A fictitious name is used.

[2] Names of specific individuals discussed in this case are concealed due to the sensitivity of the issues addressed. Fictitious names are used.

This work was previously published in Journal of Cases on Information Technology, Vol. 8, Issue 4, edited by M. Khosrow-Pour, pp. 24-34, copyright 2006 by IGI Publishing, formerly known as Idea Group Publishing (an imprint of IGI Global).

Chapter 4.34
The Next Big RFID Application:
Correctly Steering Two Billion Bags a Year Through Today's Less-Than-Friendly Skies

David C. Wyld
Southeastern Louisiana University, USA

ABSTRACT

This chapter examines the adoption of radio frequency identification (RFID) technology in the commercial aviation industry, focusing on the role of RFID systems for improved baggage handling and security. The chapter provides a timely overview of developments with regard to the implementation of RFID technology in commercial aviation, which promises distinct advantages over the currently used bar-code system for baggage handling. The chapter focuses on how RFID technology can improve customer service through better operational efficiency in baggage handling, which has been demonstrated to be an integral component of the airline's customer service equation. Developments with RFID technology can dramatically improve the accuracy of baggage handling, which can enable air carriers to close an important service gap among customers in an increasingly turbulent operating environment. Other service industries can certainly benchmark the airline industry's use of RFID technology in luggage tracking as a way to improve their own operational capabilities.

INTRODUCTION

To put this chapter in perspective, consider this scenario: You have just landed in Alexandria, Egypt, or Alexandria, Louisiana. You are standing at the baggage carousel, having flown in on the last flight arriving that night. A constant stream of bags of all shapes, sizes, and colors circle past you, disappearing one by one as your "lucky" fellow passengers claim their prizes. After about 15 minutes, the carousel stops spinning. At that point, you realize that your checked roller-bag has not arrived on the same flight as you.

Now, you are in "lost luggage hell," and while the airline may do its best to accommodate you, no amount of compensation from the air carrier—whether in money, miles, or drink coupons—can change one simple fact: How are you going to make that winning presentation to a major new client at 8:00 the next morning? You realize that the only clothing you have in your possession is the warm-up suit you wore to be comfortable all day as you traveled; your "killer suit" and "confidence tie" are likely sitting on an airport tarmac thousands of miles away, with no clothing store in the city that will open before the meeting (unless you happen to be in Las Vegas).

The system that you are dependent upon to correctly track your checked luggage to either the Memphis in Tennessee or in Egypt, or wherever else it may be, is based on correct readings along the line of a bar-coded label, bearing a 10-digit IATA (International Air Transport Association) number. Gartner's Research Director, Jeff Woods, commented that "bags are very well tracked right now" by the airlines and their bar code-based systems (cited in Morphy, 2004). Yet, this is little consolation when it is *your* bag that is lost. The baggage tracking systems of the world's airlines are mature, and even under the best of conditions, bar code technology works in correctly reading only eight or nine bags out of every 10. This means that the airlines continue to devote considerable time and energy to manually intervene to correctly direct the right bags onto the right flights, while spending great amounts of money to reunite passengers with their bags when the system breaks down.

Today, savvy airlines, even in their precarious financial positions, are seeing the shift to RFID (radio frequency identification)-based baggage tracking systems as a solid operational investment that can produce significant cost savings and demonstrated return on investment (ROI). Airports as well are taking the initiative to shift to RFID-based systems, sensing the opportunity to produce greater traveler satisfaction with their experience at a specific airport. In a deregulated world of airline and airport choices, these entities are combining forces to enhance customer service and give them a competitive advantage, perhaps for a significant window of time until such RFID-based systems are made mandatory.

In this chapter, we will examine the mechanics of how RFID-based baggage tracking works and the benefits it can provide. After a brief overview of RFID technology, we will look at the experience of Delta Air Lines, which is the first airline to publicly commit to taking the technological leap forward to implementing RFID-based baggage tracking. We will then examine the confluence of technology, terrorism, and yes, marketing, that will likely drive the adoption of RFID-based tracking of checked baggage throughout the world. The RFID movement is also being spearheaded by the U.S. government. It is clearly interested in securing the safety of the traveling public and with it, what financial viability the airline industry has left in the wake of the after-effects of September 11, 2001, and the decline in travel spurred by that awful tragedy, an economic recession, and record fuel prices. We will examine the government push in this area and concerns over passenger privacy. Finally, we will look at an alternative vision of the future of airline customer service, which may preclude the need for baggage service as part of the air passenger experience altogether.

WHAT IS RFID?

In brief, radio frequency identification uses a semiconductor (microchip) in a tag or label to store data. Data is transmitted from, or written to the tag or label when it is exposed to radio waves of the correct frequency and with the correct communications protocols from an RFID reader. Tags can be either *active* (using a battery to broadcast a locating signal) or *passive* (using power from the RFID reader for location). A firm may use a combination of fixed and handheld readers for reading RFID tags to gain as complete a picture as has ever been possible on exactly what is where in their operations. Reading and writing distances range up to 100 feet, and tags can be read at high speeds (Booth-Thomas, 2003). For a detailed explanation of the technology, see Jones and Wyld (in press), McFarlane (2002), Kambil and Brooks (2002), and Reed Special Supplement (2004).

The advantages of RFID over bar code technology are summarized in Table 1.

RFID tags have been described as being a "quantum leap" over bar codes. *Inc. Magazine* characterized RFID vs. bar codes as "like going from the telegraph to the Internet" (Valentine, 2003).

As noted in an interview last year with the *Harvard Business Review*, William Copacino, group chief executive officer for Accenture's Business Consulting Capability Group, interest in RFID is picking up significantly throughout the global business community today. This is due not only to the fact that prices are rapidly dropping for both the RFID tags themselves and for the readers to sense them, but more importantly, the technology is providing significant improvements in operations and efficiency over traditional methods, while affording companies the concomitant opportunity to improve their customer service strategies (opinion cited in Kirby, 2003). From the perspective of Deloitte Consulting (2004), if RFID is viewed as simply an alternative means of identification and labeling to bar code technology, then businesses will have a "lost opportunity" on their hands. This is because RFID technology potentially offers wide-ranging opportunities for transformative change (a change of the highest magnitude) in internal business processes, supply chain management, security threat management, and customer service. Innovative applications of RFID technology are being seen in myriad industries today, including such critical areas as pharmaceuticals (Wyld & Jones, in press) and livestock tracking (Wyld, Juban, & Jones, 2005).

BAGGAGE AND AIRLINE CUSTOMER SERVICE

The critical link in customers' minds between seeing their luggage on the baggage carousel upon arrival and their perception of the quality of an airline's service offering has been empirically proven. Each year, professors Brent D. Bowen (University of Nebraska Omaha) and Dean E. Headley (Wichita State University) produce their

Table 1. RFID vs. bar code technology

• Bar codes require line of sight to be read.	• RFID tags can be read or updated without line of sight.
• Bar codes can only be read individually.	• Multiple RFID tags can be read simultaneously.
• Bar codes cannot be read if they become dirty or damaged.	• RFID tags are able to cope with harsh and dirty environments.
• Bar codes must be visible to be logged.	• RFID tags are ultra thin, and they can be read even when concealed within an item.
• Bar codes can only identify the type of item.	• RFID tags can identify a specific item.
• Bar code information cannot be updated.	• Electronic information can be over-written repeatedly on RFID tags.
• Bar codes must be manually tracked for item identification, making human error an issue.	• RFID tags can be automatically tracked, eliminating human error.

Airline Quality Rating report. These researchers' analytical methodology ranks airline performance in the United States, based on a weighted average of four key performance measures. These benchmarks have been validated as key in determining consumer perceptions of the quality of airline services. The four measures, drawn from data that the airlines are mandated to report to the U.S. Department of Transportation, include:

1. on-time arrivals,
2. mishandled baggage,
3. involuntary denied boardings, and
4. 12 areas of customer complaints.

Several airlines in the U.S. that have performed well in the quality survey, including Southwest, JetBlue, and Midwest Express, have touted their rankings in Bowen and Headley's (2004) report in their advertising campaigns.

Such has not been the case with Atlanta, Geor-

Table 2. 2004 airline quality ratings (adapted from Bowen & Headley, 2004)

RANK	AIRLINE	AQR SCORE
1	JETBLUE AIRWAYS	-0.64
2	ALASKA AIRLINES	-0.74
3	SOUTHWEST AIRLINES	-0.89
4	AMERICA WEST AIRLINES	-0.89
5	US AIRWAYS	-0.96
6	NORTHWEST AIRLINES	-1.02
7	CONTINENTAL AIRLINES	-1.04
8	AIRTRAN AIRWAYS	-1.05
9	UNITED AIRLINES	-1.11
10	ATA AIRLINES	-1.17
11	AMERICAN AIRLINES	-1.24
12	*DELTA AIR LINES*	*-1.24*
13	AMERICAN EAGLE AIRLINES	-2.10
14	ATLANTIC SOUTHEAST AIRLINES	-5.76

gia-based Delta Air Lines. Based on the recently released *Airline Quality Rating 2004* report (as seen in Table 2), Delta has now fallen to *last* among the 12 major U.S. airlines in consumer perceptions of service quality. To put this in perspective, while the airline's composite quality rating has actually *improved* over time since 2000, in that same timeframe, Delta's competition has been making marked improvements in the service components that matter most to airline customers.

Today, Delta is a firm embroiled in the turmoil that makes up the airline industry in America. Facing rising fuel costs, a downturn in business travel, an uncertain economy, and discount competition, *all* the established, legacy carriers in the U.S. are struggling financially and operationally today, with prominent carriers such as US Airways and United barely surviving (e.g., see Tully, 2004). Delta itself has been the subject of bankruptcy rumors, and it has conducted layoffs and closed its major hub at the Dallas/Fort Worth International Airport to stave off its demise (Perez, 2004). In September, CEO Gerald Grinstein announced a comprehensive overhaul plan, including laying off thousands of employees, and received initial agreement from its pilots' union to the recall of retired pilots on a limited basis (Fein, 2004; Weber, 2004). The airline industry is finding that without the ability to raise fares or to spend lavishly to improve customer service, it must improve its operational efficiencies and performance to survive today.

One particular area of weakness for Delta has been its handling of air travelers' checked-in luggage. In fact, according to the recently released 2004 report (which uses annual data as of the close of 2003), Delta's mishandled baggage rate increased from 3.57 in 2002 to 3.84 in 2003. As can be seen in Table 3, Delta still remains below the industry average rate of four lost bags per 1,000 passengers. However, Delta's own performance is impacted by that of Atlantic Southeast Airlines (ASA), Delta's regional partner throughout much of the United States. ASA "earned" *the* lowest

Table 3. Mishandled baggage reports for U.S. airlines—June 2004 (adapted from U.S. Department of Transportation, Air Travel Consumer Report, August 2004; http://airconsumer.ost.dot.gov/reports/2004/0408atcr.doc)

RANK	AIRLINE	REPORTS PER 1,000 PASSENGERS
1	JETBLUE AIRWAYS	2.81
2	AIRTRAN AIRWAYS	3.02
3	SOUTHWEST AIRLINES	3.16
4	HAWAIIAN AIRLINES	3.18
5	ALASKA AIRLINES	3.32
6	CONTINENTAL AIRLINES	3.32
7	AMERICA WEST AIRLINES	3.55
8	NORTHWEST AIRLINES	3.80
9	ATA AIRLINES	3.80
10	UNITED AIRLINES	3.83
11	US AIRWAYS	4.10
12	*DELTA AIR LINES*	*4.23*
13	AMERICAN AIRLINES	4.66
14	EXPRESSJET AIRLINES	5.29
15	AMERICAN EAGLE AIRLINES	9.00
16	COMAIR	10.21
17	SKYWEST AIRLINES	10.71
18	ATLANTIC COAST AIRLINES	13.42
19	ATLANTIC SOUTHEAST AIRLINES	13.97

quality rating of *all* airlines operating in the United States, regardless of size. Luggage service is a particularly sore point for Delta's code-sharing partner, as ASA's rate of 15.41 mishandled bags per 1,000 passengers is almost *four times* the industry average.

Despite years of trying to improve the quality of its baggage-handling systems, Delta has seen the performance of its current bar code-based system flat-line, with bar-coded labels being successfully read by scanners only 85% of the time. According to Delta spokesman Reid Davis, the airline faced the fact that it had "reached the end of the improvements that could be accomplished without new technology" (cited in Rothfeder, 2004). Of course, just because a bag is not scanned correctly does not mean that your bag will end up in Wichita Falls when you were heading to Wichita. In the end, Delta estimates that only 0.7% of all checked luggage is actually "lost." However, the airline spends upwards of $100 million each year to return these bags to their rightful owners and provide compensation to passengers whose luggage is never found (Collins, 2004).

Delta's top management has decided to tackle its "bag problem" head-on, looking to RFID technology as the means to an end of providing far-better luggage service to its passengers. In the fall of 2003, Delta implemented a pilot test of an RFID tracking system for checked luggage on flights between Jacksonville, Florida, and its hub in Atlanta, Georgia. In this testing program, Delta tracked 40,000 passenger bags equipped with radio frequency identification (RFID) tags from check-in to loading on an aircraft. As can be seen in Table 4, the RFID-enabled system provided far superior reading accuracy than the legacy bar code-based system. In the spring of 2004, Delta implemented another pilot RFID baggage-tracking system at its Cincinnati, Ohio, hub, producing similar results (Murray, 2004).

Through the two test programs, Delta learned several valuable lessons. It saw that tag antennas could be damaged by the static electricity generated along the conveyor systems (Collins, 2004). It also found that the lowest scanner accuracy rate (96.7%) was found when attempting to scan bags inside the unit load devices (ULDs), the large containers pre-loaded with checked luggage that are then loaded onto the plane. The ULDs are made of metal with canvas doors, and the metal housing impeded the radio signals. Delta plans to coat the ULDs with a material that can better reflect the radio waves (Brewin, 2004a). While the test programs were conducted in rather neutral weather environs, concerns were raised over the ability of the tagging systems to function in harsher environments, such as at Delta's western hub in Salt Lake City, Utah (Murray, 2004). Finally, there is a famous American commercial from Samsonite that shows a gorilla in his cage, tossing the bag around and eventually stomping on the suitcase. The obvious message is that checked bags are not always handled "delicately" by the humans or the machinery as it passes through baggage systems. Thus, it must be noted that baggage handling itself can damage or detach labels/tags, and concerns over the durability of the RFID tag are genuine.

Even with limited capital to invest in IT projects, in July 2004 Delta became the first airline to commit to having RFID-enabled baggage tracking in place system-wide by 2007. Delta plans to use passive tags, which will cost the airline 25 cents each initially. However, the airline hopes that the cost of the tags will drop to approximately 5 cents a unit by the time the system is fully implemented in 2007 (McDougall, 2004). Delta estimates that the full implementation cost of its RFID-based tracking system will ultimately fall somewhere between $15 and $25 million for its 81 airport locations. Delta has not yet announced plans for deploying the RFID-based system with its code-sharing partners, which would greatly raise the number of airports worldwide for implementation and the cost and complexity of the overall project (Murray, 2004). While this represents a significant investment, the ROI equation shows that this cost can be recouped in far less than a single year. This makes Delta unique, as it is one of the few examples to date in *any* industry where the decision to invest heavily in automatic identification technology is based on the desire to dramatically improve customer service.

Delta's RFID-enabled baggage system will give the company the ability to track a bag from the time a passenger checks it in at his/her departing airport till the time the bag is claimed at the baggage carousel at the arrival airport. At check-in, the RFID tag's serial number will be associated with the passenger's itinerary. Delta will position fixed readers at check-in counters and on conveyor belts where the bags are sorted. The airline will also equip baggage handlers with portable readers and outfit aircraft cargo holds with readers built into them. RFID readers can also be positioned to scan bags as they are loaded and unloaded from the unit load devices (ULD—the large containers that are loaded onto the plane). Through this surveillance system, Delta should be able to all but eliminate the problem of mis-loaded and misdirected checked luggage, and the attendant costs of reuniting the lost bag with the passenger. Ramp and flight crews will be able to make certain that the right luggage is on board before an aircraft takes off. And, in the event a passenger's bag is misdirected, Delta can instantly locate the bag through its RFID reader and more quickly route it to the passenger's destination. Pat Rary, a Delta bag systems manager, illustrated the fact that RFID will allow the airline to take proactive customer service steps on baggage problems. He observed that:

With this technology, we won't have to wait for the customer to come tell us that the bag is lost. We can tell the customer it's on the wrong plane and start responding before it's a crisis. Eventually, RFID should be able to signal an arriving passenger's cell phone with news of how long it will be before the bag is on the carousel. (cited in Field, 2004, p. 61)

Rob Maruster, Delta's director of airport strategy, recently commented in *Airline Business* that RFID tracking "will transform the airline on the ramp as much as radar did to transform air traffic control. When that happened, it was as if a light was turned on and people said, oh, so that's where the planes are. This technology will do that for bags. People will say, oh, so that's where the bags are" (cited in Field, 2004, p. 60). Delta's ultimate goal is to have a baggage tracking system that will have a "zero mishandling rate" (Brewin, 2004a).

RFID AND BAGGAGE SECURITY

Unfortunately, in our post-September 11 world, there are worse things that can happen in the air or at the airport than losing one's luggage or even eating the "Chef's Surprise" at the airport restaurant. The twin, nearly simultaneous jet crashes in Russia in August 2004 have now been attributed to in-flight bomb detonations by Chechen female suicide bombers, raising fears that suicidal terrorists could use similar methods to attack the

West (Hosenhall & Kuchment, 2004). While enhanced physical passenger screening, such as that just announced by the Transportation Security Administration (TSA) in the U.S., can deter such would-be suicidal terrorists, since September 11, the airline industry and national governments have placed renewed vigilance on screening both carry-on and checked bags for explosives and on making sure that all checked bags are matched to passengers who have actually boarded the aircraft. Writing in *Management Services*, Collins (2004) observed that one of the very real near-term applications for RFID technology is the prospect that a passenger's checked bag will be able to tell security personnel and the airline if it has not been properly screened.

The need for matching passengers with checked luggage has been at the forefront of anti-terrorism concerns ever since the in-flight bombings in the 1980s that took down a Pan American 747 over Lockerbie, Scotland, and an Air India jumbo jet over the Atlantic. Out of this concern, airlines must routinely remove bags from aircraft when a passenger fails to board, out of fear that a homicidal, rather than suicidal, terrorist would attempt to down an airliner with a bomb in an unaccompanied, checked suitcase (AIM Global, 2004).

Often, this is a time-intensive, laborious process, which can delay flight departures indefinitely, as ramp workers face the daunting task of finding the bags in question out of the hold of an aircraft or from the unit load devices. Airport operations managers and airline flight crews will often tell horror stories of how the inability to find the one or two targeted bags of a non-boarding passenger in and amongst the bags of 300-400 passengers on a jumbo jet has caused flights to be delayed for hours, costing the airline countless amounts of goodwill amongst the passengers, even if such measures are done precisely to safeguard their transit and their very lives. Thus, airports are also very interested in providing better baggage tracking as part of their customer service equation.

In Florida, the Jacksonville International Airport installed an RFID-based system in 2003 to direct checked luggage through their newly installed baggage handling system. The city's airport authority and the TSA jointly funded the Jacksonville system. The contractors for the Jacksonville Airport project included FKI Logistex and SCS Corporation. The Jacksonville system was designed to only handle outbound luggage, directing checked bags from the check-in counter through explosive detection screening and on to the correct terminal serviced by the respective airlines. All checked bags have a bar code label affixed to them, with approximately 12% receiving an additional RFID tag, due to their being selected for special screening attention by a computer-assisted passenger profiling system (CAPPS) (Trebilcock, 2003).

The Jacksonville pilot program tested the effectiveness of both disposable and reusable tags. Passengers checking in on the north side of the airport who were selected by the CAPPS had a disposable tag attached to their luggage, while those checking in on the airport's south side had a reusable, credit card size tag affixed to their checked bags. Each reusable tag costs $2.40, and each disposable tag costs 63 cents. Van Dyke Walker, Jr., director of planning and development for the Jacksonville Airport Authority, believes that his airport's system is a precursor of what is to come. He commented that "RFID is the future of airline baggage tracking, and we want to be ready" (cited in Trebilcock, 2003, p. 40).

Las Vegas' McCarran International Airport is considered to be an ideal proving ground for RFID baggage tracking. This is due to the fact that the vast majority of the passengers using the airport either begin or end their journeys there. In fact, as Las Vegas sees only 8% of its passengers connecting to other flights at its airport, a rate that is only second to Los Angeles International Airport (Anonymous, 2003a), Las Vegas' system is designed to track all checked luggage, routing bags through bomb detection screening and on to the proper aircraft. From the perspective of Randall H. Walker, McCarran International Airport's director of aviation, the RFID-enabled baggage handling system "becomes a win for all concerned: the traveler, the airport, the TSA and the airlines" (cited in Anonymous, 2004a). In 2005, the TSA is slated to have similar systems in place at both LAX and Denver International as well (AIM Global, 2004). Alaska Airlines also uses the tags on its international flights out of San Francisco International Airport (Woods, 2004).

Internationally, RFID-based baggage tracking systems are being tested in Narita, Japan, Singapore, Hong Kong, and Amsterdam (CNETAsia, 2004; Atkinson, 2002). In fact, the RFID baggage tracking system being installed at Hong Kong International Airport is regarded as the largest automatic identification system to be developed and deployed to date in Asia. Hong Kong's airport is one of the busiest in the world, handling approximately 35 million passengers each year. Y. F. Wong, who heads Technical Services and Procurement at the Airport Authority of Hong Kong, believes that the airport's investment in RFID technology is essential, as it addresses the need for improved customer satisfaction, while also enabling increased levels of security assurances (cited in Anonymous, 2004a). According to John Shoemaker, senior vice president of corporate development at Matrics, which will supply the airport with upwards of 80 million smart labels over the next five years, "What is key about Hong Kong International is that it is deploying this system to also save money" (quoted in Collins, 2004).

RFID baggage tracking is thus a means to an end for airports—with the end being improved baggage security. Simon Ellis, a supply-chain futurist at Unilever, recently observed that: "Security is just a sub benefit of visibility. Knowing exactly what is where gives you better control…and if you have better control you have better security" (cited in Atkinson, 2002).

RFID IN THE NEAR FUTURE AT THE AIRPORT

In a widely read article in *Scientific American*, Roy Want predicted that airline baggage tracking would be one of the first commercially viable RFID applications (Want, 2004). The potential market size is outstanding, as the world's airlines currently handle approximately two billion checked bags annually (Anonymous, 2003b). In the view of AIM Global (2004), with the proven accuracy and effectiveness of RFID-enabled baggage tracking, it may just be a matter of time before the TSA mandates that such automatic identification technology-based systems be employed in the U.S. However, such mandates, whether in the U.S. alone or in conjunction with other civil aviation authorities worldwide, would raise a multitude of issues. These include who will bear the costs of such systems, the need for standards, and the need for international airlines that fly to the U.S. and/or interconnect with U.S.-based carriers to employ such RFID tagging.

Paul Coby, chief information officer of British Airways, believes that members of the airline industry need to work together to ensure that investments in technologies such as RFID will yield the fullest possible ROI and customer service benefits. He suggested that the International Air Transport Association (IATA) should play a leading role in driving this technology, so as to ensure that the industry adopts common information systems standards. Coby commented, "For technology to fully bring business change, the whole industry needs to move forward" (cited in Thomas, 2004). In June, 2004, Delta and United jointly proposed an RFID-specification for baggage to the IATA (Collins, 2004).

The need for a unique air transport standard is obvious for the not-so-distant future, looking to the day when luggage will contain items with their own RFID tags, say on Gillette razors, Benetton shirts, and items purchased from Target, Wal-Mart, Metro, or countless other retailers. Wal-Mart mandated the use of tags on merchandise it purchases from key suppliers by January 2005 (RFID Journal, 2003), thus prompting other retailers to follow suit, or at least begin investigating the technological investment such a move to RFID will require. For example, the retailer Boscov's (U.S.) sees customer service benefits in terms of reduced stock-outs, yet worries about the tag and infrastructure costs (Sullivan, 2004a). Tesco (UK) announced plans to expand its RFID test project to include eight big-name packaged-goods manufacturers like Proctor & Gamble (Sullivan, 2004b). Others, like Federated's Lazarus store in Columbus, Ohio, and restaurants in Texas have seen improvements in customer service in terms of improved sales transactions (Coupe, 2003; Dunne & Lusch, 2005, p. 405). However, retailers will need to address the issue of consumer privacy, much like the airlines must do (Dunne & Lusch, 2005, p. 306; Lacy 2004).

It is even more important when one considers that the aircraft itself will likely have key parts tagged with RFID sensors in the near future. Boeing and Airbus are taking the lead in outfitting their new passenger jets, the 7E7 and A380 respectively, with RFID-tagged parts to provide a new level of historical and performance information on the key components. The two dominant commercial aircraft manufacturers are cooperatively working to produce industry standards, which is especially important since they share 70% of their supplier base (Tegtmeier, 2004). Likewise, Federal Express and Delta have pilot tested, equipping both flight deck electronics and engine parts, with RFID sensors (Brewin, 2004a). Thus, in only a matter of a few years, commercial airliners will be perhaps one of the most concentrated locations for RFID tags, making standards a necessity for avoiding problems with signal collision and information overload.

Tracking luggage with RFID may not be the only automatic identification technology we will see in use at the airport. By 2015, the International Civil Aviation Organization (ICAO) has proposed putting RFID chips in the over a billion passports worldwide. This move, while drawing fire from civil rights groups around the globe, may become a reality, all in an effort for the airlines and civil authorities to have better insights into who exactly to let on their aircraft (Jones, 2004). Likewise, the U.S. Transportation Security Administration has begun looking at how to use RFID-tagged boarding passes to improve airline security. The goals would be both to enhance airport security by giving facility security the ability to track passengers' movements within the airport and to speed passengers through airport security lines. The latter would be accomplished by linking the issuance of boarding passes to the proposed "registered traveler" program. This would allow frequent fliers who have been through a background check to be given specially tagged boarding passes, which they could then use to be directed through special "fast lanes" at security checkpoints (Brewin, 2004b).

The TSA is investigating the RFID-enabled boarding pass concept in concert with a number of other airport security initiatives in the United States. However, working in conjunction with the Federal Aviation Administration's Safe Skies for Africa Initiative, RFID-tagged boarding passes are already being deployed in an undisclosed number of African states (Brewin, 2004b). There are concerns however as to how this data will be utilized in airport security. From a practical standpoint, critics have scoffed at the jumble of data that would be created by trying to track thousands of passengers simultaneously in an airport. Privacy advocates also object to the invasiveness of the tracking, leading one to ask, "Are they going to track how long I spend in the ladies' room?" (cited in Brewin, 2004b).

There is also concern that airports, in their push to provide wireless access for patrons, may find that such Wi-Fi systems can conflict with RFID tracking innovations. In fact, in mid-2004, Northwest Airlines discovered that the wireless communication system used by its baggage han-

dling operators was overwhelmed by a new Wi-Fi antenna installed by AT&T Wireless Services. The problem was alleviated after AT&T agreed to adjust its power levels, but it seriously impinged on Northwest's own wireless systems for a time (Schatz, 2004).

A mid-September survey in 2004 by software supplier Wavelink found that approximately four out of five Frontline Conference and Expo attendees were currently piloting the technology or planned to do so in the next two years. Key concerns of the company executives included cost, lack of standards, and an early, untested market. Yet they expect adoption of the technology to grow, as it matures and benefits become reality (Gonsalves, 2004). However, as supply chain consultant Scott Elliff argues, all the new technology "simply isn't a substitute for superior business practices" (Elliff, 2004). The airline industry needs to remember this and, better yet, implement better business practices.

CONCLUSION AND FUTURE DIRECTIONS

This chapter has discussed the application of RFID in numerous airline applications across the world. The chapter has particularly discussed the advantages in using such applications for the benefit of all parties concerned. As has been shown, there is much promise for RFID to be applied in the airline industry to produce competitive advantage for airlines that are willing to implement the technology in a time of great competitive and economic turmoil in the industry. Both air carriers and airports themselves can leverage the technology to provide better customer service and heighten the security of air travel.

On a final note, moving to RFID may be the only way airlines may be able to even continue handling checked luggage in the future, both from a security and a cost standpoint. In fact, one company, the British-based low-fare carrier,

Ryanair, has announced its intention to eventually stop providing checked baggage service altogether. Michael O'Leary, Ryanair's maverick CEO, believes that by banning checked luggage, the cost of flying each passenger could be cut by at least 15%. This would be due to the elimination of the staff needed at check-in counters and in baggage handling operations. Not only would there be a direct cost savings for Ryanair, but there is the very real prospect for improved service, as passengers would get through the airport much faster and that their aircraft could be utilized more productively. The latter would be due to the quicker turnarounds that the airline could achieve by not having to load outbound and unload inbound aircraft luggage holds (Noakes, 2004).

Over the next few years, Ryanair has planned to take steps to modify its passengers' mindsets regarding their baggage to encourage them to carry more of their baggage with them on board. The airline has already raised the weight limits for carry-on bags, while hiking its fees (up 17%) for overweight checked luggage. O'Leary even intended for the airline to begin giving passengers a small rebate if they choose to not check a bag sometime in 2005. While Ryanair's competition scoffs at O'Leary's luggage-ban plan, he notes that other innovations in the airline industry, including the elimination of paper tickets and Web-based travel booking, drew similar derision when they were first introduced (Noakes, 2004; Johnson & Michaels, 2004).

While the Ryanair gambit may prove to be prescient, for the near term, passenger luggage service will continue to be a cost of doing business for airlines. As such, Gene Alvarez, an analyst with Meta Group, predicts that RFID-based baggage tracking will become standard throughout the airline industry over the next decade (as cited in Brewin, 2004c). By assuring us that it is our black roller bag that ends-up on the luggage carousel at the end of our long journey home, airlines like Delta can seek a competitive advantage through improved baggage service. In the end, we will likely see air carriers, airports, commercial aircraft manufacturers, and national transport and security agencies working cooperatively to smarten baggage handling through RFID tracking through common systems, while looking at other potential applications for automatic identification technology throughout the air transport industry.

REFERENCES

AIM Global. (2004, January). Flying high. *RFID Connections*. Retrieved from http://www.aim-global.org/technologies/rfid/resources/articles/jan04/0401-bagtag.htm

Anonymous.(2003a). Tag tracking. *Airline Business, 19*(12), 14.

Anonymous. (2003b, July). Luggage tracking trial by Delta Air Lines. *Smart Packaging Journal, 11*, 6.

Anonymous. (2003c, November 10). Wal-Mart lays out RFID roadmap. *RFID Journal*. Retrieved from http://www.rfidjournal.com/article/articleprint/647/-1/9/

Anonymous. (2004a, May 26). Hong Kong airport picks RFID baggage tracking. *Smart Travel News*. Retrieved from http://www.smarttravelnews.com/news/2004/05/ hong_kong_airpo.html

Anonymous. (2004b, May 20). Delta rolls out wireless baggage transfer system. *Smart Travel News*. Retrieved from http://www.smarttravelnews.com/news/2004/05/ delta_rolls_out.html

Atkinson, H. (2002). The allure of radio frequency. *Journal of Commerce Week, 3*(16), 28-30.

Booth-Thomas, C. (2003). The see-it-all chip: Radio-frequency identification—With track-everything-anywhere capability, all the time—Is about to change your life. *Time, 162*(12), A8-A16.

Bowen, B. D., & Headley, D. E. (2004). *Airline*

quality ratings 2004. Retrieved from http://www. unomaha.edu/~unoai/aqr/2004%20synopsis. htm

Brewin, B. (2003a, December 18). Delta has success in RFID baggage tag test, but a wide-scale rollout of RFID technology is being slowed by lack of money. *Computerworld*. Retrieved from http://www.computerworld.com/mobiletopics/mobile/technology/story/ 0,10801,88390,00. html?f=x10

Brewin, B. (2003b). Delta's RFID trial run has airport predecessors. *Computerworld,* (June 23). Retrieved from http://www.computerworld.com/printthis/2003/0,4814,82381,00.html

Brewin, B. (2004a). Delta to test RFID for parts tracking: Meanwhile, Boeing and Airbus are both pushing for common RFID standards. *Computerworld*. Retrieved from http://www. computerworld.com/mobiletopics/mobile/technology/story/ 0,10801,93611,00.html?f=x10

Brewin, B. (2004b, April). TSA eyes RFID boarding passes to track airline passengers: Privacy groups view the idea as a "nightmare" for civil liberties. *Computerworld*. Retrieved from http://www.computerweekly.com/articles/article. asp?liArticleID=127364&liFlavour ID=1&sp=1

Brewin, B. (2004c, January 6). RFID bag-tag test proves a soaraway success. *Computer Weekly*. Retrieved from http://www. computerweekly. com/articles/article.asp?li ArticleID=127364& liFlavourID= 1&sp=1

CNETAsia Staff. (2004, July 17). Japan firms to test radio-tagged luggage. *CNETNews.com*. Retrieved from http://news.com.com/2102-1009_3-1026860.html?tag=st.util.print

Collins, J. (2004, July 2). Delta plans U.S.-wide RFID system: The airline carrier will spend up to $25 million during the next two years to roll out an RFID baggage-handling system at every

U.S. airport it serves. *RFID Journal*. Retrieved from http://www.rfidjournal.com/article/articleview/1013/1/1

Collins, P. (2004). RFID: The next killer app? *Management Services, 48*(5), 20-23.

Coupe, K. (2003, May 15). Customer loyalty initiative being tested by Texas restaurants. *MorningNewsBeat.com*. Retrieved from http://morningnewsbeat.com/archives/2003/05/15.html

Deloitte. (2004). *Tag, trace, and transform: Launching your RFID program*. Retrieved from http://www.deloitte.com/ (registration required).

Dunne, P. M., & Lusch, R. F. (2005). *Retailing* (5th ed.). Mason, OH: South-Western.

Elliff, S. A. (2004, September 6). RFID: Maybe *not* the "next big thing". *The Journal of Commerce, 56*(28), 46.

Fein, A. (2004, September 8). Delta airlines to layoff thousands, outlines plan. *Axcessnews. com*. Retrieved from http://www.axcessnews.com/business_090804a.shtml

Field, D. (2004). Radio waves. *Airline Business, 20*(7), 60-62.

Gonsalves, A. (2004, September 23). Companies adopting RFID despite challenges, survey finds. *Information Week*. Retrieved from http://www.rfidinsights.com/showArticle.jhtml? articleId=47902028&printableArticle=true

Hosenhall, M., & Kuchment, A. (2004, September 6). Crashes: Did "black widows" bring down the planes? *Newsweek, 144*(10), 6.

Johnson, K., & Michaels, D. (2004, July 1). Big worry for no-frills Ryanair: Has it gone as low as it can? *The Wall Street Journal*, A1, A10.

Jones, K. (2004). Are you chipped? *PC Magazine, 23*(15), 21.

Jones, M. I., & Wyld, D. C. (in press). Smart tags + smart professors = smart students. *The Journal of the Association of Marketing Educators.*

Kambil, A., & Brooks, J. D. (2002, September 1). *Auto-ID across the value chain: From dramatic potential to greater efficiency & profit—A white paper from the Auto-ID Center at the Massachusetts Institute of Technology.* Retrieved from http://www.autoidcenter.org/publishedresearch/SLO-AUTOID-BC001.pdf

Kirby, J. (2003). Supply chain challenges: Building relationships—A conversation with Scott Beth, David N. Burt, William Copacino, Chris Gopal, Hau L. Lee, Robert Porter Lynch, and Sandra Morris. *Harvard Business Review, 81*(7), 64-74.

Lacy, S. (2004, August 31). Inching toward the RFID revolution. *Business Week Online.* Retrieved from http://www.businessweek.com/ (subscription required).

McDougall, P. (2004, July 5). No more lost luggage. *InformationWeek, 996,* 14.

McFarlane, D. (2002, May 1). *Auto-ID based control: An overview—A white paper from the Auto-ID Center at the Institute for Manufacturing of the University of Cambridge.* Retrieved from http://www.autoidcenter.org/publishedresearch/CAM-AUTOID-WH-004.pdf

Morphy, E. (2004, July 2). Delta ups service bar with RFID luggage tracking. *CRM Daily.* Retrieved from http://www.newsfactor.com/story.xhtml?story_id=25711

Murray, C. (2004, July 12). Airline clears RFID luggage tags for takeoff. *EE Times,* Retrieved from http://www.embedded.com/showArticle.jhtml?articleID=22104613

Noakes, G. (2004, July 16). Ryanair bids to banish baggage. *Travel Trade Gazette, 2623,* 20.

Perez, E. (2004, August 16). Flight upgrade: With Delta reeling, chief plans unusual bet on premium routes; as losses mount, Mr. Grinstein pairs cost cuts with extras; leather seats in coach; big risks in crowded skies. *The Wall Street Journal,* A1, A6.

Reed Special Supplement. (2004). RFID: Powering the supply chain. *Logistics Management, 43*(8), R3-R16.

Rothfeder, J. (2004, August 1). What's wrong with RFID? *CIO Insight.* Retrieved from http://www.cioinsight.com/print_article/0,1406,a=133044,00.asp

Schatz, A. (2004, June 8). Airports clash with airlines over Wi-Fi. *The Wall Street Journal,* B1-B2.

Sullivan, L. (2004a, September 20). Retail: General merchandising: Stores look for service with ROI. *Information Week.* Retrieved from http://www.rfidinsights.com/showArticle.jhtml?articleId=47212239&printableArticle=true

Sullivan, L. (2004b, September 29). U.K. grocer expands RFID initiative. *Information Week.* Retrieved from http://www.informationweek.com/story/showArticle.jhtml?article ID=48800020

Tegtmeier, L. A. (2004). RFID knowledge enabled logistics. *Overhaul & Maintenance, 10*(5), 24-28.

Thomas, D. (2004, June 28). Airline industry needs to back IT. *Information World Review.* Retrieved from http://www.iwr.co.uk/News/1156239

Trebilcock, B. (2003). Ready to fly? *Modern Materials Handling, 58*(3), 40-42.

Tully, S. (2004, June 14). Airlines: Why the big boys won't come back. *Fortune,* 101-102, 104.

U.S. Department of Transportation, Office of Aviation Enforcement and Proceedings, Aviation Consumer Protection Division. (2004). *Air travel consumer report—August 2004.* Retrieved from http://airconsumer.ost.dot.gov/reports/2004/0408atcr.doc

Valentine, L. (2003, September 26). The new wireless supply chain. *CRM Daily.* Retrieved from http://cio-today.newsfactor.com/story.xhtml?story_id=22376

Want, R. (2004). RFID: A key to automating everything. *Scientific American, 290*(1), 56-66.

Weber, H. R. (2004, September 21). Delta pilots agree to recalls. *The [New Orleans] Times-Picayune,* C-1, C-7.

Woods, L. (2004). The fail-proof luggage finder. *Kiplinger's, 58*(10), 34-35.

Wyld, D. C., & Jones, M. I. (in press). A magic pill?: The emergence of radio frequency identification (RFID) technology in the pharmaceutical supply chain. *Journal of Pharmaceutical Marketing & Management.*

Wyld, D. C., Juban, R., & Jones, M. I. (2005). Dude, where's my cow?: The United States Automatic Identification Plan and the future of animal marketing. *Academy of Information and Management Sciences Journal, 8*(1), 107-120.

Chapter 4.35
Policy–Based Access Control for Context–Aware Services over the Wireless Internet

Paolo Bellavista
University of Bologna, Italy

Antonio Corradi
University of Bologna, Italy

Cesare Stefanelli
University of Ferrara, Italy

ABSTRACT

The spreading wireless accessibility to the Internet stimulates the provisioning of mobile commercial services to a wide set of heterogeneous and limited client terminals. This requires novel programming methodologies to support and simplify the development of innovative service classes. In these novel services, results and offered quality levels should depend on both client location and locally available resources (context). In addition, it is crucial to manage the frequent modifications of resource availability due to wireless client movements during service provisioning. Within this perspective, the chapter motivates the need for novel access control solutions to flexibly control the resource access of mobile clients depending on the currently applicable context. In particular, it discusses and exemplifies how innovative middleware for access control should support the determination of the client context on the basis of high-level declarative directives (profiles and policies) and distributed online monitoring.

INTRODUCTION

Recent advances in wireless networking and the growing number of wireless-enabled portable devices create new promising commercial opportunities. In-Stat/MDR estimates that more than 465 million mobile device units will be built and shipped in 2004, with an annual increase of more than 7%, and a similar rise expectation for the next years (Reeds, 2003). A primary commercial challenge is to exploit this enlarging market to ubiquitously provide mobile users with both traditional Internet services and innovative location-dependent mobile commerce applications.

Service providers and wireless network operators have to face new and challenging technical issues toward the seamless integration of wireless clients with the traditional fixed Internet. This scenario, called *wireless Internet* in the following, already starts to exhibit research and commercial solutions to support network connectivity (Bos, 2001; Perkins, 1999). However, provisioning commercially mature mobile services over the global and open wireless Internet requires addressing complex and different issues, such as configuration management, service content adaptation, access control, accounting, dynamic un/installation of infrastructure/service components, and interoperability. The research in several of these areas is still at its beginning; it starts to recognize the need for novel and flexible middleware solutions (Bellavista, 2002a).

In particular, the wireless Internet calls for novel methodologies to support and simplify the development of innovative service classes where results and offered quality levels depend on the *context*; that is, the logical set of resources that a client can access due to provisioning environment properties, such as current client location, security permissions, access device capabilities, user preferences and trust level, runtime resource state, and mutual relationships with currently local users/terminals/resources (Bellavista, 2003a). Some simple forms of context determination, such

as the ones associated with traditional security permissions, are not new for distributed systems. The novelty here is that the frequent mobility of wireless Internet clients makes it crucial to manage the recurrent context variations, and the consequent service reconfiguration at provision time. In fact, the context depends on both quite static aspects, for example, the local authorization rules and the client device characteristics, and very dynamic aspects, for example, the client location and the provision-time state of involved resources.

In other words, the wide heterogeneity, the changing network topology/connectivity and the resource shortage/discontinuities typical of the wireless Internet stress the relevance of context awareness and of developing context-adaptive services. However, the complexity of designing, implementing, and deploying context-aware mobile services potentially limits the rapid emergence of this new service market. Therefore, there is a growing request for highly flexible and innovative middleware to facilitate the development and runtime support of context-aware wireless Internet services. In particular, in this chapter we motivate and discuss the necessity of novel security middleware solutions to perform enhanced forms of access control. Such an access control exploits the flexible definition and the dynamic determination/update of user contexts during service sessions.

For instance, a mobile stock trading service should allow its mobile users to operate via laptops connected to Wi-Fi hotspots, via PDAs connected to Bluetooth Local Infotainment Points (BLIP), and via GSM phones receiving simple SMS-based communication. Access control middleware should assign differentiated contexts depending on differentiated classes of users, access terminals and connectivity technology. On the basis of context, clients should have visibility of alternative trading service interfaces. In addition, access control solutions should update contexts (and service provisioning accordingly) in response to client mobility and user class of service. If a bronze user moves to a very congested wireless cell, she should simply lose visibility of the trading service. A gold user, instead, should have priority and transparently access a service gateway that downscales the service results to either text files or SMS messages. The result is a reduced modality of service provisioning that does not aggravate too much the network congestion situation.

The chapter aims at identifying the main requirements, functions and technical challenges associated with innovative context-aware security middleware for wireless Internet access control. In particular, it claims that flexible access control should determine the client context depending on different types of high-level declarative metadata (profiles and policies) and on the runtime state of the provisioning environment. Profiles and policies can represent, respectively, the characteristics of users/terminals/resources and the resource/service management strategies, in a cleanly separated way from the service implementation. The online resource monitoring is crucial to enable the runtime shaping of contexts in response to the frequent modifications of resource availability due to wireless client mobility. Access control middleware based on both metadata and online monitoring can determine and impose differentiated contexts (and consequently differentiated and tailored service behaviors) with no need to modify the application logic. As a relevant side effect, this favors middleware/service component reusability in different deployment scenarios (Bellavista, 2003b).

As an example of context-aware access control solution, the chapter presents the architecture and the most relevant implementation aspects of Wireless Internet Context-aware access Control (WICoCo). WICoCo is the Java-based security solution for access control in CARMEN (Bellavista, 2003b). WICoCo addresses two primary state-of-the-art challenges for context-aware access control: how to enforce user/service requirements expressed at a high level of abstrac-

tion in terms of declarative metadata, and how to achieve full visibility of monitoring information in a portable way.

In addition, to smooth the relevant discontinuities in resource availability at the wired-wireless edges of the wireless Internet, WICoCo provides mobile clients with mobile middleware proxies that work over the fixed network infrastructure on their behalf (and in their vicinity). WICoCo proxies determine the client contexts and mediate any client access to resources. They are implemented in terms of mobile agents (MAs) and can follow the provision-time movement of clients, where and when needed (Fuggetta, 1998).

CONTEXT-AWARE SERVICE PROVISIONING OVER THE WIRELESS INTERNET

The wireless Internet scenario exhibits several peculiar characteristics that need to be considered in service provisioning. Mobility of users and access devices is pushed to the extreme. Users can connect to the network from ubiquitous points of attachment and wireless portable devices can roam by maintaining continuous connectivity (Bos, 2001). Frequent disconnections of users/devices are rather common operating modes that can occur either voluntarily to reduce connection costs and to save battery or accidentally due to the loss of wireless connectivity.

Moreover, the wireless Internet exhibits a high degree of heterogeneity of both access devices (in terms of screen size and resolution, computing power, memory, storage, operating system, and supported software) and networking technologies (IEEE 802.11a/b/g, Bluetooth, IrDA, GPRS, and UMTS). In addition, this heterogeneity seems not only a temporary aspect due to the novelty and immaturity of the technology, but is expected to last in the open and global wireless Internet.

These distinctive features of mobility and heterogeneity pose new challenging issues and undermine several assumptions of traditional distributed services. Traditional service provisioning relies on a relatively static characterization of the context. For instance, resource availability is typically independent of both the user current location and the access device properties (location and heterogeneity transparency). Changes in the set of accessible resources are relatively small, rare, or predictable (Roman, 2000). On the contrary, in the wireless Internet, it is crucial to consider rapidly changing contexts and to frequently reorganize service provisioning in response to context modifications. Client mobility requires solutions that properly and promptly handle changes of client location, modifications in locally accessible resources, temporary disconnection, and changing network topology. In addition, users can change their portable access devices, with different wireless technologies, even at runtime. All the above elements require context-aware service management at provision time.

Service provisioning in the wireless Internet requires the full visibility of location information. For instance, middleware/service components should be aware of the location of both users and involved resources to forward stock trading transaction requests to the server, instances that minimize the current client/server distance. Middleware/service components should also have visibility of different kinds of system-level data, such as the access device characteristics and the currently available wireless bandwidth, respectively, to customize service provisioning and to guarantee effective resource usage. These aspects are particularly crucial in wireless provisioning environments because of the scarcity and the high cost of resources. System-level data should be propagated up to the middleware/application level to dynamically determine the applicable context for the user during her session and to perform service configuration and delivery accordingly. For instance, middleware/service components should be aware of the congestion state of both the replicated stock trading service components

and the local wireless network. This awareness enables the forwarding of transaction requests to the server instances by balancing the network/service load and, therefore, by minimizing the client connection time.

In summary, the handling of context information in the wireless Internet is complicated by the frequent variations in the provisioning environment, primarily due to client mobility and heterogeneity at provision time. Context variability significantly increases the complexity and the costs of designing, developing and deploying wireless Internet services, thus slowing down their widespread diffusion. As a consequence, context-aware services call for middleware support infrastructures. There is the need for non-traditional middleware with full context visibility and capable of automating service reconfiguration depending on dynamic context changes. These middleware should interact with the underlying execution environment to collect relevant information for context determination, for example, current location of users/devices, resource state, user preferences, and device characteristics. This information should be processed at provision time to identify the applicable contexts, their evolution, and the most appropriate service management operations.

CONTEXT-AWARE ACCESS CONTROL: REQUIREMENTS AND SOLUTION GUIDELINES

Traditional security solutions for access control, in both centralized and distributed systems, are all based on the main concept of associating permission information with either the potentially accessible resources (as in access control lists) or the potentially accessing clients (as in capabilities) (Sandhu, 1996). These permissions rule resource accesses in a simple way, by denying/allowing different access modes, for example, read/write/execute, to different clients depending on the client identity or grouping. In traditional systems, access control solutions are usually provided at the operating system level. They evaluate the applicable permissions at runtime, typically at any client access request in the case of access control lists and at the starting of the client session when adopting capabilities.

We claim that the traditional security solutions for access control are not flexible enough for mobile commerce services over the wireless Internet, where it is crucial to distinguish access control on the basis of a wide variety of information, and not only to consider the client identity. For instance, the set of resources that a client can access should also depend on user preferences, characteristics of currently used access terminals, subscribed services, and associated trust level (Bellavista, 2003a). In addition, resource accessibility should also take into account the congestion state of the provisioning environment at resource request time. When addressing quality of service issues for mobile commerce services over best-effort networks, it is crucial to operate access control decisions that depend on the expected quality perturbations produced by newly accepted requests. This is necessary to avoid compromising the established service level agreements on the already admitted active sessions.

Moreover, novel security solutions should support the possibility to modify access control decisions and with the maximum degree of flexibility, even by affecting already established service sessions. Let us think about the case of a gold user who enters a congested wireless cell. It could be reasonable to reduce the set of accessible resources of "already-in" bronze users, even if they have already achieved the access to those resources. For instance, bronze users could be automatically rebound to downscaled service components, which are less resource-consuming.

Last, but not least, we claim that access control decisions should also impact on the resource visibility itself provided to the client, in order to suggest (and simplify) the most suitable client-resource binding depending on the client characteristics and the provision-time conditions. This customized visibility could significantly reduce the complexity of developing mobile commerce services for the wireless Internet. It is the access control support that becomes in charge of proposing only the resource bindings that best fit the specific management goals chosen, for example, best-effort quality support, resource load balancing, and limitation of the client connection time.

In other words, we claim that access control solutions for mobile commerce over the wireless Internet should be context-aware. Security supports for the wireless Internet should also assume the burden of dynamically establishing the user context, of determining the applicable resource visibility, and of automatically reconfiguring the provided services with no (or little) impact on the implementation of mobile commerce clients and servers. Let us note that context-aware access control middleware can significantly simplify the realization of context-dependent mobile services by allowing developers to continue to implement context-transparent traditional service components (Bellavista, 2003b).

Providing such an access control middleware is particularly challenging and complex. The client mobility, the wide heterogeneity of clients and wireless technologies, and the openness of the provisioning environment are only the most evident among the numerous tricky aspects to address. This multiplicity of issues is producing a plethora of research projects and prototypes, each one proposing different partial solutions in the general area of context-aware resource visibility in mobile computing environments (Schilit, 2002). Most important, some first common guidelines of solution are starting to emerge. On the one hand, there is a growing interest in specifying access control rules and resource management strategies in a cleanly separated way from the service implementation. This can be done by adopting different kinds of high-level metadata to describe clients, resources, and service management requirements, and by interpreting/enforcing them at service provision time, as introduced in the third section. On the other hand, the significant discontinuity in resource availability (and costs) between the wired infrastructure and the wireless access cells is pushing towards the exploitation of proxy middleware components, as illustrated in the third section.

Profile and Policy Metadata

The need for a clean separation of concerns between context determination (and context-based service management) and application logic implementation starts to be widely recognized (Roman, 2000). Two main types of approaches are possible to achieve such separation in a flexible way. The first is to define separated programming meta-levels in charge of mobility management and service adaptation. These meta-levels interwork with the actual service implementation by exploiting reflection techniques (Capra, 2003). The second possibility is to specify high-level metadata describing the characteristics of the involved service entities and the goals of service management. The evaluation and enforcement of these metadata require middleware facilities for monitoring and event distribution. Reflection represents an interesting solution guideline for context-aware mobile commerce services, but is difficult to integrate with legacy systems usually implemented in non-reflective programming languages. On the contrary, profile/policy-based approaches, as the WICoCo one extensively described in the fourth section, can apply also to legacy services, independently of their implementation language. For these reasons, in the following we will only focus on metadata-based solutions for context management.

Context-aware access control solutions can significantly benefit from the adoption of metadata to represent both the context characteristics and the choices in service behavior at a high level of abstraction, with a clean separation between service management and service logic (Huber, 1996). Among the different possible types of metadata, profiles and policies are considered of increasing interest (Heflin, 2003). Profiles represent characteristics, capabilities and requirements of users, devices, resources, and service components. They should guide the determination of the applicable context, for example, by allowing a client device to have visibility of a service component if and only if the client can visualize the format of the results produced by that component. Several research efforts are attempting to identify well accepted formats for the most common access devices. They are encouraging the adoption of standards for profile representation, in order to favor resource reusing and sharing in the open wireless Internet (W3C, 2002).

Policies express the choices ruling system behavior, in terms of the actions that subjects can/must perform upon resources. Policies are maintained completely separate from system implementation details; they are expressed at a high level of abstraction to simplify their specification by system administrators, service managers, and even final users. Some recent policy-based systems distinguish two different kinds of policies (Moffett, 1993): authorization policies and obligation ones. The former specify the actions that subjects are allowed to perform on resources depending on various types of conditions, for example, subject identity and resource state. The latter define the actions that subjects must perform on resources when triggered by the occurrence of specified conditions.

Figure 1 shows a possible metadata taxonomy, and two examples of obligation policy and device profile. The depicted taxonomy is the one adopted in the WICoCo solution, as more extensively described in the fourth section, where we will show how the different types of metadata are relevant to determine the applicable context and to update it flexibly during service provisioning.

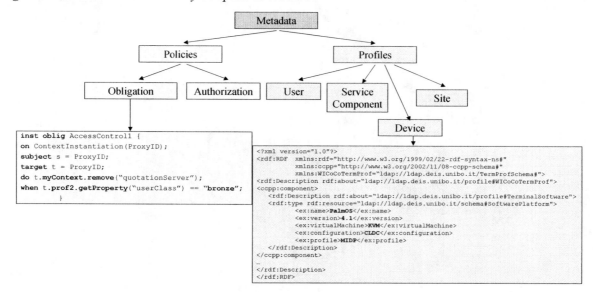

Figure 1. The metadata taxonomy adopted in WICoCo

Middleware Proxies

In context-aware security solutions for access control, it is crucial to adopt middleware proxies that execute over the fixed Internet on the behalf of wireless mobile clients. Middleware proxies are located along the service flow path between the clients and the server, typically in the proximity of the clients they work for, as depicted in Figure 2 (Bellavista, 2003a).

Proxies are demonstrating their effectiveness in playing the general role of assisting mobile clients in their current access locality, by smoothing the problems due to both intermittent and limited bandwidth wireless connections. For instance, proxies can asynchronously perform complex queries on wired resources and can downscale service results to fit the access device visualization capabilities (Hwang, 2003). In particular, by focusing on context-aware access control, proxies can perform, over the wired network, the possibly complex computations needed to determine the applicable contexts, and should work as intermediaries in the client access to any resource currently included in its context.

Mediating service accessibility via proxies, however, requires any participating wireless locality to enable the proxy-based support for any possible visiting client. This could be impracticable in the open wireless Internet where highly heterogeneous unpredictable types of clients are willing to access different and statically unforeseen mobile commerce services. In fact, these clients usually require differentiated support behaviors and different capabilities to interpret the applicable metadata. Any a priori installation of all possible middleware proxies in all possible access localities is to be considered definitely unfeasible in an open provisioning environment. For these reasons, there are a few state-of-the-art research projects that propose the adoption of the mobile agent (MA) technology to implement wireless Internet middleware proxies (Bellavista, 2003b; IKV, 2003). MA-based proxies can follow the client movements from a wireless access locality to another one during service provisioning, also by preserving the session state thanks to the MA peculiar capability to migrate both behavior and reached state of execution at runtime (Fuggetta, 1998).

Figure 2. Middleware proxies mediating the mobile client access to wireless Internet services

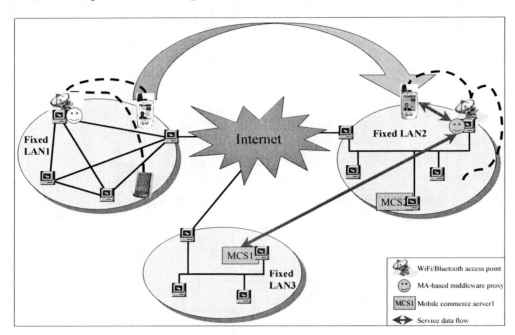

In the next section, we will exemplify how the proxy-based WICoCo middleware can dynamically determine and update the applicable context depending on different forms of metadata, and how WICoCo proxies use the applicable context to rule the client access control to mobile commerce services over the wireless Internet.

WICOCO MIDDLEWARE

Along the previously sketched design guidelines, we have developed WICoCo, a flexible and portable middleware for context-aware access control in the wireless Internet. This section describes the main characteristics of WICoCo primarily to point out how the combined adoption of different kinds of metadata, mobile code, and portable implementation technologies can lead to very flexible access control solutions. This flexibility is needed to fit the specific properties of the open and heterogeneous wireless Internet provisioning

environment. In our opinion, the WICoCo design and implementation can represent a useful experience to exemplify, with an actual middleware prototype, the state-of-the-art guidelines of solution emerging in this novel challenging field.

WICoCo is the access control security solution adopted in CARMEN, an MA-based flexible middleware for adaptive service provisioning to mobile wireless clients (Bellavista, 2003b). The CARMEN middleware is designed according to the layered architecture shown in Figure 3. CARMEN is based on a general-purpose MA platform called SOMA, which supports the mobility of both code and reached execution state of middleware components. The CARMEN facilities provides mechanisms and tools to address the most common issues in context-aware service provisioning to wireless clients: a rich and articulated naming system (the *identification*, *discovery* and *directory* facilities) (Bellavista, 2001); a *location* facility that integrates heterogeneous tracking solutions for IEEE 802.11b and Bluetooth; a *monitoring* facility that allows observing indicators at the application and system level to achieve full visibility of context changes (Bellavista, 2002b); and an *event manager* facility to distribute context-related events to interested CARMEN components, even mobile (Bellavista, 2003b).

WICoCo works on top of the above facilities, and consists of two main components: the context manager (CM) and the metadata manager (MM). CM determines dynamically the client context, mediates the client access to resources in the applicable context via specialized MA-based proxies, and transparently performs service adaptation in the case of context modifications. MM supports the specification, modification, and checks for correctness, installation, and evaluation of the different kinds of WICoCo metadata. To better understand how WICoCo performs context-aware access control, in the following we will focus on the description of the two WICoCo components, CM and MM, and of the monitoring/location facilities responsible for sensing context changes.

Context Manager

CM is the WICoCo component responsible for dynamically establishing the context of any client, thus determining its resource visibility. In particular, WICoCo exploits MA-based mobile proxies,

working over the fixed network on behalf (and in proximity) of their wireless clients, to determine the applicable contexts and to mediate any client access to resources.

To dynamically determine the applicable context object for a client, CM firstly merges the list of resources in the client access locality, obtained via the discovery facility, and the list of globally available resources, retrieved via the directory facility. Then, CM discards resources from the merged set depending on the metadata included in the applicable user/device/service component profiles (see the fourth section). For instance, if the device profile specifies that the Web browser on the access terminal can visualize only c-HTML pages, stock trading service components that provide only XML-based stock information are automatically removed from the context.

The obtained resource set is the result of the combination of local/global resource availability and applicable profile metadata, that is, user desiderata, access device capabilities, and service component characteristics. To obtain the applicable context, this resource set is subject to further restrictions and discarding due to the enforcement of the access control policies (see the fourth section). The result is a context object listing all the resources currently accessible to one client. CM represents a context object as a

Figure 3. The CARMEN layered architecture

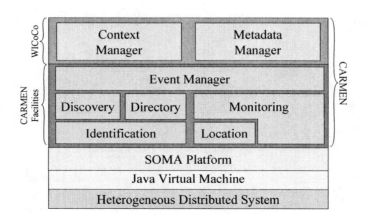

container of tuples, any tuple corresponding to an accessible resource and including a unique resource identifier, a resource descriptor, and additional information to properly manage the resource binding in case of client mobility. The context object is automatically updated anytime a client requests a resource access and anytime an event in the provisioning environment triggers a modification in the applicable context. In fact, events may trigger the enforcement of WICoCo access control policies, thus affecting the resource visibility, as detailed in the following.

The WICoCo MA-Based Proxies

WICoCo provides any user, at the starting of her service session, with a personal mobile proxy that migrates over the fixed network and follows the user movements among wireless localities at service provision time. The mobile proxy acts as the intermediary between the user wireless device and the accessed resources. The access permission/denial depends on the currently applicable context, which the proxy determines by exploiting the CM facilities.

We claim the suitability of the MA technology to implement mobile proxies for context-aware access control. WICoCo exploits SOMA to implement proxies as SOMA agents and to provide them with execution environments, called places, which offer the basic services for MA communication and migration. Places typically model nodes and can be grouped into domains that correspond to network localities, for example, local area networks with IEEE 802.11b/Bluetooth access points providing wireless connectivity to WiFi/Bluetooth portable devices (Figure 4a). CARMEN middleware facilities are available in any domain. Proxies run on places in the domain where the associated users and the corresponding wireless companion devices are currently connected.

WICoCo associates one proxy for each user, with a 1-to-1 mapping; proxies follow their associated users in their movements among different domains, carry the applicable context and the reached service state, and make it possible to migrate whole service sessions. As shown in Figure 4b, proxies retrieve the profiles of their companion devices (and of the profile associated users) at their instantiation via MM (see the fourth section). Let us note that the proxies need to ask for profiles only once, at the starting of the service session, being the profiles part of their state, which is maintained even after migration.

Figure 4.

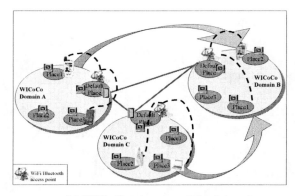

(a) WICoCo places and domains

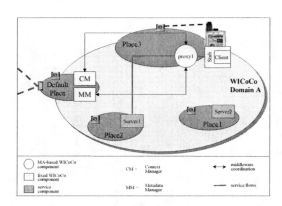

(b) the deployment of WICoCo middleware components in one wireless access locality

Only the modification of the associated profiles triggers a corresponding event and a new profile request.

Proxies are designed to refer, at start up, only to CM and MM, without any direct resource access. They request their contexts by passing profile information to the CM component in their domain, as depicted in Figure 3b. After context determination, CM returns back to the proxy a context object listing the identifiers of all accessible resources, either active or passive. At the beginning, all resources in the context are passive. A resource becomes active when the user requests to access it. For any active resource, the context object includes a resource identifier (the only information maintained for passive resources), the binding management strategy to apply in case of client migration, and a reference object that implements the chosen binding. WICoCo supports four different binding strategies (resource movement, copy movement, remote reference, and rebinding). The proxies dynamically re-qualify resource bindings, with no impact on the client/server implementation (Bellavista, 2003b). Any modification of interest in the provisioning environment produces the notification of a monitoring event to both CM and the involved proxies; the notified proxies usually react by interrogating their local CM to update their context objects.

Proxies interact with an additional type of middleware components: device-specific stubs. The stub is the only middleware component required to run on the wireless device, locally wraps the service-specific client, and connects to the responsible proxy to send/receive service requests/results. Let us observe that the adoption of proxies over the fixed network and of lightweight clients on the portable devices permits to exploit the MA-based access control also when providing mobile commerce services to limited devices that cannot host MA execution environments.

Metadata Manager

MM is in charge of supporting the specification of all the different kinds of metadata depicted in the taxonomy of Figure 1. User profiles maintain information about personal preferences, interests, security requirements, and subscribed services for any WICoCo registered user. Device profiles report the hardware/software characteristics of the supported access terminals. Service component profiles describe the interface of available service components as well as their properties relevant for dynamic binding to mobile clients, for example, type/format of provided results. Site profiles are a resource group abstraction, and list all the resources available at one WICoCo host. WICoCo adopts standard formats for profile representation: the W3C Composite Capability/Preference Profiles (CC/PP) for user/device profiles (W3C, 2002), the Web Service Description Language (WSDL) for the service component interface description (Curbera, 2002), and the Resource Description Framework (RDF) for the site collections of resources (Decker, 2000).

In addition, MM permits to specify access control policies as high-level declarative directives that affect the context determination and its runtime modification. WICoCo access control policies include not only traditional authorization policies, but also obligation policies. Authorization policies define the actions that clients are allowed to perform on resources and are triggered by resource access requests. Obligation policies, instead, specify the actions that clients and middleware/service components must perform on resources when specified conditions occur. The enforcement of obligation policies is event-triggered. For instance, a NetworkOverload (threshold) event, notified by the CARMEN Event Manager in response to the request of the monitoring facility (described in the following section), can trigger an obligation that updates the contexts of clients in the network locality, by removing the mobile stock trading service from bronze user contexts. WICoCo policies are written in the Ponder language and maintained completely separate from both application logic and middleware implementation details (Imperial, 2003).

MM supports not only the metadata specification/update but also the dynamic distribution, installation and enforcement of the access control policies. It is organized in two logical modules: the specification module, and the policy enforcer. The specification module exploits the tools developed within the Ponder project for editing, distributing, updating, removing, and browsing policies (Imperial, 2003). In addition, it provides tools for transforming high-level policy specifications into platform-enforceable Java policy objects. When a new policy object is created, it is registered in the directory facility and distributed to the interested MA-based proxies. The policy enforcer retrieves newly instantiated policy objects and parses them to retrieve relevant information: events, subjects, targets and actions. Then, on behalf of policy subjects, it registers the significant events to the event manager. It actually enforces the policies, when needed, by interpreting the applicable policy specifications. Policy interpretation consists in policy parsing, controlling the dynamic conditions for policy applicability, extracting the policy actions, and accordingly activating the specified context management operations.

Portable Middleware Facilities for Monitoring and Location

For any context-aware middleware, it is definitely crucial to have full visibility of the whole information that characterizes the provisioning environment, for example, the state of distributed resources and service components. This full visibility is difficult when operating on global scenarios with highly heterogeneous access terminals, communication technologies, and resources. The visibility goal further complicates in an open deployment scenario where the middleware por-

tability must be considered essential.

The WICoCo access control aims at full portability, if possible not depending on the heterogeneous characteristics of the resources and of the operating systems involved. In addition, WICoCo has the objective of dynamically installing and propagating its middleware infrastructure (primarily its proxies) where and when needed at runtime, and to this purpose operates on top of a Java-based MA platform. The choice of Java simplifies dynamic portability. Almost all the recent MA platforms are built on top of the standard Java Virtual Machine (JVM) both to exploit the Java class loading features and to enable the MA portable migration in open environments (Bellavista, 2001). However, the Java choice can make it very hard to achieve the needed level of system state visibility. In the following, we show how WICoCo achieves the full awareness of monitoring and location information in a portable way, without imposing any modification to the standard JVM. The monitoring/location visibility solution in WICoCo is presented as an example, also applicable to other context-aware middlewares and to other application domains. The primary solution guideline is to achieve some forms of portability through the design of modular middleware infrastructures consisting of dynamically selected plug-ins.

Monitoring Facility Implementation

The monitoring facility enables the online observation of the state of resources and service components. It achieves the visibility of different kinds of monitoring data at different levels of abstraction. At the application level, it dynamically interacts with the JVM to gather detailed information about the execution of Java-based service components. At the kernel level, it enables the access to system indicators at the monitored target, such as CPU/memory usage of active processes and available network bandwidth. To overcome the transparency imposed by the JVM, the monitoring facility exploits extensions of the Java technology: the JVM Profiler Interface (JVMPI) (SUN, 2003a) and the Java Native Interface (JNI) (Gordon, 1998). In addition, it integrates with external standard monitoring entities of large adoption in network management, that is, Simple Network Management Protocol (SNMP) agents (Stallings, 1998).

JVMPI provides an interface to indicate to the JVM which are the application-level events of interest for monitoring purposes. After this initialization phase, JVMPI can be exploited to collect, filter and analyze the events produced by Java applications, for example, method invocation and object allocation. On the contrary, WICoCo obtains kernel-level monitoring data, such as CPU usage and incoming network packets, via SNMP agents that export local monitoring information in their standard management information bases (MIBs). To enable also the monitoring of non-SNMP hosts, the monitoring facility exploits JNI to integrate with platform-dependent monitoring mechanisms. Details about how to perform Java-based online monitoring by exploiting JVMPI, SNMP, and JNI, together with details about the implementation of the monitoring facility are available elsewhere (Bellavista, 2002b).

Here, instead, we focus on the fact that, in absence of a standard uniform support for online monitoring in Java, the monitoring portability is achieved via a modular architecture. The facility integrates three different components (ProfilerAgent, SNMPAgent, and *ResManager) and dynamically links the mechanisms and plug-ins fitting the monitoring target (see Figure 5). ProfilerAgent provides the JVMPI-based monitoring of Java resources and is portable on any host with the standard JVM. SNMPAgent acts as an SNMP manager that interrogates the monitored target to obtain the state of non-Java resources (Bellavista, 2002b). The *ResManager classes achieve kernel-level monitoring visibility via the JNI-based integration with native monitoring libraries, implemented with the same interfaces for different platforms. The monitoring facility binds to the correct monitoring mechanisms (and possibly loads the correct native library) for the monitored target. At middleware deployment time, the facility exploits the site profile to choose which monitoring modules to install. In that way, the

Figure 5. The architecture of the portable monitoring facility

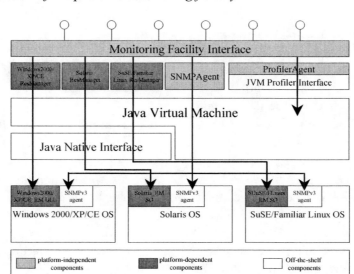

modular implementation of the facility achieves portability over a large set of deployment scenarios and permits the installation of the middleware components only where specifically needed. The result is to provide a uniform monitoring interface independently of the platform heterogeneity.

Location Facility Implementation

Similar considerations about portability via dynamic composition of alternative modules apply to the location facility. At the state of the art, there is no application-level API for cell location visibility in wireless networks accepted by any vendor and spread across the most common operating systems. This is producing vendor/technology-specific solutions, which significantly slow down the emergence of a wide market of location-dependent wireless Internet services. Our approach is to develop a portable location facility via the dynamic composition of different implementation mechanisms, automatically downloaded and deployed depending on the system characteristics of wireless access points and client devices.

The WICoCo Location provides online visibility of the associations between access terminals and WiFi/Bluetooth wireless cells. On the one hand, middleware-level location visibility is required to enable the development of location-dependent services, without affecting the client/server implementation (Bellavista, 2002a). In the case of Wi-Fi connectivity, the location facility exploits the monitoring information that IEEE 802.11 access points make available via standard SNMP MIBs (Gast, 2002). In particular, the access point is configured to notify an intra-domain SNMP trap anytime a new portable device associates with the local wireless locality. This permits the location component to have the online visibility of all the associated wireless access devices, and, in particular, to sense any new device entering the controlled domain. In the case of Bluetooth-based access points, the facility exploits the portable Java API for Bluetooth to obtain the list of the devices

currently connected to the network locality (JCP, 2003; Johansson, 2001).

On the other hand, it is sometimes useful to have portable location visibility also at the client side, that is, at client stubs. In the case of WiFi-enabled clients hosting Linux, the location facility provides a Java API, based on the Linux Wireless Extensions, to obtain the access points currently in visibility and some related communication-level information, such as received signal strength (Debian, 2003). If the clients host Windows CE3.0/CE.NET, the facility exploits the Network Driver Interface Specification User-mode I/O (NDISUIO), which is platform-dependent but portable on any network vendor implementation, to obtain the same information as in Linux (MSDN, 2003). Finally, in the case of Bluetooth connectivity, the facility takes advantage of the Java API for Bluetooth.

As for the monitoring facility, at middleware deployment time the facility exploits the terminal and site profiles to choose which location mechanisms to install at either the fixed network or the access terminal, depending on the type of wireless connectivity and on the operating system. Specialized MAs dynamically install the needed location modules over the fixed network; at the wireless devices, the client stubs exploit the standard code upload mechanisms of the Java 2 Micro Edition.

MOBILE STOCK TRADING CASE STUDY

To exemplify how the WICoCo access control operates during a service session and how it facilitates the development of context-aware services, this section provides some design and implementation insights of a mobile stock trading service (MSTS). MSTS allows mobile users with their wireless devices to roam among different wireless localities while continuing to operate on up-to-date stock quotations. In addition, MSTS can immediately notify abrupt quotation changes to interested users independently of their current location. It is the WICoCo middleware that handles all the complexity associated with access control and changing resource visibility: the access control support is in charge of context determination and modification in response to user mobility, terminal heterogeneity, and time-evolving resource availability. Context management does not affect the implementation of MSTS-specific clients and servers, which are transparently realized as in traditional distributed systems.

The WICoCo-based MSTS prototype allows users to browse stock quotations and to buy/sell stocks. The transactional properties of buying/selling operations are not the primary focus of the prototype and are not currently supported. We have deployed MSTS in a distributed environment consisting of several local area networks with either IEEE 802.11b or Bluetooth access points. Each locality is modeled as a WICoCo domain that hosts the middleware facilities and an MSTS server, called "quotationServer," that maintains updated stock quotations. In addition, each domain provides execution environments for the proxies of the MSTS users currently connected to that locality.

Let us observe that in the MSTS case the "quotationServer" instances in the different domains are exact replicas of the quotation information. In different application scenarios, WICoCo can easily support the deployment of location-dependent services by exploiting domain servers with different domain-related data, for example, tourist information about local buildings and restaurants.

Users can access MSTS via wireless devices where only the device-specific MSTS clients and the associated client stubs are installed. We have currently implemented clients and client stubs for portable devices with either the J2ME/CLDC/MIDP suite and Wi-Fi connectivity, or PalmOS and Bluetooth. MSTS clients allow the users to subscribe to the service, to specify the list of

stock quotations of primary interest, and to successively modify the profile information. In order to start the service session, the users must pass an authentication phase. A successful authentication associates the user with both a unique user identifier and a unique device identifier corresponding to the currently used terminal. User and device identifiers are cleanly separated in WICoCo to allow the same user to change her access device (nomadic user mobility) by maintaining the same active service session.

After the authentication, the MSTS user is associated with a newly instantiated and personal WICoCo proxy. Figure 6 shows an excerpt from the simple and reusable code of the MSTSProxy, which subclasses the general-purpose WICoCoProxy. At the instantiation, the proxy executes the init() method to retrieve the profiles of both the user and her current device from the directory facility. Examples of CC/PP-compliant profiles for users and terminals are reported in the annex. We have used the CC/PP standard XML schemas to represent the device software platform characteristics and the supported data formats, while we had to define our schema extensions to maintain the user information of interest for MSTS, for example, the user belonging to the silver class and her stocks of primary interest. After the profile retrieval, the proxy commands CM to determine the context object myContext. As described in the previous sections, CM dynamically determines the context by applying different kinds of metadata. Starting from the set of locally and globally visible resources, CM removes the items with resource profiles incompatible with the user/terminal ones. For instance, in the case of the device profile in the annex, service components providing only XML-based results are removed from the context because the access terminal only supports txt, c-HTML, and mp3-based data formats.

Then, all the obligation policies for access control triggered by the *ContextInstantiation* event are enforced. For instance, the enforcement of AccessControl1 in Figure 7a forbids bronze users to access MSTS by removing quotation server resources from their contexts. After the policy enforcement, the determination of the session-start context is completed, and the context is sent to the proxy. Let us observe that access control actions such as the one specified in AccessControl1 could have been obtained also in a more traditional way, by defining an equivalent authorization policy to deny the access of bronze users to quotation servers. Even if the access control result is the same, the two alternative solutions have some differences. In the case of authorization policies, the user context would have included the quotation server instances; an access request to a quotation server would have produced a runtime evaluation of the access control permission. By enforcing AccessControl1, the resource visibility itself is completely hidden to the proxy (and therefore to the client). Thus, the MSTS client cannot even try to request that resource during the service session. This results in a little increase in the context determination overhead at session initialization, but reduces the runtime overhead for access denial. Most important, this intrinsically provides context-aware differentiated

views of available resources, thus simplifying the resource binding decisions to the proxy and avoiding useless denials at runtime.

Once the context is determined, the proxy invokes the getResource("quotationServer") method on myContext. If the context includes a resource called "quotationServer," the invocation makes that resource active in the context, and returns back the resID resource descriptor to the proxy. If there is no resource with the given name in the applicable context, the exception handling produces a pop-up window in the MSTS client. The pop-up tells the user that the MSTS service is not accessible in her current wireless locality.

After the initialization and after any migration to a new domain, the proxy executes its run() method: if the user device is connected, the proxy requests the downloading of all stock quotation information from resID and then invokes visualizer() to push the received results to the client. Figure 6 shows that the update of an MSTS resource triggers the same actions described above. Obviously, it is reasonable to think also to alternative lighter solutions that assign to the user the responsibility of pulling the possibly updated results when desired. To this purpose, it is suf-

Figure 6. Excerpts from the MSTSProxy code

```
class MSTSProxy extends WICoCoProxy {
  …
void init() {
… UserProfile prof1 = Directory.getProfile(userID);
  DeviceProfile prof2 = Directory.getProfile(deviceID);
  Context myContext = CM.getContext(prof1,prof2);
  StockInfoList resID;
  try {
      resID = (StockInfoList) myContext.getResource(
        "quotationServer"); }
  catch (NotInContextException exception) { … }
… }
void run() {
… if (isConnected==true) results = resID.downloadAll();
  visualizer(results);
  … }
void onMSTSResUpdate() {
… if (isConnected==true) results = resID.downloadAll();
  visualizer(results);
  … }
… }
```

ficient to specify a void on MSTSResUpdate() method. Other proxy threads, not shown in the code excerpt, serve in the visualization of the stock quotations of primary interest indicated in the user profile and in the handling of user-entered queries/purchases/sales for specific stocks.

Without any impact on the design and implementation of the MSTS server, client and proxy, WICoCo permits to flexibly specify different access control policies, for different deployment domains, even depending on the resource state at policy enforcement time. All these policies are evaluated dynamically when triggered by either a resource access request or an event notified by the monitoring/location facility, and possibly modify

the applicable context during a service session. For instance, Figure 7b reports AccessControl2, which is triggered by the *NewLocation* event notified by the location facility when the user connects to the new domain LocalityID. By simply specifying that policy, a system administrator obtains that, in the LocalityID domain, silver users cannot access MSTS when the average network bandwidth is lower than a threshold. Let us note that, to reduce the overhead due to policy enforcement, in MSTS this potential context update is performed only at the user entrance in a new domain and not at any sensed variation in the local network bandwidth. Similarly, it is possible to simply associate service re-configuration operations at the user entrance

Figure 7. Examples of MSTS access control policies

```
inst oblig AccessControl1 {
on ContextInstantiation(ProxyID);
subject s = ProxyID;
target t = ProxyID;
do t.myContext.remove("quotationServer");
when t.prof2.getProperty("userClass") == "bronze";
        }
```

(a) AccessControl1 enforced at context instantiation time

```
inst oblig AccessControl2 {
on NewLocation(ProxyID,LocalityID)
subject s = ProxyID;
target t = ProxyID;
do t.myContext.remove("quotationServer");
when ((t.prof2.getProperty("userClass") == "silver") &&
        (Monitoring.getAvgBand() > threshold));
        }
```

(b) AccessControl2 triggered by the user change of domain

```
inst oblig AccessControl3 {
on AvgBandUnderThreshold();
subject s = getOneLocalProxy();
target t = s;
do t.myContext.remove("quotationServer");
when t.prof2.getProperty("userClass") == "silver";
        }
```

(c) AccessControl3 enforced in response to a local network traffic change

```
inst auth- AccessControl4 {
subject s = ProxyID;
target quotationServerID;
action downloadAll(), query(),
        onlyPrimaryStocks();
when s.prof2.getProperty("userClass")=="silver";
        }
```

(d) AccessControl4 triggered by a proxy access request to an MSTS resource

```
inst oblig AccessControl5 {
on QuotationServerOverload(QSID);
subject s = getOneLocalProxy();
target t = s;
do t.myContext.remove(QSID) ->
    t.myContext.add("quotationServerBackup") ->
    t.resID = (StockInfoList) myContext.getResource(
        "quotationServerBackup");
when ((t.prof2.getProperty("userClass") == "silver")
&& (Monitoring.getCPULoad(QSID.host()) > t1)
&& (Monitoring.getMemoryOcc(QSID.host()) > t2));
        }
```

(e) AccessControl5 enforced when the local quotation server is overloaded

in a network locality, by specifying other policies triggered by the *NewLocation* event. The change of domain of attachment is usually one of the most important reasons of context update in wireless Internet services (Bellavista, 2003b).

However, when necessary, it is also possible to specify access control policies that immediately update the contexts in the domain as soon as something changes in the local resource availability. Figure 7c shows AccessControl3 triggered by the *AvgBandUnderThreshold* event notified by the monitoring facility. AccessControl3 denies the MSTS access to one randomly-chosen proxy in the domain if the associated user is silver class, by producing an exception handling similarly to the failure of getResource(). If the local network bandwidth keeps too low even after the policy enforcement, another *AvgBandUnderThreshold* event will be notified, and possibly another proxy will have the MSTS access denied. Alternatively, a system administrator could have decided to update the context of a silver user only when her proxy requests to access the MSTS resource. Access-Control4 in Figure 7d specifies the same actions of AccessControl3 but in terms of an authorization policy triggered by the proxy explicit request of operating on resID. Here we can apply the same performance considerations about the differences between obligation and authorization policies that we previously made for context initialization.

Finally, also server state modifications can trigger context modifications and consequent context-aware service adaptations. The Access-Control5 policy in Figure 7e automatically rebinds silver user proxies to an alternative local quotation server, which acts as a slow backup copy of the master quotation server. The policy is triggered when the CPU and the memory usage of the master overcome the thresholds, with the goal of preventing the degradation of the service quality achieved by the gold clients in the locality.

RELATED WORK

Several research efforts have addressed the general issue of middleware to support different forms of mobility in the wireless Internet (user, device, resource, and service component mobility). They face very diverse aspects, from the provisioning of virtual home environments to 3G roaming users, to the effective synchronization of data replicas on mobile devices, and to profile-based content tailoring (Davies, 2002; Mascolo, 2002; Moura, 2002; Roman, 2000). It is relevant to observe that, notwithstanding the wide spectrum of challenges addressed, most solutions recognize the need to consider some forms of context. To this purpose, they propose the adoption of different kinds of metadata to drive the service behavior at runtime, for example, to maintain replica modification flags and multimedia presentations with alternative contents (Agarwal, 2002; Bulterman, 2002). We do not intend to provide here a general survey of the state-of-the-art middleware for context awareness in mobile computing, but only to focus on the access control research that explicitly deals with the primary design guidelines proposed in the chapter, that is, the profile/policy-driven context management, and the exploitation of MA-based middleware proxies.

By focusing on metadata for context-aware access control, a few first research proposals are appearing due to the novelty of the approach. All these projects agree on the crucial relevance to cleanly separate the context-aware access control issues from the application logic implementation, both to favor component reusability and to facilitate service development. Some proposals exploit reflection techniques to define separated programming meta-levels (Capra, 2003). Tanter and Piquer use reflection to define customizable access control strategies to rearrange the associations among service components and needed resources depending on meta-objects (2001). However, the determination of the applicable context is performed only at execution start, and cannot change at provision time. Another interesting approach is FarGo, which supports the programming of context determination rules as separate components (Holder, 1999). Similarly to Tanter (2001), the context is computed and associated to FarGo service components only at the application start. WICoCo has several points in common with the above approaches: it exploits middleware intermediaries to mediate the client access to resources, and it adopts some forms of metadata to separately specify how to determine the applicable context. The primary distinguishing feature, however, is that WICoCo can specify context determination rules in terms of high-level profiles and policies and that these rules can be modified during service provisioning, without any impact on the service implementation.

About policy representation, a wide spectrum of languages with different purposes, expressiveness, and formats have been defined, especially in the network management area, for example, the routing-oriented RPSL, the service monitoring-oriented SRL, and the service path management-oriented PPL (Stone, 2001). Several recent proposals exploit XML as their representation language, to facilitate the adoption in open environments. Among them, the eXtensible Access Control Markup Language (XACML) is the most significant effort of standardization and permits to represent both access control policies and resource access requests/responses (OASIS, 03). Differently from these approaches, Ponder allows the specification not only of authorization policies but also of obligation ones, essential in WICoCo to trigger the context update in response to environment modifications. In addition, Ponder is object-oriented and supports high-level abstractions to model collections of subjects/targets, based on either groups or roles. Let us note that a recent research hot topic is the definition of semantic-based policy languages, for example, KaoS and Rei, which have a further extended expressive

power (Tonti, 2003). The Ponder adoption in WICoCo is a reasonable compromise between the very rich expressiveness (and considerable overhead) of semantic-based languages and the simplicity (and reduced expressiveness) of XML-based solutions.

Regarding the adoption of proxies, the solution guideline of interposing security mediators between users and resources is recently emerging in different areas. For instance, in Ajanta, any MA access to resources is controlled by using a proxy-based mechanism at the client side (Karnik, 2000). In a different domain, Foster et al. propose the exploitation of proxies to secure the access to the resources offered by a computational grid (1998). In particular, proxy-based solutions seem suitable for wired-wireless integrated environments to smooth the discontinuities in available resources at the wired-wireless edges. Yoshimura et al. propose statically placed middleware components that perform local monitoring and multimedia adaptation (2002). Ross et al. exploit security proxies to determine the customized resource visibility of wireless clients; device-specific scripts, embedded in the proxy code, determine the visibility decisions (2000). However, also due to the novelty of the MA technology, few researches have proposed MAs to implement access control proxies. The ACTS OnTheMove project has developed a mobile application support environment that provides a statically installed proxy that manages laptop mobility between fixed and wireless networks (Kovacs, 1998). Other MA proposals mainly concentrate on proxies for profile-based virtual home environments (Lipperts, 1999). To the best of our knowledge, WICoCo is original in adopting MA-based mobile proxies working in the fixed network to perform context-aware access control also for resource-constrained terminals that cannot host any version of the JVM.

LESSONS LEARNED AND CONCLUDING REMARKS

The provisioning of mobile commerce services over the wireless Internet motivates flexible security solutions with full context awareness and capable of properly handling context modifications at runtime. On the one hand, the complexity of context handling and of context-based service management suggests a clear separation of concerns between access control strategies and service logic implementation. This is primary to simplify the implementation of context-dependent adaptive mobile commerce and to promote the reusability of service components. Novel programmable security middleware, integrated with profiles and policies, can provide the required adaptability, while hiding low-level implementation mechanisms. Notwithstanding their high level of abstraction, the metadata evaluation at runtime is demonstrating to introduce an acceptable overhead when coupled with effective and decentralized support solutions that exploit code/state mobility to maintain access control proxies in proximity of their wireless clients.

On the other hand, context-aware access control in an open environment calls for portable mechanisms for online monitoring. Java-based technologies are mature to integrate heterogeneous monitoring solutions within a uniform portable framework with performance results compatible with most mobile commerce applications for the wireless Internet. The SUN attention for the integration of the JVM with monitoring mechanisms is confirmed by the novel management features of the forthcoming JVM1.5 edition, which are expected to further improve the performance of Java-based monitoring (SUN, 2003c).

ACKNOWLEDGMENT

Work supported by the FIRB WEB-MINDS Project "Wide-scale Broadband Middleware for Network Distributed Services" and Strategic IS-MANET Project "Middleware Support for Mobile Ad-hoc Networks and their Application".

REFERENCES

Agarwal, S., Starobinski, D., & Trachtenberg, A. (2002). On the scalability of data synchronization protocols for PDAs and mobile devices. *IEEE Network, 16*(4), 22-28.

Bakic, A., Mutka, M.W., & Rover, D.T. (2000). BRISK: A portable and flexible distributed instrumentation system. *Software - Practice and Experience, 30*(12), 1353-1373.

Bellavista, P., Bottazzi, D., Corradi, A., Montanari, R., & Vecchi, S. (2004). Mobile agent middlewares for context-aware applications. In I. Mahgoub & M. Ilyas (Eds.), *Handbook of mobile computing.* CRC Press, to be published.

Bellavista, P., Corradi, A., Montanari, R., & Stefanelli, C. (2003a). Dynamic binding in mobile applications: A middleware approach. *IEEE Internet Computing, 7*(2), 34-42.

Bellavista, P., Corradi, A., Montanari, R., & Stefanelli, C. (2003b). Context-aware middleware for resource management in the wireless Internet. *IEEE Transactions on Software Engineering, 30*(2), 1086-1099.

Bellavista, P., Corradi, A., & Stefanelli, C. (2001). Mobile agent middleware for mobile computing. *IEEE Computer, 34*(3), 73-81.

Bellavista, P., Corradi, A., & Stefanelli, C. (2002a). The ubiquitous provisioning of Internet services to portable devices. *IEEE Pervasive Computing, 1*(3), 81-87.

Bellavista, P., Corradi, A., & Stefanelli, C. (2002b). Java for on-line distributed monitoring of heterogeneous systems and services. *The Computer Journal, 45*(6), 595-607.

Bos, L., & Leroy, S. (2001). Toward an all-IP-based UMTS system architecture. *IEEE Network, 15*(1), 36-45.

Bulterman, D.C.A. (2002). SMIL 2.0: Examples and comparisons. *IEEE Multimedia, 9*(1), 74-84.

Capra, L., Emmerich, W., & Mascolo, C. (2003). CARISMA: Context-aware reflective middleware system for mobile applications. *IEEE Transactions on Software Engineering, 29*(10), 929-945.

Curbera, F., Duftler, M., Khalaf, R., Mukhi, N., Nagy, W., & Weerawarana, S. (2002). Unraveling the Web services: An introduction to SOAP, WSDL, and UDDI. *IEEE Internet Computing, 6*(2), 86-93.

Davies, N., & Gellersen, H.-W. (2002). Beyond prototypes: Challenges in deploying ubiquitous systems. *IEEE Pervasive Computing, 1*(1), 26-35.

Debian. (2003). Tools for Manipulating Linux Wireless Extension. Retrieved October 2003, from *http://packages.debian.org/stable/net/wireless-tools.html*

Decker, S., Mitra, P., & Melnik, S. (2000). Framework for the semantic Web: An RDF tutorial. *IEEE Internet Computing, 4*(6), 68-73.

Foster, I., Kesselman, C., Tsudik, G., & Tuecke, S. (1998). A security architecture for computational grids. *5th ACM Conference on Computer and Communications Security* (pp. 83-92). ACM Press.

Fuggetta, A., Picco, G.P., & Vigna, G. (1998). Understanding code mobility. *IEEE Transactions on Software Engineering, 24*(5), 342-361.

Gast, M. (2002). *802.11Wireless networks: The definitive guide.* O'Reilly.

Gordon, R. (1998). *Essential Java native interface.* Prentice Hall.

Heflin, J., & Huhns, M.N. (2003). The Zen of the Web. *Special Section of IEEE Internet Computing, 7*(5), 30-59.

Holder, O., Ben-Shaul, I., & Gazit, H. (1999). Dynamic layout of distributed applications in FarGo. *21st Int. Conf. on Software Engineering (ICSE'99)* (pp. 163-173).

Huber, H., Jarke, M., Jeusfeld, M.A., Nissen, H.W., & Zemanek, G.V. (1996). Managing multiple requirements perspectives with metamodels. *IEEE Software, 13*(2), 37-48.

Hwang, Y, Kim, J., & Seo, E. (2003). Structure-aware Web transcoding for mobile devices. *IEEE Internet Computing, 7*(5), 14-21.

IKV++ Technologies AG. (2003). enago mobile. Retrieved October 2003, from *http://www.ikv.de*

Imperial College. (2003). Ponder Toolkit. Retrieved October 2003, from *http://www-dse.doc.ic.ac.uk/Re-search/policies/ponder.shtml*

Java Community Process (JCP). (2003). Java APIs for Bluetooth (JSR-82). Retrieved October 2003, from *http://www.jcp.org/en/jsr/detail?id=82*

Johansson, P., Kazantzidis, M., Kapoor, R., & Gerla, M. (2001). Bluetooth: An enabler for personal area networking. *IEEE Network, 15*(5), 28-37.

Karnik, N.M., & Tripathi, A.R. (2000). A security architecture for mobile agents in Ajanta. *20th Int. Conf. Distributed Computing Systems (ICDCS'00)* (pp. 402-409). IEEE Computer Society Press.

Kovacs, E., Rohrle, K., & Reich, M. (1998). Integrating mobile agents into the mobile middleware. *Mobile Agents Int. Workshop (MA'98)* (pp. 124-35). Springer-Verlag LNCS.

Lee, J. (2000). Enabling network management using Java technologies. *IEEE Communications Magazine, 38*(1), 116-123.

Lipperts, S., & Park, A. (1999). An agent-based middleware: A solution for terminal and user mobility. *Computer Networks, 31,* 2053-62.

Mascolo, C., Capra, L., & Emmerich, W. (2002). Middleware for mobile computing. *Networking 2002 Tutorial papers* (pp. 20-58). Springer-Verlag LNCS 2497.

Microsoft Software Developer Network (MSDN). (2003). *NDIS Features in Windows CE.* Retrieved October 2003, from *http://msdn.microsoft.com/ library*

Moffett, J., & Sloman, M. (1993). Policy hierarchies for distributed systems management. *IEEE Journal on Selected Areas in Communications, 11*(9), 1404-1414.

Moura, J.A., Oliveira, J.M., Carrapatoso, E., & Roque, R. (2002). Service provision and resource discovery in the VESPER VHE. *IEEE Int. Conf. on Communications (ICC'02).* IEEE Computer Society Press.

Organization for the Advancement of Structured Information Standards – OASIS. (2003). eXtensible Access Control Markup Language Standard 1.0 (normative) Specification Document. Retrieved December 2003, from *http://www. oasis-open.org/committees/download.php/2406/ oasis-xacml-1.0.pdf*

Perkins, C. (Ed.). (1999). Special section on autoconfiguration. *IEEE Internet Computing, 3*(4), 42-80.

Reed Electronics Group - In-Stat/MDR - Mobile Devices and Components. (2003). Live another day: Year-end review & 2003 handset forecast. Retrieved December 2003, from *http://www. instat.com*

Roman, G.-C., Picco, G.P., & Murphy, A.L. (2000). Software engineering for mobility: A roadmap. *22nd Int. Conf. on Software Engineering (ICSE'00)* (pp. 241-258). IEEE Computer Society Press.

Ross, S.J., Hill, J.L., Chen, M.Y., Joseph, A.D., Culler, D.E., & Brewer, E.A. (2000). A composable framework for secure multi-modal access to Internet services from Ppst-PC devices. *3rd IEEE Workshop on Mobile Computing Systems and Applications* (pp. 171–182).

Sandhu, R., & Samarati, P. (1996). Authentication, access control, and audit. *ACM Computing Surveys, 28*(1), 241-243.

Schilit, B.N., Hilbert, D.M., & Trevor, J. (2002). Context-aware communication. *IEEE Wireless Communications, 9*(5), 46-54.

Schroeder, B.A. (1995). On-line monitoring: A tutorial. *IEEE Computer, 28*(6), 72-78.

Stallings, W. (1998). *SNMP, SNMPv2, SNMPv3, and RMON 1 and 2* (3rd ed.). Addison Wesley.

Stone, G.N., Lundy, B., & Xie, G.G. (2001). Network policy languages: A survey and a new approach. *IEEE Network, 15*(1), 10–21.

SUN Microsystems. (2003a). Java Virtual Machine Profiler Interface (JVMPI). Retrieved October 2003, from *http://java.sun.com/ products/jdk/1.3/docs/guide/jvmpi/jvmpi.html*

SUN Microsystems. (2003b). Java Management Extensions (JMX). Retrieved October 2003, from *http://java.sun.com/products/JavaManagement/*

SUN Microsystems. (2003c). A Roadmap for Java 2 Platform, Standard Edition (J2SE) 1.5. Retrieved October 2003, from *http://developer. java.sun.com/developer/technicalArticles/Road-Maps/J2SE_1.5/ j2se_1_5.html*

Tanter, E., & Piquer, J. (2001). Managing references upon object migration: Applying separation of concerns. *21s Int. Conf. Chilean Computer Science Society (SCCC'01)* (pp. 264-272).

Tonti, G., Bradshaw, J.M., Jeffers, R., Montanari, R., Suri, N., & Uszok, A. (2003). Semantic Web languages for policy representation and reasoning:

A comparison of KAoS, Rei, and Ponder. *2nd Int. Semantic Web Conf. (ISWC2003).*

World Wide Web Consortium. (2002). Composite Capability/Preference Profiles (CC/PP). Retrieved December 2002, from *http://www. w3.org/Mobile*

Yoshimura, T., Ohya, T., Kawahara, T., & Etoh, M. (2002). Rate and robustness control with RTP monitoring agent for mobile multimedia streaming. *IEEE Int. Conf. on Communications (ICC'02).* IEEE Computer Society Press.

APPENDIX

Examples of CC/PP-compliant profiles for WICoCo users and terminals:

Code excerpts from an MSTS silver user profile

```
<?xml version="1.0"?>
<rdf:RDF  xmlns:rdf="http://www.w3.org/1999/02/22-rdf-syntax-ns#"
          xmlns:ccpp="http://www.w3.org/2002/11/08-ccpp-schema#"
          xmlns:WICoCoTermProf="ldap://ldap.deis.unibo.it/UserProfSchema#">
<rdf:Description rdf:about="ldap://ldap.deis.unibo.it/profile#WICoCoUserProf">

<ccpp:component>
   <rdf:Description rdf:about="ldap://ldap.deis.unibo.it/profile#UserID">
   <rdf:type rdf:resource="ldap://ldap.deis.unibo.it/schema#Identity">
        <ex:name>Paolo Bellavista</ex:name>
        <ex:nickName>Paolo</ex:nickName>
        <ex:city>Bologna</ex:city>
        <ex:userClass>silver</ex:userClass>
        …
   </rdf:Description>
</ccpp:component>

<ccpp:component>
   <rdf:Description rdf:about="ldap://ldap.deis.unibo.it/profile#StockPrefs">
   <rdf:type rdf:resource="ldap://ldap.deis.unibo.it/schema#Stock">
        <ex:primaryStocks>  <rdf:Bag>
                <rdf:li>HP</rdf:li>
                <rdf:li>DaimlerChrisler</rdf:li>
                <rdf:li>IBM</rdf:li>
        </rdf:Bag>  </ex:primaryStocks>
   </rdf:Description>
</ccpp:component>
…
</rdf:Description>
</rdf:RDF>
```

Code excerpts from a WindowsCE device profile

```
<?xml version="1.0"?>
<rdf:RDF  xmlns:rdf="http://www.w3.org/1999/02/22-rdf-syntax-ns#"
          xmlns:ccpp="http://www.w3.org/2002/11/08-ccpp-schema#"
          xmlns:WICoCoTermProf="ldap://ldap.deis.unibo.it/TermProfSchema#">
<rdf:Description rdf:about="ldap://ldap.deis.unibo.it/profile#WICoCoTermProf">

<ccpp:component>
   <rdf:Description rdf:about="ldap://ldap.deis.unibo.it/profile#TerminalSoftware">
   <rdf:type rdf:resource="ldap://ldap.deis.unibo.it/schema#SoftwarePlatform">
        <ex:name>WindowsCE</ex:name>
        <ex:version>4.0</ex:version>
        <ex:vendor>Microsoft</ex:vendor>
   </rdf:Description>
</ccpp:component>

<ccpp:component>
   <rdf:Description rdf:about="ldap://ldap.deis.unibo.it/profile#TerminalBrowser">
   <rdf:type rdf:resource="ldap://ldap.deis.unibo.it/schema#Browser">
        <ex:name>Mozilla</ex:name>
        …
        <ex:formatSupported>  <rdf:Bag>
                <rdf:li>txt</rdf:li>
                <rdf:li>c-HTML</rdf:li>
                <rdf:li>mp3</rdf:li>
        </rdf:Bag>  </ex:formatSupported>
   </rdf:Description>
</ccpp:component>
…
</rdf:Description>
</rdf:RDF>
```

This work was previously published in Advances in Security and Payment Methods for Mobile Commerce, edited by W.-C. Hu, C.-w. Lee and W. Kou, pp. 81-108, copyright 2005 by IGI Publishing, formerly known as Idea Group Publishing (an imprint of IGI Global).

Chapter 4.36
Data and Application Security for Distributed Application Hosting Services

Ping Lin
Arizona State University, USA

K. Selçuk Candan
Arizona State University, USA

ABSTRACT

The cost of creating and maintaining software and hardware infrastructures for delivering web services led to a notable trend toward the use of application service providers (ASPs) and, more generally, distributed application hosting services (DAHSs). The emergence of enabling technologies, such as J2EE and .NET, has contributed to the acceleration of this trend. DAHSs rent out Internet presence, computation power, and data storage space to clients with infrastructural needs. Consequently, they are cheap and effective outsourcing solutions for achieving increased service availability and scalability in the face of surges in demand. However, ASPs and DAHSs operate within the complex, multi-tiered, and open Internet environment and, hence, they introduce many security challenges that have to be addressed effectively to convince customers that outsourcing their IT needs is a viable alternative to deploying complex infrastructures locally. In this chapter, we provide an overview of typical security challenges faced by DAHSs, introduce dominant security mechanisms available at the different tiers in the information management hierarchy, and discuss open challenges.

INTRODUCTION

In an e-businessess setting, distributed computation with multiple parties' participation is typical. Most business tasks, for example calculating the collective financial health of a group of independent companies, are inherently distributed (Franklin et al., 1992). Consequently, most businesses need an information technology (IT) infrastructure capable of providing such distributed services. For most businesses, investing in a local, privately owned infrastructure is not economically meaningful. For instance, an e-commerce company may find deploying an infrastructure that can handle peak demand volumes, while sitting idle most other times wasteful. Therefore, businesses are willing to pay premium prices for third-party solutions that can help them reduce their infrastructural needs while providing them appropriate quality of service guarantees. Consequently, application service providers (ASPs) and distributed application hosting services (DAHSs), which rent out storage, (Internet) presence, and computation power to clients with IT needs (but without appropriate infrastructures) are becoming popular. Especially with the emergence of enabling technologies, such as J2EE (J2EE, 2003) and .NET (.NET, 2003), there is currently a shift toward services hosted by third parties.

Most DAHSs typically deploy a large number of servers to host their customers' business logic and data. They employ hardware- or software-based load balancing components to provide

quality of service guarantees to customers. In addition, DAHSs can also place or replicate applications and data in servers closer to the end-users to eliminate network delays. Examples include Akamai and MirrorImage.

A typical application hosting infrastructure (*Figure 1*) consists of three major components: database management systems (DBMSs), which maintain business data, application servers (ASs), which encode business logic of the customers, and web servers (WSs), which provide the web interface between end-users and the business applications that are hosted by the DAHS. Although there are various modes of DAHS operation, a common way hosting services are used is as follows: (1) the customer (or application owner) with an application program publishes this application along with the relevant data onto the servers of the host. (2) Whenever they need, the customers (or its clients) access this application remotely by passing appropriate parameter variables to the host using the web interface. (3) User requests invoke appropriate program scripts in the application server, which in turn issue queries to the underlying DBMS to dynamically generate and

Figure 1: Components of a distributed application infrastructure

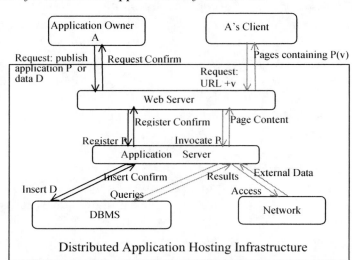

construct responses. In other words, the host runs the application with the local or provided data and sends the result back to the requesting party. (4) The host charges the application owner based on the resources (such as bandwidth, CPU, or storage) required for the processing of the request. *Figure 1* shows a typical application hosting infrastructure and its operation flows.

Distributed application hosting services, on the other hand, pose various security challenges due to their inherently distributed and mostly open natures. Without proper security provisions, customers will not choose to outsource services, hence DAHS will not survive. In this chapter, we provide an overview of various security challenges faced by DAHSs, discuss the techniques developed to address these challenges, introduce the security technologies and protocols used at different tiers in the Internet information management hierarchy, and discuss still-open issues.

The structure of the chapter is as follows. In the next section, we give an overview of the basic data and application security services and security tools. We also enumerate the security challenges faced by DAHSs. Then, we discuss security mechanisms adopted by widely used information management architectures. In the subsequent sections, we discuss the techniques available to DAHS to tackle these challenges and highlight the open problems.

OVERVIEW OF DATA AND APPLICATION SECURITY

In data, content, and information delivery systems, security generally refers to the ability of a system to manage, protect, and distribute sensitive information so that information is free from eavesdropping, tampering, and spoofing and the service is available to all legitimate users. Therefore, security plays an essential role in e-commerce and e-business applications, where quality of information and service delivery means money,

and military systems, where secure information and service links directly to national safety and human life.

Basic data, application, and system security services needed by such systems can be categorized as follows:

- *Authentication*: All entities in the system should be properly identified.
- *Authorization and confidentiality*: Access to applications or information should be restricted only to those entitled entities. Data or application code should be unintelligible to any non-entitled entity.
- *Integrity*: Data or applications should be free from unauthorized modification and damage.
- *Availability*: Data, application, and the system should be available to users despite attacks or damages.
- *Auditing*: Records of security relevant events (such as authentication, authorizing decisions, or abnormal events) should be kept for assessing attacks and intrusions or for evaluating effectiveness of security policies and mechanisms.

Although they address different security challenges, at their foundations, all these services rely on basic cryptography techniques. For a comprehensive background in cryptographic protocols and tools refer to Section I of this book. In this chapter, we focus on the security challenges peculiar to DAHSs.

Security Challenges and Security Mechanisms in Distributed Application Hosting Services

Distributed application hosting services (DAHSs) face a number of security challenges. In small, closed local area networks, the mutual trust between clients and hosts is high. Clients can fully trust all hosts and the communications are reliable.

However, in open, wide area networks, such as the Internet, where hosts are added and removed dynamically, it is very possible that clients and hosts have little mutual trust. In an environment where servers may not always be honest, data security constitutes a major concern to users. Executing an application remotely exposes the application code and data to non-trusted, potentially malicious, distributed computing infrastructures. A malicious host may make use of clients' private information to gain illegal profits or cause damages to systems by tempering. Certain applications, such as business transactions and military applications, do not lend themselves well to the risks involved in simple outsourcing computation tasks to third parties. How to protect application code and input data from malicious executing environments, therefore, is a critical challenge.

As discussed earlier, techniques for data security occupy a wide spectrum. Most mechanisms aim at protecting data from unauthorized accesses. On the other hand, users' queries to data servers or private inputs to outsourced applications may also be of value and, without proper protection, important information may be leaked to the untrusted or compromised servers. For example, in a stock database, the type of stock a user is querying is sensitive information and may need to be kept private, sometimes even from the database server. Hence, traditional network-level encryption schemes may not be enough.

The security concerns in DAHSs can be broadly categorized as follows:

- System resources may be accessed by malicious or illegal clients so that sensitive information is leaked.
- Legal clients may access more system resources than they are entitled to, hence damaging these resources or preventing other clients from accessing these resources.
- Clients' application, data, or requests may be leaked, modified, or lost when they are being transported by insecure communication channels or executed by malicious hosts.

A qualified application hosting infrastructure should provide proper mechanisms to tolerate any faulty or malicious actions listed above. Although these mechanisms have already been briefly introduced earlier in this section, in the remainder of the chapter we focus on the DAHS specific challenges in *authentication, authorization,* and *confidentiality.*

- **Authentication in DAHSs:** Authentication means verification and validation. Identity authentication enables verifying the identities of the entities participating in the application hosting services (either the clients or the hosts) to make sure that both ends at the communicating channel have the right to perform their tasks. Services will be denied to unauthorized clients.

   Data authentication, on the other hand, verifies the origin and the integrity of data. In DAHSs, data owners usually outsource their data and delegate their services to untrusted third-parties. Hence DAHSs should provide mechanisms to enable clients to verify query answers. Application can be delivered across networks for remote execution. This gives rise to two authentication issues: (1) to authenticate that the application is safe and does not contain malicious code; and (2) to authenticate that the application has been correctly executed on untrusted remote sites.

- **Authorization in DAHSs:** In order to protect resources of DAHS hosts, security policies should be specified by hosts to restrict clients' access to resources. If any violation occurs, proper action will be taken by hosts, including the termination of service.

- **Confidentiality in DAHSs:** Private information of DAHS clients (including outsourced application code and data) is not leaked to or modified by any third party when transported through the Internet, nor DAHS hosts when the code is executed or the data is stored. Confidentiality can be achieved by encryption, private information retrieval, computation hiding, and information hiding: noticing that in some cases, users' queries also need to be kept private, private information retrieval prevents query as well as results from being disclosed to the host; computation hiding seeks to hide users' private input data or code from partially trusted hosts; and information hiding is used to hide not only the content but also the existence of communication from possible attackers.

Traditional security mechanisms like authentication, access control, and cryptography have been well studied and established through various industry standards. On the other hand, some of the required technologies, such as private information retrieval, computation hiding, and information hiding are new research areas and the underlying techniques are not standardized yet. We will revisit authentication, authorization, and confidentiality challenges in DAHSs and discuss the related technologies in greater detail. Having covered the background in security technologies, however, we now proceed to compare security challenges and provisions of popular data and information management architectures that form the basis of DAHSs.

COMPARISON OF SECURITY PROVISIONS OF VARIOUS ENABLING SYSTEMS

The diversity of distributed application environments and usage scenarios of computer systems contribute to the diversity of the security concerns faced by DAHSs. Since many applications, such as those involved with e-commerce, contain common modules, independent software developers can save a great deal of time by building their applications on top of existing modules that already provide required functionalities. This calls for a distributed architecture, where different modules can locate each other through directory services and can exchange information through messaging systems. J2EE and .NET are two popular distributed application architectures, and Chapter 9 of this book provides a detailed comparison of the security measures these architectures provide. In this section, we discuss security concerns and mechanisms in various enabling software and hardware systems.

Web Services and XML

Web services are standardized ways of integrating web-based applications. The primary function of web services is to allow independent web entities to communicate with each other without considering the underlying IT systems. Web service integration is done through programmatic interfaces, which are operating system independent and programming language neutral. Currently, there are various standards that enable web service integration. Extensible Markup Language (XML), Simple Object Access Protocol (SOAP), Web Service Description Language (WSDL), and Universal Description, Discovery and Integration (UDDI) are open enabling standards. XML is used to organize the data with tags enabling applications to understand the structures of each other's data; SOAP is a light-weight protocol, based on XML, to encode the data for exchange between web applications; WSDL is an XML-based language to describe web services so that web applications can identify services that they need; and UDDI is a directory that lists available services on the Internet and enables applications to discover each other.

- *Hierarchical structure:* XML data has a graph structure explicitly described by user-defined tags. The basic objects of XML

Figure 2: (a) An XML DTD, (b) A matching XML document, and its (c) graph representation

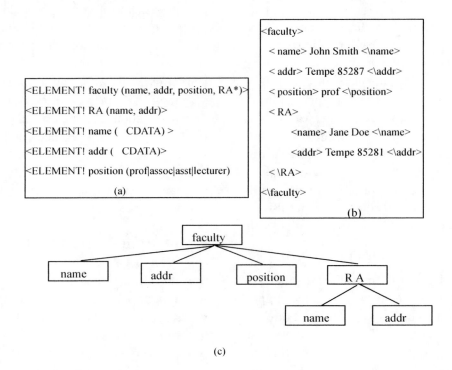

(a)

(b)

(c)

data are elements, attributes, and references (idrefs). An element is a semantically whole unit. It may include subelements as components as well as attributes describing its relevant features. An idref links an element to another. Objects of an XML document are connected via element-subelement, element-attribute, element-link relationships and, therefore, form a graph (*Figure 2*). If references are removed, the graph is degraded into a tree structure; hence the structure of any XML object may be regarded as a hierarchy.

• ***Declarative structure:*** XML data may be *validated* or *well formed*. A validated XML data conforms to a structure defined by a given Data Type Definition (DTD). A well-formed XML data follows grammar rules of XML but has no associated DTD file to define its structure. A well-formed XML data may partially conform to some DTD or not conform to any DTD.

XML encryption is the standard process specified by W3C to encrypt any XML web resource (Reagle, 2003). It supports symmetric and asymmetric encryption as well as super-encryption (i.e., encryption of data that has already been encrypted). It can also support block encryption (encryption algorithms, such as DES, that divide plaintext into fixed-length blocks and then encrypt each block respectively) and stream encryption (encryption algorithms, such as SEAL, that manipulates the plaintext in the units of bits). It supports various key exchange protocols, such as RSA-v1.5, RSA-OAEP (Fujisaki et al., 2000), and Diffie-Hellman. With XML encryption, both the schema and the content of XML documents can be hidden from non-entitled entities.

Transport layer security protocols, such as SSL/TSL or network layer security protocols

(IPsec) lay the foundation for secure messaging in web services. These protocols enable client/server authentication, data integrity, and confidentiality as discussed before. XML signature (Section AUTHENTICATION) and XML encryption can be used within SOAP to provide message-level authentication and persistent confidentiality. IBM, Microsoft, and VeriSign proposed WS-Security specification to describe how to attach signatures and encryption headers to SOAP messages (Atkinson, 2002).

At the higher levels, there is a need for service-level security models. For example, IBM provides a general security model for web services in .NET (2003). In this model, a web service is accessed by requiring each requester to carry with the request messages some proof that certain specified claims are satisfied. The associated claims and relevant information constitute the policy for the web service. A security token for an entity encodes security information, such as user name or digital certificate. The requester proves required claims by attaching its security token to request messages or by asking the security token from a special web service called Security Token Service (which may ask for its own claims). IBM and Microsoft are developing WS-Policy to describe capabilities and constraints of the security policies on entities, WS-Trust to describe the trust models for Web services, WS-Privacy to enable web services and requesters to declare privacy requirements and practices, WS-Secure Conversation to describe message exchange authentication and management, WS-Federation to describe the management of trust among heterogeneous systems, and WS-authorization for describing how to manage authorization data and security policies (.NET, 2003).

Although most web applications reside in and above the application server tier that use these two technologies, data storage and management is usually left to database management systems (DBMSs). Next, we will consider security provisions of two popular DBMSs.

Database Management Systems (Oracle and DB2)

Views, private virtual databases, access control, and encryption have long been practiced by back-end database systems to achieve security. In *Table 1* we compare security mechanisms used by two popular database management systems: Oracle (Oracle, 2003) and DB2 (DB2, 2003).

- Oracle's security mechanisms are embedded into the database. For DB2, there are also various tool suites to help secure DB2 data. Oracle and DB2 both provide authentication. DB2's authentication works closely with the underlying operation system's security features to verify user IDs and passwords.
- Both of their access controls are role based. Oracle can provide access control explicitly to row level data. In DB2, access control can be explicitly granted to tables or views and row level access control is gained implicitly by defining views on rows.
- Both of them provide database encryption. Through GUI interface provided by the Encryption Wizard of Oracle, encryption can be conducted at schema, table, or column levels. With application tools such as IBM DATA Encryption, encryption for DB2 data

Table 1. Oracle and DB2 comparison [sources (Oracle, 2003; DB2, 2003)]

	Oracle	DB2
Authentication	Provided	Provided
View	Provided	Provided
Access Control	Row level access control	Table (view) level access control
Encryption	Row level encryption	Table level encryption
Auditing	Fine grained	Less granular

can be conducted at table levels.

- A view is a specific way of looking at a database. Generally, a view is constructed by arranging data in some order and making only some parts of the data visible. Views can hence be used as a mechanism to grant various types of access rights on the same data. Oracle and DB2 both provide views and view-based access control.

- Oracle and DB2 both provide auditing to capture relevant data. Oracle provides session auditing at the schema, table, and column levels to trace users' encryption/decryption operations. DB2's auditing facility acts at the instance level, where an instance is a database manager that maintains a set of databases that cannot be accessed by other instances.

While application and database servers are dominant architectural components for e-businesses and web service providers, they also form the basis of *grid*s that integrate scientific as well as business applications and data.

Data and Computation Grids

Grid computing refers to the system design approach that benefits from resources available from various devices in a network to solve a complicated problem that usually needs a huge number of processing cycles or a large amount of data from different origins. Grid computing makes all heterogeneous systems across an enterprise or organization virtually shared and always available to any legal members. Consequently, through sharing of computing capabilities and data, grid computing accelerates processing of problems that are too complicated for a single machine to handle. Hence, it enables complex business problems, computing intensive scientific problems, or large data analysis problems to be solved rapidly. The need to share resources and to execute untrusted code from any member of

the grid introduces various security concerns for grid computing. In grid systems, authentication and authorization should always be present. Data grids should integrate a variety of databases regardless of which operating system they reside on. Although each database may have its own security requirements and provisions, the data grid should provide access control that respects each data source's policy while satisfies users' data needs to the greatest possible extent. Although, there are no established standards, Butt et al. (2002) proposed a technique, which uses run time monitoring and restricted shells, to enable maximum legitimate use permitted by security policies of a shared resource. The application architectures, DBMSs, and resources on a grid are connected with each other as well as the end users through wired or wireless networks. Hence, network security is essential.

Wired and Wireless Networks

Firewalls and secure socket layer (SSL) communication are two typically used techniques to achieve network security. Firewalls isolate to-be-protected servers from the open Internet so that only messages from authenticated sources can penetrate through. Firewall authentication relies on package filtering or stateful package inspection to check the originating and destination address associated with messages. The main deficiency of the firewall technique is that it does not inspect the content of the messages. An attacker who achieves access by misrepresenting his/her identity may exploit this security hole by sending malicious content. SSL is an open protocol, developed by Netscape, to provide secure HTTP connection and data transmission between web browsers and web servers. Theoretically, it is a protocol at the transport layer of network protocol stack. Its function is to establish secure communication sessions between clients and servers. Before data communication starts, by a handshake protocol, SSL allows a client and a server to authenticate each other through asymmetric cryptography and X.509 certificates, as well as to negotiate the encryption algorithm and cryptographic keys to be used during secure data communication. From that moment on, all data is encrypted by symmetric cryptography. To check data integrity, data is transported along with keyed MAC checksum. The SSL version often used in wired networks is TLS.

In wireless networks, the counterpart of TLS is WTSL. A mobile device can establish secure communication session to a wireless access protocol (WAP) gateway through WTSL. Then, on behalf of the mobile device, this WAP gateway can establish secure communication session to the target server through TSL over wired networks (*Figure 3*). Since WTSL is not compatible with TSL, the WAP gateway has to do translation between them. Therefore, data is encrypted all the way between the mobile client and the server except on the WAP gateway where the translation occurs. If the WAP gateway is compromised, confidential data may be leaked. Two possible ways to achieve end-to-end security are to eliminate the WAP gateway or to add application level encryption. *Table 2* gives a comparison of TSL and WTSL.

- TSL is a *de facto* standard to establish secure session between clients and servers in the Internet. WTSL is its counterpart in wireless networks (WAP). Both of them are transport layer protocols. They both support encryption, public key infrastructure, digital signature, certificate, etc.

- TSL relies on reliable network connection (TCP). WTSL can be established on unreliable network connection (UDP).

- To adapt for mobile environments where connection is not stable and may be lost easily, WTSL supports suspended or resumable sessions. Support for resumable session is also an option for TSL.

- TSL is derived from SSL. WTSL, on the other hand, is not compatible with SSL.

Having covered the security challenges and

Table 2. Comparison of TSL and WTSL [source (Wright, 2000)].

	TSL	WTSL
Usage Environment	Wired networks	Wireless networks (WAP)
Protocols	TCP	TCP or UDP
Support for session suspend and resume?	YES	YES
Compatible with SSL	YES	NO

Figure 3: TSL and WTSL

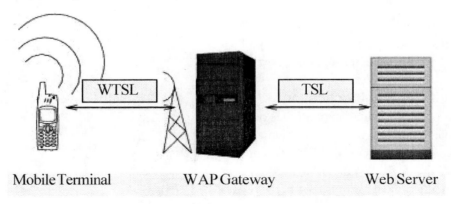

Mobile Terminal   WAP Gateway   Web Server

provisions in enabling architectures, in the remainder of the chapter we will focus on authentication, authorization, and confidentiality related challenges and provide an overview of the solutions proposed and techniques developed to address these issues. We will review the state-of-the-art as well as state-of-the-practice, highlight open challenges and directions, and discuss impact of data and code security on various applications.

AUTHENTICATION

Authentication involves verification of the claims made by parties in a secure environment. A common authentication task is (a) the verification of the identity of a communicating entity: without knowing for certain the identity of a client, for example, it is not possible to decide whether to accept or deny the access request. In addition, (b) data exchanged within a DAHS also needs to be authenticated to verify that it is really from the claimed origin and that its content is really what the source claims to have sent. In such an untrusted environment, answers to database queries should also be verified. Finally, (c) application authentication involves verifying whether execution of the application on untrusted DAHS servers is correctly performed or not. In this section, we will consider various authentication tasks in DAHSs.

Identity Authentication

Identity authentication protocols may be classified into two: (1) trusted third party authentication and (2) authentication without a trusted third party.

Trusted Third Party Authentication

Trusted third party authentication relies on a third party that is trusted by both communicating parties. Kerberos protocol (Kohl & Neuman, 1993), which is the *de facto* standard for network authentication, is a typical example. Kerberos re-

lies on symmetric cryptography. In this protocol, the trusted third party is called the Key Distribution Center (KDC). Authentication protocol consists of three steps (as shown in *Figure 4*):

i)   The client sends a request, which includes its and the server's identities (*c* and *s* respectively), together with a nounce *t*, to the KDC. The nounce is used to prevent replay of the request and should be a value, such as a timestamp, that cannot be changed.

ii)   KDC creates a session key $K_{c,s}$, and sends the session key and the nounce that are encrypted with the client's secret key K_c, back to the client. The KDC also issues credentials with which the client can access the server. A credential is a ticket, $T_{c,s} = <c,$ $K_{c,s}$, *expiration_time*>, that can be used to identify the client at the server. The ticket is encrypted with the server's secret key K_s, to prevent the client from tempering with it.

iii) Finally, the client sends to the server an authenticator which includes

(1)   the current timestamp t_c, encrypted using the session key, and

(2)   The ticket $T_{c,s}$ which was encrypted by the KDC with the server's   secret key.

The server, after receiving the authenticator in Step 3, can establish the identity of the client by

Figure 4: Kerberos authentication

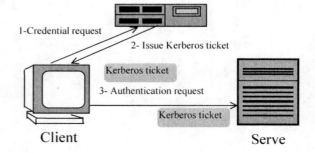

(1) decrypting the ticket, (2) extracting the identity of the client and the session key, and then (3) using the session key to decrypt the authenticator to see if the timestamp is current. If so, under the assumption that the KDC is trustworthy, the request is known to come from the stated client. If the identity of the server is also required to be authenticated to the client, (4) the server will respond with an incremented timestamp encrypted with the session key. This will enable the client to know that the server is able to read the timestamp, which means that the server has access to the session key, thus it is indeed the target server. After the authentication is over, the client may confidently communicate with the server using the session key.

Note that, in the above protocol, each time a client communicates with a server, trust between the client and the server has to be established using server's and client's secret keys. To reduce the probability of disclosure of the secret keys, the Kerberos protocol can be enhanced by allowing a Ticket Granting Server (TGS). In the enhanced protocol KDC has access to client's and TGS's secret keys, whereas the server's secret key is only known to the TGS.

One major advantage of the Kerberos protocol is that it only involves efficient symmetric encryption. On the other hand, it relies on the absolute security of KDC. If KDC is corrupted, the security system will be compromised. In order to prevent a corrupt third party to break the security of the system, other protocols aim to eliminate the need for a trusted third party.

Authentication without a Trusted Third Party

Public key cryptography can serve as an authentication protocol (Nace & Zmuda, 1997). Let us assume that there are two communicating parties, S_a and S_b. Each party has a key pair (*Pub*, *Priv*), which includes a public key and a private key, respectively. Let us denote S_a's key pair as

$(Pub_a, Priv_a)$ and S_b's key pair as $(Pub_b, Priv_b)$. The authentication procedure is as follows:

i) S_a and S_b exchange their public keys.

ii) S_a generates a random number R_a, sends it to S_b.

iii) S_b responds with $Priv_b(R_a)$, and another random number R_b.

iv) S_a decrypts $Priv_b(R_a)$ with Pub_b. If she obtains R_a, she knows the other party is S_b, for only S_b can sign it with $Priv_b$.

v) S_a responds with $Priv_a(R_b)$.

vi) S_b decrypts $Priv_a(R_b)$ with Pub_a. If he obtains R_b, he knows the other party should be S_a, for only S_a can sign the number with her private key.

After the trust has been established, S_a and S_b can communicate with each other in this way: before sending a message, each party encrypts the message with the other party's public key. The other party, after receiving the encrypted text, decrypts it with his/her own private key to retrieve the plain text.

The main advantage of the public cryptography authentication is that its security depends only on the two communication parties themselves. One main disadvantage of public cryptography authentication, however, is that it utilizes the inefficient asymmetric cryptography. Also, if a malicious third party intercepts the public keys being exchanged, it can replace them with different public keys and pose as one of the communication parties. A key exchange protocol, like Diffie-Hellman, may serve as a solution to this problem.

Data Authentication

Data authentication involves verifying data's origin and integrity. Digital signatures can be used to prove the origin of a data message and hash (or digest) values can be used to check the integrity of the data being exchanged. In fact, by signing on the checksum hash value, both the origin and integrity can be verified. Basic tools for data authentication, therefore, include signature algorithms (such as DSA and RSA/SHA-1) and digest algorithms (such as MD5, MAC, and SHA). However, different types of data have different structures or usage contexts; hence the ways to digest or sign them may vary.

In DAHSs, data owners make their database available at third party servers. Since a single database contains more than one data object and since accesses to the database are through declarative queries (instead of explicit object ids), authenticating database accesses require techniques more elaborate than simple digests and signatures.

A correct database answer to a given query should be complete and inclusive. A complete answer must include all data elements that satisfy the query and an inclusive answer should not include any data that does not satisfy the query. If the server hosting the database is trusted, then one possible authentication solution is to let the server certify answers by signing on them using a private key. However, in a DAHS, data owners may outsource their databases to untrusted third party publishers; hence, new protocols that authenticate database query results from untrusted publishers are needed. Some of these techniques are discussed next.

Authentic Database Publication

Devanbu et al. (1999) propose a generic model for authentic third party data/database publication (*Figure 5*). The model consists of the following steps: (1) the data owner sends the database to the third party publisher; (2) the data owner signs the database digest and sends it to its clients; (3) a client queries the database stored at the publisher; (4) the publisher processes the query, sends the answer and some verification information to the client; and (5) using the verification information and the digest, the client verifies whether the answer it received is correct or not.

Query results can always be verified by submitting the whole database as the verification information to the client. Clearly, this would be very expensive. Hence it is crucial to develop proper database digest techniques that enable exchange of minimal verification information.

Devanbu et al. (1999) show that Merkle Hash Trees can be used to efficiently verify answers to selection, projection, join, and set operation queries that are common in relational databases. This protocol relies on the existence of database index trees, which are used for providing efficient access to the contents of the database. A trusted party (e.g., the data owner) recursively digests nodes of the index tree such that every leaf digest

Figure 5: Third party data publishing

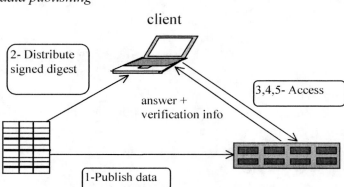

is a hash over the corresponding data value and every non-leaf digest is a hash over its children's digests (*Figure 6*). Merkle hash trees have two properties that enable authentication: Given the correct root digest,

- any modification to the tree structure can be detected; and
- the existence of a given subtree can be verified.

These two properties are fundamental for the verification of the inclusiveness of query answers. By requiring leaves of the tree being sorted according to some total order, it possible to enhance the Merkle hash tree with a third property: Given the correct root digest and a sequence of leaf values, $q = <t_i, ..., t_j>$,

- the completeness of the sequence can be verified.

This enhanced property is fundamental in verifying the completeness of query answers. Based on these results, Merkle hash trees can be used for authenticating inclusiveness and completeness of relational query results.

As discussed in the subsection on web service and XML, on the other hand, in DAHSs and the web, the de facto standard to organize data

is XML. Hence, next we look into mechanisms for authenticating data and databases published in XML format. First, we concentrate on signing XML data and documents and then we will discuss authentication procedures for third party XML database publication.

XML Data Signatures

World Wide Web Consortium (W3C), which develops interoperable technologies and standards for the Web, has established an XML signature standard (Eastlake, 2003). This standard includes:

- a digest algorithm (SHA-1),
- a signature algorithm (DSA or RSA/SHA-1),
- a message authentication code (a hash function with a shared secret key), and
- transform algorithms to be applied to XML documents before they are digested. Transform algorithms add flexibility to the XML signature. For example, with path filtering transformations, the signer can choose to sign only nodes on a specified path in a given XML document.

W3C also specifies a progressive digesting procedure called DOMHASH (Maruyama et al.,

Figure 6: A balanced binary Merkle hash tree

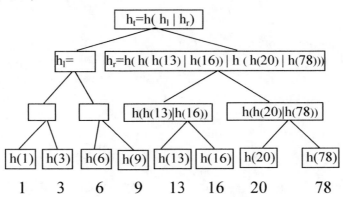

2000) to recursively digest a DOM tree (Hégaret et al., 2003) (the native tree presentation of an XML document) from the leaf to the root, so that each node (element or attribute) has a digest value and the digest of an non-leaf element is a hash over its subelements and attributes' digests and its content. This strong version of the digest enables efficient comparison of two versions of an XML document to find the different parts.

XML signatures can be used to verify the integrity of a given XML document or some selected parts of it, but it cannot be used to verify the inclusiveness and completeness of answers to XML queries. Next, we discuss techniques for authentication of results to a query executed on an XML database published at an untrusted third party.

Authentic Third-Party XML Database Publication

Merkle hash trees work well for node selection queries (as discussed earlier), however, is not directly applicable for XML path queries, which require identification of all paths in a given XML document that match a given condition. Devanbu et al. (2001) proposes the following approach for creating XML digests using the DTD of a given XML document:

i) The XML document owner builds an enhanced Merkle hash tree for each path type in the DTD and associates the root digest of the resulting Merkle hash tree with the corresponding path type.
ii) The owner builds another enhanced Merkle hash tree from all path type digests and associates the root digest of this second tree with the given XML document.
iii) The owner then signs the document digest and sends it to clients for verifying query results.

This enables efficient verification of the results

to simple path queries in addition to the selection queries. For each path query, the publisher finds all path types that match the query and for each matching path type, it constructs a certificate. Using the XML digest provided by the owner, the client can verify whether the certificate provided by the publisher includes all and only the results of the correct path type. Furthermore, the client can pre-calculate all path types that match the query and see whether for each matching path type, a certificate is received. Hence the client can verify the completeness and inclusiveness of the answer. This protocol, however, has the following limitations:

- It is computationally costly. Besides the cost of building Merkle hash trees, the owner needs to pre-calculate all subtrees for each path type. To verify each query, the client needs to find all matching path types.
- It has a large space overhead for the publisher: for each possible path type, a large certificate has to be maintained.
- It requires clients to know the DTD of the document to verify answers.
- It can not handle complicated path queries and queries over XML data that do not have a corresponding DTD.

Bertino et al. (2002) propose an alternative protocol that is cheaper and that does not need DTDs. This protocol utilizes DOMHASH to calculate root digest. See Chapter 6 of the book for a detailed discussion. Since this protocol is based on only one DOMHASH value for the entire XML document, it is cheaper than the previous protocol, which needs hashing for every path type. Also, since the path types do not need to be known in advance, this protocol does not need the DTDs. One disadvantage of the protocol, however, is that it lacks the ability to verify answers to selection queries, hence it is less flexible.

Application Authentication

In distributed environments, application code can move among various distributed entities: (1) application code (such as Java applets) can be distributed from servers to clients for local execution; (2) application code can travel from thin mobile clients to powerful servers for execution; (3) in DAHSs, application code can be published and outsourced to remote server by the application owners; and (4) the code can travel between DAHS servers to achieve load balancing and process migration. For application code distribution, the recipient (either the client or the server) must validate the origin and the integrity of the code before loading, installing, and executing it. Otherwise, the recipient can be subject to a malicious or tampered source, which can gain unauthorized access to the recipient's resources or can receive a virus which can break down the recipient's machine and spy for sensitive information. The source also should use authentication techniques; otherwise, a malicious recipient may try to deceive the owner by providing false results. Furthermore, if the application code and the associated data visit multiples servers to conduct steps of a computation, a malicious server can modify the state of the code or the data it carries before the code moves To Whom It May Concern: the next server. For example, a malicious airline server may raise the lowest airfare a mobile airfare agent code has computed from all prior visited airlines to cheat the client.

As in data authentication, checksums and digital signatures once again constitute the set of basic tools for application code authentication. Prior to transmission, the code owner can sign the code with its digital certificates. Upon receipt, the recipient can verify the signature and decide whether the origin and integrity of the code can be trusted. If the code is verified, the recipient then has to determine the execution permissions for the code. Although checksums and digital signatures can be used to identify the owner and recipient of the code, if these entities are themselves not trusted, we need additional mechanisms to verify the application code and the execution results. To prove that an application does not contain any malicious code as to damage internal data structure of the host, or overuse resources of the host, the application owner can provide an encoding of a proof that the code complies with the security policy of the recipient. Application code augmented as is called a *proof-carrying code*. To prove that the application is executed properly, on the other hand, the owner can benefit from *replicated execution* or *execution traces*. In a multi-agent system where there are multiple agents interacting, in order to prove that an agent is secure for interactions (i.e., the agent will not access services or data that it is not entitled to), the service provider can utilize agent's current state, records of previous interactions with other agents, and the analysis of possible consequences of the interaction. Next, we discuss proof carrying codes, replicated execution approaches, execution traces, and secure agent interactions individually.

Proof-Carrying Codes

Proof-carrying code protocol (Necula & Lee, 1998), for proving that an application does not contain any malicious code, consists of two phases:

i)   The recipient of the code extracts from the untrusted application code safety predicates that can be proved if and only if the code conforms to the security policy defined by the recipient. Generally, a security policy defines (1) the language in which the application should be written, (2) the conditions under which the application can be trusted, (3) the interface between the recipient and the application code, and (4) the methods for inspecting application code and discovering potential security violations. The safety predicate is constructed by inspecting the instructions of the application to find ones that may violate the security policy and generating for each such instruction a predicate that proves the safe execution of the instruction. The recipient sends the safety predicates to a proof producer (such as the application owner) and the proof producer returns the proof back to the recipient.

ii) The recipient, then, checks the proof via a proof checker. If the recipient verifies the correctness of the proof, it can safely install and execute the application. This protocol is general and the recipient does not have to trust any party (either the owner or the proof producer). However, the proof size can be very large: it usually grows linearly with the size of the application code, but it can grow exponentially in worst cases.

Replication

One way to ensure the correct execution of the application code is via server (or recipient) replication and voting (Minsky et al., 1996). In this protocol, the execution of the code is divided into stages and each stage is executed at multiple servers:

i) The owner dispatches the stage one execution to multiple server replicas. Every replica sends the stage one output to all replicas of stage two.

ii) In the following stages, each replica chooses its input to be the majority of the outputs received from the previous stage. It then conducts its computation and sends the output to all replicas of the next stage. At the last stage, the replicas send their outputs back to the client.

iii) Finally, the client determines the output to be the majority of the outputs it received from the replicas corresponding to the last stage of the execution.

In addition to the high network and computation bandwidth requirements, this protocol fails if the majority of the servers at a certain stage are malicious or compromised. To prevent a third-party server from spoofing as one of the replicas, this protocol can be extended with authentication schemes to verify each replica.

Yee (1997) proposes a code replication scheme in which a copy of the code is executed by visiting the sequence of servers in the reverse order of stages. This scheme is capable of detecting certain types of tampering with the results. For example, given a mobile agent code that searches the lowest airfare by visiting airline servers in a particular order, one copy of the agent can travel the same servers in the reverse order. In this case, any inconsistency between two results implies tampering. This protocol is simple and introduces low overhead (only a copy of the original execution required). However, it is effective only when the order in which the servers are visited does not make any difference in the final result.

Cryptographic Traces

Verifying the execution trace of an application on a given server is another way to authenticate results (Vigna, 1998). An execution trace for an application on a given server records the statements executed by the server and the values of the data obtained. The traces are protected via the server's certified digital signature; hence the server cannot disown the trace. By retrieving the traces from suspected servers and using them to simulate the overall execution, the client can identify any tampering.

One main disadvantage of this protocol is that it is a post-execution method and cannot offer timely authentication. Another disadvantage is that it does not provide any mechanism to detect tampering a priori, so the client does not have any indication regarding when to ask for traces from a server.

Secure Agent Interactions

Bonatti et al. (2003) present a framework intended for multi-agent environments with authenticated the secure interaction between agents. The system keeps track of all agents' (1) histories, actions they performed, and messages they exchanged; (2) states that contain their current knowledge about the system; and (3) consequence operations, which describe what knowledge an agent can derive from its state and its reasoning capability. A secret is specified by the service provider agent in terms of actions and data forbidden to be accessed. Based on these, secure interaction in a multi-agent system is defined in terms of secure histories that do not leak any information via messages that are exchanged and consequences that do not violate any secrets. Maintaining correct and accurate information about an agent's state and consequence is almost impossible in practice. Hence, Bonatti et al. (2003) suggest using approximate information and proposes a rule-based logic language with which an agent can specify how to approximate the available information about other agents.

AUTHORIZATION

Even when identities of the parties in a DAHS environment have been verified through authentication, there is still possibility of other forms of attacks by malicious entities. For instance, available resources should be protected and the access should be restricted, otherwise untrusted users may break down the system purposefully or even trusted users may, without any malicious intention, cause damage to the system by improper operations. Therefore, proper access control mechanisms that can ensure that the operations that an authenticated user (or an application program on behalf of the user) can invoke on a server lie within the limits of server's security policies are essential.

Security Policies

Security policies specify what actions are allowed and what are not allowed. A policy has three dimensions: subjects, objects, and access types. Subjects are users or programs that work on behalf of the users. Objects represent resources to be protected from subjects. Access types include actions, such as read or update that subjects can execute on objects. There are various security policy models (Sandhu & Samarati, 1994). In this section, we briefly discuss discretionary, mandatory, and role based policies.

Discretionary Policies

A set of authorization rules defines the access mode for each subject and object pair. Every access is checked against this set of authorization rules. This model is simple and good for cooperative but independent environments, however, it cannot restrict what subjects will do with the information after they fetch it from the servers.

Mandatory Policies

In this model, each subject and object is assigned a security level. For example, the security level of an object may reflect the sensitivity of the information associated with the object to unauthorized disclosure. The security level of a subject is called clearance and it may reflect the trustworthiness of the subject. Access is granted only if the security levels of the target object and the subject satisfy certain relationship. Generally, to read an object, the clearance level of the subject should be higher than or equal to the security level of the object; whereas, to write an object, the object being written must have equal or higher security level than the subject (Sandhu & Samarati, 1994). In this way, the information flow is guided in a way to prevent sensitive information flowing to lower level objects. This model fits well with stricter, such as military, environments.

Role Based Policies

This model mediates subjects' access to objects according to subjects' activities (or roles). The model identifies all roles in the system and, with each role, it associates a set of operations and responsibilities. Access authorizations for objects are defined in terms of roles. Subjects are given permissions to play roles. A subject playing one role is granted all operations that are authorized for that particular role. Role based model is flexible. It does not assign access rights to subjects directly, but indirectly through roles. Hence, it avoids the cumbersome task of assigning and re-assigning access rights as the system evolves. This model is also space saving, as redundant specification of access rights assigned to users playing the same role is diminished.

Data Authorization

In a DAHS environment, the sensitive information contained in each data source, managed on the behalf of the data owners, must be protected from unauthorized user accesses. Especially in a data grid, the underlying system should provide authorization mechanisms for the databases that are being federated. Considering XML's role in distributed data and information exchange, special attention should be given to how the structure of XML data affects authorization.

Authorizing Federated and Mediated Databases

DAHSs and data grids usually host applications that integrate heterogeneous packages (including application software and associated databases) outsourced from origins with different security policies.

Therefore, they need to enforce global security policies while respecting the local security policies of each individual data source. Different security models have been developed for federated and mediated databases. Idris et al. (1994) introduce a security model for federated systems where security levels may continuously change. Jonscher & Dittrich (1994) propose a decentralized authorization security model for tightly controlled federated databases. Blaustein et al. (1995) propose a security model that relies on bilateral agreements between data sources to identify how each party protects others' data. Wiederhold (1992; 1993) introduces a centralized model, based on mediators, which integrate heterogeneous databases with different security policies. Candan et al. (1996) introduce two co-operation principles that may be implemented by a mediated system:

- ***Cautious cooperation:*** If a user's query only needs to access information that the user is entitled to, the mediator will answer the query unless the global security policy directly forbids so, while each participating database's security policy is always respected.

- ***Conservative cautious cooperation:*** If a user's query only needs to access information that the user is entitled to, the mediator will answer the query unless from such query the user can infer information he or she is not allowed to access by global security policies, while each participating database's security policy is always respected.

Based on a rule-based mediator model that consists of a mediator M, a set of data sources $\{d_1, d_2, ..., d_n\}$ integrated by M, a global security policy G, and a set, V, of local security policies, Candan et al. (1996) further propose a formal approach for secure mediated databases. Global security constraints in G are modeled as:

- a set of facts of the form *secret*(A,i), denoting users with security level i has no access right to the information (atom) A and
- a set of rules of the form *secret*(A,i) ←

secret$(A,j) \land i < j$, enforcing that if A can not be accessed by certain security level, it can not be accessed by lower levels either.

Local security constraints, V, on the other hand, are modeled as:

- boolean functions of the form $viol_d(d: f(<argument>))$, which identify whether executing function f with specified arguments on date source d for users of security level i violates d's local security policy or not.

In order to prevent a malicious user from inferring unauthorized information through knowledge about the implemented security policy, Candan et al. (1996) adopt query transformation methods to ensure that the query simply fails (without raising violation alerts) if it violates any local security constraints.

Participating databases may have different security orderings; for example, the classification labels of security levels in different databases may be different or security levels with the same label may have different security orderings in different databases. To integrate such heterogeneous databases, there is a need for mechanisms to merge heterogeneous security orderings in a way that each individual security ordering is preserved and the constraints between security orderings of different databases are satisfied, while a maximal level of global security is maintained when there are conflicts. Bonatti et al. (1996) give a formal definition of this problem and propose two solutions: rule-based and graph-based approaches. The rule-based approach represents the semantics of security orderings and inter-database constraints using logic rules, while the graph-based approach represents them using a graph. Both methods can find a combined security ordering, for a given non-conflicting set of individual orderings, in polynomial time.

Authorization of XML Data

As discussed in Section Security Challenges and Security Mechanisms in Distributed Application Hosting Services, XML security is an essential part of web-based information architectures. Therefore, developing access control mechanisms that understands the structure and properties of data in XML form to enforce selective dissemination of information over the web is essential for DAHSs. According to Bertino et al. (2001), an XML access control mechanism should at least:

- consider XML's rich, hierarchical structure and provide fine-grained authorization to components of a given XML data;
- provide both DTD-level and data-level authorization. DTD-level authorization applies to a set of data objects conforming to the same DTD, while data-level authorization applies to one particular document or its components;
- handle authorization to XML objects that are not conforming or partially conforming to a particular DTD;
- devise proper authorization propagation rules that refer to hierarchical relationships (such as DTD-data, element-subelement, element-attribute, and element-link) to propagate authorization policies of higher level components to lower level components. These rules should also provide mechanisms to solve propagation conflicts when a component has multiple inconsistent authorizations propagated from higher levels.

Due the rich structure of XML, a standard authorization mechanism for XML data remains an open challenge. Author-X (Bertino et al., 2001) is a tool that provides access control to XML data. Author-X satisfies the minimal requirements mentioned above. It adopts the discretionary access control model; the policies have the following format: $<U, O, P, R, S>$. U denotes a user or a group of users to whom the authorization applies. O describes the object (DTD, XML data, or portions of them) to be protected. P denotes the access privilege (browsing or authoring) to be permitted or restricted. R provides the propagation rules (cascade the authorization to all descendants, limit the propagation to first-level descendants, or no-propogation). Finally, S denotes whether this is positive or negative authorization. Using negative authentication, a security manager can efficiently define authentications with exceptions (e.g., defining an authorization applying to a whole document except for some few elements).

Author-X defines the following conflict-resolution rules: (1) explicit authorizations override propagated ones; (2) if there are multiple propagated authorizations, the most specific one (lowest level in the hierarchy overrides the others; (3) if there are conflicts due to propagated rules at the same level, the negative authorizations override.

The process of authorization in Author-X is as follows: For the target XML data object, Author-X

- finds the associated DTD. If the XML document does not have an associated DTD, Author-X finds the DTD that the target document mostly conforms to (hence it handles the partially conforming documents);
- propagates all possible DTD-level and document-level authorizations and resolves all conflicts;
- prunes from the document all elements that do not have required positive authorizations (explicit or implicit); and
- evaluates the user query against the pruned document and extracts the target data.

The IBM alphaWorks XML Security Suite (XML Security Suite, 1999) is another tool that provides access control mechanism for XML documents. It shares some common features with Author-X: authorization propagation based on structure hierarchy and conflicting authorization resolution, implementation of an XML-based language (XACL) for specifying security policies, and fine grained authorization. On the other hand, unlike Author-X, IBM alphaWorks utilizes role-based access control, which is more suitable for e-commerce environments. It also accommodates context and provisional actions into the access control model. Hence the extended authorization policy can specify whether a given subject, under certain context (access request time or some other conditions), is allowed to access the given protection object in a given way or not. It can also specify provisional actions (such as logging the access decisions, encrypting specified elements, verifying signatures, reading, writing, or deleting specified elements) that have to be performed whether the access is granted or not. With this extended semantics, XML Security Suite integrates authorization and non-repudiation mechanisms for accessing XML documents and data objects; i.e., a subject cannot deny that it made an access attempt. IBM alphaWorks has two propagation directions, up and down, and when there are conflicting propagations, it arbitrarily selects one. This differs from the most specific based conflict resolution of Author-X.

Cho et al. (2002) propose a simple mandatory XML data security model in which XML elements may have associated security levels or inherit them from their parents. A user is allowed to access only those elements whose security levels are no more than her clearance level. To minimize the cost of checking security levels, for each query, the system rewrites a given XML query by identifying the appropriate amount of checking. Cho et al. (2002) achieve an optimal rewriting of the query. In general, checking whether or not a user has access right to a particular object from a given set of access control rules can be inefficient. Maintaining an explicit accessibility map that lists all users that can access a given object, on the other hand, is space-inefficient. Yu et al. (2002) introduce compressed accessibility maps to efficiently enforce authorization policies over XML data. The compression is achieved by taking advantages of the feature that XML data items grouped together have similar accessibility properties.

Open networks like the Internet are inherently insecure despite authentication and authorization schemes. Sensitive data or application code may be leaked to or compromised by attackers eavesdropping on the communication link between clients and hosts or disclosed to malicious hosts. The business logic or query results may be altered to cheat clients.

In the Section CONFIDENTIALITY, we discuss underlying confidentiality issues and related technologies.

Application Authorization

Karnik (1998) summarizes several ways to authorize accesses to server resources by outsourced application programs in mobile agent-based systems. Similar approaches can also be implemented for application authorization in DAHSs:

- **Direct reference approach:** The server supplies the mobile agent with reference to the resource and screens all accesses via a security manager. The security manager checks against the security policies to see if each application method (or procedure) under execution is allowed to access the associated resources.

- **Proxy approach:** The server builds a specific resource proxy when a mobile agent asks for some resource. The proxy provides a safe interface to the resource. This safe interface looks the same as the original interface, but certain methods are disabled to prevent the agent from accessing the resource via methods that the security policy does not permit.

- **Capabilities approach:** This mechanism has been adopted in several distributed systems.

Every agent, before accessing a resource, presents a credential containing its access rights to the server. Only after the server grants its approval can the agent access the resource. The credential is issued to the agent after its identity has been authenticated.

- **Wrapper approach:** The resource is encapsulated with a wrapper and agents have references only to this wrapper. The wrapper maintains access control lists and decides whether an agent has the authority to access the resource or not.

- **Protection domain approach:** There are two execution environments: one safe environment to host the agents and one trusted environment to provide access to the resource. The safe environment processes each potentially unsafe request of an agent according to its own security policy and screens unsafe requests. For safe requests, it calls methods of the trusted environment that provides access to the resource. The trusted environment can only be called by methods within this safe environment.

The proxy and capabilities approaches are flexible: an instance of a proxy or a capability can be generated dynamically and specifically to satisfy each application or agent code. The dynamicity of the capabilities approach, on the other hand, introduces various challenges: an application may propagate its capability to others or, if security policies change, capabilities may need to be revoked. The wrapper approach is simple and more static: there is only one wrapper for each resource object and all applications share the same wrapper for that resource.

CONFIDENTIALITY

Confidentiality (or privacy) means that private information of DAHS customers (including outsourced application code and data) is not leaked to or modified by any party. The degree of confidentiality of security schemes can be categorized into the following two classes:

- *Information theoretic privacy:* These schemes are built without any cryptographic assumptions and, hence, cannot be broken even with unlimited computation power.
- *Computational privacy:* These schemes are built on various cryptographic assumptions, usually about certain hard-to-compute problems. In these schemes, the goal is to ensure that there are no efficient computations (conducted by a randomized algorithm bounded by a polynomial time in the length of inputs) that can break the scheme. Cryptographic assumptions used by computational privacy schemes are based on one-way functions that are easy to compute but hard to inverse. The most popular one-way functions, such as integer factorization, Φ-assumption, and quadratic residuosity problem, come from number theory (Goldreich, 1997).

Encryption schemes are the basic tools to achieve confidentiality. Besides the common data encryption methods that hide sensitive data, there have been some techniques for hiding other kinds of secret information from untrusted servers:

- Information hiding hides not only the communication content, but also the existence of communication between two parties, so that no suspicion arises that a secret communication exists.
- Computation hiding prevents host sites from gaining unauthorized information about the content of the published code, the data it executes on, or the outputs produced as a result of the computation.
- Private information retrieval aims to let users query a database without leaking to the database what data is queried.

In this section, we report on the state-of-the-art techniques for hiding applications, data, data distribution, and user's query from application and database servers. In Subsection Computation Hiding, we focus on how to keep data or application confidential from untrusted hosts and we describe solutions to the problem of computing encrypted functions with encrypted data. In Subsection Private Information Retrieval, we give a general introduction to private information retrieval and in Subsection Private Informational Retrieval in XML Databases we specifically focus on private information retrieval in XML databases.

Information Hiding

Cryptography deals with concealing the content of information. Information hiding, on the other hand, seeks to hide the existence of information. For some highly sensitive applications, such as military or intelligence agencies, even the existence of communication arouses suspicion. Hence to provide information hiding services, a DAHS should be able to hide the communication traffic itself, which cannot be achieved with ordinary cryptography.

Information hiding technologies include spread spectrum radio, which is used to hide wireless transmission; temporary mobile subscribers, which are used in digital phones to hide a given user's location; and digital watermarks, which are used to imperceptibly insert copyright information in digital images, video, and audio. As they are not heavily used in DAHSs and data grids, in this chapter, we will not discuss information hiding techniques in detail.

Computation Hiding

In distributed computation environments, such as DAHSs, input data owners, application owners, and computation providers (servers) may be different parties distributed over networks. Computation hiding involves hiding secret data, propriety code, or secret outputs during a distributed computation.

Secure Distributed Computing

Secure distributed computing is also called fault-tolerant distributed computing or oblivious circuit evaluation. The basic underlying mechanism aims evaluating a function (or a circuit) to which each party has one secret input, so that the output becomes commonly known to all parties but all inputs remain secret. If there is a trusted agent, secure distributed computing is a trivial problem: each party can securely send its private input with the help of cryptographic protocols; the agent computes the function and then distributes the result. Secure distributed computation intends to solve the problem without the assumption of any trusted agent, i.e., to simulate a trusted agent over a set of mutually untrusted parties. Secure distributed computing protocols are built on various basic protocols:

- *Bit commitment:* A bit commitment protocol simulates the function a sealed opaque envelope used for committing a bit of information: once the bit is sealed and committed by the committer, the content of the bit can not be changed (the envelope is closed and sealed); the receiver, upon receiving the sealed bit, cannot read it until the content is revealed by the committer (the envelope is opened and letter now can be read). Bit commitment schemes can be built on one-way functions (Naor, 1989). In secure distributed computing, bit commitment schemes are utilized to enable a party to commit to some information.

- *Oblivious transfer:* Oblivious transfer is a protocol to transfer a bit among the involved parties in a way that the information held by the sender and the receiver about the transfer is asymmetric. A simple version of the oblivious transfer protocol resembles an undependable post service: *A* wants to send a bit *b* to *B*. Let us assume that the bit is successfully transferred to *B* with a probability of 0.5. *A* does not know whether the bit is successfully transferred or not but *B* always knows the result of transfer; hence the overall information transfer is asymmetric. The importance of oblivious transfer is that it is a basic protocol from which more complicated secure distributed computing protocols can be built and to which all secure distributed computing protocols can be reduced (Kilian, 1988).

- *Zero-knowledge proofs:* An interactive proof system is a two-party protocol in which a prover owns a secret and wants to convince a verifier that it really has the secret through interaction with the verifier. An interactive proof system is computationally zero-knowledge if from the interaction a computationally bounded verifier knows nothing about the secret except the validity of the proof. Every language in NP has a computationally zero-knowledge proof system if a one-way function exists (Goldreich, 1997). This fact is very useful in constructing multi-party secure distributed computing protocols that can tolerate active attackers.

- *Secret sharing protocol:* A secret sharing protocol, with threshold *t*, enables a dealer to distribute a secret among several players such that each player has an individual share of the secret (called a *t*-share) and coalition of any group of maximum *t* players cannot reconstruct the secret from their shares. A verifiable secret sharing scheme is a scheme that, despite the cheating of a dishonest dealer and some of the players, honest players can still receive valid shares and identify when the dealer cheats. The general idea is to let the dealer distribute primary shares of the secret to all players and each player distributes subshares (called secondary shares) of its primary share to all other players. Inconsistency of primary share and secondary shares of any player would invoke a challenge-response process and all challenge-response reduce to a conclusion whether the dealer is repudiated (more than a certain number of players accuse it of cheating) or upheld (less than a certain number of players accuse it of cheating). Verifiable secret sharing schemes are fundamental in constructing fault-tolerant secure computation protocols.

- ***Byzantine agreement:*** In the Byzantine agreement problem, each party has an initial bit and wants to find if initial bits held by all parties have the same value. The challenge is to ensure that even when there are parties who are dishonest and act as if they have different initial values, all non-faulty parties are able to draw correct conclusions for their initial values. This challenge can be solved if no more than one-third of the parties are faulty (Lamport et al., 1982). Because of the fault-tolerance it provides, Byzantine agreement protocols are employed as backbones to construct sophisticated fault-tolerant secure computing schemes (Bazzi & Neiger, 1991).

Secure distributed computing protocols may involve only two parties (two-party secure computing) or more (multi-party secure computing). Most two-party secure computing protocols are built on cryptographic assumptions, such as oblivious transfer, and are based on one of the following two techniques (Franklin et al., 1992): In the first approach, one party scrambles the code and its secret input; after scrambling, this party interacts with the second party to transfer the scrambled code and input; the second party then evaluates the scrambled code with the scrambled input values and sends the output to the first party. In the second one, the two parties interact for every logical component of the code in a secure and interactive fashion.

In multiparty secure computing, much attention has been given on fault tolerance, i.e., resilience against active attacks. An active attacker can cause some of the parties to behave against the protocol. Most multiparty secure computing protocols follow three stages. In the input sharing stage, each party distributes shares of its private input to other parties, in the computation stage each party performs the required computation on shares of private inputs and generates the shares of the ultimate result, and, finally, in the output reconstruction stage shares of the final result are combined by individual parties to recover the result. Zero-knowledge proofs and verifiable secret sharing are essential tools for multiparty secure computing. Zero-knowledge proofs enable the misconduct of any party to be detected. Verifiable secret sharing (which enables each party to verifiably share its secret input with all other parties) guarantees that, if a party is caught cheating, the remaining honest parties can reconstruct its private input and simulate messages it would have sent in the later stages of the protocol. Collectively, these two protocols prevent honest parties involved in a multiparty secure computing from suffering.

Secure computing protocols that can withstand passive attackers are called private secure computing protocols. Secure computing protocols that can withstand active attackers are called resilient secure computing protocols. Two-party secure computing protocols are generally private protocols, as some basic fault-tolerance techniques, such as Byzantine agreement and verifiable secret sharing, used for handling active attacks and requires more than two parties' engagements (Franklin et al., 1992).

Instance Hiding

Instance hiding deals with the problem of computing with encrypted data; therefore, it can be regarded as a special case of secure distributed computing. In instance hiding, there is a weak party (e.g., a DAHS client) who has some secret input and wants to compute a function that requires a large amount of computation resources, with the help of strong parties (e.g., DAHS servers): the weak party sends each strong party its encrypted data, and from the partial results computed by the strong parties it reconstructs the actual output with minimal effort. Instance hiding is especially required in DAHSs, where a computation center enables weak, private computing devices, such as mobile terminals, compute hard problems.

Like many cryptography techniques, most instance hiding schemes are built on hard number theory problems, such as primitive root, quadratic residuosity, and discrete logarithm problems (Abadi et al., 1987).

Not all functions have information theoretic one-server (or one-oracle) instance hiding schemes. For instance, Abadi et al. (1987) prove that no NP-Hard problem has such a scheme. This result is also consistent with the related results that "there exists no information theoretic two-party secure distributed computing protocols for some functions" and that "there exists no information theoretic one-server private information hiding scheme (Subsection Private Information Retrieval) without sending the whole database."

It has been proven, on the other hand, that for any function, even for NP-Hard functions, there always exists information theoretic multi-server (multi-oracle) instance hiding schemes, as long as servers are forbidden from communicating with each other.

Function Hiding

Function hiding deals with the problem of computing with an encrypted function. Function hiding has crucial DAHS applications: the owner of a secret algorithm can make its code available at a DAHS server in a way that the algorithm of the program and its execution are prevented from disclosure despite intensive code analysis and reverse engineering. In this subsection, we describe various techniques for function hiding:

- *Matrix modification method:* This method is specifically for hiding polynomial functions that have matrix representations. Hiding is achieved by modifying the function matrix in a randomized way such that the real output can be decrypted from the randomized output. Typical examples include Error Correcting Codes (ECCs) modification and similarity transform modification.

ECCs modification technique uses an ECC based cryptosystem, such as McEliece public key cryptosystem (Loureiro & Molva, 1999), to hide matrix of polynomial functions. ECC-based security relies on the difficulty of decoding a large linear code with no visible structure.

Similarity transform modification technique transforms a function matrix, F, into its similarity matrix KFK^{-1} and the input x into Kx, where K is a random invertible matrix serving as the secret key. With similarity transform modification technique, the owner can hide a function with a loop structure within which there is a polynomial calculation. The security of this approach relies on the difficulty of finding the secret key (Badin et al., 2003).

- *Decomposition method:* This method hides polynomial functions. By asking the server to evaluate all possible terms of a given polynomial, the client can locally construct the result by selecting and merging the relevant components. This way, the server can not learn the polynomial.
- *Homomorphism encryption:* This method uses a homomorphism encryption function E such that, it is possible to compute $E(x+y)$ directly from $E(x)$ and $E(y)$ (Sander & Tschudin, 1998).
- *Redundant computation:* This method uses dummy computation and dummy data to hide the real computation and real data.

In general, the types of functions that can be protected via function hiding are very limited, for it is very hard to find encryption schemes for general functions such that the encrypted functions remain executable. Up to now, most function hiding protocols are restricted to hiding polynomial functions.

Note that instance hiding and function hiding are closely related. Theoretically, instance hiding and function hiding problems are equivalent. In some instance hiding schemes, in order to compute with encrypted data, the function is also scrambled in a matching way. If the scrambling hides the original function, function hiding is achieved at the same time. Similarity transform modification technique mentioned above is a good example to this type of hiding. Such symmetric hiding schemes have very important applications in DAHSs: to hide both the private data and code from remote hostile executing environments the owner can publish secret algorithms on untrusted servers and let those servers provide computation service with the privacy of secret input data also preserved.

A more practical and hence more promising way to protect code and data from leakage and tempering is to provide a certified safe executing environment to the secret code (Smith et al., 1999). Such safe executing environments cannot be inspected or tampered with and, hence, are called temper proof environments (TPEs). A TPE is provided and certified by a trusted manufacturer (TM). The security of TPE cryptographic protocol relies on the trust between the code owner and the trusted manufacturer as well as the security of TPE. To alleviate these requirements, some independent authority can periodically verify and certify the TPE. The TPE is generally a temperproof hardware; hence, its private keys cannot be leaked without actually destroying it. IBM has a product called "secure co-processor" that can serve as a TPE (Dyer et al., 2001). When it is turned on, the secure co-processor generates public/private key pairs and outputs the public

key that can be used for encrypting the code and the data. Since the host does not know the private key to decrypt the code or the data, the only thing it can do is to upload the hidden messages to the TPE, which internally decrypts the code and data before execution.

Private Information Retrieval

Private Information Retrieval (PIR) is a family of encryption protocols seeking to protect users' private queries from malicious data hosts. This is a relatively new research area in database security. Traditional database security mainly deals with preventing, detecting, and deterring improper disclosure or modification of information in databases. When the database services are made available through third party hosts that cannot be fully trusted, users' queries may be improperly utilized to achieve certain malicious goals. For example, users may not trust their queries being executed on a third party stock database server. Through PIR, users can query the untrusted data source while protecting the confidentiality of their queries and the answers.

The basic idea behind any information theoretic PIR scheme is to replicate the database to several non-communicating servers and ask from each copy of the database a subset of the data that is independent of the target data in a way that the user can reconstruct the target data from query results. Chor et al. (1995) show that PIR can be translated into an oblivious transfer problem and that, if one copy of database is used, the only way to hide the query in the information theoretic sense is to send the whole database to the user. In order to reduce even one bit in communication between the server and the user, replication of the whole database is required.

In PIR schemes, communication is the major cost; hence, in order to achieve practical use, it is crucial to reduce the communication cost as well as the number of replicas required. The best-known k-server scheme requires $O(n^{2k-1})$ communication (Chor et al., 1995) (where is the database size). However, to achieve communication to a subpolynomial in the size of the database, more than a constant number of servers are needed (Chor et al., 1995).

In DAHSs, replication is not a preferable solution to reduce communications in PIR. It is very likely that database owners are reluctant to replicate databases to other servers that they can not keep in contact. Moreover, it may not be possible to prevent third party servers from communicating with each other. In computationally private PIR schemes, therefore, the user privacy requirement is relaxed so that what the servers can see with respect to any two retrieval indexes are indistinguishable for any polynomial time server. PIR schemes built on cryptographic assumptions can further reduce the communication and the number of replicas. If a one-way function exists, then there is a two-server scheme, such that the communication is f for any $\varepsilon > 0$ (Chor et al., 1997). Under the quadratic residuosity assumption, a one-server scheme can be constructed with sub-polynomial communication (Kushilevitz & Ostrovsky, 1997). Under the Φ-hiding assumption, a one-server scheme with a poly-logarithmic communication is possible (Beimel et al., 1999).

Private Informational Retrieval in XML Databases

As discussed earlier, XML has an inherent tree-like structure. Queries over trees are generally expressed in the form of tree path descriptions. XQuery, the standard for XML query language proposed by W3C, is a typical example. Its core is Xpath, the W3C standard for addressing parts of an XML document by describing path patterns.

XML documents can be queried in a navigational manner, i.e., traversing documents along paths described by these patterns and performing join operations on the resulting paths when necessary. However, navigation is often inefficient. Using index mechanisms on the XML structures (i.e., path information) or element values and traversing index trees instead of traversing XML document can reduce query processing time.

On the other hand, if the tree (XML tree or index tree) is traversed in plain to identify the matching paths, the query as well as the result is revealed to the server. Thus hiding the traversal of the tree is necessary for hiding data and queries from untrusted XML servers.

Lin and Candan (2003) propose a protocol to hide tree traversal paths. This protocol allows clients to outsource their sensitive data on servers without any prior trust. In this protocol, tree

Figure 7: The intersection property and the movement of the target node

Big circles represent retrieval of a redundancy sets. Small circles denote the target nodes.

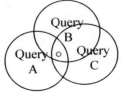

(a) Repeated accesses for a node reveal its location due to intersection

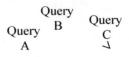

(b) Movement of the node reduces information leakage by intersection.

nodes are encrypted before being outsourced; hence, their contents (if the nodes are XML elements, also the element types) are hidden from the untrusted data store. Furthermore, to hide the XML tree structure, each time a user wants to retrieve a node, he or she asks for a set of nodes called the redundancy set including the target node and additional random nodes. The redundancy set hides the requested node from the server. However, repeated accesses for a particular node can reveal its location, since the node is always within the intersection of the redundant sets of these queries. *Figure 7(a)* demonstrates this situation. To prevent the server from inferring the locations of the nodes based on repeated node accesses, after each node is retrieved, the node is swapped with a randomly chosen empty node. Thus the node moves with respect to each retrieval, making any correct guessing of its location temporary and of no permanent use. *Figure 7(b)* depicts the movement of target node. In this figure, there are three consecutive queries A, B, C all of which wants to retrieve the same node. As shown in the figure, the protocol moves the location of the target node after each retrieval. It does so without violating the XML tree structure.

For a reasonable security level, the size of the redundancy set need not be large to hide long paths. If the size of the redundancy set is m, then the probability of finding the target node from a given set is $<U, O, P, R, S>$, the probability of finding the parent-child relationships in a tree is $1/m^2$, and the probability of finding a given path from root to a leaf is $1/m^{path\ length}$. Hence this protocol is sufficient to hide tree-structured data and queries from any polynomial computation-bounded servers. To enable multiple users to query a tree simultaneously, which is mandatory for an open and public data store, we also devised deadlock free concurrency control mechanisms (Lin & Candan, 2003). Unlike the information theoretic private information retrieval schemes, the proposed technique requires no replication of the database and the communication cost is $O(m$

$\times$ *tree depth*) which is adaptable and generally much less than the size of the database. Compared with general computationally private information retrieval schemes, the proposed technique is much simpler and does not rely on any cryptographic assumptions except for the ones on which the underlying encryption schemes are built.

A detailed study of the security guarantees provided by this protocol requires proper modeling of the user queries as well as the interaction between clients and the server. A request for a redundancy set constitutes a call. Each query path retrieval then can be represented as an ordered set of calls. If there are multiple users accessing the system, calls of concurrent queries can be intermixed. Supposing that there is a transport layer security mechanism that hides the identity of owner of each call, we can model DAHS server's view of data accesses as a stream of calls from unknown origins. The server might still be able to infer the tree structure by (a) observing the call stream it receives, (b) guessing which calls in the stream belong to the a single query, (c) guessing which queries it observes are identical or similar, and then (d) looking at the intersection of the redundancy sets of the corresponding calls in each identical query. That is, the server can analyze the calls and intersections of their redundant sets to learn about the tree structure.

Figure 8 depicts a possible attack. This figure shows the hypothetical case where a query is posed twice consecutively; i.e., without interference from any other queries. In this case, the corresponding calls (e.g., A2 and B2) of the two queries intersect. Hence the query path (depicted by bold black line) is revealed.

In order to measure the degree of security that can be provided by the private information retrieval system, it is necessary to understand the probabilities with which the server can use correlations between queries to break the information retrieval security. The server can use the following analyses to attack the system:

Figure 8: Consecutive queries for the same data reveal the path

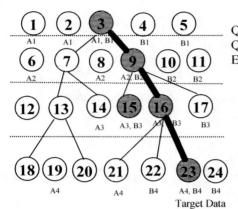

Query A consists of calls A1, A2, A3, A4,
Query B consists of calls B1, B2, B3, B4.
Each call retrieves a set of nodes:

A1{1,2,3},
A2{6,8,9},
A3{14,15,16},
A4{19,21,23},
B1{3,4,5},
B2{9,10,11},
B3{15,16,17},
B4{22,23,24}.

Note that A_i intersects B_i

- Given two sequences of calls, the server can try to calculate the likelihood of these two sequences containing identical (or similar) queries.
- Given two sequences of calls that are known to contain two identical queries, the server can try to identify the individual calls of them.
- Given the calls of two identical queries, the server can try to discover the query path.

These attacks by the server would rely on the intersection property mentioned above. Intuitively, such an attack by the server can be prevented by ensuring that intersections do not reveal much information. This is achieved by modifying the client/server protocols such that the redundant sets intersect at multiple nodes as well as by inserting appropriate dummy/interfering calls. As shown in *Figure 9*, these methods destroy the relationship between queries and intersecting calls, preventing attackers from exploiting the intersection property.

In *Figure 9*, each axis tracks the time when calls are posed. An arrow from one call to another represents intersection between them. *Figure 9(a)* shows that, when there are no interfering calls, the intersection property can be used by a mali-

cious server to identify the existence of identical queries in a given sequence of calls. In addition, if the sizes of the intersections are small, the server can also learn the actual data nodes. *Figure 9(b)*, on the other hand, shows how by adding dummy calls (D1, ... D4) and by increasing the sizes of the intersections, one can limit the information the server can learn studying the intersection of redundant sets. Intuitively, each D_i call adds ambiguity and reduces the probability with which the server can identify the calls that correspond to identical queries. Note that in order to provide efficient and provable security, the process of introducing dummy calls have to follow a strategy that randomizes the intersections with minimal overhead.

This private information retrieval scheme requires legal clients to have access to encryption/decryption keys and be able to perform encryption and decryption operations. Where encryption and decryption constitute heavy computation costs for clients with very limited computation power and memory, we suggest the use of assistant hardware, such as smart cards, to reduce the encryption/decryption execution costs as well as to securely disseminate keys.

Figure 9: Increased size of intersection and dummy/interfering calls reduce information leaked through the intersection of redundant sets

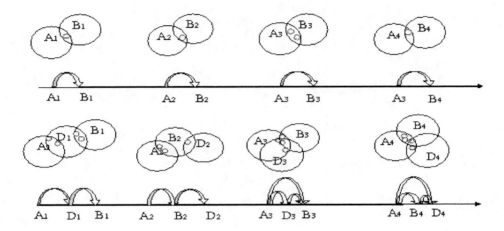

CONCLUSION

In this chapter, we provided an overview of the security mechanisms and tools for Distributed Application Host Services (DAHSs) that rent out Internet presence, computation power, and data storage space to clients with infrastructural needs. ASPs and DAHSs operate within the complex, multi-tiered, and open Internet environment and, hence, they introduce many security challenges that have to be addressed effectively. In this chapter, we discussed security challenges in DAHS from three main aspects: authentication, authorization, and confidentiality. For each aspect, we surveyed current techniques and tools to address these security challenges and discussed open research challenges.

REFERENCES

Abadi, M., Feigenbaum, J., & Kilian, J. (1987). On hiding information from an oracle. In Proceedings of the 19th ACM Symposium on Theory of Computing (pp. 195-203).

Atkinson, B., Della-Libera, G., & Hada, S., et al. (2002). Specification: Web Service Security (WS-Security), version1.0.05. Retrieved September 15, 2003, from the World Wide Web: http://www-106. ibm.com/developerworks/library/ws-secure/.

Badin, R., Bazzi, R. A., Candan, K. S., & Fajri, A. (2003). Provably secure data hiding and tamper resistance for a simple loop program. *Proceedings of 2003 AeroSense Technologies and Systems for Defense and Security*, (pp. 21-25).

Bazzi, R.A., & Neiger, G. (1991). Optimally simulating crash failures in a Byzantine environment. In Proceedings of the Fifth International Workshop on Distributed Algorithms (pp. 108-128).

Beimel, A., Ishai, Y., Kushilevitz, E., & Marlkin, T. (1999). One way functions are essential for single-server private information retrieval. In Proceedings of the 31st Annual ACM Symposium on Theory of Computing (pp. 89-98).

Bertino, E., Castano, S., & Ferrari, E. (2001). Securing XML documents with Author-X. IEEE Internet Computing, 5 (3), 21-31.

Bertino, E., Catania, B., Ferrari, E., Thuraisingham, B. M., & Gupta, A. (2002). Selective and authentic third-party distribution of XML documents (MIT Sloan working paper No. 4343-02).

Blaustein, B. T., McCollum, C. D., Notargiacomo, L., Smith, K. P., & Graubart, R. D. (1995). *Autonomy and confidentiality: Secure federated data management*. The 2nd International Workshop on Next Generation Information Technologies and Systems.

Bonatti, P. A., Kraus, S., & Subrahmanian, V. S. (2003). Secure agents. *Annuals of Mathematic and Artificial Intelligence, 37* (1-2) 169-235.

Bonatti, P. A., Sapino, M. L., & Subrahmanian, V. S. (1996). Merging heterogeneous security orderings. In *European Symposium on Research in Computer Security* (pp. 183-197).

Butt, A. R., Adabala, S., Kapadia, N. H., Figueiredo, R., & Fortes, J. A. B. (2002). Fine-grain access control for securing shared resources in computational grids. Retrieved September 15, 2003, from the World Wide Web: http://computer.org/proceedings/ipdps/1573/symposium/15730022babs.htm.

Candan, K. S., Jajodia, S., & Subrahmanian, V. S. (1996). Secure mediated databases. In *IEEE Conference on Data Engineering* (pp. 28-37).

Cho, S., Amer-Yahia, S., Lakshmanan, L. V. S., & Srivastava, D. (2002). Optimizing the secure evaluation of twig queries. In *Proceedings of the 28th Very Large Data Bases Conference* (pp. 490-501).

Chor, B., & Gilboa, N. (1997). Computationally private information retrieval. In *Proceedings of the 29th Annual ACM Symposium on the Theory of Computing* (pp. 304-313).

Chor, B., Goldreich, O., Kushilevitz, E., & Sudan, M. (1995). Private information retrieval. In *Proceedings of 36th IEEE Conference on the Foundations of Computer Sciences* (pp. 41-50).

DB2. (2003). *DB2 relevant information*. Retrieved May 15, 2003, from the World Wide Web: http://www7b.boulder.ibm.com/dmdd/.

Devanbu, P. T., Gertz, M., Kwong, A., Martel, C. U., Nuckolls, G., & Stubblebine, S. G. (2001). Flexible authentication of XML documents. In *ACM Conference on Computer and Communications Security* (pp. 136-145).

Devanbu, P. T., Gertz, M., Martel, C. U., & Stubblebine, S. G. (1999). *Authentic third-party data publication, 14th IFIP 11.3 Conference on Database Security*.

Dyer, J. G., Lindemann, M., Perez, R., Sailer, R., Doorn, L. V., Smith, S. W., & Weingart, S. (2001). Building the IBM 4758 secure coprocessor. *IEEE Computer, 34* (10), 57-66.

Eastlake, D., & Reagle, J., et al. (2003). *W3C XML Signature WG*. Retrieved on September 15, 2003, from the World Wide Web: http://www.w3.org/Signature.

Franklin, M., Galil, Z., & Yung, M. (1992). *An overview of secure distributed computing* (Technical Report, TR CUCS-008-92). Columbia University.

Fujisaki, E., Okamoto, T., Pointcheval, D., & Stern, T. (2000). *RSA-OAEP is still alive!* Retrieved September 15, 2003, from the World Wide Web: http://eprint.iacr.org/.

Goldreich, O. (1997). On the foundations of modern cryptography. In B. Kaliski (ed.), *Advances in Cryptology Crypto '97* (pp. 46-74). Berlin and Heidelberg: Spring-Verlag.

Hégaret, P. L., et al. (2002). *Document Object Model (DOM)*. Retrieved September 15, 2003, from the World Wide Web: http://www.w3.org/DOM/

Idris, N. B., Gray, W. A., & Churchhouse, R. F. (1994). Providing dynamic security control in a federated database. In *Proceedings of the 20th Very Large Data Bases Conference* (pp. 13-23).

J2EE. (2003). *J2EE relevant information*. Retrieved September 15, 2003 from the World Wide Web: http://java.sun.com on Java security APIs, such as JAAS, JSSE, JCE.

Jonscher, D., & Dittrich, K. R. (1994). An approach for building secure database federations. In *Proceedings of the 20th Very Large Data Bases Conference* (pp. 24-35).

Karnik, N. M. (1998). *Security in mobile agent systems* (Ph.D. Thesis). University of Minnesota. Retrieved September 15, 2003, from the World Wide Web: http://www.cs.umn.edu/Ajanta.

Kilian, J. (1988). Founding cryptography on oblivious transfer. In *Proceedings of 20th ACM Symposium on Theory of Computing* (pp. 20-31).

Kohl, J., & Neuman, C. (1993). *The Kerberos network authentication service*. Retrieved September 15, 2003, from the World Wide Web: http://www.faqs.org/rfcs/rfc1510.html.

Kushilevitz, E., & Ostrovsky, R. (1997). Replication is not needed: single database, computationally-private information retrieval. In *Proceedings of the 38th IEEE Symposium on Foundations of Computer Sciences* (pp. 365-373).

Lamport, L., Shostak, R., & Pease, M. C. (1982). The Byzantine generals problem. *ACM Transactions on Programming Languages and Systems, 4*, 382-401.

Lin, P., & Candan, K. S. (2003). Hiding traversal of tree structured data from untrusted data stores. In H. Chen et al. (eds.), *Intelligence and Security Informatics* (pp. 385). New York: Springer-Verlag.

Loureiro, S., & Molva, R. (1999). Function hiding based on error correcting codes. In *Proceedings of Cryptec'99 International Workshop on Cryp-*

tographic techniques and Electronic Commerce (pp. 92-98).

Maruyama, H., Tamura, H., & Uramoto, N. (2000). *Digest Values for DOM* (DOMHASH), RFC2803. Retrieved September 15, 2003, from the World Wide Web: http://www.faqs.org/rfcs/rfc2803.html.

Minsky, Y., Renesse, R. V., Schneider, F. B., & Stoller, S. D. (1996). Cryptographic support for fault-tolerant distributed computing. In *Proceedings of the 7th ACM Special Interest Group on Operating Systems European Workshop* (pp.109-114).

Nace, W. A., & Zmuda, J. E. (1997). *PPP EAP DSS public key authentication protocol*. Retrieved September 15, 2003, from GlobeCom IETF library.

Naor, M. (1989). Bit commitment using pseudo-randomness. In G. Brassard (ed.), *Advances in Cryptology - Crypto '89* (pp. 128-136). Berlin and Heidelberg: Springer-Verlag.

Necula, G. C., & Lee, P. (1998). Safe, untrusted agents using proof-carrying code. In G. Vigna (ed.), *Mobile Agents and Security* (pp. 61-91). Berlin and Heidelberg: Springer-Verlag.

.NET. (2003). *.NET relevant information*. Retrieved September 15, 2003, from the World Wide Web: www.microsoft.com/net/technical/security.asp, www.microsoft.com/net/business/security_net.asp.

Oracle. (2003). *Oracle relevant information*. Retrieved September 15, 2003, from the World Wide Web: http://otn.oracle.com/deploy/security/content.html.

Reagle, J., et al. (2003). *W3C XML Encryption WG*. Retrieved September 15, 2003, from the World Wide Web: http://www.w3.org/Encryption/2001/.

Sander, T., & Tschudin, C. F. (1998). Protecting mobile agents against malicious hosts. In G. Vigna (ed.), *Mobile Agent Security* (pp. 44-61). Berlin and Heidelberg: Springer-Verlag.

Sandhu, R. S., & Samarati, P. (1994). Access control: principles and practice. *IEEE Communications Magazine, 32* (9), 40-48.

Smith, S. W., Perez, R., Weingart, S., & Austel, V. (1999). *Validating a high-performance, programmable secure coprocessor.* 22nd National Information Systems Security Conference.

Vigna, G. (1998). Cryptographic traces for mobile agents. In G. Vigna (ed.), *Mobile Agents and Security* (pp.137-153). Berlin and Heidelberg: Springer-Verlag.

Wiederhold, G. (1992). Mediators in the architecture of future information systems. *IEEE Computer, 25* (3), 38-49.

Wiederhold, G. (1993). Intelligent integration of information. *Proceedings of the ACM Special Interest Group on Management of Data International Conference on Management of Data, 22* (2), 434-437.

Wright, T. (2000). *Proposal for WAP-IETF co-operation on a wireless friendly TLS.* Retrieved September 15, 2003, from the World Wide Web: http://www.ietf.org/proceedings/00jul/SLIDES/tls-wtls/.

XML Security Suite. (1999). Retrieved September 15, 2003, from the World Wide Web: http://www.alphaworks.ibm.com/tech/xmlsecuritysuite.

Yee, B. S. (1999). A sanctuary for mobile agents. In J. Vitek & C. Jensen (eds.), *Secure Internet Programming: Security Issues for Distributed and Mobile Objects* (pp.261–273). Berlin and Heidelberg: Springer-Verlag.

Yu, T., Srivastava, D., Lakshmanan, L. V. S., & Jagadish, H. V. (2002). Compressed accessibility map: efficient access control for XML. In *Proceedings of the 28th Very Large Data Bases Conference* (pp. 478-489).

This work was previously published in Information Security Policies and Actions in Modern Integrated Systems, edited by M. Fugini and C. Bellettini, pp. 273-316, copyright 2004 by IGI Publishing, formerly known as Idea Group Publishing (an imprint of IGI Global).

Chapter 4.37
Information Privacy
in a Surveillance State:
A Perspective from Thailand

Pirongrong Ramasoota Rananand
Chulalongkorn University, Thailand

ABSTRACT

This chapter examines information privacy as manifested and understood in Thai society. Multidisciplinary perspectives—philosophical, anthropological, historical, legal, policy-oriented, and communicative—are used to explore information privacy, which arguably is emerging as an ethic in Thailand. While the diffusion of ICTs along with the country's aspiration toward an information society may have given rise to this conceptual emergence, the longstanding surveillance that characterizes the Thai state is reckoned to be a major hindrance to a meaningful realization of this ethic in Thai society.

BUDDHISM AND PRIVACY:
AN INCONGRUENCE (?)

In studying normative concepts in Thai society, many scholars, foreign as well as local, have turned to one preeminently potent philosophical force that has shaped Thai culture for centuries: Buddhism. Thailand is a predominantly Buddhist culture with more than 95% of the population professing the religion. As far as the ethic of privacy is concerned, Buddhism may shed some light on the existence or lack of it in Thai society, as will be discussed.

By some philosophical accounts, Buddhism is said to bear resemblance to liberalism, upon which the theory of privacy originally was founded. This is with particular regard to both philosophies' emphases on the individual capacity to seek and attain emancipation. However, the two philosophical traditions diverge in their goals and concepts of human emancipation in accordance with the different social contexts in which they evolve. While liberalism emphasizes emancipation as the creation of individuals who struggle to achieve rights and freedom in secular and material terms, Buddhism teaches the transience of matter and being and encourages individuals to discard material belongings and worldly comforts in order to achieve spiritual freedom, as embodied in the ultimate condition of nirvana.

Likewise, on a philosophical plane, privacy appears to be incongruent with Buddhism in at least two important ways. First, the philosophical environment of Buddhism is anchored in the idea of interrelatedness rather than in a model of the individual vs. the society or the state. In this regard, the problem is the relationship between the inner and the outer rather than the private vs. the public. The fact that Buddha himself left the household life behind to seek enlightenment may indicate that Buddhism leaves the liberal problematique behind or is fundamentally indifferent to it.

Second, unlike liberalism, which focuses on individualism, natural rights, and human dignity, Buddhist thinking sees the obsession with one's individual self and one's possessions, material or not, as the root cause of suffering. Emancipation, according to Buddhist teaching, means disillusionment with and relinquishing of preoccupation with the self and worldly desires. Therefore, individuality can be seen as both the beginning and the end to human emancipation in Buddhism.

To put it another way, Buddhist philosophy operates on a different level from that of liberalism. Aside from its relatively modest contribution to promoting rights-oriented political culture, Buddhism also pays little attention to physical freedom, which is a crucial basis for privacy.

In any case, it ought to be noted that these philosophical interpretations are filtered mainly from classical Buddhist teaching, which may not necessarily reflect the behavior of relatively secularized Buddhists in contemporary Thai society.

ANTHROPOLOGICAL EVIDENCE OF PRIVACY IN THAI SOCIETY

The Thai language does not have a word for privacy but refers to it by descriptively translating it from English as *khwam pen suan tua* or *khwam pen yu suan tua*, meaning "the state of being private."

According to a prominent Thai anthropologist,[1] the Thai public-private divide is inherently distinct from that of the West. Citing the example of an interior design of traditional Thai houses in the Northeast, this anthropologist points out how the room that is considered most private—the spirit room—can be shared by all members of the family. This spirit room, he explains, usually is located at the center or in the least accessible corner (from outsiders) in the house and is considered a sacred space that needs to be protected from outside intervention. Meanwhile, this room also is designated as a space where all family members perform religious rituals and functions together, since it is where the ancestral shrines and the ashes of ancestors are kept. What this signifies, he says, is that the traditional Thai concept of privacy is fundamentally collectivistic. It is the kind of privacy that is shared by intimate members of the household. By this token, individualistic privacy is said to have no place in traditional Thai culture.

Similar to this interpretation is an anthropological study at a local university, which finds privacy implications in the evolution of house forms and habitation patterns of Thai peasants in the Central Region over the past 100 years. When peasants first settled in this region, their habitation units featured a large common space, which was used for several purposes (social rituals, workspace, and playground) and relatively small living space (kitchen and sleeping areas). Most of these traditional houses do not have separate bedrooms, since family members usually sleep together in one big central room. Most of the common space, regarded as social space, was located outdoors so that neighbors could join in the activities.

But as the capitalist economy grew and took over the peasant community, traditional farming was no longer adequate to cope with the modern way of life. Many farmers became migrant laborers in the city, and new farming technologies were adopted by those who still farmed to increase production. With more time freed up and with the penetration of television, many farmers found themselves spending more time indoors. This directly affected the house forms. Most evident was the way private space increased at the expense of common space. Separate rooms with doors are now common in peasants' houses, and so are rooms with new functions. For instance, the emergence of the TV/living room has become a norm for architectural patterns across the peasant community in the Central Plains.

Clearly, privacy in the physiological sense has increased in the peasant community. However, this did not have bearing on the ethic of privacy in the sense of private rights against the intrusion of others and an aspect of human dignity. This claim will be substantiated in the ensuing accounts on the history of state surveillance in Thailand and the perception of privacy by Thais, particularly in the context related to information and communication technologies (ICTs).

HISTORY OF STATE SURVEILLANCE IN THAILAND: FROM WRIST TATTOOING TO SMART CARDS

Thailand, formerly Siam, has had a long heritage of the state controlling people through different means of surveillance. In the ancient period (13th to mid-19th centuries) when human power was scarce, a majority of the male population (the commoners) had to have their wrists tattooed with codes that would signify their subordination to a certain noble.[2] The nobles, on the king's behalf, would control these men and extract from them forced levies of produce or taxes, *corvée* labor and soldiering forces. This system of manpower control and wealth mobilization also was comple-

mented with periodic population surveys and detailed recordkeeping of each male commoner and his family. However, such traditional methods of surveillance were not very successful in coping with the commoners' various subterfuges to avoid *corvée* recruitment and to avoid being tattooed.[3]

When the first wave of Western modernization reached Siam in the mid-19th century, the country underwent a major reform known as the Chakkri Reformation.[4] Then, more rational and bureaucratic means of surveillance replaced the brutal wrist tattooing. Registration documents and surveys became new practices of "civil registration," which later was established as a major institutional component of the newly constructed Ministry of Interior.

Since the early 20th century, all Thais have been required to report the births, deaths, and moves in their families to local offices of the Ministry of Interior. From the 1950s to the early 1970s, two identification cards were launched in response to wartime crisis and dictatorial rule that insisted on identifying Thai citizens from those immigrants who fled from neighboring war-torn countries in Indochina. In addition to the identification card, the household registration paper was another crucial identification item for Thai citizens. Gradually, the two documents became indispensable documents in the lives of Thais. They are mandatory for almost all transactions from education, banking, employment, and conscription to getting a home and a cellular phone. Over the years, Thai people have become accustomed to the use of both documents, hence contributing much to the social control that the state desires. Nevertheless, the actual surveillance capacity of the state still was marred by several factors, including red-tape bureaucracy, traditional clientele relationship, inherent inefficiency, and rampant corruption.[5]

In 1983, some of these difficulties were overcome partly by the application of ICTs to the management of civil registration information. The Population Information Network (PIN), as the much-prided project of the Ministry of Interior was called, consisted of two major phases of operation. The first phase (1983-1988) primarily involved the issuing of personal identification numbers and the creation of a central population database (CPD) that hosts basic personal information on all citizens within one centralized computer storage. The second phase (1996-2001), partly inspired by the inefficiency of PIN I,[6] featured the establishment of online linkage between the CPD and all civil registration offices nationwide and the issuance of new personal identification cards with a magnetic stripe capable of storing more information than before. This card, which is the third generation of ID cards in Thailand, contains basic registration data, a photo, and a digital scan of both thumbprints of the cardholder.[7]

In the closing year of PIN II, a new government led by telecommunications tycoon Thaksin Shinawatra took office. In 2002, the Thaksin government staged a bureaucratic reform and introduced a new ministry called the Ministry of Information and Communication Technology (MICT). One of the tasks assigned to the newly founded ministry was to be in charge of a new multipurpose ID card, or smart card. In 2003, the cabinet asked the MICT to oversee the procurement and management of the new smart card, including the cooperation among other government bodies concerning smart cards. The main collaboration for the smart card, however, was between the MICT and the Ministry of Interior, or, more specifically, the Department of Local Administration, which has been in charge of the PIN project and the CPD.

The new smart card will contain a microchip capable of storing numerous fields of information that are relevant to all the participating record-keeping organizations. These organizations, which will be data sources for the new card, include the Ministry of Interior's civil registra-tion bureau, the social security department, the health and welfare ministries, the land transport department (for driver's licenses), the civil servant bureau, and the agriculture ministry, among others. The information on the card will include the cardholder's name, addresses, date of birth, religion, nationality, blood type, allergies, medical conditions, biometric images (fingerprints, face, and iris), parents' names, marital status, social security details, health insurance, driving license details, taxation data, the Bt 30 healthcare scheme, and details of those officially registered as poor.[8]

The smart card project, as approved by the cabinet in 2004, is divided into three phases. The first phase aims to produce 12 million smart cards with the budget of Bt 1.67 billion for the fiscal year 2004. The second phase, with the budget of Bt 3.12 billion for the 2005 fiscal year, will distribute 26 million cards. The third phase has the budget of Bt 3.12 billion for the remaining 26 million smart cards in 2006. By the end of the project, it is expected that all of Thailand's 64 million people will have a smart card.[9]

The smart card plan has sparked some, although not widespread, criticisms mainly from the civil society. Much of the criticism centers on the lack of legislation on privacy or personal data protection in Thailand and the plausible misuses of personal information stored in the card.[10] Some critics voiced concerns about the inclusion of sensitive information, such as blood group and genetic information in the healthcare segment of the card, while others expressed worries about the transparency of government agencies in handling and managing databases of information contained in the card. Due partly to these criticisms and technical problem, the smart card project was delayed in its implementation.

Prompted by recent insurgency movements and rampant violence that intensified in the Muslim-majority provinces bordering Malaysia,[11] PM Thaksin in October 2005 pushed the long-delayed smart ID card to be issued first to 1.2 million residents of three provinces: Yala, Pattani, and Narathiwat.[12] According to the premier, this is a way to curb the violence in these provinces, since it is believed that militants are abusing dual citizenship to escape across Thailand's border with Malaysia after committing attacks. Once the cards are issued, Thaksin hopes Malaysia will share information about its citizens so that Bangkok can determine which people are claiming dual citizenship and force Thai Muslims to choose one nationality. In effect, the smart card is foreseen to end the long-existing dual citizenship problem with Malaysia.

Interestingly, since the smart card was reintroduced and urgently launched in association with the security crisis in the South, there has been no criticism against it whatsoever. The media's seeming indifference to the issue may be attributed partly to their reluctance to clash with the outspoken prime minister, who often likened media criticisms on the handling of the Southern issue to lack of patriotism.[13]

Prior to the urgent issuance of the smart card, the prime minister in July 2005 pushed for the passing and immediate implementation of the executive decree on administrative rule in emergency situations, which gives him absolute power while restricting people's freedoms. The law, as widely criticized and opposed by academics and the press, echoes edicts issued in earlier times, such as Revolutionary Order No. 17, the National Administrative Reform Council's Order No. 42, and the Press Act of 1941.[14] These critics are concerned that the government is exploiting the Southern violence as a reason to issue the law to curb press freedom and the rights of the public. Aside from severely restricting freedom of expression, the law also infringes on the right to privacy. For instance, Article 11(5) of the decree allows government officials to investigate, intercept, or terminate any letter, print, telegraph, telephone, or other means of communication, as

deemed necessary. This newly granted authority must be viewed in the context absent any legal measures that would provide a check on excessive or unjustified use of government power.

In addition to new aggregate surveillance mechanisms like the smart card, the present government is also notorious for other, more targeted, big-brother practices. According to the 2003 annual report of the Office of Official Information Committee, for instance, the disclosure of telephone use and phone tapping practices by government agencies was listed as issues that urgently need to be considered. As stated in the report, such practices have clear privacy implications, and they frequently were publicized in the news. Telecommunications operators were cited as saying that they were constantly approached by security organizations and law enforcement agencies to tap or intercept telephone communication of individuals.[15]

Similarly, Internet service providers and network providers routinely revealed caller ID of their subscribers when they were contacted by the police who wanted to investigate individuals and organizations on the Internet.[16] In the legal vacuum of cybercrime, the Internet has been exploited for many unlawful ends, hence giving law enforcement officials legitimacy to probe into any Internet user's personal information. Such practices were done entirely without a warrant and went unchecked by any regulatory authority, even though they clearly violated information privacy of the investigated parties.

PRIVACY AND DATA PROTECTION IN THAI LAWS

Until now, Thailand has had no coherent legislation that directly and exclusively regulates privacy, or *khwam pen (yu) suan tua* in Thai. Although there are a number of articles on different legislation and the constitution that address matters related to privacy in its multifarious dimensions, these provisions mainly deal with privacy in conjunction with other rights and legal protections. There are no direct stipulations about violation of privacy, per se, since abuses typically have been framed in terms of trespass, defamation, or breach of trust or confidence instead.

Insofar as data protection is concerned, there has been evidence of legal protection of government information since the ancient period of Ayutthaya.[17] However, the protection of personal data belonging to individual citizens was not legally recognized until sometime in the early 20th century after the Chakkri Reformation. With the introduction of new information and communication technologies (e.g., radio and telegraph), a legislation to govern their use, the Radio and Telegraph Act, was passed in 1914. This law contains a section that prohibits and sets forth penalties for unauthorized opening of documents or telegraphs that belong to others. In 1934, the Telegraph and Telephone Act was passed, which regulated against unauthorized opening, eavesdropping, and disclosure of information transmitted by telegraph or telephone. Notably, the legal trend then had been toward a concept of privacy focusing on ownership and property rights rather than on personal freedom. A slight shift occurred in 1949 with the amendment of the constitution to incorporate the new section on rights and liberties, which followed the Thai government's adoption of the UN Universal Declaration of Human Rights. Article 47 in this section lays down the first constitutional protection of a set of rights that are akin to the rights of privacy in the West. It reads:

The rights of individuals in their families, dignity, honors, reputation and privacy are recognized and shall be protected. Public communication and dissemination of personal information, using whatever means, which may affect the rights of individuals in their families, dignity, honors, reputation, and privacy are prohibited unless they are done in the public interest.[18]

This provision remained unchanged for the next 60 years and was adopted again in the section on rights and liberties of Thai citizens in the latest constitution promulgated in 1997 as part of political reform. From it, one can deduce that privacy is understood not as a separate category of right but as one that is recognized in conjunction with other types of rights.

Following the 1949 constitutional amendment, a number of laws were passed with contents addressing matters relating to privacy and data protection. These are mostly civil and criminal laws that regulate information between private parties. Very few deal with the protection of people's information privacy from government interference.[19] Despite the existence of these legal provisions, information privacy is hardly given adequate recognition and protection in practice. While it may be unfair to blame this deficiency solely on the lack of implementation, given the general apathy toward the issue in Thai society, there undeniably are shortcomings in existing privacy-related laws that need to be rectified.

First, the penalties for violation are usually minimal. For instance, in the Juvenile Justice System Act, the penalty prescribed in cases of abuses involves a maximum fine of 500 Baht (about US$ 15) or a maximum six-month jail term. In the past, it was quite commonplace to see the identity of juvenile suspects revealed in newspaper coverage. It was only with the strong and consistent campaigning of child rights NGOs and activists that newspapers discontinued this practice in recent years.

Second, civil and criminal law causes of action as well as appeals to constitutional law are not adequate to protect privacy, especially when it comes to the regulation of computerized files. As mentioned, the protection of privacy under civil and criminal law depends upon litigation brought under torts of trespass, defamation, or breach of confidence. To establish a civil or criminal wrong against a person or his or her property, it is essential to prove that the wrong was either intentional or that an injury arose from negligence. In the case of defamation, for instance, the truth of a statement is the basis for litigation. In the context of computerized recordkeeping, use, and transfer, a file could be true but nevertheless could cause injury when used in a different context or when combined with other data. With the now common practice of computer matching across different databases and interagency record linkage, an individual's privacy can be invaded without causing harm, as recognized by law. Furthermore, within the routine environment of automated data practices, it would be very difficult to demonstrate the intention to cause harm.[20]

In addition, like most legal statutes on rights and freedoms in Thailand, these privacy-related laws are subject to limitations usually on the basis of collective public interests—national security, public safety, and so forth. In fact, such exceptions even gravitate toward a norm in Thailand, given the country's extensive history of dictatorial rule, its security situation during the Cold War, and the constant threat of a *coup d'etat* under civilian governments. During the problematic period of the late 1960s and early 1970s, national security became a shorthand for the government's suppression of suspected insurgents and dissidents. Many repressive laws were passed in the name of protecting national security, in effect undermining the constitutional protection of people's rights and liberties.

Insofar as laws that regulate the collection and use of personal information by government agencies are concerned, a similar trend of making exceptions in the interest of national security is also evident. The 1991 Civil Registration Law, which was enacted in response to the introduction of computerized recordkeeping and data processing, is a case in point. Apart from making such exceptions, this law also allows other government departments to share in the use of civil registration information through requests for copies of information as well as through computer linkage. Such a provision surely helps to facilitate computerized manipulation of personal data, which are growing by leaps and bounds in the Thai bureaucracy.

In 1997, when the historic Freedom of Official (Government) Information Act B.E. 2540 was passed, information privacy emerged under the section Personal Information and Data.[21] This section contains five articles that clearly imitate the eight basic fair information practice principles of the OECD's Guidelines for the Protection of Privacy and Transborder Flow of Personal Data.[22] While these regulations follow internationally recognized principles of data collection, they still contain some loopholes, which, again, appear in the form of exceptions. For instance, Article 24 of the law articulates the principles of use limitation and disclosure limitation. This article forbids government agencies to disclose personal information in their recordkeeping systems to other government agencies or to third parties without first obtaining the informed consent of the data subject, albeit with the following exemptions: internal use, planning, statistics, census, research, national archives, criminal investigation and litigation, and matters of life and death. Furthermore, the court, government officials, and/or government agencies and departments that are identified as the appropriate authority by other laws are allowed to obtain information about data subjects from any government database. This lengthy list of exemptions closes with an open-ended provision to allow as exceptions any other cases that may be stipulated in subsequently enacted royal decrees.

Nevertheless, the section on data protection in this relatively new bill is not without merit. First, the technique used in information storage—manual vs. computerized—is not an issue. Personal information is defined broadly to cover both manual and computerized personal records. That both types of records are subject to regulation is a good thing, since tampering with manual records can be just as dangerous. Also, the contained data protection principles definitely represent an improvement over the previous status quo, since they recognize, in principle, that the individual citizen has a legitimate legal interest in the information pertaining to him or her contained in government files.

It deserves mentioning that the introduction of data protection within the freedom of official information law was, indeed, strategic. According to a well-respected lawmaker who had been involved in the enactment of this law, the inclusion of personal data protection was an initial step toward further legislative action in the future. Since public awareness about data protection was still minimal, it made sense to introduce the issue to the legislature under the umbrella of access to government information, which was a more timely topic and one that had significant public support. For the same reason, defensive governments would be more likely to let their guards down due to the pressure from representatives of the public who had been vying for a greater access to government information.[23]

In another development, as Thailand was joining the rest of the world in the information society/economy bandwagon in the early to mid-1990s, a new direction of policy and planning that emphasized widespread diffusion of ICTs emerged. To accommodate this, it was deemed necessary by the responsible policy unit—the National Information Technology Committee (NITC)[24]—that information laws be created, particularly those that address automatic information processing and electronic commerce. As a result, six ICT laws were drafted, including a data protection law, starting in 1998.[25] It deserves mentioning that these legislative concerns were taken mostly at face value. They are void of any

political or philosophical grounding and are meant to be instruments to meet the requirements of the envisioned information society only.

In the case of the data protection law, one of the NITC's rationales in drafting the new law was to accommodate the European Union's Direction on Transborder Data Flow and on the Protection of Individuals in relation to the Processing of Personal Data. Article 25 of the Directive notably prohibits the transfer of data to a third country that does not provide an adequate level of protection. Since Thailand has had quite close trade relationship with the EU, it was obliged to adopt this legal requirement into its policy agenda. The emergence of a data protection legislation in Thailand thus may follow the model described by Colin Bennett (1998), who writes extensively on information privacy policy, as a penetrative process of policy convergence.

After the bureaucratic reform in 2005, which gave birth to the Ministry of Information and Communication Technology (MICT), the drafting of ICT laws was transferred to the new Ministry, while NECTEC was relegated to be only a center for ICT research. The draft law, which was drawn up twice, followed the guidelines used by the EU Directive on data protection and data protection laws in Australia, Hong Kong, and New Zealand. The completed draft law underwent a review by related agencies, including the Office of Official Information Commission (OOIC)[26], who disagreed with many of its provisions. From then on, the OOIC has assigned a legal research center at Thammasart University to research data protection laws overseas in order to develop another version of the data protection law.

According to recent research (Serirak, 2004), the two draft laws on data protection have many similarities. For instance, both of them serve as general provisions on data protection and recommend that a special regulatory body be set up and assigned the task of implementing the new law in the same fashion as the OOIC for the preceding

Freedom of Official Information Law. Also, the stipulations contained in both drafts are meant to protect individuals as well as legal entities. Both draft laws also recommend that all organizations, public and private, develop a clear data protection policy that is in line with the provisions in the new law.

Meanwhile, the two drafts differ on a few points. First, the OOIC's draft rules that all data controllers and processors be registered with a regulatory committee to be set up, while the ICT's draft does not make this compulsory but places it under the consideration of the committee. Second, the OOIC's draft also proposes that there be only one regulatory body, which will be known as the Office of National Information Committee, to oversee all information-related issues, including freedom of information and data protection. This new office, as the OOIC envisioned, will function as another department within the government's bureaucracy under the care of the Ministry of Prime Minister's Office. The ICT's draft, however, recommends that the Office of the Data Protection Committee be set up as a separate regulatory agency that specializes only in regulating data protection. The new office will be under the MICT and will be outside the government's bureaucracy in order to allow for greater work efficiency and flexibility.

Despite the development in both draft laws, the data protection act is yet to be passed. With the insurgency crisis looming in the South, it is likely that more state surveillance measures will be introduced, hence undermining the importance of privacy and the need to pass a data protection law in the near future.

THAI PERCEPTION OF INFORMATION PRIVACY

While data protection law has emerged in the context of globalizing policy convergence and international diffusion of the Internet, it is quite questionable whether the general Thai public indeed considers information privacy important. Here, information privacy is defined as "control over the circulation of one's personal information, including access to, transfer, exchange, and communication of that information."[27]

As far as information privacy on the Internet is concerned, local research found that 92% of Internet users surveyed were aware of and gave importance to their right to information privacy in that context. Age and income were found to positively influence their level of awareness; that is, the older and more economically established a person is, the more will he or she realize the importance of information privacy on the Internet. When it comes to violation of information privacy in cyberspace, the studied Internet users interestingly placed the least importance on looking up an IP address by law enforcement officers while giving the most emphasis to making personal data that may have moral implications publicly available. Meanwhile, they ranked private information collectors higher in their potential big-brother list than government recordkeeping organizations. Data from the same research also show that information privacy was not understood as an intrinsic value, desired for its own sake. The surveyed Internet users were found to regard privacy more as an instrumental value that was necessary to achieve other important ends, such as security, employment, and legal protection (Khananithinand, 2002).

Correspondingly, focus group interviews of subsets of the Thai public on the issue of information privacy and state surveillance found that participants in the higher socioeconomic strata were more apprehensive about the application of new ICTs in organizational recordkeeping and were more definite in maintaining a boundary between public and private realms. They also exhibited less trust in the handling of personal information in government files than those from lower socioeconomic backgrounds. The latter group was apt to see government's documentary activities as a benign force that benefits the collective interests of the public. As would be expected, participants who were Internet users, mostly from higher socioeconomic groups, expressed a greater awareness and understanding of information privacy than those who were nonusers, mostly from lower socioeconomic groups.

Meanwhile, there was a clear reflection of indifference and economic utilitarianism in evaluating information privacy and government surveillance from the participants in lower socioeconomic groups. So long as surveillance practices benefited them economically, they would tend to accept it as part of the status quo. These participants did not value privacy much, because they saw it not as a part of their basic need. They could get by with less of it in their daily lives. To them, the greater priority was to make ends meet. Their tendency to not question government information practices was reinforced by their feelings of powerlessness vis-à-vis the state and its ignorance of the ramifications of new surveillance technologies that were in widespread use.

In addition, the study found that personal experiences and vulnerability played a crucial role in helping to crystallize the participant's orientation to aspects of privacy. Participants who were HIV-positive and those who had worked with HIV-positive persons were more critical of the government's approaches toward health surveillance and were more cognizant of the importance of a reliable body of laws that could restrict serious invasions of information privacy. Interestingly, unlike the participants in the lower socioeconomic groups, the HIV-positive participants, who came from relatively similar backgrounds, felt that they were in a position to politically mobilize against unfair government information practices or in support of legal measures that would restrict a serious invasion of privacy (Ramasoota, 2000).

EMERGENCE OF PRIVACY ETHIC ON THE INTERNET

As far as regulation of Internet content in Thailand is concerned, the ICT Ministry, since its inception in 2002, has been the central authority in legal enforcement with strong support from the Office of National Police. Meanwhile, self-regulatory efforts are emerging in the industry as well as in civil society circles. At the forefront of self-regulation is the so-called Thai Webmaster Association (TWA) (formerly the Thai Webmaster Club), which was established in 2002 by a group of Thai Webmasters with social concerns. In 2002, the TWA defined a set of ethical rules and guidelines to ensure safe access to the Internet and to serve as measures in dealing with different types of content provision. This code of ethics is to be enforced by the newly constructed self-regulatory body called the Webmaster Council of Thailand (WCT), which comprises selected members from the TWA and a number of appointees from the public and private sectors.

Interestingly, the TWA's code of ethics holds striking resemblance to that of the more established Press Council of Thailand (PCT). Eighteen out of 24 articles in the TWA's code echo those in the PCT's code. This includes the following ethical principles:

- Accuracy and completeness of information
- Information authenticity and copyright
- Right of reply
- Prompt correction of information
- Language decency
- Specification of information source and protection of source anonymity
- Respect of human dignity, especially the rights of juveniles, women, and the underprivileged
- Clear measure against obscene materials

- Fairness in criticism and commentary remarks
- Clarity in presenting advertising information (not advertorial in disguise)
- Avoidance of misleading information
- Avoidance of privacy violation except for public interest
- Professionalism and integrity
- Public order and morale
- Avoidance of dispute and conflict with others in the same profession.

The ethics that are not borrowed from the PCT's code include the following:

- No spreading of viruses
- No spreading of information that causes personal damage
- Clear privacy policy
- Clear identification on the Web site of a Webmaster's contact address
- Good judgment in balancing public interest with employers' demands, professionalism, and the Webmaster

There are three major explanations for this cross-media transfer of ethical standards. First, the Webmaster of a few online newspapers holds a prominent role in the TWA and was a leading force in the drafting of the TWA's code of ethics. Second, and related to the first, it is a known fact that the newspaper industry now represents the most established form of self-regulation in all information-related industries. So, their code of ethics readily may serve as a blueprint for other forms of mass media. In addition, most Webmasters in Thailand, particularly the more technocratic IT professionals in the TWA, had little knowledge about such a loaded concept like ethics. So, they most likely rendered the responsibility in the drafting of the code to those with journalistic backgrounds.

Notably, this cross-media transfer of ethics is done within a philosophical vacuum and with little recognition of the technical differences between print media and the Internet and, thereby, associated implications for privacy. Also, the code contains a similar tendency toward exception, as would be the case of other information-related laws, as discussed earlier.

CONCLUSION

Information Privacy Ethic and the Surveillance State: Strange Bedfellows in the Age of Globalization

While globalization and the internationalization of information society ideology may have given rise to the emergence of information privacy on the legislative agenda and as a professional code of ethics, these two forces (i.e., referring to globalization and internationalization of information society) to implant it in the Thai value system. If ethics is to be construed as "beliefs regarding right and wrong behavior in accordance with generally accepted social norms" (Reynolds, 2003, p. 4), then information privacy may only be a pseudo-ethic in a surveillance society like Thailand. It is not so much the lack of realization by the general public about the critical importance of privacy ethic applied to ICTs as it is their insensitivity and ignorance toward social-scale surveillance practices that made this implantation of value very difficult. What lies deeper than this habituation and conformity to surveillance are the philosophical underpinnings of Thai culture that may be incongruent with the concept of privacy. In the absence of critical scholarship and public learning that could create avenues for resistance to the growing technological surveillance, what is certain is that information privacy in Thai society always will have uneasy bedfellows.

REFERENCES

Bennett, C. J. (1998). Convergence revisited: Toward a global policy for the protection of personal data. In P. E. Agre & M. Rotenberg (Ed.), *Technology and privacy: The new landscape.* Cambridge, MA: MIT Press.

Fried, C. (1968). Privacy. *Yale Law Journal, 77*(3), 475-493.

Khananithinand, N. (2002). *Awareness of information privacy by Thai Internet users.* Unpublished master's thesis, Chulalongkorn University, Bangkok, Thailand.

Miller, A. (1971). *The assault on privacy: Computers, data banks and dossiers.* Ann Arbor, MI: University of Michigan Press.

Phongphaichit, P., & Baker, C. (1995). *Thailand, economy and politics.* Oxford: Oxford University Press.

Ramasoota, P. (1997). Information technology and bureaucratic surveillance: A case study of the population information network (PIN) in Thailand. *Information Technology for Development, 8.*

Ramasoota, P. (2000). *State surveillance, privacy and social control in Thailand* (1350-1998). Unpublished doctoral thesis, Simon Fraser University, Canada.

Ramasoota, P. (2003). *Internet content regulation.* A research report submitted to the Thailand Research Fund (TRF) under the Media Reform Project.

Ramasoota, P. (2004). Communication rights in Thailand: Towards whose information society. In *Proceedings of the Regional Symposium on Communication Rights in Asia,* Manila, The Philippines.

Reynolds, G. (2003). *Ethics and information technology.* Boston: Thompson.

Serirak, N. (2004). *Data protection law and implications towards good governance.* Unpublished doctoral thesis, Thammasart University, Thailand.

Westin, A. (1967). *Privacy and freedom.* New York: Atheneum.

Wilson, K.G. (1988). *Technologies of control: New interactive media for the home.* Madison, WI: University of Wisconsin Press.

ENDNOTES

[1]   Dr. Nithi Aeusriwongse, former professor of Anthropology and Sociology, Chiang Mai University, interview by author, October 13, 1996, Chiang Mai University, Chiang Mai.

[2]   This is a different system from slavery. All free commoners were supposed to report to a certain noble or to the king in order to be entitled to basic legal protection. The commoners usually had the right to choose the noble with whom they wanted to be, while the slaves would always be tied to one noble because of debt bondage.

[3]   Some commoners co-opted with the nobles through a patron-client relationship to avoid arduous *corvée*, while others bribed officials who carried out the tattooing to exempt them or to make an invisibly minuscule tattoo.

[4]   The reform, named after the ruling Chakkri dynasty, began formally in 1892 and took more than two decades to complete. Aside from a major bureaucratic reform, king Chulalongkorn, who initiated it, also launched a series of other reforms, including the emancipation of slaves, the abolition of the *corvée* system and outdated customs, the establishment of a modern military force, legal reform, educational reform, and the creation of new and modern means of transportation and communication such

as highways and the telegraph. See more in Pasuk Phongphaichit and Chris Baker's (1995) *Thailand, Economy and Politics.* Oxford: Oxford University Press.

[5] Pirongrong Ramasoota (1998). Information Technology and Bureaucratic Surveillance: A Case Study of the Population Network (PIN) in Thailand. *Information Technology for Development, 8,* 53.

[6] After PIN I was completed, a proposal for PIN II was raised in 1992. Due to discontinuity in governments, limited budget, and the need to pass a new civil registration law, however, PIN II was significantly delayed and did not take off until 1996.

[7] Ibid., 54.

[8] http://www.boingboing.net/2002/11/25/Thailand

[9] http://www.thaipro.com/news_00/201_Thai-smart-cards.html

[10] Personal data protection draft law has been in the process for a number of years but has never passed. According to a newspaper analysis dated November 2003, it would take at least one more year for the drafting of the law to be ready. The article also commented that the draft legislation focuses only on data possessors and ignores the issues of data controllers and processors, who might be capable of misusing personal data stored in the databases.

[11] As a result of insurgency attacks in the three provinces, more than 960 people have been killed since January 2004.

[12] This number only accounts for residents aged 15 to 70 out of a total of 2.2 million people that reside in the three provinces.

[13] Prime Minister Thaksin Shinawatra was quite (in)famous for his outspokenness, particularly with regard to his critics and the media. In September 2003, there were news reports about 130 Muslims in the problematic Southern provinces who fled to Malaysia in political exile. The PM was furious and openly asked the local media to stop reporting this news. His exact words were, "Aren't you media people Thai? If so, stop reporting this news immediately."

[14] These laws imposed dictatorial control on freedom of the press and the people's rights and liberties. As a result of strong campaigning by the press and its civic alliance in the early 1990s, the former two were abolished. As for the Press Act of 1941, many of its provisions were made obsolete by articles that addressed freedom of expression and freedom of the press in the new Constitution promulgated in 1997. See more details about the protest by the press against the new executive decree in "Press Up in Arms Against Decree," *The Bangkok Post,* July 21, 2005.

[15] See more in Pirongrong Ramasoota (2004), "Communication Rights in Thailand: Towards Whose Information Society," Proceedings of the Regional Symposium on Communication Rights, Manila, August 7-9, 2004.

[16] Pirongrong Ramasoota (2003), "Internet Content Regulation," a research report submitted to the Thailand Research Fund (TRF) under the Media Reform Project.

[17] The Ayutthaya period—named after Ayutthaya, kingdom's capital—spanned more than 417 years from 1350 to 1767.

[18] Article 47 of the Thai Constitution 2534 B.E. (1991), amended version (No. 5), section 3: Rights and Liberties of Thai citizens.

[19] See an inclusive review of these laws in Pirongrong Ramasoota, State Surveillance, Privacy, and Social Control in Thailand (doctoral thesis, Simon Fraser University, 2000), 258-259.

[20] See more detailed discussion on the issue of computer-related litigation in Wilson (1988, p. 54).

[21] The movements that gave rise to the passing of this new law came from the civil society. A group of academics, NGOs, and activists

argued on grounds that existing laws did not provide adequate public access to official information while politicizing instances of social injustice and negative consequences in the cases of denied access. The movements coincided with the rising democratic sentiments in the aftermath of the crackdown on pro-democracy demonstrators by a military-led government in 1992.

22 The OECD Guidelines were a result of collaborative work by experts at the Washington, D.C.-based World Peace through Law Center and its affiliated organizations of lawyers, judges, and jurists. The eight fair basic information principles could be summarized in the following terms: collection limitation, data quality, purpose specification, use limitation, security safeguards, openness or transparency, individual participation, and accountability.

23 Dr. Borvornsak Uwanno, former dean of Faculty of Law, Chulalongkorn University, interview by author, October 11, 1998, Vancouver, Plazcek Residence.

24 The NITC was hosted by the technocratic National Electronics and Computer Technol-

ogy Center (NECTEC) of the Science and Technology Ministry.

25 The areas addressed by the six draft laws include computer crime, electronic data interchange (EDI), digital signature, electronic fund transfer, information infrastructure, and data protection.

26 The OOIC was created in 1997 to oversee and help enforce the newly enacted Freedom of Official Information Act. Housing a 30-member staff, the office is headed by a full-time director and a part-time committee that convenes periodically to decide on various information-related topics. Apart from receiving complaints from the public on access to government information, it also acts as ombudsmen and coordinator between members of the public and government agencies on issues related to government information.

27 This definition derives from a review of prominent definitions given to privacy by Westin (1967, p. 7), Fried (1968, pp. 475-493), and Miller (1971, pp. 211-216).

This work was previously published in Information Technology Ethics: Cultural Perspectives, edited by S. Hongladarom and C. Ess, pp. 124-137, copyright 2007 by Information Science Reference, formerly known as Idea Group Reference (an imprint of IGI Global).

Chapter 4.38
An Integrated Security Verification and Security Solution Design Trade–Off Analysis Approach

S. H. Houmb
Norwegian University of Science and Technology, Norway

G. Georg
Colorado State University, USA

J. Jürjens
TU Munich, Germany

R. France
Colorado State University, USA

ABSTRACT

This chapter describes the integrated security verification and security solution design trade-off analysis (SVDT) approach. SVDT is useful when there is a diverse set of requirements imposed upon a security critical system, such as a required security level, time-to-market and budget constraints and end users' expectations. Balancing these needs requires developers to evaluate alternative security solutions, and SVDT makes this evaluation effective. UMLsec, an extension to UML for secure systems development, is used to specify security requirements, and UMLsec tools are used to verify if the alternative design solutions satisfy security requirements. Verified design alternatives are then evaluated by the security solution design trade-off analysis. The trade-off analysis is implemented using Bayesian belief nets (BBN) and makes use of a set of trade-off parameters, such as budget, business goals, and time-to-market constraints, to support design decisions regarding how to best meet security requirements while also fulfilling other diverse system requirements.

INTRODUCTION

Security critical systems must perform at the required security level, make effective use of available resources, and meet end-user expectations. Balancing these needs, while fulfilling budget and time-to-market constraints, requires developers to design, and evaluate alternative security solutions. Standards and techniques exist to aid in this work, but most address a single facet of a system, such as its development, or rely on specially trained assessors. For example, ISO 15408 Common Criteria for Information Technology Security Evaluation (ISO 15408, 1999) is based on a qualitative assessment, performed by one or a few certified assessors, and focuses on system development activities. The Common Criteria certify security critical systems against seven Evaluation Assurance Levels (EAL) that define the security level of a target system. The Common Criteria do not capture the notion of a system's operational security level. This is the security level observed during its operation at a particular point in time, as described by Littlewood (1993). Trade-off techniques, such as ATAM (Kazman, Klein, & Clements, 2000) and CBAM (Kasman. Asundi, & Klein, 2002) provide well-tested approaches to aid decision making at the architectural level. CBAM also takes economical implications into consideration during the analysis. However, these techniques rely on the presence of an assessor who is familiar with the technique and who has proper experience in multiple areas of architectural trade-off analysis. This makes it difficult for developers with little experience in the security domain, or with trade-off analysis processes, to consider alternative security solutions during system design. Evaluating solution alternatives during design is critical to providing security by design within budget constraints. Security and architectural evaluations are also, in many cases, time-consuming and resource intensive, which precludes their use in situations where time-to-market, budget and rapid incremental development constraints exist.

The integrated security verification and security solution design trade-off analysis (SVDT) approach described in this chapter takes into consideration both development and operational security level concerns by integrating security verification, risk assessment, design trade-off analysis, and relevant parts of the Common Criteria. SVDT consists of four main steps: (1) identify potential misuses and assess their risks, (2) identify alternative security solutions for misuses that must be addressed, (3) perform UMLsec security verification of these security solutions to ensure they prevent the target misuse, and (4) perform security solution design trade-off analysis among the alternative solutions.

This chapter focuses on steps (3) and (4), using UMLsec and its related tool-support to verify that potential security solutions do meet their intended requirements, and using a trade-off analysis tool that evaluates the relative ability of different solution designs to meet the complete set of system constraints. The trade-off tool incorporates the notion of a static security level to address the security level derived from development activities, and a dynamic security level to address the security level derived from predicting events when the system is operating. Determination of the static security level is based on the Common Criteria recommendations, while the dynamic security level is derived from information regarding both normal use and potential misuse of the system. The dynamic security level is estimated using a prediction model (Houmb, Georg, Reddu, France, & Bieman, 2005b) that uses the following parameters: misuse frequency (MF), misuse impact (MI), security solution cost (SC) and security solution effect (SE).

The static security level, dynamic security level, standards, policies, laws and regulations, priorities, business goals, security risk acceptance criteria, and time-to-market (TTM) and budget constraints are all parameters to the trade-off analysis, which computes the return on security investment (RoSI) for each security solution. To better facilitate the trade-off analysis and security verification, an aspect-oriented modelling (AOM) technique is used to separate security solutions from system core functionality. Security solutions are specified and analysed in isolation before examining their influence on the system. Inappropriate or insufficient solutions that fail security verification can be quickly discarded from continued consideration, while complete analysis is reserved for the most promising alternatives. The results of trade-off analysis of different design alternatives are compared using their return on security investment (RoSI) value, and developers can make decisions regarding which alternatives best meet security requirements while also meeting other diverse system constraints.

The chapter is organised as follows. Background information on the techniques used in SVDT and related techniques is presented in the next section. This is followed by a discussion of the SVDT approach, concentrating on security verification and security solution design trade-off analysis. Both of these topics are presented in detail, in the context of a running example of the design of a portion of an e-commerce prototype platform. Future trends in the design of security critical systems follow this discussion, and the chapter concludes with a discussion of the controlled development of secure systems.

BACKGROUND

Techniques used in SVDT to facilitate security verification and security solution design trade-off analysis are presented in this section. We also discuss other techniques often used in these areas and their relation to the SVDT approach.

The SVDT approach is based on model-driven development (MDD). MDD is a development method proposed by the object management group (OMG) in which software development activities are carried out on models (OMG, 2003). The goal

is to obtain the implementation of a system by transforming models from high levels of abstraction to lower levels of abstraction and eventually into code. Analysis and refinement can occur at any level of abstraction. Risk-driven development is used in conjunction with MDD to combine development and security risk management throughout system development. Model-based risk-driven development uses models to identify security risks, assess alternative treatments to these risks, and document the resulting design. The goal of model-based risk-driven development is to cost-effectively achieve a required level of security.

The two steps of the SVDT approach that are discussed in detail in this chapter are security verification of potential solutions and security solution design trade-off analysis among these potential designs. Both steps require that alternative design solutions be easily analysed and interchanged in the system design. For this reason, the SVDT approach uses AOM techniques. AOM allows the separation of security solutions from system core functionality. Security solutions can then be analysed to verify their security properties without the added complexity of other system components. The security solutions must be integrated (or composed) into the core system design for trade-off analysis, and AOM techniques also support this integration. Analysing an alternative solution is easily achieved by integrating it with the core system and performing the analysis again.

The AOM technique allows reuse of previous experience and domain knowledge since the security solution design aspects are completely reusable in their generic form. Aspects are UML template patterns specified using a specialised role-based modelling language and must be instantiated in the context of a system prior to composition (France, Kim, Ghosh, & Song, 2004a). The instantiation step includes binding the names of model elements in the aspect to those of comparable model elements in the core design. Model elements that are targets of composition are unrestricted as long as they are specified as targets in the aspect. Thus, classes, methods, attributes, relations, arguments, sequence fragments, messages, stereotypes, and tags are all potential points where composition can occur. Composition consists of merging two models using default merging rules. Composition can result in adding model elements, deleting model elements, replacing model elements, or augmenting, deleting or replacing behaviour (France, Ray, Georg, & Ghosh, 2004b). Composition directives can be used when it is necessary to change the default merging rules to obtain correct behaviour in the composed model (Straw et al., 2004). We have developed composition techniques for UML static structure diagrams and sequence behaviour diagrams. The composition of sequence diagrams is used in the SVDT approach. Our AOM techniques differ from others in two respects. First, many AOM techniques require that an aspect contain information regarding where and how in the system core functionality it will be applied (Jacobson, 2003a; Jacobson, 2003b; Kiczales et al., 2001), whereas our generic aspect models have no knowledge of any core system and are thus completely reusable. We create context-specific aspect models to specify system-specific information regarding where the aspect will be applied through model element name bindings. Secondly, other AOM techniques typically provide composition mechanisms to augment or replace model elements and behaviour (Clarke, 2002; Clarke & Banaissad, 2005), but we have also found the need to delete model elements and behaviour, as well as interleave behaviour. These capabilities are included in our AOM techniques.

Recall that in step (3) of the SVDT approach, security verification is performed on potential security solutions. SVDT uses security verification for two purposes. The first purpose of security verification is to verify that potential security design solutions fulfil their respective security requirements. The second purpose is to verify that these potential designs prevent the targeted misuse scenarios. Security requirements and potential design solutions must therefore be specified using a method that supports verification. Although there are many possible security verification approaches, we have chosen UMLsec because of its link to UML and the tool-support it provides (Jürjens, 2004). UMLsec eases the task of integrating AOM techniques, security verification, and security solution design trade-off analysis through its capabilities. AOM techniques, UMLsec security verification, and trade-off analysis are linked together in such a way that each builds on the other to make the process as efficient as possible. Security design solutions and security requirements are both specified using UMLsec, and this allows us to use UMLsec tool-support to verify whether potential designs meet their requirements. UMLsec is also used to model adversary behaviour in a misuse scenario, and again its tool-support can be used to verify whether a potential design solution prevents the adversary from successfully achieving the misuse. The security verification is thus used to ensure that only those security solutions that will fulfil the security requirements and sufficiently solve the misuse scenarios are evaluated in the trade-off analysis.

The security solution design trade-off analysis step of the SVDT approach utilises a specialised trade-off analysis tool that is based on Bayesian belief networks (BBN). Related trade-off analysis techniques exist, but none are tailored to the security domain. This does not mean that one cannot use these techniques when performing security solution design trade-off analyses, but rather that a specialised technique is more efficient, particularly for developers unfamiliar with the security domain. The main reason for this is that the effects of a series of security solution decisions are conceptually hard for humans to analyse due to the interrelations and dependencies between the security solutions. The two most often used software design trade-off analysis methods are the architecture trade-off analysis method (ATAM) and the cost benefit analysis method (CBAM). In addition, there are variations on these two methods available. Both ATAM and CBAM were developed by the Software Engineering Institute (SEI). The focus of ATAM is to provide insight into how quality goals interact with and trade off against each other. ATAM consist of nine steps and aids in eliciting sets of quality requirements along multiple dimensions, analysing the effects of each requirement in isolation, and then understanding the interactions of these requirements. This uncovers architectural decisions, which are then linked to business goals and desired quality attributes.

CBAM is an extension of ATAM and looks at both the architectural and the economic implications of decisions. The focus in CBAM is on how an organisation should invest its resources to maximise gains and minimise risks. CBAM is still an architecture-centric method, but incorporates cost, benefit, and schedule implications of decisions into the trade-off analysis.

The security solution design trade-off analysis presented in this chapter is a security specific design trade-off analysis. It incorporates ideas from both ATAM and CBAM and is extended to use security solution and misuse-specific parameters, in addition to the economic implications, as input to the trade-off analysis. It is also extended to evaluate the required security level by combining both static and dynamic security levels. Analysing the consequence of security solution design decisions is also supported, because a composed model containing both the system and security solution is utilised. Because the security solution design trade-off analysis is coupled with AOM techniques, analysing several different alternatives is easy to do and developers can test a wide range of possible alternatives in order to find the design that presents the best fulfilment of competing requirements.

THE APPROACH

System security consists of defining, achieving, and maintaining the following properties: confidentiality, integrity, availability, non-repudiation, accountability, authenticity, and reliability, as defined by the security standard ISO/IEC 13335: Information technology — Guidelines for management of IT Security (ISO/IEC 13335TR, 2001). The integrated SVDT approach targets all security properties, however the example given in this chapter only considers the security property confidentiality, which is also referred to as secrecy.

SVDT consists of the following four steps: (1) identify potential misuses and assess their risks, (2) identify alternative security solutions for misuses that must be addressed, (3) perform UMLsec security verification of these security solutions to ensure they prevent the target misuse and (4) perform security solution design trade-off analysis among the alternative solutions. This chapter focuses on step (3), the security verification of security solutions, and step (4) security solution design trade-off analysis. Step (1), identify potential misuses and assess their risk, and step (2), identify alternative security solutions, are performed using the CORAS risk assessment platform (CORAS Platform, 2005). This platform is based on the CORAS model-based risk assessment methodology (Stølen et al., 2002). For the reminder of the chapter we therefore assume that potential misuses, their associated risk, and potential alternative security solutions are already identified and assessed. Figure 1 shows an overview of the SVDT approach for steps (3) and (4). The alternative security solutions for a particular misuse are represented by the set A, where a represents one of the security solutions in A. Security solutions are modelled as security aspects using UMLsec notation and security verification is performed using UMLsec tools. Design trade-off analysis is only performed on

Figure 1. Overview of the security verification and security solution design trade-off analysis (SVDT) approach

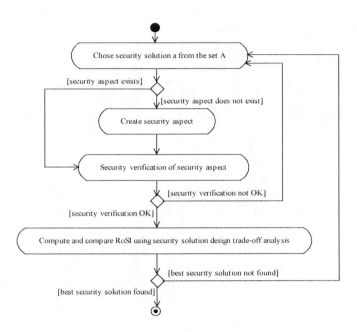

a security solution if it passes the verification by the UMLsec tools.

Security Verification

The security verification performed in step (3) of the SDVT approach uses the UMLsec profile and tools (Jürjens, 2005). Potential security design solutions must be modelled as security aspects using the profile.

UMLsec

The UMLsec profile allows a developer to specify security-related information within the diagrams of a UML system specification. The profile uses the standard UML extension mechanisms *stereotypes, tagged values,* and *constraints*. *Stereotypes* are used together with *tags* to formulate security requirements and assumptions

related to the system environment, and *constraints* give criteria used to determine whether the requirements are met by the system design. Stereotypes define new types of modelling elements and extend the semantics of existing types or classes in the UML metamodel. Stereotype names are written in double angle brackets and are attached to a model element. The model element is then interpreted according to the extended meaning ascribed to the stereotype.

Properties are explicitly defined by attaching a *tagged value* to a model element. A tagged value is a name-value pair, where the name is referred to as the *tag*. The notation is *{tag=value}* with *value* to be assigned to the tag. Information can also be added to a model element by specifying *constraints* to refine its semantics. Stereotypes are used to attach tagged values and constraints as pseudo-attributes of the stereotyped model elements. Table 1 presents a fragment of the

Table 1. A subset of the UMLsec profile

Stereotype	Base Class	Tags	Constraints	Description
critical	object, subsystem	secrecy, integrity, authenticity		critical object or subsystem
data security	subsystem	Adversary	secrecy, integrity and authenticity	basic data security requirements
secure links	subsystem	Adversary	secrecy, integrity and authenticity matched by links	enforces secure communication links
LAN	link, node			LAN connection
Internet	link			Internet connection

UMLsec stereotypes, together with their tags and constraints. More details can be found in Jürjens (2004).

Each stereotype in Table 1 can be applied to particular types of model elements. For example, the *critical* stereotype can be applied to an object or a subsystem, whereas the *LAN* stereotype must be applied to a link or a node. Specific tags can be associated with the stereotypes, e.g., *secrecy* can be associated with a *critical* subsystem, or *adversary* can be associated with a *secure links* subsystem. The *adversary* tag specifies a type of attacker (e.g., *default* or *insider*) and thus what type of adversary model should be used when verifying that a design meets its UMLsec specification. An adversary model specifies what capabilities an attacker has; for example, a default adversary has the ability to read, delete, insert, and access information passed across an unencrypted Internet link.

Security Requirements for ACTIVE Modelled Using UMLsec

The example used in this chapter is an e-commerce platform prototype that provides electronic purchase of goods over the internet. The ACTIVE e-commerce platform prototype was developed by the consortium of the EU project EP-27046-ACTIVE (ACTIVE, 2001). The design models presented here are a combination of refined models based on design descriptions provided by the ACTIVE project and new design models that take into consideration the result of the three risk assessments performed by the EU-project IST-2000-25031 CORAS (CORAS Project, 2005). For details on ACTIVE, the reader is referred to the publications of the two EU projects.

The infrastructure of the e-commerce platform consists of a Web server running Microsoft Internet Information Server (IIS), a Java application server (Allaire JSP Engine) and a database server RDBMS running Microsoft SQL server. The communication between the application server and the database is handled using the JDBC protocol. Potential customers access the Web server from a Java enabled Web browser using the HTTP protocol. The system deployment architecture is shown in Figure 2.

UMLsec, as described in the previous section, is used to model the security requirements. The security requirements can either be developed directly or derived from the results of a risk assessment giving misuses that need to be treated. In Figure 2 the communication link l_1 between the User PC and the e-commerce Site is over the *Internet* using the communication protocol TCP/IP. The communication link l_2 between server-side components (e.g., Web server and application server) occurs over a *LAN*. The UMLsec defined stereotypes <<*secure links*>>, <<*Internet*>> and <<*LAN*>> are used to indicate

Figure 2. E-commerce platform deployment diagram (Refined from ACTIVE designs)

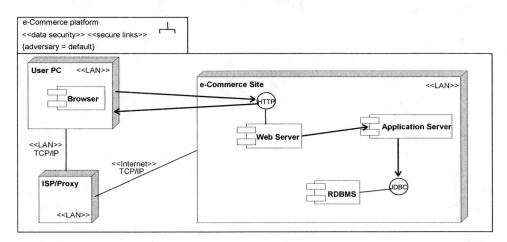

the type of communication link between nodes, and the stereotype <<*data security*>> is, as defined in the previous section, used to specify the requirements for data transmitted over the communication links. The meaning ascribed to the stereotype <<*data security*>> is specified in the class diagram in Figure 3.

The example in this chapter uses the login mechanism of the ACTIVE platform. To access any of the services in the e-commerce platform a user must either login as a visitor or as a registered user. The UMLsec stereotype <<*data security*>>, specified for the subsystem *S* in the deployment diagram in Figure 2, is refined using the associated *tagged values* in the class diagram shown in Figure 3. The security requirement *"login information must be kept secret"* means that the user name,

modelled as *uname* in the class diagram, and password, modelled as *pword* in the class diagram, must be kept secret. In order to preserve <<*data security*>> the communicating parties also need to know the authenticity of the other party, which is modelled using the associated tagged values *{authenticity=loginManager}* and *{authenticity = eCommerceclient}*.

After specifying the system using UMLsec, the list of misuses in need of treatment is modelled as adversary models. Adversary models describe potential adversary behaviour and thus the set of concrete threats against the system. Adversary models are functions of the form $\text{Threats}_M(s)$ that take an *adversary type M* and a *stereotype s as inputs* and return a subset of *{delete, read, insert, access}* as adversary

Figure 3. E-commerce platform login service class diagram

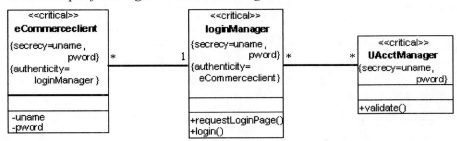

capabilities. These capabilities are defined as follows: delete means that the adversary is able to delete data specified as protected by the UMLsec stereotypes, read means that the adversary is able to read these data, insert means that the adversary is able to insert additional data, and *access* means that the adversary is able to access protected data. These functions are derived from the specification of the physical layer of the system, which in this example is the deployment diagram in Figure 2. The risk assessment of the ACTIVE user authentication mechanism (Dimitrakos et al., 2002) identified the ACTIVE login process as being vulnerable to man-in-the-middle attacks. During this kind of attack, user names and passwords can be intercepted by an attacker and used later to impersonate a valid user. This means that a default adversary (i.e., an attacker able to perform standard attacks) M, with communication stereotype s, has the set $\text{Threats}_M(s) = \{\text{read}\}$ for $s=Internet$ and $\text{Threats}_M(s)=\varnothing$ for $s=LAN$. Thus for communication link $l_1=Internet$ in Figure 2, the result is that the default adversary M can *read* the secret data, *uname* and *pword*, that are specified in the class diagram of Figure 3.

One potential security solution for this misuse or adversary behaviour is to use transport layer security (TLS). Since the original TLS sequence includes potential vulnerabilities (Jürjens, 2004), a variant of TLS described by Jürjens (2004) is used. This security solution is then modelled as a security aspect using UMLsec, and the UMLsec tools are used to verify that it meets the security requirements and prevents the attack. This security verification occurs prior to evaluating the TLS security solution in the security solution design trade-off analysis.

TLS Aspect Security Verification

Security verification of the TLS aspect means checking whether the default adversary M will be able to obtain secret information. Figure 4 depicts the interaction template for the security aspect variant of TLS. More information on the TLS aspect can be found in Houmb, Georg, France, Bieman, and Jürjens (2005c).

The TLS aspect model contains two class templates; client and server, which are shown as instances in the sequence diagram in Figure 4. For the purposes of this example, certificate creation and certificate authority public keys are assumed to be obtained in a secure manner. The client must have the certificate authority's public key and the server must have a certificate, signed by the certificate authority (CA), containing its name and public key. Primed variables are used to distinguish between sent and received values. For example, the guard $[|S' = |S]$ tests the received value of $|S$ against the previously sent value of the same variable. Other assumptions include the fact that both nonces (message sequence identifiers) and session keys must change each time the protocol is initiated.

Security verification of the aspect model is performed by transferring the UML diagram in Figure 4 to UMLsec formal semantics, which are expressed in terms of Abstract State Machines (ASMs). These ASMs are built on the UML statechart semantics described by Börger, Cavarra, and Riccobene (2000). Since the security aspect is analysed against the adversary behaviour, both the security aspect and the default adversary behaviour are modelled as an ASM adversary machine. The security aspect is executed in the presence of an adversary type M. The adversary machine models the actual behaviour of an adversary type M as part of the security aspect a. This is accomplished with an ASM consisting of two sets of information: (1) the set of control states, $control \in State$, where *State* is the complete set of states in the ASM and *control* is the set of control states; (2) the set of adversary knowledge $K \subseteq EXP$, where *Exp* consists of all possible information that an adversary might gain, i.e., all UMLsec stereotyped data in the system specification. In this example we are only interested in whether an adversary can gain the secret data *uname* and

Figure 4. TLS mechanism aspect; interaction template

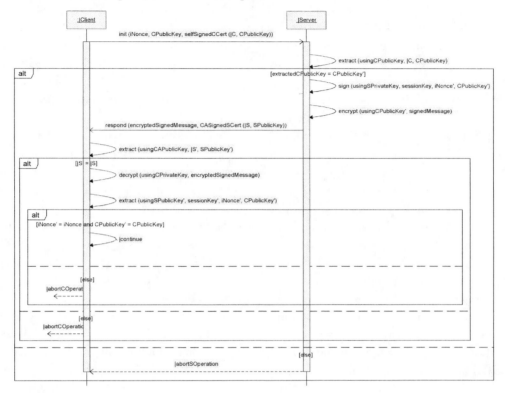

pword. The UMLsec tool iteratively executes the ASM according to the following schema:

- Specify the initial state **control = control$_0$** and the initial adversary knowledge K$_0$.
- Perform security analysis by checking the data in the link queues and, if the data of any of the link queues (in-queue and out-queue of link *l* connected to the current state) belonging to a link *l* with read $\in \text{threats}_M^S (l)$, where *S* denotes the subsystem being analysed, the data is added to K, else K is unchanged.
- Chose the next **control** state non-deterministically from the set of **control** states.

The verification stops when all control states have been visited or if the secret knowledge has been gained, in our example that {*uname, pword*}$\in$K. Since the UMLsec tool analyses link

queues, these must be specified for each message in Figure 4. Message link queues are specified by first placing the content of the message in the out-queue *(outQu)* of the sending object. Next the content of the message is sent on the communication link *l* by removing it from the out-queue of the sender and inserting it into the in-queue *(inQu)* of the receiver. For example, for the *init* message in the TLS aspect, the content of the message is put in the out-queue of the Client, *outQu$_C$*={iNonce, CPublicKey,selfSinedCCert(|C,CPublicKey)}. The message is sent on the communication link *l$_I$* (since the communication between *client=eCommerceclient* and *server=loginManager* is over the *Internet* as specified in the deployment diagram in Figure 2) by removing the content from the out-queue for the client *outQu$_C$* and inserting it into the in-queue of the Server *inQu$_S$*. Since this message does not contain the secret data *uname* and *pword*, the adversary does not gain the data. Each control state is visited, and each message is processed as described above. None of the messages in the TLS aspect contain the secret data *uname* and *pword*, so this information is never added to K. Thus, the security of the aspect is verified, and the tool gave this result in five seconds.

Security Solution Design Trade-Off Analysis

When choosing among alternative security solutions the decision-maker needs a measurable and relational expression of the security level of the alternative security solutions. The security solution design trade-off analysis supports this by computing and comparing the expected RoSI of the security solutions. RoSI is computed using a set of trade-off parameters, such as priorities, security risk acceptance criteria, standards, laws and regulations, and in particular, business goals, budget, TTM and policies. RoSI for a particular solution is derived by evaluating the effect and cost of the solution against the security requirements, or the misuse impact and frequency, if the solution is intended to treat a misuse. Figure 5 gives an overview of the security solution design trade-off analysis. The parameters on the left side of the figure (security requirement, solution effect, solution cost, misuse cost and misuse impact) are input parameters, meaning the information that is traded off. The parameters on the right side of the figure (security risk acceptance criteria, standards,

policies, laws and regulation, priorities, business goals, TTM and budget) are trade-off parameters, meaning the information that is used to trade-off the input parameters. There might be other input and trade-off parameters that are important and should be included, which can be done by tailoring the trade-off analysis, as discussed later in the chapter.

Potential misuses may reduce the security level of a security solution and are measured in terms of misuse frequency or probability and misuse impact. Misuse impact is given in terms of loss of asset value, and misuse frequency refers to the anticipated number of times within a time period p that the misuse might occur. Asset is something to which an organisation directly assigns value and, hence, for which the organisation requires protection (AS/NZS 4360, 2004). The value of assets is given in terms of their importance to the business. Security solutions address misuses by either reducing their impact, frequency or both and include mechanisms such as encryption, security protocols, authentication protocols, security extensions to applications and protocols and other similar techniques. Each security solution is characterised by its security properties, its effect, and its cost.

Structure of the Trade-Off Analysis

For each security solution, the solution treatment effect SE and the solution cost SC need to be estimated. This is done using appropriate estima-

Figure 5. Overview of the trade-off analysis

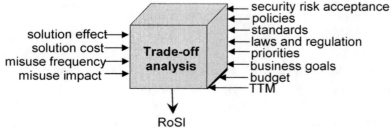

tion sets (Houmb & Georg, 2005a). If estimation information does not exist, one may collect and combine such information using different information sources as described by Houmb (2005). The structure of the trade-off analysis is constructed such that it is easy to tailor, change and maintain. The structure supports a step-wise trade-off procedure and is hierarchically constructed. The step-wise trade-off procedure is as follows:

1. Estimate the input parameters in the set *I*, where *I={MI,MF,SE,SC}* and *MI* is misuse impact, *MF* is misuse frequency, *SE* is security solution effect, and *SC* is security solution cost.
2. Estimate the static security level using information from the development for part 3 of Common Criteria, the security assurance requirements.
3. Estimate the dynamic security level or the operational security level by computing the risk level, using the prediction model described in Houmb et al. (2005b), based on the parameters *MI* and *MF*.
4. Estimate the treatment level, using the prediction model in Houmb et al. (2005b), based on the parameters *SE* and *SC*.
5. Estimate the trade-off parameters in the set *T*, where: *T={SAC,POL,STA,LR,BG,TTM,BU}* and *SAC* is security acceptance criteria, *POL* is policies, *STA* is standards, *LR* is law and regulation, *BG* is business goal, *TTM* is time-to-market and *BU* is budget.
6. Compute RoSI by a) combining the static and dynamic security level, b) evaluating the treatment effect on the combined security level by considering both the security solution effect and the security solution cost and c) Compute RoSI by evaluating the result of a) using the trade-off parameters.
7. Evaluate RoSI for a particular security solution against the rest of the potential security solutions in the security solution set *A*.

Figure 6 shows the hierarchical structure of the trade-off analysis. The structure consists of four levels and follows the step-wise description from above. The AND gates in the figure mean that all incoming events linked to the incoming arches are combined. The out-going arches from an AND gate carry the result of the combination to the next level of the analysis. Each of the squares in the figure represents a set of information, for example the set of information that contributes to the static security level.

BBN Implementation of the Trade-Off Analysis

The security solution design trade-off analysis is implemented using Bayesian Belief Networks (BBN). BBN handles large scale conditional probabilities and has proven to be a powerful technique for reasoning under uncertainty. BBN is used for various uncertainty problems, such as support of disease determination based on a set of symptoms in the medical domain, and for the help function in Microsoft Office. It has also been successfully applied when assessing the safety of systems (SERENE Project, 1999).

The BBN methodology is based on Bayes rule and was introduced in the 1980s by Pearl (1988). HUGIN (Hugin Expert A/S, 2004) is the leading tool supporting BBN. Bayes rule calculates conditional probabilities. A BBN is a connected and directed graph consisting of a set of nodes or variables and directed arches. Nodes correspond to events or concepts and are represented in a set of states. The potential states of a node are expressed using probability density functions (pdf). Pieces of information or evidence are inserted into the leaf nodes and propagated through the network using the pdfs. A pdf describes one's confidence in the various outcomes of the node and depends conditionally on the status of the connected nodes. There are three types of nodes: (1) target nodes, which represent targets of the assessment,

Figure 6. Hierarchical overview of the structure of the trade-off analysis

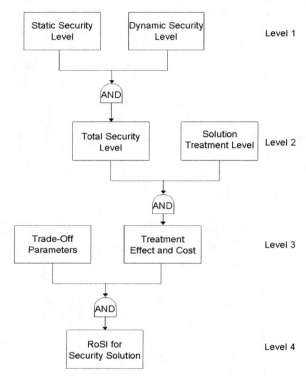

Figure 7. BBN topology for security solution trade-off analysis

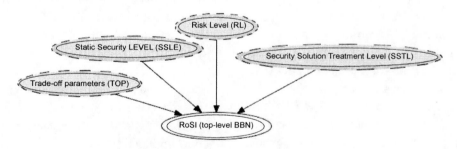

(2) intermediate nodes, that are nodes for which one has limited information or beliefs (the intermediate level) and (3) observable nodes, which represent information and evidence that can be directly observed (e.g., the number of people on a particular bus at a particular time) or in other ways obtained. Application of the BBN method consists of three tasks: (1) construction of the BBN topology, (2) elicitation of probabilities to nodes and edges and (3) making computations.

Further information on BBN, and in particular on the application of BBN for software safety assessment, can be found in Gran (2002) and the SERENE Project (1999).

The BBN Topology of the Security Solution Design Trade-Off Analysis

Figure 8 gives an overview of the BBN topology of the trade-off analysis. The topology consists

Figure 8. Top-level net in the BBN topology

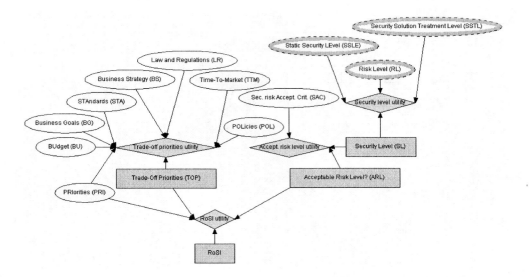

of four levels (as illustrated in Figure 6). Here the focus is on the two upper levels of the topology. Evidence and information can be inserted at any level, because the levels are linked together as input and output nodes that carry information between the different levels. In Figure 7 the four nodes *trade-off parameters, static security level, risk level* and *security solution treatment level* are input nodes (they hide the three other levels), and are indicated by dotted ovals. Each of the input nodes actually consists of additional subnets, but information or evidence can be inserted directly into the input nodes that exist at any particular level.

Figure 8 shows the top-level net in the BBN topology. The network consists of four main parts: (1) trade-off variables, which are combined by the *trade-off priorities utility*; (2) security level variables, which are combined by the *security level utility*; (3) security risk acceptance variables, which are combined with the security level variables by the *accept risk level utility*; and (4) RoSI variables, which are combined with the variables from the other parts, using the *RoSI utility*. The

utility functions (the diamonds in the figure) define the relationship between the nodes on the incoming edges. They are specified using pdfs and can be simple lookup tables or more sophisticated relational expressions (such as if-then-else expressions). The decision variables (the squares in the figure) specify the output from the utility functions. In some cases these variables work as helper variables (e.g., the security level decision variable and the trade-off priorities decision variable). The security level utility computes the security level based on the static security level variable, risk level variable, and security solution treatment level variable. Each of these variables is computed from its associated subnet. Since the HUGIN propagation algorithm (Jensen, 1996), which is used for the computations, starts with the leaf nodes and propagates one level at the time, the security level and the trade-off priorities are the first to be computed. These two sets of variables are independent and can be computed separately. The next part computed is the acceptable risk level, since it depends on the security level utility, and all other variables depend on this part of

Table 2. Nodes, states and variables of the top-level BBN

Node/variables	States
RoSI	Conf, Integr, Avail, NonR, Accnt, Auth and Relia
PRI	BU, BG, LR, BS and POL
BU	BU_costlimit
TTM	[min_date,max_date]
BG	Conf, Integr, Avail, NonR, Accnt, Auth and Relia
BS, LR, POL and SAC	Conf, Integr, Avail, NonR, Accnt, Auth and Relia
SL, ARL and TOP	Conf, Integr, Avail, NonR, Accnt, Auth and Relia

Figure 9. Static security level subnet

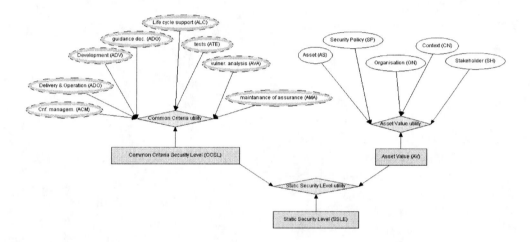

the network. Last the RoSI is computed based on the trade-off priorities, acceptable risk level, and the variable priorities (PRI). PRI is used as input both when computing the trade-off priorities and when computing RoSI. The reason for this is that the variable are used to determine the outcome of the trade-off priorities utility function, and then used to ensure that those priorities are fulfilled when computing RoSI. PRI represent company or domain-specific issues that must be preserved and, therefore, determines how the other trade-off variables are handled.

The target node RoSI represents the objective of the assessment. The trade-off variables each represent different issues that influence which security solution is best for the problem under consideration. The node BU denotes the budget available for mitigating security risks and is given as the interval [min, max], where *min* is the minimum budget available for mitigating security risks (in many cases set to 0) and *max* is the maximum budget available for mitigating risks. The variable BG specifies business goals regarding security issues. BG consists of seven states: confidentiality, integrity, availability, authenticity, accountability, non-repudiation and reliability, according to the security definition of the security standard ISO/IEC 13335. The variable STA is used to include standards to which the system must adhere. BS covers security issues related to the business strategy. LR covers laws and regulations for security issues that the system must meet. SAC represents security risk acceptance criteria and specifies acceptable and non-acceptable risks. PRI is used to prioritise the other trade-off variables and makes the BBN topology company, system, and domain specific. TTM is given as the interval /min_date, max_date], where *min_date* is the earliest TTM date, and *max_date* is the latest TTM date. Table 2 depicts the nodes/variables and states for the top-level BBN.

Figure 9 shows the static security level subnet, which feeds evidence into the SSLE node in the top-level BBN. This network consists of two parts in three levels: (1) the security assurance requirements of Common Criteria (part 3 of CC) that has three levels and (2) assets and their environment. Part 3 of Common Criteria, the security assurance requirements, describe different general and security specific aspects of a development process and target the evaluation of system against the seven Evolution Assurance Levels (EAL) of Common Criteria. Each EAL determines a set of security assurance requirements that needs to be validated by the evaluator during the certification process. We use these criteria rather than part 2 of Common Criteria, the functional security requirements, since such requirements are domain specific and also evolve over time. Certification according to Common Criteria is achieved using the documentation provided during system development and covers the requirement, design and implementation phases. By including the assurance class AMA, maintenance of assurance, the BBN hierarchy also covers the maintenance phase of a system's life-cycle.

The asset and asset environment portion of the BBN is used to specify assets that need to be protected and the related security policies, organisational issues, context in which the assets exist, and the stakeholder that either owns or is related to the assets by assigning them a value. A stakeholder is an individual, team, or organisation (or classes thereof) with interest in, or concerns relative to, one or more assets. The context is the strategic or organisational environment in which

an asset exists. An organisation is a company, firm, enterprise or association, or other legal entity that has its own function(s) and administrations. Security policy concerns the rules, directives, and practices that govern how assets are managed, protected and distributed within an organisation and its systems.

The computation order for this subnet is that the common criteria utility and the asset value utility are computed first, since their variables are independent. The static security level is then computed based on the results from the common criteria and asset value utilities.

Figure 10 shows the risk level subnet. This subnet represents the dynamic security level and feeds evidence into the RL node in the top-level BBN. The subnet consists of three parts in two levels. First the operational risk level and the security risk level are computed. The operational risk level is computed based on the variables MTTM and METM, while the risk level is computed based on the variables MUSE, MF, and MI. Last, the risk level is computed using the result of the operational risk level/risk level computation, and MC.

Figure 11 shows the security solution treatment level subnet. This subnet feeds input into the SSTL node in the top-level BBN. The treatment level is computed based on the variables SE, SC and SS. SE and SS use the seven security attributes of ISO 13335 as states. The node SC consists of one state, the *sc_costlimit*, which is given as the interval [min,max], where *min* is the minimum expected cost for the security solution and *max* is the maximum expected cost for the security solution.

Each subnet has at least one output node that represents the information being transferred to the level above in the BBN topology. Similarly, input nodes represent information given as input from associated subnets. Input nodes are modelled using grey dashed lines. If there are no observations or information available for some of the observable nodes, they are left empty. An example is when the security solution does not target a misuse. In

Figure 10. Risk level subnet

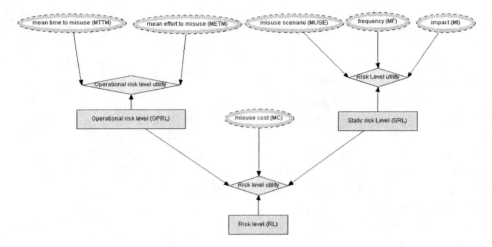

Figure 11. Security solution treatment level subnet

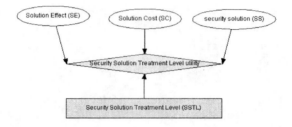

this case the related variables are left empty and not taken into consideration when computing RoSI. Due to space restrictions, we only discuss the security solution treatment level subnet in the example given in the next section.

Demonstration of Security Solution Design Trade-Off Analysis for TLS

Earlier we described the e-commerce platform ACTIVE, described a misuse scenario and described a potential security solution treating the misuse; a variant of TLS. In this section, the SSTL part of the BBN topology is used to demonstrate how to use the security solution trade-off analysis.

Recall that the BBN methodology consists of construction of the BBN topology, elicitation of

probabilities to nodes and edges, and making computations. The previous section described the BBN topology for the security solution design trade-off analysis. This topology is an implementation of the trade-of analysis and is a general topology for computing RoSI for security solution evaluation. The elicitation of probabilities and computations is, however, domain specific and needs to be assessed in each case.

Before evidence can be entered into the subnet, the utility function for SSTL needs to be defined. Tables 3, 4, and 5 show parts 1, 2, and 3 of the SSTL utility function used in this example. The state *category_a* of the variable SS refers to the situation when the TLS variant is separate from the Web application and works as an add-in to the Web application. This means that TLS is not integrated into the application. This also means that the login

Table 3. SSTL utility function part 1

Variable	State							
SSTL	Low							
SS	category_a				category_b			
SC	min		max		min		max	
SE	Conf	Integr	Conf	Integr	Conf	Integr	Conf	Integr
Utility	0.2	0.2	0.4	0.4	0.5	0.5	0.7	0.7

Table 4. SSTL utility function part 2

Variable	State							
SSTL	Medium							
SS	category_a				category_b			
SC	min		max		min		max	
SE	Conf	Integr	Conf	Integr	Conf	Integr	Conf	Integr
Utility	0.7	0.7	1.0	1.0	0.7	0.7	1.0	1.0

Table 5. SSTL utility function part 3

Variable	State							
SSTL	High							
SS	category_a				category_b			
SC	min		max		min		max	
SE	Conf	Integr	Conf	Integr	Conf	Integr	Conf	Integr
Utility	0.8	0.8	1.0	1.0	0.9	0.9	1.0	1.0

information is not encrypted between the add-in and the Web application, which makes it possible for an attacker to gain the secret information by using directed software sniffers. The state *category_b* of the variable SS refers to the situation when the TLS variant is integrated into the Web application. The different utilities assigned for min and max for the variable SC, related to each of the states of SS, determines the effect of the cost spent on the solution. For example, when the variable SSTL is *high*, the utility for min is set to 0.9. This value of min reflects that not thoroughly checking the implementation (e.g., due to lack of time or money) leads to a small probability that there are mistakes in the implementation, even if the security solution itself is proven to be completely secure and non-modifiable. The

reader should treat the utilities given in Tables 3, 4, and 5 as a simple example of how utilities can be used. They do not reflect a general and actual effect and relational specification. Figure 12 shows an example of a computation on the SSTL subnet for the TLS variant when the pdf for *SC* is set to *P(min)=0.7* and *P(max)=0.3*. Figure 13 shows the effect on the computation when the pdf for *SE* is set *to P(Conf)=0.7* and *P(Integr)=0.3*. By inserting evidence in the observable nodes the effects can be observed in the network.

As shown in the SSTL utility functions and by the two example figures, elicitation of probabilities and computation requires information regarding the relation between the different variables, as well as values of the variables themselves. The elicitation of probabilities refers to establishing

Figure 12. Result of computation when pdf for SC is P(min)=0.7 and P(max)=0.3

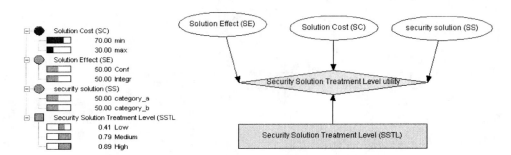

Figure 13. Result of computation when pdf for SE is P(Conf)=0.7 and P(Integr)=0.3

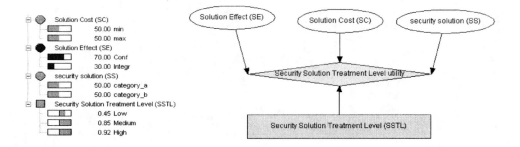

the prior pdf, $P_{prior}(X_i)$, for each state for each node/variable in the network. To compute the effect of information or evidence entered into the network likelihood functions need to be defined, which is done in the utility functions. The utility functions then define the relationship between all sets of states in the network. This is necessary in order to propagate the evidence through the network. Propagate means computations, which is done using the HUGIN propagation algorithm described earlier. The utility functions, or likelihood functions, are used to update the network. This means that the utility functions are a critical part of the network, but it also means that a BBN topology can be tailored for a particular case by changing the utility functions. As argued by both Gran (2002) and SERENE Project (1999), the construction of the network is critical to the outcome of the propagation. One way to aid the construction of the topology and the specification

of the utility functions is by using ontologies. We are currently exploring this subject in order to perform topology verification. The current version of the security solution design trade-off analysis is constructed using domain knowledge and is analysed to find the critical parts and the sensitive nodes in the network.

Evidence or information to feed into the network can come from various sources. Houmb (2005) discusses types of information sources and techniques that can be used to combine these sources. There are two main information sources available for estimating the variables in the BBN topology: empirical or observable information and subjective information, such as subjective expert judgments. Observable sources are sources that have directly or indirectly observed the phenomena. Such sources have not been biased by human opinions, meaning that the source has gained knowledge or experience by observing facts. One type of observable information source is real-time information sources, such as intrusion detection systems (IDS), log-files from Firewalls, and honeypots. Other observable information sources are company experience repositories, public experience repositories, domain knowledge, recommendations (best practise), and related standards. Examples of public repositories are the quarterly reports from Senter for Informasjonssikkerhet (SIS) in Norway, CERT.com, reports from the Honeynet-project, and other attack trend reports.

Subjective information sources can be direct or indirect, meaning that the expert may have direct or indirect knowledge or experience that he or she uses when offering information or evidence. For example, direct knowledge consists of actual events that the expert has observed. Indirect knowledge refers to events observed by another expert or an observable information source. Here the subjective information source interprets the information given by other sources before providing information. Examples of subjective information sources are subjective expert judgment and expert judgment on prior experience from similar systems. When considering experience from similar systems, the experts need to provide a description of their reasoning about the differences between the systems and the effect of those differences on the configuration being assessed. For more information see Houmb (2005). There might also be situations where there is no information or evidence available. In such situations the symbol $\perp$ is used to indicate lack of information. The variable is still included in the computation, however, to distinguish between no relation, which is denoted *P(event)=0*, and no information available.

RELATED WORK

Our work is related with the approaches presented in the other chapters of this book. In particular,

the UMLsec security verification is comparable with the work presented in Chapter II. Their approach uses 3 steps; identify security goals, identify security requirements, and construction of satisfaction argument, to establish security argumentation. The SVDT approach is based on the safety case approach and use a goal-claim-evidence structure to argue for the satisfaction of the security requirements. In the integrated approach a more formalised and tool-supported verification is used. This is, due to the UMLsec notation and the translation module in the tool, a strong and efficient verification approach for separate security mechanism, but do not handle interrelated security mechanism very well, for which this more informal approach is more suitable. The same goes for the SQUARE method (Chapter III), which focuses on security requirements, and provides techniques for security requirement capturing that the SVDT approach does not support. By including parts of SQUARE and the security goal argumentation technique the integrated approach would be able to provide better support for security requirements capturing, in addition to the misuse identification and requirement transformation that is already included, as well as handle situations where formal security verification is not possible or unnecessary costly.

Another aspect with secure systems development is that such system does not exist in isolation and are influenced by both the people using it and the environment it exist in. The work presented in Chapter IV, looks into the social factors that influences such systems and facilitates security requirement capturing and analysis from the user, administrator, and designer point of view. Our approach would benefit from including a broader user-spectre when evaluating which countermeasure (security solution) to implement.

The approach presented in Chapter V has a lot in common with the SVDT approach. They both use security patterns to capture security specific knowledge, and thus makes it easier for developers not familiar with the security domain to include security as part of the development. The SVDT approach does this through separation of concerns and techniques for weaving security specific patterns (aspects) into the core functionality before coding. This makes it possible to evaluate alternative security patterns and find the most appropriate one, which is done by the security solution design trade-off analysis. Both approaches provide analysis of security patterns; UMLsec security verification for the integrated approach, and Semantic Analysis Pattern (SAP) using security constraints for the security pattern approach. Both approaches provide means for identifying potential misuses using risk analysis, for modelling these misuses and for identifying countermeasures. However, the SVDT approach does also consider the economical implications of both misuses and countermeasures when evaluating potential security patterns.

The work by Weiss (Chapter VI) looks at dependencies between security patterns by combining them using the NFR framework. By doing so, security patterns are put into a framework where one can analyse their effect on each other and on the system. This is one of the weaknesses of the SVDT approach. The SVDT approach does support the analysis of dependencies between security patterns (called security aspects) through the security solution design trade-off analysis, but do not provide any guidelines in its current version. Its strengths, however, are that it supports formal verification of security patterns, while the work by Weiss is an informal reasoning about the dependencies.

The SVDT approach does not support agile software development directly. The idea behind our trade-off analysis is cost-effective development, but it is currently based on a traditional development process. Rapid increments, such as those in Web development and so forth, have other requirements to the development process than larger and more complex systems. The feature driven development method that is presented in Chapter VII has a lot in common with the SVDT

approach concerning the role of risk analysis and misuse modelling, but does not provide any concrete guidelines and formalised support for, for example, misuse cost estimation and security evaluation. However, for smaller systems with a short TTM rigid processes and formalism are in many cases too time consuming and costly to be justified.

Our approach can be combined with the secure Tropos approach (Chapter VIII). These two approaches look at the security verification from two different angles, and thus can be combined to provide a formal analysis of the fulfilment of a security goal by a security mechanism in its environment from Tropos complimented with the SVDT formal verification of the actual behaviour of the mechanism.

The work presented in Chapter XI has similar goals, such as formal security verification and analysis of the system during operation, as our approach. Their claim is that security is partly a social and not only a technical problem, and their work aims at a security analysis that includes a variety of factors, such as social context and human behaviour. The SVDT approach looks at the technical aspect of the system, but it does not provide sufficient techniques for analysing human behaviour and looking at security from a social context. The focus of the SERENITY approach is on greater user-friendliness, while the SVDT approach looks at potential and necessary trade-offs between security, functionality, and cost, to derive at the correct security level. The SERENITY approach do also intend to look into how to analyse the interrelations between security mechanisms, which the SVDT approach currently does not support. The common focus on the semantics of security patterns (called aspects in the SVDT approach) and formal verification of these makes the two approaches complementary. Hence, techniques from both can be integrated to strengthen both the integrated and the SERENITY approach. The dynamic verification of security during operation from the SERENITY approach, for example, would be useful to include in the SVDT approach to target a better analysis of the actual implementation of a system.

It is also worth mentioning that the techniques described in this chapter compliment the model-driven development (MDD) paradigm. However, for a wide acceptance and application of MDD techniques they must make efficient use of resources and be easy to use across all facets of development. Frameworks that combine MDD techniques and provide tool-support for these techniques must be available to guide the developer in all steps of development of a secure system. An example of such a framework is the Aspect-Oriented Risk-Driven Development (AORDD) framework (Houmb & Georg, 2005a). The security verification and security solution design trade-off analysis techniques described in this chapter are part of the AORDD framework. The framework consists of an iterative risk-driven development process that uses AOM techniques and two repositories with associated rules that support the BBN implementation of the security solution design trade-off analysis. The repositories store experience for reuse, such as security aspects and their related estimation sets. (Recall that estimation sets include estimations of misuse impacts and frequency, as well as security solution effectiveness and cost.) The rule sets guide annotation of design models (currently UML models) and how information is transferred from those models to the BBN topology. Once the system design is completed, MDD techniques that generate code can be used to realise the system (Jürjens & Houmb, 2005).

Frameworks such as AORDD will help developers unfamiliar with the security domain successfully develop secure systems using the MDD paradigm.

CONCLUSION

The chapter describes an approach for effective and controlled development of secure systems. SVDT addresses conflicting issues, such as fulfilling a required security level, making effective use of available resources, and meeting end-user expectations. Security verification using UMLsec tool-support and security solution design trade-off analysis are two techniques of SVDT. Security verification is used to verify that security requirements are fulfilled by analysing a security solution design that is modelled as a security aspect using UMLsec. The security solution design trade-off analysis is implemented using BBN. The BBN topology consists of four levels that interact through input and output nodes. The topology covers the static security level, risk level, security solution treatment level, and trade-off parameters. The topology is organised using subnets to ease the propagation of evidence. Elicitation of probabilities is achieved using available empirical or observable information sources combined with subjective information sources. Probabilities are obtained from experience and stored in the repositories described in the previous section. Computations are performed using the HUGIN propagation algorithm. The trade-off analysis is demonstrated using an example.

The BBN topology used in the security solution design trade-off analysis is a general topology and is not limited to security solution evaluation. However, it is security-specific in its current version, since the variables used are security-related variables. Tailoring the topology for other types of decision support is possible if other trade-off variables are added. Modifying or changing the security level and risk level nodes and subnets may also be necessary. The topology can also be tailored to a particular security policy or made company-specific by modifying the priorities in the PRI node and by tailoring the TOP, ARL, SL and RoSI utilities in the top-level BBN.

It is important to note that even though the BBN topology automates part of the decision process, it is still merely a representation of the combination of domain knowledge and human interpretation of what is important to take into consideration in such decisions. This means that both a different structure of the BBN topology and different estimation sets will influence the outcome of the computation.

REFERENCES

ACTIVE. (2001). *EP-27046-ACTIVE, Final Prototype and User Manual.* Version 2.0. Deliverable 4.2.2.

AS/NZS 4360. (2004). *AS/NZS 4360:2004: Australian/New Zealand Standard for Risk Management.* Standards Australia, Strathfield.

Börger, E., Cavarra, A., & Riccobene, E. (2000). Modeling the dynamics of UML state machines. In Y. Gurevich, P. Kutter, M. Odersky, & L. Thiele (Eds.), *Abstract state machines: Theory and applications* (Vol. 1019, pp. 223-241). LNCS, Springer.

Clarke, S. (2002). Extending standard UML with model composition semantics. *Science of Computer Programming, 44*(1), 71-100.

Clarke, S., & Banaissad, E. (2005). *Aspect-oriented analysis and design.* Reading, MA: Addison-Wesley Professional.

CORAS Platform. (2005). *CORAS risk assessment platform, version 2.0.* Retrieved September 26, 2005, from http://sourceforge.net/project/showfiles.php?group_id=88350&package_id=133388&release_id=276903

CORAS Project. (2005). *IST-2000-25031 CORAS: A platform for risk analysis of security critical systems.* Retrieved October 28, 2005, from http://coras.sourceforge.net/

Dimitrakos, T., Ritchie, B., Raptis, D., Aagedal, J. O., den Braber, F., Stølen, K., & Houmb, S. (2002). Integrating model-based security risk management into Ebusiness systems development: The CORAS approach. In J. Monteiro, P. Swatman, & L. Tavares (Eds.), The *2nd IFIP Conference on E-Commerce, E-Business, E-Government (I3E 2002)* (pp. 159-175). Volume 233 of IFIP Conference Proceedings, Kluwer.

France, R. B., Kim, D. K., Ghosh, S., & Song, E. (2004a). A UML-based pattern specification technique. *IEEE Transactions on Software Engineering, 30*(3), 193-206. IEEE Computer Society.

France, R. B., Ray, I., Georg, G., & Ghosh, S. (2004b). An aspect-oriented approach to design modeling. *IEE Proceedings on Software, Special Issue on Early Aspects: Aspect-Oriented Requirements Engineering and Architecture Design, 151*(4), 173-185. IEEE Computer Society.

Gran, B. A. (2002). *The use of Bayesian Belief Networks for combining disparate sources of information in the safety assessment of software based systems.* Doctoral of engineering thesis 2002:35, Department of Mathematical Science, Norwegian University of Science and Technology.

Houmb, S. H. (2005). Combining disparate information sources when quantifying operational security. In N. Callaos, W. Lesso, & E. Hansen (Eds.), *Proceeding of 9th World Multi-Conference on Systemics, Cybernetics and Informatics (SCI 2005)* (Vol. 1, pp. 228-235), Orlando, Florida.

Houmb, S. H., Georg, G., Reddu, R., France, R. & Bieman, J. (2005b). Predicting availability of systems using BBN in aspect-oriented risk-driven development (AORDD). The 2nd Symposium on Risk Management and Cyber-Informatics (RMCI '05). In N. Callaos, W. Lesso, & E. Hansen (Eds.), *Proceeding of the 9th World Multi-Conference on Systemics, Cybernetics and Informatics (SCI 2005)*, Orlando, Florida.

Houmb, S. H., & Georg, G. (2005a). The Aspect-Oriented Risk-Driven Development (AORDD) Framework. In O. Benediktsson, P. Abrahamsen, D. Dalcher, E. T. Hannberg, R. O'Connor, & H. Thorbergsson. (Eds.), *Proceedings of the International Conference on Software Development (SWDC/REX)* (pp. 81-91), Reykjavik, Iceland. Gutenberg.

Houmb, S. H., Georg, G., France, R., Bieman, J., & Jürjens, J. (2005c). Cost-benefit trade-off analysis using bbn for aspect-oriented risk-driven development. *Proceedings of 10ᵗʰ IEEE International Conference on Engineering of Complex Computer Systems (ICECCS 2005)* (pp. 185-195). Shanghai, China.

Hugin Expert A/S. (2004). *BBN-tool HUGIN Explorer™, ver. 6.3*. Alborg, Denmark. Retrieved August 24, 2005, from http://www.hugin.dk

ISO 15408. (1999). *ISO 15408 Common Criteria for Information Technology Security Evaluation*. Retrieved from http://www.commoncriteria.org/

ISO/IEC 13335. (2001). IGuidelines for management of IT Security—Part 1: Concepts and models. Retrieved from http://www.iso.org

Jacobson, I. (2003a. October). Case for aspects–Part I. *Software Development Magazine, 32-37*. Retrieved from http://www.jaczone.com/papers/10sd.Jacobson32-37.pdf

Jacobson, I. (2003b, November). Case for aspects–Part II. *Software Development Magazine, 42-48*. Retrieved from http://www.jaczone.com/papers/11sd.Jacobson44-48.pdf

Jensen, F. (1996). An introduction to Bayesian Network. London: UCL Press.

Jürjens, J. (2004). *Secure systems development with UML*. Berlin Heidelberg, New York: Springer-Verlag.

Jürjens, J. (2005). *UMLsec-Webinterface: Tool support for security verification using UMLsec*. Retrieved November 8, 2005, from http://www4.in.tum.de/~umlsec/csduml/interface/

Jürjens, J., & Houmb, S. H. (2005). Dynamic secure aspect modeling with UML: From models to code. In L. Briand, & C. Williams (Eds.), *Proceedings of 8ᵗʰ International Conference on Model Driven Engineering Languages and Systems (MoDELS 2005)* (pp. 142-155). Montego Bay, Jamaica.

Kasman, R., Asundi, J., & Klein, M. (2002). *Making architecture design decisions: An economic approach*. Technical report CMU/SEI-2002-TR-035. Retrieved from http://www.sei.cmu.edu/pub/documents/02.reports/pdf/02tr035.pdf

Kazman, R., Klein M., & Clements, P. (2000). *ATAM: Method for architecture evaluation*. Technical report CMU/SEI-2000-TR-004. Retrieved from http://www.sei.cmu.edu/pub/documents/00.reports/pdf/00tr004.pdf

Kiczales, G., Hilsdale, E., Hugunin, J., Kersten, M., Palm, J., & Griswold, W. (2001). Getting started with AspectJ. *Communications of the ACM, 10*(44), 59-65. ACM.

Littlewood, B., Brocklehurst, S., Fenton, N., Mellor, P., Page, S., Wright, D., Dobson, J., McDermid J., & Gollmann, D. (1993). Towards operational measures of computer security. *Journal of Computer Security, 2*(2/3), 211-229.

Object Management Group. (2003). *OMG MDA guide*. OMG. Version 1.0.1. Retrieved from http://www.omg.org

Pearl, J. (1988). *Probabilistic reasoning in intelligent systems: Network for plausible inference*. Cambridge, UK: Cambridge University Press.

SERENE Project. (1999). *SERENE: Safety and Risk Evaluation using Bayesian Nets*. ESPIRIT Framework IV no 22187. Retrieved October 30, 2005, from http://www.hugin.dk/serene/

Stølen, K., den Braber, F., Dimitrakos, T., Fredriksen, R., Gran, B. A., Houmb, S. H., Stamatiou, Y. C., & Aagedal, J. Ø. (2002). Model-based risk assessment in a component-based software engineering process: The CORAS approach to identify security risks. In F. Barbier (Ed.), *Business component-based software engineering* (pp. 189-207). Kluwer.

Straw, G., Georg, G., Song, E., Ghosh, S., France, R., & Bieman, J. (2004). Model composition directives. In T. Baar, A. Strohmeier, A. Moreira, & S. Mellor (Eds.), *Proceedings UML 2004, the 7th International Conference on UML* (pp. 84-97). Volume 3273 of LNCS. Springer-Verlag.

Chapter 4.39
M–Payment Solutions and M–Commerce Fraud Management

Seema Nambiar
Virginia Tech, USA

Chang-Tien Lu
Virginia Tech, USA

Chung-wei Lee
Auburn University, USA

ABSTRACT

Mobile security and payment are central to m-commerce. The shift from physical to virtual payments has brought enormous benefits to consumers and merchants. For consumers it means ease of use. For mobile operators, mobile payment presents a unique opportunity to consolidate their central role in the m-commerce value chain. Financial organizations view mobile payment and mobile banking as a way of providing added convenience to their customers along with an opportunity to reduce their operating costs. The chapter starts by giving a general introduction to m-payment by providing an overview of the m-payment value chain, lifecycle and characteristics. In the second section, we will review competing mobile payment solutions that are found in the marketplace. The third section will review different types of mobile frauds in the m-commerce environment and solutions to prevent such frauds.

INTRODUCTION

Mobile commerce (m-commerce) grows dramatically. The global m-commerce market is expected to be worth a staggering US$200 billion by 2004 (Durlacher Research, n.d.; More Magic Software, 2000). M-commerce can be defined as any electronic transaction or information interaction conducted using a mobile device and mobile networks, for example, wireless or switched public network, which leads to transfer of real or perceived value in exchange for information, services or goods (MobileInfo.com). M-commerce involves m-payment, which is defined as the process of two parties exchanging financial value using a mobile device in return for goods or services. A mobile device is a wireless communication tool, including mobile phones, PDAs, wireless tablets, and mobile computers (Mobile Payment Forum, 2002).

Due to the widespread use of mobile phones today, a number of payment schemes have emerged which allow the payment of services/goods from these mobile devices. In the following sections an overall view of the m-payment value chain, the m-payment life cycle and the m-payment characteristics is given. Also the operational issues are analyzed, which are critical to the adoption level of a payment system. The operational issues or characteristics will help in the unambiguous identification of the payment solutions.

M-Payment Value Chain

Many different actors can be involved in mobile payment process (McKitterick & Dowling, n.d.; Mobile Payment Forum, 2002). For example, there is a consumer who owns the mobile device and is willing to pay for a service or product. The consumer initializes the mobile purchase, registers with the payment provider and authorizes the payment. A content provider or merchant sells product to the customer. In the mobile payment context, content can range from news to directory services, shopping and ticketing services, entertainment services, and financial services. The provider or merchant forwards the purchase requests to a payment service provider, relays authorization requests back to the customer and is responsible for the delivery of the content. Another actor in the payment procedure is the payment service provider, who is responsible for controlling the

flow of transaction between mobile consumers, content providers and trusted third party (TTP) as well as for enabling and routing the payment message initiated from the mobile device to be cleared by the TTP. Payment service provider could be a mobile operator, a bank, a credit card company or an independent payment vendor. Another group of stakeholders is the trusted third party, which might involve network operators, banks and credit card companies. The main role of the TTP is to perform the authentication and the authorization of transaction parties and the payment settlement.

Finally there are mobile operators who are more concerned with the standardization and interoperability issues. They may also operate mobile payment procedure themselves and provide payment services for customers and merchants. One thing that needs to be considered is who receives the customer data. Customers rarely wish to divulge any information, whereas the same customer information might be important for merchants or content providers for their business. Payment procedures need to ensure that none of the players receive the data, for example, when customers use a prepaid payment solution to buy goods but also need to require divulging customer information to any of the players considered.

M-Payment Lifecycle

Payment transaction process in a mobile environment is very similar to typical payment card transaction. The only difference is that the transport of payment detail involves wireless service provider. WAP/HTML based browser protocol might be used or payment details might be transported using technologies such as blue tooth and infrared (Mobile Payment Forum, 2002).

Mobile payment lifecycle shown in Figure 1 includes several main steps (Telecom Media Networks, 2002):

1. *Registration*: Customer opens an account with payment service provider for pay-

Figure 1. M-payment life cycle

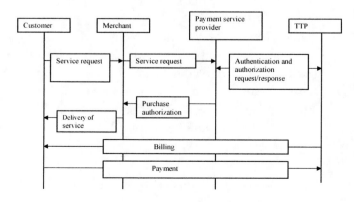

ment service through a particular payment method.

2. *Transaction*: Four steps are identified in an m-payment transaction.

(a) Customer indicates the desire to purchase a content using a mobile phone button or by sending an SMS (short message service).

(b) Content provider forwards the request to the payment service provider.

(c) Payment service provider then requests the trusted third party for authentication and authorization.

(d) Payment service provider informs content provider about the status of the authentication and authorization. If customer is successfully authenticated and authorized, content provider will deliver the purchased content.

3. *Payment settlement*: Payment settlement can take place during real-time, prepaid or postpaid mode (Xiaolin & Chen, 2003). A real-time payment method involves the exchange of some form of electronic currency, for example, payment settlement directly through a bank account. In a prepaid type of settlement customers pay in advance using smart cards or electronic wallets. In the post-pay mode, the payment service provider sends billing information to the trusted third party, which sends the bill to customers, receives the money back, and then sends the revenue to payment service provider.

Operational Issues in M-Commerce Payment

Payment schemes can be classified as account based and token based. In the account-based scheme, consumers are billed on their account. This scheme is not suitable for small value transactions. In the token-based scheme, a token is a medium of payment transaction representing some monetary value and requires the support

of the payment provider or TTP. Customers have to convert the actual currency to tokens. There are three different billing methods. One is real time, in which some form of electronic currency is exchanged during the transaction. The payment settlement can also be prepaid where customers pay in advance to have a successful transaction. Another method is the postpaid method in which customers pay after they receive the service/good.

Customers will choose a new payment method only if it allows them to pay in an accustomed method. The different payment settlement methods offered by the provider will hence play a crucial role. Based on payment settlement methods, the payment solutions can also be categorized as smart and prepaid cards solution, electronic cash or digital wallets solution, direct debiting and off-line-procedure solution, and credit cards and payments via the phone bill solution. In the payment using smart card or prepaid card solution, customers buy a smart card or prepaid card where the money-value is stored and then pay off for goods or services purchased. Customers can also upload a digital wallet with electronic coins on a prepaid basis. The smart cards, prepaid cards and digital wallets are thus used for prepaid payment solution. Another form of payment settlement is direct debit from the bank, which is a real-time payment method, since the purchase amount will be deducted as soon as the customer authorizes the payment. Payment method can also be using the phone bill or the credit card, where the customer pays for the good or services purchased at a later time. Payment by phone bill is one of the simplest methods of payment in which a special merchant-specific phone number is called from the mobile phone, which causes a predefined amount to be billed to callers' telephone bill. These types of payment schemes are applicable only to a single payment amount, providing limited security, and requiring users and merchants to share the same mobile operator (Pierce, 2000).

Smart cards can be used for all the three types of payment methods, for example, credit, debit and stored value as well as in authentication, authorization and transaction processing (Shelfer & Procaccino, 2002). A smart card thus enables the storage and communication of personal information such as value of goods and identity. A smart card can be either a memory card or processing enabled card. Memory cards are one type of prepaid cards, which transfer electronic equivalent of cash to the merchant electronic register. Processor cards, on the other hand, can be used as a debit card, credit card or a stored value card. A major drawback is the large costs associated with replacement of the existing infrastructure. In addition, the model lacks technical interoperability among existing smart card architectures.

The adoption of various payment frequencies in payment process is also a critical factor to make m-commerce payment succeed. It can be paid per view where consumers pay for each view, or increment, of the desired content; for example, downloading Mp3 files, video file or ring tones. It can also be paid per unit, where consumers pay once for each unit successfully completed with the content provider. A consumer would spend a certain number of units during each session, which is subsequently billed to the customer; for example, customer participating in an online game. The third type is a flat rate payment where consumers pay a recurring amount to access content on an unlimited basis for a certain period of time; for example, customer being charged to have access to an online magazine (McKitterick & Dowling, n.d.). The success of a payment solution will also depend on whether it can pay for a wide range of products and services. The payment can be a micro-payment, which refers to a payment of approximately $10 or less. In a micropayment system the number of transactions between each payer and the merchant is large as compared to the amount of each individual transaction. As a result transaction-processing cost grows for such systems. This kind of setting is addressed by a subscription scheme where a bulk amount is paid for which the use of a service is bought for a certain period of time. Traditional account

based systems are not suitable for these kinds of transactions and hence the need for third-party payment processors arises which accumulate the transactions that can be paid for at a later time. The payment can also be macro-payments, which refers to larger value payments such as online shopping. It is also important to consider the technical infrastructure required by the customers to participate in a payment system (Krueger, 2001; Mobey Forum Mobile Financial Services Ltd, 2001). Some solutions do not require any changes to the hardware or software, which will then have a trade-off on the security aspect of payment. Some solutions require a sophisticated technology, which may be very secure but may not have taken the user's convenience into consideration. Most current payment solutions are SMS or WAP (Wireless Application Protocol) based. Some of the solutions use dual chip. In addition to SIM (Secure Identification Module), a second chip, such as WIM (Wireless Identity Module), standard smart cards and memory flash cards, is integrated into mobile device to provide the security functionality. The dual slot technology can also be used for payment services. This technology uses a regular SIM-card to identify the mobile device and also provide a second card slot for a credit or debit card integrated within a mobile phone. Payment solutions relying on an external chip card reader, which is connected to the mobile terminal using Bluetooth, infrared technologies or a cable, also come under the dual slot category.

In addition, software based payment solutions have been considered. A software agent based wireless e-commerce environment has been proposed (Maamar et al., 2001), called Electronic Commerce through Wireless Devices (E-CWE). The environment associates users with user-agents, embodies user-agents with personalization and mobility mechanisms, and relates providers to provider-agents. Initially a J2ME application has to be downloaded which provides the interface to credit card information, including merchant and payment data. Then credit information is posted via HTTPS connection to the payment service provider. All business logic is fetched from the Web server and usually no new software or hardware is required on the device.

MOBILE PAYMENT SYSTEMS OR SOLUTIONS

This section will portray current mobile payment solutions and compare them from user perspective of cost, security and convenience. The Electronic Payment Systems Observatory (ePSO) identified over 30 different mobile payment solutions, each with its own particular set of technologies (ePSO, n.d.). Mobile operators provide many solutions: some by financial players and others involving alliances between operators and financial organizations. Most of the solutions involve a relatively similar process.

Existing mobile solutions are categorized based on the payment settlement methods that are prepaid (using smart cards or digital wallet), instant paid (direct debiting or off-line payments), and post paid (credit card or telephone bill). The three payment settlement options may vary in their requirements, process of payment and technologies used. The only requirement to a prepaid type of payment solution is a PIN for authorizing a transaction and a smart card value or stored value card for making payment. The technological requirements range between just a mobile phone to a smart card with a dual slot phone and smart card reader. The payment procedure starts with customers selecting a product or service and the mode of payment. Next, customers authorize the transaction using PIN number and then the payment amount is deducted from the stored value card.

Payment solutions based on payment direct from credit or bank accounts require an agreement between customer and payment provider that authorizes the payment provider to divulge the customer information to merchant and charge the customer. Customers have to divulge their credit card information or bank account number to payment service providers. The transaction also requires a PIN or a password. The technologies in use today for this type of solutions are a dual slot phone with a smart reader, dual chip phones (SIM+WIM), and payment provider calling back the customer's mobile phone. In general the solutions in this category follow the same high-level process. Customers select a product or service and the payment mode and authorize the transaction by entering a PIN or password. The payment provider forwards the card/bank information to the merchant. The payment amount is deducted from bank account or credited to customers' account and paid to the merchant.

The solutions based on charging the customer through phone bill require an agreement between customer and payment provider to charge the customer's phone bill. Such solutions require infrared or bluetooth technologies for establishing connection to the point of sale. In some cases a premium rate is enough. If the mobile phone uses a bluetooth/infrared technology, the point of sale contacts the mobile phone using the technology. Customers will then choose the product or service and authorize the payment with a button click on the mobile phone. Subsequently, the amount is charged to the phone bill. If the mobile phone uses just a premium rate to select a product or service, the mobile network calls the point of sale to authorize the sale and subsequently the amount is charged to the phone bill.

The following section portrays some current payment solutions such as Paybox, iPIN, m-PayBill, m-Pay and Jalda. A general analysis of the payment solutions based on customer requirements of cost, security and convenience is also provided.

Payment Solutions

Paybox

One of the most widespread mobile phone payment applications is Paybox (Paybox.net, 2002), which was launched in Germany in May 2000. Later it

Figure 2. Paybox transaction

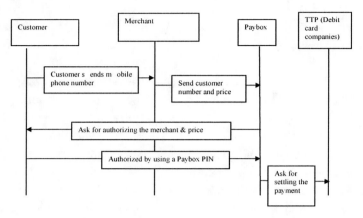

was launched in Austria, Spain, Sweden and the UK. This service enables customers to purchase goods and services and make bank transactions via mobile phone. The value of purchases or credit transfers is debited from customers' bank account. The infrastructures needed to use Paybox are a mobile phone, a bank account and a paybox registration. A typical real-world mobile transaction using Paybox is given in Figure 2. Customers send their phone number to a merchant. The merchant communicates this phone number and the price. The Paybox system calls the customer and asks for payment authorization. Payers authorize by their PIN. Paybox informs the trusted third party to settle the payment.

Paybox is very simple and easy to use because of the very limited infrastructures needed and only costs a small annual fee for customers. M-payment is independent. For example, it allows services to customers of any bank or mobile operator. A key advantage of the independent payers is that they enable every mobile user to use the service upon registration, regardless of their mobile service provider. This independency of Paybox is also helpful to merchants since teaming up with such a payer is more efficient than teaming up with three or more separate mobile operators. Paybox also promises to provide a fraud protected cost effective system. The disadvantages are that the operation of Paybox is expensive since the system has to

make voice calls using integrated voice recognition system (IVR) to the customer, which could range over various durations. In addition, there is no data privacy and customer and merchant have no proof of transaction, which might be a possible cause of fraud. The high latency also restricts it to high value transactions (Fischer, 2002). Most of all the transaction can be done only using a GSM enabled phone.

An annual fee is charged to customers, but there is no transaction fee involved. Paybox can be used with any mobile phone. Hence infrastructure costs are low. Peer to peer transactions come with an extra cost. Customers need to know only the PIN number to participate and the IVR system will then guide them through the rest of the payment process. Processing of transactions is fast. Paybox is suitable for macro as well as small payments. Paybox can also be used for peer-to-peer transactions where customers can send and receive money to other participants. Paybox owns customers' data and does not give the personal data to any other parties involved in the process. However, one drawback is that both customers and merchants do not have any proof of the transaction. Some fraud prevention techniques are promised by Paybox (Paybox.net, 2001), including address checking and correction using fuzzy logic tools, using checksums for credit card numbers and bank account numbers, checks on the demographic data, credit history checks, and address verification by sending the final PIN.

iPIN

iPIN is a privately held corporation based in Belmont, CA (USA) (ePSO, n.d.; Cap, Gemini, Ernst &Young, 2002). iPIN's Enterprise Payment Platform (EPP) is a leading end-to-end electronic and mobile commerce payment technology. It allows virtual point of sale and peer-to-peer payments over fixed as well as wireless networks. Seven software components have been identified in iPIN (Cap, Gemini, Ernst &Young, 2002). The main component of the iPIN payment system is the commerce router, which manages transactions throughout the payment lifecycle. It serves the user-interface pages and manages all end-user customer account activity. The repository is used for managing configurations and merchant information. Billing engine does the transaction fee calculation and facilitates account settlement. The merchant POS controller connects to the merchant's point of sale. The payment gateway connects to financial providers such as banks and credit card companies. The business intelligent module of iPIN keeps track of the success and returns on investments. The usage of the iPIN multiple payment instruments enables a customer to choose prepaid, debit or credit solution.

A typical transaction using the iPIN payment system is shown in Figure 3. Customers initiate purchase requests to merchant. The merchant sends an authorization request to the issuer's commerce router. Customers are redirected to the commerce router for authenticating themselves after a secure session is established with the commerce router. After successful authentication is complete, the commerce router authorizes the transaction. Then the router establishes a transaction record in the database and sends the authorization response to the merchant. The merchant then sends a clearing message to the commerce router, confirming the transaction.

iPIN offers users a secure and efficient way to purchase virtual goods and services with a variety of connected devices including Web, WAP, SMS and IVR. Throughout the purchase process, the enterprise houses the user's personal profile and guarantees payment to merchants without actually transferring customers' private financial information. Fees are based on transactions. There is no setup fee for the customer. The only effort by consumers is to open or activate an account. Users are afforded several payment options including micro payment, and can choose to associate these charges to a prepaid account, monthly bill, and bankcard or loyalty program. Available via a mobile handset, self-care tools let users access detailed transaction histories, set account preferences such as spending limits and preferred account details, and receive answers to frequently asked questions. iPIN provides for interoperability between a group of individual payment networks, allowing merchants from one network to sell to users from other networks, while giving users access to a larger group of merchants and products.

Vodafone m-PayBill

m-PayBill supports virtual POS for micro and small payments (ePSO, n.d.; Vodafone M-Pay bill, n.d.). The bill is charged to customers' phone bill or from the prepaid airtime. The requirements for this payment solution are a WAP phone or a Web browser to settle the payment. Figure 4 shows a typical micro payment transaction using Vodafone. The Vodafone customers register for m-PayBill online by entering their mobile phone number, choosing a username, a password, and a four-digit PIN. When using a WAP phone the user is asked to enter the PIN for identification. Purchase amount is then charged to the phone bill or deducted from prepaid airtime.

m-PayBill membership is free; there are no basic or transaction fees. No extra infrastructure needed to perform the transaction except for a

Figure 3. Transaction in an iPIN payment solution

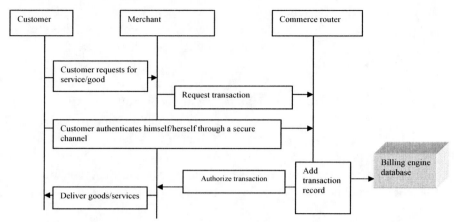

Figure 4. Transactions in Vodafone-mPayBill solution

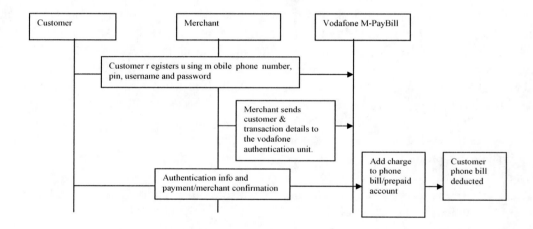

WAP phone. m-PayBill provides interoperability by having service providers outside of European Union plus Norway, Iceland and Liechtenstein. The personal information is transferred to the service providers in other countries for purchases outside the European Union. The security of the information will then depend on the privacy policy of that country. Payment information is maintained on the server and does not change hands, thus preventing any chances of fraud. The process is basically easy to understand and provides faster transactions. Customers who already registered with the Vodafone network operator need not register again to use the procedure. Payment solution, however, is only applicable to micro-payments.

m-Pay

m-Pay is a mobile payment solution developed in corporation between PBS, Orange and Gem plus (PBS ,n.d.). It is a server-based credit/debit card payment solution via mobile phone for goods ordered via telephone sales and on the Internet through the PC or a WAP mobile phone. To use this application the user sends a written applica-

Figure 5. Payment transaction in an m-Pay solution

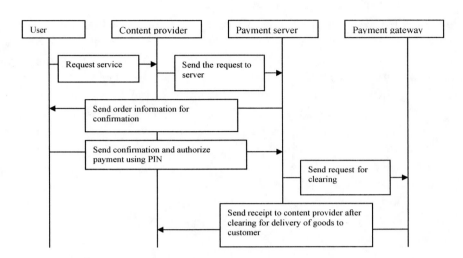

tion to Orange asking to link the payment data to the GSM data in a payment server. Activating the payment function on the mobile phone requires an individually allocated PIN-code, which is connected to the SIM-card in the mobile phone. A typical transaction using m-Pay is given in Figure 5.

Customers request a service or product from the content provider. This request in the form of an SMS message is sent to payment server, which takes care of authorizing the payment request. Payment server sends the order information to customers for confirmation, which customers do by using a personal identification number presented in the SIM card. The server will then translate the mobile phone number into a valid card number and conduct a debit/credit card transaction. This confirmation is sent to the payment gateway for clearing, after which a receipt is generated by the gateway and sent to the content provider.

Customers must first register with Orange to use m-Pay. The registration is free but a new "Orange" SIM card required and payment confirmation service provided comes with a cost. An advantage with regards to cost is that customers need not buy new handsets to use the solution.

None of the sensitive information is put on air. A payment receipt will be sent, whereupon customers receive notification in the form of an SMS message. The payment is carried out by exchange of e-payment certificates. The PBS payment server verifies any transaction from the SIM card, which ensures that the merchant is approved to trade and also that the card has not been reported stolen or stopped from further transactions. To use this payment application, users have to download a script over the air to activate the dormant payment application in their SIM card. The payment transaction will take less than 10 seconds. After the PIN code has been accepted by the SIM application, customers are able to buy airtime and the amount will automatically be drawn from their credit/debit card account.

Jalda

Jalda is an account-based system wherein both consumers and retailers are connected to a special account managed by a payment provider, who usually acts as the certificate authority (Dahlström, 2001; ePSO, n.d.). For payments using mobile phones, the certificate is stored centrally with the payment provider. Users authorize a transaction through a PIN-code. It can also be used for Internet transactions, in which case the certificate is stored in the hard drive. Jalda is a session-based Internet payment method that enables payment by the second, item, quantity, mouse click, search, character, page, or practically any other parameters. Jalda consists of two parts: an application program interface (API) and a payment server that administers user data and keeps track of transactions. The Jalda actors are consumers who use Jalda API applications to purchase via the mobile phone and the content provider who uses the Jalda API to charge consumers for service.

The system enables customers to be charged by whatever parameter the content provider desires. The content provider deducts a small transaction fee from the customer phone bills. The infrastructure required is a WAP phone. Security of payments is guaranteed by using strong authentication and non-repudiation protocols. Self-administration interface enables users to control their account. A payment receipt is sent to users, which may be stored in the WAP phone. Jalda is an account-based payment method, enabling both prepaid and credit-based payments. The accounts are managed and held by the payment provider and the payment provider usually acts as the certificate authority. Jalda can also be used for normal payments as well as micro-payments. The Jalda micropayment protocol is based on a concept of a payment session that is initiated by the payer by accepting and electronically signing a session contract with the merchant. The payment provider will then verify the contract for the vendor. After successful verification the vendor can then start keeping track of the service used by sending periodic indications when the consumer is consuming the service.

Jalda supports interoperability but does not enforce it as a global standard. Hence two payment providers need to make an agreement before the respective users can purchase goods from the other payment provider's merchants.

Other Solutions

Nokia launched a dual chip solution called EMPS (Electronic Mobile Payment Services). One chip was a usual SIM (subscriber identity module) card and the other was a WIM (WAP Identity module) for making mobile payments. Parkit is used in some cities of Finland to pay for parking. In this solution a service number of the parking area is called after which parking is registered and customers end the parking by calling again to a nationwide "ending number". The parking fee will be included on customers' telephone bill, credit card bill or a separate bill.

General Analysis of the Payment Solutions

Payment solutions can be categorized on the basis of the payment settlement methods, which are instant-paid, postpaid, prepaid or a combination of these. In the prepaid solution, customers buy a smart card where the amount equivalent is stored and then pay of this for goods or services desired. Subscription of services can also be considered as prepaid type of payment. The prepaid type of solutions allows privacy to users since at no point of the process is required to disclose any personal data. The instant paid solution is that payment settlement is done as soon as users confirm the payment as in direct debiting systems. In the postpaid solution customers pay for goods or services later. Payment by credit card and phone bill is an example. Table 1 shows this categorization for Paybox, iPIN, m-PayBill, m-Pay and Jalda.

The key to the acceptance of a mobile payment procedure is in the hands of customers. The determinants affecting the adoption of a payment solution are cost, security and convenience. Cost includes direct transaction cost, fixed cost of usage and cost for technical infrastructure on the part of the customer. *Security* is evaluated by confidentiality of data and confirmation of the payment. *Convenience* means ease, comfort, fast

Table 1.The categorization of payment solutions

Payment Solutions	Instant Paid	Prepaid	Postpaid
Paybox	X		
IPIN	X	X	X
m-PayBill	X	X	
m-Pay	X	X	
Jalda	X	X	

Table 2. Summary of the payment solutions

Payment Model	COST	CONVENIENCE	SECURITY
Paybox	An annual fee is charged to customer, but no transaction fee is involved. Peer-to-peer transaction comes with extra cost. Infrastructure costs are low.	Useful for macro, micro and peer-to-peer transactions. Customer is required to know only the PIN number to participate.	Customer personal data is kept in the Paybox server and not exchanged with other participants. Fraud prevention techniques are employed.
iPIN	No setup fee. Fees are based on transactions. Infrastructure costs are low.	Several payment options including micro-payments are offered. Interoperability between groups of individual payment networks is provided.	Enterprise houses users' personal data and guarantees privacy.
Vodafone m-PayBill	Membership is free. No basic or transaction fees. Infrastructure cost does not exist except that the customer might require a WAP enabled phone.	Only applicable to micro-payments. Payment process is more customer friendly. Customer who registered with Vodafone operator can automatically use the solution.	Interoperability between various countries is provided, but requires transfer of personal information. The privacy of the data will depend on the countries' privacy policy.
m-Pay	Registration is free. A new Orange SIM card is needed, which comes with a cost. Payment confirmation is also provided with a cost.	Customers need to download a script to activate applications on SIM card. Payment transaction is fast.	Payment is carried out by exchange of certificates. Customer receives payment confirmation in the form of SMS. Server verifies every transaction from SIM card.
Jalda	Content provider charges a small transaction fee from customers' phone bills. The customer might require a WAP enabled phone.	It can be used for normal as well as micro-payments, and supports interoperability but has not been enforced as a global standard.	Usage of strong authentication and non-repudiation protocols guaranteed. Payment receipt is sent to user.

processing and number of accepting merchants and interoperability. Table 2 gives a summary of the payment solutions based on the customer requirements.

FRAUD MANAGEMENT SYSTEMS IN M-COMMERCE

Fraud is defined as access or usage of the network with the intent of not paying for the service accessed. It can be either external or internal to the operator's network, and often involves both. Telecommunication fraud is estimated at 22 billion US dollars (USD) per year and growing annually at 2 billion USD (18 billion to fixed line fraud and 4 billion attributed to cellular). The convergence of voice and data communications, which has been driven by the tremendous uptake of the Internet and mobile phone ownership, has made fraud a high priority item on the agenda of most telecommunication operators. The advent of e-commerce activity further compounds the problem as industry analysts predict phenomenal growth in e-commerce over the next 3 years, with 40% of all e-commerce transactions expected to occur using mobile devices such as phones and personal assistants.

Many mobile payment solutions failed since they were unable to accumulate critical user mass. Merchants and consumers expressed their distrust in the electronic payment systems (Dahleberg & Tuunainen, 2001). The possible modes of fraud that will be experienced within m-commerce payment activity will encompass frauds related to security breaches in the underlying payment model, as well as in the underlying carrier network. A number of technologies are being used to prevent and detect these kinds of frauds. The frauds that can occur in the m-commerce environment have thus been categorized as mobile phone fraud, mobile network fraud and fraud specific to the m-commerce transaction process.

Mobile Phone Fraud

Criminals and hackers have devoted time and money to develop and refine their techniques, applying them to mobile phones as well. Not only is mobile phone fraud profitable, the stolen handsets have also provided anonymity to callers engaged in criminal activities. The various types of mobile phone fraud may be classified into two categories: subscription fraud and cloning fraud. Subscription fraud occurs from obtaining a subscription to a service, often with false identity details and no intention of paying. Cases of bad debt are also included in this category. In subscription fraud, all the calls for an account are fraudulent so there is no fraud-free period. Rules that are good for one time period may not be relevant for future time periods because calling behavior changes over time.

A signature-based system has been proposed in Cahill, Lambert et al. (2000). This system is event-driven rather than time driven so that fraud can be detected as it is happening and not at fixed intervals of time. It is based on the concept of account signatures, which may describe call durations, times between calls, days of week and times of day, terminating numbers, and payment methods for the particular account. All fraud records for particular kind of fraud are put into a fraud signature. For detecting a possible fraud, the call is scored by comparing its probability under the account signature to its probability under a fraud signature. Calls that are unexpected under the account signature and expected under the fraud signature receive higher scores and will be considered as more suspicious.

Cloning is the complete duplication of a legitimate mobile identification, namely, the MIN/ESN pair. Cloned phones can be identified with a technology called call pattern analysis. When a subscriber's phone deviates from its normal activity, it triggers an alarm at the service provider's fraud management system. It is put into queue where a fraud analyst ascertains whether the customer has been victimized and then remedies the situation by dropping the connection.

Location awareness of the mobile phone can be used to detect clones within a local system and to detect roamer clones (Patel, 1997). The success of these techniques is based on the assumption that the legitimate phones will stay powered up most of the time. Clones, by definition, will exist at a different location from the legitimate mobile phone. Clone detection within a user's current system can be recognized by "too many locations" and "impossible locations". A phone cannot be making a call from one cell site, and sending a registration message from another. In the cases of too many locations, fraud can be detected when getting registration messages from two different locations at almost the same time or getting two registration messages in an interval shorter than the re-registration period. Impossible location or velocity violation occurs when after a registration message at a location, another registration attempts from a location that is impossible to reach in the time elapsed. For the roaming, fraud is detected by monitoring handsets locations at the Home Location Register (HLR) and registration messages from Mobile Switching Center at Visitor Location Register (MSC/VLR) when mobiles enter a new system.

Mobile Network Fraud

A mobile wireless network is vulnerable due to its features of open medium, dynamic changing network topology, cooperative algorithms, lack of centralized monitoring and management point, and lack of a clear line of defense. There are many techniques to prevent mobile network intrusion such as secure MAC, secure routing and encryption. Intrusion detection approaches can be broadly classified into two categories based on model of intrusions: misuse and anomaly detection. Misuse detection refers to attempting

to recognize the attacks of previously observed intrusions in the form of a pattern or signature, and monitor the occurrence of these patterns; for example, frequent changes of directory or attempts to read a password file. Anomaly detection refers to establishing a historical normal profile for each user, and then using sufficiently large deviation from the profile to indicate possible intrusions.

Anomaly detection is a critical component of the overall intrusion detection and response mechanism. Trace analysis and anomaly detection should be done locally in each node and possibly through cooperation with all nodes in the network. In the anomaly detection model (Zhang & Lee, 2003), the attack model consists of attack on routing protocols wherein attacks behave by acting on routing protocols, or it may be a traffic pattern distortion. The audit data of the model are comprised of the local routing information and position locator of the mobile node. Classifiers are used as intrusion detectors and features are selected from the audit data. There are five steps to detect a possible intrusion in the network: selecting audit data, performing appropriate data transformation, computing classifier using training data, applying the classifier to test data, and post-processing alarms to produce intrusion reports.

A technique called Trace modulation has been used in Nobile, Satyanarayanan, and Nguyen, 1997), where the end-to-end characteristics of a wireless network are recreated. Trace modulation is transparent to applications and accounts for all network traffic sent or received by the system under test. These techniques can be used to detect possible bugs in the mobile network system

M-Commerce Payment Specific Fraud

Various types of frauds may arise due to security breaches in the payment model. With the mobile Internet, a fraudster can pick sensitive information out of the air. The vulnerabilities may include infection of the mobile device by a virus, use of PINs and passwords, which are easily guessable, possibility of messages getting lost, spoofing on cardholder or the payment provider and message replay. The requirements for protecting m-commerce transactions are similar to those for protecting fixed-line transactions. Sensitive data, for example, must be secured during transmission. The following sections state various frauds that may occur during the payment life cycle and the availability of the prevention and management schemes.

Fraud Prevention During Payment Authentication

Just as with the fixed line Internet, authenticating a user's identity may be the hurdle at which demand for m-commerce services could fall. Authentication is a process of associating a particular individual with an identity. Two different techniques have been used for authorization. One is a knowledge-based approach in which individuals use the "personal knowledge" about something, like a password or a PIN to identify themselves. The other is a token based approach in which the identification is done based on something a person has, like a driver's license number and credit card number. Both these approaches are susceptible to fraud due to lost or stolen tokens and also due to personal identifications that are used by fraudsters (Miller, 1994). A distributed scheme that solves the problem of uncovering the PIN has been proposed by Tang, Terziyan, and Veijalainen (2003). The authors suggest that instead of storing the entire PIN digits in the SIM of the mobile device, a part of the PIN is stored in the remote machine in the network. The PIN verification then involves both the mobile device and the remote machine, each verifying their respective parts of the PIN.

The increased use of wireless devices in m-commerce makes the need for identity verification even more important yet difficult to ensure; hence the need of biometrics in this field becomes more important. A biometric identification process for smart cards has been proposed by Jain, Hong, and Pankanti (2000). A biometric system has been defined as a system that makes personal identification based on some physical or behavioral characteristics of the person. In the enrollment phase a characteristic feature of the individual is scanned and converted to a digital representation. This digital form is then processed to a compact but expressive form called a template, which is stored in the smart card. During the recognition phase the biometric reader captures the characteristic and converts it into a digital form. The generated template is compared with the one stored in the smart card to establish the identity of the individual. In voice biometric systems mobile phone speakers are identified and verified based on their voice. The significant difference between a regular biometric system and the voice biometric system is that the regular one processes an image for identification whereas the voice biometric system processes acoustic information. This difference in processing results in a major difference in their acceptance since the regular biometric system requires extra infrastructure like image scanner whereas the voice biometric system can be deployed in the existing telecom systems using specialized applications (Markowitz, 2000). Radio frequency fingerprinting has been used to identify mobile phones. The Supervisory Audio Tones (SAT) tone frequency, SAT tone deviation, maximum deviation, frequency error, supervisory frequency, and supervisory tone deviation are used to fingerprint or individualize a mobile phone (Boucher, 2001).

It is being observed that the mobile phone is vulnerable to malicious software like viruses, which might be capable of creating unauthorized copies of the PIN or password when the user creates an authentication response to the payment provider. Therefore the various possibilities of virus infection in mobile phones should also be addressed. Two kinds of applications infected by virus can be downloaded. One is the signed application, which is authenticated by checking the signature using the public key stored in the mobile phone. The other is an unsigned application, which is basically un-trusted, and is the basic cause of identity fraud. To prevent such a fraud it would be appropriate to limit the access of the application to a sensitive resource on the mobile device by systematic denial or by sending a prompt to the user for validation.

Fraud During Payment Transaction and Settlement

A fraudulent transaction requires the fraudster to be in possession of the customer signature, such as PIN or password, and also to be able to send the response message to the payment provider. A possible way to prevent such a fraud is to send an authentication request number from authentication server to customer together with the authentication request, which should be unique for the transaction and should only be used for the message exchange with the cardholder.

The authentication gateway in a mobile commerce environment injects messages into the mobile network through a Short Message Switching Center for SMS as the transport or Unstructured Supplementary Services Data Center (USSDC) when using USSD as the transport. The messages pass through the Signaling System 7 (SS7) based network associated with the mobile network. This is the signaling network used for control of the mobile network. It is possible that SMS messages can be read or manipulated if the SMS switching center is accessible to the user. The capture of the messages is a source of mass fraud attacks. Hence mobile operators involved in the payment process should be encouraged to review their procedures

for protecting all the vulnerable parts of their network, including the BSSs, SS7 networks and the SMSC/USSDC and their interfaces.

To decrease the probability of fraud, prepaid solutions were introduced which allow users to access specific services for which they pay in advance. In GSM mobile networks the prepaid solutions are intelligent network, which allows automatic call termination when the prepaid value reaches zero. Fraud prevention during payment settlement generally involves supporting the non-repudiation property of mobile networking. Zhou and Lam proposed an efficient technique for non-repudiation of billing using digital signatures and hashing mechanisms (Zhou & Lam, 1998). In this scheme a mobile user needs to submit a digital signature when requesting a call along with a chained hash value. After this, a series of hashed values are released at predefined intervals, which allows at most the last unit of service in dispute. The problem of uncollectible debt in telecommunication services is addressed by using a goal-directed Bayesian network for classification, which distinguishes customers who are likely to have bad debt (Maamar et al., 2001). Digital data can be copied and a user can spend a valid electronic coin several times. Requiring the vendors to contact the financial institution during every sale, in order to determine whether the dollar spent is still good, can prevent double spending. Double spending can also be prevented using tamper resistant smart cards, which contain a small database of all transactions. Double spending can also be detected, in which case a double spender is identified when the cash is settled in the bank. In another detection mechanism tamper resistant device, "Observer" is used to prevent double spending physically. This allows the owner to spend the coin once in an anonymous manner, but the identity of the owner would be revealed if he or she tries to use it again (Chaum & Pedersen, 1992). The detection schemes thus do not prevent but deter double spending and also do not require any specific hardware.

RESEARCH ISSUES AND CONCLUSIONS

Research Issues

Without a wide popularity and usage, any given payment solution will not survive, regardless of its different attractive features. The disappearance of some innovative electronic payment procedures like eCash serves as an example of this fact. A mobile payment procedure today should not only consider the option of low to medium macro-payments, but also include at least the potential for further development in the direction of cost-effective micro payments.

Apart from the widespread acceptance of the solution by customers, another issue that remains to be solved is an issue of different mobile payment service providers. Because of their existing customer base, technical expertise and familiarity with billing, mobile telephone operators are natural candidates of the service providers. However, risk management and the need to ensure the cooperation of different providers for interoperability in an efficient m-payment system may complicate the issue. Future payment models may be the bank-dominated models where the mobile phones will provide just another way for customers to access their bank account. The PKI security standard, which is now widespread in the e-commerce scenario, can be applied to the m-commerce scenario as well. Integrating PKI into a single SIM handset needs further study. Finally, EMV, a standard for debit and credit bankcards, deserves consideration.

Conclusions

Mobile security and payment are central to m-commerce. Today, a number of competing mobile payment solutions have already found their way into the marketplace. In this chapter we surveyed several payment solutions and listed some fraud management schemes, which are central to a successful payment solution.

An important point which influences the establishment of the mobile payment procedure is the technical infrastructure needed on the customer side. A sophisticated technology may fail if the customer is not able to handle it with ease. On the other hand, simple procedures based on simple message exchange via short messaging services (SMS) may prove profitable. Thus, at present and in the future the important payment solutions will be SMS-based, which can easily be charged to the mobile phone bill of customers. Some other procedures may integrate two or more solutions. An important observation is that m-payments are still in their infancy. The m-payment solutions are still being developed with standards defined on individual business segments, which is a major reason for market fragmentation in this area even though the mobile marketplace is global. Other interesting areas related to m-commerce payment not mentioned in this chapter are issues of standardization and interoperability. These issues will have to be resolved for these solutions to reach their full potential, especially in places like Europe, where there are a large number of mobile operators and users who tend to roam into different areas.

Mobile commerce can only be conducted if all parties believe that there is adequate security. The majority of users of mobile commerce technologies are concerned about security. A sound security policy includes identifying security risks, implementing effective security measures, and educating users on the importance of security procedures. Fraud management systems are becoming increasingly important for wireless carriers. The challenge is to monitor and profile the activity of the users and to be alert to the changing nature of fraud.

REFERENCES

Boucher, N.J. (2001). *The cellular radio handbook: A reference for cellular system operation* (4th ed.). New York: A Wiley-Interscience Publication, John Wiley & Sons Inc.

Cahill, M.H., Lambert, D., Pinheiro, J.C., & Sun, D.X. (2000). Detecting fraud in real world. In J. Abello, P. Pardalos & M. Resende (Eds.), *Handbook of massive datasets*. New York: Kluwer Press.

Chaum, D., & Pedersen, T. (1992). Wallet databases with observers. In E. Brickell (Ed.), *Proceedings of Crypto 92* (vol. 0740 of LNCS, pp. 89-105).

Dahleberg, T., & Tuunainen, V. (2001). Mobile payments: The trust perspective. Workshop Sollentuna September 2001. Retrieved September 14, 2003, from *http://web.hhs.se/cic/seamless/Portal/Documents/Sollentuna/Abstract_Dahlberg_Tuunainen.doc*

Dahlström, E. (2001). The Jalda payment method. *ePSO-Newsletter, 5*(5). Retrieved September 13, 2003, from *http://epso.jrc.es/newsletter/vol05/5.html*

Fischer, I.M. (2002). Towards a generalized payment model for Internet services. Masters thesis. Technical University of Vienna.

Jain, A., Hong, L., & Pankanti, S. (2000). Biometric identification. *Communications of the ACM, 43*(2). Retrieved September 14, 2003, from the ACM Digital Library.

Krueger, M. (2001). The future of m-payments - business options and policy issues. Electronic Payment Systems Observatory (ePSO) Institute for Prospective Technological Studies. Retrieved September 2003, from *http://www.e-pso.info/epso/index.html*

Maamar, Z., Yahyaoui, H., Mansoor, W., & Heuvel, W. (2001). Software agents and wireless e-commerce. *ACM SIGecom Exchanges, 2*(3). Retrieved September 14, 2003, from the ACM Digital Library.

Markowitz, A.J. (2000). Voice biometrics. *Communications of the ACM, 43*(9). Retrieved September 14, 2003, from the ACM Digital Library.

McKitterick, D., & Dowling J. (*2003*). State of the art review of mobile payment technology. Retrieved September 14, 2003, from Trinity College Of Dublin, Department of Computer Science Web site: *http://www.cs.tcd.ie/publications/tech-reports/reports.03/TCD-CS-2003-24.pdf*

Miller, B. (1994). Vital signs of identity [biometrics]. *IEEE Spectrum Magazine, 31*(2), 22-30. Retrieved September 14, 2003, from the IEEE Xplore Online Delivery System.

Mobey Forum Mobile Financial Services Ltd. (2001). The preferred payment Architecture Technical Documentation. Retrieved September 2003, from *http://ipsi.fraunhofer.de/mobile/teaching/m-commerce_ws0203/payment/MobeyTechnical.pdf*

Mobile Commerce Report. Retrieved September 9, 2003, from *http://www.durlacher.com/downloads/mcomreport.pdf*

MobileInfo.com: M-Commerce. Retrieved September 9, 2003, from *http://www.mobileinfo.com/Mcommerce/index.htm*

Mobile Payment Forum. (2002). Enabling secure, interoperable, and user-friendly mobile payments.

Retrieved September 9, 2003, from *http://www.mobilepaymentforum.org/pdfs/mpf_whitepaper.pdf*

Mobile Payments in M-Commerce, White paper. (2002). Retrieved September 2003, from Cap, Gemini, Ernst and Young Web site: *http://www.cgey.com/tmn/pdf/MobilePaymentsinMCommrce.pdf*

More Magic Software (2000, November 24). Payment transaction platform. Retrieved September 9, 2003, from *http://www.moremagic.com/whitepapers/technical_wp_twp021c.html*

Nobile, B.D., Satyanarayanan, M., & Nguyen, G.T. (1997). Trace-based mobile network emulation. *Proceedings of the ACM SIGCOMM '97 Conference on Applications, Technologies, Architectures, and Protocols for Computer Communication.* Retrieved September 14, 2003, from the ACM Digital Library.

Patel, S. (1997). Location, identity and wireless fraud detection. *IEEE International Conference on Personal Wireless Communications, 17-19 Dec.* (pp. 515-521). Retrieved September 14, 2003, from the IEEE Xplore Online Delivery System.

Paybox: ePSO Inventory Database (n.d.). Retrieved September 13, 2003, from *http://www.e-pso.info/epso/index.html*

Paybox.net. (2001). Paybox security, Whitepaper, business and technical information regarding the security at paybox. Retrieved September 2003, from *http://www.paybox.net/publicrelations/public_relations_whitepapers.html*

Paybox.net. (2002). Mobile commerce delivery made simple: Whitepaper. Retrieved September 13, 2003, from *http://www.paybox.net/publicrelations/public_relations_whitepapers.html*

Payment Technology. Retrieved September 13, 2003, from Trinity College Of Dublin, Department of Computer Science Web site: *http://www.cs.tcd.ie/publications/tech-reports/reports.03/TCD-CS-2003-24.pdf*

PBS. (n.d.). *Mobile payment.* Retrieved September 14, 2003, from *http://www.pbs.dk/english/produkter/mbetaling.htm*

Pierce, M. (2000). *Multi-party electronic payments for mobile communications.* Doctoral dissertation. University of Dublin.

Shelfer, K.M., & Procaccino, J.D. (2002). Smart card evolution. *Communications of the ACM, 45*(7). Retrieved September 14, 2003, from the ACM Digital Library.

Tang, J., Terziyan, V., & Veijalainen, J. (2003). Distributed PIN verification scheme for improving security of mobile devices. *Mobile Networks and Applications, 8*(2). Retrieved September 14, 2003, from the ACM Digital Library.

Telecom Media Networks. (2000, September). Mobile payments-commerce. Retrieved September 13, 2003, from *http://www.cgey.com/tmn/pdf/MobilePaymentsin MCommrce.pdf*

Vodafone M-Pay Bill. (n.d.). What is Vodafone m-pay bill? Retrieved September 2003, from *http://mpay-bill.vodafone.co.uk/w_mpay.html*

Xiaolin, Z., & Chen, D. (2003). Study of mobile payment systems. *IEEE International Conference on E-commerce* (pp. 24-27). Retrieved September 14, 2003, from the IEEE Xplore Online Delivery System.

Zhang, Y., & Lee, W. (2003). Intrusion detection techniques for mobile wireless networks. *Wireless Networks, 9*(5). Retrieved September 14, 2003, from the ACM Digital Library.

Zhou, J., & Lam, K. (1998). Undeniable billing in mobile communication. *Proceedings of the 4th Annual ACM/IEEE International Conference on Mobile Computing and Networking* (pp. 284-290).

Retrieved September 14, 2003, from the ACM
Digital Library.

Chapter 4.40
Secure Agent for E-Commerce Applications

Sheng-Uei Guan
National University of Singapore, Singapore

INTRODUCTION

One hindrance to the widespread adoption of mobile agent technology (Johansen et al., 2002) is the lack of security. SAFER, or Secure Agent Fabrication, Evolution and Roaming, is a mobile agent framework that is specially designed for the purpose of electronic commerce (Guan & Yang, 2002, 2004; Yang & Guan, 2000; Zhu, Guan, Yang, & Ko, 2000). By building strong and efficient security mechanisms, SAFER aims to provide a trustworthy framework for mobile agents. Although such an agent transport protocol provides for the secure roaming of agents, there are other areas related to security to be addressed.

Agent integrity is one such area crucial to the success of agent technology. The integrity protection for agent code is relatively straightforward. A more complex code integrity scheme to handle code-on-demand is also proposed in Wang, Guan, and Chan (2002). Agent data, however, is dynamic in nature and will change as the agent roams from host to host. Despite the various attempts in the literature (Chionh, Guan, & Yang, 2001), there is no satisfactory solution to the problem so far.

Some of the common weaknesses of the current schemes are vulnerabilities to revisit attack and illegal modification (deletion/insertion) of agent data.

DESCRIPTION OF SADIS

SADIS has been designed based on the following assumptions:

1. Entities including agents, agent butlers, and hosts should have globally unique identification number (IDs).
2. Each agent butler and host should have a digital certificate that is issued by a trusted CA. These entities will be able to use the private key of its certificate to perform digital signatures and encryption.
3. Whereas the host may be malicious, the execution environment of mobile agents should be secure and the execution integrity of the agent can be maintained.
4. Entities involved are respecting and cooperating with the SADIS protocol.

Key Seed Negotiation Protocol

The proposed key seed negotiation protocol defines the process for key seed negotiation and session key and data encryption key derivation. When an agent first leaves the butler, the butler generates a random initial key seed, encrypts it with the destination host's public key, and deposits it into the agent before sending the agent to the destination host. It should be noted that agent transmission is protected by the agent transport protocol (Guan and Yang, 2002), thereby protecting the system from being compromised by malicious hosts.

The key seed negotiation process is based on the Diffie-Hellman (DH) key exchange protocol (Schneier, 1996), with a variation. The agent will first generate a private DH parameter a and its corresponding public parameter x. The value x, together with the ID of the destination host, will be encrypted using a communication session key and sent to the agent butler.

The agent butler will decrypt the message using the same communication session key (discussed later). It, too, will generate its own DH private parameter b and its corresponding public parameter y. With the private parameter b and the public parameter x from the agent, the butler can derive the new key seed and use it for communications with the agent in the new host. Instead of sending the public parameter y to the agent as in normal DH key exchange, the agent butler will encrypt the value y, host ID, agent ID and current timestamp with the destination host's public key to get message M. Message M will be sent to the agent after encrypting with the communication session key.

$$M = E(y + \text{host ID} + \text{agent ID} + \text{timestamp}, H_{pubKey})$$

At the same time, the agent butler updates the agent's itinerary and stores the information locally. This effectively protects the agent's actual itinerary against any hacking attempts related to itinerary, thereby protecting against the data deletion attack.

When the agent receives the double-encrypted DH public parameter y, it can decrypt with the communication session key. Since the decrypted result M is parameter y and some other information encrypted with the destination host's public key, the current host will not be able to find out the value of y and thus find out the new key seed to be used when the agent reaches the destination host. It should be noted that this does not prevent the host from replacing M with its own version M' with the same host ID, agent ID, timestamp but different y. The inclusion of host ID, agent ID inside M can render such attack useless against SADIS. A detailed discussion on this attack can be found in the security analysis section.

Subsequently, the agent will store M into its data segment and requests the current host to send itself to the destination host, using the agent transport protocol (Guan & Yang, 2002).

On arriving at the destination host, the agent will be activated. Before it resumes normal operation, the agent will request the new host to decrypt message M. If the host is the right destination host, it will be able to use the private key to decrypt message M, and thus obtain the DH public parameter y. As a result, the decryption of message M not only completes the key seed negotiation process but also serves as a means to authenticate the destination host. Once the message M is decrypted, the host will verify that the agent ID in the decrypted message matches the incoming agent, and the host ID in the decrypted message matches that of the current host. In this way, the host can ensure that it is decrypting for a legitimate agent instead of some bogus agent. If the IDs in the decrypted messages match, the decrypted value of y is returned to the agent.

With the plain value of y, the agent can derive the key seed by using its previously generated private parameter a. With the new key seed derived, the key seed negotiation process is completed.

The agent can resume normal operation in the new host.

Whenever the agent or the butler needs to communicate with each other, the sender will first derive a communication session key using the key seed and use this communication session key to encrypt the message. The receiver can make use of the same formula to derive the communication session key from the same key seed to decrypt the message.

The communication session key K_{CSK} is derived using the following formula:

$$K_{CSK} = Hash(key\_seed + host\ ID + seqNo).$$

The sequence number is a running number that starts with 1 for each agent roaming session, and is reset to 1 whenever the agent reaches a new host. Each message communicated will therefore be encrypted using a different key. As this means that the butler and agent will not be able to communicate if messages are lost without detection, SADIS makes use of TCP/IP as a communication mechanism. Once the communication is reestablished after a send failure, the sender will resend the previous message (encrypted using the same communication session key). The agent and the butler can therefore synchronize on communication session key calculations.

The agent encrypts host information with a data encryption key K_{DEK}. The data encryption key is derived as follows:

$$K_{DEK} = Hash(key\_seed + hostID)$$

The details on encryption will be discussed in the next section.

Data Integrity Protection Protocol

The key seed negotiation protocol lays the necessary foundation for integrity protection by establishing a session-based key seed between the agent and its butler. Digital certificates also help protect the agent data integrity.

Our data Integrity Protection protocol is comprised of two parts: chained signature generation and data integrity verification. Chained signature generation is performed before the agent leaves the current host. The agent gathers data provided by the current host d_i and construct D_i as follows:

$$D_i = E(d_i + ID_{host} + ID_{agent} + timestamp, k_{DEK})$$

or

$$D_i = d_i + ID_{host} + ID_{agent} + timestamp$$

The inclusion of host ID, agent ID and timestamp is to protect the data from possible replay attack, especially when the information is not encrypted with the data encryption key, thereby creating an unambiguous memorandum between the agent and the host. The construction of D_i also gives the flexibility to encrypt the data or keep it in plain. After constructing D_i, the agent will request the host to perform a signature on the following:

$$c_i = Sig(D_i + c_{i-1} + ID_{host} + ID_{agent} + timestamp, k_{priv}),$$

where c_0 is the digital signature on the agent code by its butler.

One design focus of SADIS is not only to detect data integrity compromise, but also, and what is more important, to identify malicious hosts. To achieve malicious host identification, it is an obligation for all hosts to verify the incoming agent's data integrity before activating the agent for execution. In the event of data integrity verification failure, the previous host will be identified as the malicious host.

Data integrity verification includes the verification of all the previous signatures. The verification of signature c_0 ensures agent code integrity, the verification of c_i ensures data provided by host

h_i is intact. If any signature failed the verification, the agent is considered compromised.

While the process to verify all data integrity may seem to incur too much overhead and somewhat redundant (e.g., why need to verify the integrity of d_1 in h_3 while host h_2 already verifies that), it is necessary to ensure the robustness of the protocol and to support the function of malicious host identification. Although the agent butler can eventually detect such data integrity compromise (since agent butler has to verify all signatures), but there is no way to establish the identity of malicious host(s).

Security Analysis

To analyze the effectiveness and reliability of SADIS, a detailed security analysis is performed subjecting SADIS to a variety of attacks. Based on the attack targets, the various attacks to SADIS can be classified into data attack, key attack, signature attack, itinerary attack, and composite attack. Composite attack refers to attacks that are combinations of two or more of the aforementioned attacks. The security analysis will be organized according to the previously mentioned classifications.

Data Attack

Data attack refers to any attempt that aims to compromise the data carried by an agent. Compromise can be in the form of data modification, deletion, or insertion.

Considering the data modification scenario, let us assume that the data targeted is D_i provided by host i, because the agent itinerary is protected by the butler and cannot be changed, only host i can produce a valid signature if the data were to be modified. However, even if the malicious party (or even host i) can produce a valid signature $c_i{}'$ corresponding to $D_i{}'$, since c_i is chained to the signature of the next host c_{i+1}, signature verification for host $(i+1)$ will fail. Therefore, in order to perform a successful data modification attack, the malicious host must be able to forge the signatures for all hosts in the itinerary since host i. As the only way to achieve this is to obtain the private keys of all the following hosts, data modification attack is extremely difficult under SADIS.

A number of the existing data integrity protocols suffer from data deletion attack. After analyzing the root cause of the vulnerabilities, it is realized that it is extremely important to protect the agent's itinerary. If the agent's itinerary is closely guarded by the butler, any data deletion will result in modification to the agent's itinerary and thus be detected.

Key Attack

Besides direct attack on data integrity, a malicious host may attempt to attack the various keys in order to compromise data integrity. There are three different types of keys in SADIS. They are session-based key seed, communication session key, and data encryption key. In SADIS, the key seed is kept by the agent and the butler separately. Attacks to the key seed can only target at the key seed negotiation protocol. As all communication in key seed negotiation is protected by the communication session key, we can safely rule out the possibility of any third-party malicious attempts to break the protocol. We can focus on the scenario where the current host attempts to break the key exchange to obtain the key seed to be used in the subsequent host.

First, as the DH public parameter is encrypted using the destination host's public key, the current host will not, without manipulation, be able to complete DH key exchange to find out the new key seed. Without the private key from the destination host, no one can obtain y to complete the key exchange. Furthermore, as the encrypted message contains the agent ID and destination host ID, the current host won't be able to send a bogus agent carrying this encrypted y to the destination host for decryption.

If the current host attempts to manipulate any one or both of these parameters, it is able to manipulate the key seed derived when the agent reaches the destination host. However, the change in key seed will be immediately detected when the agent communicates with the butler or vice versa. In order to perform a successful attack, the current host must therefore be able to obtain the key seed in the butler so that it can intercept and replace message communicated between the butler and the agent. Unfortunately, as illustrated earlier, there is no way the current host can find out the value of DH public parameter from butler y. Thus, the key seed will not be compromised.

Besides key seed, SADIS makes use of communication session key and data encryption key in the protocol. These two keys are directly derived from the session-based key seed using a hash function. As far as any third-party host is concerned, attack to communication session key or data encryption key is equivalent to attacking the encryption key given only the cipher text. Even in the extreme case when such a key is compromised, the loss is limited to the message it encrypts.

Signature Attack

Usually a malicious host would need to forge digital signature when it attempts to compromise data integrity. If data integrity is not compromised, there is no need to attack the chained signature at all.

Itinerary Attack

If the agent itinerary is not carefully protected, it may lead to compromise to data integrity, especially in the case of data deletion as illustrated earlier in the section. In SADIS, as the agent updates the butler of its next destination host as part of the key seed negotiation protocol, there is no additional overhead related to the itinerary protection mechanism. Therefore, there is no way a malicious host can perform any attack on the itinerary (except, of course, if it breaks into the agent butler).

Composite Attack

At times, in order to perform a successful attack, more than one area is targeted simultaneously. In addition to attacks with specific targets, there are certain general hacking techniques such as man-in-the-middle attack and replay attack. The design of SADIS employs a mechanism to protect the protocol against these hacking techniques. Through the use of communication session key, man-in-the-middle attack can be avoided. On the other hand, the use of sequence number in communication session key generation effectively protects the protocol from replay attack by a third party host. In addition, the inclusion of host ID, agent ID, and timestamp during the key seed negotiation process prevents the current host from performing a replay attack with the next destination host.

The design of SADIS does not have dependency on any specific encryption/hashing algorithm. In an unlikely scenario when one algorithm is broken, SADIS can always switch to a stronger algorithm.

Implementation

In order to verify the design of SADIS and assess its applicability, a prototype of SADIS is developed. The prototyping language is chosen to be Java, because of its platform independent feature.

Just like any other security mechanism, there is certain overhead associated with SADIS. The overhead is incurred as additional time required for processing as well as additional data carried by the agent. To assess the efficiency of SADIS, a study is performed on the prototype.

The result of this experimental study on SADIS is broken down, based on functionality and is shown in Table 1 and Table 2. It can be seen that the bulk of the overhead is incurred during key

Table 1. SADIS time efficiency (time taken for operations in milliseconds)– Performance without SADIS

Key Seed Negotiation (butler timing)	40	50	50	40	40	44.0
Key Seed Negotiation (destination host)	41	41	40	40	40	40.4
Agent Butler Communication (agent timing – send)	40	40	50	40	40	42.0
Agent Butler Communication (butler timing – send)	30	30	31	40	30	32.2
Agent Butler Communication (agent timing – receive)	10	10	10	10	10	10.0
Agent Butler Communication (butler timing – receive)	10	30	10	10	20	16.0

Table 2. SADIS time efficiency (time taken for operations in milliseconds) – Performance comparison with SADIS

Operation	1 (ms)	2 (ms)	3 (ms)	4 (ms)	5 (ms)	Avg (ms)	Overhead (ms)
Key Seed Negotiation (butler timing)	250	260	250	220	260	248.0	204.0
Key Seed Negotiation (destination host)	290	281	260	280	290	280.2	239.8
Agent Butler Communication (agent timing – send)	60	60	70	50	60	60.0	18.0
Agent Butler Communication (butler timing – send)	41	50	40	40	40	42.2	10.0
Agent Butler Communication (agent timing – receive)	10	20	10	10	10	12.0	2.0
Agent Butler Communication (butler timing – receive)	30	30	30	20	20	26.0	10.0

Table 3. SADIS data overhead

	Original Data Size	Maximum Overhead	Overhead	OKGS Overhead
1	1800	96	5.33%	33.87%
2	2001	96	4.80%	37.73%
3	5000	96	1.92%	N/A
4	10000	96	0.96%	N/A
5	100000	96	0.10%	N/A

seed negotiation where the key exchange protocol and the public key operation is performed. Despite the relatively high overhead, this will not impact the overall performance of SADIS significantly because the frequency of agent roaming is low compared to the frequency of some other agent operations (such as agent-to-butler communication). As a result, the overhead incurred at this stage is "one-time" in nature. Other than in the key seed negotiation, the time overhead incurred elsewhere in the protocol is negligible.

Other than overhead in terms of processing time, there is certain overhead to the data size as well. SADIS is designed to produce almost fixed data overhead regardless of the data size. SADIS therefore tends to be more efficient when actual data size is higher. This ability to limit the size of overhead data regardless of actual data size is an improvement in efficiency over existing work. The last and most significant overhead is the digital signature created by the host. The overhead of digital signature is a fixed length of 64 bytes. Altogether, SADIS has a maximum data overhead of 96 bytes.

As the statistics show, SADIS is optimized to improve time efficiency and data efficiency compared with related work in the literature. The feasibility and practicality of SADIS is thus demonstrated through the prototype.

IMPACT OF SADIS

Various techniques have been developed to protect agent integrities (Borselius, 2002), based on trusted hardware, trusted host, and conventional contractual agreements. SADIS addresses the problem of data integrity protection via a combination of techniques such as execution tracing, encrypted payload, environmental key generation, and undetachable signature. The security of SADIS is completely based on its own merits without making any assumption about the integrity of external hosts. SADIS also makes use of a negotiated key seed to generate data encryption key. Therefore, no random value needs to be encrypted and stored with the agent. With SADIS, the data and the communication keys undergo one time encryption. Thus, even if some of the keys are compromised, the key seed will still remain secret.

CONCLUSION

In this article, SADIS—a new data integrity protection protocol—has been proposed. Besides being secure against a variety of attacks and robust against vulnerabilities of related work in the literature, the research of SADIS includes the objective of efficiency. Unlike some existing literature, the data integrity protection protocol aims not only to detect data integrity compromise, but more important, to identify the malicious host. With security, efficiency, and effectiveness as its main design focuses, SADIS works with other security mechanisms to provide mobile agents with a secure platform.

REFERENCES

Borselius, N. (2002). Mobile agent security. *Electronics & Communication Engineering Journal, 14*(5), 211-218.

Chionh, H. B., Guan, S-.U., & Yang, Y. (2001). Ensuring the protection of mobile agent integrity: The design of an agent monitoring protocol. *Proceedings of IASTED International Conference on Advances in Communications* (pp. 96-99).

Guan, S-.U., & Yang, Y. (2002). SAFE: Secure-roaming agents for e-commerce. *Computers & Industrial Engineering Journal, 42*, 481-493.

Guan, S-.U., & Yang, Y. (2004). Secure agent data integrity shield. *Electronic Commerce and Research Applications, 3*(3), 311-326.

Guan, S-.U., & Zhu, F. (2004). Ontology acquisition and exchange of evolutionary product-brokering agents. *Journal of Research and Practice in Information Technology, 36*(1), 35-46.

Guan, S-.U., Zhu, F., & Maung, M-.T. (2004). A factory-based approach to support e-commerce agent fabrication. *Electronic Commerce and Research Applications, 3*(1), 39-53.

Johansen, D., Lauvset, K. J., Renesse, R., Schneider, F. B., Sudmann, N.P., & Jacobsen, K. (2002). A Tacoma retrospective. *Software—Practice and Experience,* 605-619.

Schneier, B. (1996). *Applied cryptography: Protocols, algorithms, and source code in C* (2nd ed.). New York: Wiley.

Wang T., Guan, S-.U., & Chan, T. K. (2002). Integrity protection for code-on-demand mobile agents in e-commerce. *Journal of Systems and Software, 60*(3), 211-221.

Yang, Y., & Guan, S-.U. (2000). Intelligent mobile agents for e-commerce: Security issues and agent transport. In S. M. Rahman & M. S. Raisinghani (Ed.), *Electronic commerce: Opportunity and challenges* (pp. 321-336). Hershey, PA: Idea Group Publishing.

Zhu, F., Guan, S-.U., Yang, Y., & Ko, C. C. (2000). SAFER e-commerce: Secure agent fabrication, evolution and roaming for e-commerce. In S. M. Rahman & M. S. Raisinghani, *Electronic commerce: Opportunity and challenges.* Hershey, PA: Idea Group Publishing.

KEY TERMS

Agents: A piece of software, which acts to accomplish tasks on behalf of its user.

Cryptography: The art of protecting information by transforming it (*encrypting* it) into an unreadable format, called "cipher text." Only those who possess a secret *key* can decipher (or *decrypt*) the message into plain text.

Flexibility: The ease with which a system or component can be modified for use in applications or environments other than those for which it was specifically designed.

Protocol: A convention or standard that controls or enables the connection, communication, and data transfer between two computing endpoints. Protocols may be implemented by hardware, software, or a combination of the two. At the lowest level, a protocol defines a hardware connection.

Security: The effort to create a secure computing platform, designed so that agents (users or programs) can only perform actions that have been allowed.

This work was previously published in Encyclopedia of E-Commerce, E-Government, and Mobile Commerce, edited by M. Khosrow-Pour, pp. 962-967, copyright 2006 by Information Science Reference, formerly known as Idea Group Reference (an imprint of IGI Global).

Chapter 4.41
A Case Study on a Security Maturity Assessment of a Business-to-Business Electronic Commerce Organization

Shirley Ann Becker
Northern Arizona University, USA

Anthony Berkemeyer
Texas Instruments, Inc., USA

ABSTRACT

GlobalUBid.com is a B2B (business-to-business) e-commerce company offering excess and obsolete inventory to online customers. GlobalUBid is rapidly expanding into the global online marketplace; but recently, its Web site crashed due to a denial-of-service (DOS) attack. A lack of security awareness at an organizational level has left GlobalUBid's online system vulnerable to internal and external attacks. Though informal security policies are in place, many employees are not aware of them nor are they enforced on a regular basis. Unsecured aspects of the physical workplace make the organization vulnerable to disgruntled employees, hackers, and unscrupulous competition. GlobalUBid has hired URSecure consultants to conduct a security assessment in uncovering internal and external vulnerabilities. URSecure has made recommendations for improved security, though the organization must develop most of the implementation details. GlobalUBid management recognizes the need for improved security, though there is a concern about the financial implications of implementing a security plan.

ORGANIZATIONAL BACKGROUND

GlobalUBid.com[1] became a startup company in March of 1998 in order to provide online auction capabilities to U.S. companies getting rid of excess inventory. GlobalUBid is one of the first online auction sites in the business-to-business (B2B) e-commerce industry. Inspired by the skyrocketing stock values of 1997 IPOs (initial public offerings), local venture capitalists backed the company with an initial investment of $1.5 million for building the online B2B auction site. The strategic plan was to build the system as quickly as possible with an expenditure of $1,000,000 during the first year.

In May 1998, 10 Web developers, two database administrators (DBAs), and a system administrator (SA) were hired to apply both Oracle and Microsoft software technologies in building the system. The technology staff worked an average of 98 hours per week (14-hour days, seven days a week) with the promise of stock options significantly increasing in value when the company went public. The company had announced plans for an IPO offering in the spring of 1999. Approximately half of the Web developers left within the first three months because of the burnout associated with the mandatory overtime to complete the online system. These employees were replaced immediately but at a higher cost for salaries and increased stock options.

Management and the technical staff knew that when the venture capital ran out, the company would have to declare bankruptcy without an opportunity of going public. They were aware of the dot com IPO offerings that made employees with stock options instant millionaires. They were also aware of the increasing number of failed dot coms littering the Internet, many of which had insufficient venture capital to sustain development efforts.

By April 1999, the company had developed the Web technology to support online auction capabilities. The online site became available for public use in July with limited domestic support. Though the online auction site was deemed successful by GlobalUBid's management team, more customers were needed to increase inventory sales. Inventory turnover was less than 10% per month with customer growth rate increasing 2% each month. Many of the sellers were expressing their dissatisfaction with the inventory turnover rate. It was decided that the IPO would be moved back by at least one year in order to increase the customer base and the inventory turnover rate.

GlobalUBid expanded its customer base by entering the global B2B marketplace primarily through acquisitions. GlobalUBid acquired GCB. com (Global Customer Base) in December 1999 in order to double its site traffic and add more than 5,000 new sellers in the European market. In February 2000, GlobalUBid acquired an online transaction system called StaticPrice from a company in Frankfurt, Germany. This B2B software component provided a powerful search engine and expanded GlobalUBid's business model to include fixed quote pricing in addition to the auctioning component. Customers could now purchase inventory that was offered at a fixed price in order to expedite the purchasing process. This acquisition provided an opportunity to expand GlobalUBid's global presence in the Asia Pacific area and Northern Africa. By the end of the 2000 fiscal year, the number of global customers exceeded 1,600 and the rate of inventory turnover doubled.

By the spring of 2000, a marketing manager was hired to manage a newly created marketing department composed of 100 employees. The objective was to have an online support system in place by early September in order to grow international sales and handle customer service enquiries. The marketing manager would take advantage of customer and seller data in order to predict inventory sales and identify potential customer growth areas. The confidential information stored in the system's databases would be used to personalize the company's relationships with both sellers and buyers to increase sales and inventory offerings. This confidential data, though password protected, was readily accessible by management, technology personnel, and the sales staff.

A recent crisis occurred when a denial of service (DOS) attack crashed GlobalUBid's online server. For over 14 hours, none of its customers could access the system while the SA tried to bring the server back online. Though lost sales are projected to be over $18,000, management's primary concern is the reaction of customers and sellers over the breach of system security. The long-term impact of a DOS attack could be devastating if customers or sellers thought confidential data were at risk of being stolen. The online auction component, in particular, requires anonymity in order to secure bids. Management agreed that a consultant team should be brought in to assess the potential for more security breaches within or external to the company.

SETTING THE STAGE

GlobalUBid is hierarchically structured, as shown in Figure 1. Four vice-presidents report to Ms. Susan Dawson, who is the president and chief executive officer (CEO). The CEO reports directly to the venture capitalist team who visits the company site on a quarterly basis. During each visit, the chief financial officer (CFO) presents a summary of the financial standing of the company in terms of venture capital spent, international and domestic sales by auction and fixed price quotes, and operational expenses. The venture capitalist team has final approval over any acquisitions or major expenditures until after the IPO.

Management Team

Ms. Susan Dawson, the CEO, has more than 22 years of sales experience, primarily in mail-order consumer products. She has an MBA and a Bachelor of Science degree in electrical engineering.

Figure 1. The organizational structure of GlobalUBid

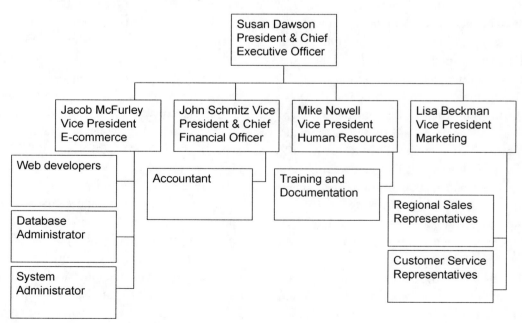

Before joining GlobalUBid, she was president and CEO of a $20 million annual sales mail-order catalog company targeting middle class consumers. During her tenure, she increased mail-order sales by 25% while reducing shipping and handling costs by 5%. So far, Ms. Dawson's leadership in formulating GlobalUBid's corporate strategy has proven to be successful. She was primarily the one responsible for the strategic acquisitions that allowed GlobalUBid to become a major player in the international B2B marketplace.

Mr. Jacob McFurley, vice-president of e-commerce, has extensive experience in managing government contracts for software systems. He has worked as a project manager for 15 years on satellite systems, focusing on telecommunications software components. He also worked as a project manager for a Fortune 500 company managing an inventory control system using COBOL[2] business software. Mr. McFurley is new to the e-commerce area of software development, though he is knowledgeable in software processes, the C++ programming language, and large database systems. He received a Master of Science degree in computer science and a Bachelor of Science in physics.

Mr. John Schmitz, vice-president and chief financial officer, worked in the banking industry for over 20 years. Most recently, he was the bank president of a small town bank in Illinois. Mr. Schmitz has an MBA and a Bachelor of Science degree in mathematics. He has a close working relationship with the venture capitalists, as one of them was his college roommate at Illinois State University.

Mr. Mike Nowell, vice-president of human resources, is fairly new to GlobalUBid. He was hired after the first year of operations in order to formalize the benefits package including stock options. He was also hired to staff up in the marketing and customer services areas. Mr. McFurley highly recommended Mr. Nowell, as they had worked together for a government contractor during the early 1980s. Mr. Nowell has an MBA and a Bachelor of Science degree in management.

Ms. Lisa Beckman is the newest addition to the management team, as she was hired in March 2000 to manage the sales and customer support staff. She has five years of experience in managing telemarketers for the Democratic National Committee. She is a sister of the same venture capitalist who is a colleague of Mr. Schmitz.

None of the executive staff has experience in managing security risks in an organization. Though Mr. McFurley has extensive knowledge in computing and information technology, he lacks expertise in the security of online systems.

Overview of GlobalUBid

The overall objective of GlobalUBid is to provide customers ready access to inventory that may be difficult to find, obsolete, military, or special order components. Sellers have an opportunity to liquidate inventory that otherwise might be difficult to dispose. Currently, there are over five million inventory items that are available for sale either through the auction or the fixed price quoting system. The customer is able to conduct sophisticated searches of hard to find inventory given the powerful search engine capability that was provided by the acquisition of StaticPrice. com.

Customer and seller confidentiality is guaranteed by GlobalUBid, as stated in the privacy policy statement on its Web site. The auction component requires anonymity between each buyer and seller, which is maintained even after the purchase has been made. Inventory is initially offered to a customer at an opening bid with a specified time period for placing bids. Each customer places a bid on an inventory item until the bidding time period lapses. The customer can place an unlimited number of bids during the bidding time period. The seller is able to monitor the bidding process throughout the bidding time period, though at no time is any type of communication allowed in terms of bidding activity. The customer may ask the seller questions via an anonymous e-mail system that is maintained by GlobalUBid.

The fixed price quoting system allows a seller to offer inventory at a fixed price. There is no bidding component, though the customer may ask the seller questions about the inventory via the GlobalUBid e-mail system. This system component also offers the customer an opportunity to list inventory items and request price quotes from potential sellers. This is also an anonymous selling and buying system such that fixed price quotes are made through GlobalUBid's e-mail system.

GlobalUBid handles all transactions in terms of payment processing. The customer is required to submit payment to GlobalUBid within 24 hours of winning a bid or accepting a fixed price offer from a seller. The customer is also rated internally by GlobalUBid in order to track the payment history of a customer. The customer is flagged "yellow" when failing to make a valid payment within the specified time period. A second occurrence changes the flag to "red" and the customer is suspended from using GlobalUBid's online system unless a cash account is established for future payments.

Recently, Mr. Schmitz made a recommendation to include an electronic payment system to the GlobalUBid site in order to expedite the payment process. However, it would require a secure environment that would guarantee credit card data could not be stolen. Mr. McFarley is responsible for identifying the system requirements for adding an electronic payment system, which would protect all transaction data in the customer database system.

Security & Organization

The management team discusses risk primarily from a financial perspective during the executive meeting held on Friday afternoons. The primary concern is that venture capital will run out before the online auction and fixed price quoting systems make a profit. Management has not addressed any specific security issues including external attacks by hackers or security breaches due to disgruntled employees. However, they have identified natural disasters including tornadoes, snowstorms, and floods, which pose risks to the daily operations of GlobalUBid. To protect from natural disasters, system backups are to be made quarterly with all operational data downloaded from the server. The backup copy is stored in a local bank vault approximately 20 miles from GlobalUBid.

This lack of security awareness at an organizational level is not unusual given that much of the emphasis is on the technological aspects of developing defenses against security breaches (Gordon & Loeb, 2002). Many companies lack a security vision that goes beyond a defensive mentality, such as downloading Microsoft patches when a virus attack is imminent. This was the case with the recent MSBlast worm where organizations could have prevented the disaster simply by installing a patch that was made available to them. A security plan with supporting processes would protect organizations from many security hazards, but too few have them. As a result of this neglect, information and software systems are far more vulnerable than need be in terms of damages that can be caused by security attacks (Straub & Welke, 1998). Many organizations are left vulnerable to attacks, especially given the rise in cyber crime activities. As long as hacking know-how is easily transferable, its costs are low, technology is readily available, and industry remains reactive to security attacks, cyber crime will continue to flourish (Siponen, 2001).

Whitman (2003) points out that a security policy is perhaps the most important layer of security available to an organization. Yet, many organizations do not understand their vulnerabilities; and as such, they neither have a policy nor a plan for the prevention, detection, and correction of threats (Wood, 2000).

Security & Personnel

The executive team promotes few security measures within and external to the operational environment of GlobalUBid. Mr. Nowell was overheard telling Ms. Beckman that he disabled virus protection software on his laptop in order to download e-mail attachments. Managers often forget to log off computer workstations not only in their offices but also in the conference rooms. All managers rely heavily on remote e-mail access using their laptop computers to connect to GlobalUBid's server. The SA has been trying to keep up with Microsoft patches and virus protection updates, with laptops taking precedence over all other personal computers and workstations.

The technical staff in general agrees that security policies must be defined and adhered to. However, the database administrators have conflicting opinions regarding database backup and security policies. The system administrator has established security policies in terms of user-IDs and passwords, but he lacks the authority to ensure that they are followed.

GlobalUBid personnel are only moderately concerned about following the security policies that are in place. It is not uncommon to see yellow notes on workstations with userID, password, and customer information. All personnel are trained in security measures regarding password protection, maintaining confidentiality of customer data, and securing workstations. However, accountability is sporadic in ensuring these policies are followed.

The news about the "I love you" virus disabling computer systems around the world spread like wildfire across news sources. Mr. McFurley held an emergency meeting with his technical staff regarding virus software protection. It came as a surprise that 45% of the personal computer workstations and 90% of the laptops did not have the latest version of virus software. The cost of the virus, from an industry perspective, was devastating (refer to Appendix A). Fortunately, the love bug did not infiltrate GlobalUBid's e-mail system and the technical staff gave each other "high-fives" for updating the virus protection software just in time.

Security & Existing Processes

The SA, Mr. Bill Jones, primarily follows the book in ensuring user profiles are set up correctly, firewall software is current, and virus software is updated. This is the extent of securing the server to eliminate vulnerabilities associated with DOS and virus attacks.

Ms. Wei Choi and Mr. Raj Tripathy, the Oracle DBAs, have system administration access to the database systems. They provide full access rights to both Mr. Jones and Mr. McFurley in order to resolve database problems when the DBAs are not available. Mr. Tripathy sets up user profiles for each of the Web developers such that they have access to operational database components including customer, seller, inventory, and sales data. The sales and customer service staff have restricted access to customer and seller data, though they could insert new data and update existing data as long as they enter a user identifier and password code.

User identification codes and passwords are distributed among all personnel both electronically and as a hardcopy report. Each user is asked to change his or her password upon receiving the list, though no formal process exists to ensure that this is done.

The organization has a formal policy on shredding documents. Letterhead is available with "confidential" boldly appearing on the top of it. The personnel policy to be followed is that any customer, financial, or employee content requires the use of this letterhead. There is one shredder by the copy machine for employee use, and the letterhead paper is to be kept in a locked storage cabinet with the key made available by Ms. Arthur.

Security & Physical Environment

Each employee wears a badge with his or her picture, employee identification number, and title. An employee takes an elevator to the second floor of the Marshall building and gains access to the GlobalUBid work area via a badge reader. The secretary, Ms. Evelyn Arthur, sits at a front desk facing the elevator door from 8 a.m. to 5 p.m. At times, there is no one at the front desk when Ms. Arthur runs internal errands, attends executive meetings, or takes her one-hour lunch break. Each visitor is expected to sign-in at the front desk, whereby Ms. Arthur issues a temporary badge to be returned at the end of the visit.

Before leaving the building, each employee secures his or her workstation by closing all electronic files, logging out, placing the computer on standby, and storing confidential documents. About 20% of the employees fail to secure workstations on a regular basis. It mostly is unnoticed by management because of the screen reader software that automatically places the computers on standby. An employee is provided a handbook during a one-day "new employee" orientation. The handbook discusses workstation maintenance, including procedures on changing passwords, closing applications, and placing a computer on standby. Ms. Jessica Antony, the human resource trainer, thoroughly covers these policies during orientation.

The server machines and the physical data and log files are separated from other work areas by divider walls. All administrators have workstations in this area, and they are responsible for securing all operational data. Unauthorized employees are not to enter this area without being accompanied by the SA or DBAs.

Security & System Architecture

The system architecture for GlobalUBid is shown in Figure 2. The system is comprised of both internally and externally accessible components. All components have access to "the outside world" through a proxy server and a firewall. The inter-

Figure 2. System architecture

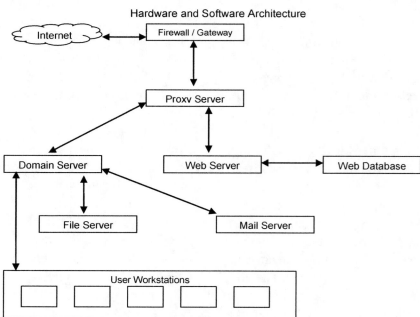

nally accessible components of the architecture include the domain, file, and mail servers and user workstations. The externally accessible components of the system architecture include the Web server and Web database.

A key part of the system architecture is that the externally accessible components can only be accessed by the internal components from the outside. That is, user workstations access the outside Internet in order to connect to and update the Web site and Web dataset. Only the SA has direct access to the Web server and Web database (externally accessible components) by physically using the systems. The belief is that this increases security of company sensitive information.

CASE DESCRIPTION

Denial of Service (DOS) Attack

A DOS attack took place on Monday, May 22, at 6 a.m. When Mr. Jones arrived for work at 8 a.m., panicked sales personnel were trying to locate him. None of the staff could access software applications necessary to answer customer questions or to monitor inventory bids. International phone calls were inundating the staff regarding the unavailable Web site. Mr. Jones was able to recover from the attack around 8 p.m. such that all system applications were operational.

The management staff, lead by Mr. McFurley, called an emergency meeting about the security breach. Mr. McFurley expressed concern about a subsequent breach with little or no recourse for ensuring system availability. Mr. Nowell expressed another concern about security and a disgruntled sales person who recently quit. The employee had unsecured access to both customer and seller files. Mr. Nowell read an article about disgruntled employees accounting for much of the online theft and security breaches that occur in organizations (refer to Appendix B). Mr. Schmitz pointed out that the financial impact of the DOS is

currently unknown. He stated that there might be financial consequences as the result of customer mistrust in the security of GlobalUBid's online system.

Management agreed that the consultant company, URSecure, Inc., should be contracted to conduct a full security assessment. The overall objective would be to identify potential security risks both internally and externally. Dr. Timothy Berger, the lead assessor of URSecure, Inc., proposed to GlobalUBid that a security assessment be conducted, followed by a formal presentation of findings.

Security Assessment

Dr. Berger met with GlobalUBid management to explain the security assessment process followed by his team. He recommended that they visit Carnegie Mellon Software Engineering Institute's CERT Coordination Center (www.cert. org) to learn about cyber crime, which is anticipated to reach 80,000 reported incidents by 2002. Dr. Berger explained that security threats are internal due to disgruntled or dishonest employees gaining easy access to online systems, and external due to malicious hackers or persons no longer employed. He provided them with a handout on cyber crime terminology (Appendix C). Management was told that these attacks could be devastating when the organization has few security processes.

Dr. Berger explained that the security assessment was based on recommendations made by online security resources provided by the CERT Coordination Center (www.CERT.org), the (CSI) Computer Security Institute (http://www.gocsi. com), and National Institute on Standards and Technology (www.nist.gov).

Mr. McFurley met with the technical staff in order to get support for conducting a security assessment by URSecure, Inc. Mr. McFurley explained that the assessment process would uncover high risk factors, including: incomplete or missing security processes, lack of training and documentation on existing security processes, a failure to enforce security processes, no reward and recognition system for employees, and a missing feedback mechanism for security improvements.

Mr. Jones scowled at Mr. McFurley while expressing his view that the security assessment is a waste of time. Mr. Jones pointed out that he is constantly updating the virus protection and firewall software; and as such, he felt there is no need for consultants poking around in his server files. Ms. Choi also expressed her concern regarding data integrity if the consultants inadvertently made changes to the database. Mr. McFurley assured everyone that the consultant's work is strictly confidential and that at no time would they have unsupervised access to GlobalUBid data.

Security Areas

Dr. Berger outlined several areas to be included in the security assessment conducted by the URSecure team. Dr. Berger pointed out that in addition to these areas there are others that need to be included in a comprehensive security assessment plan.

- **Physical security.** Physical security is assessed in terms of the building perimeter, cubicles, halls, offices, conference rooms, doors, and other public areas. The physical work area is evaluated for unsecured copiers, faxes, and printers, confidential documents, passwords and userIDs.
- **Database security.** Database security is evaluated in terms of user profiles and access rights. Oracle scripts are assessed in terms of unauthorized data access by software applications. Database log files are audited for unauthorized user access to data.
- **Desktop and Group Policies.** Individual and group policies are audited in terms of desktop access rights, remote administration, hardware configuration, software backups, user privileges, virus protection, and software downloads.

Security Audit Form

Table 1 illustrates part of a security audit form that is used by URSecure team. Each question is based on security information obtained from the CERT Web site, as extracted by the URSecure team. The form is completed by an URSecure team member while conducting an interview with employees, observing informal policies and employee behavior, auditing logs, or reviewing

Table 1. Part of the physical security questionnaire

Security Item	Root Cause	Risk Rating	Security Actions
Badge is worn at all times.	NT IP NB	High	There is an informal process of wearing a badge while in the work area, but it is not consistently enforced. Badge does not distinguish an employee from a visitor.
Temporary badges for visitors.	NT IP NB	High	There is an informal process for visitor sign-in, but it is not consistently enforced. A badge is issued to a visitor when a secretary is at the front desk. Visitors roam the building without being escorted by an employee.
Badge request to replace lost or stolen one.	NT NP NB	Severe	There is no process for replacing stolen or lost badges. A new badge can be requested without an explanation.
Controlled access to physical areas on second floor.	NT NP NB	Severe	There are no employee restrictions on the conference room, server area, offices, or other workspaces. Employees often share multiple workstations and desktops without logging in.

documents. The "root cause" is noted for each potential security violation. Root cause values are "no," "informal," or "formal" for the three areas of training, formal processes, and baseline data. Root cause values are shown in Table 1.

For each item on the questionnaire, a "risk rating" factor is assigned to it. The risk ratings are severe, high, moderate, low, or none. A severe rating means that due to a lack of security processes, the company is highly vulnerable to an attack. A high rating means that the probability of a breach is significant because security processes are informal. A moderate rating means that the breach is less likely to occur because security processes have been formalized. A low risk means that security processes have been formalized and supported with training and documentation.

Security audit forms are to be developed for each of the security assessment areas that comprise the security assessment plan. These forms need to specify questions that are objective and can be readily evaluated for compliance. In addition, baseline data need to be defined in quantitative terms whenever possible. Baseline data are important for comparing improvements made by the organization in each of the security assessment areas.

Assessment Results

Physical Security

There are numerous security risks associated with the physical layout of GlobalUBid (refer to Figure 3). The peripheral of the building has windows for which the blinds are not drawn. Confidential material, including an entity-relationship diagram of the customer database, could be seen externally.

Figure 3. GlobalUBid's physical layout

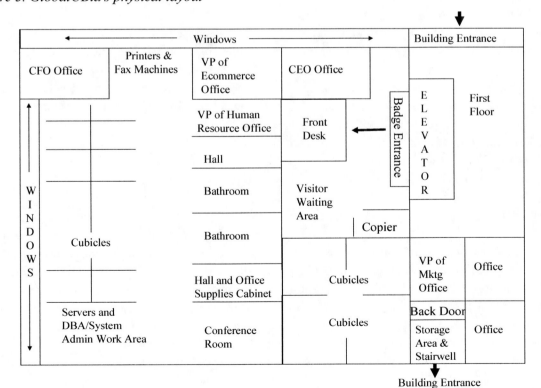

Several vice-presidents have unlocked doors leading from their offices to a patio where sensitive data are visible.

The front desk is sporadically vacated; and as such, visitors can access the GlobalUBid premises without signing in. On the first visit to GlobalUBid, two URSecure team members accessed the second floor without badges and they were not questioned by any employees. The copier, readily accessible by visitors, had confidential documents lying unattended.

The server machine is somewhat vulnerable to a security breach because it is accessible to anyone on the second floor. It is located in a secured cubicle next to the SA's work area; it is secured in the sense that no one is allowed in the area unaccompanied by the technical staff. Desktop computers in cubicles are also vulnerable given that many are not logged off. Several desktops are left unattended with open e-mail messages displayed. Approximately 20% of the sales staff has customer data stored as icons on the desktop. The conference room computer has not been logged off after an executive meeting. A history of Web pages with sensitive buyer and seller data is accessible using the history button in Internet Explorer.

Both the front and back entrances appear to be secure, though further assessment is needed to determine whether there are undetected security risks. The consultants acknowledged that further investigation is needed to uncover security issues associated with the physical environment.

Database Security

Mr. Tripathy, one of the database administrators, identified a security risk associated with GlobalUBid's databases in that the system administrator has unsecured access to both the operating system and databases. The SA can perform database administration functions without notifying the DBAs. As such, there is no accountability for unauthorized database access. This security breach also exists for the production database system, as Mr. McFurley, Web developers, DBAs, and the SA have unsecured access to production data. Though these data are for development use only, if stolen, they would compromise GlobalUBid's competitive advantage.

Another security risk appears to be a lack of formal procedures for backup and recovery of operational data, though further investigation is needed. Mr. Tripathy explained that backup is typically done by Ms. Choi at the end of the workweek. However, last week's backup was not performed because the developers were fixing a software bug associated with the online bidding system. Ms. Choi explained that last week's backup was only delayed. She is confident that an in-house backup occurs each week, as documented in the database log files.

In terms of database recovery, both DBAs rely on Oracle defaults to store data in recovery logs. Neither of the DBAs knows the contents of these logs and they rely on Oracle software to backup the logs periodically. Mr. Tripathy is somewhat concerned about the loss of operational data because he has never performed a database recovery. However, Ms. Choi is confident in fully recovering from a database failure if it were to occur. She has implemented recovery procedures many times in her previous DBA position and has relied extensively on Oracle software for 100% recovery of operational data.

Desktop Security

The URSecure team members interviewed staff from international sales, customer service, human resources, and management regarding desktop security. The questionnaire in Table 2 illustrates some of the findings uncovered during the interview activities.

The consultants found that about 25% of those surveyed employees writes userIDs and passwords on notes attached to monitors, desks, and walls. These unsecured data are readily ob-

Table 2. Questionnaire results from desktop security assessment

Is the user required to change the password for his/her account?			
Yes	No	Not Sure	
54%	31%	15%	
Can the same password be used more than once?			
Yes	With Restrictions	Never	Not Sure
23%	8%	23%	46%
Are there requirements on password content? Check all that apply			
Minimum length			50%
Maximum length			17%
Requirement on letter, digit, special character combinations			17%
What are the requirements? (No response) Not sure			16%
What happens when I forget my password? Check all that apply			
I ask the System Administrator			46%
I don't know			0%
I use a word that I won't forget			23%
I ask a coworker because he/she will remember it			0%
I look it up (I have it stored)			0%
Other (please explain)			23%

tainable by anyone near the employee workstation. Almost a third of the employees stated that they were unaware of the company policy to change the user password on a regular basis.

GlobalUBid personnel were asked about userID and password sharing and the results are shown in Figure 4. Only one third stated that they would not provide their passwords to anyone, including the system administrator. Mr. McFurley told the team that all employees are informed of keeping passwords secure and changing them, as disseminated regularly in a "keeping passwords secure" e-mail note.

Recommendations

Dr. Berger was asked to present the findings, make recommendations for security improvements, and identify the current level of security maturity as a basis for setting future goals.

During the presentation, Dr. Berger showed management a chart whereby GlobalUBid was rated for security maturity. He proposed a security plan, as shown in Table 3, in order to manage security risks. Dr. Berger suggested that management implement a reward and recognition system in order to obtain buy-in from all employees. He did not provide the details, stating that management needs to address this issue.

Dr. Berger recommended the formation of a Security Response Team (SRT) comprised of personnel from various departments. He did not specify a manager to lead the team, but did mention that human resources should play an active role. He stated that the roles and responsibilities of each SRT member should be formalized. Dr. Berger also suggested that the company establish an auditing process that would be performed by the SRT. Thus, employees would be accountable for their security actions and rewarded for security innovation and improvement.

Figure 4. Employee responses to password protection

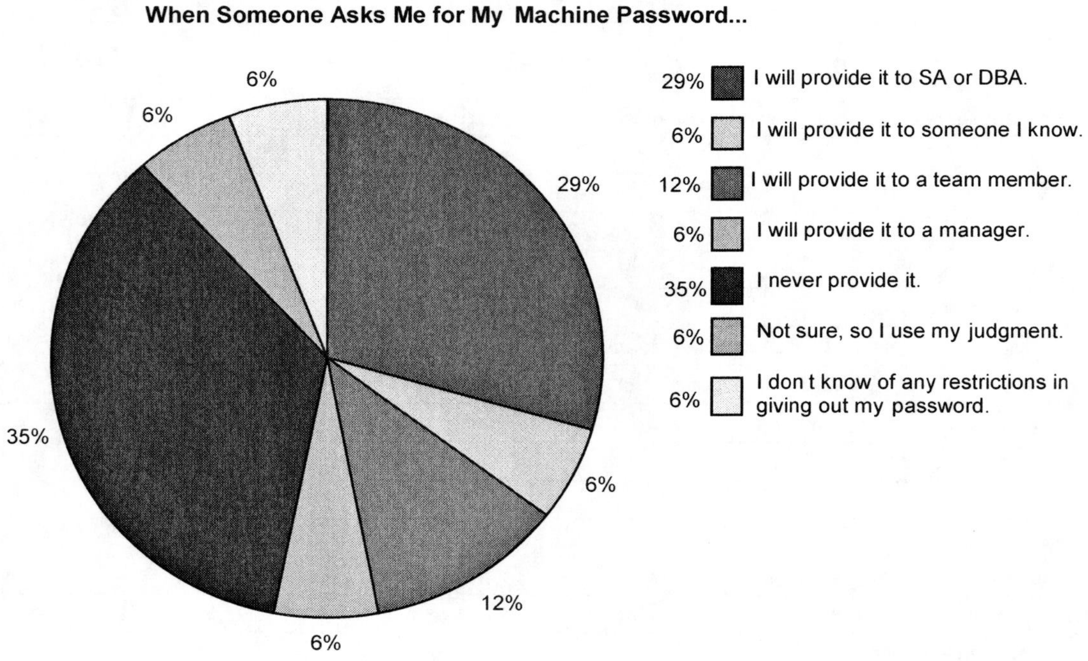

When Someone Asks Me for My Machine Password...

29% ■ I will provide it to SA or DBA.

6% □ I will provide it to someone I know.

12% ▨ I will provide it to a team member.

6% ▨ I will provide it to a manager.

35% ■ I never provide it.

6% ▨ Not sure, so I use my judgment.

6% □ I don t know of any restrictions in giving out my password.

Dr. Berger summarized the improvements for both physical and database security illustrated. He notes that there are improvements to be made in the other security areas, with the details to be provided in a follow-up meeting with management.

Improved Physical Security

Many of the physical security recommendations formalize processes for securing sensitive data both electronically and in hardcopy form. The following recommendations are made to the management team.

- Develop processes for displaying and disseminating confidential data, including userIDs and passwords, customer and seller data, database schemas, and software code.
- Develop a confidentiality rating for company documents.

- Develop a process for disposing of documents based on the confidentiality rating.
- Develop a process for securing unoccupied offices, conference rooms, halls, closets, and exit doors.

Dr. Berger reminded the management team that physical security requires a commitment by all employees. However, he did not specify what measures should be taken to obtain a commitment by all employees.

Improved Database Security

The consultant team made recommendations for improving database security, emphasizing backup and recovery processes to protect the company's most valuable asset — operational data. The following illustrate database security recommendations made by the URSecure team.

Table 3. Security plan

Activity	Description
Security Vulnerabilities	Each vulnerability is identified in terms of ease of exploitation, likelihood of occurrence, speed of recovery, and monetary damages.
Security Process	Security processes are formalized in terms of implementing, managing, and maintaining security in each area.
Process Improvement	Lessons learned from each incident are used to improve security processes.
Measurement System	A measurement system is established to identify costs associated with maintaining each security process, and to calculate direct and indirect costs for each incident reported.
Incident Costs	For each security incident, direct and indirect costs are calculated. Direct costs include labor, lost sales, and overhead expenses. Indirect costs include reputation and lost customers and sellers.
Security Assessment	For each security incident, data is collected on security processes used, their effectiveness, cost of using them, and those that were by-passed.
Security Monitoring	Each global security incident is monitored. Data is recorded about vulnerabilities and recovery mechanisms used. Lessons learned from each incident are used to improve security processes.
Security Awareness	Each employee is continuously trained on security processes and consequences of not following processes. Reward and recognition system is in place for security improvements suggested by employee.

- Define and document user roles and responsibilities for system administration, database administration, Web developers, and management.
- Conduct audits of database logs comparing user access rights and data manipulation in terms of inserts, deletions, and updates.
- Develop backup and recovery procedures in order to ensure 100% recovery capability for all database systems.
- Perform periodic "recovery" drills to determine the success rate of recovery. These drills include levels of severity inclusive of natural disaster, intrusion, non-malicious data corruption, and system failure.

After listening to Dr. Berger's initial findings, Ms. Dawson expressed her concern regarding the lack of leadership in securing the organization. She also expressed concern that the financial cost and resources necessary to implement a full-scale security plan outweigh the benefits. She set a date for an executive meeting in order to discuss what would be financially feasible in terms of improved security.

CHALLENGES FACING GlobalUBid

There are several challenges facing GlobalUBid, as it continues to expand into the international marketplace. One of its biggest challenges is to improve organizational awareness of security issues associated with internal and external attacks. It may be difficult to change the laissez faire attitude towards security because of the competitive nature of the dot com industry and the software challenges facing GlobalUBid. Though management recognizes the need for increased security, their focus is on what they perceive as issues that are more critical. There are 12 online competitors who have entered the B2B international marketplace for inventory disposal. International sales continue to drop as the world economy faces a growing recession, oil prices continue to rise, and the threat of terrorist activity remains high.

In addition, the executive management team is concerned about the financial cost of implementing a security plan and the resources needed to form an SRT. Given only one DOS attack occurred since GlobalUBid has become operational, management feels that the financial costs outweigh the security benefits.

Many desktops remain vulnerable to malicious attacks because Microsoft software patches, virus protection, and firewall updates are not done on a regular basis. Database backups appear to be scheduled around software development deadlines, which could leave the data vulnerable to failures. Employees fail to secure their workstations, thus leaving them vulnerable to unauthorized access to sensitive data. One of the major challenges is to develop security policies that are strictly adhered to by all personnel. A reward and recognition system needs to be developed that would promote the implementation of security policies as well as identify improvements to them.

Personnel resistance to implementing security policies must be overcome in order to ensure a high level of security is maintained. Several employees expressed a concern about the additional effort required to secure desktops and documents. The customer service staff has complained that their workload would significantly increase if shared userIDs and passwords are banned.

Employee dissatisfaction may be an underestimated security risk, especially given the amount of overtime required by many of the employees. Over 30% of the developers have recently quit and several more are threatening to boycott the mandatory Saturday overtime. The organization remains vulnerable to internal security breaches until this issue is addressed.

REFERENCES

Blakley, B., McDermott, E., & Geer, D. (2001). Information security is information risk management. *Proceedings of the 2001 Workshop on New Security Paradigms,* Cloudcroft, New Mexico, (pp. 97-104).

Cambanis, T. (2003, May 22). Worker vengeance makes its way online. *Information Security News.* Retrieved July 25, 2003: http://lists.insecure.org/lists/isn/2003/May/0106.html

Cnn.com. (2000, May 11). Former student: Bug may have been spread accidentally. *Cnn.com Technology.* July 25, 2003: http://www.cnn.com/2000/ASIANOW/southeast/05/11/ilove.you.02/#1

Gordon, L.A., & Loeb, M.P. (2002). The economics of information security investment. *ACM Transactions on Inf. and System Security,* 5(4), 438-457.

OnlineSecurity.com. (2001). Recent computer forensic case studies from the Online Security files. Retrieved July 25, 2003: http://www.onlinesecurity.com/Email_Files/onlinesecurity_email_v2.html

Siponen, M.T. (2001). Five dimensions of information security awareness. *ACM SIGCAS Computers and Society,* 31(2), 24-29.

Straub, D.W., & Welke, R.J. (1998). Coping with systems risk: Security planning models for management decision making. *MIS Q.,* 22(4), 441–469.

Verton, D. (2001, July 11). Analysis: Insiders a major security threat. *Cnn.com Sci-Tech.* Retrieved July 25, 2003: http://www.cnn.com/2001/TECH/industry/07/11/insider.threat.idg/?related

Whitman, M. (2003). Enemy at the gate: Threats to information security. *Communications of the ACM,* 46(8), 91-95.

Wood, C.C. (2000). Integrated approach includes information security. *Security,* 37(2), 43-44.

ENDNOTES

[1] The .com associated with each online company discussed in this paper is dropped after it has been initially introduced (e.g., GlobalUBid.com is referred to as GlobalUBid).

[2] COBOL (Common Business Oriented Language) was the first widely used programming language for business applications. COBOL was used in the 1960-1970s to develop many automated payroll, inventory, customer service, employee, accounting, and other business applications. There are still many COBOL programs that are operational, though they are typically viewed as "legacy" software.

[3] These steps are based on Blakley, McDermott, and Geer's (2001) security risk management activities.

APPENDIX A: LOVE BUG VIRUS

The "Love Bug" virus spread worldwide with surprising speed, as millions of unsuspecting victims opened the e-mail, which had the subject line "ILOVEYOU" and often came from someone known to the user (cnn.com, 2000). The virus devastated e-mail programs and damage from the bug and variations of it were estimated at $7 - $10 billion. Once activated on a computer, the love bug virus destroyed files. Then, it replicated itself, accessed a program that searched for login names and passwords, and mailed them back to the bug's author.

APPENDIX B: DISGRUNTLED EMPLOYEES & CYBER CRIME

According to Verton (2001), cyber crime can be devastating when knowledgeable employees become disgruntled, causing damage to online systems. One company fired two knowledgeable employees for demanding pay increases and stock options to avoid software development problems. The next day, the company was hit with a DOS (denial of service) attack that allowed external access to the company's server. Two minutes after being brought online, it was attacked again.

In another case, an executive downloaded proprietary information that would help him in his new job with the company's competitor (OnlineSecurity.com, 2001). The executive zipped the files and sent them via a dial up Internet connection to the competitor's office. E-mail retrieved from the executive's laptop discussed his cyber crime intentions to the competition.

A disgruntled employee who had been fired from a travel agency hacked into his former employer's computer system, canceling 60 customer airline tickets (Cambanis, 2003). The cost of this cyber crime was estimated to be over $90,000, not including damage to its reputation.

APPENDIX C: MALICIOUS CODE

Virus – Source code that replicates or copies itself in order to spread to other files. Its destruction can range from a harmless message to file corruption or reformatting of a hard drive.

Worm – Often combined with a virus, source code designed to spread to other computers. The ILOVEYOU virus contained a worm sending itself to addresses in the Microsoft Outlook address file.

Trojan Horse – Source code designed to behave unexpectedly, often for purposes of stealing user login and password data or destroying files. "ExploreZip" Trojan horse relied on Microsoft Outlook to infect other computers. It reduced file sizes to zero, making them unrecoverable.

Sniffing – Source code monitoring information traveling over a network. Sniffer software can be used legitimately to monitor network flow or illegitimately to steal confidential data.

Cyber Attacks

Hacker – A user attempting to gain unauthorized access to computing systems.

Cracker – A hacker with malicious intent in gaining access to computing systems. Malicious intent includes crashing or defacing Web sites or accessing, stealing, or destroying unauthorized files.

White Hats – Hackers attempting to gain unauthorized access with the purpose of uncovering security breaches. They are typically employed to uncover a company's security vulnerabilities. They may also be hackers who uncover security flaws and report them to software vendors.

Black Hats – Hackers attempting to gain unauthorized access to computing systems with the intent to cause damage.

Grey Hats – Hackers attempting to gain unauthorized access based on some justification. These hackers often look for weaknesses and then publish them. They are not White Hats because they may supply information to both software vendors and crackers.

Spoofing – Hackers hiding their identities by using fake e-mail addresses or pretending to be valid e-mail addresses.

Phishing – Hackers pretending to be company representatives in e-mail notes to users requesting password or credit card data. The user is directed to a Web site that masquerades as the company site in order to steal confidential data.

Denial of Service (DOS) Attacks – Hackers flooding a Web site with traffic to cause a network overflow. The network is shut down, resulting in a corporate Web site to be inaccessible by users.

This work was previously published in Journal of Electronic Commerce in Organizations, Vol. 2, No. 4, edited by M. Khosrow-Pour, pp. 1-19, copyright 2004 by IGI Publishing, formerly known as Idea Group Publishing (an imprint of IGI Global).

Chapter 4.42
Trustworthy Web Services:
An Experience–Based Model for Trustworthiness Evaluation

Stephen J. H. Yang
National Central University, Taiwan

Blue C. W. Lan
National Central University, Taiwan

James S. F. Hsieh
Ulead Systems Inc., Taiwan

Jen-Yao Chung
IBM T. J. Watson Research Center, USA

ABSTRACT

Web service technology enables seamless integration of different software to fulfill dynamic business demands in a platform-neutral fashion. However, the adoption of loosely-coupled and distributed services will cause trustworthiness problems. In this article, we present an experience-based evaluation of service's trustworthiness based on trust experience (understanding) and trust requirements (policy). We utilize ontology to specify past experiences of services and trustworthy requirements of the requester. Before invoking found services, the addressed method can help the requester evaluate the trustworthiness of the services based on his or her trustworthy requirements and past experiences of the services. Furthermore, we also present an evaluation method for composite services by taking the structure of the composite services into account. The main contribution of the paper is providing evaluation methods for Web services such that the service requester can make better decisions in selecting found services in terms of service's trustworthiness.

INTRODUCTION

The evolution of Internet and Web-based technologies energize enterprises to conduct worldwide business transactions with greater ease than before. Various B2C and B2B applications have been developed to provide continuing business services for customers and partners. However, tightly-coupled applications only enable enterprises a static business pattern, which cannot fulfill a great deal of diverse demands in today's fast-moving business environment. How to deliver adapted business services to customers and partners in a timely manner becomes a hot issue for e-business development now. Web service is an emerging solution that aims to support cross-functional integration beyond organizational boundaries. A number of de facto standards including SOAP (Mitra, 2003), WSDL (Chinnici, Moreau, Ryman, & Weerawarana, 2004), UDDI (Bellwood, Clement, & Riegen, 2003) and BPEL4WS (Andrew, Curbera, Dholakia, Goland, Klein, & Leymann, et al, 2003) are proposed for service communication, description, advertisement, and orchestration, respectively. By providing a uniform framework to solve the heterogeneity of programming languages and platforms, Web services can help e-business utilize virtual service components to build Web-based enterprises information systems that automate business processes in an inter-enterprise manner. Web services will not only make enterprises be more responsive, efficient, and productive, but will also make it easier to conduct B2B e-commerce via standard interface. Gartner Group (Pezzini, 2003) predicts that there are more than 60% of businesses that will adopt Web services by 2008. Furthermore, some enterprises have adopted Web services to conduct their businesses among their partners and customers now, for example, Galileo International (2006) and Triple A (2006).

However, delegating a computing task to dynamically-found services has to undertake the risk of unknown service providers and unknown services qualities. The uncertainties in such a distributed, loosely-organized, flexible, and dynamic computing environment will cause a lot of trustworthiness problems including: (1) Quality of service (QoS): What are the service's availability, reliability, scalability, performance, and integrity? From service requesters' perspective, they care about not only the functionality of a service but also its QoS issues. How can service requesters ensure that a found service will be available and will work reliably? Can a service deliver its functionality consistently under different loading? How does a service rollback its execution state if it fails in the middle? (2) Security of message-based communications: How do service requesters and service providers keep confidentialities of transmitted data over secured or unsecured communication channels? They have to prevent classified information from internal and external eavesdropping. How can service requesters and service providers maintain data integrity? All interactions and data exchanging between the service requester and the service provider should comply with some kind of agreements. Any unauthorized modifications may lead to violations of agreements or misunderstanding of original intendment (3) Management of trust relationships: Can service requesters trust service advertisements? What is the reputation of the corresponding service provider? How to measure the service's functional and non-functional performances is the key for evaluating the trustworthiness of the service advertisements and the service provider. It is also helpful for both service requesters and service providers to maintain trust relationships among them such that they can have higher confidence in choosing the service provider or service requester based on collected past experiences.

The trustworthiness concern can be classified into three levels, infrastructure, understanding, and policy. Infrastructure is the first level focusing on keeping the trust of service's infrastructure. In other words, the essence of a trustworthy Web service is that the underlying system of the Web service is trusted (Grandison & Sloman, 2000). For example, the underlying software and hardware of a Web service must be trustworthy to ensure the trustworthiness of the service. The network should guarantee that network transmission is reliable and secure. Recently, most of research efforts focused trustworthiness problems on fundamental security issues. W3C is presently developing XML Signature, XML Encryption and P3P projects. Moreover, many researchers also have proposed some related specifications to enhance the trustworthiness of Web services such as WS-Security (Anthony, Chris, Phillip, & Ronald, 2004), WS-Policy (Bajaj, Box, Chappell, Curbera, Daniels, & Hallam-Baker, et al., 2004), WS-Trust (IBM, 2002), Web Service Level Agreements (IBM Corporation, 2003) and WS-Quality (Mani & Nagarajan, 2002). Understanding is the second layer. Huhns and Buell (2002) pointed out that we are more likely to trust something if we understand it. That means that you will not trust what you do not understand. We need to confirm that services, which are performed by service providers or agents, are trusted when we invoke them. An active approach is to analyze the behaviors of services based on abstract behavior models of service providers and agents. A passive approach is to analyze experiences and estimate degree of trust based on requester's experiences of the service (Singh, 2002). Passive approaches such as rating service, reputation mechanism, referral network, and social network are technologies for exchanging experiences and reputation based on a third-party certification group (Grandison & Sloman, 2000) or a peer-to-peer sharing mechanism (Yolum & Singh, 2002). The third layer, policy, is used to describe requirements of trust, security, privacy, and societal conventions to reach high-level trustworthy objectives (Huhns & Buell, 2002; Singh, 2002). In general, the policy provides many specific description-methods for requesters to define what states and situations we could accept. In other words, policy works like a rule set used to decide what behaviors and states could acquire authorizations.

In this article, we present an experience-based evaluation of service's trustworthiness based on understanding and policy levels. We utilize ontology to specify past experiences of services and trustworthy requirements of the requester. Before invoking found services, the addressed method can help the requester evaluate the trustworthiness of the services based on his trustworthy requirements and past experiences of the services. Furthermore, we also present an evaluation method for composite services by taking the structure of the composite services into account. The main contribution of the article is providing evaluation methods for Web services such that service requester can make better decisions in selecting found services in terms of the service's trustworthiness.

The rest of this article is organized as follows. An overview of related works is given, then follows the architecture of our experience-based trust management. The method of evaluating single service's trustworthiness and the evaluation method of composite service's trustworthiness are shown then. Finally, the concluding remarks and future works are presented.

RELATED WORKS

In order to improve the reliability of modern computer systems and promise to develop more trustworthy computing environments, both industrial vendors and academic institutes spend a lot of efforts on trust computing studies and form a number of open organizations such as Trusted Computing Group ([TCG] 2005) and TRUST (2005), dedicated to providing various solutions with joint efforts. Trusted Computing Group is a not-for-profit organization formed to develop, define, and promote open standards for hardware-enabled trusted computing and security technologies across multiple platforms, peripherals, and devices. From TCG's viewpoint, trust is the expectation that a device will behave in a particular manner for a specific purpose. A trusted platform should provide at least three basic features, namely, protected capabilities, integrity measurement, and integrity reporting. Hence they design Trusted Platform Module (TPM) as the basis for enhancing the security of computing environment in disparate platforms including mobile devices, PC clients, servers and storage systems, and so forth. TPM is the root of trust, which indicates that it is the component that must be trusted without external oversight, and it provides numerous cryptographic capabilities such as encryption/decryption, digital signature and integrity measurement, and so forth. With the combination of transitive trust and TPM, the trust boundary can be extended from trusted execution kernel up to OS loader codes, OS codes, and application codes by proving system's integrity to the remote party. Generally, TPM is implemented as a micro-controller to store keys, passwords, and digital certificates such that it can be used in different computing platforms to assist in performing protected capabilities, integrity measurement, and integrity reporting, and IBM 4758 cryptographic coprocessor (Doorn, Sailer, Perez, & Dyer, 2006) shows how to use TPM in an open way.

Team for Research in Ubiquitous Secure Technology (TRUST) is a new science and technology center established by U.S. National Science Foundation. TRUST brings a lot of top U.S. universities in security research together, including Berkeley, Stanford, Carnegie Mellon, San Jose State University, and so forth. Due to a rapid increase in computer security attacks at all levels in the last decade, TRUST recognizes that computer trustworthiness is a pressing scientific, economic, and social problem. They try to solve the problem from three directions: (1) security science – includes software security, trusted platforms, applied cryptographic protocols and network security; (2) system science – includes complex inter-dependency modeling and analysis, secure network embedded systems, model-based integration of trusted components, and secure information management software tools; and (3) social science – includes economics, public policy and societal challenges, digital forensics and privacy, and human computer interfaces and security. Besides, TRUST will have an education and outreach component that focuses not only on integrating research and inquiry-based education, but also on transferring new and existing knowledge to undergraduate colleges, educational institutions serving under-represented populations, and the K-12 community. For the long-term considerations, such activities can help lay the groundwork for training the scientists and engineers who will develop the next generation of trustworthy systems as well as help prepare the individuals who will ultimately become the users and consumers in the future.

There are also many different attempts on offering trustworthy solutions in the service level, including QoS-aware service delivery, trustworthy service selections, reliable service compositions, validation-based access control, and so forth. wsBus (Erradi & Maheshwari, 2005) is an enhanced service registry as well as an intermediary that augments and manages the delivery of Web services by providing run-time support for reliable messaging, securing, monitoring, and managing of Web services. It acts as a mediator between service requesters and service providers. All messages are intercepted by a messaging gateway, and messages are placed onto a queue for follow-up processing if they succeed in passing three reliability checks of message's expiration, duplication, and ordering. In the meantime, wsBus will keep all messages in a persistent storage to provide fault tolerance and reliable message delivery such that messages can be re-sent when communication failures occur. Besides, wsBus also supports multiple transport protocols such as MSMQ, TCP, JMS, and HTTP/R, and thus it can offer reliable service delivery by taking advantage of the underlying protocol's reliable communications capabilities. Wang, Chen, Wang, Fung, & Uczekaj (2004) proposed an integrated quality of service (QoS) management in service-oriented enterprise architectures. The integrated QoS management is to provide QoS support in a consistent and coordinated fashion across all layers of enterprise systems, ranging from enterprise policies, applications, middleware platforms, and down to network layers. They classified QoS characteristics into four categories, as well as developed an XML-based language for service requesters to express QoS requirements: performance—response time, message throughput, payload size and end-to-end delay; reliability—delivery guarantee, duplication elimination, message ordering, loss probabilities, error rate, retry threshold, message persistency and criticality; timeliness—time-to-live, deadline, constant bit-rate, frame time and priority; and security—message signing and encryption. The integrated QoS management architecture consists of various component services to help service providers determine whether QoS requirements of required services from a client can be satisfied based on evaluations of current work loadings and resource allocations. In addition, the architecture supports run-time QoS monitoring and adaptations as well.

Tosic and Pagurek (2005) tried to assist service requesters in selecting appropriate Web services with comprehensive contractual descriptions. From technical contract perspective, they claimed that comprehensive descriptions of Web services require several different types of contracts, and they classified all kinds of contractual descriptions into three broad categories: functionality contracts—syntactic contract, behavioral contract, synchronization contract, and compositional contract; quality contracts – QoS contract and pricing contracts; and infrastructure contracts—communication contract, security contract, and management contract. Based on the categories, they examined a number of existing Web service languages including WSDL (Chinnici et al., 2004), BPEL4WS (Andrew et al., 2003), WS-CDL (Kavantzas, Burdett, Ritzinger, Fletcher, & Lafon, 2004), WS-Policy (Bajaj et al., 2004), WSLA (Keller, & Ludwig, 2003), WSOL (Tosic, Pagurek, Patel, Esfandiari, & Ma, 2003) and OWL-S (OWL Services Coalition, 2006) to check what types of contracts can be specified with them. However, none of the previous specifications can provide comprehensive description capabilities. On the other hand, Zhang, Zhang, & Chung, (2004) presented another method to help service requesters select trustworthy Web services. They proposed a user-centered, mobile agent-based, fault injection-equipped and assertion-oriented approach to assist service requesters in selecting trustworthy Web services. Upon their UMFA approach, the service requester can employ mobile agents with test data and predefined semantic assertions to determine whether targeted services can fulfill both functional and trustworthy requirements thoroughly.

In the case of Web services compositions, the QoS and trustworthiness problems are more complex than the problems in individual services due to various compositional patterns. Jaeger, M.C., Rojec-Goldmann, G. & Muhl, G. (2005) provided a mechanism to help service requesters determine the overall QoS of a Web services composition by aggregating the QoS of the individual services. Based on defined composition patterns including Sequence, Loop, XOR-XOR, AND-AND, AND-DISC, OR-OR and OR-DISC, they gave the corresponding aggregation rules for mean execution time, mean cost, and mean fidelity. In order to get a closer estimation of the service composition, the aggregation method will take dependencies into account if dependencies between particular services exist. The effectiveness of such considerations is obvious when services of a particular dependency domain are integrated within different composition patterns of the whole composition.

EXPERIENCE-BASED TRUSTWORTHINESS EVALUATION

In this section, we present our experience-based trustworthiness evaluation architecture based on CMU's RETSINA agent architecture (http://www.cs.cmu.edu/~softagents/) by incorporating three additional modules including *inquiry module*, *evaluation module*, and *choice module* as shown in Figure 1.

The *inquiry module* queries past experience data of services in a task plan from reputation system or social network. It computes confidence of services based on requirement hypothesis, which will be explained in detail in the next section. The *evaluation module* is an extension of the original scheduler module, which generates appropriate schedules (workflow or process) to coordinate service's executions. The *evaluation module* retrieves confidence of services from the *inquiry module* and then performs trustworthy evaluation with Petri nets-based modeling and verification, which will be presented in detail in the next section. The *choice module* is an extension of the original execution module, and is designed to choose the most suitable task plan and schedule based on the evaluation results of *evaluation module*. *Execution module* will coordinate all services

with the selected schedule. There are six steps in our experience-based trust management: (1) A service requester issues a request with functional and trustworthy requirements. The trustworthy requirement contains policies in the forms of rule set to specify the requester's acceptable risk degree represented by two ontologies of general aspects and domain aspects. (2) The functional requirement will be analyzed to discover the requested services, while the trustworthy requirement will be evaluated by the extended *evaluation module*. (3) The service provider delivers offered service functionality with service instances according to invocations of the execution module, and the results will be reported to the communication module. (4) The requester consumes the service instances. (5) The requester sends feedbacks of his experiences regarding the consumed service instances. (6) The experiences received in step 5 will be saved in the reputation and social network inside the trust management system so that the system can refer to the experiences when some other requesters issue a similar request of trust evaluation later.

Figure 1. Architecture of experience-based trustworthiness evaluation

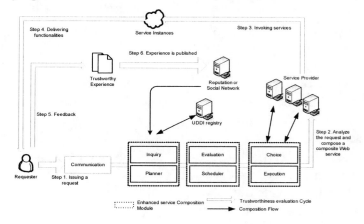

INQUIRY MODULE FOR EXPERIENCE SPECIFICATION

We have utilized ontology to specify experience of trust. Ontology employs classes to describe concepts (Maximilien & Singh, 2004) so that we construct instances from classes and describe past experiences with facts. For example, we list the experiences from two aspects, general and domain-specific samples for online bookstore services as shown in Table 1.

The experiences regarding bookstore services can be modeled by several "trustworthy aspect ontologies" as shown in Figure 2. We define a class "Experience of Trust" to represent the abstract model of experiences. The "Experience of Trust" class consists of two abstract classes:

"general aspect" and "domain aspect" to express multi-dimensional aspects and concepts of the experiences. The general aspect describes the general functionality and non-functional properties with functional and non-functional classes, and domain aspect considers different domain specific properties such as selling, booking, and others. The experience instance will be shown in detail in the next subsection.

Table 2 is an experience instance of the "Experience of Trust" class based on the class diagram in Figure 2 and the description of experience in Table 1.

Trustworthy requirement is a kind of rule-based policy that we utilize to determine whether described experiences are acceptable to meet service requester's trustworthy requirement. The

Table 1. Description of experience regarding bookstore services

General aspect Functional	
	Has the service request been fulfilled?
Non-Functional	
Network performance	What is the response time of the service instance in this service? What is the turnaround time of service instance in this service? What is the packet miss rate of service instance in this service?
Security	Does the service use RSA technology? Does the service use DES technology?
Quality	What is the availability of this service? What is the usability of this service?
Domain aspect Selling	
Bookstore	How long will it take to deliver a requested book in this service? Has the book been damaged during delivery in this service? What is the list price of the requested book in this service?

Figure 2. Trustworthy aspect ontology

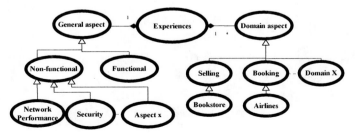

rules for trustworthy requirements are similar to sentences appearing in propositional logic. There are two examples of trustworthy requirement rules in Box 1. The trustworthy requirement rules are constructed by the requester's requirements.

By adopting a propositional logic-based inference engine, we can issue two queries *TELL* and *ASK* to knowledge base *KB* with. *TELL* is used to query whether some experience instance *tr* meets requester's trustworthy requirements. *ASK* is used to determine whether a service can satisfy the request.

We utilize experiences to infer whether a trustworthy requirement is acceptable. For example, based on experience instance *tr* in Table 2, we can infer that requirement s_1 is non-acceptable but requirement s_2 is acceptable with knowledge base *KB*. Therefore, the experience instance *tr* meets the requester's trustworthy requirement.

EVALUATION MODULE FOF TRUSTWORTHINESS EVALUATION

Evaluating Single Service

We utilize sampling of binomial probability to calculate the confidence, which is used to determine whether a service conforms to the requester's trustworthy requirements, based on a 95% confidence interval in terms of probability (Mitchell, 1997). The following terms are defined:

- *S* is defined as a set of service instances representing samples of total past service instances for one service, and is denoted by $S=\{s_1, s_2,...s_n\}$.

- *Tr* is defined as a set of trust evaluation values of past experience instance, and is denoted by $Tr=\{tr_1, tr_2,...tr_n\}$.

- *Rating: S→TrRatings(s)*: The Rating function maps the service instance *s* to past experience instance, *tr*. In other words, the function associates past service instance with past experience instance, and the experiences are collected by past requesters. For example, the function *Ratings(s)=tr* represents a trust evaluation *tr* of instance *s* ($s∈S∈tr∈Tr$).

- *Accept:Tr→{0,1}* A requirement hypothesis can be denoted as *Accept* function. The output of Accept function is 1 when past

Table 2. Description of experience instance tr regarding bookstore service

Aspect	Property	Value
Functional	Reach	True
Non-Func-tional		
Network perfor-mance	Response time	510 ms
	Turnaround time	2100 ms
	Packet miss rate	1.5 %
Security	RSA technology	True
	DES technology	True
Bookstore	Book delivery time	2 Days
		3 Hours
	Damage	False
	Price	$ 53.5

Box 1.

$S_1 : Accept ⇐ Functional.Reach ∧ Smaller(Network\ performance.Response\ time, 700ms) ∧$
$Smaller(Bookstore.Book\ delivery\ time, 2\ Days) ∧ Smaller(Bookstore.Price, \$50)$
$S_2 : Accept ⇐ Functional.Reach ∧ Security.RSA\ technology ∧ ¬Bookstore.Damage ∧$
$Smaller(Network\ performance.Packet\ miss\ rate, 2\%)$

experience instance is accepted by requester, otherwise it is 0. The *ASK* function is a query for the knowledge base *KB*.

$$Accept\left(tr\right) \equiv \begin{cases} 1 & ASK\left(KB, tr\right) = Accept \\ 0 & otherwise \end{cases}$$

Based on the usage of Large-Sample of Hypothesis for a Binomial Proportion to evaluate the simple error and true error of a hypothesis addressed in Mitchell (1997) and Mendenhall (1999), the result of the hypothesis assesses the sample as a Boolean value (true or false). Thus we can see that the hypothesis assesses the sample as a Bernoulli trial, and the distribution of Bernoulli trial is a binomial distribution. The binomial distribution approximates the normal distribution when the number of sample is enough. Simple error is the correct rate in samples, and true error is the correct rate in population. We will get a confidence interval according to the simple error and the area of confidence interval represents a probability which true error falls in the interval. In the normal distribution, the true error is 95% probabilities falling within the range of *mean±1.96×SD* (Standard Deviation) in compliance with the experience rule. In other words, we can utilize the confidence interval to evaluate lowest true error of the evaluating hypotheses.

Let *Accept* function be the hypothesis and then we can evaluate the possible true error of the hypothesis based on the past instances S according to the Evaluating Hypotheses theory (Mitchell, 1997). Whether the *tr (tr∈E)* is accepted by *Accept* is a binomial distribution which approximates the normal distribution when the number of samples is large enough. Thus we can utilize the normal distribution to calculate that the sample error closes with the true error. The true error is of 95% probabilities falling within a confidence interval, which will be approved as a trustworthy service in the general application.

We define the confidence symbol as the lowest bound of the true error. The trust of service conforms to the request's requirement when the confidence is higher.

$$p = \frac{1}{n}\sum_{s \bullet S} Accept\left(Rating(s)\right)$$

$$SD = \sqrt{\frac{p \times \left(1 - p\right)}{n}}$$

$$z_{95\%} = 1.96$$

$$Confidence \equiv \max\left\{p - z_{95\%} \times SD, 0\right\}$$

As the number of samples increases, the standard deviation decreases relatively, and the confidence will be closer to the true error. For example, the past instances of the bookstore service are *S, |S|=256*. Requester proposes a Requirement Hypothesis *Accept*. If the result of calculation is *p=0.6*, the confidence can be calculated from the following equation.

$$p = \frac{1}{256}\sum_{s \in S} Accpet\left(Rating(s)\right) = 0.6$$

$$z_{95\%} = 1.96$$

$$Confidence = p - z_{95\%} \times \sqrt{\frac{p \times \left(1 - p\right)}{256}}$$

$$\cong 0.6 - 0.060012 = 0.539987$$

The calculated confidence is 53.99%, which means the value is of the service has 53.99% probability to meet the trustworthy requirement based on 95% confidence interval. Hence we can assert that trust of the service have 53.99% probability of conforming to the requester's requirements.

Evaluating Composite Services

We define Trustworthy Web Service Evaluation Petri Net (TWSEPN), which is extended from Petri nets to model composite Web service. Furthermore, we applied the coverability graph of TWSEPN to simulate states of service execution (behavior analysis) (Narayanan & McIlraith, 2002). Based on the simulation, we can compute the variation of trustworthy confidence in a composite Web service.

Trustworthy Web Service Evaluation Petri Nets (TWSEPN)

Petri nets are characterized by its graphical modeling and mathematical computation power, which is very suitable for Web service modeling and simulation. In addition, Petri nets are more powerful than state machine-to-model-concurrent and distributed systems, and it can verify both structural and behavioral properties of the system. Petri nets can also be represented as mathematical models such as state equations so it is able to apply different mathematical techniques such as matrix operations to calculate system's behaviors. The details of TWSEPN are defined as follows:

$$TWSEPN = (P, T, F, M_{initial}, M_{finial}, Conf)$$

1. $P=\{p_1, p_2,...p_j\}$ is a finite set of places; each place represents a pre-condition and post-condition in a service.
2. $T=\{t_1, t_2,...t_k\}$ is a finite set of transitions; each transition represents a *sub-service* or *control-service* in a composite service. The transitions of sub-services are represented services, which organize the composite service, and the transitions of control-services are represented flow control in the TWSEPN.
3. $F\subseteq(P\times T)\cup(T\times P)$ is a set of arcs; each arc represent the control flow between *sub-services* in a service.
4. $M_{initial}\in\{0,1\}^j$ represents the initial marking in the *TWSEPN*.
5. $M_{final}\in\{0,1\}^j$ represents the final marking in the *TWSEPN*.
6. *Conf:T→Confidence* is a mapping function which maps the *sub-services* to these confidences.

We use the *Requirement Hypothesis Accept* to compute the *Confidence* of *sub-services*.

$$Conf(t)\equiv$$
$$\begin{cases} Confidence \text{ of the } t & t \text{ } is \text{ a sub-service} \\ 1 & t \text{ is a control-service} \end{cases}$$

In order to model different workflow patterns, we define several useful control constructs and their corresponding confidences, including sequence, split, split-join, if-then-else, iterate, and so forth, as illustrated in Figure 3.

Trustworthy Evaluation with TWSEPN

According to the $M_{initial}$ and firing rules, we deduce all covered markings into a coverability graph to express the transformation of markings (states). The classical coverability graph algorithm was proposed by Murata (1989). It was optimized later by Finkel (1993), who proposed an algorithm to construct the minimal coverability graph. We have used the algorithm to construct the coverability graph of the TWSEPN. Based on TWSEPN's definitions and control patterns, we parse a composite service, generate the corresponding model, and derive its coverability graph easily as shown in the following and Figure 4.

CHOICE MODULE FOR SELECTING TRUSTWORTHY COMPOSITE SERVICES

Every arc in a coverability graph represents a confidence value denoted by formula *Conf(t)(t∈T)*. Hence, it is easy to find out the *minimum confidence* of a TWSEPN model by investigating all possible product values (firing sequences). Since a coverability graph is a directed graph, which might contain cycles, we need to consider the two different cases: The first one is that the coverability

Figure 3. Control patterns in TWSEPN

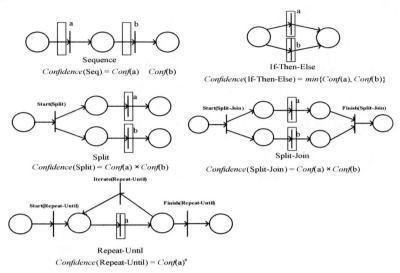

graph is a directed acyclic graph, and the other is that the coverability graph contains cycles.

Find Minimum Confidence

If the coverability graph is a directed acyclic graph (DAG), the graph is an Activity on Edge Network (AOE). In an AOE, every activity is attached to the arcs, and AOE can be serialized by topological order. Every arc represents a state transformation, and the confidence value of the transformation is attached to the arc. The algorithm of calculating minimum confidence of all possible product values is presented in Algorithm 1.

In order to determine the minimum confidence of all possible product values in a cyclic graph, we present a method based on Cormen (1999) to determine the Strongly Connected Components (SCC) of the coverability graph in linear time (Tarjan's algorithm). Then we can compress the SCC into two vertexes and one arc to transform the directed cyclic graph into a DAG. The vertexes which construct the SCC, and the weights of edges which are in the SCC are denoted as:

$$M^{SCC} = \{M_a, M_b \ldots\},$$

and

$$T^{SCC} = \{t_\alpha, t_\beta \ldots\} \ (T^{SCC} \subseteq T).$$

Two of the compressed vertexes are denoted as $M_{a,b\ldots}$ and $M'_{a,b\ldots}$. A special symbol δ is defined to represent the infinite property. The lower bound of the confidence is:

$$\left(\prod_{t \in T^{SCC} \text{ and } t \in T} Conf(t)\right)^\delta \text{ in the compressed SCC.}$$

We substitute for the confidence values of arcs between $M_{a,b\ldots}$ and $M'_{a,b\ldots}$. Then we must ensure that the lower bound of the confidence is:

$$\left(\prod_{t \in T^{SCC} \text{ and } t \in T} Conf(t)\right)^\delta \text{ in the SCC.}$$

The lowest confidence loop is formed by the set T' $(T' \subseteq T^{SCC})$ in the SCC. The confidence of the loop is denoted as C and:

Figure 4. The TWSEPN model of program 1 and its coverability graph

```
Program 1
  ignore

<process:CompositeProcess rdf:ID="CompositionService">
  <process:composedOf>
     <process:If-Then-Else>
        <process:ifCondition>    </process:ifCondition>
        <process:then>
           <process:AtomicProcess rdf:about="#ser1"/>
        </process:then>
        <process:else>
           <process:SplitJoin>
              <process:AtomicProcess rdf:about="#ser2"/>
              <process:Repeat-Until>
                 <process:untilCondition>    </process:untilCondition>
                 <process:untilProcess>
                    <process:AtomicProcess rdf:about="# ser3"/>
                 </process:untilProcess>
              </process:Repeat-Until>
           </process:SplitJoin>
        </process:else>
     </process:If-Then-Else>
  </process:composedOf>
</process:CompositeProcess>

  Ignore
```

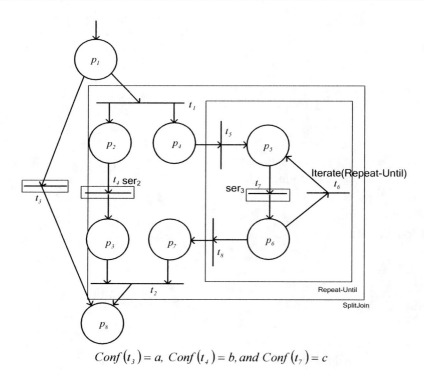

$Conf(t_3) = a,\ Conf(t_4) = b,\ and\ Conf(t_7) = c$

$$c = \prod_{t \in T' \text{ and } t \in T} Conf(t)^{\gamma_i}, \gamma_i \in N$$

Let $\gamma = \max\limits_{t \in T' \text{ and } t \in T} \{\delta_i\}$.

A special symbol δ is defined to represent the infinite property, and the symbol δ exists for each integer n, $\delta > n \times \gamma$. Thus the following formula can be derived:

$$c = \prod_{t \in T' \text{ and } t \in T} Conf(t)^{\gamma_i} \geq \left(\prod_{t \in T' \text{ and } t \in T} Conf(t) \right)^{\gamma}$$
$$\geq \left(\prod_{t \in T^{SCC} \text{ and } t \in T} Conf(t) \right)^{\delta}$$

There are two kinds of arcs in the original incoming ones. An arc e connects to M ($M \in M^{SCC}$) and the graph contains an arc e' which connects M with M' ($M' \in M^{scc}$). Otherwise, the arc e is connected to $M'_{a,b...}$. Finally, the minimum confidence of all possible product values can be determined by the following formula:

$$\min \begin{cases} CompositeConf(M_x) \times \\ Conf(t), CompositeConf(M_y) \end{cases}$$

Choose Best Schedule of Service Execution

As the production of the confidence values includes an exponential variable δ, we have to decide which the minimum is. The evaluation of two composite confidences cc and cc' is shown as follows:

- If both cc and cc' do not include the variable δ, scalar comparison is used to evaluate the situation;
- If both cc and cc' include the variable δ, the comparison of the confidences, which include the variable, δ is performed. If the confidences are equal, the comparison of the confidences, which do not include the

variable, δ is performed;
- If one of cc and cc' includes the variable, δ, the smaller of two confidences is the one, which includes variable, δ; and
- The system decides a scalar and use scalar comparison to evaluate the situation.

The aforementioned method can be used to choose the best schedule. For example, according to Figure 4, the SCCs are detected as shown in Figure 5. Based on the addressed method, the coverability graph can be transformed into a DAG as shown in Figure 6. In accordance with algorithm #1, we can evaluate the *composition confidence* of a composite Web service. In the final step, we could decide whether this composite service conforms to the trustworthy requirements. In the scenario, the minimal composition confidence of this service is $min\{a, b \times c^{\delta}\}$. If some composite services can reach the same goal and the minimal composition confidence is greater than $min\{a, b \times c^{\delta}\}$, we will choose the greater one to ensure that the choice is the most trustworthy one.

CONCLUSION AND FUTURE RESEARCHES

In this article, we have presented an experience-based trustworthy evaluation model based on trust experience (understanding) and trust requirement (policy). In *inquiry model*, we utilize ontology to describe experiences and requirements to infer individual confidence degree of all sub-services. In *evaluation module*, we have presented TWSEPN to model a schedule (workflow or process) of a composite Web service and evaluate the whole confidence degree of the composite Web service with TWSEPN's coverability graph and individual confidence of sub-services. Finally, we developed a *choice module* to import various trust requirements in order to determine the best plan of a composite Web service for service execution.

In the near future, we will introduce concepts of penalty and insurance to improve evaluation of trustworthy degree in Web services. If a service provider ever provided a failed service, his trustworthy degree will degrade due to the penalty. In addition, service providers need to address service insurance with a digital agreement, and service requesters can file a damage claim based on the digital agreement if the offered service fails to meet the agreement.

ACKNOWLEDGMENT

This work is supported by National Science Council, Taiwan under grants NSC 94-2524-S-008-001.

REFERENCES

Andrew, T., Curbera, F., Dholakia, H., Goland, Y., Klein, J. & Leymann, F. et al. (2003). *Business Process Execution Language for Web Service Version 1.1*. Retrieved June 1, 2006, from http://www.ibm.com/developerworks/library/ws-bpel

Anthony, N., Chris, K., Phillip, H., & Ronald, M. (2004). *Web Services Security: SOAP Message Security 1.0 (WS-Security 2004)*. Retrieved June 1, 2006, from http://docs.oasis-open.org/wss/2004/01/oasis-200401-wss- soap-message-security-1.0

Bajaj, S., Box, D., Chappell, D., Curbera, F., Daniels, G. & Hallam-Baker, P. et al. (2004). *Web Services Policy Framework (WS-Policy)*. Retrieved June 1, 2006, from http://www-106. ibm.com/developerworks/library/specification/ ws-polfram/

Bellwood, T., Clement, L. & Riegen, C.V. (2003). *UDDI Version 3.0.1*. Retrieved June 1, 2006, from http://uddi.org/pubs/uddi_v3.htm

Chinnici, R., Moreau, J-J., Ryman, A. & Weerawarana, S. (2004). *Web Services Description Language (WSDL) Version 2.0 Part 1: Core Language*. Retrieved June 1, 2006, from http://www.w3.org/TR/wsdl20/

Cormen, T. H., Leiserson, C. E., & Rivest, R. L. (1999). Introduction to algorithms. The MIT Press and McGraw-Hill.

Doorn, L. v., Sailer, R., Perez, R. & Dyer, J. (2006). *4758/Linux Project*. Retrieved June 1, 2006, from http://www.research.ibm.com/ secure_systems_department/projects/linux4758/index.html

Erradi, A., & Maheshwari, P. (2005). wsBus: QoS-aware middleware for reliable Web services interactions. *Proceedings of IEEE EEE05* (pp. 634-639).

Finkel, A. (1993). The minimal coverability graph for petri nets. *Advances in Petri Nets 1993, Lecture Notes in Computer Science,* 674, 210-243.

Galileo International (2006). Retrieved June 1, 2006, from http://www.galileo.com/galileo/

Grandison, T., & Sloman, M. (2000). A survey of trust in Internet applications. *IEEE Communications Surveys,* 2-16.

Huhns, M. N., & Buell, D. A. (2002). Trusted autonomy. *IEEE Internet Computing,* 92-95.

IBM Corporation (2003). *Web Services Level Agreements*. Retrieved June 1, 2006, from http://www.research.ibm.com/wsla/WSLASpecV1-20030128.pdf

IBM, BEA Systems, Microsoft, Layer 7 Technologies, Oblix, VeriSign, Actional, Computer Associates, OpenNetwork Technologies, Ping Identity, Reactivity and RSA Security (2004). *Web Services Trust Language*. Retrieved June 1, 2006, from http://www-128.ibm.com/developerworks/ webservices/library /specification/ws-trust/

Jaeger, M. C., et al. (2005). QoS aggregation in Web service compositions. *Proceedings of IEEE EEE05* (pp. 181-185).

Kavantzas, N., Burdett, D., Ritzinger, G., Fletcher, T. & Lafon, Y. (2004). *Web Services Choreography Description Language Version 1.0.* Retrieved June 1, 2006, from http://www.w3.org/TR/2004/WD-ws-cdl-10-20041217/

Keller, A., & Ludwig, H. (2003). The WSLA framework: Specifying and monitoring service level agreements for Web services. *Journal of Network and Systems Management, 11*(1), 57-81.

Mani, A., & Nagarajan, A. (2002). *Understanding quality of service for Web services.* Retrieved June 1, 2006, from http://www-106.ibm.com/developerworks/webservices/library/ws-quality.html

Maximilien, E. M., & Singh, M. P. (2002). Conceptual model of Web service reputation. *SIGMOD Record, 31*(4), 36–41

Maximilien, E. M., & Singh, M. P. (2004). A framework and ontology for dynamic Web services selection. *IEEE Internet Computing, 8*(5), 84–93

Mendenhall, W., & Beaver, R. J. (1999). *Introduction to probability and statistics.* Duxbury Press.

Mitchell, T. (1997). *Machine learning.* WCB McGraw-Hill.

Mitra, N. (2003). *SOAP Version 1.2 Part 0: Primer.* Retrieved June 1, 2006, from http://www.w3.org/TR/ 2003/REC-soap12-part0-20030624/

Murata, T. (1989). Petri nets: Properties, analysis, and applications. In *Proceedings of the IEEE, 77*(4), 541-580.

Narayanan, S., & McIlraith, S. A. (2002). Simulation, verification, and automated composition of Web services. In *Proceedings of ACM WWW 2002* (pp. 77-88).

Pezzini, M. (2003). Composite applications head toward the mainstream. *Gartner Group,* ID Number AV-21-1772.

Shadbolt, N. (2002). A matter of trust. *IEEE Intelligent Systems,* 2-3.

Singh, M. P. (2002). Trustworthy service composition: Challenges and research questions. In *Proceedings of the Autonomous Agents and Multi-Agent Systems Workshop on Deception, Fraud and Trust in Agent Societies* (pp. 39-52).

The OWL Services Coalition. (2006). *OWL-S: Semantic Markup for Web Service Version 1.0.* Retrieved June 1, 2006, from http://www.daml.org/services/owl-s/1.0/owl-s.html

Tosic, V., Pagurek, B., Patel, K., Esfandiari, B., & Ma, W. (2003). Management applications of the Web service offerings language (WSOL). In *Proceedings of CAiSE03* (pp. 468-484). Springer-Verlag.

Tosic, V., & Pagurek, B. (2005). On comprehensive contractual descriptions of Web services. In *Proceedings of IEEE EEE05* (pp. 444-449).

Triple A (2006). Retrieved June 1, 2006, from http://www.infoworld.com/articles/hn/xml/02/08/12/020812hntriplea.html?0814wewebservices

TRUST (2005). *Team for Research in Ubiquitous Secure Technology (TRUST).* Retrieved June 1, 2006, from http://trust.eecs.berkeley.edu/

Trusted Computing Group (2005). *Trusted Computing Group.* Retrieved June 1, 2006, from https://www.trustedcomputinggroup.org/

Wang, G., Chen, A., Wang, C., Fung, C. & Uczekaj, S. (2004). Integrated quality of service (QoS) management in service-oriented enterprise architectures. In *Proceedings of IEEE EDOC04* (pp. 21-32).

Yolum, P., & Singh, M. P. (2002). An agent-based approach for trustworthy service location. In

Proceedings of 1st International Workshop on Agents and Peer-to-Peer Computing (AP2PC) (pp. 45-56).

Zhang, J., Zhang, L. & Chung, J. (2004). An approach to help select trustworthy Web services. In *Proceedings of IEEE CEC-East* (pp. 84–91).

This work was previously published inInternational Journal of Information Security and Privacy, Vol. 1, Issue 1, edited by H. Nemati, pp. 1-17, copyright 2007 by IGI Publishing, formerly known as Idea Group Publishing (an imprint of IGI Global).

Chapter 4.43
Perceptions of End–Users on the Requirements in Personal Firewall Software:
An Exploratory Study

Sunil Hazari
University of West Georgia, USA

ABSTRACT

Information security is usually considered a technical discipline with much attention being focused on topics such as encryption, hacking, break-ins, and credit card theft. Security products such as anti-virus programs and personal firewall software, are now available for end-users to install on their computers to protect against threats endemic to networked computers. The behavioral aspects related to maintaining enterprise security have received little attention from researchers and practitioners. Using Q-sort analysis, this study used students as end-users in a graduate business management security course to investigate issues affecting selection of personal firewall software in organizations. Based on the Q-sort analysis of end-users in relation to seven variables identified from review of the information security literature, three distinct group characteristics emerged. *Similarities and differences between groups are investigated and implications of these results to IT managers, vendors of security software and researchers in information security area are discussed.*

INTRODUCTION

Information must be readily available in organizations for making decisions to support the organizational mission. Murphy, Boren, and Schlarman (2000) state that due to increased connectivity and the urgency to exchange information and data among partners, suppliers, and customers on a real time basis, the need to protect and secure computer resources is greater than ever. As a result, this has created the possibility of exposing sensitive corporate information to competitors as well as hackers who can now access organizational computer resources from remote sites. The potential loss of such information to an organization goes beyond financial losses and includes the possibility of corrupted data, denial of services to suppliers, business partners and customers, loss of customer confidence, and lost sales. Security in business processes (i.e., maintaining proper authentication, authorization, non-repudiation, and privacy) is critical to successful e-business operations. Enabling business functions over the Internet has been recognized as a major component for the success of businesses and, by mitigating risks in a cost-effective manner, security is now being viewed as a component of business operations (Deise, Nowikow, King, & Wright, 2000). Decisions about information systems made by managers are vital to the success, and even survival, of a firm (Enns, Huff, & Golden, 2003).

Despite increased security threats, organizations have traditionally allocated very little of the total IT budget to information security. Forrester Research estimates that in Fortune 500 companies, the average amount of money as a percent of revenue that is spent on IT security is 0.0025 percent or slightly less than what they spend on coffee (Clarke, 2002). Organizations must evaluate and prioritize the optimum mix of products and services to be deployed for protecting confidentiality (maintaining privacy of information), integrity (maintaining information is not altered in transit), and availability (maintaining access to information and resources) of corporate assets. The decision to deploy certain technology is based on variables such as the organizational business model, level of risk, vulnerability, cost, and return on investment (Highland, 1993).

There are several ways in which information can be protected. One method to safeguard information is by using controls. The concept of controls can be applied to financial auditing as well as technical computer security. General controls include personnel, physical and organizational

controls as well as technical security services and mechanisms (Summers, 1997). Computer security controls can be hardware or software-based and may include biometric devices, anti-virus software, smart cards, firewalls, and intrusion detection systems that can be used to build the enterprise security infrastructure. Additionally, these controls may be preventive, detective, or corrective. This paper will focus on one such computer security control — Personal Firewalls. Firewalls intercept traffic and make routing and redirection decisions based on policies. Some firewalls can also inspect packets and make transformation and security decisions; therefore, they are critical components in maintaining security in organizations. There are different types of firewalls, such as hardware, software, enterprise, and personal firewalls. Personal firewalls are client-based solutions that are installed on desktop/laptop computers and may be administered individually from a central location. Successful selection and adoption of firewalls (enterprise as well as personal) is based on various factors, some of which are technical while others may be behavioral. This exploratory study looks at the new genre of personal firewalls and, based on review of the literature, attempts to identify factors that could result in successful selection of personal firewalls in organizations and further provide empirical evidence to support deployment of firewall software.

The purpose of this paper is to investigate self-referent perceptions of end-users, and use Q-Sort analysis to investigate factors affecting deployment of security firewall software in organizations. The paper is organized as follows: review of research on information security is presented to the reader along with extraction of variables from the literature that may determine firewall deployment in organizations; The Q-Sort Factor Analysis method used for the study is explained and the research design is provided; Along with data analysis, results of the study are then explained, which is followed by discussion and applications to practice. Due to the nature of research design used in this study, limitations are also explained. The study also sheds light on behavioral aspects of information security, which may be tied to perceptions of end-users who may influence technology selection in their organization. This will provide empirical evidence to an area that has been identified as lacking in research (Dhillon & Blackhouse, 2001; Troutt, 2002) and provide directions and guidance for future studies.

INFORMATION SECURITY RESEARCH

In the area of information security, research has often lagged practice. Dhillon & Blackhouse (2001) have stressed the need for "more empirical research to develop key principles for the prevention of negative events and therefore to help in the management of security." Despite known vulnerabilities in applications and operating systems, companies continue to deploy software to stay competitive, and steps taken to secure products and services are knee-jerk reactions to media stories that are more reactive than proactive in nature. Most IT managers lack a coherent framework and concrete methodology for achieving enterprise security. A security plan that includes technology, personnel, and policies would be a much better approach to developing an enterprise security strategy. One such model is the Enterprise Security Framework Price Waterhouse Coopers (PWC) model. The PWC model is comprehensive because it addresses the entire enterprise of security architecture. The model emphasizes information security strategies within the organization using a holistic rather than a piecemeal approach. The framework is based on four pillars: *security vision and strategy, senior management commitment, information security management structure*, and *training and awareness*. Within the pillars are *decision drivers, development,*

and *implementation* phases. Firewalls are placed in the *development* phase since they are used to provide interpretation of corporate standards at the technical level. For a detailed discussion of the PWC model, the reader is referred to Murphy, Boren, and Schlarman (2000).

Firewalls can be considered a last line of defense in protecting and securing information systems. Wood (1988) provided a context for information security systems planning and proposed that reactive and incremental improvement approaches to address security are harbingers of a more serious problem. Other factors identified in Wood's model are the lack of top management support, information overload, insufficient staffing, and limited resources. Straub and Welke (1998) advocate using deterrence, prevention, detection, and recovery security action cycle to mitigate systems risk and use prioritized security controls. Data on computer crimes is often under-reported because companies are not willing to risk public embarrassment and bad publicity. Most companies choose to handle these incidents internally without keeping documentation or reporting to local, state or federal authorities (Saita, 2001). There is a need for unbiased empirical studies in the information security area that will provide insight into problems affecting today's technology dependent corporations and industries. With a strong need to collect and analyze computer security data, the CSI/FBI Computer Crime and Security Survey is published yearly (see http://www.gocsi.com). This study provides descriptive statistics but does not attempt to identify relationship between variables, as is expected in analytical surveys. Also, results reported in this annual survey have been identified by the publishers themselves to be potentially misleading due to the limited number of respondents and their accuracy as a result of anonymous nature of the surveys. These results have also been called into question because of lack of statistical or scholarly rigor and self-serving interest (Heiser, 2002). Despite these limitations, the CSI/FBI survey provides a useful role in comparison of yearly data for similar parameters.

To provide better evidence of factors that affect deployment of technology tools that create awareness of security issues and produce better informed employees, research into behavioral factors also needs to be conducted to gain insight into programs and processes that will lead to the development of a robust enterprise security strategy. Information security awareness research has been mostly descriptive and has not explored the possibilities offered by motivation/behavioral theories, or the related theory of planned behavior and the technology acceptance model, specifically in the information security domain (Mathieson, 1991; Siponen, 2000; Legris, Ingham, & Collerette, 2003). Since security has been deployed at the perimeter of electronic network and on servers by system administrators, the area of information security has ignored users of information systems since software developers are far removed from how the user will interact with security software. Human compliance with information security rules require an understanding of how people work and think (Highland, 1993). Lane (1985) considers the human factor to be the first and most important component of security and a critical part of the risk analysis process. This is especially true in personal firewall software since the burden of maintaining a secure environment is being shared by the user and the system administrator.

The area of *human computer interface* provides a link between the user and software applications. User satisfaction is a function of features, user interface, response time, reliability, "installability," information, maintainability, and other factors. "If a product's user interface catches a user's attention and is simple to learn and use, and has the right price and features, then the product may gain competitive advantage" (Torres, 2002, p. 15). The theory of user interface design and user involvement in completing task-based actions related to Internet and security software has been substantiated by two studies in which user interaction with

peer-to-peer software (Good & Kerkelberg, 2002), and PGP software (Whitten & Tygar, 1999) were examined. Good and Krekelberg (peer-to-peer study) found that applications connecting to the Internet need better usability and software design to maintain integrity of information stored on a user's computer. In this study, individuals assumed responsibility of keeping firewalls operational at all times. This contributed in large part to maintaining effective enterprise security. Whitten and Tygar (PGP study) found that user errors are a significant portion of computer security failures, and further concluded that user interfaces for security programs require a usability standard much different from other consumer software. (Although this study is not directly concerned with user satisfaction, but is more focused on factors that affect deployment rather than development of end-user software in a specific area, some factors may be directly tied to user satisfaction as will be shown by correlational analysis).

An important reason to look at end-user perception is that it may affect how well the user does his or her part in staying vigilant to combat threats posted by hackers to organizational assets. The end-user may be a conduit to organizational data being compromised. Proper software selection as well as positive user attitude and motivation for using the software are therefore important to ensure ongoing use of personal firewall software. Kettinger and Lee (2002) address the fact that the proliferation of personal computing and individualized software, and popularity of the Internet in organizations have resulted in users playing an important role in driving IT implementation. Their study found that for users selecting their own IT applications (such as desktop software programs), there is greater user satisfaction after implementation. Grantham and Vaske (1985) also state that positive user attitudes are important predictors in continued system use. This is especially important for personal firewall use because computers are at risk at all times when connected to the Internet. In reference to software selection, Chiasson and

Lovato (2001) emphasize: "Understanding of how users form perceptions of software innovation would help software designers, implementers and users in their evaluation, selection, implementation and ongoing use of software. However, with the exception of some recent work, there is little research examining how a user forms his or her perceptions of innovation over time" (p. 16). The area of information security as it relates to maintaining confidentiality and integrity of data stored on personal computers can benefit from identification of factors that would make it possible to safeguard corporate assets that are at risk as a result of remote data access by employees. Software selection for deployment on company computers cuts across different user levels in terms of knowledge and level of expertise of the user. Selection of software therefore must be done to accommodate all types of users ranging from novices to experts. The latter category of users may have higher tacit knowledge of tasks to be able to compensate for the interface without realizing it (Gery, 1997).

Due to increasing mobile and off-site access by employees using cable modems, DSL connections, and wireless devices to access corporate resources, personal firewalls are a necessary component to maintain overall enterprise security in an organization. Because of the nature and availability of personal firewall software, most companies choose to acquire it rather than develop it in-house. Software acquisition that results in productivity gains and strategic advantage is of critical concern to organizations, and factors that relate to these benefits must be correctly identified and understood for software acquisition decisions (Nelson, Richmond, & Seidmann, 1996). Purchase of commercial software includes identifying requirements, evaluating packages from different vendors, configuring, installing, and evaluating it either as server or client-based solution. This may further involve requirements acquisition that leads to product selection (Maiden, Ncube, & Moore, 1997). As a method of selection, professionals in

charge of evaluating personal firewall software could draft a feature requirements document, and evaluate vendor products by comparing available features as well as using demonstration versions of software. This would be followed by user experience with the software. As mentioned earlier, the need for user involvement in information systems has been considered an important mechanism for improving system quality and ensuring successful system implementation. It is further believed that the user's satisfaction with a system leads to greater system usage (Baroudi, Olson, & Ives, 1986). The requirements for software though must be as measurable as possible to enable product selection and may also use repertory grids in which stakeholders are asked for attributes applicable to a set of entities and values for cells in an entity-attribute matrix. This would produce representation of requirements in a standardized, quantifiable format amenable even to statistical analyses (Maiden, Ncube, & Moore, 1997). In relation to the security area, Goodhue and Straub (1991) found company actions and individual awareness to be statistically significant in a study of perceptions of managers regarding controls installed in organizations.

RESEARCH DESIGN

Subjects in this exploratory research study were 31 MBA students enrolled in a Security and Control of Information Systems course. The students came from different backgrounds, such as finance, liberal arts, nursing, and computer science. From a business perspective, the course examined implications of information security risks faced by organizations. Although technical issues of security, such as authentication, authorization, and encryption that make electronic commerce sites successful in processing business transactions securely were also explored in the course, the primary focus in the course was from a business perspective. There was no structured lab work during class, but to gain a better understanding of security issues, students were expected to complete hands-on exercises outside class. During initial weeks, topics covered included the PWC model, TCP/IP vs. OSI models, network, e-mail, database security, digital certificates and signatures, risk assessment, and privacy issues. Also, during Week 5, students had been previously tested on the topics using short-answer type questions to determine learning competency of factual information and applications related to information security in organizations. The test score counted towards 15% of overall course grade. With coverage of the aforementioned topics, it was safe to assume that students had knowledge of current security issues facing organizations in today's economy. Because there is no consensus on the *common body of knowledge* acceptable for all security professionals, and since this was an exploratory study, the study was conducted in a controlled environment with a homogenous population of students to minimize confounding by extraneous variables. Using MBA students as surrogates for professionals or executives in reference to use and evaluation of technology has also been found to be acceptable (Briggs, Balthazard, & Dennis, 1996).

The hands-on firewall assignment in this course covered installation, configuration, and use of one standard personal firewall software (ZoneAlarm). After students had a chance to use the software, they were asked to participate in the study. No class discussion was conducted on results of the firewall tests in case it affected students' perceptions about the software, which could have influenced their response. Therefore, the data reflected individual student perception without class discussions. Students were given instructions to visit a Web site that explained the nature of the study and provided information on how the Q-sort statements should be sorted. This was important since students are more used to completing questionnaires in a survey format that use Likert scale, open-ended, or close-ended

questions (such as those used during end of term class evaluation of instruction), but may not be familiar with the peculiarities of the Q-sort procedure. To reduce data errors and extract usable data, instructions were presented in detail before the respondents were shown the statements for the study. This was an exploratory study for the purpose of investigating and contributing to research in the relatively new domain of user-centered security products that are being deployed by businesses to increase enterprise security.

Q-Sort Analysis

Q-sort analysis uses a technique for studying human subjectivity (Stephenson, 1953; Brown, 1980; McKeown & Thomas, 1988). It is useful in exploratory research and a well-developed theoretical literature guides and supports its users (Thomas & Watson, 2002). Q-sort methodology is suited for small samples and relies on theories in the domain area being researched to develop items for analysis. A disadvantage of the Q-sort methodology is that it is not suitable for large samples, and it forces subjects to conform to certain expectations (such as fitting responses within a normal distribution). Brown (1986) suggests that 30 to 50 subjects are sufficient for studies investigating public opinion. Q-sort uses an ipsative (self-referenced) technique of sorting participant's statements about subjective conditions. It is a variation of factor analysis technique that uses Q-methodology theory to analyze correlation measure (Brown, 1980). Respondents to Q-sort studies are required to sort statements into predefined normal distribution type scale in which a fixed number of items fall under each category. The rankings provide clusters of perceptions of individuals' consensus and conflict, which can be used to place individuals with similar characteristics into groups for further study. In the past, the Q-sort technique used index cards for sorting, but now Web-based data collection programs (such as WebQ) are common. Initially the statements are presented to respondents in random order, and each respondent organizes statements into predefined categories. To view entered data, the respondent also can update statement rankings to see where the statements fall under each category. One advantage of using the WebQ method is that data submission errors are reduced since the program verifies that the statements are sorted according to predefined requirements.

In this personal firewall study, the statements were to be classified by respondents as "Most Important" (+2), "Important" (+1), "Neutral" (0), "Less Important" (-1), and "Least Important" (-2). To provide a forced distribution that is expected in the Q-Sort methodology, respondents were given instructions to identify one statement as "Most Important," two statements each as "Important" and "Less Important," and three statements as

"Neutral." The instrument used is shown in Figure 1.

DATA ANALYSIS

Q-Sort analysis is a type of inverse factor analysis in which the cases (subjects) rather than statement variables (features) are clustered. As recommended by Brown (1980), a procedure that arranged statements based on responses of a single individual was used for data analysis. The responses involved statements of opinion (also called Q-sample) that individuals rank-ordered based on the feature requirements in personal firewall software. The arrayed items (Q-sort) from the respondents were correlated and factor-analyzed. The factors indicated clusters of

Figure 1. WebQ questionnaire

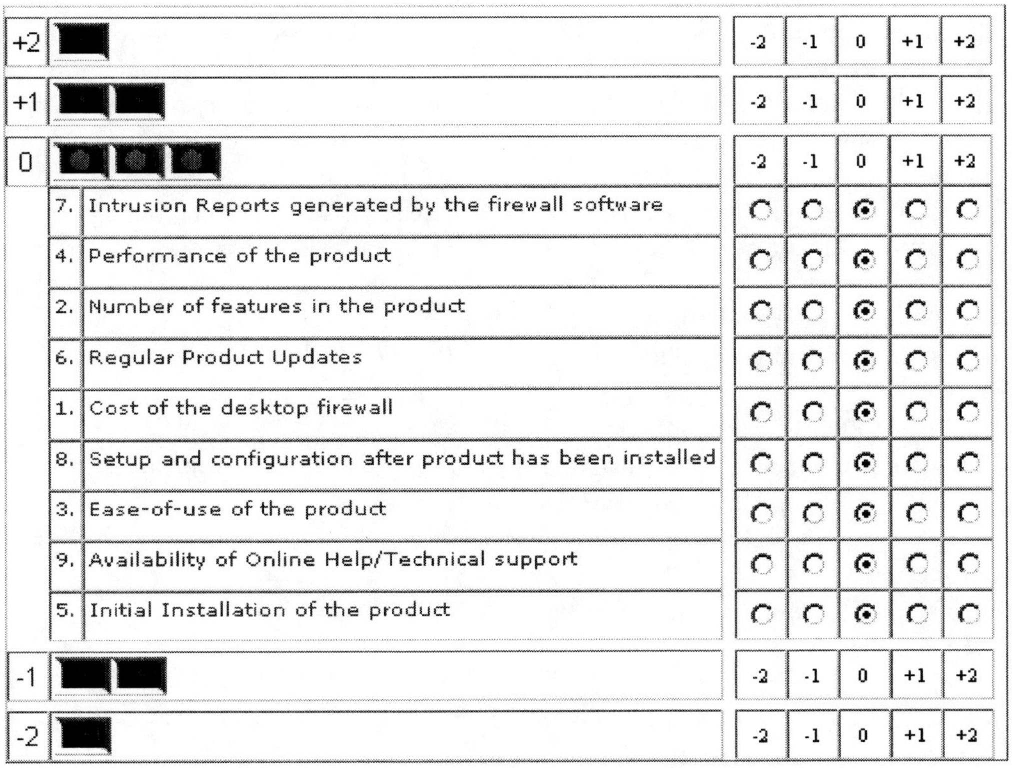

subjects who had ranked the statement in the same fashion. Explanation of factors was then advanced in terms of commonly shared attitudes or perspectives.

A review of security literature (Hazari, 2000; Northcutt, McLachlan, & Novak, 2000; Scambray, McClure, & Kurtz, 2001; Strassberg, Rollie, & Gondek, 2002; Zwicky, Cooper, Chapman, & Russell, 2000) was used to extract the following statement variables relating to requirements in personal firewall software: performance, ease-of-use, updates, features, reports, cost, configuration, and support. Operational definition of these variables as it relates to the study are provided:

Performance [PERF]: Refers to how well the software operates under various conditions (such as high traffic, types of data, port scans, etc.)

Ease-of-use [EOU]: Refers to usability of the product (such as screen design and layout, access to features using tabs, buttons, etc.)

Updates [UPDTS]: Refers to product updates at regular intervals after product has been installed and used

Features [FEATR]: Refers to the number of program options and features available in software

Reports [RPORT]: Refers to Intrusion Reports and log files generated by the firewall software

Cost [COST]: Refers to price paid for the product (either as shrink wrapped package or as a download)

Configuration [CONFIG]: Refers to setup and configuration after product has been installed

Support [SUPPRT]: Refers to availability of online help and technical support either by phone or e-mail

Installation [INSTLL]: Refers to initial installation of the product

Prior to conducting the Q-sort analysis, ranked scores of all participants (before identifying factor groups) on each statement variable were calculated for preliminary descriptive statistics. These are shown in Table 1, where a mean score of 5 = Most Important and 0 = Least Important).

Correlation between the nine feature variables shows a low level of correlation between statements. This indicates there is a high degree of independence between the statement categories as used in the analysis. This finding is important since it supports the assertion that the statements represent relatively independent factors obtained from the review of the literature.

In the correlation matrix shown, Table 2 shows significant correlation ($p < 0.05$) between cost and updates, cost and reports, ease-of-use and performance, ease-of-use and updates, and installation and support.

As mentioned earlier, in Q-factor analysis, the correlation between subjects rather than variables are factored. The factors represent grouping of people with similar patterns of response during sorting (Brown, 1980; Thomas & Watson, 2002). Following guidelines for Q-factor analysis, eight factors were initially identified with eigenvalues > 1 (an eigenvalue is the amount of variance in the original variable associated with the factor). These factors and their percentage of variance are shown in Table 3.

Factors selected were rotated to maximize the loading of each variable on one of the extracted

Table 1. Participant ranked scores

Variable	Mean	SD
PERF	4.45	0.77
EOU	3.39	1.08
UPDTS	3.23	0.88
FEATR	3.06	0.93
RPORT	3.00	1.03
COST	2.97	1.20
CONFIG	2.55	0.85
SUPPRT	2.35	0.98
INSTLL	2.00	0.89

Table 2. Correlation matrix between variables

	COST	FEATR	EOU	PERF	INSTLL	UPDTS	RPORT	CONFIG	SUPPRT
Cost	1.00	-0.21	0.27	-0.18	-0.13	-0.43*	-0.49*	-0.08	-0.10
FEATR		1.00	-0.29	0.35	-0.16	0.06	-0.17	-0.13	-0.25
EOU			1.00	-0.44*	0.00	-0.37*	-0.27	-0.20	-0.04
PERF				1.00	-0.10	-0.11	-0.13	0.13	-0.14
INSTLL					1.00	-0.13	-0.04	0.18	-0.53*
UPDTS						1.00	0.26	-0.30	0.17
RPORT							1.00	-0.15	0.03
CONFIG								1.00	-0.24
SUPPRT									1.00

Table 3. Eigenvalues of unrotated factors

	Eigenvalues	%	Cumul. %
1	11.56	37.28	37.28
2	6.03	19.45	56.73
3	3.91	12.61	69.34
4	2.98	9.61	78.95
5	2.14	6.92	85.87
6	1.93	6.23	92.10
7	1.43	4.61	96.71
8	1.02	3.29	100.00

factors while minimizing loading on all other factors. Factors selected for rotation are usually identified by taking those with eigenvalue greater than one (Kline, 1994). However, in this study, the more rigorous Kaiser rule of selecting factors whose eigenvalue is at or above the mean eigenvalue (in this case 3.85) was used. Factors 1, 2, and 3, which represented almost 70% of total variance in data, were then subjected to principal component analysis with varimax rotation.

Following rotation, a Factor Matrix indicating defining sort (i.e., respondents in agreement) identified three factor groups with similar pattern of responses. The correlation of individual respondents with factors is shown in Table 4.

From Table 4 it can be observed that for Factor 1, respondents 4, 12, 13, 15, 18, 20, 22, and 27 were in agreement and are highly loaded on this factor. Similarly, respondents 6, 10, 14, 16, 21, 24, 26, 29, and 30 were in agreement in Factor 2, and respondents 5, 7, 8, 9, 11, 17, 19, and 23 were in agreement in Factor 3.

The statements in which these three factor groups were ranked are shown in Table 5.

Table 6 shows correlation between the factors. Similar to the findings earlier about variable independence, the factor groups also show a high degree of independence.

The normalized factor scores for each factor were examined next. This provided a measure of

Table 4. Factor matrix of respondents (* indicates defining sort)

Q-Sort	Factor Loadings		
	1	2	3
1	0.2386	-0.0398	0.8988
2	0.0227	0.1971	0.8158*
3	0.4975	-0.3790	0.5458
4	0.8575*	-0.2912	0.0811
5	-0.2639	0.0196	0.7993*
6	-0.0614	0.7524*	-0.2289
7	0.4014	-0.1587	0.4678*
8	0.1367	0.0728	0.9054*
9	0.5351	0.1183	0.6886*
10	0.5065	0.5665*	0.1764
11	0.5351	0.1183	0.6886
12	0.8192*	0.3263	0.1035
13	0.6495*	0.3357	-0.0844
14	-0.0464	0.7321*	0.5845
15	0.6535*	0.3450	0.3053
16	0.2052	0.8598*	0.2453
17	-0.1340	0.0127	0.9512
18	0.7553*	0.2324	0.2987
19	0.2431	0.4049	0.6946
20	0.5983*	0.5865	-0.0334
21	0.4660	0.6533*	0.4573
22	0.5672*	0.1057	-0.3342
23	0.3501	-0.1001	0.8185
24	0.1008	0.9240*	0.0038
25	0.3329	0.0999	0.2194
26	0.2254	0.6545*	0.1329
27	0.7660*	0.1246	0.5677
28	-0.1210	-0.3611*	0.2307
29	0.3850	0.7032*	0.0144
30	0.4656	0.5605	-0.3196
31	-0.1987	0.8988*	0.2470
% explained variance	21	22	26

relative strength of importance attached by a factor to each statement on the scale used during sorting. Tables 7(a), 7(b), and 7(c) show these scores.

From the Table 7(a) it can be seen that adherents of Factor 1 feel strongly in favor of statement 4 (Performance) and oppose statements 8 and 5. This indicates for Factor 1 group, performance is preferred over initial installation, setup and configuration of the product.

The results of Factor 2 group are consistent with Factor 1; that is, performance of the product is the highest rated criterion. Ease-of-use also rated highly in Factors 1 and 2. Perceived ease-of-use in an information systems product has been shown to play a critical role in predicting and determining a user's decision to use the product (Hackbarth, Grover, & Yi, 2003). The largest dissension between Factor 1 and 2 groups involved statements 9 (Availability of Online Help), 7 (Intrusion Reports generated), and 6 (Regular Product Updates).

The results of Factor 3 are consistent with Factors 1 and 2 with Performance criteria once again being highly rated. The most dissension between Factors 2 and 3 involved statements 1 (Cost) and 3 (Ease-of-use). The most dissension between Factors 1 and 3 involved statements 1 (Cost), 3 (Ease-of-use), and 9 (Availability of Online Help).

DISCUSSION AND APPLICATIONS FOR PRACTICE

The Q-sort analysis classified subjects into three groups. Eight subjects were classified under Factor 1, and 10 subjects each were included in Factors 2 and 3. There were three subjects in the study that were not distinguished in any group. These subjects were excluded from further analysis. The classification into factors gave a better idea of group characteristics. Since Factors 1 and 2 were similar and shown to include subjects who considered Performance, Ease-of-use, and

Table 5. Ranked statement totals with each factor

No.	Statement	Factor 1		Factor 2		Factor 3	
1	COST	0.31	5	0.91	2	-1.45	9
2	FEATR	-0.45	7	0.10	5	0.70	2
3	EOU	0.91	2	0.63	3	-0.55	6
4	PERF	1.26	1	1.72	1	1.80	1
5	INSTLL	-1.92	9	-0.31	6	-0.63	7
6	UPDTS	0.52	3	-0.54	7	0.61	3
7	RPORTS	0.03	6	-1.28	8	0.55	4
8	CONFIG	-1.07	8	0.12	4	-0.17	5
9	SUPPRT	0.41	4	-1.34	9	-0.87	8

Table 6. Correlation between factors

Factor	1	2	3
1	1.0000	0.3218	0.2970
2	0.3218	1.0000	0.2298
3	0.2970	0.2298	1.0000

Table 7.

No.	Statement	z-score
4	PERF	1.258
3	EOU	0.910
6	UPDTS	0.524
9	SUPPRT	0.409
1	COST	0.314
7	RPORT	0.032
2	FEATR	-0.454
8	CONFIG	-1.071
5	INSTLL	-1.922

No.	Statement	z-score
4	PERF	1.717
1	COST	0.905
3	EOU	0.626
8	CONFIG	0.116
2	FEATR	0.102
5	INSTLL	-0.313
6	UPDTS	-0.535
7	RPORT	-1.276
9	SUPPRT	-1.343

No.	Statement	z-score
4	PERF	1.805
2	FEATR	0.702
6	UPDTS	0.606
7	RPORT	0.553
8	CONFIG	-0.170
3	EOU	-0.547
5	INSTLL	-0.632
9	SUPPRT	-0.872
1	COST	-1.446

(a) Normalized Factor 1 score   *(b) Normalized Factor 2 score*   *(c) Normalized Factor 3 score*

Availability of Online Help as the most important characteristics, this group can be considered to be comprised of non-technical users who place more emphasis on the product performing as expected in achieving goals for security. Factor 3 subjects emphasized technical characteristics and were more interested in number of features in the product, updates to the product on a regular basis, intrusion reports generated by personal firewalls, and setup/configuration of the product after installation. This group had characteristics of technical users.

The normalized factor scores provided a measure of relative strength of importance attached by factors to each statement on the scale used during sorting. As mentioned earlier, adherents in Factor 1 felt strongly in favor of statement 4 (Performance) and opposed statements 8 (Setup/ configuration) and 5 (Installation). The results of Factor 2 are consistent with Factor 1, that is, Performance of the product is the highest rated criterion. Ease-of-use also rated highly in Factors 1 and 2. The largest dissension between Factor 1 and 2 groups involved statements 9 (Availability of Online Help), 7 (Intrusion Reports generated), and 6 (Regular Product Updates). The most dissension between Factors 2 and 3 involved Statements 1 (Cost) and 3 (Ease-of-use). Results of Factor 3 were consistent with Factors 1 and 2, with Performance criteria once again being highly rated. The largest dissension between Factors 1 and 3 involved statements 1 (Cost), 3 (Ease-of-use), and 9 (Availability of Online Help). Extreme differences between all factors appeared in Cost, Intrusion Reports generated, and Availability of Online Help. There was only one statement, Performance of the product, that showed consensus among all factors; that is, it did not distinguish between any pair of factors, which indicates Performance of the desktop firewall software is an agreed upon criterion irrespective of group characteristics.

The managerial implications of this study can be assessed at the level of selecting appropriate software for use on computers in organizations to maintain security. There is evidence of user satisfaction being a useful measure of system success (Mahmood et al., 2000). While the end-user may not purchase individually preferred software for installation on company owned computers, the user can influence decisions for selection by making known to IS managers the features that would contribute to regular use of security software such as personal firewalls. Given access of these machines to corporate resources, appropriate and regular use of software would contribute to maintaining enterprise security. For technical professionals (e.g., programmers) who install firewalls on their desktop, programs

could emphasize the statements that are defining characteristics shown in Factor 3. For an industry that has non-technical professionals (such as Factor 1 and 2), other non-technical characteristics of the product could be emphasized thus achieving maximum effectiveness in program deployment. Increased awareness should minimize user related faults, nullify these in theory, and maximize the efficiency of security techniques and procedures from the user's point of view (Siponen, 2000).

The results of this study could also benefit vendors who develop software for end-users. In this study it was found that performance of the software is the most important factor that affects selection of software, irrespective of group characteristics. Due to project deadlines and market competition, software is often shipped without being fully tested as secure, and standard industry practice is to release incremental service packs that address security issues in the product. In a case of security software, this may adversely affect the reputation of a vendor once its products have been shown to have high vulnerability to being compromised. The findings of this study could provide a better understanding of importance of personal firewall security software on organizational client computers. The decision to install an information system necessitates a choice of mechanisms to determine whether it is needed, and once implemented, whether it is functioning properly (Ives, Olson, & Baroudi, 1983). More research needs to be done in the area of selection of software for implementation on user's computers that are owned by corporations and given to employees for off-site work. This can include regular employees vs. contractors who may connect to employer and client networks from the same computer. If the findings are to have wider applicability, qualified industry professionals and security officers responsible for maintaining secure infrastructure in corporations should be included in the analysis. The study provides management and security professionals a basis for making decisions related to enterprise security.

It provides personal firewall vendors an insight into feature requirements of the personal firewall market, and provides academic researchers interested in security, a more focused approach on various dimensions of security software from the behavioral perspective. Future studies could be industry and product specific in order to assess differences in selecting general-purpose software versus security specific products.

In many cases, management has looked at the need for implementing information security programs and products as a necessary encumbrance, something akin to paying taxes or insurance premiums (Highland, 1993). But organizations are increasingly becoming aware of the potential for legal exposure via lawsuits, and are deploying countermeasures (such as personal firewalls) to reduce vulnerability and mitigate risk. The chief information security officer in today's organizations should have the responsibility of managing organizational risks by using empirical models and analysis to determine strategies for protecting corporate assets. Firewalls are the last line of defense in the corporate network and therefore play a critical role in information security. With personal firewalls being a new product genre, this study was conducted since there is no research available that specifically looks at determinants for selection of security software in a corporate environment to protect organizational assets. As the information security field evolves further, decisions for security software acquisitions need to be researched further. Selection and deployment of appropriate firewalls can make a significant difference in an organization's enterprise security strategy. It is therefore also important to understand the variables (as shown in this study) that may affect decisions to select and deploy personal firewall software in a corporate environment.

LIMITATIONS OF THE STUDY

Due to the exploratory nature of this study, there are several limitations. The sample used in the study comprised of all students enrolled in a security course at the same university, and was further limited to the firewall topic among a wide range of technical and behavioral information security topics. Students worked with only one type of firewall software and characteristics of this particular program may have heightened their awareness of certain strengths and weaknesses in the software. Since the purpose of information security implementation in an organization is to support business objectives of the organization, information security departments are sometimes placed under the chief financial officer recognizing the direct relationship between information assets and monetary assets. Software acquisition decisions may therefore be made by the finance department with limited input from the IT department. The purpose of this study was to explore an important topic for research on information security and determine operant subjectivity in a field where empirical research is severely lacking. The Q-sort technique itself is suitable for small sample populations (Thomas & Watson, 2002), but the correlations obtained in smaller samples tend to have considerable standard errors (Kline, 1994). The exploratory nature of this study was not intended to prove some general proposition but to seek a better understanding of group characteristics that directly relate to maintaining a secure network environment (in this case by deploying personal firewalls to plug possible vulnerabilities that might exist in a network through use of computers by employees either on-site or at remote locations). The perceptions of end-users will therefore guide the selection and deployment of security technologies in an organization to provide a secure corporate environment.

CONCLUSION

In this study, Q-methodology was used to define participant viewpoints and perceptions, empirically place participants in groups, provide sharper insight into participant preferred directions, identify criteria that are important to participants, explicitly outline areas of consensus and conflicts, and investigate a contemporary problem relating to desktop firewalls by quantifying subjectivity. Similar to other IT areas, security software selection and deployment in today's environment faces many challenges, such as staying current with new threats, project deadlines, implementation issues, and support costs. Quality drives customer satisfaction and adoption of software. Human factors are important in contributing to successful software deployment in organizations, especially when it relates to desktop software applications. Organizations are now viewing security and controls as business enablers and desktop firewall technology plays a critical role in safeguarding corporate assets. In a fast-paced area where the new generation of applications and services are growing more complex each day, it is critical to understand characteristics that affect selection of end-user security products in enterprises.

This study addresses a small but important area of safeguarding enterprise information security by using personal firewalls. As has been previously noted, limited research exists beyond the current study that explores behavioral aspects of information security. This study holds importance for professionals tasked with evaluating and selecting security products for company wide deployment. As the area of information security gains increased importance due to the strategic role of technology in organizations, and current events impact areas such as disaster recovery and enterprise continuity planning, a study of end-users to determine their perceptions about selection of technology controls in organizations is critical for protecting organizational assets. More research needs to be done in the area of perception of users towards other security software (such as anti-virus, intrusion detection, virtual private network software, and encryption products), and, due to varying security needs in different industries, studies could also be industry and product specific. While the findings should be considered preliminary, the results raise interesting observations about issues uncovered regarding security perceptions of feature requirements in personal firewalls. Information security is a dynamic area and, in this environment, this exploratory study contributes to evolving research by identifying variables from theoretical literature and using an empirical technique to study issues that affect safeguarding vital assets of an organization from internal and external threats.

REFERENCES

Baroudi, J., Olson, M., & Ives, B. (1986). An empirical study of the impact of user involvement on system usage and information satisfaction. *Communications of the ACM, 29*(3), 785-793.

Briggs, R.O., Balthazard, P.A., & Dennis, A.R. (1996). Graduate business students as surrogates for executives in the evaluation of technology. *Journal of End-user Computing, 8*(4), 11-17.

Brown, S.R. (1980). *Political subjectivity: Applications of Q methodology in political science.* New Haven, Connecticut: Yale University Press.

Brown, S.R. (1986). Q-technique and method: Principles and procedures. In W.D. Berry & M.S. Lewis-Beck (eds.), *New Tools for Social Scientists: Advances and Applications in Research Methods.* Beverly Hills, CA: Sage Publications.

Chiasson, M., & Lovato, C. (2001). Factors influencing the formation of a user's perceptions and use of a DSS software innovation. *ACM SIGMIS Database, 32*(3), 16-35.

Clarke, R. (2002, February). *Forum on technology and innovation: Sponsored by Sen. Bill Frist (R-TN), Sen. Jay Rockefeller (D-WV), and the Council on Competitiveness.* Retrieved October 28, 2003, from *http://www.techlawjournal.com/security/20020214.asp*

Deise, M., Nowikow, C., King, P., & Wright, A. (2000). *Executive's guide to e-business: From tactics to strategy.* New York: John Wiley & Sons.

Dhillon, G., & Blackhouse, J. (2001). Current directions in IS security research: Toward socio-organizational perspectives. *Information Systems Journal, 11*(2), 127-153.

Enns, H., Huff, S., & Golden, B. (2003). CIO influence behaviors: The impact of technical background. *Information and Management, 40*(5), 467-485.

Gery, G. (1997). Granting three wishes through performance-centered design. *Communications of the ACM, 40*(7), 54-59.

Good, N., & Krekelberg, A. (2002). *Usability and privacy: A study of Kazaa P2P file-sharing.* Retrieved November 12, 2003, from *http://www. hpl.hp.com/shl/papers/kazaa/*

Goodhue, D.L., & Straub, D.W. (1991). Security concerns of system users: A study of perceptions of the adequacy of security measures. *Information & Management, 20*(1), 13-27.

Grantham, C., & Vaske, J. (1985). Predicting the usage of an advanced communication technology. *Behavior and Information Technology, 4*(4), 327-335

Hackbarth, G., Grover, V., & Yi, M. (2003). Computer playfulness and anxiety: Positive and negative mediators of the system experience effect on perceived ease-of-use. *Information and Management, 40*(3), 221-232.

Hazari, S. (2000). *Firewalls for beginners.* Retrieved December 17, 2003, from *http://online. securityfocus.com/infocus/1182*

Heiser, J. (2002, April). Go figure: Can you trust infosecurity surveys? *Information Security,* 27-28.

Highland, H.J. (1993). A view of information security tomorrow. In E.G. Dougall (ed.), *Computer Security.* Holland: Elsevier.

Ives, B., Olson, M., & Baroudi, J. (1983). The measurement of user information satisfaction. *Communications of the ACM, 26*(10), 785-793.

Kettinger, W., & Lee, C. (2002). Understanding the IS-User divide in IT innovation. *Communications of the ACM, 45*(2), 79-84.

Kline, P. (1994). *An easy guide to factor analysis.* London: Rutledge

Lane, V.P. (1985). *Security of computer based information systems.* London: Macmillan.

Legris, P., Ingham, J., & Collerette, P. (2003). Why do people use information technology? A critical review of the technology acceptance model. *Information and Management, 40*(3), 191-204.

Mahmood, M.A., Burn, J.M., Gemoets, L.A., & Jacquez, C. (2000). Variables affecting information technology end-user satisfaction: A meta-analysis of the empirical literature. *International Journal of Human-Computer Studies, 52*, 751-771.

Maiden, N., Ncube, C., & Moore, A. (1997). Lessons learned during requirements acquisition for COTS systems. *Communications of the ACM, 40*(12), 21-25.

Mathieson, K. (1991). Predicting user intentions: Comparing the technology acceptance model with the theory of planned behavior. *Information Systems Research, 3*(2), 173-191.

McKeown, B., & Thomas, D. (1988). *Q Methodology.* California: Sage Publications Inc.

Murphy, B., Boren, R., & Schlarman, S. (2000). *Enterprise security architecture*. CRC Press. Retrieved November 2, 2003, from *http://www. pwcglobal.com*

Nelson P., Richmond W., & Seidmann A., (1996). Two dimensions of software acquisition. *Communications of the ACM, 39*(7), 29-35.

Northcutt, S., McLachlan, D., & Novak, J. (2000). *Network intrusion detection: An analyst's handbook* (2nd ed.). IN: New Riders Publishing.

Saita, A. (2001, June). Understanding peopleware. *Information Security*, 72-80.

Scambray, J., McClure, S., & Kurtz, G. (2001). *Hacking exposed* (2nd ed.). CA: Osborne/McGraw-Hill.

Siponen, M.T. (2000). A conceptual foundation for organizational information security awareness. *Information Management & Security, 8*(1), 31-41.

Stephenson, W. (1953). *The study of behavior*. Chicago, IL: University of Chicago Press.

Strassberg, K., Rollie, G., & Gondek, R. (2002). *Firewalls: The complete reference*. NY: Osborne McGraw-Hill.

Straub, D.W., & Welke, R.J. (1988). Coping with systems risk: Security planning models for management decision making. *MIS Quarterly, 22*(4), 441-469.

Summers, R. (1997). *Secure computing: Threats and safeguards*. New York, NY: McGraw-Hill.

Thomas, D., & Watson, R. (2002). Q-sorting and MIS research: A primer. *Communications of the AIS, 8,* 141-156.

Torres, R.J. (2002). *Practitioner's handbook for user interface design and development*. NJ: Prentice-Hall.

Troutt, M.D. (2002). IT security issues: The need for end-user oriented research. *Journal of End-user Computing, 14*(2), 48.

Whitten, A., & Tygar, J. (1999). Why Johnny can't encrypt: A usability evaluation of PGP 5.0. In *Proceedings of the Eigth USENIX Security Symposium*.

Wood, C. (1988). A context for information systems security planning. *Computers & Security, 7*(5), 455-465.

Zwicky, E., Cooper, S., Chapman, D., & Russell, D. (2000). *Building Internet firewalls* (2nd ed.). CA: O'Reilly.

This work was previously published in the Journal of Organizational and End User Computing, Vol. 17, No. 3, edited by M. A. Mahmood, pp. 47-65, copyright 2005 by IGI Publishing, formerly known as Idea Group Publishing (an imprint of IGI Global).

Chapter 4.44
Determining the Intention to Use Biometric Devices:
An Application and Extension of the Technology Acceptance Model

Tabitha James
Virginia Polytechnic Institute & State University, USA

Taner Pirim
Mississippi Center for Supercomputing Research, USA

Katherine Boswell
Middle Tennessee State University, USA

Brian Reithel
University of Mississippi, USA

Reza Barkhi
Virginia Polytechnic Institute & State University, USA

ABSTRACT

Protection of physical assets and digital information is of growing importance to society. As with any new technology, user acceptance of new software and hardware devices is often hard to gauge, and policies to introduce and ensure adequate and correct usage of such technologies are often lacking. Security technologies have widespread applicability to different organizational contexts that may present unusual and varied adoption considerations. This study adapts the technology acceptance model (TAM) and extends it to study the intention to use biometrics devices across a wide variety of organizational contexts. Due to the use of physiological characteristics, biometrics present unique adoption concerns. TAM is extended in this study to include constructs for perceived need for privacy, perceived need for security and perceived physical invasiveness of biometric devices as factors that influence intention to use. The model is shown to be a good predictor of intention to use biometric devices.

INTRODUCTION

Property theft, violent crimes, theft and misuse of digital information, terrorism, and threats to privacy, including identity fraud, in today's digitally connected, mobile society necessitate the development of tools to protect digital information and physical assets by both individuals and corporate entities. According to findings from the National Crime Victimization Survey, approximately 24 million U.S. residents were victims of crime in 2003, including both property crime and violent criminal acts (Bureau of Justice, 2003). The 2003 CSI/FBI Computer Crime and Security Survey reported that 56% of their participants reported unauthorized computer use. Out of the respondents that were willing or could quantify the financial implications, the amount of losses reported exceeded $200 million (Richardson, 2003). The Federal Trade Commission (FTC) reported 86,168 cases of identity fraud in 2001 and stated that they believe this figure does not capture all the cases (FTC, 2001). Identity fraud categories included credit card fraud, telecommunications/utility fraud, bank fraud, employment fraud, fraudulent loans, government documents or benefits fraud, evasion of legal sanctions and criminal records, medical services, opening of Internet accounts, leasing of a residence, bankruptcy filings, trading of securities or investments, among others (FTC, 2001).

The need to secure both digital and physical assets is apparent from these statistics, yet it is often difficult for technology to keep pace with the growing number of threats and the increasing number of vulnerabilities that exist in traditional methods of security. A method of identification that has been growing in popularity is the use of physical or behavioral traits, such as fingerprints or DNA, to identify and authenticate individuals. Certain physical and behavioral traits are unique to each individual and therefore may provide methods of identification that are more successful than traditional approaches. Technological devices that utilize these unique traits to identify and authenticate an individual are known as biometrics. These devices have the obvious advantage of not falling prey to many of the well known vulnerabilities of traditional methods. Since a biometric device uses a unique biological trait to distinguish an individual, it is very difficult and often impossible for the identifier to be lost, stolen, duplicated, or given away (Liu & Silverman, 2001). This advantage makes biometric devices an appealing option for individuals and corporations that wish to adopt a new security technology.

The Technology Acceptance Model (TAM) has received wide acceptance for studying the usage behavior of new technologies (Davis, 1989). We extend TAM to determine the intention to use security technologies, specifically biometric devices. We utilize a vignette-based survey design to study the user behavior toward biometrics and the intention to use these devices. This approach provides a general overview of individual's perceptions of biometrics regardless of the application area or device type; hence, providing insight into possible barriers of adoption of biometric technologies for security purposes. By focusing on factors that influence an individual's intention to use biometric technologies, we can explore the possible modes of adoption that may smooth the transition to new forms of security and authentication technologies. The literature suggests that barriers to adoption of biometric devices can be grouped into the following categories: physical invasiveness, information invasiveness, ease of use, privacy, and the perceived level of benefit from the device (Deane, Barrelle, Henderson, & Mahar, 1995; Liu & Silverman, 2001; Woodward, 1997). We posit that an individual's need for privacy and security along with the perceived invasiveness of the device and the original TAM constructs of perceived usefulness and ease of use, will impact the intention to use biometric devices. This model is generalizable to a wider range of security/privacy technologies which will aid in our understanding of barriers to adoption to these technologies so that appropriate policies and marketing strategies may be designed to aid in their implementation and use.

In the following section, the relevant literature is presented, along with the theoretical foundation for the proposed constructs. Section 3 discusses the methodology used to test the proposed model and section 4 presents the findings. Section 5 provides a discussion of the results, as well as the limitations and directions for future research, and section 6 provides the conclusions.

LITERATURE REVIEW AND RESEARCH MOTIVATION

Biometrics

Biometrics can be defined as "the application of computational methods to biological features, especially with regard to the study of unique biological characteristics of humans" (Hopkins, 1999). More generally, a biometric system can be referred to as "a pattern recognition system that makes a personal identification by establishing the authenticity of a specific physiological or behavioral characteristic possessed by the user" (Jain et al., 2000). Interest in using biometrics is rising, and adoption of these technologies is penetrating corporations and governments. The International Biometric Group predicts the market for biometrics to rise from \$815 million in 2004 to \$2.08 billion by 2006 (BTT, 2005). These numbers indicate that biometric devices will emerge as an important security tool over the next several years. Biometric devices fall into two main categories: physiological, which includes fingerprint, retinal, hand geometry and facial scanners and behavioral such as signature biometrics.

There are several areas of usage for biometric devices. These application areas can be loosely grouped into four categories: physical access, virtual access, e-commerce, and covert surveillance (Liu & Silverman, 2001). Applications in the physical access category include any situation where restricted availability of a facility or mode of transportation is necessary (Beiser, 1999; BTT, 2001; Liu & Silverman, 2001; McMillian, 2002; Wayman, 2000; Woodward, 1997). Physical access control holds the major share of the biometrics market, accounting for approximately 50% of the biometrics market (Norton, 2002).

Security devices used for this category have received increased scrutiny as the importance of authenticating individuals for security purposes grows, yet, often conflicts with personal privacy issues. The tradeoff between maintaining a desired level of security while maintaining a sufficient level of privacy for an individual has received a new level of importance. Privacy advocates often argue that new security infrastructures often encroach upon an individual's privacy by providing means by which characteristics and movements may be more easily tracked and information on individuals more easily exchanged. However, in light of heightened awareness in the United States and other countries due to recent security threats and breaches (e.g., September 11th plane highjackings and London subway bombings), there has been a renewed interest in means of security that may better protect public places and transportation.

Virtual access includes biometric protection of information, that is, network and computer security. This provides protection of data that is stored on a company's computer systems and traverses the corporate network (Suydam, 2000). A major use of biometrics in the virtual access category is the replacement of passwords, or as an additional level of security on top of a password (Dean, 2002; Liu & Silverman, 2001). Since passwords can be easily forgotten or given away, this alternative may not only improve security it may also ease administrative tasks.

Credit card, online banking, online trading, ATMs, and online purchasing provide many e-commerce applications to which biometrics may be applied (Liu & Silverman, 2001). Some companies hope that the use of biometric technologies for authentication may reduce the amount of money spent for fraud cases. Devices in this category can help prevent unlawful financial transactions, identity theft, and help provide security for an individual's credit cases (Arent, 1999; Herman, 2002; Jain, Hong, & Pankanti, 2000; Jeffords, Thibadoux, & Scheidt, 1999; Liu & Silverman, 2001; Woodward, 1997).

Covert surveillance forms the last category. Devices in this category are intended to identify possible criminals. Applications in this area are often the most controversial, yet are growing in popularity due to increased interest in providing additional levels of security by monitoring, for example: passengers in public transportation, people attending large public events, buildings with public access, or traffic. Biometrics may be used, for example, to compare individuals against databases of known criminal offenders in airports or casinos (Scheeres, 2001; Titsworth, 2002). Biometric devices are being used by several states in attempts to avoid issuance of fraudulent driver's licenses (Atkinson, 2002; Titsworth, 2002; Wayman, 2000). The use of mobile biometric devices by police departments are being explored as a way to decrease the number of fraudulent IDs used (Dale, 2001). As these systems advance, they should help provide personal security for individuals and help find criminals.

As with many security technologies, biometric devices have widespread applicability. Unlike many traditional technologies, they are not specialized in their usage setting or purpose and their usefulness is often associated with their function rather than their stand-alone implementation, as would be the case with a software package. Biometric devices may be adopted for use in a variety of settings for a myriad of functions by different types of entities. The adoption decision for biometrics, not unlike many security technologies, may be an individual decision or an organizational decision. That is, these devices may be marketed as devices that can be obtained by an individual for general purposes such as securing one's home or may be implemented as an additional security device on a vehicle which is then sold as a package. They may also be implemented by an organization where compliance for use is mandatory such as entry to a facility by employees or where the implementation and usage may be regarded as a choice. A determination of the general acceptance of the device is useful to any entity considering the adoption of these types of security devices regardless of context. The purpose of this study is to develop a general model of user acceptance for biometric devices, regardless of the context of their use or the physiological or behavioral traits they use for identification.

Technology Acceptance Model

Determining the factors influencing acceptance of technologies provides useful insight for entities both wishing to market a technology or those attempting to successfully adopt a technology. An understanding of possible barriers to successful adoption and usage of a technology can enable parties to put in place techniques that will aid the process, thus lessening possible financial losses from an unsuccessful adoption attempt. There have been significant advances in predicting usage and determining factors influencing adoption. The technology acceptance model (TAM), developed by Davis (1989), has gained much popularity in the literature due to its success in determining intention to use and usage of technologies (Venkatesh & Davis, 2000).

The TAM model is an adaptation of the theory of reasoned action (Ajzen & Fishbein, 1980) intended to focus on acceptance and usage behavior specifically for information systems. TAM postulates that the two most important determinants of user acceptance of computing technologies are ease of use and usefulness (Davis, 1989; Davis, Bagozzi, & Warshaw, 1989). The TAM model looks at these two determinants and their relationship to behavioral intention to use and actual system usage. Significant empirical research has shown positive results in using TAM to predict acceptance and usage behavior of end users in several areas. Application areas include end-user software adoption (Szajna, 1994), e-commerce (Chen, Gillenson, & Sherrell, 2002; Koufaris, 2002), digital libraries (Hong, Thong, Wong, & Tam, 2002), telemedicine technologies (Hu, Chau, Sheng, & Tam, 1999), smart cards (Plouffe, Hulland, & Vandenbosch, 2001), and building management systems (Lowry, 2002).

As has been shown in previous TAM studies, we expect perceived usefulness and perceived ease of use to positively impact intention to use. If an individual believes the device to be useful and easy to use we assume that they will be likely to submit to the use of the device. We also expect the perceived ease of use of the technology to impact the perceived usefulness of the technology.

Hypothesis 1 – The perceived usefulness of the security technology will have a positive impact an individual's intention to use the technology.

Hypothesis 2 – The perceived difficulty/ease of use of the security technology will have a positive impact an individual's intention to use the technology.

Hypothesis 3 – The perceived ease of use of the security technology will have a positive impact on the perceived usefulness of the technology.

The current research extends and adapts the original technology acceptance model to study security technology implemented as biometric devices. As the purpose of security technologies is to protect physical assets and digital information, the perception of the importance of securing digital and physical assets should influence the beliefs and behaviors of the participants. To study biometric technology, we need to extend the TAM model to account for the level of physical invasiveness that is not included in the original TAM model. While we focus on biometric technology,

physical invasiveness is not completely unique to biometrics but also applicable to other security technologies such as microchip implantation. Approaches such as biometric identification and microchip implantations are technologies that avoid some of the well-known vulnerabilities in identification and authentication methods. Physical invasiveness adds a new dimension to the acceptance and use of security devices.

This study extends the TAM model with the addition of constructs for perceived need for security and privacy as well as perceived invasiveness to provide a robust model of technology acceptance for biometrics which could be easily adapted for any class of security device. These added constructs take into account the user's perceptions and beliefs in the areas of security, privacy and physical invasiveness which are not captured in the original TAM model. The resulting model, therefore, provides further insight into the usage intentions of the end users or security technologies. Due to the rising importance of security and privacy in today's society, a closer examination of the acceptance of advanced technologies such as biometrics is warranted. These extensions are further justified in the following sections. The resulting conceptual model developed for this study including the hypothesized relationships is shown in Figure 1.

Physical Invasiveness

The perception of physical invasiveness is relatively new to the computing technologies area. Invasiveness in the medical technologies area has been an area of concern but the application for these technologies is drastically different in type (e.g., medical technologies for treatment purposes). Recent discussions of using implanted microchips for identification and tracking purposes have raised some concerns. Although discussed, the use of this technology in humans has not currently reached the market.

Biometric devices require the use of physiological traits and in some cases may be perceived

Figure 1. Conceptual model

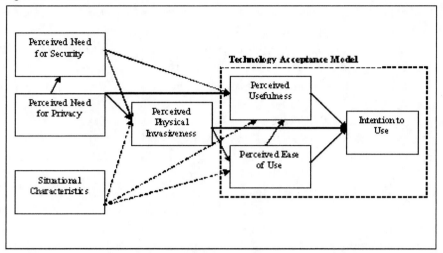

as physically invasive. Many biometric devices can be intimidating to use for many individuals, especially initially. Many people have a natural aversion to using devices that require a scan of their eyes and fingerprint biometrics can have negative associations (Kim, 1995). Due to the personal nature of this identification method, individuals may view the devices as invasive which may present an obstacle to user acceptance (Liu & Silverman, 2001). The use of fingerprint biometrics and especially retinal biometrics are often encumbered by the perception of physical invasiveness (Kim, 1995). Due to the newness of physical invasiveness to security devices, little research has been conducted to determine the impact of this characteristic on usage. Kim (1995) point out that certain biometric devices may be perceived as more physically invasive or hold a more negative connotation than others.

"For example, fingerprint scanners may be associated with the criminal bookings. Similarly, due to the inherent self-protection of the eyes, most people are likely to feel uncomfortable with the idea of having a laser directed at their eye retina every time they want to make a financial transaction. In contrast, hand recognition where the palm is placed on the plate, appears not to bother people so much (probably because hand-shaking

is common behavior). Also, dynamic signature verification would be acceptable to people of all ages and social groups who are literate, since signature is already widely used as a means of personal identification" (Kim, 1995).

The perception of physical invasiveness of biometric devices may affect the usage behavior for the technology as well as impact the perception of ease of use of the device. Invasiveness can be perceived as an intrusion or encroachment to one physically and/or from a privacy standpoint. As can be seen from the proceeding quote, biometric devices can have negative connotations as to their use as well as a level of physicality that may provide levels of discomfort (both physically and mentally) than traditional security devices. In this study, we are concerned with the physical invasiveness of the devices. That is, the perception of discomfort or fear from the physicality of the device use. The perceived physical invasiveness construct is defined for the current study as, one's perception of the invasiveness of the technology to their person.

We expect the perceived invasiveness of the devices should negatively impact their perceived ease of use. If an individual perceives these technologies to be highly invasive then they may think they are more difficult to use.

Hypothesis 4 – The perceived physical invasiveness of the security technology will have a negative impact on the perceived ease of use of the technology.

The perceived invasiveness of the biometrics should also directly negatively impact an individual's intention to use. When they perceive the devices to be highly physically invasive they should be more reluctant to submit to their use and more likely to avoid or object to their adoption or use.

Hypothesis 5 – The perceived invasiveness of the security technology will have a negative impact an individual's intention to use the technology.

Security

Security in a broad sense encompasses the protection of assets, both physical and digital. These assets may be physical, your person or a building, or informational, a company's financial records or a person's medical records. Perceived need for security is therefore defined as, one's perceived need for the safekeeping of physical or informational assets.

Physical asset security has long been protected by the use of traditional methods such as restricted entry to areas by the use of locks. Digital security has become increasingly important as the connectedness of society grows with the use of the Internet. Various security measures have been implemented in the attempt to thwart an ever-increasing number of threats from viruses or malicious invasions of digital information.

Traditionally, devices to assure that only authorized individuals can access restricted areas fall into two categories: something an individual has, such as a key or a smart card or something the user knows, such as a pin or password (Jain et al., 2000). The major downfalls to these practices are the possibility of theft of the entry token or intentional (unintentional) compromise of the knowledge necessary to gain access. Physical as-

set security is often one measure used to protect digital information. Restricted access to areas that house the equipment used to store data has long been of primary concern for information security practitioners (Loch, Carr, & Warkentin, 1992).

The reliability and protection of data has long been an issue. Physical protection of data and the reduction of data errors have been compounded by the increased reliance on networks which frequently introduces new information security threats on top of the traditional ones. Threats to information security include accidental and intentional entry of bad data, accidental and intentional destruction of data, unauthorized access to data, inadequate control over media, poor control over manual I/O, access to data or systems by outsiders (both hackers and competitors), computer viruses/worms, weak or inadequate physical control, and natural disasters (i.e., fire, flood, power loss; Loch et al., 1992). Development and adoption of new technologies to attempt to prevent and detect new types of information security breaches are extremely important in today's computing environment and the topic of much research.

There has been a lack of research to study an individual's perception of the importance of or need for security. Behavioral studies have focused on security awareness in information security (Siponen, 2000) or organizational security practices (Straub, 1990). However, of increasing importance is an individual's perception of the importance of securing their physical assets and digital information as this may impact their perception of the importance of security devices and thereby influence their usage behavior. As biometric devices by design are targeted towards securing digital and physical assets, an individual's perceived need for security should influence the perception of usefulness of the device. If an individual has a high perceived need for security, the perceived usefulness of a security tool to protect themselves as well as their assets should increase. This leads us to the following hypothesis:

Hypothesis 6 – An individual's desire for the security of their person and his/her personal information will have a positive impact on the perceived usefulness of the technology.

Although the requirements for use of biometric technologies may be perceived as more invasive than traditional security technologies, a high perceived need for security may counteract the perception of invasiveness and therefore have a negative impact on the perceived physical invasiveness of biometrics. If an individual places major importance on their security and/or the security of their assets, the physicality of using the biometrics may be perceived as less of a factor than otherwise.

Hypothesis 7 – An individual's desire for the security of their person and his/her personal information will have a negative impact on the perceived invasiveness of the technology.

Privacy

Privacy refers to the ability of an individual to "control the terms under which personal information is acquired and used" (Westin, 1967, p. 7). Information privacy has been defined as, "the ability of the individual to personally control information about one's self" (as quoted in Smith, Milberg, & Burke, 1996, p. 168). For the current study, perceived need for privacy will be defined as the importance to an individual of being able to control the acquisition and usage of personal information.

The reliance on the collection and use of data in today's technology dependent society has increased privacy concerns. Hence, privacy has been listed as one of the biggest ethical issues of the information age (Mason, 1986). Mason argues that there exist two major threats to an individual's right to privacy: an increased ability to collect data due to the growth of information technology in areas such as surveillance, communication, computation, storage and retrieval and

an increase in the value of this information for decision making (Mason, 1986). Henderson and Snyder (1999) describe three major forces driving an increased focus on personal information privacy: (1) new technological capabilities, (2) an increased value of information, and (3) confusion over what is ethically right and wrong.

Research in the information systems area on privacy has focused on organizational use of collected data. Smith et al. (1996) developed an instrument to measure an individual's concern over an organization's information privacy practices which was later reexamined by Stewart & Segars (2002). Their study identified four primary dimensions of an individual's concern of organizational information privacy practices: collection, unauthorized secondary use, improper access, and errors (Smith et al., 1996).

Security tools are often used as a means of protecting an individual's privacy and therefore if an individual has a high perceived need for privacy, this should have a positive impact on the perceived usefulness of the devices. We propose that an individual's need for privacy will positively impact perceived usefulness.

Hypothesis 8 – An individual's perceived need for privacy will have a positive impact on the perceived usefulness of the technology.

Security is often tied into privacy due to the use of security devices to protect personal information. The protection of information considered sensitive, especially in digital form, is a major concern for both individuals and corporations. The use and security of personal information released to a secondary party is also of rising concern in society due to the increased ability to collect and process such information. In many cases however, the use of security devices raises its own set of privacy concerns. It is often necessary to collect data considered personal from individuals in order to enforce user authentication to facilities and digital information. Along with the possibility of perceived invasion of privacy from monitoring and surveillance security systems, the technologies themselves often give rise to privacy issues (Kim, 1995).

It has been shown that an individual's perception of the importance of their privacy has a positive impact on their need for security as shown in Pirim, James, Boswell, Reithel, and Barkhi (2004). If an individual places a high importance on privacy, that individual will place a high importance on securing their privacy. Therefore, it is expected that an individual's need for privacy will positively impact their perceived need for security.

Hypothesis 9 – An individual's perceived need for privacy will have a positive effect on his/her need for security.

Complications for the use of security tools arise due to the fact that methods of providing security can be viewed as invasions of privacy. Identification and verification are the primary means of providing security. In order to protect assets and individuals it is necessary to know the identity of the individuals who are granted access to physical locations as well as digital information and to be able to verify that an individual is who he or she claims to be. To accomplish this task, a certain amount of information that may be considered private is necessary. Privacy advocates often object to the collection of personal information and to appease society's need for privacy, it is necessary to collect the minimum amount of information necessary and to protect the information that is collected from misuse or theft. Biometrics present an even more unique characteristic in the collection of personal information as the data needed to implement the devices are physiological or behavioral traits of an individual, rather than typical data collected to identify an individual such as a name, birth date, or identification number.

Biometric devices may be viewed as invasions

of privacy due to the personalized physical usage requirements. Therefore, the more private an individual perceives themselves to be, the more invasive the biometric devices may be perceived. This leads to the following hypotheses:

Hypothesis 10 – An individual's desire for privacy will have a positive impact on the perceived invasiveness of the technology.

METHOD

Smith et al. (1996) developed a survey instrument to measure information privacy, focusing on corporate information privacy. The construct for perceived need for privacy utilized in our study is more general. This study uses an instrument developed to measure an individual's perceived need for privacy in a general context. The set of

Table 1. Factor loadings for the perceived need for privacy and security instrument (S1-S9 correspond to Questions 1-9 in Appendix A and P1-P9 correspond to Questions 10-18 in Appendix A)

Item	Factor	
	1	2
S1	**.731**	.056
S2	**.761**	.086
S3	**.801**	.148
S4	**.753**	.119
S5	**.721**	.159
S6	**.631**	.223
S7	**.648**	.378
S8	**.652**	.384
S9	**.625**	.379
P1	.420	**.591**
P2	.444	**.616**
P3	.192	**.770**
P4	.473	**.571**
P5	.380	**.617**
P6	.305	**.619**
P7	−.077	**.725**
P8	−.034	**.688**
P9	.435	**.488**

items to measure the perceived need for security are intended to look at an individual's general feelings on security. The instrument for both the perceived need for privacy (see Appendix A, Questions 1–9) and perceived need for security constructs (see Appendix A, Questions 10–18) was developed in prior research where it was pretested and refined (Pirim et al., 2004). Cronbach's alphas obtained for the current study were 0.90 for the perceived need for security construct and 0.85

for the perceived need for privacy construct. The Cronbach's alphas obtained for both constructs were higher than the recommended levels of 0.70. Table 1 shows the result of the confirmatory factor analysis for these instruments, and Table 2 provides means and standard deviations for the items.

Perceived physical invasiveness, perceived usefulness, perceived ease of use, and intention to use, were examined through the use of a series

Table 2. Descriptive statistics for perceived need for security and privacy

Item No.	Question	Mean	S.D.
S1	I feel that the safeguarding from potential external threats of my physical being is important to me.	1.56	.76
S2	I feel that my personal security at my home or in my vehicle is important to me.a	1.39	.67
S3	I feel that my personal security at my place of work or other work related places is important to me	1.51	.71
S4	My security at places of public access, such as a mall or airport, or special public events, such as the Olympics or the Super Bowl, is important to me.	1.48	.64
S5	I feel that the security of my tangible assets (such as my home, vehicle, etc.) is important to me.	1.53	.70
S6	I feel that keeping my personal possessions, such as jewelry, money, electronics, etc. safe is important to me.	1.66	.74
S7	I feel that the safekeeping of my informational assets contained in digital or paper format is important to me (such as financial records, medical records, etc.)	1.53	.72
S8	I feel that the security of my personal information, such as my PC files or personal records (financial, medical, etc.) is important to me.	1.56	.72
S9	I feel that the safekeeping of information I have provided to a corporation or other entity is important to me.	1.66	.78
P1	I feel my privacy is very important to me.	1.47	.68
P2	I feel that my control over my personal information is very important to me.	1.51	.69
P3	I feel that it is important not to release sensitive information to any entity.	1.92	.97
P4	I feel it is important to avoid having personal information released that I think could be financially damaging.	1.48	.70
P5	I feel it is important to avoid having personal information released that I think could be socially damaging to me.	1.65	.76
P6	I feel it is important to avoid having personal information about me released that may go against social morals and attitudes.	1.80	.86
P7	I feel that the release of personal information to individuals with whom I have a high comfort level is unacceptable.	2.62	1.19
P8	I feel that the release of personal information to entities where I feel as though I am anonymously providing the information is unacceptable.	2.27	1.11
P9	I feel that the use of personal information that has been released by me but is used in a manner not intended by me is unacceptable.	1.61	.86

of vignettes. The vignettes (see Appendix A) were designed to include a selection of various application areas for biometrics devices along with a selection of different device types. The application areas include situations where biometric devices were used in each of the following categories: physical access, virtual access, e-commerce, and covert surveillance (Liu & Silverman, 2001). A variety of biometric devices were included in the vignettes, from both the behavioral and physiological categories including retinal scanners, fingerprint scanners, hand geometry scanners, signature biometrics, and facial recognition devices. The amount of time required to use the device was also varied slightly. Along with varying the device type, usage time, and application area, the vignettes were also varied as to the implementation. That is, the situations described not only had various purposes but various requirements as to choice of use. For example, in some situations the adoption involved an individual choice, such as employing a device to enter one's home; in other situations the adoption involved an organization where the usage requirement could be viewed as either mandatory (e.g., entrance into a corporate facility), or not mandatory (e.g., use of a biometric at an ATM). The variations in security technology and the situations were an attempt to generalize the findings.

The purpose of the study was not to determine which contexts or device types impacted the attitudes of the users, rather to develop a generalizable model of technology acceptance for this category of devices. In order to control for potential situational confounds and biases, the vignettes were developed to include all of the application areas discussed above. In addition, we selected a sample of devices to represent both the behavioral and physiological categories. All vignettes were presented to each study participant to be able to generalize the findings of the research over all usage categories and device types. The subjects were asked the same questions after reading each of the vignettes (see Appendix A) and all vignettes

were presented to each survey participant. For each vignette, the same set of questions was asked for each of the following constructs: perceived physical invasiveness, perceived usefulness, perceived ease of use, and intention to use. All items were measured by a five point scale (1 = *strongly agree*, 5 = *strongly disagree*).

The survey was administered to faculty, staff, and students at the University of Mississippi. A total of 298 usable responses were collected. Table 3 shows the demographic information for the sample used.

To analyze the model, a series of linear regressions were performed to obtain path coefficients for the proposed model. Situational differences in the usage scenarios of the devices were introduced through the use of vignettes in the instrument. As described above, the vignettes were varied by changing the device type, usage context, and application area as well as the length of time associated with using the device. To test the impact of varying the situational characteristics on the model, dummy variables were introduced in some

Table 3. Profile of survey participants

Total Number of Participants	298
Sex	
Male	144
Female	154
Age	
17-21	98
22-36	97
Over 36	103
Major	
CS	6
Engineering	16
Finance	31
Management	23
MIS	13
Marketing	47
Other	162
Highest Level of Education	
High School	78
2-Year Associates	51
4-Year Undergraduate	67
Masters	42
PhD	60

of the regressions. In this manner, we were able to observe if any vignette had an undue influence while the number of vignettes introduced to each subject and the variation of their contexts allowed for an overall view of the impact of the additional constructs. The regression equations for these tests are shown below.

$$PI = \beta_0 + \beta_1 P + \beta_2 S + \beta_3 D_1 + \beta_4 D_2 + \beta_5 D_3 + \beta_6 D_4 + \beta_7 D_5 + \beta_8 D_6 + \beta_9 D_7 \qquad (1)$$

$$PJ = \beta_0 + \beta_1 P + \beta_2 S + \beta_3 PEU + \beta_4 D_1 + \beta_5 D_2 + \beta_6 D_3 + \beta_7 D_4 + \beta_8 D_5 + \beta_9 D_6 + \beta_{10} D_7 \qquad (2)$$

$$PEU = \beta_0 + \beta_1 P + \beta_2 D_1 + \beta_3 D_2 + \beta_4 D_3 + \beta_5 D_4 + \beta_6 D_5 + \beta_7 D_6 + \beta_8 D_7 \qquad (3)$$

Where PI = perceived invasiveness, P = perceived need for privacy, S = perceived need for security, PEU = perceived ease of use, PU = perceived usefulness, and D_1 through D_7 are dummy variables associated with the vignette scenarios (where $D_i = 1$ if vignette i is used, $D_i = 0$ otherwise).

The proposed relationship between perceived need for privacy and perceived need for security was found to be significant in prior research (Pirim et al., 2004). We tested this relationship again in the current study using a regression to obtain path coefficients for the constructs in the model related to intention to use. These regression equations are shown below.

$$S = \beta_0 + \beta_1 P \qquad (4)$$

$$IU = \beta_0 + \beta_1 PU + \beta_2 PEU + \beta_3 PI \qquad (5)$$

Where P = perceived need for privacy, S = perceived need for security, IU = intention to use, PU = perceived usefulness, PEU = perceived ease of use, and PI = perceived invasiveness.

RESULTS

The hypotheses were tested to determine the model's capability of predicting user acceptance of biometric devices and the operationalized model is presented in Figure 2. Table 4 presents the regression coefficients, t values, and significance levels for the model.

Both perceived usefulness and perceived ease of use had significant effects on intention to use ($\beta = 0.50$; $\beta = 0.30$), supporting hypotheses 1 and 2. The implication here is that if the individual feels that the biometric device is useful in a particular situation they will be more likely to use the technology. An individual may also be more likely to use the device if they feel that it is easy to use.

The perceived ease of use of the device was found to have a significant impact on perceived usefulness ($\beta = .65$), supporting hypothesis 3. An individual's perception of how easy the device will be to use may be a large determining factor on its perceived usefulness. This implies that the complexity of use of the device will significantly impact whether or not said device is perceived as being useful.

Perceived invasiveness has a negative significant impact on the ease of use of the device ($\beta = -.187$), supporting hypothesis 4. This result implies that the more invasive the biometric is perceived to be, the less easy it will be viewed to use.

Perceived physical invasiveness impacted negatively an individual's intention to use the biometric device ($\beta = -0.12$), supporting hypothesis 5. This implies that the more invasive a biometric is perceived to be the less likely are the chances of the individual actually using the device if a choice is given.

An individual's perceived need for security was found to have a significant impact on perceived

Table 4. Regression coefficients for extended technology acceptance model

Dependent Variable	Construct	Standardized Coefficient		t	Sig
Security (R2 = .408)	Privacy		.638	14.272	.000
Invasiveness (R2 = .027)	Privacy		.108	4.087	.000
	Security		-.125	-4.753	.000
	D1	-.027		-.999	.318
	D2	-.116		-4.330	.000
	D3	-.126		-4.709	.000
	D4	-.071		-2.650	.008
	D5	-.078		-2.918	.004
	D6	-.070		-2.595	.010
	D7	-.128		-4.777	.000
EOU (R2 = .058)	Invasiveness		-.187	-9.288	.000
	D1	.004		.170	.865
	D2	.018		.698	.486
	D3	.106		4.014	.000
	D4	-.024		-.901	.368
	D5	.001		.029	.977
	D6	.004		.148	.882
	D7	.095		3.591	.000
Usefulness (R2 = .471)	EOU		.649	41.274	.000
	Security		.121	6.204	.000
	Privacy		-.006	-.301	.763
	D1	.082		4.160	.000
	D2	-.054		-2.731	.006
	D3	-.099		-4.980	.000
	D4	.011		.579	.562
	D5	-.016		-.820	.412
	D6	-.022		-1.110	.267
	D7	-.050		-2.534	.011
Intention (R2 = .595)	EOU		.301	17.259	.000
	Usefulness		.500	28.472	.000
	Invasiveness		-.117	-8.678	.000

alpha = .05 for all regressions

usefulness (β = .12), supporting hypothesis 6. The results of the regression imply that an individual's perceived need for security will positively impact how useful they feel the biometric device will be.

Perceived need for security has a negative significant impact on perceived invasiveness (β = −.125), supporting hypothesis 7. This implies that the more secure an individual feels he or she needs to be, the less invasive the technology will be viewed.

Perceived need for privacy did not have a significant impact as expected on perceived usefulness, therefore not supporting hypothesis 8. However, perceived need for privacy impacts perceived need for security, thus indirectly affecting the perceived usefulness of the device.

The results obtained show a significant effect (β = 0.64) of perceived need for privacy on the perceived need for security. The implication of this relationship is that if an individual feels a high perceived need for privacy he or she will have a high perceived need for security. This finding supports hypothesis 9.

Perceived need for privacy is shown to have a significant positive affect on perceived invasiveness of the device ($\beta = .108$), supporting hypothesis 10. Biometric devices may be viewed as invasions of privacy due to the personalized physical usage requirements. Therefore, the implication of the results obtained is that the more private an individual perceives themselves to be, the more invasive the biometric device may be perceived.

DISCUSSION, LIMITATIONS, AND DIRECTIONS FOR FURTHER RESEARCH

The results of the statistical tests of the hypotheses indicate that the additional constructs do significantly impact the intention of a user towards biometric devices. Invasiveness is shown to have, as expected, a significant negative impact on ease of use as well as intention to use security technology. As was mentioned in previous research, negative connotations associated with biometric devices as well as the obvious physicality of using the technology will influence the adoption behaviors of the users. When examining the invasiveness construct, the influence of the situational contexts were more apparent. There was a noticeable impact from the vignettes where a retinal biometric device was employed and to the use of a biometric device in a public arena where identification could be viewed with a negative connotation. Although not explicitly tested for, this implies that there is the possibility that the eye may be viewed as a more sensitive or invasive area of a person than the areas subjected to other biometric devices. Kim (1995) addressed this issue as described in the literature review. This indicates that further research as to the area of the body that is subject to appraisal by different device types may be an interesting avenue to explore in future research.

The addition of the perceived physical invasiveness construct in the current model provides an important addition to the adoption literature as it has not been explored in terms of non-medical technology in a rigorous way due to the lack of its presence in most mainstream technologies. With the development and exploration of technologies for identification that require unusual usage requirements (e.g., that a person must submit to a scan of a body part or to the implantation of a chip in order for the device to be used for its intended purpose), perceived physical invasiveness determining the impact of this construct on the adoption behaviors of end users will increase in importance. By gauging this impact, organizations considering implementing these types of devices for use by consumers or employees as well as companies marketing such tools will be able to carefully consider their device choice as well as develop informational and training sessions tailored to the concerns of the users that may help ease fears and smooth adopting.

Perceived need for security positively impacted the usefulness of the device, but perceived need for privacy did not. However, perceived need for privacy is shown to impact perceived need for security. These results imply that an individual's perception of their need for privacy did not directly impact the device's perceived usefulness but is closely tied to their perceived need for security forming an indirect relationship. These results imply that security and privacy are strongly linked. An individual with a strong desire for privacy may therefore view security technologies as a means to protect this privacy. Privacy could thus be viewed as something an individual wishes to protect therefore providing additional utility to security devices. There does exist a conflicting issue, as can be seen with the impact of perceived need for privacy on perceived physical invasiveness, in that all security devices typically require some relinquishing of personal "data" in order to properly identify and verify (or secure) the individual, facility, or digital information.

The study was limited due to the number and

variation of survey participants. The sample was restricted to faculty, staff and students at one major university located in an area with a small population. While providing a good sample due to the variation of backgrounds, educational level and employment opportunities that are present in a university environment, a larger sample size with greater variation in physical location and place of employment may be a direction for future research. Another direction of future research is to use Structured Equation Modeling (SEM) to evaluate this model. Due to the substantial number of constructs in the model, a larger number of subjects would be required to employ SEM. The methodology employed in the current study still tests the relationships in the model and provides key insights about the relationships between the constructs in the model. However, the model could be further investigated in later studies utilizing SEM or other techniques that test all relationships between constructs in the model simultaneously.

CONCLUSION

The model developed in this study is shown to be a good predictor for intention to use biometric devices. The instrument developed in this research could be used as an indicator of adoption success of biometric technologies for both an adoption company and entities wishing to market and sell these technologies for different security situations. Obtaining an idea of adoption success could be useful in preventing unsuccessful attempts to utilize a biometric technology prior to adoption and prevent or mitigate financial losses due to unsuccessful adoption attempts or underutilized technology.

The results of testing the model show that an individual's perceived need for security and the perceived ease of use of the device significantly impact the individual's perception of the usefulness of the biometric device. This would imply that the more security conscious an individual is the more likely they would be to accept the use

of a biometric technology. This implies that they would perceive the device as being useful as a means to protect their security. Both perceived usefulness and perceived ease of use impact an individual's intention to use the biometric device. Perceived physical invasiveness of the device was shown to have a significant negative impact on intention to use. Perceived physical invasiveness of the device is also shown to have a significant negative impact on the ease of use of the technology. These results are especially important in the biometrics arena as several of the devices may produce strong feelings of physical invasiveness that many other technologies in the security environment are exempt from. They are also useful from the perspective of the choice of biometric type to implement. Since physical invasiveness is shown to have an impact, more attention may need to be paid to this concern in the decision making process.

The results outline two major areas of managerial significance related to the adoption of biometric devices. First, the careful consideration as to the specific biometric technology implemented is important as physical invasiveness may produce unwanted adoption behavior. This perceived invasiveness may also impact the perceived ease of use of the device in an unexpected way possibly requiring the use of different approaches for adoption procedures or more extensive training on the technology. Secondly, it is also useful to note that an individual's perceived need for security plays an important role in the intention to use the biometric device. Therefore, as security concerns become more important in the current state of the world, adoption procedures that emphasize this benefit of the technology may aid in improving the adoption procedure.

The model proposed and tested in this project could be modified and applied to other technologies in the security area. As concern over privacy and security issue increase, the ability to obtain an overall picture of security technology adoption becomes more important not only to help increase the level of security of crucial assets but to aid in the prevention of unsuccessful attempts to adopt new technologies.

REFERENCES

Ajzen, I., & Fishbein, M. (1980). *Understanding attitudes and predicting social behavior.* Upper Saddle River, NJ: Prentice Hall.

Arent, L. (1999, July). ATM wants to be your friend. *Wired.* Retrieved August 30, 1999, at www.wired.com

Atkinson, R. (2002, May). Biometrics drivers' licenses on the cards. *Biometric Technology Today, 10*(5), 1-2.

Beiser, V. (1999, August). Biometrics breaks into prisons. *Wired.* Retrieved from www.wired.com

BTT. (2001, February 3). Biometrics secure Internet data centres worldwide. *Biometric Technology Today.*

BTT. (2005, January 1). 2004 market review. *Biometric Technology Today, 13*(1), 9-11.

Bureau of Justice. (2003). Bureau of Justice statistics – Criminal victimization. Retrieved February 14, 2006, from http://www.ojp.usdoj.gov/bjs/cvictgen.htm

Chen, L., Gillenson, M., & Sherrell, D. (2002). Enticing online consumers: An extended technology acceptance perspective. *Information and Management, 39,* 705–719.

Dale, L. (2001, September 6–7). Mobile biometric devices help in law enforcement. *Biometric Technology Today, 9*(8), 6-7.

Davis, F. (1989, September). Perceived usefulness, perceived ease of use, and user acceptance of information technology. *MIS Quarterly,* 319–340.

Davis, F., Bagozzi, R., & Warshaw, P. (1989). User acceptance of computer technology: A comparison of two theoretical models. *Management Science, 35*(8), 982–1003.

Dean, K. (2002, August). College seeks security in thumbs. *Wired.* Retrieved September 1, 2002, from www.wired.com

Deane, F., Barrelle, K., Henderson, R., & Mahar, D. (1995). Perceived acceptability of biometric security systems. *Computers and Security, 14,* 225–231.

FTC. (2001). Identity theft complaint data: Figures and trends on identity theft January 2001 thru December 2001. Retrieved February 14, 2006, from http://www.ftc.gov/bcp/workshops/idtheft/trends-update_2001.pdf

Henderson, S., & Snyder, C. (1999). Personal information privacy: Implications for MIS managers. *Information and Management, 36,* 213–220.

Herman, A. (2002, January). Major bank signs up for digital signature verification technology. *Biometric Technology Today, 10*(1), 1.

Hong, W., Thong, J., Wong, W., & Tam, K. (2002). Determinants of user acceptance of digital libraries: An empirical examination of individual differences and system characteristics. *Journal of Management Information Systems, 18*(3), 97–124.

Hopkins, R. (1999). An introduction to biometrics and large scale civilian identification. *International Review of Law Computer and Technology, 13*(3), 337–363.

Hu, P., Chau, P., Sheng, O., & Tam, K. (1999). Examining the technology acceptance model using physician acceptance of telemedicine technology. *Journal of Management Information Systems, 16*(2), 91–112.

Jain, A., Hong, L., & Pankanti, S. (2000). Biometric identification. *Communications of the ACM, 43*(2), 91–98.

Jeffords, R., Thibadoux, G., & Scheidt, M., (1999, March). New technologies to combat check fraud. *The CPA Journal, 69*(3), 30-34.

Kim, H. (1995). Biometrics, is it a viable proposition for identity authentication and access control? *Computers and Security, 14,* 205–214.

Koufaris, M. (2002). Applying the technology acceptance model and flow theory to online consumer behavior. *Information Systems Research, 13*(2), 205–223.

Liu, S., & Silverman, M. (2001, January/February). A practical guide to biometric security technology. *IT Professional*, 27–32.

Loch, K., Carr, H., & Warkentin, M. (1992). Threats to information systems: Today's reality, yesterday's understanding. *MIS Quarterly, 16*(2), 173–186.

Lowry, G. (2002). Modeling user acceptance of building management systems. *Automation in Construction, 11,* 695–705.

Mason, R. (1986). Four ethical issues of the information age. *MIS Quarterly, 10*(1), 5–12.

McMillian, R. (2002, August). The myth of airport biometrics. *Wired.*

Norton, R. (2002, October). The evolving biometric marketplace to 2006. *Biometric Technology Today,* 7–8.

Pirim, T., James, T., Boswell, K., Reithel, B., & Barkhi, R. (2004). *An empirical investigation of an individual's perceived need for privacy and security* (Working paper). Virginia Polytechnic Institute and State University. Available online from tajames@vt.edu

Plouffe, C., Hulland, J., & Vandenbosch, M. (2001). Research report: Richness versus parsimony in modeling technology adoption decisions – Understanding merchant adoption of a smart card-based payment system. *Information Systems Research, 12*(2), 208–222.

Richardson, R. (2003). 2003 CSI/FBI computer crime and security survey. Retrieved February 14, 2006, from http://www.gocsi.com

Scheeres, J. (2001, March). Smile, you're on camera. *Wired.* Retrieved March 30, 2001, from www.wired.com

Siponen, M. (2000). A conceptual foundation for organizational information security. *Information Management and Computer Security, 8*(1), 31–44.

Smith, H., Milberg, S., & Burke, S. (1996). Information privacy: Measuring individuals' concerns about organizational practices. *MIS Quarterly, 20*(2), 167–196.

Stewart, K., & Segars, A. (2002). An empirical examination of the concern for information privacy instrument. *Information Systems Research, 13*(1), 36–49.

Straub, D. (1990). Effective IS security: An empirical study. *Information Systems Research, 1*(3), 255–276.

Suydam, M. (2000, March). Taking (health) care. *Information Security, 54.*

Szajna, B. (1994). Software evaluation and choice: Predictive validation of the technology acceptance instrument. *MIS Quarterly, 18*(3), 319–324.

Titsworth, T. (2002). More than face value: Airports and multimedia security. *IEEE Multimedia, 9*(2), 11–13.

Venkatesh, V., & Davis, F. (2000). A theoretical extension of the technology acceptance model: Four longitudinal field studies. *Management Science, 46*(2), 186–204.

Wayman, J. (2000, February). Federal biometric technology legislation. *Computer*, 76– 80.

Westin, A. (1967). *Privacy and freedom.* New York: Atheneum.

Woodward, J. (1997). Biometrics: Privacy's foe or privacy's friend? *Proceedings of the IEEE, 85*(9), 1480–1492

APPENDIX A

The following scale was presented for all questions (1–58):

1	3	5
Strongly agree		Strongly disagree

Choose the best response to the following statements by circling either a 1 (strongly agree), 2 (agree), 3 (neither agree nor disagree), 4 (disagree), or 5 (strongly disagree).

1. I feel that the safeguarding from potential external threats of my physical being is important to me.
2. I feel that my personal security at my home or in my vehicle is important to me.
3. I feel that my personal security at my place of work or other work related places is important to me.
4. My security at places of public access, such as a mall or airport, or special public events, such as the Olympics or the Super Bowl, is important to me.
5. I feel that the security of my tangible assets (such as my home, vehicle, etc.) is important to me.
6. I feel that keeping my personal possessions, such as jewelry, money, electronics, etc., safe is important to me.
7. I feel that the safekeeping of my informational assets contained in digital or paper format is important to me (such as financial records, medical records, etc.).
8. I feel that the security of my personal information, such as my PC files or personal records (financial, medical, etc.) is important to me.
9. I feel that the safekeeping of information I have provided to a corporation or other entity is important to me.
10. I feel my privacy is very important to me.
11. I feel that my control over my personal information is very important to me.
12. I feel that it is important not to release sensitive information to any entity.
13. I feel it is important to avoid having personal information released that I think could be financially damaging.
14. I feel it is important to avoid having personal information released that I think could be socially damaging to me.
15. I feel it is important to avoid having personal information about me released that may go against social morals and attitudes.

16. I feel that the release of personal information to individuals with whom I have a high comfort level is unacceptable.

17. I feel that the release of personal information to entities where I feel as though I am anonymously providing the information is unacceptable.

18. I feel that the use of personal information that has been released by me but is used in a manner not intended by me is unacceptable.

Vignettes

Please read the following vignettes and then respond to **each statement** below. Your responses should fall between 1 (strongly agree) and 5 (strongly disagree).

Vignette 1:

Jimmy returns home from work. To enter his residence, he places his hand on a biometric hand geometry scanner located by the door instead of using a key for entrance. He holds his hand on the pad for a few seconds.

19. I think this biometric device is useful.
20. I think this biometric device is easy to use.
21. I think one of the reasons this device is useful is because of its ease of use.
22. I think that this device would be physically invasive.
23. I think I would use this device.

Vignette 2:

Birsel goes to the airport to visit Turkey. A facial scanner is used upon entering the airport, where the image is compared against a database of known criminal offenders, to prevent the entry of undesirable persons to the sterile area of the airport. She has to step on a marked spot and look at a camera for a few seconds in order to have her face scanned to compare it with this database.

24. I think this biometric device is useful.
25. I think this biometric device is easy to use.
26. I think one of the reasons this device is useful is because of its ease of use.
27. I think that this device would be physically invasive.
28. I think I would use this device.

Vignette 3:

Ken works at a biochemical company where sensitive research on cloning practices is taking place. This area of the company contains computers and sensitive research information that is restricted to certain employees. He needs to be authorized to enter the area every time access is needed by using a retinal scanner at the door. He has to place his face in a frame, with his chin in a chin slot. He has to look in a scanning device for a few seconds without blinking.

29. I think this biometric device is useful.
30. I think this biometric device is easy to use.
31. I think one of the reasons this device is useful is because of its ease of use.

32. I think that this device would be physically invasive.
33. I think I would use this device.

Vignette 4:

Jane goes to the bank to get cash out of the ATM machine. In lieu of a passcode and ATM card, the transaction is authorized and her identity authenticated by the use of a fingerprint scanner. She has to press her thumb on a biometric device and the device scans her thumbprint instantaneously to access the records pertaining to her.

34. I think this biometric device is useful.
35. I think this biometric device is easy to use.
36. I think one of the reasons this device is useful is because of its ease of use.
37. I think that this device would be physically invasive.
38. I think I would use this device.

Vignette 5:

Peter works for a data center that contains highly sensitive information and expensive equipment. The data center tracks the times that the individual enters and exits the data center. Peter enters the data center by using a hand geometry scanner and to exit the data center he has to also use a hand geometry scanner. To use the device, Peter has to place his hand on the hand geometry scanner for a few seconds upon entry and exit to the data center.

39. I think this biometric device is useful.
40. I think this biometric device is easy to use.
41. I think one of the reasons this device is useful is because of its ease of use.
42. I think that this device would be physically invasive.
43. I think I would use this device.

Vignette 6:

Ken is one of the system administrators for a company. As a system administrator, Ken has access to all files on the computer. The company tracks administrator access to the server. The company is implementing a fingerprint biometric to authenticate onto the server as administrator. Ken has to place his index finger on a biometric device, which instantly authenticates him into the server.

44. I think this biometric device is useful.
45. I think this biometric device is easy to use.
46. I think one of the reasons this device is useful is because of its ease of use.
47. I think that this device would be physically invasive.
48. I think I would use this device.

Vignette 7:

A hospital keeps medical records on all its patients. In the past, this information was protected by a password that was freely passed around when information was needed. For liability reasons, the hospital wants to restrict access to the medical records to only doctors and nurses. The hospital decides to implement a retinal scanner biometric device to ensure that only authorized individuals access the medical records. The doctor or nurse has to stand in front of the retinal scanner staring at a marked spot for a few seconds to authenticate into the system.

49. I think this biometric device is useful.
50. I think this biometric device is easy to use.
51. I think one of the reasons this device is useful is because of its ease of use.
52. I think that this device would be physically invasive.
53. I think I would use this device.

Vignette 8:

Katherine wants to use a credit card at a store to pay for her purchases. Normally, she would have to present an official photo id and sign a credit slip. To increase security, a digital signature device is used to authenticate the person. Katherine has to sign a digital pad instead of signing a credit slip.

54. I think this biometric device is useful.
55. I think this biometric device is easy to use.
56. I think one of the reasons this device is useful is because of its ease of use.
57. I think that this device would be physically invasive.

This work was previously published in Journal of Organizational and End User Computing, Vol. 18, Issue 3, edited by M. A. Mahmood, pp. 1-24, copyright 2005 by IGI Publishing, formerly known as Idea Group Publishing (an imprint of IGI Global).

Chapter 4.45
Security System for Distributed Business Applications

Thomas Schmidt
Vienna University of Technology, Austria

Gerald Wippel
Vienna University of Technology, Austria

Klaus Glanzer
Vienna University of Technology, Austria

Karl Fürst
Vienna University of Technology, Austria

ABSTRACT

Internet-focused application components of cooperating enterprises need comprehensive security technologies that go far beyond simple Internet authentication and authorization mechanisms. Basically, authentication is the process of determining the identity of a user or system, whereas authorization is the process of specifying who is allowed to access which resources. XML-based Web services is an upcoming and very promising technology. It enables the communication among Internet application components regardless of their implementation language. A major drawback of existing Web service approaches is the missing security conventions. Therefore, we concentrated all our effort on developing a holistic extended enterprise authentication and authorization system to facilitate agile and secure enterprise-spanning business processes with Web service-enabled application components.

INTRODUCTION

Collaboration between independent enterprises with different core competencies is a very important way to seize opportunities very fast in agile business environments (Goldman, 1991; Camarinha-Matos, 1999). To distinguish the approach described in the following from the general term "business-to-business," the more specific term "extended enterprise" (*Figure 1*) will be used.

The following definition for extended enterprises is new but influenced by other related definitions and approaches: extended enterprises (EE) are temporary or permanent networks of independent enterprises including a coordinator cooperating with the aim to design, manufacture, and sell a product or service in a project-oriented way independent of enterprise borderlines, automated inter-enterprise communication through the usage of information technology, and communicating via Internet-related technologies like XML-based Web services.

The extended enterprise coordinator mentioned above is often described as an enterprise, which extends its boundaries to incorporate business partners. This coordinator has to provide specific resources for operating the extended enterprise. As a matter of course, the same enterprise can be involved in various extended enterprises. Thus it may happen that two enterprises cooperate in one business segment and compete in other business segments at the same time.

INTEGRATION CONCEPT FOR EXTENDED ENTERPRISES

The common goal of the extended enterprise members is the support of the whole product life cycle composed of product design and development, process planning, logistics, production, marketing and sales, and etcetera. There is a need for several information systems to automate the particular life cycle steps. Different from isolated enterprises, the supporting information system functionalities are widespread in all participating enterprises. Therefore, a very extensive horizontal integration and collaboration between these enterprises is necessary (Zhang, 2003) so that each enterprise is able to contribute their part to the information systems inside the extended enterprise (*Figure 2*). The business value from such collaboration extends across the entire concept development, design planning, engineering, and supplier relationship management (Sayah, 2003).

Figure 1. Principle of extended enterprises

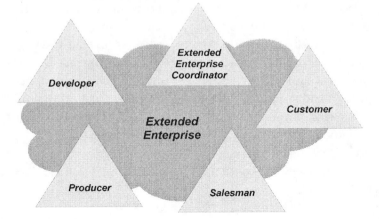

Figure 2. Extended enterprise integration concept

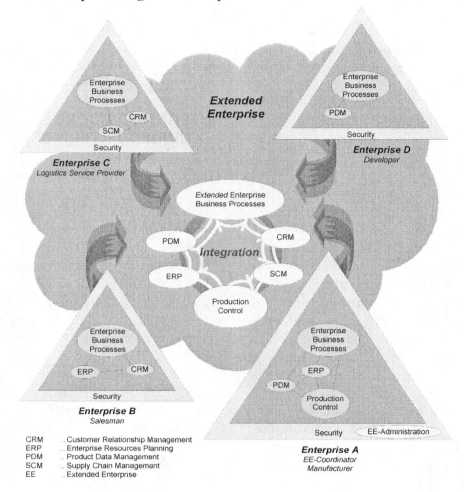

CRM	.. Customer Relationship Management
ERP	.. Enterprise Resources Planning
PDM	.. Product Data Management
SCM	.. Supply Chain Management
EE	.. Extended Enterprise

All business processes that support the product life cycle — summarized into the term "extended enterprise business processes" — interact with the enterprise business processes of the respective company. One precondition for such a closely horizontal integration is the existence of a vertical integration inside the company to provide all internal business processes and business system functionalities to the business partners.

A very important ingredient for a successful software system enabling extended enterprises is security, particularly if the Internet is used as the communication technology. In *Figure 2* each

participating company is enveloped with a security layer to guarantee a secure information exchange, authorization, authentication, and other security mechanisms. One enterprise, in the majority of cases the extended enterprise coordinator, has to do the extended enterprise administration including choosing of the business partners and assigning partners to projects and roles.

Due to the fact that security issues are manifold, in this paper the main focus lies on authorization and authentication measures for extended enterprises. The major issue here is to assure that only authorized people or systems have access to extended enterprise resources.

PRESENT SECURITY APPROACHES

Role-Based Access Control

The concept of role-based access control (RBAC) (Sandhu, 1999; Ferraiolo, 2001) is a suitable mean to simplify administration of privileges. The core idea here is not to grant a specific user privileges to access resources but to introduce an abstraction layer: the roles (e.g., the role "salesman"). Privileges are assigned to each role (e.g., "salesman" has access to a customer database). Roles are assigned to users (e.g., the role "salesman" is assigned to the user "Bob"). This enables a simplified administration of roles because there are three separate activities, which can be carried out by different people (or roles): assigning roles to roles to establish a hierarchy, assigning privileges to roles, and assigning users to roles.

The RBAC approach has been widely accepted and implemented for enterprise wide access control. First research has been conducted in the field of distributed role-based access control (Sandhu, 2000; Johnston, 1998) to delegate administration to the departments of one enterprise. But, so far, there has been no holistic approach, which provides a solution for extended enterprises.

Public Key Infrastructure and Privilege Management Infrastructure

The public key infrastructure (PKI) approach is often used to establish security in a distributed environment. Basically, both a public and a private key are used. The private key is kept secret by an entity (e.g., a person or an enterprise). The public key has to be distributed. Another central element of PKI is the certification authority (CA), which

can certify (like a passport office) the identity of a specific user or entity. This certificate is similar to a passport in the real world. By using the public key infrastructure approach, a trust network can be built. A very important PKI-concept is the certification path. If someone has a certificate from a CA, which is trusted by your own CA, then you can trust this certificate.

The privilege management infrastructure (PMI) is used for authorization. It uses so-called attribute certificates and enables privileges, roles, and delegation mechanisms. Similarly to the PKI CA, an attribute authority (AA) is defined. The attribute authority and certification authority are logically (and, in many cases, physically) completely independent from each other. The creation and maintenance of "identity" can (and often should) be separated from the PMI. Thus the entire PKI, including CAs, may exist and operate prior to the establishment of the PMI.

DRBAC-EE APPROACH

In addition to the RBAC approach, the new approach of distributed role-based access control for extended enterprises (DRBAC-EE) introduces a supplementary abstraction layer, the extended enterprise roles (*Figure 3*). Legally defined roles are a feature of the legal security framework and are defined contractually. In addition, the property if a role is a must-have or a can-have role is also contractually defined. An enterprise that collaborates in an extended enterprise within the scope of a specific project has to provide must-have roles. Additionally, the extended enterprise administrator assigns the can-have roles. To give an example: the roles "member of the advisory board" and "member of the steering committee" are must-have roles. The roles "software developer" and "marketing manager" are can-have roles.

The extended enterprise project administrator centrally controls projects in the security domain (in both the legal and technical sense), including

Figure 3. Role mapping within extended enterprises

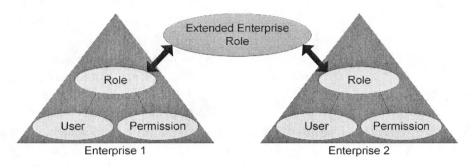

assigning can-have roles to the enterprises. The legal administrator adds and removes participating enterprises.

Figure 4 shows two extended enterprises, each with a single leader (enterprises 1 and 5) that controls resources and operations. It is extremely important to have an automated translation between internal and extended enterprise ontologies. This is especially true for enterprise 4, which has to deal with three different ontologies: its own and the two of the different extended enterprises. In practice, we can observe this problem with component suppliers in the automobile industry for example. They have to deal with different ontologies of their big customers. An automated translation from one "world" into the other is a must. A heterogeneous but coherent business space

(extended enterprise A and extended enterprise B in *Figure 4* has to be established with each partner of an extended enterprise.

Depending on the complexity of the service, we have developed two different approaches for extended enterprise authorization and authentication: indirect and direct access. The indirect access approach adds an abstraction layer and can deal with ontology translation problems more effectively, whereas the direct access approach can be more efficient and is used mainly to access simple services.

Figure 5 shows the collaboration diagram for the indirect approach, where user X of enterprise A wants to access a resource of enterprise B. A central component is the "access management." The main responsibilities are privilege verification

Figure 4. Extended enterprise administration

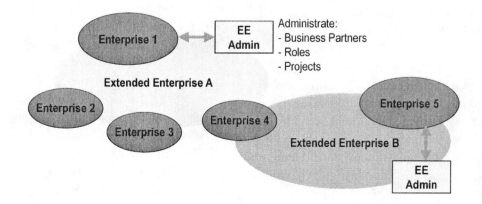

Figure 5. Managing indirect access with DRBAC-EE

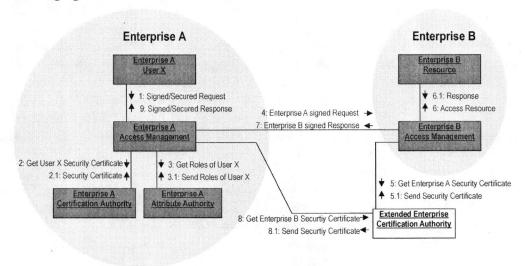

for internal and extended enterprise roles, ontology translation of internal to extended enterprise roles and processes, and logging for documentation, data mining, and legal actions.

Having gained access (*Figure 5*), all communication is done using the access management component. The collaboration diagram shows a request submitted to the access management component by user X (1). This request can be signed (e.g., using XML digital signature) and/or secured (e.g., using the SSL protocol). The access management component uses a security certificate to check this request (2 and 2.1). The attribute authority of enterprise A is accessed to realize the translation between the user X and his extended enterprise roles (3 and 3.1). Subsequently, the enterprise A access management component signs the request with the signature of enterprise A and sends it with the complete role information to the access management component of enterprise B (4). The roles in this request are the extended enterprise roles and are therefore valid only in the context of this specific extended enterprise. The certification authority of the extended enterprise is accessed to check the signature of the request (5 and 5.1). The request is logged for documentation, billing

and data mining. After that, the resource is accessed (6 and 6.1) and the response is signed and sent back to enterprise A (7). This response is also checked (8 and 8.1) and transferred to user X (9). The response to the user could also be signed and/or secured to assure security (certificate check by the user is not shown here).

IMPLEMENTATION

The implementation of the DRBAC-EE approach is based on the Service Oriented Architecture (SOA) and consists of several services as mentioned in the above collaboration diagram. The authentication service of this approach uses an attribute-based authentication with a privilege management infrastructure. In contrast to X.509 (ITU-T, 2000), XML is used to handle the data needed. The necessary attributes are included in the header of the SOAP message:

- extended enterprise
- enterprises that will act as business partners
- projects to be carried out in the scope of the extended enterprise, and

- legally defined, shared, and project-specific roles.

The SOAP envelope is enriched with additional headers based on the Security Assertions Markup Language (SAML) (SAML, 2002) and Web Service Security (WSS) (WSS, 2002) specification.

SAML, an open standard of Organization for Advancement of Structured Information Standards (OASIS), is an XML-based specification for exchanging security information. One major design goal for SAML was Single Sign-On (SSO), the ability of a user or service to authenticate in one domain and use resources in other domains without re-authenticating. SAML defines XML-encoded security assertions, an XML-encoded request/response protocol, and rules for using assertions with standard transport and messaging frameworks. An assertion is a declaration of fact according to someone.

WSS specification, originally developed by IBM, Microsoft and VeriSign, is now a public draft standard of OASIS that describes enhancements to the SOAP messaging to provide quality of protection through message integrity and single message authentication. The goal of the specification is to enable applications to conduct secure SOAP message exchanges. The WSS specification provides three main mechanisms: security token propagation, message integrity, and message confidentiality. Among other things the WSS specification specifies an extension mechanism of the SOAP header with SAML security token, which is used by the DRBAC-EE approach.

The central access management service of this approach is mainly responsible for authorization of subjects and for routing of messages. As the authentication service it uses SAML to wrap security attributes. Furthermore, the service utilizes XACML (eXtensible Access Control Markup Language) for the authorization check and for expressing security policies (XACML, 2003).

XACML is an XML-based language for access control that has been standardized within OASIS. It provides an access control model and it is a common language to express and to enforce security policies in a variety of environments. XACML allows primarily developers to describe access control policies for XML objects, but also other objects like Web services or files.

The access management service consists of the following sub-services (see *Figure 6*):

Figure 6. Basic services of the access management service

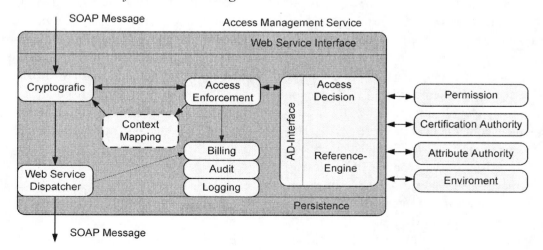

- The cryptographic service is responsible for encryption of messages and for the generation and verification of signatures attached to messages. The used APIs, which are based on XML Encryption and XML Signature specification, enable the encryption of total or several parts of messages, offering a secure and unbroken security channel between different services. This service uses the certification authority service to fulfill its task.

- The access enforcement service enforces an access decision from the access decision service and permits or denies access to the service based on returned results. To fulfill this task, it extracts the needed information from the incoming message or/and from the attribute authority. Attributes concerning the requestor (e.g., user, service) are wrapped by a SAML structure in the header of the message and attributes concerning service operation are direct extracted from the body of the message. The access enforcement service can also be part of the target service to restrict access.

- The access decision service makes the access decision based on the obtained attributes from the message and the permissions respectively rules stored in the XACML policies. The internal reference engine of this service uses XACML policies for the fine-grained access protection of services and resources. At present these policies are either XML files or build up from a database. This service offers a Web service and Java interface based on the ISO/IEC 10181-3 standard. To support the direct approach as mentioned above an external party can send SAML requests to this XACML-based service to enforce access decision. For the decision process the access decision service uses the attribute authority, the certification authority, the permission and rule store, and the environment.

- The context mapping service is part of the attribute authority service and provides the proper mapping of the internal enterprise attributes to the external extended enterprise attributes and vice versa.

- The dispatcher service routes received message to the target service. The routing information are extracted from the received message header and/or requested from a local or global directory services (e.g., UDDI).

- The billing, audit and logging services are collecting data for billing, data mining, documentation and maintenance of the system.

- A SOAP header enriched with additional security attributes needed for the authorization is shown in *Figure 7*. Like the SOAP body, this header has to be signed for security reasons (not shown here).

The <wsse:Security> SOAP header block of the WSS specification provides the mechanism for attaching security-related information targeted at a specific recipient. SAML assertion element <saml:Assertion> are attached to the SOAP message using WSS by placing assertion elements inside the <wsse:Security> header. Attributes of the <saml:Assertion> element specify the version of SAML, id of the assertion, issuer of the assertion, time of the instantiation. Sub-Element <saml:Conditions> specifies the time span at which the assertions are valid.

The element <saml:Authentication Statement> declares a statement that its subject, specified using sub-element <saml:Subject> was authenticated by particular means at a particular time using its attributes AuthenticationMethod and AuthenticationInstant. The example above specifies authentication by means of X.509 PKI. Sub-element <saml:NameIdentifier> of element <saml:Subject> declares the name and the domain of the subject. In our case the name of extended enterprise roles are declared. Sub-element <saml:SubjectConfirmation> of element <saml:Subject> specifies the protocol to be used to authenticate the subject and additional authentication information using the sub-elements <saml:ConfirmationMethode> and <saml:SubjectConfirmationData>.

Figure 7. Added information in the header of the SOAP request

```
<soap-env:Header>
  <wsse:Security >
    <saml:Assertion MajorVersion="1" MinorVersion="0"
            AssertionID="2sxJu9g/vvLG9sAN9bKp/8q0NKU="
            Issuer="www.floci-ee.com" IssueInstant="2003-02-14T16:58:33.173Z">
      <saml:Conditions NotBefore="2003-02-14T16:53:33.173Z" NotOnOrAfter="2003-02-15T16:53:33.173Z"/>
      <saml:AuthenticationStatement
            AuthenticationMethod="urn:oasis:names:tc:SAML:1.0:am:X509-PKI"
            AuthenticationInstant="2003-02-14T16:53:33.173Z">
        <saml:Subject>
          <saml:NameIdentifier NameQualifier="www.floci-ee.com" Format="">
              EELogisticManager</saml:NameIdentifier>
          <saml:SubjectConfirmation>
            <saml:ConfirmationMethod>
                urn:oasis:names:tc:SAML:1.0:cm:holder-of-key</saml:ConfirmationMethod>
            <ds:KeyInfo><ds:X509Data>    </ds:X509Data></ds:KeyInfo>
          </saml:SubjectConfirmation>
        </saml:Subject>
      </saml:AuthenticationStatement>
      <saml:AttributeStatement>
        <saml:Subject>
          <saml:NameIdentifier NameQualifier="www.floci-ee.com" Format="">
              EELogisticManager</saml:NameIdentifier>
          <saml:SubjectConfirmation>
            <saml:ConfirmationMethod>
                urn:oasis:names:tc:SAML:1.0:cm:holder-of-key</saml:ConfirmationMethod>
            <ds:KeyInfo><ds:X509Data>    </ds:X509Data></ds:KeyInfo>
          </saml:SubjectConfirmation>
        </saml:Subject>
        <saml:Attribute AttributeName="ExternalContext"
                AttributeNamespace="http://www.floci-ee.com/drbac-ee/2003-01">
          <saml:AttributeValue>
            <f:RequestAttributes>
              <f:User>
                <f:Id>312983</f:Id><f:Name>MrSample</f:Name></f:User>
              <f:ExtendedEnterprise>
                <f:Id>23</f:Id><f:Name>EE2</f:Name></f:ExtendedEnterprise>
              <f:Service>
                <f:WsdlUrl>http://host/wsdl/Timetable.wsdl</f:WsdlUrl>
                <f:URL/>
                <f:EndPoint>http://host:8080/TasksWS/jaxrpc/TimetableIF</f:EndPoint>
              </f:Service>
              <f:Enterprise>
                <f:Id>234876</f:Id><f:Name>ACIN</f:Name></f:Enterprise>
              <f:EERolesToEEProjects>
                <f:EERolesToEEProject>
                  <f:EEProject>
                    <f:Id>127746</f:Id><f:Name>Project</f:Name></f:EEProject>
                  <f:EERoles>
                    <f:EERole>
                      <f:Id>154</f:Id><f:Name>EEManager</f:Name></f:EERole>
                  </f:EERoles>
                </f:EERolesToEEProject>
              </f:EERolesToEEProjects>
            </f:RequestAttributes>
          </saml:AttributeValue>
        </saml:Attribute>
      </saml:AttributeStatement>
      <ds:Signature>    </ds:Signature>
    </saml:Assertion>
    <ds:Signature>    </ds:Signature>
  </wsse:Security>
</soap-env:Header>
```

The <saml:AttributeStatement> associates the specified subjects using sub-element <saml:Subject> with the specified attributes using the element <saml:Attribute>. The element <saml:Subject> identifies a subject using element <saml:Name Identifier> specifying role name and an element <saml:SubjectConfirmation> supplying data that allows secure authentication of the subject. The example above uses a signature for the confirmation.

The element <saml:Attribute> and its sub-element <saml:AttributeValue> specify all attributes names and values like extended enterprise, enterprise, extended enterprise roles and projects required by the target service.

The last element <ds:Signature> in the SOAP Header contains a signature with a reference to a SAML assertion.

CONCLUSION

The ability to create agile business value networks from independent enterprises in an effortless and secure way will be the crucial point of success for next generation business-to-business software. Especially the establishment and maintenance of security are extremely important requirements of the industry for agile business value networks.

Within the scope of an international research and development project, design and implementation of a holistic security system for the complex extended enterprise environment have been done successfully. Considering as example business case, a proof-of-concept prototype has been realized in close collaboration with the industrial end-users within the project consortium.

ACKNOWLEDGMENTS

This work was partly supported by the European Commission within the scope of the Growth project FLoCI-EE, G1RD-CT-2000-00324.

REFERENCES

Camarinha-Matos, L.M., & Afsarmanesh, M. (eds.). (1999). *Infrastructures for virtual enterprises.* Boston: Kluwer Academic Publishers.

Ferraiolo, D.F., Sandhu, R.S., Gavrila, S., Kuhn, D.R., & Chandramouli, R. (2001). Proposed NIST standard for role-based access control. *ACM Transactions on Information and System Security,* 4 (3), 224-274.

Goldman, S., Preiss, K., Nagel, R., & Dove, R. (1991). *21st century manufacturing enterprise strategy, Infrastructure.* (Vol. 2). Bethlehem, PA: Iacocca Institute, Lehigh University.

ITU-T. (2000, March). *ITU-T Recommendation X.509: Information technology. Open systems interconnection. The Directory: Public-key and attribute certificate frameworks. ITU: International Telecommunication Union.*

Johnston, W., Mudumbai, S., & Thompson, M. (1998). Authorization and attribute certificates for widely distributed access control. In *Seventh International Workshop on Enabling Technologies: Infrastructure for Collaborative Enterprises.*

SAML (Security Assertions Markup Language) 1.0. (2002, May 31). Committee Specification OASIS (Organization for Advancement of Structured Information Standards). Retrieved from *www.oasis-open.org/committees/security/*

Sandhu, R.S., & Coyne, E.J. (1999, February). Role-based access control models. *IEEE Computer,* 38-47.

Sandhu, R.S. (2000). Engineering authority and trust in cyberspace: The om-am and rbac way. In *Proceedings of the Fifth ACM Workshop on Role-Based Access Control* (pp. 111-119).

Sayah, J., & Zhang, L.J. (2003, September 30). *On-demand business collaboration enablement with Web services.* IBM Research Report, No. RC22926 (W0309-191). IBM T.J. Watson Research Center.

WSS (Web Service Security) 0.9. (2002, January 26). Working Draft OASIS (Organization for Advancement of Structured Information Standards). Retrieved from *www.oasis-open. org/committees/wss/*

XACML (eXtensible Access Control Markup Language) 1.0. (2003, September). Committee Specification OASIS (Organization for Advancement of Structured Information Standards). Retrieved from *www.oasi-sopen.org/committees/tc_home. php? wg_abbrev=xacml*

Zhang, L.J., & Jeckle, M. (2003). The next big thing: Web services collaboration. In *Proceedings of the 2003 International Conference on Web Services Europe (ICWS-Europe03)* (pp. 1-10). Spring-Bergle, LNCS 2853.

This work was previously published in the International Journal of Web Services Research, Vol. 2, No. 1, edited by Zhang, pp. 77-88, copyright 2005 by IGI Publishing, formerly known as Idea Group Publishing (an imprint of IGI Global).

Chapter 4.46
Incident
Preparedness and Response:
Developing a Security Policy

Warren Wylupski
University of New Mexico, USA

David R. Champion
Slippery Rock University, USA

Zachary Grant
New Mexico Mounted Patrol, USA

ABSTRACT

One of the emerging issues in the field of digital crime and digital forensics is corporate preparedness in dealing with attacks on computer network security. Security attacks and breaches of an organization's computer network can result in the compromise of confidential data, loss of customer confidence, poor public relations, disruption of business, and severe financial loss. Furthermore, loss of organizational data can present a number of criminal threats, including extortion, blackmail, identity theft, technology theft, and even hazards to national security.

This chapter first examines the preparedness and response of three southwestern companies to their own specific threats to corporate cybersecurity. Secondly, this chapter suggests that by developing an effective security policy focusing on incident detection and response, a company can minimize the damage caused by these attacks, while simultaneously strengthening the existing system and forensic processes against future attacks. Advances in digital forensics and its supporting technology, including intrusion detection, intrusion prevention, and application control, will be imperative to maintain network security in the future.

INTRODUCTION

On 12 April 2005, LexisNexis acknowledged that personal information on as many as 310,000 U.S. residents may have been stolen from its databases. The company had announced in March that information on approximately 30,000 persons had been stolen, but an internal investigation increased the estimate. LexisNexis is informing affected individuals by mail that they may be at risk of identity theft from unknown persons who illegally accessed the passwords and identity information of legitimate customers of Seisint, which LexisNexis bought in September 2004. (Litan, 2005)

Information is crucial. Those armed with information have the ability to do great good or cause great harm. Corporations and organizations that harbor personal, sensitive, or proprietary information can no longer take a passive approach to computer network and data security. Even while companies strive to apply the evolving field of digital forensics to their overall network security, external and internal threats to corporate cyber-security have grown tremendously. External threats consist of *malware* such as *viruses* and *Trojan horses*, *spyware*, and *adware*. Malware is malicious software that designed to disrupt or damage systems. Other external threats include, *script kiddies*, *social engineering*, *spam*, and *hacking*. (See Table 1 for definitions of these terms.) Internal threats stem from disgruntled employees and non-compliant (non-malicious) employees. These activities can lead to a loss of network integrity and loss of data. Worse, criminals can use proprietary organizational data for a number of dangerous or illegal activities, including extortion, fraud, theft or national security threats.

Attempted computer intrusion has become a common occurrence for businesses, regardless of their size or nature of their industry. Even the familiar and ubiquitous e-mail venue has become a thoroughfare for malicious entry into organizations. One southwestern healthcare company receives over 70,000 e-mail messages a month, of which 17,000 are legitimate messages, while the others are spam. Another southwest organization estimated that 70% to 75% of the incoming e-mail was unwanted. While most of these e-mail messages cause no harm, the cost to prevent a breach in computer security from this and other methods increases every year, according to Ware (2004).

Additional security challenges can come from the installation of wireless routers, unauthorized downloads and installation of software, and the loss and theft of computer desktops, laptops, and portable storage media. Loss of hardware or storage media can cause considerable damage to an organization's reputation. In 2005, Bank of America disclosed that in late December 2004 it lost unencrypted computer backup tapes containing Social Security numbers and other personal data belonging to government employees based on 1.2 million federally issued credit cards. At the time of the announcement, there was no evidence that any fraudulent activity had occurred due to information that existed on those tapes. In 2001, the Federal Bureau of Investigation announced that it was missing 184 laptop computers; three computers held information considered sensitive, and one computer held confidential information (Weyden, 2001).

Given the increase in intensity and severity of system intrusion attempts, most organizations today are without sophisticated protection systems or an effective security policy or process that addresses prevention, detection, and response to attempted network intrusion (Strahija, 2003).

Among the key findings of a Congressional report prepared by the Office of National Counterintelligence Executive was the integral role of digital forensics in combating economic and industrial espionage. The report notes that the vulnerability of technological and business secrets constitutes a threat to national security, as foreign governments or other individuals delve into corporate structures in order to secure sensitive

Table 1. Definition of key terms

Term	Definition
Malware	Short for malicious software. Malware is designed to disrupt computers and systems. Examples of Malware include viruses or Trojan horses. (Webopedia, n.d.)
Virus	A program that is easily reproducible, which spreads quickly within and across networks. Viruses can be disguised as or embedded within legitimate programs. Viruses quickly multiply and cause systems to slow down and stop functioning. (Webopedia, n.d.)
Trojan Horse	A program that is in the form of a non-malicious program. Trojan horses act as a shell for malicious payloads such as a virus or spyware. (Webopedia, n.d.)
Spyware	A program that becomes hidden on a system that captures the user's activities such as email and credit card numbers, and logs websites visited. This spyware then relays this information back to another unauthorized individual. (Webopedia, n.d.)
Adware	This program displays unwanted advertisements to the user based on user's web-browsing activity. (Webopedia, n.d.)
Script Kiddies	A person who is not technologically sophisticated, such as a "kiddie", who randomly seeks out a specific weakness over the Internet. (Webopedia, n.d.)
Social Engineering	Collecting private information by using tricks in order to gain the trust of victims. Social security numbers are often by convincing the victim that something is wrong with their account, and they need verification in order to correct the problem. (Webopedia, n.d.)
Spam	"Electronic junk mail or junk newsgroup postings" (Webopedia, n.d., para. 1).
Hacking	"Unauthorized access to or use of data, systems, server or networks, including any attempt to probe, scan or test the vulnerability of a system, server or network or to breach security or authentication measures without express authorization of the owner of the system, server or network" (Terms of Use Agreement, n.d., para. 20).

technologies, collect profiles on potential human sources, and exploit industry conferences and seminars (Office of the National Counterintelligence Executive, 2005). Moreover, the exposure of medical, financial, legal, and other personnel data due to security breaches leaves corporations open to blackmail, theft or fraud. The threats associated with the loss of sensitive or proprietary corporate data are limited only by the imagination of the perpetrator. Furthermore, much of the nation's infrastructure hinges upon the effectiveness of both private and public institutions, such as those in the transportation, information and technology, chemical and hazardous materials, finance, energy, and telecommunications industries, to name a few. Criminal or terrorist breaches into these systems represent a potentially devastating threat to national security (The National Strategy to Secure Cyberspace, 2003). Therefore, not only is an effective preparedness and response plan integral to the network security policy of any company or organization, it is also important to the national infrastructure.

The loss of sensitive or proprietary data to criminal or otherwise illegitimate parties should be a primary concern for any organization. *Network intrusion, security breach,* and *security incidents* all relate to unauthorized access to computer data and systems. Security incidents are broken into three distinct types of activities:

1. Any breach or unauthorized access of corporate data which may or may not result in losses or damage. Individual computer hardware (such as laptops and desk top machines), storage media, or entire network systems are all potential targets.
2. Any use of corporate computer systems for malicious activity by internal or external forces.
3. Any event, malicious or accidental, which results in damages or losses to the company such as a virus or worm (*CIO Magazine,* 2004).

Examples of network threats include external and internal hacking and unauthorized entry, malicious code, and denial of service (DOS). The effects of network intrusion attempts can include the slowing or disrupting of network and software applications, hijacking of systems to send out unauthorized Spam, and damage or erasure of operating systems and computer files. The financial cost to an organization of responding to a one-time computer intrusion and its damage typically exceeds the organization's annual security budget, in some cases these costs exceeding $500,000 (*CIO Magazine,* 2004). These threats are no longer a petty annoyance. They are potentially disastrous and costly, and organizations should take steps to prevent and minimize their effects. The forensic process to collect, examine, analyze, and report intrusion attempts should be embedded within a company's network security policy through intrusion detection, intrusion prevention and application control.

This chapter focuses on three organizations' existing preparedness and responses to computer and network security incidents. The identity of these organizations has been obscured, so that the material presented will not be used in an attempt to access their systems. These three organizations shall be referred to in this work as follows: the health care company will be referred to as *Healthcare Company*; the school district will be referred to as *School District*; and the county government as *The County*. This analysis is provided in order for the reader to understanding the challenges to providing a secure network. Through the discussion of breach prevention and detection, as well as appropriate incident response, our intent is to (a) provide information about the real challenges involved in defending against system compromises, (b) to provide a foundation for the reader, and an ideal security policy against which his or her own network security policy can be compared. Lastly, (c) we look to future trends in the area of network security.

ISSUES, CONTROVERSIES, PROBLEMS

The amount of money that organizations choose to spend on network security, and its corresponding complexity, varies greatly among organizations. Some companies believe in a comprehensive system for breach prevention and detection, with a physical separation of systems including utilizing a Demilitarized Zone (or DMZ) for access to the Internet, while others rely on their hardware for multiple purposes and systems with a direct connection to the outside world. There is also significant variability in organizations' security policy and planned response/ data collection. Some of the reasons for this variability include the organization's size, industry, and exposure to the internet companies that prevent external e-mail and Web-surfing have lower chance of intrusion attempt than a company that allows those activities. Other reasons for variability in network security are the requirement to comply with certain regulatory legislation such HIPAA or Sarbanes-Oxley; risk of catastrophe—will the impact of a successful intrusion attempt be extreme or minimal; does the organization have a disaster recovery systems in place, and how quickly will the organization be able to recover; and the history of severe intrusion attempts.

Breach Prevention/Detection

Organizations aiming to maximize their protection against computer breaches should first do self-assessments to determine their attractiveness as targets, and to identify their primary assets. Companies must determine "What kind of a target am I?" Financial, government, or government support agencies would take different approaches to security, than would smaller, local business such as a mom and pop bagel shop. In the same way, organizations must understand their assets that they are trying to protect. Is an operational network used for normal data-collection and processing most important, or is it protection of the already existing data? Answering this question should help the company to determine where they should allocate their resources. This analysis includes actual breaches as well as detecting/recording of blocked attempts. This collected information helps organizations understand the actual threats and detect patterns. For example, in 2003 experts were able to forecast the blaster worm by patterns they had seen of intrusions blocked.

In reference to the security breach at Lexis-Nexis presented earlier in the chapter, Avivah

Litan from the Gartner Group (2005) suggests three specific actions that should be implemented immediately by companies that possess sensitive customer information:

- Implement two-factor authentication for access for systems and databases. This will deter unauthorized sharing of simple user IDs and passwords in organizations that have access to such data.
- Implement activity-monitoring tools, at the application or database level, to detect patterns of unusual activity that may indicate fraud.
- Consider security practices as a key criterion when selecting information services providers.

The Security Policy

Dancho Danchev is a security consultant focusing on the implementation of security solutions, research and development of marketing concepts. Danchev (2003) stated that at a minimum, an organization's security policy should at a minimum address some of these following elements:

- How sensitive information must be handled.
- How to properly maintain user ID(s) and password(s), as well as any other accounting data.
- How to respond to a potential intrusion attempt.
- How to use workstations and Internet connectivity in a secure manner.
- How to properly use the corporate e-mail system. (p. 4)

Cisco Systems, a provider of Internet protocol-based (IP) networking solutions, identify three types of policy statements that should cover all network systems and data within an organization—the usage policy statement, partner acceptable use statement, and administrator acceptable use statement (Network Security Policy: Best Practices White Paper, 2003). They suggest that the usage policy statement should describe the users' roles and responsibilities and provide for punitive or disciplinary actions against an employee. The partner acceptable use statement should describe the use of data and appropriate conduct as well as what constitutes a security intrusion attempt and what actions will be taken should that occur. The administrator "acceptable use" statement should describe network administration, privilege review, and policy enforcement. Each of these policy statements should complement the other, without conflict or ambiguity. An aid in developing these statements and the underlying network security policy document is being able to draw upon the experiences of other organizations. In the remainder of this section we share successes and ongoing challenges faced by organizations trying to maintain their network security.

Planned Response/Data Collection

Larger companies should have certified forensic specialists on staff, to capture the appropriate information. Smaller organizations can use software such as EnCase Forensic Software by Guidance Software to preserve the electronic evidence, analyze it, and report on it. Companies specializing in forensic analysis can be found in most major US cities, and often they will assist in litigations. Each organization should make every attempt to prosecute these intrusions; however, these decisions are often made at the federal level. Because of legislation such as the HIPAA, Gramm-Leach-Bliley Act, and Sarbanes-Oxley require data collection, documentation and reporting, most organizations are mandated to collect this information and act on it regardless of prosecution.

The following section provides a brief description of how three different organizations

had prepared for, and subsequently dealt with their own security breaches. The first, Healthcare Company, is a fairly detailed case study. The second two cases, School District and County, are shorter and are based on the limited information available at the time of this writing. However, all three of these cases demonstrate integral aspects of incident preparedness in digital forensics.

Case I: Healthcare Company

In early 2005, Healthcare Company was alerted to an outage on an internal firewall. The firewall bridged the companies "remote network" from their core campus network. The internal firewall had stopped responding to all management requests and any type of electronic communication.

The initial troubleshooting steps indicated that there may be hardware failure on the firewall itself. Engineers from the company worked with their hardware vendor and after several hours of troubleshooting, it was decided that there was a flood of data packets that caused the firewall to utilize 100% of its resources. The utilization was so high that utilities such as packet dumps or management analysis were not possible. A physical disconnect of the interfaces was required to determine where the traffic utilization was originating from. It was later found to be a single host sending an extremely large number of very small packets, and in effect caused a denial of service attack on the firewall. The attack was not directed at the firewall, but as the firewall inspected each packet, it overloaded its capabilities. Though the bandwidth capabilities of the firewall were not affected, the interrupt process utilization was at 100%.

The network service was degraded for three days. It was later found that the single host had connected to the network via a dialup connection into a remote access server. Further analysis determined that the host was not foreign, but actually was a company asset that was assigned to a field employee. Further investigation of the host found a great amount of unwanted software that may have caused the network interruption, but it was unknown which software was actually malicious. After comparing data to firewall logs and other key security devices, the most suspicious application was called "view toolbar".

Company staff researched the view toolbar and found it to be a somewhat harmless application that came with the standard adware features. The company set up a laboratory environment to download the application to test their research. The results from a Google search with the verbiage "view toolbar download" were a page full of Web sites from which the toolbar could be downloaded. The first Google result appeared to be a page to download the toolbar. Within three to eight seconds of launching that Web site and opening the Web page, the computer hung, that is its processing ceased, and the lab firewall went down. Immediately the staff realized they were dealing with a malicious Web site, not a malicious toolbar. Later, through trial and error, it was determined that the first five results from their Google search were all malicious sites.

The company contacted the major security companies such as Symantec, Microsoft, and Checkpoint to discover if what they had found was a known vulnerability. None had seen this new type of exploit.

Healthcare Company contacted SecureWave, a Luxembourg company. SecureWave advertised a product that gave administrators complete control of both hardware and software. In late January 2005, SecureWave gave a demonstration of their software capabilities to the management of Healthcare Company. Though impressed, the engineers from the healthcare organization wanted to truly test the product. They advised the SecureWave representative of their latest security exploit and asked if SecureWave would be willing to install their product in a lab environment and visit the malicious Website. SecureWave agreed; their representative stated, "If there is vulnerability on an operating system that our product can't stop, we want to know about it."

The laboratory was set up and SecureWave software installed on a host provided by the healthcare company. The host was pointed to the known malicious Web site. The results were astounding. SecureWave not only stopped the vulnerability, but gave the onlookers a peek into how the malicious site worked. SecureWave logs detailed exact steps of how the Web site operated, including the files is placed on the host and registry changes it tried to make. Initially a java script was run that disabled all ActiveX security that was on the browser. An ActiveX session was then started and nine DLL application files were loaded to miscellaneous directories on the host. Multiple registry changes were attempted, but stopped by SecureWave. "View Tool Bar" replica appeared, but turned out to be nothing more than a Java IFrame posing as a toolbar.

Once again the major security companies were given the information found in the SecureWave logs. Three weeks later, Microsoft released nine critical operating system and explorer patches that are believed to be linked to the type of exploit stopped by SecureWave.

Though Healthcare Company experienced a network impact, the story is still a success. They were able to find a true zero day protection software for their host and server assets along with additional benefits to assist them in safeguarding their patient information and exceed their HIPAA requirements for electronic security.

Security Policy

In addition to their published security policy, Healthcare Company uses six techniques for breach prevention and detection: (1) *Firewalls* are deployed throughout the network to interface between the private network and the public Internet. All traffic and breach attempts are logged and stored on a security server for historical evaluation. All computers that can be taken off of the network, such as laptops, should also have firewall software installed, which blocks and logs intrusion attempts. Traffic auditing should also be enabled on the firewalls to capture what traffic is being allowed through and what traffic is being blocked as well as determining if the firewall settings have changed. Healthcare Company uses information gained by auditing firewall traffic to gather information about employees' network habits and bandwidth utilization. This information is reviewed on a monthly basis looking at from which it is determined what sites should be blocked based on amount of traffic and subsequent bandwidth utilization. (2) *Intrusion Detection Systems (IDS)* are strategically placed throughout the network. IDS systems watch for signatures of vulnerabilities, and their databases of intrusion patterns are updated periodically to insure networks against the latest intrusion attempts. (3) *IDS Reporting* records the data in the historical logs and prepares daily/weekly/monthly reports. These reports are analyzed and for traffic patterns or policy violations. (4) *Router / Switch fail Attempt Alerts* are used to notify security staff when a router or switch has three or more failed attempts at login. Notification is logged and sent to the security staff via e-mail. (5) *Network Filters* are put in place on the majority of remote Wide Area Network devices. These devices have filters that limit network traffic. For example, Internet Control Message Protocol (ICMP) or PING is often used by support staff. The ICMP is allowed from the support staff subnet, but is not allowed from any other network. Hackers often use ICMP to assist in network discovery and denial of service attacks. There is a vulnerability of *Teardrop attack* on computers running Windows NT 4.0, among other operating systems. In a Teardrop attack, the receiving network is unable to handle certain erroneous packets causing the network to crash. This vulnerability has been closed years ago as most systems have migrated to Windows 2000 or Windows XP. The ongoing problem with PING is that an outside person is able to guess the company's network topology. Using PING using tools such as traceroute or tracert for windows an individual can determine how many hops (such firewalls and routers) are present, and name of the company's ISP. Although organizations are able to block external ICMP, internal ICMPs can still be accomplished by an organization's guests if the individuals are given access to the network for print, Internet, e-mail or file access. (6) *Operating System Hardware/Software lockdown* is a key in securing a network. SecureWave is an IO control software that can lock down any IO device so physical security breaches can be prevented. SecureWave also allows software control, so that only approved files can be loaded to memory. This prevents Trojan horses, viruses, spyware, and other malicious vulnerabilities from being launched on a computer.

As a proactive intrusion detection tool, Healthcare Company uses *honey pots* in an unsecured area of the Internet. A *honey pot* (also spelled honeypot) is a host computer that is purposely left vulnerable, but with some minimum security in order to entice an intruder. The techniques of hackers and activities of viruses are monitored and adjustments to the network are made in response. Spernow (2000) has identified how Microsoft uses the honeypot as an important aspect of intrusion detection and prevention.

The honeypot-network approach to intrusion detection has recently emerged as one of the most important trends in enterprise information security. In setting up a honeypot network, security administrators design a section of an enterprise's network to make it attractive to intruders. This section will contain false information that appears to be, for example, application source code or future marketing plans. Once an intruder enters this area—which no authorized user would have reason to enter—the system automatically alerts security staff, who begin tracking the intruder's activities and may even feed him disinformation for the purpose of learning more about his identity and location.

Understanding the nature and motivation of intrusion attempts is critical to enhancing information security procedures. A hack by a teenager hoping to impress his friends can have serious consequences for an enterprise but usually poses less of problem—and almost always calls for a different degree and type of response—than corporate espionage or politically motivated "information terrorism." The honeypot network offers enterprises the most important element they need in identifying intruders and their motives: time. Time is especially critical when—as perhaps with the Microsoft hack—the intruders work in foreign countries, where identifying and apprehending intruders may require high-level cooperation between governments. (para. 5&6)

Only the larger companies typically use honeypots, although only a few companies in fact actually need them—the others are able to use the information gathered by the hosts of the honeypots. The following section addresses what to do in the event of intrusion detection.

Planned Response/Data Collection

The key to network security is the response plan. Though each breach is different, simple yet comprehensive plans can keep a breach minimized or contained.

As a part of its planned response and data collection activities, Healthcare Company considers reporting authority and reporting formats. The kind of breach and data accessed must be reviewed to determine the nature of incident reporting required. Reporting is encouraged, if not mandated, to internal company legal, risk management and compliance designees, law enforcement, and federal government. Patients are to be notified if protected information is disclosed due to HIPAA, and finally notification should be made to customers, if their personal information has been exposed.

Prosecution of intrusion is encouraged, although cost is often a barrier for small companies.

Forensic analysis and even the data capture and imaging of the affected hardware can become costly. While many organizations cannot afford proper analysis needed for prosecution, they prefer to patch the hole and move on. Prosecution in general is a complex problem due to multiple jurisdictions and the nature of the crime. These types of crimes often occur from a distance, either across state lines or internationally. The collection of credible evidence is therefore an important task for any criminal investigation of network breaching. We will look at specific steps to be taken to preserve evidence in the discussion of Data Collection below.

1. **Planned Response.** Healthcare Company has an emergency response team (ERT) consisting of information technology staff that respond to security breaches. Because each breach is different, the team analyzes the effect and severity of the breach to help them determine the appropriate response. General guidelines are set within the team to know how to respond in general. One guideline is "if the attack is a denial of service, but the security and data of a host system is intact, filtering countermeasures should be employed to prevent the attacker's source address from getting through." Another such guideline is "to isolate and disconnect infected systems, and disable ports if necessary. Test your system to determine if the virus is still spreading."

   The ERT team has the endorsement from upper management to shut down any and all systems necessary to prevent protected health information (PHI) or financial information from being accessed. Normally, any planned outage must have executive authority, but during such crises the ERT has full authority to stop any vulnerability to save critical information.

2. **Data Collection.** Data collection is an important piece in vulnerability assessment and

recovery. Any time a system is suspected of being breached, the machine is secluded and a bit for bit replica is created. The replica is created so IT staff or investigators can go through the information without damaging evidence of the breach. Network logs from firewalls and IDS systems are captured and copied for examination.

Data is examined with the following intent:

- Method of the breach.
- What information was revealed?
- Is there still vulnerability on a different system?
- What was left behind, such as a *rootkit* or a Trojan horse? A rootkit is a set of tools allowing an intruder to collect user IDs and passwords.

These findings would be used for determining the next step. For example, if a violation of federal law occurred, federal law enforcement would be notified. If patient information was breached, the appropriate patients would be notified immediately.

Documenting incidents is very important, not only as an aid for solving the intrusion problem, but also to develop an audit trail that may be used in criminal proceedings. It is critical to capture as much information as possible and create forms enabling users who are not ID specialists to provide as much information as possible. Some of the important elements of incident reporting forms are:

1. Contact information for person(s) discovering problem and/or responsible parties.
2. Target systems and/or networks. Know all about the systems under attack, including operating system versions, IP addresses and so on.

3. Purpose of systems under attack. What are the systems used for (Payroll, Research and Design, Patient Records, and so on), as well as some kind of a ranking of the importance of the system.
4. Evidence of intrusion. Discover anything that is known about the intrusion.
   a. Method of attacks used
   b. Source IP address of attacker
   c. Network contact information for this address
5. List of parties notified. This can include the technical contacts, internal legal contacts and possibly the legal authorities.

Healthcare Company had its computer network infected with the Nimda-D virus in 2002, which cause a full network outage for five days. The cost to repair the damage caused by the virus, excluding lost productivity and revenue, was in excess of $150,000. The cost to repair the damage from this virus was 2.5 times the amount the organization budgeted for security for all of 2002. This organization plans to spend approximately $1.8 million over two years 2004 and 2005, due to the requirements of Sarbanes-Oxley Act and Health Insurance Portability and Accountability Act (HIPAA). The current year annual budget for security in 2005 is approximately $700,000, more than a ten-fold increase over their 2002 security budget.

Case II: School District

In its current state, network security at the School District is heavily slanted toward the end user and decentralized site management. Each site is able to purchase equipment and software and establish e-mail and Web presence autonomously with little mandate to follow guidelines provided by the technology department. One school installed its own e-mail system, which was hacked into and taken over as an e-mail forwarding service for illegitimate e-mail. Since spam is blocked by the

IP Address from which it is sent, using the school district's IP address gave the hacker the ability to temporarily bypass e-mail filtering software. Once the e-mail forwarding was realized and shut down by the School District's technology department, the hacker was then able to use the e-mail system as a proxy to deliver pornography. If the technology department had been involved in setting up the e-mail system, it would have been standardized to another, more secure system.

Security Policy

School District does not have an official computer and network security policy. Their informal policies are driven by funding and legality. As their federal funding mandates content filtering, School District is obligated to comply. Likewise, illegal peer-to-peer file sharing such as the old Napster and Kaaza, are also prevented. While the technology department manager wrote and submitted a formal security policy to the administration for approval, it was subsequently returned for clarification. After additional rewrites and resubmission attempts, which were met with additional and requests for clarification by the administration, the policy was abandoned by the technology manager.

School District's management staff identified that ideally, their security policy would include a number of aspects including (1) an override to the existing site-based IT management, (2) establishing a DMZ, (3) centralized purchasing and standardization on applications and hardware, (4) control of wireless access points, and (5) limit network access to School District owned equipment only.

Planned Response/Data Collection

School District has not considered a planned response to network intrusion, or how data are to be collected. In contrast to Healthcare, School District (with over 100 schools) spends only a little more per year on network security than the salary of their security manager. The answer to why one organization's security is more inclusive than another's can be demonstrated in four areas. These are: (1) *liability* (HIPAA, Sarbanes-Oxley), (2) *risk of catastrophe*—impact of intrusion attempt, (3) *existence of disaster recovery*, and (4) *history of severe intrusion attempt*, or loss. Should their network become affected and unusable, the schools can continue to function until they can activate their disaster recovery plan, using tape backups at an offsite location. Therefore, while School District has yet to experience a network intrusion, their risk of catastrophe is minimal. These schools also have little exposure with regard to Sarbanes-Oxley due to their non-for-profit organizational structure. HIPAA liability, while present due to student medical information, remains relatively minimal in contrast to a typical medical provider.

Case III: The County

Due to heightened security concerns, the County divulged comparatively few details about their intrusion event. What is known is that the County gave little attention to the importance of their network security, until they had a major security incident in which their 600 employees' and seven councilors' payroll and personal information were lost. A data storage device was stolen from an office, and this device held the payroll and personnel information.

Security Policy

At the time that this theft occurred, the county did not have an effective, written policy in place. The County implemented their security policy two months after their security breach.

Planned Response/ Data Collection

The County did not have a planned response or data collection plan. They did however pay for credit monitoring for these individuals for one year, at considerable cost. The presence of an effective security policy may have helped prevent the loss and subsequent liability incurred by the County.

We will now look at existing security policies, and the challenges faced in developing effective policies.

Lessons Learned

From the descriptions of how three different organizations prepared for and responded to security threats, three clear lessons emerge: have a clear policy, engage in continuous reassessment, and learn from past mistakes.

Clear Policy

A lucid and effective policy that is widely disseminated and familiar to employees is essential. Healthcare Company's clearly defined policy enabled it to respond effectively to network intrusion. Their policy is as follows:

1. User IDs and passwords must be kept confidential and cannot be displayed.
2. Employees cannot connect company equipment to other networks or to wireless networks without IT involvement.
3. The loading of any software without IT involvement on company computer systems or on the network can cause network disruptions and the loss of productivity or data. Such unauthorized action is unlawful and subject to monetary penalties.
4. Personal software, unauthorized software or unlicensed software cannot be loaded on company equipment.
5. Copies of company owned software cannot

be made or loaded on personal computers.
6. The IT User Administrator form must be completed for all terminated employees.
7. If an employee has patient health information, company proprietary information or employee ID information on a mobile device, such as a laptop, PDA or USB drive, or on any form of media, such as a CD or floppy drive, the file must be password protected or encrypted.
8. Patient health information, company proprietary information or employee ID information should not be maintained on personal computer systems (non-company-owned systems).
9. Employees may not disable virus protection or any other software running on company equipment without IT involvement.
10. Computer or system hardware and software must be purchased through IT.
11. Managers are responsible for ensuring their employees adhere to this policy.

However, although they have a written policy that is specific in nature and covers many of the aspects that should be included, there are few repercussions for employees that are in non-compliance with the standards provided. A written policy that can be ignored is as ineffective as no policy at all, as we shall see later in the chapter, in the Attacks and Outcomes section.

Continuous Reassessment

As threats evolve to overcome defenses, cybersecurity demands an ongoing testing and evaluation of existing systems. School District surprisingly reported only the one security incident involving the takeover of an unsecured e-mail server. Their liability so far has been minimal, given their absence of a written security policy, and ineffective topology. While continuing their existing site based IT management and decentralized purchasing of software and hardware,

School District moves forward integrating their systems. As their systems become more easily accessible, with connectivity through the Internet, we expect this to drastically increase their number and severity of intrusion attempts, both internally and externally generated. Even while they seek to improve their topology by adding a DMZ and additional intrusion detection systems, the absence of a security policy will probably lead to additional, more serious security breaches.

After their system became impacted due to an employee downloading unauthorized and malicious software, Healthcare Company was able to respond quickly, identify the problem, and identify and report a new type of exploitation. Reassessments of network security are an ongoing effort.

Learn from Past Mistakes

As an ongoing practice, Healthcare Company examines network breaches and case studies from other companies to insure their network is secure. They also write a detailed report of any system intrusion and use the information to find ways to improve the long-term security of the network. Their goal is to learn from their mistakes and find ways to patch the holes. The employee that downloaded an unauthorized program that was unknowingly malicious was not sanctioned, which exposes a large gap in Healthcare Company's policy. Healthcare Company is aware that threat of sanctions and punishment for non-compliance of their security policy, is not followed up with imposed sanctions and penalties, such as reprimands and suspension from work. While they acknowledge that their policy is ineffective as a threat of sanctions or punishment to employees for non-compliance, they have no plans to fix this problem. As non-compliance with the security policy continues to be tolerated, lapses in security and intrusions will continue as a result.

The County's security incident, a lost laptop computer containing employee personal data,

was extremely costly in terms of both dollars and reputation. In response, the county implemented their 21-page security policy. Their policy provides specifics relating to physical security and asset management, account access and control, prohibited and personal use, as well as specific enforcement and sanctions. There have been no further employee causes security lapses since this policy was enacted.

SOLUTIONS AND RECOMMENDATIONS

Effective intrusion preparedness and response relies on a combination of policies and processes, organizational commitment, and employee accountability. An Ideal Security Policy and an Ideal Security Topology are presented as the ideal model of organizational security.

Ideal Security Policy

There are many challenges to formulating a comprehensive and effective computer and network security policy. External customers, internal customers and employees, organizational goals, and emerging security threats must all be considered. Organizations must weigh the cost of protecting the network against the possibility of a serious security incident. Internal political considerations must be taken into account. For example, Healthcare Company had to overcome the disparity between its executive's needs and wishes, and operational security. Executives demanded Web-based e-mail such as HotMail or Yahoo Mail, although these e-mail pathways are unprotected by the organization's e-mail filters. Other political considerations must also be weighed, such as how to spend the limited IT budget; should the organization purchase new desktop computers, or upgrade their virus protection. As a network becomes breached by a hacker, the IT department may decide to shut down access to other applications or systems, in order to observe the ongoing intrusion to learn how to make the network more secure in the future. This exploration is often necessary, especially when dealing with an unknown or new threat, although the organization's executives might disapprove. The following is a framework or model of an ideal security policy.

Purpose /Goal

According to Robert J. Shimonski (2004), the purpose of the security policy is to formally state the "objectives, goals, rules and formal procedures that help to define the overall security posture and architecture for said organization" (para. 5). In addition to that basic framework, Shimonski goes on to say that security policies must address seven important functions: (1) it must be understandable; (2) it must be realistic; (3) it must be consistent; (4) it must be enforceable; (5) it must be documented, distributed, and communicated properly; (6) it must be flexible; and (7) it must be reviewed periodically (2004).

Customization

Security policy should be customized to the organization's unique characteristics. A policy should provide reasonable expectations of privacy for employees. List procedures used by IT to review security especially when it impacts the productivity or privacy of employees. It should, for instance, include the people who need to be notified when reviewing an employee workstation (the employee's manager, and others in the chain of command) or shared file system.

Asset Defining/ Risk Analysis

Danchev (2003) suggests a strategy for asset definition and risk analysis. He suggests identification of company assets and determination of potential risks and an ongoing process. Assets must be de-

fined to ensure that they are properly protected. Consider who the assets are protected from, and then identify the potential risks. Set up a process for continuous or at a minimum, periodic review to identify new assets.

List and prioritize the organization's critical assets (categories, systems, processes). Hardware, networks and software, should all be included in the risk analysis process. In reviewing hardware, all servers, desk top and laptop machines, and removable media such as CD's and USB drives should be considered.

Networks provide outside access for employees, vendors, and clients. Security of the point of entry, whether it is via VPN or dialup, should be considered. Restriction of access to specific applications or systems, and setting limits to the duration which a password will be active.

Outdated software and patches may lead to vulnerabilities, and should be identified. Unencrypted software and file sharing applications (Kazaa, Sharereactor, E-Donkey, etc.) also represent potential vulnerabilities, as do Instant Message (chat) software, entertainment or freeware software coming from unknown and untrustworthy sources.

Threat Management

The organization must perform a risk analysis, identifying company assets and determining who should access them using the principal of *least privilege*, or minimum access necessary to perform required activities. Assets could include proprietary information, customer data, intellectual property, or simply access to e-mail or access to the Internet. These assets may be used by employees, partners (for instance, an extranet), vendors (servicing large-scale mainframe or storage), customers (registered users to receive service information or upgrades), or general Internet users. The access policy should define these groups, and define roles within these groups; for instance an employee can be an accountant, manager, or administrator roles. Access to the assets should be defined for each role, including access to the Internet and e-mail. Third-party policy enforcement tools Netegrity's eTrust Identity and Access Management tools look at (1) Who are you? (authentication), (2) What do you want? (authorization), and (3) Why do you want it? (role—defines reading/writing/executing policies).

Threat management is separated between on-site physical security threats, and Internet threats. Physical security threats exploit passwords, virus protection, removable media, and incident handling. Creation of passwords is an important task that often is given little thought, due to the increasing of systems and accounts that requiring password protection. Care should be taken so an individual's login consists of a password unique to only one account. The same password should not be used across systems, as once that password is compromised, complete access is available. Do not use common or familiar words as passwords, such as a child's name or birthday, or social security number. As a rule, passwords should be no longer than seven characters, and should contain some numbers and symbols. New passwords should not consist of a previous password with a "1" added to the end, i.e. the old password is FL&3RX and the new password then becomes FLY&3RX1.

Automatic aging of passwords should be turned on for every application or system. Users are encouraged to change their password prior to the aging expiration, at which time they are forced to change it. Users should only be allowed to reuse a password after the fifth time they change passwords. The new password should following the creation process listed above. When practical, organizations should consider using two-factor authentication mechanisms such as RSA's SecurID to secure VPNs, and requiring public-key signatures for authenticating the source of e-mail.

Danchev (2003) suggests that organizations structure their security policy to explicitly instructing employees how to work on the computer and in the cyber world, in order to avoid exposure to computer viruses. He suggests never opening files and programs received from unknown sources. At a minimum, all file and program should be scanned with an updated virus scanner before they are opened, regardless of the file extension (.exe, .bat, .com, .doc, etc.). Full system scans should be scheduled to run at least once a week using updated virus signatures. Virus protection should never be deactivated, unless it is done so temporarily by the IT or security department.

Removable media (CD's, floppies, tapes, USB drives, etc.) should be controlled so that their use is restricted to only company owned machines. Media brought in from outside the organization should never be accessed. If it is required that this media be used, care must be taken to ensure that no malicious programs are present in them. A process for conducting periodic system back up and testing as well as system maintenance should be included in the security policy.

Since every situation of security intrusion will vary, organizations should predefine and implement an intrusion response plan that provides general overview of how to respond to vulnerabilities. Within the response plan should exist prior authorization to shut down systems if necessary to protect critical data and systems. The organization should have at the ready, trained personnel with the ability to user forensic technology to track the steps of an exploit. The organization should use security incidents as a training tool, refocusing policy or topology as necessary.

Danchev (2003) identified Internet-based threats to security that include Web browsing, e-mail, instant messaging (IM), and downloading software and opening files. He suggests that organizations determine acceptable use for each of these activities that could lead to a security breach. Companies need to define when and how individuals are allowed to browse the Web, download and open files, and communicate using e-mail and IM. The potential threats posed by each of these activities should be clearly communicated, in addition that their activities monitored for inappropriate or illegal activity.

Additional Internet-based threats include Web conferencing tools, remote computing, and employee owned equipment. Web conferencing tools and their access remote control tools also expose organizations to vulnerability. Networks should default to prevent access to conferencing and remote control applications such as WebEx. Then networks are configured to allow for Web conferencing, it provides vulnerability for hackers to come in and take over using the remote control tools.

Remote access can take the form of Virtual Private Network (VPN) or wireless Internet access. VPN solutions are good for productivity, but without control of what is done allow for network vulnerability. Systems using VPN are still connected to the Internet, and Internet activities should be regulated with this in mind. Systems using VPN must be protected with an updated firewall; without a firewall, the system and network is vulnerable to intrusion attempt.

By using Wi-Fi, laptop users are vulnerable to hackers who could steal data, introduce viruses, launch spam or attacks other computers. This type of vulnerability is easily exploited in public hotspot locations. In January 2005, the total number of public hotspots exceeded 50,000 internationally, with approximately 25,500 of these locations in the U.S. (Worldwide WiFi Hotspots Reach 50,000 Milestone, 2005). With the total number of hotspots is expected to double in 2005, Wi-Fi vulnerability will continue to grow (ibid).

And finally, employee owned equipment should never be used to gain access the network.

Balance

Organizational security must be balanced against external customer needs, internal customer requirements, and employee privacy issues. At the same time, organizations must determine their risk for a security breach versus how much

they should expend to prevent and detect such intrusions. Balancing the need to allow software vendors access to perform maintenance against keeping the network and attached systems secured is not an easy decision, nor are the other balancing questions. The decisions of access by customers, employees, and internal customers must be carefully weighed in favor of organizational security. These decisions will not be popular, and will often require further and frequent review.

Implementation/Distribution

Post the security policy centrally, so that it is available to all employees both electronically and in paper form. The policy should be reviewed on a regular basis, with changes made as necessary. Send out important changes, additions, and deletions when warranted. Other notification of changes can be made via e-mail, memo, or voicemail.

Distribute policy to employees, having then sign and return their promise to comply with the policy. Annually thereafter, employees should review the entire policy and sign that they promise to comply. Definitions of terms should be included in the policy's glossary.

Enforcement and Sanctions

List and enforce disciplinary action for lapses in the security policy. Appropriate use, prohibited use, and personal use should all be defined, in addition to listing types of activities requiring management approval, and approval hierarchy. Define disciplinary action up to and including termination, for violations of the security policy. In addition, contractors may be liable to damages and penalties allowed under law. Illegal activity should be reported to the appropriate legal authorities.

Supervisors are responsible for ensuring employee's compliance with the security policy. Employee's usage can be monitored based on request by the employee's supervisor, department head, or Human Resources. An account can be immediately suspended with reasonable suspicion of a security breach or misuse. The employee's supervisor and Human Resources will be notified, and analysis of the account and records completed. Disciplinary action should result if warranted.

Revisions

Set a goal, perhaps annually, to revise the security policies. Understand and know where vulnerabilities exist. Set goals to correct them vulnerabilities, neutralizing as many of them as possible. Learn from each incident and response. Create and implement audit and test policies, including these in the revised versions of the security policy.

Ideal Security Topology

Every network will be unique, but core techniques can be utilized to minimize vulnerabilities. Hackers and scripted vulnerabilities use many techniques to not only penetrate the network, but gather information that could be used to infiltrate a network. There are basic measures that can be implemented, which would enhance network protection and force malicious attackers to move on to their next victim. If a company does not have the resources to employee network security staff, they should hire an outside company or service provider that would help to secure their network. The following is a comprehensive list of basic protective measures included in an ideal security topology.

1. **Edge Network**
   a. Service Provider—Many Internet service providers provide denial of service (DOS) attacks and pattern alerts. Though a firewall is designed to fend of DOS attacks, this option allows the firewall to operate with out the additional load of DOS attacks. Limiting

any unnecessary traffic to the network equipment will enhance your quality of service to the organization and its customers. Receiving alerts from the service provider about possible vulnerabilities and traffic patterns can assist in foreseeing large scale vulnerabilities.

   b. Perimeter Equipment—Separate the firewall function from the perimeter routers. A perimeter router should have a minimal number of services. Services such as FTP, TFTP, Telnet, should only be utilized if absolutely necessary. Console access is the most secure way to manage a network device, allowing all IP access to be minimized. Applications such as IP-Reach by Raritan, allow management of an access point that must be physically connected to the router.
      i. Security—Perimeter routers should contain access lists or filters to only allow management from a small range of IP's, preferably from the organization's private network. If remote access is needed encrypted communications should be utilized such as SSH. Filters should shut down top vulnerabilities ports that are not used. For example, few companies actually utilize TCP and UDP ports 135 – 139 to the Internet. Filters should shut these ports down. ICMP should also be used only if mandatory. Shutting ICMP down will further assist in hiding the network from some of the basic intrusion attempts.
   c. Firewall—A firewall should be capable of stateful packet inspection, tracking each connection traversing all interfaces of the firewall and makes sure they are valid. This allows packet inspection for vulnerabilities and exploits.
      i. The network between the firewalls

and perimeter routers should be as minimized as possible. If there is only one single router and a single firewall, a 30 bit mask (255.255.255.252) should be used to minimize the available network space within that zone.

ii. Security—Outbound ports should be limited. Many companies secure inbound connections, but open most outbound ports. This topology can empower exploits and open gaps within security. Only outbound ports needed for legitimate business purposes should be opened. Auditing and logging of the traffic will also help identify patterns and possible exploits.

d. Traffic Monitors / IDS / IPS

i. Services such as Websense should monitor and report Web traffic and block known malicious Websites that deliver code to computers via Web surfing. Spyware and adware can have an adverse affect on operating systems and provide information useful for potential hackers. Generated reports can also be used by administrators to enforce company policies regarding Web surfing and in return provide a better quality of service to their customers and employees.

ii. IDS and IPS systems are an integral piece in network security. Never rely solely on a firewall for protection. Placing IDS & IPS systems strategically within the network will allow enable the organization to see what vulnerabilities are getting past the firewall. Free IDS systems are available, such as Snort (www.snort.org) to allow real-time monitoring of data. LanCope offers

a StealthWatch product that offers excellent functionality for quick monitoring of vulnerabilities and network analyzation.

2. **DMZ**

a. A DMZ is recommended. A zone that has a physical or virtual separate assignment with a structured topology to limit its communications to other company assets. DMZ or exposed hosts should be monitored very closely. Any server or computer that has a Static Public IP, NATed or not, should have all unnecessary services shut off. The host should have minimal purpose. Limit the amount of allowed traffic to this host.

b. Inbound and outbound e-mail should utilize two different hosts. Allowing a single host to act as inbound and outbound gateways, single use servers allow for the possibility that it will be used as a gateway for unwanted e-mail.

3. **Internet Network Hosts & Network Topology**

a. Servers and PC's cannot be ignored. Updated security patches and correct configuration is an important step in securing the network. Having a firewall in and IDS in place is only a piece of the puzzle. A poorly configured computer can have all the security bypassed and expose the network to malicious intrusion attempts.

i. Patch Management—Keeping Servers and PC's up to date with the current patches can help alleviate the possibility of a vulnerability being exploited. Unfortunately, many patches from the OS vendor are released weeks or months after vulnerability is discovered.

ii. Install Lockdown—Normal users should not be administrators on hosts. Administrator level functions should be handled by IT personnel. In addition, unauthorized applications and I/O devices should be controlled. Many companies have paper policies but no enforcement actions.

1. SecureWave has a product that allows full I/O and Application control. This allows administrators to deny items such as thumb drives, CD-ROMs, and floppy drives. SecureWave allows encryption of certain I/O devices and also allows only certain types or brands to be utilized. SecureWave also allows application control. No files can be loaded to memory, unless it is approved on a white list. This allows complete protection from spyware, adware, Trojans, and unwanted applications from being installed on company hosts. The *white list* concept is a paradigm shift in administration theories. Many products offer control and will have a list of unapproved applications or files. A white list is a list of approved applications or files. This provides a smaller more comprehendible list to manage.

iii. File Encryption—Encryption on hard drives of servers and hosts of important or proprietary information can prevent information from being stolen if a computer is ever stolen. This information can be easily accessed, without a system password. Even bios passwords cannot protect the data, as the hard drive.

b. Internal Protocols and network management should be limited as much as possible. For example, only allow ICMP from a subnet designated to IT staff. ICMP is used in many Trojans as a discovery to pass vulnerabilities on a mass scale.

Alternative Solutions

One example of trying a variety of approaches is the *New Mexico Mounted Patrol*. This organization is an unfunded law enforcement agency that utilizes officers with a range of experience from the private sector. All of their officers volunteer on a part-time basis to provide the state of New Mexico with thousands of hours of policing with no cost to New Mexico taxpayers.

One of the focuses in the recent years is digital crime. Each year statistics of digital crime increases and the resources for law enforcement are limited. The New Mexico Mounted Patrol has been working with several companies in the private sector to help understand and defeat intruders of digital crime.

During an evaluation of software, officers from the New Mexico Mounted Patrol were able to test an effective product from LanCope called StealthWatch. StealthWatch is a utility that monitors network traffic and alerts to any vulnerabilities or anomaly within a network. "The demo was setup within a ten minute period, and shortly after an intruder was found on the test environment" explained Chief Erwin. "The demonstration was meant to give an overview of the product; we didn't expect to actually find an intruder on the test network that we thought was secure!"

This software demonstration provided law enforcement with a good example of the tools that the private industry uses for protection. It is critical that law enforcement understand these types of tools so they may partner with the private industry to defeat system intruders.

FUTURE TRENDS

There is no end in sight to the increasing number and varieties of computer network intrusions taking place. While the awareness of computer based crime increases, the complexity of prosecuting offenders across jurisdictions or internationally does little to deter these types of crime. Fortunately, technology continues to advance with regard to intrusion prevention, detection, and response.

Adaptive Behavioral Intrusion Detection

The concept of behavioral intrusion detection is comparing activity across a network to a pre-established baseline. The organization establishes some access points in the network, such as at the firewall, and determines a normal level of activity, around which ongoing activity is compared. The baseline is set during a designated learning period, after which the system only then evaluates ongoing system data. By this comparison of ongoing activity to the static baseline, deviations from the baseline would be investigated for potential security threats. The limitation of the one-time learning period is that the baseline becomes quickly obsolete due to business changes, network updates, and emergent security threats. Resetting the baseline can remediate the problem, until the next internal or environmental change.

Adaptive behavioral intrusion detection collects data from the network to sets its baseline continuously, rather than a one-time basis. Using real-time network data provides a higher level of security. The system continuously analyzes network data, which allows it to "identify previously unknown threats, covert channel attacks and sophisticated evasion techniques" (Paly, 2004, para. 29). Using this methodology allows the system to respond to changes in network traffic and evolving security threats. The system monitors both inside and outside of the firewall, so that attempted intrusions as well as actual intrusions can be monitored.

Network Cloaking

Network cloaking prevents network intrusions by making protected networks invisible to malicious external users. It does so by responding to an intrusion attempt while the attack is in progress. This occurs as the technology recognizes the intrusion attempt and stops it before any malicious packets penetrate the network. Hiding the ports prevents unauthorized users from discovering other potentially damaging information about the protected network such as applications. It is believed that the use of cloaking eliminates the risk of port service attacks from unauthenticated users.

Application Control

While most organizations work off a prohibited or *black list*, it is now possible for these same organizations to restrict unauthorized and malicious programs using application control via a *white list* of centrally approved program files. Only those programs appearing on the white list are enabled for execution. By restricting which programs are authorized for execution, it is possible to eliminate the launching of games, shareware, malicious programs, and any other unauthorized and unwanted programs. Each allowed program is assigned a signature algorithm, which is verified prior to its execution. Should a program not be approved or is approved but contains any type of modification, it will be prevented from running unless it receives specific approval.

These three security advancements within intrusion detection, intrusion prevention, and application control continue the fight for network security. We expect to see more complex and effective developments in the area as a direct response to the number and severity of network intrusions increase.

CONCLUSIONS

One integral component of digital forensics is the safeguarding of corporate and organizational data that can lead to identity theft, technology theft, monetary larceny, fraud, blackmail, extortion, and even threats to national security if it falls into the wrong hands. Continuous organizational vigilance is required in order to maintain security against network intrusion. A business owner, manager, and network security administrator has many tools that allow him or her to adequately protect their vital computer systems and databases. Unfortunately, as we have shown above, organizations and the people within them do not always act as they should. Companies fail to develop, implement, and enforce their policy. Employees circumvent established procedures and processes, and equipment frequently becomes lost or stolen. We discussed these and other challenges to network security, and provide guidance as to creating an effective network topology and security policy. Finally, we reviewed newer and emerging technologies, which companies can now employ to prevent data loss and network intrusion. Safeguarding organizational data is a key component in the forensic application of cyber technology, given the risks to personal, corporate, and even national security.

REFERENCES

Danchev, D. (2003). *Building and implementing a successful information security policy.* Retrieved April 15, 2005, from http://www.windowsecurity. com/articles/Building_Implementing_Security_ Policy.html

Litan, A. (2005). *Latest security breach shows need to tighten data access.* Retrieved April 19, 2005, from http://www.gartner.com/ DisplayDocument?doc_cd=127287

National strategy to secure cyberspace. (2003). Retrieved July 25, 2005 from http://www.white-house.gov/pcipb/

Network security policy: Best practices white paper. (2003). Retrieved April 18 2005, from http://www.cisco.com/warp/public/126/secpol. html

Office of the National Counter Intelligence Executive. (2005). *Annual report to Congress on foreign economic collection and industrial espionage.* Retrieved July 26, 2005, from http://www.nacic. gov/publications/reports_speeches/reports/fe-cie_all/fecie_2004/FecieAnnual%20report_ 2004_NoCoverPages.pdf

Paly, S. (2004). *Adaptive and behavioral approach to new threats.*

Global DataGuard, Inc., Retrieved April 18, 2005, from http://www.net-security.org/article. php?id=751

Shimonski, R. (2004). *Defining a security policy.* Retrieved April 29, 2005, from http://www. windowsecurity.com/articles/Defining_a_Secu-rity_Policy.html

Spernow, W. (2000). *Microsoft hack may really be a sweet success for honeypot networks.* Retrieved April 19, 2005, from http://www.gartner.com/ DisplayDocument?ref=g_search&id=316940

Strahija, N. (2003). *Lack of security policy in companies.* Retrieved April 18, 2005, from http:// www.xatrix.org/article2891.html

Terms of use agreement (n.d.). Retrieved April 27, 2005, from http://takeaction.worldwildlife. org/terms.html

Ware, L.C. (2004). *State of information security.* Retrieved April 25, 2005, from http://www2.cio. com/research/surveyreport.cfm?id=75

Webopedia. (n.d.). Retrieved April 27, 2005, from http://www.webopedia.com/TERM/

Weyden, J. (2001). *FBI 'loses' hundreds of laptops and guns.* Retrieved April 27, 2005, from http://www.theregister.co.uk/2001/07/18/fbi_loses_hundreds_of_laptops/

Worldwide WiFi hotspots reach 50,000 milestone. (2005). Retrieved April 28, 2005, from http://www.jiwire.com/press-50k-milestone.htm

Chapter 4.47
Applying Directory Services to Enhance Identification, Authentication, and Authorization for B2B Applications

Yuan-Yuan Jiao
Nankai University, China

Jun Du
Tianjin University, China

Jianxin (Roger) Jiao
Nanyang Technological University, Singapore

ABSTRACT

System-to-system integration is an essential aspect of Business-to-Business (B2B) organizations. This chapter proposes a common infrastructure model for B2B applications, referred to as the IAAIBB model. It aims to centralize the Identification, Authentication and Authorization (IAA) infrastructures and to provide easy interoperability among business partners. The key technique is to incorporate the directory service into business applications. The directory service acts as the core repository of the IAAIBB model to support all functions associated with identification, authentication and authorization. The chapter illustrates how IAAIBB enables a sound trust relationship for B2B applications, as well as the implementation of the IAAIBB model. Also reported is the evaluation of the IAAIBB model, which reveals a number of advantages. The IAAIBB model leverages on the strength of XML, the directory service, the PKI cryptography and role-based access control.

INTRODUCTION

Business entities face tough challenges nowadays. Companies are pressured to reduce costs and work with fewer resources, while at the same time develop marketing campaigns that hit the market faster, generate better leads, drive higher revenues and increase customer retention rates. It is widely accepted that business automation and integration would be a solution to meet these challenges. As observed by Olsen (2000), system-to-system integration is an essential aspect of the B2B segment that brings company internal business applications over the Internet, while interfacing with business partners electronically.

Advanced companies are going beyond simply specifying software architectures and creating a *business model* that provides a framework for all corporate applications. For example, unified modeling language (UML) is widely used for such modeling purposes (Li, Cao, Castro-Lacouture, & Skibniewski, 2003). Nevertheless, trust and interactivity are critical success factors throughout any business process (Wilson & Abel, 2002). A good B2B relationship implies that both organizational and personal needs should be addressed coherently (Tellefsen, 2002). This issue should be addressed as early as at the system definition and design phase. A directory service, which is tightly bound to a company's and its suppliers' structures, would be employed, for example, to address a purchasing manager's personal needs for dealing with various users by varying sense of control.

Related Work

Konstantopoulos, Spyrou and Darzentas (2001) pointed out that efforts should be given to the development of standard infrastructures for deploying directories and the use of public key infrastructure (PKI). B2Bexchange.com developed a hub-and-spoke concept to enable numerous communication protocols to be "translated" at the central exchange hub without overloading the end system at the company side. Oracle proposed a B2B integration technology architecture that consists of two repositories for interactions with pre-defined business processes (Bussler, 2002). IBM developed a conversation model providing conversation policy-based support, which performs as an exchange "glue" to handle message-centric B2B interactions (Hanson, Nandi, & Kumaran, 2002).

RosettaNet has been widely recognized as a B2B process standard in addition to B2B data standards (Lewis, 2000), but it focuses exclusively on the public business processes. Built upon the OSI 7 layer standard, all RosettaNet standards are at the application layer, and thus their extensibility is limited. By comparing different types of commercial business applications, Chen (2003) suggested that "using *standards* to facilitate the communications between two different systems is the most promising approach to facilitating e-business integration." Popular standard-related technologies for e-business systems include HTTP, XML, SOAP, WSDL, UDDI and PKI (Sheldon, Jerath, & Pilskalns, 2002). Electronic Data Interchange (EDI) is a set of standards for controlling the transfer of business documents, such as purchase orders and invoices, between computers. But it is too costly, complex and rigid for small and medium enterprises (SMEs) to take advantage of it (Stefansson, 2002).

It is reported that XML greatly impacts business applications, such as integrating ERP packages, communications, database systems, standards, as well as security (David, Shi, & Cheng, 2002). Li et al. (2003) proposed an "e-union" model using XML to improve the interoperability. The model first converts database tables into XML documents, then uses them as a standard data-exchange format. It is difficult, however, to support customized XML standards for specific industrial sectors.

Online B2B transactions involve four important issues: data confidentiality, authentication, non-repudiation and integrity (Engel, 2001). Technology-wise, PKI can be used to meet these requirements. PKI has potential for supporting multiple applications. To achieve this, this chapter introduces the directory service technique.

For an efficient integration of business applications, organization should define the objectives (i.e., roles) clearly, and ensure the decentralization of decisions according to responsibilities (i.e., assigning roles to individuals properly) (Doumeingts, Ducq & Kleinhans, 2000). A directory service can be used for storing management information, such as rules and company policies. Then, role-based access control (RBAC) can be enabled to facilitate the management of access control lists (ACLs) with more flexibility and reduced workload of IT staff (Sandhu, Coyne, Feinstein, & Youman, 1996; Songwan, Gail, & Joon, 2002).

Although a few ubiquitous B2B architectures exist, there is rarely a common infrastructure for running business applications (Lewis, 2000). Software components such as "glue" or agent and enterprise application integration (EAI) are commonly used nowadays to enhance those applications with information exchange (www. B2Bexchange.com). The need for extra data manipulation not only reveals security threats, but also increases the error rate.

With the increasing adoption of B2B applications, more and more pairs of user IDs and passwords need to be managed. Much time and effort have to be devoted to user identification and authorization, which is not value-added at all. It is imperative in the first place to minimize the number of logins for end-users. The prerequisite for this is to find a reliable and unified mechanism for end-users to identify and authenticate themselves.

X.500 was defined as a completed directory service to operate over an ISO/OSI network (CCITT, 1988). However, X.500 does not support TCP/IP, and its specification is too complex for commercial applications. A simplified version of access-protocol for X.500 was introduced in 1997 and approved by the Internet Engineering Task Force (IETF) as a lightweight directory access protocol (LDAP) (UoM, 2002). Jamhour (2001) pointed out that the LDAP is a lighter version of X.500, which is a bit misleading.

Interoperability among directories requires common object schemas and understandable communication protocols. LDAP is the well-known directory accessing protocol and is widely supported by commercial software vendors; directory service markup language (DSML) is an emerging, effective high-level protocol to access directories (Songwan et al., 2002; OASIS, 2002).

In a directory service-enabled distributed data-provisioning environment, end-users may have problems with where to find the data (location) and how to get the data (query mechanisms). Marquina, Ramos, and Taddei (1998) developed a metadata advertising protocol to deal with these problems. Similar to XML, their proposed mechanism establishes user data descriptions to avoid predefining strict data regulations. However, this is impossible nowadays, in a heterogeneous network environment. Since XML has emerged to become a de facto standard for data exchange over the Internet, the adoption of XML would hopefully help keep the system more open.

Both LDAP and XML have been used as the communication protocols for directory services. Kuz (2002) uses LDAP as the communication protocol for GIDS. Some people proposed to use SSL and PKI as a means to ensure the confidentiality for transmitting data. LDAPS (www.ldaps. net) is a refined version of LDAP that caters to security needs. Hash algorithm is also used to safeguard directory service nodes' credentials (Berger, 1998).

Strategy for Solution

Current work on directory service mostly focuses on intra-organizational applications, but rarely on B2B integration. While European researchers have contributed substantially to data exchange, security and enterprise modeling, a very limited number of papers deal with the integration of directory services with business applications. The application of directory services to the identification, authentication and authorization infrastructures is yet to come.

This chapter proposes a directory service-enabled infrastructure model for B2B applications (referred to as IAAIBB model) for centralizing the identification, authentication and authorization infrastructures. It aims to provide a smooth interoperability among business partners. The key technique is incorporating directory services into business applications. The directory service acts as the core repository of the infrastructure model to support all functions related to identification, authentication and authorization. In addition, it should be platform independent, open, extensible and secure. The IAAIBB model leverages on the advantages of XML, directory services, the PKI cryptography and RBAC.

OVERVIEW OF IAAIBB MODEL

The IAAIBB model employs the directory service as its supporting infrastructure. The working principle of the IAAIBB model is illustrated in Figure 1. The model reduces end-users' login times to one for all applications. It also simplifies system connections and lessens the number of high-level application servers. With reference to the layered network model, the interactions within the IAAIBB model are demonstrated in Figure 2.

This model consists of two major components: the directory service, and the IAA layer, which talks to the directory service. The directory service holds user information and critical business rules, and deals with data fusion. Adapted from conventional network reference models, the IAA layer seeded in every computer is an executant that guarantees the business rules be followed strictly. The IAA layer may query a business partner's directory services for authenticating a remote user.

This model provides a single management interface for a user to sign on. Managers do not

Figure1. The IAAIBB model in view of connectivity

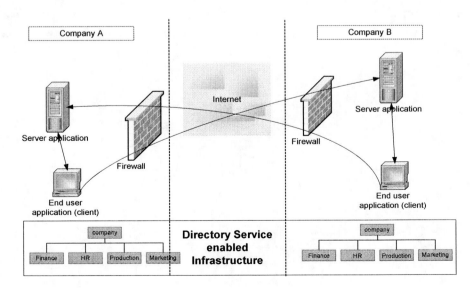

Figure 2. The IAAIBB model

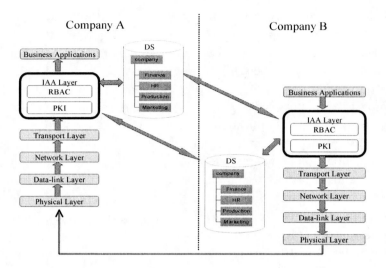

have to bother IT staff to enable access in ubiquitous systems, nor is it necessary for end-users to remember many ID and password pairs. Data encryption and advanced user authentication mechanics are built in the model, thus contributing to the robustness of B2B application systems.

Directory Service

A directory service is the core technology that supports IAA layer and provides essential security information. It is not an internal component of the IAA layer, but a relatively standalone computer system. Separation of these two parts helps make the system neat and flexible, as different companies may use different directory services.

Mapping Organizational Structure In Computer

Assume a company is named "manufacturer_company." For illustrative simplicity, only the production and sales departments are expanded. A typical organizational chart is shown in Figure 3.

This organizational structure is then mapped into a computerized directory service, as shown in Figure 4, where the Novell Netware NDS

Figure 3. Organizational chart of "manufacturer_company"

Figure 4. Company directory structure in the computer system

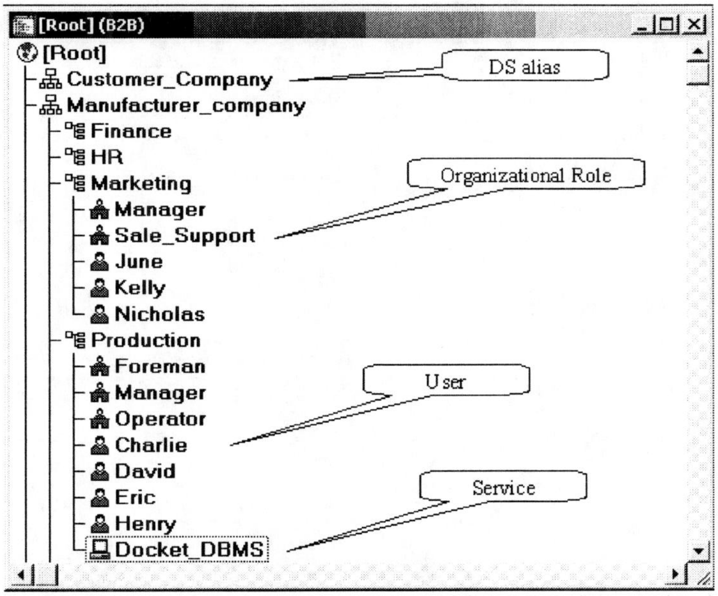

console is used for demonstration. There are four important objects, namely, the user, organizational role, service and directory service alias.

The user object represents a computer user, which stores user information, both administrational and organizational. A user's key attributes are listed in Table 1. The organizational role object represents a collection of job functions, such as a production manager or sales support personnel. Its attributes are shown in Table 2. The service object represents a particular business application, which can be considered as a software service, such as a database management system (DBMS).

Its attributes are listed in Table 3. The directory service alias object holds information about other directory services, which may be a directory service of a business partner or of another department. The directory service alias holds the network information about the remote directory services, as well. Its attributes are shown in Table 4.

IAA Layer

The directory service-enabled IAA infrastructure is essentially an improved network application reference model that employs a new layer called

Table 1. Attributes of a user object

Key administrational attributes	Key organizational attributes
Common name (user ID)	Workforce ID
Login disabled (Boolean)	Manager workforce ID
User's Public Key	Role
Trustees (administrators)	Organizational Unit (department)
Object hash code (for fast indexing and searching)	

Table 2. Attributes of an organizational role object

Key administrational attributes	Key organizational attributes
Role ID	Role name (position equivalent)
Role description	Description of the role
Role disabled (Boolean)	Restrict whether the role is enabled
Object hash code	For fast indexing and searching

Table 3. Attributes of a service object

Key administrational attributes	Key organizational attributes
Service ID	Service name (e.g., production daily docket system, customer order tracking system)
Service description	The description of the service
Service disabled (Boolean)	Restrict whether the service is enabled
Service public key	Public key for the service
Access rules (in Well-Formed-Formula (WFF) format)	Indicate which organizational role is eligible for data-access

Table 4. Attributes of a directory service alias object

Key administrational attributes	Key organizational attributes
DS alias Name	Company name
DS server's IP address	Businesses category
DSML V2.0 support (Boolean)	Indicate whether it supports version 2

Table 5. Basic APIs for directory service operations

Function	Explanation
Boolean authRequest(ID);	False: object does not exist, authentication fail True: object exists, authentication succeed
String retrievePublicKey(ID);	ID could be serviceID or a userID, return null means that object does have a public key stored in directory service
Role retrieveRole(userID);	Query directory service to get user object's role property.
Boolean ModifyRequest (modification);	All these functions are meant for administration purpose, and they have been explained in detail in OASIS (2002).
Object searchRequest(search criteria);	
Boolean addRequest(newobject, context);	
Boolean delRequest(objectID, context);	
Boolean modifyDNRequest(old DN, new DN);	

IAA as the core functional component, standing on top of the transport layer and below the business application layer, as illustrated in Figure 2. Such a dedicated layer structure facilitates the standardization of B2B applications running in the IAA infrastructure. Since the IAA layer is separated from business applications and functions below the application layer, interoperability is dramatically enhanced. Therefore, system developers gain much flexibility in developing business application logics without paying much attention to IAA matters.

System Description

The IAA model is a synthesized software component by integrating directory service access, RBAC, PKI and DSML, as shown in Figure 5. The input to the IAA layer is an IAA header and user data, as given in Table 6. The IAA header consists of the encryption algorithm the user data is supposed to apply, for example, 64-bit encryption or 128-bit encryption. The user data part comprises a sender's fully qualified distinguished name (FQDN) and the destination's FQDN, along with application data. The last two are encrypted by the sender's private key. The output is a decrypted message containing the sender's FQDN and user data, as given in Table 7. This information is then sent to the upper application layer for processing.

Components of the IAA Layer

The IAA layer comprises three components: public key-based cryptography, RBAC and DSML v2.0. The public key cryptography is used to decrypt incoming messages from the lower layer (i.e., the network layer) or to encrypt outgoing messages from the higher layer (i.e., the applica-

Figure 5. System diagram of the IAA layer

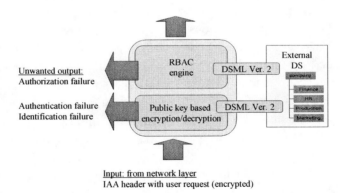

Table 6. The content of an input data gram

IAA header: encryption method	Sender's FQDN	Destination's FQDN (encrypted)	User data (encrypted)

Table 7. The content of an output data gram

Sender's FQDN	User data

Figure 6. The data flow of an IAA layer

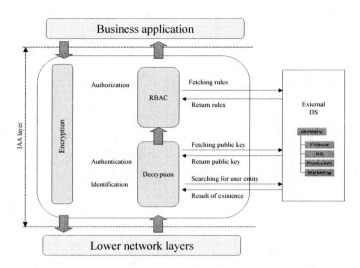

tion layer). The private keys of users or business entities are kept securely with themselves, either in their local PCs or a security device. All public keys are stored in the directory service, available for others to retrieve.

The RBAC component acts as an inference engine. After receiving a decrypted message, the RBAC component queries the directory service for the user's role and all rules pertaining to that role. The protocol used is DSML. First-order logics are used to infer whether a user's request should be granted. Depending on the results, the user's request may be denied or forwarded to the application layer. As an inference engine, the RBAC component calls other components' APIs.

The DSML component performs as a connector to the directory service. The LDAP can perform the same function, as well. The reason for not choosing LDAP is that the LDAP requires additional software components (i.e., LDAP clients) on both the user and the server sides. In particular, as business software is adopting XML as a standard for data exchange, the DSML, a type of XML, suggests itself as a superior solution. As a result, the same XML parser engine can be shared by the DSML component.

B2B INTERACTIONS WITHIN AND BETWEEN COMPANIES

Application Interactions within a Company

B2B applications within a company constitute two types of interactions: (1) A user sends his request to the server; and, in turn, (2) The server responds to the user's request and sends the result back to the user. Figure 7 shows the data flow from a user's computer to the server. Basically, the data is generated from the user computer's application layer, then passed to the IAA layer, encrypted and passed down to the network layer, and further forwarded to the remote server. Afterwards, the server receives the data, parses the message through its lower-network layers, decrypts the data in the IAA layer, judges accessibility and then passes it on to the server application if it is successful. The general flow chart of the server's response is illustrated in Figure 8.

Setting Rules in the Directory Service

Managers can use a single interface to assign or remove the accessibility of the subordinates, as all

Figure 7. System flow chart of a user sending request to the server

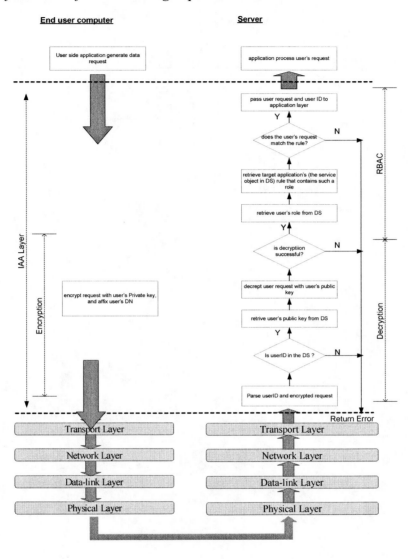

the rules are centralized in the directory service under either the service object or the user object. The single-interface mode performs as a directory service configuration utility with enhanced functionality on rule configuration. The interaction between the directory service and a manager is enacted at the IAA layer using the directory service's own key pairs and the manager's key pair. Through the single interface, managers can access the directory service, and retrieve and

modify the rule set of a specific object, be it a user or service.

The IAA layer uses a role-based mechanic (i.e., RBAC) to safeguard an end-user's accessibility to server applications. This enables managers and administrators to assign a user's duty effectively. The RBAC component imposes certain constraints to the assignment of duties to individual employees. Specification of such

Figure 8. System flow chart of the server responding to the user

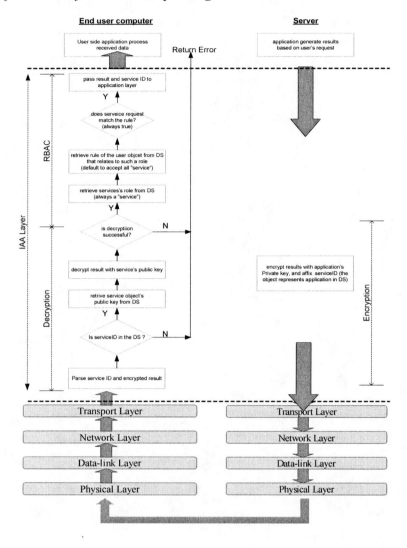

constraints forces managers away from "thinking and acting personally."

Minimizing the Times of End-Users' Logins

With the IAA infrastructure, users need not to key in any ID and password to access other applications. Rather, this is handled by making use of the user's private keys autonomously to process any user request. A user needs to type an ID and password only once, at the first time of accessing his or her local PC. Every private key, stored either in a computer's hard disk or security device, is unlocked upon a user's login, and is locked again when the user logs out.

Application Interactions Between Two Companies

One of the difficulties of B2B applications is the management of trust relationships and data fusion (meaning who can access data and to what extent). The IAAIBB model alleviates these problems without compromising security. Any B2B application implies such a scenario that all participants have a priori agreement about certain access rights to individual data. Organizational trust is suitable to such applications (Pavlou, 2002).

Most directory service products on the market support DSML v2.0. In practice, it seldom happens that two companies' B2B systems are not compatible when they choose different directory service software. The RBAC engine of the IAA infrastructure can always query about the other company's directory service for remote user information.

A directory service alias object is added into the directory service for name resolution of remote directory services. This is very necessary, otherwise a local machine may not know where to retrieve a remote user's information. In this way, the process flow of IAA within each company remains intact. A remote user encrypts his request with his or her private key, affixes with his or her FQDN, then sends the combined message to the business partner's application server (considered as local).

In a local application server, whenever the decryption component finds a remote user, it starts to check its local directory service for the address of that remote directory service. Then it queries the corresponding remote business partner's directory service for this user's existence and possible public key. This is similar to the TCP/IP DNS service process. If any error occurs at this stage, then identification and authentication fail. Upon success of a decryption by the remote user's FQDN, the decrypted service request is passed on to the RBAC engine. The RBAC engine queries the remote directory service again for that user's

organizational role predefined in his directory service. The RBAC engine further queries the local directory service (as the requested service—i.e., server application—is in the local directory service) and searches for all rules pertaining to the requested action of this particular user. If the remote user's role satisfies the rules (handled by the first-order logic algorithm), the request is handed over to the server application. If this procedure fails, it leads to service denial. Figure 9 shows the data flow using two companies' directory services for a cross-organizational transaction.

Once a request is granted and the server responds, a server application generates the result, encrypts it using its own private key, affixes it with the server's FQDN and sends it back to the remote user's machine (achieved by lower-network supporting layers).

When the remote user's PC receives the message, it processes the parsed source FQDN by querying its own local directory service for the network address of the partner's directory service associated with the server application. After getting the network address, the PC queries the partner's directory service for existence of the said FQDN and fetches the public key pertaining to that FQDN. Afterwards, decryption takes place in light of the retrieved public key. Any failure of this process leads to the failure of identification and authentication. If it succeeds, the decrypted message with the user's FQDN is passed to the RBAC engine of the user's PC. After a successful inference by RBAC, the message and the server's FQDN are further forwarded to the end-user's application layer for processing.

IMPLEMENTATION OF IAAIBB MODEL

Injecting IAA Layer

There is no change to lower supporting layers. The TCP/IP protocol is still valid. The IAA layer

Figure 9. Interactions between the IAA layer and an external directory service

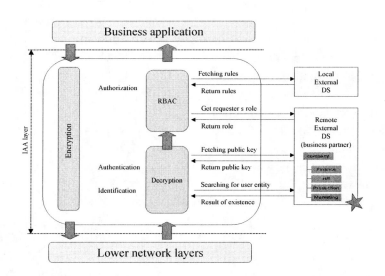

calls APIs of TCP/IP, and also receives incoming data streams from the TCP/IP layer. As for a new business application, it needs to be designed to call APIs that the IAA layer can provide, other than calling TCP/IP APIs directly. With regard to legacy systems, three approaches are used to inject the IAA layer: (1) Rewrite the whole legacy system to talk to the IAA layer for data transmission. This is a neat approach but incurs much cost; (2) Write glue software to translate data between the IAA layer and a legacy system, meanwhile keeping the existing communication channel for a graceful migration; and (3) Inject wrappers to incorporate the communication ability inside the legacy system. But this costs the most, as existing low-level network components cannot be reused.

Setting Up a Directory Service

Selecting a Directory Service

According to industry analysts, such as Michael Hoch, Aberdeen Group senior analyst of Internet Infrastructure, many companies think that selecting a directory service has to be a secondary choice. But with the proposed IAAIBB model, the selection of a directory service is of the first priority. As most directory services in the market support DSML v2.0, technical compatibility is not an issue.

The Gartner Group (www.gartner.com), a market research firm, found out that large companies often maintain 100 or more directories attached to their networks, many of which possess duplicate information. The full service directory (FSD) model might be turned to for choosing a directory service. Alternatively, a company can choose a directory service according to the company's specific needs, provided that the company can understand the directory's capabilities well. For example, a human resource-oriented company may use the directory service provided by PeopleSoft, whereas a new startup company may choose Microsoft Active Directory for fast implementation and cost savings. A large company may choose to use Novell e-directory for fast response and reliable replications over different regions. A company largely depending on groupware "Lotus Notes" may choose the Lotus Notes' directory component as its core directory service. Moreover, a company may purchase a multipurpose directory service, which can facilitate the integrations of existing internal directory services.

Constructing Rules

The rules under the service object in a directory service highly depend on particular B2B applications. In general, rules for the DBMS can be set using TABLE, FORM, VIEW and SQL actions, including ADD, DELETE and UPDATE operations. Rules for document-based databases like Lotus Notes may be constructed based on each individual document database with internal FORM, VIEW and ACTION operations. All in all, the more the rules are defined, the more controllability the IAAIBB model provides.

EVALUATION OF THE IAAIBB MODEL

Leveraging Productivity

End-User Single Sign-On

For end-users, the IAAIBB model can save time, as users do not have to remember diverse user IDs and passwords. All they need to remember is a single password to unlock the access to their private key the first time they access the computer. An end-user no longer needs to type in a password for each individual B2B application. User intervention by identification is released for further data transaction. The application always picks up the user's private key to encrypt data autonomously.

With the IAAIBB model, the private key is maintained as a digital data stream stored in elec-

tronic media, and thus is always available. And the password to unlock the private key need not be changed frequently, unless both the private key and the unlock password are stolen. An end-user is totally free from memorizing and keeping track of various passwords.

Easy Control Configuration for Managers

The IAAIBB model helps corporate systems to function as an organizational role instead of individual employee. For example, even if the purchasing manager is changed to another person, as long as the new person's role is set as a "purchasing_manager," all configurations need not to be changed and the new manager is still able to access a partner's docket data immediately.

The IAAIBB model provides a single interface for managers to configure access rules for different organizational roles. This is because all the access rules are consolidated inside a unified directory service. The single configuration interface is probably a directory service configuration utility with enriched functionality on rule construction and assignment.

A company's system can easily integrate or extend its data access into another company's systems as long as the new partner has adopted the same IAA layer and provided directory services for public access. The IAAIBB model also helps managers improve the productivity of a new employee on the first day. A manager can use the single interface to add access rules for the new employee if he or she is to hold a new organizational role. As for an existing role, everything becomes much simpler. The manager only needs to assign it to the new employee and, in turn, this new employee immediately has access to all necessary network services because they already have been set up. This also applies to the case of job relocation.

Enhancing Security

Local Processing of Passwords

It is safe to use a password to unlock a local private key, because the unlocking procedure is done locally. An end-user uses the password to unlock his or her private key the first time he or she accesses the computer. Because the unlocking process is done within the local computer, there is no means for a network hacker to capture the password over the network wire. The password can only be revealed within the workplace. Hence, the end-user has more confidence in securing a password.

Secured Transactions

To enhance data confidentiality, the IAAIBB model encrypts data using advanced PKI cryptography techniques for every transaction. It is very difficult to crack such an encryption algorithm, because there are a large number of possible combinations of key pairs, which requires a very sophisticated algorithm for decoding. And the cost of cracking such a public key-based cryptography is much higher than the benefits of getting the encrypted information. In addition, superior executives can set strict rules in the directory service that the RBAC engine must refer to. Once a user is demoted from an eligible role, that user is no longer able to access data pertaining to his or her previous role.

Authentication in IAAIBB is more advanced than that using plain text passwords. A plain text password only needs a simple comparison with a stored password at the server side. But with the IAAIBB model, a user's private key is always kept locally, not in the server. Hence, as long as the user keeps his or her private key properly, other people have no way to fraud the system by impersonating the legal user. Hackers also have no chance to get the private key even if they have managed to access the server via lower-level security black holes. Furthermore, a person's directory service object (i.e., the user object) can be removed immediately after he resigns. Therefore, even though the user keeps his or her private key, the user's request will never pass the authentication phase at the IAA layer, as there is no item in the directory service to match with the user's FQDN. Hence, the application layer will never receive a request from the ex-employee.

The IAAIBB model also enhances data integrity. The data going through the network wire is encrypted. Because the receiving computer is not able to decrypt the data using the sender's public key, any change to the encrypted data stream will lead to decryption failure at the receiver's computer, and thereby the request will be rejected.

Table 8. Data source for cost calculation

Data item	Description	Resource
1	IT admin staff's salary	"Singapore salary guide 2003" www.businesstrends.com.sg
2	Resignation rate and recruitment rate	"Statistics on Productivity" Standards, Productivity and Innovation Board of Singapore www.spring.gov.sg/portal/stats/productivity/productivity.html
3	Data-entry time for handling resignation	"I-Login – one Net for Novell Employees" Linda Kennard. 2002. Novell Connection, Feb, 10-12 www.novell.com/connectionmagazine/2002/02/ilogin22.pdf

Cost Savings

The calculation below is based on a reasonable assumption of a SG$2,000 average salary in Singapore in year 2003 in a medium-sized company (around 500 employees). Assume that an employee has to key in a user ID and password four times a day on average. Sources of data used in cost calculation are summarized in Table 8.

Cost Savings from Reduction of End-users' Keying in User IDs and Passwords

Considering such scenarios as a password that a user has already memorized or one that is rarely used but the user has written it down somewhere, the input of a user ID and a password takes 40 seconds on average. The non-value added cost for all users to key in passwords per year is thus given as:

(Number of employees)*(Annual Salary)*(hours used in keying in password)/(working hours a year) = 500*(SG$2,000/month*13 months)*(4*40/3600*250 days)/(250 days*8 Hours/day) = SG$72,222.

If using the IAAIBB model, the cost figure is given as:

500*(SG$2,000/month*13 months)*(10/3600*250 days)/(250 days*8 Hours/day) = SG$4,514.

The rate of cost savings is:

(72,222-4514)/72,222 = 92.5%.

In the above cost analysis, the indirect cost has not been counted. The indirect cost may include password recovery cost, password re-issuing cost, as well as manpower and materials related to recording and tracking passwords.

Cost Savings from Service Provisioning and De-Provisioning

Service provisioning means the process for providing a new employee with access to all necessary network resources. Accuracy and time are the measure for the effectiveness of service provisioning. In a dispersed network application environment, line managers have to talk to IT staff to grant access to the new employee's ID in each system. If using the IAAIBB model, once the new user ID is activated associated with an existing organizational role, the new user immediately possesses all access to the systems available to that particular role.

Service de-provisioning means that when a person leaves a company, all network services and data services assigned to that user should be terminated immediately. But it is hard to achieve this in today's dispersed network application environments. It takes much time, because managers and IT staff have to scan through all the systems. If that person is a network administrator, the IT department may have a headache to change all passwords, because the ex-administrator probably knows all users' passwords. With the IAAIBB model, this security threat is eliminated. Once a user leaves the company, that user's name will be deleted from the directory service immediately. Even if the ex-employee tries to access a system application using the private key that he or she still keeps, the IAA layer will never let the ex-employee's request pass through.

The cost savings using the IAAIBB model can also be projected. The total cost before adopting the IAAIBB model is given as:

(number of workforce)*((resignation rate)+(recruitment rate)+(intra firm relocation rate))*(hours for data entry for every case)*(hour pay for IT admin staff) = 500*(2.2% + 2.6% + 0%) *1.13 hrs*(SG$4,000*13/(250*8)) = SG$705.

With the IAAIBB model, the deletion of a user object in the directory service costs the maximum of 1 minute. The cost is to be:

500*(2.2% + 2.6% + 0%)*(1 minute/60 minutes/ hour)*(SG$4,000*13/(250*8)) = SG$10.4.

Therefore, the rate of cost-saving is: (705-10.4)/705 = 98.5% .

Extended Network Access

An Open Infrastructure

As long as the participating business partners have adopted the IAA layer in their networks and set up their own directory services, they can be allowed to access another company's network services (i.e., server applications) with only a few policy settings. No extra client software is needed. External users can use the existing internal client software without any modification. Whether the other party can access data is controlled by the local directory service. This saves time and effort for developing extra client software for external users, and thus helps to standardize business processes. In this sense, the IAAIBB model breaks down the barriers between the Intranet, Extranet and Internet in a B2B commerce environment.

Integrating Heterogeneous Systems

Different companies use different internal application systems. And even their internal connection topologies are different. To integrate them, a common acceptable infrastructure performing as a standard to speak both technological and managerial languages would be a best solution. The IAAIBB model fits into this niche. It is based on a hierarchical directory structure that executives are familiar with. It uses sound technologies like RBAC and PKI cryptography that professionals in the computer networks and system development areas understand well. The difficulties in coordinating system developers and corporate executives are thus alleviated. This facilitates the achievement of successful system integration.

SUMMARY

This chapter introduces the idea of integrating the directory service to business applications. An infrastructure model, called IAAIBB, is proposed. The significant contribution of the IAAIBB model is the achievement of *single sign-on* for end-users. It also provides an open infrastructure for business applications in terms of identification, authentication and authorization. With the support of the IAAIBB model, each end-user no longer needs to remember and keep track of a user ID and password for every application, but simply provides a single password to unlock his or her private key the first time the user accesses the computer. After that, all applications will make use of the unlocked private key autonomously. Moreover, the IAAIBB model separates the IAA security module from the application layer by taking advantage of advanced computer technologies. It makes it easier to leverage on system interoperability, while keeping existing business logics valid and intact. This merit lends the IAAIBB model to the potential of being extended as an open-infrastructure standard for B2B applications.

REFERENCES

Berger, A. (1998). Privacy protection for public directory services. *Computer Networks and ISDN Systems, 30*, 1521-1529.

Bussler, C. (2002, June 26-28). B2B integration technology architecture. *IEEE Proceedings of the 4th IEEE International Workshop on Advanced Issues of E-Commerce and Web-Based Information Systems*, Newport Beach, CA.

CCITT. (1988). *Recommendation X.500: The directory—Overview of concepts, models and service*. Place des Nations: International Telecommunications Union.

Chen, M. (2003). Factors affecting the adoption and diffusion of XML and Web services standards for e-business systems. *International Journal of Human-Computer Studies, 58*(3), 259-279.

David, C.Y., Shi, M.H., & Cheng, Y.K. (2002). The impact and implementation of XML on business-to-business commerce. *Computer Standards & Interfaces, 24*, 347-362.

Doumeingts, G.Y., Ducq, B.V., & Kleinhans, S. (2000). Production management and enterprise modeling. *Computers in Industry, 42*, 245-263.

Engel, F. (2001). Why e-business will be good for business. *Card Technology Today*, July/August.

Hanson, J.E., Nandi, P., & Kumaran, S. (2002, September 17-20). Conversation support for business process integration. *Proceedings of the 6th IEEE International Enterprise Distributed Object Computing Conference*, Lausanne, Switzerland.

Jamhour, E. (2001, November 7-9). Distributed security management using LDAP directories. Computer Science Society, *Proceedings of XXI International Conference of the Chilean Computer Science Society*, Santiago & Punta Arenas, Chile.

Konstantopoulos, M., Spyrou, I., & Darzentas, J. (2001). The need for academic middleware to support advanced learning services. *Computer Networks, 37*, 773-781.

Kuz, I. (2002). The globe infrastructure directory service. *Computer Communications, 25*, 835-845.

Lewis, M. (2000). Supply chain optimization: An overview of RosettaNet e-business processes. *eAI Journal, 2*(6), 12-18.

Li, H., Cao, J., Castro-Lacouture, D., & Skibniewski, M. (2003). A framework for developing a unified B2B e-trading construction marketplace. *Journal of Automation in Construction, 12*(2), 201-211.

Marquina, M., Ramos, P., & Taddei, A. (1998). A taxonomically distributed data retrieval model. *Computer Physics Communications, 110*(1-3), 198-205.

OASIS. (2002). *Directory Services Markup Language (DSML)*. Organization for the Advancement of Structured Information Standards. Retrieved 2005 from www.oasis-open.org/cover/dsml.html

Olsen, G. (2000). An overview of B2B integration. *eAI journal*, May, 28-36.

Pavlou, P.A. (2002). Institution-based trust in inter-organizational exchange relationships: The role of online B2B marketplaces on trust formation. *Journal of Strategic Information Systems, 11*(3-4), 215-243.

Sandhu, R., Coyne, E.J., Feinstein, H.L., & Youman, C.E. (1996). Role based access control models. *IEEE Computer, 29*(2), 38-47.

Sheldon, F.T., Jerath, K., & Pilskalns, O. (2002, December 11-13). Case study: B2B e-commerce system specification and implementation employing use-4-case diagrams, digital signatures and XML. *Proceedings of IEEE the 4th International Symposium on Multimedia Software Engineering*, Newport Beach, CA.

Songwan, S., Gail, J.A., & Joon, S.P. (2002, August 26-29). An application of Directory Service Markup Language (DSML) for Role-based Access Control (RBAC). *Proceedings of IEEE the 26th Annual International Computer Software and Applications Conference*, Oxford, UK.

Stefansson, C. (2002). Business-to-business data sharing: A source for integration of supply chains.

International Journal Production Economics, 75, 135-146.

Tellefsen, T. (2002). Commitment in business-to-business relationships: The role of organizational and personal needs. *Industrial Marketing Management, 31*(8), 645-652.

University of Michigan. (2002). *Lightweight directory access protocol*. Retrieved 2005 from www.umich.edu/~dirsvcs/ldap/ldap.html

Wilson, S., & Abel, I. (2002). So you want to get involved in e-commerce. *Industrial Marketing Management, 31*(2), 85-94.

Chapter 4.48
Risk Factors to Retrieve Anomaly Intrusion Information and Profile User Behavior

Yun Wang
Yale University and Yale-New Haven Health System and Qualidigm, USA

Lee Seidman
Qualidigm, USA

ABSTRACT

The use of network traffic audit data for retrieving anomaly intrusion information and profiling user behavior has been studied previously, but the risk factors associated with attacks remain unclear. This study aimed to identify a set of robust risk factors via the bootstrap resampling and logistic regression modeling methods based on the KDD-cup 1999 data. Of the 46 examined variables, 16 were identified as robust risk factors, and the classification showed similar performances in sensitivity, specificity, and correctly classified rate in comparison with the KDD-cup 1999 winning results that were based on a rule-based decision tree algorithm with all variables. The study emphasizes that the bootstrap simulation and logistic regression modeling techniques offer a novel approach to understanding and identifying risk factors for better information protection on network security.

INTRODUCTION

Statistically based anomaly intrusion detection systems analyze audit trail data to detect anomaly intrusion and profiling use behavior. Although the idea behind intrusion detection is simple (i.e., using normal patterns of legitimate user behavior to identify and distinguish the behavior of an anomalous user) (Anderson, 1972, 1980; Denning, 1987; Helman & Liepins, 1993; Stallings, 2003), abnormal behavior detection is a difficult task to implement because of unpredictable attacks. The ideal intrusion detection system has four goals: (1) to detect a wide variety of intrusions; (2) to detect intrusions in a timely fashion; (3) to present the analysis in a simple format; and (4) to be accurate (Bishop, 2003). Over the past two decades, statistical methods have been used for developing various intrusion detection systems, and achieving these goals has been attempted. Some previously studied methods include, for example, adaptive detection model (Teng, Chen, & Lu, 1990), principal component analysis (Shyu, Chen, Sarinnapakorn, & Chang, 2003), cluster and multivariate analysis (Taylor & Alves-Foss, 2001; Vaccaro & Liepins, 1989), Hidden Markov Model (Cho & Park, 2003; Gao, Ma, & Yang, 2002), data mining (Anderson, Frivold, & Valdes, 1995; Qu, Vetter, & Jou, 1997; Lee, Stolfo, & Mok, 1999), Bayesian analysis (Barbard, Wu, & Jajodia, 2001), and frequency and simple significance tests (Masum, Ye, Chen, & Noh, 2000; Qin & Hwang, 2004; Ye, Emran, Li, & Chen, 2001; Zhou & Lang, 2003). However, most previous studies have been focused mainly on the first two goals and have been conducted based on the use of all possible variables as independent variables to fit a model. Mukkamala et al. (2003) briefly addressed the data reduction issue, but the knowledge about the degree of significance of an individual variable associated with an attack still remains unclear, and accuracy of such association has not been addressed. A statistical model with a large number of independent variables may not guarantee a high ability of predicting power, and unnecessary variables could cause biases and could lead the model either to overestimate or to underestimate the predicted values. To address these gaps in knowledge, this study, using the bootstrap resample method (Efron & Tibshirani, 1994) and multiple stepwise logistic regression modeling technique (Hosmer & Lemeshow, 2000) sought to identify a small set of risk factors that are robust, statistically significant, and stable to use in detecting anomaly intrusion and profiling user behavior.

METHODS

Data Source

The study sample was drawn from the Third International Knowledge Discovery and Data Mining Tools Competition 1999 data (KDD-cup, 1999),

which was created, based on the 1998 Defense Advanced Research Projects Agency (DARPA) Intrusion Detection Evaluation off-line database developed by the Lincoln Laboratory at Massachusetts Institute of Technology (Cunningham et al. 1999). The full KDD-cup data, which included seven weeks of TCP dump network traffic as training data that were processed into about five million connection records, two weeks of testing data, and 34 attack types, were generated on a network that simulated 1,000 Unix hosts and 100 users (Lippmann & Cunningham 2000). The test data do not have the same probability distribution as the training data and include additional specific attack types that were not in the training data. The data unit is a connection that consists of about 100 bytes of information and represents a sequence of TCP packets starting and ending at a fixed time window, between which data flow to and from a source IP address to a destination IP address under predefined protocols. Each connection record is identified as either normal or as a specific attack type. This study used 10% of the training data as a derivation dataset and the full test data as a validation dataset to identify and examine the risk factors.

Outcome and Independent Variables

The outcome of interest was a binary variable that labeled a connection as anomalous (yes/no), which could be any one of the included 38 attack types (24 in the derivation sample and an additional 14 new types in the validation sample). The independent variables included 41 initial variables or features (Stolfo, 2000) across four groups: (1) basic features of individual TCP/IP connections; (2) content features within a connection suggested by domain knowledge; (3) traffic features computed using a two-second time window; and (4) destination features. The type of protocol was categorized into three dummy variables: ICMP (yes/no), TCP (yes/no), and UDP (yes/no); normal or error status of the connection was divided into four dummy variables: REJ (yes/no), S0 (yes/no), SF (yes/no), and RSTO/RSTOS0/RSTR (yes/no) (Table 1); number of data bytes from source to destination and number of data bytes from destination to source were condensed by dividing the original values by 1,000 to match the scale for the other variables. The final number of potential independent variables, including the dummy variables, was 46.

Bootstrap Resample Method

A fundamental challenge in network anomaly intrusion detection area is to make probability-based inferences about a set of population characteristics (e.g., θ and σ that represent the true user behavior pattern based on the entire network traffic) based on a set of estimators (e.g., $\hat{\theta}$ and $\hat{\sigma}$ that represent an observed user behavior pattern) using a sample acquired from the population. The bootstrap is a computer-based nonparametric simulation statistical method that aims for making better statistical inferences and addresses the sample variability issue; it has been used widely in sta-

tistics and quantitative social science since 1979, when Bradley Efron published his first article on this method (Efron, 1979). Bootstrapping differs from the traditional parametric approach to inference in that it involves resampling the original data with replacement numerous times in order to generate an empirical estimate of the entire sampling distribution of an estimator rather than strong distributional assumptions and analytic formulas (Efron & Tibshirani, 1986; Mooney & Guval, 1993). This unique attribute allows researchers to make inferences in cases where such analytic solutions are unavailable and where such assumptions are untenable in anomaly detection. During bootstrapping, a new sample is generated by drawing n observations with replacement from the original data, and a new estimate is calculated. The resulting empirical distribution based on bootstrap analysis approximates the true user behavior pattern, which provides an approach to obtain an approximation of the estimate pattern in the absence of prior information about the true distribution of the estimate or the original data, a common situation of retrieving information in anomaly detection.

Table 1. Protocol and connection states

Name	Meaning
Protocol	
TCP	Transmission control protocol
UDP	User datagram protocol
ICMP	Internet control message protocol
Connection	
REJ	Connection attempt rejected
RST0	Connection established, originator aborted
RSTR	Connection established, responder aborted
S0	Connection attempt, no reply seen
S1	Connection established, not terminated
SF	Normal establishment and termination

Multiple Logistic Regression Model

A logistic regression model, also known as logit model, is used for data in which the outcome variable is binary or dichotomous and is coded as 1 for the presence of an event and 0 for the absence of an event, and independent variables are binary, continuous, or categorical predictors. Its use has grown significantly during the past decade and has become the standard method for regression analysis of dichotomous data in many fields, including business, finance, criminology, engineering, and life science. Suppose that y_i, which has a 1 or 0 value, is the outcome variable for individual subject i, and p_i, is the probability that $y_i = 1$, for k independent variables and $i = 1,...,$ n individuals. The logistic regression model can be represented as:

$$\log\left[\frac{p_i}{1-p_i}\right] = \beta_0 + \beta_1 x_{i1} + \beta_2 x_{i2} + \cdots + \beta_k x_{ik}$$

$$(1)$$

$$p_i = \frac{\exp(\beta_0 + \beta_1 x_{i1} + \beta_2 x_{i2} + \cdots + \beta_k x_{ik})}{1 + \exp(\beta_0 + \beta_1 x_{i1} + \beta_2 x_{i2} + \cdots + \beta_k x_{ik})}$$

$$(2)$$

The expression on the left-hand side of the equation is usually referred to as the logit or log-odds, and has the desired property that no matter what the values of β_k and x_{ik}, p_i always ranges from 0 to 1. The parameter, β_k, is a logit coefficient that indicates the log-odds increase by β_k for every unit increase in the independent variable, x_{ik}. Exponentiating β_k yields an odds ratio (OR) that measures how much more likely (or unlikely) it is for the outcome to be present among those with $x_{ik} = 1$ than among those with $x_{ik} = 0$ for a binary independent variable or for every unit increase in which the independent variable is continuous. For example, assuming the outcome is an attack (yes = 1, no = 0), if x_{i1} denotes whether a connection is UDP, then OR = 1.5 estimates that an attack is 1.5 times as likely to occur among UDP connections than among non-UDP connections.

Statistical Analysis

The study was accomplished sequentially in three steps. The first step involved conducting a bivariate analysis for checking the frequency and association with the outcome for each of the 46 variables. Continuous variables with uneven distribution were normalized through the standardized z score transformation (observed value minus the mean value divided by the standard deviation of the values). The second step fitted 3,000 stepwise logistic regression models with 3,000 iterations of the bootstrapping simulation based on the derivation sample. Variables with a frequency > 0.1% that demonstrated a significant association with the outcome variable in the first step were eligible for loading into the forward stepwise logistic regression modeling process. A significance threshold of 0.01 for adding variables and an insignificance threshold of 0.05 for removing variables were used to select potential risk factors detecting potential attacks from the independent variable set. These thresholds ensure that a variable to be added into the model will be statistically significantly associated with the outcome at least 99% of the time, and a variable to be removed from the model will not be statistically significantly associated with the outcome at least 95% of the time.

The third step aimed to select final risk factors from the bootstrapping results. During each iteration of bootstrapping in the second step, a new sample was generated by drawing n observations with replacement from the original sample, and a stepwise logistic model was fitted, yielding a set of variables that were statistically significantly associated with the outcome. Thus, 3,000 iterations of the simulation yielded 3,000 sets of p-values, indicating the significance level for each variable's association with the outcome. A variable that was statistically significant at least

85% of the time (i.e., it ensured that a variable will have at least 0.85 probability of truly holding a significant association with the outcome for a given network traffic population) and had a Wald Chi-square absolute value of 10 or higher (i.e., it ensured that the significance level will be at least 0.001) was considered a robust risk factor for predicting attacks. The area under the receiver operating characteristic (ROC) curve was calculated for each fitted model per iteration to evaluate its discriminating power (Hosmer & Lemeshow, 2000). All of the statistical analyses were conducted using STATA version 8.0 (STATA Corporation, College Station, TX) and SAS version 8.12 (SAS Institute Inc. Cary, NC).

Classification

Risk factors identified by the bootstrap and stepwise logistic regression procedures were used to construct a final logistic model based on the derivation sample. The model yielding a set of parameters corresponding to each risk factor was used to calculate a probability of being an anomalous connection for each connection in both derivation and validation samples. By determining an appropriate threshold of being anomalous, this probability provided a standard to classify and profile user behavior into different groups (e.g., normal or anomalous). Sensitivity, specificity, ROC area, and correctly classified rate were used to measure the discrimination power and stability of the risk factors in classification and profile. Sensitivity measures the probability that a statistical test is positive for a true positive statistic, and specificity measures the probability that a statistical test is negative for a true negative statistic. In this study, a sensitivity value of 0.95 means that 95% of the detected events have been recognized correctly as normal connections, and a specificity value of 0.95 means that 95% of the abnormal activities have not been classified as normal. The relationship between values of

sensitivity and specificity tends to be nonlinear and inversely proportional; increasing one value will systematically decrease the other. The ROC area, which measures the discriminating power of a model fitted by the predicted probability, ranges from 0.5 to 1.0. A model with no predictive power has a value of 0.5, and a perfect model has a value of 1.0. The correctly classified rate measures the proportion of connections that are normal and correctly identified as normal, and the proportion of connections that are anomalous and are correctly classified as anomalous. It is scaled as 1 when all the observed normal and abnormal connections are correctly classified, and 0 when there is 100% misclassification. The top KDD-cup 1999 winning entry (Elkan, 1999) that was conducted by using the C5 decision trees software was used as a benchmark to compare with classification results yielded by risk factors.

RESULTS

Characteristics of Data

The study sample included 805,050 network connections, within which the derivation sample had 494,021 (61.4%) connection records, and the validation sample had 311,029 (38.6%) records. Since each connection represented a two-second window, most records in both the derivation and the validation samples had exactly the same values across the 46 variables longitudinally. Most of these variables had very uneven distributions across the outcome, and 10 variables (19.6%), including connection from/to the same host/port, number of wrong fragments, number of urgent packets, number of hot indicators, number of failed login attempts, root shell is obtained, successfully root command attempted, number of shell prompts, number of outbound commands in an FTP session, and host login, were excluded from further stepwise modeling processes, because they had either zeros or very low frequencies or means. An additional five variables, including number of operations on access control files (ID = 16), rate of connections that have REJ errors (ID = 20), rate of the connection to the same service as the current connection that have SYN errors (ID = 24), rate of connections to the current host with RST errors (ID = 35), and rate of connections to the current host and specified service with RST errors (ID = 36), also were not eligible for stepwise regression analysis, because they had no statistically significant association with the outcome in the bivariate analysis (Table 2). The number of connections labeled *normal* was similar between the derivation and validation samples (19.7% vs. 19.5%). The abnormal connections were categorized into four major attack types: *probe* — surveillance and other probing; *DoS* — denial of service; *U2R* — unauthorized access to local super user (root) privileges; and *R2L* — unauthorized access from a remote machine of connections. All these attack types had unbalanced distributions: 79.2% of the records were *DoS*; 19.7% represented *normal*; and the remaining 1.1% of the records was split among *Probe*, *R2L*, and *U2R*. The validation sample showed a remarkable difference in the distribution of the attacks with the initial derivation set after including the new attack types. Although the order of the most frequent attack types remained the same as the validation sample, there were remarkable frequency differences between the two samples throughout all attack types. The largest difference was *R2L*, increasing from 0.2% (n = 1,126) in the derivation sample to 5.2% (n = 16,189) in the validation sample; the next was *U2L*, from 0.01% (n = 52) to 0.07% (n = 228). The distributions in *normal* and *probe* were similar between the two samples (19.7% vs. 19.5% and 0.8% vs. 1.3%, respectively). *DoS* was reduced approximately 5.3 absolute percent points in the validation sample. The overall connections were distributed as 19.6% for *normal*, 1.0% for *probe*, 77.2% for *DoS*, 0.03% labeled *R2L*, and 2.2% labeled *U2R* (Table 3).

Risk Factors for Anomaly Intrusion

With non-parametric bootstrapping, 3,000 multiple logistic regression models have been fitted, based on random sampling with replacement from the original derivation data. These models yielded a mean ROC area value of 0.999 (95%CI, 0.99-1.00) and a mean Chi-square value of 516,490. Using the frequency rate of 85% as a threshold, 16 variables that were statistically significantly associated with the outcome and had a Wald Chi-square absolute value of 10 or higher were identified as robust risk factors. These variables were used to fit the final model to obtain the corresponding parameters for calculating the risk score for each connection (Figure 1). Among these factors, the frequency rate of being a robust risk factor range was from 85.2% (rate of connections to different services) to 100.0% (TCP, HTTP, RST, guest login, connections to the same host as the current connection, connections having the same destination host, connections having the same destination host and using the same service, rate of connections to the current host having the same source port, and rate of connections to the same service coming from different hosts). Overall, these risk factors demonstrated great associations with the outcome. Table 4 illustrates the coefficient, odds ratio, and a standardized estimate of each factor yield by the final model. A factor with a standardized estimate less than 0 or an odds ratio less than 1 indicates that the factor had a negative association with the outcome, and a connection with this characteristic was unlikely to be an *anomaly*. Compared with Figure 1, which shows the likelihood of each risk factor being statistically significantly associated with the outcome, Table 4 shows the strength of each factor associated with the outcome. The areas under the ROC curve were 1.00 with an r-squared of 0.96 and a goodness-of-fit of 0.06 for the final model. Predictive ability ranged from 0.00 in the lowest deciles to 1.00 in the highest deciles, indicative that the model had good discrimination.

Table 2. Bivariate analysis based on the derivation sample

ID	Variables	Anomaly		Normal	
	Basic features of individual TCP connections				
1	Length (number of seconds) of the connection (mean, SD)	6.62	402.56	216.66	1359.21
	Type of protocol				
2	ICMP (yes/no [%, #])	71.16	282,314	1.32	1,288
3	TCP (yes/no [%, #])	28.55	113,252	78.96	76,813
4	UDP (yes/no [%, #])	0.30	1,177	19.71	19,177
5	Network service on the destination, HTTP (yes/no [%, #])	0.61	2,407	63.62	61,886
6	Number of data bytes from source to destination (per 1,000) (mean, SD)	3.48	1102.60	1.16	34.23
7	Number of data bytes from destination to source (per 1,000) (mean, SD)	0.25	31.80	3.38	37.58
	Normal or error status of the connection				
8	REJ (yes/no [%, #])	5.43	21,534	5.49	5,341
9	S0 (yes/no [%, #])	21.92	86,956	0.05	51
10	SF (yes/no [%, #])	72.27	286,731	94.28	91,709
11	RSTO or RSTOS0 or RSTR (yes/no [%, #])	0.35	1,395	0.10	98
	Content features within a connection suggested by domain knowledge				
12	Login successfully (yes/no [%,#])	0.83	3,298	71.9	69,939
13	Number of compromised conditions (mean, SD)	0.01	0.11	0.03	4.05
14	Number of root accesses (mean, SD)	0.00	0.11	0.06	4.53
15	Number of file creation operations (mean, SD)	0.00	0.04	0.00	0.20
16	Number of operations on access control files (mean, SD)	0.00	0.01	0.01	0.08
17	Guest login (yes/no, [%, #])	0.08	314	0.38	371
	Traffic features computed using a two-second time window				
18	Connections to the same host as the current connection (mean, SD)	411.76	156.27	8.16	17.71
19	Rate of connections that have SYN errors (mean, SD)	0.22	0.41	0	0.03
20	Rate of connections that have REJ errors (mean, SD)	0.06	0.23	0.06	0.23
21	Rate of connections to the same service (mean, SD)	0.74	0.42	0.99	0.09
22	Rate of connections to different services (mean, SD)	0.02	0.71	0.02	0.12
23	Connections to the same service as the current connection (mean, SD)	362.04	226.19	10.94	21.80
24	Rate of connections that have SYN errors (mean, SD)	0.22	0.41	0	0.03
25	Rate of connections that have REJ errors (mean, SD)	0.06	0.23	0.06	0.23
26	Rate of connections to different hosts (mean, SD)	0	0.05	0.13	0.28

continued on following page

Table 2. continued

Destination

27	Connections having the same destination host (mean, SD)	253.06	21.13	148.51	103.40
28	Connections having the same destination host and using the same service (mean, SD)	185.38	109.98	202.06	86.91
29	Rate of connections having the same destination host and using the same service (mean, SD)	0.73	0.43	0.84	0.31
30	Rate of different services on the current host (mean, SD)	0.02	0.08	0.06	0.18
31	Rate of connections to the current host having the same source port (mean, SD)	0.72	0.45	0.13	0.28
32	Rate of connections to the same service coming from different hosts (mean, SD)	0.00	0.04	0.02	0.05
33	Rate of connections to the current host with S0 errors (mean, SD)	0.22	0.41	0.00	0.03
34	Rate of connections to the current host and specified service with S0 errors (mean, SD)	0.22	0.41	0.00	0.02
35	Rate of connections to the current host with RST errors (mean, SD)	0.06	0.23	0.06	0.22
36	Rate of connections to the current host and specified service with RST errors	0.06	0.23	0.06	0.22

Table 3. Frequencies of major attacks by samples

Attack Types	Derivation (N=494,021)		Validation (N=311,029)		P value
	Total (#)	Rate (%)	Total (#)	Rate (%)	
Anomaly					
Surveillance and other probing (probe)	4,107	0.8	4,166	1.3	<0.001
Denial of service (DoS)	391,458	79.2	229,853	73.9	<0.001
Unauthorized access to local super user (root) privileges (U2R)	52	0.0	228	0.1	<0.001
Unauthorized access from a remote machine (R2L)	1,126	0.2	16,189	5.2	<0.001
Normal	97,278	19.7	60,593	19.5	0.021

Classification

Based on Figure 1 and Table 4, an abnormal probability was calculated for each connection in both the derivation and the validation samples. The derivation sample-based probability had a mean of 0.35 with a standard deviation of 0.38 and a range of 0.00 to 1.00; the validation sample-based probability had a mean of 0.36 with a standard deviation of 0.44 and ranged from 0.00 to 1.00. The correlation coefficient of the probabilities between the two samples was 0.99. There were 70,600 (14.3%) connections that had a unique probability value in the derivation sample. Figure 2 illustrates the overall distributions of the risk factors-based probability of anomaly by the derivation and the validation samples, emphasizing

Figure 1. Percentage of risk factors significantly associated with anomaly intrusion

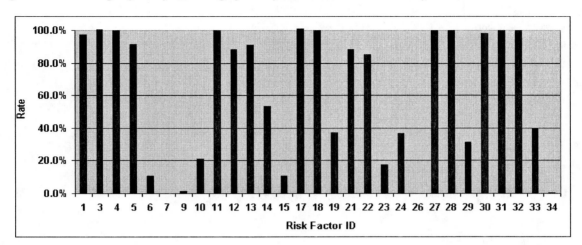

that by choosing an appropriate threshold, the risk factors are robust to distinguish the normal and anomaly groups. Figure 3 shows the association of different thresholds among sensitivity, specificity, and correctly classified rate based on the derivation sample. Note that these relationships were not linear — specificity was affected more than sensitivity and correctly classified rate by changes in classification threshold, and sensitivity tends to decrease as specificity increases, which is a common circumstance in traditional information retrieval. This figure clearly demonstrated the importance of a threshold in classification,

and showed that the probability of 0.70 is the optimum value that provides an excellent sensitivity (98.9%), specificity (98.8%), and correctly classified (98.8%) values in the derivation sample. When applying this threshold to the validation sample, the sensitivity, specificity, and correctly classified value were 91.4%, 94.8%, and 92.1%, respectively. Compared with the KDD-cup 1999 top winning results, the risk factors-based classification showed similar ROC area (1.00 vs. 1.00), higher sensitivity (98.9% vs. 91.8%), similar specificity (98.8% vs. 99.5%) values, and higher correctly classified rate (98.8% vs. 93.3%)

Table 4. Selected risk factors significantly associated with the outcome based on the derivation sample

ID	Risk Factors	Coefficient	Odds Ratio	95% Confidence Interval	P value	Standardized Estimate
	Intercept (β_0)	7.0326				
1	Length (number of seconds) of the connection	-0.1109	0.90	0.88 - 0.91	<0.001	-0.0611
2	ICMP (reference)		1.00			
3	TCP	-0.3732	0.69	0.60 -0.79	<0.001	-0.1001
4	UDP	-2.5541	0.08	0.07 -0.09	<0.001	-0.2799
5	HTTP	0.4891	1.63	1.47 -1.81	<0.001	0.0907

continued on following page

Table 4. continued

8	REJ (reference)		1.00			
11	RST	4.6891	108.61	81.16 -145.34	<0.001	0.1419
12	Login successfully	-0.3492	0.71	0.64 -0.78	<0.001	-0.0684
13	Number of compromised	0.0288	1.03	1.01 -1.05	<0.001	0.0159
17	Guest login	2.1580	8.65	7.26 -10.32	<0.001	0.0443
18	Connections to the same host as the current connection in the past two seconds	4.4714	87.48	73.69 -103.84	<0.001	2.4652
21	Rate of connections to the same service	-2.0776	0.13	0.12 -0.14	<0.001	-1.1455
22	Rate of connections to different services	-0.3198	0.73	0.71 -0.74	<0.001	-0.1763
27	Connections having the same destination host	0.7734	2.17	2.10 -2.23	<0.001	0.4264
28	Connections having the same destination host and using the same service	-1.2429	0.29	0.27 -0.30	<0.001	-0.6852
30	Rate of different services on the current host	-0.28880	0.75	0.73 -0.77	<0.001	-0.1588
31	Rate of connections to the current host having the same src port	1.2126	3.36	3.18 -3.56	<0.001	0.6686
32	Rate of connections to the same service coming from different hosts	0.3106	1.36	1.35 -1.38	<0.001	0.1712

Figure 2. Distributions of anomalous probability by the derivation and the validation samples

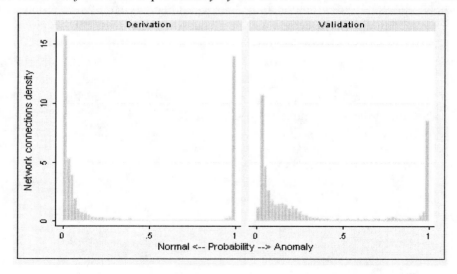

than the top winning results in the derivation sample, and similar sensitivity (91.4% vs. 91.8%), slightly low specificity (94.8% vs. 99.5%), ROC area (0.96 vs. 1.00), and comparable correctly classified rate (92.1% vs. 93.3%) with the winning results in the validation sample. Overall, this study demonstrated similar classification performances in comparison with the KDD-cup 1999 winning results but in a remarkably simple format, and it emphasized that the 16 risk factors are robust for better information retrieval on network security.

Figure 3. Impact of different thresholds on classification results

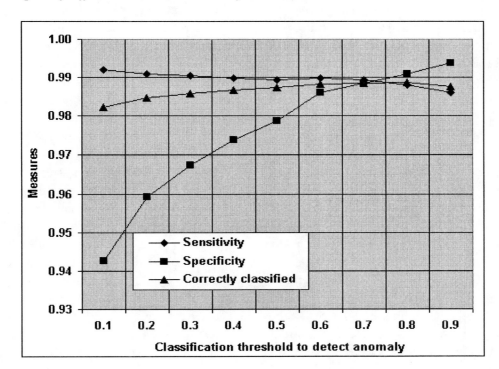

Table 5. Comparison with KDD-cup 1999 winning entry

Measure of classification	Predicted probability based on risk factors		KDD-cup 1999 winning entry
	Derivation sample	Validation sample	
ROC area	0.9974	0.9494	0.9960
Sensitivity (%)	98.90	91.44	91.81
Specificity (%)	98.84	94.77	99.45
Correctly classified rate (%)	98.80	92.10	93.30

DISCUSSION

Anomaly intrusion detection is a communication process; an intrusion detection system can be considered a particular type of information retrieval system that acquires a set of symbols (information) from network traffic audit data and determines that one set of symbols has the same or a similar meaning as another. With the rapid advancement in computer and network technology and increased information and national security threats, the demand for better analysis of network traffic data and being able to improve interpretability of the structure of its symbols has intensified significantly. The primary contribution of the present study is that it applied the bootstrapping simulation and stepwise logistic regression modeling approaches to the intrusion detection area for meeting this demand. It demonstrated that the combination of using such modern statistical techniques could provide a novel solution for better information protection.

Furthermore, with the stepwise logistic regression model and bootstrap methods, the study identified and validated 16 risk factors for predicting and assessing the risk of being an anomalous intrusion for data stream exchanging in network traffic. Such risk factors are easy to collect and are available through network traffic in real time; they have been validated with a test dataset with novel attack types that were not present in the derivation sample, yielding predictive performance for anomaly events that were comparable to the original derivation results. Overall, these risk factors, reducing approximately 65% of the initial data dimension demonstrated, had similar performances in sensitivity, specificity, and correctly classified rate in comparison with the full dimension data and the KDD-cup 1999 winning results but in a remarkably simple format.

The benefit of using statistical methods is that they offer a wide availability of approaches, ranging from simple significance tests to complex analyses, including multidimensional scaling, multiple regression, cluster analysis, and factor analysis, to seek various solutions in retrieving anomaly intrusion information and profiling user behavior. However, the development of a sound statistical model and the identification of a set of robust risk factors to retrieve anomaly intrusion information present many challenges. There is no one gold-standard model that can be used to compare the performances; a stream of network traffic data with many positive risk factors might not represent a true attack, and a look-alike normal stream could present a novel attack due to uncertain factors and users changing their behavior. In general, increasing the sensitivity could reduce the false positive alarm rate, and increasing the specificity could reduce the false negative alarm

rate. The objective of a good statistical model is to demonstrate high values in sensitivity, specificity, and correctly classified rate. To achieve this goal, the process of selecting risk factors must consider the issues of sampling variability and stability of variables' statistical significance, which were addressed by the stepwise logistic modeling and bootstrap simulation techniques in the present study. This is one of strengths of this study. Another strength relies on the use of KDD-cup 1999 data to identify the risk factors, which is the most comprehensive and widely used public benchmark for testing intrusion detection systems available today. Since risk factors can influence the results in several ways, an ideal risk factor should be unaffected by scientific interpretation, widely accepted, and available on audit processes. Most of the 16 risk factors uphold these criteria and have been used widely in many intrusion detection studies.

Despite the strengths, the study has a number of limitations. First, the analyses were conducted based on cross-sectional but not longitudinal data, and, therefore, the estimated parameters may or may not perform well over time. Longitudinal statistical modeling techniques, which take into account changes in user behavior over time, should be considered as a future research direction. Second, despite the fact that KDD-cup intrusion detection evaluation data are the most widely used public benchmark for testing intrusion detection systems and the most comprehensive data available today, they have been criticized for lacking some important variables, such as timestamp and user-level information. The distribution of attack types (e.g., 79.2% of DoS vs. 19.7% of normal, and only 1.0% of data split among other attack types) also seems unrepresentative of real populations about which most researchers are aware. Thus, the performance of the risk factors and the corresponding parameters could be different in a new dataset that includes the missing variables and a fair distribution of attack types.

Finally, this study did not take into account the between-system variance, since the KDD-cup data does not provide information at the individual network system level. The logistic regression model treated the between-system variance as zero. A disadvantage of this solution is that connections in one system tend to have similar outcomes and time-homogeneity but may not be representative of user behavior on other network systems (e.g., the data exchanging rate could be different between two network systems due to differences in network traffic or hardware configurations, and such differences could increase the variation of the connection time and impact on user behavior). A hierarchical random effects logistic regression modeling approach, which takes into account variation across different systems by allowing each system to have its own intercept, should be considered as a further direction when new benchmark data that include traffic from different networks become available.

This study could impact information retrieval at the network intrusion detection level in several aspects. The analysis approach to simplify the structure of information and to present the analysis in a simple format could be applied to different datasets and outcomes. The risk factors can be used as key elements to develop a neural network-based intrusion detection system; the risk factors and the corresponding parameters-based probability can be used as a principal solution to detect intrusion and profile users as a primary threshold to filter network traffic or as a key component assisting other intrusion detection techniques to develop a variety of hybrid-based detection systems. Since the probability risk score can be accomplished through common computer languages without interfacing with any typical software and statistical tool, it therefore can be widely adapted in a mobile computing environment and presents better intrusion detection information to network administrators for making more informed decisions in computer security.

ACKNOWLEDGMENT

The authors thank the anonymous reviewers and the editor-in-chief, for help with the manuscript, which has benefited greatly from their suggestions and comments. The authors also thank Dr. James Cannady at Nova Southeastern University for his comments, and Allyson Schulz, Director of R & D at Qualidigm, for her editorial commentary.

REFERENCES

Anderson, D., Frivold, T., & Valdes, A. (1995). *Next-generation intrusion detection expert system (NIDES): Summary report.* SRI International.

Anderson, P. J. (1972). *Computer security technology planning study volume II.* Bedford, MA: Air Force Systems Command.

Anderson, P. J. (1980). *Computer security threat monitoring and surveillance.* Fort Washington, PA: James P. Anderson Co.

Barbard, D., Wu, N., & Jajodia, S. (2001). Detecting novel network intrusions using Bayes estimators. In *Proceedings of the 1st SIAM International Conference on Data Mining* (pp. 24-29).

Bishop, M. (2003). *Computer security: Art and science.* Boston, MA: Addison-Wesley.

Cho, S. B., & Park, H. J. (2003). Efficient anomaly detection by modeling privilege flows using hidden Markov model. *Computer and Security, 22*(1), 45-55.

Cunningham, R. K., Lippmann, R. P., Fried, D. J., Garfinkle, S. L., Graf, I., Kendall, K. R., et al. (1999). Evaluating intrusion detection systems without attacking your friends: The 1998 DARPA intrusion detection evaluation. *SANS.*

Denning, D. (1987). An intrusion-detection model. *IEEE Transaction on Software Engineering, 13*(2), 222-232.

Efron, B. (1979). Bootstrap methods: Another look at the jackknife. *Annals of Statistics, 7,* 1-26.

Efron, B., & Tibshirani, E. R. (1986). Bootstrap methods for standard errors, confidence intervals, and other measures of statistical accuracy. *Statistical Science, 1*(1), 57-77.

Efron, B., & Tibshirani, E. R. (1994). *An introduction to the bootstrap.* London: Chapman & Hall.

Elkan, C. (2000). Results of the KDD'99 classifier learning contest. *ACM Transactions on Information and System Security, 3*(4), 262-294.

Gao, B., Ma, H., & Yang, Y. (2002). HMMS (hidden Markov models) based on anomaly intrusion detection method. In *Proceedings of the First International Conference on Machine Learning and Cybernetics* (pp. 381-385).

Helman, P., & Liepins, G. (1993). Statistical foundations of audit trail analysis for the detection of computer misuse. *IEEE Transactions on Software Engineering, 19*(9), 886-901.

Hosmer, D. W., & Lemeshow, S. (2000). *Applied logistic regression* (2nd ed.). New York: John Wiley & Sons.

KDD Cup. (1999). *Data available on the Web.* Retrieved February 19, 2005, from http://kdd.ics. uci.edu/databases/kddcup99/kddcup99.html

Lee, W., Stolfo, S., & Mok, K. (1999). A data mining framework for building intrusion detection models. In *Proceedings of the IEEE Symposium on Security and Privacy* (pp. 120-132).

Lippman, R., & Cunningham, S. (2000). Improving intrusion detection performance using keyword selection and neural networks. *Computer Networks, 34*(4), 594-603.

Masum, S., Ye, E. M., Chen, Q., & Noh, K. (2000). Chi-square statistical profiling for anomaly detection. In *Proceedings of the 2000 IEEE Workshop on Information Assurance and Security* (pp. 182-188).

Mooney, C. Z., & Duval, R. D. (1993). *Bootstrapping: A nonparametric approach to statistical inference.* Newbury Park, CA: Sage Publications.

Mukkamala, S., Tadiparthi, G. R., Tummala, N., & Janoski, G. (2003). Audit data reduction for intrusion detection. In *Proceedings of the IEEE 2003 International* Joint Conference on Neural Networks (pp. 456-460).

Qin, M., & Hwang, K. (2004). Frequent rules for intrusive anomaly detection with Internet datamining. In *Proceedings of the 13th USENIX Security Symposium* (pp. 456-462).

Qu, D., Vetter, B. M., & Jou, Y. F. (1997). Statistical anomaly detection for link-state routing protocols. In *Proceedings of the 1997 IEEE Symposium on Security and Privacy* (pp. 62-70).

Shyu, M., Chen, S., Sarinnapakorn, K., & Chang, L. (2003). A novel anomaly detection scheme based on principal component classifier. In *Proceedings of the IEEE Foundations and New Directions of Data Mining Workshop, in Conjunction with the 3rd IEEE International Conference on Data Mining (ICDM)* (pp. 172-179).

Stallings, W. (2003). *Network security essentials, applications and standards* (2nd ed.). NJ: Pearson Education.

Taylor, C., & Alves-Foss, J. (2001). "Low cost" network intrusion detection. In *Proceedings of the New Security Paradigms Workshop* (pp. 89-96).

Teng, H., Chen, K., & Lu, S. (1990). Adaptive real-time anomaly detection using inductively generated sequential patterns. In *Proceedings of the 1990 IEEE Symposium on Research in Security and Privacy* (pp. 278-284).

Vaccaro, H. S., & Liepins, G. E. (1989). Detection of anomalous computer session activity. In *Proceedings of the 1989 IEEE Symposium on Security and Privacy* (pp. 280-289).

Ye, N., Emran, S. M., Li, X., & Chen, Q. (2001). Statistical process control for computer intrusion detection. In *Proceedings of the DARPA Information Survivability Conference & Exposition (DISCEX II)* (pp. 397-343).

Zhang, Z., Li, J., Manikopoulos, C. N., Jorgenson, J., & Ucles, J. (2001). HIDE: A hierarchical network intrusion detection system using statistical preprocessing and neural network classification. In *Proceedings of the 2001 IEEE Workshop Information Assurance and Security* (pp. 85-90).

Zhou, M., & Lang, S. D. (2003). Mining frequency content of network traffic for intrusion detection. In *Proceedings of the IASTED International Conference on Communication, Network, and Information Security* (pp. 101-107).

This work was previously published in the International Journal of Business Data Communications and Networking, Vol. 2, Issue 1, edited by J. Gutierrez, pp. 44-60, copyright 2006 by IGI Publishing, formerly known as Idea Group Publishing (an imprint of IGI Global).

Chapter 4.49
Information Security for Legal Safety

Andreas Mitrakas
European Network and Information Security Agency (ENISA), Greece

INTRODUCTION

The growing use of information technology in sensitive daily transactions highlights the significance of information security to protect information assets. Vulnerabilities associated with public and private transactions pose challenges that government, private organizations, and individuals are compelled to respond to by adopting appropriate protection measures. Information security responds to the need of transacting parties for confidentiality, integrity, and availability of resources (Pfleeger, 2000). Information security is required in transactions carried out among, businesses, public administrations, and citizens. An organizational response to information security threats includes setting up and implementing appropriate policy frameworks that are typically endorsed by agreement. Beyond organizational objectives lies an emerging legal framework instigated by the role of information security as a means to safeguard information assets that are socially significant. Organizations are often required to implement information security measures mandated by industry regulations or

legislation, such as in electronic banking transactions. The scope of these legal and regulatory requirements is to mitigate potential risk that entails liabilities for shareholders, employees, customers, trading partners, or other third parties involved in a transaction. Information security and its subsequent regulation are equally important for public services. In e-government services made available to citizens and businesses, information security ensures e-government transactions. The remainder of this article presents an overview of the prevailing legal and policy issues that are currently associated with information security.

BACKGROUND

Electronic transactions typically require a high level of assurance with respect to the content and management of the transaction, the authentication of the trade partners, threats against enterprise resources, and so forth. The following presents a brief and non-exhaustive overview of the regulatory background on information security. If not properly treated, security risks may nurture liability risks for the parties who fail to adopt security countermeasures. Liability in this regard might emanate from general legal requirements or as it has become increasingly apparent from specific legislation that addresses specific security matters. The evidential value of electronic documents, for example, can be challenged as long as the contents of the transaction and the conditions under which it was carried out cannot be ascertained (Mitrakas, 1997). Information security can also function as negative proof of actions that are under investigation in a digital forensics process.

The *U.S. National Information Systems Security Glossary* defines information security as "the protection of information systems against unauthorized access to or modification of information, whether in storage, in processing, or in transit, and against the denial of service to authorized users or the provision of service to unauthorized users, including those measures necessary to detect, document, and counter such threats" (1992, p. 38). Information security threats can be distinguished in categories such as the following:

- **Natural threats**, which are described by terms such as *acts of God*, sometimes described as *force majeure*; for example, unforeseen events such as a flood or an earthquake.
- **Accidental threats** caused by the actors involved, such as, for example, missing out in a plan or a procedure.
- **Intentional threats** by actors directly or indirectly involved, such as, for example the deletion of data with the intent to transfer funds without authorization.

Although threats might carry liability or criminal consequences to the implicated parties, the basis for information security in law is the legal duty of care that transacting parties must show in their daily or business dealings (Lindup & Lindup, 2003). The duty of care is yet more significant in situations where a party acts under a certain capacity or in a trade. There are situations, however, whereby the law mandates certain information security measures in order to protect against information threats, such as, for example, in the case of processing personal data. In such cases, there is a set of duties of the implicated personal data controller to implement security safeguards on personal data stored or processed (Directive 95/46/EC of the European Parliament and of the Council of 24 October 1995 on the protection of personal data and on the free movement of such data, p. 31).

Information security objectives must be associated with the acts at hand and strive to detect the implementation of the following principles with the evidence in hand:

- Confidentiality ensuring that information is accessible only to those authorized to have access, according to the International Standards Organization (ISO). Confidentiality is typically ensured through encryption.
- Integrity is the condition that exists when data are unchanged from their sources and have not been modified, altered, or destroyed at any operation according to an expectation of data quality.
- Availability of data is the degree to which a system is operable and in a committable state at the start of an assignment.
- Accountability of parties involved for acts performed being held to account, scrutinised, and required to give an account. Especially in white collar crime, accountability is often associated with governance.

Whereas the aforementioned principles might only be fully observed within highly organized environments that operate on the basis of audited security policies and practices (e.g., in white-collar crime investigated in a corporation) in other less organized environments odd data has to be put in context through social methods and mundane practices to pinpoint actions in the crime under investigation. To determine information security measures, it is typically required that a risk assessment is carried out by measuring two quantities of risk the magnitude of the potential loss, and the probability that the loss will occur. Prior to a risk assessment, it is advisable to carry out a vulnerability assessment by identifying and quantifying vulnerabilities in a system that seeks network and information security measures (Dunn & Wigert, 2004).

Information security is an enabler to ascertain basic rights, such as the right to confidentiality, personal data protection, trade secrets, and so forth. In information society, information security is gradually becoming a significant factor upon which basic rights depend in order to be exercised by all members of the society. Information security as such is not a right in itself; there is no such thing as a right to information security. This article argues that although information security is an instrument to exercise and enjoy other basic rights and freedoms, it should be encouraged and afforded protection in a meaningful way (Dworkin, 1977). Within the European Union, internal market rules that sometimes depend on information-society services rely on information security in order to take meaningful effect. Conditions regarding the encouragement and exercising of information security include, for example, exceptions with regard to crime investigation through digital forensics, lawful interception, and so forth. A balance, however, must be sought to ensure that legitimate users are granted sufficient access to information security resources and that they are not unnecessarily constrained in the choice of information security resources that evolved over time. The commercial use of public networks has resulted in a surge of regulation concerning an array of issues, among which information security plays a lynchpin role (Rathmell & Valeri, 2002). It is important to stress that information security regulation is twofold in the following situations:

- Addressing risks associated with an attacker carrying out an illegal act, such as hacking or spreading viruses.
- Setting out the requirements for the party that is attacked to take out appropriate measures mitigating risks or face the consequences.

LEGAL CONSIDERATIONS

Information security has emerged as a legal requirement in order to ensure, for example, the legitimate use of computer resources; protection against cyber-crime, and compliance in critical areas such as electronic signatures, personal data protection, and so forth. At an international level, the legal framework of information security includes the UNCITRAL Model Law on Electronic Signatures (United Nations, 2001), which recommends that countries adopt laws allowing the enforceability of electronic signatures, subject to a risk assessment with regard to reliability and trustworthiness. Similarly, the OECD Information Security Guidelines (2002) aim at creating a culture of security by effectively managing risk (Ward, 2003). When carrying out risk assessments, it is necessary to consider legal risks in the audit processes.

Information security is necessary to control risk in transactions. An information security approach and information security rules allow for the assessment of threats and mitigation of risk. Whereas a threat is the possibility of hindering the operation of an information system, risk is the probability that a threat might materialize. The principles of proportionality and reasonableness have been enshrined in the EU Directive 95/46/EC on the protection of individuals with regard to the processing of personal data and on the free movement of such data. Privacy protection requires the setup of discreet environments to process personal data in a way that leaking such data to another environment can never go undetected. An example includes the use of social security numbers; for example, as a business identifier or as reliable input in building identification profiles that are merged into comprehensive databases. The duty to maintain the confidentiality of data that is stored within or exchanged between information systems is another necessary condition that concerns service providers and users of data alike because failure to protect implies liability consequences for the implicated parties.

Regarding data protection, Directive 2002/58/EC of the European Parliament and Council, concerning the processing of personal data and the protection of privacy in the telecommunications sector, has introduced new rules for an array of issues associated with information security in electronic communications. Although the scope of the Directive is to warrant an equivalent level of protection of fundamental rights and freedoms to ensure the free movement of such data, equipment, and services across the European Union, the protection of the legitimate interests of subscribers is equally observed. The directive prohibits wiretapping and eavesdropping without the prior consent of the users concerned, with the exception of legally authorized interceptions.

Another pertinent issue for privacy is related with the use of cookies that can reveal user behavior; Directive 2002/58/EC stipulates that member states must ensure that the use of electronic communications networks to store information or to gain access to information stored in the terminal equipment of a subscriber or user, is only allowed on condition that the subscriber or user concerned is provided with clear and comprehensive information and is offered the right to refuse such processing by the data controller. The ability to treat cookies remotely implies that, if cookies are used as tracking devices, the end user must have exclusive control over them.

Cybercrime law protects certain rights and assets such as privacy by making interception and unauthorized access illegal. To investigate cybercrime and crimes carried out with the help or by information technology, law enforcement agencies seek access to content of communications, data in transit, stored data, and authentication data. In terms of legislation, the efforts of the Council of Europe and the Organisation for Economic Cooperation and Development (OECD) can be highlighted. The Convention on Cybercrime of the Council of Europe stipulates in Article 15 that investigative powers and procedures are subject to conditions and safeguards provided for under its domestic law in a way that provides for adequate protection of human rights and liberties (Council of Europe, 2001). The protection afforded to citizens must be commensurate with the procedure or power concerned. This convention is currently nonbinding, pending ratification by national parliaments; however, it makes significant steps towards defining crimes related to computer systems.

The *OECD Cybersecurity Guidelines* stipulate that security should be implemented in a manner consistent with the values recognized by democratic societies including the freedom to exchange thoughts and ideas, the free flow of information, the confidentiality of information and communication, the appropriate protection of personal information, openness and transparency.

Some countries, however, have already initiated data retention schemes that might be further extended, in spite of concerns regarding their success. The issue of data retention requires addressing security threats such as spam because, for the time being, it is not necessarily clear whether service providers have to retain all data or selected portions of them. In the latter option, privacy considerations have to be addressed along with a duty to implement spam filters at the service-provider level.

INFORMATION SECURITY THROUGH SELF-REGULATION

In addition to the legal framework, information security is addressed through voluntary frameworks imposed by trade partners. Voluntary frameworks include policies and agreements that aim at setting out the conditions for information security safeguards within an organisation, or in transaction frameworks. A security policy lays down the rules for network information access, determines the process to enforce policies and lays out the architecture of the security environment of an organisation. At a bilateral level, the parties use service level agreements to specify the quality service they seek from their provider and ensure availability rates for their applications. Quite often, however, parties might set up security frameworks, which are activated by means of subscriber agreements that are executed individually. In this case, the service can be a generic one that does not necessarily allow for a high degree of customization (Kiefer, Wu, Wilson, & Sabett, 2004).

Additional measures such as internal policy drafting and mapping, audit, and control of enforcement are also essential to support a security framework (Caelli, Longley, & Shain, 1991; Clarke, 2004). An approach to information security includes

- Detecting and recognizing of a threat and the risks it poses through an appropriate threat analysis, a vulnerability analysis, and risk assessment;
- A strategy on a security plan and subsequent implementation; and
- An audit of the implemented security plan.

Information security can be assured through security policies that are drafted on the basis of international standards (ISO, 2000). Regardless of the form that information takes, or means by which it is shared or stored, it should always be appropriately protected. The International Standards Organisation (ISO) standard known as ISO 17799 provides recommendations and guidance for information security management. This standard provides a shared basis to develop organizational security standards and effective security management practice. Beyond businesses and financial institutions, the ISO 17799 has also been recognized as appropriate for use in government environments (Deprest & Robben, 2003).

A security policy identifies the rules and procedures that parties accessing computer resources must adhere to in order to ensure the confidentiality, integrity, and availability of data and resources as well as accountability, if required. Furthermore, a security policy formalizes an organization's security posture, describes and assigns functions and responsibilities, and identifies the incident response procedures. Voluntary security frameworks are binding to the extent that this is the intent of the parties involved. Breach of warranty in a publicized or otherwise security policy is a breach of an obligation that is likely to result into the party involved paying damages. From a legal viewpoint a security policy supports the following requirements:

- Communicates security information in binding manner by ensuring management involvement;
- Makes enforcement of a security framework possible;
- Identifies the areas of responsibility for users, administrators, and management by means of which the consequences of non-compliance are determined and is enacted by senior management; and
- Meets the requirement to protect certain rights (e.g., privacy) while contributing to enterprise productivity goals.

The components of a security policy are adapted to the type and corporate goal of an organization. Typical elements of a security policy include the following:

- **Security Definition:** A security policy includes a well-defined security vision for the organization. The security vision should convey to the readers the intent of the policy in ensuring the confidentiality, integrity, and availability of data and resources through the use of effective and established security processes and procedures. The security policy definition addresses why the security policy is implemented and what it entails in terms of the mission and the business goals of the organization.

- **Enforcement:** A security policy identifies how a security policy is enforced and how a breach is managed. This requirement is necessary in order to ensure that incidents are handled in an appropriate manner while the security policy remains binding across the organization.

- **User Access to Computer Resources:** A security policy regards the roles and responsibilities of users accessing resources on the organization's network. This section ties organizational procedures to individual roles and aims at controlling the acts or omissions of the human factor in secure processes. Additionally, some organizations may require that other organizations meet the terms and conditions identified in the organization's security policy before granting access.

It is necessary to ensure that security policies are consistent with other applicable policies within the organisation concerned. Additional requirements of the security policy framework involve the definition of the conditions to deliver services in areas of particular interest, such as electronic signatures and data protection, for example ETSI

(2001) and IETF (2003). Standards in this area provide guidance and set the framework in order to deliver services, control and rely upon electronic signatures (Mitrakas, 2005). European Union regulatory initiatives highlighted the significant effort is beginning to take shape in the European Union with regard to information security. The European Network Information Security Agency (ENISA) aims at providing support to member states, the E.U. Commission, and stakeholders with regard to information security management and policy. The Network Information Security Standardisation (NIS) Steering Group aims at liaising with the industry and ENISA in order to provide an appropriate forum for standardisation in the European Union (ETSI, 2003).

FUTURE TRENDS

Beyond legislation, the evolution of case law is expected to enhance and determine the admissibility and evidential value of data that are protected, according to specific information security policies, in those application areas in which they emerge as a requirement. Remarkably, to date there has been little done to address in a uniform manner the requirements pertaining to the legal value of information security policies. Additional requirements might seek to cover the mapping and methods on the reconciliation of information security policy frameworks in overlapping transactions especially in the field of outsourcing services. An additional area of future attention could address information security policy frameworks as they relate to applications. As present day requirements for transparency within organizations instigated by the requirements for greater corporate accountability are likely to be further raised, it is expected that online applications will increasingly become more demanding in explaining to the end user what they do and actually warranting the performance and trustworthiness of a system or service (Mitrakas, 2005). To date, general conditions and service agreements cover part of this requirement; however, a comprehensive description of the technical features and functionality of the application in a way that allows the end user to gain some insight, while protecting the vital security interests of the service provider, is needed. Tailoring information security policies further to meet the needs of particular groups of organizations is an additional expectation.

Additional requirements of a framework for information security require the definition of the conditions to deliver services in applications. Standards in this area provide guidance and set the framework in order to deliver services and control and rely upon electronic signatures (Mitrakas, 2005). In emerging technologies, and applications the definition of security threats must addresses the requirements on organizational responsibility and transparency. Additionally, self-imposed frameworks, through agreement or best practices, must also be put in place in an effort to provide guidance to trade parties and confidence to citizens. Cybercrime prevention can further extend to awareness programs as well as the development of industry specific threat and risk assessment methodologies in order to deal with current information security risks emanating from malicious attacks as well as terrorism. Additional attention can be dedicated to areas that affect large populations, such as, for example, e-government, where public interest is high.

CONCLUSION

Information security has emerged as a way to ensure the integrity, confidentiality, and availability of certain assets that are necessary to carry out transactions in an information society. Information security is a necessary instrument to allow members of the society to exercise and enjoy basic rights. Political and legal initiatives, aimed at encouraging and protecting in a meaningful way the evolution of security to protect those rights. Cross-border cooperation becomes essential to ensure the applicability and robustness of measures adopted and practices employed. An essential requirement for business level applications is to gain a common understanding of the legal implications of security in electronic communications and transactions especially with regard to threats and vulnerabilities that are successfully exploited to the detriment of a trade party that might carry liability or bear penal consequences.

Further efforts are necessary to clarify the boundaries of the legal framework application with regard to information security. Especially in new or emerging technologies and applications, further definition of security threats is needed that addresses the requirements of organizational responsibility and transparency. Additionally, self-imposed frameworks, through agreement or best practices, must also be put in place in an effort to provide guidance to trade parties and confidence to citizens. Penal law aspects can further extend to awareness programs and the development of industry-specific threat and risk assessment methodologies in order to deal with current information security risks emanating from malicious attacks and terrorism. Special emphasis can be dedicated to areas that affect large populations, such as e-government.

Harmonizing the requirements for cross-border cooperation can be facilitated by initiatives aiming at effective mutual assistance arrangements. There is an urgent need to ease the reporting and investigation of suspicious incidents and to provide information to help investigations without facing legal sanctions or complex processes. Information security is necessary as an instrument that puts into practice legal requirements; there is, however, a way to go before it can be fully leveraged in legal processes.

REFERENCES

Caelli, W., Longley, D., & Shain, M. (1991). *Information security handbook*. London: Macmillan.

Clarke, R. (2004). *Introduction to information security*. Retrieved December 10, 2004, from www.anu.edu.au/people/Roger.Clarke/EC/IntroSecy.html

Council of Europe. (2001). *Convention on cybercrime and explanatory memorandum*. Strasbourg: European Committee on Crime Problems.

Deprest, J., & Robben, F. (2003). *E-government: The approach of the Belgian federal government*. Brussels: FEDICT and CBBSS.

Dunn, M., & Wigert, I. (2004). *Critical information infrastructure protection*. Zurich, Switzerland: Swiss Federal Institute of Technology.

Dworkin, R. (1977). *Taking rights seriously*. London: Duckworth.

ETSI. (2001). *Policy requirements for CSPs issuing qualified certificates*, Sophia-Antipolis.

(ETSI) European Telecommunications Standards Institute. (2003). *Response from CEN and ETSI to the Communication from the Commission to the Council, the European Parliament the European Economic and Social Committee and the Committee of the Regions: Network and Information Security: Proposal for a European Policy Approach*. Sophia-Antipolis, France.

IETF RFC 3647. (2003). *Internet X.509 public key infrastructure—Certificate policies and certification practices framework*. Retrieved January 10, 2005, from www.faqs.org/rfcs/rfc2647.html

ISO (International Standards Organization). (2000). *Information technology: Code of practice for information security management*. Geneva: author.

Kiefer, K., Wu, S., Wilson, B., & Sabett, R. (2004). *Information security: A legal, business and technical handbook*. Chicago: American Bar Association.

Lindup, K., & Lindup, H. (2003). The legal duty of care—A justification for information security. *Information Security Bulletin, 8*(1), 14.

Mitrakas, A. (2005). Policy frameworks for secure electronic business. In M. Khosrow-Pour (Ed.), *Encyclopedia of information science and technology: Volume I-V*. Hershey, PA: Idea Group Reference.

Mitrakas, A. (2004). *Open EDI and law in Europe: A regulatory framework*. The Hague, The Netherlands: Kluwer Law International.

National Security Telecommunications and Information Systems Security Instruction (NSTISSI) No. 4009. (1992). *National Information Systems Security (INFOSEC) Glossary*.

OECD (2002). *Guidelines for the security of information systems and networks: Towards a culture of security*. Paris.

Pfleeger C. (2000). *Security in computing*. Upper Saddle River, NJ: Prentice Hall.

Rathmell, A., & Valeri, L. (2002). *Handbook of legislative procedures of computer and network misuse in EU countries* (Study for the European Commission Directorate-General Information Society). London: Rand Europe.

United Nations. (2000). *Guide to enactment of the UNCITRAL uniform* rules on electronic signatures. New York: Author.

Ward, J. (2003, February). Towards a culture of security. *Information Security Bulletin, 8*(6), 15.

KEY TERMS

Accountability: Accountability of parties means holding to account, scrutinising, and being required to give an account; especially in white-collar crime, accountability is often associated with governance.

Availability: Availability of data is the degree to which a system is operable and in a committable state at the start of an assignment.

Confidentiality: Confidentiality ensures that information is accessible only to those authorized to have access and it is typically ensured through encryption.

Information Security: Information security is the protection of information systems against unauthorized access to or modification of information, whether in storage, processing or transit, and against the denial of service to authorized users or the provision of service to unauthorized users, including those measures necessary to detect, document, and counter such threats.

Integrity: Integrity is the condition that exists when data is unchanged from its source and has not been modified, altered, or destroyed at any operation according to an expectation of data quality.

Risk Assessment: Risk assessment is determined by measuring two quantities of risk, the magnitude of the potential loss, and the probability that the loss will occur.

Security Policy: Security policy is a document that lays out the rules for network information access, determines the process to enforce policies and lays out the architecture of the security environment of an organisation.

Vulnerability Assessment: Vulnerability assessment is the identification and quantification of vulnerabilities in a system that seeks network and information security measures.

NOTE

This article expresses the author's personal views.

This work was previously published in Encyclopedia of E-Commerce, E-Government, and Mobile Commerce, edited by M. Khosrow-Pour, pp. 620-625, copyright 2004 by Information Science Reference, formerly known as Idea Group Reference (an imprint of IGI Global).

Section 5
Organizational and Social Implications

This section includes a wide range of research pertaining to the social and organizational impact of information security technologies around the world. Chapters introducing this section critically analyze the links between computing and cultural diversity as well as the natural environment. Additional chapters included in this section examine the link between ethics and IT and the influence of gender on ethical considerations in the IT environment. Also investigating a concern within the field of information security is research which provides an introductory overview of identity management as it relates to data networking and enterprise information management systems. With 32 chapters, the discussions presented in this section offer research into the integration of security technology as well as implementation of ethical considerations for all organizations.

Chapter 5.1
We Cannot Eat Data:
The Need for Computer Ethics to Address the Cultural and Ecological Impacts of Computing

Barbara Paterson
Marine Biology Research Institute, Zoology Department, University of Cape Town, South Africa

ABSTRACT

Computer ethicists foresee that as information and communication technology (ICT) increasingly pervades more and more aspects of life, ethical issues increasingly will be computer-related. This view is underpinned by the assumption that progress is linear and inevitable. In accordance with this assumption, ICT is promoted as an essential component of development. This notion ignores the cultural origin of computing. Computer technology is a product of the Western worldview, and consequently, the computer revolution is experienced differently by people in different parts of the world. The computer revolution not only threatens to marginalize non-Western cultural traditions, but the Western way of life also has caused large-scale environmental damage. This chapter argues that computer ethics has to critically analyze the links between computing and its effects on cultural diversity and the natural environment and proposes that the Earth Charter can function as a framework for such holistic research.

INTRODUCTION

Computer ethics is a fast-growing and increasingly important field of practical philosophy. Deborah Johnson (1999) predicts that because the majority of moral problems will be computer ethics issues, computer ethics will cease to be a special field of ethics (Bynum, 2000). Kristina Gòrniak-Kocikowska (1996) predicts that the computer revolution will give rise to a revolution of ethics and that computer ethics will become a global ethics relevant to all areas of human life. Bynum and Rogerson (1996) and Moor (1998) suggest that the second generation of computer ethics should be an era of global information ethics. These views seem to ignore the reality that the effects of the computer revolution are experienced differently by people in different parts of the world. While for some the challenge is to keep up with the continuous new developments, others are still struggling to put in place the infrastructure that may allow them to ride the waves of the information tide and participate in its benefits.

Nelson Mandela has stated that the gap between the information rich and the information poor is linked to quality of life and that, therefore, the capacity to communicate is likely to be the key human right in the 21st century (Ng'etich, 2001). However, at the beginning of the new century, the digital divide between industrialized nations and the developing world is immense. Eighty percent of worldwide Internet activity is in North America and Europe (Gandalf, 2005), although these areas represent 19% of the worldwide population. The ratio of Internet users to nonusers in developing countries is 1:750, compared to 1:35 in developed countries (Ng'etich, 2001). Although Internet usage in Africa grew by 429.8 % between 2000 and 2005, it only represents 2.5 % of worldwide usage, and only 2.7% of Africans are Internet users (World Internet Usage Statistics, 2005). In Africa, poverty and illiteracy prevent many people from accessing computer technology.

Many believe that these hurdles are simply a question of income per capita and infrastructure (Anyian-Osigwe, 2002; Grant, Lewis, & Samoff, 1992). In the first world, computing is experienced as a crucial element in the competitive market and, therefore, also is promoted in the third world as a vital part of development. The notion that computers are the solution to bridge the gap between the rich and the poor overlooks the fact that computers are the product of a particular worldview promoting values such as efficiency, speed, and economic growth (Berman, 1992; Bowers, 2000).

Computer use requires people to act and think in a prescribed unified way (Heim, 1993, as cited in Gorniak-Kocikowska, 2001, 2004; Kocikowski, 1999, as cited in Gorniak-Kocikowska, 2001,

2004). Not only is there the danger that the computer revolution will marginalize cultural traditions other than the Western one, but the Western way of life also has precipitated environmental degradation to the extent that we are now facing an environmental crisis of global warming, natural resource depletion, and accelerated species extinction.

The term *West* can have different meanings, depending on its context. *Western* is no longer simply a geographical distinction but also a cultural and economic attribute. Here, *West* is used to refer to societies of Europe and their genealogical, colonial, and philosophical descendants, such as the United States, Australia, or Argentina. The term *Western culture* will be used to refer to the common system of values, norms, and artefacts of these societies, which has been shaped by the historic influence of Greco-Roman culture, Christianity, the Renaissance, and the Enlightenment.

Different cultures have unique ways of storing, representing, and transmitting knowledge, such as mythologies, storytelling, proverbs, art, and dance. These modes cannot all be equally well-represented through computerization, but all are equally valid and deserve to be preserved (Hoesle, 1992). We cannot assume that computer technology will solve the complex social and environmental problems at hand. In order to adequately address these complex issues, a diverse body of knowledge is required, and we simply cannot afford to lose any sources of knowledge.

Although there is an increasing gap between the first and third worlds, and the environmental crisis presents some of the most pressing and difficult moral issues (Hoesle, 1992), there is only a small body of research in computer ethics that addresses the problem of the digital divide between the first and third worlds and the relationship between computing and the environmental crisis (Capurro, 1990; Floridi, 2001; Gòrniak-Kocikowska, 2004). Just as computerization is a product of the West, most computer ethics is explored and defined by Western scholars.

Although writers such as Johnson (1997) and Gòrniak-Kocikowska (2004) acknowledge that computer technology was created from within a particular way of life, most current computer ethics research ignores the cultural origins of the technological determinist stance. This stance is prevalent in writing on computing and also affects computer ethics (Adam, 2001; Winner, 1997). The evolutionary view of progress and its impact on the human world leaves other cultures no choice but to adopt computerization and to assimilate the values that are embedded in computerization (Bowers, 2000). Moreover, current computer technology adopts a logico-rational paradigm that often relies on convergences by eliminations and aggregations. It is not clear that computers will develop in such a way so as to mimic or represent values or value choices that invoke those elements at the core of any human being. This consequence might not only lead to information colonialism but also may arguably reinforce a worldview that is ecologically unsound.

In this chapter, it is argued that computer ethics has to critically address the links between computing and its effect on cultural diversity and the natural environment. A framework for global ethics is being provided in the form of the Earth Charter, which has been developed in a decade-long global process in order to realize a shared vision of a sustainable global society. It is suggested that computer ethics make use of this framework in order to carry out the holistic research that is required to see how information and computer technology can be used responsibly to create a future that is ecologically and economically sustainable and socially and culturally just.

BACKGROUND

The field of computer ethics is underpinned largely by the assumption that technological progress is linear and inevitable. This observation has been made by Adam (2001) for the more popular writings and those dealing with professionalism, but it is equally true for the more academic computer ethics research. For example, James Moor (1998) states that the "computer revolution has a life on its own. ... The digital genie is out of the bottle on a world-wide scale." Kristina Gòrniak-Kocikowska (1996) predicts that the computer revolution will affect all aspects of human life and that, consequently, computer ethics will become the global ethics of the future not only in a geographic sense but also "in the sense that it will address the totality of human actions and relations."

The notion of a computer revolution carries the theme of a technology out of control, continuously developing while humans are limping along, hardly able to keep up with the innovations but always looking forward to the inevitable next step in computing power (Curry, 1995). In this view, technological progress is unavoidable and determines society rather than being determined by human need. Innovation becomes a goal in its own right (Veregin, 1995). This technological determinism takes the objectivity of the world for granted and ignores the complex relationships between society and technology, thus obstructing analysis and critique of technological development (Adam, 2001).

Technological determinism is supported by the tool-based model of technology, which carries the implication that technology develops independently of social and scientific contexts, thus ignoring that technological innovation takes place against a background of social context and profit motives and that every technology imposes limits on thought and action (Pickles, 1995; Veregin, 1995; Winograd & Flores, 1986). The more technology becomes an integral and indispensable part of life, the greater is its influence (Veregin, 1995). The determinist stance is further reinforced by the increasing complexity of information systems and the increasing dependency on the technical knowledge of experts who understand them. For the average person, a computer system resembles a black box whose inner workings remain a mystery.

Furthermore, technological determinism informs an evolutionary view of progress that places different cultures in a competitive struggle. Seeing computerization as inevitable means that nontechnological cultures must adopt computerization or become extinct (Bowers, 2000). The Declaration of Principles formulated at the World Summit on the Information Society affirms that "the Information Society should be founded on and stimulate respect for cultural identity, cultural and linguistic diversity, traditions and religions, and foster dialogue among cultures and civilizations" (WSIS, 2004). Nonetheless, Gòrniak-Kocikowska (2004, p. 3) predicts that the computer revolution will lead to "a takeover and ruthless destruction of traditional values of local cultures by the new digital civilisation." The computer is a product of Western civilization, and the field of computer ethics is dominated by Western scholars who tend to overlook problems outside their cultural experience. This ethnocentrism marginalizes the need to consider the long-term implications of displacing diverse cultural narratives.

THE COMPUTER AS A PRODUCT OF WESTERN CULTURE

The computer has its roots in 16th- and 17th-century Europe, an era of increased mechanization and increased focus on mathematics. The mechanic philosophy, which emerged during the Renaissance and the scientific revolution, was based on the assumption that sense data are discrete and that problems can be analyzed into parts that can be manipulated by mathematics. For Hobbes, the human mind was a machine, and to reason was to add and subtract (Merchant, 1980). The binary system and its significance for machines were advocated by Leibniz in the latter half of the 17th century (Freiberger & Swaine, 2003). As more and more processes of daily life were being mechanized, the desire also to automate cogni-

tive processes such as calculation came naturally. The computer is the result of the effort to achieve both high-speed and high-precision automatic calculation and a machine capable of automatic reasoning (Mahoney, 1988).

The classical view of reality is still influential in Western common sense thought and in the notion that Western science produces objective, value-free, and context-free knowledge (Merchant, 1980). Although "it is an inherent characteristic of common-sense thought … to affirm that its tenets are immediate deliverances of experience," common sense is an organized cultural system composed of conclusions based on presuppositions" (Geertz, 1983, p. 75). The mechanistic metaphor has shaped Western culture's view of nature, history, society, and the human being (Merchant, 1980). This metaphor has influenced the birth of economics with Smith's (1976) "The Wealth of Nations," which analyzed market economies as self-governing mechanisms regulated by laws and giving rise to an orderly society. The scientific revolution has brought about a strong focus on quantification and computation. The industrial revolution and its emphasis on increasing production through mechanization has given rise to a strong focus on economics attested by the development of both capitalism and Marxism.

Twentieth-century information theory, the mathematical representation of transmission and processing of information, and computerization manifest the view that problem solving is essentially the manipulation of information according to a set of rules (Merchant, 1989, p. 231). The method of computer science is formalization (i.e., symbolization of real-world phenomena so they can be subjected to algorithmic treatment. The computer is thus a result and a symptom of Western culture's high regard for abstraction and formalization; it is a product of the mathematician's worldview, a physical device capable of operation in the realm of abstract thought.

Epistemological Issues of Computerization

One cornerstone of the rationalistic tradition is the correspondence theory of language (Winograd & Flores, 1986). This theory has influenced thinking about computers and their impact on society. Quantification and computer representations are taken as models of an objective reality. Whereas humans have developed a complex system of languages to interpret, store, copy, or transmit information that they receive in analog format through their senses, computers facilitate the external processing of information in digital format by representing it in binary form. Thus, computers reduce experience to numerical abstraction. As a consequence, the natural and social worlds are treated as being made up of discrete and observable elements that can be counted and measured. Reality is reduced to what can be expressed in numbers (Berman, 1992).

Using a computer is an isolated activity of the individual. Although computers have revolutionized communication in terms of scope and speed, computers are not conducive to cooperation and teamwork. Human-computer interaction generally is characterized by a one-user-per-computer ratio. Collaboration with other computer users generally means division of a task into a linear sequence of subtasks, which can be addressed by single individuals. Furthermore, computer-based experience is a partial experience predominantly limited to the visual. The manipulation of objects displayed on the screen emphasizes the interaction between the active subject and the passive object, which is characteristic of a scientific mind that has been exposed as being male and disembodied (Keller, 1985). This interaction is underpinned further by a domination logic that objectifies both the natural world and people as other (e.g., women or indigenous people) to justify their exploitation (Merchant, 1980).

The disengagement between subject and object reinforces a psychological distance between the individual and the social and natural environment (Veregin, 1995; Weizenbaum, 1976). Computer-based experience is individualistic and anthropocentric and no longer influenced by geographic space. Computerization creates an alternative, unnatural environment, or infosphere (Floridi, 2001). The computer has created a different world in which most activities involve information technology; in addition, the concepts regarding these activities are shifting and becoming informationally enriched (Moor, 1998). Digitization has become a worldview in itself (Capurro, 1990). Such views may adequately describe the experiences of people whose lives are permeated by computerization but emphasize how different these experiences are from the realities of the majority of people on the planet. The value dualism of hard vs. soft information ignores the reality that the computerized abstraction of the world is not absolute but rather dependent on cultural context, scientific paradigm, and technological feasibility. The digital world excludes and obscures important aspects of the realms of society and natural environment.

Contrary to the individualism of computerized experience, African thought emphasizes the close links among knowledge of space, of self, and one's position in the community. Although African traditions and cultural practices are diverse, there are underlying affinities that justify certain generalizations (Wiredu, 1980). In African philosophy, a person is defined through his or her relationships with other persons, not through an isolated quality such as rationality (Menkiti, 1979; Shutte, 1993). African thought does not know the sharp distinction between the self and a world that is controlled and changed. The world is a place in which people participate in community affairs. In fact, participation is the keystone of traditional African society. Participation integrates individuals within the social and natural networks of the world. The members of a community are linked by participation, which becomes the meaning of personal and collective unity and connects people both horizontally and vertically, the living and the dead as well as the physical environment that surrounds them (Mulago, 1969). Setiloane (1986) calls participation "the essence of being"; "I think, therefore I am" is replaced by "I participate, therefore I am" (Taylor, 1963, p. 41). The individual's personhood is dependent on the community, but the continuation of the community depends on the individual. The life of the ancestors is continued through the individual; the individual life is continued through the dependents (Mulago, 1969). Unlike the Western concept of community, the African meaning of community does not refer to an aggregation of individuals (Menkiti, 1979) but prioritizes the group over the individual while still safeguarding the dignity and value of the individual (Senghor, 1966). Shutte (1993) explains that the notions of a person as a free being and that of being dependent for one's personhood on others are not contradictory. Through being affirmed by others and through the desire to help and support others, the individual grows, personhood is developed, and personal freedom comes into being. African thought sees a person as a being under construction whose character changes as the relations to other persons change. To grow older means to become more of a person and more worthy of respect. In contrast to Western individualism and its emphasis on the rights of the individual Menkiti (1979) stresses that growth is a normative notion: "personhood is something at which individuals could fail" (p. 159). The individual belongs to the group and is linked to members of the group through interaction; conversation and dialogue are both purpose and activity of the community. Consequently, African socialism aims to realize not the will of the majority but the will of the community (Apostel, 1981) and, therefore, rejects both European socialism and Western capitalism because both are underpinned by subject-object dualism, which produces relationships between a person and a thing rather than a meeting of forces. Subject-object dualism, as is reinforced through computerization, alienates the individual from others. While Western rational thought values individuality, African tradition is afraid of solitude and closed individuality, and values solidarity, consensus, and reconciliation.

Users who share the cultural assumptions embedded in computer technology are not aware of the inherent bias, but members of other cultures are aware that they have to adapt to different patterns of thought and culturally bound ways of knowing (Bowers, 2000; Duncker, 2002; Walton & Vukovic, 2003; Winschiers & Paterson, 2004). The uncritical acceptance of the computer obscures its influence on the user's thought patterns. The digital divide is seen as a problem of providing access to technology. However, it may be that the digital divide is an expression of the dualisms inherent in the cultural concepts underpinning computerization. Hoesle (1992) stresses that the main issue of contrast between industrialized countries and the third world is cultural. Capurro (1990) warns that a critical awareness of how information technology is used to manipulate both ourselves and the natural environment is necessary. Such awareness must include the linkages between progress in developing countries, which goes hand-in-hand with more widespread use of computers and the emergence of Western individualism and subjectivism (Bowers, 2000) and impacts on the environment.

THE LINGKAGES BETWEEN INFORMATION TECHNOLOGY, DEVELOPMENT, AND THE ENVIRONMENT

Information technology generally is seen as an essential component of development and strongly promoted by international development agencies. It is assumed that information technology enhances both economic development and democratic practices. This promotion implies that unless developing countries apply information technology and join the fast train of the computer revolution, they will be left behind (Berman, 1992). Publications on ICT development in Africa describe African societies as "lagging behind" (Schaefer, 2002), while ICT structures in Africa are compared to "the North American picture ... in the first half of the twentieth century" (Kawooya, 2002). This line of argument not only supports technological determinism but also subscribes to a development ideology that is based on a particular concept of history. This concept is as linear as the concept of technological progress, assuming that every society has to go through the same stages until they reach the same economic levels as countries considered developed.

Information Technology and Democracy

The notion that information technology contributes to a more democratic society is based on the assumption that information technology is nondiscriminatory in that it potentially provides equal opportunities to everyone. However, equal access does not ensure equal benefit (Neelameghan, 1981). In addition, this assumption ignores the existing imbalances and asymmetric societal structures that do not allow everyone to participate equally (Adam, 2001; Grant Lewis & Samoff, 1992; Veregrin, 1995). Information technology is not inherently neutral but is linked to power from which moral implications arise: "Those who filter and package information for us in the [global information infrastructure] will hold enormous power over us" (Johnson, 1997). As a study by Introna and Nissenbaum (2000) suggests, the criteria by which search engines filter information are not transparent, and particular sites systematically are excluded. This conclusion runs counter to the democratic value associated with the Internet.

As long as the public sphere continues to prioritize information from the North over information generated in the South (Lor & Britz,

2002), it is questionable whether people in Africa and other developing nations actually do have access to appropriate and useful information. Simply providing the infrastructure to tune in to the North-to-South information flow cannot bridge the gap between the information-rich and the information-poor. The information-poor have to generate information for themselves and about themselves. Thus, the issue raised by Johnson (1997) of power being exercised by those who filter and package information over those who receive this information is a pertinent one for Africa and other non-Western countries whose voices are marginalized in the global information scenario.

Although the scope of online communication allows people to engage with a vast number of other people all over the world, Bowers (2000) argues that the learning of moral norms is of higher importance to democratic decision making than is access to information. Global communication, although spanning a much broader geographic scope, tends to join like-minded people who share a common interest. Online communities provide little opportunity for participants to understand the needs of others and one's responsibility to them (Adam, 2001; Bowers, 2000; Johnson, 1997). The more time people spend communicating online with like-minded people, the less time is spent communicating with those whose geographic space they share. As a result, people engage less in debate and tend toward already formed biases. The paradox of growing insularity through increasing connectivity prompts Johnson (1997) to raise an old question: Is democracy possible without shared geographic space? In the African context in which multi-ethnicity is the norm rather than the exception, and tribalism and ethnic discrimination are a major obstacle for democracy, the question is extremely pertinent. In the light of Johnson's and Bowers' analyses, there seems to be the danger that computer-mediated communication may exacerbate the existing ethnic divide in many African countries by harboring insularity.

Information Technology and Economic Development

Ogundipe-Leslie (1993) argues that development itself is characterized by cultural imperialism and ethnocentrism and interferes with the natural internal processes in the society to which it is introduced. Development is based on the assumption that every society shares the same values that characterize developed societies, such as efficiency, speed, and competitiveness. These values are evoked through references to the super information highway that will lead African countries into a future of material security and possession of particular goods and services that are typical of industrial societies. This eurocentric point of view is used as a standard of measurement so that societies who do not conform are not perceived as different but as primitive, traditional, or underdeveloped (Ogundipe-Leslie, 1993). The notion of development as an economic upliftment ignores a nation's values, aspirations, beliefs, and patterns of behavior. As a consequence, measures to develop according to the Western economic model interfere with the natural internal processes in society and uproot the individual and collective lives of the people. Ogundipe-Leslie (1993) criticizes development not only for its cultural imperialism and ethnocentrism but also for ignoring the social costs that people have to pay for the interruption of their social dynamics.

Computerization and particularly the global information infrastructure increasingly enforce Western ideology onto other cultures. Computerization is shaping consciousness and bodily experience to accept computer mediation as normal; consequently, computer illiteracy is considered socially abnormal and deficient, and those who do not use computers are less-developed and less-intelligent. Capurro (1990) confirms that the influence of modern information technology is shaping all aspects of social life. For example in the industrialized world in which computerization is permeating society, it is becoming apparent that computerization rationalizes humans out of work processes (Bowers, 2000). Increasingly fewer people do more complex tasks in a shorter time, thus excluding more people from this process. One of Africa's hidden and untapped assets is its human resources (Britz, 2002). Computerization is seen as a means to provide information, education, and economic opportunity to all people to overcome the problem of unemployment. There is, however, the danger that computer technology in Africa might further enforce and enlarge the gap between the advantaged and the disadvantaged.

Berman highlights the origins of computer technology by stressing that during and after World War II and the subsequent period of expansion of the welfare state, economic planning data were used by the state to gain control over people. African countries inherited the concept of authoritarian state control in colonial rule. The computer's logical structure, which emphasizes hierarchy, sequence control, and iteration, reflects the structure of bureaucratic organizations. This focus on control is obscured by the assumption of scientific objectivity. Hence, the power, which is exercised through computer application, is hidden behind the appearance of expert decision. The computer is a technology of command and control (Berman, 1992). Not only do computers reinforce authoritarianism, but they also become a symbol of advanced development and efficiency. But because computers narrow the scope to quantifiable information, indigenous knowledge is further marginalized, which makes it difficult for the state to take the qualitative aspects of social structure and culture into account.

While some level of ICT may be important for development in the sense of improved well being and decreased suffering of African people, no level of ICT will be a sufficient condition for these hopes. The perception that ICTs are necessary for economic development ignores that technology invents its own need. The multitude of new consumer products and the rate at which they are introduced indicate that producers create needs where none existed (Veregin, 1995). The global ICT market is characterized by ever-decreasing intervals of software releases that force African countries continuously to invest in new software in order to avoid a further widening of the digital gap (Winschiers & Paterson, 2004).

The Environment

Bowers (2000) warns that the globalization of computer-based culture is not only a form of colonialism but that the cultural assumptions and lifestyles reinforced by the digital culture are ecologically problematic. Merchant (1980) stresses that the mechanistic view of nature sanctions exploitative environmental conduct. The mechanistic philosophy renders nature dead instead of a living, nurturing organism. As a consequence, cultural constraints, which previously restricted destructive environmental conduct, lost impact and were replaced with the machine metaphor (i.e., images of mastery and domination that sanctioned the exploitation of nature). While rural communities are aware that environmental conditions are unpredictable and that scarcity is a possibility, the modern Western way of life is based on the false assumption that progress does not depend on the contingencies of natural systems. Thus, the predominant challenge of the 21st century will be the environment.

The notion of knowledge and information as strategic resources points toward the link between computerization and the industrial revolution and its main characteristic: the transformation of utility value into exchange value (Capurro, 1990). Computerization commodifies information and anything else that falls under its domain. In this sense, the computer revolution "represents the digital phase of the Industrial revolution … it perpetuates the primary goal of transferring more aspects of everyday life into commodities that can be manufactured and sold, now on a global basis" (Bowers, 2000). There are "connections between computers, cultural diversity and the

ecological crisis" (Bowers, 2000). The market has become a universal principle encompassing all forms of human activity and commodifying the relationships among people and between human beings and the environment. The mapping and subdivision of lived space based on national or global grids nullify places of local meaning while playing an important part in the functioning of capitalist economy by creating space as an exploitable resource (McHaffie, 1995). Geographic information systems (GIS) have further depersonalized this process. The parallel between information and nature is not accidental; both are considered resources. Nature is a shared resource that is vital for human survival, and information is a resource that is shared among people. Critics of Western-style development, such as Vandana Shiva (1989), have pointed out how the commodification of natural resources, which is typical of the Western paradigm, excludes natural systems from the economic model. In this paradigm, a river in its natural state is not considered productive unless it is dammed. The natural system has to be modified in order to produce value; the use value of the river has to be transformed into exchange value. The preoccupation with quantification contributes not only to the commodification of nature but also to the widespread acceptance of data as the basis of thought. Unless information can be computerized, it is not considered valuable and, hence, undermines the importance of indigenous knowledge.

The global computer revolution perpetuates the assumption underlying development ideology that it is merely a question of time until developing countries will reach the level of industrialized nations. Hoesle (1992) asserts that this assumption cannot possibly be fulfilled. The ecological footprint of the so-called developed nations is not only far heavier than that of the third world but also is unsustainable. It therefore would become an ecological impossibility for the whole world to adopt the same lifestyle. Hoesle (1992) infers that because "the [Western] way of life is not universalizable [it is] therefore immoral." He questions the legitimacy of a world society built according to Western values that have brought humankind to the verge of ecological disaster.

Computerization is instrumental in shaping the ecological problems we are facing, because computerization decontextualizes knowledge and isolates it from the ambiguities and complexities of reality.

The rationalistic tendency to fraction complex holistic processes into a series of discrete problems leads to the inability to address ecological and social issues adequately. Popular cyberlibertarian ideology wrongly assumes that information technology provides free and equal interactions and equal opportunities that neutralize asymmetric social structures (Adam, 2001; Winner, 1997). ICT can only be truly beneficial to Africans if they support the African concept of community and counteract insularity. Besides focusing on the advantages of ICTs, the negative consequences of computerization, such as the rationalization of labor, which are observable in industrialized nations, must be avoided. The current patterns of production (i.e., the high frequencies of hardware and software releases) are ecologically and socially unsustainable and need to change (Winschiers & Paterson, 2004).

Hoesle (1992) therefore stresses the need to bring values back into focus and to recognize humans as part of the cosmos. Modern subjectivism and the sectorial and analytic character of scientific thinking have almost forgotten the advantages of a holistic approach to reality (Hoesle, 1992). The value and legitimacy of Africa's rich tacit knowledge has been undermined because this knowledge is largely informal and does not fit the computer-imposed data formats (Adeya & Cogburn, 2001; Harris, Weiner, Warner, & Levin, 1995). Cultures are reservoirs of expression and symbolic representations with a truth claim of their own and, thus, need to be preserved (Hoesle, 1992). However, Lor and Britz (2002) call attention to the limited contribution that information generated

in the South is making to the global knowledge society and point to the bias of the public sphere toward information generated in the North. Only a minute proportion of Internet hosts is located in Africa, although most countries on the continent have achieved connectivity to the Internet (Maloka & le Roux, 2001). The pressing issue is not providing access to technology in order to turn more people into receivers of information that was created elsewhere and may not be useful to them, but, as suggested by Capurro (1990), it is to find ways that African countries can promote their identities in information production, distribution, and use. In terms of a global information ecology, he stresses the importance "of finding the right balance ... between the blessings of universality and the need for preserving plurality" (Capurro, 1990, p. 130). In order to find this balance, a great conversation is necessary that transcends limitations of discourse among members of particular social groups (Berman, 1992; Moor, 1998). Such a global dialogue must be cross-sectoral, cross-cultural, and transdisciplinary. Capurro (1990) reminds us that the electronic revolution is only a possibility that has to be inserted responsibly into existing cultural and social contexts in order to produce the necessary knowledge pluralism to address the complex social and ecological issues we are facing.

In order to fill the need for such global dialogue that addresses the ethical requirements for development that is truly sustainable, a global ethical framework has been developed in the form of the Earth Charter.

THE EARTH CHARTER

The Earth Charter (www.earthcharter.org) development began in 1987 with the Brundtland Report, "Our Common Future," calling for a Charter for Nature (WCED, 1987) that would set forth fundamental principles for sustainable development. The Earth Charter was addressed again during the 1992 Rio Earth Summit and taken forward when Maurice Strong and Mikhail Gorbachev launched the Earth Charter Initiative in 1994. In a decade-long participatory and consultative process involving all major religions and people from different cultures and all sectors of society, the present list of principles of the Earth Charter was developed and finalized in 2000. The Earth Charter consists of a preamble, 18 principles, numerous subprinciples, and a conclusion suggesting "the way forward." The preamble expresses that the future depends on the choices we will make and that "we must join together to bring forth a sustainable global society founded on respect for nature, universal human rights, economic justice, and a culture of peace." The Earth Charter locates humanity as part of the cosmos and stresses the interdependencies among people and between people and nature. The preamble emphasizes that the foundations of global security are threatened by patterns of consumption and production, which undermine communities and cause environmental degradation. The Earth Charter emphasizes that every individual shares the "universal responsibility" of facing the challenges of using knowledge and technologies to build a just, democratic, and ecologically sound future. The Earth Charter principles address four themes: respect and care for the community of life; ecological integrity; social and economic justice; and democracy, non-violence, and peace. As the "way forward," the Earth Charter calls for the development of a sustainable way of life based on a "collaborative search for truth and wisdom" in which cultural diversity is valued.

The Earth Charter and Computer Ethics

Because computing is the product as well as the extension of a way of life and worldview that largely has caused the environmental crisis, and because computers are directly linked to the concept of third-world development, computer

ethics has to locate itself more explicitly within the broader context of the environmental issues on the one hand and development ethics on the other.

The Earth Charter framework not only helps to address particular issues in light of their compliance with ecological integrity and respect for nature, but also stresses the gap between rich and poor and global responsibility to address poverty. By stating that "when basic needs have been met, human development is primarily about being more, not having more," the Earth Charter prioritizes qualitative criteria to measure development over quantitative criteria.

The Earth Charter and the WISIS declaration subscribe to the same values: peace, freedom, equality, solidarity, tolerance, shared responsibility, and respect for nature. The two documents do not replace each other but are compatible. While WISIS focuses on ICT development, the Earth Charter is much broader in scope, thus complementing and strengthening the WISIS declaration. Being global both in terms of content and scope (Dower, 2005), the Earth Charter is a proposal for a system of global ethics. It encompasses both human rights as well as less formalized principles for ecological, social, and political development. If ICTs are to be an integral part of this future, it is vital that computer ethics takes cognizance of the existence of this global ethical framework and examines how computing can be inserted into this vision of a sustainable and just future. The Earth Charter asserts the interconnectedness of people and the environment and affirms the wisdom of different cultural traditions, while at the same time confirming the contribution of humanistic science and sustainable technology. The preamble to the Earth Charter highlights the current environmental and social crisis but sees "these trends are perilous—but not inevitable." In other words, the Earth Charter does not subscribe to technological determinism but rather declares that "the choice is ours." The choices we are making as individuals as well as communities determine the future. To change the course of current patterns of thought and behaviors is a matter of human will power and creative energy. It involves a change of attitudes, worldviews, values, and ways of living, such as consumption and production habits.

Unlike the WISIS declaration, the Earth Charter addresses not only states but also the broader public. The global ethic formulated in the Earth Charter provides guidelines for behavior and action. But it is important to realize that the Earth Charter is not to be understood as final. It provides a framework and catalyst for reflection and discussion. As such, this framework is of value to computer ethics. It is the role of computer ethics to guide ICT development toward a sustainable future. By addressing whether the Earth Charter can be endorsed by computer professionals, computer ethics can examine the Earth Charter's justification. The results of such an examination will be fruitful for both the Earth Charter and Computer Ethics. The vision for a sustainable future that is set forth in the preamble to the Earth Charter can guide the development of a vision for the role of computing and ICT in the future. The Earth Charter can be an ethical values framework for improving progress toward sustainability, designing codes of conduct for both professionals and education, and designing accountability systems. The Earth Charter principles set out under the heading Ecological Integrity can help to guide computing and ICT development in terms of environmental performance, which, for example, would refer to issues concerning energy and emissions, both in the production and the use of computer technology; the materials used; the use of resources in production cycles; and the disposal of computing technology, hazardous substances, and so forth. The social impacts of computing (e.g., the danger of increased insularity of users or the rationalization of labor) can be addressed by the principles under the heading Social & Economic Justice and Democracy. The Earth Charter principles grouped under "Democracy, Non violence and Peace" provide guidance to address issues such as the impact of computing for community participation, the impact of computing on the well being of the community, the impact on community environment, and quality of life.

Today's globalized world is a multicultural world. However, the field of computer ethics is dominated by Western perspectives. It is necessary to overcome this eurocentric tendency by examining the implications of computer technology from different cultural paradigms. The Earth Charter, on the other hand, has been developed by people from various cultural contexts. Computer ethicists may examine how computing either can support or violate the principles and values stated in the Earth Charter. Using the Earth Charter as a framework for addressing ethical issues arising in computing will enable computer ethicists to examine these issues from the perspectives of different cultural backgrounds as well as the implications for the environment and the development of a sustainable global society. Using the Earth Charter to address particular computer ethics issues will help to put them in a larger global context, supporting a more critical and inclusive examination without giving in to technological determinism or information colonialism.

Rather than accepting the current destructive tendencies of industrial civilization and imposing them on developing nations, the Earth Charter encourages the reinvention of industrial civilization through changes of cultural orientation and extensive revision of systems, practices, and procedures. As such, the Earth Charter is closely linked to development ethics (Dower, 2005). Computer ethics needs to acknowledge the linkages between computing, development, and environmental conduct. The Earth Charter provides a tool for the development of a computer ethics that is global in both content and scope and contributes toward a sustainable future for all.

CONCLUSION

There are several positions in computer ethics that purport the global character of computer ethics. These views, however, ignore the observation that the digital divide is a divide between a minority of people whose lives are permeated by computerization and a majority of people whose lives largely are unaffected by the computer. These views also seem to ignore that computerization itself is a product of a particular culture and worldview. In spite of the advantages that computerization and information technology have to offer, there is the danger of traditional worldviews and cultural practices being transformed and replaced with Western values embedded in the technology. This replacement is a form of information colonialism and a threat to the environment endangering human survival. Gòrniak-Kocikowska (2004) predicts that although it would be desirable that the emergence of a new global ethic is a participatory process of dialogue and exchange, it is more likely that Western cultural values and worldviews will be imposed through computerization. It is the responsibility of computer ethics to prevent such ethnocentrism.

To avoid that computerization enforces the adoption of a Western worldview, a broad cross-cultural dialogue is necessary. Such dialogical ethical research requires a balanced framework that takes cultural diversity and the need for ecological sustainability into account. A suitable framework for global ethical dialogue is already in place in the form of the Earth Charter, a set of principles that lays down an inclusive ethical vision that recognizes the interdependencies of environmental protection, human rights, equitable human development, and peace.

ACKNOWLEDGMENTS

Les Underhill, Britta Schinzel, Tim Dunne, and John Paterson read earlier drafts of this chapter.

REFERENCES

Adam, A. (2001). Computer ethics in a different voice. *Information and Organization, 11,* 235-261.

Adeya, C. N., & Cogburn, D. L. (2001). Globalisation and the information economy: Challenges and opportunities for Africa. In G. Nulerns, N. Hafkin, L. Van Audenhoven, & B. Cammaerts (Eds.), *The digital divide in developing countries: Towards an information society in Africa* (pp. 77-112). Brussels: Brussel University Press.

Anyiam-Osigwe, M. C. (2002). Africa's new awakening and ICT. Toward attaining sustainable democracy in Africa. In T. Mendina & J. J. Britz (Eds.), *Information ethics in the electronic age. Current issues in Africa and the world* (pp. 36-46). Jefferson, NC: McFarland.

Apostel, L. (1981). *African philosophy: Myth or reality.* Gent, Belgium: Story-Scientia.

Berman, B. J. (1992). The state, computers, and African development: The information non-revolution. In S. Grant Lewis & J. Samoff (Eds.), *Microcomputers in African development: Critical perspectives* (pp. 213-229). Boulder, CO: Westview Press.

Bowers, C. A. (2000). *Let them eat data: How computers affect education, cultural diversity, and the prospects of ecological sustainability.* Athens: The University of Georgia Press.

Britz, J. J. (2002). Africa and its place in the twenty-first century. A moral reflection. In T. Mendina & J. J. Britz (Eds.), *Information ethics in the electronic age: Current issues in Africa and the world* (pp. 5-6). Jefferson, NC: McFarland.

Bynum, T. W. (2000, Summer). A very short history of computer ethics. *Newsletter of the American Philosophical Association on Philosophy and Computing.* Retrieved July 2005, from http://www.

southernct.edu/organizations/rccs/resources/research/introduction/bynum_shrt_hist.html

Bynum, T. W., & Rogerson, S. (1996). Introduction and overview: Global information ethics. *Science and Engineering Ethics, 2,* 131-136.

Capurro, R. (1989). Towards an information ecology. In I. Wormell (Ed.), *Information quality. Definitions and dimensions. Proceedings of the NORDINFO International Seminar "Information and Quality,"* (pp. 122-139) Copenhagen.

Curry, M. R. (1995). Geographic information systems and the inevitability of ethical inconsistencies. In J. Pickles (Ed.), *Ground truth* (pp. 68-87). London: The Guilford Press.

Dower, N. (2005). The earth charter and global ethics. *Worldviews: Environment, Culture, Religion, 8,* 15-28.

Duncker, E. (2002). Cross-cultural usability of the library metaphor. In *Proceedings of the Second Joint Conference on Digital Libraries (JCDL) of the Association of Computing Machinery (ACM) and the Institute of Electrical and Electronics Engineers Computer Society (IEEE-CS) 2002,* Portland, Oregon (pp. 223-230).

Floridi, L. (2001). Information ethics: An environmental approach to the digital divide. *Philosophy in the Contemporary World, 9*(1). Retrieved June 2005, from www.wolfson.ox.ac.uk/~floridi/pdf/ieeadd.pdf

Freiberger, P. A., & Swaine, M. R. (2003). Computers. In *Encyclopædia Britannica 2003.* [CD-ROM]. London: Encyclopedia Britannica.

Gandalf. (2005). *Data on Internet activity worldwide (hostcount).* Retrieved July 2005, from http://www.gandalf.it/data/data1.htm

Geertz, C. (1983). *Local knowledge. Further essays in interpretive anthropology.* New York: Basic Books.

Gòrniak-Kocikowska, K. (1996). The computer revolution and the problem of global ethics. *Science and Engineering Ethics, 2,* 177-190.

Gòrniak-Kocikowska, K. (2004). The global culture of digital technology and its ethics. *The ETHICOMP E-Journal, 1*(3). Retrieved May 2005, from http://www.ccsr.cse.dmu.ac.uk/journal

Grant Lewis, S., & Samoff, J. (1992). Introduction. In S. Grant Lewis & J. Samoff (Eds.), *Microcomputers in African development: Critical perspectives* (pp. 1-24). Boulder, CO: Westview Press.

Harris, T. M., Weiner, D., Warner, T. A., & Levin, R. (1995). Pursuing social goals through participatory geographic information systems. Redressing South Africa's historical political ecology. In J. Pickles (Ed.), *Ground truth* (pp. 196-222). London: The Guilford Press.

Heim, M. (1993). *The metaphysics of virtual reality.* New York: Oxford University Press.

Hoesle, V. (1992). The third world as a philosophical problem. *Social Research, 59,* 227-263.

Introna, L., & Nissenbaum, H. (2000). Shaping the Web. Why the politics of search engines matter. *The Information Society, 16,* 169-185.

Johnson, D. G. (1997). Is the global information infrastructure a democratic technology? *Computers and Society, 27,* 20-26.

Johnson, D. G. (1999). Computer ethics in the 21st century. In *Proceedings of ETHICOMP99,* Rome, Italy.

Kawooya, D. (2002). The digital divide. An ethical dilemma for information professionals in Uganda? In T. Mendina, & J. J. Britz (Eds.), *Information ethics in the electronic age: Current issues in Africa and the world* (pp. 28-35). Jefferson, NC: McFarland.

Keller, E. F. (1985). *Reflections on gender and science.* New Haven, CT: Yale University Press.

Kocikowski, A. (1999). Technologia informatyczna a stary problem totalitaryzmu. *Nauka, 1,* 120-126.

Lor, P. J., & Britz, J. J. (2002). Information imperialism. Moral problems in information flows from south to north. In T. Mendina & J. J. Britz (Eds.), *Information ethics in the electronic age: Current issues in Africa and the world* (pp. 15-21). Jefferson, NC: McFarland.

Mahoney, M. S. (1988). The history of computing in the history of technology. *Annals of the History of Computing, 10,* 113-125.

Maloka, E., & le Roux, E. (2001). *Africa in the new millennium: Challenges and prospects.* Pretoria: Africa Institute of South Africa.

McHaffie, P. (1995). Manufacturing metaphors. Public cartography, the market, and democracy. In J. Pickles (Ed.), *Ground truth* (pp. 113-129). New York: The Guilford Press.

Menkiti, I. A. (1979). Person and community in African traditional thought. In R. A. Wright (Ed.), *African philosophy* (pp. 157-168). New York: University Press.

Merchant, C. (1980). *The death of nature: Women, ecology, and the scientific revolution.* San Francisco: Harper and Row.

Moor, J. (1998). Reason, relativity, and responsibility in computer ethics. *Computers and Society, 28,* 14-21.

Mulago, V. (1969). Vital participation: The cohesive principle of the Bantu community. In K. Kickson & P. Ellinworth (Eds.), *Biblical revelation and African beliefs* (pp. 137-158). London: Butterworth.

Neelameghan, A. (1981). Some issues in information transfer. *A third world perspective. International Federation of Library Associates (IFLA) Journal, 7,* 8-18.

Ng'etich, K. A. (2001). Harnessing computer-mediated communication technologies in the unification of Africa: Constraints and potentials. In E. Maloka & E. le Roux (Eds.), *Africa in the new millennium: Challenges and prospects* (pp. 77-85). Pretoria: Africa Institute of South Africa.

Ogundipe-Leslie, M. (1993). African women, culture and another development. In S. M. James (Ed.), *Theorising black feminism: The visionary pragmatism of black women, A.P.A. Busia* (pp. 102-117). London: Routledge.

Pickles, J. (1995). Representations in an electronic age. Geography, GIS, and democracy. In J. Pickles (Ed.), *Ground truth* (pp. 1-30). New York: The Guilford Press.

Schaefer III, S. J. (2002). Telecommunications infrastructure in the African continent. 1960-2010. In T. Mendina & J. J. Britz (Eds.), *Information ethics in the electronic age: Current issues in Africa and the world* (pp. 22-27). Jefferson, NC: McFarland.

Senghor, L. (1966). Negritude—A humanism of the 20th century. *Optima, 16,* 1-8.

Setiloane, G. M. (1986). *African theology: An introduction.* Johannesburg: Skotaville Publishers.

Shiva, V. (1989). *Staying alive: Women, ecology, and development.* London: Zed Books.

Shutte, A. (1993). *Philosophy for Africa.* Cape Town: University of Cape Town Press.

Smith, A. (1976). *An inquiry into the nature and causes of the wealth of nations* (R. H. Cambell & A. S. Skinner, Eds.). Oxford, UK: Clarendon Press.

Taylor, J. V. (1963). *The primal vision: Christian presence amid African religion.* London: S.C.M. Press.

Veregin, H. (1995). Computer innovation and adoption in geography: A critique of conventional technological models. In J. Pickles (Ed.), *Ground truth* (pp. 88-112). London: The Guilford Press.

Walton, M., & Vukovic, V. (2003). Cultures, literacy, and the Web: Dimensions of information "scent." *Interactions, 10,* 64-71.

WCED (1987). *Our common future. Report of the World Commission on Environment and Development (WCED)* (pp. 323-333). New York: Oxford University Press.

Weizenbaum, J. (1976). *Computer power and human reason: From judgement to calculation.* New York: W.H. Freeman.

Winner, L. (1997). Cyberlibertarian myths and the prospect for community. *ACM Computers and Society, 27,* 14-19.

Winograd, T., & Flores, F. (1986). *Understanding computers and cognition.* Norwood, NJ: Arlex Publishing Corporation.

Winschiers, H., & Paterson, B. (2004). Sustainable software development. *Proceedings of the 2004 Annual Research Conference of the South African Institute of Computer Scientists and Information Technologists on IT Research In Developing Countries (SAICSIT 2004)—Fulfilling the promise of ICT,* Stellenbosch, South Africa (pp. 111-115).

Wiredu, K. (1980). *Philosophy and an African culture.* London: Cambridge.

World Internet Usage Statistics. (2005). *Data on Internet usage and population.* Retrieved November 2005, from http://www.internetworldstats.com/stats1.htm

WSIS. (2004). *The world summit on the information society: Declaration of principles.* Retrieved November 2005, from http://www.itu.int/wsis

Chapter 5.2
Privacy and Property in the Global Datasphere

Dan L. Burk
University of Minnesota Law School, USA

ABSTRACT

Adoption of information technologies is dependent upon the availability of information to be channeled via such technologies. Although many cultural approaches to information control have been identified, two increasingly ubiquitous regimes are battling for dominance in the international arena. These may be termed the utilitarian and deontological approaches and may be identified roughly with the United States and the continental European tradition. Each approach has been aggressively promulgated by its respective proponent via international treaty regimes in the areas of privacy and intellectual property, to the virtual exclusion of other alternatives. Absent a drastic shift in international treaty dynamics, these dominant conceptions likely will curtail the development of alternate approaches that might otherwise emerge from local culture and tradition.

INTRODUCTION

Technology, like all human artifacts, bears the value-laden imprint of its makers, including embedded cultural assumptions as to how technology should or should not be used. These embedded values may differ from the values of cultures outside that of the originators of the technology and may lead to cultural disruption when the technology is put to uses outside its original cultural milieu. For example, many of the controversies surrounding the proliferation of Internet technology—controversies over pornography, intellectual property, privacy, bulk e-mail, or hate speech—may be viewed as cultural clashes between the values embedded in the technology and the values of those now using the technology (Burk, 1999b).

Law, considered a formalized expression of values, similarly embodies cultural norms and also may clash with the values embedded in alien technologies. But as Lessig (1999) and Reidenberg (1998) have shown, embedded technological rule sets in information technologies are contiguous with the explicit legal and normative rule sets of their originating culture; that is, both law and technology constrain behavior according to the value system that they express. This relationship has important implications for the proliferation and adoption of information and communication technologies (ICTs) around the globe. Development of these technologies presupposes the existence of informational content to be stored, communicated, or processed. Adoption of such technologies is, therefore, necessarily dependent upon the legal and normative regime that determines the availability and control of the information to be stored, manipulated, and disseminated via that technology. The ability to specify the legal and technical parameters for use of information is necessarily the ability to control the adoption and use of ICTs that process such information.

Consequently, as ICTs become more widely available, the provision of informational content increasingly has become a matter of intense interest, both among nations that are net information producers and among nations that are net information consumers—although perhaps for different reasons. As nations that develop information technologies export those technologies, they have consciously exported along with it particular legal and normative models for informational control, effectively spreading their value systems alongside their technologies. Issues of informational control have tended to arise in two separate sectors, contemplating, respectively, development of creative informational content and gathering of personal information. Legal regimes regulating control of these informational genres typically are labeled under the rubrics of "intellectual property" and "data privacy." In each area, the late 20th and early 21st centuries have seen a clear trend toward off-the-shelf regimes derived from the economic and political dominance of the United States and the European Union. Each of these economic powers has aggressively promoted its own approach to information control, and in doing so, have largely displaced and overwhelmed the development of local or indigenous from-the-ground-up informational regimes.

In this chapter, I examine the nature and proliferation of these off-the-shelf models that now dominate international provision of information. I shall first sketch the general outlines of the dominant approaches toward information ownership and toward control of personal information, showing how the philosophies from each side of the Atlantic parallel one another for each of these respective information denominations. Specifically, I show how both information ownership and data privacy are dominated by parallel regimes of Western utilitarian and deontological ethics. I then turn to a description of the political and legal strategies by which the dominant information regimes have been internationally promulgated and indicate the effect that these ethical juggernauts have had in an era of globalization. I then survey the type of localized or indigenous approaches that are being extinguished by the dominant Western approaches and conclude that, absent some unexpected and drastic change in the near term, prospects for any cultural diversity in approaches to informational control is relatively bleak.

INTELLECTUAL PROPERTY

The economic character of digital communication and data processing technologies hold profound implications for any regime of informational control. Once the infrastructure of these technologies is in place, they allow the reproduction and dissemination of digitized content at essentially zero marginal cost. Additionally, the equipment used to engage in such activity is increasingly available at a relatively modest cost, which continues to decline with technological advances in the fabrication of semiconductor devices for processing and storage capacity. These economic trends diminish or largely remove the economic impediments that in the past have naturally constrained the creation and dissemination of creative informational works. Consequently, any control that is to be exercised over such works must increasingly come from legal constraints. Nations that are net information exporters have a vested interest in such legal constraints, typically in the form of intellectual property regimes, in order to capture the value of the content they produce.

The American Approach

The legal constraint of intellectual property law necessarily imposes costs upon consumers of creative content; by imposing such constraints, access to creative works that digital technology might make freely available is diminished when legal controls are imposed. In the United States, these constraints are justified under a rationale that is unabashedly utilitarian, which presumes that the long-term benefits of legal constraints will justify the short-term cost. Most frequently, this calculus of cost and benefit is couched in the language of economics. Creative works are characterized as economic public goods, which may be underproduced because they can be appropriated at a cost below the cost of production. Intellectual property rights constitute an incentive to creation that allows the creator to charge for certain uses of the work and so recoup the investment required to develop such work (Landes & Posner, 1989).

Under this approach, intellectual property rights are justified only to the extent that they benefit the public in general. The constraints imposed by intellectual property rights, deterring certain uses by the public, are permissible only if outweighed by the benefit of new works that they prompt. The individual rights of authors are secondary. In copyright, the specific legal regime covering creative informational works, authors certainly may benefit from the incentives offered,

but this is merely a corollary benefit. The rights of the author should at least in theory extend no further than necessary to benefit the public and conceivably could be eliminated entirely if a convincing case against public benefit could be shown.

As a practical matter, of course, those industries with a pecuniary interest in strong copyright protection essentially always can make a case for public benefit from such incentives. In contrast, much as predicted by public choice theory, the needs of the general populace remain inchoate, unrepresented by any well-organized or well-financed constituency that might argue the potential harms or downside of increasing incentives. As a consequence, little actual balancing occurs, resulting in a one-way jurisprudential ratcheting of intellectual property rights toward continual expansion. However, the rights are not absolute, as the grant of rights to one group may adversely affect the costs of another politically cogent group, which may exercise political leverage to obtain an exemption. Hence, while the overall approach of the American system may be utilitarian, the rights system is complex and riddled with special exceptions not necessarily justified by efficiency or welfare considerations.

The European Approach

While the American approach to copyright is based almost exclusively on a utilitarian rationale, the European model is based largely upon a tradition that has been characterized as author-centered or personality-based (Drahos, 1996; Ginsburg, 1990). Under this approach, copyright is justified as an intrinsic right of the author, a necessary recognition of the author's identity or personhood. Although there are variations on this rationale, with slight difference of philosophical nuance between different European nations (Dietz, 1995), the general rationale for copyright in this tradition regards creative work as an artifact that has been invested with some measure of the author's personality or that reflects the author's individuality. Out of respect for the autonomy and humanity of the author, that artifact deserves legal recognition.

Central to this jurisprudence of authorial autonomy is the provision of so-called moral rights, which specify certain uses and characteristics of creative works as a recognition of the inherent dignity and personality of the author (Stromholm, 1983). Typical moral rights accorded to authors include the right of attribution (formerly known in a more gendered form as the *right of paternity*) under which the author has the right to have the work associated or not associated with his or her name; the right of integrity, by which the author has the right not to have his or her creation altered by another; and an economic right or *droit de suite*, under which the author has the right to benefit from future resale of the work. Such rights tend toward inalienability; often, the author cannot waive, sell, or disclaim them (Netanel, 1993).

This approach might be generally termed *deontological*, based in a strong notion of absolute rights accorded to the individual. In contrast to the American cost-benefit approach, the deontological approach declines consideration of instrumental incentives as a means to an end, focusing instead on what may be necessary to honor the personhood of the individual (Hughes, 1988). Under this approach, authors should be accorded moral rights, no matter what the resulting calculus of general utility or harm. This is not to say that rights under the European system are any less complex or rife with political exceptions than under the American system. But certain features relating to authorial prerogative, which could not be justified under the U.S. system, remain under the European approach.

INFORMATION PRIVACY

The ease with which automated digital media allow collection, reproduction, and distribution of information has affected not only the law and practical governance of creative works but also other types of informational control regimes. Data related to individual transactions, movements, and activities are also easily captured, stored, and manipulated, raising issues of information privacy and data protection. Much as in the case of intellectual property, two primary models for privacy regulation have emerged on the international scene, paralleling the models previously discussed for intellectual property: an American and a European approach, grounded respectively in utilitarian and deontological considerations.

The American Approach

The United States has adopted a so-called *sectoral* approach to informational privacy, eschewing comprehensive data protection laws in favor of piecemeal treatment of the issue (Cohen, 2000; Reidenberg, 2000). Thus, personal information records in certain industries, such as credit reporting or healthcare, may be covered nationally by specific federal regulation. States or local governments may regulate particular aspects of retention, storage, and transfer of personal data within their geographic jurisdiction. Some industries may self-regulate through trade organizations or associations, or may adopt aspirational models of good practice. This fragmented approach results in a patchwork of regulations that can only be described as maddeningly haphazard, sometimes contradictory, and frequently confusing.

This approach has been largely adopted to keep the data collection environment as business-friendly as possible, limiting the imposition of privacy regulation to specific situations in order to minimize the potential financial and administrative burden on firms. This effectively produces a regime in which individual data belongs to the firms that capture or generate it in the course of consumer transactions. The default for usage of individual data is typically set as an implied blanket permission whereby individuals must take some affirmative action to opt out of data collection or usage. Actual regulation is indirect, such as governmental imposition of sanctions for fraudulent misrepresentation upon firms that promise consumers particular data protection and then fail to deliver.

While not as explicitly utilitarian as the U.S. approach to intellectual property, this American approach to privacy has clear instrumentalist roots, arising from particular economic considerations. Much of the business-friendly sectoral approach arises out of a historical American distrust of governmental solutions and a preference for market-based behavioral incentives. Perhaps paradoxically, this preference arises from a conviction that decentralized ordering via market forces will result in greater individual autonomy than would state intervention. This entails an assumption that the coercive power of the state is to be feared, whereas the coercive power of a given business naturally will be disciplined by market forces.

Consequently, the sectoral approach avoids comprehensive regulation and relegates governmental intervention to a bare minimum. Rather, the market is expected to supply privacy protection: if consumers desire privacy protection, then it is anticipated that businesses will voluntarily supply it in order to capture their patronage. Indeed, to the extent that recognition of individual rights in private data has been discussed, market-based approaches such as propertizing individual information have been proposed. Of course, the market for privacy is notoriously prone to market failure, as no individual datum is likely to be of sufficient worth to bargain over; it is only in the aggregate the data has value. Thus, no individual consumer will have sufficient bargaining power to exploit property rights in his or her individual data, and no market is likely to emerge that would allow decentralized control over personal information.

The European Approach

In contrast to the American sectoral approach to data collection, the European Union has adopted an approach based on comprehensive legislation, and grounded in strong, even inalienable individual rights (Reidenberg, 2000). This approach is spelled out under a data privacy directive requiring EU member states to adopt conforming legislation. The directive subjects individually identifiable or sensitive data to certain legal safeguards regarding the handling of such data. Notice of data collection must be given to the affected individual as well as the opportunity to review and correct individualized records. Certain types of personal data considered especially sensitive, such as data relating to health or religion or sexuality, receive special protection. Release or dissemination of the data for purposes other than that for which it was initially collected is restricted. Perhaps most importantly, the system hinges upon consent of the individual; people must opt in before individualized data can be collected. Notwithstanding the opt-in rule for collection, many of the rights accorded to individuals with regard to notice and data handling are inalienable; individuals cannot waive them, even if they wish to do so.

Such mandatory and inalienable rights, residing with the individual, are the hallmarks of a deontological approach. Paralleling the European tradition in intellectual property, EU privacy law elevates considerations of regard for personal autonomy over considerations of cost and benefit. Indeed, compliance with EU data protection requirements imposes a substantial financial and administrative burden on a broad array of businesses that may handle personalized data. Nonetheless, the EU data directive accords strong privacy rights not only despite the cost and inconvenience to EU businesses but, indeed, despite the cost and inconvenience to businesses outside the EU, including businesses operating within the U.S. This sets the stage for direct international conflict of the deontological EU approach and the U.S. utilitarian approach.

INTERNATIONAL PROMULGATION

The deliberate international propagation of the U.S. and EU models may be largely explained by the economic characteristics of information technologies already mentioned. As such technologies are adopted, both creative content and personal data can be quickly and cheaply distributed from jurisdictions with lax regulation or oversight into jurisdictions with more stringent regulation and oversight. This creates an incentive for more stringent jurisdictions to encourage greater stringency outside their borders, effectively expanding the territory covered by their regulatory regimes to other nations.

In general, stringent informational control jurisdictions will tend to be developed nations that are net exporters of information; less stringent jurisdictions will tend to be less-developed nations that are net importers of information (Burk, 1999a). The result is a gradient of informational stringency that to some extent reflects tension between developed nations and underdeveloped or developing nations. The economic and political position conferred by information export entails the economic and political leverage to impose information control policies that are advantageous to the developers.

Copyright Treaties

International promulgation of information control models has occurred in part through standard international coercive mechanisms—unilateral treaty negotiations, diplomatic pressure, direct imposition or threat of economic sanctions, and even occasional veiled threats of military force. For the most part, however, the dominant information ownership models have been internationally promulgated via multilateral treaty negotiations.

These formal agreements under international law predate the age of digital technologies, but have gained increased importance since the advent of such technology.

The Berne Convention

The oldest international treaty regarding copyright is the Berne Convention, now well over a century in existence (Ricketson, 1987). Neither this treaty nor, indeed, any other creates an international system of copyright; thus, copyright protection exists country-by-country according to the provisions of national law. But although it does not create a worldwide right for authors, the Berne Convention instead harmonizes copyright law by requiring signatory nations to provide at least a specified minimum standard of protection for creative works. The provisions of this treaty are situated firmly within the European authorial model, requiring signatory nations to accord authors with moral rights, including rights of integrity and attribution.

Because of this, the United States remained for many years a holdout to Berne membership, acceding to the treaty only in 1989 after American businesses determined that they might benefit from harmonized international copyright protection. Prior to 1989, the United States attempted to promulgate and rely on a Berne alternative, the Universal Copyright Convention (UCC), which lacked Berne's moral rights provisions. But the UCC also lacked Berne's international appeal, and U.S. businesses clamored for accession to Berne as globalization awakened them to the value of widespread international copyright uniformity. This ultimately resulted in U.S. accession to Berne, but with significant reservations. Even after joining Berne, the United States declined to enact conforming moral rights legislation, relying instead upon a patchwork of specific visual artists' rights, trademark law, and state unfair competition law to constitute the nominal equivalent of its obligations under the treaty.

WTO TRIPs

Despite the success of the Berne Convention in attracting nations to implement a harmonized minimum standard of copyright protection, the treaty falls well short of the results desired by information exporting nations. A major impediment to implementation of the Berne Convention has been the lack of any credible enforcement mechanism. Berne is, at best, aspirational; although nations acceding to the treaty promise to abide by certain standards, the treaty lacks any functional provision to punish or discipline noncompliance.

Consequently, in an era of globalization, copyright proponents sought more robust international mechanisms for advocating strong control over creative informational works. They turned to the most rapidly developing instruments and institutions of international law, integrating intellectual property into multilateral trade negotiations under the General Agreement on Tariffs and Trade (GATT) (Reichman, 1995). Ongoing rounds of treaty negotiations, intended to lower international trade barriers, culminated in the creation of the World Trade Organization (WTO), an institution intended to ensure and advance the principles of the GATT agreements. To this end, the WTO houses a dispute resolution procedure that allows signatory governments to submit treaty noncompliance disputes to the decision of adjudicatory panels (Komuro, 1995). By moving intellectual property under the umbrella of international trade, this adjudicatory mechanism could be used to enforce compliance with copyright treaty standards.

Consequently, a new agreement on Trade-Related Aspects of Intellectual Property Rights (TRIPs) was attached to the GATT treaty framework. Agreement to the provisions of the TRIPs agreement is required for admission to the WTO. TRIPs sets minimum standards for intellectual property protection in WTO signatory nations, including compliance with the major provisions of the Berne Convention (Helfer, 1998; Reichman, 1995). As a consequence, the majority of the world's nations is rapidly falling under the regime of the Berne Convention, either by explicitly becoming Berne signatories or by acceding to Berne via TRIPs. The number of nations in the latter category continues to grow as nations seek admittance to the WTO trade treaty to which TRIPs is tied. Although at the time of this writing a few jurisdictions remain outside the WTO membership, most have either joined the WTO or are working toward membership.

This nearly universal application of Berne might appear to herald the international victory of the European model, but the appearance is deceptive. There is one important caveat to the incorporation of Berne into TRIPs: at the insistence of the United States, TRIPs does not require signatories to comply with the moral rights provisions of Berne. This effectively strips the implementation of deontological copyright from the treaty and accomplishes the goal that the United States long had sought both domestically and internationally: strong global copyright protection without strong authorial rights. Consequently, under the TRIPs regime, the utilitarian model of information control dominates the international regime of information ownership.

Privacy Law

The international profile for privacy law has developed in a strikingly different fashion than that for intellectual property. Unlike the field of intellectual property, where the United States has been highly aggressive in asserting an affirmative utilitarian position, the field of privacy and data protection has seen the United States remaining relatively passive. As a result, the utilitarian position in this area has been manifest primarily because the United States as a major international player has maintained its own domestic sectoral stance. The more assertive role has been left to the European Union, but even so, the EU has not directly advanced its position under the kind of international treaty instruments or institutions that have been so conspicuous in the contest to shape international intellectual property law.

Instead, the EU model for data privacy has proliferated by virtue of a self-replicating feature in the EU data privacy directive. This directive might be considered *viral* in the sense that this term has been applied to certain forms of legal license provisions; that is, it infects follow-on users with some aspect of its own purpose and restrictions. In this particular case, the contagion is accomplished by means of a reciprocity provision that forbids member states from releasing personalized data to users in nations whose law lacks data privacy provisions equivalent to those in the European Directive (Swire & Litan, 1998). This places other nations in an awkward position as their native businesses attempt to engage in transactions with EU-based firms; if those nations lack EU-type data protection, doing business with the EU becomes nearly impossible. In other words, the reward for adopting the European privacy model is the privilege of conducting business with EU firms.[1]

Consequently, the economic importance of the EU bloc has driven the adoption of the rights-based approach in much of the world and has, in fact, left the United States in the position it once occupied with regard to the Berne Convention: a prominent holdout against a widespread international model. Indeed, lacking privacy laws substantially equivalent to those of the EU, the U.S. has had to negotiate safe harbor provisions that allow U.S. firms to conduct business with the EU on the basis of individual data protection compliance. This in some sense co-opts the sectoral approach as individual businesses individually adopt the tenets of EU data protection, since the benefits of adopting the deontological approach outweigh the costs.

ALTERNATIVES LOST

The international dynamic described here reveals competing utilitarian and deontological models, the utilitarian model holding a dominant edge in intellectual property law, the deontological model holding an edge in data privacy. But as both models ultimately arise out of the Western European intellectual tradition, imposition of either the American or European model on the rest of the world may smack somewhat of colonialism (Hamilton, 1996). Indeed, it should; the promulgation of these models is to some degree an extension of the promulgation of intellectual property and related laws by the great powers throughout their colonial empires during the 19th and 20th centuries (Geller, 1994). Local, non-Western cultures have developed their own norms and expectations for the control of information; these cultural approaches may share some features with the dominant international models, or they may differ substantially. When off-the-shelf information control models are imposed from outside, local customs and expectations regarding the treatment of information may be neglected or even eradicated.

Ownership Alternatives

Indigenous approaches to ownership and control of creative activity may differ radically from that formulated under either the American or European approaches, which, despite their philosophical differences, share fundamental assumptions regarding individuality and the nature of the creative act that law might recognize. Thus, Alford (1995) suggests that the problem long seen by Western powers as copyright piracy in China stems, in fact, from the Confucian cultural heritage in that region. The Confucian tradition largely denied the value or desirability of novel creative contribution, instead promoting respect for the classical work of revered sages and cultural icons. Under this approach, the most desirable contribution to present culture would arise by emulating the venerable work of the past, rather than by fostering original creations in the present or future. Thus, original expression—the entire purpose of Western systems of literary ownership—is viewed as undesirable under Chinese tradition, while copying—the cardinal sin in Western systems of literary ownership—becomes the cardinal virtue under a Confucian mindset.

Chinese antipathy toward intellectual property was additionally long reinforced by a communist ideological suspicion of the U.S. market-based approach of propertization, in some cases transforming the local appropriation of Western content into a sort of geopolitical statement. Communal approaches to creative works are by no means limited to Chinese or other politically communist systems. Numerous other ethnic groups have displayed a preference for communal rather than individual control of such works, although typically on cultural grounds rather than on political ideologies. Thus, to indigenous peoples such as the New Zealand Maori, the copyright concept of "author" seems outlandish or peculiar, as creative works are deemed to belong to the tribe or group (Geller, 1994). In other cases, such as that of the North American Hopi, individuals cannot claim ownership of creative works because creativity is deemed to stem from the inspiration of a divine spirit or higher power, not from the human artisan (Gana, 1995).

Individual ownership of cultural objects or folklore is also foreign to many other indigenous communities. Among the indigenous cultures of sub-Saharan Africa, control of cultural properties may be restricted to certain families that are designated the guardians for preservation or transmission (Kuruk, 1999). In addition to situating informational control with a particular lineage rather than with an individual, the concept of ownership or control itself may differ substantially from Western concepts of property. In many African communities, guardianship or custody of cultural properties entails responsi-

bility for the preservation and transmission of a song, chant, icon, or artifact, but not the right to exclude others in the relevant community from access to the property. In a similar vein, aboriginal Australians likewise designate certain persons as custodians or stewards of culturally significant designs, as do many Native American tribes (Gana, 1995). In such societies, the goal of ownership is largely to maintain the meaning of cultural objects within their society, rather than to generate new works.

Indeed, to the extent that dominant Western proprietary approaches affirm individual contribution and ownership, rather than collective control of cultural properties, it has been suggested that nonappropriable works are cast into the public domain for free appropriation by individual follow-on creators (Chander & Sunder, 2004). This raises the concern that the dominant models transform indigenous knowledge into a virtual resource of raw material to be mined by artists in the developed world, whose recast creative product will be fully protected against appropriation or use by those who supplied the basis for the new work (Boyle, 1996; Coombe, 1998). This outcome fuels developing world suspicion that the dominant Western models are purposefully designed to systematically disenfranchise developing world creators. But even setting aside concerns over intentional exploitation, the ownership models drawn from the Western philosophical tradition may fit poorly with indigenous cultural expectations.

Privacy Alternatives

Unlike intellectual property, where alternative local conceptions of ownership have been increasingly documented and examined, studies of indigenous privacy or data protection preferences are almost nonexistent. While scattered studies of non-Western cultural privacy considerations exist, only recently have any of them been related to the subject of data protection. The sparse literature that exists indicates that privacy practices outside the developed world may differ markedly from the individualist practices of the developed West. Privacy researchers long have recognized that Western concepts of privacy are relatively recent and highly culture-specific, arising in large measure from the social and sexual mores of Western lifestyles (Posner, 1978). To the extent that a taste for privacy stems from actual or metaphorical physical seclusion, it presupposes an industrialized asset base that would allow different groups of people to be segregated by class, gender, or age, and perhaps segregated yet again by types of activity or bodily function. Such segregation requires not only a relatively affluent lifestyle but also certain cultural assumptions as to the proper criteria for sequestering or publicizing any particular activity.

Neither of these conditions is necessarily present in the history or development of personal information treatment by other cultures. Concrete examples of alternative data protection preferences in non-Western settings remain to be documented, but extrapolating from the scattered studies of diverse cultural approaches to privacy and sensitive information, it seems plausible to expect that attitudes toward data protection also would diverge from the dominant models. In some cultures, it is likely that the basis for privacy is radically shifted away from the deontological assumption of individual autonomy and personal dignity. In many cultures, family identity may take precedence over that of the individual. In yet other cultures, the relational boundary is yet wider, and communal or group identity may take precedence. Such cultural norms may sit uncomfortably within the Western deontological model of data protection.

For example, Lü (2005) notes that while China has at present no comprehensive data protection law, some internal discussion of such laws has begun. The literature comprising these preliminary discussions appears to reflect a different balance of values than those surrounding Western data protection laws; in particular, Chinese commentators appear to give greater weight to social responsibilities than to individual rights or desires for privacy. Other sociological studies suggest that while traditional Chinese culture fosters an interest in solitude and personal reserve that parallel Western notions of privacy, concern over anonymity and government collection of data is minimal (Chan, 2000). The emphasis on social obligation and de-emphasis on state action may reflect both recent Chinese political history and more general Chinese cultural norms emphasizing social values at the expense of individual autonomy. Moreover, empirical studies of Chinese familial relations suggest that traditional Chinese interests in the control of information may lie at the boundary of the family rather than that of the individual (Chan, 2000).

Recent commentary on the indigenous norms of South Africa suggests a similar cultural pattern at odds with the Western concept of privacy. One of the guiding precepts of post-apartheid South African political, public, and private initiatives has been the philosophy of *ubuntu*, a cultural worldview that emphasizes communal values of connectedness and that places community welfare over individual welfare (Broodryk, 2002; Kwamwangamalu & Nkonko, 1999; Louw, 2001). Olinger, Britz, and Olivier (2005) observe that the communal and interpersonal philosophy of *ubuntu* leaves little purchase for concepts of individual privacy as defined in the developed world. Under *ubuntu*, personal identity is dependent upon and defined by the community. Within the group or community, personal information is common to the group, and attempts to withhold or sequester personal information is viewed as abnormal or deviant. While the boundary between groups may be less permeable to information transfer, *ubuntu* lacks any emphasis on individual privacy.

Recent analysis of Japanese cultural norms shows an analogous pattern in the disposition of personal information. Mizutani, Dorsey, and Moor (2004) argue that Japanese cultural norms of information access rely on the context of the individual within certain groups. In Japanese culture, loyalty to the group is emphasized over individuality; proper conduct is defined by situated community—the workplace, the neighborhood, age category, and so forth. Privacy within a particular group is maintained by the norm of *enryo*, or appropriate restraint in handing personal information in that context. A given individual may rely on others in the context of the group to exercise appropriate discretion, or *amae* toward handling of personal information in the context of the group. Here again, the boundary for information access lies in the context of particular groups rather than with the individual, as the dominant data protection model assumes.

A data protection model adapted to such cultural attitudes might recognize familial or community interests in reviewing and controlling data pertinent to the family group or the community, rather than being oriented toward individual data protection rights. Rather than excluding all but the individual and those authorized by the individual to access personal data, restrictions on access might exclude those outside the relevant group, or might condition access to certain information upon group affiliation. Access requirements might anticipate and rely upon cultural norms, such as *enryo*, or they might even formalize these norms, requiring handlers of personal data to act with appropriate restraint toward the information. Or, in a normative environment such as that created by the South African *ubuntu* worldview, data protection may be seen as irrelevant for many situations considered pressing in the developed nations.

At the same time, such cultural differences may reflect traditional norms that may be changing under the influence of globalized media. Mizutani et al. (2004) note that younger Japanese people are more likely to demand individual privacy over the demands of the group. Lü (2005) similarly notes that Chinese attitudes toward personal and familial privacy are changing rapidly under increasing

Westernization, and legal instantiation of data protection norms similarly is being shaped by international treaty obligations. Thus, it appears that the promulgation of Western information ethics paradigms via formal treaty obligation is only a component, if nonetheless a key component, of a broader cultural shift toward Western individualism in the wake of globalization.

CONCLUSION

The developed world's paradigms of utilitarian and deontological informational control are rapidly overgrowing other indigenous models around the globe in much the same way that exotic species introduced into local ecosystems may crowd out indigenous species. To some extent, this trend comes as a general result of globalization, as the normative and ethical assumptions carried by Western media consciously or unconsciously are adopted in other sectors of the world. But to the extent that these models are promulgated by legal instruments, the imposition of the developed world's models is deliberate and calculated.

Much as in the case of lost biological species, we have only poor records of the indigenous cultural models that are being overwhelmed and forgotten by the rapid proliferation of the dominant information models. In the case of intellectual property, scholars critical of copyright and patent maximalism have documented several examples of non-Western or indigenous cultural approaches that reject or differ from the deontological or utilitarian assumptions of the developed world. But in the case of privacy and data protection, the scholarly record is sparse. Scattered accounts of non-Western privacy norms can be found in the literature on anthropology and cultural studies, but little has been done to relate these accounts to the question of data protection. This marked disparity between cultural analyses of privacy and of intellectual property may reflect the economic disparity between the two fields. The value of personal data is primarily personal, while the business value of indigenous knowledge and cultural objects raises the profile of issues related to their ownership and makes the need for analysis of those issues seem more immediately compelling.

Thus, intellectual property scholars have already analyzed the potential for application of non-Western ownership systems to intellectual property. Similar analysis is needed in the area of data protection. Studies of non-Western and indigenous cultures similarly may suggest additional misalignments with the dominant data protection models. In some cases, the cultural line between public and private may shift away from that assumed by the dominant models; it is likely that in some cultural settings, information considered highly personal by Western standards, such as wealth or spending habits, may be deemed open and public, whereas information considered relatively innocuous in Western settings, such as a nickname, might be considered extremely private. As in the examples of China, Japan, and South Africa, privacy as a matter of individual autonomy may be relatively unimportant in cultural settings in which communal or group obligations take precedence; instead, protection of communal information might be deemed more appropriate. In such cultures, access to personal information or assent to the collection of personal information might more appropriately be sited with the family, the local community, or the reference group than with the individual.

But such approaches to personal or communal information control are unlikely to be accommodated within the data protection juggernaut now sweeping across the globe. Ironically, the imposition of either dominant model is troublesome from the internal perspective of each model. From a deontological standpoint, it is unclear that the autonomy of individuals is accorded respect by imposing upon them rights to which they object or with which they disagree. From a utilitarian standpoint, there may be substantial benefits to standardization of legal regimes, including legal regimes for information control, but this comes at the high and perhaps unacceptable cost of suppressing or deterring competitive alternatives. Nonetheless, absent a radical change in current trends, it is unclear whether the benefits of indigenous information alternatives, or the respect due their originators, will be realized in the foreseeable future.

REFERENCES

Alford, W. P. (1995). *To steal a book is an elegant offense: Intellectual property law in Chinese civilization*. Palo Alto, CA: Stanford University Press.

Boyle, J. (1996). *Shamans, software and spleens*. Cambridge, MA: Harvard University Press.

Broodryk, J. (2002). *Ubuntu: Life lessons from Africa* (2nd ed.). Pretoria: National Library of South Africa.

Burk, D. (1999a). Virtual exit in the global information economy. *Chicago-Kent Law Review, 73*, 943-995.

Burk, D. (1999b). *Cyberlaw and the norms of science*. Boston College Intellectual Property and Technology Forum 1999. Retrieved October 15, 2006, from http://infoeagle.bc.edu/bc_org/avp/law/st_org/iptf/commentary /content/burk.html

Chan, Y. (2000). Privacy in the family: Its hierarchical and asymmetric nature. *Journal of Comparative Family Studies, 31,* 1-17.

Chander, A., & Sunder, M. (2004). The romance of the public domain. *California Law Review, 92*, 1331-1374.

Cohen, J. E. (2000). Examined lives: Informational privacy and the subject as object. *Stanford Law Review, 52*, 1373-1438.

Coombe, R. J. (1998). *The cultural life of intellec-*

tual properties: Authorship, appropriation, and the law. Durham, NC: Duke University Press.

Dietz, A. (1995). The moral right of the author: Moral rights and the civil law countries. *Columbia-VLA Journal of Law & the Arts, 19,* 206-212.

Drahos, P. (1996). *A philosophy of intellectual property.* Brookfield, UK: Dartmouth.

Gana, R. L. (1995). Has creativity died in the third world? Some implications of the internationalization of intellectual property. *Denver Journal of International Law & Policy, 24,* 109-144.

Geller, P. E. (1994). Legal transplants in international copyright: Some problems of method. *UCLA Pacific Basin Law Journal, 13,* 199-230.

Ginsburg, J. C. (1990). A tale of two copyrights: Literary property in revolutionary France and America. *Tulane Law Review, 64,* 991-1031.

Hamilton, M. A. (1996). The TRIPs agreement: Imperialistic, outdated, and overprotective. *Vanderbilt Journal of Transnational Law, 29,* 613-634.

Helfer, L. (1998). Adjudicating copyright claims under the TRIPs agreement: The case for a European human rights analogy. *Harvard Journal of International Law, 49,* 357-437.

Hughes, J. (1988). The philosophy of intellectual property. *Georgetown Law Review, 77,* 287-291.

Komuro, N. (1995). The WTO dispute settlement mechanism: Coverage and procedures of the WTO understanding. *Journal of International Arbitration, 12,* 81-171.

Kuruk, P. (1999). Protecting folklore under modern intellectual property regimes: A reappraisal of the tensions between individual and communal rights in Africa and the United States. *American University Law Review, 48,* 769-849.

Kwamwangamalu, N. M., & Nkonko, M. (1999). Ubuntu in South Africa: A sociolinguistic per-

spective to a Pan-African concept. *Critical Arts Journal, 13,* 24-42.

Landes, W. M., & Posner, R. A. (1989). An economic analysis of copyright law. *Journal of Legal Studies, 18,* 325-363.

Lessig, L. (1999). *Code and other laws of cyberspace.* New York: Basic Books.

Louw, D. J. (2001). Ubuntu and the challenges of multiculturalism in post-apartheid South Africa. *Quest: African Journal of Philosophy, XV*(1-2), 15-36.

Lü, Y. (2005). Privacy and data privacy issues in contemporary China. *Ethics and Information Technology, 7*(1), 7-15.

Mizutani, M., Dorsey, J., & Moor, J. (2004). The Internet and Japanese conception of privacy. *Ethics and Information Technology, 6*(2), 121-28.

Netanel, N. (1993). Copyright alienability restrictions and the enhancement of author autonomy: A normative evaluation. *Rutgers Law Journal, 24,* 347-442.

Olinger, H.N., Britz, J.J., & Olivier, M.S. (2005). Western privacy and ubuntu: Influences in the forthcoming data privacy bill. Ethics of new information technology. *Proceedings of the 6th International Conference on Information Ethics: Philosophical Inquiries,* Twente, The Netherlands (pp. 292-306).

Posner, R. (1978). The right of privacy. *Georgia Law Review, 12,* 393-422.

Reichman, J. H. (1995). Beyond the historical lines of demarcation: Competition law, intellectual property rights, and international trade after the GATT's Uruguay round. *The International Lawyer, 29,* 388-483.

Reidenberg, J. R. (1998). Lex informatica: The formulation of information policy rules through technology. *Texas Law Review, 76,* 553-593.

Reidenberg, J. R. (2000). Resolving conflicting international data privacy rules in cyberspace. *Stanford Law Review, 52*, 1315-1371.

Ricketson, S. (1987). *The Berne Convention for the protection of literary and artistic works: 1886-1986.* London: Kluwer.

Stromholm, S. (1983). Droit moral—The international and comparative scene from a Scandinavian viewpoint. *International Review of Industrial Property and Copyright Law, 14*, 1-35.

Swire, P., & Litan, R. (1998). *None of your business: World dataflows, electronic commerce, and the European privacy directive.* Washington, DC: Brookings Institution Press.

ENDNOTES

[1] Although the topic lies beyond the scope of this chapter, it is worth noting that the EU has adopted with some success a similar strategy in the case of proprietary database protection; the benefit of EU database protection statutes is available only to businesses from jurisdictions with equivalent protection.

This work was previously published in Information Technology Ethics: Cultural Perspectives, edited by S. Hongladarom and C. Ess, pp. 94-107, copyright 2007 by Information Science Reference, formerly known as Idea Group Reference (an imprint of IGI Global).

Chapter 5.3
A Social Ontology for Integrating Security and Software Engineering

E. Yu
University of Toronto, Canada

L. Liu
Tsinghua University, China

J. Mylopoulos
University of Toronto, Canada

ABSTRACT

As software becomes more and more entrenched in everyday life in today's society, security looms large as an unsolved problem. Despite advances in security mechanisms and technologies, most software systems in the world remain precarious and vulnerable. There is now widespread recognition that security cannot be achieved by technology alone. All software systems are ultimately embedded in some human social environment. The effectiveness of the system depends very much on the forces in that environment. Yet there
are few systematic techniques for treating the social context of security together with technical system design in an integral way. In this chapter, we argue that a social ontology at the core of a requirements engineering process can be the basis for integrating security into a requirements driven software engineering process. We describe the i* agent-oriented modelling framework and show how it can be used to model and reason about security concerns and responses. A smart card example is used to illustrate. Future directions for a social paradigm for security and software engineering are discussed.

INTRODUCTION

It is now widely acknowledged that security cannot be achieved by technological means alone. As more and more of our everyday activities rely on software, we are increasingly vulnerable to lapses in security and deliberate attacks. Despite ongoing advances in security mechanisms and technologies, new attack schemes and exploits continue to emerge and proliferate.

Security is ultimately about relationships among social actors — stakeholders, system users, potential attackers — and the software that are instruments of their actions. Nevertheless, there are few systematic methods and techniques for analyzing and designing social relationships as technical systems alternatives are explored.

Currently, most of the research on secure software engineering methods focuses on the technology level. Yet, to be effective, software security must be treated as originating from high-level business goals that are taken seriously by stakeholders and decision makers making strategic choices about the direction of an organisation. Security interacts with other high-level business goals such as quality of service, costs, time-to-market, evolvability and responsiveness, reputation and competitiveness, and the viability of business models. What is needed is a systematic linkage between the analysis of technical systems design alternatives and an understanding of their implications at the organisational, social level. From an analysis of the goals and relationships among stakeholders, one seeks technical systems solutions that meet stakeholder goals.

In this chapter, we describe the *i** agent-oriented modelling framework and how it can be used to treat security as an integral part of software system requirements engineering. The world is viewed as a network of social actors depending on each other for goals to be achieved, tasks to be performed, and resources to be furnished. Each actor reasons strategically about alternate means for achieving goals, often through relationships with other actors. Security is treated as a high-level goal held by (some) stakeholders that need to be addressed from the earliest stages of system conception. Actors make tradeoffs among competing goals such as functionality, cost, time-to-market, quality of service, as well as security.

The framework offers a set of security requirements analysis facilities to help users, administrators, and designers better understand the various threats and vulnerabilities they face, the countermeasures they can take, and how these can be combined to achieve the desired security results within the broader picture of system design and the business environment. The security analysis process is integrated into the main requirements process, so that security is taken into account from the earliest moment. The technology of smart cards and the environment surrounding its usage provides a good example to illustrate the social ontology of *i**.

In the next section, we review the current challenges in achieving security in software systems, motivating the need for a social ontology. Given that a social modelling and analysis approach is needed, what characteristics should it have? We consider this in the following section. The two subsequent sections describe the ontology of the *i** strategic actors modelling framework and outline a process for analyzing the security issues surrounding a smart card application. The last section reviews several areas of related work and discusses how a social ontology framework can be complementary to these approaches.

BACKGROUND

Despite ongoing advances in security technologies and software quality, new vulnerabilities continue to emerge. It is clear that there can be no perfect security. Security inevitability involves tradeoffs (Schneier, 2003). In practice, therefore, all one can hope for is "good enough" security (Sandhu, 2003).

But how does one determine what is good enough? Who decides what is good enough? These questions suggest that software and information security cannot be addressed by technical specialists alone. Decisions about security are made ultimately by stakeholders — people who are affected by the outcomes — users, investors, the general public, etc. — because the tradeoffs are about how their lives would be affected. In electronic commerce, consumers decide whether to purchase from a vendor based on the trustworthiness of the vendor's business and security practices. Businesses decide how much and where to invest on security to reduce exposure to a tolerable level. In healthcare, computerized information management can streamline many processes. But e-health will become a reality only if patients and the general public are satisfied that their medical records are protected and secure. Healthcare providers will participate only if liability concerns can be adequately addressed.

Tradeoffs are being made by participants regarding competing interests and priorities. Customers and businesses make judgments about what is adequate security for each type of business, in relation to the benefits derived from online transactions. Patients want their personal and medical information to be kept private, but do not want privacy mechanisms to interfere with the quality of care. In national defense, secrecy is paramount, but can also lead to communication breakdown. In each case, security needs to be interpreted within the context of the social setting, by each stakeholder from his/her viewpoint.

Current approaches to security do not allow these kinds of tradeoffs to be conveyed to system developers to guide design. For example, UML extensions for addressing security (see Chapter I for a review) do not lend themselves well to the modelling of social actors and their concerns about alternate security arrangements, and how they reason about tradeoffs. Access control models can specify policies, but cannot support reasoning about which policies are good for whom and

what alternate policies might be more workable. They cannot explain why certain policies meet with resistance and non-compliance.

Each of the common approaches in security modelling and analysis focuses on selective aspects of security, which are important in their own right, but cannot provide the guidance needed to achieve "good enough" overall security. Most approaches focus on technical aspects, neglecting the social context, which is crucial for achieving effective security in practice. The technical focus is well served by mechanistic ontology (i.e., concepts that are suitable for describing and reasoning about automated machinery — objects, operations, state transitions, etc.). The importance of social context in security suggests that a different set of concepts is needed. From the previous discussion, we propose that the following questions are important for guiding system development in the face of security challenges:

- Who are the players who have an interest in the intended system and its surrounding context? Who would be affected by a change?

- What are their strategic interests? What are their business and personal objectives? What do they want from the system and the other players?

- What are the different ways in which they can achieve what they want?

- How do their interests complement or interfere with each other? How can players achieve what they want despite competing or conflicting interests?

- What opportunities exist for one player to advance its interests at the expense of others? What vulnerabilities exist in the way that each actor envisions achieving its objectives?

- How can one player avoid or prevent its interests from being compromised by others?

These are the kind of questions that can directly engage stakeholders, helping them uncover issues and concerns. Stakeholders need the help of technical specialists to think through these questions, because most strategic objectives are accomplished through technological systems. Stakeholders typically do not know enough about technology possibilities or their implications. Technologists do not know enough about stakeholder interests to make choices for them. In order that stakeholder interests can be clarified, deliberated upon, and conveyed effectively to system developers, a suitable modelling method is needed to enable stakeholders and technologists to jointly explore these questions. The answers to these questions will have direct impact on system development, as they set requirements and guide technical design decisions.

We argue therefore that a social ontology is needed to enable security concerns to become a driving force in software system development. In the next section, we explore the requirements for such a social ontology.

APPROACH

If a treatment of security requires attention to the social context of software systems, can the social analysis be given full weight in a software engineering methodology that is typically dominated by a mechanistic worldview? How can the social modelling be reconciled and integrated with mainstream software modelling?

It turns out that a social paradigm for software system analysis is motivated not only by security concerns, but is consistent with a general shift in the context of software and information systems. The analysis of computers and information systems used to be machine-centric when hardware was the precious resource. The machine was at the centre, defining the human procedures and structures needed to support its proper functioning. Today, hardware and software are commoditized

and distributed everywhere. Human practices and imagination determine how hardware and software are put to use, not the other way round. Pervasive networking, wired and wireless, has also contributed to blurring the notion of "system." Computational resources can be dynamically harnessed in ad hoc configurations (e.g., through Web services protocols in service-oriented architectures) to provide end-to-end services for a few moments, then dissolved and reconfigured for another ad hoc engagement. Even computational entities, in today's networked environment, are better viewed as participants in social networks than as fixed components in a system with pre-defined structure and boundary. Increasingly, the computational services that we desire will not be offered as a single pre-constructed system, but by a conglomeration of interacting services operated by different organisations, possibly drawing on content owned by yet other providers.

The questions raised in the previous section arise naturally from today's open networked environments, even if one were not focusing on security concerns. The relevance of a social ontology is therefore not unique to security. Competing interests and negative forces that interfere with one's objectives are ever present in every organisation and social setting. They are accentuated in an open network environment. In security scenarios, the negative forces are further accentuated as they materialize into full-fledged social structures, involving malicious actors collaborating with other actors, engaging in deliberate attacks, possibly violating conventions, rules, and laws. Security can therefore be seen as covering the more severe forms of a general phenomenon. Competing and conflicting interests are inherent in social worlds. Negative forces do not come only from well identified malicious external agents, but can be present legitimately within one's organisation, among one's associates, and even among the multiple roles that one person may play. It may not be possible to clearly separate security analysis from the analysis of "normal" business. We conclude, therefore, that a social ontology would serve well for "normal" business analysis, recognizing the increasingly "social" nature of software systems and their environments. A social ontology offers a smooth integration of the treatment of normal and security scenarios, as the latter merely refer to one end of a continuum covering positive and negative forces from various actors.

Given this understanding, the social ontology should not be preoccupied with those concepts conventionally associated with security. For example, the concepts of asset, threat, attack, counter-measure are key concepts for security management. In the social ontology we aim to construct, we do not necessarily adopt these as primitive concepts. Instead, the social ontology should aim to be as general as possible, so that the concepts may be equally applicable to positive as well as negative scenarios. The general ontology is then *applied* to security. Special constructs unique to security would be introduced only if the expressiveness of the general constructs is found to be inadequate. The principle of Occam's razor should be applied to minimize the complexity of the ontology. If desired, shorthand notations for common recurring patterns can be defined in terms of the primitives. The premises behind a social ontology are further discussed in Yu (2001a, 2001b).

BASIC CONCEPTS OF THE *i* STRATEGIC MODELLING FRAME-WORK

The *i** framework (Yu, 1993, 1997) proposes an agent oriented approach to requirements engineering centering on the intentional characteristics of the agent. Agents attribute intentional properties such as goals, beliefs, abilities, commitments to each other and reason about strategic relationships. Dependencies give rise to opportunities as well as vulnerabilities. Networks of dependencies are analyzed using a qualitative reasoning approach.

Agents consider alternative configurations of dependencies to assess their strategic positioning in a social context. The name *i** (pronounced eye-star) refers to the concept of multiple, distributed "intentionality."

The framework is used in contexts in which there are multiple parties (or autonomous units) with strategic interests, which may be reinforcing or conflicting in relation to each other. The *i** framework has been applied to business process modelling (Yu, 1993), business redesign (van der Raadt, Gordijn, & Yu, 2005; Yu et al., 2001), requirements engineering (Yu, 1997), architecture modelling (Gross & Yu, 2001), COTS selection (Franch & Maiden, 2003), as well as to information systems security.

There are three main categories of concepts: actors, intentional elements, and intentional links. The framework includes a strategic dependency (SD) model — for describing the network of relationships among actors, and a strategic rationale (SR) model — for describing and supporting the reasoning that each actor has about its relationships with other actors.

Actor

In *i**, an *actor* (○) is used to refer generically to any unit to which intentional dependencies can be ascribed. An actor is an active entity that carries out actions to achieve its goals by exercising means-ends knowledge. It is an encapsulation of intentionally, rationality and autonomy. Graphically, an actor is represented as a circle, and may optionally have a dotted boundary, with intentional elements inside.

Intentional Elements: Goal, Softgoal, Task, Resource and Belief

The intentional elements in *i** are goal, task, softgoal, resource and belief. A goal (◯) is a condition or state of affairs in the world that the stakeholders would like to achieve. A goal can be achieved in different ways, prompting alternatives to be considered. A goal can be a business goal or a system goal. Business goals are about the business or state of the affairs the individual or organisation wishes to achieve in the world. System goals are about what the target system should achieve, which, generally, describe the functional requirements of the target system. In the *i** graphical representation, goals are represented as a rounded rectangle with the goal name inside.

A *softgoal* (⬭) is typically a quality (or non-functional) attribute on one of the other intentional elements. A softgoal is similar to a (hard) goal except that the criteria for whether a softgoal is achieved are not clear-cut and *a priori*. It is up to the developer to judge whether a particular state of affairs in fact sufficiently achieves the stated softgoal. Non-functional requirements, such as performance, security, accuracy, reusability, interoperability, time to market and cost are often crucial for the success of a system. In *i**, non-functional requirements are represented as softgoals and addressed as early as possible in the software lifecycle. They should be properly modelled and addressed in design reasoning before a commitment is made to a specific design choice. In the *i** graphical representation, a softgoal is shown as an irregular curvilinear shape.

*Task*s (⬡) are used to represent the specific procedures to be performed by agents, which specifies a particular way of doing something. It may be decomposed into a combination of sub-goals, subtasks, resources, and softgoals. These sub-components specify a particular course of action while still allowing some freedom. Tasks are used to incrementally specify and refine solutions in the target system. They are used to achieve goals or to "operationalize" softgoals. These solutions provide operations, processes, data representations, structuring, constraints, and agents in the target system to meet the needs stated in the goals and softgoals. Tasks are represented graphically as a hexagon.

A *resource* (▭) is a physical or informational entity, which may serve some purpose. From the viewpoint of intentional analysis, the main concern with a resource is whether it is available. Resources are shown graphically as rectangles.

The *belief* (◯) construct is used to represent domain characteristics, design assumptions and relevant environmental conditions. It allows domain characteristics to be considered and properly reflected in the decision making process, hence facilitating later review, justification, and change of the system, as well as enhancing traceability. Beliefs are shown as ellipses in *i** graphical notation.

Strategic Dependency Model

A strategic dependency (SD) model consists of a set of nodes and links. Each node represents an actor, and each link between two actors indicates that one actor depends on the other for something in order that the former may attain some goal. We call the depending actor the *depender*, and the actor who is depended upon the *dependee*. The object around which the dependency relationship centers is called the *dependum*. By depending on another actor for a dependum, an actor (the depender) is able to achieve goals that it was not able to without the dependency, or not as easily or as well. At the same time, the depender becomes vulnerable. If the dependee fails to deliver the dependum, the depender would be adversely affected in its ability to achieve its goals. A *dependency* link (———D———) is used to describe such an inter-actor relationship. Dependency types are used to differentiate the kinds of freedom allowed in a relationship.

In a *goal dependency*, an actor depends on another to make a condition in the world come true. Because only an end state or outcome is specified, the dependee is given the freedom to choose how to achieve it.

In a *task dependency*, an actor depends on another to perform an activity. The depender's goal for having the activity performed is not given. The activity description specifies a particular course of action. A task dependency specifies standard procedures, indicates the steps to be taken by the dependee.

In a *resource dependency*, an actor depends on another for the availability of an entity. The depender takes the availability of the resource to be unproblematic.

The fourth type of dependency, *softgoal dependency*, is a variant of the goal dependency. It is different in that there are no *a priori*, cut-and-dry criteria for what constitutes meeting the goal. The meaning of a softgoal is elaborated in terms of the methods that are chosen in the course of pursuing the goal. The dependee contributes to the identification of alternatives, but the decision is taken by the depender. The notion of the softgoal allows the model to deal with many of the usually informal concepts. For example, a service provider's dependency on his customer for continued business can be achieved in different ways. The desired style of continued business is ultimately decided by the depender. The customer's softgoal dependency on the service

provider for "keep personal information confidential" indicates that there is not a clear-cut criterion for the achievement of confidentiality. The four types of dependencies reflect different levels of freedom that is allowed in the relationship between depender and dependee.

Figure 1 shows a SD model for a generic smart card-based payment system involving six actors. This example is adapted from Yu and Liu (2001). A Card Holder depends on a Card Issuer to be allocated a smart card. The Terminal Owner depends on Card Holder to present the card for each transaction. The Card Issuer in turn depends on the Card Manufacturer and Software Manufacturer to provide cards, devices, and software. The Data Owner is the one who has control of the data within the card. He depends on the Terminal Owner to submit transaction information to the central database. In each case, the dependency means that the depender actor depends on the dependee actor for something in order to achieve some (internal) goal.

The goal dependency New Account Be Created from the Card Issuer to the Data Owner means that it is up to the Data Owner to decide how to

Figure 1. Strategic dependency model of a generic smart-card system

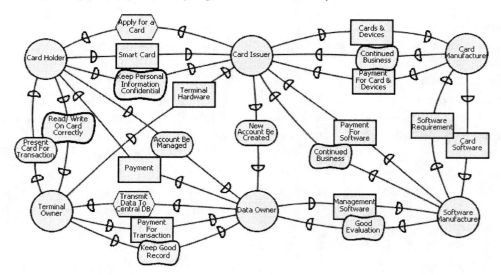

create a new account. The Card Issuer does not care how a new account is created; what matters is that, for each card, an account should be created. The Card Issuer depends on the Card Holder to apply for a card via a task dependency by specifying standard application procedures. If the Card Issuer were to indicate the steps for the Data Owner to create a new account, then the Data Owner would be related to the Card Issuer by a task dependency instead.

The Card Issuer's dependencies on the Card Manufacturer for cards and devices, the manufacturer's dependencies on Card Issuer for payment are modelled as resource dependencies. Here the depender takes the availability of the resource to be unproblematic.

The Card Holder's softgoal dependency on the Card Issuer for Keep Personal Information Confidential indicates that there is not a clear-cut criterion for the achievement of confidentiality. In the Manufacturer's softgoal dependency on Card Issuer, Continued Business could be achieved in different ways. The desired style of continued business is ultimately decided by the depender.

The strategic dependency model of Figure 1 is not meant to be a complete and accurate description of any particular smart card system. It is intended only for illustrating the modelling features of *i**.

In conventional software systems modelling, the focus is on information flows and exchanges — what messages actors or system components send to each other. With the social ontology of *i**, the focus is on intentional relationships — what are the actors' expectations and constraints on each other. Since actors are intentional, strategic, and have autonomy, they reflect on their relationships with other actors. If these relationships are unsatisfactory, they will seek alternative ways of associating with others.

Security concerns arise naturally from this perspective. A social ontology therefore provides a way to integrate security into software system engineering from the earliest stages of conception, and at a high level of abstraction.

Intentional Links

Dependencies are intentional relationships between actors. Within each actor, we model intentional relationships in terms of means-ends, decomposition, contribution, and correlation links.

- **Means-ends** links (—▷—) are used to describe how goals can be achieved. Each task connected to a goal by a means-ends link is one possible way of achieving the goal.

- **Decomposition** links (——) define the sub-elements of a task, which can include sub-tasks, sub-goals, resources, and softgoals. The softgoals indicate the desired qualities that are considered to be part of the task. The sub-tasks may in turn have decomposition links that lead to further sub-elements. Sub-goals indicate the possibility of alternate means of achievement, with means-ends links leading to tasks.

- A **contribution** link (→) describes the qualitative impact that one element has on another. A contribution can be negative or positive. The extent of contribution is judged to be partial or sufficient based on Simon's concept of satisficing (Simon, 1996), as in the NFR framework (Chung, Nixon, Yu, & Mylopoulos, 2000). Accordingly, contribution link types include: *help* (positive and partial), *make* (positive and sufficient), *hurt* (negative and partial), *break* (negative and sufficient), *some+* (positive of unknown extent), *some-* (negative of unknown extent). *Correlation* links (dashed arrows) are used to express contributions from one element to other elements that are not explicitly sought, but are side effects.

Strategic Rationale Model

The strategic rationale (SR) model provides a detailed level of modelling by looking "inside" actors to model internal intentional relationships. Intentional elements (goals, tasks, resources, and softgoals) appear in SR models not only as external dependencies, but also as internal elements arranged into a predominantly hierarchical structure of means-ends, task-decompositions and contribution relationships.

The SR model in Figure 2 elaborates on the rationale of a Card Manufacturer. The Card Manufacturer's business objective Manufacture Card Hardware is modeled as a "hard" functional goal (top right corner). Quality requirements such as Security and Low Cost are represented as softgoals. The different means for accomplishing the goal are modeled as tasks. The task Provide Total Card Solution can be further decomposed into three sub-components (connected with task-decomposition links): sub-goal of Get Paid, sub-task Develop Card Solution, and sub-task

Manufacture Card & Devices. To perform the task Manufacture Card & Devices, the availability of Materials need to be taken into consideration, which is modeled as a resource.

In the model, task node Provide Simple Card Solution (such as the Millicent solution), and Provide Total Card Solution (such as the Mondex solution) are connected to the goal with means-ends links. This goal will be satisfied if any of these tasks is satisfied. Provide Total Card Solution will help the Security of the system (represented with a *Help* contribution link to *Security*), while Provide Simple Card Solution is considered to have no significant impact on security if it is applied to cards with small monetary value. The Simple Card Solution is good for the goal of Low Cost whereas the Total Card Solution is bad. This is supported by the belief that "Total Card Solution, such as Mondex, is expensive." Beliefs are usually used to represent such domain properties, or design assumption or environmental condition, so that

Figure 2. Strategic rationale model of card manufacturer

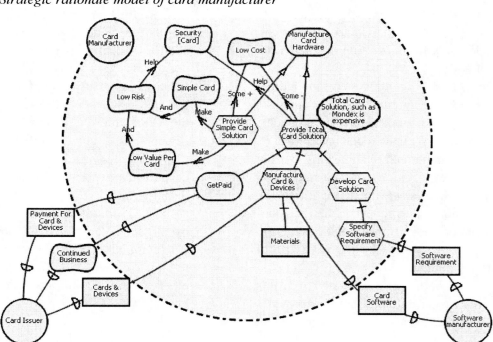

traceability of evidence of design decision could be explicitly maintained with the model.

During system analysis and design, softgoals such as Low Cost and Security [card] are systematically refined until they can be operationalized and implemented. Unlike functional goals, nonfunctional qualities represented as softgoals frequently interact or interfere with each other, so the graph of contributions is usually not a strict tree structure (Chung et al., 2000).

Agents, Roles, and Positions

To model complex relationships among social actors, we further define the concepts of agents, roles, and positions, each of which is an actor, but in a more specialized sense.

A *role* ( ) is an abstract actor embodying expectations and responsibilities. It is an abstract characterization of the behavior of a social actor within some specialized context or domain of endeavor. An *agent* ( ) is a concrete actor with physical manifestations, human or machine, with specific capabilities and functionalities. A set of roles packaged together to be assigned to an agent is called a position. A *position* ( ) is intermediate in abstraction between a role and an agent, which often has an organisational flavor. Positions can COVER roles. Agents can OCCUPY positions. An agent can PLAY one or more roles directly. The INS construct is used to represent the instance-and-class relation. The ISA construct is used to

express conceptual generalization/specialization. Initially, human actors representing stakeholders in the domain are identified together with existing machine actors. As the analysis proceeds, more actors are identified, including new system agents, when certain design choices have been made, and new functional entities are added.

Figure 3 shows some actors in the domain. At the top, six generic abstract roles are identified, including the Card Holder, the Terminal Owner, the Data Owner, the Card Issuer, the Card Manufacturer, and the Software Manufacturer. These actors are modeled as roles since they represent abstractions of responsibilities and functional units of the business model. Then concrete agents in smart card systems are identified. For instance, actors in a Digital Stored Value Card system include Customer, Merchant, Subcontractor Company, and their instances. These agents can play one or more roles in different smart card systems. Here, Financial Institution is modeled as a position that bridges the multiple abstract roles it covers, and the real world agents occupying it. Initially, human/organisational actors are identified together with existing machine actors. As the requirements analysis proceeds, more actors could be added in, including new system agents such as security monitoring system, counter-forgery system, etc., when certain design choices have been made, and new functional entities are added.

An *agent* is an actor with concrete, physical manifestations, such as a human individual. An

Figure 3. Actor hierarchy (roles, positions, and agents) in a smart card system

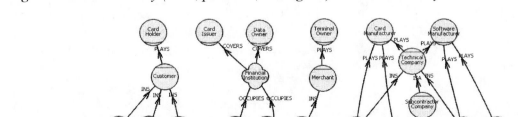

agent has dependencies that apply regardless of what role he/she/it happens to be playing. For example, in Figure 3, if Jerry, a Card Holder desires a good credit record, he wants the credit record to go towards his personal self, not to the positions and abstract roles that Jerry might occupy or play. We use the term agent instead of person for generality, so that it can be used to refer to human as well as artificial (hardware, software, or organisational) agents. Customer and Merchant are represented as agent classes and groups. Dependencies are associated with a role when these dependencies apply regardless of who plays the role. For example, we consider Card Holder an abstract role that agents can play. The objective of obtaining possession of the card, and deciding when and whether to use it, are associated with the role, no matter who plays the role.

The INS construct represents the instance-and-class relation. For example, Mr. Lee's Convenience Store is an instance of Merchant, and Jerry is an instance of Customer. The ISA construct expresses conceptual generalization/ specialization. For example, a Subcontractor Company is a kind of Technical Company. These constructs are used to simplify the presentation of strategic models with roles, positions, and agents. There can be dependencies from an agent to the role it plays. For example, a Merchant who plays the role of Terminal owner may depend on that role to attract more customers. Otherwise, he may choose not to play that role.

Roles, positions, and agents can each have subparts. In general, aggregate actors are not compositional with respect to intentional properties. Each actor, regardless of whether it has parts, or is part of a larger whole, is taken to be intentional. Each actor has inherent freedom and is therefore ultimately unpredictable. There can be intentional dependencies between the whole and its parts (e.g., a dependency by the whole on its parts to maintain unity).

DOMAIN REQUIREMENTS ANALYSIS WITH *i**

We now illustrate how the social ontology of *i** allows security issues to be identified and addressed early in the requirements process. We continue with the example of smart card systems design. Security in smart card systems is a challenging task due to the fact that different aspects of the system are not under a single trust boundary. Responsibilities are split among multiple parties. The processor, I/O, data, programs, and network may be controlled by different, and potentially hostile, parties. By discussing the security ramifications of different ways of splitting responsibilities, we aim to show how the proposed modelling framework can help produce a proper understanding of the security systems that employ smart cards. Figure 4 shows the basic steps to take during the process of domain requirements analysis with *i**, before we consider security. The process can be organised into the following iterative steps.

Actor Identification

In step (1), the question "who is involved in the system?" will be answered. According to the definition given above, we know that all intentional units may be represented as actors. For example, in any smart card based systems, there are many parties involved. An actor hierarchy composed of roles, positions, and agents such as the ones in Figure 3 is created.

Goal/Task Identification

In the step (2) of the requirements analysis process, the question "what does the actor want to achieve?" will be answered. As shown in the strategic rationale (SR) model of Figure 2, answers to this question can be represented as goals capturing the high-level objectives of agents. During system analysis and design, softgoals such as low cost and security are systematically refined until they can be operationalized and implemented. Using the SR model, we can reason about each alternative's contributions to high-level non-functional quality requirements including security, and possible tradeoffs.

The refinements of goals, tasks and softgoals (step (3) in Figure 4) are considered to have reached an adequate level once all the necessary design decisions can be made based on the existing information in the model. The SR model in Figure 3 was created by running through steps (1), (2), (3) in Figure 4 iteratively.

Strategic Dependency Identification

In the step (4) of the requirements analysis process, the question "how do the actors relate to each other?" will be answered. Figure 1 shows the SD model for a generic smart card-based payment system. By analyzing the dependency network in a Strategic Dependency model, we can reason about opportunities and vulnerabilities. A Strategic Dependency model can be obtained by hiding the internal rationales of actors in a Strategic Rationale model. Thus, the goal, task, resource, softgoal dependencies in a Strategic Dependency model can be seen as originating from SR models.

The kinds of analysis shown above answers questions such as "who is involved in the system? What do they want? How can their expectations be fulfilled? And what are the inter-dependencies between them?" These answers initially provide a sketch of the social setting of the future system, and eventually result in a fairly elaborate behavioral model where certain design choices have already been made. However, another set of very important questions has yet to be answered (i.e., what if things go wrong)? What if some party involved in the smart card system does not behave as expected? How bad can things get? What prevention tactics can be considered?" These are exactly the questions we want to answer in the security requirements analysis.

SECURITY REQUIREMENTS ANALYSIS WITH *i**

We now extend the process to include attacker analysis, vulnerability analysis, and countermeasure analysis. The dashed lines and boxes on the right hand side of Figure 5 indicate a series of analysis steps to deal with security. These steps are integrated into the basic domain requirements engineering process, such that threats from poten-

Figure 4. Requirements elicitation process with i*

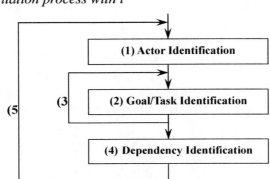

Figure 5. Security requirements elicitation process with **i***

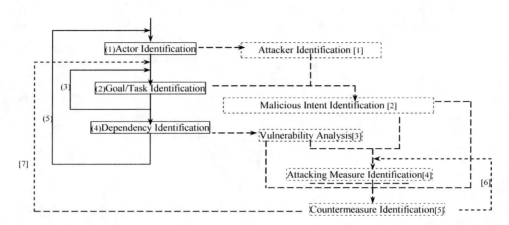

tial attackers are anticipated and countermeasures for system protection are sought and equipped wherever necessary. Each of the security related analysis steps (step [1] to [7]) will be discussed in detail in the following subsections.

Attacker Analysis

The attacker analysis steps aim to identify potential system abusers and their malicious intents. The basic premise here is that all the actors are assumed "guilty until proven innocent." In other words, given the result of the basic *i** requirements modelling process, we now consider any one of the actors (roles, positions, or agents) identified so far can be a potential attacker to the system or to other actors. For example, we want to ask, "In what ways can a terminal owner attack the system? How will he benefit from inappropriate manipulation of the card reader, or transaction data?"

In this analysis, each actor is considered in turn as an attacker. This attacker inherits the intentions, capabilities, and social relationships of the corresponding legitimate actor (i.e., the internal goal hierarchy and external dependency relationships in the model). This may serve as a starting point of a forward direction security analysis (step [1]

in Figure 5). A backward analysis starting from identifying possible malicious intents and valuable business assets can also be done.

Proceeding to step [2] of the process, for each attacker identified, we combine the capabilities and interests of the attacker with those of the legitimate actor. For simplicity, we assume that an attacker may be modeled as a role or an agent. To perform the attacker analysis, we consider that each role may be played by an attacker agent, each position may be occupied by an attacker agent, and that each agent may play an attacker role (Figure 6). The analysis would then reveal the commandeering of legitimate resources and capabilities for illicit use. The intents and strategies of the attackers are explicitly represented and reasoned about in the models.

This approach treats all attackers as insider attackers, as attacks are via associations with normal actors. We set a system boundary, then exhaustively search for possible attackers. Random attackers such as Internet hackers/crackers, or attackers breaking into a building can also be dealt with by being represented as sharing the same territory with their victim. By conducting analysis on the infrastructure of the Internet, we may identify attackers by treating Internet resources as resources in the *i** model. By conduct-

Figure 6. Modelling attackers in strategic actors model

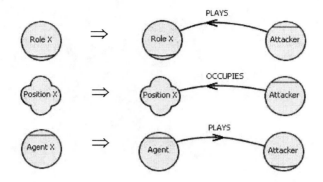

ing building security analysis, break-in attackers, or attackers sharing the same workspace can be identified. Alternatively, we could adopt an opposite assumption, i.e., assume there is a trusted perimeter for each agent, all the potential threat sources within this trusted perimeter are ignored, measures will only be taken to deal with threats from outside of the perimeter.

As shown in the Strategic Rationale model in Figure 7, the motives of Attacker in the smart card system may be modeled as intentional elements in an i* model. An attacker may be motivated by financial incentives (softgoal Be Profitable), or by non-financial ones (e.g., Desire for Notoriety). These malicious intents may lead to various attack strategies, such as Financial Theft, Impersonation Attack, Gain Unauthorized Access, Attack on Privacy, and Publicity Attack.

Dependency Vulnerability Analysis

Dependency vulnerability analysis aims at identifying the vulnerable points in the dependency network (step [3] in Figure 5). A dependency relationship makes the depender inherently vulnerable. Potential attackers may exploit these vulnerabilities to actually attack the system, so that their malicious intents can be served. *i** dependency modelling allows a more specific vulnerability analysis because the potential failure of each dependency can be traced to a depender and to *its* dependers. The questions we want to answer here are "which dependency relationships are vulnerable to attack?", "What are the chain

Figure 7. Motives of attacker in a smart card system

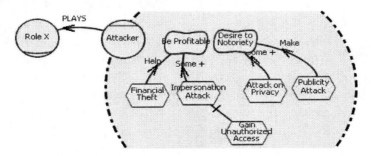

Figure 8. Dependencies (in other words, vulnerable points) in a smart card system

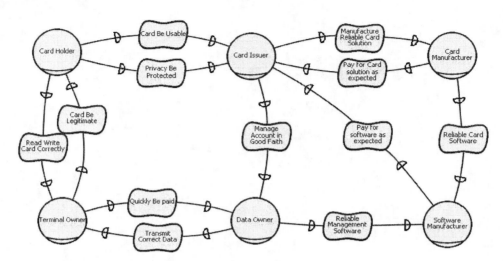

effects if one dependency link is compromised?" The analysis of dependency vulnerabilities does not end with the identification of potential vulnerable points. We need to trace upstream in the dependency network, and see whether the attacked dependency relationship impacts other actors in the network.

Figure 8 is a simplified version of the SD model of Figure 4, showing only the softgoal dependencies. We assume that each of the actors in the SD model can be a potential attacker. And as an attacker, an actor will fail to deliver the expected dependencies directed to it, of whom it is the dependee.

For instance, the Card Holder depends on the Terminal Owner to Read/Write Card Correctly. To analyze the vulnerability arising from this dependency, we consider the case where the terminal owner is not trustworthy. And we try to identify the potential attacks by answering question of "In what possible ways could the attacker break this dependency relationship?" To do this, we elaborate on the agent Attacker Playing Terminal Owner. Starting from attacker's potential motivations, we refine the high-level goals of the attackers

(and possible attack routes) based on analysis of the SD and SR models of the normal operations of the smart card (e.g., what resources an actor accesses, what types of interactions exist, etc.). In this way, we may identify a number of potential attacks that are sufficient to make this dependency not viable (*Break*).

Proceeding to step [4], we now focus on how an attacker may attack the vulnerable points identified above by exploring the attacker's capacities. We model potential attacks (including fraud) as negative contributions from the attackers (from their specific methods of attack) toward the dependee-side dependency link. A *Break* contribution indicates that the attack is sufficient to make the softgoal unviable. For clarity of analysis, we place the attack-related intentional elements into agents called "Attacker Playing Role X." Details of the attack methods (e.g., Steal Card Information, Send Falsified Records) can be elaborated by further means-ends and decomposition analysis. Thus, the steps and methods of the attack can be modeled and analyzed. Other internal details of the Terminal Owner are not relevant and are thus not included in the model. Negative contribution links are used to show attacks on more specific vulnerabilities of the depender (e.g., refinements of Transact with Card).

The dependencies that could be broken are highlighted with a small square in Figure 9. When a dependency is compromised, the effect could propagate through the dependency network upstream along the dependency links. For example, if the Terminal Owner is not Quickly Be Paid, he may stop accepting card as a payment option.

Countermeasure Analysis

During countermeasure analysis, system designers make decisions on how to mitigate vulnerabilities and set up defenses against potential attackers. This type of analysis covers general types of attacks, and formulates solutions by selectively applying, combining, or instantiating prototypical solutions to address the specific needs of various stakeholders. The general types of attacks and the prototypical solutions can be retrieved from a taxonomy or knowledge repository.

Necessary factors for the success of an attack are attacker's motivations, vulnerabilities of the system, and attacker's capabilities to carry out the attack. Thus, to counteract a hypothetical attack, we seek measures that will sufficiently negate these factors. Based on the above analysis, we already understand the attackers' possible malicious intents and system vulnerabilities. As shown in Figure 5, countermeasure analysis is an iterative process. Adding protective measures may bring new vulnerabilities to the system, so a new round of vulnerability analysis and countermeasure analysis will be triggered (step [6]).

With the knowledge of some potential attacks and frauds, the depender may first look for trustworthy partners, or change their methods of operation, or add control mechanisms (countermeasures) to protect their interests. A countermeasure may prevent the attack from happening by either making it technically impossible, or by eliminating the attacker's intent of attack.

Figure 9. Attacks directed to vulnerable dependencies in a smart card system

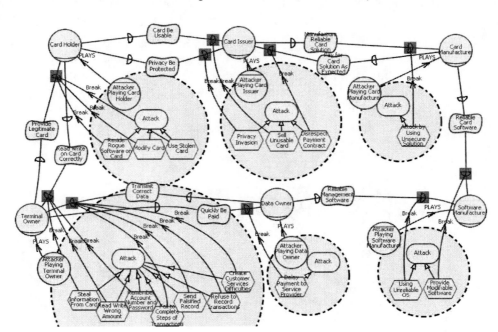

Figure 10. Resistance models defeating hypothetical attacks

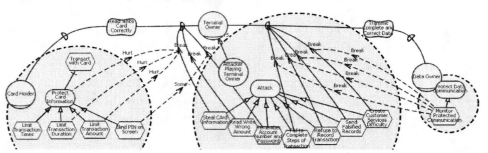

Figure 10 shows a SR model with defensive actions as well as attacks. Protection mechanisms are adopted to counteract specific attacks. In some cases, the protections are sufficient to defeat a strong attack (defense *Break* link (dotted arrow) pointing to an attack *Break* link). In other cases, countermeasures are only partially effective in defending against their respective attacks (through the *Hurt* or *Some-* contribution types).

Qualitative Goal-Reasoning Mechanism

A qualitative goal-reasoning process is used to propagates a series of labels through the models. A label (or satisficing status) on a node is used to indicate whether that intentional element (goal, task, resource, or softgoal) is viable or not (e.g., whether a softgoal is sufficiently met). Labels can have values such as Satisfied "✔," Denied "✗

," Weakly Satisfied "✔ " and Weakly Denied "✗," Undecided "？," etc. (Liu et al., 2003). Leaf nodes (those with no incoming contributions) are given labels by the analyst based on judgment of their independent viability. These values are then propagated "upwards" through the contribution network (following the direction of the contribution links, and from dependee to depender). The viability of the overall system appears in the high level nodes of the various stakeholders. The process is an interactive one, requiring the analyst to make judgments whenever the outcome is inconclusive given the combination of potentially conflicting contributions.

To begin, the analyst labels all the attack leaf nodes as Satisfied since they are all judged to be possible (Figure 11). Similarly, all the defense leaf nodes are judged to be viable, thus labelled Satisfied. The values are then propagated along contribution links. Before adding defense nodes,

Figure 11. Countermeasure effectiveness evaluation model

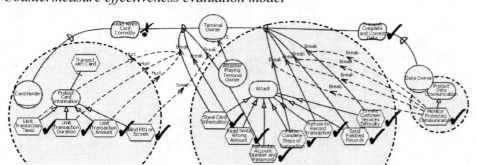

the Card Holder's dependency on the Terminal Owner for Read Write Card Correctly softgoal was labelled as Denied, because of the potentially strong attacks from Terminal Owner. However, as countermeasures are added, the influences of the attacks will be correspondingly weakened.

Regarding Read Write Card Correctly, three possible attacks are identified. One of them Steal Card Info is counteracted by three defense measures, though each one is partial (Hurt). Another attack Remember Account Number & Password has a defense of unknown strength (*Some-*). The third attack has no defensive measure. The softgoal dependency Read Write Card Correctly is thus judged to be weakly unviable ($\digamma$). On the other side, as the Data Owner's protection mechanism could sufficiently defeat the four possible attacks, the Transmit Complete and Correct Data softgoal dependency is thus judged to be viable (✔). Potential attacks lead to the erosion of viability of the smart card system. Incorporating sufficient countermeasures restores viability.

A prototype knowledge-based tool is being constructed to support this framework for analyzing information systems security.

Trust Analysis Based on System Configuration

In the models previously given, the various participants in a smart card system were modelled as abstract roles and analyzed generally. However, in real world smart card systems, various concrete physical or organisational parties play or occupy these roles. These are shown in Table 1. Thus, to actually understand their trust and security situations, we have to apply the generic model to the real world configurations. We consider two representative kinds of smart card based systems. One is the Digital Stored Value Card, the other is the Prepaid Phone Card (Schneier & Shostack, 1998).

Table 1. Actors (roles, positions, and agents) in various smart card system configurations

Generic Smart Card Model	Card Holder	Terminal Owner	Card Issuer	Data Owner	Card Manufacturer	Software Manufacturer
Digital Stored Value card	Customer	Merchant	Financial Institution		Technology Company	
Digital Check Card	Customer	Merchant	Financial Institution	Customer	Technology Company	
Prepaid Phone Card	Customer	Phone Company				
Account-based Phone Card	Customer	Phone Company		Customer	Technology Company	
Key store card	User		Technology Company			
Employee Access Token	Employee	Employer				
Web browsing card	Customer		Financial Institution		Technology Company	

Digital Stored Value Card System

These are payment cards intended to be substitutes for cash. Both Mondex and VisaCash are examples of this type of system. The Customer is the Card Holder. The Merchant is the Terminal Owner. The Financial Institution that supports the system is both the Data Owner and the Card Issuer. The Smart Card Technology Company, such as Mondex, is both the Card Manufacturer and the Software Manufacturer.

In such a configuration, the previously separated roles of Data Owner and Card Issuer are Played by the same physical agent, namely, Financial Institution. Similarly, Card Manufacturer and Software Manufacturer are combined into one physical agent — the Smart Card Technology Company. Figure 12 describes the threat model of a digital stored value card. Here the Software Manufacturer's attack on Card Manufacturer can be ignored since they belong to the same agent — the Smart Card Technology Company. Also the attack from Data Owner to Card Issuer can be ignored since they both played by the Financial Institution. These two attacking-defending relationships are highlighted in Figure 11 with little squares.

Prepaid Phone Card System

These are special-use stored value cards. The Customer is the Card Holder. The Phone Company plays all the four roles of Terminal Owner, Data Owner, Manufacturer, and Card Issuer. Figure 13 shows the threat model of a prepaid card system. Under such a system configuration, more attack-defense pairs disappear. Only four possible attacks need to be considered now. Three of them are from the phone company, which includes violating privacy, to issue unusable card, to read write card incorrectly. The other attack is from the Card Holder, who might use an illegitimate card.

Note that each time new roles are created, the possibility of new attacks arises. These models reflect Schneier's observation that the fewer splits we make, the more trustworthy the target system is likely to be (Schneier & Shostack, 1998).

RELATED WORK

Each approach to security and software engineering has an ontology, whether explicitly defined or implied. We expect that a social ontology can be complementary and beneficial to various approaches to integrating security and software engineering. We begin with work from the security

Figure 12. A threat model of digital stored value card system

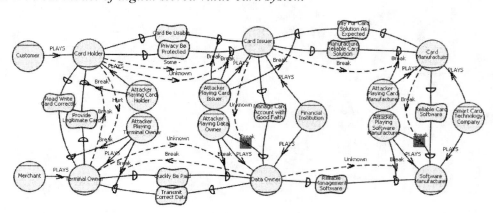

Figure 13. A threat model of prepaid phone card system

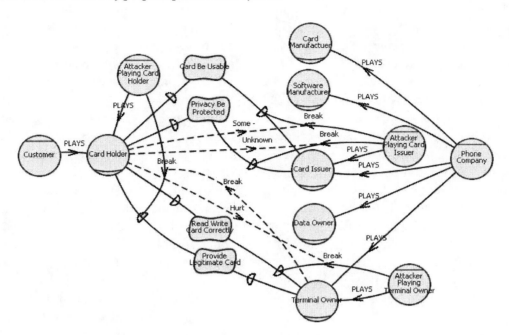

community, followed by software engineering approaches that have paid special attention to security.

Security Models

Formal models have been an important part of computer security since mainframe computing (Samarati & Vimercati, 2001). Security policies originate from laws, regulations, or organisational practices, and are typically written in natural language. Security models using mathematical formalisms can provide a precise formulation of the policies for implementation. More importantly, formally specified policy models can be mathematically verified to guarantee security properties. As mathematical abstractions, they provide unambiguous specifications that are independent of implementation mechanisms. Some concepts in security models include: subject, object, action, clearance level, user, group, role, task, principal, owner, etc.

Since security models are idealized abstractions, their application in real life requires a series of translations, involving interpretation and decision making at each stage. Organisational structures must be analyzed so as to select the appropriate models, or a combination of models. Policies need to be interpreted and codified properly to achieve the desired results. Real world entities and relationships are mapped to the model abstractions. Finally, the security model is mapped to security implementation mechanisms. The levels of abstractions used in security requirements, design, and implementation therefore mirror those in software system development and provide a basis for integration.

The social ontology outlined in this chapter can facilitate and augment an integrated security development process by enriching the reasoning support needed to arrive at decisions at each stage in the process. The ontology in existing security models are intended for the automated enforcement of specified security rules (e.g., to decide whether to give access). They do not support reasoning about why particular models or policies are appropriate for the target environment, especially when there are conflicting objectives and interpretations. Furthermore, many of the simplifying assumptions that formal models rely on do not hold in real life (Denning, 1999). The social ontology of strategic actors provides a framework for reasoning about the use of such models from a pragmatic, broader perspective.

In the development of new security models, there is a trend towards ontologies that are more closely aligned with the ontology of organisational work. For example, role based access control (RBAC) (Ferraiolo, Sandhu, Gavrila, Kuhn, & Chandramouli, 2001; Sandhu, Coyne, Feinstein, & Youman, 1996) allows privileges to be organised according to organisational roles such as loan officer or branch manager. These trends are consistent with the proposed social ontology approach, though RBAC models, like other access control models, are meant for enforcement, not strategic organisational reasoning.

Security Management Frameworks

While formal computer security models focus on policies built into the automated system, the overall security of information and software systems depends very much on organisational practices. Security practices have existed long before the computer age. Many of the principles continue to apply and have been adapted to software systems. Standards have been defined to promote best practices (e.g., ISO 17799, 1999).

OCTAVE (Alberts & Dorofee, 2002), CRAMM, and FRAP (Peltier, 2001), are oriented toward decision making from a business perspective, leading to management, operational, and technical requirements and procedures. Although few frameworks have explicit information models, they do have implicit ontologies revolving around key concepts such as asset, attack, threat, vulnerability, countermeasure, and risk.

The main focus of these frameworks is on prescriptive guidelines. Tables and charts are used to enumerate and cross-list vulnerabilities and threats. Potential countermeasures are suggested. Risks are computed from potential losses arising from estimated likelihood of threats. Since quantitative estimates are hard to come by, most assessments rely on ratings such as low, medium, high.

While formal computer security models attempt to guarantee security (requiring simplifying assumptions that may depart from reality), security management frameworks acknowledge that security breaches will occur, and suggest countermeasures to reduce risk. This pragmatic stance is very much in the spirit of the social ontology proposed in this chapter. Security management frameworks can be augmented by the modelling of strategic actor relationships and reasoning about how their goals may be achieved or hindered.

Another drawback of checklists and guidelines is that they tend to be too generic. Experience and expert judgment are needed to properly apply them to specific systems and organisational settings. Such judgments are hard to trace or maintain over time as the systems evolve.

The explicit modelling of strategic relationships can provide a more specific analysis of sources of vulnerabilities and failures, thus also allowing countermeasures to be targeted appropriately. Using the strategic dependencies and rationales, one can trace the impact of threats along the paths to determine which business goals are affected. The impact on goals other than security can also be determined through the model since they appear in the same model. One can see how security goals might compete with or are synergistic with non-security goals, thus leading to decisions that take the overall set of goals into account. Using an agent-oriented ontology, one can determine which actors are most affected by which security threats, and are therefore likely to be most motivated to take measures. Tradeoffs are done from the viewpoint of each stakeholder. This approach provides a good basis for an ontology of security, which can mediate between business reasoning from an organisational perspective and system design reasoning from a technical perspective.

Some preliminary work have been done to integrate the *i** modelling ontology with risk-based security management approaches (Gaunard & Dubois, 2003; Mayer, Rifaut, & Dubois, 2005). Further extensions could incorporate economic theories and reasoning (e.g., Anderson, 2001; Camp & Lewis, 2004). The ontology of *i** can provide the structure representation of social relationships on which to do economic reasoning.

Software Systems Design Frameworks

Having considered work originating from the security side, we now turn to contributions from the software engineering and system development perspective.

Extensions to UML (see Chapter I for information of such approaches).The ontology of UML, consisting of objects and classes, activities, states, interactions, and so forth, with its security-oriented extensions, are useful for specifying the technical design of security features and functionalities, but does not support the reasoning that lead up to those requirements and designs. As indicated in the second section of this chapter, technical design notations are useful for recording the results of decisions, but do not offer support for arriving at those decisions. The social ontology proposed in this chapter can therefore complement UML-based approaches, such as the one presented in Chapter IX, by supporting the early-stage requirements modelling and reasoning that can then be propagated to the technical design stage, resulting in design choices expressed in UML-like design notations. Stakeholder deliberations and tradeoffs therefore

are effectively conveyed to technical designers. Conversely, the effect of technical choices can be propagated upstream to enable stakeholders to appreciate the consequences as they appear in the stakeholders' world.

Extensions to information systems modelling and design. In the information systems area, Pernul (1992) proposes secure data schemas (extension of entity-relationship diagrams) and secure function schemas (extension of data flow diagrams). In Herrmann and Pernul (1999) and Röhm and Pernul (1999), these models are extended to include a business process schema, with tasks, data/material, humans, legal bindings and information flow, and an organisational schema with role models and organisation diagrams to describe which activities are done where and by whom. Other information systems security approaches include the automated secure system development method (Booysen & Eloff, 1995) and the logical controls specification approach (Baskerville, 1993; Siponen & Baskerville, 2001).

These approaches illustrate the extension of conventional information systems ontologies to incorporate security-specific ontologies. Different concepts are added to each level of modelling (e.g., database schemas, process or function schemas, workflow schemas, and organisation diagrams). As with UML extensions, these approaches tend to emphasize the notation needed to express security features in the requirements specification or design descriptions and how those features can be analyzed. However, the notations (and the implied ontology) do not provide support for the deliberations that lead up to the security requirements and design. A social ontology that supports explicit reasoning about relationships among strategic actors, as outlined in this chapter, can be a helpful extension to these approaches.

Responsibility modelling. A number of approaches center around the notion of responsibility. In Strens and Dobson (1994), when an agent delegates an obligation, the agent becomes a responsibility principal, and the receiver of the delegation process is a responsibility holder. An obligation is a high-level mission that the agent can fulfill by carrying out activities. Agents cannot transfer their responsibilities, only their obligations. Three kinds of requirements are derived from responsibilities: need-to-do, need-to-know and need-for-audit. The need-to-know requirements relate to security policies — which subjects (e.g., users) should be allowed to access which objects (e.g., files, etc.) so that they are able to fulfill their responsibilities.

Backhouse and Dhillon (1996) also adopt a responsibilities analysis approach, incorporating speech acts theory. The model for automated profile specification (MAPS) approach (Pottas & Solms, 1995) uses responsibilities and role models to generate information security profiles (such as access control) from job descriptions and organisational policies.

This group of work has a more explicit ontology of social organisation. The emphasis is on the mappings between organisational actors and the tasks or activities they have to perform. While actors or agents have responsibilities, they are not viewed as having strategic interests, and do not seek alternate configurations of social relationships that favor those interests. The focus of attention is on functional behaviors and responsibilities. Security is treated as additional functions to be incorporated, and there are no attempts to deal with interactions and tradeoffs between security and other non-functional objectives such as usability or maintainability. The social ontology of *i** can therefore be quite complementary to these approaches. Other socio-organisational approaches are reviewed in Dhillon and Backhouse (2001).

Requirements Engineering Approaches to Security

While security needs to be integrated into all stages of software engineering, there is general agreement that integration starting from the earliest stages is essential. It is well known that mistakes early in the software process can have far reaching consequences in subsequent stages that are difficult and costly to remedy. Fred Brooks (1995) had noted that the requirements stage is the most difficult, and suggested that software engineering should focus more on "building the right system," and not just on "building the system right."

In requirements engineering research, a large part of the effort has been devoted to verifying that the requirements statements are precise, unambiguous, consistent, and complete. Recently, more attention has been given to the challenge of understanding the environment and context of the intended system so that the requirements will truly reflect what stakeholders want.

Goal-oriented requirements engineering. Traditional requirements languages for software specification focus on structure and behavior, with ontologies that center around entities, activities, states, constraints, and their variants. A goal-oriented ontology allows systems to be placed within the intentional setting of the usage environment. Typically, goal-oriented requirements engineering frameworks employ AND/OR tree structures (or variants) to analyze and explore alternate system definitions that will contribute to stakeholder goals in different ways. Security can be readily integrated into such a framework since attacks and threats interfere with the normal achievement of stakeholder goals. Security controls and countermeasures can be derived from defensive goals to counteract malicious actions and intents.

The NFR framework: Security as softgoal. The NFR framework (Chung, 1993; Chung et al., 2000) is distinctive from most of the above cited approaches to security in that it does not start with vulnerabilities and risks, nor from security features and functions. It starts by treating security as one among many non-functional requirements. As with many other non-functional requirements such as usability, performance, or information accuracy, security is viewed as a goal whose operational meaning needs to be interpreted according to the needs of the specific application setting. This interpretation is done by a series of refinements in a goal graph until the point (called operationalization) where subgoals are sufficiently concrete as to be accomplishable by implementable actions and mechanisms, such as access control mechanisms or protocols. At each stage in the refinement, subgoals are judged to be contributing qualitatively to the parent goals in different ways. Because the nature and extent of the contribution requires judgement from experience and possibly domain expertise, the term softgoal is used, drawing on Simon's notion of satisficing (Simon, 1996).

The NFR framework thus offers a systematic approach for achieving "good enough" security — a practical objective in real life (Sandhu, 2003; Schneier, 2003) that have been hard to achieve in conventional mathematical formalisms. A formal treatment of the satisficing semantics of softgoals is offered in Chung et al. (2000).

The NFR framework is also distinctive in that it allows security goals to be analyzed and understood at the same time as other potentially competing requirements, for example, usability, performance, maintainability, and evolvability. In the past, it has been difficult to deal with these non-functional requirements early in the development life cycle. Typically functional requirements dominate the design process. Experienced and expert designers take non-functional requirement into account intuitively and implicitly, but without support from systematic frameworks, languages, or tools. The softgoal graph approach acknowledges that security needs to compete with other goals during requirements analysis and during design. Different aspects of security may also compete with each other. The NFR goal-oriented approach supports reasoning about tradeoffs among these competing goals and how they can be achieved.

Beyond clarifying requirements, the NFR softgoals are used to drive subsequent stages in system design and implementation, thus offering a deep integration of security into the software engineering process.

A related body of work is in quality attributes of software architecture, for example, the ATAM approach (Kazman, Klein, & Clements, 2000) for architectural evaluation. Many of the basic elements are similar to the NFR framework. The classification of quality attributes and mechanisms (for security and other attributes), however, are viewed from an evaluation viewpoint. The taxonomy structure of quality attribute is not seen as goals to be elaborated based on tradeoffs encountered in the particular system. Quality attributes are concretized in terms of metrics, which are different for each quality, so trade-offs are difficult across different metrics.

The KAOS framework: Goals, obstacles, and anti-goals. KAOS (Dardenne, van Lamsweerde, & Fickas, 1993; van Lamsweerde, 2001, 2004; van Lamsweerde, Brohez, Landtsheer, & Janssens, 2003) is a goal-oriented requirements engineering framework that focuses on systematic derivation of requirements from goals. It includes an outer layer of informally specified goals, and an inner layer of formalized goal representation and operations using temporal logic. It is therefore especially suitable for real-time and safety critical systems. Refinement patterns are developed making use of temporal logic relationships.

The KAOS ontology includes obstacles, which impede goal achievement. The methodology provides techniques for identifying and resolving obstacles. To incorporate security analysis, attackers present obstacles to security goals. New security requirements are derived from attack generation and resolution.

Tree structures have been used in the security community for analyzing the structure of threats (Schneier, 1999), and in the safety community for the analysis of faults and hazards (Helmer et al.,

2002). Experiences from these approaches can be incorporated into goal-oriented frameworks.

Agent-Oriented Requirements Engineering

The agent-oriented approach adopts goal-oriented concepts and techniques, but treats goals as originating from different actors. The *i** modelling framework views actors as having strategic interests. Each actor aims to further its own interests in exploring alternative conceptions of the future system and how the system will affect its relationships to other actors. This may be contrasted with other frameworks which may include some notion of actor which are non-intentional (e.g., in use case diagrams in UML) or non-strategic (e.g., in KAOS, where agents are passive recipients of responsibility assignments at the end of a goal refinement process).

*i** adopts the notion of softgoal from the NFR framework, but makes further distinctions with goal, task, and resource. Softgoals are operationalized into tasks, which may in turn contain decompositions that include softgoals.

Security issues are traced to antagonistic goals and dependencies among attackers and defenders. As in the NFR framework, security is treated as much as possible within the same notational and reasoning framework as for other non-functional requirements (as softgoals), but extended to include functional elements (as goals, tasks, and resources). Security is therefore not treated in isolation, but interacts with other concerns at all steps throughout the process. The illustration of *i** in this chapter is based on the example in Yu and Liu (2000, 2001). Further illustrations are in Liu et al. (2002), Yu and Cysneiros (2001), Liu et al. (2003), Liu and Yu (2003, 2004).

The *i** approach has been adopted and extended in a number of directions. The Tropos framework (Bresciani, Perini, Giorgini, Giunchiglia, & Mylopoulos, 2004; Castro, Kolp, & Mylopoulos, 2002) further develops the *i** approach into a full-fledged software engineering methodology, using the agent-oriented social ontology originating from requirements modelling to drive architectural design, detailed design, and eventual implementation on agent-based software platforms. Formal Tropos incorporates formalization techniques similar to KAOS, so that automated tools such as model checking can be applied to verify security properties (Liu et al., 2003).

A number of extensions to *i** have been developed to address specific needs of security modelling and analysis. Mouratidis et al. (2003a, 2003b, 2004, 2005, also Chapter VIII) introduced the concepts of security reference diagram and security constraints. Common security concepts such as secure entities, secure dependencies, and secure capabilities are reinterpreted within the *i** ontology. The security constraint concept attaches a security-related strategic dependency to the dependency that it applies to. An intuitive benefit of this concept is that the association between the two is indicated without having to refer to the internal rationale structures of actors. An attack scenarios representation structure that aims to support the analysis of specific attacking and protecting situations at a more detailed design stage is developed. New language structures developed include secure capability, and attacking link.

Giorgini et al. (2003, 2005; also Chapter VIII) introduced four new primitive relationships related to security requirements: trust, delegation, offer and owner relation. These new primitives offer an explicit treatment of security concepts such as permission, ownership, and authority, which allows a more detailed analysis.

In Crook, Ince, and Nuseibeh (2005), the problem of modelling access policies is addressed by extending the Tropos approach (Liu et al., 2003), to ensure that security goals can be achieved and that operational requirements are consistent with access policies.

Misuse/Abuse Cases

Misuse and abuse cases techniques (Alexander, 2001; Sindre & Opdahl, 2000, 2001; see also Review in Chapter I) are complementary to goal-oriented techniques as they offer different ways of structuring requirements knowledge (Rolland, Grosz, & Kla, 1999). Use cases are action-oriented and include sequence and conditionals. Goal refinements are (mostly) hierarchical covering multiple levels of abstraction. In addressing security requirements, the development of misuse/abuse cases can be assisted by using goal analysis. Conversely, goal analysis can be made concrete by considering positive and negative use cases and scenarios. Note that use cases are better suited to later stages in requirements analysis since they assume that the system boundary is already defined. Unlike the strategic actors in *i**, actors in use cases are non-intentional and serve to delineate the boundary of the automated system.

CONCLUSION

In this chapter, we have argued that a social ontology can provide the basis for integrating security and software engineering. We presented the social ontology of *i** and illustrated how it can be used to include security goals when designing a smart card system. We have outlined how a social ontology is complementary to a number of techniques in security engineering and in software engineering, thus building common ground between the two areas.

ACKNOWLEDGMENT

The authors (1 & 3) gratefully acknowledge financial support from the Natural Sciences and Engineering Research Council of Canada, Bell University Laboratories, and author (2) the National Key Research and Development Plan (973, no.2002CB312004) and NSF China (no. 60503030).

REFERENCES

Alberts, C., & Dorofee, A. (2002, July). *Managing information security risks: The OCTAVE (SM) approach.* Boston: Addison Wesley.

Alexander, I. (2002, September). Modelling the interplay of conflicting goals with use and misuse cases. *Proceedings of the 8th International Workshop on Requirements Engineering: Foundation for Software Quality (REFSQ-02)*, Essen, Germany (pp. 9-10).

Alexander, I. (2003, January). Misuse cases: Use cases with hostile intent. *IEEE Software, 20*(1), 58-66.

Anderson, R. (2001). *Security engineering: A guide to building dependable distributed systems.* New York: Wiley.

Backhouse, J., & Dhillon, G. (1996). Structures of responsibilities and security of information systems. *European Journal of Information Systems, 5*(1), 2-10.

Baskerville, R. (1993). Information systems security design methods: Implications for information systems development. *Computing Surveys, 25*(4), 375-414.

Boehm, B. W. (1988). A spiral model of software development and enhancement. *IEEE Computer, 21*(5), 61-72.

Booysen, H. A. S., & Eloff, J. H. P. (1995). A methodology for the development of secure application systems. *Proceeding of the 11th IFIP TC11 International Conference on Information Security.*

Bresciani, P., Perini, A., Giorgini, P., Giunchiglia, F., & Mylopoulos, J. (2004) Tropos: An agent-oriented software development methodology. *Autonomous Agents and Multi-Agent Systems, 8*(3), 203-236.

Brooks, F. (1995, August). *The mythical man-month: Essays on software engineering, 20th Anniversary Edition* (1ˢᵗ ed.). Boston: Addison-Wesley.

Castro, J., Kolp, M., & Mylopoulos, J. (2002). Towards requirements driven information systems engineering: The Tropos project. *Information Systems, 27*(6), 365-389.

Chung, L. (1993). Dealing with security requirements during the development of information systems. In C. Rolland, F. Bodart, & C. Cauvet (Eds.), *Proceedings of the 5ᵗʰ International Conference Advanced Information Systems Engineering, CAiSE '93* (pp. 234-251). Springer.

Chung L., Nixon, B. A., Yu, E., & Mylopoulos, J. (2000). *Non-functional requirements in software engineering.* Kluwer Academic Publishers.

CRAMM – CCTA (Central Computer and Telecommunications Agency, UK). *Risk analysis and management method.* Retrieved from http://www.cramm.com/cramm.htm

Crook, R., Ince, D., & Nuseibeh, B. (2005, August 29-September 2). On Modelling access policies: Relating roles to their organisational context. *Proceedings of the 13ᵗʰ IEEE International Requirements Engineering Conference (RE'05),* Paris (pp. 157-166).

Dardenne, A., van Lamsweerde, A., & Fickas, S. (1993). Goal-directed requirements acquisition. *Science of Computer Programming, 20*(1-2), 3-50.

Denning, D. E. (1998). *The limits of formal security models.* National Computer Systems Security Award Acceptance Speech. Retrieved October 18, 1999, from www.cs.georgetown.edu/~denning/infosec/award.html

Dhillon, G., & Backhouse, J. (2001) Current directions in IS security research: Toward socio-organizational perspectives. *Information Systems Journal, 11*(2), 127-154.

Ferraiolo, D., Sandhu, R., Gavrila, S., Kuhn, R., & Chandramouli, R. (2001, August). Proposed NIST standard for role-based access control. *ACM Transactions on Information and Systems Security, 4*(3), 224-74.

Franch, X., & Maiden, N. A. M. (2003, February 10-13). Modelling component dependencies to inform their selection. *COTS-Based Software Systems, 2ⁿᵈ International Conference, (ICCBSS 2003)* (pp. 81-91). Lecture Notes in Computer Science 2580. Ottawa, Canada: Springer.

Gaunard, P., & Dubois, E. (2003, May 26-28). Bridging the gap between risk analysis and security policies: Security and privacy in the age of uncertainty. *IFIP TC11 18ᵗʰ International Conference on Information Security (SEC2003)* (pp. 409-412). Athens, Greece. Kluwer.

Giorgini, P., Massacci, F., & Mylopoulos, J. (2003, October 13-16). Requirement engineering meets security: A case study on modelling secure electronic transactions by VISA and Mastercard. *The 22ⁿᵈ International Conference on Conceptual Modelling (ER'03)* (LNCS 2813, pp. 263-276). Chicago: Springer.

Giorgini, P., Massacci, F., Mylopoulos, J., & Zannone, N. (2005). Modelling social and individual trust in requirements engineering methodologies. *Proceedings of the 3ʳᵈ International Conference on Trust Management (iTrust 2005).* LNCS 3477. Heidelberg: Springer-Verlag.

Gross, D., & Yu, E. (2001, August 27-31). Evolving system architecture to meet changing business goals: An agent and goal-oriented approach. The *5ᵗʰ IEEE International Symposium on Requirements Engineering (RE 2001)* (pp. 316-317). Toronto, Canada.

Helmer, G., Wong, J., Slagell, M., Honavar, V., Miller, L., & Lutz, R. (2002). A software fault tree approach to requirements analysis of an intrusion detection system. In P. Loucopoulos & J. Mylopoulos (Ed.), *Special Issue on Requirements Engineering for Information Security. Requirements Engineering* (Vol. 7, No. 4, pp. 177-220).

Herrmann, G., & Pernul, G. (1999). Viewing business-process security from different perspectives. *International Journal of Electronic Commerce, 3*(3), 89-103.

ISO 17799. (1999). *Information security management — Part 1: Code of practice for information security.* London: British Standards Institution.

Kazman, R., Klein, M., & Clements, P. (2000). *ATAM: Method for architectural evaluation (CMU/SEI-2000-TR-004).* Pittsburgh, PA: Software Engineering Institute, Carnegie Mellon University.

Liu, L., & Yu, E. (2003). Designing information systems in social context: A goal and scenario modelling approach. *Information Systems, 29*(2), 187-203.

Liu, L., & Yu, E. (2004). Intentional modelling to support identity management. In P. Atzeni et al. (Eds.), *Proceedings of the 23rd International Conference on Conceptual Modelling (ER 2004)* (pp. 555-566). LNCS 3288. Berlin, Heidelberg: Springer-Verlag.

Liu, L., Yu, E., & Mylopoulos, J. (2002, October 16). Analyzing security requirements as relationships among strategic actors. The *2nd Symposium on Requirements Engineering for Information Security (SREIS'02).* Raleigh, NC.

Liu, L., Yu, E., & Mylopoulos, J. (2003, September). Security and privacy requirements analysis within a social setting. *Proceedings of International Conference on Requirements Engineering (RE'03)* (pp. 151-161). Monterey, CA.

Lodderstedt, T., Basin, D. A., J, & Doser, R. (2002). SecureUML: A UML-based modelling language for model-driven security. *Proceedings of UML '02: Proceedings of the 5th International Conference on The Unified Modelling Language,* Dresden, Germany (pp. 426-441).

Mayer, N., Rifaut, A., & Dubois, E. (2005). Towards a risk-based security requirements engineering framework. *Workshop on Requirements Engineering For Software Quality (REFSQ'05), at the Conference for Advanced Information Systems Engineering (CAiSE),* Porto, Portugal.

McDermott, J., & Fox, C. (1999). Using abuse case models for security requirements analysis. *Proceedings 15th IEEE Annual Computer Security Applications Conference,* Scottsdale, USA (pp. 55-67).

Mouratidis, H., Giorgini, P., & Manson, G. A. (2003a). Integrating security and systems engineering: Towards the modelling of secure information systems. *Proceedings of the 15th Conference on Advanced Information Systems Engineering (CAiSE 03)* (Vol . LNCS 2681, pp. 63-78). Klagenfurt, Austria: Springer.

Mouratidis, H., Giorgini, P., & Manson, G. (2004, April 13-17). Using security attack scenarios to analyse security during information systems design. *Proceedings of the 6th International Conference on Enterprise Information Systems,* Porto, Portugal.

Mouratidis, H., Giorgini, P., & Schumacher, M. (2003b). Security patterns for agent systems. *Proceedings of the 8th European Conference on Pattern Languages of Programs,* Irsee, Germany.

Mouratidis, H., Kolp, M., Faulkner, S., & Giorgini. P. (2005, July). A secure architectural description language for agent systems. *Proceedings of the 4th International Joint Conference on Autonomous Agents and Multiagent Systems (AAMAS05).* Utrecht, The Netherlands: ACM Press.

Peltier, T. R. (2001, January). *Information se-*

curity risk analysis. Boca Raton, FL: Auerbach Publications.

Pernul, G. (1992, November 23-25). Security constraint processing in multilevel secure AMAC schemata. The *2nd European Symposium on Research in Computer Security (ESORICS 1992)* (pp. 349-370). Toulouse, France. Lecture Notes in Computer Science 648. Springer.

Pottas, D., & Solms, S. H. (1995). Aligning information security profiles with organizational policies. *Proceedings of the IFIP TC11 11th International Conference on Information Security.*

Röhm, A. W., & Pernul, G. (1999). COPS: A model and infrastructure for secure and fair electronic markets. *Proceedings of the 32nd Annual Hawaii International Conference on Systems Sciences.*

Rolland, C., Grosz, G., & Kla, R. (1999, June). Experience with goal-scenario coupling in requirements engineering. *Proceedings of the IEEE International Symposium on Requirements Engineering*, Limerick, Ireland.

Samarati, P., & Vimercati, S. (2001). Access control: Policies, models, and mechanisms. In R. Focardi & R. Gorrieri (Eds.), *Foundations of security analysis and design: Tutorial lectures* (pp. 137-196). LNCS 2171.

Sandhu, R. (2003, January/February). Good enough security: Towards a business driven discipline. *IEEE Internet Computing, 7*(1), 66-68.

Sandhu, R. S., Coyne, E. J., Feinstein, H. L., & Youman, C. E. (1996, February). Role-based access control models. *IEEE Computer, 29*(2), 38-47.

Schneier, B. (1999). *Attack trees modelling security threats.* Dr. Dobb's Journal, December. Retrieved from http://www.counterpane.com/attacktrees-ddj-ft.html

Schneier, B. (2003). *Beyond fear: Thinking sensibly about security in an uncertain world.*

New York: Copernicus Books, an imprint of Springer-Verlag.

Schneier, B., & Shostack, A. (1998). *Breaking up is hard to do: Modelling security threats for smartcards.* First USENIX Symposium on Smart-Cards, USENIX Press. Retrieved from http://www.counterpane.com/smart-card-threats.html

Simon, H. (1996). *The sciences of the artificial* (3rd ed.). MIT Press.

Sindre, G., & Opdahl, A. L. (2000). Eliciting security requirements by misuse cases. *Proceedings of the 37th Conference on Techniques of Object-Oriented Languages and Systems* (pp. 120-131). TOOLS Pacific 2000.

Sindre, G., & Opdahl, A. L. (2001, June 4-5). Templates for misuse case description. *Proceedings of the 7th International Workshop on Requirements Engineering, Foundation for Software Quality (REFSQ2001)*, Switzerland.

Siponen, M. T., & Baskerville, R. (2001). A new paradigm for adding security into IS development methods. In J. Eloff, L. Labuschagne, R. von Solms, & G. Dhillon (Eds.), *Advances in information security management & small systems security* (pp. 99-111). Boston: Kluwer Academic Publishers.

Strens, M. R., & Dobson, J. E. (1994). Responsibility modelling as a technique for requirements definition. *IEEE, 3*(1), 20-26.

van der Raadt, B., Gordijn, J., & Yu, E. (2005). Exploring Web services from a business value perspective. To appear in *Proceedings of the 13th International Requirements Engineering Conference (RE'05),* Paris (pp. 53-62).

van Lamsweerde, A. (2001, August 27-31). Goal-oriented requirements engineering: A guided tour. The *5th IEEE International Symposium on Requirements Engineering (RE 2001)* (p. 249). Toronto, Canada.

van Lamsweerde, A. (2004, May). Elaborating security requirements by construction of intentional anti-models. *Proceedings of ICSE'04, 26ᵗʰ International Conference on Software Engineering* (pp. 148-157). Edinburgh: ACM-IEEE.

van Lamsweerde, A., Brohez, S., Landtsheer, R., & Janssens, D. (2003, September). From system goals to intruder anti-goals: Attack generation and resolution for security requirements engineering. *Proceedings of the RE'03 Workshop on Requirements for High Assurance Systems (RHAS'03)* (pp. 49-56). Monterey, CA.

Yu, E. (1993, January). Modelling organizations for information systems requirements engineering. *Proceedings of the 1ˢᵗ IEEE International Symposium on Requirements Engineering* (pp. 34-41). San Diego, CA.

Yu, E. (1997, January 6-8). Towards modelling and reasoning support for early-phase requirements engineering. *Proceedings of the 3ʳᵈ IEEE International Symposium on Requirements Engineering (RE'97)* (pp. 226-235). Washington, DC.

Yu, E. (2001a, April). Agent orientation as a modelling paradigm. *Wirtschaftsinformatik, 43*(2), 123-132.

Yu, E. (2001b). Agent-oriented modelling: Software versus the world. *Agent-Oriented Software Engineering AOSE-2001 Workshop Proceedings* (LNCS 222, pp. 206-225). Springer Verlag.

Yu, E., & Cysneiros, L. (2002, October 16). Designing for privacy and other competing requirements. *The 2ⁿᵈ Symposium on Requirements Engineering for Information Security (SREIS'02)*. Raleigh, NC.

Yu, E., & Liu, L. (2000, June 3-4). Modelling trust in the i* strategic actors framework. *Proceedings of the 3ʳᵈ Workshop on Deception, Fraud and Trust in Agent Societies,* Barcelona, Catalonia, Spain (at Agents2000).

Yu, E., & Liu, L. (2001). Modelling trust for system design using the *i** strategic actors framework. In R. Falcone, M. Singh, & Y. H. Tan (Eds.), *Trust in cyber-societies--integrating the human and artificial perspectives* (pp. 175-194). LNAI-2246. Springer.

Yu, E., Liu, L., & Li, Y. (2001, November 27-30). Modelling strategic actor relationships to support intellectual property management. The *20ᵗʰ International Conference on Conceptual Modelling (ER-2001)* (LNCS 2224, pp. 164-178). Yokohama, Japan: Spring Verlag.

This work was previously published in Integrating Security and Software Engineering: Advances and Future Visions, edited by H. Mouratidis and P. Giorgini, pp. 70-106, copyright 2007 by Information Science Reference, formerly known as Idea Group Reference (an imprint of IGI Global).

Chapter 5.4
Computer Security in E-Learning

Edgar R. Weippl
Vienna University of Technology, Austria

INTRODUCTION

Although the roots of e-learning date back to 19th century's correspondence-based learning, e-learning currently receives an unprecedented impetus by the fact that industry and universities alike strive to streamline the teaching process. Just-in-time (JIT) principles have already been adopted by many corporate training programs; some even advocate the term "just-enough" to consider the specific needs of individual learners in a corporate setting.

Considering the enormous costs involved in creating and maintaining courses, it is surprising that security and dependability are not yet considered an important issue by most people involved including teachers and students. Unlike traditional security research, which has largely been driven by military requirements to enforce secrecy, in e-learning it is not the information itself that has to be protected but the way it is presented. Moreover, the privacy of communication between teachers and students.

For a long time students and faculty had few concerns about security, mainly because users in academic areas tended not to be malicious. Today, however, campus IT-security is vital. Nearly all institutions install firewalls and anti-virus soft-

ware to protect campus resources. Even the most common security safeguards have drawbacks that people often fail to see. In Stanford the residential computing office selected an anti-virus program. However, the program can be set to collect data that possibly violates students' privacy expectations; therefore many students declined using it (Herbert, 2004).

Whenever servers that store personal data are not well protected, they are a tempting target for hackers. Social security numbers and credit card information are valuable assets used in identity theft. Such attacks were successful, for instance, at the University of Colorado (Crecente, 2004). A similar incident happened at the University of Texas; the student who committed the crime was later indicted in hacking (Associated Press, 2004).

The etymological roots of *secure* can be found in *se* which means "without", or "apart from", and *cura*, that is, "to care for", or "to be concerned about" (Landwehr, 2001). Consequently, *secure* in our context means that in a secure teaching environment users need not be concerned about threats specific to e-learning platforms and to electronic communication in general. A secure learning platform should incorporate all aspects of security and dependability and make most technical details transparent to the teacher and student. However, rendering a system "totally secure" is too ambitious a goal since no system can ever be totally secure and still remain usable at the same time. The contribution of this chapter is to

- Define and identify relevant security and dependability issues.
- Provide an overview of assets, threats, risks, and counter measures that are relevant to e-learning.
- Point to publications that address the issues in greater detail.

BACKGROUND

While there a many definitions of the primary requirements of *security*, we will start with the classical *CIA requirements*. CIA is the acronym for confidentiality, integrity, and availability. All other requirements can be traced back to these three basic properties. Confidentiality is defined (Avizienis, Laprie, Randell, & Landwehr, 2004) as *the absence of unauthorized disclosure of information*, integrity as *the absence of improper system alterations* and availability as *readiness for correct service*.

Dependability is a broader concept that encompasses all primary aspects of security save confidentiality:

- Availability
- Reliability refers to the continuity of correct service
- Safety is defined as the absence of catastrophic consequences on the user(s) and the environment
- Integrity
- Maintainability is the ability to undergo modifications and repairs

For many universities e-learning systems have become production critical assets. It is therefore essential that all of the aforementioned generic requirements are evaluated during a process of risk assessment. The first step in such a process is to understand security and dependability as enabling technology. Only when systems work reliably will users trust and use them.

The obvious ultimate goal of an assessment is to implement cost-effective controls to avoid faults. Looking at all possible threats of a given application and subsequently mitigating the most important ones is a process that is called *threat modeling* (Swiderski & Snyder, 2004). The first step is to *decompose* the application and to determine how data is processed. This can best be done by creating data flow diagrams (Baskerville, 1993).

The second step is to *enumerate all threats*. There are eight dimensions along which faults can be categorized (Avizienis et al., 2004). Even though it is not required to categorize threats in this stage the eight dimensions are helpful to cover many different aspects and to avoid forgetting some.

1. **Phase of Creation:** Development faults vs. operational faults
2. **System Boundaries:** Internal faults vs. external faults
3. **Phenomenological Cause:** Natural faults vs. human-made faults
4. **Dimension:** Hardware faults vs. software faults
5. **Objective:** Malicious faults vs. non-malicious faults
6. **Intent:** Deliberate faults vs. non-deliberate faults
7. **Capability:** Accidental faults vs. incompetence faults
8. **Persistence:** Permanent faults vs. transient faults

The third step is to *rank the threats* according to the probability and potential damage. The forth and final step is planning and implementing *mitigation strategies* (Swiderski & Snyder, 2004).

RELEVANCE TO E-LEARNING

In this section we will first look at all requirements and highlight typical threats that are relevant in the context of e-learning. The final subsection highlights solutions and points to publications that address specific areas in greater detail.

Requirements

Availability

Attacks by insiders on servers delivering e-learning content are not as likely as on servers used for examinations. Students are in general interested in learning and will thus have little incentive to actively attack the system; non-malicious faults, however, might still occur. Obviously this does not mean that students will never attack an e-learning system used for studying, but examination systems are certainly more attractive targets. During learning, availability is not as important as, for instance, during online exams. A downtime of a few hours is acceptable for content servers but clearly not for exam servers.

For exams, the threat profile is different because students are likely to attack the system once they realize they might fail the exam. If they could crash the server their exams cannot be graded and they will have a second chance. Even if students cannot crash the server they might try to attack the availability of the local PC they use during the exam. Briefly unplugging it will cause a reboot and give them a good excuse for not being graded.

Reliability

When exams or assignments are graded automatically reliability is important; while multiple choice questions can be evaluated easily, reliability is more difficult to address the more sophisticated the evaluation algorithm is.

Keyword-based grading of free text answers will generally work well for technical exams that require precise answers but not for subjects with long and very free answers such as studies of literature.

Safety

In most cases there will be very little safety considerations required when introducing e-learning programs unless the subject taught is inherently critical. For instance, wrong instruction on how to operate certain machinery will in consequence create safety hazards once people operate the machinery.

Confidentiality

In many cases confidentiality is not a major requirement when creating e-learning content. The knowledge taught is generally widely available in text books. It is the way the content is presented and the effort of creating simulations and other interactive learning environments that are worth protecting.

For exams and assessments, confidentiality, however, is essential. Exam questions need to be kept secret until the exams commences; the correct answers need to be concealed until the exams are handed in.

Even if learning content contains few secrets, there are still elements that require protection against unauthorized read access. Discussion boards and forums are commonly used not only to discuss organizational issues but also course content. When controversial topics—such as pro-life vs. pro-choice—are discussed students' privacy needs to be protected.

Integrity

Data integrity is one of the most important requirements. During the learning process content should not be modified by unauthorized people as minor modifications might be difficult detect. For exams the integrity of questions, students' answers and correct answers clearly needs to be protected—before, during, and after the exam.

Secondary security attributes such as non-repudiation require system and data integrity. Non-repudiation refers to the fact that users cannot plausibly deny having performed an operation. For instance, students should not be able to deny having handed-in an exam.

Maintainability

As e-learning systems become part of the critical infrastructure maintainability is important. Not only needs the system to be maintained but also exit scenarios are required. Once a lot of e-learning content has been created it is too late to evaluate whether a migration can be made to another platform. It makes little difference whether a commercial or an open-source e-learning platform is used, one has to carefully plan how content can be extracted and migrated to another platform. Even if both the new and the old platform support e-learning standards such as SCORM a migration is not necessarily easy.

Human-Made Faults

Since the majority of system faults are human-made it is necessary to distinguish them further. Human-made faults are either *non-malicious* or *malicious*. All malicious faults or obviously deliberate.

Non-malicious faults can be either caused by mistakes (*non-deliberate*) or by bad decisions (*deliberate*). Non-deliberate mistakes can occur because of accidents or incompetence. Deliberate faults can also be traced back either to accidents or incompetence (Avizienis et al., 2004).

Solutions and Related Publications

Being aware that security and dependability are relevant is the first important step. However, all the mentioned issues need to be addressed in detail. In this section we will point to related publications that touch all of these issues in the context of e-learning. Since Web-based e-learning applications all run on a server, we assume that security measures typical for any server maintenance are implemented. This includes software updates and installing patches, data backups, and redundant hardware.

Security Risk Analysis

Weippl (2005b) provides a first introduction to a security risk analysis for e-learning. Similarly, (Weippl, 2001c) argues why security is an enabling technology in the move to m-commerce. With the rise of m-learning the rationale for improving security for mobile devices is important for e-learning as well. Even though e-learning may in many aspects be seen as just another form of e-commerce there are special requirements regarding security. In (Weippl, 2005a) the requirements specific to e- and m-learning are elaborated in detail.

Privacy

In Weippl and Essmayr (2003) an improved model to manage security and privacy of personal data on mobile devices is presented. The main idea is to keep data separated in different compartments and only allow a limited number of system functions to transfer data between these compartments. Threats to students' privacy when using e-learning applications are analyzed in Weippl and Tjoa (2005).

Mobile Security

As mobile devices are being widely used by students and faculty, they can also be used as authentication tokens. In Weippl, Essmayr, Gruber, Stockner, and Trenker (2002) a concept for mobile authentication is proposed that allows personal devices with wireless connectivity to identify and authenticate their owners to other services.

Database Security

With the proliferation of PCs in all departments of universities, local databases are used by numerous staff and faculty to manage students, courses, registrations, etc. It may seem very inefficient to store data multiple times and disregard integrity.

However, unlike tightly controlled companies, universities should enable and even promote decentralized and heterogeneous environments, even for organizational processes. Nonetheless, central administration, registrar's offices, etc., require some information on students' activities (e.g., which courses a student really attends).

When integrating databases, it is advantageous if administrators of existing databases are not required to change the schema of their local database. As owners of databases (i.e., individual lecturers, professors, etc.) are most probably not willing to give up their autonomy, they want to have control over who has access to which information in their database (Weippl, 2003a).

Database agents (Weippl et al., 2003) can be used to solve this problem (i.e., to integrate heterogeneous databases). Agents are especially well suited to address the issue of security which is even more relevant in distributed environments. While migrating, DB agents are wrapped into Java agents that take care of many issues regarding security and migration.

Role-Based Access Control

Role-based access control (RBAC) is a widely used in database systems. In programming environments, however, RBAC and other access control models are often not well supported. Application programmers regularly have to implement the controls from scratch. The GAMMA framework allows programmers to specify arbitrary access control policies in XML. Programmers only need to derive their classes from specific base classes to automatically protect access to restricted method calls.

Weippl (2001a) proposes to wrap content in cryptographic containers and use RBAC mechanisms to permit or deny operations such as reading, printing, modifying, or distributing content. Weippl (2001b) goes into detail and shows an architecture to securely distribute course content and enforce access control even when distributing content over the Internet.

If different systems are integrated as described in Weippl et al. (2003) it is essential to provide a way of mapping identities and roles of one system to another system. The challenge is to correctly map groups and roles into (legacy) systems that do not support such mechanisms and vice versa. To minimize user errors when setting up access rights, mandatory access control mechanisms can be used. In Weippl (2005a) a security model for e-learning is introduced to model a MAC approach in an RBAC environment—similar to Osborn et al. (2000).

Availability

When delivering e-learning content for asynchronous studying, availability is not as important as during real-time interaction (i.e., chats, broadcast sessions, online exams, etc.).

To avoid frustrated users, downtime of self study section should obviously not be too high. Nonetheless, by clearly communicating how long a site might be unavailable user will usually accept this without problems. For periods with real-time communication, other channels of communication should be provided as a backup. By giving students, for instance, a telephone number to call when they experience problems during a chat or broadcast session user acceptance can be greatly increased.

Backups are essential to ensure availability of data after system failures. While backups are a routine task of server maintenance there are some specific requirements in the context of e-learning. Typically an entire server is backed up and monthly backups are archived for quite some time. For effective learning, however, privacy of personal communication in e-learning platforms can be essential (Weippl & Tjoa, 2005). Backups and log files are threats to the individual learner's privacy. By clearly stating the privacy preferences of a system, users know how personal data is used and for how long it is archived; they can thus decide what information to post on the platform and when to use other means of communication.

FUTURE TRENDS

Recently, security in the context of learning and teaching receives more attention. In most cases security of campus networks is improved to protect personal information of students and faculty and to discourage copyright infringements through P2P file sharing.

Moreover, Moodle, a major open-source e-learning platform, recently launched a security initiative[1] that makes systematic code reviews to improve code security. Increasingly, researchers and practitioners attend tutorials on security in e-learning.[2] The author of the chapter anticipates that within the next few years security considerations will be essential when decisions about implementing e-learning programs will be made.

CONCLUSION

During the last few years, e-learning systems became widely-used system not only to support distance learning but also to supplement and improve presence teaching. Increasingly, users and administrators become aware that large e-learning systems need be secured and dependability is an issue. Many requirements are similar to those of other Web-based services; however, privacy and freedom of academic research and teaching also requires new approaches. Content authors want to protect their e-learning content from copyright infringements, while teachers need to protect systems from students who may undermine their evaluation system by cheating. Students should not be too closely monitored by their teachers when using e-learning software. Since these intertwined requirements are not met by existing systems, new approaches are needed; this article provides many references for interested readers to follow. The book *Security in E-Learning* (Weippl, 2005c) contains many more details.

REFERENCES

Associated Press. (2004). Former student indicted in computer hacking. *USA Today*. Retrieved from http://www.usatoday.com/tech/news/computersecurity/hacking/2004-11-05-ut-hack-charge_x.htm

Avizienis, A., Laprie, J. C., Randell, B., & Landwehr, C. (2004). Basic concepts and taxonomy of dependable and secure computing. *IEEE Transactions of Dependable and Secure Computing*, *1*(1),11-33.

Baskerville, R. (1993). Information systems security design methods: Implications for information systems development. *ACM Computing Surveys*, *25*(4), 375-414.

Crecente, B. D. (2004). *Hacker breaks into computer at cu.* RockyMountainNews.com. Retrieved from http://rockymountainnews.com/drmn/local/article/0%2C1299% 2CDRMN_15_3300285%2C00.html

Herbert, D. (2004). *Bigfix may be big risk, say rccs.* The Stanford Daily. Retrieved from http://daily.stanford.edu/tempo?page=content&id=15170&repository=0001_article

Landwehr, C. (2001). Computer security. *International Journal of Information Security, 1*(1), 3-13.

Osborn, S., Sandhu, R., and Munawer, Q. (2000). Configuring role-based access control to enforce mandatory and discretionary access control policies. *ACM Transaction on Information and System Security, 3*(2), 85-206.

Schneier, B. (2003). *Beyond fear: Thinking sensibly about security in an uncertain world.* New York: Springer-Verlag.

Swiderski, F., & Snyder, W. (2004). *Threat modeling.* Redmond, WA: Microsoft Press.

Weippl, E. (2001a). An approach to role-based access control for digital content. In *Proceedings of the International Conference on Information Technology: Coding and Computing (ITCC), Current Trends in Multimedia Communications and Computing* (pp. 290-295). Las Vegas, NV: IEEE Computer Society Press.

Weippl, E. (2001b). An approach to secure distribution of Web-based training courses. In M. Oudshoorn (Ed.), *Proceedings of the Australasian Computer Science Conference, Australian Computer Science Communications.* Gold Coast, Australia: IEEE Press.

Weippl, E. (2001c). The transition from e-commerce to m-commerce: Why security should be the enabling technology. *Journal of Information Technology Theory and Application (JITTA), 3*(4), 17-19. Retrieved from http://peffers.net/journal/volume3_4/ecpreface.pdf

Weippl, E. (2005a). Security in e-learning. In H. Bidgoli (Ed.), *The handbook of information security.* New York: John Wiley & Sons.

Weippl, E., & Essmayr, W. (2003). Personal trusted devices for ebusiness: Revisiting multilevel security. *Mobile Networks and Applications, 8*(2), 151-157. Retrieved from http://www.kluweronline.com/issn/1383-469X

Weippl, E., Essmayr, W., Gruber, F., Stockner, W., & Trenker, T. (2002). Towards authentication using mobile devices: An investigation of the prerequisites. In B. Jerman-Blazic & T. Klobucar (Ed.), *Proceedings of the 6th IFIP Communications and Multimedia Security Conference (CMS): Advanced Communications and Multimedia Security* (pp. 91-105). Portoroz, Slovenia: Kluwer Academic Publishers.

Weippl, E., Klug, L., & Essmayr, W. (2003). A new approach to secure federated information bases using agent technology. *Journal of Database Management, 14*(1), 48-68.

Weippl, E., & Tjoa, A. (2005). Privacy in e-learning: Anonymity, pseudonyms and authenticated usage. *Technology and Smart Education (ITSE), 2*(4), 247-256.

Weippl, E. R. (2003a). Integrity in student databases. *Proceedings of EDMEDIA 2003.* Honolulu: AACE.

Weippl, E. R. (2005b). Security in e-learning. *ACM ELearn Magazine.* Retrieved from http://www.elearnmag.org/subpage/sub_page.cfm?section=4&list_item=19& page=1

Weippl, E. R. (2005c). *Security in e-learning (Advances in Information Security).* New York: Springer-Verlag. Retrieved from www.e-learning-security.org

KEY TERMS[4]

Dependability: Is a broader concept that includes availability, reliability, safety, integrity, and maintainability but not confidentiality. A system is *available* if it is ready to perform a service. It is *reliable* if it continues providing a correct service. *Safety* refers to the absence of catastrophic consequences for users and the environment. A system's *integrity* guarantees no unauthorized modifications. When systems can be modified and repaired easily they are *maintainable. Confidentiality* means that information is not disclosed to unauthorized subjects.

E-Learning: Dating back to the hype of the term e-commerce, e-learning is widely used in different ways; for instance, E-Learners Glossary[3] defines e-learning as any form of learning that utilizes a network for delivery, interaction, or facilitation. E-learning covers a wide set of applications and processes, such as Web-based learning, computer-based learning, virtual classrooms, and digital collaboration. It includes the delivery of content via Internet, intranet or extranet, audio- and videotape, satellite broadcast, interactive TV, and CD-ROM. The "e" in e-learning stands for electronic and thus all forms of learning that involve electronic components should be considered to be e-learning in the broadest sense; obviously e-commerce mainly refers to commerce conducted via electronic networks, and e-learning therefore has strong ties with communication networks. Because computers no longer exist without networks, however, these stand-alone learning applications will eventually cease to exist. For instance, today,

even the simplest CD-ROM courses contain links to the Web. Trainings can either be *self-based* or *instructor-led* (ILT). E-learning is *computer-based* (CBT) if a computer is used. If the computer is connected to the Internet and a Web browser is used to access the e-learning platform, it is considered to be *Web-based* (WBT).

Exploit: An exploit is a program that uses a vulnerability to attack the system's security mechanisms. Exploits usually compromise secrecy, integrity or availability and often lead to elevation of privilege.

Risk: A risk is the relative likelihood that a bad thing will happen (Schneier, 2003). In other words, risk is defined as the probability that a vulnerability is exploited and results in a damage.

Security: Encompasses the primary aspects of availability, integrity, and confidentiality.

Threat: A threat is a bad thing that can happen (Schneier, 2003), such as a server being stolen.

Vulnerability: A vulnerability is system's weakness or error that might allow to penetrate the security barriers.

ENDNOTES

[1] http://security.moodle.org/
[2] http://www.e-learning-security.org/
[3] http://security.moodle.org/
[4] The most recent authority for definitions of security- and dependability-related concepts is Avizienis et al. (2004).

Chapter 5.5
Trust in Virtual Communities

Eun G. Park
McGill University, Canada

INTRODUCTION

Trust is one of the key factors that emerged as a significant concept in virtual communities. Trust is so complicated that it is hard to define in one standardized way. Trust issues have evolved into two major ways in the fields of virtual community and security. Among a huge literature concerning trust in virtual communities, a majority of literature addresses technical solutions on trust-building by providing new Web-based applications. They range from human users authorization, semantic Web, agent technologies and access control of network to W3C standardization for content trust and security. Some examples include AT&T's Policymaker or IBM's Trust Establishment Module (Blaze, Feigenbaum, & Lacy, 1996; Herzberg, 2000). Only a minority deals with understanding the concept of trust and sources of trust-building from social and cultural aspects. It appears to miss the essence of trust in virtual communities, although an integrated approach is needed for building trust in communication and the use of virtual communities. This article aims to present the definition of trust and relevant concepts for recognizing sources of trust-building in virtual communities. This article also presents future research implications for further development on trust and trust-building in virtual communities.

BACKGROUND: DEFINITION OF TRUST

Trust has been defined by several researchers in many disciplines. One definition of trust is "the confidence that a person has in his or her favorable expectations of what other people will do based on previous interactions" (Gefen, 2000, p.726). Trust is also defined as the firm belief in the competence of an entity to act dependably, securely and reliably within a specified context (Grandison & Solomon, 2000). The common features of trust from these definitions is that trust is a notion of manifestation in reasoning and judging processes that has originated in psychology (Trcek, 2004). It is understood as an implicit set of beliefs that the other party will refrain from opportunistic behavior and will not take advantage of the situation (Hosmer, 1995; Moorman, Zaltman, & Deshpande, 1992). Ridings (Ridings, Gefen, & Arinze, 2002) asserts that trust is working as a subjective substitute to rules on participants' behaviors and creates the necessary atmosphere that makes engagement with others frequently. Especially in virtual communities, where rules of social behavior are absent, the most common agreement is that trust is essential and noteworthy for the continuity of the community (Ridings et al., 2002).

Trust is understood as complicated and problematic in the literature on computer-mediated communication or group support systems (Hosmer, 1995; Rousseau, Sitkin, Burt, & Camerer, 1998). It depends on the situation where participants' contact is possible in person and/or in face-to-face contact. Trust in virtual communities occurs as a conversation to one or many individuals as well as to a general audience, as posted at bulletin board. That is, trust is the concept of the generalized and collective level in the context of interpersonal relationships (Rotter, 1971; Jarvenpaa, Knoll, & Leidner, 1998). The mutual interest and sharing of experience bring closeness to the community for the common and shared topic, which fosters trust to the community. Repeated and accumulated interactions between participants increase trust. In contrast, lack of face-to-face contact and visibility causes loss of trust in communications. Easy camouflage to mask one's identity, gender, age or race, as well as to create multiple aliases bring suspect to participants and result in decreasing trust in virtual communities.

SOURCES OF TRUST-BUILDING

A literature on trust-building from the traditional communities addresses the characteristics of trust that can be also applied to virtual communities. The concept of trust was considered as an assessment, not as en entity, that is measurable in some ways (Denning, 1993). Denning thought that the assessment resulted from past experience and interactions. Since the 1990s, several researches on trust-building have made efforts to measure factors of trust-buildings. For example, trust is considered as multidimensional, consisting of three factors in an intertwined mode: ability, benevolence and integrity (Butler, 1991; Mayer, Davis, & Schoorman, 1995). Ability indicates skills or competencies that enable an individual to influence to a certain topic, such as mutual interest, event or hobby in virtual communities. Benevolence is the expectation that others support to do good to the trustee, such as posting to the ongoing discussion to encourage or to help. Integrity is the expectation that another will act in accordance with socially accepted standards of rules or honesty, such as the norms of reciprocity that the community needs to function. Jarvenpaa's research groups adopted the three factors for surveys of virtual communities and demonstrated that trust consists of three separate dimensions in virtual community contexts, as well (1998). Another subsequent research group merged the three factors into two scales—ability and the combination of benevolence and integrity—and conducted a survey to examine what factors build trust and how they are related in trust-building (Ridings et al., 2002). The result of this survey present that trust is a significant predictor of virtual communities members who join to exchange information, especially to get information; and their belief of trust increases by their responsiveness and confiding behavior.

Lynch asserts that the level of trust is the binding of *identity* with *behavior* (2001). Identity alone does not provide trust for the provider of given information. Trust is built over the knowledge of past behavior and subjective assessment of the character of an identity. Possession of identity, therefore, creates some accountability for behavior, and observation of behavior over time allows one to form expectations about the behavior association with an identity (Lynch, 2001). With this identity, people can exercise control over their self-presentation by choosing names, signature files or personal descriptions and aliases. The differing levels of an invented self-representation can be possible from anonymity, pseudonymity and real identity (Wood & Smith, 2001). In a virtual community, anonymity is a state of communicating where the identity of the communicator is not readily apparent. Pseudonymity lies at the one end of real-life identity and the other end is anonymity with some degree of protection.

One problem relating to identity arises in judging what identities are authentic by shifting to multiple selves and involving the fragmentation of many selves (Tuckle, 1995). The *authenticity* of the identity and content is tied to the authoritative identity performed by and for authorizing sources. This naturally produces an emphasis on the attribution of sources as a means to enhance the apparent authenticity of information. The judging of authenticity is a dynamic process, with accounts being presented and undermined by participants in an ongoing interaction. In virtual communities, several elements are required to be considered authentic: personal testimony, objective statement and externally attributed sources combined with the choice of images, fonts and layouts (Hine, 2000).

Another approach to understanding trust-building in virtual communities is taken from a perspective of *authority*. Based on Wilson's concept of cognitive authority, which means influence on one's thoughts as one would consciously recognize as proper (1983), Fritch and Cromwell examined how people assess trust and authority over the contents of information in a networked world (2001). Since there is no filtering of information in virtual communities, determining authority of information is important in assessing trust. Authority over information is determined by authorship (i.e., who authored the information), ownership (i.e., who is actually responsible for information) and affiliation (i.e., who sponsors the information). Fritch and Cromwell provided

a theoretical model of specific criteria as sources of authority: author competence and trustworthiness (by author identity and author credentials); document validity (accuracy of information, presentation and formats of information, organizational identity and authority); overt affiliation with an institution; and covert affiliation with an institution.

Trcek also provided basic relevant factors as a means for assessing trust from the following criteria: irrationality, context dependence, action binding, temporal dynamics, feedback dependence and trust differentiation. He argued that these factors can be used for evaluating systems in a standardized way (2004). Although there have been many attempts to understand and measure trust, there is no one framework most commonly accepted to measure trust in the context of virtual communities.

FUTURE TRENDS AND CONCLUSION

As long as trust is one of the important issues in virtual communities, the idea of formalizing trust is complicated. Its specific identifying criteria are getting more complicated to identify to participants in virtual communities. As we integrate trust into virtual communities, understanding sources of trust-building is clearly going to be necessary and inevitable. A plethora of future research for further development exists in relation to trust and trust-building in virtual communities. Although a common standard model for evaluating trust does not exist, technical solutions on trust management applications will be increasing. At the same time, social and cultural aspects of trust-building in virtual communities will continue to be developed. Comparative approaches to understanding trust in different communities or from different types of information sources will be interesting, feasible areas for further research. Investigating the relationship of trust and frequency of use of the community can be studied, as well.

REFERENCES

Blaze, M., Feigenbaum, J., & Lacy, J. (1996). The role of trust management in distributed systems security. *IEEE Conference on Security and Privacy*, Oakland, CA.

Butler, J.K. (1991). Toward understanding and measuring condition of trust: Evolution of conditions of trust inventory. *Journal of Management, 17*(3), 643-663.

Denning, D. (1993). A new paradigm for trusted systems. *Proceedings of ACM SIGSAC New Security Paradigms Workshops* (pp, 36-41).

Fritch, J., & Cromwell, R. (2001). Evaluating Internet resources: Identity, affiliation, and cognitive authority in a networked world. *Journal of the American Society of Information Science and Technology, 52*(6), 499-507.

Gefen. (2000). E-commerce: The role of familiarity and trust. *Omega, 28,* 6, 725-737.

Grandison, T., & Solomon, M. (2000). A survey of trust in internet applications. *IEEE Communications Surveys*, 2-13. Los Alamos, NM: ICCC Society Press.

Herzberg, A. (2000). Access control meets public key infrastructure. *IEEE Conference on Security and Privacy*, Oakland, CA.

Hine, C. (2000). *Virtual ethnography.* Thousand Oaks, CA: Sage Publications.

Hosmer, L.T. (1995). Trust: The connecting link between organizational theory and philosophical ethics. *Academy of Management Review, 20*(2), 379-403.

Jarvenpaa, S.L., Knoll, K., & Leidner, D.E. (1998). Is anybody out there? Antecedents of trust in global virtual teams. *Journal of Management Information systems, 14*(4), 29-64.

Lynch, C. (2001). When documents deceive: Trust and provenance as new factors for information retrieval in a tangled Web. *Journal of the American Society of Information Science and Technology, 52*(1), 12-17.

Mayer, R.C., Davis, J.H., & Schoorman, F.D. (1995). An integrative model of organizational trust. *Academy of Management Review, 20*(3), 709-734.

Moorman, C., Zaltman, G., & Deshpande, R. (1992). Relationships between providers and users of market research: the dynamics of trust within and between organizations. *Journal of Marketing Research, 29,* 413-328.

Ridings, C. M., Gefen, D., & Arinze, B. (2002). Some antecedents and effects of trust in virtual communities. *Journal of Strategic Information Systems, 11,* 271-295.

Rotter, J.B. (1971). Generalized expectancies for interpersonal trust. *America Psychologist, 26,* 443-450.

Rousseau, D.M., Sitkin, S.B., Burt, R.S., & Camerer, C. (1998). Not so different after all: A cross discipline view of trust. *Academy of Management Review, 23*(3), 393-404.

Trcek, D. (2004). Towards trust management standardization. *Computer Standards & Interfaces, 26,* 543-548.

Tuckle, S. (1995). *Life on the screen: Identity in the age of the Internet.* London: Weidenfeld and Nicolson.

Wilson, P. (1983). *Second-hand knowledge: An inquiry into cognitive authority.* Westport, CT: Greenwood Press.

Wood, A.F., & Smith, M.J. (2001). *Online communication: Linking, technology, identity & culture.* Mahwah: Lawrence Erlbaum Associates.

KEY TERMS

Accountability: A responsibility to account for and/or explain actions undertaken; obligation of government, public services or funding agencies in compliance with agreed rules and standards.

Authenticity: Undisputed credibility of being genuine, honest with oneself as well as others; an absence of hypocrisy or self-deception.

Authority: The power, right or control to give orders or to make decisions.

Identity: A thing to represent or identify oneself to the other party or audience.

Sources of Trust-Building: Factors, elements or relevant concepts to support trust-building during mutual communication and interactions of participants in virtual communities.

Trust: A set of beliefs that one party will render accountability over the other party in communication or interactions.

Virtual Community: A collection of people sharing common interests, ideas and feelings over the Internet or other collaborative networks.

Chapter 5.6
Online Communities, Democratic Ideals, and the Digital Divide

Frances S. Grodzinsky
Sacred Heart University, USA

Herman T. Tavani
Rivier College, USA

ABSTRACT

We examine some pros and cons of online communities with respect to two main questions: (1) Do online communities promote democracy and democratic ideals? and (2) What are the implications of online communities for information justice and the digital divide? The first part of the chapter will examine online communities in general and will attempt to define what we mean by "community" and more precisely, "online communities." It will then examine ways of building online communities, that is, what brings people together online. The second part of the chapter will look at the positive and negative contributions of online communities in light of democratic ideals and will address the issue of information justice and the digital divide. In examining these questions, we also consider the effects of the Internet for community life at both the local and global levels.

ONLINE COMMUNITIES

Before examining some of the pros and cons of online community life, we begin by elucidating the notion of a virtual or online community. First, however, we consider what *community* means in general.

What is a Community?

According to *Webster's New World Dictionary of the American Language, community* is defined as "people living in the same district, city, etc., under the same laws" (1996, p. 269). The first part of this definition stresses the geographical aspects of community via an association with concepts such as *district* and *city*. In the past, community life typically was constrained by geographical limitations. In the 20th century, various forms of transportation, including the automobile, made it possible to extend, even if only slightly, the geographical boundaries of a community. However, traditional communities for the most part have continued to remain limited by physical constraints such as geography.

The advent of the Internet and the forms of social interaction it makes possible causes us to reexamine our thinking about the concept of a community. Individuals who are separated physically by continents and oceans can participate daily in electronic communities. As a result, more recent definitions of community tend to focus on the second part of the definition—"under the same law"—which can include common rules and common interests that one or more groups of people share, rather than on criteria involving geographical districts and physical constraints. In order for a community to exist, there must be some degree of shared beliefs, values, and goals among members who share a common vision and who desire to perpetuate it through the socialization of new members. Two values that traditionally have been associated with strong communities are trust and commitment.

We should point out that communities do not need to be homogenous in population, even though many are. Consider that, in many cases, individuals with diverse backgrounds participate and belong to communities because of their commitment to the shared values of the community, which often manifest themselves in a set of rules that embodies these beliefs.

What is an Online Community?

Howard Rheingold (2001) suggests that online communities can be understood as "computer-mediated social groups." He describes his initial experience in joining the WELL (the Whole Earth

'Lectronic Link), one of the earlier electronic communities, in which norms were "established, challenged, changed, reestablished, rechallenged, in a kind of speeded-up social evolution." The WELL was a community, Rheingold maintains, because of the kinds of social contracts and collaborative negotiations that happened in that setting. The WELL and other early electronic communities, including listservs, were instrumental in the initial formation of women's groups online. For example, WOW (Women on the Well) was a forum for women who belonged to the WELL, creating a community within a community. And SYSTERS-l, formed in 1990, was an early online community that supported women working in science and technology (Shade, 2002).

Michelle White (2002) notes that in cyberspace, the term *community* is a popular way of describing synchronous online settings because it suggests that they offer "social exchange, emotional support, and learning environments." Synchronicity, in this definition, can apply to location in cyberspace as well as to time, because, while chat rooms and instant messaging services—two forms of technology that facilitate online communities—are synchronous in terms of time and space, listservs and newsgroups are only synchronous in space and not time. (This point supports our emphasis on the latter part of the definition of community in the preceding section.) White also points out that describing online settings as communities acknowledges the "complex and important activities that people engage in through those sites." In effect, it also legitimizes these structures by making them seem as if they are physical and real.

Building Online Communities

In the preceding section, we noted that common interests can bring people together to form an online community. But what exactly are some of the common interests that define these individuals as members of a given community? Traditionally, people have been inclined to think of themselves in terms of factors related to national heritage, religious and political affiliations, gender, and so forth. Many of our traditional notions of identity, including the concept of nationality, are becoming antiquated in the age of the Internet. For example, young people who have grown up using the Internet may prefer to define themselves in terms of their consumer interests rather than in terms of some particular country or state that they happen to inhabit in the off-line world. Geographic and national boundaries may mean far less to this group of persons than they have to those who came of age in the era preceding the Internet, when distance and geographical remoteness precluded the formation of natural communities that included international participants.

Yet, for other groups, the Internet has facilitated connections that would have been impossible in physical space. A young gay teenager, for example, who may feel isolated in his or her local community, can find support and encouragement from other gay teens online. Women can connect to other women on the Web and can access information not always readily available in physical space. There are online communities that support cyberfeminism, women's health issues, anti-cyberstalking, and anti-harassment actions. There also are parenting chat rooms as well as groups dealing with the glass ceiling and work-related issues, date rape, incest, divorce, and so forth. As more and more women embrace cybertechnology and as women begin to trust those in their particular online communities, they are more likely to self-represent and identify as part of the group in a way that they already do in physical space.

Another form of online community has been the weblog or blog. Blogs typically are initiated by an author as a form of online journal, yet they fall under White's definition of online community (see previous section) because they attract people of like-minded interests who read, learn, and communicate in the blog through postings. A

recent Google search for women's blogs offered up among others: Christian women, technology, finance, clothes, body image, relationships, health, and feminism. In the past few years, blogging has become more popular, and people often have blogs to which they contribute regularly. Blogging has become what "meetings" were in the age prior to the Internet: a place to discuss and share ideas and opinions on certain issues.

DO ONLINE COMMUNITIES PROMOTE DEMOCRATIC IDEALS?

In the first section, we suggested that many of the new possibilities for social interaction made possible by online communities could be viewed as positive contributions. Also consider that on the Internet, people can meet new friends and future romantic partners; can form medical support groups; can join chat rooms, list-servers, and discussion forums to disseminate material to like-minded colleagues; and can communicate by e-mail with individuals with whom they otherwise would not likely bother to correspond by physical mail or telephone. However, we also need to examine some negative effects of these new forms of interaction, especially in terms of their implications for democracy and social justice. For example, hate speech has proliferated; harassment and stalking incidents have occurred (see Grodzinsky & Tavani, 2004); and there has been at least one incident involving a virtual rape in cyberspace (see Dibbell, 1993). Also, the Internet has minimized the need for face-to-face communications and has made it much easier to deceive people about who actually is communicating with them. These concerns lead us to ask whether the Internet also threatens some of the important values underlying community life.

Overall, have online communities had a positive effect on communication and interaction? Gordon Graham (1999) points out that the Internet enables a "reconfiguration of human communities" based on individual choices provided users. So, one advantage of online communities is that they empower the individual to choose a community in which to interact instead of simply having to accept the default community or society in which he or she is already situated. Graham believes that online communities also further promote freedom in the sense that members, if they choose, can disregard more easily certain kinds of personal properties or attributes, such as gender and ethnicity, which are more obvious in traditional communities.

If Graham is correct, then the Internet has provided individuals with greater choice and freedom with respect to joining communities. Values involving freedom, choice, openness, and so forth, certainly would seem to favor demo-cratic ideals. However, others see the relation-ship between the Internet and democracy quite differently. Richard Sclove (1995), for instance, believes that technologies—and, by implication, Internet technologies—tend to undermine rather than facilitate democracy and community life. Cass Sunstein (2002) argues that the Internet has both democracy-enhancing and democracy-threatening aspects. He believes that the Internet enhances democracy in the sense that it provides greater access to information by lowering the costs involved in finding and getting information. Because that information also can be filtered so easily, however, he suggests that the Internet threatens what he calls "deliberative democracy" (see Thorseth, 2005, for a detailed discussion of deliberative democracy and the Internet). Gra-ham (1999) has also suggested that the Internet, perhaps unwittingly, might strengthen the worst aspects of democracy, because Internet technology facilitates political and social fragmentation by isolating individuals and insulating groups. These factors tend to increase polarization.

To appreciate the level of polarization and fragmentation made possible by technology, consider a hypothetical scenario envisioned by Richard Epstein (2000) set in the year 2028, in

which our personal (electronic) agents prepare a personalized electronic newspaper for us each morning. The newspaper contains information about only those topics that we individually have selected; and the information is presented to us from an ideological perspective that we choose. In other words, our electronic agents have been carefully instructed to filter information to meet all of our specifications and tastes. Contrast this kind of personalized newspaper of the future, which Nicholas Negroponte (1995) refers to as *The Daily Me*, with conventional newspapers of today. Imagine what it would be like to have your daily newspaper tailored to your own individual interests and tastes.

Epstein describes a (hypothetical) dinner party in which the guests, all of whom subscribe to personalized newspapers, assemble around the dinner table. The guests soon discover that they have no common vocabulary, no common shared memories, and no common conceptual framework in which to share their conversations. For example, one guest reads only news about sporting events, while another reads only about the virtual economy. And even if two or more guests happen to read news reports about the same general topic, the perspectives from which the information is disseminated to them via their electronic agents is so radically different that they still would likely be unable to find any common ground for conversation. Not surprisingly, there is complete silence at the dinner party.

Epstein asks how we could maintain a de-mocracy in a world in which there is no shared vocabulary of civic concepts and principles. The character in Epstein's story who describes the conversation at the dinner party laments, "We have the frightening proliferation of extremists groups who have their own private vocabularies and ideologies." Epstein also asks how the "public square," which has been fragmented into "tens of thousands of highly specialized communities that do not communicate with one another," can be recreated. So, we have seen that while the

Internet may promote democratic ideals such as choice and freedom, it also seems to undermine those ideals by fragmenting society and polarizing individuals.

INFORMATION JUSTICE AND THE DIGITAL DIVIDE

We have examined the growing emergence of online communities and their implications for democracy and democratic ideals. Will the notion of physical community become obsolete in the future? In order to investigate this question, we need to examine local and global communities through the perspective of information justice, an aspect of social justice. Information justice is tied to questions about whether the digital network can help people to better manage their lives through an access to technology, while avoiding the dangers of exploitation and discrimination that often exist in physical space. In an article entitled "Reconceptualizing the Digital Divide," and in his book, *Technology and Social Inclusion*, Mark Warschauer (2002, 2003, respectively) observes that technology projects around the world too often focus on providing hardware and software and pay insufficient attention to the human and social systems that also must change in order for technology to make a difference. According to Warschauer (2002):

[Access to ICT] is embedded in a complex array of factors encompassing physical, digital, human, and social resources and relationships. Content and language, literacy and education, and community and institutional structures must all be taken into account if meaningful access to new technologies is to be provided.

To understand the impact of the Internet for questions involving information justice at both the local and global levels, it is important to understand issues surrounding the digital divide.

According to Benjamin Compaine (2001), the phrase *digital divide* is essentially a new label for an earlier concept: information haves and have-nots. It describes the disparity that exists between those who have access to information and communication technology (ICT) and those who do not. Compaine (2001) defines the digital divide as the perceived gap between those who have and do not have access to information tools *and* the ability to use those tools. Hence, the digital divide can be understood as the gap, perceived or real, between those who have and do not have either (a) access to ICT or (b) the knowledge and ability to use that technology, or both.

To speak of *the* digital divide might suggest that there is one overall divide—that is, a single divide as opposed to many divides or divisions. Although multiple divisions exist, we limit our discussion to two broad categories: a divide *within nations* and a divide *between nations*. Within nations, divisions exist between rich and poor persons, racial majority and minority groups, men and women, young and old, disabled and nondisabled persons, and so forth. On the other hand, there is a division that sometimes is referred to as the global digital divide that exists between information-rich and information-poor nations. We examine some of the effects of the digital divide at the local and global levels, respectively in the next two sections.

Some Effects of the Digital Divide at the Local Level

In response to concerns about a growing digital divide at the local level, we briefly consider some issues in the U.S. In 1993, the Clinton administration announced its plans for a National Information Infrastructure (NII). One objective of the NII was to ensure that all Americans would have access to ICT. To accomplish this goal, the National Telecommunications and Information Administration (NTIA) was charged with investigating the status of computer and Internet access among Americans. In 1995, the NTIA issued its first report, *Falling through the Net*, which confirmed the commonly held belief that Internet access was related to socio-economic factors. This report also noted that a disproportionate number of information have-nots lived in rural areas and inner cities. The NTIA's 1999 report, *Falling through the Net: Defining the Digital Divide*, noted that while more Americans were accessing the Internet, significant discrepancies in access still existed with respect to socio-demographic factors involving race, education, income, and marital status. According to the NTIA's 2000 report, *Falling through the Net: Toward Digital Inclusion*, the rate of digital inclusion is increasing in the U.S. across all socio-demographic sectors. Some have interpreted this report to imply that the divide between ICT haves and have-nots in the U.S. is narrowing; others, however, dispute this interpretation.

A key issue in the debate about the digital divide in the U.S. is the question whether some kind of universal service policy is needed to ensure that all Americans will have the appropriate level of access to computer and Internet technologies. Prior to the Internet era, the issue of universal service in America had been debated in the context of telephony (or telephone technology). When telephones became available in the early part of the 20th century, there was some concern that people living in less-populated rural areas in the U.S. would not be able to afford this new technology. Because having a telephone was considered essential for one's well being, the Communications Act of 1934 was enacted into law, and telephone usage rates were subsidized in order to ensure that all Americans would have affordable telephone service. A question currently debated is whether having Internet access also is or soon will be at the point of becoming essential for one's well being.

Recent proposals have recommended special e-rates in the form of federal technology discounts to subsidize the cost of Internet access for public

schools and libraries. Whereas prior universal service policies involving telephony aimed to provide telephone access at the residential level, e-rates are targeted for public schools, libraries, and other community points of access. In effect, e-rates aim to provide universal Internet access for Americans, but critics point out that those rates do not ensure universal service. Why is a policy that ensures universal service, as opposed to universal access, to ICT necessary? Gary Chapman and Marc Rotenberg (1995), representing Computer Professionals for Social Responsibility (CPSR), have argued not only that everyone must have access to the Internet but also that pricing should be structured so that full Internet service is affordable to everyone. In their view, merely providing community points of access to the Internet, such as at public schools and libraries, would not be sufficient. Chapman and Rotenberg argue that just as placing telephones in public locations would not meet the requirements for a universal telephone service policy, simply providing Internet access in public places cannot satisfy the conditions needed for universal Internet service.

Whereas advocacy groups such as CPSR have lobbied the U.S. Congress for a universal Internet service policy, others have opposed such legislation. Opponents generally have used three kinds of arguments (Tavani, 2004). One type of objection is based on the notion that a universal Internet service policy would create an entitlement that could grow out of control and possibly set a precedent for entitlements for other kinds of government-subsidized services in the future. Another kind of objection is based on the concern that the revenue needed to implement a universal Internet service policy would have to be generated by tax subsidies. Here, it is argued that a tax of this type would be unfair to taxpayers in moderate-income brackets who would shoulder the greatest burden, as well as to the telephone and utility companies who also would be taxed. A third type of objection is based on the view that issues concerning Internet access for poorer citizens are, at bottom, issues involving personal priorities and values for those citizens. Critics who appeal to this line of reasoning point out that nearly everyone in the U.S. who wishes to own a television and subscribe to TV cable service can find a way to purchase those items and pay for those services. Hence, they conclude that no universal service policy for ICT is needed. Supporters of universal service, however, argue that their opponents have either overly simplified or greatly underestimated the problems faced by those who are unable to afford Internet access in their homes. This brings up the underlying philosophical issue of whether Internet access should be viewed as a positive right.

What are positive rights, and how are they different from negative rights? Negative rights are like liberties in the sense that we have a (legal) right not to be interfered with in exercising them. So if I have a (negative) right to own a computer and purchase Internet access, then no one is permitted to interfere with my purchasing these items and services. Can one's legal rights involving Internet access also possibly be understood as a positive right in which full Internet service must be provided to everyone? There are very few positive rights. In the U.S., for example, one's right to have access to healthcare is considered a negative rather than a positive right because the government is not required to provide citizens with healthcare. In the European Union countries, on the other hand, access to healthcare generally is considered a positive right. One of the few positive rights enjoyed by U.S. citizens is the right to receive a free public education through high school (grades 1-12). This is a positive right in the sense that the U.S. government legally is required to provide each citizen with access to such an education.

Perhaps the rationale used for determining why one has a right to receive a free public education in the U.S. can help us to frame an argument for why universal Internet access also should be required by law. We can begin by asking why

public education is a positive and not merely a negative right. One answer is that without adequate access to an education, a child will not have equal access to opportunities involving jobs, careers, and so forth. If it also could be shown that having Internet access at home is essential in order for students to participate adequately in the educational process, then it would seem that students should have a positive right to Internet access. But why would not having access to ICT necessarily deprive someone of access to goods that are important or vital to one's well being? Jeremy Moss (2002) has argued that not having access to a form of technology that is "instrumentally vital for access to other goods (employment, knowledge about one's health outcomes or access to democratic institutions)" is essentially a "threat to one's well being." It is for this reason that Moss believes that persons who do not have access to ICT are "constrained through not having the resources to do *something important*" (2002, p. 162; emphasis added).

What does Moss mean when he suggests that having access to ICT is important because it provides a means for certain resources that are "vital for one's well-being"? He argues that without access to ICT, people are unfairly disadvantaged for three reasons: (1) their access to knowledge is significantly limited; (2) their ability to participate fully in the political process and to receive important information is greatly diminished; and (3) their economic prospects are severely hindered. We elaborate briefly on each point. First, Moss claims that because access to knowledge is lessened or prevented by the digital divide, people who are deprived of access to ICT are not able to benefit from the increasing range of information on the Internet and, thus, are falling further behind. Second, because of barriers to participation in the decision-making process in developing countries, people in remote areas may have no other means to participate in national debates or to receive information about important developmental matters and policies that can affect them significantly. Third, not having access to digital resources can severely hinder the prospects that developing countries have for economic growth. Moss believes that because so much of world growth is driven by the information and communication sector, people living in countries that are not part of this sector will be disadvantaged. If Moss is correct, then it would seem that a strong case could be made for declaring that universal Internet access should be construed as a positive right (Tavani, 2003). Doing so also would help to bridge the global digital divide between developed and developing nations.

Some Effects of the Digital Divide at the Global Level

Most people in the non-Western world do not have Internet access. Those in many developing countries who are fortunate to have Internet access often are required to deal with technical problems involving poor connectivity and low bandwidth. Consider, for example, some of the challenges faced by Internet users in Malawi, given the current state of telecommunications in that African nation. Levison, Thies, and Armarasinghe (2002) point out that people living in this developing country must contend with a very expensive form of telephone service (and corresponding Internet access) that is metered in terms of minutes used. Not only is Internet access prohibitively expensive in Malawi, but also those who can afford access must cope with many practical difficulties and limitations. For example, telephone connections there are so slow and telecom failures so frequent that using the Internet for conventional purposes (e.g., for interactive searches that most Internet users residing in North America and Western Europe take for granted as part of a Web interface) is generally impractical. The kinds of problems experienced by Internet users in Malawi should not be viewed as isolated or as peculiar to countries in sub-Saharan Africa. Rather, they are typical of those encountered by users in many developing nations.

Efforts to address problems involving the ICT divide between industrialized and developing countries can be traced back to the early 1990s, when the idea of a Global Information Infrastructure (GII) emerged. Al Gore described the initial plan for a GII in an address to the International Telecommunication Union in Brazil on March 21, 1994. A principle objective of Gore's plan was to develop a global infrastructure that would support universal access to ICT. Critics argue that very little has resulted from this and other earlier proposals aimed at addressing global concerns about unequal access to ICT. Recently, however, there have been signs suggesting that concerns about a global digital divide are being taken seriously. In the summer of 2000, for example, the Okinawa Charter on Global Information was announced at an annual Group of Eight (G8) summit in Japan. At that summit, the G8 leaders formed the Digital Opportunities Task Force (DOT), which some see as a first step in a serious effort to narrow the global digital divide or what some now refer to as the international information and knowledge divide. Leslie Regan Shade (2002) refers to "globalizing from below" in describing the way women in the Philippines, Latin America, Africa, and Asia have developed grass roots initiatives for democracy and social justice. At the second global knowledge conference in Malaysia in 2000, there were two initiatives introduced: a gender and ICT replication and learning fund that promotes an exchange of initiatives on gender equity and women's empowerment using ICT; and support to women entrepreneurs, which provides incentives either through ICT businesses, online mentoring, or financing (Shade, 2002).

In an article titled "Equity of Access: Adaptive Technology," (Grodzinsky, 2000), the author addressed the problems faced by users with disabilities. She argued that in the age of information technology, the computer equipped with adaptive devices can be the equalizer that allows people with disabilities to participate in and compete for jobs that require computer access, because it supports autonomous learning and empowers the user. Since the publication of that article, there have been several advances in assistive devices and interface design that address disability issues. There is now a disability setting, for example, in the Windows Control Panel. Sun Systems (a computer company) has developed an accessibility program and in March 2001, "the American Foundation for the Blind cited the achievements of Sun's Accessibility Team, recognizing Sun with the 2001 Access Award. The Java Accessibility API provides a complete and consistent interface that makes it easy for mainstream developers and for assistive technology vendors to make fully accessible applications available to users with disabilities" (Sun, 2001). For those with vision impairments, Sun's products are compatible with a number of specialized assistive technologies, including freeware and open source solutions. Gnome 2.0 provides software to make the desktop user-accessible and customizable.

While these technologies have moved in the right direction, accessibility on the Web has remained a problem. Since the mid-1990s, the world of Internet computing has expanded significantly. With the advent of e-commerce, shopping has moved online, and library access and research are now available through large online databases and accessed through search engines. Web sites invite us into their domains with applications that include movie clips, animations, hyperlinks, and shopping carts. But are these applications accessible to all? How useful is the movie clip to the hearing impaired user? Can the blind user find the hyperlink to get to the next page of a Web site?

Given that the infrastructure of the information age is the Internet, why aren't all Web sites accessible to everyone? The World Wide Web Consortium (W3C) has a Web Accessibility Initiative (WAI) whose technical activity section is dedicated to ensuring that the core technologies of the Web are accessible to those with disabilities (World Wide Web Consortium). Then why haven't

Web designers taken advantage of the free expertise and built their sites to be accessible to those with disabilities? There are several issues: a lack of mandate for the private sector, cost, speed, and sensitivity to the problem of accessibility for the disabled. Because Section 508 of the Americans with Disabilities Act only applies to organizations receiving government funds, those in the private sector can ignore the mandate on accessibility. But even universities that receive federal monies have been slow to make their sites accessible to disabled persons. In terms of cost, it is more expensive to create a Web site with a multimodal interface. Developers have to become familiar with accessibility issues and how to overcome them. It takes longer to develop these Web sites, because it is often difficult to translate into accessible code all the bells and whistles that make a Web site interesting. Sometimes, these must be limited as a developer builds in text redundancy so that accessibility can be realized. Also, some companies perceive that these Web sites generally are larger and take longer to load, which translates into a speed issue. In general, this is not the case. Given the current processor speeds, network capabilities, and memory capacity of personal computers, we must ask if these are real issues or simply excuses. Slowly but surely, computer developers are recognizing that users with disabilities form a viable international community that has joined the professional ranks of not only computer programmers, engineers, and scientists, but also computer users with purchasing power.

CONCLUSION

Assuming that the digital divide can be bridged at both the local and global levels, important questions still remain. One question has to do with whether increased online communities at the global level threaten our traditional community life, especially as it exists in the off-line world. Philosopher Hans Jonas (1984) speaks of "neighbor ethics." Traditionally, we have had a presumptive responsibility to consider our neighbors as people deserving special moral consideration. Historically, we have banded together with our neighbors in the face of external threats, and we have enjoyed and benefited from the mutual support and reciprocal relationships with our neighbors in physical communities. But who are our neighbors in the global community? If we band together in online communities comprised of people living on several different continents, we can offer our "electronic neighbors" support in some sense and to some degree. But, in so doing, do we also risk the possibility that we will lessen our commitment to our neighbors in physical space? If so, we can ask whether this tradeoff is one worth accepting or is one that needs to be reevaluated.

ACKNOWLEDGMENT

This chapter draws from and expands upon material in two previously published works:

Grodzinsky, F. S., & Tavani, H. T. (2006). The Internet and community building at the local and gloabl levels: Some implications and challenges. In J. Frühbauer, R. Capurro, & T. Hausmanninger (Eds.), *Localizing the Internet: Ethical issues in intercultural perspective.* Munich: Fink Verlag.

Tavani, H. T. (2004). *Ethics and technology: Ethical issues in an age of information and communication technology.* John Wiley & Sons.

REFERENCES

Chapman, G., & Rotenberg, M. (1995). The National information infrastructure: A public interest opportunity. In D. G. Johnson & H. Nissenbaum (Eds.), *Computers, ethics & social values* (pp. 628-644). Englewood Cliffs, NJ: Prentice Hall.

Compaine, B. (2001). *The digital divide: Facing a crisis or creating a myth.* Cambridge, MA: MIT Press.

Dibbell, J. (1993, December 21). A rape in cyberspace. *Village Voice,* pp. 36-42.

Epstein, R. G. (2000). The fragmented public square. *Computers and society.* Retrieved from http://www.cs.wcupa.edu/~epstein.fragmented.htm

Graham, G. (1999). *The Internet: A philosophical inquiry.* New York: Rutledge.

Grodzinsky, F. S. (2000). Equity of access: Adaptive technology. *Science and Engineering Ethics, 6*(2).

Grodiznsky, F. S., & Tavani, H. (2004). Ethical reflections on cyberstalking. In R. A. Spinello & H. T. Tavani (Eds.), *Readings in CyberEthics* (2nd ed.) (pp. 561-570). Jones and Bartlett.

Jonas, H. (1984). *The imperative of responsibility: In search of an ethics for the technological age.* Chicago: University of Chicago Press.

Levison, L., Thies, W., & Amarasinghe, S. (2002). Providing Web search capability for low-connectivity communities. In J. R. Herkert (Ed.), *Proceedings of the 2002 International Symposium on Technology and Society (ISTAS'02)* (pp. 87-92). Los Alamitos, CA: IEEE Computer Society Press.

Moss, J. (2002). Power and the digital divide. *Ethics and Information Technology, 4*(2), 159-165.

National Telecommunications and Information Administration (NTIA). (1995). *Falling through the net: A survey of the have-nots in rural and urban America.* Washington, DC: US Department of Commerce. Retrieved November 15, 2005, from http://www.ntia.doc.gov/ntiahome/fallingthru.html

National Telecommunications and Information Administration (NTIA). (1999). *Falling through the net: Defining the digital divide*. Washington, DC: US Department of Commerce. Retrieved November 15, 2005, from http://www.ntia.doc. gov/ntiahome/fttn99.html

National Telecommunications and Information Administration (NTIA). (2000). *Falling through the net: Toward digital inclusion*. Washington, DC: US Department of Commerce. Retrieved November 15, 2005, from http://www.ntia.doc. gov/ntiahome/fttn00/contents00.html

Negroponte, N. (1995). *Being digital*. New York: Alred Knopf Books.

Rheingold, H. (2001). *The virtual community: Homesteading on the electronic frontier* (rev. ed.). Cambridge, MA: MIT Press.

Scolve, R. E. (1995). *Democracy and technology*. New York: Guilford Press.

Shade, L. R. (2002). *Gender and community in the social construction of the Internet*. New York: Peter Lang.

Sun Microsystems. (2001). *Java's support for accessibility*. Retrieved November 16, 2005, from http://www.sun.com/access/java.access. support.html

Sunstein, C. R. (2002). *Republic.com*. Princeton, NJ: Princeton University Press.

Tavani, H. T. (2003). Ethical reflections on the digital divide. *Journal of Information, Communication and Ethics in Society, 1*(2), 99-108.

Tavani, H. T. (2004). *Ethics and technology: Ethical issues in an age of information and communication technology*. Hoboken, NJ: John Wiley and Sons.

Thorseth, M. (2005, March 18). *IT, multiculturalism and global democracy—ethical challenges*. Paper presented at the Workshop on Positive Discrimination. Institute for Philosophy, Pedagogy, and Rhetoric, Copenhagen University. Retrieved November 16, 2005, from http://trappe13.dynamicweb.dk

Warschauer, M. (2002). Reconceptualizing the digital divide. *First Monday, 7*(7). Retrieved December 21, 2002, from http://www.firstmonday. dk/issues/issue7_7/warschauer

Warschauer, M. (2003). *Technology and social inclusion: Rethinking the digital divide*. Cambridge, MA: MIT Press.

Webster's New World Dictionary of the American Language. (1996). World Publishing Company.

White, M. (2002). Regulating research: The problem of theorizing research in LambdaMOO. *Ethics and Information Technology, 4*(1), 55-70.

World Wide Web Consortium. Retrieved from http://www.w3.org/WAI/Technical/Activity. html

Chapter 5.7
Security and Privacy in Distance Education[1]

George Yee
National Research Council Canada, Canada

INTRODUCTION

Many applications and tools have been developed to support the design and delivery of distance learning courses. Unfortunately, many of these applications have only cursory provisions for security and privacy, such as authentication based only on user id and password. Given the increased attacks on networked applications and the increased awareness of personal privacy rights, this situation is unacceptable. Indeed, electronic services of all kinds, including distance learning, will never be fully successful until the users of these services are confident that their information is protected from unauthorized access and their privacy assured.

In the literature, there are few papers dealing specifically with security and privacy for distance education. El-Khatib, Korba, Xu and Yee (2003) discuss security and privacy for e-learning in terms of legislative requirements, standards and privacy-enhancing technologies. Korba, Yee, Xu, Song, Patrick and El-Khatib (2004) investigate how security and privacy can promote user trust in agent-supported distributed learning. Yee and Korba (2003, 2004) discuss the use and negotiation of privacy policies for distance education. Lin, Korba, Yee and Shih (2004) describe the application of security and privacy technologies to distance learning tools. Yee, Korba, Lin and Shih (2005) present an approach for using context-aware agents to implement security and privacy in distance learning. Holt and Fraser (2003) discuss the psychological and pedagogical motivation for security and privacy.

This chapter provides an overview of security and privacy requirements and solutions for distance education. To provide context for the requirements, the Background section examines a set of tools typically employed in the authoring and delivery of course material. The Security Requirements section discusses security requirements and solutions. Likewise, the Privacy Requirements section discusses privacy requirements and solutions. Following these, the Future Trends section presents some likely future trends in this area. The Conclusion, References and Terms and Definitions sections follow the Future Trends section.

BACKGROUND

This section provides an overview of some of the major tools used in distance education and their purposes. The security implications of the use of these tools are addressed in the sections following the description of the tools.

Distance Education Tools

Distance education practitioners typically employ software tools that provide the following functionality:

Administration Tool

The purpose of this tool is to manage the administrative information of an institute/organization that relates to distance education. This information is very sensitive, as it relates to personal information. Examples of administrative information include the student's marks, address, date of birth, tuition fees still owing, and so on.

Courseware Authoring Tools

Most courseware for distance education is designed to be Internet accessible. As a result, there is a demand for rapid multimedia course development tools and many such tools have been developed. A highly desirable feature of such tools is the ability to take portions of existing courseware from different courses or the same course and recombine them to produce courseware for a new course or to improve courseware effectiveness. From the security point of view, courseware-authoring tools should incorporate copyright protection for the courseware that they produce (see copyright discussion below).

Course Content Delivery Tools

After an online course has been designed, it requires proper tools to deliver it. These tools allow students to synchronously or asynchronously access online courses through the Internet. Since students may have different kinds of computing devices, different tools are available for different platforms.

Synchronous and Asynchronous Communication Tools

Some tools are designed for supporting synchronized activities between instructors and students. A typical example is a video conferencing tool designed for activities such as face-to-face visual and voice communication. This requires synchronization between the communicating parties. Other tools are designed only for supporting asynchronous activities between instructors and students. A typical example is online course delivery that can be done at the student's convenience, without the synchronous online presence of the instructor.

Multimedia Lecturing Tools

Video and slide-show synchronization tools improve slide presentations. They allow for synchronized instructor explanation of the course slides while students are browsing through them. Asynchronous instructor explanations are also possible, where such explanations are pre-packaged and triggered by the page the student has reached.

Student Performance Assessment Tools

Assessing how students perform within online courses is a challenge for instructors. Various tools have been developed for online assessment. These tools tend to focus on creating online exams or tracing a student's online learning logs. Some of the assessment tools monitor student behavior while browsing the course material to generate more effective quizzes. For example, monitoring how much time a student takes on a particular portion of the material may be an indicator of its degree of difficulty for the student.

Figure 1 provides a summary of these distance education tools. In Figure 1, the synchronized communication between instructors refers to online discussion between instructors. The synchronized communication between students refers to online discussion between students such as is commonly done in a chat room.

SECURITY REQUIREMENTS

Authentication

For both instructors and students, it is important that they are authenticated before they join distance education activities.

Authentication of Students

The identity of the student must be authenticated upon logon to the distance education system. The system must make sure that the student accessing it is who he/she claims to be.

Authentication of Instructors

Ensuring the identity of the online instructor is very important, since the instructor has access to many components of the online learning system, including course material, student information and student performance records. Instructors will also have different roles and access privileges as compared to laboratory assistants or students.

Access Control

To make the output of online exams or quizzes worthy of trust, the exam needs to be protected from unauthorized access.

Exam Access Protection

In traditional education, exams are generally administered in the classroom. Instructors are physically present to monitor the students during the exam. However, distance education online exams must be handled differently. Many different modes of testing have evolved for distance education. In some instances, there will be no instructor physically present to monitor the students during the exam, leaving open, for example, the possibility of the student having someone else do the exam. Controls must be in place to ensure that the student accepting credit is the person completing the exam.

Data Integrity, Storage Confidentiality

To make the outcome of online exams or quizzes worthy of trust, the student's exam answers must be protected.

Exam Results Protection

Attackers may see, steal or even modify the students' answers during the transmission or storage of completed exams.

Copyright Protection

Distance education courseware is deemed valuable property that belongs to the organization or instructor. Digital material is easy to reproduce. Since all online courseware is digital material, the protection of courseware copyright must be in place.

Courseware Copyright Protection

Protecting courseware copyright is an important issue in both traditional education and distance education. In the digital world, protecting copyright is more difficult because it is easy to make copies of digital material. In some cases, the distance education system protects courseware from unauthorized copying during storage, transmission or presentation (e.g., screen scraping). This may be true for those institutions where the courseware generated by the instructors is considered highly valued. However, another vital issue is tracking the use of copyrighted material from other sources. Educational organizations spend a great deal of time and effort tracking this material in the process of adhering to their copyright requirements. Any approach that simplifies copyright maintenance for third-party materials would be extremely valuable.

Presentation Copyright Protection

Some instructors may not want their presentation reproduced or shown to people who are not part of a class discussion group. In addition, instructors may wish to make use of presentation content owned by other instructors. There is, thus, a need to allow some of this exchange and sharing to occur without infringing on the rights of the content owners.

Security Solutions

Student authentication can be done with user id and password if the course is not highly sensitive. If more stringent authentication is required, Public Key Infrastructure (PKI, 2002) and digital signatures might be used. However, deployment of such systems and the inherent issues of key management make this approach costly. Instructor authentication may employ a PKI solution quite effectively, since the number of instructors is typically small, which decreases the number of keys that must be managed.

Ensuring that the right student completes an exam can be a difficult problem. Promising approaches employ continuous monitoring of the student using biometrics. Protection of exam answers during transmission of the completed exams may be obtained through the use of the security protocol, Secure Sockets Layer (SSL). The exam answers may be protected while in storage through the use of symmetric encryption (e.g., AES or triple DES).

Protection of the courseware during storage and transmission may be achieved using encryption. Protection during presentation of the courseware is very challenging, since a student can simply record the sessions using a screen capture application, cut-and-paste actions or even a camcorder. The presentation tool running on the student's computer may have built-in functions to defeat digital replication of the courseware material (e.g., the tool will not run if a screen capture process is running at the same time).

For presentation copyright protection, a Digital Rights Management (DRM) solution can be employed that enforces permissions associated with the presentation material. One permission might be associated with reproduction. Another might state that the material can only be shown to people in the discussion group. There are companies that specialize in providing DRM solutions for digital media (e.g., Authentica, at www.authentica.com).

PRIVACY REQUIREMENTS

Privacy requirements for distance education are driven primarily by legislation and personal feelings about what information should be kept private.

Privacy Legislation

The following is a brief overview of privacy legislation in three geographical areas, the European Union, the United States (U.S.), and Canada.

Data privacy in the European Union is governed by a very comprehensive set of regulations called the Data Protection Directive (European Union). Some key provisions include requiring the explicit and "unambiguous" consent of individuals before collecting or processing their personal data (Article 7), and prohibiting the collection of certain "sensitive" data (e.g., pertaining to racial or ethnic origins) except in certain cases (Article 8). The European Union has the most detailed and comprehensive legislation of all three geographical areas.

In the U.S., privacy protection is achieved through a patchwork of legislation at the federal and state levels. Privacy legislation is largely sector-based (Banisar, 1999). At the federal level, there are presently more than a dozen privacy laws. Some of these laws are: Privacy Act of 1974 as amended (5 USC 552a), Electronic Communications Privacy Act of 1986 and Right to Financial Privacy Act of 1986. Laws applicable to the private sector include: Family Educational Rights and Privacy Act of 1978, Privacy Protection Act of 1980 and Video Privacy Protection Act of 1988. As can be seen, the laws typically apply to specific technologies or privacy threats to, for example, bank records, government databases or video rental history. The laws serve as operational boundaries rather than requirements, and there is no national all-encompassing code for privacy protection. As such, the U.S. laws are less effective at protecting personal privacy than either the legislations of the European Union or Canada. The U.S. is not the leader in privacy protection (Hurley, 1999; Milberg, Burke, Smith, & Kallman, 1995; Banisar, 1999).

In Canada, privacy legislation is enacted in the Personal Information Protection and Electronic Documents Act (PIPEDA) (Department of Justice) and is based on the Canadian Standards Association's *Model Code for the Protection of Personal Information* (Canadian Standards Association), recognized as a national standard in 1996. This Code consists of 10 Privacy Principles (Canadian Standards Association). The Canadian provisions are less comprehensive than those of the European Union, but more effective than those of the U.S., due to its all-encompassing and pre-

scriptive nature. Moreover, they contain the same main features as the legislation of the European Union. Since the Canadian Privacy Principles (Table 1) are representative of privacy legislation in other countries and are prescriptive and all encompassing, they may serve as a useful guide to privacy requirements for software systems, including distance education systems.

In Canada, as of January 1, 2004, all service providers (organizations) are required to follow this set of principles when handling consumer private information. Principles 2, 3, 4 and 5 apply directly to a distance learner's private information. Principle 6 is the responsibility of the learner. Principle 7 requires security protection for private information. A distance learner's private information includes home address, telephone number, date of birth, learning preferences, marks and so on.

Student Performance Assessment

Tools that assess student performance need to collect data on the student's learning performance while he/she is browsing the course material. The tool requires this information for automatic generation of personalized tutorials. However, this information collection might be considered an infringement of the student's privacy. In this case, depending on privacy laws, the learning system operator may require student agreement to collect the learning performance information.

Communication Privacy

A student should be able to ask the instructor a question online in private. Any ensuing online discussion should also be private if desired.

Privacy Solutions

An effective approach to protecting privacy for distance education, to comply with privacy legislation, is the use of privacy policies (Yee & Korba, 2003, 2004). A privacy policy is a document that spells out the privacy preferences of the owner of the policy, in terms of what information the owner is willing to share, with whom the information can be shared, for what purposes can the information be used and for how long it can be retained by the receiving party. Each distance learner would have his/her own privacy policy. The educational institution would have corresponding privacy policies that spell out what private information it needs and under what conditions. In order for a distance learner to take part in distance learning activities that involve the disclosure of the learner's private information, the learner's privacy policy must be compatible with the institution's privacy policy. Where the two policies are not compatible, the two parties may negotiate their policies. To ensure that the educational institution complies with the learner's privacy policy, various compliance engines and mechanisms can be employed.

The student's agreement for the collection of his/her performance information for student performance assessment may be reflected in the student's privacy policy.

Communication privacy may be achieved by using SSL (Chou, 2002) to set up a secure channel between the student and the instructor. All communication that flows through this channel would be encrypted, ensuring privacy.

FUTURE TRENDS

With consumers becoming more and more aware of their privacy rights and the vulnerability of these privacy rights on the Internet, the future of electronic services will require more security and privacy features and capabilities. Distance education, as an electronic service, is no exception. This trend can be seen in the new security protocols being developed for Web services (Geer, 2003; Chappell, 2003). The increasing focus on

privacy is evidenced by the advent of privacy legislation, the use of P3P (Platform for Privacy Preferences Project) privacy policies for Web sites (www.w3.org/P3P/), and by developments such as the Liberty Alliance Project that seeks to protect personal information through federated identity management (Liberty Alliance Project) (www.projectliberty.org/).

The need for security and privacy is also being accelerated by the expansion of distance learning from universities to government, military and private enterprises. Government and military applications of distance learning will require greater security, as the subject matter could be top secret. Private enterprises may require better data protection, since knowledge of what employees are being trained on may reveal strategic or competitive secrets.

CONCLUSION

For distance education to be fully successful, distance education systems must provide for security and privacy. Instructors and students alike need to feel confident that their data and privacy are fully protected from malicious attack. Distance education requirements for security and privacy can be fulfilled with existing technology. Vendors and developers of distance education systems need to pay more attention to designing their systems to ensure security and privacy.

REFERENCES

Banisar, D. (1999, September 13). Privacy and data protection around the world. *21st International Conference on Privacy and Personal Data Protection.*

Canadian Standards Association. Model code for the protection of personal information. Retrieved Sept. 5, 2003, from *www.csa.ca/standards/pri-*

vacy/code/Default.asp?articleID=5286&langu
age=English

Chappell, D. (2003). WS-security – New technologies help you make your Web services more secure. *MSDN Magazine*, April. Retrieved July 26, 2004, from *http://msdn.microsoft.com/msdn-mag/issues/03/04/WS-Security/default.aspx*

Chou, W. (2002). Inside SSL: The Secure Sockets Layer protocol. *IEEE Computer Society IT Pro*, July/August, 47-52.

Department of Justice. *Privacy provisions highlights.* Retrieved April 4, 2002, from *http://canada.justice.gc.ca/en/news/nr/1998/attback2.html*

El-Khatib, K., Korba, L., Xu, Y., & Yee, G. (2003). Privacy and security in e-learning. *International Journal of Distance Education Technologies*, *1*(4), October-December, NRC Paper Number: NRC 45786.

European Union. Directive 95/46/EC of the European Parliament and of the Council of 24 October 1995 on the protection of individuals with regard to the processing of personal data and on the free movement of such data. Unofficial text retrieved Sept. 5, 2003, from *http://aspe.hhs.gov/datacncl/eudirect.htm*

Geer, D. (2003). Taking steps to secure Web services. *IEEE Computer*, October, 36, 10.

Holt, P., & Fraser, J. (2003). Anxiety and design issues for e-learning. *Proceedings of Ed-Media 2003*, Honolulu, Hawaii.

Hurley, D. (1999, September 13). A whole world in one glance: Privacy as a key enabler of individual participation in democratic governance. *21ˢᵗ International Conference on Privacy and Personal Data Protection.*

Korba, L., Yee, G., Xu, Y., Song, R., Patrick, A., & El-Khatib, K. (2004). *Designing distributed learning environments with intelligent software agents.* Hershey: Idea Group.

Liberty Alliance Project. Retrieved July 26, 2004, from *www.projectliberty.org/*

Lin, N.H., Korba, L., Yee, G., & Shih, T.K. (2004, March 29-31). Security and privacy technologies for distance education applications. *Proceedings of the 18th International Conference on Advanced Information Networking and Applications (AINA 2004)*, Fukuoka, Japan. NRC Paper Number: NRC 46540.

Milberg, S.J., Burke, S.J., Smith, H.J., & Kallman, E.A. (1995). Values, personal information, privacy, and regulatory approaches. *Communications of the ACM*, December, 38, 12.

Public-Key Infrastructure (X.509) (pkix). (2002). Retrieved Sept. 3, 2003, from *www.ietf.org/html.charters/pkix-charter.html*

W3C. Platform for Privacy Preferences (P3P) Project. Retrieved July 26, 2004, from *www.w3.org/P3P/*

Yee, G., & Korba, L. (2003, May 18-21). The negotiation of privacy policies in distance education. *Proceedings of the 14th IRMA International Conference*, Philadelphia, PA. NRC Paper Number: NRC 44985.

Yee, G., & Korba, L. (2004). *Instructional technologies: Cognitive aspects of online programs.* Hershey: Idea Group.

Yee, G., Korba, L., Lin, N.H., & Shih, T.K. (2005). Context-aware privacy and security agents for distance education. To appear in a special issue of the *International Journal of High Performance Computing and Networking (IJHPCN)*.

KEY TERMS

The definitions provided here pertain to usage in this chapter and may not be applicable in every other domain.

Access Control: Preventing unauthorized use of a resource; that is, controlling who can access the resource, under what conditions the access can occur and what those accessing the resource are allowed to do.

Asynchronous Communication: People communicate online asynchronously if they are not online at the same time.

Authentication: Proving that a party is who he/she claims to be.

Communication Privacy: A communication that cannot be listened in on by unauthorized parties.

Copyright Protection: Providing the means for artists or publishers to control the use and reproduction of their original materials.

Data Integrity: The assurance that data received are exactly as sent by an authorized party. In other words, the data contains no modifications, insertions, deletions or reproductions.

Distance Education Tools: Software applications that are used for the design, implementation and delivery of course materials; also includes software applications for distance education administration, communication during a distance education session and student performance assessment.

Storage Confidentiality: The confidential nature of data in storage.

Student Performance Assessment: Evaluation of how well the student performed or learned in distance education courses. Such evaluation can lead to more effective quizzes and tutorials as aids to student learning.

Synchronous Communication: Online communication between two or more parties, where all parties are online at the same time.

ENDNOTES

[1]   NRC Paper Number: NRC 47172

This work was previously published in Encyclopedia of Distance Learning, Vol. 4, edited by C. Howard, J. Boettcher, L. Justice, K. Schenk, P.L. Rogers, and G.A. Berg, pp. 1599-1606, copyright 2005 by Information Science Reference, formerly known as Idea Group Reference (an imprint of IGI Global).

Chapter 5.8
Ethics and Privacy of Communications in the E-Polis

Gordana Dodig-Crnkovic
Mälardalen University, Sweden

Virginia Horniak
Mälardalen University, Sweden

INTRODUCTION

The electronic networking of physical space promises wide-ranging advances in science, medicine, delivery of services, environmental monitoring and remediation, industrial production and the monitoring of persons and machines. It can also lead to new forms of social interaction. However, without appropriate architecture and regulatory controls, it can also subvert democratic values. Information technology is not, in fact, neutral in its values; we must be intentional about design for democracy (Pottie, 2004).

Information and communication technology (ICT) has led to the emergence of global Web societies. The subject of this article is privacy and its protection in the process of urbanization and socialization of the global digital Web society referred to as the e-polis. Privacy is a fundamental human right recognized in all major international agreements regarding human rights, such as Article 12 of the Universal Declaration of Human Rights (United Nations, 1948), and it is discussed in the article "Different Views of Privacy".

Today's computer network technologies are sociologically founded on hunter-gatherer principles. As a result, common users may be possible subjects of surveillance and sophisticated Internet-based attacks. A user may be completely unaware of such privacy breaches taking place. At the same time, ICT offers the technical possibilities of embedded privacy protection obtained by making technology trustworthy and legitimate by design. This means incorporating options for socially acceptable behavior in technical systems, and making privacy protection rights and responsibilities transparent to the user.

The ideals of democratic government must be respected and even further developed in the future e-government. Ethical questions and privacy of communications require careful analysis, as they have far-reaching consequences affecting the basic principles of e-democracy.

VALUES OF THE E-POLIS

In our post-industrial age, we are witnessing a paradigm shift from techno-centrism to human-centrism and the emergence of an entirely new value system that holds out the prospect of a new Renaissance epoch. Arts and engineering, sciences and humanities are given a means whereby they can reach a new synthesis (Dodig-Crnkovic, 2003). This meeting of cultures is occurring to a great extent in cyberspace, making issues of cyber ethics increasingly important.

One expression of a new rising human-centrism is the emergence of e-government, which changes the citizen-government relation, making the political system transparent and more accessible to the citizen in the participatory democracy. It is, therefore, argued that a rethinking of the idea of development in the contemporary globally networked civilization is necessary (Gill, 2002). Networking at the global level must be seen in a symbiosis with local resources. Social cohesion in this context results from the ability to participate in the networked society through mutual interaction, exchange of knowledge and sharing of values. The problem of promoting e-government in developing countries via virtual communities' knowledge-management is addressed by Wagner, Cheung, Lee, and Ip (2003).

PRIVACY MATTERS

Before the advent of ICT, communication between people was predominantly verbal and direct (Moore, 1994; Agre & Rotenberg, 1997). Today, we increasingly use computers to communicate. Mediated by a computer, information travels far and fast to a virtually unlimited number of recipients, and almost effortlessly (Weckert, 2001). This leads to new types of ethical problems, including intrusion upon privacy and personal integrity. Privacy can be seen as a protection of two kinds of basic rights:

- **Priority in Defining One's Own Identity:** (This implies the right to control the use of personal information disclosed to others, as personal information defines who you are for the others. As a special case, the freedom of anonymity can be mentioned. In certain situations we are ready to lend our personal data for statistical investigations, for research purposes and similar, under the condition that anonymity is guaranteed.)

- **The Right to Private Space:** (This is generalized to mean not only physical space but also special artifacts exclusively associated with a certain individual, such as a private diary or private letters – or disk space.) The privacy of one's home is a classic example of a private space that, moreover, is related to one's own identity. It is also an instructive archetype because it shows the nature of a private space as a social construction. You are, in general, allowed to choose whom you wish to invite to your home. However, under special circumstances, it is possible for police, for example, to enter your home without your consent, this being strictly regulated by law.

Historically, as a result of experiences within different cultures, a system of practices and customs has developed that defines what is to be considered personal and what is public (see Warren & Brandeis, 1890; Thompson, 2001). A basic distinction in human relations is, consequently, that between the private (shared with a few others) and the common (shared with wider groups) (DeCew, 2002). Fried (Rosen, 2000) claims that only closely related persons can have true knowledge of an individual.

According to Mason (2000), privacy can be studied through the relationships of four social groups (parties): (1) the individual; (2) others to whom the first party provides specific personal information for the sake of creating or sustaining a personal relationship or in return for services; (3)

all other members of society who can get access to an individual's private information, but who have no professional relation to the individual and no authority to use the information; and (4) the general public who are in no direct contact with the individual's private space or information. During the interaction between parties, individuals invoke different levels of privacy. The advantages of close relationships are compared with the risks of the release of information and its inappropriate use, which could result in a loss of personal space or harm to one's identity.

DIFFERENT VIEWS OF PRIVACY

The acquisition, storage, access to and usage of personal information is regulated and limited in most countries of the world by legislation. However, each part of the world has its own laws. In the United States (U.S.), separate laws apply to different kinds of records. Individual European countries have their own specific policies regarding what information can be collected and the detailed conditions under which this is permissible. (For an international survey of privacy laws, including country-by-country reports, see Privacy and Human Rights 2004; see also Briefing Materials on the European Union Directive on Data Protection).

The current political situation in the world and the threat of terrorist attacks has led to governmental proposals in the European Union requiring Internet Service Providers to store personal information—for example, data relating to Internet traffic, e-mails, the geographical positioning of cellular phones and similar—for a period of time longer than is required of them at present (ARTICLE 29 Data Protection Working Party).

Although relevant legislation is in effect locally, there are difficulties with respect to the global dissemination of information. To avoid conflicting situations, there is a need for interna-

tional agreements and legislation governing the flow of data across national borders.

COMPUTER ETHICS

ICT is value-laden, as is technology in general, and is changing our ways of conceptualizing and handling reality (Bynum & Rogerson, 2003; Spinello, 2003). It is not always easy to recognize intrinsic values incorporated in an advanced technology. Specialized technical knowledge is often needed for an understanding of the intrinsic functionality of a technology; for example, how information is processed in a computer network.

The need for a specific branch of ethics for computer and information systems, as compared with a straightforward application of a general ethical theory to the field of computing, is discussed by Bynum (2000), Floridi and Sanders (2002) and Johnson (2003). Tavani (2002) gives an overview of this so-called uniqueness debate. While the philosophical discussion about its nature continues, computer ethics/cyber ethics is growing in practical importance and is establishing itself as a consequence of the pressing need for the resolution of a number of acute ethical problems connected with ICT.

The changing resources and practices appearing with ICT both yield new values and require the reconsideration of those established. New moral dilemmas may also appear because of the clash between conflicting principles when brought together unexpectedly in a new context. Privacy, for example, is now recognized as requiring more attention than previously received in ethics (Moor, 1997). This is due to reconceptualization of the private and public spheres brought about by the use of ICT, which has resulted in the recognition of inadequacies in existing moral theory about privacy. In general, computer ethics can provide guidance in the further development and modification of ethics when the existing is found to be inadequate in the light of new demands generated by new practices (Brey, 2000).

For Moor (1985), computer ethics is primarily about solving moral problems that arise because there is a lack of policy (policy vacuum) about how computer technology should be used. In such a case, the situation that generates the moral problem must first be identified, conceptually clarified and understood. On the other hand, Brey claims that a large part of work in computer ethics is about revealing the moral significance of the existing practices that seem to be morally neutral. ICT has implicit moral properties that remain unnoticed because the technology and its relation to the context of its use are not sufficiently understood. Disclosive computer ethics has been developed to demonstrate the values and norms embedded in computer systems and practices. It aims at making computer technology and its uses transparent, revealing its morally relevant features.

FAIR INFORMATION PRACTICES

One of the fundamental questions related to the expansion of community networks is the establishment of fair information practices that enable privacy protection. At present, it is difficult to maintain privacy when communicating through computer networks, which are continually divulging information. An example of a common concern is that many companies endeavor to obtain information about the behavior of potential consumers by saving cookies on their hard disks. Other possible threats against citizens' privacy include the unlawful storage of personal data, storage of inaccurate personal data and abuse or unauthorized disclosure of such data; these are issues surrounding government-run identity databases. Especially interesting problems arise when biometrics is involved (for identity documents, such as passports/visas, identity cards, driving licenses). Remote electronic voting is dependent on the existence of a voters' database, and there are strong privacy concerns if the same database is used for other purposes, and especially if it contains biometric identifiers.

Many countries have adopted national privacy or data protection laws. Such laws may apply both to data about individuals collected by the government and to personal data in the hands of private sector businesses. The OECD has defined *fair information practices*, which include the following principles: collection limitation, data quality, purpose specification, use limitation, security, openness, individual participation and accountability (see OECD Guidelines on the Protection of Privacy).

The exceptions to these principles are possible in specific situations, such as law enforcement investigations, when it might not be appropriate to give a suspect access to the information that the police are gathering. Nonetheless, the principles of fair information practices provide a framework for privacy protection.

LEGITIMACY BY DESIGN AND FUTURE TRUSTWORTHY COMPUTING

Legitimacy is a social concept developed during human history, meaning "socially beneficial fairness." It concerns classical social problems, such as the prisoner's dilemma and the "tragedy of the commons," in which individuals may profit at the expense of society. Social interactions without legitimacy lead society into an unsustainable state.

However, traditional mechanisms that support legitimacy, such as laws and customs, are particularly ineffective in the cyberspace of today with its flexible, dynamic character, (Whitworth & de Moor, 2003). The remedy is the incorporation of legitimacy by design into a technological system. That process begins with a legitimacy analysis that can translate legitimacy concepts, such as freedom, privacy and intellectual property into specific system design demands. At the same time, it can translate technological artifacts, such as computer programs, into statements that can be understood and discussed in terms of ethical theory.

Legitimate interaction, with its cornerstones of trustworthiness and accountability, seems a key to the future of the global information society. This implies that democratic principles must be built into the design of socio-technical systems such as e-mail, collaborative virtual environments (CVEs), chats and bulletin boards, electronic voting systems and similar. As the first step towards that goal, the legitimacy analysis of a technological artifact (software/hardware) is suggested.

Trust is a broad concept, and making something trustworthy requires a social infrastructure as well as solid engineering. All systems fail from time to time; the legal and commercial practices within which they're embedded can compensate for the fact that no technology will ever be perfect. (Mundie, de Vries, Haynes, & Corwine, 2003)

In any computer-mediated communication, trust ultimately depends not on personal identification code numbers or IP addresses, but on relationships between people with their different roles within social groups. The trust necessary for effective democracy depends on communication, and much of the communication is based on interaction over computer networks. Trust and privacy trade-offs are normal constituents of human social, political and economic interactions, and they consequently must be incorporated in the practices of the e-polis. The bottom line is, of course, the transparency of the system and the informed consent of all parties involved.

CONCLUSION

ICT supports and promotes the formation of new global virtual communities that are socio-tech-

nological phenomena typical of our time. In an e-democracy government, elected officials, the media, political organizations and citizens use ICT within the political and governance processes of local communities, nations and on the international stage. The ideal of e-democracy is greater and more direct citizen involvement. For the modern civilization of a global e-polis, the optimal functioning of virtual communities is vital. What are the basic principles behind successful virtual community environments? According to Whitworth, there are two such principles:

- Virtual community systems must match the processes of human-human interaction
- Rights and ownership must be clearly defined

It is technically possible for ICT to incorporate these principles, which include privacy protection via standards, open source code, government regulation, and so forth (Pottie, 2004; Tavani & Moor, 2000), including also trustworthy computing (Mundie et al., 2003).

A process of continuous interaction and dialog is necessary to achieve a socio-technological system that will guarantee the highest standards of privacy protection. Our conclusion is that trust must be established in ICT, both in the technology itself and in the way it is employed in a society.

REFERENCES

Agre, P. E., & Rotenberg, M. (Ed.). (1997). *Technology and privacy: The new landscape.* MIT Press.

Brey, P. (2000). Method in computer ethics: Towards a multi-level interdisciplinary approach. *Ethics and Information Technology, 2*(3), 1-5.

Briefing materials on the European Union Directive on data protection. Retrieved December 11,

2004, from www.cdt.org/privacy/eudirective/The Center for Democracy & Technology

Bynum, T. W. (2000). Ethics and the information revolution. In G. Collste (Ed.), *Ethics in the age of information technology* (pp. 32-55). Linkoeping, Sweden: Center for Applied Ethics Linkoeping Universitet.

Bynum, T. W., & Rogerson, S. (Eds.). (2003). *Computer ethics and professional responsibility.* Malden, MA: Blackwell.

Data protection working party. Retrieved December 11, 2004, from http://europa.eu.int/comm/internal_market/privacy/workingroup_en.htm

DeCew, J. (2002). *Privacy, the Stanford encyclopedia of philosophy.* Retrieved December 11, 2004, from http://plato.stanford.edu/archives/sum2002/entries/privacy

Dodig-Crnkovic, G. (2003). Shifting the paradigm of the philosophy of science: The philosophy of information and a new renaissance. *Minds and Machines: Special issue on the philosophy of information, 13*(4), 521-536.

Floridi, L., & Sanders, J. (2002). Mapping the foundationalist debate in computer science, a revised version of Computer ethics: Mapping the foundationalist debate. *Ethics and Information Technology, 4.1*, 1-9.

Gill, K. S. (2002). Knowledge networking in cross-cultural settings. *AI & Society, 16*, 252-277.

Johnson, D. G. (2003). Computer ethics. In L. Floridi (Ed.), *Blackwell guide to the philosophy of computing and information.* Malden, MA: Blackwell Publishing.

Mason, R. O. (2000). *A tapestry of privacy, a meta-discussion.* Retrieved December 11, 2004, from http://cyberethics.cbi.msstate.edu/mason2/

Moor, J. H. (1997). Towards a theory of privacy for the information age. *Computers and Society, 27*, 3.

Moor, J. H. (1985). What is computer ethics? *Metaphilosophy, 16*, 4. Availble from www.ccsr.cse.dmu.ac.uk/staff/Srog/teaching/moor.htm

Moore, B., Jr. (1994). *Privacy: Studies in social and cultural history.* Armonk: M. E. Sharpe.

Mundie, C., de Vries, P., Haynes, P., & Corwine, M. (2003). *Trustworthy computing white paper.* Retrieved from www.microsoft.com/mscorp/twc/twc_whitepaper.mspx

Privacy and human rights 2004, an international survey of privacy laws and developments. Retrieved December 11, 2004, from www.privacy-international.org/survey/phr2004

OECD. (1980, September 23). *Guidelines on the protection of privacy—Recommendation of the Council Concerning Guidelines Governing the Protection of Privacy and Transborder Flows of Personal Data.* Retrieved April 20, 2006, from http://www.oecd.org/document/53/0,2340,en_2649_34255_15589524_1_1_1_1,00.html

Pottie, G. J. (2004). Privacy in the global village. *Communications of the ACM, 47*(2), 2-23.

Rosen, J. (2000). Why privacy matters. *Wilson Quarterly, 24*(4), 32.

Spinello, R. A. (2003). *Cyberethics. Morality and law in cyberspace.* Sudbury, MA: Jones and Bartlett Publishers.

Tavani, H. T. (2002). The uniqueness debate in computer ethics: What exactly is at issue, and why does it matter? *Ethics and Information Technology, 4*, 37-54.

Tavani, H. T., & Moor, J. H. (2000). Privacy protection, control of information, and privacy-enhancing technologies. *SIGCAS Computers and Society, 31*(1), 6-11.

Thompson, P. B. (2001). Privacy, secrecy and security. *Ethics and Information Technology, 3.*

United Nations. (1948). *Universal declaration of*

human rights, general assembly resolution 217 A (III). Retrieved from www.un.org/Overview/rights.html

Wagner, C., Cheung, K., Lee, F., & Ip, R. (2003). Enhancing e-government in developing countries: Managing knowledge through virtual communities. *The Electronic Journal on Information Systems in Developing Countries, 14*(4), 1-20.

Warren, S., & Brandeis, L. D. (1890). The right to privacy. *Harvard Law Review, 4,* 5.

Weckert, J. (2001). Computer ethics: Future directions. *Ethics and Information Technology, 3.*

Whitworth, B., & de Moor, A. (2003). Legitimate by design: Towards trusted virtual community environments. *Behaviour and Information Technology, 22*(1), 31-51.

KEY TERMS

Computer Ethics: A branch within applied ethics dealing with ethical questions concerning ICT. Computer ethics includes application of ethical theories to issues regarding the use of computer technology, together with standards of professional practice, codes of conduct, aspects of computer law and related topics.

Cookies: Information about a user stored by the server on the user's hard disk. Typically, a cookie records a user's preferences when using a particular site, which often happens without the user's knowledge, even though they must nominally agree to cookies being saved for them.

CVEs: Collaborative Virtual Environments.

Cyber Ethics: See computer ethics. Broadly speaking, cyber ethics deals with the conduct of individuals with respect to the information world; in the words of Moor: "the formulation and justification of policies for the ethical use of computers." Narrowly, cyber ethics refers to computer ethics discipline in cyberspace.

Cyberspace: A virtual space that consists of resources available through computer networks. It also refers to the culture developed by electronically connected communities. The term was first coined by William Gibson in the book *Neuromancer.*

Design for Democracy: The incorporation of options for socially acceptable behavior in technical systems, making the basic principles of privacy protection, rights and responsibilities transparent to the user.

Disclosive Ethics: A multi-level interdisciplinary approach concerned with the exposition of embedded values and norms in computer systems, applications and practices.

Policy Vacuum: James Moor has defined this term, meaning the absence of policies for governing conduct in new situations resulting from the use of new technologies. The central task of computer ethics is to fill the policy vacuums resulting from the use of computers by formulating guidelines for their use.

Privacy, Right of: The right of a person to be free from intrusion into or publicity concerning matters of a personal nature; also called right to privacy.

Technology Legitimate by Design: Technology designed in such a way as to promote its legitimate use and prevent its misuse.

Uniqueness Debate: A discussion among ethicists whether computer ethics is a unique field of ethics or merely a straightforward application of existing ethical theories to the specific technology (computers).

Chapter 5.9
A Process Data Warehouse for Tracing and Reuse of Engineering Design Processes

Sebastian C. Brandt
RWTH Aachen University, Germany

Marcus Schlüter
RWTH Aachen University, Germany

Matthias Jarke
RWTH Aachen University and Fraunhofer FIT, Germany

ABSTRACT

The design and development processes of complex technical systems are of crucial importance to the competitiveness of an enterprise. These processes are characterised by high creativity and strong non-deterministic dynamics. Traditional information science methods, however, are intended for more deterministic work processes. They cannot be effectively applied to support creative activities like conceptual synthesis, analysis, and decision making. Therefore methods of experience management need to be exploited here. This paper presents a new integrated approach to such design process guidance based on capturing the process traces in a Process Data Warehouse (PDW). Both the products to be designed and the process steps corresponding, are structured and stored as extended method traces. This trace capture facilitates the processing and subsequent reuse of the information through a process-integrated development environment. The concept of the PDW has been evaluated in an engineering design case study which focuses on the phases of conceptual design and basic engineering in designing a chemical production plant.

INTRODUCTION

In designing and developing complex technical systems, the design engineers are confronted with the high dynamics of the processes and the many degrees of freedom in designing technical structures, in addition to the complexity of the structures themselves. The difficulties of their tasks result from the use of utilities like different design and simulation tools, and the planning and distribution of resources, such as personnel. In such a creative engineering process, any restriction of the experts in their options would greatly affect their productivity and might even lead to project failure. Today, these tasks frequently involve experts from several disparate disciplines, for example, computer science, electrical and mechanical engineering, and control engineering. Their complex and *non-deterministic* work processes need to be supported by thorough and integrated information science methods and systems. Presently, the possibilities of such support are widely being researched in computer science.

Solutions have been established so far mainly for *deterministic* work processes. They are often found in the domains of business, economics, or management. These solutions cannot be directly transferred due to the non-determinism found in complex technical design processes. The design processes involve the intricate interplay of *eliciting* complex requirements, *synthesising* solution possibilities, *analysing* the alternative models by simulations and other methods, and *deciding* on alternatives by discussing the analysis results. The software environments currently found in these areas are usually very heterogeneous. Each tool has been developed for a separate step of these processes, yet these software tools are seldom able to cooperate. While they are able to support the evolution of *product* data, only a few tools also comprise *process* support. It is important not to separate the products or artefacts created as part of these design processes—documents, diagrams, and other products—from the processes themselves. Any kind of integrated support needs to take both aspects of products and processes into account. Yet the design processes treated here are not sufficiently well understood to allow applying prescriptive and deterministic approaches to process support. They usually involve activities of multi-objective decision making based on incomplete information. This is especially true for the early phases of basic chemical engineering as described in this paper, where only qualitative conclusions about processes and process quality are possible.

The interdisciplinary collaboration of the various experts involved in a design process is usually based on informal structures. This disallows most of the common approaches of information technology-based support. In the case of cooperative processes that involve multiple companies, aspects like organisational boundaries, incongruous work processes, and the need for intellectual property protection create additional complexity.

On this background, the aim of the research presented here is to improve the work situation of the system developers participating in these design and development processes. Hence the authors of this paper have developed the concept of the *Process Data Warehouse* as an engineering product and process repository, to allow the tracing and reuse of complex design processes.

This paper is organised as follows. The next section will investigate the possibilities of supporting technical design processes by experience management. In the section afterwards, the concept of the Process Data Warehouse for trace capture and experience reuse will be explained in more detail. The following section will illustrate how these concepts have been applied in a case study in the domain of chemical engineering. Finally, conclusions are provided including further on-going and future research.

SUPPORT FOR DYNAMIC DESIGN PROCESSES

The inherent dynamics of the work processes pose one of the main problems in engineering design and development. In these processes, the requirements and other parameters change from one project to the next, and can also evolve during the lifetime of a single project. As no methods in the sense of "best practice" are known, the driving influence in engineering design is the personal experience of the system designers. Transferring this tacit knowledge from one expert to another is often needed. This transfer normally requires a long-term process which prominently consists of more or less successful trials and errors.

For solving the problems of different steps or phases of a design project, different specialised software tools need to be employed. Each of these tools is normally based on its own proprietary model and contains only some generic import and/or export functions. Possibilities of converting or integrating the data directly between the different internal tool models rarely exist. Their hard-wired usage processes are enacted independently of each other. A similar, yet even more problematic situation arises if the project needs the synergetic cooperation of experts from different domains, and possibly companies. Again, methods of knowledge management can be successfully applied here.

A common approach to knowledge management is based on offering information to the expert which has been recorded in earlier executions of the same or a similar task. In this way, each expert can use his own experience and that of his colleagues to improve both his work situation and the quality of his work, while also enhancing his autonomy. This information allows the construction of some kind of best practice rules by analysing the different steps of previous or finished design processes. Knowledge management is usually applied in processes where no algorithms or other kinds of well-defined problem solving processes

are available, no complete domain models have been—nor can be—established, and specific expert knowledge is more important than large amounts of common sense (Bergmann 2002).

For some domains, technical solutions have already been established. During the last decade, many manufacturing enterprises have started using Product Data Management (PDM) systems, and/or the successor systems for Product Lifecycle Management (PLM). The aim of these systems is to integrate the manufacturing processes (usually CAM, CIM) with product design activities on the one hand, and Enterprise Resource Planning (ERP) processes on the other hand. Yet most of these existing systems still lack essential aspects needed for supporting phases of conceptual design, such as knowledge or experience management. Some more recent approaches exist to extend these systems by integrating concepts of artificial intelligence (Kim, Kang, Lee, & Yoo, 2001), or by using ontological models and tools (Gao, Aziz, Maropoulos, & Cheung, 2003).

Common to all the approaches described so far is their placement in domains like automotive engineering where the design processes are relatively well-documented, strict, and deterministic, allowing prescriptive definition of the activities to be executed. This stands in contrast to chemical process engineering (CAPE) where the process dynamics inhibit deterministic modelling approaches.

Because of these problems, it would be helpful to offer to the experts fine-grained support for these non-deterministic processes. For some time it has been known that experience and understanding of one's own work is necessary to enable process evolution and improvement (Humphrey, 1990). This insight has resulted in several approaches based on the basic concept of knowledge management and *experience reuse*. For example, as part of the TAME project, Basili and Rombach (1988) propose a process model for supporting creative software development processes which is based on their own experiences in software requirements engineering. Their approach focuses strongly on quantitative and metrics-based method evaluation for the later steps of software engineering. In the *Experience Factory* approach, an independent logical organisation is responsible for gathering the knowledge and core competencies of a development group and offering this information for reuse (Basili, Caldiera, & Rombach, 1994). The concept of *organisational memory*, as described, for example, by Conklin (1993), also formed the basis for a set of approaches to knowledge and experience management.

Some similar research approaches exist in the area of engineering design processes. In Grabowski, Lossack, and Leutsch (2001), a knowledge-based approach for product design is examined, based on integrating partial domain models and using patterns to represent the non-deterministic behaviour of design processes. Another project is developing a process platform which supports the experience-based management and reuse of coarse-grained aspects of software development processes (Münch & Rombach, 2003). A different approach to reuse the experience of product development is shown in Wagner and Aslanidis (2002). This case stresses the manual processing of expert knowledge and its reuse by less experienced colleagues, by storing the knowledge and the contact information of experts who know more about it, in a corporation-wide experience portal.

A set of well-researched methods for the domain of artificial intelligence is based on the definition and reuse of *cases* which represent knowledge, based on certain problem characterisations and the lessons applicable for reusing this knowledge. The possibilities offered by this Case-Based Reasoning (CBR), and their limitations, are described in Aamondt and Plaza (1994).

DATA WAREHOUSES FOR PROCESS TRACING AND DECISION SUPPORT

Process Tracing and Decision Logging

Beyond the approaches described so far, there is the need of *integrated* technical support for the early phases of creative system design, specifically concerning complex technical systems. Therefore, the authors' research group has examined the possibilities offered by recording and reusing the traces of work *processes* in technical design. The project activities have been performed as part of the Research Centre on Cooperative Computer-Aided Process Engineering (SFB 476 IMPROVE, Marquardt & Nagl, 2004) which started in 1997, and has been funded by the German National Science Foundation (DFG) since then. The research deals with the product-based views as well as the concepts of direct process support, already investigated in previous projects. It has led to supporting creative design and development processes by integrated method guidance (Pohl et al., 1999). These views have been extended and adapted to the domain of process engineering. This strategy resulted in the model of the *Process Data Warehouse* (PDW). It captures and analyses the traces of design processes: products, process instantiations, and their interdependencies (Jarke, List, & Köller, 2000). The main concept has been to capture the artefacts (the technical system) to be designed and modified during the processes, and to relate them to the processes which perform these modifications. From these semantically structured product and process traces, the relevant information can be extracted in an *analysis* step, and then *reused* in further process executions. This information can be presented to the experts as experience knowledge in order to solve the problems of later development cycles more easily, efficiently, and autonomously.

The central problem of this approach is how to support traceability. To enable traceability, first of all the conceptual relations between products, processes and their dependencies need to be examined. Therefore, Ramesh and Jarke (2001) abstracted the *traceability reference model* shown in Figure 1 from a large number of industrial case studies. This model distinguishes between product-oriented and process-oriented trace objects.

The *product-oriented* traces describe the properties and relationships of concrete design objects. A high-level object defines some goal or constraint that needs to be *satisfied* by a number of *product objects* on a more fine-grained level of modelling. This implies dependencies (*depends-on*) between these lower-level objects which also comprise the special cases of generalisation and aggregation.

The *process-oriented* traces represent the history of actions that led to the creation of the product objects. Two link types exist between those process objects: *evolves-to* which describes the temporal evolution of a lower-level design object towards a higher level, and *rationale* which captures the reason for this evolution. The integrated presentation of the product and process traces in this "onion-shell" meta model symbolises the fact that they cannot be reasonably separated as one strongly depends on the other.

As visible in the left part of Figure 1, the role of the *stakeholder* during product creation or documentation is of importance as well. It is also necessary to record and connect the *sources* which contain and display the information.

The description of this reference model shows that recording the process traces needs to include all related influence factors, like the actual problem situation, the resulting artefacts, and the decisions that led to the final results.

From these traces the semantically relevant information can be extracted in an *analysis* step. Due to the complexity of the traces, automated analysis is impossible in most cases. When working on complex processes with only few repetitions and few concrete product instances, this analysis step can often be left out. The decision between the available information can be done in the moment of reuse. If there are too many data to be retraced this way, a so-called *method engineer* is responsible for extracting and explicitly modelling method fragments and situations, often supported by methods of data mining.

When an expert needs to solve a certain problem, the current process and product situation is analysed by the PDW to find matching solutions from the recorded (and analysed) traces. If an adequate method or product fragment is found, it can be offered to the expert for *reuse* through a *guidance* mechanism. Yet it is his or her own decision whether to adapt and use this information, to request more details, or to discard it. In many cases a small hint should suffice that the

Figure 1. Traceability reference model from Ramesh and Jarke (2001)

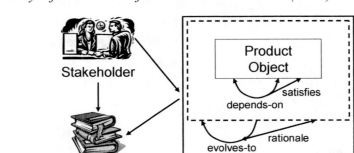

step currently enacted, conforms to the experience gathered up to now or, even more important, conflicts with it.

It also has to be recorded whether the problem was successfully solved, and how far the process support provided was appropriate, as a final *feedback* information. By using this information the system and the support it offers, can be evaluated and improved.

The Process Data Warehouse

The Process Data Warehouse (PDW) has been defined by Jarke et al. (2000) as a knowledge-based metadata repository for tracing and driving heterogeneous work processes in engineering. It stores the history of processes and products to enable experience reuse with the aid of situated process support.

In the well-known area of Data Warehouses (Jarke, Lenzerini, Vassiliou, & Vassiliadis, 2003), large amounts of fixedly structured data (e.g. from sales or accounting) are aggregated, normally based on relational schemata. More flexible structures are necessary for a PDW to support creative design processes. Firstly, all models of the PDW are explicitly defined in an ontology-based language. Secondly, the complete model consists of loosely connected *partial models*, each of them modelling a certain conceptual area or usage environment. Apart from incorporating the *process* aspect, this also allows to integrate the complex and often changing domain models. Thus the conceptual model of the PDW is composed of a number of models (or ontology modules) which are held together by a central model, the so-called *Core Ontology*.

The recording of *product* information is normally realised inside the tools contained in a development environment. Special steps need to be taken for recording and relating *process* traces and supplementary information like decisions and arguments. It is necessary to enrich the application environment with tools to enable a consistent

automated and partially manual trace capture. This enrichment has been realised based on the idea of *a-posteriori integration*. The experts can still use the tools they are accustomed to, while additional value is provided by the integration.

Over the last decade, the authors' research group has developed the process-integrated development environment PRIME which implements the vision of *integrating* development tools, product data, process guidance, and trace capture. The concept of process integration was derived from the idea of process-centred environments (PCE, see Dowson & Fernström, 1994) which are based on the three domains of modelling, enactment, and performance. The concepts of PRIME enhance the interaction between these domains. Especially a tight integration between the enactment domain (where method fragments are executed) and the performance domain (where the user interacts with the tools) was realised. More information about this topic can be found in Pohl et al. (1999).

The PDW forms a central part of this process-integrated environment. It records the development traces based on the concepts offered by the partial models for processes, products, and application domains. This way, the information from diverse tools, workplaces and disciplines is integrated into one central storage. Other external data sources and repositories are indirectly integrated, with the PDW taking the role of a semantic data mediator. To find and reuse experience traces, the current process state, the situation of the selected products and the attributes of other objects in their vicinity can be used to formulate queries on the experience base. It is possible to use semantic search mechanisms on the integrated model of the PDW, as it is based on ontological concepts and ontology- and logic-based languages. This enables the retrieval of objects and their attributes based on relationships, attribute values, classifications, and other constraints. Due to the explicit definition of the concepts and their relationships in the ontology modules, classifications, subsumption, and other properties can be automatically inferred. Attribute ranges and other concepts can also be used to achieve similarity comparisons and searching.

The Conceptual Framework of the Process Data Warehouse

As already mentioned, the conceptual model of the Process Data Warehouse is based on a set of loosely connected partial models. These are interconnected through the *Core Ontology* which will be introduced in this paragraph. It comprises the process models, the product and dependency models, models for decision support and documentation, for the description of content and categorisations, and other integration models. Around these fundamental and domain-independent models, *extension points* are placed that can be used to add the models of a specific application domain or other specialisations. Theses partial models, or ontology modules, are explicitly implemented in a modelling language similar to the realisation of ontologies as part of the Semantic Web effort (RDF, OWL, see Berners-Lee, Hendler, & Lassila, 2001). The

concrete data is then stored as instances of the appropriate concepts. This allows modifications and extensions of the partial models used, even during project execution.

Four prominent areas of conceptualisation are arranged around the *object* as the abstract central concept. They are shown in Figure 2:

- The *product* area (top) contains basic models for the artefacts created or modified during the design processes—documents and other information resources, including their structural composition and version histories.
- The *descriptive* area (left) contains basic concepts for describing the content or role of documents and products on a high semantic level. This includes content descriptions, sources, and categorisations which are grouped into categorisation schemes. The vocabulary necessary for content-based retrieval is mostly provided here.
- The *process* area (bottom) contains the concepts needed to describe the process steps which produce or modify the artefacts. This comprises process definitions which can be enacted (method fragments), process

Figure 2. Overview of the four modelling areas

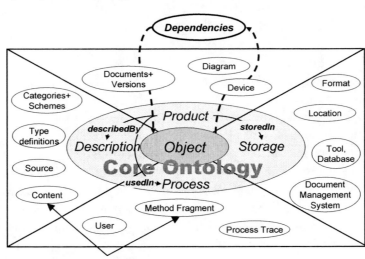

Partial Models/Ontologies

traces resulting from enactment, and users which guide the enactment. Organisational structures like companies and workgroups are also placed here.

- In the *storage* area (right), external stores and repositories like are integrated into the PDW. When integrating active stores like document management systems or external tools, changes of documents or other data can be automatically propagated into the PDW.

Dependencies are explicitly modelled as a global concept to enable specialised relations between elements independent of their concrete relationships. They were also described in the traceability reference model earlier in this paper. This hierarchy of relationship types is modelled inside an additional area which can be seen as orthogonal to the four areas.

Three primary relationships between the elements of the partial models are shown in the figure. *DescribedBy* relates the product objects with descriptive elements that describe their type, content or category; *storedAt* represents the storage of products and documents in physical places like file systems or repositories; and *usedIn* describes how the product objects are created, used, and modified by the users in process activities.

All areas offer the *extension points* which have been mentioned above. Here, the partial models of an application domain or other specialisations can be added. For example, the storage area offers the basic models for file storage inside a document management system, relating file-based documents with their conceptual representation inside the Process Data Warehouse. This allows accessing the documents' contents and their physical storage places, including the visualisation or modification inside appropriate tools. The PDW is notified of any document change, enabling further processing and annotation based on the semantic models of the other three areas. To apply the concepts of the storage area, an integration of the EMC

Documentum© system (Documentum, 2006) has been developed by extending the concepts, and implementing specialised functionality.

Sometimes it is necessary to work with documents which have no formal structure, or a structure which is not known. In this case, the PDW offers the possibility to semantically annotate, categorise and structure the documents according to an appropriate domain model. This approach has already been investigated in a previous project concerning the multimedia artefacts of plastics engineering simulations.

So far, the Process Data Warehouse has been described as it has been developed by the authors' research group. In the following section, this approach is applied to the process of designing a chemical production plant.

A CASE STUDY IN CHEMICAL ENGINEERING

Designing a Chemical Plant

The sample scenario described in this section is a simplified version of designing a plant for polyamide 6 (nylon) production. The scenario was developed in an industrial workshop with several German partners (e.g., Bayer AG). The elaboration of the cooperative scenario, the requirements for the productions processes and the product itself, are described in Nagl, Westfechtel, and Schneider (2003).

At the beginning of plant design, various constraints are written down concerning the chemical process itself. For example, the residue for some of the input components must not rise above a certain limit, or the finished and cooled product must have a certain size. The complete recycling of any catalyst or input component is required. During the phase of basic engineering, an initial process concept is stepwise refined into more detailed functional elements, the so-called "process steps" and "unit operations".

The Process Data Warehouse for Designing the Plant

In Figure 3, the Process Data Warehouse is shown as it has been used in the application scenario of chemical plant design. A brief overview of the realisation of the PDW for this specific application domain follows here. The partial models integrated into the extension points are based on the Conceptual Life Cycle Process model CLiP (Bayer & Marquardt 2004) which contains all fundamental concepts of the domain of basic (chemical) engineering. This model is constructed out of the four modelling levels common for this kind of information models. The meta meta model mainly consists of the concepts System and its Aspects whereas the concrete instances created and/or recorded in the development process can be found three levels below, on the token level. The role of a central connecting concept is taken by the flowsheet which forms the centre of the design process, both as a diagram and as a data model. The model level of CLiP has been transformed into an ontology-based version (Yang & Marquardt 2004), realised in the Ontology Web Language (OWL, see McGuiness & van Harmelen 2004). This allowed the direct integration into the PDW. The structural components of the chemical plant (like diagrams, devices, and streams) have been derived from the product and document concepts. The functional aspects extend the descriptive area by adding content and source concepts, in other words, the mathematical or physical model which generated a certain simulation result, the kind of reaction it models, or the chemical components which react with each other.

As shown in Figure 3, this case study deals with the situation where a certain process step, the *Reaction*, is to be realised by one or more different reactor equipments. This step can be seen as the starting point in Figure 3, item 1.

Figure 3. The application scenario of chemical plant design with PDW support

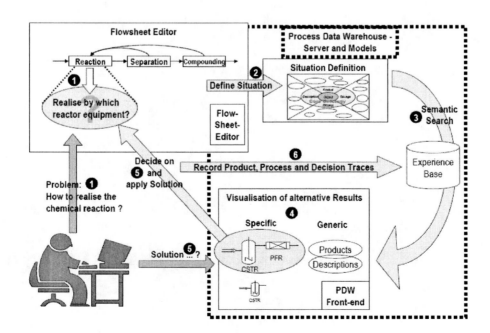

The experience reuse framework consists of the Process Data Warehouse, the process-integrated development environment PRIME and the flow-sheet editor which has been integrated into this environment. This framework is able to specify the current problem situation based on the integrated rules, and tries to find a matching process trace or a recurring method fragment in the experience base of the PDW (Figure 3, item 2).

The required problem definition consists of elements of several of the four areas introduced in the previous section, each of the elements being the concrete instance of one of the semantic concepts contained in the PDW's ontologies. This can also be seen in Figure 4:

- The *product* part of the situation is composed of the design elements displayed in the flow-sheet editor, such as the reaction, the streams of chemical elements flowing into and out of it, their relationships, and attributes like temperature or pressure. Their states—in other words, being selected in the graphical user interface—also need to be taken into consideration.
- Some of the relations and dependencies reach into the *description* area, as chemical components, reaction types, and other

categorisations can be found here.
- The most important *process* element is the user's intention in this situation, otherwise known as "Refine the selected Reaction". This is normally determined by a user interface element being activated, for example, a menu item being clicked. The current activity type of "Extend the Flowsheet with Reaction Alternatives"—synthesising a model, in contrast to analysing a number of alternatives or deciding on one of them—is also part of the situation.

This situation definition can then be passed on to the Process Data Warehouse to search for matching experience information (item 3 in Figure 3). In the example scenario, several different realisations are found and returned. These include using or combining two different kinds of polymer reactors (Plug Flow Reactor [PFR], Continuous Stirred Tank Reactor [CSTR]). This information is then presented to the expert in the PDW client front-end, as visible in item 4. Two different visualisations can be applied here. A generic representation shows the concept instances, their attributes and relations in UML instance notation, while the specific representation in this case shows

Figure 4. The instances of the situation definition and their concepts

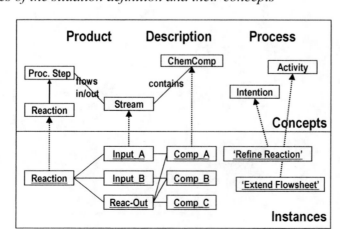

a graphical snapshot of the reactor equipments and their streams (see Figure 5).

Now the expert needs to decide which realisation to use. He may decide on reusing one of the alternatives offered. Then a method fragment inside PRIME is activated that directly executes the steps in the flowsheet editor which are needed to add the new refinement and to insert the selected alternative (see item 5). If he wants to create a new realisation, this can be done using the normal functionality of the flowsheet editor.

In any case, the solution is recorded in the Process Data Warehouse (item 6). Apart from the product information (the selected refinement alternative), the intermediate process steps and situations are traced and related to the decision that led to this alternative, including some additional arguments the expert may want to enter manually.

This is only a preliminary decision, as the chosen realisation still has to be analysed. The process-integrated flowsheet editor and the PDW also serve as the starting and integration points for simulation runs in the appropriate tool(s). After the simulation, the same cycle will have to be

repeated for other, alternative refinements. This is also supported by the flowsheet editor mentioned above. In the end, the expert can decide—and document—which of the alternatives should be kept for further steps in the development process. This might also include a cooperative discussion. In any case, the arguments entered earlier and the simulation results related to them will be needed for supporting the decision process here. This information is only kept in the PDW.

The repeated cycles of choosing a reactor realisation, furthermore simulating the realisation, documenting the results, and entering some notes or arguments, and the concluding decision making may be recognised as a single recurring method fragment, through analysing the process traces. In this analysis phase, the method engineer may decide to add a loosely modelled method fragment into the experience base that can be activated by the expert when facing this or a similar problem situation again, to guide him or her efficiently through these tasks.

A similar product reuse solution has already been realised in the area of plastics engineering. The 3-dimensional simulation of a section of

Figure 5. The specific (top) and the generic (bottom) visualizations of the search results

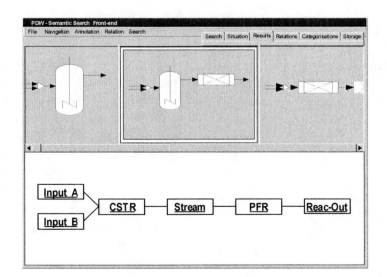

a compounding extruder has been process-integrated to support the expert in his decisions. Other aspects, like the visualisation and handling of multimedia-based simulation results and cross-organisational cooperation, have been treated there as well (Jarke, Miatidis, Schlüter & Brandt, 2004).

CONCLUSION AND OUTLOOK

In this paper, a traceability-based approach for supporting creative design processes has been described. By integrated and interrelated capture of the product and process artefacts of the work processes, their subsequent reuse as experience traces is enabled. The Process Data Warehouse (PDW) is constructed as a set of loosely connected ontology modules that are arranged around the four areas of the Core Ontology, namely products, processes, descriptions, and storage. Domain models and other extension are placed around the concepts of these four areas. Based on the PDW, information and computer science support for engineering design and development processes has been facilitated. The approach has been validated in a case study of designing a plant for the production of polyamide 6 (nylon) by hydrolytic polymerisation. The case study was successfully concluded as part of the Cooperative Research Centre IMPROVE.

During the case study, it has been found that common ontology languages lack essential features necessary for the projected functionality. Some simple aspects of meta modelling need to be integrated. Treating concepts as instances would also allow to relate concepts and instances, or to define attributes and their values on concepts. OWL-DL, as defined by the W3C standard, does not offer this functionality; OWL full does, yet reasoning on such models is no longer decidable (McGuiness & van Harmelen, 2004). Thus, a different platform like ConceptBase (see Jarke, Gallersdörfer, Jeusfeld, Staudt, & Eherer, 1995)

needs to be used as basis for the PDW repository.

For supporting similar processes in other domains, several extensions are being planned and under development. By adding methods for data acquisition, visualisation, and retrieval, an integrated view on different information sources is to be achieved. Among those, techniques of data mining are especially important to enable explorative data analysis. Also, document mining methods can be used to cluster large numbers of documents according to content similarities, and to integrate the resulting document and feature maps with the ontology-based view of the PDW. Thus, a multi-view-based user interface approach is created that is able to display, explore, and search the information according to different visualisation and usage paradigms.

Furthermore, the PDW is presently being extended and transferred by the authors into other industrial application areas, based on the experience gained in the described case study:

In plastics engineering, it has been found that certain kinds of continuous production processes for rubber profiles show characteristics similar to those of design processes. Today the operator is only able to efficiently start and control such a production line after having gained a lot of personal experience. Methods of automation control do not suffice. For the research presented here, these processes offer the advantage that process parameters and production quality can be automatically registered and measured quantitatively. Using the concepts and models of the PDW described in this paper, a system for supporting production operators driving such a production line is being installed. It is being evaluated at the site of the cooperation partner, Meteor rubber productions (Meteor, Bädje, Co, 2006). Apart from improving the work situation, the aim is to reduce the time spent in producing rejects, thus saving money and reducing environmental impact.

Two other research areas are being pursued based on applying this experience-based approach. The application scenario will be extended to include cross-organisational cooperation processes, positioned in the intersection of chemical engineering and plastics engineering design. As the protection of intellectual property is of utmost importance in any industrial application domain, a major topic is controlling the selective transfer of information following the principle of need-to-know.

Finally, in the domain of chemical engineering, the workflows of the full plant life cycle are going to be examined, from the design phase through plant operation, modifications and redesign or reengineering. The "freezing" and later restarting or continuing of design processes is also to be researched.

ACKNOWLEDGMENT

This work was supported by the German National Science Foundation (Deutsche Forschungsgemeinschaft, DFG) within the Collaborative Research Centre CRC/SFB 476 "Informatics Support for Cooperative Chemical Engineering - IMPROVE". Thanks are due to our colleagues from the project, and to our students who implemented the Process Data Warehouse and PRIME.

This is an extended version of the publication: Brandt, S.C., Schlüter, M., & Jarke, M. (2005). A Process Data Warehouse for Tracing and Reuse of Engineering Design Processes. In *Proceedings of the Second International Conference on Innovations in Information Technology (IIT'05)*, Dubai, United Arab Emirates, September 2005.

REFERENCES

Aamodt, A., & Plaza, E. (1994). Case-based reasoning: Foundational issues, methodological variations, and system approaches. *AI Communications, 7*(1), 39-59.

Basili, V.R., Caldiera, G., & Rombach, H.D. (1994). The Experience Factory. In J.J. Marciniak (Ed.), *Encyclopedia of software engineering, Volume 1* (pp. 469-476). John Wiley & Sons.

Basili, V.R., & Rombach, H.D (1988). The TAME project: Towards improvement-oriented software environments. *IEEE Transactions on Software Engineering, 146,* 758-773.

Bayer, B., & Marquardt, W. (2004). Towards integrated information models for data and documents. *Computers and Chemical Engineering, 28,* 1249-1266.

Bergmann, R. (2002). *Experience management* (LNAI 2432). Springer-Verlag.

Berners-Lee, T., Hendler, J., & Lassila, O. (2001). The Semantic Web—A new form of Web content that is meaningful to computers will unleash a revolution of new possibilities. *Scientific American, 17.*

Brandt, S.C., Schlüter, M., & Jarke, M. (2005). A process data warehouse for tracing and reuse of engineering design processes. In *Proceedings of the Second International Conference on Innovations in Information Technology (IIT'05)*, Dubai, UAE.

Conklin, E.J. (1993). Capturing organisational memory. In *Readings in groupware and computer-supported cooperative work: Assisting human-human collaboration* (pp. 561-565). San Mateo, CA: Morgan Kaufman.

Dowson, M., & Fernström, C. (1994). Towards requirements for enactment mechanisms. In *3rd European Workshop on Software Process Technology (EWSPT-3), LNCS 772,* Villard de Lans, France (pp. 90-106).

Documentum. (2006). *Enterprise content management.* EMC Corporation. Retrieved February 2006, from http://www.documentum.com/

Gao, J.X., Aziz, H., Maropoulos, P.G., & Cheung, W.M. (2003). Application of product data management technologies for enterprise integration.

International Journal Computer Integrated Manufacturing, 16(7-8), 491-500.

Grabowski, H., Lossack, R., & Leutsch, M. (2001). A design process model. In *Proceedings of the 3rd International Workshop on Strategic Knowledge and Concept Formation*, Sydney, Australia.

Humphrey, W.S. (1990). *Managing the software process.* Boston: Addison-Wesley Longman Publishing Co.

Jarke, M., Gallersdörfer, R., Jeusfeld, M.A., Staudt, M., & Eherer, S. (1995). ConceptBase—A deductive object base for meta data management. *Journal of Intelligent Information Systems, 4*(2), 167-192.

Jarke, M., List, T., & Köller, J. (2000). The challenge of process data warehousing. In *Proceedings of the 26th International Conference on Very Large Databases (VLDB)*, Cairo, Egypt.

Jarke, M., Lenzerini, M., Vassiliou, Y., & Vassiliadis, P. (2003). *Fundamentals of data warehouses* (2nd ed.). Berlin: Springer-Verlag.

Jarke, M., Miatidis, M., Schlüter, M., & Brandt, S. (2004). Media-assisted product and process traceability in supply chain engineering. In *37th Hawaii International Conference on System Sciences (HICSS)*, Big Island, Hawaii, USA.

Kim, Y., Kang, S., Lee, S., & Yoo, S. (2001). A distributed, open, intelligent product data management system. *International Journal of Computer Integrated Manufacturing, 14*(2), 224-235.

Marquardt, W., & Nagl, M. (2004). Workflow and information centered support of design processes—The IMPROVE perspective. *Computers and Chemical Engineering, 29*(1), 65-82.

McGuiness, D.L., & van Harmelen, F. (2004). *Web Ontology Language (OWL) overview* (W3C Recommendation). Retrieved February, 2006, from http://www.w3.org/TR/owl-features/

Meteor Gummiwerke K.H. Bädje GmbH&Co.KG. (2006). 31167 Bockenem, Germany. Retrieved February, 2006, from http://www.meteor.de

Münch, J., & Rombach, D. (2003). Eine Prozessplattform zur erfahrungsbasierten Softwareentwicklung. In M. Nagl, & B. Westfechtel (Eds.), *Modelle, Werkzeuge und Infrastrukturen zur Unterstützung von Entwicklungsprozessen* (pp. 93-106). Wiley-VCH.

Nagl, M., Westfechtel, B., & Schneider, R. (2003). Tool support for the management of design processes in chemical engineering. *Computers and Chemical Engineering, 27*(2), 175-197.

Pohl, K., Weidenhaupt, K., Dömges, R., Haumer, P., Jarke, M., & Klamma, R. (1999). PRIME: Towards process-integrated environments. *ACM Transactions on Software Engineering and Methodology, 8*(4), 343-410.

Ramesh, B., & Jarke, M. (2001). Toward reference models for requirements traceability. *IEEE Transactions on Software Engineering, 27*(1), 58-93.

Wagner, K., & Aslanidis, S. (2002). Prozessorientierte Nutzung von Erfahrungswissen in den frühen Phasen der Produktentstehung. In *Proceedings of the 4th Conference on Application of Knowledge Management in Industry and Public Administrations—Knowtech*, München, Germany.

Yang, A., & Marquardt, W. (2004). An ontology-based approach to conceptual process modelling. In A. Barbarosa-Póvoa, & H. Matos (Eds.), *European Symposium on Computer Aided Process Engineering, 14* (pp. 1159-1164). Elsevier.

This work was previously published in the International Journal of Intelligent Information Technologies, Vol. 2, Issue 4, edited by V. Sugumaran, pp. 57-76, copyright 2006 by IGI Publishing, formerly known as Idea Group Publishing (an imprint of IGI Global).

Chapter 5.10
The Impact of Sarbanes–Oxley (SOX) Act on Information Security Governance

Gurpreet Dhillon
Virginia Commonwealth University, USA

Sushma Mishra
Virginia Commonwealth University, USA

ABSTRACT

This chapter discusses the impact of Sarbanes-Oxley (SOX) Act on corporate information security governance practices. The resultant regulatory intervention forces a company to revisit its internal control structures and assess the nature and scope of its compliance with the law. This chapter reviews the organizational implications emerging from the mandatory compliance with SOX. Industry internal control assessment frameworks, such as COSO and COBIT, are reviewed and their usefulness in ensuring compliance evaluated. Other emergent issues related to IT governance and the general integrity of the enterprise are identified and discussed.

INTRODUCTION

Accounting scandals at some of the big corporations like Enron, HealthSouth, Tyco, and WorldCom had a devastating impact on investor confidence. Clearly, it was possible to engage in frauds of such magnitude because of the inability of auditors to detect early signs of such possibilities. In the case of Enron, an accounting loophole allowed the company to use gross instead of net value to calculate profits from energy contracts (Ackerman, 2002). Many shareholders lost their confidence in corporate reporting of company financial statements and generally in the integrity of the auditors. Issues such as lack of independence of auditors providing higher margin consulting services to audit clients, limited independence by corporate directors, increased use of stock options as a means of compensation, and inadequacy of the *generally accepted accounting principles* (GAAP) came to the fore.

The resultant crisis in the financial markets and massive media coverage of the frauds created a situation where government's interference was inevitable. The main reason cited, leading to such a situation, was a lack of accountability of top management to government and shareholders. Measures like assessment of internal controls on the part of corporations to restore investor confidence did not seem enough (Agarwal & Chadha, 2004). Investor protection needed radical changes in the legal system as form of assurance. Thus, the U.S. government intervened by passing the Sarbanes-Oxley Act in 2002.

This chapter reviews the impact of legal controls on *information technology* (IT) governance practices, especially in the case of the SOX Act. The chapter is organized into four sections. The first section describes the concepts of corporate governance, IT governance, and internal controls. A review of the definitions is followed by a rationale for good corporate governance practices. The next section discusses specific titles of SOX Act that impact IT governance practices. Interpretations of those areas of SOX that relate to increased importance of IT Governance are then presented and emerging issues associated with compliance with this law are identified and addressed. The concluding section presents a discussion of the future challenges and implications.

CORPORATE GOVERNANCE AND IT MANAGEMENT

Corporate governance, as defined by the *Certified Information Systems Auditor* (CISA) Review Manual (2004), is ethical corporate behavior by directors or others charged with governance in the creation and presentation of wealth for all stakeholders. The ethical issues of an organization are fostered through corporate governance practices. The practice of corporate governance is further defined by the *Organization for Economic Cooperation and Development* (OECD, 2004) as:

the distribution of rights and responsibilities among different participants in the corporation, such as board, managers, shareholders and other stakeholders, and spells out the rules and procedures for making decisions on corporate affairs. By doing this, it also provides the structure through which the company objectives are set and the means of attaining those objectives and monitoring performance. (in CISA Review Manual, p. 52)

Thus, corporate governance lays the ground for all other types of management functions focused on different areas of specialization, for example, IT governance.

Information Technology Governance

IT governance is a structure of relationships and processes to direct and control the enterprise to achieve its goal by adding value while balancing risk and return over IT and its processes (ISACA, 2004). The amount of investment in IT projects is seemingly high today. It has become increasingly important to clearly define the value derived from these investments and present justification to the shareholders. Effective management of IT and good IT governance practices do not necessarily have the same purpose. Though both these functions cater to the effectiveness of IT in an organization, there lies a subtle difference in the domain of each.

IT management has a much narrower focus and ensures effective supply of the IT products and services for operational efficiency. It is primarily concerned with the management of IT operations. IT management could be looked upon as a subset of the IT governance process. Successful implementation of a strategic IT project to meet the objectives of an enterprise is an example of good IT management techniques (Haes & Grembergen, 2004).

The domain of IT governance is much broader and concentrates on envisioning the IT requirements of the business in the future for strategic advantage and better performance. Deciding upon a strategic IT project to meet business goals, defining implementation techniques, and allocating optimal resources for effective management of IT projects could be examples of effective IT governance in use.

The objective of IT governance is to plan how the organization could meet its goals in the future through optimal use of IT resources. IT governance is concerned with objectives that focus on areas such as: alignment of IT with business, assessment of the value and benefit that IT provides to business, management of the risks associated with IT, and performance measures for IT services to the business (Anantha, 2004). This can be achieved by setting up IT governance frameworks with practices best suited for an organization. Corporate governance can be effectively implemented by having strong IT governance and a method of objective assessment and implementation of internal controls in a company. IT is the backbone of effective internal controls. Hence, internal controls play an important role in achieving a healthy corporate governance culture in an organization.

Role of Internal Controls

The importance of identifying, establishing, and maintaining the integrity of internal controls has been felt by organizations for a rather long period of time. It was the *Committee of Sponsoring Organizations of the Treadway Commission* (COSO) that first introduced a framework for assessing internal controls in 1992. Subsequently, other frameworks, such as *Control Objectives for Information and related Technology* (COBIT),

were developed and are now being extensively used by businesses.

Internal Control Objectives

Internal controls are a means to provide reasonable assurance that an organization will achieve its business objectives while avoiding undesired risks. Internal controls are policies, procedures, practices, and organizational structures put in place to reduce risks. At the heart of internal controls lies routinization of organizational processes. Any problem in the company ought to be corrected based on compliance or management- initiated concerns. Internal control activities and supporting processes are either manual or supported by computers. They operate at all levels in an organization and help in reducing risks involved at various stages of the operation, thus helping the organization reach its business objectives.

In 1992, the American Institute of Certified Public Accountants, the Institute of Internal Auditors, the American Accounting Association, the Institute of Management Accountants, and the Financial Executives Institute issued a jointly prepared statement. This authoritative document identified the fundamental objectives of any business unit (General Masters, Inc., 2004). Accordingly, objectives of internal control have to be achieved in three broad areas:

- Economy and efficiency of operations, including safeguarding of assets and achievement of desired outcomes. This comprises an entity's basic business objectives, along with performance and profitability.
- Reliability of financial and operational data and management reports.
- Well-guided compliance efforts directed to all laws and regulations.

The responsibility of implementing and monitoring these controls lies with the management of the firm. The board of directors and the senior executives of the organization establish an appropriate culture in workplace where each individual takes part in the control process. This can be achieved through effective and explicit communication of internal control objectives.

The internal control objectives are a statement of the desired result or vision that is to be achieved by implementing the control procedures in a particular activity. These objectives vary with functionalities implementing it. Some of the examples of these objectives could be:

- **Internal accounting controls**: These are primarily concerned with accounting operations, such as safeguarding assets and reliability of financial records.
- **Operational controls**: These objectives are directed at the daily operations, functions, and activities that ensure operations are meeting the business objectives of the firm.
- **Administrative controls**: These are concerned with operational efficiency in a functional area and adherence to management policies. They support the operational controls.

The effectiveness of internal control has been an ongoing debate across industries. Yet, there is no consensus on a common definition of the term among business executives, auditors, or regulators. Due to this prevalent ambiguity, executives have been able to define internal controls in manner convenient to them.

COSO

It is indeed difficult to assess the effectiveness of internal controls of different organizations, as each has its own standard definition. Organizations are different in many aspects: size, business philosophy, nature of the industry to which they belong, and corporate culture, to name a few.

With combination of such factors, each organization has a unique environment and thus different measures for effectiveness of its internal controls. To overcome these problems, the Committee of Sponsoring Organizations of the Treadway Commission framework was developed. Effectiveness of internal controls in business processes must be measured and evaluated to identify obstacles to success and quality. The COSO framework describes a unified approach for evaluation of the internal control system that a management designs to provide reasonable assurance of achieving the fundamental business objectives. The original COSO framework contains five control components that assure sound business objectives. These are:

1. **Control environment:** The control environment defines the tone of an organization and the way it operates, providing both discipline and structure. Organizations with effective control environments set a positive example from the "top management" and try to create integrity and control consciousness. The management sets formalized and clearly communicated policies and procedures, encouraging shared values and teamwork. This objective primarily provides the ethics, direction, and philosophy to the organization. It focuses on the integrity of the people in the organization and their competence. Management, through its human resources development practices, conveys these values. The standard set by the management is reflected in the ways in which it assigns responsibility and authority to employees. Basically, if the employees can align their value system with that of the organization and see their future with it, then management is successful in passing down its core values to employees. As Ramos (2004) puts it, "The control environment is the foundation for all other components of internal controls and provides discipline and structure" (p. 29).

2. **Risk assessment:** Through the process of risk assessment, management identifies the potential threats that can prevent it from meeting business objectives. Management should be aware of the possible risks involved in business, identify them, and analyze the likelihood and impact of these risks on the business. It is management's discretion to decide how risk averse it is and also to determine how these tolerance levels can be achieved. Organizations are vulnerable to various kinds of risks because they are in a state of flux in a dynamic environment. Thus they need mechanisms to identify and deal with risks resulting from such changes. An organization is anchored to its mission and goals through objective setting.

3. **Control activities:** These include the operationalization of policies and procedures that are created and established to show management's intention of addressing all the risk elements. Such activities cover the entire organization, at different levels and different functionalities. These could include activities like approvals, authorizations, verifications, and segregation of duties, to name a few. Essentially, these activities fall under any one of the three objectives: operational, financial reporting, and compliance. Whatever the nature of the activities, there has to be awareness and responsibility among the people who undertake the tasks. Ethical consideration of these responsibilities cannot be documented. These activities are usually less formal or structured in small organizations, and in some cases, there may be no need for certain activities due to the direct involvement of the manager, owner, or CEO. Nevertheless, the intent of such activities is that these must exist to provide the system of checks and balances necessary for effective internal control.

4. **Information and communication:** Computer-based systems are required to run an enterprise because they produce reports containing operational, financial, and compliance information. These systems contain internally generated data as well as information about external events, developments, and conditions required for informed decisions. Surrounding the control activities, there should be systems in place that can capture and communicate relevant information in a timely manner and help in ensuring integrity of the internal controls. Information thus obtained could be critical to the processes of conducting, managing, and controlling the operations of the organization. To facilitate the communication process, there should be adequate open channels for information flow. These channels are needed to reinforce the message to personnel that internal control responsibilities are a priority and should be taken seriously (Steinberg & Tanki, 1993). It is the responsibility of the management to clearly articulate the role of each individual in the internal controls system and the way it impacts other activities in the company.

5. **Monitoring:** In today's Internet age, the pace and rate of change of information needs of an organization is fast. Thus to perform effectively all systems must be evaluated to ensure that they are performing as intended, particularly internal control systems. This kind of monitoring can be accomplished either by ongoing checks and balances that occur during normal operations or through separate evaluations by management, often with the assistance of the internal audit function. The extent of ongoing monitoring usually determines the need for separate evaluations. When deficiencies in internal control are discovered, they should be reported immediately to higher management levels in the organization, including the board of directors if the need arises, for appropriate remedial action to be taken. In such cases, management should obtain input from third

parties, such as the external auditor or those not part of the internal control systems.

A detailed understanding of the COSO framework does not guarantee that a complete assessment of effective internal controls system would be possible. The COSO framework, however, does highlight the importance of identifying and managing risks across the enterprise. A newer version of the COSO framework is now available that consists of eight components. In addition to the existing five controls, three new controls have been added. These are: objective setting, event identification, and risk response.

Measuring the effectiveness of internal control is a difficult task since it is an ongoing process. Three primary business objectives and the eight COSO components needed to achieve those objectives constitute the internal control framework. To evaluate the effectiveness of the controls, it is necessary to know the intent of having a control in the first place. "Elements of controls that should be considered when evaluating control strength include whether the controls are classified as preventive, detective, or corrective in nature" (ISACA, 2004, p. 30). Given the particular nature of the control, its effectiveness can be determined.

COBIT

Strong IT support is required to effectively manage the internal controls. Even though companies realize the importance of the general IT controls, they need formal guidelines for effective IT governance. To address this requirement, Control Objectives for Information and related Technology have been created. It is a rich, robust, and the most widely used IT governance framework. This framework is considered a standard across industries for developing and maintaining IT controls. It is positioned to be more comprehensive for management, as it is at a higher level than

technology standards for information systems management.

The idea behind the COBIT framework is that information is needed to support business objectives and requirements. Companies should be able to assess the nature and extent of IT controls required to integrate their internal control objectives. Basically, it is important for a company to demonstrate how its IT controls support COSO and whether IT controls are appropriately documented in all COSO components.

In COBIT, control objectives are defined in a manner consistent with COSO. It is a process-oriented framework following the concept of business reengineering. COBIT is comprised of four domains, 34 IT processes or high-level control objectives, and 318 detailed control objectives. A control objective has been identified and the rationale to link the document to business objectives has been provided at all identified processes and domains. It is a comprehensive framework for managing risk and control of information and related technology. COBIT 3rd edition, released in 1996, is the latest version available.

COBIT was developed to align IT resources and processes with business objectives, quality standards, monetary controls, and security needs. COBIT is composed of four domains:

1. **Planning and organization:** This domain covers the strategic importance of IT and assesses how IT would be best able to meet business objectives. It reaffirms the importance of planning and organizing effectively for the company's strategic vision to be realized. To achieve this, a proper technological infrastructure is required.

2. **Acquisition and implementation:** In this domain, the importance of methods and tools to bring strategic goals to the operational level is highlighted. IT solutions have to be developed or acquired to meet the objectives and integrated with the business process.

Continuous improvement in existing systems and its maintenance is the goal in this domain.

3. **Delivery and support:** This domain considers the delivery of required services for proper functioning of the systems as its core function. To deliver services, necessary support processes must be set up to help in processing data or support application controls.

4. **Monitoring:** This domain monitors all IT processes for their quality and compliance with control requirement. Continuous monitoring ensures that all the controls are in place and working effectively. It also addresses any oversight on behalf of management in control process.

Each of these domains has a series of sub-domains that extensively cover all the control points for governance. The relationship of COSO with IT-control guidelines like COBIT has to be understood properly to achieve the goals of effective internal control. Figure 1 shows the relationship between COSO and COBIT objectives.

COBIT assumes three levels of IT efforts when considering the management of IT resources. At the lowest level, there are activities and tasks required to achieve measurable results. The next level is defined by processes, which are a series of joined activities or tasks where controls can be placed. At the highest level, processes are naturally grouped together to form domains. These domains are in alignment with the management cycle or life cycle applicable to IT processes. This conceptual framework of three levels can be approached from three vantage points: information criteria, IT resources, and IT processes.

Figure 1.

COBIT Control Objectives	COSO Component				
	Control Environment	Risk Assessment	Control Activities	Information and Communication	Monitoring
Plan and Organize (PO)					
Define a strategic IT plan.		•		•	•
Define the information architecture.			•	•	
Determine technological direction.					
Define the IT organization and relationships.	•			•	
Manage the IT investment.					
Communicate management aims and direction.	•			•	•
Manage human resources.	•			•	
Ensure compliance with external requirements.			•	•	•
Assess risks.		•			
Manage projects.					
Manage quality.	•		•	•	•

continued on following page

Figure 1. continued

Acquire and Implement (AI)					
Identify automated solutions.					
Acquire and maintain application software.			•		
Acquire and maintain technology infrastructure.			•		
Develop and maintain procedures.			•	•	
Install and accredit systems.			•		
Manage changes.			•		
Deliver and Support (DS)					
Define and manage service levels.	•		•		•
Manage third-party services.	•	•	•		•
Manage performance and capacity.			•		
Ensure continuous service.			•		•
Ensure systems security.			•	•	•
Identify and allocate costs.					
Educate and train users.	•			•	
Assist and advise customers.					
Manage the configuration.			•	•	
Manage problems and incidents.			•	•	•
Manage data.			•	•	
Manage facilities.			•		
Manage operations.			•	•	
Monitor					
Monitor the processes.				•	•
Assess internal control adequacy.					•
Obtain independent assurance.	•				•
Provide for independent audit.					

THE SARBANES-OXLEY ACT

The Sarbanes-Oxley Act is the popular name for the *Public Company Accounting Reform and Investor protection Act*. By a nearly unanimous vote in July 2002, the U.S. Congress passed this law, which has been termed as most radical redesign of federal securities laws since the 1930s. This 131-page law is intended to protect investors by improving the accuracy and reliability of corporate disclosures and plugging loopholes in existing stocks and securities laws. SOX was enacted in response to public anger at accounting fraud and corporate governance failures. It mandates that companies use stringent policies and procedures for reporting financial information accurately and timely. These mandates break new ground in the fight against corporate fraud and require a wide variety of information technologies to sustain compliance in perpetuity. To ensure compliance, violators of any rule of the U.S. *Security and Exchange Commission* (SEC) issued under this act may face civil or criminal sanctions.

Even though SOX is a U.S. law, it has international implications. International companies with offices in the U.S. must comply with its requirements (Nash, 2003). SOX impacts European companies, many of which are dually listed on exchanges in Europe and the U.S. or have subsidiaries headquartered in the U.S. Specifically, Section 106 of the Act states that its jurisdiction includes any foreign public accounting firm that prepares or furnishes an audit report to a publicly traded U.S. company. Volonino, Kermis, and Gessner (2004) note:

Key to achieving sustainable compliance with SOX is an IT infrastructure that satisfies mandated levels of internal control, corporate governance, and fraud detection. Compliance will require seamless integration of properly implemented and documented information systems (IS). Data passed from events and transactions to financial statements must be controlled — and preserved so as to not destroy the details. (p. 1)

The Security and Exchange Commission rule for SOX Section 404 mandated that a company's internal control over financial reporting should be based upon a recognized internal control framework. The SEC recommends COSO as the model of choice for ensuring that proper internal controls are in place.

The Act called for the formation of a powerful *Public Company Accounting Oversight Board* (PCAOB). It significantly alters corporate and accounting requirements in six important areas: (1) auditor oversight, (2) auditor independence, (3) corporate responsibility, (4) financial disclosures, (5) analyst conflicts of interest, and (6) civil and criminal penalties for fraud and document destruction (Anderson & Black, 2002).

Auditor oversight has often been cited as a common source of error in accounting records. This act does not allow companies to get away with such mistakes. Auditor involvement at every stage of assessment of business effectiveness is mandatory according to SOX. Auditors' independence has also been emphasized in this act. Companies should check the internal controls and report as part of compliance.

Firms must be able to produce unaltered e-records and other documents in a timely manner when summoned by PCAOB (Patzakis, 2003).

The corporation is responsible for assuring that ethical practices are followed by the corporation and that information shared with outsiders is accurate and trustworthy (Coates, 2003). The financial disclosures made by companies should be checked, verified by auditors, and attested by top management. Endorsement of the reports by top management is a unique feature of this act, and this exercise is intended to increase investor confidence in the financial reports of the company. Any endeavor to manipulate data or transactions by analysts, therefore, is under the direct scrutiny of top management. This reduces analysts' conflict of interests and they are forced to present correct and accurate picture of the company's finances. Any negligence in financial reporting could result in criminal or civil charges against the company. This helps to ensures ethical practices.

Sarbanes-Oxley Sections Impacting IT

Internal Controls: Title III–Corporate Responsibility

Section 302. Corporate Responsibility for Financial Reports applies to financial statements and related financial information. It requires CEOs and CFOs to certify ("sign") the following in each annual and quarterly report filed with the SEC:

- that the report has been reviewed; and
- that, to the best of their knowledge, the report does not contain an untrue statement or omit any material fact.

This means that the report fairly presents the issuer's financial condition and results of operation. The CEOs are responsible for establishing and maintaining internal controls and have designed *disclosure control procedures* (DCP) in such a way that all material information relating to the issuer and its consolidated subsidiaries is made known to them during the reporting period. The section ensures that the CEOs have evaluated the effectiveness of internal DCP within the 90 days prior to the report and that the report reflects their conclusions about the effectiveness their DCP as of that date.

It implies that they have disclosed to the company's auditors and to the audit committee all significant deficiencies in the design or operation of internal controls, as well as any fraud–whether or not material–that involve management or other employees who have a significant role in the issuer's internal controls. It also implies that there have been no significant changes in internal controls that could affect statements in the future. If there are such changes, then the type and importance of such changes must be reported (Coffee, 2002).

Internal Controls: Title IV–Enhanced Financial Disclosures

Section 401. Disclosures in Periodic Reports requires the company to disclose "all material off-balance sheet transactions, arrangements, obligations (including contingent obligations) and other relationships" that might have a "material current or future effect" on the financial health of the company. As per this section, each annual report of the company must include management's opinion regarding the effectiveness of the issuer's internal control procedures and a description of management's role in establishing and maintaining those procedures.

Section 401 restricts the use of pro forma information. This section states that information contained in a public company's reports must be "presented in a manner that reconciles it with the financial condition and results of operations of the issuer under generally accepted accounting principles."

Section 404. Management Assessment of Internal Controls is another primary thrust of SOX. Most companies focus on Section 404 because it requires that CEOs and CFOs certify the effectiveness of the financial controls they have in place (Hoffman, 2003). It requires a new disclosure document referred to as an *internal control report*. An internal control report, which is also included in every annual report, must "state the responsibility of management for establishing and maintaining an adequate internal control structure and procedures for financial reporting" [Section 404(a)]. Management assessment of "the effectiveness of the internal control structure and procedures of the issuer for financial reporting," which the audit firm must "attest to and report on" [Section 404(b)], should also be included.

Section 404 addresses the design and operational effectiveness of financial reporting controls of the organization by making it mandatory that internal control processes, procedures, and practices must be documented and tested. The SEC maintains that the purpose of Section 404 is to provide investors and others with reasonable assurance that companies have designed processes to help ensure that transactions are properly authorized, recorded, and reported (Gallagher, 2003), and that assets are safeguarded against unauthorized or improper use. As such, the intent of Section 404 is to prevent fraud and demonstrate adequate control.

Section 409. Real Time Issuer Disclosures requires companies to disclose any event that may have a material impact on their financial condition or operations on a "rapid and current basis." While what is meant by *timely* has yet to be defined, it might be as soon as 48 hours after an event. This section states that disclosure may need to "include trend or qualitative information and graphic presentations, as the Commission determines . . . is necessary or useful for the protection of investors and in the public interest."

Corporate Governance: Title IX–White Collar Crime Penalty Enhancements

Section 906. Corporate Responsibility for Financial Reports holds CEOs, CFOs, and corporate directors both accountable and liable for the accuracy of financial disclosures. In contrast to Section 302, Section 906 penalties apply only if the officer knows of the problem or error when certifying a report. According to this section, certifying a report while being knowledgeable that it does not meet the requirements of this section results in a fine of up to $1,000,000, or imprisonment for not more than 10 years, or both. Willfully certifying a statement not meeting the requirements results in a fine of up to $5,000,000, or imprisonment of not more than 20 years, or both.

Fraud and Records Retention: Title VIII – Corporate and Criminal Fraud Accountability

Section 802. Criminal Penalties for Altering Documents applies to the retention and protection of corporate audit documents and related records, including e-records. This section establishes new criminal penalties for document alteration and destruction. Section 802 imposes a fine and/or imprisonment of up to 10 years for noncompliance of any accountant who conducts an audit of a publicly traded company. Auditors are required to maintain all audit and review work papers for at least five years.

Procedures for preserving e-records that comply with SOX requirements are needed since they will be subject to greater scrutiny. This legislation demands proper e-records management, particularly when they could be used for electronic evidence.

EMERGENT ISSUES

SOX came into effect in 2004, with the larger companies having to show compliance by November 2004. The issues that arise from enactment of the law are manifold. The primary challenge to IT companies today is driven by SOX compliance. The Act is exerting tremendous pressure on IT organizations to attest to the control of IT processes related to financial reporting. Only recently has the daunting scope of these requirements become apparent to them, and a majority of IT organizations are struggling to cope with these overwhelming compliance demands. These new responsibilities add significant effort to the already daunting IT business management challenges — pressure on IT to drive more business value, lower costs, and maintain high-service levels. The IT approach to SOX compliance could typically include the following actions:

- The IT division of the company should work with the CFO or Sarbanes Steering Committee to understand the specific business processes determined to be within Sarbanes' scope.
- The IT team should identify the related computerized applications directly impacting the business processes. This would lead to a proper documentation of the processes.
- Management should also understand the control requirements of the firm's external financial attestation auditors on what is called the "acceptable IT general controls."
- IT managers should identify the specific IT general control components that impact the significant computerized applications (i.e., security).
- Management should identify and document those control techniques that achieve the objectives of the IT general controls components.
- The IT division should identify deficiencies in the control environment and/or com-

pensating controls on the business process end to enhance the control environment as needed.

- IT managers should test the IT controls identified to ensure their functionality and operating effectiveness.

The requirements of the act, such as enhanced disclosure of off-balance sheet items and necessity for companies to present pro forma "operating" earnings reconciled to GAAP earnings, are necessary steps toward eliminating some of the techniques that unscrupulous corporate executives have used to mislead investors. While useful, these provisions are only patching holes in the financial reporting process rather than dealing with any underlying structural issues. The commitment of the directors to the financial issues of the company in ways that are ethical and moral is important for the success of SOX.

The act commissions the study of potential impact of a shift from rules-based to principles-based accounting standards. Rules-based accounting standards are filled with specific details in an attempt to address as many potential contingencies as possible. This has made standards longer and more complex. Under these standards, there is provision for arbitrary criteria for accounting treatments that allows companies to structure transactions to circumvent unfavorable reporting. Thus companies can present financial reports in a way desirable to them.

Principles-based accounting is inherently more flexible. It provides a conceptual basis for accountants to follow instead of a list of detailed rules. It is expected that it would better enable financial reporting to evolve and keep pace with new financial instruments and techniques. It would require more judgment calls by auditors and management, as it is well known that investors' desire for a more consistent application of accounting principals is what led to the proliferation of transaction-oriented rules to provide implementation guidance to management. GAAP is a principles-

based system. In addition, principles-based accounting standards allow accountants to apply professional judgment in assessing the substance of a transaction. This approach is substantially different from the "checkbox" approach common in rules-based accounting standards.

The Sarbanes-Oxley Act will create new avenues of concern for organizations having to cope with pressures to improve the quality of information for the sake of compliance in the coming years. The tools for automatic control mapping, evaluating online and real-time control functioning will greatly facilitate compliance. It will fuel further research to meet the demands of the law. There are numerous research issues emerging from these challenges, including behavioral factors for facilitating collaborative policy development and technological factors for automating data flows (Volonino et al., 2004). Some of these avenues could be: process simplification and standardization, data simplification and standardization, technology standardization and integration. The Act can impact various aspects of IT, and thus many emergent issues would have to be dealt with as the understanding of the legislation improves with time. Some of the areas that would need attention in future by the companies could be:

- **Data integrity and electronic records retention policy:** SOX links e-record management accountability between internal and external record managers in a supply-chain fashion — as electronic data interchange (EDI) and e-commerce link data, documents, and records in commercial transactions. "This chain-of-accountability imposes several requirements" (Volonino et al., 2004, p. 6). Some of these responsibilities could be deployment of e-record storage methods to make sure that organizational knowledge is documented and preserved. The companies are required to develop more reliable and verifiable means for e-record management and retrieval techniques than are available today. This could be a potential area of concern for companies in future.

- **Integrity of communications:** In order for the compliance objectives to be effective, there has to be a better way of communicating faster and reliably through electronic medium. This could help in faster reporting of problems in data security, thus helping to prevent future frauds. Research into how to reduce exposure of critical data and how to prepare to respond to e-record requests (or demands) by the oversight board is urgently needed. This area needs further exploration.

- **Process/work flows:** Real-time update of information could be a challenge for the companies. Recording each and every transaction and retrieving the information at a short notice would need a lot of system planning and reorganizing. Creating reports from transactions and showing quarterly compliance is also a daunting task. Thus interdependencies among transactions and processes (including where transactions start and stop) must be identified. Technologies are needed to specify what can go wrong in data processing, where controls are needed, how to prevent and detect control problems, and who is responsible for monitoring the controls. Section 404 of the Act requires organizations to test and document processes and procedures designed to prevent fraud and demonstrate adequate control. This area needs future attention from companies showing compliance.

- **Disaster recovery practices and security policies:** Information security assurance policies in companies would be a critical area to look into in the future. Disaster recovery policies need to be made transparent to outsiders who can become potential stakeholders of the company. To show compliance, companies need to develop and deploy effective information security threat response and investigation policies. Those policies will require collaboration between corporate IT security teams and IT auditors. Methods to identify policy requirements and facilitate collaboration need to be devised.

- **Improved anti-fraud techniques across industries:** Data integrity has been a main thrust of SOX. Systems employed to control, record, and report data have to ensure that no manipulation has been done. New systems to meet this demand have to be developed. "Data passed from events and transactions to financial statements must be controlled — and preserved so as not to destroy the details essential for fraud detection" (Volonino et al., 2004, p. 6). In order to detect fraud, the computer systems of the company must be capable of linking both the sales estimates and sales reality to the financial function. If we simply look at historic accounting information, it will be difficult to detect fraud, much less detect it before another financial report is issued. Methods for IS integration and fraud detection are needed, as well as an understanding of the nature and warning signs of fraud. This could be a potential area of concern and has to be addressed by the corporations.

- **Rigorous checking for effectiveness of internal controls:** Managers should address the design and operating effectiveness of internal controls. In doing so, internal controls will be tested. Top management should encourage this practice. The nature of testing that has to be done to check the effectiveness of internal controls depends on the computer-based systems of the company and type of control being validated. It is important to note that testing must be done to establish a basis for management's conclusion. Simply asking whether controls are adequate is not sufficient. This suggests an active role for senior management in evaluating IT and audit processes. Involvement of top management will revive research into systems to facilitate horizontal and vertical communication throughout the organization.

- **Cost of compliance:** The cost of compliance to companies is overwhelming. In an annual survey of compliance in IT by businesses, the estimated cost of compliance for the year 2006 is more than $6.0B, almost equal to the amount spent in 2005 which was $6.1B (Hagerty & Scott, 2005). This could be detrimental for small companies since they will be unable to justify the benefits of the act against the cost of compliance. Some of the small publicly traded companies have gone private just to avoid this cost. Besides the monetary aspects, other cost in terms of time invested by company personnel or effort (in form of traveling and explaining control areas in their branch offices all across the globe) are placing significant demands on the resources of companies. This could be a concern if the companies have to keep paying so much for compliance.

CONCLUSION

SOX has created challenges and set new standards for IT governance in companies. To fully comply with the law, companies will need to improve information quality to insure transparency and reliability. Investors (individual or institutional) are outsiders for the most part and can only rely on the good faith of corporate insiders for insight into effectiveness of the companies. To protect such investors, SOX attempts to legislate ethics and integrity into the public management process.

Government's determination to increase corporate responsibility has ushered in new legislation that impacts IT directly. With increased disclosures, new enforcement schemes, and emphasis on corporate accountability, SOX delivers significant reforms and places significant demands on IT. The Sarbanes-Oxley Act has the potential to reshape the role of IT in business. The role of IT governance, within the broader context of corporate governance, demands new attention and efforts on the part of the executives, shareholders, and government.

Improvement in technology to meet the requirements would be a driving factor to make the law successful. Technology, such as enterprise resource planning systems, has the potential to meet such demands. Other upcoming technologies like XML, especially the XBRL and XBRL-GL derivatives, could provide firms with the possibility of cost-efficient, online, real-time systems (Alles, Kogan, & Vasarhelyi, 2004). These facilities could help in posting the financial statements on the Web as soon as they are completed. The last recorded corporate transactions, contracts, and commitments in process could be made available to public through the company's Web site even prior to their realization in traditional accounting.

Compliance with legislations like SOX would appear to be a necessary condition for corporate responsibility, but it is insufficient. Public policy merely addresses the manifestations of corporate social pathology. Top executives will have to set an example to other employees in the company by sticking to good corporate practices. A law cannot make people moral or ethical in behavior.

In today's scenario, the organizational dynamics have reasonably changed from what they were even 20-25 years ago, and the dependency of the organizations on technology has been accelerating. Management practices have to be flexible in terms adopting new technologies. Making use of new technologies for corporate governance practices is cost effective for the companies in the long run. Currently, there is much apprehension about this legislation and it would not be surprising if SOX, like many other complicated laws, has unforeseen results that will dampen the spirit of introducing this law (Alles et al., 2004).

Sarbanes-Oxley was created to restore investor confidence in public markets. This Act has literally rewritten the rules for accountability, disclosure, and reporting of good corporate governance. Ethical practices are no longer optional. The responsibility of making this Act a success lies with the managers and auditors of each and every firm. Such legislation can act as a watchdog, but morality cannot be legislated.

REFERENCES

Ackman, D. (2002, January 15). Enron the incredible. *Forbes.com.* Retrieved February 22, 2004, from http://www.forbes.com/2002/01/15/0115enron_print.html

Agrawal, A., & Chadha, S. (2004). Corporate governance and accounting scandals. AFA 2004 San Diego Meetings. *Journal of Law and Economics* (forthcoming 2005).

Alles, M., Kogan, A., & Vasarhelyi, M. (2004). The law of unintended consequences? Assessing the costs, benefits and outcomes of the Sarbanes-Oxley Act. *Information Systems Control Journal, 1*, 17-20.

Anantha, S. (2004). Auditing governance in ERP projects. *Information Systems Control Journal,* (2),19.

Anderson, P. J., & Black, A. R. (2002, October 23). Accountants' liability after Enron. *S&P's: The Review of Securities & Commodities Regulation, 35*(18), 227.

Coates, B. E. (2003). Rogue corporations, corporate rogues & ethics compliance: The Sarbanes-Oxley Act, 2002. *Public Administration and Management, 8*(3), 164-185.

Gallagher, S. (2003, August 1). Gotcha! Complying with financial regulations. *Baseline Magazine.* Retrieved November 29, 2005, from http://www. baselinemag.com/article2/0,3959,1211224,00. asp

General Masters, Inc. (2004). *COSO framework and Sarbanes Oxley* [Electronic Version]. Retrieved July 2, 2005, from http://www.gmasterinc. com/coso/cosomain.htm

Haes, S., & Grembergen, V. (2004). IT Governance and its mechanisms. *Information Systems Control Journal, 1*.

Hagerty, J., & Scott, F. (2005). SOX spending for 2006 to exceed $6B. *AMR Research.* Retrieved November 29, 2005, from http://www.amrresearch.com/content/view.asp?pmillid=18967

Hoffman, T. (2003). Users struggle to pinpoint IT costs of Sarbanes-Oxley compliance. *Computerworld,* December 1. Retrieved November 29, 2005, from http://www.computerworld. com/managementtopics/management/itspending/story/0,10801,87613,00.html

Information Systems Audit and Control Association (ISACA)(2004). *CISA Review Manual, 2004 Edition.* Rolling Meadows, IL: ISACA.

La Porta, R. et al. (2000). Investor protection and corporate governance. *Journal of Financial Economics*, 58, 3-27.

Nash, E. (2003, November 7). Compliance must be top of your agenda. *Computing,* 33.

Organisation for Economic Cooperation and Development (OECD) (2004). *Principles of corporate governance.* Paris: Organisation for Economic Cooperation and Development.

Patzakis, J. (2003, Spring). New accounting reform laws push for technology-based document retention practices. *International Journal of Digital Evidence, 2*(1), 1-8.

Ramos, M. (2004, September/October). Just how effective is your internal control? *The Journal of Corporate Accounting and Finance*, 29-33.

Steinberg, R., & Tanki, F. (1993). Internal control-integrated framework: A landmark study. *The CPA Journal Online*. Retrieved November 29, 2005, from http://www.nysscpa.org/cpajournal/old/14465853.htm

Volonino, L., Kermis, G., & Gessner, G. (2004, August 5-8). Sarbanes-Oxley links IT to corporate compliance. In *Proceedings of the Tenth Americas Conference on Information Systems*. New York: Association for Information Systems.

Chapter 5.11
Privacy Implications of Organizational Data Mining

Hamid R. Nemati
University of North Carolina at Greensboro, USA

Charmion Brathwaite
University of North Carolina at Greensboro, USA

Kara Harrington
University of North Carolina at Greensboro, USA

ABSTRACT

Technological advances and decreased costs of implementing and using technology have allowed for vast amounts of data to be collected, used and manipulated for organizations to mine. If correctly deployed, Organizational Data Mining (ODM) offers companies an indispensable decision-enhancing process that optimizes resource allocation and exploits new opportunities by transforming data into valuable knowledge (Nemati & Barko, 2001). These tools have the potential to significantly reduce a company's costs by helping to identify areas of potential business, areas that the company needs to focus its attention on or areas that should be discontinued because of poor sales or returns over a period of time. However, this information, if used in the wrong context, can be very harmful to an individual. As a result, ODM may "pose a threat to privacy" in the sense that discovered patterns can reveal confidential personal attributes about individuals. This paper examines a number of issues related to the privacy concerns that are inherent with the use of ODM.

PURPOSE OF ODM

Companies' interactions with their customers have changed dramatically over the years. There is no longer the guarantee of a customer's loyalty. Factors such as niche marketing, the decreased attention spans of customers, the availability of alternative products as well as others complicate the situation even more. "Your customers are not your customers. You are merely their caretaker until one of your competitors can provide and communicate a better offer" (Berson et al., 1997). As a result, many companies have realized that in order to remain competitive, they need to understand their customers better and to quickly respond to their customers' wants and needs. To succeed, these companies must anticipate customer desires, satisfy these desires and, at the same time, encourage continued business.

Gone are the days where the shopkeeper would simply keep track of all of his customers in his head, and would know what to do when a customer walked into the store. Today shopkeepers are faced with a much more complex situation: more customers, more products, more competitors and less time to react. Thus, understanding customers is now much harder to do. Also, in this new technology age, with businesses moving at "Internet speed," uncertainty over a business' sustainability has increased significantly: Competition is global, and businesses are trying to minimize costs while customers and prospective customers want to negotiate their own terms. To remain competitive in this environment involves using the best tools available that will allow the company to take care of customers better than its competition. As a result, both the customer and the company will benefit from the successful analysis and determination of customer needs. The customer will be satisfied that he/she is being served in a timely manner, and the company will reduce costs associated with providing products or services that are of little interest to the customer. Improved customer service and reducing costs, exemplify the importance of collecting data for analysis.

TECHNOLOGY IMPROVING DATA MINING

Technological advances and decreased costs of implementing and using technology have allowed for vast amounts of data to be collected, used and manipulated for data mining. Traditionally, data collection was done manually through market surveys conducted by companies. This data was then summarized and categorized for use by the company to assess their clientele's needs. The questions usually focused on the usage of particular products and comparisons to competitors' products. Because these surveys tended to be anonymous (at least initially), consumers had few, if any, reservations about providing data. By analyzing sales records (provided either through the stores or directly from salespeople) companies knew which areas had greater sales and which needed additional marketing or support to increase market share. This type of analysis, however, tended to be long and laborious producing large volumes of paperwork because almost everything was done manually.

With automation, work became more efficient and less labor intensive. Vast amounts of data could be processed in shorter time spans so analyses became more accurate and up-to-date. As transaction processing became more automated, it became easier for companies to collect and store vast amounts of transactional data on their customers. The cost of data storage also decreased further fueling the data collection frenzy. The data was stored for future analysis in repositories or databases called data warehouses.

With increasing use of the Internet, especially for online purchasing, companies are able to collect this data instantaneously and track users' movements with or without their knowledge.

The advent of the Internet and the associated explosive growth in databases has thrust business intelligence into the forefront of many corporate technology initiatives — from internal business reporting to direct marketing to Web traffic analysis. For the modern organization, business intelligence, often defined as the process of turning raw data into insightful, consumable pieces of information, has never been more prevalent throughout organizations than it is today. (MicroStrategy, www.microstrategy.com, 2001)

Data that the user previously had the option of providing could now be collected without the user's permission. This new data, called clickstream data, adds a new dimension to the individual profile. Companies can now track user interests and can target their marketing campaigns directly at the user before purchases are even made. Clickstream data is obtained from Web sites as the user/consumer browses. It is an important source of data collection for the data warehouse because of its detailed nature. It allows companies to better complete the customer profile because companies can integrate Web-based data with traditional data. Due to its large volume, this data can be very difficult to sort through in order to determine valuable information. There are many tools available that make sorting through this clickstream data easier. These tools provide extraction, transformation and load facilities to combine the desired data from the clickstream with the traditional data. The clickstream data dimensions are combined with traditional data dimensions for analysis in data marts/warehouses. The most important sources of the clickstream data are query strings and cookie fields, which are used to gather customer data. Clickstream data, however, can be collected from many other Internet sources through background processes built into the technology. Technology also automates the mining process, presenting it in a relevant way for business users. The data warehouse is the foundation of and the means for data integration

that leads to a strategic data usage (Berson et al., 1997). Data mining techniques are applied to the cleaned and rationalized data stored in a data warehouse, which can lead to effective customer relationship management.

There are a number of different ODM techniques (Nemati & Barko, 2001). The first method utilizes statistics. Statistical techniques are driven by the data and are used to discover patterns and build predictive models. Through regression analysis a model is created that maps values from predictors, so that the fewest errors occur when making a prediction.

Two of the oldest techniques, clustering and the nearest neighbor prediction, are often used in data mining. Clustering is described as the grouping or clustering of like records together. Clustering is usually done to give the end user a high-level view of what is going on in the database. It can also mean segmentation, which is useful to marketing people for coming up with a birds-eye view of the business. Sometimes, however, clustering is performed not so much to keep records together, but to make it easier to see when one record sticks out from the rest. These "outsiders" could spark new areas of business or can help identify failing areas of the business. When clustering is used in business, the clusters are often dynamic, changing weekly to monthly, and decisions concerning which cluster a record should be placed in can be difficult. The nearest neighbor technique is quite similar to clustering. In order to predict what a prediction value is in one record, the nearest neighbor method looks for records with similar predictor values in the historical database and uses the prediction value from the record that is "most similar" to the unclassified record. The nearest neighbor prediction algorithm works in very much the same way except that nearness in a database may consist of a variety of factors, such as where a person lives or their gross income. Nearest neighbor techniques are among the easiest to use and understand, because they work in a way similar to the way that people think by detecting closely matching examples. They also perform quite well in terms of automation, because many of the algorithms are robust with respect to dirty data and missing data. Finally, they are particularly adept at performing complex return on investment (ROI) calculations because the predictions are made at a local level, where business simulations could be performed in order to optimize ROI. Because they enjoy similar levels of accuracy compared to other techniques, the measures of accuracy, such as lift, are as good as from any other technique (Berson et al., 1997).

As its name implies, a decision tree is a predictive model that can be viewed as a tree. Each branch of the tree is a classification question, and the leaves of the tree are partitions of the data set with their classification. Because of their tree structure and capability to easily generate rules, decision trees are the favored technique for building understandable models. Because of this clarity, they also allow for more complex profit and ROI models to be added easily in on top of the predictive model (Berson et al., 1997).

Neural networks have probably been of greatest interest through the formative stages of data mining technology. True neural networks are biological systems (that is, they function like human brain) that detect patterns, make predictions and learn. The artificial neural networks are computer programs that implement sophisticated pattern detection and machine-learning algorithms on a computer to build predictive models from large historical databases. Artificial neural networks derive their name from their historical development, which started off with the premise that machines could be made to "think," if scientists found ways to mimic the structure and functioning of the human brain on the computer. Neural networks are very powerful predictive modeling techniques that can be applied to a variety of different types of problems, but some of the power comes at the expense of ease-of-use and ease-of-deployment, since it requires all of the predictor values to be in numeric form. The output of the neural network is also numeric and needs to be translated if the actual prediction value is categorical. Neural networks, however, are used in a wide variety of applications. They have been used in all facets of business, from detecting the fraudulent use of credit cards and credit risk prediction to increasing the hit rate of targeted mailings. They also have a long history of application in other areas: the military (for the automated driving of an unmanned vehicle at 30 miles per hour on paved roads) and biological simulations (learning the correct pronunciation of English words from written text).

Rule induction is one of the major forms of data mining and is a common form of knowledge discovery in unsupervised learning systems. It represents the idea of "mining" for gold through a vast database. The gold, in this case, would be a rule that is interesting — a rule that tells you something about your database that you did not already know and probably were not able to explicitly articulate. Rule induction on a database can be a huge undertaking, where all possible patterns are systematically pulled out of the data, and then accuracy and significance are added to them to tell the user how strong the pattern is and how likely it is to occur again. In general, however, the rules that are "mined" are relatively simple.

ODM is defined as leveraging data mining tools and technologies in an organizational context to acquire and maintain a competitive advantage (Nemati & Barko, 2001). ODM techniques have had widespread appeal and are implemented in most industries around the world. If correctly deployed, ODM offers companies an indispensable decision-enhancing process that optimizes resource allocation and exploits new opportunities by transforming data into valuable knowledge (Nemati & Barko, 2001). These tools have the potential of significantly reducing a company's costs by helping to identify areas of potential business, areas that the company needs to focus its attention on or areas that should be discontinued because of poor sales or returns over a period of time. ODM, therefore, helps the decision makers make informed, and hopefully timely, decisions on where the business should be. It provides facts or information that can help the company focus or direct the company along the most profitable path, and, at the same time, provide better management and service to customers.

FOOD FOR THOUGHT

Whereas the idea behind using this information to target advertising specifically to suit the needs of the consumer is advantageous, this information, if used in the wrong context, can be very harmful to an individual. Focused marketing saves a company money they would have otherwise spent on general, blanket advertising, and the return on investment would be minimal. The information obtained from tracking user preferences allows the company to utilize targeted advertising. The company knows beforehand that the consumer is interested in a particular product, so they target the customer with a product that they are more likely to purchase, increasing the opportunity for a sale. For example, Amazon.com uses this technique for recommending books to readers based on their previous purchases; Blockbuster Entertainment uses it to recommend video rentals to individual customers based on their rental history and American Express uses it to suggest products to its cardholders based on an analysis of their monthly spending patterns (Information and Privacy Commissioner, 1998).

This technique is not only beneficial to retailers' suppliers can also use the data to their advantage. For example, Wal Mart captures point-of-sale transactions from over 2,900 stores in six countries and continuously transmits this data to its massive 7.5 terabyte data warehouse. Wal Mart allows more than 3,500 suppliers to access data on their products and perform data analyses. These suppliers use this data to identify customer buying patterns at the store-display level. They use this information to manage local store inventory and identify new merchandising opportunities (Information and Privacy Commissioner, 1998).

However, because companies collect data from so many different sources, not all of the data may be correct and/or available, and, as companies substitute default values for data not available, the individual profile may become skewed and produce undesired results. For example, a company may purchase a list of consumers that are likely to buy a particular product. If that data is inaccurate, the company could end up wasting resources targeting unlikely consumers. There are all kinds of stories of pets, children, etc., receiving marketing information that they cannot possibly act upon. Differences in culture and legal requirements can also influence results. What may be acceptable in one culture may have the completely opposite effect in another. In light of the recent terrorist attacks, an inaccurate profile could have legal ramifications, as well as influence public perception, and have an adverse affect on opportunities available to that person. What financial, emotional and social affects would occur if someone was inaccurately profiled as a terrorist? Data mining "poses a threat to privacy, in the sense that discovered patterns classify individuals into categories, revealing in that way confidential personal information with certain probability. Moreover, such patterns may lead to generation of stereotypes, raising very sensitive and controversial issues, especially if they involve attributes such as race, gender or religion. An example is the debate about studies of intelligence across different races" (Estivill-Castro, Brankovic & Dowe, 1999).

In this new economy, it is not uncommon for a company's data to be a major asset. The existing market of personal data postulates that the gathering institution owns the data. Thus, many companies, such as the Gartner Group, base their business on the sale of data and related information. The sale of data, in this case, can be a good revenue earner; however, there can also be some negative outfall from its sale. In 1989, the Californian Department of Motor Vehicles earned over $16 million by selling the driver-license data of 19.5 million Californian residents. A deranged man used this data to obtain the home address of actress Rebecca Schaeffer and killed her in her apartment. The sale of driver-license data ended after this tragedy. In 1990, Lotus Development Corp. announced a release of a CD-ROM with the data on 100 million U.S. households. The data was so detailed that it generated strong public opposition, and Lotus abandoned the project. However, this mostly affected small business, as large companies already had access and continued to use Lotus data sets. At least 400 million credit records, 700 million annual drug records, 100 million medical records and 600 million personal records are sold yearly in the U.S. by 200 superbureaus. Among the records sold are bank balances, rental histories, retail purchases, criminal records, unlisted phone numbers and recent phone calls. When combined, this information provides data images of individuals that are sold to direct marketers, private individuals, investigators and government agencies (Estivill-Castro et al., 1999). A company may choose not to sell the data and only use it internally. They may have a privacy policy that protects a consumer's personal data; however, if the company files bankruptcy, then the asset (data) can be sold to satisfy debt obligations. The consumer whose data has been collected has no control over the use of the data once it is sold. Concerns about informational privacy generally relate to the manner in which personal data is collected, used and disclosed. When a business collects, discloses or uses data without the knowledge or consent of the individual to whom the data relates, the individual's privacy may be violated (Information and Privacy Commissioner, 1998).

Regulations

Consumers are concerned about the collection and use of their personal data (FTC survey, 1998). They are concerned that the data will be manipulated (data mined), and the resulting information will be used in ways that may be detrimental to them. For example, medical information located in databases has been accessed by persons who were able to mine the data and combine it to identify individuals' private medical data and contact information. A Florida abortion clinic sued Compuserv for providing access to a database that allowed users to mine information. The users were able to compile personal data to create a list of clinic patients along with their contact information, such as addresses and telephone numbers (obtained from driver's license data). A pro-life supporter used the information to contact many of the clinic's patients. This egregious violation of individual privacy resulted in a lawsuit and the database base being shut down (CNET News Staff, 1999). Legislators are aware of the need to update current laws and create new ones to accommodate changing technology and to protect personal privacy.

LAWS AND ENFORCEMENT

Data mining and accompanying technologies have advanced at a rapid rate and have outpaced legislation designed to protect consumers. The Federal Trade Commission (FTC) is the primary federal agency responsible for the enforcement of various laws governing the privacy of an individual's information on the Internet. The FTC Act (FTCA), 15 U.S.C. § 45(a), gives the FTC investigative and enforcement authority over businesses and organizations engaged in interstate commerce. While waiting on the enactment of new legislation, the FTC utilizes existing laws to protect consumers from unfair and deceptive trade practices. The FTC has allowed most businesses to self-regulate. However, the government has regulated some industries, such as healthcare and financial services. They also require Web sites to follow specific rules when obtaining information from children.

Health information is subject to Health Insurance Portability and Accountability (HIPPA) Act of 1996. The original legislation went into effect in 2001, and the final modifications take effect in April 2003. The act applies to health information created or maintained by health care providers who engage in certain electronic transactions, health plans and health care clearinghouses. The Office for Civil Rights (OCR) is responsible for implementing and enforcing the HIPPA privacy regulation (OCR Web site, 2002). The act sets standards to protect privacy in regards to individuals' medical information. The act provides individuals access to their medical records, giving them more control over how their protected health information is used and disclosed and providing a clear avenue of recourse if their medical privacy is compromised (HHS, 2002). Data miners must take care not to violate this regulation, or they will face stiff penalties, which may include fines and/or imprisonment.

Financial information is routinely minded to improve customer service and marketing and to increase an organization's bottom line. It is essential that this data be adequately protected from fraudulent use. The illegal and fraudulent use of financial information is widespread, causing harm to individuals and opening the organization and individual(s) responsible for the lapse in security to liability for the damage and hardship caused for not adequately protecting personal financial data. Financial information is subject to the Gramm-Leach-Bliley Act (15 U.S.C. §§ 6801 et seq.). The act requires financial institutions to protect data collected from routine transactions (i.e., names, addresses and phone numbers; bank and credit card account numbers; income and credit histories; and social security numbers). Financial institutions must develop a written information

security plan that describes their program to protect customer information. All programs must be appropriate to the financial institution's size and complexity, the nature and scope of its activities and the sensitivity of the customer information at issue (FTC, 2002). Experts suggest that three areas of operation present special challenges and risks to information security: employee training and management: information systems, including network and software design; information processing, storage, transmission and retrieval and security management, including the prevention, detection and response to attacks, intrusions or other system failures. The rule requires financial institutions pay special attention to these areas (FTC, 2002).

Special care must be taken when dealing with information obtained from children. The Children's Online Privacy Act of 1998 (COPPA) (15 U.S.C. §§ 6501 et. seq.) governs the online collection of personal information from children under the age of 13. The regulation requires that Web sites get parental consent before collecting personal data from children. Web sites are also required to post a privacy statement detailing what information will be collected, how it will use that information, if it will make the information available to third parties and a contact at the site. When utilizing data mining, one should be aware of how the data to be used for mining was obtained. The user can be held responsible for utilizing data that was illegally obtained. This is not limited to solely to children and pertains to all data.

The FTC would like to see self-regulation of industries. However, if businesses don't effectively comply with the FTC, the agency is prepared to step in and apply existing laws to protect consumers. FTC Chairman Robert Pitofsky, on July 21, 1998, stated that, "new laws may be needed to eliminate concerns raised by the online collection of personal information. ... While some industry players may form and join self-regulatory programs, many may not. ... This would result in a lack of uniform privacy protections that the Commission believes are necessary for electronic commerce to flourish. The Commission believes that unless industry can demonstrate that it has developed and implemented broad-based and effective self-regulatory programs by the end of 1998, additional governmental authority in this area would be appropriate and necessary" (Consumer Privacy on the World Wide Web, 1998). The FTC proposed the following four fair information practices that Web sites collecting information on consumers should comply with:

Notice and Awareness: notify consumers of their data collection practices and how they use the information.

Choice and Consent: online users must be given the choice and give permission regarding how their data is used.

Access and Participation: consumers must have "reasonable" access to their data to be able to correct inaccuracies.

Security and Integrity: sites must take "reasonable steps" to ensure the security and integrity of the data they collect.

These regulations were prescribed to protect the privacy of personal information collected from and about individuals on the Internet, to provide greater individual control over the collection and use of that information and other purposes. However, how well these self-regulatory programs work is very questionable. In the space of six months, TRUSTe, a nonprofit privacy initiative, had three of its licensees — RealNetworks, Microsoft and Deja News — investigated for privacy violations. In 1998, just the year before, yet another TRUSTe licensee, Geocities (now owned by Yahoo Inc.), settled with the FTC after being cited for improperly collecting data from children under 13 (Lemos, 1999a). Organizations, such as TRUSTe, provide Web site owners with seals once they meet certain criteria relating to consumer privacy. Sites qualify for the seals by agreeing to post their privacy policies online, and

allowing the seal providers to audit their operations to ensure they're adhering to the policy. When violations are discovered, TRUSTe and other privacy services "come in after the fact and say what the company did was bad, but they don't do anything to solve the problems," said Richard Smith, an independent Internet consultant, who has uncovered several of the worst incidences of online privacy infringement (Lemos, 1999b). Can the consumer really trust that his or her privacy is being protected? Is the government really doing enough? Can they do more? The government is enacting regulations and is trying to monitor the situation, but it is unclear when, if ever, the legislation will be able to keep pace with the technology.

New Legislation: The Patriot Act

The events of September 11, 2001, have led to new legislation designed to help the authorities combat terrorism. The Patriot Act (Uniting and Strengthening America by Providing Appropriate Tools Required to Intercept and Obstruct Terrorism Act, H. R. 3162, Oct. 24, 2001) covers a broad range of topics including: wiretapping and intelligence surveillance, criminal justice, student privacy, financial privacy and immigration. The legislation increased law enforcement's powers, lowered the burden of proof needed for searches and surveillance and decreased checks and balances that protect individual rights and privacy.

Both the surveillance provision in the 'Patriot' Act and Attorney General Ashcroft's new domestic spying guidelines opens up the very real prospect that the FBI will return to the pre-Watergate days, when political dissenters ranging from Dr. Martin Luther King to average largely unknown Americans, were routinely spied on or had their lives disrupted. (Steinhardt, 2002)

Due to the Patriot Act, the government has been given easier access to individuals' records.

These records could be personal, such as medical, educational, mental health, as well as financial. All the FBI needs to do to gain access is to certify that the records may be relevant to an investigation. The FBI will undoubtedly be collecting more data than it has in the past, and the government will be more active in applying data mining technology in the hunt for suspected terrorists. The government is actively investing in data mining, providing research grants and leading the effort to increase the ability of technological tools to be used for law enforcement and surveillance:

...the tool that probably has the most potential to thwart terrorism is data mining. Think of it as a form of surveillance that casts its eye on computer networks. (Businessweek, 2001)

Governmental Use of Data Mining and Surveillance Tools

Technologists will need to assist investigators with the current technology and develop new or improve current data mining tools. The U.S. government utilizes some very powerful surveillance tools. There are legitimate concerns regarding accuracy of data and privacy of the material these tools produce. This material is often the subject of analysis using data mining or other techniques. It is imperative that those who utilize data mining and other technologies be aware of the potential abuses and limitations of the technology. The concern is that if the tools are blindly relied upon, then costly mistakes could occur, such as missing something vital to national security and perhaps allowing another attack or the guilty to go free, or, on the other hand, wrongly accusing an innocent person.

The chasm between pre- and post-September 11, 2001 views on privacy and what is acceptable government intrusion into our lives is significant. What was once unacceptable is now, not only being considered, but also being implemented. Judicial requirements for searches and wiretapping are being lessened and in some instances virtually removed. The idea of "Big Brother watching us" has become more real as technological advances provide the tools to conduct surveillance (Carnivore, Echelon, facial recognition software, etc.). There were considerable concerns regarding the use of surveillance tools by privacy advocates prior to the terrorist attacks. The government, judiciary and law enforcement struggled to keep up with the technological changes, and the debate raged on about how and what could be monitored. This changed substantially after September 11, 2001. There are still many concerns with privacy and civil liberties; however, a shift towards security and increasing law enforcement power has occurred. The government is allocating resources to improve its technology and change legal procedures to allow them to conduct investigations appropriate for the technology. Data mining is a key technology that will undoubtedly be utilized for national security purposes. The government has several tools in its arsenal to obtain personal data for mining. It is important for those using data mining techniques to understand how the data is obtained. They should ask questions such as: Was the data legally obtained? Was it taken in violation of an individual's privacy? What context? The results of the data mining could have a profound effect on an individual, or society as a whole, if the predictions, relationships or correlations are not accurate. In our current environment of heightened tensions, the data miner should be aware of the possibility of abusing the additional powers granted to law enforcement and violating individuals' right to privacy.

Government Tools

The government has a number of tools for electronic eavesdropping. They are reluctant, of course, to share how these tools work beyond basic concepts. The most prominent of these tools are Carnivore (DCS 1000), Data Interception by Remote Transmission (DIRT), Echelon and Transient Electromagnetic Monitoring Pulse Standard (Tempest). There are serious concerns for proper oversight to be maintained when utilizing these technologies so that abuses do not occur. There must be a balance between the individual's rights and national security. It is essential for those who will be conducting analysis to understand the issues surrounding the collection of data. The analysts and technologists will be part of this process and must be aware of the legal, privacy, security and ethical concerns, and also the ramifications their results may have on individual lives.

Carnivore

The FBI developed Carnivore to monitor the Internet for illegal activity. The FBI describes Carnivore as a software-based tool that examines all Internet IP packets on an Ethernet and records only the packets with very specific parameters. These parameters refer to the data, which is subject to lawful order, and disregards communications that are not allowed to be intercepted. The FBI refers to this as Carnivore's "surgical ability" to intercept and collect data. Prior to September 11, the FBI stated that law enforcement needed to get high-level authorization from the Department of Justice (DOJ) to apply for judicial approval for the use of Carnivore. They also point out that there are significant penalties for those who misuse the system. However, there are concerns about the FBI's description and implementation of Carnivore. Since it is a secretive tool, the FBI will not disclose the source code or how the system actually works. How do we know that its "surgical ability" works? Can it really discern and separate communications approved by the court from those that are not allowed? Who will oversee law enforcement to make certain there is no misuse? Is the intercepted data secure? Are businesses willing to allow the FBI to install unknown software on their systems?

The DOJ requested an independent technical review of Carnivore, which was conducted by the Illinois Institute of Technology Research Institute (IITRI). The DOJ's own review (only the draft was available) stated that Carnivore does not adequately protect the data it is intercepting. Academics and technical personnel from AT&T Laboratories, University of Pennsylvania, SRI International and Purdue University reviewed the IITRI's report. Their paper entitled, "Comments on the Carnivore System Technical Review" identified several concerns with the DOJ report and its results. The review summed up its results in the following statement: "Unfortunately, serious technical questions remain about the ability of Carnivore to satisfy its requirements for security, safety and soundness" (Illinois Institute of Technology, 2000).

Aside from technical concerns, there were other issues addressed by the reviewers. They were troubled by the fact that a single agent determines what data is collected and deleted. (This seems to contradict the FBI's "surgical ability" to separate communications.) Also, the FBI states that Carnivore is not intended to collect all data, but the researchers disagreed with that characterization. They also questioned the FBI's reliance on the "pen register statute" — the law that allows agents to obtain the phone numbers a suspect has called — as the basis of using Carnivore to capture e-mail headers. "The statute falls short of such use because headers could reveal the correspondence of two parties not included in a search warrant, if they carbon copy a third, suspected, person" (Lemos, 2000).

DIRT

DIRT has the ability to monitor and intercept data from any Windows PC in the world. This tool is only available to law enforcement and military. The DIRT Bug operates as a Trojan horse and sneaks inside a Windows PC by an attachment, macro or program. Once inside the system, it allows law enforcement complete control of the system without the user's knowledge. It has the ability to track each keystroke and transmit logs to law enforcement monitoring the PC. When the PC is online, it will invisibly behave like an anonymous File Transfer Protocol (FTP) server, giving the monitor 100 percent access to all resources on the targeted computer (Schwartau, 1998). Encrypted files can be opened because DIRT is able to capture passwords and decrypt the files. The manufacturer, CODEX Data Systems, claims that if you have a PC at home there is very little you can do to keep DIRT out (Schwartau, 1998).

Echelon

Echelon is a satellite surveillance system developed during the Cold War, primarily by the U.S. and Great Britain. The UKUSA Alliance also includes Canada, New Zealand and Australia. Individual states in the UKUSA Alliance are assigned responsibilities for monitoring different parts of the globe, providing surveillance coverage of the entire earth. They achieve this coverage by using satellites, ships, planes, radar and communication-interception sites located around the world. It is believed that Echelon has the capability to intercept every international telephone call, fax, e-mail and radio transmission. The fact that Echelon can intercept any phone conversation, e-mail, etc., is impressive, but what is more remarkable, is that they can make sense out of it all. Imagine all the telephone conversations that occur everyday and in every language. How does any agency sift through that amount of data and produce worthwhile results and useful data?

"The UKUSA states have positioned electronic-intercept stations and deep-space satellites to capture all satellite, microwave, cellular and fiber-optic communications traffic. The captured signals are then processed through a series of supercomputers, known as dictionaries that are programmed to search each communication for targeted addresses, words, phrases or even individual voices" (Goodspeed, 2000). It is mind boggling to conceptualize the amount of data these

computers must sift through to identify keywords and identify pertinent data. Echelon must utilize incredibly powerful data and knowledge mining tools to accomplish this task. The data compiled naturally contains data outside of the scope (searching for terrorists) of the original search. This data may contain confidential economic or private matters, and the temptation will exist to inappropriately use this data.

Echelon is very powerful and has the capability of being incredibly intrusive. This has prompted cautious comments regarding proper oversight from members of the government. A primary concern is how can there be proper oversight on a secretive system. Sen. Frank Church was quoted as saying:

...the capability at any time could be turned around on the American people and no American would have any privacy left, such is the capability to monitor everything: telephone conversations, telegrams, it doesn't matter. There would be no place to hide. If this government ever became a tyranny, if a dictator ever took charge in this country, the technological capacity the intelligence community has given the government could enable it to impose total tyranny, and there would be no way to fight back ... I don't want to see this country ever go across that bridge ... we must see to it that this agency and all agencies that possess this technology operate within the law and under proper supervision, so that we never cross over that abyss. That is the abyss from which there is no return. (Poole, 1999/2000)

Concerns are justified due to prior abuses of the system. The following are examples of past inappropriate usage of Echelon:

Mike Frost, a former Communications Security Establishment employee and author of Spyworld, which is about his career in Canada's secret service, claims that as far back as 1981 Canada was using its U.S.-produced spy technology to *eavesdrop on the American ambassador to Ottawa. In one instance, Canadian spies managed to overhear the ambassador discussing a pending trade deal with China on a mobile telephone and used that data to undercut the Americans in landing a $2.5-billion Chinese grain sale.* (Goodspeed, 2000)

On another occasion, in 1983, Mr. Frost says British intelligence officials invited their Canadian counterparts to come to London to eavesdrop on two British cabinet ministers whose political loyalty was doubted by Margaret Thatcher, then the British prime minister. Since it would have been illegal for British officials to do the surveillance themselves, they had the Canadians do the job using eavesdropping equipment in the Canadian embassy. After three weeks of snooping, the Canadians quietly turned over all their findings to the British, Mr. Frost says. (Goodspeed, 2000)

After the end of the cold war, the concerns of other nations, especially in the European Union (EU) focused on whether Echelon was being used for economic espionage or to violate individual rights. The EU commissioned reports regarding Echelon in 1997 and, again, in 2001 to first prove Echelon's existence and then to consider the economic ramifications of the system on their industries. Although its existence has been known for years, it has not been officially sanctioned. This system was established to spy on other countries, particularly the former Soviet Union. The EU report found evidence of Echelon and routine U.S. spying and interception of communication between firms. The U.S. justifies this eavesdropping by stating that they are trying to combat bribery.

The U.S. operation is believed to be run by the National Security Agency (NSA). The NSA does admit it collects intelligence but says it does not violate individual citizen's rights in the U.S. or abroad. The privacy issue is tricky because laws generally only protect individuals of a particular

state. Therefore, the EU would like to see rules established to protect against industrial and economic espionage and assure individuals right to privacy. The NSA's position regarding surveillance is that they provide the U.S. government with valuable intelligence data on terrorism and narcotics and weapons trafficking, stating that, because of the intrusive nature of their job, they are subject to strict regulations and oversight from different governmental bodies. In light of recent events and expanded governmental powers, the question that arises is of the degree of oversight and what is the proper balance between individual rights and national security.

Tempest

Tempest is a classified government program, based on the knowledge that all electronic devices emit low-level electromagnetic radiation that can be remotely captured and later displayed. Compromising emanations radiate from many sources including computer monitors, tape drives, scanners, printers and power cables, which can be captured. There is no way to detect Tempest surveillance, and it is unclear whether a court order would be needed to collect Tempest data.

The NSA has some limited data regarding the tool on their Web site, which confirms the existence of the tool. The NSA did not disclose if, how or which agencies use this tool.

OTHER AREAS OF CONCERN

Wiretapping and Intelligence Surveillance

The role of a judge in wiretapping is to ensure that surveillance is conducted legally and with proper justification. This role is now minimized. Under the new legislation, Foreign Intelligence Surveillance Act (FISA) surveillance can be used in a criminal investigation. FISA authority had been reserved for matters of national security. Internet tools, such as Carnivore, can be utilized with a lower burden of proof to obtain a court order. Searches can be conducted without probable cause. A pen register or trap and trace order can be obtained by law enforcement by simply certifying that it is relevant to an ongoing investigation.

Criminal Justice/Legal Concerns

The government can request to keep searches secret. In the past, they were required to notify those subjects of the search.

The government can now share data between agencies without guards for future use or dissemination of that information. The data included can be obtained from wiretaps and other searches. Once that data is spread out among agencies, it is difficult to recall. Who else will have access to it? How long will it be available? Who is responsible for certifying accuracy of the data or error correction and updating data among agencies? As it stands now, there are no measures in place to address these concerns. This data would be a prime candidate for data mining by combining data from these different sources and evaluating it. For these results to be credible, it is essential to use accurate and up-to-date data.

Proposal of a National Identification Card

A national identification card was proposed, but quickly rebuffed by many diverse factions because it raised concerns about the potential of the card to collect vast amounts of personal data. Although it does not have enough support currently, it is still on the table as an option.

Why not have an ID card? Many other countries have national ID cards. In our political culture, the thought of being tracked by an ID number or card and listed in an official registry (database) is not appealing. This may appear to be a contradic-

tion because we have Social Security numbers and are often tracked by them. However, having an official registry and a database that can track our actions is a frightening thought to many. Some questions that should be considered when discussing the viability of adopting a card are: What data would be required?; Who would have access?; and Would the card include a computer chip capable of tracking use.

In Malaysia the government is issuing a "multipurpose card" for their citizens. The card will include a computer chip (smart chip). The chip will allow the card to be used as a driver's license, cash card, National Health Service card and a passport (*Businessweek*, 2001).

This will allow the Malaysian government to track an incredible amount of data on each citizen. In the U.S., if a card was enabled with a smart chip and the data stored in a database, how long would it take before other government agencies or companies would want to tie into the database? The Social Security number is a prime example. It was originally intended for tax purposes, but over time, other government agencies, health care providers and companies began using it as an identifier. The number's usage is so widespread that even simple transactions require a person to give his Social Security number. For example, it is common when applying for video store membership that a person will be asked to supply her Social Security number. The video store has no legal right to require it, but it is so commonplace that most people supply it without even thinking it inappropriate.

There are additional concerns that would also need to be addressed such as: cost, fraud (counterfeiting and identity theft), the potential threat of tracking and monitoring people's actions and movements (internal passports), the establishment of a data base of all Americans, increased harassment and discrimination (non-native looking people would be asked at greater rates to provide their card) and, most importantly, would it solve the problem it was developed for: the prevention of terrorism.

CONCLUSION

The gathering of data for data mining purposes was initially an attempt by companies to learn as much as possible about their customers so that they could provide customized or personable service and increase sales. The development and use of computer/data technology helped speed this process, as it made the gathering and analyzing process easier. However, recent developments have caused individuals to lose control over that data about them. As technology advanced, the tools became more invasive and thorough and accuracy increased. It is possible that this data, available to anyone (individuals, businesses, governments), can be manipulated in such a way as to produce an in-depth profile of an individual or group.

Concerns have arisen regarding the use of data mining, because an individual has to interpret the results and data and knowledge gained can be taken out of context. For example, if Echelon picked up a phone conversation where a person stated they are picking up a kilo of Columbian, someone would have to determine what that would mean. Are they trafficking drugs or picking up coffee? Individuals have their own preconceptions and bias, which must be acknowledged and taken into consideration when interpreting and analyzing data. Profiles may be misleading, for example, in many countries military service is obligatory for certain individuals. These countries may also have a state religion. An innocent person could easily be considered suspect, because they fit some predetermined profile of a terrorist by having military experience and religious ties.

The U.S. government utilizes some very powerful surveillance tools to gather data. There are legitimate concerns regarding accuracy of data and privacy of the material these tools produce. The data mining technology is limited and can

produce inaccurate results. What is the cost of a mistake? Is it a type-one or type-two error? What if you wrongly accuse an innocent person or allow a guilty person to go free? What percentage of accurate results is acceptable? Is an 85 percent accuracy rate good? If you are sending out a flyer or picking a stock, then yes it is. If you are deciding if a person should be questioned and possibly detained by the police, is that percentage still acceptable? What if you are one of the 15 percent wrongly accused? What are the implications? (Under the Patriot Act, if the accused is an immigrant, they may be detained indefinitely.) These are questions that must be seriously considered. The end users of the technology must understand these concerns and the limitation of the technology they employ.

There are serious concerns that current technology and technology being developed will allow governments extraordinary abilities to monitor their citizens. There is a legitimate concern that "Big Brother" has arrived. Proper oversight and usage is essential to limit abuses:

All of these technologies are built on ones and zeros so it is possible to blend them together — just as TV's computers, video games, and CD players are converging — into one monster snooping technology. In fact, linking them together makes each one exponentially more effective. Unifying the various surveillance systems makes sense from a technological standpoint, and there is likely to be strong pressure, once the tools are in place to try to make them work better. It is useful to keep this scenario in mind, if only as a warning beacon of some of the hazards ahead. Left unchecked, technologists could create a nearly transparent society," says David J. Farber, a pioneering computer scientist who helped develop the Net. "All the technology is there," he says. "There is absolutely nothing to stop that scenario — except law." Surveillance can be checked by laws that require regular audits, that call for citizens to be notified when they are investigated and that give people the right to correct data collected about them. That's the best way of guaranteeing in our efforts to catch the next terrorist, we don't wind up with Big Brother instead. (BusinessWeek, 2001)

Concerns about surveillance tools were abundant prior to September 11, since then they have lessened with the understanding that the technology will be used for national security. However, the new legislation increasing law enforcement and governmental powers are not limited solely to terrorism. In our rush to protect ourselves, we must be certain not to trample on individual rights in such a way that we regret it in the future. The balance between individual rights vs. national security should be carefully weighed. Those mining data obtained by business or governmental surveillance tools need to consider how the data is obtained, its accuracy and the limitations of the tools. They must be especially aware of the potential use of their analysis. Reliance on inaccurate results could have profound effects on individuals or our society as a whole.

REFERENCES

Berson, A. & Smith, J. (1997). *Data warehousing, data mining, and OLAP*. McGraw-Hill.

Computer Professionals for Social Responsibility. (2001, May). *Privacy and civil liberties*. Retrieved December 2002 from http://www.cpsr.org/cpsr/privacy.

Estivill-Castro, V., Brankovic, L., & Dowe, D. L. (1999, August). *Privacy in data mining*. Retrieved October 15, 2002 from Australian Computer Society—NSW Branch at: http://proxy-mail.mailcity.lycos.com/bin/redirector.cgi?c lass=1&url =http%3a%2f%2fwww%2eacs%2eorg%2eau% 2fnsw%2farticles%2f1999 082%2ehtm&uuid=13 622&partner_key=mailcity"\t"newwin"—http:// www.acs.org.au/nsw/articles/1999082.htm.

Federal Trade Commission (FTC). (2000, May). *Privacy online: Fair information practices in the electronic marketplace*. Retrieved Fall 2001 from the FTC website: http://ftc.gov/bcp/conline/pubs/alerts/safealrt.htm.

France, M., Green, H., Kerstetter, J., Black, J., Salkever, A. & Carney, D. (2001, November 5). Privacy in an age of terror. McGraw-Hill. *BusinessWeek*, 83-91.

Goodspeed, P. (2000, February 19). The new space invaders spies in the sky. *National Post Online*. Retrieved Fall 2001 from http://www.fas.org/irp/program/process/docs/000219-echelon.htm.

Illinois Institute of Technology (2000, December 3). *Comments on the carnivore system technical review*. Retrieved November 27, 2001 from http://www.crypto.com/papers/carnivore_report_comments.html. Section 2.

Information and Privacy Commissioner/Ontario. (1998, January). *Data mining: Staking a claim on your privacy*. Retrieved October 18, 2002 from http://www.ipc.on.ca/english/pubpres/papers/datamine.htm#examples.

Lemos, R. (1999a, November 2) *Can you trust TRUSTe?* Retrieved October 14, 2002, from ZDNet News at http://zdnet.com.com/2100-11-516377.html?legacy=zdnn.

Lemos, R. (1999b, October 31). *RealNetworks rewrites privacy policy*. Retrieved October 14 from ZDNet News at http://zdnet.com.com/2100-11-516330.html?legacy=zdnn.

Lemos, R. (2000, December 4). *Experts: Carnivore review limited*. Retrieved Fall 1999 from www.zdnet.com.

Macavinta, C. (1999, January 6), CNet News Staff. (1999, January 8). *Florida clinic sues Compuserv*. Retrieved October 15, 2002 from http://news.com.com/2100-1023-219927.html?tag=bplst.

Magouirk, J. (2001, September 18). *Partners in*

privacy. Intelligent Enterprise MicroStrategy. *Investor information.* Retrieved from http://www. microstrategy.com.

Microstrategy (2001, Fall). http://www.corporate-ir.net/ireye/ir_site.zhtml?ticker=mstr@script=100.

National Broadcasting Company. (1975, August 17). *Meet the press.* Washington DC: Merkle Press. Quoted in *Puzzle Palace, 477.*

Nemati, H. R., & Barko, C. D. (2001, Winter). Issues in organizational data mining: A survey of current practices. *Journal of Data Warehousing, 6*(1), 25-36.

Online Discussion. (2002, June 19). Steinhardt, *Homeland Security and Digital Privacy.* Retrieved from www.washingtonpost.com/wp-srv/technology/transcripts/archive_steinhardt_061902.htm.

Prepared Statement of the Federal Trade Commission (1998, July). *Consumer privacy on the World Wide Web.* Retrieved September 16, 2002 from the FTC website. http://www.ftc.gov/os/1998/9807/privac98.htm.

Safeguarding customers' personal information: a requirement for financial institutions. Retrieved from the FTC at http://www.ftc.gov/bcp/conline/pubs/alerts/safealrt.htm.

Schwartau, W. (1998, July 6). It's getting easier to dig up DIRT on criminals. *Network World.* Retrieved Fall 2001 http://www.nwfusion.com/forum/0706schwartau.html.

U.S. Deparment of Health and Human Services. (2002, August). *Issues first major protections for patient privacy.* Retrieved from the U.S. Dept. of Health and Human Services website from http://www.hhs.gov/news/press/2002pres/20020809a.html.

ZDNet News. (2000, December 4). Lemos Report. *Experts: Carnivore review limited.* Retrieved from http://zdnet.com.com/2100-11-526074.html.

This work was previously published in Organizational Data Mining: Leveraging Enterprise Data Resources for Optimal Performance, edited by H. Nemati and C.D. Barko, pp. 61-78, copyright 2005 by IGI Publishing, formerly known as Idea Group Publishing (an imprint of IGI Global).

Chapter 5.12
Patents and Standards in the ICT Sector:
Are Submarine Patents a Substantive Problem or a Red Herring?

Aura Soininen
Lappeenranta University of Technology and
Attorneys-at-Law Borenius & Kemppinen, Ltd, Finland

ABSTRACT

Multiple cases have been reported in which patents have posed dilemmas in the context of cooperative standard setting. Problems have come to the fore with regard to GSM, WCDMA, and CDMA standards, for example. Furthermore, JPEG and HTML standards, as well as VL-bus and SDRAM technologies, have faced patent-related difficulties. Nevertheless, it could be argued that complications have arisen in only a small fraction of standardization efforts, and that patents do not therefore constitute a real quandary. This article assesses the extent and the causes of the patent dilemma in the ICT sector through a brief analysis of how ICT companies' patent strategies and technology-licensing practices relate to standard setting and by exemplifying and quantifying the problem on the basis of relevant articles, academic research papers, court cases and on-line discussions. Particular attention is paid to so-called submarine patents, which bear most significance with respect to the prevailing policy concern regarding the efficacy of the patent system.

INTRODUCTION

Background

Our society is filled with various types of standards, commonly agreed ways of doing things. Standards may be sociocultural, political, economic, or technical. Language is a standard, the metric system is a standard, and so is our social etiquette (Cunningham, 2005). Technical standards could be defined as any set of technical specifications that either provide or are intended to provide a common design for a product or a process. They range from a loose set of product characterizations to detailed and exact specifications for technical interfaces. Some of them control product interoperability, some ensure quality or safety, and some are so-called measurement standards (Grindley, 2002).

Particularly interoperability/compatibility standards are paramount in industries such as information and communications technology (ICT) that are dependent on interconnectivity. In fact, the telecommunications industry has relied on them throughout its history. These standards define the format for the interface, allowing different core products, often from different manufacturers, to use the same complementary goods and services, or to be connected together as networks (Grindley, 2002; Teece, 2000). Thus, interoperability standards enable gadgets to work together and thereby they further the goal of increased communicative potential. This follows that their use may also lead to financial benefits due to so-called network externalities (Cunningham, 2005; Shurmer & Lea, 1995). These strong network effects are present when a product or a service becomes more valuable to users as more people use it. Examples of products that benefit from network effects include e-mail, Internet access, fax machines, and modems (Shapiro & Varian, 1999).

A further economic effect of interoperability standards is that they reduce the switching costs from one supplier to another by preventing producers and consumers from being locked into a proprietary system. Standards, however, do not totally eliminate switching costs. When producers and users become committed to a particular system or standard, and the longer they stay with it, the more expensive and difficult it is for them to switch to another that is comparable (Blind, 2004). Consequently, due to these strong economic effects, control of the outcome of standard setting may yield significant economic advantage on the sale of both core and related products (Hjelm, 2000). Patents that provide their holders with a defined right to prevent others from making, using and selling an invention can be used to gain that leverage or to control the adoption of a standard. Therefore, potential conflicts between patent rights and the need for standardization affect the ICT industry and the consumers at large, and these economic effects need to be bared in mind when examining the deficiencies of prevailing standard-setting procedures and the legal framework.

This article studies the patent-related dilemmas that may arise both in the course of standard setting and after the standard has been established. Potential conflicts and their causes are identified and exemplified on specific case studies, and the study of Blind, Bierhals, Thumm, Hossain, Sillwood, Iverser, et al. (2002) is used to quantify the problems further. The aim is to find out whether the problem with patents, particularly with so-called submarine patents, is substantial, or whether it is only a minor concern that has attracted undeserved attention. Term "submarine patent" is used here for patent applications and patents that may yield significant economic power because they "read on" a standard and come to the fore after it has been established.

Standardization and Patents in General

Standards can be established in many ways: the markets determine *de facto* standards, and organized standards bodies agree upon *de jure* standards. These bodies could be said to include government legislators, official standards organizations, various industry committees, and consortia. Unlike de facto standards, de jure standards are usually established in advance and are later implemented by multiple vendors (Grindley, 2002; Messerschmitt & Szyperski, 2003; Mueller 2001).

Standards emerge from all the sources in the ICT sector listed previously. The Internet Society (ISOC), the Organization for the Advancement of Structured Information Standards (OASIS), the World Wide Web Consortium (W3C), and the Internet Engineering Task Force (IETF) could be mentioned as examples of bodies active in the field of software and the Internet. Then again, the European Telecommunications Standardization Institute (ETSI), the American National Standardization Institute (ANSI), the International Telecommunications Union (ITU), and the International Organization for Standardization (ISO) could be mentioned as organizations operating in the telecommunications industry (Rahnasto, 2003).

A further distinction is that between open and proprietary standards. The purpose of open standards is to provide an industry with well-documented open specifications that could be implemented without prior business and legal arrangements (Caplan, 2003; Messerschmitt & Szyperski, 2003). Furthermore, with open standards, unlike proprietary standards, development of the specification is open to participants without restrictions. The openness may not always be absolute, however, and as a consequence the term "open standards" has various interpretations in practice (Caplan, 2003; Messerchmitt & Szyperski, 2003). In fact, although patent-free standards have traditionally been preferred in the interests of ensuring their success and promoting their use, it has become more difficult to design standards that do not contain any patentable inventions. This holds true particularly when the aim is to choose pre-eminent technology for a standard (Frank, 2002; Soininen, 2005). Therefore, it is not rare to call a standard open even if it includes patented technology providing that licenses are accessible to all. This definition has been adopted in this article as well.

As to the connection between de facto and de jure standards and open and proprietary standards, privately set de facto standards are typically proprietary in nature (Lemley, 2002) meaning that the patent holder controls their utilization. Then again, official standards organizations typically promote open standards, and those originating from various industry groups and consortia may fall in either category or somewhere in between depending on whether everyone has been able to participate in the selection of the technical specification, or whether the standard has been agreed upon by a handful of companies having the technical knowledge in the area and who then have it adopted throughout the industry (Rahnasto, 2003). The focus of this article is on open, commonly agreed de jure standards.

As said earlier, although open standards are in principle available for anyone to use proprietary technology may be involved in their implementation, and using the specification may require a license (Rahnasto, 2003). Consequently, many official standards organizations and also some consortia have policies that permit their members to contribute proprietary technology under certain conditions: disclosure of the contributor's essential patents may be required, and before the technology is elected, patent holders are asked whether they are willing to offer a license at least on a non-discriminatory basis and on fair and reasonable terms (Frank, 2002). The purpose is to protect the patent holder's interests while fostering standards that incorporate the best technology and have the capacity for worldwide promulgation (Berman, 2005; Soininen, 2005). These organizations are called together as "standards bodies" or "standards organizations" from now on.

From the companies' perspective the dilemma

between patents and open standards arises from the need to ensure returns on R&D investments through the exclusion of others while interoperability requires the inclusion of other parties. In fact, patent holders are free to refuse licensing altogether or they may choose the licensees and the licensing terms freely as long as the practice complies with relevant legislation, such as competition regulation/ antrust regulation. Thus, companies appear not to be very willing to license their patented technologies to everyone, particularly not to their competitors, on a royalty-free basis or for low returns. It seems, however, that in the context of common standards a limited exception can often be made for business reasons (Interview data U.S., 2004). Indeed, the use of common protocols and interfaces may expand the markets for networks of products that implement them, and producers then compete by innovating on top of the standardized functions (Peterson, 2002a). Nonetheless, even if a company decided to take part in standard setting, the interests of firms, individual contributors and users participating diverge and patents may be utilized strategically to achieve patent holder's objectives. Consequently, the standardization process may turn out to be burdensome as the mere existence of vested interests, for example, intellectual property rights (IPRs), complicates matters (Farrell, 1996; Shurmer & Lea, 1995; Soininen, 2005). Identifying relevant patents and agreeing on their beforehand cause complications and delays to the standardization process.

The relationship between ICT companies' patent strategies and technology licensing practices discussed earlier in general and in respect to open standards is one of the main questions that need to be addressed further in order to find an explanation to why it is that patents may raise such thorny issues in respect to standards. Moreover, attention has to be paid to the standards organizations' practices and bylaws aimed at reducing that tension in practice.

Standardization and Submarine Patents

As mentioned earlier, different types of standards bodies play an important role in establishing standards in the ICT sector, and many of them allow patented or patentable technology to be submitted, but specifically require disclosure of the patents and occasionally even of pending patent applications during the standardization process, as well as their licensing. This is to clarify relevant rights during the process of standard development and reduce the risks of submarine patents so that patent holders cannot claim infringements afterwards, and thereby prevent others from using a standard, or to extract overly high licensing fees. If all essential, relevant rights are clarified during the process, a well-informed decision can be made (Kipnis, 2000). It might also be possible to design around the identified patents and patent applications, or to choose another technology for a standard. In fact, since patent-free standards are often the first choice, disclosure may have a negative effect on what technology is chosen (Soininen, 2005). For instance, when selecting the GSM standard another viable option was apparently rejected because it was considered too proprietary (Bekkers, Verspagen, & Smits, 2002).

Since proprietary technology may easily be discriminated, companies may even have an incentive to manipulate the standardization process and hide the fact that they have relevant patents. Standardization namely gives patents market power they did not have before (Rahnasto, 2003), which in turn improves the holder's negotiation position following the election and adoption of a standard. Furthermore, the disclosure requirement has its shortcomings and therefore companies may not even need to break the rules to capture an industry standard. The disclosure requirement is not necessarily extended beyond the personal knowledge of the individual participant, it may not be practically possible for a company to clarify all the patents and patent applications, and the obligation does not always cover pending patent applications, especially unpublished ones (Lemley, 2002). Consequently, a large share of the rights is not necessarily considered during the standardization process. Moreover, since standard setting may take a long time, many years in some cases, undertakings usually continue their R&D projects and file more and amend their existing patent applications during that period. Therefore, if the obligation to disclose does not hold throughout the standard setting, it is even more likely that patents will surface after it has been established (Soininen, 2005).

The optimal scope of the disclosure requirement, what happens if the guidelines are breached, and what course of action should be taken if there was no contractual duty or even a recommendation to disclose patents or pending applications and a patent surfaces after the adoption of the standard, remain matters for debate both outside and inside the courts. The submarine patent risk stemming partially from non-disclosure also involves third-party patents. Indeed, as Lemelson's submarine patent tactic has demonstrated, it is ideal from the patent holder's perspective to have a patent claiming technology that becomes widely adopted within an industry (Soininen, 2005). In fact, the submarine patent scenario could be said to have become more probable in recent years as numerous cases have been reported in which, despite efforts to identify relevant patents, claims have surfaced after the standard has been agreed upon (Blind et al., 2002). Furthermore, the importance of patents in business has increased in many respects and the legal framework constituting of patent laws and competition/antitrust regulation that may pose limits to the utilization of patents could also be described as pro-patent even though the system has been severely criticized (FTC, 2003; OECD, 2004). This has resulted not only in a higher number of applied-for and granted patents, but also in more aggressive enforcement and increases in

technology licensing, bare patent licensing and cross-licensing, which in turn has the potential of generating more conflicts (Peterson, 2002). In fact, it appears that there is an increase in all types of patent claims and charges that relate to standards, and particularly in telecommunications, negotiations over such matters cause delays in the development of standards worldwide (Krechmer, 2005). Therefore it is essential to study the patent landscape in the ICT sector further, take a closer look at realized disputes and examine the loopholes of the system. Only by understanding how it is failing, it is possible to implement better practices.

Standardization and Licensing

There is another quandary involving patents and standards in addition to the submarine patent dilemma described earlier, and that has to do with licensing. This dilemma relates mainly to the mainstream obligation to license one's essential patents on fair, reasonable and non-discriminatory terms (RAND). The problem is that this problem may be limited in firms' patent statements in various ways, resulting in unexpected hold-ups. Companies may, for example, agree to license only patents that are essential for using that portion of the standard they have suggested, or they may impose limits by stating that licenses are available to any qualified applicants (Frank, 2002; Rahnasto, 2003; Soininen, 2005). One typical qualification is that licenses are offered only to companies that offer reciprocal treatment or promise not to threaten patent litigation against the licensing company (Berman, 2005). Moreover, specific licensing terms are not typically agreed upon during the standardization process so that the standards organization would play a role in it (Kipnis, 2000). Each company negotiates terms separately, which allows it to apply its own interpretations of what is considered fair, reasonable and nondiscriminatory (Frank, 2002; Rahnasto, 2003). In fact, it is for this reason that manufacturers participating in standards committees may even be forced to delay the standards development in order to negotiate acceptable terms before the final vote. The worst-case scenario is that the sum of license fees exceeds the total profit available to a product manufacturer, and that the standard never becomes adopted (Krechmer, 2005). Ultimately, consideration of the fairness, reasonableness and nondiscriminatory nature of the terms is left to the courts (Soininen, 2005). So far, however, the courts have not provided proper guidelines on how to determine what is fair, reasonable and nondiscriminatory (Rahnasto, 2003).

Thus, the problems related to the adoption of standardized technology may have to do with disagreement over the content of a company's licensing statement, even in the absence of submarine patents. One might even wonder, considering the large number of patents that are being reported as essential in the course of standardization, whether the disclosure obligation bears any significance in practice. Therefore, it is not enough to concentrate merely on the submarine patent problem and its causes when there is a possibility that limiting that particular risk might have only minimal effect.

Research Objective and Methodology

Standard setting is the cornerstone of today's economy, and it is essential particularly in the ICT sector. The most important feature of open standards is that they have the potential to become widely promulgated and used without undue restriction: this is essential to their success and to the very idea of something being or becoming a standard. Patents may, however, be used exclusively and therefore they may jeopardize the purpose for which standards have been created. Indeed, submarine patents as well as perplexity regarding proper licensing terms may result in increased costs in the form of excessive licensing fees, or they may force the industry to abandon the standard altogether meaning that the societal

benefits may be lost. Since patents help companies to gain leverage over the standard-setting procedure and the adoption of the standard, potential dilemmas addressed in this article are also a policy concern. One may ask particularly in the context of so-called submarine patents whether the patent system fulfils its goal. These patents have factually been hidden and thus they have not contributed to technological development of that specific industry, as is the purpose of the patent system.

This article examines the patent-related dilemmas and analyses their causes by exemplifying and quantifying them on the basis of newspaper stories, online articles, research papers, and trial documents. Further data was collected from interviews with eleven Finnish ICT companies and eight U.S. ICT companies in order to illustrate the relationship between patent strategies and licensing practices in general and in the context of standard setting. The interviews with the Finnish companies focused on patent strategies and were conducted by the author in 2003. Those with U.S. companies based in the Bay Area, CA, were more general and related to their innovation models, appropriability strategies and licensing practices. They were conducted by the author in cooperation with Pia Hurmelinna-Laukkanen and were completed in 2004. The interviewed firms included different types of ICT companies operating in the fields of information technology (software, hardware and related services for different purposes), chip interface technology, audio technologies, and digital entertainment products designed for computers and the Internet, and telecommunications. It should be noted that most of the U.S. case companies were larger than the Finnish companies, their revenues spanning from $60 million to $19,000 million. Furthermore, the size of their patent portfolios was substantially larger and varied mostly between 300 and 2,000 issued patents (one of the companies did not have patents at all). Only one Finnish company had a substantial portfolio of over 5,000 issued patent families, two of them had a medium-sized portfolio of approximately 60 issued patent families and close to 200 pending applications, and the rest had less than 10 issued patents/pending patent applications. The U.S. companies were also more actively involved in standard setting than the Finnish companies.

Obviously, it is difficult to make generalizations on the basis of such limited data. Thus, the data are used to complement other studies and views presented in the literature. In some cases, however, there were common features applicable to all of the firms, or several of them were found to have certain common denominators. Then again, some of the results are presented as examples of corporate operational models. One reason for this is that the interviews were in-depth in nature, meaning that the discussion was sometimes focused more on certain areas, and it would not therefore be possible to say whether the expressed views were common to all of the companies or not. Furthermore, in some situations less than 8 (U.S.) or 11 (Finnish) companies yielded relevant data: only a few companies in the Finnish sample were involved in setting standards. In the following, I refer to the interview data as interview data U.S. (2004) and interview data Finland (2003).

I will start by re-examining the submarine patent concept because the original meaning of submarine patents has largely disappeared as a result of legislative amendments. Nevertheless, certain aspects of the current patent law still contribute to their existence. I will then study ICT companies' patent strategies and technology licensing practices in order to demonstrate the general developments in the area and tensions between proprietary and open operation models and their implications on standardization. After that I will review the disclosure and licensing challenges that have been reported in the context of standardization and patents, and examine the likelihood of such conflicts. I conclude the article by considering the extent of the problems and whether the submarine patent problem really exists

and can be limited, or whether it is merely a red herring that needs no further attention. It should however be noted that the sufficiency and flexibility of the prevailing legal framework applicable to solving potential conflicts is not particularly examined in this article even though it is clear that applicable legal tools influence companies' negotiation power, and thereby their behavior during and after standard setting. These legal tools could also prove helpful in minimizing the harmful societal effects of submarine patents. This type of in-depth analysis would be the next phase following the recognition of the prevailing problem, its magnitude and main causes.

THE ORIGINS OF SUBMARINE PATENTS

The term submarine patent has been traditionally used to refer to (U.S.) patents that are issued after a long, intentionally delayed pendency at the patent office. The purpose of prolonging the application period by filing continuation applications, for example, has been to keep the invention secret as long as necessary for the industry to mature on the basis of the technology. When the industry is faced with the challenge of changing the technology, the patent is allowed to be issued, and the patent holder is in a position to prevent others from utilizing the invention and to demand royalties from those who began to use the technology while the application was pending (Heinze, 2002). Indeed, in the U.S. it is possible to file continuation applications and to preserve the priority date of the parent application as long as the parent application and the following continuation application disclose the same invention. There are no limitations on how many times a parent application can be continued (Graham & Mowery, 2002). The application period may thus last over a decade, and all this may happen even if the patent has not made any contribution to the development of the technology it covers: if it has been secretly pending for a long time, no-one has had the opportunity to find out about the invention, design alternative technologies, or develop the patented technology further. Thus, the trade-off between the inventor (the right to exclude others) and society (detailed information about the invention), the keystone of the patent system, is not in balance (Soininen, 2005). Figure 1 illustrates the popularity of continuations in relation to software and other patents in the U.S.

It is clear from the statistics in Figure 1 that continuations are filed frequently. Nevertheless, submarine patents as defined earlier are rare. In many cases it is inefficiency in the patent office that causes long delays rather than intentional postponement on the patentee's part (Ferguson, 1999). Nonetheless, Jerome Lemelson's patents in particular, issued after decades of pendency at the patent office, have attracted a lot of public attention (Stroyd, 2000; Vanchaver, 2001). Lemelson, who was above all a visionary who anticipated where technology was heading, applied for patents for inventions that he did not himself implement, and amended his applications when necessary to prevent them from being issued. Some of his applications were continued half a dozen times, potentially adding years to the process each time (Varchaver, 2001). He claimed a total of more than

500 patents on basic technologies used nowadays in industrial robots and automated warehouses, as well as in fax machines, VCRs, bar-code scanners, camcorders, and the Sony Walkman. His "machine vision" patent No. 5,283,641 was issued after 42 years of pendency (Stroyd, 2000; Ferguson, 1999; The Lemelson Foundation, n.d.; Soininen, 2005).

Lemelson was active in enforcing his rights. Once someone had developed a product that had some relation to one of his patents, the potential violator was confronted and reasonable compensation was demanded. Aggressive enforcement continues even today, after the death of Lemelson himself. Although quite a few of his patents have been challenged in court, over 750 companies paid royalties for them in 2001 (Soininen, 2005; Stroyd, 2000; Varchaver, 2001). Lemelson is not the only one to have used submarine patenting tactics, however. Another famous example is Gilbert Hyatt, whose patent for a single-chip microcontroller was issued in 1990 after 20 years of pendency. It was successfully challenged by Texas Instruments, but by that time Hyatt had already been able to collect approximately $70 million in royalties. Submarine patentees also include Olof Soderblom, whose patent for token-ring technology was pending in secrecy in the USPTO

Figure 1. Continuation patents as a proportion of issued patents: Software patents compared with all other patents, 1987-1999 (Graham & Mowery, 2002)

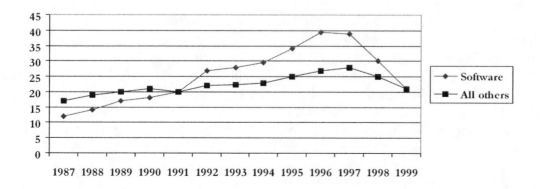

for 13 years until it was granted in 1981 (Heinze, 2002). While the application was pending, other companies developed token-ring technologies independently. This development took place in connection with a public-standard-setting process carried out by the Institute of Electrical and Electronic Engineers (IEEE). Since Soderblom's patent surfaced companies have been forced to pay him more than 100 million dollars in royalties (IPO, n.d; Soininen, 2005).

Legal Changes and the Tactics of Submarine Patenting

Since Lemelson's, Hyatt's, and Soderblom's times the U.S. Congress has taken action and amended patent laws in order to discourage submarine patenting. The change from the 17-year patent term counted from the day of issuance to a 20-year term starting from the application date took place in 1995 in accordance with the GATT agreement (Graham & Mowery, 2002). Consequently, a prolonged application period reduces the life of an issued patent. Another amendment made in 1999 was related to the publication of patent applications within 18 months from filing. Although there are exceptions to this rule, the change has reduced the prospect of surprising an industry before 1999 all patent applications filed in the U.S. remained secret until the patent was issued (Graham & Mowery, 2002; Heinze, 2002; Soininen, 2005). A further modification to the Patents Act that would obligate disclosure of all patent applications within 18 months has also been proposed recently before Congress. The introduced bill, H.R. 2795: Patent reform Act of 2005, is currently in the committee hearing phase (GovTrack.us, n.d.).

Furthermore, the U.S. Court of Appeal for the Federal Circuit held some years ago in the Symbol Technologies et al. v. Lemelson case that the equitable doctrine of prosecution laches, which is one of the defenses that can be used in patent infringement cases in order to demonstrate that even though there was a patent infringement, the patent should be held unenforceable, can be applied when the patent is issued following an unreasonable and unexplained delay by the applicant during the patent prosecution. Here, it does not matter whether the patentee's practice of keeping the application pending for many years has been accomplished strictly in accordance with the rules or not (Calderone & Custer, 2005; Soininen, 2005; Symbol Technologies Inc. v. Lemelson Medical, Education & Research Foundation, 277 F.3d 1361, 1363 (Fed. Cir. 2002); *See also* Symbol Technologies, Inc et al. v. Lemelson Medical, Education & Research Foundation, LP et al., 422 F.3d 1378 (Fed. Cir. 2005)).

Thus, it has been confirmed that the doctrine of laches, a defense based on prolonged patent application period, can sometimes be used for protecting an infringer from the harmful effects of submarine patents. Moreover, it is not only after the patent has been granted that the doctrine of prosecution laches can be applied. The Federal Circuit made it clear in the In re Bogese case that it is possible for the USPTO to address the issue before the patent is granted, and to reject it on this basis (In re Bogese II, 303 F.3d 1362, 1367 (Fed. Cir. 2002)). As far as Europe is concerned, patent applications have traditionally been automatically published within 18 months from filing, and the 20-year patent term has begun from the filing date. Moreover, although it is possible to file divisional applications, continuations are not allowed (Graham & Mowery, 2002; Soininen, 2005).

Submarine Patents Today

If submarine patents are defined narrowly as meaning patents issued after a long, intentionally delayed, secret pendency at the patent office, they do not seem to exist. Nonetheless, despite the legal amendments, circumstances in which patent applications are concealed long enough for the industry to start using a technology without knowing about the lurking patent arise particularly in fields characterized by fast technological development. In some parts of the ICT industry, for example, 18 months of secrecy may already be too long, and prolonging the application phase intentionally is not required for achieving the intended result (Soininen, 2005). Furthermore, patent applicants filing only in the U.S. may currently opt out of the 18-month publication rule and file continuations in order to detect industry developments and to postpone the grant of the patent for five years or so. Since the U.S. is a large and relatively lucrative market, particularly in the computer and software sector (Mueller, 2001), many companies do not even seek international patent protection. Also, provided that the numbers of filed ICT patent applications and granted patents continue their upward trend (OECD, 2005; OECD, 2004), it is getting more and more difficult to be aware of all relevant patents and applications. Especially if inventions are systemic, and innovation is fast and cumulative, multiple patented or patentable inventions may be incorporated into one innovation (Bessen, 2003; FTC, 2003), and therefore infringement is not merely a coincidence that can be avoided but is likely no matter how well the patents and pending patent applications are screened (Interview data U.S., 2004; Watts & Baigent, 2002). For this reason, published patent applications and granted patents may, in reality, be hidden (Soininen, 2005).

Another issue that has to be taken into account is that the scope of a patent typically changes during prosecution. Patent examiners often come up with patentability bars during examination, and require that the scope is limited in some way. Furthermore, as mentioned, the applicant may be able to add and amend patent claims during prosecution so that the scope will better reflect developments in the industry. Here the original application sets the limits for such changes, as its claims must support the new claim and no new matter can be included (EPC, Art 123; Mueller,

2001). As a consequence, although patent application might have been deemed non-essential at the time it was first published, the situation may change before it is granted. Certainly, one element of surprise relates to claim interpretation. Although a patent is a relatively well-defined right, the boundaries are never exact. The scope is not clear until it has been tested in court.

The concept of the submarine patent is understood in this article as broadly referring to patent applications and patents that surface after the standard has been established and take the industry by surprise. Here it does not matter, whether the patent application has been secretly pending or not, even though this possibility certainly contributes to the problem.

Tensions between patents and standards are examined in the following, and the problem of submarine patents and its causes are identified and exemplified further. ICT companies patent strategies and technology-licensing practices are analyzed briefly at first in order to place the dilemmas between patents and standards into a broader context and to find those practical elements that may contribute to them.

PATENT STRATEGIES AND TECHNOLOGY LICENSING PRACTICES IN THE ICT SECTOR

General Developments

With the shift from an industrial economy toward an information economy, the importance of intellectual property rights (IPRs) has increased. Today, a large proportion of companies' assets constitute intangibles, and IPRs are used to protect and profit from certain of these. Patents, for instance, provide their holders with the right to forbid others from utilizing patented inventions. Holders may thus gain competitive advantage due to their ability to stand out from the competition, or they may use their position to choose their licensees, which is one of their core rights due to the exhaustion doctrine (Kipnis, 2000). Then again, if the patent holder issues a license, as a rule he is entitled to secure any monetary or other compensation he is able to extract from the licensee (Shurmer & Lea, 1995) as long as the licensing terms are coherent with relevant regulation. The objective of licensing is to generate more revenue for the undertaking than it would be able to produce if it manufactured the patented products or utilized patented methods only by itself. Indeed, a well-reasoned licensing program helps a company to position itself favorably in the market place (Megantz, 2002; Soininen, 2005).

Obviously, there are differences between industries with respect to licensing tendencies, but generally speaking, the markets for technology licensing the component of which patents have grown. In fact, in a survey conducted by the OECD/BIAC, 60% of the responding companies reported increased inward and outward licensing, and 40% reported increased cross-licensing. Other types of knowledge sharing have become more common too, and collaboration takes place in the form of sponsored and collaborative research, strategic alliances, as well as in mergers and acquisitions. This has been said to stem from the growing technological complexity, increased technological opportunities, rapid technological change, intense competition, and the higher costs and risks of innovation. As a consequence, companies have namely become more focused on certain areas while they acquire complementary technologies increasingly from other undertakings and universities (OECD, 2004).

The features mentioned previously apply also to the ICT sector, and companies lean heavily on cooperation and networks. Contemporary academic literature refers to this type of innovation as the open innovation model, in contrast to the closed model that used to dominate. Companies applying the closed model seek ultimate control and do everything themselves, while those adopting open innovation realize that valuable ideas do not only originate within their firms, and that it does not have to be the company itself that releases these ideas in the market. Whereas making innovation proprietary and exclusive is a central feature of the closed innovation model, open innovation is characterized by the exploitation of intellectual property in order to create value. The boundary between the company and its environment is said to have become more permeable, enabling ideas and knowledge to flow more freely (Chesbrough, 2003).

One further characteristic of the competitive environment of the ICT sector is so-called coopetition that was pointed out by one of the U.S. interviewees. Coopetition basically means that companies may very well be business partners in some fields and compete aggressively in others (Interview data U.S., 2004). Naturally, all the elements mentioned before signaling the importance of networks, openness in innovation, and coopetition are reflected in ICT firms' patenting practices, the use of patents in their business, enforcement and infringement avoidance. Furthermore they affect the technology licensing tendencies and licensing terms. Similarly it is possible to detect their implications on standardization and also on settling of disputes as some of the example cases discussed later on demonstrate.

The U.S. Patent Landscape

The patent landscape of the U.S. ICT sector could be described as a thicket to the birth of which strong patent system, technological complexity and fast technological development have contributed. Thus, although a reading of the patent laws gives the impression that there is a correspondence between a product and a patent, this is not necessarily the case: patents may overlap, and the manufacture of one product may require access to hundreds or thousands of patents, or one patent may "read on" many types of products, not just one (FTC, 2003). Therefore, in order to avoid the resulting hold-up problem, many U.S. ICT companies employ defensive patent strategies, and if they have the resources to do so they build large patent portfolios in order to guarantee that others cannot prohibit them from innovating. This in turn increases the number of relevant patents in the industry. Naturally, in addition to the better negotiation position and increased ability to agree on the licensing and cross-licensing they facilitate, patents also provide the means to prevent outright imitation in these cases (FTC, 2003; Interview data U.S., 2004; Soininen, 2005).

In general, the significance of patents as protection mechanisms used to exclude others and thus to generate competitive advantage appears not to be very high in the ICT field, and it is rather competition that spurs innovation in this sector (FTC, 2003). This was reflected in the patent-enforcement activities of the U.S. companies that were interviewed, and which operated on the basis of a defensive patent strategy. Unlike the company that employed an offensive patent strategy and attempted to generate its revenues from technology and patent licensing, defensively operating firms focused more on their core businesses of making and selling products rather than devoting resources to detecting infringements (Interview data U.S., 2004). Similarly, Messerschmitt and Szyperski (2003) have observed that the exclusionary use of patents is less common in the software industry than in some other industries such as biotechnology and pharmaceuticals. In their opinion this is in part because patents tend to be less fundamental and they can be circumvented easily. Furthermore, according to a quantitative study of U.S. manufacturing firms conducted by Cohen, Nelson, and Walsh (2000), compared to other appropriability mechanisms such as secrecy, other legal tools, lead time, complementary sales, services and manufacturing, patents ranked rather low in effectiveness in fields such as the manufacture of electrical equipment and electronic components, semiconductors and communications equipment, all of which are connected to the ICT sector. Moreover, there were substantial

variations between industries: patents appeared to be most important in the chemical industry. This does not mean that they are not acquired for other purposes, such as those indicated earlier, and naturally all of their functions are based on the patent holder's ability to prevent others from utilizing the invention.

Since many ICT companies are dependent on one another as indicated earlier and patents are not vital for protection, they generally have no reason to complicate their business relationships by claiming patent infringement. However, while particularly large U.S. ICT firms seem to be aggressive in building patent portfolios mainly for defensive purposes, offensive patent strategies tend to predominate for individuals and small software companies (Messerschmitt & Szyperski, 2003). Indeed, various sources have reported an increase in companies that derive their revenue purely from patents. These companies, also called patent trolls, do not typically have any R&D of their own, nor do they manufacture any products themselves: unlike most ICT companies therefore, they are not dependent on other firms. Their business is to force companies involved in manufacturing to license their patents by claiming patent infringement (FTC, 2003; Interview data U.S., 2004; Peterson, 2002b; Surowiecki, 2006). Patent trolls seek for direct licensing revenues and do not usually benefit from a cross-license. Therefore a defensive patent strategy that might otherwise help certain ICT companies to maintain their freedom-to-operate, and that has proven successful also in the context of standards as will be illustrated later has only minimal influence on them.

It is not only patent trolls that seek to make better use of their patent portfolios, however. The prevailing trend in the U.S. has been to found patent-licensing programs, sometimes by forming a separate patent-licensing unit, for the purpose of generating extra revenues mainly from inventions that are not considered core to the company's main operations (Rivette & Kline, 2000). This trend is likely to have an effect also on standardization as standards are becoming more and more vital for the ICT industry and thus they also carry a lot of economic significance. Consequently, having a patent that claims a broadly adopted standard may be a dream come true for a company seeking licensing revenues and not operating in that particular technology area.

Basically, patents are viewed as core elements of corporate business strategies in the U.S. ICT sector. They are employed for multiple purposes in different contexts. They may be used as protection measures and as components in joint ventures, in patent pools, and technology licensing arrangements. A license may also be a pure patent license or a broad cross-license providing a company with not-to-sue coverage. Furthermore, patents may be used to attract other types of resources to the company. They serve as indicators of innovativeness, and can be helpful in attracting financing: they can be used as collateral and are seen as a positive indication in the eyes of venture-capital investors and potential buyers. In fact, one trend that is detectable in the U.S. is the increased tendency of selling and buying patent portfolios and individual patents (FTC, 2003; Interview data U.S., 2004). This may happen in conjunction with the acquisition of an entire company, or patents may be bought from bankrupt firms. This follows that it is not easy to avoid patent infringement as patents may easily find their way to unknown parties meaning that a notification of potential patent infringement may practically come from anyone.

There is one further feature about the U.S. patent landscape that should be noted. It has been claimed that a substantive number of patents are being granted particularly in new areas such as software and the Internet that do not actually fulfill the patentability requirements. These so-called bad patents have contributed to various patent-related difficulties and they have been deemed to be one of the main reasons why the U.S. patent system is not in balance (FTC, 2003).

The European Patent Landscape

So far Europe has not faced patent trolling on a large scale, which could be explained by the fact that the consequences of litigation and infringement are less severe: while the average cost of patent litigation in the U.S. amounts to more than $2 million per side (Vermont, 2002), in Finland the figure for hearing an infringement the case in the district court is closer to EUR 150 000 per side. Of course the total amount of litigation costs may be fundamentally higher if the case involves various phases such as a precautionary measure claim, and both infringement and annulment actions. Moreover, the damages issued are substantial in the U.S. For instance, in 1990 the Federal District Court awarded $910 million in damages to Polaroid in its patent-infringement litigation against Kodak, Alpex Computers was awarded $260 million for patent infringement (litigation against Nintendo) in 1994, and in 2003 Microsoft was forced to pay Eolas $521 million for infringement of an Internet browser patent (PwC Advisory, 2006). By way of comparison, the largest amount of damages ever awarded in Finland was EUR 252,282 (Labsystems Oy v. Biohit Oy, HO S 94/1922, Court of Appeal).

Furthermore, the patent web in the ICT sector appears to be less complex in Europe than in the U.S., although there are certainly variations between different technology areas. For instance, the European mobile-phone industry and the electronics field are areas in which large patent portfolios are common (OECD, 2004; Watts & Baigent, 2002). However, with the exception of the large telecommunications and electronics companies, patents seem to be regarded not so much as strategic assets, but rather as legal tools applied and used for protecting the results of the company's own R&D efforts, and occasionally for licensing (DLA, 2004; Interview data Finland, 2003).

It was evident, for instance, from the interviews with the Finnish companies that were not involved in the mobile-phone area as manufacturers, and had less than 70 issued patent families, that small-scale portfolio building was the preferred strategy for avoiding otherwise weak patent protection. There were no cross-licenses, however, and the companies appeared to be able to operate freely without paying much attention to the patents of others (Interview data Finland, 2003). In general, the patent application part of the patent strategy was well thought out, although it should be noted that the process was technology-oriented and lacked the type of business acumen that was present in the U.S. (Interview data Finland, 2003). In fact, this is a conclusion that has been shared also by others. For instance Kratzman (2005) pointed out in his research:

Finnish patents tend to be academic and not written to generate revenue. They are not commercial nor do they cover multiple applications, an essential element in generating licensing interest. (p. 14)

With respect to the utilization of the patents in the company's business transactions and the infringement surveillance, they could be described as incidental, perhaps because patents were not regarded as important contributors to the company's revenue stream, and most Finnish companies had so few of them. Lead time, constant innovation and, in the area of software, copyright protection, were considered more important (Interview data Finland, 2003). Furthermore, attitudes towards patents appear to be largely negative, even indifferent, in the software industry in particular (Interview data Finland, 2003), which, based on Blind et al. (2001), applies not only to Finland but also to the rest of the Europe as far as independent software developers are concerned. It should be noted, though, that even small and medium-sized companies are beginning to realize the importance of strategic patent management, perhaps partially as a response to the attention

paid to patents by investors. Generally speaking, there is a steady increase in the propensity of filing patents in the European ICT sector (OECD, 2005), which in turn will probably increase the likelihood of patent-based conflicts, and make it more difficult to design around the patents when selecting a standard, for instance. Currently, however, European companies appear not to be employing their patents as aggressively as U.S. undertakings and therefore there is a chance that even though European companies had patents that could be characterized as submarines, this would not create substantial hindrances to the industry. On the other hand, markets for technology are international and as the case with GSM standard that will be discussed in the licensing section of this article illustrates, also patent strategies of U.S. companies tend to influence European standardization efforts.

Licensing Practices in the ICT Sector

As regards to companies licensing practices, some companies tend to be more open in their operations than others. Usually it is rather easy to outsource the manufacturing of products, their distribution and marketing, but it is the development that R&D-intensive companies prefer to keep to themselves. This could be detected in the technology-licensing practices of the U.S. ICT companies, which, given the reported increase of 4000% in licensing revenues from 1980 to 1990 (Vermont, 2002) and the recent fascination surrounding the success of open-source software licensing, were surprisingly closed, particularly in terms of licensing in external technologies.

One of the interviewees explained the situation by saying that it was difficult to find useful technologies, and counting on outside technologies was usually considered risky due to potential problems with third-party rights and quality issues, for example. In-house R&D was simply trusted more. When companies did rely on external technologies, they rather acquired the entire company than licensed-in the technology. If they did license-in it was largely limited to non-core elements and design tools. As for licensing-in open-source software, the companies were very careful, and typically had tools in place to make sure that they audited what came in (Interview data U.S., 2004).

When it comes to licensing out their technologies interviewed companies tended to be more open, and there was one company whose business model was based mainly on this. Furthermore, licensing out was used in order to integrate in-house technologies into other companies' products and to make them compatible so that the market for that technology would expand. The licensing models adopted in the interviewed software companies were basically very broad for distribution purposes, and they licensed software to their customers as a package and to other companies to be used as embedded in their products. However, with the exception of commonly established standards, other types of technology licensing that did not involve a complete product were limited (Interview data U.S., 2004).

The licensing terms companies follow naturally vary depending on the subject matter, the business model adopted for the particular product or technology, and the parties involved. Nevertheless, there are certain typical configurations that reflect the extent of control the licensor or the licensee has. The scope of the license is paramount: the licensor retains more control over the technology if he or she grants only non-exclusive rights, which appears to be the most common form in the ICT sector. The possibility to define the degree of exclusivity, for example, in terms of geographic areas or certain uses, and the ability to assign and sublicense the rights are other key elements in determining the scope of a license (Poltorak & Lerner, 2004). Incorporating technical assistance also gives the licensor control over the licensed technology. In the case of trademarks in particular, the licensor has good reason to control the quality of the licensed products, and to put

in place certain procedures for testing them and inspecting the licensee's production facilities (Megatz, 2002). It is also advisable to include a termination clause to enable either party to get out of the contractual relationship if necessary. One of the most intriguing termination clauses that reflects the atmosphere in the ICT industry relates to patent peace: such clauses are frequently used in open-source licenses, for instance, and in their broadest form they provide the licensor with the right to terminate the license in the face of claims by the licensee regarding infringement on any of its patents. Representations, warranties, and indemnification clauses related to risk allocation, as well as royalty rates, also affect the balance of the contractual relationship.

Most importantly, however, attention needs to focus on terms relating to modifications, improvements, and therefore also grant-backs. From the licensor's perspective, it is often advantageous to obtain the rights to any improvements developed by the licensee, preferably including the right to sublicense the improvements to other licensees. This would prevent the licensee from using a fundamental improvement or an extensive new development to gain control over the licensor's core technology. Then again, access to improvements developed by the licensor is important for the licensee in ensuring the continued viability of the licensed product or technology (Megantz, 2002).

Some of the companies interviewed had adopted a very restrictive approach to modifications, allowing them only rarely and even then often requiring grant-back terms. Control was maintained through the heavy involvement of the licensor's engineers in the implementation phase, and through quality control. The licensor also typically maintained the right to modify the license terms. Then again, in the context of software licenses, the licensees had very few rights, the source code was seldom provided, and reverse engineering was typically prohibited. Obviously, this depended on whether it was an end-user license, an OEM agreement or a VAP bundle agreement. On the other hand, some companies had adopted a more open approach and operated on a more flexible and market-driven basis. Interfaces were opened up, for instance, and one of the companies even licensed out its software under various open-source agreements (Interview data U.S., 2004).

It could be concluded from previous discussion that R&D intensive ICT companies have rather control-seeking licensing models, but they may be flexible too if it suits the company's business model. Thus, since standards are of crucial importance in this industry, exceptions are often made for the essential purpose of securing product compatibility, interoperability and interconnection (Interview data U.S., 2004). In fact, since many companies may be developing equipment or software for the same systems and platforms, for example, and there are inevitably huge numbers of relevant patents involved (Watts & Baigent, 2002), standardization may prove effective in providing access to essential patents held by various firms. On the other hand, it must be remembered that companies' prevailing licensing practices tend to show also in the standard-setting context, and although the patent policies of standards organizations typically give specified options to the patent holder, different licensing terms can be used to maintain control over the technology as indicated already in the background section of this article. Furthermore, it is only the essential patents need to be licensed when a company participates in setting a standard. As one of the interviewees pointed out, this constitutes a fairly thin layer. Only patents that are technically or commercially necessary to ensure compliance with the standard must be licensed, and only to the extent that it is necessary. Therefore, if the patent holder has waived its rights, for instance, patents cannot be asserted for complying with the standard, but they can be asserted if something extra is being done (Interview data U.S., 2004). Then again those companies that do not benefit from a common

standard or are after royalties have generally no interest in taking part in standard setting because doing so could require the licensing of their rights under royalty-free or RAND terms.

The licensing quandaries will be discussed later on, and I will now turn to a more detailed analysis of the submarine patent risk stemming from deficient identification of essential patents to which some of the factors presented in this and the earlier section clearly contribute. Generally speaking the highlighted importance of intellectual property rights and their substantial role as part of companies' business strategies has made it more difficult to avoid conflicts of interests.

STANDARDIZATION AND SUBMARINE PATENTS

Both patents providing their holders with exclusive rights, and open standards expected to be widely promulgated without exclusive control are important to the ICT sector. As they both want different things resolution is not always easy (Cunningham, 2005). From the perspective of this article the core element contributing to the tension between patents and standards, is that it is not always known in advance whether undertakings have patents or pending patent applications that might cover the standards technology. This complicates matters, since patents that surface after the adoption of the standard may, in the worst case, result in no other choice than abandoning it. Although both licensing and patent identification quandaries that were introduced briefly already in the background section may lead to significant economic losses, it is more difficult to anticipate the consequences and to avoid problems in the latter case. Therefore, submarine patents that surface after a standard has been elected and adopted are not only a practical dilemma but also a policy concern. Submarine patents may face the industry with unpredictable predicaments, and ultimately harm consumers. Cases in which unidentified patents of standard setters have caused concern and resulted in legal disputes include Dell and Rambus litigations. Third-party submarines contain the patents of Forgent Networks, Inc and Eolas Technologies, Inc among others.

The most effective way to reduce the possibility of hidden patents that have the potential to cause complications with respect to the adoption of a standard is to conduct a proper patent due diligence periodically and to agree upon the contravening issues beforehand. This is where the patent policies of standards organizations that are aimed at creating shared expectations among standardization participants with respect to licensing and disclosure rules come to the fore (Interview data U.S., 2004; Ohana, 2005). Indeed, if companies participate in setting a standard they usually do their best to follow the standardization organization's patent policies, and consider any deviation unethical (Interview data U.S., 2004; Ohana, 2005). Sometimes the rules are simply not very transparent, and since different standardization organizations have different types of policies it may be burdensome to be aware of and to comply with them all, particularly if the company is involved in many standards organizations. In fact, about 40% of companies in Blind et al. (2002) sample group reported that they had problems due to the unclear IPR structure, resulting, for instance, in the late identification of the patent holders. There is a need for rules that hold as few surprises as possible (Interview data U.S., 2004; Ohana, 2005).

The standards organization's patent policies and their shortcomings with respect to the disclosure obligation are examined in subsequent paragraphs. Since companies adopting the standard ultimately bear the responsibility for patent infringement, there is then a brief glimpse into that part of companies' patent strategies that is aimed at reducing that risk. Combined with what has been said earlier about the patent system and the patent landscape in the ICT sector, these sections constitute the analysis of the causes contributing to the likelihood of infringing others' essential patents in the ICT sector and the challenges companies face in settling these disputes particularly due to the emergence of so-called patent trolls. Case studies illustrate the situation further and give examples of actualized disagreements. The fact that many disputes have been handled in court demonstrates that it has not been possible to settle the issues amicably and that there are significant economic interests involved.

Patent Policies

Many, although not all, standards bodies that are responsible or involved in coordinating the development of standards have implemented explicit IPR or patent policies for handling issues to do with standardization and patents. These policies aim at discouraging the manipulation of the process in order to gain market power, and at easing the tension between the open nature of standards and the proprietary nature of IPRs (Feldman & Rees, 2000; Kipnis, 2000; Soininen, 2005). The policies guide the participant's behavior, and from the legal point of view their nature and content affect the determination of whether a company participating in standard setting and failing to disclose its relevant rights has breached a contract, defrauded, competed unfairly or deceptively or abused its dominant position, for example. Therefore, if the patent policy is deficient, it is difficult to challenge the patent holder's right to prevent all others from using his invention, discriminate among licensees or to condition the license however he wants to as long as this is done in accordance with relevant laws. In the following attention is paid to the nature, extent, scope and timeframe of the prevailing disclosure obligations of different organizations such as ITU, ANSI, ETSI, W3C, OASIS, and IETF and their ability to reduce the risk of submarine patents is assessed.

Nature of the Policy

It has been argued that without legally binding policies standards could easily become the subject of "hold-up" because once a standard has been established, all the patents necessary to comply with it become truly essential. The more widely the standard is adopted, the more power the patent holders gain (Shapiro, 2001). Nonetheless, not all standards organizations aspire to control their participants through imposing on them explicit contractual obligations, and many use their policies more as a "code of practice" (e.g., ITU-T Patent Policy, n.d.). ANSI, for example, has taken the position that it does not mandate disclosure or impose licensing obligations on patent holders because this would overburden the process. It relies more on its participants to voluntarily act in accordance with the policy. Nevertheless, according to Marasco (2003) it has not so far faced abuse of the process. Actually, even though the guideline-nature of the disclosure requirement may narrow down the possibilities to enforce it in court and to claim damages in case of an infringement, non-obligatory rules may also bear significance when it is determined whether a certain participant has operated in good faith under some other principle of law, such as Federal Trade Commission Act, Section 5 that prohibits unfair and deceptive business practices. The case studies of Dell and Rambus examined later will demonstrate this issue further.

The Duty to Disclose

The patent policies of standardization organizations differ in their approach to disclosure in terms of duty to disclose, the scope of the disclosure and its timing. For the most part, they tend to rely on their participants (submitters or members [Perens, n.d.]) to voluntarily disclose all patents that could influence the standard. This is by no means a simple task, and failing to disclose patents that are essential for using the standard may happen by accident. Searching the portfolio is time-consuming and expensive, and therefore companies may not want to make the expense of searching them. Also, it is not always easy to recognize all essential patents and patent applications. This follows that particularly in big companies with large portfolios a company's representative in a standard-setting process may not know whether a proposed standard incorporates a patent within his company's portfolio (Kipnis, 2000; Peterson, 2002b; Soininen, 2005).

It is probably for this reason that standards organizations generally take no responsibility for finding all relevant IPRs, or for verifying the information disclosed by the contributors (e.g., ANSI, 2003b; IETF, 2005; OASIS, 2005), and they are not keen on imposing such obligations on their participants. Thus, many of them do not require disclosure that goes beyond the personal knowledge of the discloser (e.g., IETF, 2005; OASIS, 2005), nor do they require their participants to carry out patent searches (e.g., ANSI, 2005a; ETSI, 2005; ITU-T, 2005; OASIS, 2005; W3C, 2004), which in turn increases the probability that relevant patents remain undisclosed (Soininen, 2005).

Scope of the Disclosure Requirement

Another contributing factor to the submarine patent risk is that it is not necessarily required for companies to disclose their pending, particularly unpublished, patent applications (e.g., ANSI, 2003b: ANSI, 2003a; Kipnis, 2000; Lemley, 2002). The W3C disclosure requirement is an exception, however. It also extends to the unpublished patent claims that were developed based on information from a W3C Working Group or W3C document (W3C, 2004). The OASIS policy also requires the disclosure of all patents and/or patent applications known to the technical committee member (OASIS, 2005). The problem with announcing pending patents is that, although the protection provided by a patent is always unclear until confirmed in court, the scope is even more ambiguous until the patent is issued, and it is therefore not possible to assess whether it will be essential in order to use the technology. It is also possible that it will never be granted. The problem is, however, that if there is no obligation to disclose pending patent applications, waiting until the standard has been agreed upon before allowing the patent to be issued does not constitute a policy breach. In fact, given the need to make informative decisions about standard "characteristics," there has been discussion on whether participants should also be obliged to disclose their potential patenting activity. The U.S. patent system includes a so-called grace period, which allows the inventor to file for a patent up to one year after disclosing it in a printed publication. Thus, it is possible for a company that has submitted a technical proposal to the standards body to then file for a patent covering it after the standard has been elected.

Opinions on the scope of the disclosure obligation are divided. Some people feel that, although companies were required to state their possible interest in patenting their technology, it is never certain that they will apply these patents in reality, or that they will be granted or even essential. On the one hand, if companies had to announce their potential pending patents, other committee members could take them into account when decisions about standardized technology were made (Kipnis, 2000). At the same time, there might be a risk of "sham" announcements in these cases (Soininen, 2005).

Timing of the Disclosure

The timeframe of the disclosure requirement also bears significance in respect to the causes of the submarine patent problem. Since standardization may be valid for years and companies' R&D development is definitely not frozen during that time, it is likely that pending patent applications will be modified and new applications filed during the process. Therefore, although a company may

have no pending patent applications or granted patents at the beginning, it might have them when the standard is finally set. For this reason, some standards bodies, such as W3C, have patent policies that incorporate an obligation to disclose essential patents throughout the entire process (W3C, 2004). The ETSI IPR Policy also requires each member to make reasonable efforts to inform the ETSI in good time about any essential patents, both its own and third-party, of which it becomes aware at any stage (ETSI, 2005). Then again, the IETF policy encourages contributors to update their disclosures if the claims are modified, or if a patent is granted or abandoned (IETF, 2005).

Third-Party Patents

Standards organizations patent policies can never bind third parties and even though some patent policies do encourage also other interested parties as well as contributors to bring attention to potential third-party patents (e.g., IETF, 2005; ITU-T, n.d.; ITU-T, 2005; OASIS, 2005), this is not enough to record all of them. One option to increase the awareness of third-party rights would be to conduct a patent search. Standards bodies are not typically involved in such an activity, however (e.g., IETF, 2005; OASIS, 2005). On the other hand, ETSI is now considering an ex ante approach to declaring relevant patents with respect to the Long-term Evolution (LTE) standard (Informamedia.com, 2006). This would at least diminish the likelihood that new essential patents emerge after the standard has been elected and it remains to be seen whether this approach will be adopted on a broader scale.

It could be concluded that patent policies are helpful in reducing particularly the risk of standard setters' submarine patents and even though they could be strengthened in many ways to narrow down the possibility of manipulating the process in order to gain market power, some of the difficulties are mainly practical. Therefore it might not be possible to avoid them even if companies were posed an obligation to disclose their potential patenting activity, for instance. The only effect of doing so could be that companies are discouraged from participating which in turn would increase the risk that patents remain undisclosed and generate problems at a later stage.

Patent Strategies to Avoid Infringement

There may be a room for improvement in standards bodies patent policies but it is not only loopholes in them but also deficiencies in companies' own patent strategies that contribute to the fact that relevant rights may remain unnoticed and standard adopters may face predicaments due to them. Obviously, it is the company incorporating a standard into its products and services that ultimately bears the risk of infringing others' patents, and therefore identifying relevant rights is not by any means only the responsibility of standards organizations. Indeed, in addition to enhancing a company's own patenting, licensing and enforcement activities, a proficient patent strategy also helps in avoiding patent infringements.

A major goal in managing corporate patent liability is to avoid being sued and paying substantial royalties to other patent holders. What is even more important is to avoid being prevented from using a particular technology, which could force the company out of a lucrative market (Miele, 2000). Furthermore, the costs of patent litigation, particularly in the U.S., could be substantial and a drain on financial and human resources (Knight, 2001). Thus, if it is necessary to prevent significant liability, the company should consider refraining from using technology that infringes others' rights. In some cases this is not possible, and the company has to employ such technology that has been patented by others in order to operate in a particular market. Keeping both situations in mind, there are certain steps that could be taken in order to reduce the liability, the likelihood that patent holders will assert their rights against the

company, and the amount of royalties that should be paid in cases in which patent liability cannot be avoided (Miele, 2000). One of these steps includes identifying patent problems early in the product cycles. For instance, a freedom-to-operate search conducted on the basis of patent classification numbers and certain keywords might be useful for identifying close references, which could then be examined in more detail (Knight, 2001) before the product is released onto the market. Another step is to monitor the patent activities of the company's closest and biggest competitors because companies are often particularly sensitive to infringing activities that originate from their competitors (Miele, 2000).

In practice avoiding infringements is not that easy and companies' patent strategies are not flawless. No patent search is or can be 100% thorough (Knight, 2001), and as many Finnish interviewees mentioned, it may be difficult to identify relevant rights and to make sense of the scope of patent rights (Interview data Finland, 2003). Sometimes, a company may not even have any specialized infringement surveillance. Indeed, in Finnish companies infringement checkpoints were rarely incorporated into R&D projects. This does not indicate, however, that there was no knowledge whatsoever about the patent landscape: information regarding other companies' patent position can be obtained as a side product when the company is considering patenting its own inventions and conducts prior art searches for that purpose (Interview data Finland, 2003). As far as the U.S. companies were concerned, the extent of due diligence with regard to others patents varied depending on the situation: some technology areas were more important, and some were known to be more heavily patented than others, thus requiring more thorough clarification. Nevertheless, these companies typically did not have any systematic patent clearance (Interview data U.S., 2004).

A further risk-reducing alternative to freedom-to-operate analysis and other types of patent surveillance is to use the porcupine approach discussed earlier in the section on patent strategy in the ICT sector. This means that a company builds a defensive patent portfolio aimed at reducing potential infringement allocations and making settlement easier. It may also have broad cross-licenses in place, thereby removing a huge block of patents from its surveillance list (Interview data Finland, 2003; Interview data U.S., 2004). This is a strategy that has been favored by large U.S. and multinational Finnish ICT companies, but unfortunately it does not work well against individual patent holders or so-called patent trolling companies. The fact that patents are being assigned more than before, further increases the risk that they find their way to such parties that do not come up in competitor surveillance and remain unnoticed for that reason.

In sum, companies may take certain precautions to prevent patent liability, but even if they do, the risk of patent infringement remains particularly high in areas in which it is simply not possible to keep track of new filed applications and issued patents. As one of the U.S. interviewees stated, there is always a risk that others' patents will read on your product. You can do all the clearance work and look at all the patents that are out there, but the next week a new patent may be granted (Interview data U.S., 2004). Nevertheless, there are many improvements that could be made in order to strengthen the infringement surveillance, and instead of fighting only their own battles during the standard-adoption phase, companies could pool their expertise and resources and help to limit the submarine patent risk already before the standard is established.

Case Studies of Standard-Setters' Submarine Patents

Standards organizations' IPR policies related to disclosure do not cover every situation, which is understandable, since weight must also be given to the flexibility of the process. Also the means ICT companies have currently implemented in order to avoid infringement of other companies' patents do not help much in identifying relevant rights. The unfortunate consequences are that despite the efforts there still is a high risk that patents surface after the establishment of the standard, and these (essential) patents are much more valuable then than they would have been previously: it gets more difficult to change the specification as time passes and the technology becomes adopted. Therefore, particularly if they are not breaching IPR policy, some patent holders may seize the opportunity and seek to hide the fact that they have essential patents, or pending applications—otherwise the standard could be modified so that it no longer covers them.

The problem with standard-setters' submarine patents is not only theoretical, because the risk has actualized also in reality. Cases that have involved undisclosed patenting activities and have resulted in legal disputes include Dell, Rambus and Unocal from which Dell and Rambus cases are discussed in the following. These examples demonstrate further the importance and role of a proficient patent policy since it does not merely help to reduce the submarine patent risk beforehand but it also influences the possibilities to solve the problem later on. The previously-mentioned example cases indicate, for instance, that competition authorities do not take misbehavior during standard setting lightly and are keen on examining doubtful situations even though the merits of the case may not be sufficient in order to find fault from the defendant's side. In the end the result is dependent on the wording of the policy and proof of misbehavior. In a way legal tools that are available provide the last means to solve actualized conflicts. Luckily, litigation is not always needed. For instance IBM's behavior in relation to ebXML standard implies that consequences of the failure to disclose are not always detrimental. Since many ICT companies are largely dependent on one another it may be possible to reach an amicable solution rather easily in some situations.

Federal Trade Commission v. Dell Computer Corp. (1995)

In the Dell (1995) case the Federal Trade Commission (FTC) accused Dell Computer Corporation, on the basis of Section 5 of the FTC Act which prohibits unfair or deceptive business practices, of intentionally concealing its patent during the Video Electronics Standards Association (VESA) VL-bus technology standardization process. Although VESA's IPR policy required that its members disclose any potentially conflicting patents, Dell certified that it did not have such patents. After the standard had been widely adopted in the marketplace, Dell sought to enforce its patent against VESA members. The Commission found that even if Dell's actions were not strictly speaking intentional, the company had failed to act in good faith. It also stated that had Dell disclosed its patents properly, VESA would have incorporated different technology into the standard. Dell's misrepresentation therefore caused restraints on competition resulting in the hindrance of industry acceptance and increased costs in terms of implementing the bus design (Federal Trade Commission v. Dell Computer Corp., FTC File No. 931 0097 (2 November 1995)) (Soininen, 2005).

In the end, a consent decree was agreed upon and Dell promised not to assert its patents against computer manufacturers that complied with the standard (Balto & Wolman, 2003; Hemphill, 2005; Lemley, 2002). It should be noted, however, that even though a satisfactory result was reached through a settlement the case was not decided in court leaving the industry with ambivalence about the proper interpretation. In fact, the Rambus litigation discussed later indicates that the conclusion could have been different if the case had been litigated further.

Rambus, Inc v. Infineon Technologies AG (Fed. Cir. 2003) and Federal Trade Commission v. Rambus, Inc

Rambus has faced two litigations due to its actions in the Joint Electronics Devices Engineering Council (JEDEC). The first one, Rambus, Inc v. Infineon Technologies AG (2003), arose when Rambus sued Infineon for synchronous dynamic random access memory (SDRAM) patent infringement. Infineon counter-claimed that Rambus had defrauded it when it failed to disclose patents and pending patent applications during its membership of JEDEC and while JEDEC was developing the industry standard for SDRAM. More specifically, Rambus had filed for a patent '898 for Rambus DRAM technology in 1990, it cooperated in forming the standard from 1992 until 1996 when it resigned from the standards body just before the final vote, and both during and after its participation it had filed continuation and multiple divisional applications based on the original 898 application, and by doing so it amended its patent protection to cover the SDRAM technology. Later, it allowed these patents to be issued, and began to defend its own patents aggressively, requiring companies to pay royalties. Nonetheless, the Federal Circuit came to the conclusion that Rambus had not fraudulently failed to disclose its patent applications, but held that its duty to disclose as a JEDEC participant applied only to those containing claims that could reasonably be considered necessary in order to practice the proposed standard, and that this obligation arose only when the work had formally begun. The court held further that the duty to disclose did not cover the participant's future plans or intentions, that is, filing or amending patent applications, and criticized JEDEC's patent policy for its staggering lack of defining details. It thereby left its members with vaguely defined expectations as to what they believed the policy required. (Rambus, Inc v. Infineon

Technologies AG, No. 01-1449 [Fed. Cir. 2003]; Soininen, 2005).

The second litigation, FTC v. Rambus, Inc was based on Section 5 of the FTC Act, and it is still pending. The FTC has accused Rambus of a series of anti-competitive acts and practices, claiming that through deliberate and intentional means it has illegally monopolized, attempted to monopolize, or otherwise engaged in unfair methods of competition in certain markets related to the technological features necessary for the design and manufacture of a common form of digital computer memory. It further claims that Rambus's anti-competitive behavior has, among other things, increased the royalties associated with the manufacture, sale, or use of synchronous DRAM technology, and has reduced the incentive to produce memory using it and to participate in JEDEC or other industry standard-setting organizations or activities (Administrative Complaint, 2002; Soininen, 2005).

The difference between FTC v. Rambus and the Dell case is that in the former the FTC is attempting to demonstrate that Rambus gained market power through its misbehavior, and thus that the industry is locked into the JEDEC's SDRAM standard. According to the FTC, "It is not economically feasible for the industry to attempt to alter or work around the JEDEC standards in order to avoid payment of royalties to Rambus" (Administrative Complaint, 2002). In its initial decision released on 24 February 2004, Judge MacGuire stated that the FTC "failed to sustain their burden of establishing liability for the violations alleged," and dismissed the complaint. In her opinion there was no evidence, for example, that Rambus had violated JEDEC patent policy, or that the challenged conduct had had anti-competitive effects (Initial Decision, 2004; Soininen, 2005). To conclude, even though a standard setter has operated unethically and the other participants disapprove his conduct, it may be difficult to challenge it in court particularly if proper guidelines are lacking.

IBM and the ebXML Standard

Even though Dell and Rambus attempted to enforce their rights against those who had adopted the standard, patent holders do not always seek royalties although a patent emerges after the standard has been established. One reason for a submarine patent holder to comply with the standards organization's policy is the bad publicity, which may result in the loss of credibility as a fair standardization participant (Sarvas & Soininen, 2002). For example, IBM claimed in April 2002 that it had one patent and one patent application that were relevant for implementing the open, royalty-free ebXML standard developed by OASIS in cooperation with the United Nations, and that it was willing to license them on RAND terms. IBM's announcement caused strong reactions in the public and in the industry, particularly because IBM had participated in the design of the standard. Furthermore, IBM had previously announced that it was willing to contribute to the standard without any restrictions, but had nevertheless made comments regarding the licensing terms and conditions of the two patents. However, soon after the news reached the public, IBM agreed to license the patents royalty-free (Berlind, 2002a; Berlind, 200b; Wong, 2002).

Case Studies of Third-Party Submarines

Those companies that do not benefit from a specific standard simply do not participate in setting it and therefore it may happen that third parties who are not covered by patent policies have patents that "read on" the standard, and do not appear before its adoption. If the patent holder then decides to enforce his rights, the benefits of the standard may be lost. In fact, many businesses that received patents during the technology boom were either purchased by other companies or landed in holding companies. Thus, in some cases a standards organization may adopt a standard believing it is royalty-free, and then find out that the new owner, which did not participate in the standard-setting process, is aggressively trying to enforce its IPRs (Clark, 2002). For instance, the director of intellectual property at Jupiter Networks Inc has observed a sudden surge in these types of third-party patent-infringement assertions, some of which are valid and some are not. This surge is understandable in his opinion, because patent holders hope to profit from the wide deployment of products that must implement Internet standards. He described a typical patent-assertion scenario in which a patent holder dusts off issued patents directed to old but related technologies or modifies claims in pending patent applications to read on published standards, and then targets standards-compliant networking-equipment manufacturers (Lo, 2002). The case studies presented in subsequent paragraphs illustrate the type of legal disputes that may arise if a third-party patent holder attempts to enforce his rights. Basically, the accused infringer can defend itself by claiming non-infringement or unenforceability, or by attempting to invalidate the patent. These are the strategies followed also in the case studies presented.

Forgent Networks and the JPEG Standard

A third-party claim arose in 2002 when Forgent Networks Inc searched its portfolio of 40 patents and found that it had a patent (US Patent 4,698,672) related to the implementation of a baseline version of the ISO/IEC 1098-1 standard, that is, the JPEG image standard that is one of the most popular formats for compressing and sharing files on the Internet, and is also used in various industries in products such as digital cameras, personal digital assistants, cellular phones, printers and scanners. In its desperate search for profits, Forgent estimated the solidness of its infringement claim and entered into a multi-million-dollar licensing agreement with the Japanese companies Sony and Sanyo before making a public announcement in

July 2002 of potential JPEG patent infringement and starting to pursue licensing fees from a range of companies. Forgent had, in fact, obtained the patent in question through the acquisition of Compression Albs Inc. in 1997. Since the inventors who originally filed for the patent in 1986 had not participated in the JPEG standardization process that was going on around that time, according to Forgent, no abuse of the standardization process had taken place (Clark, 2002; Lemos, 2002; Markoff, 2002; Reingold, 2006).

As a result of Forgent's aggressive patent enforcement, many U.S., European, and Asian companies agreed to license the '672 patent, and by April 2004 it had generated approximately $90 million in licensing fees. Those who did not agree to license willingly were sued for patent infringement. Indeed, on 22 April 2004 Forgent's subsidiary Compression Labs, Inc sued 31 major hardware and software vendors, including Dell and Apple Computers, for patent infringement, and on 6 August 2004 it initiated litigation against 11 companies (Asaravala, 2004; Forgent Networks, 2006).

Professionals in the field of compression technology and representatives of the JPEG committee doubted the validity of the patent and stated that there could be prior art available that would render it invalid. These doubts have been manifested in legal actions, such as those taken by 24 companies that filed a counter-complaint against Forgent and its subsidiary in the Delaware District Court seeking declaratory relief as to non-infringement, invalidity, and unenforceability of the patent. Even Microsoft, which had not been sued by Forgent at that time, filed a complaint against it on 15 April 2005, claiming that the patent had been obtained fraudulently. Furthermore, the non-profit Public Patent Foundation has filed a request for re-examination of the '627 patent in November 2005. In late January 2006 the U.S. Patent and Trademark Office (USPTO) made a decision to review the patent, which will in any case expire in October

2006 (Forgent Networks, 2006; Lemos, 2002; Reingold, 2006; Red Herring, 2006).

EOLAS and HTML Specification

Another third-party submarine example is the EOLAS case. Here, the dispute arose when Eolas Technologies Inc, which had licensed a patent from the University of California, sued Microsoft for the use of the patented invention, that is, the widely used feature of HTML, the format that describes the format of Web pages. After a long stream of litigation the Federal Circuit (2005) also found the patent valid and infringed (Eolas Technologies Incorporated and the Regents of the University of California v. Microsoft Corporation, Case Nr. 04-1234 (Fed.Cir, 2005)), and the Supreme Court refused to hear the case (Malone, 2005). At the request of W3C the Eolas patent was also re-examined by the USPTO, which released two preliminary findings claiming that it was invalid. Ultimately, the patent office kept the patent in force, however (Perens, n.d.).

Although a patent holder has a very strong negotiating position if the patent accidentally "surfaces" after the adoption of the standard and those who are accused of patent infringement can mainly defend themselves by trying to invalidate the patent, third-party patents do not always create problems. In many cases reasonable licensing terms can be agreed upon. As with the cases in which the patent holder had participated in the standard setting, business relationships and bad publicity may also be reasons why third-party patent holders comply with a standardization organization's policy and license the patents royalty-free, for instance, although they may have no obligation to do so.

The Risk of Patent Problems and How to Reduce It?

It could be concluded from previous discussion that it is important to implement proficient patent policies that are clear, concise and transparent and hold as few surprises as possible. These policies should be drafted with an intention of influencing companies' behavior both during and after standard setting so that misconduct could be diminished and potential problems solved. The nature, extent, scope and the timeframe of the disclosure requirements are examples of such disclosure terms that could be clarified in order to reduce the submarine patent problem, which taking into account the recent litigations and the fact that 40% of companies in Blind and Thumm's sample group reported problems regarding unclear IPR structure (Blind et al., 2002) is not only theoretical. Furthermore, one way of reducing the problems that may result when not all patents are known prior to the establishment of a standard could be to require that essential patents granted in the future will be identified and potentially licensed under the same terms as the disclosed patents. In fact, it is a common requirement in patent pools for essential future patents to be subject to grant-back and thus to contribute to the pool. This requirement may occasionally have anticompetitive effects, however, Balto and Wolman (2003) and patent holders would probably consider this type of requirement too restrictive.

As regards to third-party patents that are becoming a more and more relevant concern there is a lot that could be done in order to reduce the risk they may pose to the adoption of a standard. First of all, the standard-setting participants could be encouraged to conduct more thorough patent searches already during the standardization procedure, and to let the standards organizations know about potential third-party claims. Secondly, third parties could be reserved an opportunity to make a patent statement early on, and thirdly, standards organizations could take a more active role in finding relevant patents themselves. Otherwise, if dealing with the increasing number of third-party patents was only left to companies implementing the standard, they would be in different positions and the openness of the standard could be endangered: only those companies that already have cross-licensing agreements in place, have enough leverage in order to negotiate a good deal with the patent holder, or have the resources to fight the patent in court might be able to adopt the standard.

A further way to limit the risk of submarine patent-related troubles arising from both standard-setters and third parties, and to help companies to solve the conflicts better and therefore to reduce the harmful consequences of such patents would be to renovate the legal framework. The possibilities and the need to do so have not been estimated in this article, however. Obviously, when considering the actions needed, the advantages and disadvantages should be estimated and balanced carefully. Therefore, it is in place to examine also the other patent and standard related quandary that has to do with licensing. These problems are similar to those experienced with submarine patents, and in fact, the GSM example presented later is in essence a submarine patent case. What basically differentiates submarine patent cases and those in which a patent has been properly disclosed is, however, the possibility to make informative decisions about the adoption of a standard, and to design around it or agree upon licensing terms in advance, and thus avoid great societal losses that would occur had the standard been already broadly adopted and if the parties were not able to solve the conflicts.

LICENSING OF PATENTS AND STANDARDIZATION

In case a patent holder has disclosed that it may have patents or pending patent applications that are essential for using a standard, standards bodies typically pose certain licensing alternatives for that company. The patent holder's options are usually the following: (1) the patent holder may state that it is willing to license its essential patents on royalty-free terms, (2) the patent holder

may refuse from licensing altogether, (3) the patent holder may promise to license, but negotiate the terms separately, or (4) the patent folder may make a statement of licensing on fair, reasonable and nondiscriminatory terms (RAND). These alternatives are discussed further in subsequent paragraphs, and case studies are used to illustrate the licensing perplexities. The necessity and effects of addressing the submarine patent problem are estimated on this basis.

Royalty-Free Licensing

Royalty-free standards often have more chances of being broadly accepted and widely used than standards requiring licensing payments. For instance, the Internet has been said to require freely available standards in order to work effectively. Patent-based standards requiring royalty payments inhibit its development because they slow down or discourage the adoption of new technologies. As a consequence, companies frequently agree to make their patented technology available on a royalty-free basis, and hope to generate more profits by selling products that use their standardized technology (Clark, 2002; Interview data U.S., 2004).

As mentioned, given the benefits, standardization participants are often willing to license their patents on a royalty-free basis for the specific purpose of using the standard. This holds true particularly if they are able to make sure that the patents could nevertheless be utilized for defensive purposes if the need arose (Interview data U.S., 2004). Naturally, participation and agreement to license to everyone require that such conduct is in accordance with the firm's commercial interests: having its superior technology chosen for a standard may provide it with a head start in incorporating that technology into its products, for example. Then again, companies seeking licensing revenues through incorporating their proprietary inventions into a standard do not typically have a business motivation to participate in designing royalty-free standards (Soininen, 2005).

Refusal to License

If a royalty-free licensing scheme cannot be negotiated, and the patented technology cannot be designed around, it may nevertheless be in the interests of the public to get the patent holder to agree to license it at least on RAND terms. If the patent holder refuses to license on these vague terms, the standardization process is halted and other solutions are sought (Hjelm, 2000). Refusing to license at all is rare, however, although it is the most influential form of leveraging one's patent rights (Rahnasto, 2003). As the following case study demonstrates it has nevertheless played a major role in making the ETSI Wideband Code Division Multiple Access (WCDMA) standard backward compatible with the IS-95 standard favored by Qualcomm Inc, for instance (Soininen, 2005).

What happened in the WCDMA dispute was that Qualcomm accused ETSI of intentionally excluding Qualcomm's technology from its standards, thereby creating an unfavorable position for Qualcomm in the European third-generation telecommunications market. In order to make its voice better heard, the company claimed that the key technologies needed for WCDMA infringed its patents, and refused to license this technology unless the WCDMA was made backward compatible with the IS-95 standard. It seems that Qualcomm expected that a harmonized standard would increase its licensing revenues fundamentally (Hjelm, 2000; Westman, 1999; Soininen, 2005).

Ericsson, who was another key patent holder in the technology involved, was of the opinion that Qualcomm's patents were not infringed, and to gain a better negotiation position it also sued Qualcomm for the infringement of Ericsson's CDMA patents (one of the U.S. standards) Qualcomm was employing. Finally, consensus was reached as a result of cooperation between Qualcomm and Ericsson. The companies entered into a series of definitive agreements that resolved all disputes relating to CDMA technology, and as a part of the settlement Ericsson acquired Qualcomm's terrestrial CDMA wireless infrastructure business, including its R&D facilities. Furthermore, the companies gave a promise to license essential WCDMA patents (Hjelm, 2000; Westman, 1999). The standardization process was practically frozen during this period, which lasted roughly a year (Sarvas & Soininen, 2002).

Indeed, as the previous example demonstrates companies operating in the ICT sector are dependent on each other and therefore conflicts in one area may result in complex legal battles in another. Nevertheless refusing to license may be a feasible strategy for a company that opposes a certain standard. A firm may also wish to delay the acceptance of a standard to give it more time to develop products that incorporate it.

Blank Promise to License

Firms typically agree to license their patents royalty-free, or on RAND or other terms, or they may merely agree to license but make no statement of the the terms and conditions. Particularly if the last-mentioned option is available and chosen, there is likely to be a fight over the proper licensing conditions. One example of a disagreement over proper licensing terms was the one that arose during the formation of the European GSM standard in the 1980s, which was first coordinated by CEPT (Conference Europeenne des Administrations des Postes et des Telecommunications) and later by ETSI. In fact, this particular licensing dilemma, which involved Motorola, contributed to the change in patent culture that took place in the European telecommunications sector in which patenting had until that time been regarded as a secondary issue—specifically among the national telecommunications service providers whose markets had previously been monopolized but were now deregulated (Bekkers, Verspagen, & Smits, 2002; Granstrand, 1999).

What basically has been presented in literature to have happened in the context of the GSM standard was that a U.S. company, Motorola, for which patenting was a natural and integral part of doing business, entered the European scene and employed the aggressive patent strategy it was used to. While other standard setters operated in accordance with a "gentleman's agreement", shared their ideas and specifications during the standardization process in an open atmosphere, and refrained from patenting once the basic technical decisions had been made, Motorola pursued patent protection in the course of the process (Granstarand, 1999). Furthermore, Bekkers, Verpagen & Smits (2002) have argued that while most other companies agreed on licensing their essential rights on fair, reasonable and nondiscriminatory terms, Motorola refused to make general declarations. It declined monetary compensation and was only willing to cross-license its patents to certain companies. Although Siemens, Alcatel, Nokia and Ericsson were able to negotiate cross-licenses, Motorola's licensing strategy effectively prevented various other companies from entering the market. When a number of non-European companies finally managed to obtain all the necessary licenses to built GSM terminals in the late 1990s, the cross-licensees had already built up a strong market position. Moreover, since the cumulative licensing fee paid for a GSM handset was very high as confirmed by studies of Bekkers, et al., the price made it difficult to compete if the company was not part of a cross-licensing agreement. In fact it has been argued that the licensing fees have totaled as much as 29% of the costs of the GSM handset (Bekkers et al. 2002)

RAND-Licensing

Even under the RAND system, specific licensing terms are typically not agreed upon during the standard setting. Revealing the terms after adoption can generate conflicts and hamper the parties' ability to compete in the affected market. Peterson (2002b) lists the following situations that could arise in this context: (1) the patent holder seeks a broad grant-back that appears non-discriminatory but has different effects on different parties; (2) the patentee requires a minimum annual royalty based on "administrative costs", which may have the effect of excluding smaller rivals and new entrants; (3) the patentee seeks royalties from downstream providers such as manufacturers of finished goods, and refuses to license to suppliers of upstream inputs such as IC vendors, and thus to increase its income, which however may increase competitors' costs and time to market; (4) the patent holder acquires admissions of infringement and validity, and/or retains the right to immediately terminate a license if the licensor challenges infringement or validity; (5) the patentee requires acceptance of venue, which might constitute a major problem for small companies or foreign competitors; and (6) the patent holder seeks a royalty that it considers "fair" but that exceeds the average profit margin of all the parties who need licenses. For instance, one of the U.S. interviewees mentioned that his company had been approached with a royalty requirement as high as 10% (Interview data U.S., 2004).

Furthermore, even though the company may have made it clear in its licensing statement that the license was only available under certain conditions it considered as fair, reasonable and nondiscriminatory, these terms may come as a surprise to some and cause disputes. For instance, the Townshend v. Rockwell International Corp. and Conexant Systems (N.D.Cal.2000) litigation arose when Townshend, whose patents "read on" the V.90 standard for 56K chipset modems and who had promised to license them on certain terms, filed a patent-infringement suit against Rockwell and its successor Conexant. In response Rockwell and Conexant asserted two antitrust counterclaims based on the Sherman Act Sections 1 (conspiracy) and 2 (monopolization and its attempt) among others, and claimed that Townshend and 3Com had conspired to restrain trade by deceiving the ITU into incorporating Townshend's patent into the industry standard, denying competitors access to the technology, and filing a patent-infringement lawsuit to prevent Conexant from using Townshend's technology. Furthermore, Townshend and 3Com were accused of having attempted to monopolize the market for 56K modem chipset products (Kirsch, 2000; Townshend v. Rockwell International Corp. and Conexant Systems, Inc., 55 U.S.P.Q.2d 1011 (N.D.Cal.2000)).

I am not going to go into the legal specialties of the case here, but the Court found all Rockwell's and Conexant's counterclaims unfounded. With regard to the antitrust-based claims it noted, among other things, that there had been no collusion, and since 3Com—to which Townshend had non-exclusively licensed its essential patent prior to the setting of the ITU V.90 standard—had declared during the standardization procedure that Townshend had relevant patents pending, ITU had not been deceived. Since 3Com had also made a proposition prior to the acceptance of the standard to license those patents for a per-unit royalty fee, or to cross-license them in return for technologies that were specified in the standard, or related to it and were otherwise practically necessary or desirable for technical or economic reasons in order to make a commercially viable product compliant with the standard, and further that it had not been shown that Rockwell and Conexant could not have obtained a license under those terms, Townshend's actions could not be held anticompetitive (Kirsch, 2000; Townshend v. Rockwell International Corp. and Conexant Systems, Inc., 55 U.S.P.Q.2d 1011 (N.D.Cal.2000)).

The previous case illustrates that it is particularly difficult to defend oneself against such patent holders that have disclosed their patents properly and declared their licensing terms during the standard-setting procedure. Indeed, due to the flexibility in the interpretation of RAND,

having patents in standardized technology could also become a valuable source of royalties or other resources. For instance, Qualcomm relies on a royalty stream resulting from others utilizing its patented technology incorporated into various standards. In fact, the pricing of Qualcomm's licenses has led to huge disagreement between Qualcomm and six other companies involved in the WCDMA 3G standard. Basically, Broadcom, Ericsson, NEX, Nokia, Panasonic Mobile Communications and Texas Instruments have all claimed that Qualcomm, who promised to license its essential WCDMA patents on RAND terms, is charging excessive and disproportionate royalties for them. Qualcomm has been claimed to charge the same royalty rate on the WCDMA 3G standard as it does for the CDMA2000 standard adopted in the U.S., although it has fewer essential patents in it. Furthermore, it offers lower royalty rates to handset customers who buy chipsets exclusively from Qualcomm than to manufacturers of chipsets for mobile phones, making entry into the market more difficult for chip makers (Nokia, 2005a; Outlaw.com, 2005; Nokia, 2005b).

As a result of this disagreement, all six of the previously-mentioned companies filed complaints to the European Commission in October 2005 requesting it to investigate and to put an end to Qualcomm's anticompetitive conduct (Nokia, 2005a, 2005b; Out-law.com, 2005). Qualcomm has responded to the allocations stating that they are legally without merit, and appear to be nothing more than an attempt by these licensees to renegotiate their license agreements. In a separate move, Qualcomm then filed a patent-infringement action against Nokia claiming that Nokia was infringing 12 of its patents that related to GSM, GPRS, and EDGE standards (Jacobs, 2005; Nokia, 2005c; Wireless Watch, 2005b).

This is not the end of Qualcomm's legal disputes, however. Previously, in July and again in October, the company had filed infringement suits based on the previously-mentioned patents against Broadcom. These actions were a follow-up of Broadcom's claims that included a patent-infringement action filed against Qualcomm in May 2005, a complaint with the U.S. International Trade Commission (ITC) suggesting that Qualcomm was unfairly importing products that infringed Broadcom's patents and requesting that the ITC investigate Qualcomm's imports, and a separate antitrust suit raised in July. This U.S. antitrust claim was based on similar grounds as the complaint made to the European Commission. In its antitrust complaint Broadcom charged Qualcomm with abuse of the wireless technology standards-setting process, failure to meet its commitments to license technology for cellular wireless standards on RAND terms, and various anticompetitive activities in the sales and marketing of chipsets based on CDMA technology (Gohring, 2005a, b; Regan, 2005).

As can be seen from the volume of suits and counter-suits discussed earlier, Qualcomm's strategy of using its essential patents as revenue generators is challenging and particularly litigation-sensitive, and it is not considered viable by all technology/patent-licensing firms even though their business model would support such activity. One of the U.S. interviewees stated, for example, that taking into consideration the current legal situation and the IPR policies adopted by many standards bodies, it was not beneficial for it to take any part in the standardization. Its business was based on technology and patent licensing, not on manufacturing products, and there was simply not enough monetary compensation involved in standards (Interview data U.S., 2004).

Cross-Licensing

As mentioned earlier, agreeing upon exact licensing terms is not part of the standard-setting procedure, and negotiations are held between the companies interested in using the standard. This follows that another reason beyond the technological benefits for promoting the selection of patented technology for a standard is the possibility to cross-license patents with those of other participants that also "read on" the standard. The more patents companies have, the less they have to pay others for using the standard. Cumulative royalties might otherwise reach the point of unprofitable manufacture (Alkio, 2003; Soininen, 2005). For this reason, companies have an incentive to obtain patents that are essential for using the standardized technology. They may therefore amend their pending patent applications and file for new ones during the standardization process in order to make sure that if a certain technology is chosen for a standard, their patents cover some of its elements. For example, with regard to the CDMA 2000 standard, Qualcomm held 28%, Nokia 16%, NTT DoCoMo 13%, Ericsson 8%, Motorola 7% and Hitachi 5% of the essential patents involved. Then again, Ericsson has 30%, Nokia 21%, Qualcomm 20% and Motorola 14% of the essential patents included in the WCDMA standard (Alkio, 2003). In fact, it has been estimated that some of these major patent holders will end up with a total royalty of 7% of costs or less, while a nonpatent holder could pay 25% of the wholesale price in GSM and WCDMA royalties (Wireless Watch, 2005a).

In order to diminish the problem with too high royalties, some manufacturing firms and operators have declared that they would prefer to agree upon cumulative royalty caps beforehand (Wireless Watch, 2005a). For instance, Nokia was behind such a proposal in respect of 3G patents (Naraine, 2002a). Nevertheless, there are different views on whether agreeing on licensing terms is the job of the standards organization at all, and Qualcomm, in particular, has opposed the royalty-cap proposition actively (Naraine, 2002b). Also one of the U.S. interviewees pointed out during the interview, that in the end, the markets determined whether a product was feasible at a certain price or not. This was not the licensor's responsibility. He further noted that the game in the industry seems to have turned into a price competition rather than the building up of value to customers and communicating that value to them

(Interview data U.S., 2004). However, as far as the next version of the 3GPP-based radio standard, Long Term Evolution (LTE), is concerned, ETSI is considering getting all relevant patent holders to sign up to a pre-agreed cumulative cap of approximately 5% for royalties on the cost of LTE equipment (Informamedia.com, 2006).

Licensing and Submarine Patents

As explained earlier, standardization participants have diverging business interests that, combined with control over certain aspects of technology, complicate the standardization process and the adoption of standards particularly if monetary or other licensing compensation is pending. In fact, quantitative research conducted by Blind et al., (2002) has indicated that the dilemma is not rare at all: over 30% of European companies reported that they had faced dilemmas involving the high licensing fees demanded by the IPR/patent holders, and approximately 25% had had problems with cross-licensing (Blind et al., 2002; Soininen, 2005). However, if there were no compensation, fewer patent holders might be inclined to allow anyone to utilize their patented inventions, and technologically inferior technology might be chosen for the standard. In fact, it has been suggested that incentives offered to patent holders are not sufficient given the positive effects of standardization. Another quantitative study also conducted by Blind and Thumm (2002) demonstrated that the tendency to join standardization processes is lower if an undertaking has intense patent activity than if it does not. It is suggested that this could be an indicator that the use of IPRs, reflecting the success of the company's own R&D activities, and participation in standardization are, to certain extent, alternative innovation strategies (Blind et al., 2002, Soininen, 2005). Unfortunately this finding also indicates that a large chunk of patents may fall into the category of third-party patents that have a high likelihood to remain unnoticed.

What basically differentiates submarine patent cases and those in which a patent has been properly disclosed is the possibility to make informative decisions about the adoption of a standard, design around it or to agree upon licensing terms in advance. However, standards organization's patent policies only require a general promise to license on RF or RAND terms. Exact licensing conditions are negotiated separately between the parties and this is often done after the standard has been elected. Therefore, with an exception of the fact that a licensing statement has been given and therefore there are more changes of challenging the company's licensing terms, these situations bear a lot of similarities to submarine patent cases. Obviously, if licensing terms were specified better and RAND terms were determined in accordance with the situation that has prevailed prior to the establishment of the standard, there would be less room for interpretation, and the patent holder would not be in such a good negotiation position. This follows that, even though it was possible to diminish the dilemma with submarine patents discussed earlier, licensing perplexities would probably continue to prevail. On the other hand early disclosure could at least diminish those significant economic losses that would occur if the submarine patent surfaced after the standard had been used broadly and various complementary products and services had been based on it. It should be pointed out, however, that the advantages of clearing all relevant patents beforehand also depends on whether the standard is such that it is constantly evolving as new features are incorporated into the system after the original standard has been set, or whether it remains unchanged after its establishment. In the former situations it would be important to be able to gain information also on those rights, which are essential for the purposes of implementing the standard in its amended form, while those rights that were initially essential may no longer be relevant at this phase.

DISCUSSION

In the previous sections I have identified multiple situations in which patents have caused concern during and after cooperative standard setting. These situations could basically be divided into those in which the holder of the disputed patent has participated in setting the standard and those in which the patent holder is a third party. Furthermore, a distinction could be made between patents that have been properly disclosed to the other participants, and the rights that come as a surprise either because the patent policy has not required their disclosure and no attention has been drawn to them, the patent holder has intentionally concealed them despite the patent policy, or the rights holder has accidentally neglected to disclose them.

The number-one reason for the disputes that have arisen in the previously-mentioned situations is that patent holders use their position of being able to prevent others from using an invention that is essential for operating the standard to require licensing fees or other terms that are unacceptable to companies operating in the industry. When talking about properly disclosed patents, the patent holder may have made a declaration prior to the publication of the standard specification to the effect that it was willing to license its essential patents royalty-free, or that it was willing to license them on fair, reasonable and non-discriminatory terms. Here, the patent holder may have posed certain limitations, or the patent holder may have made only a blank promise of RF or RAND licensing, and a dispute may arise afterwards over what the correct interpretation of such a promise is. Sometimes, there may not be any kind of a promise.

The consequences of the patent holder refusing to license at all, or on terms accepted by most companies, depend on when the dilemma comes to light. The longer it takes for the dispute to arise the worse are the consequences from a societal perspective. Before the standard is set it may well

be possible to design around the patents or to choose other technologies over heavily patented ones, and even after the standard specifications have been published, the abandoning of the standard altogether, or its modification, may not be detrimental as companies may have alternative standards to choose from. Of course, the time and the money invested in setting a standard would be lost. On the other hand, if the standard has already been broadly adopted it may be difficult and very costly to change the specifications without losing the network benefits. Ultimately, doing so would harm consumers who are already using a system in which various products are interchangeable and interoperable. Obviously, from the patent holder's perspective, the situation is reversed: the later his patent comes to the surface, the more leverage he gains.

I posed the question in the title of this article whether especially the submarine patent problem truly existed or whether it was a red herring. Although the evidence is largely anecdotal and further quantitative research is needed, I have to conclude that problems to do with unidentified patents do come to the surface after the standard has been established. Obviously, even though there is a high likelihood that plenty of relevant patents remain unnoticed, it is only a minor aspect of the variety of conflicts that patents give rise to during or after standardization, and plenty of standards can be adopted without actually having to face troubles with submarine patents. Particularly those situations in which it can be proven that a standard-setting participant breached the patent policy and purposefully concealed the existence of relevant patents or patent applications and thus misled the industry and manipulated the process in order to gain market power, appear to be rare. Companies typically try to do their best to comply with the patent policy.

Avoiding problems with submarine patents seems to be getting more challenging all the time, however. This is because ICT patents, some of which are valid and some of which are not, are increasing in number making it more difficult to avoid infringement. Furthermore, patents are being assigned more often than before and therefore they may end up in companies that did not participate in setting the standard. Patents are also utilized more aggressively in the field, and the more patent-holding companies are seeking to extract as high royalties as they can get from those implementing a standard the less likely it is that an amicable solution can be reached. As a consequence, particularly the U.S. red herring population seems to be growing quickly in number, even though certain legal provisions such as the U.S. Sherman Act, sections 1 and 2, which prohibit conspiracy and monopolization or its attempt, and the FTC Act, section 5, which prohibits the use of unfair and deceptive business practices, have been and could be used in an attempt to wipe out the most colorful individuals. Other legal tools include fraud, equitable estoppel that prevents a party that has not operated fairly from enforcing his rights, the doctrine of prosecution laches applicable to patents that have been issued following an unreasonable and unexplained delay during patent prosecution phase, and the implied-license and patent-misuse doctrines (Lemley, 2002; Mueller, 2001). Furthermore, non-infringement clarification and patent invalidation either in court or as an opposition (EPO) or re-examination (USPTO) procedure in the patent office could be attempted. In Europe the EC treaty, Art 81 (prohibits agreements and concerted practices that prevent, distort or restrict competition) and 82 (prohibits the abuse of dominant position) could offer limited help as well. Unfortunately, the legal means have not appeared to be very effective so far. The fact that legal disputes have arisen demonstrates that the dilemmas are serious and that they bear significant economic weight, however.

What makes particularly the submarine patent problem interesting from the societal and patent policy perspective is that in this case companies implementing the standard have not, for some reason or other, been able to identify the rel-evant rights or to plan their operations so as to avoid infringement. Moreover, the consequences of not being able to continue to use a specific standard may have far-reaching effects not only on the competition in a certain field but also on consumers. Therefore, the purpose of the patent system—to promote innovation and facilitate technology transfer through granting the inventor an exclusive right in return for publishing his invention—may not merely restrain trade in the traditional sense, that is, legal monopoly versus free competition, but may also contravene the public interest in a way that is no longer reasonable given the role of patents in enhancing innovation. This, incidentally, has been seriously questioned in areas such as software and semiconductors. In fact, patents and standards are a policy concern linked to a more general concern regarding IPR protection and the possibility of using it in order to control product interoperability.

This article suggests that further attention should be paid to analyze the efficacy of the legal framework and the need for legislative amendments particularly in the context of standards and so-called submarine patents that come to surface after the standard has been established and adopted. As a practical matter for diminishing potential conflicts, clarifying patent policies in respect to disclosure and licensing obligations, conducting more thorough patent due diligence, and developing guidelines on how to determine RAND terms are recommended. It is further noted that limiting only the risk of submarine patents will not get us far in reducing the conflicts between patents and standards.

REFERENCES

Administrative Complaint (2002), Docket No 9302, 18 June 2002.

Alkio, M. (2003, March 9). Kovaa peliä patenteilla. *Helsingin Sanomat*, p. E3.

ANSI. (2003a). *Guidelines for implementation of the ANSI Patent Policy.*

ANSI. (2003b). *Patent policy.*

Asaravala, A. (2004, April 24). Forgent sues over JPEG patent. *Wired News.* Retrieved August 29, 2006, from http://www.wired.com/news/business/0,1367,63200,00.html

Balto, D.A., & Wolman, A.M. (2003). Intellectual property and antitrust: General principles. *IDEA The Journal of Law and Technology, 43*(3), 396-474.

Bekkers, R., Duysters, G., & Verspagen, B. (2002). Intellectual property rights, strategic technology agreements and market structure. The case of GSM. *Research Policy, 31,* 1141-1161.

Bekkers, R., Verspagen, B., & Smits, J. (2002). Intellectual property rights and standardization: The case of GSM. *Telecommunications Policy, 26*(3-4), 171-188.

Berlind, D. (2002a, April 16). IBM drops Internet patent bombshell. *Tech Update.*

Berlind, D. (2002b, April 25). The hidden toll of patents on standards. *Tech News on ZDNet.* Retrieved August 29, 2006, from http://news.zdnet.com/2100-9595_22-891852.html

Berman, V. (2005, January-February). Is it time to reexamine patent policy for standards? *IEEE Design & Test of Computers,* 71-73.

Bessen, J. (2003). *Strategic patenting of complex technologies* (Working Paper). Research on Innovation.

Blind, K. (2004). *The economics of standards.* Edward Elgar.

Blind, K., Bierhals, R., Thumm, N., Hossain, K., Sillwood, J., Iverser, E., et al. (2002). *Study on the interaction between standardisation and intellectual property rights* (EC Contract No G6MA-CT-2000-02001, 2002).

Blind, K., Edler, J., Nack, R., & Strauß, J. (2001). *Micro- and macroeconomic implications of the patentability of software innovations. Intellectual property rights in information technologies between competition and innovation* (Study on Behalf of German Federal Ministry of Economics and Technology).

In re Bogese II, 303 F.3d 1362, 1367, Federal Circuit (2002).

Initial Decision (2004). Docket No 9302, 23 February 2004.

Calderone, L.L., & Custer, T.L. (2005, November). *Prosecution laches as a defense in patent cases.* Flaster Greenberg Attorneys at Law. Retrieved August 29, 2006, from http://www.flastergreenberg.com/pdf/PatentArtic_prf3.pdf

Caplan, P. (2003). *Patents and open standards* (White paper prepared for the National Information Standards Organization).

Chesbrough, H. (2003). *Open innovation.* Harvard Business School Press.

Clark, D. (2002, October). Do Web standards and patents mix? *Computer,* pp. 19-22.

Clark, R. (2002, July 19). *Concerning recent patent claims.* Retrieved August 29, 2006, from http://www.jpeg.org/newsrel1.html

Cohen, W.M., Nelson, R.R., & Walsh, J.P. (2000, February). *Protecting their intellectual assets: Appropriability conditions and why U.S. manufacturing firms patent (or not)* (NBER Working Paper Series).

Cunningham, A. (2005). Telecommunications, intellectual property, and standards. In I. Walden, & J. Angel (Eds.), *Telecommunications law and regulation.* Oxford.

DLA. (2004). *European intellectual property survey.*

Eolas Technologies Incorporated and the Regents

of the University of California v. Microsoft Corporation, Case Nr. 04-1234, Federal Circuit, 2 March 2005.

ETSI. (2005). *IPR policy.*

Farrell, J. (1996). *Choosing the rules for formal standardization.* UC Berkeley.

Federal Trade Commission v. Dell Computer Corp., FTC File No. 931 0097, 2 November 1995.

Feldman, R.P., & Rees, M.R. (2000, July). The effect of industry standard setting on patent licensing and enforcement. *IEEE Communications Magazine*, pp. 112-116.

Ferguson, K. (1999). 20/20 foresight. Retrieved August 29, 2006, from http://www.forbes.com/1999/04/19/feat.html

Forgent Networks. (2006). *Intellectual property, '672 patent cases.* Retrieved August 29, 2006, from http://www.forgent.com/ip/672cases.shtml

Frank, S.J. (2002, March). Can you patent an industry standard? *IEEE Spectrum.*

FTC. (2003). *To promote innovation: The proper balance of competition and patent law and policy.*

Graham, S.J.H., & Mowery, D.C. (2002, June 6-8). *Submarines in software? Continuations in U.S. software patenting in the 1980s and 1990s.* Paper presented at the DRUID Summer Conference on Industrial Dynamics of the New and Old Economy—Who is Embracing Whom?, Copenhagen/Elsinore.

Granstrand, O. (1999). *The economics and management of intellectual property.* Edward Elgar Publishing.

Grindley, P. (2002). *Standards, strategy and policy.* Oxford.

Gohring, N. (2005a). Qualcomm files a second suit against Broadcom. *InfoWorld.* Retrieved August 29, 2006, from http://www.infoworld.com/article/05/10/21/HNqualcommsecondsuit_1.html

Gohring, N. (2005b). Qualcomm files patent infringement suit against Nokia. *InfoWorld.* Retrieved August 29, 2006, from http://www.infoworld.com/article/05/11/07/hnqualcommsuit_1.html

GovTrack.us. 109th Congress, H.R. 2795: Patent Act of 2005. Retrieved August 29, 2006, from http://www.govtrack.us/congress/bill.xpd?bill=h109-2795

Hahn, R.W. (2001, March). Competition policy and the new economy. *Milken Institute Review*, 34-41.

Heinze, W.F. (2002, May). Dead patents walking. *IEEE Spectrum,* 52-54.

Hemphill, T.A. (2005, January). Technology standards development, patent ambush, and US antitrust policy. *Technology in Society, 27*(1), 55-67.

Hjelm, B. (2000). Standards and intellectual property rights in the age of global communication: A review of the international standardization of third-generation mobile system.

IETF. (2005). Intellectual property rights in IETF technology.

Informamedia.com. (2006, March 1). ETSI acts on unfair, unreasonable and discriminatory IPRs. *Informamedia.com.*

IPO. (n.d.). *21st Century Patent Coalition: "Submarine patents" ARE a significant problem.* Retrieved August 29, 2006, from http://www.ipo.org/contentmanagement/contentdisplay.cfm?contentid=7334

ITU-T (n.d.). *Patent policy.*

ITU-T (2005). *Patent policy implementation guidelines.*

Jacobs, P. (2005, December). Qualcomm defends patent licensing programme. *wirelessweb*. Retrieved August 29, 2006, from http://wireless.iop.org/articles/news/6/12/6/1

Kipnis, J. (2000, July). Beating the system: Abuses of the standards adoption process. *IEEE Communications Magazine*, pp. 102-105.

Kirsch, E.D. (2000). International standards participation: Lessons from Townshend & Dell. *International Lawyers Network. The bullet"iln"*, *1*(2). Retrieved August 29, 2006, from http://www.ag-internet.com/push_news_one_two/internationalstandards.htm

Knight, H.J. (2001). *Patent strategy for researchers and research managers*. John Wiley & Sons.

Kratzman, V.A. (2005). *Technology transfer mid-term report next step recommendations*. FINPRO.

Krechmer, K. (2005, January). *Communications standards and patent rights: Conflict or coordination?* Paper presented at the Economics of the Software and Internet Industries Conference, Tolouse, France.

Labsystems Oy v. Biohit Oy. HO S 94/1922. Finnish Court of Appeal.

The Lemelson Foundation. (n.d.). Jerome H. Lemelson. Retrieved August 29, 2006, from http://www.lemelson.org/about/bio_jerry.php

Lemley, M.A. (2002). *Intellectual property rights and standard setting organizations* (UC Berkeley Public Law and Legal Theory Research Paper Series, Research Paper No. 84).

Lemos, R. (2002, July 23). Finding patent truth in JPEG claims. *CNET News.com*. Retrieved August 29, 2006, from http://news.com.com/Finding+patent+truth+in+JPEG+claim/2100-1001_3-945686.html

Lo, A.M. (Jupiter Networks, Inc). (2002). *A need for intervention: Keeping competition alive in the networking industry in the face of increasing patent assertions against standards*. FTC/DOJ Hearings on Competition and Intellectual Property Law and Policy In the Knowledge-Based Economy—Standard Setting and Intellectual Property, 18 April 2002.

Malone, S. (2005, November 1). *Microsoft loses Eolas Supreme Court appeal*. PC Pro. Retrieved August 29, 2006, from http://www.pcpro.co.uk/news/news/79431

Marasco, A. (ANSI). (2003, October 30). *IPR and standards*. Presentation at AIPLA.

Markoff, J. (2002, July 29). Patent claim strikes an electronics nerve. *The New York Times*.

Megantz, R.C. (2002). *Technology management. Developing and implementing effective licensing programs*. John Wiley & Sons.

Messerschmitt, D.G., & Szyperski, C. (2003). *Software ecosystem*. The MIT Press.

Miele, A.L. (2000). *Patent strategy: The manger's guide to profiting from patent portfolios*. John Wiley & Sons.

Mueller, J.M. (2001). Patenting industry standards. *John Marshall Law Review, 34*(897).

Naraine, R. (2002a, May 8). Nokia calls for 5% cap on 3G patent royalties. *internetnews.com*. Retrieved August 29, 2006, from http://internetnews.com/wireless/article.php/1041561

Naraine, R. (2002b, May 10). Qualcomm rejects Nokia patent cap proposal. *internetnews.com*. Retrieved August 29, 2006, from http://www.interetnews.com/wireless/article.php/1116381

Nokia. (2005a, October 28). *Leading mobile wireless technology companies call on European Commission to investigate Qualcomm's anti-competitive conduct*. Retrieved August 29, 2006, from http://press.nokia.com/PR/200510/1018639_5.html

Nokia. (2005b, October 28). *Leading mobile wireless technology companies call on European Commission to investigate Qualcomm's anti-competitive conduct.* Retrieved August 29, 2006, from http://europe.nokia.com/BaseProject/Sites/NokiaCom_CAMPAIGNS_57710/CDA/Categories/PressEvents/_Content/_Static_Files/transcript.pdf

Nokia. (2005c, November 7). *Nokia responds to reports of Qualcomm GSM patent infringement suit.* Retrieved August 29, 2006, from http://press.nokia.com/PR/200511/1019958_5.html

OASIS. (2005). *IPR policy.*

OECD. (2004). *Patents and innovation: Trends and policy challenges.* Retrieved August 29, 2006, from http://www.oecd.org/dataoecd/48/12/24508541.pdf

OECD. (2005). *Compendium of patent statistics.* Retrieved August 29, 2006, from http://www.oecd.org/dataoecd/60/24/8208325.pdf

Ohana, G. (Cisco Systems, Inc). (2005. October 6). Intellectual property rights: Policies in standard-setting: Areas of debate. In *Proceedings of From A to Veeck: Standardization and the Law, 2005 ANSI Annual Conference.* Retrieved August 29, 2006, from http://public.ansi.org/ansionline/Documents/Meetings%20and%20Events/2005%20Annual%20Conference/Legal%20Conference/Ohana-Panel%20I.pdf

Out-law.com. (2005, November 31). Mobile-makers say 3G patent licensing breaks antitrust laws. Retrieved August 29, 2006, from http://www.out-law.com/page-6280

Peterson, S.K. (Hewlett-Packard Company). (2002a). *Consideration of patents during the setting of standards.* For FTC and DOJ Roundtable, Standard Setting Organizations: Evaluating the Anticompetitive Risks of Negotiating IP Licensing Terms and Conditions Before A Standard Is Set, 6 November 2002.

Peterson, S.K. (Hewlett-Packard Company). (2002b). *Patents and standard-setting processes.* FTC/DOJ Hearings on Competition and Intellectual Property Law and Policy in the Knowledge-Based Economy, 18 April 2002.

Perens, B. (n.d.). *The problem of software patents in standards.* Retrieved August 29, 2006, from http://perens.com/Articles/PatentFarming.html

Poltorak, A.I., & Lerner, P.J. (2004). *Essentials of licensing intellectual property.* John Wiley & Sons.

PwC Advisory. (2006). *2006 patent and trademark damages study.*

Rahnasto, I. (2003). *Intellectual property rights, external effects, and anti-trust law.* Oxford University Press.

Rambus, Inc v. Infineon Technologies AG. No. 01-1449. Federal Circuit, 29 January 2003.

Red Herring. (2006, February 3). JPEG patent reexamined. Retrieved August 29, 2006, from http://www.redherring.com/Article.aspx?a=15582&hed=JPEG+Patent+Reexamined&sector=Industries&subsector=Computing

Regan, K. (2005, July 5). Broadcom suit accuses Qualcomm of antitrust tactics. *E-Commerce Times.* Retrieved August 29, 2006, from http://www.ecommercetimes.com/story/44395.html

Reingold, J. (2006, January). *Patently aggressive.* 102. Retrieved August 29, 2006, from http://www.fastcompany.com/magazine/102/patents.html

Rivette, K., & Kline, D. (2000). *Rembrandts in the attic.* Harvard Business School Press.

Sarvas, R., & Soininen, A. (2002, October). *Differences in European and U.S. patent regulation affecting wireless standardization.* Paper presented at the International Workshop on Wireless Strategy in the Enterprise, Berkeley, California.

Shapiro, C. (2001). *Navigating the patent thicket:*

Cross licenses, patent pools and standard setting.

Shapiro, C., & Varian, H.R. (1999). *Information rules.* Harvard Business School Press.

Shurmer, M., & Lea, G. (1995, June). Telecommunications standardization and intellectual property rights: A fundamental dilemma? *Standardview, 3*(2).

Soininen, A. H. (2005).Open Standards and the Problem with Submarine Patents. Proceedings SIIT 2005 pp. 231-244 4th International conference on standardization and innovation in information technology.

Stroyd, A.H. (2000). *Lemelson bar coding patents: Attempting to sink the submariner.* Retrieved August 29, 2006, from http://www.mhia.org/PSC/pdf/Lemelson.PDF

Surowiecki, J. (2006, December 26/January 2). Blackberry picking. *The New Yorker*, Financial Page.

Symbol Technologies Inc. v. Lemelson Medical, Education & Research Foundation. 277 F.3d 1361, 1363. Federal Circuit, 2002.

Symbol Technologies, Inc et al. v. Lemelson Medical, Education & Research Foundation. LP et al., 422 F.3d 1378. Federal Circuit, 2005.

Teece, D.J. (2000). *Managing intellectual capital.* Oxford University Press.

Townshend v. Rockwell International Corp. and Conexant Systems, Inc., 55 U.S.P.Q.2d 1011. Northern District of California, 2000.

Varchaver, N. (2001, May 3). *Jerome Lemelson the patent king.* Retrieved August 29, 2006, from http://www.engin.brown.edu/courses/en90/fall/2003/Lemelson%20Fortune%20may%2014%202001%20article.pdf

Vermont, S. (2002). The economics of patent litigation. In B. Berman (Ed.), *From ideas to assets. Investing wisely in intellectual property.* John Wiley & Sons.

Watts, J.J.S., & Baigent, D.R. (2002). Intellectual property, standards and competition law: Navigating a minefield. *IEEE*, 837-842.

Westman, R. (1999, October). The battle of standards—And the road to peace. *On—The New World of Communication*, pp. 26-30.

Wireless Watch. (2005a, November 29). Mobile patents war shifts to email. *The Register.* Retrieved August 29, 2006, from http://www.theregister.co.uk/2005/11/29/mobile_email_patents_war/

Wireless Watch. (2005b, November 15). *The Register.* Qualcomm IP battle hots up. Retrieved August 29, 2006, from http://www.theregister.co.uk/2005/11/15/qualcomm_ip_battle/

Wong, W. (2002, April 18). IBM ebMXL patent plan royalty-free. *Tech Update.*

W3C (2004). *Patent policy.*

This work was previously published in International Journal of IT Standards and Standardization Research, Vol. 5, Issue 1, edited by K. Jakobs, pp. 84-102, copyright 2007 by IGI Publishing, formerly known as Idea Group Publishing (an imprint of IGI Global).

Chapter 5.13
Gender Influences on Ethical Considerations in the IT Environment

Jessica Leong
Ernst & Young, New Zealand

INTRODUCTION

We become just by performing just actions.
—Aristotle, Nichomachean Ethics, 4th century,
B.C. (Miner & Rawson, 2000)

From the opening statement, it is evident that ethics has played a part in our everyday lives since the beginning of time, and still continues to do so. Another aspect of our lives that has become increasingly widespread is the use of information technology. In the Information Age, it is not often that we link ethics and information technology (IT).

This article examines the link between ethics and IT, and the influence of gender on ethical considerations in the IT environment.

BACKGROUND

Definitions

Ethics have been defined as, "The behavioural manners and norms of a group or society" (Takala & Urpilainen, 1999). Are males and females classified as one group? Or do their ethical considerations differ?

Multi-Dimensional Scale

A multi-dimensional ethics scale (Reidenbach & Robin, 1990) was used, as opposed to a single-item scale. A single-item measurement scale is inadequate for complex phenomena such as ethics. Ethical decision-making is not always affected by a single factor. In some situations, individuals might consider only one dimension, whereas in other situations, they consider a few dimensions (Grupe et al., 2002). It should be noted however, that this multi-dimensional ethics scale can only assess community standards, and is not able to assess right versus wrong.

PREVIOUS STUDIES

Previous studies have been conducted on ethical attitudes. In a study examining whether a group of MBA students, when asked if they would attempt an illegal act that would net them or their company a profit of more than $100,000 if given a 1% chance of being caught, more than one-third responded "yes". (Liberman & Etzioni, 2003).

Previous studies have also been conducted on gender influences on ethical attitudes. Christie et al. (2003) investigated the influence of personal characteristics of business managers from India, Korea, and United States. Characteristics included age, gender, personal beliefs and the values of on one's ethical perceptions, attitudes and conduct. It was found that there was a significant difference in ethical attitudes of business managers due to gender.

Ross and Robertson (2003) also found gender to be statistically significant in effecting the ethical attitudes of professionals. It was noted that some studies on gender differences found females more ethical than males (Arlow, 1991), while other studies found males to be more ethical than females (Fritzsche & Becker, 1983).

Upon review of research conducted on ethical conduct, one study noted that almost half (49%) of respondents said that ethical conduct is *not* rewarded in business today (Anonymous, 2003). However, in the same study, 79% of the respondents said their organizations have written ethics standards, and believed that top management supports those ethics (Anonymous, 2003).

These statistics indicate that the adoption of ethical behaviour is viewed favourably, but yet findings reveal that many do not believe that ethical conducts reaps benefits in the long run.

Further study on ethics is important as there are many benefits in acting ethically such as retaining employees. Studies have found that employees are more likely to remain loyal to organizations who they believe are ethical (Smith, 2000). Ultimately, good employees add to the bottom line. Studies have also found that there are associated cash costs to unethical behaviour, for example, internal fraud (Morse, 2003). Other intangible benefits of ethical behaviour are increases in trust levels (Keefe, 2002), and good reputation (Sheffert, 2001).

A greater understanding of ethics will provide an insight into how ethical behaviour relates to various factors such as educational background and income levels. This study looks at how ethical attitudes are affected by gender differences. This research contributes to the existing body of knowledge by examining differences in ethical attitudes, employing quantitative statistical methods. This enables the significance of differences due to gender to be quantified. Such analyses is lacking in literature today. The quantitative method employed is further detailed in the Data Analysis section below.

RESEARCH OBJECTIVES AND RESEARCH QUESTIONS

As we can see from previous studies, varying results were found when gender was examined as a factor for ethical considerations. What role does gender then play in the ethics of the IT environment? This study seeks to understand the differences in attitudes of IT practitioners due to gender, to see if they are consistent with previous findings on other populations.

The objective of this research is to understand IT practitioner attitudes to ethics. Therefore, the research question that drives this study is, "Is there a difference in attitudes of IT practitioners to ethics due to their *gender?*"

The next section addresses the methodology used for the evaluation of the data.

METHODOLOGY

Data Collection Method

This study uses a quantitative approach for evaluating data collected. Surveys were used as the data collection method. An online electronic questionnaire was selected as the survey instrument.

The hypothesis for this study is:

H₀1: There is a difference in attitudes of IT practitioners to ethics due to *gender*.

The dependent variables are the *scale items* (fair, just, acceptable, etc). The independent variable is *gender*.

Items on Multi-Dimensional Scale

Questionnaires were used together with an accompanying scenario written as a series of four vignettes. Online electronic questionnaires, housed by an online questionnaire-hosting site, Informis (2005) were used. A link to the survey was presented on the Project Management Institute (PMI)'s Web site. As the site is visited by project management practitioners worldwide, a wide variety of respondents were captured from all parts of the world, at no additional cost. The drawback to this is that the exact response rate cannot be determined, as there is no way of ascertaining the number of readers that responded to the survey.

A link to the survey was also included in Harrison International Limited's Web site[1]. Harrison International Limited is an international consulting company, providing consulting services in project management and strategic management to organizations around the world. This was deemed a highly appropriate way of recruiting respondents for the study, as respondents would be business professionals, closely related to the target respondents for this study.

The survey and associated scenarios were developed from earlier studies carried out by Reidenbach and Robin (1990) and Tuttle et al. (1997). The associated scenarios were written for business circumstances and based on scenarios that could be present in software development projects. The questions in the questionnaire were adapted to encompass other factors that influence ethical considerations. The Codes of Ethics of IT Professional Bodies stress that ethical decisions should be made with reference to the duties of care to: colleagues, clients, society, employer, profession, and professional affiliation (ACM, 1992; IEEE, 1990; NZCS, 2003). Hence, the statement pertaining to family in Reidenbach and Robin (1990)'s scale is replaced by duties owed to colleagues, clients and the society. This is displayed graphically in Table 1.

Thus the scale looks like this:

- **Dimension One:** A broad-based moral equity dimension
  - Fair/Unfair
  - Just/Unjust
  - Acceptable/Unacceptable
  - *Acceptable/Unacceptable to colleagues*[2]
  - *Acceptable/Unacceptable to clients*[2]

Table 1.

Duties of Cared Owed: (ACM, 1992; IEEE, 1990; NZCS, 2003)	Replace *Family* item in the multidimensional scale with:
• Society • Clients • Colleagues • Profession • Professional affiliation	• *Acceptable to colleagues* • *Acceptable to clients* • *Acceptable to society*

- *Acceptable/Unacceptable to society*[2]
- Morally/Not morally right
- **Dimension Two:** A relativistic dimension
  - Traditionally Acceptable/Unacceptable
  - Culturally Acceptable/Unacceptable
- **Dimension Three:** A contractualism dimension
  - Does not violate/Violates an unspoken promise
  - Does not violate/Violates an unwritten contract

The Four Scenarios

Four scenarios were developed specifically for this research study. The four scenarios used are:

- Project Initiation
- Project Development
- Project Staffing
- Project Termination

Each case vignette details a scenario commonly encountered in the IT environment. The vignettes follow the software development life cycle closely, such that there is a project beginning (e.g., Initiation), middle (e.g., Development and Staffing) and end (e.g., Termination). Respondents are asked to rate the action taken in the scenario from different viewpoints (e.g., fair/unfair, acceptable/unacceptable to clients, acceptable/unacceptable to society, etc.). They rate the action taken on a scale of 1 to 10, with 1 being most fair, and 10 being most unfair.

Project Initiation

The first case vignette, Project Initiation, is about presenting complete information when tendering for a project. It describes that there is ambiguity in the specifications provided by the client for a software development project. However, the software development team needs the job, so they need to consider if they are to reveal potential cost overruns to the client, or to tender at a lower than realistic cost, knowing that they will be able to charge more later. The respondents are then told that the software development team under quotes on the price of the contract, in hope of getting the contract, and making up for any shortfalls by variation orders later in the contract.

Project Development

The second case vignette, Project Development, is about professional honesty and communication of issues. It describes a situation where the software development company tendered and obtained the job at a low cost. However, the job turned out to be more complex than expected. The client has agreed that the original specifications they provided were imprecise and omitted needed functionality. The project was then re-evaluated and an additional set of requirements agreed to and priced. The respondents are then told that the software developer continues to work on the project despite knowing that there will be cost overruns and the project will most likely fail.

Project Staffing

The third case vignette, Project Staffing, is about being to right socio-economical imbalances. It describes how the project manager had to advertise for additional staff for the project. There had recently been an equal employment opportunities (EEO) directive to employ more females. Very few females applied for the job. Of those who did, none were strong candidates for the position, but the Human Resources department is insisting that they be employed and be given on the job training to rectify any perceived shortcomings in their qualifications and skills. If they are employed, it could jeopardise the project budget even further. Respondents are then told that the project manager employed a female, even though she was not best qualified for the job.

Project Termination

The fourth and last case vignette, Project Termination, is about the integrity of lower-level team members who are under direction of managers. It describes how the project was eventually completed. It cost five times the original price and took twice as long. The client representative has told the software developer that he knew all along that the original set of requirements and specifications were inadequate, but he wanted them to get the job, so he encouraged the project to go ahead. He now wants a $15,000 sweetener for this project, bearing in mind that there are other projects in the pipeline for the now expanded team. The software developer approached his project manager about this and the project manager has told him to work it into the budget somehow, and that in fact, he went to school with the client who gave them the opportunity to quote for the job as a much-needed favour. Respondents are then told that the client representative was paid the sweetener, and asked to rate the action taken in the scenario.

Data from the questionnaires were then collated and analyzed for patterns. This study analyzes the gender effect on respondent attitudes to ethics. While attitudes to ethics may be affected by other influential effects such as income, work experience, and educational background, the separation of the gender effect from other influential effects is outside the scope of this study. For further details, refer to Leong (2003).

DATA ANALYSIS

Two hundred usable responses were received for the survey. The demographic distribution of the sample is detailed in the Table 2.

Before embarking on detailed analysis, a check was made to see that there does appear to be some pattern in the questionnaire responses. With this in mind, the response patterns for each of the 11 items used in the four scenarios were visually inspected. This will indicate if all items act in the same way and if each of the four scenarios meets with a similar response. Data was also checked for normality to confirm that the data collected was of normal distribution.

Having tested if there is indeed a pattern in the responses and that it does depend on the attitudes

Table 2. Demographic distribution of sample

	Sample Respondent Groups	Sample
Gender	Male	64.7%
	Female	35.3%
Age	Under 20	2.0%
	20-29	50.0%
	30-39	22.0%
	40-49	14.7%
	50+	11.3%
Highest Education Level	Primary School	0.0%
	High School	10.7%
	Undergraduate Student	54.4%
	Postgraduate Student	34.9%
Ethnicity	European	56.0%
	Chinese	27.3%
	Indian	6.0%
	Other	10.7%
Household Annual Income	Less than $36,000	12.7%
	$36,001-$50,000	27.1%
	$50,001-$70,000	22.9%
	$70,001-$90,000	10.2%
	Over $90,000	27.1%

to the various dimensions of ethical behaviour, the hypothesis was tested. The hypothesis was tested using analyses of variance (ANOVA), as to whether gender might account for individual differences in attitudes to project management ethics.

RESULTS

The sum of scores received for the four case vignettes were calculated. A comparison of scores was performed for male and female respondents for the four case vignettes.

It was found that there were no significant differences in mean scores due to gender in all four scenarios. Although not statistically significant, in the Project Initiation and Project Development scenarios, the female scores were higher, whereas in the Project Staffing and Project Termination scenarios, the male scores were higher. This indicates a higher concern for ethical considerations in females in the Project Initiation and Project Development scenarios, and a higher concern for ethical consideration in males in the Project Staffing and Project Termination scenarios. Scoring higher meant that the respondents viewed the scenario as being more unethical than those who scored lower.

DISCUSSION OF RESULTS

Results from the analyses shows that while there is no difference between the scoring patterns of male and female respondents, the scoring pattern depended on the scenario.

It is not surprising that males would express more concern in the Project Staffing and Project Termination scenarios, as it could be interpreted that females are to be preferentially selected in the Project Staffing scenario as a form of positive discrimination.

Findings for the Project Initiation and Project Development scenarios were also consistent with

Arlow (1991), where females were found to be more ethical than males. However, findings for the Project Staffing and Project Termination scenarios were consistent with Fritzsche and Becker (1983), where males were found to be more ethical than females.

It was noted that while female scores were higher in the first two scenarios, when scores in the four scenarios were compared against the two genders, there were no significant differences found. This suggests that gender affects ethical considerations in the environment presented, depending on the nature of the situation encountered.

CONCLUSION

Limitations

There is a limitation to studies on ethics in general. Ethics has been said to be the connection between morals and the telling of truth. According to Bok (1981), the "whole truth" is unattainable to a human being Takala and Urpilainen (1999). Therefore, it is difficult to place a right or wrong answer on any studies conducted on ethics. An evaluation of real-life situations may be at variance with hypothetical scenarios.

Value of this Study

This research study has come up with some findings that would be of interest not only to practitioners, but researchers alike. This study has provided further insight to the effect gender has on our ethical considerations, by not just presenting a set of conceptual theories, but quantifying the significance of difference in ethical attitudes using the quantitative methods detailed above. The subject of ethics is quite hard to define and much empirical analysis could be conducted to gain a better understanding of this subject area.

FUTURE TRENDS

There has been a sharp increase in interest on gender differences in IT. From recent statistics, it has been advocated that there is a shortage of females in the IT discipline. Further research on gender differences in IT may shed some light on the key factors contributing to this situation. Future studies may want to examine if male practitioners in IT believe that there is a gender imbalance. Further research could be done on male IT practitioners' behaviour toward females in the industry, and to examine if males have a positive or negative perception toward their female counterparts. Results from these studies will enhance our understanding on this subject area.

REFERENCES

ACM. (1992). *ACM Code of Ethics and Professional Conduct*. Retrieved November 30, 2003, from http://www.acm.org/constitution/code.html

Anonymous. (2003). Ethics: How to set the tone in today's turbulent times. *Accounting Office Management & Administration Report, 3*(6), 1.

Arlow, P. (1991). Personal characteristics in college students: Evaluation of business ethics and corporate social responsibility. *Journal of Business Ethics, 10*(1), 63-69.

Bok, S. (1981). *Lying—A moral choice*. Gummerus Osakeyhtion Kirjapaino.

Christie, P. M. J., Kwon, I. G., et al. (2003). A cross-cultural comparison of ethical attitudes of business managers: India, Korea, and the United States. *Journal of Business Ethics, 46*(3), 263.

Fritzsche, D. J., & Becker, H. (1983). Ethical behaviour of marketing managers. *Journal of Business Ethics, 2*(4), 291-299.

Grupe, F. H., Garcia-Jay, T., et al. (2002). Is it time for an IT ethics program? *Information Systems Management, 19*(3), 51-57.

IEEE. (1990). *IEEE Code of Ethics*. Retrieved November 30, 2003, from http://www.ieee.org/

Informis. (2005). *Informis Connected Research*. Retrieved from http://www.informis.co.nz

Keefe, P. (2002, June). Trustworthy IT. *Computerworld*.

Leong. (2003). *A study on attitudes of project management practitioners to project management ethics. Information systems and operations management*. Auckland: University of Auckland.

Liberman, V., & Etzioni, A. (2003). Right vs. wrong: The bottom line on ethics. *Across the Board, 40*(4), 59-63.

Miner, M., & Rawson, H. (2000). *The new international dictionary of quotations*. New York: Signet.

Morse, J. R. (2003). The economic costs of sin. *The American Enterprise, 14*(7), 14.

NZCS. (2003). *New Zealand computer society codes of ethics and professional conduct*. Retrieved from http://www.nzcs.org.nz/SITE_Default/about_NZCS/code of ethics.asp

Reidenbach, R. E., & Robin, D. P. (1990). Toward the development of a multidimensional scale for improving evaluations of business ethics. *Journal of Business Ethics, 9*, 639-653.

Ross, W. T., & Robertson, D. C. (2003). A typology of situational factors: Impact on salesperson decision-making about ethical issues. *Journal of Business Ethics, 46*(3), 213-234.

Sheffert, M. W. (2001, September). The high costs of low ethics. *Financial Executive*, 56-58.

Smith, C. (2000). The ethical workplace. *Association Management, 52*(6), 70-73.

Takala, T., & Urpilainen, J. (1999). Managerial work and lying: A conceptual framework and an explorative case study. *Journal of Business Ethics, 20*, 181-195.

Tuttle, B., Harrell, A., et al. (1997). Moral hazard, ethical considerations and the decision to implement an information system. *Journal of Management Information Systems, 13*(4), 7-27.

KEY TERMS

Dependent Variable: The observed variable in an experiment or study whose changes are determined by the presence or degree of one or more independent variables.

Ethical Consideration: What would or would not be ethical behaviour under specified circumstances.

Gender: The condition of being female or male.

Independent Variable: A manipulated variable in an experiment or study whose presence or degree determines the change in the dependent variable.

Information Age: The period beginning in the last quarter of the 20th century and noted for the abundant publication, consumption, and manipulation of information, especially by computers and computer networks.

IT: Abbreviation for information technology.

Practitioner: One who practices something, especially an occupation, profession, or technique.

Systems Development Life Cycle: Any logical process used by a systems analyst to develop an information system including requirements, validation, training, and user ownership.

Vignettes: To describe in a brief way.

ENDNOTE

[1] http://www.harrison.co.nz/HTML/Overview/LinksExternalEvents.htm

[2] added variables

This work was previously published in Encyclopedia of Gender and Information Technology, edited by E. Trauth, pp. 649-655, copyright 2006 by Information Science Reference, formerly known as Idea Group Reference (an imprint of IGI Global).

Chapter 5.14
Radio Frequency Identification Technology in Digital Government

Les Pang
National Defense University, USA

INTRODUCTION

Following technical strides in radio and radar in the 1930s and 1940s, the 1950s were a period of exploration for radio frequency identity (RFID) technology as shown by the landmark development of the long-range transponder systems for the "identification, friend or foe" for aircraft. Commercial use of RFID appeared in the 1960s, such as electronic article surveillance systems in retail stores to prevent theft. The 1970s were characterized by developmental work resulting in applications for animal tracking, vehicle tracking, and factory automation.

RFID technology exploded during the 1980s in the areas of transportation and, to a lesser extent, personnel access and animals. Wider deployment of RFID tags for automated toll collection happened in the 1990s. Also, there was growing interest of RFID for logistics and having it work along side with bar codes. In the beginning of the 21st century, the application of RFID technology has been ubiquitous and now it is practically part of everyday life (Landt, 2001).

BACKGROUND

Similar to bar coding, RFID tags provide information about goods, products, conveyances, animals, and people in transit. However, unlike bar coding which tracks product lines, RFID technology uses radio frequencies to automatically detect individual units and the information about these units. Use of radio frequency eliminates line-of-sight requirements and permits wireless detection.

RFID offers a number of advantages over the current bar-code technology which uses universal product codes (UPC). Codes in RFIDs are long enough so that each tag may have a unique code whereas a specific line of products are limited to a single UPC code. The distinctive nature of RFID tags results in an object that can be individually tracked as it moves from location to location. For product items, this characteristic can help retailers reduce theft of specific units and other forms of loss. Although functionalities provided by this technology far surpass those provided by bar coding, it does not mean that RFID will replace bar codes because of cost considerations.

RFID technology ensures better inventory control which leads to improved supply chain operations. The U.S. Department of Defense (DOD) has required its roughly 40,000 suppliers to put RFID tags on pallets and cases as well as on single items costing $5,000 or more beginning January 1, 2005. Wal-Mart has required that its top-100 suppliers provide the tags by 2005 for tracking merchandise, materiel, and goods.

RFID technology extracts information from tags, also known as transponders, wirelessly and automatically. Consider an arrangement of antennas connected to reader, which in turn is connected to a computer. When a tag enters the radio frequency field, it derives power from radio frequency signal. This energy allows a tag to transmit data, typically an identity, often in the form of an electronic product code (EPC). Unlike bar codes which tell you that a carton contains product XYZ, EPCs can specifically identify one box of product XYZ from another box of product XYZ.

This information is fed to a reader via the antenna. The reader interprets the information and translates it into binary format before relaying it to the connected computer. The computer can perform an action based on data received—this could be simply identifying existence of an item or adding or deleting it from its inventory. In some cases, the computer can also send a message back to the tag (Shahi, 2004).

RFID technology has clearly emerged as an approach to support e-government strategies aimed at improving citizen services, security operations, government-to-business interactions, and internal government operations. This article explores the potential of RFID technology in achieving quantum-level improvements in the realm of digital government particularly at the federal sector.

APPLICATIONS OF RFID

Applications of RFID technology were researched and actual and potential uses of the technology for digital government were identified and categorized into the following functions:

- Delivery of citizen services
- Security applications
- Business-to-government interactions
- Internal government operations

Applications identified were specifically those that have been or can be implemented by a government entity including the military.

Delivery of Citizen Services

Improving Drug Safety

The Food and Drug Administration is investigating attaching RFID tags onto pharmaceutical drug labels. These tags will help pharmacists and technicians find where on the shelf a drug is stored and the length of time the drug has been there. This system can also help when there are drug recalls and for verifying expiration dates (Sun Microsystems, 2003).

In another application, RFID tags are being embedded in lids of medication bottles and vials to ensure patient medication compliance. The RFID can be programmed to remind the patient when the next dose is due and tracks and records the time the patient opens the bottle to remove the tablet or capsule. The data can then be retrieved by a reader for review by the physician, researcher, or pharmacist. This approach can be applied to Veterans Administration hospitals, military hospitals, and other government medical facilities (Information Mediary Corporation, 2004).

Reducing Traffic Congestion

Toll facilities operated by state government transportation agencies are equipped to read RFID tags mounted on vehicles. Examples of electronic toll collection systems include Virginia's Smart-Tag system, the EZ-Pass system in the northeast United States, and California's FasTrak system. The tag is linked to a prepaid replenishable account that is debited when paying the toll. These tag-equipped vehicles no longer need to stop and pay the toll, thereby reducing traffic congestion at these locations.

Improving Postal Services

RFID tags can be used to improve the flow of mailed packages. An RFID-enabled conveyor system was developed that is able to sort packages with 100% accuracy and at a speed of 200 packages per minute. This success shows that RFID can be used instead of bar codes for this type of operations (Collins, 2003b). Also, the U.S. Postal Service is investigating the placement of RFID technology on postage stamps in order to track and locate mail quickly (Sun Microsystems, 2003).

Preventing Auto Theft

German companies developed a holographic windshield label that will make it difficult to conceal the identity of a stolen car. The high-security windshield label is difficult to counterfeit because of the hologram technology. This label allows police to view electronic data verifying the ownership and operating status of a vehicle. If a criminal attempts to transfer a label to a stolen car, the RFID label is disabled because the connection between the antenna and chip will be decoupled (Anonymous, 2002a).

Ensuring Tire Safety

Michelin, the tire manufacturing company, has begun testing RFID tags embedded in tires for tracking purposes to ensure compliance with the United States Transportation, Recall, Enhancement, Accountability and Documentation Act (TREAD Act) in the wake of the Firestone and Ford Explorer fiasco. The Act requires carmakers to closely monitor tires starting with the 2004 model so the tires can be recalled promptly if a problem occurs (Anonymous, 2003a).

Improving Transit Operations

Washington, DC's public transit system uses an RFID-based smart-card system called SmarTrip. Used by more than 360,000 of its Metrorail travelers, a card-carrying passenger can stroll by a reader at the entrance kiosk of one station and the value of the card is displayed. When it is scanned past the exit kiosk of another station, the cost of the trip is automatically calculated and deducted from a prepaid account. This helps the passenger avoid waiting in line for purchasing paper fare cards. These cards can also be used to pay commuter parking lot fees and bus trips within the regional network.

In Bogotá, Colombia, 23,000 transit buses carry RFID tags ensure that the buses are distributed throughout the city and avoiding congestion located at major thoroughfares (Collins, 2004e).

Improving Highway Safety

The Federal Highway Administration is looking at using RFID technology in its goal to reduce road fatalities in the United States by 50%. The agency has funded companies to develop dedicated short-range communications (DSRC) technology, a complement to RFID systems, for issuing alerts to drivers about impending intersection collisions, rollovers, weather-related road hazards, or warning a driver that his or her vehicle is going too fast to safely negotiate an upcoming curve. This high-bandwidth technology can also be used for downloading road maps and a possible replacement for automatic toll collection systems (Collins, 2004b).

Improving Food Safety

One of the futuristic uses of RFID tags has been its capability to work with "smart" appliances. For example, RFID technology will allow a refrigerator to track the expiration dates of the food it contains and notify its owner when it does expire. This is an area that may be of interest to the Food and Drug Administration for ensuring food safety at commercial sites (Brown, 2002).

Facilitating Financial Transactions

The use of RFID technology to facilitate payments can be used at government-operated recreational areas and parks, museums, food concessions, and other government-sponsored facilities. The private sector has been pioneers in this area with their novel applications of tag technology particularly in retail establishments.

Improving Luggage Flow

McCarran International Airport in Las Vegas is applying RFID tags as part of its effort to over-hauling its baggage-handling systems to support federal security regulations and reduce incidences of lost baggage. The system which currently uses bar-coded labels is expected to improve in terms of expediting the flow of baggage using RFID (Joachim, 2004).

Security Applications

Access Control

Many buildings and other secure locations are using contactless RFID tags as physical access cards. Often in the form of smart cards, these credit card-sized systems contain a microprocessor embedded in it.

Anticounterfeiting

The Internal Revenue Service is investigating embedding RFID tags into currency to reduce counterfeiting. In addition, euros may get RFID tags to stop counterfeiting. These tags will also have the ability of recording data such as details of the transactions involving the subject paper note. This would prevent money laundering, track illegal transactions, and also prevent kidnappers demanding unmarked bills (Sun Microsystems, 2003).

Personal Identification

China will issue over a billion RFID-based personal identification cards to each of its citizen. Three million handheld RFID readers would be issued to the police to give them the ability to scan the information contained in the cards (Winer, 2004).

Another way personal identity can be ascertained is through VeriChip, a small RFID chip about the size of a grain of rice. Each VeriChip contains a unique identification number which is used to access a database consisting of personal information. It is implanted just under the skin not unlike receiving a shot and it is scanned with a scanner. Because of this approach, the developers claim that the VeriChip cannot be lost, stolen, misplaced, or counterfeited. This chip can be used for personal identification. In October 2004, the Federal Drug Administration approved the device to give medical personnel instant access to patient records (Feder, 2004).

Livestock Tracking

Vermont Senator Patrick Leahy told a Georgetown University audience that he had firsthand experience with RFID technology from his own involvement in a Vermont pilot program tracking cattle to thwart outbreaks such as mad cow disease (Swedberg, 2004).

Improving Port Security

Pilot studies are being conducted that test RFID technologies in combination with satellite tracking systems, gamma ray image scanning devices, and Web-based software to make sure containers at U.S. ports hold what they are supposed to contain (Rosencrance, 2002).

Making Children Safe

RFID tags embedded in wristbands have been used in various amusement parks in the United States and Europe to track the location of children. Parents who can rent these wrist bands for their children can locate their children to 5 feet of their actual location using a distributed network of sensors. This child-tracking system relies on a combination of active RFID tags and Wi-Fi access-point triangulation (Anonymous, 2004e). This approach can be used at government-run facilities frequented by children such as art galleries, museums, and zoos.

Improving Firearm Safety

A Belgian subsidiary of the firearm company, Smith and Wesson, implemented a RFID firearm system which would make a firearm operational only to the individual implanted with a corresponding microchip (Gossett, 2004).

Detecting Counterfeit Drugs

The Food and Drug Administration recommended the use of RFID technology to create a "pedigree" for a drug—a secure record documenting that the drug was manufactured and distributed under safe and secure conditions. The agency predicts that

RFID can be used to track all individual drugs by 2007 (Food and Drug Administration, 2004).

Tracking Inmate Movements in Prisons

RFID technology promises to locate prisoner movements in real time. At the Ross Correctional Facility in Chillicothe, Ohio, inmates wear wristwatch-sized transmitters that track them within the prison. These devices can also detect whether prisoners have removed them and can send an alert to prison computers (Best, 2004).

Securing Library Books

San Francisco Public Library system approved plans to tag library books with RFID chips to prevent theft of the books and track its use (Stanley, 2004).

Business-to-Government Interactions

Improving Supply Chain Management

RFID technology promises improved product availability and reduce processing costs. Private sector retailers Wal-Mart, Target, and Albertson are mandating its suppliers to put RFID tags on cases and pallets. The DOD is requiring suppliers to place passive RFID tags on pallets and cases starting in 2005. As an incentive to suppliers that tag their shipments, the agency is introducing a fast-track billing process enabled by the faster processing of deliveries (Collins, 2004c).

Tracking Airline Parts

The Air Force and the Federal Aviation Administration might want to consider what Boeing and Airbus are planning to do with RFID technology. These two major airline manufacturers are initiating a number of forums for customers and suppliers to prepare the airline industry for the use of RFID technology to identify major airplane parts (Roberti, 2004a).

Improving Asset Management in Hospitals

Managers in military hospitals and other government medical facilities may want to look at RFID-based asset-management solutions. One RFID provider will tag and track 10,000 pieces of mobile medical equipment at three Virginia hospitals (Collins, 2004d).

Tracking Vehicles in Secure Areas

A new RFID-enabled yard management system is being developed that will let operators of shipping yards and quarries automatically track vehicles as they enter, travel through, and exit facilities (Maselli, 2004).

Tracking Containers

A provider of wireless asset-management systems is integrating optical character recognition technology with RFID tags to replace the manual processes terminal operators now use to track the container from ship to terminal and vice versa. The provider expects to process a container more efficiently, at a higher volume and with lower costs (Anonymous, 2003b).

Internal Government Operations

Tracking Wounded Soldiers

RFID technology was used for tracking wounded soldiers who were involved in the war in Iraq. The U.S. Navy's Fleet Hospital in Pensacola, Florida, tested a system involving RFID wristbands which store the soldier's identification and medical information regarding his or her condition and treatment as he or she moves from the battlefield to a hospital. The U.S. Navy is also using RFID technology to track the status and location of prisoners of war, refugees, and others arriving at the hospital (Anonymous, 2003).

Tracking Combat Rations

The Department of Defense simulated the tracking of combat rations throughout the entire supply chain from "vendor to foxhole." The agency showed how data could be aggregated and encoded on a special tag with a temperature sensor for the quality control of the combat rations (Anonymous, 2004c).

Improving Internal Services Management

The U.S. General Services Administration mandated RFID technology to assist in managing data on government buildings, fleets of cars, and products. The driving factors are cost reduction and improved efficiency. The agency intends to cut cycle times and provide rapid response to customers through the use of this technology (Sun Microsystems, 2003).

Tracking Media

Government agencies have a tremendous storehouse of media that it must track for retrieval purposes. Playboy TV is deploying RFID to track master tapes at its British headquarters where tapes are edited for broadcast over the English and European cable and satellite networks. Tracking tapes in the library used to be a difficult task at Playboy—they spent hours searching for tapes throughout the building. By tagging each of its 11,000 videos, Playboy is experiencing highly reduced search times (Collins, 2003a).

ISSUES

With the implementation of any new technology, issues can arise stemming from its use. RFID technology is no exception. This section will focus on four key concerns surrounding the tags—privacy, system reliability, interoperability, and cost.

Privacy

The issue of privacy revolves around retail use of RFID technology. There is concern that RFID tags affixed to consumer products remain operational after the purchase of the product. Although intended for short-distance use, these tags have the potential of being interrogated from great distances by someone with a high-gain antenna, thereby allowing, for example, the contents of a house to be scanned at a distance according to some experts. Therefore, key concerns involve the consumer not being aware of an affixed tag, the consumer not being able to deactivate the tag, and the capability of reading the tag at a distance without the knowledge of the consumer. If the purchased item was paid by credit card, theoretically it would be possible to link the items purchased to the consumer's identity.

German retailer Metro came under fire by privacy advocates who discovered that RFID tags were embedded in the store's loyalty cards. They also found that RFID tags on products sold at their store cannot be completely deactivated after purchase. "Customers are misled into believing that the tags can be killed at a special deactivation kiosk, but the kiosk only rewrites a portion of the tag, while leaving the unique ID number intact." Outraged German citizens were demanding that Metro put an immediate end to the trials (Associated Press, 2004).

Privacy groups such as Consumers Against Supermarket Privacy Invasion (C.A.S.P.I.A.N) are trying to get legislation introduced into Congress to outlaw RFID tagging. Others are applying market pressures to encourage businesses to behave responsibly.

Government is responsible for maintaining the public trust of the citizens. If the government uses RFID tags in ways that violate of privacy standards, public trust is breached and there will be considerable ramifications.

System Reliability

Some observers indicate that antitheft RFID systems are capable of being set off by odd things such as items of personal electronics or bits of metal. One claim was that a child activated these systems because he happened to generate the exact frequency of electromagnetic energy.

Early applications of RFID technologies were not successful. Early tests conducted for the Department of Defense showed that tags on liquid-filled containers could not be read reliably but this problem has been corrected. Tagging liquid-filled containers (such as cartons of bottled water or shampoo) is still a challenge but tags that will work on virtually any surface or container are now available (Anonymous, 2004c).

Practitioners have identified other problems with RFID technology. There is considerable delay when an encoded tag cannot be read. Some imply that it is not ready for high-volume processes yet. There are also middleware issues that need to be addressed in order that the RFID tag system to be compatible with the database management system (Sliwa, 2004).

Activists against the technology state that RFID could be bad for health reasons. In a future world where RFID readers are ubiquitous, people would be continually bombarded with electromagnetic energy. The long-term health effects of chronic exposure to this constant energy are not clearly known to researchers (Anonymous, 2003b).

Interoperability

Based on interviews with senior executives across the globe, the system infrastructure presented by the diverse and competing RFID vendors are often incompatible. Many countries have not agreed on common standards, frequencies, and power levels for RFID tags and readers (Collins, 2004c).

Significant differences in the numbering scheme for the RFID tags have surfaced. The EPCglobal, the industrial consortium for RFID technology, envisioned that all companies would use a single EPC numbering scheme. However, the DOD, the biggest customer migrating to RFID technology, prefers using its "Unique ID" numbering system accepted as one of the EPC standards. Other industries are also seeking to use their own unique numbering systems so that companies within those industries will not have to spend much to modify their software systems (Anonymous, 2004d).

One of the biggest challenges involves integrating the data received by the RFID with an organization's back-end systems. This occurred to 7-Eleven when the company piloted an effort to use a RFID stored-value card inside the corporate headquarters in Dallas and at a store in Plano, Texas (Levinson, 2004).

Cost

Companies are also concerned about the cost of RFID tags and how much they will have to spend to comply with mandate such as those posed by Wal-Mart and the DOD. A related question is how to allocate the cost of deploying RFID systems and tagged products among the different players in the supply chain (Collins, 2004d).

The cost of the tag is roughly $0.50 to a dollar; many in the industry say that the price must come down to $0.05 for it to be economically viable (Carroll, 2004).

FUTURE TRENDS

RFID, as with many other technologies, proceeds through a maturation cycle. It is now being over-hyped as the solution to many problems. It may not prove to have a place within an organization's infrastructure, culture, or financial budget.

Nonetheless, it is exciting to see the number of actual and potential ways this technology can help in improving and streamlining business processes. The future looks very bright for RFID technology. For example, RFID promises to bring a new level of usability and functionality to cell phones. By inserting an RFID reader into the unit, it will allow mobile services, ticketing, payment transactions, and exchanging business cards by simply touching two cell phones together. Employees can send real-time attendance logs and automate routine reporting tasks over the cellular network.

CONCLUSION

As this technology matures, sufficient attention must be made toward the issues identified here, namely, privacy, system reliability, interoperability, and cost. People need to feel confident that their personal privacy is protected whenever RFID tags are used and that information is not being distributed to unauthorized parties. People need to know that RFID systems are reliable enough for mission-critical applications such as financial transactions. Instead of a multitude of incompatible standards, there needs to be a common basis for RFID systems to work with each other without going through tedious effort. The RFID tags should be economical so that they could be used on a widespread basis and offer substantial value to both businesses and ultimately consumers.

REFERENCES

Anonymous. (1999). Mobil speedpass goes global as Mobil Singapore rolls out Asia's first RFID-based pay-at-the-pump system. Retrieved May 2, 2004, from http://www.ti.com/tiris/docs/news/news_releases/90s/rel04-05-99.shtml

Anonymous. (2001). Radio Frequency Identification: A basic primer. The Association of the Automatic Identification and Data Capture Industry. Retrieved April 5, 2004, from http://www.aimglobal.org/technologies/rfid/resources/RFIDPrimer.pdf

Anonymous. (2002). Smart license may cut car theft. *RFID Journal,* October 11.

Anonymous. (2003a). Michelin embeds RFID tags in tires. *RFID Journal,* January 17.

Anonymous. (2003b). A basic introduction to RFID technology and its use in the supply chain. Retrieved April 11, 2004, from http://admin.laran-rfid.com/media/files/WhitePaperRFID.pdf

Anonymous. (2003c). RFID tag privacy concerns. *Watching Them, Watching Us.* Retrieved July 2003, from http://www.spy.org.uk/cgi-bin/rfid.pl

Anonymous. (2004a). Frequently asked questions. *RFID Journal,* 2004. Retrieved October 22, 2004, from http://www.rfidjournal.com/article/articleview/207#Anchor-Are-63368

Anonymous. (2004b). Dockside cranes get brains. *RFID Journal,* October 29.

Anonymous. (2004c). DOD completes successful pilot. *RFID Journal,* March 12.

Anonymous. (2004d). EPCglobal chief resigns. *RFID Journal,* April 14.

Anonymous. (2004e). RFID connections. *AIM GLOBAL Newsletter,* March.

Anonymous. (2004f). RFID tracked casualties in Iraq. *RFID Journal,* May 19.

Anonymous. (2004g). RFID technology helps kids play it safe at Florida's Wannado City Theme Park. Retrieved October 15, 2004, from http://www.govtech.net/?pg=magazine/channel_story&channel=27&id=91563

Associated Press. (2004). *German retailer halts radio chip practice.* March 1. Retrieved May 5, 2006, from http://www.informationweek.com/story/showArticle.jhtml?articleID=18201214

Best, J. (2004). Ohio to track prisoners with radio tags. *CNET News,* August 2. Retrieved May 5, 2006, from http://news.zdnet.com/2100-9584_22-5293154.html

Brown, T. (2002). Presentation to the Association of Coupon Professionals. *Stratapult,* March 22.

Carroll, J. (2004). The wonders of RFID. *ZDNet,* January 12. Retrieved May 5, 2006, from http://zdnet.com.com/2100-1107_2-5139151.html

Collins, J. (2003a). Playboy uses RFID to track tapes. *RFID Journal,* July 28. Retrieved May 5, 2006, from http://www.rfidjournal.com/article/articleview/516/1/1/

Collins, J. (2003b). RFID speeds sorting of packages. *RFID Journal,* August 6. Retrieved May 5, 2006, from http://www.rfidjournal.com/article/articleview/526/1/26/

Collins, J. (2004a). Automotive RFID gets rolling. *RFID Journal,* April 13. Retrieved May 5, 2006, from http://www.rfidjournal.com/article/articleview/866/1/1/

Collins, J. (2004b). DOD updates RFID policy. *RFID Journal,* April 1. Retrieved May 5, 2006, from http://www.rfidjournal.com/article/articleview/856/1/14/

Collins, J. (2004c). Estimating RFID's pace of adoption. *RFID Journal,* December 3. Retrieved

May 5, 2006, from http://www.rfidjournal.com/article/articleview/675/1/1/

Collins, J. (2004d). Hospitals get healthy dose of RFID. *RFID Journal,* May 27. Retrieved May 5, 2006, from http://www.rfidjournal.com/article/view/920

Collins, J. (2004e). RFID speeds up Bogotá. *RFID Journal,* February 26. Retrieved May 5, 2006, from http://www.rfidjournal.com/article/articleview/808/1/1/

Finkenzeller, K. (2003). RFID systems. In *RFID Handbook—Fundamental and Applications in Contactless Smart Cards and Identification.* Hoboken, NJ: John Wiley & Sons.

Food and Drug Administration. (2004, February). *Combating counterfeit drugs—A report of the Food and Drug Administration.* Washington, DC: Author.

Gossett, S. (2004). Paying for drinks with wave of the hand. *WorldNet Daily,* April 14. May 5, 2006, from http://worldnetdaily.com/news/article.asp?ARTICLE_ID=38038

Feder, B. (2004). Identity badge worn under skin approved for use in health Care. *New York Times,* October 14. May 5, 2006, from http://www.nytimes.com/2004/10/14/technology/14implant.html?ex=1184126400&en=0072f621842258ae&ei=5035

Fisher, D. (2004). RSA keeps RFID private. *eWeek,* February 23. May 5, 2006, from http://www.eweek.com/article2/0,1759,1536569,00.asp

Information Mediary Corporation. (2004). *Introducing the Med-ic™eCAP™Compliance Monitor.* Retrieved October 15, 2004, from http://informationmediary.com/ecap/

Joachim, D. (2004). On location: McCarran International Airport. *Network Computing,* January 22. May 5, 2006, from http://www.networkcomputing.com/showitem.jhtml? docid=1501f4

Landt, J. (2001). *Shrouds of time—The history of RFID.* Warrendale, PA: Association for Automatic Identification and Mobility.

Levinson, M. (2004). The RFID imperative. *CIO Magazine,* October 3. May 5, 2006, from http://www.cio.com/archive/120103/retail.html

Maselli, J. (2004). RFID gets more out of mines. *RFID Journal,* March 30. May 5, 2006, from http://www.rfidjournal.com/article/articleview/852/1/1/

Roberti, M. (2004a). Boeing, Airbus team on standards. *RFID Journal,* May 6. May 5, 2006, from http://www.rfidjournal.com/article/view/934/1/1/

Roberti, M. (2004b). U.S. seeks intra-agency council. *RFID Journal,* April 9. May 5, 2006, from http://www.rfidjournal.com/article/articleview/868/1/14/

Rosencrance, L. (2002). With 9/11 in mind, port operators testing security technology. *ComputerWorld,* September 6. May 5, 2006, from http://www.computerworld.com/securitytopics/security/story/0,10801,74027,00. html?from=story_package

Shahi, R. (2004). *Radio frequency identification: Future of automatic identification and data capture.*

Sliwa, C. (2004). Sara Lee wrestles with RFID, looks for benefits. *ComputerWorld,* September 13. May 5, 2006, from http://www.computerworld.com/mobiletopics/mobile/story/0,10801,95848,00.html

Stanley, J. (2004). Chip away at privacy. *San Francisco Examiner,* July 2.

Sun Microsystems. (2003). RFID streamlines processes, saves tax dollars. Retrieved October 15, 2004, from http://www.sun.com/br/government_1216/feature_rfid.html

Swedberg, C. (2004). Sen. Leahy voices RFID concerns. *RFID Journal,* March 24.

Virginia Department of Transportation. (2004). FAQs: Using Smart Tag on E-Z Pass Toll Locations. Retrieved October 15, 2004, from http://www.virginiadot.org/comtravel/faq-smart-tag-ezpass-default.asp

Winer, P. (2004). RFID in Colorado and China. Retrieved October 15, 2004, from http://radio.weblogs.com/0121943/2004/04/21.html#a95

KEY TERMS

Active Tag: A tag with a power source such as a battery that can be used as a source of energy for the tag's circuitry and antenna.

Bar Codes: A collection of lines of different weights and spacing that can be read by a computer input device.

Passive Tag: A tag that does not have a power source such as a battery. Power is supplied by the reader. When radio waves from the reader meet a passive tag, the coiled antenna within the tag forms a magnetic field. The tag draws power from the field and energizes the circuits in the tag. The tag next transmits the data encoded in the tag's memory.

Reader: A device which is capable of "interrogating" or reading data from a tag. The reader has an antenna that emits radio waves; the tag responds by sending back its data.

Tag: A portable device which is capable of receiving data from or transmitting data to a reader. It holds a microchip combined with an antenna in a compact package. The antenna picks up signals from an RFID reader or scanner and then returns the signal typically with some additional data. RFID tags can be very tiny such as the size of a large rice grain or as large as a paperback book.

Transponder: A combined receiver and transmitter whose function is to transmit signals automatically when triggered by a reader or an interrogator.

VeriChip: An implantable radio frequency identification (RFID) microchip for human use.

This work was previously published in Encyclopedia of Digital Government, edited by A. Anttiroiko; M. Malkia, pp. 1394-1401, copyright 2007 by Information Science Reference, formerly known as Idea Group Reference (an imprint of IGI Global).

Chapter 5.15
Gender Differences in the Navigation of Electronic Worlds

Sharon McDonald
University of Sunderland, UK

Lynne Humphries
University of Sunderland, UK

INTRODUCTION

Recent developments in visualization techniques coupled with the widespread use of complex graphical interfaces, frequently designed to meet the needs of a perceived homogenous set of ideal users, have served to highlight the gap between what an interface demands of its user and the user's actual capabilities (Hindmarch & McDonald, 2006). Consequently, if we are to be able to develop more usable interfaces, then a consideration of individual differences in interaction becomes increasingly important. The most fundamental individual difference of all is that of gender, yet surprisingly it is often the most overlooked. In this article, it is argued that if we are to develop more usable interfaces then individual differences such as gender are not factors that may be considered in the design process, but factors that must be considered. The issue of navigation in virtual and information spaces will be used as a vehicle for this discussion.

THE IMPORTANCE OF NAVIGATION

Navigation is a complex process, which involves determining and following a path through an environment to reach some goal or target. In the physical or virtual world, this might be to arrive at a particular place; in information worlds, this goal may be to find a particular Web page or unit of information. In recent years, navigation has become a key issue within human computer interaction (HCI) research. It has also been the focus of much research in the field of individual differences, meaning that it is one of the few areas in which there is a good corpus of work on gender-based differences in interaction. In addition to providing a forum for this discussion of gender differences on a key interaction task, navigation also provides an example of how performance differences in interaction may be an artifact of the metrics used to study a particular behaviour. The next section of this article presents the results of research studies that have investigated gender differences in navigation. The implications of this work are discussed and areas of future research are highlighted.

IMPACT OF GENDER ON NAVIGATION

A number of studies of way-finding in the physical world have demonstrated gender-based differences in terms of navigational efficiency (usually assessed by task completion times), and navigational strategy (for example, Lawton, Charleston and Zieles, 1996). The results of such studies usually end up being reported in the popular press as evidence that males are generally superior at this type of activity than females. This may serve to strengthen the stereotypical view that some careers that might draw upon this skill would be unsuitable or in some way inappropriate for women, and in so doing increasing the possibility that some women may feel discouraged to engage in these areas. These studies have also impacted on the study of navigation in virtual worlds as it is assumed that there is a direct parallel between the development of navigation knowledge in real and virtual worlds (Kim & Hirtle, 1995).

The findings of studies of gender differences in virtual worlds do seem to support the general trend that has emerged from studies of physical spaces. The general pattern of results suggest that females tend to rely much more heavily on landmark knowledge than males, who can use landmark knowledge but are more adapt at using other environmental cues. For example, Devlin and Bernstein (1995) found that males made fewer errors and were better able to use visual-spatial cues than females in a computer simulation of a real environment. Schmitz (1997) found that girls relied upon salient landmarks within a maze to guide their navigation to a greater extent than boys. Similarly, Sandstrom, Kaufman, and Huettel (1998) and Dabbs, Chang, Strong, and Milun (1998) also found that females tend to rely

predominantly on landmark information whereas males use both landmark and geometric information equally well. Previous research has also shown that females are more likely than males to refer to landmarks when asked to give directions (Miller & Santoni, 1986), and are more accurate at recalling landmarks than men (Galea & Kimura 1993). Cutmore, Hine, Maberly, Langford, and Hawgood (2000) suggest that while both males and females make good use of landmarks as navigational cues, males tended to do so with greater efficiency. They studied navigation through a virtual maze and found that male subjects were able to find their way out of the maze with fewer moves than female subjects. Cutmore et al. (2000) found that subjects' navigation of the maze improved over a series of trials suggesting that subjects were forming a mental representation of the environment, however male subjects reached a more optimum level of performance in the maze before female subjects.

The reliance upon landmarks demonstrated by female participants in these studies is of particular interest since landmark knowledge is thought to represent the primary stage of spatial knowledge acquisition in a new environment. According to Siegal and White (1975), the development of spatial knowledge of a new environment progresses through three levels of representation. Initially landmarks are recognized and are used to guide subsequent navigation. Landmark knowledge is followed by the development of route knowledge, which is characterized by the ability to navigate from one point in the environment to another, using existing knowledge of landmarks to guide decisions concerning when to take right or left turns. The final level of representation is survey knowledge. Survey knowledge allows us to give directions to others, traverse unfamiliar routes, and know the general direction of places. As such, survey knowledge is based upon a global frame of reference. This level of representation is often referred to as a cognitive map. Hence the implications of studies that have found gender differences suggest that females take longer to acquire spatial knowledge than males. However, they do not tell us about the quality of the representation once it is fully formed. It may be that while it takes longer for women to acquire this knowledge their resulting representation is much richer, as yet this has not been examined in the research literature. Moreover, it is unclear as to the extent that the environments used in these studies will have affected performance. The complex and often unrealistic environments used may only serve to heighten differences in performance.

It has been suggested that the parallel between spatial knowledge acquisition in real and virtual worlds may also extend to hypertext systems. While the results of some early studies suggest that this parallel might actual hold (Kim & Hirtle, 1995), the issue of gender differences in this domain has not been considered in much detail. McDonald and Spencer (2000) conducted a small preliminary investigation into gender-related differences in Web navigation. The study focused on the three areas in which gender differences have been previously found, user confidence, navigational efficiency, and navigational strategy. The study employed a variety of behavioural and self-report measures including rating scales for user confidence measures, and unobtrusive monitoring of the users' movements and verbal protocols. Participants were required to complete a number of search tasks and a direction giving task. Participants were asked to direct a co-experimenter to a specified area within the Web site. McDonald and Spencer found that while there were no differences in efficiency on the search task, female subjects indicated they were less confident about their ability to complete the tasks than males. In terms of verbal data, female subjects made more references to landmarks in the direction giving task than male subjects. They also tended to engage in more analysis of where a particular link might take them. In addition, female subjects were less confident about their ability to complete search tasks than male subjects.

It seems unlikely that the results obtained in these studies are due simply to differences in the rate at which males and females acquire knowledge. Navigation is a complex interactive process, which involves both the execution of actions and the evaluation of system changes; therefore it is unlikely that one single factor will have an overarching effect. Indeed, it seems that from the McDonald and Spencer study that confidence was an issue that may well have affected performance. Confidence was also found to be an issue for some of the studies on the navigation of virtual worlds, with male participants expressing a greater degree of confidence than females (Devlin & Bernstein, 1995, Schmitz, 1997). However, it may be that females' poor confidence ratings may also reflect a general tendency of women to underestimate or belittle their performance of tasks that are gender typed as masculine (Beyer, 1990). For example, Beyer found that female confidence estimates were affected not only by their actual performance on masculine typed tasks but also by their own low expectations of their performance. According to Lawton et al. (1996) environmental way-finding is stereotyped as a masculine activity. This factor may well account for differences in confidence expressed, and it is likely that confidence may well affect search times.

IMPLICATIONS FOR DESIGN

The studies discussed in this article have implications for both system design and also research studies that seek to examine the impact of individual differences such as gender on navigation. The findings suggest that parallels do exist between navigation in the real world and navigation in virtual worlds, and that gender differences are apparent in the strategies used by males and females. Therefore, as worlds grow in size, complexity, and use, there is a greater need to provide integrated support for these different strategies so that neither gender group is put at a disadvantage.

While there is no evidence regarding the ultimate quality of the mental representations male and females develop through navigational experience in an environment there is evidence to suggest that males may progress to survey knowledge faster than females. The primary areas of application of such worlds are in the areas of leisure and education. Games based on the exploration of virtual worlds are frequently used in the context of both home entertainment but also for educational purposes, a large number of which require users to navigate in a range of environments. In order to support the navigational strategies of both males and females it is essential that these environments include cues that appeal to both types of strategy. For example, an environment free of landmarks may well prove to be disadvantageous to female users. In addition, the time allowed to navigate between different sequences may also need to be extended to accommodate for the differences in the rate of spatial knowledge acquisition. Moreover, as confidence in use appears to be an issue for females there is a need for the designers of such software to ensure that their products appeal to both genders. In terms of interface options this might be achieved through the provision of extended choice in terms of character selection, environmental situations, and storylines. However, for this to happen designers must avoid the pitfall of grounding themselves in their designs that is designing for themselves rather than for the intended end users. As Ahuja (2002) points out much educational software is written for boys' interests rather than girls' interests.

An example of where a consideration of gender differences in design has led to improvements in interaction can be found in the work of Tan, Robertson, and Czerwinski (2001) and Czerwinski, Tan, and Robertson (2002). Tan, Robertson, and Czerwinski (2001) found that male subjects were able to complete navigation tasks in a virtual world faster than female subjects when both were using small displays, however, this difference was eliminated when a larger display was used.

Czerwinski et al. (2002) examined this difference further and examined the effects of providing a wider field of view on a large display they found that the use of this display brought the performance of female users up to the level of male users. The male users were also able to successfully navigate using this display and it had no ill-effects on their performance. Czerwinski et al. (2002) suggest that the wider display helps female subjects because it enables them to perceive more information through visual scanning which has the effect of facilitating the construction of a cognitive map of the information structure.

RESEARCH IMPLICATIONS

The McDonald and Spencer (2000) study suggested that females engage in more analysis of where a particular link might take them when performing their direction giving task. This behaviour may have implications for how we might measure navigation performance. Within HCI studies the most commonly used experimental metrics are time on task and the number of errors made. Clearly, if females are engaging in this type of analysis then they may also be more likely to take longer completing the task, as a consequence measures based on time may highlight differences in efficiency, which are not actually there. Moreover, an important aspect of Web navigation is link elimination. Users must match their information goals against the link categories available and select the most appropriate link to follow. It seemed that the female subjects in the McDonald and Spencer study were engaging with this process more readily than the male subjects who were more apt to follow the closest match link. Measures of the navigator's path and the method by which a navigator arrives at the task destination appear to be a more fair way of assessing differences. If enough data is collected on path measures it may indeed be possible to infer a degree of user confidence from independent measures alone as proposed by Smith (1996).

However, such independent measures need also to be supported by self-report data such as those derived from verbal protocols which provide an insight into the strategies that underlie observable behaviour. Navigation is a cognitively demanding process that involves moving oneself sequentially around an environment deciding at each step where to go next. The thinking behind those decisions may indeed be more informative than an observation of the subjects' chosen path. This is very important in the case of Web navigation where navigational errors may result from link label ambiguities rather than the user's ability to navigate per se.

The consideration of gender as a factor within HCI has received relatively little attention, despite the fact that there are frequent widespread differences in performance of subjects within research-based studies. Studies of gender differences in navigation in electronic worlds are surprisingly thin on the ground despite the fact that differences have long been demonstrated in real world studies. Researchers' failure to acknowledge the gender factor serves only to limit the validity of their work, yet in many important areas of study within HCI researchers do not strive to ensure an equal gender split among their subject base even in areas where there is known evidence that gender differences exist. For example, there are a large number of reports that spatial ability is positively correlated with navigation performance in hypertext systems, a finding that was confirmed by Chen and Rada's (1996) meta analysis of twenty three individual studies in the field. Probably the most frequently cited study in this area is Vincente and Williges (1988). Vincente and Williges found that users demonstrated enhanced search performance using a graphical interface than a text-based interface. They also found that users with high spatial ability were able to complete search tasks more quickly than users with low spatial ability in a graphical computer interface. However, only seven out of the forty subjects in their study were

female despite the fact that there is a wealth of evidence for the existence of gender differences in spatial abilities, with males demonstrating distinct advantages in spatial tasks over female subjects (Galea & Kimura, 1993).

CONCLUSION AND FUTURE WORK

While the general pattern of findings of the work discussed here suggests that gender differences in the navigation of virtual worlds parallel those existing in physical spaces there is still much research to be done. Studies are needed to examine the impact of world complexity on navigation performance over a number of interaction periods so that differences in spatial knowledge acquisition can be studied more closely. Only that way will we be able to examine differences in the ultimate quality of male and female cognitive maps. Studies are also needed to examine the type and placement of landmarks in virtual worlds to understand if they can actually lead to improvements in navigation performance of female users.

The study of individual differences in human computer interaction is growing in importance. The widespread use of computers dictates that designers can no longer assume that all computer users fit an ideal homogenous profile of skills, knowledge, and abilities. Improving the usability of computers through graphical user interfaces is a laudable aim, yet if that interface is designed on principles that meet the needs of only half of the population failure is inevitable. The importance of individual differences such as gender must also be considered within the context of the research laboratory to ensure that we are not designing experimental protocols and metrics that disadvantage particular user groups, to do so would serve to perpetuate the digital divide.

REFERENCES

Ahuja, M. K. (2002). Women and the information technology profession: A literature review, synthesis, and research agenda. *European Journal of Information systems, 11,* 20-34.

Beyer, S. (1990). Gender differences in the accuracy of self-evaluations of performance. *Journal of Personality and Social Psychology, 59,* 960-970.

Chen, C., & Rada, R. (1996). Interacting with hypertext: A meta-analysis of experimental studies. *Human-Computer Interaction, 11*(2), 125-156.

Czerwinski, M., Tan, D. S., & Robertson, G. G. (2002). Women take a wider view. In *Proceedings of CHI 2002. CHI Letters, 4*(1), 195-202.

Cutmore, T. R. H., Hine, T. J., Maberly, K. J., Langford, N. M., & Hawgood, G. (2000) Cognitive and gender factors influencing navigation in a virtual environment. *International Journal Human-Computer Studies, 53,* 223-249.

Dabbs, J. M., Chang, E. L., Strong, R. A., & Milun, R. (1998). Spatial ability, navigation strategy, and geographic knowledge among men and women. *Evolution and Human Behaviour, 19*(2), 89-98.

Devlin, A. S., & Bernstein, J. (1995). Interactive wayfinding: Use of cues by men and women. *Journal of Environmental Psychology, 15*(1), 23-38.

Galea, L. A. M., & Kimura, D. (1993). Sex differences in route learning. *Personality and Individual differences 14,* 53-65.

Hindmarch, M., & McDonald, S. (2006). The role of individual differences in human computer interaction: The case of navigation. In W. Karwowski (Ed.), *International Encycopedia of Human Factors and Ergonomics* (2nd ed.). CRC Press.

Kim, H., & Hirtle, S. C. (1995). Spatial metaphors and disorientation in hypertext browsing. *Behaviour and information technology, 14,* 239-250.

Lawton, C. A., Charleston, S. I., & Zieles, A. S. (1996) Individual- and gender-related differences in indoor wayfinding. *Environment and Behaviour, 28*(2), 204-219

McDonald, S., & Spencer, L. (2000). Gender differences in Web navigation: Strategies, efficiency, and confidence. In E. Balka & R. Smith (Eds.), *Women, work, and computerisation: Charting a course to the future* (pp. 175-181). Kluwer Academic Publishers.

Miller, L. K., & Santoni, V. (1986). Sex differences in spatial abilities: Strategic and experiential correlates. *Acta Psychologica, 62,* 225-235.

Sandstrom, N. J., Kaufman, J., & Huettel, S. A. (1998) Males and females use different distal cues in a virtual environment navigation task. *Cognitive Brain Research, 6*(4), 351-360

Schmitz, S. (1997). Gender-related strategies in environmental development: Effects of anxiety on wayfinding in and representation of a three-dimensional maze. *Journal of Environmental Psychology, 17*(3), 215-228.

Siegal, R., & White, T. (1975). The development of spatial representations of large scale environments. In H. W. Reese (Ed.), *Advances in child development and behaviour.* New York: Academic Press.

Smith, P.A. (1996). Towards a practical measure of hypertext usability. *Interacting with Computers 8*(4), 365-381

Tan, D. S., Robertson, G. G., & Czerwinski, M. (2001). Exploring 3D navigation: Combining speed-coupled flying with orbiting. In *Proceedings of CHI 2001, CHI Letters, 2*(1), 418-425

Vincente, K. J., & Williges, R. C. (1988). Accommodating individual differences in searching a hierarchical file system. *International Journal of Man Machine Studies, 29,* 647-668.

KEY TERMS

Cognitive Map: The mental representation an individual holds of an environment which is used to guide navigational choice and also for route planning.

Human Computer Interaction: An interdisciplinary subject linking computer science with many other fields to study the interaction between people (users) and computers.

Hypertext: A collection of information-based documents (e.g. Web pages) that are linked together via referential links to form a navigable structure.

Navigation: A process which involves determining and following a path through an environment to reach some goal or target.

Spatial Ability: Cognitive skills related to visualization, the ability to construct and manipulate a mental image of an object, and the ability to determine the location of objects.

Spatial Knowledge: The knowledge an individual holds about the structure of an environment. This knowledge is thought to develop through three stages, landmark, route and survey knowledge.

Virtual World: An immersive or non-immersive display environment that depicts realistic scenes.

This work was previously published in Encyclopedia of Human Computer Interaction, edited by C. Ghaoui, pp. 287-294, copyright 2006 by Information Science Reference, formerly known as Idea Group Reference (an imprint of IGI Global).

Chapter 5.16
Identity Management:
A Comprehensive Approach to Ensuring a Secure Network Infrastructure

Katherine M. Hollis
Electronic Data Systems, USA

David M. Hollis
United States Army, USA

ABSTRACT

This chapter provides an introductory overview of identity management as it relates to data networking and enterprise information management systems. It looks at the strategic value of identity management in corporate and government environments. It defines the terms, concepts, and technologies associated with identity management. This chapter is a capstone to other chapters that deal with the specific technologies (strong identification and authentication, PKI, encryption, LDAP, etc...). Federated identity management is a strategic concept that encapsulates and integrates these disparate technologies into a coordinated, comprehensive strategy to accomplish enterprise-wide goals. This chapter introduces some practical business case concepts to assists the reader in putting together their own identity management strategies using ROI and success criteria.

IDENTITY MANAGEMENT

Identity management (IdM) provides a combination of processes and technologies to securely manage and access the information and resources of an organization. IdM both protects and secures the organization and its information. It is a comprehensive approach that requires the integration of the entire network architecture—inherently providing an end-to-end solution.

With the widespread use of the Internet as a business-enabling platform, enterprises are seeing unprecedented opportunities to grow revenue, strengthen partnerships, achieve efficiencies, and win customer loyalty. The widespread use and openness of the Internet, which makes such communication in business relationships possible, also exposes core resources to corruption and inadvertent disruptions. An IdM strategy gives businesses a framework for protecting their infrastructure and incrementally addressing vulnerabilities while remaining open to new opportunities.

IdM is comprised of and supported by the full spectrum of network security technologies. IdM is the system of technologies and policies/procedures that allows the:

- identification,
- authentication,
- authorization,
- access control, and
- provisioning (secure repository)

of individuals, subsystems, objects, information, and data. It is intrinsic to the validation and secure manipulation of information and the control of individual users.

The integrity of an IdM system relies fundamentally on the validity and thoroughness of initial vetting procedures, to include identity management validity and strong authentication. This is intrinsic and provides the secure foundation for the entire infrastructure.

IdM systems technology consists of directory services, user provisioning and management, access management systems, and agents that monitor requests for resources and service. The foundation for a robust IdM system is the user data that typically resides in, preferably, a central store such as a directory server. Clean user data and well-defined business processes reduce the potential for data integrity issues and ensure that identity data across the enterprise is from an authoritative source. On this foundation is built the framework of rights and privileges that support IdM.

IdM, as noted above, is the amalgamation of business processes and technology that enable businesses, organizations, or government agencies to function as a single, secure, integrated entity with efficient, standardized processes for the management and maintenance of user rights and privileges. In an ideal world, each user possesses a single identity that can be leveraged across both the entire enterprise and an infrastructure that allows central management of users and access rights in an integrated, efficient and cost-effective way (EDS SPPS, 2004).

IdM has often been defined in different ways to support various technology trends. One such definition of identity management is the ability of a user to sign-on to a desktop once and have seamless access to *all* his or her applications (often used in conjunction with *single sign-on* (SSO) technology). This definition has historically tended to include script-based or proprietary solutions. Another definition is the ability of a user to sign-on to a desktop once and have seamless access to *many* of his or her applications. This is viewed as "reduced sign-on" that is targeted at "high-value" applications and addresses both business and security issues simultaneously. Technology companies would lead one to believe these functions are IdM. In truth, and as explained earlier, this definition is limited and doesn't fully illustrate the comprehensive solution set that IdM coherently provides.

IdM is the comprehensive strategy of managing identities (logins, profile information, etc.) across many data sources, and maintaining the relationship between those identities. Many technologies and products claim to be identity management systems but, in most cases, they are only a component and rarely address the processes and policies required for successful implementation. Identity management is *established* through company strategies, policies and processes, then *enabled* through education and technology

An important and related concept is that of federated identity. Federated identity is a means by which—through the use of a common trust model—organizations can overcome the constraints of the enterprise and facilitate business between disparate entities. Information is exchanged and accessed securely following accepted rules and policies outlined in the trust model. There are several organizations that are actively assisting in standards efforts to define and reconcile business and technical hurdles towards this vision of facilitating business between disparate organizations.

TECHNICAL FUNDAMENTALS AND FUNCTIONAL COMPONENTS

IdM is strategic, and its approach requires and encompasses several security technologies. It integrates these often disparate technologies into a comprehensive whole in order to meet defined operational and regulatory requirements in an effective and efficient manner. The following are some of the technologies that may (but do not necessarily) constitute an IdM solution:

- **Strong identification and authentication (I&A)**—this requirement is predicated by and requires strong vetting procedures to insure adequate security. It can be implemented through the use of Biometrics or time/event-based card tokens.
- **Public key infrastructure (PKI)**—inherent in secure infrastructure and generally thought of as "public," in this case we also consider "private" key exchange. For example, VPN servers, firewalls, and bulk-en-cryption devices often exchange private keys in order to authenticate data traffic between them that is organizationally internal but physically transmitted over the Internet.
- **Virtual private network (VPN)**—the necessary use of encryption to ensure confidentiality throughout the system network.
- **Access management**—the managed control of resources and their access, both from external and internal sources. This is generally managed from a central location within the infrastructure.

IdM is a holistic approach that encapsulates the functionalities of specific technologies and wraps them into a more comprehensive strategy with practical application for the business environment. Consequently, it is important to recognize that the scope of IdM within a secure architecture is comprehensive and necessitates the cohesive application and incorporation of the following:

- **Information**
  - ➤ Attributes, credentials, entitlements, work product, and so forth
  - ➤ Trusted sources of authority and sources of information
- **Lifecycle**
  - ➤ Creation and active management of identity and profile info

Figure 1. The five functional components of identity management

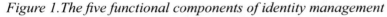
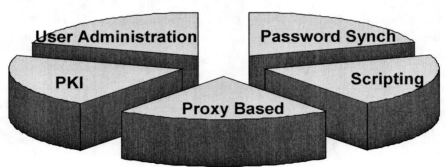

> Deactivation (removal of entitlements)
> Alumni and Retiree (for re-instatement, benefits, etc.)
> Removal of expired data related to the individual

- **Context / Role**
  > B2E, B2B, B2C
  > Employee, Client, Supplier, Partner
  > Platforms (type and ownership)
  > Locale (geography and environment)

In considering an IdM solution, an organization must consider what features are necessary to support its requirements then incorporate the relevant technologies. These features must enhance the conduct of operations and provide the following functionalities:

- Uniformly manage and enforce business policies;
- Leverage existing authoritative information sources;
- Automate administration by using workflows and approval routing;
- Reconcile and correlate account and identity information;
- Reduce security risks via identification of errant accounts;
- Provide for immediate revocation of access;

- Provide self-service of account info and password reset;
- Allow application owner a stake in the approval process;
- Ensure security within a delegated control model;
- Facilitate business by reducing time to complete requests;
- Reduce costs by gaining efficiencies in effort and operations;
- Improve service levels, productivity, and end-user experience;
- Ensure regulatory compliance and privacy of information; and
- Manage inventory, assigned resources as well as system access.

These functionalities can be divided into five basic components once adequate vetting and authentication have been ensured.

When considering the components and their incorporation, the following comparison is beneficial (Figure 2).

IDM STRATEGIC FOCUS AND DIRECTION

From a comprehensive perspective, one can readily ascertain the various components required to

Figure 2. Further discussion of components

Password Synchronization	Simplifies end-user experience	Still requires manual password entry and Varying password policies prohibit scope
Scripting	Well understood and easy to create	Some implementations can be difficult to scale and Not very secure
Proxy-based	Adds security layer	Can be difficult to include some applications
PKI	Based on standards and PKI-enabled apps increasing	Not widely deployed yet
User Administration	Simplifies administrator's work	Problem of too many passwords still exists

build an IdM solution. The following considerations must be addressed:

- **Policies, procedures, and processes—** Identity management, comprehensively is a process, supported by policy/procedures and enabled through technology, whose purpose is to efficiently, accurately, and securely manage the entire lifecycle, scope, and context of identity and entitlement information across the enterprise. Critical components include the following:
  - ➤ *Password policies*—passwords are one of the weakest links in an organization's network security system and typically require considerable attention.
  - ➤ *Approval routing/Process and required signatures*—an important but often overlooked part of the business process.
  - ➤ *Purchasing processes*
  - ➤ *Naming convention process*
  - ➤ *Security and privacy policies*—IdM is a critical part of an organization's overall security and privacy policy, which should encompass network perimeter security, incident handling, prevention of social engineering attacks, and other concerns.
  - ➤ *Employee management processes* (hiring/exit /retirement)
- **Legal and regulatory requirements—**Much of the notoriety gained by IdM in the last few years is the direct result of the many legal and regulatory statutes put in place to support information protection. HIPAA, Gramm-Leach-Bliley, FDA 21 CFR (Part 11), E-SIGN, and Sarbanes-Oxley are just a sample of the legal and regulatory requirements that impact the fielding of IdM. The aforementioned laws and regulations have one thing in common: they create new compliance pressures on CIOs and CSOs, placing new demands on an organization's security infrastructure. Fortunately, IdM solutions provide a strong, reliable technology foundation for meeting compliance requirements by tightly controlling access to resources and providing reporting tools that demonstrate compliance (EDS SPPS, 2004).

Figure 3. IdM life cycle phases

Assess
Security Office
Privacy and data protection analysis
Security assessment
Risk management services
Business continuity planning
Emergency management services

Protect
Security architecture
Technology implementation and
    integration consulting
Secure systems engineering
Secure communications and
    authentication
PKI design, implementation and
    management
Secure perimeter management
Operating system (OS) hardening
Security administration

Monitor
Security information management
Alerts and warning advisories
Intrusion detection
Intrusion response
Incident response
Computer investigations

Train
Individual training programs
Customized training program
Client-specific security aware
Training program-specific sec
Technology-specific training

Validate
Verification and validation
Certification and accreditation
Security testing and evaluation

In addition to the immediate issues to be resolved, there are longer-term considerations. Life cycle management of IdM plays a key role in the successful implementation of IdM. Figure 3 illustrates the full life cycle approach to comprehensive IdM.

Each of the IdM phases is supported by the following relevant technologies:

- Directory and data base services
- Identification, vetting, and validation
- Strong authentication
- Provisioning processes
- Information sharing (meta)
- Workflow management
- Collaboration and messaging
- Delegated administration
- Self-service applications

Given the distinct advantages to comprehensive IdM implementation, there are a number of compelling reasons to deploy comprehensive IdM. Some are self-explanatory, such as associated cost reductions. Others are not so obvious, such as the extremely important security and regulatory compliance area. The ability to ensure adherence to company security policies and procedures across business organizations, as well as identification of existing exposures, is key to managing the risk security breaches. Legislation is forcing enterprises to properly maintain their environments, assigning access on a need-to-know basis to ensure the privacy and integrity of information. Automation and self-service of an individual's identity, coupled with pervasive sharing rather than duplication of valued information, will assist with the control and reduction of overhead and operational costs. Integrating existing business processes and information systems into a uniform workflow will further reduce cost by eliminating redundant efforts and duplicate data. By elimination of human error and reducing the time to complete a request, service-level agreements can be exceeded. Improving the end-user experience and reducing idle time on redundant tasks raises productivity in the environment.

Precise, timely management of user data and access policies is required for identity management functions. This includes access management and strong, two-factor identification/authentication. There are many commercially available solutions with features such as delegated administration, ap-

Figure 4. IdM advantages

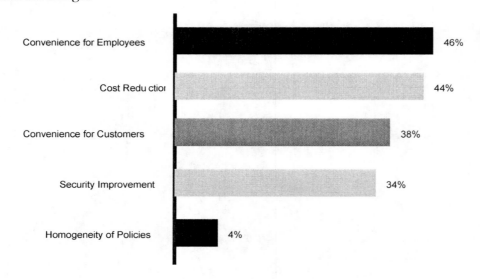

proval workflow, and user self-service that further enhance user management. There are solutions that streamline user-management tasks, enhance data accuracy and reduce technical help desk and administrative costs. Among the many benefits of IdM is its ability to improve user productivity by reducing the number of account/password combinations by providing single sign-on (SSO), password synchronization, or federated identity solutions. By eliminating the annoyance of multiple logins and passwords, IdM enhances the user experience, reduces vulnerabilities caused by lax password practices, and reduces password-related administrative and help desk costs. Additional benefits of IdM can be experienced with features such as self-service, delegated administration, portal aggregation of content/data, and the ability to remotely access systems. Finally, IdM will facilitate business. Enterprises need to provide their target audience with the ability to self-register for available services in order to easily and quickly establish new business and conduct existing transactions.

SUCCESSFUL IDM IMPLEMENTATION

An IdM strategy must be developed and deployed pervasively throughout an environment and accommodate the entire lifecycle of the identity. There must be top-to-bottom organizational buy-in and support. The approach needs to be phased in to ensure a measurable deployment and positive acceptance throughout the organization (see Figure 5 for an example of a phased approach). It must ensure accountability for identity information, adhere to local laws and government regulations, support commercial best-practices for security and privacy, and be an essential component for non-repudiation. From a business point-of-view, it must provide flexibility and process improvement and show a *return on investment* (ROI) or other defined strategic benefit.

An important first step is to identify the common processes within the enterprise. These processes will be improved during deployment by identifying the technology components within the

Figure 5. Phased implementation approach to identity management

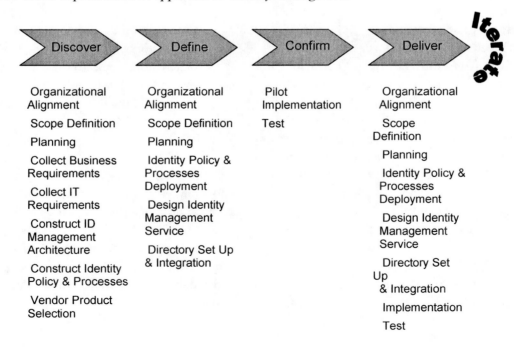

Discover	Define	Confirm	Deliver	Iterate
Organizational Alignment	Organizational Alignment	Pilot Implementation	Organizational Alignment	
Scope Definition	Scope Definition	Test	Scope Definition	
Planning	Planning		Planning	
Collect Business Requirements	Identity Policy & Processes Deployment		Identity Policy & Processes Deployment	
Collect IT Requirements	Design Identity Management Service		Design Identity Management Service	
Construct ID Management Architecture	Directory Set Up & Integration		Directory Set Up & Integration	
Construct Identity Policy & Processes			Implementation	
Vendor Product Selection			Test	

enterprise and bridge component gaps by introducing the new technology that meets the enterprise view needs, not the point-solution problem. The phases of deployment must be planned by determining the high value-added /immediate impact items that can be implemented in the shortest timeframe. This provides for early "wins" to facilitate the fielding of the IdM system.

BUSINESS CASE FOR IDM

Although often viewed as difficult to develop, it is necessary to recognize the compelling business case in support of IdM. It is immediately recognized that, from an operations perspective, the ease of systems use is vastly improved. For example, the enhanced security provided through strong identification and authentication and limited password requirements allows system administrators to enforce password policies across Web, client/server, thin client, and mainframe applications and reduces the possibility of the single authentication point being compromised. But a business case for IdM is generally a requirement of any acquisition and implementation. The foundation of that business case is the return on investment, which is often expressed in terms of the benefit/cost ratio, break-even point, and the comparison of the return from an IdM investment compared to the return from alternative business operations investments. The following discussion illustrates some of the specific items (success factors) that can be used in a typical ROI analysis.

There are four specific areas of improvement that can be used to develop metrics to define an ROI business case for IdM. In addition, success criteria can be developed, and used to baseline and justify the level of success for the IdM business case. These success factors must be defined at the beginning of the process, and progress should be measured against realistic values.

- **Users are no longer required to juggle dozens of usernames and passwords**. This eliminates the need for users to manage changing passwords and allows users to launch critical applications faster.
- **Immediate cost savings are inherent, as many help desks may be spending 40% or more of their time on password resets**. IdM frees up IT resources for more strategic work.
- **Administrators and users spend more time on productive tasks and repetitive data entry for users is eliminated**.
- **There is a quantifiable aspect to enhanced security**. The cost of a managed security service, the cost of maintaining firewalls and IDSs, and the like. Security is considerably enhanced as IdM could eliminate the requirement for passwords through the use of strong authentication (i.e., biometrics). Should passwords continue to be required, IdM eliminates user tendency to keep passwords on sticky notes, keyboards, and rolodexes. Policies are enforced that eliminate poor password management:
  - ➤ Easy to remember = "easy to guess."
  - ➤ Strong authentication mechanisms can protect the "keys to the kingdom."

These factors play a strong role in defeating social engineering attacks. The cost associated with successful attacks against corporate IdM is quickly becoming astronomical (Roth, Mehta, Boorstin, & Levinstein, 2005).

Success criteria are immediately self-evident and compelling. For example, the enhanced security provided through strong authentication and limited password requirements allows administrators to enforce password policies across Web, client/server, and mainframe applications and reduces the possibility of the single access point being compromised.

A comprehensive IdM deployment ensures continuous investment protection through managed access and the use of technologies that are reusable across multiple applications. It is also important that the technologies that are deployed adhere to published standards in order to make components modular so they can be added as needed. This ensures maximum interoperability and re-use. In this way, cost savings will be consistently realized.

In conclusion, it is imperative that we recognize the three strategic values that an IdM implementation must provide in an overall ROI business case:

- Enforcement of business and security policies;
- Foundation for IT infrastructure strategy; and
- Compliance with regulatory requirements.

CONCLUSION

In today's collaborative and interconnected e-business world, federated IdM provides a secure and effective way to share trusted user information across business boundaries—inside and outside the organization. Authenticated, portable identities improve user productivity and enable organizations to seize new business opportunities. Several early adopters in diverse industries are attempting to implement real-world capabilities for federated IdM as they lessen the need to manage accounts for external users and reduce associated administrative costs.

IdM is a security, legal, and regulatory requirement for all organizations' current and future operational frameworks, even if it is not specifically identified. In an increasingly competitive business environment, leading government agencies and industries are building new Web-based infrastructures. These organizations are seeking to gain the strategic advantages of secure collaborative networking. For those organizations that are able to build a collaborative IdM e-Business model, the door opens to a wealth of measurable benefits. IdM provides the security infrastructure necessary to ensure the appropriate authentication, resulting in secure, prescribed access and consequent strong information security.

REFERENCES

Electronic Data Systems SPPS. (2004). *Identity and Access Management: Concepts and Components*. Retrieved November 16, 2004, from http://www.eds.com

Forrester Research, Inc. (2001). *Build unified access control*. Retrieved March 15, 2001, from http://www.forrester.com/my/1,,1-0,FF.html

Hollis, K. M. (2005). *Identity management briefing*. Retrieved from http://www.eds.com

Roth, D., Mehta, S., Boorstin, J., & Levinstein, J. (2005). The great data heist. *Fortune, 151*(10), 66-72.

RSA. (2001). *RSA security briefing on identity management and single sign on (SSO)*. Retrieved June 25, 2001, from http://www.rsasecurity.com/solutionsTertiary. asp?id=1093

This work was previously published in Enterprise Information Systems Assurance and Systems Security: Managerial and Technical Issues, edited by M. Warkentin, pp. 372-383, copyright 2006 by IGI Publishing, formerly known as Idea Group Publishing (an imprint of IGI Global).

Chapter 5.17
Conducting Congruent, Ethical, Qualitative Research in Internet–Mediated Research Environments

M. Maczewski
University of Victoria, Canada

M.-A. Storey
University of Victoria, Canada

M. Hoskins
University of Victoria, Canada

ABSTRACT

Research practices in Internet-mediated environments are influenced by the dynamic interplay of online, onground and technical research spheres. This chapter illuminates the different ways in which studies can be located within these spheres and explores the resulting implications for researcher-participant relationships. Issues of participant recruitment, data collection, data use and ownership, trust and voice are discussed. The authors suggest that to conduct ethical qualitative research online, the researcher is required to develop and demonstrate awareness of the specific Internet-mediated research contexts, knowledge of technologies used and of research practices congruent with the situatedness of the study.

INTRODUCTION

The rapid adoption of the Internet has resulted in many recent changes in economic, political, social and psychological spheres of human and social interactions (e.g., Castells, 1996; Gergen, 1991; Surratt, 2001; Turkle, 1995). From conducting e-business to debating politics to exploring multiple identities online, many people using the Internet are experiencing human interactions in very different ways than they would in onground[1] communities. The medium used, in this case the Internet, both shapes and forms human and social interactions and is shaped by human and social interactions (McLuhan, 1964). Therefore, it is important to recognize how technical and social realms are connected and inform each other; and, more specifically, how research practices are shaped and being shaped by technologies used.

Denzin and Lincoln (2000) define qualitative research as:

"... a situated activity that locates the observer in the world. It consists of a set of interpretive, material practices that make the world visible. These practices transform the world. They turn the world into a series of representations, including field notes, interviews, conversations, photographs, recordings, and memos to the self. At this level qualitative research involves an interpretive, naturalistic approach to the world. This means that qualitative researchers study things in their natural settings, attempting to make sense of or interpret phenomena in terms of the meanings people bring to them" (p. 3).

But in an Internet-mediated research setting what is the "natural setting" that Denzin and Lincoln refer to? The natural setting could be conceptualized as being located in the interplays of online, onground and technical research spheres. We suggest that in order to conduct online research, awareness of the interplay of these three spheres is important for the development of ethical,

virtual research practices. Researchers need to expand their own traditional onground knowledge of research ethics to include the understanding of technologies used and an awareness of their impact on human and social interactions.

From this interplay, new conceptualizations of research practices may arise that go beyond traditional research methods and ethics, creating research practices that are congruent[2] within innovative Internet-mediated research environments. The intent of this chapter is to add to the discussion of what constitutes ethical online qualitative research by illuminating how the situatedness of both researchers and participants in technically-mediated environments actively shapes research processes. When conducting qualitative research online, it is important to ask the following questions: How are the technical characteristics of the Internet enabling research interactions? What are the human and social implications of using this new medium? Extended into the contexts of conducting qualitative research online, the questions become: How do technical characteristics of the Internet influence qualitative research? What social and ethical implications do Internet-mediated forms of human and social interactions have on qualitative research practices, specifically researcher-participant relationships?

First, the social and technical contexts of Internet-mediated research are illuminated and the implications of the interplay of three research spheres, online, onground and technical, for human and social interactions are discussed. How these changed cultural contexts impact qualitative research practices is then illustrated by exploring issues of participant recruitment, data collection, trust and voice. Later sections will provide guidelines for congruent, ethical online qualitative research practices. All explorations are grounded in cyberculture, virtual and traditional research methods literature as well as many professional conversations and research experiences.

INTERNET-MEDIATED RESEARCH CONTEXTS

When conducting research using virtual space, three spheres of interactions inform the research process: online, onground and technical (see Figure 1).

The online sphere encompasses the virtual space and all forms of actions that are completed within it, for example, a conversation in a chatroom. The onground sphere encompasses the material world and all actions grounded in physical realities, for example, the institution that employs the researcher. The technical sphere is grounded in the onground world and enables the virtual—it connects the onground and online worlds, forming the latter. The technical contexts in which the online research is embedded consist of many parts. For example: hardware, software, infrastructure, bandwidth as well as local, institutional, national and global information and communication laws and policies. In Internet-mediated research both researcher and participants are located in onground and online communities within their specific cultural parameters and their technologically-mediated interactions are influenced by the interplay of all three spheres.

When considering the growing field of Internet research, one can observe that it has been conducted in diverse quantitative and qualitative ways. Given the methodological variety seen in Internet research, the relevance of online, onground and technical spheres differs in relevance to the study. Ethical implications need to be considered within their unique contexts and primary locations within the three spheres. For example, online surveys have been conducted (e.g., Tapscott, 1998; Wellman, Quan-Haase, Witte, & Hampton, 2001), psychological experiments undertaken (e.g., Buchanan & Smith, 1999), ethnographic studies of online communities conducted (e.g., Baym, 2000; Markham, 1998; Smith & Kollock, 1999; Turkle, 1995) and Web content analyzed and archived (e.g., Schneider & Larsen, 2000). In these studies,

the spaces in which the research is conducted, the location of researchers and participants, their relationship to each other and the form of data collected, varies tremendously.

For example, in an ethnographic study of a virtual community, the researcher and participants interact directly with each other and the virtual community is the actual research focus (e.g., Baym, 1999; Markham, 1998). In this form of Internet-mediated research, the research field is primarily located online. Research findings are interpreted within the contexts of virtual communities. They are primarily written referring to online identities, actions and language use without necessarily connecting these identities with onground realities. They are located within the technical parameters that enable cyberspace.

A survey posted online, however, locates the researcher and participants primarily in their onground communities. Both parties asynchronously post and reply to the survey (e.g., Bampton & Cowton, 2002). In these surveys the virtual sphere is used as a space in which data is collected. It is not the virtual space itself that is studied but primarily people's ideas and opinions in their onground lives about a specific topic. In

Figure 1. Interplay of online, onground and technical research spheres in Internet-mediated research.

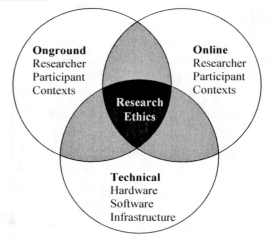

this kind of research, people's onground realities are important and the Internet is used as a technology that enables this particular study to be conducted in a specific way—very similar to research surveys conducted via telephone.

In yet other studies, the integration of the Internet into people's lives is the research focus (e.g., Kiesler, Kraut, Lundmark, Patterson, Mukopadhyay, & Scherlis, 1998; Hampton & Wellman, 1999; Wellman et al., 2001). It is explored primarily through onground contacts and inclusion of the analysis of the use of Internet-mediated interactions (e.g., e-mail, listserv, Web). Again the researcher and participants are primarily situated in onground settings, but this time the use of the Internet itself and its relevance for people's onground lives is studied.

Electronic data collection from listserv archives or from an archived website (e.g., Schneider & Larsen, 2000) represents other forms of primarily technologically-mediated research. In this research methodology, there is usually no direct interaction between the researcher and participant (listserv member or website designer)—the analysis of technologically-mediated texts and images is the focus of the study. All methodologies and spheres can overlap and are in dynamic interaction with each other. This can be seen in studies where researcher and participants initially meet in virtual space and follow up with meetings in person.

In the early years of Internet research, it seemed that traditional research methodology (e.g., ethnography, survey, discourse analysis) and research methods (e.g., interviews, participant observation) used for conducting studies in physical environments were applied in more or less the same form to study virtual interactions. As stated in the "Tri-Council Policy Statement: Ethical Conduct for Research Involving Humans," ethical principles guiding traditional research are based on the following principles: respect for human dignity, respect for free and informed consent, respect for vulnerable persons, respect

for privacy and confidentiality, respect for justice and inclusiveness, balancing of harms and benefits, minimizing of harm and maximizing of benefits (National Sciences and Engineering Research Council of Canada, 1999). In general, these remain applicable when conducting online research; however an expansion of these concepts is necessary to include human interactions in Internet-mediated environments. Existing ethical guidelines for researchers do not yet address the interplay of research spheres sufficiently. Changes in research methods are accepted and discussed, but the technical underpinnings that influence human and social interactions and create different cultural contexts are ignored.

Hine (2000) points out that "using the Internet meaningfully is about acquiring the cultural competences within which it makes sense" (p. 152). As part of understanding the "natural setting" that Denzin and Lincoln (2000) refer to, it is not only necessary for the researcher to understand the cultural codes within virtual communities but also to be able to cross the boundaries of virtual environments into the technical sphere located in digital onground realities. For ethical research to be conducted online, this would mean considering the effects of the research on participants from their online, onground and technical situatedness. For example, when a study that is conducted primarily in the virtual environment and a member of this community is quoted in the research text—whose identity needs to be protected? The online persona? The onground person? And how much does the researcher need to alter the text quoted in a document for it to become unrecognizable by search engines? The previous practice of quoting a participant's words by using a synonym may not be sufficient anymore, when considering the interplay of online, onground and technical contexts of this research. What are the specific characteristics of the Internet that create different forms of human and social interactions and innovative research spaces and forms?

As one of the author's experience lies within

research conducted primarily through virtual spaces (interviews, survey and ethnographic observations) and researcher-participant interactions, which were conducted primarily online, the following section will highlight the unique characteristics of the Internet that enable different forms of researcher-participant interactions within primarily online research contexts.

INTERNET CHARACTERISTICS AND CHANGES IN HUMAN INTERACTIONS

One of the issues most challenging in writing this chapter was to be conscious of the technical sphere informing human interactions as well as human interactions informing the technical sphere—to demonstrate the dynamic interplay of spheres instead of easily falling into technologically-deterministic language. For the purposes of this section, however, we only focus on what characterizes the virtual space and how this technologically-mediated space enables different forms of human interactions within this space.

De Kerckhove (1997) points out that the three characteristics of the Internet, "connectivity, interactivity and hypertextuality," build the basis for a sense of "webbedness" among users, which is characterized by the "mental linking of people" or the "industries of networks" (p. xxv). Technical features, such as digital data transfer, networked environments and hypertext, enable a sense of connectivity and interactivity among frequent users. These characteristics are crucial for the Internet "... to have multiple spatial and temporal orderings" (Hine, 2000, p. 114), which in turn impact forms of human and social interactions online.

Interactivity and connectivity involve information that is moved in many ways: simultaneously, quickly and in a distributed manner. In networked environments, the pattern of power is described as being less hierarchical than onground and more

distributed than linear. The power does not lie primarily within hierarchical institutions but is distributed among networked dynamic local and global interactions with new emerging organizational structures (Castells, 1996, 1997; Dobell & Neufeld, 1994). Hyperlinks and electronic mail, for example, enable people to link to each other immediately, locally and globally, asynchronously and synchronously. Consequently, time and place shift in relevance: people begin expecting quick answers to e-mail, to reach anybody at anytime and to be able to access online information 24 hours a day. Digital data transfers enable a quicker and more immediate transfer of information than previous forms of mail or fax. In comparison to traditional data storage possibilities, digital data information is easily stored and replicated. Records of all interactions are easily kept and traced. This differs from onground access to information where linearity of communication patterns is common. Convenience, accessibility, speed and interactivity are dynamics of online interactions that are commonly expected by online users (Storey, Philips, Maczewski, & Wang, 2002).

In addition, text-based environments have taken away some cues of physical interactions on which many initial judgments and assumptions are made in onground worlds. Missed physical cues, for example, gender, age and ethnicity, mean that people explore their identities and experience themselves in different ways. A different sense of identity and embodiment is facilitated, which promotes a shifting in power structures among people interacting (e.g., O'Brien, 1999; Turkle, 1995).

These Internet characteristics and resulting changes in human interaction patterns play out in research contexts and have implications for ethical research conduct as well. Important issues, such as access, privacy, informed consent, intellectual property and confidentiality, are discussed by other authors (e.g., Buchanan, 2000; Eysenbach & Till, 2001; Nosek, Banaji & Greenwald, 2002; Sharf, 1999; Suler, 2000). This chapter focuses more specifically on aspects of researcher-participant relationships in online qualitative research: participant recruitment, data collection, voice and trust[3].

IMPLICATIONS FOR RESEARCHER-PARTICIPANT RELATIONSHIPS

In qualitative studies "researchers stress the socially constructed nature of reality, the intimate relationship between the researcher and what is studied, and the situational constraints that shape inquiry. … They seek answers to questions that stress how social experience is created and given meaning" (Denzin & Lincoln, 2000, p. 8). To do so, the researcher-participant relationships are of central importance in qualitative inquiries. As described above, the cultural, Internet-mediated contexts of researcher-participant relationships have expanded and now include issues located in technical and online spheres as well.

Recruitment of Participants

The researcher is initially faced with the task of understanding how participant recruitment is changed within Internet-mediated environments. Using the Internet to recruit participants enables the researcher to use new forms of accessing and recruiting, leading to both successes and frustrations (e.g., Bampton & Cowton, 2002; Holge-Hazelton, 2002).

In Maczewski's (1999) study with young people, the impact of hyperlinks on the recruitment of participants became clear early on and quickly alerted the researcher to the implications of interactivity and connectivity. Maczewski's aim was to recruit frequent Internet users between the ages of 13 and 19 with an active presence on the Web (e.g., youth who have designed a personal website, acted as a chathost, etc.). After having become aware of their online involvement, the question became: How did the researcher interact with them and interest them in becoming participants?

In accordance with de Kerckhove's (1997) three characteristics, Maczewski recognized that the shift from onground to online participant recruitment also meant a shift from linear distribution and control over information to an environment of immediately accessible information sources that enabled potential participants to gain access to information at their time and leisure. She had initially planned to contact participants linearly through engaging in an asynchronous e-mail dialogue (as compared to a person-to-person environment), and revealing information step-by-step depending on the participant and his/her expressed interest. Upon entering the online environment, having information about the research project available to participants 24 hours a day now seemed appropriate. (All relevant information about the research project and researcher was placed on a Web information page as a resource for participants.) This enabled participants, after the researcher's initial contact by e-mail that included the information website's URL, to access the project information 24/7, to follow hyperlinks to more background information on the researcher and research project, depending on their interest, and to gain an understanding of the project without directly engaging with the researcher. Using a website as a primary information source allowed potential participants to respond in their own time, allowing for individual reflection on whether to participate or not, without the added pressure of engaging directly with the researcher. The environment of hypertextuality, interactivity and connectivity had now shifted control over what parts of information to access at what time from the researcher toward the participant.

Even prior to this step, however, the website design became an important factor in the recruitment of participants. Instead of a voice on the phone, the website now provided the first impression of the project and the researcher for the participants. Information design through text and images now conveyed the research project without personal contact and raised questions of inclusion and exclusion. Although information was accessible 24/7, what information and in what form did the researcher choose to present online? For example, if the researcher only chose clip art that represented males, it would be possible that females felt excluded. The website color choices may appeal to specific groups of people. The text style may attract or exclude certain groups of young people. Information design guidelines (Mullet & Sano, 1995) were a powerful tool in not only recruiting participants but also in establishing a respectful relationship with the participant. This was taken into account when considering the websites' design, text and structure and the presentation of information on the Web in appropriate and respectful ways. Technical knowledge of website design, knowledge of website conventions, as well as awareness of onground assumptions and online styles of interaction all played out in this initial research step. Mann and Stewart (2000) point out that the action of researchers and participants referring each other to their respective websites is part of creating a trusting relationship. The website design becomes a "social action which has meaning to them [the designers] and which they consider will have meaning for its recipients" (Hine, 2000, p. 148). As Hine continues:

"... this competence involves the conceptualization of the Web page as a means of communicating with an audience, the ability to read the temporal collage of the Web and to negotiate the space of flows, and the ability to produce appropriate displays of authenticity" (p. 148).

Understanding the Web page as a form of social action is one aspect of demonstrating cultural competence in Internet-mediated relations within the interplay of the technical, online and onground.

Data Collection

Data collection in online qualitative research presents issues for reflection that are located primarily in the technical sphere. A significant issue to be considered by the researcher is the "agency" of the technology used and how this can affect researcher-participant relations. What capabilities does the technology being used have? Although data collection tools are programmed and controlled by researchers and technicians, not all capabilities of the tool may be initially transparent to the users. Moor (2000) suggests that:

"The invisibility factor [of computer technology] presents us with a dilemma. We are happy in one sense that the operations of a computer are invisible. We don't want to inspect every computerized transaction or program every step for ourselves or watch every computer calculation. In terms of efficiency the invisibility factors is a blessing. But it is just this invisibility that makes us vulnerable. We are open to invisible abuse or invisible programming or inappropriate values or invisible miscalculation" (p. 33).

This invisibility of technological features is discussed in Storey, Philips and Maczewski's (2001) study of Web-based learning tools in which students were asked to evaluate the tools by completing three online surveys. In the signed consent form, students agreed to provide information by completing these three surveys. However, during the course of the study they discovered that the tool had also collected information on student's tool use as well as the date and time of use. This information would have been useful in relating the students' opinion of the tool to the amount of time they had spent using the tool. The information was discarded as no consent had been obtained to gather this information. In this case the time to learn all of the technical capabilities of the new tool had been limited and this tool's capability was missed. Theoretically, these kinds of capabilities could also be employed purposefully without knowledge of the participants.

Invisibility also plays a significant role in issues arising from data storage. Traditionally, the human subjects research approval form may only say that data is stored in a "locked filing cabinet." How does this apply to electronic data? Electronic data is stored on at least one computer, a server may automatically conduct backups and e-mails may be read by institutional observers, trying to hinder misuse of their system. As part of ethical research, it would be important to address appropriate ways of designing data collection tools, storing electronic data and monitoring the pathways it takes. This kind of invisibility and its possibilities of collecting data without users' knowledge are very problematic and raise ethical issues. Whose responsibility is it to ensure this doesn't happen? The tool designers or the tool users?

The Association for Computing Machinery (ACM) Code of Ethics and Professional Conduct (1992) presents some guidance for computing professionals, but what can be expected of social scientists and their institutional affiliations in this respect? What institutional policies are being developed to address these issues? What do participants need to know about how electronic data is kept safe and confidential? What is safe and confidential in a digital, networked environment? These issues need to be further discussed and reflected in ethical research guidelines for technologically-mediated research studies.

Data Use and Ownership

Data use and ownership are further important issues to consider. Digitalization of data allows for simple manufacturing and distribution of multiple data copies. For example, when Maczewski (1999) conducted interviews on ICQ[4], she realized that both the researcher and participant could save a copy of the interview transcript. This was an interesting dilemma for the researcher, as the consent form had only specified how the

researcher would use and protect the data. What were the participants' responsibilities in regards to data use? Would the participant consider posting the data on her personal website? Would she post parts of it on a bulletin board? How would this influence the research study? In this case, the researcher negotiated with the participant to not use the data in any form before the completion of the researcher's thesis. This was based on a trusting relationship, not on any consent form signed prior to the research process.

The technical possibilities of easy duplication, the online cultural contexts of interactivity and connectivity enabling many people to access this information once posted as well as researcher's and participants' onground interests needed to be recognized and negotiated within these contexts. Ideally, having recognized the interplay of the three research spheres and their implications for data collection, ownership, use, storage and accessibility would be negotiated prior to the research being conducted. Consent forms need to address the above issues and reflect the technological influences on data collection and storage.

It can be seen how the technology used adds further ethical dimensions into the research process. We consider the researchers' knowledge of tools and further Internet technical capabilities as crucial in conducting ethical research with participants and again an important element in building a trusting relationship with research participants. Many technical features of the Internet and of the tools used may initially be invisible to the researcher and/or the participants but need to be transparent in order for all research members to consent fully to the research process. So far, technologies used in qualitative research, such as tape recorders and video cameras, seem to have been more transparent to the participant and the researcher than computer-mediated technologies. With digital technologies and their "invisibility factor," the handling of technologies used becomes a significant part of the conduct of ethical online qualitative research[5].

Trust and Voice
Trust

As can be seen from the above sections, researcher-participant relations in Internet-mediated environments are altered and influenced by changed parameters of interaction. The interplay of the three research spheres also has implications for the concepts of trust, voice and power within these relations. For example, technological mediation removes the traditionally present physical cues of onground personal identity, such as age, race and gender. Turkle (1995) elaborately describes how virtual spaces allow for the experience of and play with multiple identities. The possibility of multiple identities online introduces new complexities into the building of trusting relationships. As Lincoln (1985) points out:

"The building of trust is a developmental task; trust is not something that suddenly appears after certain matters have been accomplished, but something to be worked on day to day. Moreover, trust is not established once and for all; it is fragile and even trust that has been a long time building can be destroyed overnight in the face of an ill-advised action" (p. 257).

How does this apply within online contexts when multiple identities are in play and physical identity markers are lacking? Several authors describe how trusting relationships are built online, for example, by replacing onground identity markers by relational processes, such as being open about the research project, disclosing information about oneself and using humor and tone of written text to convey personality and empathy (Baym, 2000; Mann & Stewart, 2000; Markham, 1998; Holge-Hazelton, 2002). These processes promote the building of a trusting relationship with participants—but how does the researcher "really" know with which participant identities they are interacting? Is this important and does it matter? For example, when Maczewski (1999) interviewed young people online and felt that a relationship had been built through their continuous interaction, the researcher was sure that in their physical lives they were actually young people. The different cues and dynamics of their conversations that led her to believe that these were young people still remain somewhat unclear to her. It leaves her to wonder whether it would have been possible for a 65 year old to play such a fantastic youth online and whether she could have been convincingly deceived. What implications for their relationship and the research project would this have had, if the participant's portrayed online age was different from their real age?

The concept of trust within online relationships is tightly interwoven among online and onground spheres. Researchers' and participants' identities onground, the focus of the research study (onground youth) and interactions in virtual spaces with chosen online identities made for a complex set of characteristics influencing the relation to each other.

Nosek, Banaji and Greenwald (2002) point out how the researcher's presence may hinder participants from withdrawing from the study. Online the researcher's presence is less immediate and barriers to ending the relationship therefore are perceived as lower. As with participant recruitment, a shift of power from researcher to participant can be seen.

Hine (2000) points out that researchers have to familiarize themselves with the cultural contexts into which they are entering when conducting research online. This local cultural knowledge should be acquired by the researcher to promote the building of trusting and respectful relationships with participants. If this is not done, there are many examples of how participants react negatively if a researcher does not understand the cultural codes of the research environment. For example, virtual community members may feel that their privacy has been invaded, when a researcher has not made her or his presence and intent known (Eysenbach & Till, 2001). Mann and Stewart (2000) describe how netiquette or "standards of politeness and courtesy" (p. 59) appropriate to the specific online environment are expected by users and present a beginning of an ethical framework for conducting online qualitative research.

Voice

Issues of trust are also linked with issues of voice. Within different parameters of building trusting relationships, participants' voices also need to be recognized within these same parameters. Hertz (1997) describes voice as "a struggle to figure out how to present the author's self while simultaneously writing the respondents' accounts and representing their selves" (p. xi). The question arises of which voices are presented when multiple identities are experienced online and onground by both researcher and participants. For example, participants in Maczewski's study expressed that it was easier to voice their opinions online, because they did not have to face the threat of rejection as severely as onground or of people judging them by external appearances alone:

<M> so what is it about online, that makes you be more open?

<Ky> well, it varies from person to person, reasons for opening up...

<Ky> a lot of people are shy IRL, and not having to look someone in the eye
really benefits them, makes them feel more self-assured.

<Ky> with me, it's more of my deep-rooted poetic love... I read into things a l o t more, I like to be able to express myself.

<Ky> Also, it's not that split-second judgment thing... I tend to get a few gawks IRL...hehe

<Ky> whereas online, it's all about the message, and not about the image...
(Maczewski, 1999, p. 143)

In this example, Ky's onground voice is different from her online voice, as she is more open online. This is an example of how respondents' voices are negotiated among researcher, participants and technology within the interplay of all three spheres. Joinson (2002) concurs that sometimes a higher level of self-disclosure is experienced in online than in person-to-person interviews.

Returning to the example of interacting with youth online, if a 65 year old could have a convincing youth voice online and his onground age was discovered later on, which voice would the researcher then have prioritized in this context? The physical reality? The youth voice online? In recognition of multiple voices that people own, would acknowledging the youthful voice of a 65 year old be credible in research contexts researching youth experiences? Who has voice, what is voice and how voice(s) can be represented in technologically-mediated contexts are critical questions that require further research.

Representing multiple voices in linear texts is challenging. Perhaps technologically-mediated environments could offer new opportunities for representing multiple, simultaneous voices. If the research medium allows for direct connectivity and interactivity through hypertexts[6], perhaps it would be possible to more directly include participants in presenting research findings and to illuminate multiple voices more easily than traditionally has been the case. Would it be a future role of the researcher to connect people with each other, if further knowledge would emerge from these connections? For example, with participants' consent, presenting research findings on a Web page with contact links to participants, allowing readers to directly ask further questions of research participants, could be considered. Perhaps more advanced visualization tools will be developed to assist representation of networks of research findings. Whether these changed parameters of interaction in text-based environments will be lost and missed physical cues for interaction reappear with the emergence of newer technologies, such as Voice over Internet Protocol[7], video data or digital pictures, remains to be seen.

Trust, Voice and Confidentiality

Issues of trust and voice online are further intertwined with notions of "confidentiality" and "anonymity," yet the understanding of these notions within the cultural contexts of Internet-mediated research is a complex issue. Some research participants may already have a diary of their personal life online with much of the same information as presented in a research interview. Using a synonym, for example, would not protect a participant from harm, if the reader could search the Web for interview excerpts and easily identify the page. Similar to young people using the Web to express their personal opinions as a means of empowerment and exploration of identities (Chu, 1997; Maczewski, 2002), a sense of power could perhaps be experienced by participants in acknowledging participation in a research setting. This could be achieved, for example, by transcripts being published online on participants' websites, on a common project website or the researchers' website, or by creating links among participants' websites. In networked, technologically mediated environments, there is the potential to build a different form of researcher-participant interactions in which connectivity assists the efforts of the researcher in more immediate collaboration with the participant and through different conceptualizations of confidentiality. A different form of coming to know research findings may emerge by readers exploring linked data, rather than reading text the researcher has composed (Brewer & Maczewski, 2001). How and if this would be appropriate, what form of understanding "confidentiality" and "anonymity" in contexts of interactivity, connectivity and the dynamic interaction of online and onground identities are important ethical issues for further discussion.

DEVELOPING GUIDELINES FOR CONDUCTING ETHICAL ONLINE QUALITATIVE RESEARCH

As has been demonstrated, the ethics of Internet-mediated research are located in the intersection of the online, onground and technical spheres. This intersection is characterized by interactivity, connectivity and hypertextuality and changed researcher-participant relationships. Within this interplay, the researcher is faced with the question of how to ethically conduct research that is congruent within these parameters.

Oberg (2001) suggests that in congruent research, the researcher is connected to the research topic, assessment criteria, methodology choice and epistemological assumptions. According to Oberg, continuous researcher reflexivity and mindfulness are important aspects of enabling researchers' awareness of their own assumptions and facilitating congruent research practices. When conducting Internet-mediated research, we believe these practices of congruent research to be applicable and relevant for enabling ethical research practices. Congruent, ethical online research would not depend on the researcher using onground methods online, but the researcher showing awareness of changes in cultural contexts and the implications for researcher-participant interactions. An entry point for a researcher to conduct qualitative research online would be for him/her to reflect on and answer the following questions about the research study:

1. What are the cultural contexts of the research project?
2. What kinds of technologies are used?
3. How will the interplay of online, onground and technical spheres impact the research project?
4. What are the changes in human and social interactions that occur through the specific technologies used?

5. Are my assumptions about research processes applicable within the technologically mediated research contexts?

6. Do research concepts need to be redefined to fit within new cultural contexts?

7. What changes in ethical implications arise?

These questions aim to make visible the connectedness of the online, onground and virtual research spheres. Congruent research can then be conducted when the researcher understands the complex levels of interplay of the three research spheres and adjusts the research practices used in accordance with the defining characteristics of interactivity, connectivity and hypertextuality.

As general principles for researchers, we would suggest that before conducting Internet-mediated research:

1. The researcher develops and demonstrates awareness of the specific Internet-mediated research contexts—how human and social online interactions are shaped by the medium of the Internet, differ from onground interactions and how this impacts online research processes.

2. The researcher develops and demonstrates awareness of required technological skills for operating hard- and software, including data analysis tools, to adequately conduct the research project.

3. The researcher develops and demonstrates research practices (e.g., building trusting relationships) that are congruent with the medium in which research is conducted.

In addition to the researcher personally reflecting on the above questions and gaining appropriate skills, some ethical guidelines exist that address issues raised. For example, the ACM Code of Ethics and Professional Conduct (1992) is an example of ethical guidelines that take computing technology into account. Boehlefeld (1996) discusses how ACM guidelines can be useful for social science researchers, for example, by considering computer professionals' responsibility to share their understanding of the technology with the public. This may address concerns of privacy and anonymity. For the social sciences ethical guidelines for conducting Internet research are in the process of being discussed and established (e.g., Ess, 2002; Eysenbach & Till, 2001; Jones, 1999a; Mann & Stewart, 2000).

THE FUTURE?

The processes of conducting Internet-mediated research have been discussed within today's contexts of western information societies and recognition of the novelty of Internet research for social scientists. As new technologies are rapidly developing, what different research conceptualizations and methodologies will emerge in the future? New technological media enhance processes as well as render others obsolete (McLuhan & McLuhan, 1988), for example, electronic mail reduces the need for surface mail. This dynamic leaves researchers to ponder not only which new research practices emerge but also which research practices are lost. For example, if ethnographic studies moved to explore the connections of linkages instead of in-depth field research (Wittel, 2000), what insights would be gained or lost? Qualitative research in virtual reality caves will also prove to be fascinating and yet again leave us with further complex ethical issues and show different nuances of researcher-participant relations. For example, if human physical processes, such as excitement, sadness or joy, could be externalized and projected onto screens, what research practices need to be reconceptualized in order to conduct ethical research? To ensure that technologically-mediated qualitative research is conducted in ethical ways, research practices will continually need to be critically evaluated within their unique contexts.

REFERENCES

Association for Computing Machinery (ACM) (1992). *ACM code of ethics and professional conduct.* Retrieved Jan. 27, 2003 from: http://www.acm.org/constitution/code.html.

Bampton, R. & Cowton, C. J. (2002, May). The e-interview. *Forum Qualitative Sozialforschung/Forum:Qualitative Social Research, 3*(2). Retrieved Jan. 27, 2003 from: http://www.qualitative-research.net/fqs/fqs-eng.htm.

Baym, N. (2000). *Tune In, Log On. Soaps, Fandom and Online Community.* Thousand Oaks, CA: Sage.

Boehlefeld, S. P. (1996). Doing the right thing: Ethical cyberspace research. *The Information Society, 12*(2), 119-127.

Brewer, K. & Maczewski, M. (2001, April). *Knowing in Internet-mediated-interactions: What do we know and how do we know it?* Paper presented at the 82nd Annual Meeting of the American Educational Research Association, Seattle, Washington, USA.

Buchanan, E. (2000, Fall). Ethics, qualitative research, and ethnography in virtual space. *Journal of Information Ethics, 9*(2), 82-87.

Buchanan, T. & Smith, J. L. (1999). Using the Internet for psychological research: personality testing on the World Wide Web. *British Journal of Psychology, 90,* 125-144.

Castells, M. (1996). *The Rise of the Network Society.* Cambridge, MA: Blackwell Publishers.

Castells, M. (1997). *The Power of Identity.* Cambridge, MA: Blackwell Publishers.

Chu, J. (1997). Navigating the media environment: How youth claim a place through zines. *Social Justice, 24*(3), 71-84.

De Kerckhove, D. (1997). *Connected Intelligence: The Arrival of the Web Society.* Toronto, Canada: Somerville House Publishing.

Denzin, N. K. & Lincoln, Y. S. (2000). Introduction: The discipline and practice of qualitative research. In N. K. Denzin & Y. S. Lincoln (Eds.), *Handbook of Qualitative Research* (2nd ed.) (pp. 1-17). Thousand Oaks, CA: Sage.

Dobell, R. & Neufeld, M. (1994). *Transborder Citizens. Networks and New Institutions in North America.* Lantzville, Canada: Oolichan Books.

Ess, C. (2002, October 7). Re: Draft SIX, that's it. Message posted to the Association of Internet Researchers Air-l electronic mailing list, archived at: http://www.aoir.org/pipermail/air-l/2002-October/002463.html.

Eysenbach, G. & Till, J. (2001, November). Ethical issues in qualitative research on Internet communities. *British Medical Journal, 323*(7321), 1103-1105. Retrieved Jan. 27, 2003 from: http://bmj.com/cgi/content/full/323/7321/1103.

Gergen, K. (1991). *The Saturated Self. Dilemmas of Identity in Contemporary Life.* New York, NY: Basic Books.

Gibbs, G., Friese, S., & Mangabeira, W. C. (2002, May). The use of new technology in qualitative research. *Forum Qualitative Sozialforschung/Forum:Qualitative Social Research, 3*(2). Retrieved Jan. 27, 2003 from: http://www.qualitative-research.net/fqs/fqs-eng.htm.

Hampton, K. & Wellman, B. (1999, November). Netville on-line and off-line. Observing and surveying a wired suburb. *American Behavioural Scientist, 43*(3), 475-492.

Hertz, R. (1997). *Reflexivity and Voice.* Thousand Oaks, CA: Sage.

Hine, C. (2000). *Virtual Ethnography.* Thousand Oaks, CA: Sage.

Holge-Hazelton, B. (2002, May). The Internet: a new field for qualitative inquiry? *Forum Qualitative Sozialforschung/Forum:Qualitative Social Research, 3*(2). Retrieved Jan. 27, 2003 from: http://www.qualitative-research.net/fqs/fqs-eng.htm.

Joinson, A. (2002, April). *Self-disclosure in online research: Media effects, motivated choices and the design of virtual methodologies.* PowerPoint presentation presented at ESRC Virtual Methods Series conducted at CRICT, Brunel University, Uxbridge, Middlesex, UK. Retrieved Jan. 27, 2003 from: http://www.joinson.com.

Jones, S. (1999a). *Doing Internet Research: Critical Issues and Methods for Examining the Net.* Thousand Oaks, CA: Sage.

Kiesler, S., Kraut, R., Lundmark, V., Patterson, M., Mukopadhyay, T., & Scherlis, W. (1998). A social technology that reduces social involvement and psychological well-being? *American Psychologist, 53*(9), 1017-1031.

Lincoln, Y. (1985). *Naturalistic Inquiry.* Thousand Oaks, CA: Sage.

Maczewski, M. (1999). *Interplay of online and onground realities: Internet research on youth experiences online.* Unpublished master's thesis, University of Victoria, Victoria, British Columbia, Canada.

Maczewski, M. (2002). Exploring identities through the Internet: Youth experiences online. *Child and Youth Care Forum, 31*(2), 111-129.

Mann, C. & Stewart, F. (2000). *Internet Communication and Qualitative Research. A Handbook for Researching Online.* Thousand Oaks, CA: Sage.

Markham, A. (1998). *Life Online: Researching Real Experience in Virtual Space.* London: Altamira Press.

McLuhan, M. (1964). *Understanding Media.* Cambridge, MA: MIT Press.

McLuhan, M. & McLuhan, E. (1988). *Laws of Media: The New Science.* Toronto, Canada: University of Toronto Press.

Moes, J. (2000, January). Von der Text-zur Hypertextanalyse: Konsequenzen fuer die qualitative Sozialforschung. *Forum Qualitative Sozialforschung/Forum:Qualitative Social Research, 1*(1). Retrieved Jan. 27, 2003 from: http://qualitative-research.net/fqws.

Moor, J. (2000). What is computer ethics? In R. M. Baird, R. Ramsower, & S. E. Rosenbaum (Eds.), *Cyberethics: Social and Moral Issues in the Computer Age* (pp. 23-33). Amherst, NY: Prometheus Books.

Mullet, K. & Sano, D. (1995). *Designing Visual Interfaces: Communication Oriented Techniques.* New York, NY: Prentice-Hall.

National Sciences and Engineering Research Council of Canada (1999). *Tri-council policy statement: Ethical conduct for research involving humans.* Retrieved Jan. 27, 2003 from: http://www.nserc.ca/programs/ethics/english/intro03.htm#C.

Nosek, B. A., Banaji, M. R., & Greenwald, A. G. (2002). E-research: Ethics, security, design, and control in psychological research on the Internet. *Journal of Social Issues, 58*(1), 161-176.

Oberg, A. (in press). Paying attention and not knowing. Presented at the Annual Meeting of the American Educational Research Association, Seattle, Washington, USA. In E. Hasebe-Ludt & W. Hurren (Eds.), *Curriculum Intertext.* New York: Peter Lang.

O'Brien, J. (1999). Writing in the body: Gender (re)production in online interaction. In M. Smith & P. Kollock (Eds.), *Communities in Cyberspace* (pp. 76-106). London: Routledge.

Schneider, S. & Larsen, E. (2000, September). *Campaign 2000: What's on congressional candidate Web sites? A preliminary analysis.* Paper presented at Association of Internet Researchers 1st Annual Conference, Lawrence, Kansas, USA.

Sharf, B. F. (1999). Beyond netiquette: The ethics of doing naturalistic discourse research on the Internet. In S. Jones (Ed.), *Doing Internet Research* (pp. 243-256). Thousand Oaks, CA: Sage.

Smith, M. & Kollock, P. (eds.). (1999). *Communities in Cyberspace.* London: Routledge.

Storey, M.-A., Philips, B., & Maczewski, M. (2001). Is it ethical to evaluate Web-based learning tools using students? *Empirical Software Engineering, 6*(4), 343-348.

Storey, M.-A., Philips, B., Maczewski, M., & Wang, M. (2002). Evaluating the usability of Web-based learning tool. *Educational Technology & Society, 5*(3). Retrieved Jan. 27, 2003 from: http://ifets.ieee.org/periodical/vol_3_2002/storey.html.

Suler, J. (2000). *Ethics in cyberspace research.* Retrieved Jan. 27, 2003 from: http://www.rider.edu/users/suler/psycyber/ethics.html.

Surratt, G. C. (2001). *The Internet and Social Change.* Jefferson, NC: McFarland & Company.

Tapscott, D. (1998). *Growing up Digital.* New York, NY: McGraw-Hill.

Turkle, S. (1995). *Life on the Screen.* New York, NY: Touchstone.

Wellman, B., Quan-Haase, A., Witte, J., & Hampton, K. (2001, November). Does the Internet increase, decrease or supplement social capital? Social networks, participation and community commitment. *American Behavioral Scientist, 45*(3), 437-456.

Wittel, A. (2000, January). Ethnography on the move: From field to net to Internet. *Forum Qualitative Sozialforschung/Forum:Qualitative Social Research, 1*(1). Retrieved Jan. 27, 2003 from: http://qualitative-research.net/fqws.

ENDNOTES

[1] The term "onground" is used instead of "in real life" to convey physical, material communities as the authors consider both online and onground events as part of "real life."

[2] Oberg (2001) observed students engaged in qualitative research and found that their research process excelled when "the [research] topic becomes the method through which the topic is pursued." For example, when studying mindfulness, mindfulness became an integral research method for the research process. This occurrence Oberg named "congruence." Similarly, we believe, in online qualitative research, technological capabilities and their interactions become important aspects of research methods and are integral parts of conducting ethical research. Although absolute congruency is not necessary to conduct ethical research, expanding the scope of ethical research practices to reflect characteristics of human interactions within Internet-mediated environments is necessary.

[3] We realize that given the wide range of topics described here, each topic is addressed relatively briefly. More in-depth reflection and analysis of each point raised are important issues for further research.

[4] ICQ is a widely accessible software that enables chats. For more information, see http://www.icq.com.

[5] For further reading on the process of data analysis with computer software, see Gibbs, Friese & Mangabeira (2002) as a starting point.

[6]   For a further discussion on the implications of a shift to hypertext analysis, see Moes (2000).

[7]   VoiP is a means of transmitting voice using the Internet protocol, rather than the telephone network.

This work was previously published in Readings in Virtual Research Ethics: Issues and Controversies, edited by E.A. Buchanan, pp. 62-79, copyright 2004 by Information Science Reference, formerly known as Idea Group Reference (an imprint of IGI Global).

Chapter 5.18
Electronic Banking and Information Assurance Issues:
Survey and Synthesis

Manish Gupta
State University of New York, USA

Raghav Rao
State University of New York, USA

Shambhu Upadhyaya
State University of New York, USA

ABSTRACT

Information assurance is a key component in e-banking services. This article investigates the information assurance issues and tenets of e-banking security that would be needed for design, development and assessment of an adequate electronic security infrastructure. The technology terminology and frameworks presented in the article are with the view to equip the reader with a glimpse of the state-of-art technologies that may help towards learned and better decisions regarding electronic security.

INTRODUCTION

The Internet has emerged as the dominant medium in enabling banking transactions. Adoption of e-banking has witnessed an unprecedented increase over the last few years. Twenty percent of Internet users now access online banking services, a total that will reach 33% by 2006, according to *the Online Banking Report*. By 2010, over 55 million U.S. households will use online banking and e-payments services, which are tipped as "growth areas". The popularity of online banking is projected to grow from 22 million households in 2002 to 34 million in 2005, according to Financial Insite, publisher of the *Online Banking Report*[1] newsletter.

Electronic banking uses computer and electronic technology as a substitute for checks and other paper transactions. E-banking is initiated through devices such as cards or codes to gain access to an account. Many financial institutions use an Automated Teller Machine (ATM) card and a Personal Identification Number (PIN) for this purpose. Others use home banking, which involves installing a thick client on a home PC and using a secure dial-up network to access account information, and still others allow banking via the Internet.

This article will discuss the information assurance issues (Maconachy, Schou & Ragsdale, 2002) that are associated with e-banking infrastructure. We hope that the article will allow Information Technology managers to understand information assurance issues in e-banking in a holistic manner, and help them make recommendations and actions to ensure security of e-banking components.

INTERNET/WEB BANKING

A customer links to the Internet from his or her PC. The Internet connection is made through a public Web server. When the customer brings up the desired bank's Web page, he or she goes through the front-end interface to the bank's Web server, which in turn interfaces with the legacy systems to pull data out for the customer's request. Pulling legacy data is the most difficult part of Web banking. While connection to a Direct Dial Access (DDA) system is fairly straightforward, doing wire transfer transactions or loan applications requires much more sophisticated functionality. A separate e-mail server may be used for customer service requests and other e-mail correspondence. There are also other middleware products that provide security to ensure that the customer's account information is secured, as well as products that convert information into an HTML format. In addition, many of the Internet banking vendors

provide consulting services to assist the banks with Web site design and overall architecture. Some systems store financial information and records on client PCs, but use the Internet connections to transmit information from the bank to the customer's PC. For example, the Internet version of Intuit's *BankNOW* runs offline at the client and connects to the bank via the Internet only to transmit account and transaction information (Walsh, 1999).

In this section, we discuss some of the key nodal points in Internet banking. These points are the foundations and principal aspects of e-banking: Web site and service hosting, possibly through providers; application software that includes middleware; regulations surrounding e-banking and standards that allow different organizations and platforms to communicate over the Internet.

Web Site & Banking Service Hosting

Banks have the option of hosting Web sites in-house or outsourcing to either service bureaus or core processing vendors with expertise in Internet banking. Whether outsourced or packaged, Internet banking architectures generally consist of the following components: Web servers; transaction servers; application servers; data storage and access servers. Vendors such as *Online Resources*[2] offer a package of Web banking services that include the design and hosting of a financial institution's Web site and the implementation of a transactional Web site. Online's connection makes use of the bank's underlying ATM network for transactions and real-time bill payment. In addition, optional modules are generally available for bill payment, bill presentment, brokerage, loan application/approval, small business, and credit cards. The fact that multiple options of Web hosting exist also brings with them issues in security and privacy — a topic that is considered in a later section.

Figure 1. Architectural pieces of Internet banking (Starita, 1999)

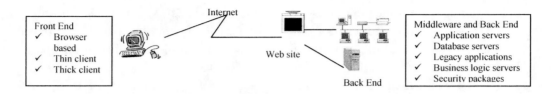

The components that form a typical Internet banking initiative are shown in Figure 1.

- *Internet Banking Front-End:* The front-end is often the client-side browser access to the bank's Web server. Client-side thin-client access to the bank's Web server: This model allows the customer to download a thin-client software product from the bank's Web site and may allow storing financial data locally. Client-side thick-client access to the bank's Web server: This is the model used when supporting personal financial management packages as tools to access account data and execute transactions. It is important to note that these models are not mutually exclusive of each other (Starita, 1999).

- *Internet Banking Transaction Platforms:* The Internet banking transaction platform is the technology component that supports transactional processes and interfaces between the front-end user interface and the back-end core processors for functions like account information retrieval, account update, and so forth. In general, the transactional platform defines two main things: (1) the functional capabilities of the Internet banking offering (e.g., whether it offers bill payment or credit card access) and (2) the method of access or interface between the front-end and back-end legacy processors (Starita, 1999).

Internet Banking Platforms & Applications

Most of the Internet plumbing to present data onto Web interfaces from data sources is of-

fered by Internet banking application software vendors, who link legacy systems to allow access to account data and transaction execution. Most players position themselves as end-to-end solution providers by including a proprietary front-end software product, integration with other front-end software, or Web design services.

Some of the solutions are middleware platforms with plug-in applications to provide bill payment, bill presentment, brokerage, loan, small business, and/or credit card functionality. Most vendors use Open Financial Exchange standard (OFX) to connect to different delivery channels such as Interactive Voice Response (IVRs), Personal Finance Managers (PFMs), and the Internet. Middleware tools are designed to handle Internet-delivered core banking and bill payment transaction (Walsh, 2002). Middleware platforms provide a link between financial institutions' legacy host systems and customers using browser-based HTML interfaces and OFX-enabled personal financial management software (Walsh, 2002).

Middleware is designed for financial institutions that require a platform that translates messages between collections of separate processing systems that house core processing functions. Core processing systems include bill payment, credit card, brokerage, loans and insurance. Electronic bill payment and presentment is widely believed to be the compelling application that brings large volumes of customers to the Internet channel to handle their finances. There are two kinds of Web sites: non-transactional and transactional. The non-transactional sites, commonly known as promotional Web sites, publish content with information about bank products and allow customers to investigate targeted areas such as college loans or retirement planning. These sites give basic information on bank products and do not allow any transactions. Banks can collect information to start to develop customer profiles by recording where a customer visits on the Web site and comparing it with demographic information to develop personalized marketing strategies.

Transactional sites link to back-end processing systems and include basic functionality such as the ability to view recent transactions and account histories, download information into Personal Financial Manager (PFM) software, and transfer funds between existing accounts. As banks become more sophisticated with transactional capabilities, such things as electronic bill payment or moving of funds outside of the bank become possible. Integrating with a third-party processor such as Checkfree or Travelers Express

most often does this. Bill presentment is also part of transactional capability; however, it is being done on a limited basis through a small number of pilots. Some banks allow customers to apply for loans, mortgages, and other products online, although much of the back-end process is still done manually. In transactional Web sites, every page must be dynamically composed and offer continual updates on products and pricing.

Standards Compliance

Standards play a vital role in seamless flow and integration of information across channels and help in reducing risk emanating from diverse platforms and standards. In addition to the challenge of integrating Internet banking products into the bank's own IT environment, many Internet banking functions involve third-party participation. This poses a significant integration question:

Table 1. Standards in e-banking models

Security issues with direct user focus	User-focused mechanisms that are available	User-transparent mechanisms/ technology
Authentication	Passwords, PINs tokens, HSDs, Biometrics	Radius, TACACS, PKI, ISAKMP
Access Control	Roles, User Discretion, Hard-coded systems	
Confidentiality	Training	Encryption
Integrity	Encryption (hashing)	
Malicious Content	Training	Mail/Spam filters, anti-virus
Non-repudiation	Use of PKI, and authentication mechanisms	
Incident Response	Training	
Social Engineering	Training	
Security issues with system-only focus		
Availability	IDSs, Firewall, redundancy, fault-tolerance, application-level security rules	
Security Event, Intrusion Detection	IDSs, probes, firewalls	
Perimeter Defense	Firewalls, IDSs,	
Administration	Depends on the system policies as well as administrators.	

What is the best way to combine separate technology systems with third parties in a cost-effective way to enable each participant to maintain control over its data, and maintain autonomy from other participants? The response from the technology marketplace has been to establish Internet banking standards to define interactions and the transfer of information between multiple parties (Bohle, 2001). The premise of a standard is that everyone would use it in the same consistent fashion; unfortunately, that is not the scenario in the current Internet banking environment. One of the problems for the lackluster performance of e-banking arguably is the industry's failure to attend to the payments infrastructure (Orr, 2002). One initiative that does show promise is by the National Institute of Standards and Technology, that has developed a proposed standard, such as "Security Requirements for Cryptographic Modules," that will require role based authentication and authorization (FIPS, 1992). Some of the standards pervasive in current e-banking models are the ADMS standard, the GOLD standard, and the OFX standard.

INFORMATION ASSURANCE

Web banking sites include financial calculators, e-mail addresses/customer service information, new account applications, transactions such as account balance checks, transfers, and bill payment, bill presentment/payment, cash management, loan applications, small business, credit card, and so forth. The modes by which they can be accessed include online service provider or portal site, direct-dial PC banking program, Internet-bank Web sites, WebTV and personal financial manager. Depending on the functionality of the Web sites, different information assurance requirements are found.

Some examples of exploitation of information assurance issues in the Web-banking arena include:

- Many ATMs of Bank of America were made unavailable in January 2003 by the SQL Slammer worm, which also affected other financial services like Washington Mutual[3,4].
- Barclays suffered an embarrassing incident when it was discovered that after logging out of its online service, an account could be immediately re-accessed using the "back" button on a Web browser. If a customer accessed their Barclays account on a public terminal, the next user could thereby view banking details of the previous customer. According to the bank, when customers join the online banking service they are given a booklet that tells them to clear the cache to prevent this from happening. However, this procedure shifts the responsibility for security to the end user[5].

Security and Privacy Issues

In their annual joint study in April 2002, the FBI and the Computer Security Institute noted that the combined financial losses for 223 of 503 companies that responded to their survey (*Computer Crime and Security Survey*) was $455 million for year 2002 (Junnarkar, 2002). Security and integrity of online transactions are the most important technical issues that a bank offering Web services will need to tackle. The Internet bank Web sites handle security in different ways. They can choose either public or private networks. The Integrion consortium, for example, uses the private IBM/AT&T Global Network for all Internet network traffic (Walsh, 1999). Server security is another important issue, usually accomplished by server certificates and SSL authentication. Banks must look at three kinds of security (Walsh, 1999): communications security; systems security — from the applications/authorization server; information security.

From a user's perspective, security must accomplish privacy, integrity authentication, access control, and non-repudiation. Security becomes an even more important issue when dealing with international banks, since only up to 128K encryption is licensed for export. Currently, most Internet bank Web sites use a combination of encryption, firewalls, and communications lines to ensure security. The basic level of security starts with an SSL-compliant browser. The SSL protocol provides data security between a Web browser and the Web server, and is based on public key cryptography licensed from security systems. Security has been one of the biggest roadblocks that have kept consumers from fully embracing Internet banking. Even after the advent of highly secure sites with the aid of 128K encryption, a virtually invulnerable encryption technology, the perception among some consumers is that Internet banking is unsafe. They apprehend privacy violations, as the bank keeps track of all transactions, and they are unsure of who has access to privileged data about their personal net worth. The basic security concerns that face financial institutions offering banking services and products through

the Internet are summarized in Figure 2 and are discussed next.

Authentication

Authentication relates to assurance of identity of person or originator of data. Reliable customer authentication is imperative for financial institutions engaging in any form of electronic banking or commerce. Strong customer authentication practices are necessary to enforce "anti-money" laundering measures and help financial institutions detect and reduce identity theft. Customer interaction with financial institutions is migrating from physical recognition and paper-based documentation to remote electronic access and transaction initiation. The risks of doing business with unauthorized or masquerading individuals in an electronic banking environment could be devastating, which can result in financial loss and intangible losses like reputation damage,

Figure 2. E-banking security infrastructure

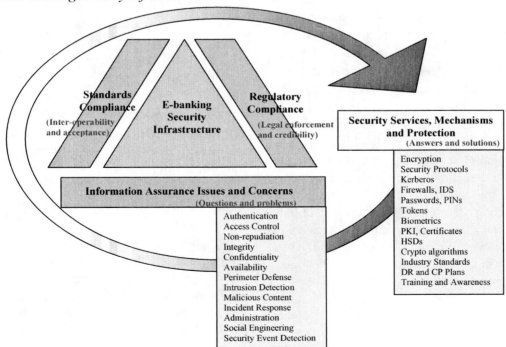

2671

disclosure of confidential information, corruption of data or unenforceable agreements.

There is a gamut of authentication tools and methodologies that financial institutions use to authenticate customers. These include the use of passwords and Personal Identification Numbers (PINs), digital certificates using a Public Key Infrastructure (PKI), physical devices such as smart cards or other types of "tokens," database comparisons, and bio-metric identifiers. The level of risk protection afforded by each of these tools varies and is evolving as technology changes. Multi-factor authentication methods are more difficult to compromise than single factor systems. Properly designed and implemented multi-factor authentication methods are more reliable indicators of authentication and stronger fraud deterrents. Broadly, the authentication methodologies can be classified based on: what a user knows (password, PINs); what a user has (smart card, magnetic card); and what a user is (fingerprint, retina, voiceprint, signature).

The issues that face banks using the Internet as a channel are the risks and risk management controls of a number of existing and emerging authentication tools necessary to initially *verify* the identity of new customers and *authenticate* existing customers that access electronic banking services. Besides, effective authentication framework and implementation provides banks with a foundation to enforce electronic transactions and agreements.

- *Account Origination and Customer Verification:* With the growth in electronic banking and commerce, financial institutions need to deploy reliable methods of originating new customer accounts online. Customer identity verification during account origination is important in reducing the risk of identity theft, fraudulent account applications, and unenforceable account agreements or transactions. There are significant risks when financial institution accepts new customers through the Internet or other electronic channels because of the absence of the

tangible cues that banks traditionally use to identify individuals (FDIC, 2001).

- *Monitoring and Reporting:* Monitoring systems play a vital role in detecting unauthorized access to computer systems and customer accounts. A sound authentication system should include audit features that can assist in the detection of fraud, unusual activities (e.g., money laundering), compromised passwords or other unauthorized activities (FDIC, 2001). In addition, financial institutions are required to report suspicious activities to appropriate regulatory and law enforcement agencies as required by 31 CFR 103.18.

Access Control

Access control refers to the regulating of access to critical business assets. Access control provides a policy-based control of who can access specific systems, what they can do within them, and when and from where they are allowed access. One of the primary modes of access control is based on roles. A role can be thought of as a set of transactions that a user or set of users can perform within the context of an organization. For example, the roles in a bank include teller, loan officer, and accountant, each of whom can perform different functions. Role based access control (RBAC) policy bases access control decisions on the functions that a user is allowed to perform within an organization. In many applications, RBAC is concerned more with access to functions and information than strictly with access to information.

The applicability of RBAC to commercial systems is apparent from its widespread use. Nash and Poland (Poland & Nash, 1990) discuss the application of role based access control to cryptographic authentication devices commonly used in the banking industry. Even the Federal Information Processing Standard (FIPS) has provisions for support for role based access and administration.

Non-Repudiation

Non-repudiation refers to the need for each party involved in a transaction to not go back on their word, that is, break the electronic contract (Pfleeger, 1997). Authentication forms the basis for non-repudiation. It requires strong and substantial evidence of the identity of the signer of a message and of message integrity, sufficient to prevent a party from successfully denying the origin, submission or delivery of the message and the integrity of its contents. This is important for an e-banking environment where, in all electronic transactions, including ATMs (cash machines), all parties to a transaction must be confident that the transaction is secure; that the parties are who they say they are (authentication), and that the transaction is verified as final. Essentially banks must have mechanisms that must ensure that a party cannot subsequently repudiate (reject) a transaction. There are several ways to ensure non-repudiation, which include digital signatures, which not only validates the sender, but also "time stamps" the transaction, so it cannot be claimed subsequently that the transaction was not authorized or not valid.

Integrity

Ensuring integrity means maintaining data consistency and protecting from unauthorized data alteration (Pfleeger, 1997). Integrity is very critical for Internet banking applications, as transactions have information that is consumer and business sensitive. To achieve integrity, data integrity mechanisms can be used. These typically involve the use of secret-key or public-key based algorithms that allow the recipient of a piece of protected data to verify that the data have not been modified in transit. The mechanisms are further presented in a later section.

Confidentiality and Privacy

Privacy and security concerns are not unique to banking systems. Privacy and confidentiality are related but are distinct concepts. Protection of personally identifiable information like banking records must be ensured before consumers. Information Privacy (NIIAC, 1995) is the ability of an individual to control the use and dissemination of information that relates to him or her. Confidentiality (NIIAC, 1995) is a tool for protecting privacy. Sensitive information is accorded a confidential status that mandates specific controls, including strict limitations on access and disclosure. Those handling the information must adhere to these controls. Information confidentiality refers to ensuring that customer information is secured and hidden as it is transported through the Internet environment. Information must not only be protected wherever it is stored (e.g., on computer disks, backup tape and printed form), but also in transit through the Internet.

Availability

Availability in our context means that legitimate users have access when they need it. With Internet banking, one of the strongest selling propositions is 24x7 availability; therefore it becomes even more critical for e-banks. Availability applies to both data and to services. Expectations of availability include presence of a service in usable form, capacity to meet service needs, timeliness of service, fair allocation, fault tolerance, controlled concurrency and deadlock management. One example where availability is compromised is the denial of service attack. On the Internet, a denial of service (DoS) attack is an incident in which a user or organization is deprived of the services of a resource they would normally expect to have. When there are enormous transactions on the Internet bank's Web site, the losses that may arise owing to unavailability are severe, in terms of financial losses and reputation losses.

Typically, the loss of service is the inability of a particular network service, such as e-mail, to be available or the temporary loss of all network connectivity and services. It becomes imperative and crucial for IT managers in the Internet banking world to better understand the kind of denial of attacks possible. Some of the common and well-known types of denial of service attacks (IESAC, 2003) are:

- *SYN Attack:* It floods the server with open SYN connections, without completing the TCP handshake. TCP handshake is a three-step process to negotiate connection between two computers. The first step is for initiating computer to send "SYN" (for "*synchronize*") packet.
- *Teardrop Attack:* It exploits the way that the Internet Protocol (IP) requires a packet that is too large for the next router to handle be divided into fragments. Here, the attacker's IP puts a confusing offset value in the second or later fragment of the packet. It can cause the system to crash.
- *Smurf Attack:* In this attack, the perpetrator spoofs the source IP address and broadcasts ping requests to multitude of machines to overwhelm the victim.

Perimeter Defense

Perimeter defense refers to the separation of an organization's computer systems from the outside world (IETF, 2000). This must allow free sharing of certain information with clients, partners, suppliers and so on, while also protecting critical data from them. A security bulwark around network and information assets of any bank can be achieved, to a certain extent, by implementing firewalls and correctly performing tuning and configuration of firewalls.

Today, with the kind of traffic generated towards Web-banking sites for all kinds of purposes, from balance enquiries to Inter-bank fund transfers, implementation of screening routers to ensure incoming and outgoing traffic would add another layer of security. In this age of systems being hijacked for cyber-attacks, it is also important that screen routers detect and prevent outgoing traffic that attempts to gain entry to systems like spoofing IP addresses. Further, the periphery of the corporate computer infrastructure can be bolstered by implementing VPN solutions to ensure privacy of data flowing through the firewall into the public domain.

Probes and scans are often used techniques that are exploited to learn about exposures and vulnerabilities on the network systems. A probe is characterized by unusual attempts to gain access to a system or to discover information about the system. Probes are sometimes followed by a more serious security event, but they are often the result of curiosity or confusion. A scan is simply a large number of probes done using an automated tool. Scans can sometimes be the result of a misconfiguration or other error, but they are often a prelude to a more directed attack on systems that the intruder has found to be vulnerable.

Intrusion Detection

Intrusion detection refers to the ability to identify an attempt to access systems and networks in a fashion that breaches security policies. The Internet banking scenario, where most of business these days is carried out over public domain Internet and where a banking Web site becomes a single point interface for information as well as transactions, gives hackers enough motivation to intrude into Internet banks' systems. To safeguard from such unwanted activities, organizations need to be able to recognize and distinguish, at a *minimum,* the following (Gartner, 1999): internal & external intrusion attempts; human versus automated attacks; unauthorized hosts connecting to the network from inside and outside the perimeter; unauthorized software being loaded on systems; and all access points into the corporate network.

Intrusion detection systems (IDS) allow organizations to protect their systems from the threats that come with increasing network connectivity and reliance on information systems. Given the level and nature of modern network security threats, the question for security professionals should not be whether to use intrusion detection, but which intrusion detection features and capabilities to use. IDSs have gained acceptance as a necessary addition to every organization's security infrastructure. IDS products can provide worthwhile indications of malicious activity and spotlight security vulnerabilities, thus providing an additional layer of protection. Without them, network administrators have little chance of knowing about, much less assessing and responding to, malicious and invalid activity. Properly configured, IDSs are especially useful for monitoring the network perimeter for attacks originating from outside and for monitoring host systems for unacceptable insider activity.

Security Event Detection

Security event detection refers to the use of logs and other audit mechanisms to capture information about system and application access, types of access, network events, intrusion attempts, viruses, and so forth.

Logging is an important link in analysis of attack and real-time alerts of any kind of suspicious activity on the Internet bank Web site. For proper tracking of unusual events and attempts of intrusion, the following logs should be collected: basic security logs, network event logging, log authentication failures, log access violations, log attempts to implant viruses and other malicious code, and log "abnormal" activity. This strongly implies that the technical department that is analyzing logs to identify "unusual behavior" must be aware of business initiatives. Besides, it has to be ensured that audit logs are retained long enough to satisfy legal requirements. Also, at a minimum, investigation of security breaches should be al-

lowed for up to 14 days after any given attack (IETF, 2000). Today, data mining techniques can interpret millions of items of log data and reveal any unobserved attempts to breach an e-bank's Web site. For this it has to be ensured that logs do not overwrite themselves causing loss of data. For analysis of events at a site, documentation of automated systems that identify what the logs mean should be maintained. Understanding the nature of attempts such as whether an attack was from within the organization or from outside or whether it was just a false alarm is critical to security.

Malicious Content

Malicious content refers to programs of any type that are introduced into a system to cause damage or steal information. Malicious content includes viruses, Trojans, hacker tools, and network sniffers. While common in multiple domains, this is as important in the e-banking world as well. Malicious code brings with it the potential to create serious technical and economic impact by crashing e-mail servers and networks, causing millions of dollars of damage in lost productivity.

Some of the common forms of malicious contents are:

- *Virus:* A *virus* is a computer program that runs on a system without being asked to do so, created to "infect" other computer programs with copies of itself. Pioneer virus researcher Fred Cohen has defined a *virus* as "a program that can 'infect' other programs by modifying them to include a, possibly evolved, copy of it".
- *Worm:* A *worm* has the ability to spread over a network and, thus, can take advantage of the Internet to do its work. Worms reside in memory and duplicate themselves throughout the network without user intervention.
- *Trojan Horse: Trojan horse* is the name applied to malicious computer program disguised as a seemingly innocent activity

such as initiating a screen saver, accessing an e-mail attachment, or downloading executable files from an un-trusted Web site. Some of the widely manifested malicious codes are Stoned, Yankee, Michelangelo, Joshi, Lehigh, Jerusalem, MBDF (for Macintosh), Melissa, Concept, LoveBug (ILOVEYOU), ShapeShift, Fusion, Accessiv, Emporer, Sircam, Nimda, Badtrans.

Protection against malicious codes like viruses, worms, Trojan horses, and so forth could be effectively dealt with by installing security protection software that thwarts and mitigates the effects of codes.

However, such software provides only a level of defense and is not by itself sufficient. Recommendations for e-banking IT infrastructure include (Noakes, 2001):

- Install detection and protection solutions for all forms of malicious code, not just an antivirus solution.
- Ensure that all users are aware of and follow safe behavior practices — do not open attachments that have not been scanned, do not visit un-trusted Web sites, and so forth.
- Ensure that users are aware of how easy data may be stolen automatically just by visiting a Web site. Install an effective solution. Keep it current with the latest signatures as new forms of malicious code are identified.
- Use anti-spammers, harden operating systems, configure stricter firewall rules, and so forth.

Security Services, Mechanisms & Security Protection

Security risks are unlike privacy risks; they originate outside the Financial Service Provider (FSP) and change rapidly with advances in technology (DeLotto, 1999). In December 2000, IATF released guidelines that require all covered institutions to secure their clients' personal information against any "reasonably foreseeable" internal or external threats to their security, confidentiality and in-

tegrity. By July 1, 2001, FSPs were expected to develop customer information security programs that: ensured the security and confidentiality of customer information, protected against any anticipated threats or hazards to the security or integrity of customer information, and protected against unauthorized access to or use of customer information that could result in substantial harm or inconvenience to customers.

The services and mechanisms that are prevalent in an e-banking environment are presented below in order to provide an understanding of key issues and terms involved.

Encryption

Encryption is the process of using a key to scramble readable text into unreadable cyphertext. Encryption on the Internet in general, and e-banking, in particular, has many uses, from the secure transmission of credit card numbers via the Web to protecting the privacy of personal e-mail messages. Authentication also uses encryption, by using a key or key pair to verify the integrity of a document and its origin. The Data Encryption Standard (DES) has been endorsed by the National Institute of Standards and Technology (NIST) since 1975 and is the most readily available encryption standard. Rivest, Shamir and Adleman (RSA) encryption is a public-key encryption system, is patented technology in the United States, and thus is not available without a license. RSA encryption is growing in popularity and is considered quite secure from brute force attacks. Another encryption mechanism is Pretty Good Privacy (PGP), which allows users to encrypt information stored on their system as well as to send and receive encrypted e-mail. Encryption mechanisms rely on keys or passwords. The longer the password, the more difficult the encryption is to break. VPNs employ encryption to provide secure transmissions over public networks such as the Internet.

Security Protocol Services

The Internet is viewed as an insecure place. Many of the protocols used in the Internet do not provide any security. Today's businesses, particularly the banking sector, must integrate security protocols into their e-commerce infrastructure to protect customer information and privacy. Some of the most common protocols are briefly discussed in Appendix A.

Firewalls & Intrusion Detection Systems

A firewall is a collection of hardware and software designed to examine a stream of network traffic and service requests. Its purpose is to eliminate from the stream those packets or requests that fail to meet the security criteria established by the organization. A simple firewall may consist of a filtering router, configured to discard packets that arrive from unauthorized addresses or that represent attempts to connect to unauthorized service ports. Firewalls can filter packets based on their source and destination addresses and port numbers. This is known as address filtering. Firewalls can also filter specific types of network traffic. This is also known as protocol filtering because the decision to forward or reject traffic is dependant upon the protocol used, for example HTTP, ftp or telnet. Firewalls can also filter traffic by packet attribute or state. But a firewall cannot prevent individual users with modems from dialing into or out of the network, bypassing the firewall altogether (Odyssey, 2001). In this age of systems being hijacked, it is also important that firewalls and screen routers detect and prevent outgoing traffic that attempts to compromise the integrity of the systems.

A Network Intrusion Detection System (NIDS) analyzes network traffic for attacks. It examines individual packets within the data stream to identify threats from authorized users, backdoor attacks and hackers who have thwarted the control systems to exploit network connections and access valuable data. NIDS add a new level of visibility into the nature and characteristics of the network. They provide information about the use and usage of the network. Host Based IDS/Event Log Viewers are a kind of IDS that monitors event logs from multiple sources for suspicious activity. Host IDS are best placed to detect computer misuse from trusted insiders and those who have infiltrated the network.

The technology and logical schemes used by these systems are often based on *knowledge-based misuse detection* (Allan, 2002). Knowledge-based detection methods use information about known security policy, known vulnerabilities, and known attacks on the systems they monitor. This approach compares network activity or system audit data to a database of known *attack signatures* or other misuse indicators, and pattern matches produce alarms of various sorts. Behavior-based detection (Allan, 2002) methods use information about repetitive and usual behavior on the systems they monitor. Also called *anomaly detection,* this approach notes events that diverge from expected (based on repetitive and usual) usage patterns. One technique is *threshold detection* (Allan, 2002), in which certain attributes of user and system behavior are expressed in terms of counts, with some level established as permissible. Another technique is to perform *statistical analysis* (Allan, 2002) on the information, build statistical models of the environment, and look for patterns of anomalous activity.

Passwords & Personal Identification Numbers (PINs)

The most common authentication method for existing customers requesting access to electronic banking systems is the entry of a user name and a secret string of characters such as a password or PIN. User IDs combined with passwords or PINs are considered a single-factor authentication technique. There are three aspects of passwords that contribute to the security they provide: secrecy, length and composition, and system controls. In the present Internet banking scenario, there are policies, for both customers as well as employees, set by banks for passwords to ensure effective authentication, like prohibiting using public e-mail IDs as user IDs, ensure that there are no user IDs with no password, ensure that policies exist and can be automatically enforced concerning minimum password length, password format (which characters make up a valid password), expiration and renewal of passwords, uniqueness of passwords, not allowing the use of "real" words for passwords, and so forth.

Tokens

The use of a token represents authentication using "something the customer possesses". Typically, a token is part of a two-factor authentication process, complemented by a password as the other factor. There are many benefits to the use of tokens. The authentication process cannot be completed unless the device is present. Static passwords or biometric identifiers used to activate the token may be authenticated locally by the device itself. This process avoids the transmission of shared secrets over an open network such as the Internet.

Digital Certificates & Public Key Infrastructure (PKI)

A financial institution may use a PKI system to authenticate customers to its own electronic banking product. Institutions may also use the infrastructure to provide authentication services to customers who wish to transact business over the Internet with other entities or to identify employees and commercial partners seeking access to the business's internal systems. A properly implemented and maintained PKI may provide a strong means of customer identification over open networks such as the Internet. By combining a variety of hardware components, system software, policies, practices, and standards, PKI can provide

for authentication, data integrity, and defenses against customer repudiation, and confidentiality (Odyssey, 2001). The *certificate authority* (CA), which may be the financial institution or its service provider, plays a key role by attesting with a *digital certificate* that a particular public key and the corresponding private key belong to a specific individual or system. It is important when issuing a digital certificate that the registration process for initially verifying the identity of customers is adequately controlled. The CA attests to the individual's identity by signing the digital certificate with its own private key, known as the *root key*. Each time the customer establishes a communication link with the financial institution, a digital signature is transmitted with a digital certificate. These electronic credentials enable the institution to determine that the digital certificate is valid, identify the individual as a customer, and confirm that transactions entered into the institution's computer system were performed by that customer. PKI, as the most reliable model for security and trust on the Internet, offers a comprehensive e-security solution for Internet banking. Unlike the other security models, PKI is a standards compliant, most credible trust framework, highly scalable and modular. PKI comprehensively satisfies the security requirements of e-banking (Odyssey, 2001).

A brief discussion on the processes and mechanisms used in PKI to address common security concerns follows:

- *Authentication:* The customer requests the Registration Authority (RA) for a certificate. The Registration Authority validates the customer's credentials. After valid credentials are ensured, the RA passes the certificate request to the Certification Authority (CA). CA then issues the certificates. A digital certificate can be stored on the browser on the user's computer, on a floppy disk, on a smart card or on other hardware tokens.
- *Confidentiality:* The customer generates a random session key at his or her end. The

session key is sent to the bank, encrypting it with the bank's public key. The bank decrypts the encrypted session key with its private key. The session key is employed for further transactions.

- *Integrity:* The message is passed through a suitable hashing algorithm to obtain a message digest or hash. The hash, encrypted with the sender's private key, is appended to the message. The receiver, on receiving the message, passes it through the same hashing algorithm. The digest he or she obtains is compared with the received and decrypted digest. If the digests are same, it implies that the data have not been tampered with in transit.

- *Non-Repudiation:* The hash is encrypted with the sender's private key to yield the sender's digital signature. Since the hash is encrypted with the sender's private key (which is accessible only to him or her), it provides an indisputable means of non-repudiation.

- The use of digital signatures and certificates in Internet banking has provided the trust and security needed to carry out banking transactions across open networks like the Internet. PKI, being a universally accepted standards compliant security model, provides for the establishment of a global trust chain (Odyssey, 2001).

Biometrics

A biometric identifier measures an individual's unique physical characteristic or behavior and compares it to a stored digital template to authenticate that individual. A biometric identifier representing "something the user is" can be created from sources such as a customer's voice, fingerprints, hand or face geometry, the iris or retina in an eye, or the way a customer signs a document or enters keyboard strokes (FDIC, 2001). The success of a biometric identifier rests on the ability of the digitally stored characteristic to relate typically to only one individual in a defined population.

Although not yet in widespread use by financial institutions for authenticating existing customers, biometric identifiers are being used in some cases for physical access control.

Banks could use a biometric identifier for a single or multi-factor authentication process. ATMs that implement biometrics like iris-scan technologies are examples of the use of a biometric identifier to authenticate users. The biometric identifier may be used for authentication, instead of the PIN. A customer can use a PIN or password to supplement the biometric identifier, making it part of a more secure two-factor authentication process. Financial institutions may also use biometric identifiers for automating existing processes. Another application would be a financial institution that allows customer to reset a password over the telephone with voice-recognition software that authenticates the customer. An authentication process that relies on a single biometric identifier may not work for everyone in a financial institution's customer base. Introducing a biometric method of authentication requires physical contact with each customer to initially capture the physical identifier, which further buttresses the initial customer verification process. But this process may increase the deployment costs.

Hardware Security Devices (HSDs)

This mechanism is an extension to usage of tokens for authentication. Using hardware devices for authentication provide "hacker-resistant" and "snooping-proof" two-factor authentication, resulting in easy-to-use and effective user identification (Grand, 2001). To access protected resources, the user simply combines his or her secret PIN (something he or she knows) with the code generated by his or her token (something he or she has). The result is a unique, one-time-use code that is used to positively identify, or authenticate the user (Grand, 2001). Some central server validates the code. Goal: provide acceleration, secure key management. A hardware security module is a hardware-based security device that generates stores and protects cryptographic keys.

There are universal criteria for rating these devices. The criteria are documented in a Federal Information Processing Standard (FIPS) called FIPS 140-1 to 140-4 — Security for Cryptographic Modules. Such hardware devices generate tokens that are dynamic one-time passwords, through the use of a mathematical function. Passwords generated by tokens are different each time the user requests one, so an intercepted password is useless as it will never be used again. Acceptance and credibility of the devices is reflected in the increasing number of devices in use.

Industry Standards & Frameworks

Industry standards for financial transactions over the Internet are an absolute necessity for ensuring various security aspects of business as well as consumer confidence. There has been a constant search and development of standards for e-banking infrastructural tenets like authentication, access control, non-repudiation, and so forth. Some of the standards developed and advocated by different industry players and their proponents are briefly discussed in Appendix B for overall understanding of the evolution and prevalence of some of the standards.

To summarize, Table 2 presents issues that user has direct control on or involvement with and issues that are commonly left for the systems to handle.

CONCLUSIONS

It should be noted that the discussion of e-banking information assurance (IA) issues has also included several generic IA issues. To illustrate this, Table 3 briefly categorizes e-banking specific information assurance issues and generic issues separately. Some issues may be more significant than in other areas. We have made an attempt to comprehensively discuss all the areas in the article.

Security for financial transactions is of vital importance to financial institutions providing or planning to provide service delivery to customers over the public Internet, as well as to suppliers of products, services, and solutions for Internet-based e-commerce. The actual and perceived threats to Internet-based banking define the need for a set of interrelated security services to provide protection to all parties that can benefit from Web banking in a secure environment. Such services may be specific to counter particular threats or may be pervasive throughout an Internet based environment to provide the levels of protection needed.

There are also requirements that the entire e-commerce environment be constructed from components that recognize the need for security services and provide means for overall security integration, administration, and management. These services that offer the security from an infrastructure standpoint are found throughout the e-commerce network and computing infrastructure. Financial institutions should carry out, as a

Table 2. End-user involvement with the security issues

E-banking Specific Issues	Generic Issues (in E-banking)
E-banking related regulations, Banking and E-banking standards and frameworks, banking-specific protocol services.	Authentication, Access Control, Integrity, Availability, Perimeter Defense, Security Event Detection, Malicious Content, Incident Response, Social Engineering, Administration.

matter of corporate security policy, identification of likely targets, which should include all systems that are open to the public network, such as routers, firewalls, and Web servers, modem banks' Web sites, and internal unsecured systems such as desktops. They should regularly revise and update their policies on auditing, risk assessment, standards, and key management. Vulnerability assessment and identification of likely targets and the recognition of systems most vulnerable to attack are critical in the e-banking arena. Accurate identification of vulnerable and attractive systems will contribute to prioritization when addressing problem areas.

ACKNOWLEDGMENTS

The authors would like to thank John Walp and Shamik Banerjee for their contributions and help with the paper, and the anonymous referees for their comments that have improved the paper. We would also like to thank the NSA for the Center for Information Assurance recognition and Department of Defense for two student fellowships. The research of the second author was supported in part by National Science Foundation (NSF) under grant 990735 and the research of the third author was supported in part by U.S. Air Force Research Lab, Rome, New York under Contract F30602-00-10505.

REFERENCES

Allan, A. (2002). *Technology Overview. Intrusion Detection Systems (IDSs): Perspective.* Gartner Research Report (DPRO-95367).

Basel Committee. (2001). *Risk management principles for electronic banking.* Basel Committee publications No. 82.

Bohle, K. (2001). Integration of Internet payment systems – What's the problem? *ePSO (E-payments systems Observatory) –Newsletter.* Retrieved on 1-Mar-2003 from http://epso.jrc.es/newsletter/vol11/ 5.html

Burt, S. (2002). Online banking: Striving for compliance in cyberspace. *Bankers Systems Inc.* Retrieved on 5-Sep-2002 from http://www.bankerssystems.com/compliance/article13.html

DeLotto, R. (1999). *Competitive intelligence for the e-financial service provider.* Gartner Group Research Report.

Dittrich, D. (1999). *Incident response steps.* Lecture series at University of Washington.

FDIC (Federal Deposit Insurance Corporation). (2001). Authentication in electronic banking. *Financial Institution Letters.*

FIPS (Federal Information Processing Standard). (1992). *Security requirements for cryptographic modules.* Federal Information Processing Standard 140-1. National Institute of Standards and Technology.

GartnerGroup RAS Services. (1999). *Intrusion detection systems.* R-08-7031.

Glaessner, T., Kellermann, T., & McNevin, V. (2002). *Electronic security: Risk mitigation in financial transactions. Public policy issues.* The World Bank.

Grand, J. (2001). *Authentication tokens: Balancing the security risks with business requirements.* Cambridge, MA: @Stake, Inc.

IESAC. (2003). *Transactional security.* Institution of Engineers, Saudi Arabian Center. Retrieved on 12-Jan-2003 from http://www.iepsac.org/papers/p04c04a.htm

Internet Security Task Force. (2000). Initial recommendations for conducting secure ebusiness. Retrieved on 12-Jan-2003 from http://www.ca.com/ISTF/recomme ndations.htm

Junnarkar, S. (2002). Online banks: Prime targets for attacks. *e-Business ZDTech News Update.*

Maconachy, W.V., Schou, C.D., Ragsdale, D., & Welch, D. (2001, June 5-6). A model for information assurance: An integrated approach. *Proceedings of the 2001 IEEE Workshop on Information Assurance and Security,* United States Military Academy, West Point, NY.

Marchany, R. (1998). *Internet security & incident response: Scenarios & tactics.* Retrieved on 2-Feb-2003 from *https://courseware.vt.edu/ marchany/InternetSecurity/Class.*

NIIAC. (The National Information Infrastructure Advisory Council). (1995). *Common ground: Fundamental principles for the national information infrastructure.*

Noakes, K. (2001). *Virus and malicious code protection products: Perspective.* Fry Technology Overview, Gartner Research Group, DPRO-90840.

OCC (Office of the Comptroller of the Currency). (1998). *OCC Bulletin 98-3 - Technology Risk Management.* PC Banking.

OCC (Office of the Comptroller of the Currency). (2001). *AL 2001-4 - OCC ADVISORY LETTER.*

Odyssey Technologies. (2001). *PKI for Internet banking.* Retrieved on 23-Aug-2002 from http:// www.odyssey tec.com

Orr, B. (2002). Infrastructure, not innovation. ABA Banking Online Journal. Retrieved on 8-Aug-2002 from http://www.banking.com/aba/ infrastructure.asp

Pfleeger, C.P. (1997). *Security in computing* (2nd ed.). Upper Saddle River, NJ: Prentice Hall.

Poland, K.R., & Nash, M.J. (1990). Some conundrums concerning separation of duty. IEEE Symposium on Computer Security and Privacy.

Starita, L. (1999). *Online banking: A strategic perspective.* Context Overview Report (R-08-7031-Gartner).

The United States Senate. (2002). *Financial Services Modernization Act: Provisions of GLB Act.* The United States Senate publication. Retrieved on 8-Aug-2002 from http://www.senate. gov/~banking/conf /grmleach.htm

Walsh, E. (1999). *Technology overview: Internet banking: Perspective.* DPRO-90293, Gartner.

Walsh, E. (2002). *Product report: S1 Corporate Suite e-Banking Software.* DPRO-95913 (Gartner Research Group.

ENDNOTES

[1] http://www.*epaynews.com/statistics/bank-stats.html*

[2] *http://www.orcc.com*

[3] Robert Lemos, Satff Writer, CNET news. com, *"Counting the cost of Slammer",* Retrieved on *March 31, 2003 from http://*news. com.com/2100-1001-982955.html

[4] Reuters, Seattle(Washington),*CNN.com, Technology news, Feb 5, 2003. Retrieved on 8-Mar-2003 from* http://www.cnn. com/2003/TECH/internet/02/05/virus. spread.reut/

[5] Atomic Tangarine Inc, *NPV: Information Security",Retrieved on 21-Mar-2003 from* www.ttivanguard.com/risk/netpresent-value.pdf

[6] The latest version of the specifications, EMV 2000 version 4.0, was published in December 2000 (*http://www. emvco.com/*).

[7] CEN/ISSS was created in mid-1997 by CEN (European Committee for Standardization) and ISSS (Information Society Standardization) to provide a comprehensive and integrated range of standardization-oriented services and products.

APPENDIX A

(Common Security Protocol services)

Protocol	Description
Secure Sockets Layer (SSL)	Originally developed by Netscape, the SSL security protocol provides data encryption, server authentication, message integrity, and optional client authentication for a TCP/IP connection. SSL has been universally accepted on the World Wide Web for authenticated and encrypted communication between clients and servers. However, SSL consumes large amounts of the Web server's processing power due to the massive cryptographic computations that take place when a secure session is initiated. If many secure sessions are initiated simultaneously, then the Web server quickly becomes overburdened. The results are slow response times, dropped connections, and failed transactions.
Secure Shell (SSH)	SSH Secure Shell is the de facto standard for remote logins. It solves an important security problem on the Internet of password hacking. Typical applications include secure use of networked applications, remote system administration, automated file transfers, and access to corporate resources over the Internet.
AS1 and AS2	AS1 provides S/MIME encryption and security over SMTP (Simple Mail Transfer Protocol) through object signature and object encryption technology. AS2 goes a step further than AS1 by supporting S/MIME over HTTP and HTTPS. Both AS1 and AS2 provide data authentication, proving that the sender and receiver are indeed the people or company that they claim to be.
Digital Certificates	Digital certificates are used to authenticate the identity of trading partners, ensuring partners are really who they say they are. In addition to data authentication, digital signatures support non-repudiation, proving that a specific message did come from a known sender at a specific time. A digital signature is a digital code that can be sent with electronically transmitted message and it uniquely identifies the sender. It is based on digital certificates. This prevents partners from claiming that they did not send or receive a particular message or transaction.
Pretty Good Privacy (PGP)	PGP is a freely available encryption program that uses public key cryptography to ensure privacy over FTP, HTTP and other protocols. PGP is the de-facto standard software for the encryption of e-mail and works on virtually every platform. But PGP suffers from absence of trust management and it is not standards compliant, though it could provide for integrity, authentication, non-repudiation and confidentiality. PGP also provides tools and utilities for creating, certifying, and managing keys.
Secure Multipurpose Internet Mail Extension (S/MIME)	S/MIME addresses security concerns such as privacy, integrity, authentication and non-repudiation, through the use of signed receipts. S/MIME provides a consistent way to send and receive secure MIME data. Based on the MIME standard, S/MIME provides authentication, message integrity, non-repudiation of origin (using digital signatures) and data confidentiality (using encryption) for electronic messaging applications. Since its development by RSA in 1996, S/MIME has been widely recognized and a widely used standard for messaging. The technology for S/MIME is primarily built on the Public Key Cryptographic Standard, which provides cryptographic interoperability. Two key features of S/MIME are the digital signature and the digital envelope. Digital signatures ensure that a message has not been tampered with during transit. Digital signatures also provide non-repudiation so senders cannot deny that they sent the message.
Secure HTTP (S-HTTP)	S-HTTP is an extension to HTTP, which provides a number of security features, including Client/Server Authentication, Spontaneous Encryption and Request/Response Non-repudiation. S-HTTP allows the secure exchange of files on the World Wide Web. Each S-HTTP file is either encrypted, contains a digital certificate, or both. For a given document, S-HTTP is an alternative to another well-known security protocol, Secure Sockets Layer (SSL). A major difference is that S-HTTP allows the client to send a certificate to authenticate the user, whereas using SSL, only the server can be authenticated. S-HTTP is more likely to be used in situations where the server represents a bank and requires authentication from the user that is more secure than a user id and password.
Simple Key management for Internet Protocols (SKIP)	It is a manifestation of IP-Level Cryptography that secures the network at the IP packet level. Any networked application gains the benefits of encryption, without requiring modification. SKIP is unique in that an Internet host can send an encrypted packet to another host without requiring a prior message exchange to set up a secure channel. SKIP is particularly well suited to IP networks, as both are stateless protocols.

continued on following page

APPENDIX A. CONTINUED

Encapsulating Security Payload (ESP)	ESP is security protocol that provides data confidentiality and protection with optional authentication and replay-detection services. ESP completely encapsulates user data. ESP can be used either by itself or in conjunction with AH. ESP may be implemented with AH, as discussed in next paragraph, in a nested fashion through the use of tunnel mode. Security services can be provided between a pair of communicating hosts, between a pair of communicating security gateways, or between a security gateway and a host, depending on the implementation. ESP may be used to provide the same security services, and it also provides a confidentiality (encryption) service. Specifically, ESP does not protect any IP header fields unless those fields are encapsulated by ESP (tunnel mode).
Authentication Header (AH)	A security protocol that provides authentication and optional replay-detection services. AH is embedded in the data to be protected (a full IP datagram, for example). AH can be used either by itself or with Encryption Service Payload (ESP). The IP Authentication Header is used to provide connectionless integrity and data origin authentication for IP datagrams, and to provide protection against replays. AH provides authentication for as much of the IP header as possible, as well as for upper level protocol data. However, some IP header fields may change in transit and the value of these fields, when the packet arrives at the receiver, may not be predictable by the sender. The values of such fields cannot be protected by AH. Thus the protection provided to the IP header by AH is somewhat piecemeal and not complete.

APPENDIX B

(Some Industry standards and frameworks in e-banking

Standard	Description
SET	Secure Electronic Transaction (SET) is a system for ensuring the security of financial transactions on the Internet. It was supported initially by Mastercard, Visa, Microsoft, Netscape, and others. With SET, a user is given an *electronic wallet* (digital certificate) and a transaction is conducted and verified using a combination of digital certificates and digital signatures among the purchaser, a merchant, and the purchaser's bank in a way that ensures privacy and confidentiality. SET makes use of Netscape's Secure Sockets Layer (SSL), Microsoft's Secure Transaction Technology (STT), and Terisa System's Secure Hypertext Transfer Protocol (S-HTTP). SET uses some but not all aspects of a public key infrastructure (PKI). SET provides authentication, integrity, non-repudiation and confidentiality.
HBCI	HBCI is a specification for the communication between intelligent customer systems and the corresponding computing centers for the exchange of home banking transactions. The transmission of data is done by a net data interface, which is based on flexible delimiter syntax.
EMV[1]	Specifications by Europay, MasterCard and Visa that define a set of requirements to ensure interoperability between chip cards and terminals on a global basis, regardless of the manufacturer, the financial institution, or where the card is used.
CEPS	The Common Electronic Purse Specifications (CEPS) define requirements for all components needed by an organization to implement a globally interoperable electronic purse program, while maintaining full accountability and auditability. CEPS, which were made available in March of 1999, outline overall system security, certification and migration. CEPS have paved the way for the creation of an open, de facto, global electronic purse standard (*http://www.cepsco.com/*).
XMLPay	XMLPay is a standard proposed/developed by Ariba and Verisign. It defines an XML syntax for payment transaction requests, responses and receipts in a payment processing network. The intended users are Internet merchants and merchant aggregators who need to deal with multiple electronic payment mechanisms (credit/debit card, purchase card, electronic check and automated clearing house payment). The supported operations include funds authorization and capture, sales and repeat sales, and voiding of transactions.
ECML	The Electronic Commerce Modeling Language ECML is a specification that describes the format for data fields that need to be filled at checkout in an online transaction. The fields defined include shipping information, billing information, recipient information, payment card information and reference fields. Version 2.0 describes these fields in XML syntax.

continued on following page

APPENDIX B. CONTINUED

W3C standard on	The W3C standard on micropayments has originated from IBM's standardization efforts. It covers the payment function for payment of digital goods. The micropayment initiative specifies how to provide in a Web page all the information necessary to initialize a micropayment and transfer this information to the wallet for processing. The W3C Ecommerce/Micropayment Activity is now closed.
Passport	Microsoft Passport is an online user-authentication service. Passport's primary service is user authentication, referred to as the Passport single sign-in (SSI) service. Passport also offers two other optional services: Passport express purchase (EP), which lets users store credit card and billing/shipping address information in their optional Passport wallet profiles to expedite checkout at participating e-commerce sites, and Kids Passport (source: Microsoft Passport Technical White Paper).
eWallet project of CEN/ISSS[2]	CEN/ISSS Electronic Commerce Workshop initiated the eWallet project in mid-2001 assuming a need for standardization in the field. CEN/ISSS has chosen a flexible working definition, considering an eWallet as "a collection of confidential data of a personal nature or relating to a role carried our by an individual, managed so as to facilitate completion of electronic transactions".
SEMPER	Secure Electronic Market Place for Europe (SEMPER) was produced by an EU supported project under a special program, undertaken by a 20-partner consortium led by IBM. It is a definition of an open and system independent architecture for electronic commerce. The project was concluded in 1999. Based on access via a browser, the architecture specifies common functions to be supported by applications, which include exchange of certificates, exchange of signed offer/order, fair contract signing, fair payment for receipt, and provision of delivery information.
IOTP	The Internet Open Trading Protocol (IOTP) is defined as an interoperable framework for Internet commerce. It is optimized for the case where the buyer and the merchant do not have a prior acquaintance. IOTP is payment system independent. It can encapsulate and support several of the leading payment systems.
SEPP	Secure Electronic Payment Process is a protocol developed by MasterCard and Netscape to provide authentication, integrity and payment confidentiality. It uses DES for confidentiality and 512, 768, 1024 or 2048-bit RSA and 128-bit MD5 hashing. RSA encrypts DES key to encrypt hash of account numbers. It uses up to three public keys, one for signing, one for key exchange, and one for certificate renewal. Besides, SEPP uses X.509 certificates with CMS at top of hierarchy [26].
STT	Secure Transaction Technology was developed by Visa and Microsoft to provide authentication, integrity and confidentiality to the Internet based transactions. It is based on 64-bit DES or 64-bit RC4 (24-bit salt) for confidentiality and 512, 768, 1024 or 2048-bit RSA for encryption with 160-bit SHA hashing. It uses two public keys, one for signing, and one for key exchange. It has credentials similar to certificates but with account details and higher-level signatures, though they are not certificates.
JEPI	(Joint Electronic Payment Initiative) CommerceNet and the W3 Consortium are jointly initiating a multi-industry project to develop an Internet payment negotiation protocol. The project explores the technology required to provide negotiation over multiple payment instruments, protocols and transports. Examples of payment instruments include credit cards, debit cards, electronic cash and checks. Payment protocols include STT and SEPP (amongst others). Payment transport encompasses the message transmission mechanism: S-HTTP, SSL, SMTP, and TCP/IP are all categorized as transport technologies that can be used for payment.

This work was previously published in the Journal of Organizational and End User Computing, Vol. 16, No. 3, edited by M. A. Mahmood, pp. 173-206, copyright 2004 by IGI Publishing, formerly known as Idea Group Publishing (an imprint of IGI Global).

Chapter 5.19
Model Driven Security for Inter-Organizational Workflows in E-Government

Michael Hafner
Universität Innsbruck, Austria

Barbara Weber
Universität Innsbruck, Austria

Ruth Breu
Universität Innsbruck, Austria

Andrea Nowak
Austrian Research Center Seibersdorf, Austria

ABSTRACT

Model driven architecture is an approach to increase the quality of complex software systems by creating high-level system models and automatically generating system architectures and components out of these models. We show how this paradigm can be applied to what we call model driven security for inter-organizational workflows in e-government. Our focus is on the realization of security-critical inter-organizational workflows in the context of Web services, Web service orchestration, and Web service choreography. Security requirements are specified at an abstract level using UML diagrams. Out of this specification security, relevant artifacts are generated for a target reference architecture based on upcoming Web service security standards. Additionally, we show how participants of a choreography use model dependencies to map the choreography specifications to interfaces for their local workflows.

INTRODUCTION

E-government refers to the use of the Internet and other electronic media to improve the collaboration within public agencies and to include citizens and companies in administrative processes. A core aim of e-government is to bring about a digital administration in order to enhance quality of service (e.g., additional online information or service offerings) as well as efficiency (e.g., reduced case processing times, fewer errors or using fewer resources to accomplish the same task).

The implementation of e-government solutions is a very complex task that can only succeed if IT-experts and domain experts cooperate with each other at a high level of abstraction right from the beginning. Security issues rooted in provisions and regulations play a very critical role. These include security requirements of public law (i.e., Austrian Signature Act [1999] and the Austrian e-government Act [2004] as well as the Federal Act concerning the Protection of Personal Data [1999]), the Austrian Security Manual [n.d.], the OECD Guidelines for the Security of Information Systems and Networks [n.d.], and internal security requirements of the municipalities.

Security requirements must not be considered as an isolated aspect, except during all stages of the software development cycle (Devanbu & Stubblebine, 2000; Ferrari & Thuraisingham, 2000). As the engineering of security into the overall software design is often neglected, different approaches for integrating security in the system development cycle have been proposed (Hall & Chapman, 2002; Breu, Burger, Hafner, & Popp, 2004). Nevertheless, they do not yet exploit the potential of a model driven approach.

Model driven software development is particularly appealing in the area of security as many security requirements adhere to certain categories (e.g., integrity) and can be described in implementation-independent models. In most cases, the development of security-critical systems is based on a set of well-known protective measures (i.e., protocols, algorithms) for which the correctness has been proved.

In this chapter, we give an overview of our approach to the model driven realization of security-critical inter-organizational workflows in the context of Web services security, Web service orchestration, and Web service choreography. The description of security requirements is performed at a high level of abstraction. Security relevant artifacts are generated for a target architecture. A description of the target architecture can be found in Hafner, Breu, and Breu (2005) and Brue, Hafner, and Web (2004).

Our approach provides a specification framework for the design of collaborating systems in the context of the platform-independent Web service technology. It also supports the systematic transition from security requirements, via the generation of security artifacts, to a secure solution based on a Web services platform. The specification of security requirements is performed in a platform-independent way and can thus be applied by domain experts without in-depth technical knowledge.

The structure of the subsequent sections is as follows. After providing an overview on Web services composition, Web services security, and Model Driven Architecture in Section 2, we present a case study in Section 3, and describe our model driven approach in Section 4. In Section 5, we describe our component-based Target Reference Architecture. Finally, Section 6 gives an overview of related work before Section 7 closes with a conclusion.

Backgrounds

This section briefly sketches the standards, technologies, and methodologies our approach is based upon.

Web Services Standards

The growing popularity of emerging Web services standards and technologies pushes the specification and implementation of powerful infrastructures based on platform-independent technology. The goal is to foster interoperability between partners who plan the realization of collaborations over networks (e.g., governmental and local authorities). Figure 1 provides a (partial) overview of existing Web services standards. The specifications and drafts cover various aspects related to the implementation of collaborations based on Web services.

Web Services Composition

Beginning at the top of the technology stack, we have the composition of Web services. Businesses provide value-added services through composition of basic or elemental Web services using service composition languages. Very often different companies offer the services. A Web services composition consists of multiple invocations of other Web services in a specific order. A composition can either take the form of an orchestration or of a choreography. An orchestra-

tion describes how Web services interact with each other at the message or application level, including the business logic and the execution order of the interactions from the viewpoint of the partner controlling the workflow execution. A choreography or a business protocol describes the interaction between business partners in terms of the sequence of messages that are exchanged in a "peer-to-peer" fashion. There is no central control of workflow execution.

WS-BPEL (2003) is a workflow orchestration language for Web services. It supports the definition of executable business processes and provides partial support for abstract business protocols. BPML (Arkin, 2002) is quite similar to WS-BPEL as it supports Web services standards, but it is considered as semantically weaker.

While an executable business process models the behavior of a partner in a specific business interaction, a business protocol standard like WS-CDL (2004) specifies the public message

Figure 1. Web services standards technology stack

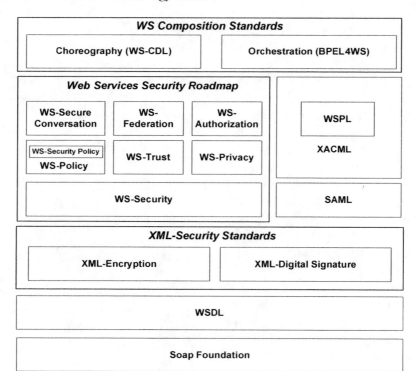

exchange between parties and abstracts from how they are internally processed. Alternative standards to describe business protocols are WSCI (n.d.) and ebXML (Bernauer, Kramler, & Kappel, 2003). ebXML additionally comprises a powerful set of standards for the specification of B2B protocols but it is not compatible to the Web services concept.

Web Services Security

As Web services are often aggregated to carry out complex business transactions, not only the Web service itself or the underlying infrastructure has to be secured, but also the message exchange between different Web services. WS-Security (n.d.) is based on XML-Encryption (Eastlake, 2002) and XML-Digital Signature (Eastlake, 2002) and specifies a mechanism for signing and encrypting SOAP messages. It is used to implement message integrity and confidentiality at the application level. WS-Security also supports the propagation of the authentication information in the form of security tokens (e.g., Kerberos tickets or X.509 certificates). XACML (Godik & Moses, 2003) provides access control mechanisms and policies within documents, while SAML (Cantor, Kemp, & Maler, 2004) represents authentication and authorization decisions in XML format and is used to exchange this information over the Internet (e.g., to support single sign-on and log-out).

WS-Policy (Bajal et al., 2004) is used for the specification of requirements for Web services in their interaction with other services in a standardized, machine-readable format. Web services endpoints negotiate the parameters and advertise the set of requirements potential service requesters have to comply with when they want to access the service (e.g., quality-of-service). WS-Security Policy (Della-Libera et al., 2002) is a complementary standard to WS-Policy and specifies how actors can assert to potential partners their policies with respect to specific WS-Security mechanisms. WS-Trust (Anderson et al., 2005) enables token interoperability. It provides

a request/response protocol for the exchange, the issuance, and the validation of security tokens by a trusted third party.

Model Driven Architecture and Security

Model driven architecture (MDA) is an approach for the design and implementation of applications that aims at cost reduction and application quality improvement (Lodderstedt, 2003). At the very core of MDA is the concept of a model (i.e., abstraction of the target system). MDA defines two types of models, a Platform Independent Model (PIM), describing the system independently from the intended platform, and a Platform Specific Model (PSM) describing the system in terms of its technical infrastructure (e.g., J2EE or .NET). The process of converting a PIM into a PSM is called transformation. Models are described using a well-defined modeling language such as UML. Model Driven Security is based upon MDA in the sense that security requirements are integrated into design models, leading to security design models. Transformation rules of MDA are extended to generate security infrastructures (Lodderstedt, 2003).

CASE STUDY

Our methodology for the systematic design and realization of security-critical inter-organizational workflows is illustrated by a portion of a workflow drawn from the use case "Processing of an Annual Statement" (Figure 2) describing the interaction between a citizen (the Client), a business agent (the Tax Advisor), and a public service provider (the Municipality).

The use case was elaborated within the project SECTINO, a joint research effort between the research group Quality Engineering at the University of Innsbruck and the Austrian Research Center Seibersdorf. It is based on a case study involving a major Austrian municipality. The

Figure 2. Processing of an annual statement (global view on workflow)

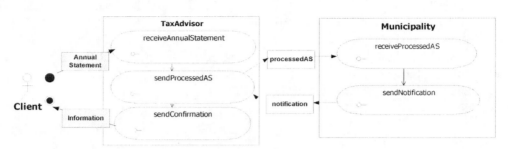

project aims at the development of a framework supporting the systematic and efficient realization and management of innovative e-government related workflows with a special focus on security requirements.

In Austria, all wages and salaries paid to employees of an enterprise are subject to the municipal tax. Businesses have to send the annual tax statement via their tax advisor to a municipality which is responsible for collecting the tax by the end of March of the following year. The municipality checks the declaration of the annual statement and calculates the tax duties. A notification with the amount of tax duties is then sent to the tax advisor by mail. Ultimately, the workflow should allow the declaration of the municipal tax via the internet.

One of the project goals is to analyze security issues that may stem from the migration of the workflow to an e-government based solution and create the necessary run-time artifacts for the target architecture through model transformation.

MODEL DRIVEN SECURITY FOR INTER-ORGANIZATIONAL WORKFLOWS

In this section, we present our approach to the management of security related aspects within the development process. We first present the model views, then proceed to the description of the mod-

els: the global workflow model, the local workflow model, and the interface model. We move on to describe model dependencies before giving an example on how to perform a risk and threats analysis and how to specify security requirements for the topmost level (global workflow) following a five step approach for security analysis called micro process for security engineering.

The requirements are transformed into run-time artifacts for the target reference architecture in Section 5.

Model Views

In the context of this chapter, a *workflow* describes a network of partners cooperating in a controlled way by calling services and exchanging documents. Our method of designing security-critical inter-organizational workflows is based on two orthogonal views: the *interface view* and the *workflow view* (Figure 3). The latter is further divided into the *global workflow model* (GWfM) describing the message exchange between cooperating partners, and the *local workflow model* (LWfM) describing the behavior of each partner.

The *interface view* represents a contractual agreement between the parties to provide a set of services based on the minimum set of technical and domain level constraints and thereby links the GWfM to the LWfM. The application of these orthogonal perspectives allows us to combine the design of components offering services that may

Figure 3. Two orthogonal views

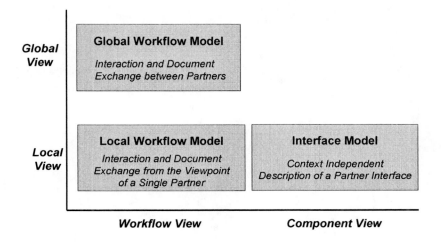

be called in different contexts. From a security perspective, the Interface View deals with security requirements from the components' point of view, while the GWfM deals with the secure exchange of documents between different partners.

Global Workflow Model

The GWfM describes an integrated abstract view of the workflow involving partners in autonomous organizations. The global workflow describes the interaction of partners abstracting from internal processing steps and does not contain any connection to the business logic.

The details of the global workflow are captured and visualized with a UML 2.0 Activity Diagram (www.uml.org) as in Figure 4 and can optionally be mapped to WS-CDL.

Since we strongly focus our approach on Web services technology, which is the most widespread technology with strong vendor support, we consider WS-CDL and WS-BPEL as appropriate top-layer standards to the Web services protocol stack (including WSDL [Christensen, Curbera, Meredith, & Weerawarana, 2001], SOAP, UDDI, and related security standards). Although we use WS-BPEL to model local, executable processes, we decided to rely on UML 2.0 for the specifica-

tion of inter-organizational collaboration protocols instead of using an "official" standard like WS-CDL. There are multiple reasons why we decided to rely on UML 2.0 instead of a specific choreography standard for the specification of the global workflow. UML 2.0 is a widespread modeling language with a comprehensive formal grounding and an intuitive visual notation. It provides all the means for modeling orchestration and choreography, it can easily be extended in various ways to provide complex workflow semantics, like security requirements at the global workflow level in our case. For a critical discussion of WS-CDL, please refer to Barros, Dumas, and Oaks (2005). In Hafner and Breu (2005) we provide a detailed account on how to map the UML 2.0 activity diagram to a choreography standard like the WS-CDL (2004).

In our example (see Figure 4), parts of the document sent from the Tax Advisor to the Municipality are meant to comply with confidentiality, integrity and non-repudiation. At runtime, the Policy Enforcement Point, acting as a security gateway, will have to sign and encrypt the document at the company's boundary according to a security policy configuration file containing the previously mentioned requirements (Section 5).

Figure 4. A sample document flow with security requirements (global workflow model)

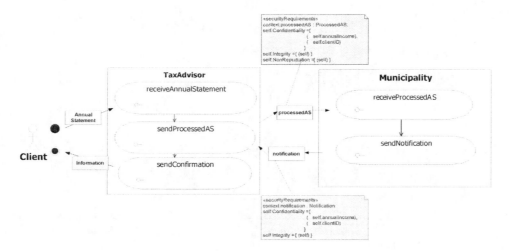

The Process of Modeling a Global Workflow

We assume that there is no central control of the inter-organizational workflow. The workflow is de The distributed process involves three actors: the local governmental authorities (e.g., municipalities), the citizens and/or the companies, and a group of tax advisors, which were mapped to generic roles: Client, Municipality, and Tax Advisor. Additionally, the process had to be realized in a peer-to-peer fashion and should ultimately integrate security requirements.

The collaboration process was roughly specified as follows:

1. The Client sends his Annual statement to his Tax Advisor
2. The Tax Advisor does some internal processing on the document (e.g., formatting, complement legal data, etc.)
3. The Tax Advisor forwards the processed annual statement on behalf of his Client to the Municipality
4. The Municipality calculates the amount of tax duties

5. The Municipality returns a notification to the Tax Advisor
6. The Tax Advisor processes the notification
7. The Tax Advisor informs his Client about his tax duties

Steps 1, 3, 5, and 7 correspond to interaction activities in the choreography, involving a peer-to-peer message flow between participants, whereas steps 2, 4, and 6 can be identified as being the "links" to the actors' local orchestrations, which would later be realized as an executable local workflow.

This first step leads to a common understanding of the structure of the "virtual" or the global workflow. Ideally, this includes the format, the structure and the sequence of the messages that are exchanged, the interfaces to the "business" or workflow logic each partner agreed to contribute to the composition, to operation semantics and to run-time constraints specification, information that is typically published in WSDL files and technical models (tModels) of UDDI Registries. From here on the participants have all information necessary to implement "interface"-compliant functionality at their nodes.

In practice, it is almost impossible to impose a straight top-down realization process on the participants for various reasons. First, it is very improbable that the partners will implement their logic from scratch. Very often partners have already implemented some kind of application logic, maybe even made it accessible to customers as a Web service. They probably want to reuse functionality of existing components running on a working infrastructure. The components reuse and their integration is a matter of cost-efficiency and requires some in-depth expertise of the technical staff.

Nor is it very likely that the partners will completely redesign the interfaces to their business logic to make them compliant to the naming conventions specified in the global workflow. Businesses and administrations can have organizational structures that may thwart a top-down approach from the very beginning (e.g., every business unit has its own IT-infrastructure, administrative units may have different reporting hierarchies, etc.).

This is why the participants of a choreography will proceed according to a hybrid approach projecting some of the interfaces of their local business logic to operations in the *interface model*, and, in turn, maybe wrap some of their local applications in order to comply with operations signatures of the *interface model*, which conforms to a uniform technical, syntactical, and semantic specification the partners agreed upon. If, for example, the partners agree to implement the global workflow based on Web services, some partners will have to provide a Web services wrapper for their application logic.

Local Workflow Model

The LWfMs define the portion of the global workflow each partner is responsible for. They are developed for each partner type. The LWfM is an executable process description that considers service calls from the outside and contains internal actions as well as connections to the business logic. It is a direct input for a local workflow manage-ment system and is typically developed internally by partners. Referring to the sample process, the GWfM captures the protocol between the online municipal tax component and the involved partners like the Municipality and the Tax Advisor, while the LWfM describes the sequence in which the component accepts and processes incoming messages based on the services described in the interface model.

The LWfM describes the necessary processing steps to calculate the tax duties. These steps are performed internally and are invisible to the outside.

Figure 5 shows an activity diagram capturing some aspects of the Tax Advisor's LWfM. The parts where the local workflow interacts with partners can be generated from the GWfM (receiveAnnualStatement sendConfirmation, and sendProcessedAS). Every actor will have to complement the part accessing his local logic (corresponding to the port InternalWebServices). With some additional specifications every actor can then generate WS-BPEL and WSDL files for his execution environment (e.g., using MDA tools like UML2BPEL [Anderson et al., 2005]).

Interface View

The *Interface View* describes the interface of every partner independently of its usage scenario and consists of four sub-models (Figure 6): the *Role*, the *Interface*, the *Access,* and the *Document Model*.

The *Document Model* is a UML class diagram describing the data type view of the partner. We talk of documents in order to stress that we do not interpret this class diagram in the usual object-oriented setting but in the context of XML schema. The *Interface* Model contains a set of abstract (UML) operations representing services the component offers to its clients. The types of the parameters are either basic types or classes in the document model. Additionally, pre- and post-conditions (in OCL style) may specify the behavior of the abstract services. The *Role Model*

Figure 5. A sample orchestration (local workflow model)

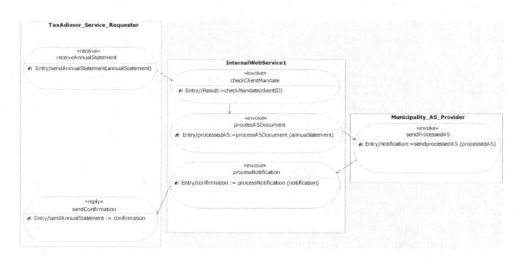

Figure 6. The sub-models of the workflow and the interface view

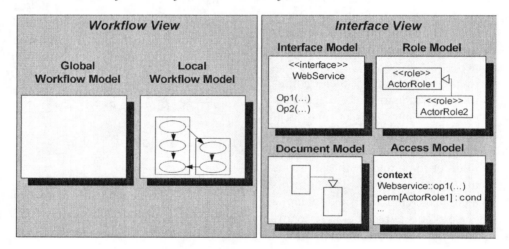

describes the roles having access to the services. The *Access Model* describes the conditions under which a certain role has the permission to call a given service. The permissions are written in SECTET-PL (Alam, Breu, & Hafner, 2006) in a predicative style over the structures of the Document Model.

The Interface Model describes a component offering a set of services with given properties and permissions. Security requirements at this level of abstraction involve the support of a role

model and the specification of access rights for particular Web service operations. A more detailed description of the Interface View can be found in Hafner, Breu, and Breu (2005).

Model Dependencies

Security requirements specified in the GWfM have to be mapped in a consistent way to the local workflows of all cooperating partners, which reflect the business logic in their local environment.

Partner A in Figure 7 is responsible for the implementation of the business logic covering Actions 1, 2, 5, and 6 in the GWfM. This can be seen as an abstract functional specification of the application logic a partner has to contribute to the global workflow. All the partners together agree on the signature format and naming conventions for the interfaces they provide to each other. These interfaces are visible to all partners and represent entry or exit points for data, messages or documents, either entering the local workflow for further processing or leaving it after processing (e.g., OP_1 (Msg1):= Msg4 in Figure 7).

In a second step, the partners map the interfaces of their local business logic to operations in the Interface Model (e.g., $LocalOP_B$ (LocalMsg1) in Figure 7). They are not visible to the partners

and are used during the execution of their own local workflows in order to perform additional workflow actions.

In the GWfM, either one or two actions are mapped to an operation in the Interface Model depending on whether the message exchange is asynchronous or synchronous. Van der Aalst et al. (2001) present a formal approach based on Petri nets for the design of inter-organizational workflows guaranteeing local autonomy without compromising the consistency of the overall process. In our terms, this means that—in a peer-to-peer fashion—the local workflows should exactly realize the behavior as specified in the global workflow.

Figure 7. Model dependencies

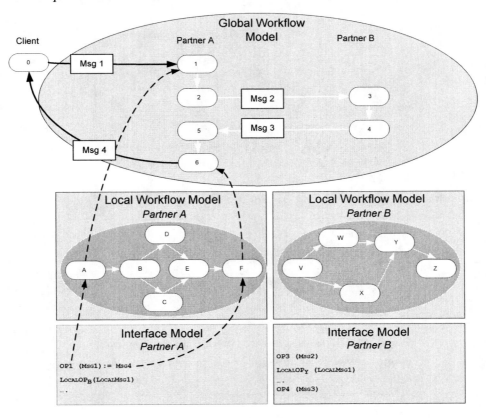

Example Security Analysis at the Global Workflow Level

In this section, we give an example of how a first iteration of a Security Analysis is performed at the level of the GWfM. Throughout further iterations, the participants of the choreography have to make sure that the security requirements, which are first defined at the GWfM level, are reliably and consistently modeled and implemented on the lower levels (this means at the local workflow level and the component level).

Security related aspects within the development of inter-organizational workflows are tackled by a five-step approach as illustrated in Figure 8 (Breu, Burger, Hafner, & Popp, 2004). The Micro Process for Security Analysis is performed iteratively at three levels of abstraction (at the global workflow level, the local workflow level, and the component level).

Requirements and measures are explored and described at the appropriate level of detail based on the corresponding artifacts (e.g., the GWfM). Table 1 illustrates the security analysis process using a sample scenario (Section 3).

Figure 8. The micro process for security analysis

Requirements Elicitation
Specify security requirements in the context of a given artifact (e.g., the global workflow model).

Threats Modeling
Gather potential threats related with the security requirements.

Risk Analysis
Estimate threat occurrence and the potential harm (quantitatively or qualitatively) to decide whether a threat has to be countered or not.

Counteractive Measures Design
Design appropriate counteractive measures based on the result of the risk analysis

Correctness Check
Check measures (formally or informally) against the requirements and decide which requirements still wait for realization.

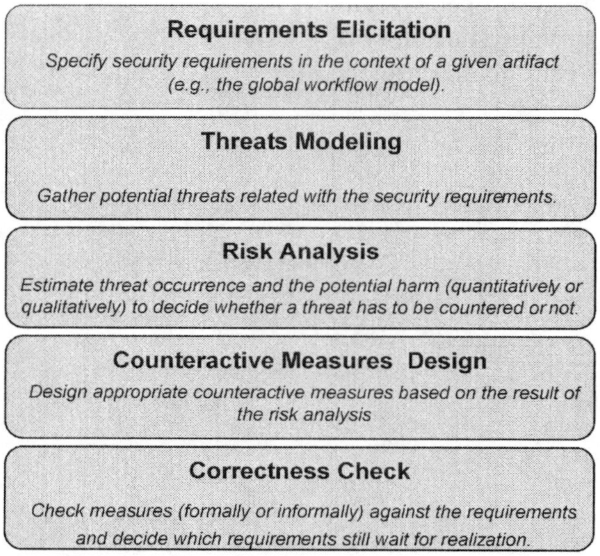

Table 1. Sample scenario of a security analysis at the global level

1.	The data exchange within the "Processing of an Annual Statement" has to comply with the requirements of integrity and confidentiality.
2.	This workflow is open to the threat that a third unauthorized party may try to read and to modify the exchanged data.
3.	The probability of occurrence is estimated as medium, the possible damage is estimated as substantial.
4.	The measures to counter the threats involve encryption and digital signatures.
5.	The proposed measures are checked. There remains the requirement that the two partners have to authenticate each other.

In the early phases of design, security requirements are expressed in a textual way (e.g., by a security relevant section within the use case specification). In the context of the UML notation, we provide extended notation techniques. Security requirements are related to each other so that they can be traced from one level of abstraction to the next (i.e., each requirement is transformed into one or several requirements or into some protective measures at the abstraction level underneath).

TARGET REFERENCE ARCHITECTURE

In this section, we present our target reference architecture for a partner, which offers a portion of a distributed workflow. We give an overview of how the various standards are integrated into the architecture.

The basic component architecture is based on the data-flow model of XACML, which is an XML based OASIS standard for a policy and access control decision language as described in Godik and Moses (2003). Figure 9 shows the target reference architecture in the view of a partner who implements his portion of the global workflow as a local workflow and offers an interface to its partners.

Workflow Engine

The core component is the workflow engine (1), which implements an orchestration language such as WS-BPEL (BEA, 2003) or BPML (Arkin, 2002) and aggregates and controls the sequence of existing Web services (2) to a composition that may be offered as a Web service of its own to external business partners. We use BPWS4J

Figure 9. Target software architecture

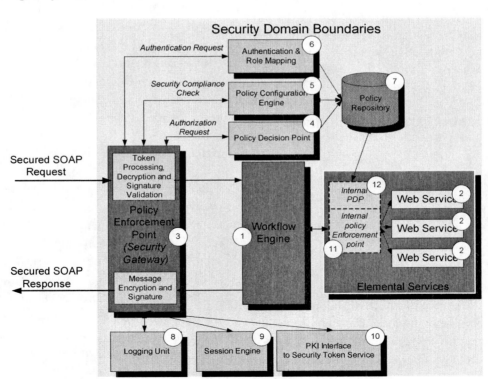

as a WS-BPEL engine (IBM, n.d.). In order to provide a trusted domain the elemental (2) and composite Web services (2) are wrapped by security components.

External Policy Enforcement Point

The external policy enforcement point (PEP) represents a single point of entry and acts as a security gateway (3). It intercepts incoming SOAP messages and applies basic security processing to the message structure. It extracts tokens from the inbound SOAP messages, decrypts elements, and checks the validity of signatures. Accordingly, the PEP adds tokens to, encrypts, and signs elements in outbound messages. This basic security-message-structure processing functionality implements standards like XML-Encryption, XML-Digital signature and WS-Security.

In case "non-repudiation-of-reception" was specified as a security requirement, the PEP returns a time-stamped and signed notification of receipt to the sender. In case of a specified "non-repudiation-of-submission," the PEP forwards a time-stamped copy of the signed message he received from the sender to the logging unit. The PEP interacts with other security components before forwarding an inbound message to the end-recipient (e.g., back-end application).

Authentication and Role Mapping Unit

The PEP first makes an authentication request to the Role Mapping Unit (6), which assigns a role to the caller. The request/response protocol is based on XACML.

Policy Configuration Engine

In a second step, the PEP checks the inbound message for compliance with security requirements by querying the Policy Configuration Engine (5). Alternatively, for outbound messages, the PEP queries the Policy Configuration Engine for security requirements to integrate into the message structure. The requirements for inbound and outbound messages are specified in a policy file based on the standards WS-Policy, XACML, and WS-Security. The security requirements, which were specified in the global workflow model, are directly translated into policy files for the configuration engine.

Policy Decision Point

The PEP finally queries the Policy Decision Point (4) for Authorization. It checks invocation requests from workflow partners to exposed services and forwards requests to the Policy Decision Points (4) or (12)—which check the requests according to some policy stored in the Policy Repository (PR) (7). The query protocol is based on XACML, whereas the policy files are based on WS-Policy, XACML, and WS-Security.

Optional: Internal Policy Enforcement Point

The external PEP (3) implements security objectives like user authentication, confidentiality, and integrity regarding data exchange with external partners, whereas the internal PEP (11) maps and enforces access rights to the local environment.

Supporting Components

The Logging Unit (8) provides application level tracing and error logging and basically implements the security requirement of "non-repudiation-of-reception." The Session Engine (9) implements a security context engine that works at the application layer and relies on WS-Trust (Della-Librera et al., 2002) and WS-Secure Conversation (Anderson et al., 2005). The PKI Interface (10) is based on WS-Trust and provides access to external security token services for token issuance, validation, or mapping.

Table 2 gives an overview of the security components, the functionality the components provide, the underlying standards and technologies, and the security requirements that are covered.

Related Work

Related work can be found in several areas. A number of approaches deal with secure document exchange and workflow management in a centrally organized environment. Among these are the Author-X system (Bertino, Castano, & Ferrari, 2001), PERMIS (Chadwick, 2002), and Akenti (Thompson, Essiari, & Mudumbai, 2003). Often a central control is appropriate, but there are also many application domains requiring a local organization.

A whole community deals with inter-organizational workflow management systems (Leyman & Roller, 2000; van der Aalst, 2000, 1999; Luo, Shet, Kochut, & Miller, 2000; Grefen, Aberer, Hoffner, & Ludwing, 2000; Casati & Shan, 2002). We do not aim to contribute a novel approach to this field. Instead, we rely on UML models for modeling workflows and existing workflow management systems based on Web services technology.

Bernauer et al. (Bernauer, Kramler, & Kappel, 2003) analyse security and workflow semantics related issues that arise when modeling B2B protocols. The chapter provides a methodical comparison of WSDL- and ebXML-based approaches. Security extensions at a low level of abstraction for workflow management systems are treated in Atluri and Huang (1996), Gudes, Oliveir, and van de Riet (1999), Huang and Atluri (1999), Wainer, Barthelmess, and Kumar (2003).

Model driven approaches that are close to the idea of our framework are Basin, Dose, and Lodderstedt (2003), Lang (2003), and Lodderstedt, Basin, and Doser (2002). Lodderstedt (2003) introduced the notion of Model Driven Security for a software development process that allows for the integration of security requirements into system models and supports the generation of security infrastructures. These approaches deal with business logic, our approach deals with workflow management.

Mantell (2003) describes an implementation, where a local workflow is modeled in a case-tool, exported via XMI-files to a development environment, and automatically translated into executable code for a WS-BPEL engine-based on Web services. Nevertheless, the approach does

Table 2. Security objectives and their implementation in the PEP component

Security Component	Provided Functionality	Implemented Technologies & Standards	Security Requirement
Security Gateway			
External PEP	SOAP Message Structure Processing	WS-Sec, XML-Encr.,XML-Sign, XACML	**Integrity** **Confidentiality** **Non-repudiation** *(Message Processing)*
Internal PEP	Internal Role Mapping	XACML, XML	**Authorization**
	Sate Dependent Permissions		
Authentication Unit	Role Mapping	XACML, WS-Policy	**Authentication**
Policy Decision Point	Authorization Request Processing	XACML, WS-Policy, WS-Security	**Authorization**
Policy Repository	Policy Archive	XACML, WS-Policy, WS-Security	
PEP Configuration Engine	Check of Compliance to Security Requirements	XACML, WS-Policy, WS-Security	*(Security Compliance)*
Suporting Components			
Logging Unit	Message Level Tracing	XML, BPEL4WS	**Non-repudiation** **Of Sender**
	Error Logging	XML, BPEL4WS	
Session Engine	Security Context Management	WS-Secure Conversation, WS-Trust	**Authentication**
PKI Interface	Access to Securtiy Token Services	WS-Trust, SAML	*(Interface STS)*

SAML	Security Assertion Markup Language
XACML	Extensible Access Control Markup Language
XML-Sign.	XML Digital Signature
XML-Encr	XML Encryption
WS-Sec	Web-Services Security Specification
XML	Extensible Mark up Language
PKI	Public Key Infrastructure
STS	Security Token Service

not provide any facilities for the integration of security requirements at the modeling level nor does it support the specification of global workflows by means of peer-to-peer interactions as suggested by the concept of abstract processes in BEA (2003).

CONCLUSION, CURRENT, AND FUTURE ACTIVITIES

In this chapter, we have presented our approach to model driven security for inter-organizational workflows. Our framework is based on the idea of specifying security requirements at the abstract level of UML models and generating executable software artifacts for the configuration of a target reference architecture, which is based on Web services technologies and (upcoming) standards.

By now, we have developed a code generator as proof-of-concept prototype, which implements the transformation functions taking the UML models and producing XML-based configuration files for some basic scenarios (confidentiality, integrity, and non-repudiation).

Current efforts are directed into several directions. We aim at the extension of the list of security requirements that can be expressed within our syntactic framework by considering additional features for basic security requirements (e.g., the distinction of documents signed by actors or by systems according to various legal requirements) and by introducing new types of complex, domain specific security requirements (e.g., transactional security requirements for electronic banking, message-level security context, and trust propagation, privacy in a distributed environment, etc.), which will be realized through "pluggable" components in the target architecture.

Our case studies in the field of e-government show us an increasing demand for high-level development of secure workflow realizations. This pushes us to tackle more complex workflow issues, like the "Qualified Signature," which requires a natural person's signature instead of a system's, the delegation of rights (e.g., a tax advisor acting on behalf of his client), and timing constraints on transactions (e.g., a notification has to returned within a two-weeks delay.

REFERENCES

Anderson, S. et al. (2005, February). *Web Services Secure Conversation Language* (WS-SecureConversation). Retrieved from ftp://www6.software.ibm.com/software/developer/library/ws-secure-conversation.pdf

Anderson, S. et al. (2005, February). *Web Services Trust Language* (WS-Trust). Retrieved from ftp://www6.software.ibm.com/software/developer/library/ws-trust.pdf

Arkin, A. (2002). *Business Process Modeling Language*. San Mateo, CA, BPMI.org, 2002. Proposed Final Draft.

Alam, M., Breu, R., & Hafner, M. (2006). Modeling permissions in a (U/X)ML world. Accepted to *ARES 2006*, Vienne, Austria.

Atluri, V., & Huang, W. K. (1996). Enforcing mandatory and discretionary security in workflow management systems. In *Proceedings of the 5th European Symposium on Research in Computer Security*.

Austrian Security Manual. Retrieved from http://www.cio.gv.at/securenetworks/sihb/

Austrian Signature Act (Signaturgesetz - SigG). (1999). Art. 1 of the Act. *Austrian Federal Law Gazette*, part I, Nr. 190/1999.

Bajal S. et al. (2004, September). *Web Services Policy Framework* (WS-Policy). Retrieved from ftp://www6.software.ibm.com/software/developer/library/ws-policy.pdf

Barros, A., Dumas, M., & Oaks, P. (2005). A critical overview of the Web Services Choreography

Description Language (WS-CDL). *BPTrends Newsletter,* Vol. 3. Retrieved from http://www.bptrends.com/publicationfiles/

03%2D05%20WP%20WS%2DCDL%20Barros%20et%20al.pdf

Basin, D., Dose, J., & Lodderstedt, T. (2003). *Model driven security for process-oriented systems.* Paper presented at the 8th ACM Symposium on Access Control Models and Technologies.

BEA, IBM, Microsoft, SAP AG, Siebel Systems. (2003, May). *Specification: Business Process Execution Language for Web Services* (Version 1.1). Retrieved from http://www.ibm.com/developerworks/library/ws-bpel

BEA, Intalio, Sun Microsystems, SAP: Web Service Choreography Interface (WSCI) 1.0. (n.d.). Retrieved from http://www.w3.org/TR/wsci/

Bernauer, M., Kramler, G., & Kappel, G. (2003). Comparing WSDL-based and ebXML-based Approaches for B2B Protocol Specification. In *Proceedings of the 1st International Conference on Service-Oriented Computing (ICSOC).*

Bertino E., Castano S., & Ferrari E. (2001). *Securing XML Documents with Author X.* IEEE Internet Computing.

Breu R., Burger K., Hafner M., & Popp G. (2004). Towards a systematic development of secure systems. *Information Systems Security.*

Breu R., Hafner M., & Weber B. (2004). Modeling and Realizing Security-Critical Inter-Organizational Workflows. In W. Dosch & N. Debnath (Eds.), *Proceedings IASSE 2004, ISCA.*

Cantor, S., Kemp, J., & Maler, E. (2004, July 13). *Assertions and Protocols for the OASIS Security Assertion Markup Language (SAML)* (V2.0, Last-Call Working Draft 17). Retrieved from http://www.oasis-open.org/committees/download.php/7737/sstc-saml-core-2.0-draft-17.pdf

Casati, F., & Shan, M. (2002). Event-based interaction management for composite e-services in e-flow. *Information Systems Frontiers.*

Chadwick, D. W. (2002). RBAC Policies in XML for X.509 based privilege management. In *Proceedings of the IFIP TC11 17th International Conference on Information Security: Visions and Perspectives.*

Christensen, E., Curbera, F., Meredith, G., & Weerawarana, S. (2001). *Web Services Description Language (WSDL) 1.1.* Retrieved from http://www.w3.org/TR/wsdl

Della-Libera, G. et al. (2002, December). *Web Services Security Policy Language* (WS-SecurityPolicy). Retrieved from http://msdn.microsoft.com/Webservices/default.aspx?pull=/library/en-us/dnglobspec/html/ws-securitypolicy.asp

Devanbu, P., & Stubblebine, S. (2000). *Software engineering for security: a roadmap.* In A. Finkelstein (Ed.), *The future of software engineering* (pp. 227-239). ACM Press.

Eastlake D. et al. (Ed.) (2002, December 10). *XML Encryption Syntax and Processing. W3C Recommendation.* Retrieved from http://www.w3.org/TR/2002/REC-xmlenc-core-20021210/

Federal Act on Provisions Facilitating Electronic Communications with Public Bodies (E-Government Gesetz - E-GovG). (2004, March 1). Art. 1 of the Act. *Austrian Federal Law Gazette,* part I, Nr. 10/2004.

Federal Act concerning the Protection of Personal Data (Datenschutzgesetz - DSG2000). (1999, August 17). *Austrian Federal Law Gazette,* part I No. 165/1999.

Ferrari E., & Thuraisingham B. (2000). *Secure database systems.* In M. Piattini & O. Díaz (Eds.), *Advanced databases: Technology Design.* London: Artech House.

Godik, S., & Moses, T. (2003, February 18). *eXtensible Access Control Markup Language (XACML)* (Version 1.0 3 OASIS Standard). Retrieved from http://www.oasis-open.org/committees/xacml/repository

Grefen, P., Aberer, K., Hoffner, Y., & Ludwig, H. (2000). CrossFlow: Cross-organizational workflow management in dynamic virtual enterprises. *International Journal of Computer Systems Science & Engineering.*

Gudes, E., Olivier, M., & van de Riet, R. (1999). Modelling, specifying and implementing workflow security in cyberspace. *Journal of Computer.*

Hafner, M., & Breu, R. (2005). Realizing model driven security for inter-organizational workflows with WS-CDL and UML 2.0: Bringing Web services, security and UML together. In L. Briand & C. Williams (Eds.), *Proceedings of the 8th International Conference MoDELS 2005*, Montego Bay, Jamaica: Model Driven Engineering Languages and Systems.

Hafner M., Breu R., & Breu M. (2005). *A Security Architecture for Inter-Organizational Workflows: Putting Security Standards for Web Services Together.* In C. S. Chen, J. Filipe, et al. (Eds.), *Proceedings ICEIS 2005.*

Hafner, M., Breu, R., Breu, M., & Nowak, A. (2005). Modeling inter-organizational workflow security in a peer-to-peer environment. In R. Bilof (Ed.), *Proceedings of the 2005 IEEE International Conference on Web Services, ICWS 2005*, Orlando, FL.

Hall A., Chapman R. (2002). Correctness by construction developing a commercial secure system. *IEEE Software, 19*(1) 18-25.

Huang, W. K., & Atluri V. (1999). *SecureFlow: A secure Web-enabled Workflow Management System.* Paper presented at the ACM Workshop on Role-Based Access Control.

IBM: BPWS4J. Retrieved from http://www.alphaworks.ibm.com/tech/bpws4j

IBM, Microsoft, VeriSign: Web services security (WS-Security). (n.d.). Retrieved from http://www-106.ibm.com/developerworks/Webservices/library/ws-secure/

Lang, U. (2003). *Access policies for middleware.* PhD thesis, University of Cambridge.

Leyman, F., & Roller, D. (2000). *Production workflow: Concepts and techniques.* Prentice-Hall. Retrieved from http://www.uml.org

Lodderstedt, T. (2003). *Model driven security: From UML models to access control architectures.* Dissertation, University of Freiburg.

Lodderstedt, T., Basin, D., & Doser, J. (2002) SecureUML: A UML-Based Modeling Language for Model-Driven Security. In J.-M. Jézéquel, H. Hussmann, & S. Cook (Eds.), *Proceedings of the 5th International Conference on the Unified Modeling Language.*

Luo, Z., Shet, A., Kochut, K., & Miller, J. (2000). Exception handling in workflow systems. *Applied Intelligence.*

Mantell, K. (2003). *From UML to BPEL. IBMdeveloperWorks.*

OECD Guidelines for the Security of Information Systems and Networks. URL: http://www.ftc.gov/bcp/conline/edcams/infosecurity/popups/OECD_guidelines.pdf.

Thompson M., Essiari A., & Mudumbai S. (2003). Certificate-based authorization policy in a PKI environment. *ACM Transactions on Information and System Security.*

Van der Aalst, W. M. P. (1999). Process-oriented Architectures for Electronic Commerce and Inter-organizational Workflow. *Information Systems.*

Van der Aalst, W. M. P. (2000). Loosely coupled interorganizational workflows: Modeling and analyzing workflows crossing organizational boundaries. *Information and Management.*

Van der Aalst, W. M. P., & Weske, M. (2001). The P2P approach to interorganizational workflows. In K. R. Dittrich, et al. (Eds.), *Proceedings of the 13th International Conference on Advanced Information Systems Engineering (CAiSE'01).* Springer, Berlin.

W3C: Web Services Choreography Description Language (Version 1.0). (2004, December 17). W3C Working Draft. Retrieved from http://www.w3.org/TR/2004/WD-ws-cdl-10-20041217/

Wainer, J., Barthelmess, P., & Kumar, A. (2003). W-RBAC—A workflow security model incorporating controlled overriding of constraints. *International Journal of Cooperative Information Systems.*

Index

encryption 256, 344, 498, 571, 572, 582, 1271, 2278, 2726, 2787, 2933, 3443, 3446, 3631
encryption cracking 1586
end node verification 1582
enforcement 156, 2427
engagement 233
Engineering and Physical Sciences Research Council 1702
ENISA 1689
enlightenment 2433
enlightenment views 3189
Enron 2958
enterprise applications 1267
enterprise deployment 3068
enterprise reconfiguration dynamics 2220, 2432, 2448, 2755, 3644
enterprise resource planning (ERP) 2133, 2949, 2962
entity extraction 1706
entrepreneur behavior 2705
entrepreneurial management 2705
entrepreneurial orientation 2705
entrepreneurial traits 2704
entry point obscuring (EPO) 3076
environmental 3434
environmental sustainability 232
e-operations 3903
EPC Network 1924
EPC. *See* electronic product code
EPCglobal 1924, 1930
ePHI (Electronic Protected Health Information) 1764
EPIC 3939
epistemological issues of computerization 2436
EPR (see electronic patient record) 1759
e-prescription 586
ERP (enterprise resource planning) 1952, 2133
error 295
E-SIGN Bill 1695
e-signatures 3447
eSocial contract 2808
espionage 1683
essential security technologies 2786
e-tailing 3903
e-teaching 3162
e-technologies 3123, 3125, 3130
ethical 3433
ethical, action 3271, 3275
ethical, action development 3279
ethical, behavior 3270
ethical, choice 2917
ethical, consideration 2615, 2622
ethical, contradictions 3178
ethical, decision-making 457, 2615
ethical, dilemmas 4001
ethical, integrity 3330

ethical, issues 3758
ethical, judgment 3271, 3275, 3277
ethical, judgment development 3278
ethical, methodology 3114
ethical, motivation 3271, 3277
ethical, motivation development 3279
ethical, norms 3493
ethical, sensitivity 3271, 3275, 3277
ethical, sensitivity development 3278
ethical, foundations 382
ethical, issues 327, 452
ethical, principles 192
ethical, problems 196
ethical, reasoning 477
ethical, standards 238
ethicist 3441
ethics 192, 212, 232, 292, 456, 463, 473, 1508, 2615, 2756, 2764, 2917, 3084, 3085, 3087, 3088, 3089, 3090, 3091, 3092, 3250, 3340, 3341, 3346, 3347, 3348, 3349, 3350, 3394, 3434, 3441, 3577, 3619, 3758, 3828
ethics, in information technology 3434
ethics, of privacy 3173
ethics, of digital government 456
ethics, of piracy 63
ethics, views on 3492
ethnographic research 3484
e-tranaction 1676
European community rights 3190
European Directive 2455
European Directive 02/58/EC 1693
European Network and Information Security Agency (ENISA) 1689
European Parliament and Council Directive 1693
European Union (EU) 1703, 1941, 3361
European Union (EU), accession process 1941
European Union Data Protection Directive 3939
evaluation agent 2017
evaluation assurance level (EAL) 1538
event data recorder (EDR) 1508
evidence based medicine (EBM) 363
evidential value 2423
evolutionary paradigms 1450
ex post investigation 1689
executive management 1398
existence of disaster recovery 2376
expert systems 1642
explicit permission seeking process 3960
exploit 2499
extensibility 158
eXtensible Access Control Markup Language (XAC-ML) 1268, 1300, 2997
Extensible Authentication Protocol (EAP) 1957, 2260
extensible markup language (XML) 1145,